# THE NUCLEAR AGE READER

# THE NUCLEAR AGE READER

**EDITED BY JEFFREY PORRO**

with

Paul Doty, Carl Kaysen, and Jack Ruina

**McGraw-Hill, Inc.**

New York St. Louis San Francisco Auckland Bogotá
Caracas Lisbon London Madrid Mexico City Milan
Montreal New Delhi San Juan Singapore
Sydney Tokyo Toronto

This book is printed on recycled paper containing 10% post consumer waste.

This book was developed for general use as the reader for the "War and Peace in the Nuclear Age" telecourse. The telecourse consists of thirteen one-hour public television programs, the study guide, this reader, and a faculty guide. The series was produced by WGBH-TV, Boston, Massachusetts, and Central Independent Television in England, in association with NHK of Japan. Major funding was provided by The Annenberg/CPB Project. Additional funding comes from the W. Alton Jones Foundation, John D. and Catherine T. MacArthur Foundation, Alfred P. Sloan Foundation, Chubb Group of Insurance Companies, Andrew W. Mellon Foundation, Corporation for Public Broadcasting, Public Broadcasting Service, Rockefeller Brothers Fund, and George Gund Foundation. "The Nuclear Age" is closed captioned for the hearing impaired.

For further information about available telecourses, telecourse licenses, and off-air taping, contact:

PBS Adult Learning Service
1320 Braddock Place
Alexandria, VA 22314-1698
1(800)-ALS-ALS-8

For information about purchases of videocassettes, off-air taping, and print materials contact:

Annenberg/CPB Project
2040 Alameda Padre Serra
Santa Barbara, CA 93140-4397
1(800)-LEARNER

First Edition
5 6 7 8 9 MAL MAL 9 9 8 7 6 5 4



**Library of Congress Cataloging-in-Publication Data**

The Nuclear age reader.

"Companion text for War and peace in the nuclear age, a prime-time television series and college-level telecourse",—
Includes bibliographies.
1. War and peace in the nuclear age (Television program) 2. Nuclear weapons. 3. Nuclear warfare. 4. World politics—1945– . 5. Nuclear arms control. 6. Antinuclear movement. I. Porro, Jeffrey D. II. War and peace in the nuclear age (Television program)
U263.N72 1988 355″.0217 87-36675
ISBN 0-07-554004-5

Manufactured in the United States of America

Credits and permissions begin on page 537.

# ABOUT THE EDITORS

**Jeffrey Porro** is a Washington writer and editor. He worked on national security issues as a staff member in the U.S. Senate and in the State Department and has been editor of *Arms Control Today* and the associate editor of *Issues in Science and Technology*.

**Paul Doty** is Mallinckrodt Professor of Biochemistry, Harvard University, and Director Emeritus of the Center for Science and International Affairs (CSIA), which he founded in 1973. He served as its director from 1973 until 1985. Doty worked on the Manhattan Project and served as a member of the President's Science Advisory Committee on Arms Control during the Carter administration. He has also chaired the Pugwash Committee and several other groups that meet regularly with Europeans and Soviets on security matters.

**Carl Kaysen** is David W. Skinner Professor of Political Economy, Massachusetts Institute of Technology, and former Director of the Program in Science, Technology, and Society at MIT. He is Director Emeritus of the Institute of Advanced Study in Princeton. He served on President Kennedy's National Security Council as Deputy Special Assistant to the President for National Security Affairs.

**Jack Ruina** is Professor of Electrical Engineering at the Massachusetts Institute of Technology and Director of the Institute's Defense and Arms Control Policy Program. He has held several Defense Department positions, including Director of the Advanced Research Projects Agency from 1961 to 1963. He has been President of the Institute for Defense Analyses in Arlington, Virginia, and was a member of the General Advisory Committee of the Arms Control and Disarmament Agency during the first Nixon administration.

# ACKNOWLEDGMENTS

The members of our Utilization Advisory Committee, listed below, provided invaluable assistance in developing this telecourse and in suggesting topics to explore. They were also instrumental in designing the telecourse materials to best meet the needs of administrators, faculty, and students.

Richard Browning
*Faculty Facilitator for Alternative Instruction*
Cuyahoga Community College
Cleveland, Ohio

Leo Flynn
*Professor of Government*
Pomona College
Claremont, California

Ruth Howes
*Professor of Physics and Astronomy*
Ball State University
Muncie, Indiana

Joyce Newman
*Telecourse Coordinator*
Governors State University
Park Forest South, Illinois

Carolyn Stephenson
*Assistant Professor of Political Science*
University of Hawaii at Manoa
Honolulu, Hawaii

Robert Woodward
*Professor of Journalism*
Drake University
School of Journalism and Mass Communication
Des Moines, Iowa

Special thanks also go to Bill Durch and Steve Miller of the Defense and Arms Control Studies Program at the Massachusetts Institute of Technology who reviewed the manuscript at several stages in its development.

Other contributors were Shannon Kile, Katherine Magraw, and Laura Reed, Ph.D. candidates in political science at the MIT Center for International Studies who worked as primary researchers for the reader, and Michael Allen Potter, a research assistant at the Center for Strategic and International Studies in Washington, D.C. Permissions editors were Eve Hall, Jane Regan, and Jeanne Harnett.

Beth Kirsch
*Staff Writer/Editor*

Ann Strunk
*Director of Print Projects*

Carol Greenwald
*Director of Instructional Programming*

WGBH Educational Foundation
Boston, Massachusetts

# PREFACE

*The Nuclear Age Reader* was developed as a companion text for "War and Peace in the Nuclear Age," a prime-time television series and college-level telecourse that will air on PBS in January 1989. "The Nuclear Age" is an introduction to the forty-year history of nuclear weapons, nuclear strategy and policy, and arms control. It is the result of an unusual collaboration among the Massachusetts Institute of Technology, Harvard University, and the WGBH Educational Foundation in Boston, Massachusetts. In addition to the thirteen-hour series, the project includes a companion book for general viewers by John Newhouse, a study guide, a faculty guide, and this reader.

"The Nuclear Age" examines the origins and evolution of the nuclear competition between the United States and the Soviet Union and its impact on the world, enabling students and viewers to draw their own conclusions on the critical issues that flow from it: the nature of deterrence; the role of science and technology; decision-making, diplomacy and negotiation in the nuclear age; and the ethical debate on nuclear weapons.

*The Nuclear Age Reader* offers readers an overview of major events of the nuclear age from 1941 to the present. The selections in this anthology include excerpts from personal diaries, memoirs, letters, and speeches of key figures who have influenced nuclear policy decisions. In addition, historical accounts, newspaper articles, government documents, and critical analyses provide readers with a sense of the public mood and political policies of the times. Its aim is to provide an insight into the reasoning of the participants and to help reconstruct the dynamics that shaped their thinking—and our world.

The threat of nuclear war is one of the few issues that can truly be said to affect us all. Not surprisingly, how to deal with this threat is one of the most controversial issues faced by political leaders, religious leaders, academics, scientists, and citizens. Do we need more weapons or fewer? Should we negotiate with the Soviet Union or strive for military superiority? What are the lessons of the nuclear age?

Our purpose in putting together this anthology is to introduce students to the basic facts and controversies of the nuclear age in order to help them form their own opinions on how best to deal with the nuclear threat. The specific group we have in mind are students who have not previously studied the nuclear age extensively. Our goal, therefore, has been to provide materials that are important but not overly technical.

In compiling the readings for this anthology, one problem we were *not* faced with was a shortage of material. Since the explosion of the first atomic weapon in 1945, an extraordinary amount has been written about almost every aspect of the nuclear age. In the 1980s alone, scores of analyses, histories, memoirs, polemics, and technical reports of varying levels of complexity have been published. Our major problem was what to choose and how to organize it to make it accessible.

The chapters are arranged for the most part in chronological order. Within each individual chapter, the readings are organized into key themes. We have tried for a mixture of the "classics," secondary sources, and material that reflect the mood of the time. The classics—primary documents and speeches—show what key decision makers did and the reasoning behind their actions. We have tried to put these in perspective for students by providing introductions to each chapter and introductory paragraphs for each set of readings. In addition, the secondary sources included analyze what went on during each period. We have also tried to include some pieces that reflect the reaction of the public and the press to the major events of the nuclear age.

Finally, although most of the material here looks at the nuclear age through American eyes, we have whenever possible included Soviet views or analysis of Soviet actions. In chapters 4 and 10 we have also emphasized important views from the NATO allies.

Although this anthology contains excerpts from more than one hundred different sources and offers more than fifty suggestions for further reading, we are quite aware that this is very much an introduction. We have only scratched the surface of the important materials available. This anthology will be a success if it improves the knowledge of students about the nuclear age and encourages them to seek out more information.

*Jeffrey Porro*

# CONTENTS

## Chapter 3 A BIGGER BANG FOR THE BUCK 80



## Chapter 4 EUROPE GOES NUCLEAR 120



## Chapter 5 AT THE BRINK 146

## Chapter 11 MISSILE EXPERIMENTAL 380



## Chapter 12 REAGAN'S SHIELD 419



## Chapter 13 VISIONS OF WAR AND PEACE 475

# *One*

# DAWN

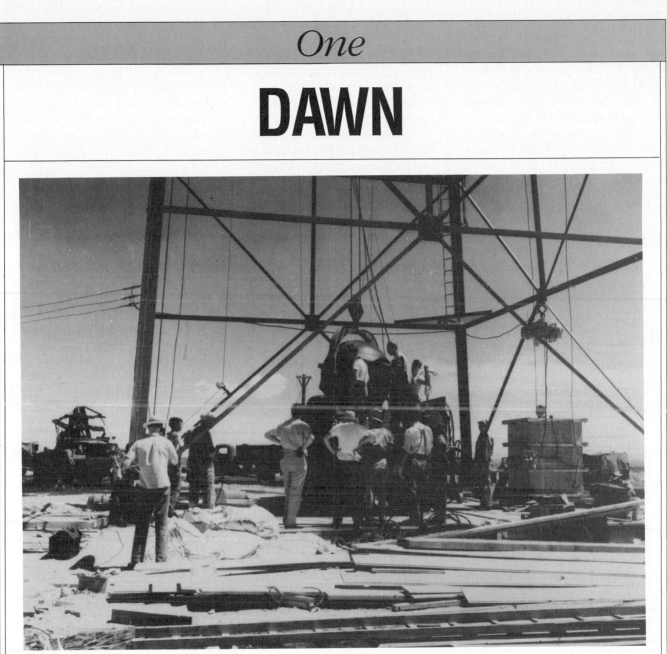

**TRINITY TEST SITE**

Scientists and workmen prepare to raise the world's first atomic bomb onto a 100-foot tower at the Trinity test site near Alamogordo, New Mexico. In the blast that followed the July 1945 test, the steel tower disappeared. Heat generated within the bomb's explosion reached nearly 100 million degrees (Fahrenheit), more than ten times the heat at the surface of the sun.
AP/Wide World Photos

# INTRODUCTION

The nuclear age began in July 1945 when the United States conducted the first successful test of an atomic weapon in the New Mexico desert. The world of 1945 was very different from the nuclear age as we know it now. In 1945, the United States and the Soviet Union were allies, though their relationship was beginning to worsen. Only the United States had nuclear weapons, and the number it had was very small. Scientists, military planners, and civilian leaders were very uncertain about the impact of the new atomic weapon on war and diplomacy.

After forty years of cold war between the United States and the Soviet Union, it is hard to imagine that the two superpowers were once allies. But during World War II they joined with Great Britain in a Grand Alliance against Hitler. However, it was not based on a wide range of U.S.-Soviet common interests. Indeed, between 1917 and 1941, relations between the United States and the Soviet Union had, on the whole, been characterized by hostility and suspicion. Only the common threat of Nazi Germany pushed the two states together.

In the twenty-five years before World War II, this hostility came from a number of sources. In the early years of its existence, the Soviet Union was ruled by revolutionaries actively committed to the overthrow of capitalism worldwide. It was no surprise that the world's largest capitalist country viewed Soviet intentions with suspicion. On the Soviet side, ideological hostility was further inflamed by the participation of U.S. forces in military action on behalf of anti-Bolshevik White Armies during the Russian civil war in 1919.

Relations between the United States and the Soviet Union improved somewhat during the 1930s. Under Josef Stalin, the Soviets seemed to turn inward and at times appeared willing to cooperate with capitalist countries such as the United States and Great Britain against the growing threat of Hitler's Germany. In 1933, the United States recognized the Soviet regime, and formal diplomatic relations began.

By 1940, however, U.S.-Soviet relations were again at a low point. In August 1939, the Soviet Union signed a nonaggression pact with Nazi Germany that seemed to open the way for Nazi aggression. In September 1939, Germany invaded Poland. Great Britain and France declared war on Germany, and World War II began. The Germans quickly seized most of Poland. The Soviets also invaded Poland, in accordance with their pact with the Germans, and annexed Poland's eastern territory. The Soviet deal with Germany and the Soviet invasion of Poland caused a great deal of hostility toward the Soviet Union in Britain and France, which now had to fight Germany alone, and in the United States.

This hostility was swept away on June 22, 1941, when the Germans launched a surprise attack on the Soviet Union. Hitler's move gave Great Britain and the Soviet Union a common enemy. Great Britain, all alone against the Nazis after the fall of France in 1940, quickly embraced this enemy of its enemy. The United States did the same when it entered the war in December 1941 after Pearl Harbor.

The Grand Alliance — Great Britain, the United States, and the Soviet Union — was born. But it must be kept in mind that it was not an alliance based on a large number of shared interests or values. It was based on a common enemy — Adolf Hitler. When that enemy was defeated, the Grand Alliance began to fall apart.

Fear of Hitler also helped to speed the development of the first atomic bomb. In December 1938, two German atomic scientists discovered nuclear fission — the splitting of the nucleus of an atom as a phenomenon that involved the conversion of mass into energy. When news of the discovery spread to the other countries, physicists realized that nuclear fission could lead to a chain reaction releasing immense amounts of energy, energy that could be used in a tremendously powerful bomb.

Many of the key atomic physicists working in Great Britain and the United States in the late 1930s were European émigrés who had fled Nazi persecution. They were very aware of the importance of the German scientists' breakthrough, and they were very fearful that Nazi Germany might develop an atomic bomb first. In the United States, Leo Szilard, a prominent émigré physicist, convinced Albert Einstein, the world's most famous physicist, to write a letter to President Franklin Roosevelt warning him about the possibility of a German bomb program. Roosevelt ordered that a special program be set up to explore the military implications of nuclear fission.

The U.S. atomic program proceeded slowly at first, and many of the early key breakthroughs were made by physicists working in Great Britain. But the U.S. effort picked up speed after the Japanese attack on Pearl Harbor in December 1941. In 1942 the top physicists in the United States were brought together to work on the Manhattan Project, whose purpose was to develop an atomic bomb. They worked feverishly and were finally successful when the first atomic bomb was tested in July 1945. Ironically, Nazi Germany had surrendered in April, and it was learned that the German scientists had made little progress toward an atomic bomb. The first atomic bomb was dropped on the Japanese city of Hiroshima on August 6, 1945. Three days later another atomic bomb was dropped on Nagasaki.

Because it was a weapons development program, the Manhattan Project was placed under the control of the military and headed by an Army general, Leslie Groves of the Corps of Engineers. The key scientists were civilians. Although all involved in the Manhattan Project were united in their dedication to building an atomic bomb, some of the scientists had worries not shared by the military or higher civilian authorities.

One prominent physicist, Niels Bohr, worried about the decision of the United States and Great Britain to share atomic information with each other but to deny it to the Soviet Union. Bohr believed that this would deepen Soviet hostility and make postwar cooperation difficult. As work on the atomic bomb progressed and it became clear that the atomic bomb would be used against Japan, some of the key Manhattan Project scientists urged the government to consider staging a demonstration of the bomb for the Japanese before attacking them. But they were overruled.

The scientists' argument in favor of a demonstration for the Japanese of the power of the atomic bomb became part of the controversy over the dropping of the bomb on Japan. In the years since Hiroshima, many historians and policy analysts have agreed with the Truman administration's argument that the atomic attacks on Japan were needed to avoid an invasion that would have cost hundreds of thousands of American lives. Others have argued that the Japanese were preparing to surrender in any case, or that a demonstration of the bomb at a remote island, as the scientists had advocated, would have been sufficient.

The Japanese surrendered five days after the bombing of Nagasaki. With Germany and Japan defeated, the old antagonisms between the United States and the Soviet Union came to the fore again. But they were made much worse by a new problem. the emerging superpowers had very different plans for what the post–World War II world should look like. In particular, Soviet leader Josef Stalin believed that to safeguard Soviet national security, Communist regimes should be imposed in the countries on his borders in Eastern Europe. The Soviets also seemed interested in extending their influence in the Far East. To the United States, Soviet plans for Eastern Europe and elsewhere were unacceptable. As the Soviets pressed forward with their plans in 1945 and 1946, the United States gradually came to believe that the expansion of Soviet power had to be stopped. U.S.-Soviet relations deteriorated badly.

Although the United States had a monopoly on nuclear weapons, it was very unclear exactly how the nation would use this monopoly. There is some evidence that Harry Truman, who became president after Roosevelt died in April 1945, tried to use the threat of the atomic bomb to pressure the Soviets to change their policy in Eastern Europe and in Asia. He was not very successful.

Some of the scientists who had worked on the bomb believed that atomic weapons were so terrible that they should never again be used as weapons of war. These scientists and other Americans urged that all atomic weapons be placed under international control. In 1946, the United States made a proposal, the Baruch Plan, to place atomic weapons under the control of the newly formed United Nations. Some of the features of the plan were unacceptable to the Soviet Union, and it was never realized. In the meantime, the Soviets were proceeding with their own program to develop atomic weapons.

In sum, by 1946 it was clear that the postwar world of the nuclear age would be very different from the prewar one. Atomic weapons were a reality, and U.S. Soviet relations had begun to unravel. But it remained very uncertain what the new world would look like and what role the United States would play in it. Some key U.S. leaders feared that the United States might retreat into isolationism as it had after World War I. U.S. military might was already evaporating as the huge U.S. armies were demobilized and the boys were sent home. It was also very uncertain exactly how atomic weapons would affect war and power.

# THE NATURE OF THE GRAND ALLIANCE

## The United States Should Support the Soviet Union

### *Document 1*

Shortly after the Nazi invasion of the Soviet Union, Joseph Davies, the U.S. ambassador to Moscow, urged Washington to support the Soviet war effort. In these excerpts from his diaries, Davies lays out the case for "vigorous and prompt" U.S. military aid, noting that aid to Moscow helps protect U.S. security. Davies also discusses Stalin's mistrust of the West.

### 1 JOSEPH DAVIES DIARY
### July 7, 1941

*Washington—July 7, 1941*
Had lunch with Sumner Welles today who is Acting Secretary in the absence of Secretary Hull. Wanted to discuss the Russian situation with him. Churchill has just announced that Britain will give "all-out" aid to Russia as allies, regardless of any conflicting ideologies and without thought of future postwar matters. I urged that the United States do likewise vigorously and promptly for two reasons: first, despite wealth and military strength, which I believe Russia had, my reports from Russia would indicate, it was nevertheless doubtful whether Russia's second line of defense — war mechanized industrial production — could in the long run stand up against German industrial war industry, and that Russia ultimately would have to have war supplies from here; second, that the Soviet leaders and the Russian people were proud and exceedingly sensitive. France and Britain had made the great mistake of flouting them in 1938 and 1939 with almost disastrous effect when they threw the Soviets into Hitler's camp. This Hitler attack, in my opinion, was a God-given break in the situation for nonaggressor nations and Soviet resistance should be stimulated in every way possible. In the event of partial success in the Ukraine, Hitler would undoubtedly make overtures of peace to them on the basis of the *status quo*. A situation where Soviet leaders might think that they had just been used to serve our purposes and to pull our chestnuts out of the fire should not be permitted to arise. Human nature was human nature. My own opinion was that the Soviet leaders were as realistic and hardheaded as any statesmen in Europe and would be disposed to reject any peace proposal of that kind because they know Hitler's promises are no good. They are not the kind who would sit on a red-hot stove the second time. Nevertheless, we should not be niggardly in our acceptance of their aid, for they were fighting Hitlerism.

Welles has a mind like a Swiss watch. He is a thoroughgoing individualist, a democrat, and naturally hostile to Communism, but he is heart and head in this fight to save this country from the menace of Nazi victory. He said that he felt that there was much force in my point of view and asked whether I had seen the statement which he had already issued — somewhat along the purpose of my discussion. I had not seen it. In principle, he said, we are in agreement, for the Soviets were fighting Hitler, and therefore are fighting to protect our security here in the United States, both in the religious world as well as in the political sphere.

## U.S.-Soviet Friendship

### *Documents 2 and 3*

Documents 2 and 3 indicate how the U.S.-Soviet alliance against Hitler also led the American public and some U.S. officials to feel quite friendly toward the Soviet Union during World War II. Document 2, from *Life Magazine*, is typical of many stories that appeared in the press. It depicts the whole struggle of the Soviet allies. In document 3, Vice President Henry A. Wallace describes the friendship and mutual admiration between the peoples of both nations.

### 2 AMERICANS SEND FOOD AND WATCHES TO HELP THEIR SOVIET ALLIES
### March 1943

Americans are bending over backwards to give needed items to their fighting Russian allies. To meet Russia's food shortage the U.S. has been shipping more and more foodstuffs to the U.S.S.R. In 1943 these shipments increased so fast that the U.S. may send more food to Russia than to hungry England this year. Like the specially requested pork product, "tushonka," shown on this page, much of the foods for Russia have been high-energy foods containing meat and animal fats. But the U.S. is also sending them dehydrated foods, many thousand tons of wheat, flour, sugar, beans, peas, rice, cereals and vegetable oil.

In addition to the vast quantities of goods obtained through lend-lease, the American people are chipping in with contributions of their own. It is about this voluntary aid that Ambassador Standley specifically charged the Russian Government with not informing the Russian people. Russian War Relief, Inc. has raised more than $9,000,000 for the Soviets since September 1941. This organization sends medical supplies, seeds to replant the scorched earth, and collects U.S. old clothing at the rate of 45,000 lb. per week. Russians get no new clothes by lend-lease except shoes. The 3,000,000 pairs of soldiers' boots convoyed to the U.S.S.R. last year had much to do with their preparedness for this winter's offensive.

Best recent example of the willingness of U.S. civilians to aid their allies with gifts is the "Watches for Russia" campaign in Seattle, Wash. In a short period of time more than 1,000 timepieces were donated. When the most accurate of them have been checked and repaired they will be turned over to the U.S.S.R. for use by doctors and nurses at the front.

## 3 SPEECH DELIVERED BEFORE THE CONGRESS OF AMERICAN SOVIET FRIENDSHIP
### Vice President Henry A. Wallace
### November 1942

It is no accident that Americans and Russians like each other when they get acquainted. Both peoples were molded by the vast sweep of a rich continent. Both peoples know that their future is greater than their past. Both hate sham. When the Russian people burst the shackles of Czarist absolutism, they turned instinctively to the United States for engineering and agricultural guidance. Thanks to the hunger of the Russian people for progress, they were able to learn in twenty-five years that which had taken us in the United States 100 years to develop.

The first person to sense the eventual significance of Russians and the Americans. . . . Their starting point is queville, who 107 years ago wrote:

"There are at the present time two great nations in the world which seem to tend towards the same end, although they start from different points. I allude to the Russians and the Americans. . . . Their starting point is different and their courses are not the same, yet each of them seems to be marked by the will of heaven to sway the destinies of half the globe."

Russia and the United States today are far closer than Tocqueville could possibly have imagined when he traveled across the United States in 1835. The continental position of both countries and the need for developing rich resources unmolested from without have caused the peoples of both nations to have a profound hatred of war and a strong love of peace. . . .

Russia and the United States have had a profound effect upon each other. Both are striving for the education, the productivity and the enduring happiness of the common man. The new democracy, the democracy of the common man, includes not only the Bill of Rights, but also economic democracy, ethnic democracy, educational democracy, and democracy in the treatment of the sexes.

### The Ferment of Today

The ferment in the world today is such that these various types of democracy must be woven together into a harmonious whole. Millions of Americans are now coming to see that if Pan America and the British Commonwealth are the warp of the new democracy, then the peoples of Russia and Asia may well become its woof.

Some in the United States believe that we have overemphasized what might be called political or Bill-of-Rights democracy. Carried to its extreme form, it leads to rugged individualism, exploitation, impractical emphasis on States' rights, and even to anarchy.

Russia, perceiving some of the abuses of excessive political democracy, has placed strong emphasis on economic democracy. This, carried to an extreme, demands that all power be centered in one man and his bureaucratic helpers.

Somewhere there is a practical balance between economic and political democracy. Russia and the United States both have been working toward this practical middle ground. In present-day Russia, for example, differences in wage income are almost but not quite as great as in the United States. The manager of a factory may be paid ten times as much as the average worker. Artists, scientists, and outstanding writers are usually paid even more than factory managers or political commissars.

The chief difference between the economic organization of Russia and that of the United States is that in Russia it is almost impossible to live on income-producing property. The Russian form of State socialism is designed not to get equality of income but to place a maximum incentive on each individual to produce his utmost.

A third kind of democracy, which I call ethnic, is in my opinion vital to the new democracy, the democracy of the common man. Ethnic democracy means merely that the different races and minority groups must be given equality of economic opportunity. President Roosevelt was guided by principles of ethnic democracy when in June of 1941 he issued an executive order prohibiting racial discrimination in the employing of workers by national defense industries.

Russia has probably gone farther than any other nation in the world in practicing ethnic democracy. From the Russians we can learn much, for unfortunately the Anglo-Saxons have had an attitude toward other races which has made them exceedingly unpopular in many parts of the world.

We have not sunk to the lunatic level of the Nazi myth of racial superiority, but we have sinned enough to cost us already the blood of tens of thousands of precious lives. Ethnic democracy built from the heart is perhaps the greatest need of the Anglo-Saxon tradition.

The fourth democracy, which has to do with education, is based fundamentally on belief in ethnic democracy. It is because Stalin pushed educational democracy with all the power that he could command that Russia today is able to resist Germany. The Russian people for generations have had a great hunger to learn to read and write, and when Lenin and Stalin gave them the opportunity, they changed in twenty years from a nation which was 90 per cent illiterate to a nation of which nearly 90 per cent are able to read and write.

### Russia May Surpass Us

Russia has had a great admiration for the American system of technical education and public libraries. If she can continue during the next twenty years the progress made in the past twenty, she will surpass the United States. If, in the future, Russia comes whole-heartedly into the family of nations, we may expect Russian scientists to make contributions to human welfare which equal those of any nation in the world. In any event, the Russian scientists will most assuredly be doing their best to place the results of science more definitely at the service of the average man and woman. Patents based on Russian scientific work will not be held out of use to benefit international cartels.

With regard to the fifth democracy, the treatment of the sexes, most of us in the United States have felt complacent. It has taken the war experience of Russia to demonstrate the completeness of our failure. Those who have visited Russia recently say that about 40 per cent of the work in the factories is being done by women. The average woman does about as much work as the average man, and is paid as much. Thousands of Russian women are in uniform, either actively fighting or standing guard. We in the United States have not yet, in the same way as the Russians, called on the tremendous reserve power which is in our women, but before this war is over, we may be forced to give women their opportunity to demonstrate that with proper training they are equal to man in most kinds of work.

The old democracy did not serve as a guarantee of peace. The new democracy, in which the people of the United States and Russia are so deeply interested, must give us such a guarantee. This new democracy will be neither communism of the old-fashioned internationalist type nor democracy of the old-fashioned isolationist sort. Willingness to support world organization to maintain world peace by justice implemented by force is fundamental to the democracy of the common man in these days of airplanes. Fortunately, the airplanes, which make it necessary to organize the world for peace, also furnish the means of maintaining peace. When this war comes to an end, the United Nations will have such an overwhelming superiority in air power that we shall be able speedily to enforce any mandate whenever the United Nations may have arrived at a judgment based on international law.

## Kennan Warns of Growing Conflicts

### *Documents 4 and 5*

**George Kennan, a senior State Department official and Soviet expert, warned early on of the basic conflicts between the United States and the Soviet Union. In document 4, an excerpt from his memoirs, Kennan discusses the growing conflict between the two powers as the war in Europe came to a close. He notes the unwillingness of the Soviets to tolerate the presence of non-Communists in Poland's postwar government. In document 5, a letter to the U.S. ambassador in Moscow, Kennan discusses the reasons why the United States cooperated with the Soviet Union during World War II. He also warns that this cooperation should not blind the United States to the dangers of Soviet expansionism.**

### 4 MEMOIRS: 1925–1950
### George F. Kennan

Before Mikolajczyk left Moscow, there began the tragic and dramatic episode of the Warsaw uprising. This, more than anything that had occurred to that point, brought the Western governments face to face with what they were up against in Stalin's Polish policy. For if the inactivity of the Red army forces as they sat, passive, on the other side of the river and watched the slaughter by the Germans of the Polish heroes of the rebellion was not yet eloquent enough as an expression of the Soviet attitude, then the insolent denial by Stalin and Molotov to Ambassador Harriman of permission for use of the American shuttle base in the Ukraine to facilitate the dropping of arms and supplies to the beleaguered Poles, and the significant demand, expressed on the same occasion, that we withdraw the shuttle bases entirely, left no room for misunderstanding. . . .

It has been my opinion, ever since, that this was the moment when, if ever, there should have been a full-fledged and realistic political showdown with the Soviet leaders: when they should have been confronted with the choice between changing their policy completely and agreeing to collaborate in the establishment of truly independent countries in Eastern Europe or forfeiting Western-Allied support and sponsorship for the remaining phases of their war effort. We no longer owed them anything, after all (if indeed we ever had). The second front had been established. The Western Allies were now on the European continent in force. Soviet territory had been entirely liberated. What was now at stake in Soviet military operations was exclusively the future of non-Soviet territories previously overrun by the Germans. We in the West had a perfect right to divest ourselves of responsibility for further Soviet military operations conducted in the spirit of, and with the implications of, the Soviet denial of support for the Warsaw uprising.

All these things occurred in the summer of 1944: five months before Yalta, eight or nine months before the crisis over Polish affairs that occurred at the time of the death of President Roosevelt. It will be understood that I, holding these views, followed only with greatest skepticism and even despair the progress of our further dealings with the Soviet leaders, in 1944 and 1945, over Poland. The Yalta Declaration, with its references to the reorganization of the existing Polish-Communist regime "on a broader democratic basis" and to the holding "of free and unfettered elections . . . on the basis of universal suffrage and secret ballot," struck me as the shabbiest sort of equivocation, certainly not calculated to pull the wool over the eyes of the Western public but bound to have this effect. With boredom and disgust I served, in the spring of 1945, as Ambassador Harriman's aide and interpreter through the many hours of unreal, repetitious wrangling with Molotov and Vyshinski as to who, among the non-Communist Poles, might be invited to participate in the discussions looking to the formation of a coalition Polish government.* I never doubted that it was all a lost cause.

## 5 LETTER TO CHARLES BOHLEN BEFORE YALTA
### George F. Kennan

I am aware of the realities of this war, and of the fact that we were too weak to win it without Russian cooperation. I recognize that Russia's war effort has been masterful and effective and must, to a certain extent, find its reward at the expense of other peoples in eastern and central Europe.

But with all of this, I fail to see why we must associate ourselves with this political program, so hostile to the interests of the Atlantic community as a whole, so dangerous to everything which we need to see preserved in Europe. Why could we not make a decent and definitive compromise with it — divide Europe frankly into spheres of influence — keep ourselves out of the Russian sphere and keep the Russians out of ours? That would have been the best thing we could do for ourselves and for our friends in Europe, and the most honest approach we could have tried to restore life, in the wake of war, on a dignified and stable foundation.

Instead of this, what have we done? Although it was evident that the realities of the after-war were being shaped while the war was in progress we have consistently refused to make clear what our interests and our wishes were, in eastern and central Europe. We have refused to name any limit for Russian expansion and Russian responsibilities, thereby confusing the Russians and causing them constantly to wonder whether they are asking too little or whether it was some kind of a trap.

* The reference here is to the several sessions of the Commission, composed of Soviet Foreign Minister Molotov and the British and American ambassadors in Moscow, that had been established by the Yalta Conference to consult with the "present [Polish] government." My disgust would have been even greater had I known that while we talked, the Soviet authorities were quietly arresting, behind our backs, some of those very Polish political figures we were discussing for inclusion in the group to be consulted, and were putting pressure on them, unbeknownst to us, to become Soviet agents.

# Roosevelt's Report on Yalta

### *Document 6*

On March 1, 1945, President Roosevelt reported to Congress on the Yalta Conference. In these excerpts, Roosevelt discusses the conference, which had a great deal to do with the shape of Europe after World War II. Roosevelt describes U.S.-Soviet discussions on Germany, Eastern Europe, and the creation of the United Nations. Although the United States, Great Britain, and the Soviet Union reached agreements at Yalta, and Roosevelt describes the conference as a success, key issues remained unresolved. These differences helped lead to the breakup of the Grand Alliance.

## 6 ADDRESS TO CONGRESS ON CRIMEAN CONFERENCE
### President Franklin Roosevelt
### March 1, 1945

It is good to be home.

It has been a long journey. I hope you will all agree that it was a fruitful one.

Speaking in all frankness, the question of whether it is entirely fruitful or not lies to a great extent in your hands. For unless you here in the halls of the American Congress — with the support of the American people — concur in the decisions reached at Yalta, and give them your active support, the meeting will not have produced lasting results. . . .

. . . First, there were the problems of occupation and control of Germany after victory, the complete destruction of her military power, and the assurance that neither

Nazism nor Prussian militarism could again be revived to threaten the peace and civilization of the world.

. . . We did, however, make it clear at the Conference just what unconditional surrender does mean for Germany.

It means the temporary control of Germany by Great Britain, Russia, France and the United States. Each of these nations will occupy and control a separate zone of Germany — and the administration of the four zones will be coordinated in Berlin by a Control Council composed of representatives of the four nations.

Unconditional surrender also means the end of Nazism and of the Nazi Party — and all of its barbaric laws and institutions.

It means the termination of all militaristic influence in the public, private and cultural life of Germany. . . .

. . . Of equal importance with the military arrangements at the Crimean Conference were the agreements reached with respect to a general international organization for lasting world peace. . . .

. . . A Conference of all the United Nations of the world will meet in San Francisco on April twenty-fifth, 1945. There, we all hope, and confidently expect, to execute a definite charter of organization under which the peace of the world will be preserved and the forces of aggression permanently outlawed.

This time we shall not make the mistake of waiting until the end of the war to set up the machinery of peace. This time, as we fight together to get the war over quickly, we work together to keep it from happening again.

As the Allied Armies have marched to military victory, they have liberated peoples whose liberties had been crushed by the Nazis for four years, and whose economy had been reduced to ruins by Nazi despoilers.

There have been instances of political confusion and unrest in these liberated areas — as in Greece and Poland and Yugoslavia and other places. Worse than that, there actually began to grow up in some of them vaguely defined ideas of "spheres of influence" which were incompatible with the basic principles of international collaboration. If allowed to go unchecked, these developments might have had tragic results.

It is fruitless to try to place the blame for this situation on one particular nation or another. It is the kind of development which is almost inevitable unless the major powers of the world continue without interruption to work together and assume joint responsibility for the solution of problems which may arise to endanger the peace of the world.

We met in the Crimea, determined to settle this matter of liberated areas. I am happy to confirm to the Congress that we did arrive at a settlement — a unanimous settlement.

The three most powerful nations have agreed that the political and economic problems of any area liberated from Nazi conquest, or any former Axis satellite, are a joint responsibility of all three Governments. They will join together, during the temporary period of instability after hostilities, to help the people of any liberated area, or of any former satellite state, to solve their own problems through firmly established democratic processes.

They will endeavor to see to it that interim governing authorities are as representative as possible of all democratic elements in the population, and that free elections are held as soon as possible.

Responsibility for political conditions thousands of miles overseas can no longer be avoided by this great nation. [Certainly I don't want to live to see another war.] As I have said, it is a smaller world. The United States now exerts a vast influence in the cause of peace throughout all the world. [What we people over here are thinking and talking about is in the interest of peace, because it's known all over the world. The slightest remark in either house of Congress is known all over the world the following day.] We will continue to exert that influence only if we are willing to continue to share in the responsibility for keeping the peace. It would be our own tragic loss were we to shirk that responsibility.

One outstanding example of joint action by the three major Allies in the liberated areas was the solution reached on Poland. The whole Polish question was a potential source of trouble in post-war Europe, and we came to the Conference determined to find a common ground for its solution. We did.

Our objective was to help create a strong, independent and prosperous nation [— that's the thing we must always remember, those words, agreed to by Russia, by Britain and by me, the objective of making Poland a strong, independent and prosperous nation —] with a Government ultimately to be selected by the Polish people themselves.

To achieve that objective, it was necessary to provide for the formation of a new Government, much more representative than had been possible while Poland was enslaved. Accordingly, steps were taken at Yalta to reorganize the existing Provisional Government in Poland on a broader democratic basis, so as to include democratic leaders now in Poland and those abroad. This new, reorganized Government will be recognized by all of us as the temporary Government of Poland.

However, the new Polish Provisional Government of National Unity will be pledged to hold a free election as soon as possible on the basis of universal suffrage and a secret ballot.

Throughout history, Poland has been the corridor through which attacks on Russia have been made. Twice in this generation, Germany has struck at Russia through this corridor. To insure European security and world peace, a strong and independent Poland is necessary.

The decision with respect to the boundaries of Poland

was a compromise [— I didn't agree with all of it by any means, but we could go as far as Britain wanted in certain areas, as far as Russia wanted in certain areas, and we could go as far as I wanted in certain areas — it was a compromise] under which the Poles will receive compensation in territory in the north and west in exchange for what they lose by the Curzon Line [in the east]. The limits of the western border will be permanently fixed in the final Peace Conference. [We know, roughly, that it will include in the new strong Poland quite a large slice of what is now called Germany.] It was agreed that a large coastline should be included. [Also that East Prussia — most of it — will go to Poland and the corner of it will go to Russia. Also . . . I think Danzig would be a lot better if it were Polish.] . . .

. . . Twenty-five years ago, American fighting men looked to the statesmen of the world to finish the work of peace for which they fought and suffered. We failed them then. We cannot fail them again, and expect the world to survive.

The Crimean Conference was a successful effort by the three leading nations to find a common ground for peace. It spells the end of the system of unilateral action and exclusive alliances and spheres of influence and balances of power and all the other expedients which have been tried for centuries — and have failed.

We propose to substitute for all these a universal organization in which all peace-loving nations will finally have a chance to join.

And I am confident that the Congress and the American people will accept the results of this Conference as the beginnings of a permanent structure of peace upon which we can begin to build, under God, that better world in which our children and grandchildren — yours and mine, the children and grandchildren of the whole world — must live.

# THE DEVELOPMENT OF THE ATOMIC BOMB

## A Warning — The Nazis May Develop an A-Bomb

### *Document 7*

Émigré physicists in the United States worried that the Germans might be the first to develop the atomic bomb. In this critically important letter from Albert Einstein to President Roosevelt, the famous scientist urges the United States to make a major effort to develop atomic weapons before the Nazis do. Einstein was urged to write to Roosevelt by another émigré physicist, Leo Szilard, who also helped draft the letter.

### 7 LETTER TO ROOSEVELT
### Leo Szilard–Albert Einstein
### August 2, 1939

Albert Einstein
Old Grove Road
Peconic, Long Island
August 2nd, 1939

F. D. Roosevelt
President of the United States
White House
Washington, D.C.

Sir:

Some recent work by E. Fermi and L. Szilard, which has been communicated to me in manuscript, leads me to expect that the element uranium may be turned into a new and important source of energy in the immediate future. Certain aspects of the situation which has arisen seem to call for watchfulness and, if necessary, quick action on the part of the Administration. I believe therefore that it is my duty to bring to your attention the following facts and recommendation.

In the course of the last four months it has been made probable through the work of Joliot in France as well as Fermi and Szilard in America — that it may become possible to set up a nuclear chain reaction in a large mass of uranium, by which vast amounts of power and large quantities of new radium like elements would be generated. Now it appears almost certain that this could be achieved in the immediate future.

This new phenomenon would also lead to the construction of bombs, and it is conceivable — though much less certain — that extremely powerful bombs of a new type may thus be constructed. A single bomb of this type, carried by boat and exploded in a port, might very well destroy the whole port together with some of the surrounding territory. However, such bombs might very well prove to be too heavy for transportation by air.

The United States has only very poor ores of uranium in moderate quantities. There is some good ore in Canada and the former Czechoslovakia, while the most important source of uranium is Belgian Congo.

In view of this situation you may think it desirable to have some permanent contact maintained between the Administration and the group of physicists working on chain reactions in America. One possible way of achieving this might be for you to entrust with this task a person who has your confidence and who could perhaps serve in an unofficial capacity. His task might comprise the following:

a) to approach Government Departments, keep them informed of the further development, and put forward recommendations for Government action, giving particular attention to the problem of securing a supply of uranium ore for the United States.

b) to speed up the experimental work, which is at present being carried on within the limits of the budgets of University laboratories, by providing funds, if such funds be required, through his contacts with private persons who are willing to make contributions for this cause, and perhaps also by obtaining the co-operation of industrial laboratories which have the necessary equipment.

I understand that Germany has actually stopped the sale of uranium from the Czechoslovakian mines which she has taken over. That she should have taken such early action might perhaps be understood on the ground that the son of the German Under-Secretary of State, von Weizacker, is attached to the Kaiser-Wilhelm-Institut in Berlin where some of the American work on uranium is now being repeated.

Yours very truly,
/ s / Albert Einstein

## An Eyewitness Account of the A-Bomb Test

### *Document 8*

This eyewitness account by a brigadier general standing 10,000 yards south of the explosion gives a sense of the reaction of the atomic bomb's creators to the first test of the weapon. The author describes the tension and then the awe felt by the scientists.

### 8 A PERSONAL ACCOUNT
### Brig. Gen. Thomas F. Farrell
### July 1945

The scene inside the shelter was dramatic beyond words. In and around the shelter were some twenty-odd people concerned with last minute arrangements prior to firing the shot. Included were: Dr. Oppenheimer, the Director who had borne the great scientific burden of developing the weapon from the raw materials made in Tennessee and Washington and a dozen of his key scientists — Dr. Kistiakowsky, who developed the highly special explosives; Dr. Bainbridge, who supervised all the detailed arrangements for the test; Dr. Hubbard, the weather expert, and several others. Besides these, there were a handful of soldiers, two or three Army officers and one Naval officer. The shelter was cluttered with a great variety of instruments and radios.

For some hectic two hours preceding the blast, General Groves stayed with the Director, walking with him and steadying his tense excitement. Every time the Director would be about to explode because of some untoward happening, General Groves would take him off and walk with him in the rain, counselling with him and reassuring him that everything would be all right. At twenty minutes before zero hour, General Groves left for his station at the base camp, first because it provided a better observation point and second, because of our rule that he and I must not be together in situations where there is an element of danger, which existed at both points.

Just after General Groves left, announcements began to be broadcast of the interval remaining before the blast. They were sent by radio to the other groups participating in and observing the test. As the time interval grew smaller and changed from minutes to seconds, the tension increased by leaps and bounds. Everyone in that room knew the awful potentialities of the thing that they thought was about to happen. The scientists felt that their figuring must be right and that the bomb had to go off but there was in everyone's mind a strong measure of doubt. The feeling of many could be expressed by "Lord, I believe; help Thou mine unbelief." We were reaching into the unknown and we did not know what might come of it. It can be safely said that most of those present — Christian, Jew and Atheist — were praying and praying harder than they had ever prayed before. If the shot were successful, it was a justification of the several years of intensive effort of tens of thousands of people — statesmen, scientists, engineers, manufacturers, soldiers, and many others in every walk of life.

In that brief instant in the remote New Mexico desert the tremendous effort of the brains and brawn of all these people came suddenly and startlingly to the fullest fruition. Dr. Oppenheimer, on whom had rested a very heavy burden, grew tenser as the last seconds ticked off. He scarcely breathed. He held on to a post to steady himself. For the last few seconds, he stared directly ahead and then when the announcer shouted "Now!" and there came this tremendous burst of light followed shortly thereafter by the deep growling roar of the explosion, his face relaxed into an expression of tremendous relief. Several of the observers standing back of the shelter to watch the lighting effects were knocked flat by the blast.

The tension in the room let up and all started congratulating each other. Everyone sensed "This is it!" No matter what might happen now all knew that the impossible scientific job had been done. Atomic fission would no longer be hidden in the cloisters of the theoretical physicists' dreams. It was almost full grown at birth. It was a great new force to be used for good or for evil. There was a feeling in that shelter that those concerned with its nativity should dedicate their lives to the mission that it would always be used for good and never for evil.

Dr. Kistiakowsky, the impulsive Russian, threw his arms around Dr. Oppenheimer and embraced him with shouts of glee. Others were equally enthusiastic. All the pent-up emotions were released in those few minutes and all seemed to sense immediately that the explosion had far exceeded the most optimistic expectations and wildest hopes of the scientists. All seemed to feel that they had been present at the birth of a new age — The Age of Atomic Energy — and felt their profound responsibility to help in guiding into right channels the tremendous forces which had been unlocked for the first time in history.

As to the present war, there was a feeling that no matter what else might happen, we now had the means to insure its speedy conclusion and save thousands of American lives. As to the future, there had been brought into being something big and something new that would prove to be immeasurably more important than the discovery of electricity or any of the other great discoveries which have so affected our existence.

The effects could well be called unprecedented, magnificent, beautiful, stupendous and terrifying. No man-made phenomenon of such tremendous power had ever occurred before. The lightning effects beggared description. The whole country was lighted by a searing light with the intensity many times that of the midday sun. It was golden, purple, violet, gray and blue. It lighted every peak, crevasse and ridge of the nearby mountain range with a clarity and beauty that cannot be described but must be seen to be imagined. It was that beauty the great poets dream about but describe most poorly and inadequately. Thirty seconds after the explosion came first, the air blast pressing hard against the people and things, to be followed almost immediately by the strong, sustained, awesome roar which warned of doomsday and made us feel that we puny things were blasphemous to dare tamper with the forces heretofore reserved to The Almighty. Words are inadequate tools for the job of acquainting those not present with the physical, mental and psychological effects. It had to be witnessed to be realized.

## A Demonstration of the A-Bomb for Japan?

### *Document 9*

After Germany was defeated, key atomic scientists argued strongly against using the atomic bomb on Japan. The excerpts here from a report signed by leading Manhattan Project physicists warn of the danger of an arms race unless the United States shares information about the bomb with other countries. The report also recommends a demonstration of the atomic bomb for Japanese leaders.

### 9 THE FRANCK REPORT June 1945

Scientists have often before been accused of providing new weapons for the mutual destruction of nations, instead of improving their well-being. It is undoubtedly true that the discovery of flying, for example, has so far brought much more misery than enjoyment and profit to humanity. However, in the past, scientists could disclaim direct responsibility for the use to which mankind had put their disinterested discoveries. We feel compelled to take a more active stand now because the success which we have achieved in the development of nuclear power is fraught with infinitely greater dangers than were all the inventions of the past. All of us, familiar with the present state of nucleonics, live with the vision before our eyes of sudden destruction visited on our own country, of a Pearl Harbor disaster repeated in thousand-fold magnification in every one of our major cities.

In the past, science has often been able to provide also new methods of protection against new weapons of aggression it made possible, but it cannot promise such efficient protection against the destructive use of nuclear power. This protection can come only from the political organization of the world. Among all the arguments calling for an efficient international organization for peace, the existence of nuclear weapons is the most compelling one. *In the absence of an international authority which would make all resort to force in international conflicts impossible, nations could still be diverted from a path which must lead to total mutual destruction, by a specific international agreement barring a nuclear armaments race.*

#### II. Prospects of Armaments Race

It could be suggested that the danger of destruction by nuclear weapons can be avoided — at least as far as this country is concerned — either by keeping our discoveries secret for an indefinite time, or else by developing our nucleonic armaments at such a pace that no other nations would think of attacking us from fear of overwhelming retaliation.

The answer to the first suggestion is that although we undoubtedly are at present ahead of the rest of the world in this field, the fundamental facts of nuclear power are a subject of common knowledge. . . . In other words, even if we can retain our leadership in basic knowledge of nucleonics for a certain time by maintaining secrecy as to all results achieved on this and associated Projects, it would be foolish to hope that this can protect us for more than a few years.

It may be asked whether we cannot prevent the development of military nucleonics in other countries by a monopoly on the raw materials of nuclear power. The answer is that even though the largest now known deposits of uranium ores are under the control of powers which belong to the "western" group (Canada, Belgium, and British India), the old deposits in Czechoslovakia are outside this sphere. Russia is known to be mining radium on its own territory; and even if we do not know the size of the deposits discovered so far in the USSR, the probability that no large reserves of uranium will be found in a country which covers ⅕ of the land area of the earth (and whose sphere of influence takes in additional territory), is too small to serve as a basis for security. *Thus, we cannot hope to avoid a nuclear armament race either by keeping secret from the competing nations the basic scientific facts of nuclear power or by cornering the raw materials required for such a race.*

We now consider the second of the two suggestions made at the beginning of this section, and ask whether we could not feel ourselves safe in a race of nuclear armaments by virtue of our greater industrial potential, including greater diffusion of scientific and technical knowledge, greater volume and efficiency of our skilled labor corps, and greater experience of our management — all the factors whose importance has been so strikingly demonstrated in the conversion of this country into an arsenal of the Allied Nations in the present war. The answer is that all that these advantages can give us is the accumulation of a large number of bigger and better atomic bombs — and this only if we produce these bombs at the maximum of our capacity in peace time, and do not rely on conversion of a peace-time nucleonics industry to military production after the beginning of hostilities.

However, such a quantitative advantage in reserves of bottled destructive power will not make us safe from sudden attack. Just because a potential enemy will be afraid of being "outnumbered and outgunned," the temptation for him may be overwhelming to attempt a sudden unprovoked blow — particularly if he should suspect us of harboring aggressive intentions against his security or his sphere of influence. In no other type of warfare does the advantage lie so heavily with the aggressor. He can place his "infernal machines" in advance in all our major cities and explode them simultaneously, thus destroying a major part of our industry and a large part of our population, aggregated in densely populated metropolitan districts. Our possibilities of retaliation — even if retaliation should be considered adequate compensation for the loss of millions of lives and destruction of our largest cities — will be greatly handicapped because we must rely on aerial transportation of the bombs, and also because we may have to deal with an enemy whose industry and population are dispersed over a large territory. . . .

## III. Prospects of Agreement

The consequences of nuclear warfare, and the type of measures which would have to be taken to protect a country from total destruction by nuclear bombing, must be as abhorrent to other nations as to the United States, England, France, and the smaller nations of the European continent, with their congeries of people and industries, would be in a particularly desperate situation in the face of such a threat. Russia and China are the only great nations at present which could survive a nuclear attack. However, even though these countries may value human life less than the peoples of Western Europe and America, and even though Russia, in particular, has an immense space over which its vital industries could be dispersed and a government which can order this dispersion the day it is convinced that such a measure is necessary — there is no doubt that Russia will shudder at the possibility of a sudden disintegration of Moscow and Leningrad and of its new industrial cities in the Urals and Siberia. Therefore, only lack of mutual *trust*, and not lack of *desire* for agreement, can stand in the path of an efficient agreement for the prevention of nuclear warfare. The achievement of such an agreement will thus essentially depend on the integrity of intentions and readiness to sacrifice the necessary fraction of one's own sovereignty, by all the parties to the agreement.

From this point of view, the way in which the nuclear weapons now being secretly developed in this country are first revealed to the world appears to be of great, perhaps fateful importance.

One possible way — which may particularly appeal to those who consider nuclear bombs primarily as a secret weapon developed to help win the present war — is to use them without warning on an appropriately selected object in Japan. It is doubtful whether the first available bombs, of comparatively low efficiency and small size, will be sufficient to break the will or ability of Japan to resist, especially given the fact that the major cities like Tokyo, Nagoya, Osaka and Kobe already will largely have been reduced to ashes by the slower process of ordinary aerial bombing. Although important tactical results undoubtedly can be achieved by a sudden introduction of nuclear weapons, we nevertheless think that the question of the use of the very first available atomic bombs in the Japanese war should be weighed very carefully, not only by military authorities, but by the highest political leadership of this country. If we consider international agreement on total prevention of nuclear warfare as the paramount objective, and believe that it can be achieved, this kind of introduction of atomic weapons to the world may easily destoy all our chances of success. Russia, and even allied countries which bear less mistrust of our ways and intentions, as well as neutral countries may be deeply shocked. It may be very difficult to persuade the world that a nation which was capable of secretly preparing and suddenly releasing a weapon as indiscriminate as the rocket bomb and a million times more destructive, is to be trusted in its proclaimed desire of having such weapons abolished by international agreement. . . .

Thus, from the "optimistic" point of view — looking forward to an international agreement on the prevention of nuclear warfare — the military advantages and the saving of American lives achieved by the sudden use of atomic bombs against Japan may be outweighed by the ensuing loss of confidence and by a wave of horror and repulsion sweeping over the rest of the world and perhaps even dividing public opinion at home.

*From this point of view, a demonstration of the new weapon might best be made, before the eyes of representatives of all the United Nations, on the desert or a barren island.* The best possible atmosphere for the achievement of an international agreement could be achieved if America could say to the world, "You see what sort of a weapon we had but did not use. We are ready to renounce its use in the future if other nations join us in this renunciation and agree to the establishment of an efficient international control."

After such a demonstration the weapon might perhaps be used against Japan if the sanction of the United Nations (and of public opinion at home) were obtained, perhaps after a preliminary ultimatum to Japan to surrender or at least to evacuate certain regions as an alternative to their total destruction. This may sound fantastic, but in nuclear weapons we have something entirely new in order of magnitude of destructive power, and if we want to capitalize fully on the advantage their possession gives us, we must use new and imaginative methods.

It must be stressed that if one takes the pessimistic point of view and discounts the possibility of an effective international control over nuclear weapons at the present time, then the advisability of an early use of nuclear bombs against Japan becomes even more doubtful — quite independently of any humanitarian considerations. If an international agreement is not concluded immediately after the first demonstration, this will mean a flying start toward an unlimited armaments race. If this race is inevitable, we have every reason to delay its beginning as long as possible in order to increase our head start still further. . . . The benefit to the nation, and the saving of American lives in the future, achieved by renouncing an early demonstration of nuclear bombs and letting the other nations come into the race only reluctantly, on the basis of guesswork and without definite knowledge that the "thing does work," may far outweigh the advantages to be gained by the immediate use of the first and comparatively inefficient bombs in the war against Japan. . . .

To sum up, we urge that the use of nuclear bombs in this war be considered as a problem of long-range national policy rather than of military expediency, and that this policy be directed primarily to the achievement of an agreement permitting an effective international control of the means of nuclear warfare.

The vital importance of such a control for our country is obvious from the fact that the only effective alternative method of protecting this country appears to be a dispersal of our major cities and essential industries.

J. Franck, Chairman
D. J. Hughes
J. J. Nickson
E. Rabinowitch
G. T. Seaborg
J. C. Stearns
L. Szilard

## Two Days After Hiroshima

### *Document 10*

This excerpt from an article in the *New York Times* that appeared two days after Hiroshima offers an early analysis of the impact of atomic weapons. The author cautions that it would be unwise to expect too much initially of the new bomb.

### 10 THE NEW FACE OF WAR AUGUST 1945

The new face of war was still veiled yesterday in the death pall above Hiroshima, but its features were chaos.

The atomic-energy bomb that fell on the Japanese homeland blasted immediately not only the enemy, but also many of our previously conceived military values.

The coupling of atomic-energy explosive with rocket propulsion marks what may be the ultimate triumph of the offensive over the defensive. There is today no apparent — certainly no immediate — answer to stratosphere rockets with "cosmic" warheads, save an answer in kind. This suggests the end of urban civilization as we know it. If they are to be preserved, cities of the future may have to burrow downward instead of upward; dispersion, rather than concentration, and tunneling into the earth rather than reaching upward into the skies may be forced in future wars.

And if it be one of the objects of armies and navies and air forces to keep war from one's own soil and to carry it to the enemy's, all of these armed forces as we now know them, become obsolete. Mass conscript armies, great navies, piloted planes, have, perhaps, become a part of history, the slow, long, tortured history of man's ascent from the mud.

### Some of the Questions Posed

Will the atomic bomb reduce the frequency of wars; or will we merely substitute push buttons for cannons? Will man disperse and go, mole-like, underground; will he seek out new methods of defense, new weapons of offense; will wars still end in the age-old way with men on foot facing men on foot?

Will armies and navies in the old sense be forever obsolete? Will wars be essentially struggles between the mass wills of civilian populations? Or will the armed forces of the ground, of the sea and of the air, armed with new weapons, employing new techniques, still bear the bloody brunt of battle?

These are questions that no man today can answer; and it is idle and harmful speculation to attempt definitive answers to them now, before the dust has even settled over Hiroshima.

It is true that in the long history of war the pendulum has swung periodically from offense to defense, from defense to offense; for every weapon there has been an answer and for every answer there has been another weapon. It is true that war has constantly become more and more destructive, more and more terrible — especially since the start of the industrial era. But it is also true that, although war has ended civilizations, it has never ended civilization; men have been slaughtered, but man, a persistent creature, goes on.

But it is precisely because with rocket propulsion we have extended the range and speed of projectiles to Wellsian figures and with atomic energy we have expanded the destructive effect of explosives to unknowable dimensions that it is futile to speculate today. At Hiroshima we unleashed nature itself, and our past experiences and accretion of knowledge cannot serve to comprehend the result.

### Effects and Limitations

But several points can immediately be made:

(1) Although the dimensions of its eventual destructiveness spell Armageddon, it would be unwise to expect too much initially of the new bomb. We do not know yet what it has done. If the enemy's will to die on a national scale remains as firm in the future as it has on a personal scale in the past, it would seem to matter little to the Japanese whether they died by the hundreds of thousands or by the scores.

(2) The difficulties of manufacturing atomic bombs probably preclude the frequent use of this form of attack. We cannot expect daily "cosmic" attacks upon Japan.

(3) We do not yet know with certainty what effect these bombs have on underground structures or caves, such as those the enemy used so successfully on Iwo and Okinawa. It may be that penetration or blast, or the bomb's aftereffects, would kill or maim all troops underground in the vicinity of the bomb's hit. But others underground, farther off, would probably escape; and caves and mountains are far more numerous than atomic bombs.

(4) Atomic attack would obviously have limited usefulness in China, Malaya and other such enemy-occupied areas unless a very large Japanese encampment or troop concentration could be spotted — for we would kill our friends as well as our enemies. In vast wooded, mountainous and jungle-covered theatres of war, like the Asiatic mainland, "cosmic" attacks might disperse an army and destroy many of its supply dumps, but not annihilate it.

(5) Armies, navies and air forces in their conventional forms as we have come to know them in this war (and that is far from "conventional") have been the solid basis of our victories. Certainly during the duration of this war we cannot dispense with them or markedly reduce them without danger of imperiling our victory. The atomic bomb is an added powerful weapon that may or may not make unnecessary future planned operations. But for prudence and safety we must prepare and plan and train — and steel ourselves psychologically as well as physically — as if there were no such weapon. We shall be very unwise if we leap to sudden conclusions and underestimate Japanese tenacity.

(6) In all post-war military planning A-1 priority must be given to Research, Development and Production — each with capitals.

# The Aftermath

## *Document 11*

**These excerpts from a book by John Hersey give a graphic description of some of the effects of the atomic bomb on Hiroshima's residents. Hersey makes clear that coping with the bomb's aftermath was a medical nightmare.**

## 11 HIROSHIMA
## John Hersey

At nearly midnight, the night before the bomb was dropped, an announcer on the city's radio station said that about two hundred B-29s were approaching southern Honshu and advised the population of Hiroshima to evacuate to their designated 'safe areas'. Mrs. Hatsuyo Nakamura, the tailor's widow who lived in the section called Nobori-cho and who had long had a habit of doing as she was told, got her three children — a ten-year-old boy, Toshio, an eight-year-old girl, Yaeko, and a five-year-old girl, Myeko — out of bed and dressed them and walked with them to the military area known as the East Parade Ground, on the north-east edge of the city. There she unrolled some mats and the children lay down on them. They slept until about two, when they were awakened by the roar of the planes going over Hiroshima. As soon as the planes had passed, Mrs. Nakamura started back with her children. They reached home a little after two-thirty and she immediately turned on the radio, which, to her distress, was just then broadcasting a fresh warning. When she looked at the children and saw how tired they were, and when she thought of the number of trips they had made in past weeks, all to no purpose, to the East Parade Ground, she decided that in spite of the instructions on the radio, she simply could not face starting out all over again. She put the children in their bedrolls on the floor, lay down herself at three o'clock, and fell asleep at once, so soundly that when planes passed over later, she did not waken to their sound.

The siren jarred her awake at about seven. She arose, dressed quickly, and hurried to the house of Mr. Nakamoto, the head of her Neighbourhood Association, and asked him what she should do. He said that she should remain at home unless an urgent warning — a series of intermittent blasts of the siren — was sounded. She returned home, lit the stove in the kitchen, set some rice to cook, and sat down to read that morning's Hiroshima *Chugoku*. To her relief, the all-clear sounded at eight o'clock. She heard the children stirring, so she went and gave each of them a handful of peanuts and told them to stay on their bedrolls because they were tired from the night's walk. . . .

As Mrs. Nakamura stood watching her neighbour, everything flashed whiter than any white she had ever seen. She did not notice what happened to the man next door; the reflex of a mother set her in motion towards her children. She had taken a single step (the house was 1,350 yards, or three-quarters of a mile, from the centre of the explosion) when something picked her up and she seemed to fly into the next room over the raised sleeping platform, pursued by parts of her house.

Timbers fell around her as she landed, and a shower of tiles pommelled her; everything became dark, for she was buried. The debris did not cover her deeply. She rose up and freed herself. She heard a child cry, 'Mother, help me!' and saw her youngest — Myeko, the five-year-old — buried up to her breast and unable to move. As Mrs. Nakamura started frantically to claw her way towards the baby, she could see or hear nothing of her other children.

In the days right before the bombing, Dr. Masakazu Fujii, being prosperous, hedonistic, and at the time not too busy, had been allowing himself the luxury of sleeping until nine or nine-thirty, but fortunately he had to get up early the morning the bomb was dropped to see a house guest off on a train. He rose at six, and half an hour later walked with his friend to the station, not far away, across two of the rivers. He was back home by seven, just as the siren sounded its sustained warning. He ate breakfast and then, because the morning was already hot, undressed down to his underwear and went out on the porch to read the paper. This porch — in fact, the whole building — was curiously constructed. Dr. Fujii was the proprietor of a peculiarly Japanese institution, a private, single-doctor hospital. This building, perched beside and over the water of the Kyo River, and next to the bridge of the same name, contained thirty rooms for thirty patients and their kinsfolk. . . .

Dr. Fujii sat down cross-legged in his underwear on the spotless matting of the porch, put on his glasses, and started reading the Osaka *Asahi*. He liked to read the Osaka news because his wife was there. He saw the flash. To him — faced away from the centre and looking at his paper — it seemed a brilliant yellow. Startled, he began to rise to his feet. In that moment (he was 1,550 yards from the centre), the hospital leaned behind his rising and, with a terrible ripping noise, toppled into the river. The Doctor, still in the act of getting to his feet, was thrown forward and around and over; he was buffeted and gripped; he lost track of everything, because things were so speeded up; he felt the water.

Dr. Fujii hardly had time to think that he was dying before he realized that he was alive, squeezed tightly by two long timbers in a V across his chest, like a morsel suspended between two huge chopsticks — held upright, so that he could not move, with his head miraculously above water and his torso and legs in it. The remains of his hospital were all around him in a mad assortment of splintered lumber and materials for the relief of pain. His left shoulder hurt terribly. His glasses were gone. . . .

. . . He was unable to move at first, and he hung there about twenty minutes in the darkened morning. Then a thought which came to him — that soon the tide would be running in through the estuaries and his head would be submerged — inspired him to fearful activity; he wriggled and turned and exerted what strength he could (though his left arm, because of the pain in his shoulder, was useless), and before long he had freed himself from the vice. After a few moments' rest, he climbed on to the pile of timbers and, finding a long one that slanted up to the river bank, he painfully shinnied up it.

Dr. Fujii, who was in his underwear, was now soaking and dirty. His undershirt was torn, and blood ran down it from bad cuts on his chin and back. In this disarray, he walked out on to Kyo Bridge, beside which his hospital had stood. The bridge had not collapsed. He could see only fuzzily without his glasses, but he could see enough to be amazed at the number of houses that were down all around. On the bridge, he encountered a friend, a doctor named Machii, and asked in bewilderment, "What do you think it was?"

Dr. Machii said, "It must have been a *Molotoffano hanakago*" — a Molotov flower basket, the delicate Japanese name for the "bread basket," or self-scattering cluster of bombs.

At first, Dr. Fujii could see only two fires, one across the river from his hospital site and one quite far to the south. But at the same time, he and his friend observed something that puzzled them, and which, as doctors, they discussed: although there were as yet very few fires, wounded people were hurrying across the bridge in an endless parade of misery, and many of them exhibited terrible burns on their faces and arms. "Why do you suppose it is?" Dr. Fujii asked. Even a theory was comforting that day, and Dr. Machii stuck to his. "Perhaps because it was a Molotov flower basket," he said.

There had been no breeze earlier in the morning when Dr. Fujii had walked to the railway station to see a friend off, but now brisk winds were blowing every which way; here on the bridge the wind was easterly. New fires were leaping up, and they spread quickly, and in a very short time terrible blasts of hot air and showers of cinders made it impossible to stand on the bridge any more. Dr. Machii ran to the far side of the river and along a still unkindled street. Dr. Fujii went down into the water under the bridge, where a score of people had already taken refuge, among them his servants, who had extricated themselves from the wreckage. From there, Dr. Fujii saw a nurse hanging in the timbers of his hospital by her legs, and then another painfully pinned across the breast. He enlisted the help of some of the others under the bridge and freed both of them. He thought he heard the voice of his niece for a moment, but he could not find her; he never saw her again. Four of his nurses and the two patients in the hospital died, too. Dr. Fujii went back into the water of the river and waited for the fire to subside.

The lot of Drs. Fujii, Kanda, and Machii right after the explosion — and, as these three were typical, that of the majority of the physicians and surgeons of Hiroshima — with their offices and hospitals destroyed, their equipment scattered, their own bodies incapacitated in varying degrees, explained why so many citizens who were hurt went untended and why so many who might have lived died. Of a hundred and fifty doctors in the city, sixty-five were already dead and most of the rest were wounded. Of 1,780 nurses, 1,654 were dead or too badly hurt to work. In the biggest hospital, that of the Red Cross, only six doctors out of thirty were able to function, and only ten nurses out of more than two hundred. The sole uninjured doctor on the Red Cross Hospital staff was Dr. Sasaki. After the explosion, he hurried to a storeroom to fetch bandages. This room, like everything he had seen as he ran through the hospital, was chaotic — bottles of medicines thrown off shelves and broken, salves spattered on the walls, instruments strewn everywhere. He grabbed up some bandages and an unbroken bottle of mercurochrome, hurried back to the chief surgeon, and bandaged his cuts. Then he went out into the corridor and began patching up the wounded patients and the doctors and nurses there. He blundered so without his glasses that he took a pair off the face of a wounded nurse, and although they only approximately compensated for the errors of his vision, they were better than nothing. (He was to depend on them for more than a month.)

Dr. Sasaki worked without method, taking those who were nearest him first, and he noticed soon that the corridor seemed to be getting more and more crowded. Mixed in with the abrasions and lacerations which most people in the hospital had suffered, he began to find deadful burns. He realized then that casualties were pouring in from outdoors. There were so many that he began to pass up the lightly wounded; he decided that all he could hope to do was to stop people from bleeding to death. Before long, patients lay and crouched on the floors of the wards and the laboratories and all the other rooms, and in the corridors, and on the stairs, and in the front hall, and under the *porte-cochère*, and on the stone front steps, and in the driveway and courtyard, and for blocks each way in the streets outside. Wounded people supported maimed people; disfigured families leaned together. Many people were vomiting. A tremendous number of schoolgirls — some of those who had been taken from their classrooms to work outdoors, clearing fire lanes — crept into the hospital. In a city of two hundred and forty-five thousand, nearly a hundred thousand people had been killed or doomed at one blow; a hundred thousand more were hurt. At least ten thousand of the wounded made their way to the best hospital in town, which was altogether unequal to such a trampling, since it had only six hundred beds, and they had all been occupied. The people in the suffocating crowd inside the hsopital wept and cried, for Dr. Sasaki to hear, "*Sensei!* Doctor!" and the less seriously wounded came and pulled at his sleeve and begged him to come to the aid of the worse wounded. Tugged here and there in his stockinged feet, bewildered by the numbers, staggered by so much raw flesh, Dr. Sasaki lost all sense of profession and stopped working as a skilful surgeon and a sympathetic man; he became an automaton, mechanically wiping, daubing, winding, wiping, daubing, winding.

## In Defense of the Bombing

### *Document 12*

This essay by Paul Fussell reviews the continuing debate on the dropping of atomic bombs on Japan. Although written thirty-six years after the fact, the essay is an eloquent defense of the bombing of Hiroshima. The author, who was due to take part in the invasion of Japan, concludes that the bomb was necessary. He argues that a U.S. invasion of Japan would have been much more terrible than the bombings.

## 12 HIROSHIMA: A SOLDIER'S VIEW
**Paul Fussell**
**August 1981**

Many years ago in New York I saw on the side of a bus a whiskey ad which I've remembered all this time, for it's been for me a model of the brief poem. Indeed, I've come upon few short poems subsequently that evinced more genuine poetic talent. The ad consisted of two lines of "free verse," thus:

> In life, experience is the great teacher.
> In Scotch, Teacher's is the great experience.

For present purposes we can jettison the second line (licking our lips ruefully as it disappears), leaving the first to encapsulate a principle whose banality suggests that it enshrines a most useful truth. I bring up the matter this August, the 36th anniversary of the A-bombing of Hiroshima and Nagasaki, to focus on something suggested by the long debate about the ethics, if any, of that affair: namely, the importance of experience, sheer vulgar experience, in influencing, if not determining, one's views about the first use of the bomb. And the experience I'm talking about is that of having come to grips, face to face, with an enemy who designs your death. The experience is common to those in the infantry and the Marines and even the line Navy, to those, in short, who fought the Second World War mindful always that this mission was, as they were repeatedly told, "to close with the enemy and destroy him." I think there's something to be learned about that war, as well as about the tendency of historical memory unwittingly to resolve ambiguity, by considering some of the ways testimonies emanating from experience complicate attitudes about the cruel ending of that cruel war.

"What did you do in the Great War, Daddy?" The recruiting poster deserves ridicule and contempt, of course, but its question is embarrassingly relevant here. The problem is one that touches on the matter of social class in America. Most of those with firsthand experience of the war at its worst were relatively inarticulate and have remained silent. Few of those destined to be destroyed if the main islands had had to be invaded went on to become our most eloquent men of letters or our most impressive ethical theorists or professors of history or international jurists. The testimony of experience has come largely from rough diamonds like James Jones and William Manchester, who experienced the war in the infantry and the Marine Corps. Both would agree with the point, if not perhaps the tone, of a remark about Hiroshima made by a naval officer menaced by the kamikazes off Okinawa: "Those were the best burned women and children I ever saw." Anticipating objection from the inexperienced, Jones, in his Book *WWII,* is careful to precede his chapter on Hiroshima with one detailing the plans already in motion for the infantry assaults on the home islands of Kyushu, scheduled for November 1945, and ultimately Honshu. The forthcoming invasion of Kyushu, he notes, "was well into its collecting and stockpiling stages before the war ended." (The island of Saipan was designated a main ammunition and supply base for the invasion, and if you visit it today you can see some of the assembled stuff still sitting there.) "The assault troops were chosen and already in training," Jones reminds us, and he illuminates the situation by the light of experience:

> What it must have been like to some old-timer buck sergeant or staff sergeant who had been through Guadalcanal or Bouganville or the Philippines, to stand on some beach and watch this huge war machine beginning to stir and move all around him and know that he very likely had survived this far only to fall dead on the dirt of Japan's home islands, hardly bears thinking about.

On the other hand, John Kenneth Galbraith is persuaded that the Japanese would have surrendered by November without an invasion. He thinks the atom bombs were not decisive in bringing about the surrender and he implies that their use was unjustified. What did he do in the war? He was in the Office of Price Administration in Washington, and then he was director of the United States Strategic Bombing Survey. He was 37 in 1945, and I don't demand that he experience having his ass shot off. I just note that he didn't. In saying this I'm aware of its offensive implications *ad hominem.* But here I think that approach justified. What's at stake in an infantry assault is so entirely unthinkable to those without experience of one, even if they possess very wide-ranging imaginations and sympathies, that experience is crucial in this case.

A similar remoteness from experience, as well as a similar rationalistic abstraction, seems to lie behind the reaction of an anonymous reviewer of William Manchester's *Goodbye Darkness: A Memoir of the Pacific War* for the *New York Review of Books.* First of all the reviewer dislikes Manchester's calling the enemy Nips and Japs, but what really shakes him (her?) is this passage:

> After Biak the enemy withdrew to deep caverns. Rooting them out became a bloody business which reached its ultimate horrors in the last months of the war. You think

> of the lives which would have been lost in an invasion of Japan's home islands — a staggering number of Americans but millions more of Japanese — and you thank God for the atomic bomb.

Thank God for the atomic bomb. From this, "one recoils," says the reviewer. One does, doesn't one?

In an interesting exchange last year in the *New York Review of Books,* Joseph Alsop and David Joravsky set forth the by now familiar arguments on both sides of the debate. You'll be able to guess which sides they chose once you know that Alsop experienced capture by the Japanese at Hong Kong in 1942 and that Joravsky made no mortal contact with the Japanese: a young soldier, he was on his way to the Pacific when the war ended. The editors of the *New York Review* have given their debate the tendentious title "Was the Hiroshima Bomb Necessary?" — surely an unanswerable question (unlike "Was It Effective?") and one suggesting the intellectual difficulties involved in imposing *ex post facto* a rational ethics on this event. Alsop focuses on the power and fanaticism of War Minister Anami, who insisted that Japan fight to the bitter end, defending the main islands with the same means and tenacity with which it had defended Iwo and Okinawa. He concludes: "Japanese surrender could never have been obtained, at any rate without the honor-satisfying bloodbath envisioned by . . . Anami, if the hideous destruction of Hiroshima and Nagasaki had not finally galvanized the peace advocates into tearing up the entire Japanese book of rules." The Japanese planned to deploy the undefeated bulk of their ground forces, over two million men, plus 10,000 kamikaze planes, in a suicidal defense. That fact, says Alsop, makes it absurd to "hold the common view, by now hardly challenged by anyone, that the decision to drop the two bombs on Japan was wicked in itself, and that President Truman and all others who joined in making or who [like Oppenheimer] assented to this decision shared in the wickedness." And in explanation of "the two bombs" Alsop adds: "The true, climactic, and successful effort of the Japanese peace advocates . . . did not begin in deadly earnest until *after* the second bomb had destroyed Nagasaki. The Nagasaki bomb was thus the trigger to all the developments that led to peace."

Joravsky, now a professor of history at Northwestern, argues on the other hand that those who decided to use the bomb on cities betray defects of "reason and self-restraint." It all needn't have happened, he asserts, "if the US government had been willing to take a few more days and to be a bit more thoughtful in opening the age of nuclear warfare." But of course in its view it wasn't doing that: that's a historian's tidy hindsight. The government was ending the war conclusively, as well as irrationally remembering Pearl Harbor with a vengeance. It didn't know then what everyone knows now about leukemia and carcinoma and birth defects. History, as Eliot's "Gerontion" notes,

> . . . has many cunning passages, contrived corridors
> And issues, deceives with whispering ambitions,
> Guides us by vanities. . . .
> Think
> Neither fear nor courage saves us. Unnatural vices
> Are fathered by our heroism. Virtues
> Are forced upon us by our impudent crimes.

Understanding the past means feeling its pressure on your pulses and that's harder than Javorsky thinks.

The Alsop-Javorsky debate, which can be seen as reducing finally to a collision between experience and theory, was conducted with a certain civilized respect for evidence. Not so the way the new scurrilous agitprop *New Statesman* conceives those favoring the bomb and those opposing. They are, on the one hand, says Bruce Page, "the imperialist class-forces acting through Harry Truman," and, on the other, those representing "the humane, democratic virtues" — in short, "fascists" opposed to "populists." But ironically the bomb saved the lives not of any imperialists but only of the low and humble, the quintessentially democratic huddled masses — the conscripted enlisted men manning the fated invasion divisions. Bruce Page was nine years old when the war ended. For a man of that experience, phrases like "imperialist class-forces" come easily, and the issues look perfectly clear.

He's not the only one to have forgotten, if he ever knew, the savagery of the Pacific war. The dramatic postwar Japanese success at hustling and merchandising and tourism has (happily, in many ways) effaced for most people important elements of the assault context in which Hiroshima should be viewed. It is easy to forget what Japan was like before it was first destroyed and then humiliated, tamed, and constitutionalized by the West. "Implacable, treacherous, barbaric" — those were Admiral Halsey's characterizations of the enemy, and at the time few facing the Japanese would deny that they fit to a T. One remembers the captured American airmen locked for years in packing-crates, the prisoners decapitated, the gleeful use of bayonets on civilians. The degree to which Americans register shock and extraordinary shame about the Hiroshima bomb correlate closely with lack of information about the war.

And the savagery was not just on one side. There was much sadism and brutality — undeniably racist — on ours. No Marine was fully persuaded of his manly adequacy who didn't have a well-washed Japanese skull to caress and who didn't have a go at treating surrendering Japs as rifle targets. Herman Wouk remembers it correctly while analyzing Ensign Keith in *The Caine Mutiny:* "Like most of the naval executioners of Kwajalein, he seemed to regard the enemy as a species of animal pest." And the enemy felt the same way about us: "From the grim and desperate taciturnity with which the Japanese died, they seemed on their side to believe they were contending with an invasion of large armed ants." Hiroshima seems to follow in natural sequence: "This obliviousness on both sides to the fact that the opponents were human beings may perhaps be cited as the key to the many massacres of the Pacific war." Since the Japanese resisted so madly, let's pour gasoline into their emplacements and light it and shoot the people afire who try to get out. Why not? Why not blow them all up? Why not, indeed, drop a new kind of big bomb on them? Why allow one more American high school kid to see his intestines blown out of his body and spread before him in the dirt while he screams when we can end the whole thing just like that?

On Okinawa, only weeks before Hiroshima, 123,000 Japanese and Americans *killed* each other. "Just awful" was the comment not of some pacifist but of MacArthur. One million American casualties was his estimate of the cost of the forthcoming invasion. And that invasion was not just a hypothetical threat, as some theorists have argued. It was genuinely in train, as I know because I was to be in it. When the bomb ended the war I was in the 45th Infantry Division, which had been through the European war to the degree that it had needed to be reconstituted two or three times. We were in a staging area near Reims, ready to be shipped across the United States for final preparation in the Philippines. My division was to take part in the invasion of Honshu in March 1946. (The earlier invasion of Kyushu was to be carried out by 700,000 infantry already in the Pacific.) I was a 21-year-old second lieutenant leading a rifle platoon. Although still officially in one piece, in the German war I had already been wounded in the leg and back severely enough to be adjudged, after the war, 40 percent disabled. But even if my legs buckled whenever I jumped out of the back of the truck, my condition was held to be satisfactory for whatever lay ahead. When the bombs dropped and news began to circulate that "Operation Olympic" would not, after all, take place, that we would not be obliged to run up the beaches near Tokyo assault-firing while being mortared and shelled, for all the fake manliness of our facades we cried with relief and joy. We were going to live. We were going to grow up to adulthood after all. When the *Enola Gay* dropped its package, "There were cheers," says John Toland, "over the intercom; it meant the end of the war. . . ."

Experience whispers that the pity is not that we used the bomb to end the Japanese war but that it wasn't ready earlier to end the German one. If only it could have been rushed into production faster and dropped at the right moment on the Reich chancellery or Berchtesgaden or Hitler's military headquarters in East Prussia or—Wagnerian *coup de théâtre*—at Rommel's phony state funeral, most of the Nazi hierarchy could have been pulverized immediately, saving not just the embarrassment of the Nuremburg trials but the lives of about four million Jews, Poles, Slavs, gypsies, and other "subhumans," not to mention the lives and limbs of millions of Allied and Axis soldiers. If the bomb could have been ready even as late as July 1944, it could have reinforced the Von Stauffenberg plot and ended the war then and there. If the bomb had only been ready in time, the men of my infantry platoon would not have been killed and maimed.

All this is not to deny that like the Russian revolution, the atomic bombing of Japan was a vast historical tragedy, and every passing year magnifies the dilemma into which it has thrown the contemporary world. As with the Russian revolution there are two sides—that's why it's a tragedy rather than a disaster—and unless we are simple-mindedly cruel, like Bruce Page, we need to be painfully aware of both at once. . . .

The predictable stupidity, parochialism, and greed in the postwar international mismanagement of the whole nuclear problem should not tempt us to mis-imagine the circumstances of the bomb's first "use." Nor should our well-justified fears and suspicions occasioned by the capture of the nuclear business by the mendacious classes (cf. Three Mile Island) tempt us to infer retrospectively extraordinary corruption, cruelty, and swinishness in those who decided to drop the bomb. Times change. Harry Truman was not a fascist, but a democrat. He was as close to a real egalitarian as we've seen in high office for a very long time. He is the only president in my lifetime who ever had the experience of commanding a small unit of ground troops obliged to kill people. He knew better than his subsequent critics what he was doing. The past, which as always did not know the future, acted in ways that ask to be imagined before they are condemned. Or even before they are simplified.

## An Assessment of the Japanese Situation

### *Document 13*

After the war ended, the United States commissioned a study of the effects of strategic bombing. This excerpt concludes that Japan could have surrendered by the end of 1945 even if the atomic bombs had not been used. This survey has been used by critics of the atomic bombing of Japan to support their case.

### 13 JAPAN'S STRUGGLE TO END THE WAR 1946

Japan's will to resist, the core target of our assault, was supported mainly by military potential, production potential, morale of the people, and such political considerations of the leadership as the preservation of the Tenno system, etc. So long as these factors supported resistance they operated, of course, as impediments to surrender. Thus affecting the determination of Japan's leaders to continue the war was not alone the actual loss of an air force capable of defending the home islands, but the loss of hope that this air force could be replaced, let alone enlarged. It was not necessary for us to burn every city, to destroy every factory, to shoot down every airplane or sink every ship, and starve the people. It was enough to demonstrate that we were capable of doing all this — that we had the power and the intention of continuing to the end. In this fashion, those responsible for the decision to surrender felt the twin-impact of our attack which made them not only impotent to resist, but also destroyed any hope of future resistance.

The will of the political leaders to resist collapsed well before the will of the people as a whole. The leaders were, however, unwilling to move too far in advance of public opinion. At the time of surrender, even though there was little pressure toward surrender from the people, their confidence in victory had been thoroughly undermined and they accepted the Imperial rescript, perhaps with surprise, but not with active resistance as some of the leaders had feared.

One further point should be developed and stressed here. The political objective which existed in Japan lay exposed and vulnerable to air attack, which fact goes far toward explaining the true basis for unconditional surrender without invasion of the home islands. That vulnerability to air attack derived in part from the basic character of the war in its decisive phases. It turned out to be essentially a war to win air control over the Japanese homeland. This concept was not merely central to much of the strategy guiding our operations, but was thoroughly understood and feared by an effective sector of Japanese leaders who sought and achieved political power to terminate the war. By the summer and fall of 1944, and throughout the remainder of the war, the validity of their fear was being persuasively demonstrated by the application of our air power in its several roles. Loss of fleet and air forces, without which, as the leaders knew, no effective defense could be mounted, was almost entirely the result of air superiority. . . .

The Hiroshima and Nagasaki atomic bombs did not defeat Japan, nor by the testimony of the enemy leaders who ended the war did they persuade Japan to accept unconditional surrender. The Emperor, the Lord Privy Seal, the Prime Minister, the Foreign Minister, and the Navy Minister had decided as early as May of 1945 that the war should be ended even if it meant acceptance of defeat on allied terms. The War Minister and the two chiefs of staff opposed unconditional surrender. The impact of the Hiroshima attack was to bring further urgency and lubrication to the machinery of achieving peace, primarily by contributing to a situation which permitted the Prime Minister to bring the Emperor overtly and directly into a position where his decision for immediate acceptance of the Potsdam Declaration could be used to override the remaining objectors. Thus, although the atomic bombs changed no votes of the Supreme War Direction Council concerning the Potsdam terms, they did foreshorten the war and expedite the peace. . . .

There is little point in attempting more precisely to impute Japan's unconditional surrender to any one of the numerous causes which jointly and cumulatively were responsible for Japan's disaster. Concerning the absoluteness of her defeat there can be no doubt. The time lapse between military impotence and political acceptance of the inevitable might have been shorter had the political structure of Japan permitted a more rapid and decisive determination of national policies. It seems clear, however, that air supremacy and its later exploitation over Japan proper was the major factor which determined the timing of Japan's surrender and obviated any need for invasion.

Based on a detailed investigation of all the facts and supported by the testimony of the surviving Japanese leaders involved, it is the Survey's opinion that certainly prior to 31 December 1945, and in all probability prior to 1 November 1945, Japan would have surrendered even if the atomic bombs had not been dropped, even if Russia had not entered the war, and even if no invasion had been planned or contemplated.

# THE END OF WORLD WAR II

## Roosevelt, Truman, and the Soviet Union

### *Document 14*

In these excerpts from *Strategies of Containment,* an analysis of postwar U.S. national security policy, historian John Lewis Gaddis examines Roosevelt's attempts to preserve the Grand Alliance. He then goes on to analyze President Truman's attempts to cope with Soviet expansionist moves in Eastern Europe. Gaddis argues that very little could have been done by the Truman administration or the West to influence Stalin's policy in Eastern Europe.

## 14 A CRITICAL APPRAISAL OF POSTWAR AMERICAN NATIONAL SECURITY POLICY John Lewis Gaddis

"My children, it is permitted you in time of grave danger to walk with the devil until you have crossed the bridge." It was Franklin D. Roosevelt's version of an old Balkan proverb (sanctioned by the Orthodox Church, no less), and he liked to cite it from time to time during World War II to explain the use of questionable allies to achieve unquestionable objectives.[1] In all-out war, he believed, the ultimate end — victory — justified a certain broad-mindedness regarding means, nowhere more so than in reliance on Stalin's Russia to help defeat Germany and Japan. Allies of any kind were welcome enough in London and Washington during the summer of 1941; still the Soviet Union's sudden appearance in that capacity could not avoid setting off Faustian musings in both capitals. Winston Churchill's willingness to extend measured parliamentary accolades to the Devil if Hitler should invade Hell is well-known;* less familiar is Roosevelt's paraphrase of his proverb to an old friend, Joseph Davies: "I can't take communism nor can you, but to cross this bridge I would hold hands with the Devil."[2]

The imagery, in the light of subsequent events, was apt. Collaboration with the Soviet Mephistopheles helped the United States and Great Britain achieve victory over their enemies in a remarkably short time and with surprisingly few casualties, given the extent of the fighting involved. The price, though, was the rise of an even more powerful and less fathomable totalitarian state, and, as a consequence, an apparently perpetual condition of precarious uncertainty that has now many times outlasted the brief and uneasy alliance that brought it about.

"Containment," the term generally used to characterize American policy toward the Soviet Union during the postwar era, can be seen as a series of attempts to deal with the consequences of that World War II Faustian bargain: the idea has been to prevent the Soviet Union from using the power and position it won as a result of that conflict to reshape the postwar international order, a prospect that has seemed, in the West, no less dangerous than what Germany or Japan might have done had they had the chance. George F. Kennan coined the term in July 1947, when he called publicly for a "long-term, patient but firm and vigilant containment of Russian expansive tendencies,"[3]† but it would be an injustice to wartime policy-makers to imply, as has too often been done, that they were oblivious to the problem. In fact, "containment" was much on the minds of Washington officials from 1941 on; the difficulty was to mesh that long-term concern with the more immediate imperative of defeating the Axis. What Roosevelt, Truman, and their advisers sought was a way to win the war without compromising the objectives for which it was being fought; it was out of their successive failures to square that circle that Kennan's concept of "containment" eventually emerged. . . .

It is also the case that Roosevelt was not above using what a later generation would call "linkage" to ensure compliance with American postwar aims. His employment of economic and political pressure to speed the dismantling of the British Empire has recently been thoroughly documented.[4] No comparably blatant requirements were imposed on the Russians, probably because Roosevelt feared that the relationship, unlike the one with London, was too delicate to stand the strain.[5] Still, he did keep certain cards up his sleeve for dealing with Moscow after the war, notably the prospect of reconstruction assistance either through Lend-Lease or a postwar loan, together with a generous flow of reparations from Western-occupied Germany, all of which Washington would have been able to control in the light of Soviet behavior.[6] Also, intriguingly, there was Roosevelt's refusal, even after learning they knew of it, to tell the Russians about the atomic bomb, perhaps with a view to postwar bargaining.[7] This combination of counterweights and linkages is not what one would expect from a statesman assuming a blissfully serene postwar environment: although Roosevelt certainly hoped for such an outcome, he was too good a poker player to count on it.

But Roosevelt's main emphasis was on trying to make the Grand Alliance survive Hitler's defeat by creating relationships of mutual trust among its leaders. The focus of his concern — and indeed the only allied leader not already in some position of dependency on the United States — was Stalin. F.D.R. has been criticized for thinking that he could use his personal charm to "get through" to the Soviet autocrat, whose resistance to such blandishments was legendary.[8] But, as with so much of Roosevelt's diplomacy, what seems at first shallow and superficial becomes less so upon reflection. The President realized that Stalin was the only man in the Soviet Union with the authority to modify past attitudes of hostility; however discouraging the prospect of "getting through," there was little point in dealing with anyone below him.[9] And it is worth noting that improvements in Soviet-American relations, when they have occurred in the past three-and-a-half decades, have generally done so when some basis of mutual respect, if not trust, existed at the top: examples come to mind of Eisenhower and Khrushchev after the 1955 Geneva summit, Kennedy and Khrushchev

* "If Hitler invaded Hell I would make at least a favorable reference to the Devil in the House of Commons." (Winston S. Churchill, *The Grand Alliance* [Boston: 1950], pp. 370-71.)

† Kennan had used the term at least once previously, assuring a State Department audience in September 1946 that his recommendations "should enable us, if our policies are wise and nonprovocative, to contain them [the Russians] both militarily and politically for a long time to come." (Quoted in George F. Kennan, *Memoirs: 1925–1950* [Boston: 1967], p. 304.)

after the Cuban missile crisis, and Nixon and Brezhnev during the early 1970's. Winning Stalin's trust may have been impossible — no one, with the curious exception of Hitler between 1939 and 1941, appears to have managed it. But making the attempt, given the uncertainties of postwar politics and diplomacy, was neither an unreasonable nor an ingenuous enterprise.

Like any statesman, though, Roosevelt was pursuing multiple objectives; building a friendly peacetime relationship with the Soviet Union was only one of them. As often happens, other priorities got in the way. For example, Roosevelt's second front strategy, designed not so much to weaken Russia as to avoid weakening the United States, could not help but create suspicions in Moscow that Washington was in fact seeking containment by exhaustion.[10] These dark misgivings survived even the D-Day landings: as late as April 1945 Stalin was warning subordinates that the Americans and British might yet make common cause with the Germans; that same month the Red Army began constructing *defensive* installations in Central Europe.[11]

Another of Roosevelt's priorities was to win domestic support for his postwar plans, and thereby to avoid Wilson's repudiation of 1919–1920. To do this, he became convinced of the need to moderate his own somewhat harsh approach to the task of peacekeeping: the country was not ready, Speaker of the House Sam Rayburn told him late in 1942, for a settlement to be enforced through blockades and bombing.[12] Roosevelt sought, accordingly, to integrate the great power condominium his strategic instincts told him would be necessary to preserve world order, on the one hand, with the ideals his political instincts told him would be necessary at home to overcome objections to an "unjust" peace, on the other.[13] Idealism, in Roosevelt's mind, could serve eminently realistic ends.

It would be a mistake, then, to write off Roosevelt's concern for self-determination in Eastern Europe as mere window-dressing. Although prepared to see that part of the world fall within Moscow's sphere of influence, he expected as well that as fears of Germany subsided, the Russians would moderate the severity of measures needed to maintain their position there. Otherwise, he was convinced, it would be impossible to "sell" the resulting settlement to the American people.* But, like Henry Kissinger in somewhat different circumstances thirty years later, Roosevelt thus found himself in a situation in which domestic support for what he had negotiated depended upon the exercise of discretion and restraint in the Kremlin. Those tendencies were no more prevalent then than later; as a consequence, a gap developed between what F.D.R. thought the public would tolerate and what the Russians would accept — a gap papered over, at Yalta, by fragile compromises.

Competing priorities therefore undercut Roosevelt's efforts to win Stalin's trust: to that extent, his strategy was flawed. And even if that had not happened, there is reason to wonder whether F.D.R.'s approach would have worked in any event, given the balefully suspicious personality of the Soviet autocrat. But there are, at times, justifications for directing flawed strategies at inauspicious targets, and World War II may have been one of these. Certainly alternatives to the policies actually followed contained difficulties as well. And there are grounds for thinking that Roosevelt might not have continued his open-handed approach once the war had ended: his quiet incorporation of counter-weights and linkages into his strategy suggests just that possibility. One is left, then, where one began: with the surface impression of casual, even frivolous, superficiality, and yet with the growing realization that darker, more cynical, but more perceptive instincts lay not far beneath. . . .

F.D.R.'s death cleared the way for a revision of strategy he himself would probably have executed in time, but not in as abrupt and confused a manner as was actually done. Harry S. Truman, totally unbriefed as to what Roosevelt had been trying to do, did the natural thing and consulted the late President's advisers. But those most directly associated with Soviet affairs, notably Harriman, had been trying to stiffen Roosevelt's position; now, with a new and untutored chief executive in the White House, they redoubled their efforts at "education." Eager to appear decisive and in command, Truman accepted this instruction with an alacrity that unsettled even those providing it, lecturing the Soviet foreign minister in person, and his distant master by cable, in a manner far removed from the graceful ambiguities of his predecessor.[14] The result was ironic: Truman embraced a *quid pro quo* approach in the belief that he was implementing Roosevelt's policy, but in doing so he convinced the Russians that he had changed it. F.D.R.'s elusiveness continued to bedevil Soviet-American relations even after his death.

In fact (and despite his 1941 remark about letting Germans and Russians kill each other off), Truman was no more prepared to abandon the possibility of an accommodation with Moscow than were Harriman and Deane. He firmly rejected Churchill's advice to deploy Anglo-American military forces in such a way as to keep the Russians out of as much of Germany as possible. He sent Harry Hopkins to Moscow in May of 1945 in part to repair the damage his own brusqueness had done. Long

* It has been pointed out, correctly, that presidents have a considerable capacity to shape public opinion: the implication is that Roosevelt could have "educated" the public to accept a settlement based on classic spheres of influences. (See Ralph B. Levering, *American Opinion and the Russian Alliance, 1939–1945* [Chapel Hill: 1976], pp. 204–7.) But what is important here is not the President's theoretical power to manipulate public opinion, but his actual *perception* of that power. And the evidence is strong that Roosevelt habitually under-estimated his influence in that regard, as far as foreign affairs were concerned.

after relations with Stalin went sour, he continued to seek the counsel of those sympathetic to the Soviet Union, notably Henry Wallace and Joseph E. Davies. The new President harbored a healthy skepticism toward all totalitarian states: ideology, he thought, whether communist or fascist, was simply an excuse for dictatorial rule. But, like Roosevelt, he did not see totalitarianism in itself as precluding normal relations. Not surprisingly in the light of his own background, the analogy of big city political bosses in the United States came most easily to mind: their methods might not be delicate or fastidious, but one could work with them, so long as they kept their word.[15]

Truman found a kindred spirit in James F. Byrnes, whom he appointed Secretary of State shortly after taking office. An individual of vast experience in domestic affairs but almost none in diplomacy, Byrnes believed in applying to this new realm an assumption that had worked well for him at home: nations, he thought, like individuals or interest groups, could always reach agreement on difficult issues if a sufficient willingness to negotiate and to compromise existed on both sides. A *quid pro quo* strategy was as natural for Byrnes as for Truman, then; the new Secretary of State observed that dealing with the Russians was just like dealing with the United States Senate: "You build a post office in their state and they'll build a post office in our state."[16]

The new administration thought it had leverage over the Russians in several respects. Harriman himself had stressed the importance of postwar reconstruction assistance, which the United States would be able to control, whether through Lend-Lease, a rehabilitation loan, or reparations shipments from its occupation zone in Germany. Roosevelt had been leaning toward use of this leverage at the time of his death; Truman quickly confirmed that unconditional aid would not be extended past the end of the fighting. Lend-Lease would be phased out, and postwar loans and reparations shipments would be tied, at least implicitly, to future Soviet political cooperation.[17]* Publicity was another form of leverage: the administration assumed that the Kremlin was still sensitive to "world opinion," and that by calling attention openly to instances of Soviet unilateralism, it could get the Russians to back down.[18] Then there was the ultimate sanction of the atomic bomb: Byrnes, though not all his colleagues in the administration, apparently believed that the simple presence of this awesome weapon in the American arsenal would make the Russians more manageable than in the past; at a minimum, he wanted to hold back commitments to seek the international control of atomic energy as a bargaining chip for use in future negotiations.[19]

But none of these attempts to apply leverage worked out as planned. The Russians were never dependent enough on American economic aid to make substantial concessions to get it: intelligence reports had long indicated that such aid, if extended, would have speeded reconstruction by only a matter of months. Another difficulty was that key Congressmen, whose support would have been necessary for the passage of any loan, quickly made it clear that they would demand in return nothing less than free elections and freedom of speech inside the Soviet Union, and the abandonment of its sphere of influence in Eastern Europe.[20] Publicity, directed against Soviet violations of the Yalta agreements in that part of the world, produced no greater success: when Byrnes warned that he might have to make public a report on conditions in Rumania and Bulgaria prepared by the American publisher, Mark Ethridge, Stalin, with understandable self-confidence, threatened to have his own "impartial" observer, the Soviet journalist Ilya Ehrenburg, prepare and release his own report on those countries.[21] The Russians dealt effectively with the atomic bomb by simply appearing to ignore it, except for a few heavy-handed cocktail party jokes by a tipsy Molotov. In the meantime, domestic pressures had forced Truman to commit the United States to the principle of international control before Byrnes had even attempted to extract a *quid pro quo* from Moscow.[22]

By the time of the Moscow foreign ministers' conference in December 1945, Byrnes had come to much the same conclusion that Roosevelt had a year earlier: that the only way to reconcile the American interest in self-determination with the Soviet interest in security was to negotiate thinly disguised agreements designed to cloak the reality of Moscow's control behind a facade of democratic procedures.* But that approach, manifested in the form of token concessions by the Russians on Bulgaria and Rumania, came across at home as appeasement: as a result, Byrnes found himself under attack from both the President and Congress, upon his return, for having given up too much.[23] The *quid pro quo* strategy, by early 1946, had not only failed to produce results; it had become a domestic political liability as well.

The *quid pro quo* approach proved unsuccessful for several reasons. One was the difficulty of making "sticks" and "carrots" commensurate with concessions to be demanded from the other side. The "sticks" the United States had available were either unimpressive, as was the case with publicity, or unusable, as in the case of the atomic bomb. The major "carrot," economic aid, was

* The Potsdam protocol, upon American insistence, specified that the Soviet Union was to receive 10 percent of such industrial equipment as was "unnecessary" for the functioning of the postwar German economy, but the Western powers would make the determination as to what was necessary and what was not. (*Foreign Relations of the United States:* [hereafter *FR:*] *Potsdam,* II, 1485–86.)

* It should be noted that the Russians, in return, extracted a token concession from the United States which appeared to broaden, but in fact did not, their role in the occupation of Japan.

important to the Russians, but not to the point of justifying the concessions that would have been required to obtain it. Another difficulty with the strategy was the problem of coordination. Bargaining implies the ability to control precisely the combination of pressures and inducements to be applied, but that in turn implies central direction, something not easy to come by in a democracy in the best of circumstances, and certainly not during the first year of an inexperienced and badly organized administration. Extraneous influences — Congress, the press, public opinion, bureaucracies, even personalities — tended to intrude upon the bargaining process, making the alignment of conditions to be met with incentives to be offered awkward, to say the least.

But the major difficulty was simply the Soviet Union's imperviousness to external influences. The *quid pro quo* strategy had assumed, as had Roosevelt's, that Soviet behavior could be affected from the outside: the only difference had been over method and timing. In fact, though, experience showed that there was remarkably little the West could do, in the short term, to shape Stalin's decisions: the Soviet dictator maintained tight control in a mostly self-sufficient country, with little knowledge or understanding of, much less susceptibility to, events in the larger world.

## Notes

1. Roosevelt to Churchill, November 19, 1942, in Francis L. Loewenhein, Harold D. Langley, and Manfred Jonas, eds., *Roosevelt and Churchill: Their Secret Wartime Correspondence* (New York: 1975), p. 282. George C. Herring credits Representative Cliffton Woodrum of Virginia with the proverb. See his *Aid to Russia, 1941–1946: Strategy, Diplomacy, the Origins of the Cold War* (New York: 1973), p. 22.
2. Quoted in Keith David Eagles, "Ambassador Joseph D. Davies and American-Soviet Relations, 1937–1941" (Ph.D. dissertation, University of Washington, 1966), p. 328.
3. "X," "The Sources of Soviet conduct," *Foreign Affairs* XXV (July 1947), 575.
4. William Roger Louis, *Imperialism at Bay: The United States and the Decolonization of the British Empire, 1941–1945* (New York: 1978); see also the appropriate chapters in Thorne, *Allies of a Kind.*
5. Herring, *Aid to Russia,* pp. 38, 47–48, 86.
6. Ibid., pp. 144–78; John Lewis Gaddis, *The United States and the Origins of the Cold War, 1941–1947* (New York), pp. 128–29, 197.
7. Martin J. Sherwin, *A World Destroyed; The Atomic Bomb and the Grand Alliance* (New York: 1975), pp. 67–140. See also two articles by Barton J. Bernstein: "The Quest for Security: American Foreign Policy and International Control of Atomic Energy, 1942–1946." *Journal of American History,* LX(March 1974), 1003–44; and "Roosevelt, Truman, and the Atomic Bomb, 1941–1945: A Reinterpretation," *Political Science Quarterly,* XC(Spring, 1975), 23–69.
8. See, for example, Gaddis Smith, *American Diplomacy During the Second World War, 1941–1945* (New York: 1965), pp. 11, 14–16.
9. This point is well made in Arthur Schlesinger, Jr., "Origins of the Cold War," *Foreign Affairs,* XLVI(October 1967), 48–49.
10. Burns, *Roosevelt: The Soldier of Freedom,* p. 374.
11. Mastny, *Russia's Road to the Cold War,* pp. 270–71. See also Bradley F. Smith and Elena Agarossi, *Operation Sunrise; The Secret Surrender* (New York: 1979), for an up-to-date account of American efforts to arrange for the secret surrender of German forces in Italy, another incident that aroused Stalin's deep suspicions.
12. Wallace diary, November 30, 1942, Blum, ed., *The Price of Vision,* p. 138.
13. Gaddis, *The United States and the Origins of the Cold War,* pp. 23–31, 149–71.
14. Gaddis, *The United States and the Origins of the Cold War,* pp. 200–6, 217–20, 230–33. See also Yergin, *Shattered Peace,* pp. 69–86; and Robert J. Donovan. *Conflict and Crisis: The Presidency of Harry S. Truman* (New York: 1977), pp. 34–42.
15. John Lewis Gaddis, "Harry S. Truman and the Origins of Containment," in Frank J. Merli and Theodore A. Wilson, eds., *Makers of American Diplomacy* (New York: 1974), pp. 503–6.
16. Quoted in Patricia Dawson Ward, *The Threat of Peace: James F. Byrnes and the Council of Foreign Ministers, 1945–1946* (Kent, Ohio: 1979), p. 22.
17. Gaddis, *The United States and the Origins of the Cold War,* pp. 215–24, 240–41; Herring, *Aid to Russia,* pp. 180–236; Thomas G. Paterson, *Soviet-American Confrontation: Postwar Reconstruction and the Origins of the Cold War* (Baltimore: 1973), pp. 33–46.
18. Ward, *The Threat of Peace,* pp. 31, 34; Davis, *The Cold War Begins,* pp. 288–334; Geir Lundestad, *The American Non-Policy Towards Eastern Europe, 1943–1947* (Oslo: 1978), pp. 235–48, 271–78.
19. Minutes, meeting of the secretaries of state, war, and navy, October 10, 1945. *FR: 1945,* II, 56. See also the Stettinius diary, September 28, 1945, in Thomas M. Campbell and George C. Herring, Jr., eds., *The Diaries of Edward R. Stettinius, Jr., 1943–1946* (New York: 1946), pp. 427–28.
20. Gaddis, *The United States and the Origins of the Cold War,* p. 260. See also OSS R & A 2060, "Russian Reconstruction and Postwar Foreign Trade Developments," September 9, 1944, Office of Intelligence Research Files, Department of State Records, Record Group 59, National Archives.

21. Memorandum, Byrnes-Stalin meeting, December 23, 1945, *FR: 1945,* II, 752–53. For the Ethridge report, see Davis, *The Cold War Begins,* pp. 322–26.
22. Ward, *The Threat of Peace,* pp. 48–49, 71; Gaddis, *The United States and the Origins of the Cold War,* pp. 268–73.
23. Yergin, *Shattered Peace,* pp. 147–62; Ward, *The Threat of Peace,* pp. 50–77; Gaddis, *The United States and the Origins of the Cold War,* pp. 273–96.

# Truman's Search for a Policy

## *Document 15*

In these excerpts from *National Security and the Nuclear Dilemma,* Richard Smoke, a national security specialist, describes the breakdown of the Grand Alliance. He focuses on the Allies' differences over Eastern Europe and on the Truman administration's search for a coherent policy for dealing with the Soviet challenge.

## 15 THE EAST-WEST DISCORD BEGINS Richard Smoke

### A New Conflict Begins to Emerge

The weakest point in this bright dream was that every thing depended upon maintaining unified purpose among the victorious wartime Allies. Each of the great powers seated on the Security Council held a veto over its decisions. Without this provision the whole concept would never have been accepted by Congress, nor by the other powers. Any permanent member could prevent the world organization from taking action that it regarded as detrimental to its own interests by wielding its veto in the Security Council. The system of collective security, therefore, would continue to work only so long as the great powers on the Council considered their interests to be in harmony and could continue to work in unison.

It took less than a year for this system to begin to break down. A rift opened and steadily widened between the USSR and the Western democracies, for many reasons. Since the democracies dominated the Council (and in those days, the UN as a whole) the Soviets feared that the international organization would take sides against them in the growing discord. To prevent it they found themselves saying "nyet" more and more often in Security Council meetings. Soon it became clear to all that the collective security concept, as conceived by the United States, was breaking on the wall of Russian vetoes. By the beginning of 1947, the United States government was looking for another approach to security.

To be sure, some conflict had begun among the Allies even before the war had ended. Churchill, who had always been staunchly anticommunist, had been suspicious of long-range Soviet motives all along. In private conversations with Roosevelt he had argued that the main American-British assault on Hitler's Europe should move up through the Balkans, rather than on the shorter path from Normandy across France, to prevent the Red Army from seizing all of Eastern Europe on its way toward Germany. Roosevelt, the final arbiter by right of commanding the larger forces, had overruled him, partly to avoid jeopardizing Allied unity.

Even so, before the end of the war Russia and the Western Allies had sharp disagreements over a number of issues, including the postwar government of Poland. Early in 1945 the Soviets established a provisional government there, a government quite different from the Polish government-in-exile that in 1939 had fled the Nazis to London, and, with Western support, claimed still to be the legitimate government of Poland. After the European war was over the Soviet-installed provisional government was made permanent despite Western objections. More and more disagreements regarding eastern Europe, Germany, and other matters began developing between the USSR and the democracies.

This is not the place to discuss in detail the many events, motives and perceptions, stretching over years, that led to a hostile and fearful state of cold war between the Soviets and the Western nations led by the United States. The story is a complicated one, with many interpretations, and even in its standard Western version demands a lengthy treatment to be presented adequately. The story is also somewhat controversial — or it has been. Two decades later an entire literature was to flower in the West, offering a "revisionist" interpretation of these events that argued that Soviet intentions were unaggressive and that the cold war was caused partly (or in some versions, entirely) by unnecessary belligerence on the part of the United States. More recent and balanced scholarship suggests that the onset of the cold war is best seen as a tragedy of misperceptions on both sides. Soviet actions probably had primarily — not exclusively — a defensive and self-protective motive. Yet these actions were such that they would inevitably be seen as dangerously aggressive by Americans and most Europeans, who were sincere in looking to their own defense. Let us sketch briefly, in the remainder of this chapter, only the bare outlines of how these misperceptions occurred and the rift between the Soviets and the Western allies developed.

### The East-West Discord Begins

When World War II ended, the Soviet Union, unlike the United States, did not demobilize its army. Instead, most of the Red Army remained in place in those portions of Europe which it had occupied. The United States enjoyed a monopoly on atomic weapons, and the United States and Britain withdrew nearly all their forces from France, Belgium, and other countries liberated from the Nazis, and kept units only in occupied Germany. The Russians continued to occupy not only their portion of Germany but also all the countries of eastern Europe, with the exception of Czechoslovakia, from which they shortly withdrew. These countries were not permitted to choose their own governments. Instead, governments controlled by local Communist parties were installed and maintained by the power of the Red Army in Hungary, Romania, Bulgaria, and Albania as well as Poland.

As the events of late 1945 and 1946 showed ever more clearly what was happening in Europe, the United States and Britain protested, to the UN and through diplomatic channels, but to no avail. The wartime Allies had worked out few definite arrangements for postwar Europe, partly because no one had known when Nazi Germany would surrender or what the European situation would be at that point. Also, no one had wanted to divert much attention from the consuming, immediate problems of winning the war to difficult and potentially divisive questions.

At the Tehran Conference and elsewhere the Allied leaders had agreed in general terms, and publicly declared, that all European countries liberated from the Nazis would be granted freedom and self-determination. Presumably this applied to eastern Europe as well. However, Roosevelt and Churchill had also informally agreed with Stalin that, by reason of geography, the Soviet Union would need regimes in eastern Europe that were friendly to the USSR. The Western leaders *hoped* that this consideration and the declarations about freedom and self-determination would not prove to be inconsistent. To Stalin, though, this informal understanding meant more than the propagandistic statements of idealistic principles, and in any case he was not about to give up, after the war, the control over eastern Europe that the Red Army's victory over the Wehrmacht had given him.

In retrospect it seems fairly clear that Stalin was mainly after a protective layer of small nations that could serve as a buffer between the USSR and the West. This essentially defensive motive was not well understood in Western countries at the time, nor for some time afterward. Russia had always been in a painfully insecure, even precarious, position. As Louis Halle points out in his insightful book *The Cold War As History*, the experience of the Russian people over the centuries had been the exact opposite of the American experience. Americans had always been unusually *secure*, whereas the Russians had always been unusually *insecure*. During the Middle Ages they had been overrun repeatedly by hordes of barbarian invaders who came out of central Asia to put the torch to Russian cities and towns, and who exacted tribute for long periods. In its formative era the Russian nation had almost been snuffed out several times.

More recently the attacks had come, time after time, from the west. Nature provided no natural defenses there; an unbroken plain stretches from France all the way across Europe and deep into Russia beyond Moscow. In the seventeenth century Poland had conquered and ruled much of Russia and burned down Moscow. When after much sacrifice the Poles were ejected and subdued, new threats had emerged — from Prussia, Sweden, the Austrian Empire, and from further west. Early in the 19th century Napoleon had invaded, and destroyed much of the capital, St. Petersburg. In World War I Russia had endured terrible casualties, worse than those of any other nation, and in 1917 had been compelled to surrender to the enemy. Only three years later the new Soviet regime found itself at war on several fronts with "armies of intervention" that were sponsored, paid for, equipped, and to some extent manned by Western countries. Ultimately these "white" armies failed to unseat the "reds" and reestablish a counterrevolutionary regime, but at several moments it was touch and go. In less than a generation Germany attacked again, more terribly than ever. Most of the industrialized part of the country was overrun and destroyed and some *twenty million* Russian soldiers and civilians lost their lives. This was a scale of death and destruction almost unimaginable for Westerners, and especially for Americans, whose homeland had scarcely ever been touched by any enemy.

In light of this history it is not surprising that after the war Stalin was determined that this should *never* happen again. By retaining a layer of nations on his border whose governments he could control, he established a barrier against new onslaughts from the west. His Communist ideology told him that the capitalist countries were bent on the destruction of the homeland of communism. The lessons of centuries of Russian insecurity and ideology together drove him to keep potential enemies as far away as possible and his neighbors under control.

Even so, had circumstances been a little different Stalin might not have insisted that the eastern European governments be entirely Communist. He did not do so in the case of Finland, which the Soviets also wished to use as a buffer state. Finland in the 1940s had a canny diplomat, and subsequently prime minister, in Juho Paasikivi. He skillfully negotiated agreements with the Soviets by which Finland was freed of Soviet occupation and permitted substantial (although not complete) freedom in its internal affairs, in return for Soviet control over its foreign policy. Stalin might have liked to find statesmen who could carry off a similar tightrope act in the other eastern European countries. He remarked at one point, discussing the problem of Poland, that what was needed was a Polish version of Paasikivi.

But the east Europeans were more thoroughly inundated with Red Army troops than were the Finns. They were also less patient and experienced with appeasement of their huge neighbor. With the exception of the Bulgarians, who are closely related to the Russians ethnically, they hated and feared the prospect of Russian hegemony. History had already given them as much taste of it as they wished: the czars had partitioned and continuously occupied Poland with troops, had ruthlessly put down the popular Hungarian revolution of 1848, and in many other ways had threatened and oppressed eastern Europe. There was no reason to expect more kindness from the new Soviet masters of a Russia grown even more preponderant in power.

A "Finnish solution" to the problem of eastern Europe was not possible. As the populations began to resist, the local Communists had to take strong-arm measures to ensure a pro-Soviet government, such as using force to limit the role of non-Communist political groups in the governmental process. These measures generated more popular resistance, hence stronger measures of control, and so on, until there was no alternative left for the Communists but totalitarian regimes, equipped with secret police and backed by the Russian army, which took up permanent residence.

This, in turn, was very different indeed from what the Americans and the other Western allies had intended. Insofar as they had thought about eastern Europe at all, they had expected it to turn out after the war somewhat as Finland did: subservient to Moscow in foreign affairs but largely free in internal affairs. Certainly they had not intended (though some pessimists had feared) totalitarian police states and a permanent Soviet occupation.

From the Western point of view this clearly was aggression. The perception was reinforced when the Soviets tried to make permanent their occupation of the northern part of Iran, begun during the war as a defensive measure with Western agreement. Again the Soviets wanted a buffer zone. In this case, strong Western protest compelled a withdrawal.

People in the West were suspicious of any events that reminded them of the history of Nazi Germany. The image of totalitarian aggression was vivid in everyone's mind, and it was easy to suppose that another totalitarian regime was behaving similarly. People began to fear that the USSR, like Nazi Germany, would never set any limit to its ambitions and would have to be stopped. The possibility of a defensive motive for Soviet behavior was overlooked. Where it was recognized, it often met the rejoinder that Hitler too had asserted defensive justifications for German aggression.

During an American tour in 1946, Churchill gave a speech in Missouri in which he declared that

> From Stettin in the Baltic to Trieste in the Adriatic an iron curtain has descended across the continent . . . I do not believe that Soviet Russia desires war. What they desire is the fruits of war and the indefinite expansion of their power and doctrines . . .

The U.S. government was still hoping at that time to make the United Nations work, and did not accept Churchill's suggestion of a Western military alliance against Russia, but his "iron curtain" phrase passed into the language.

## Truman's Meeting with Molotov About Poland

### *Document 16*

**Early in his presidency, Truman met with Soviet Foreign Minister Molotov to discuss Poland. In this selection from his memoirs, the president discusses the "get tough" stance he took with the Soviet diplomat. Sharp words were exchanged, and Molotov said, "I have never been talked to like that in my life."**

### 16 MEMOIRS
### Harry S Truman

In connection with Molotov's visit I held an important conference at two o'clock with my chief diplomatic and military advisers. Those present were Secretary of State Stettinius, Secretary of War Stimson, Secretary of the Navy Forrestal, Admiral Leahy, General Marshall, Admiral King, Assistant Secretary of State Dunn, Ambassador Harriman, General Deane, and Mr. Bohlen.

We discussed Russia and the Polish problem, and Stettinius reported that though Molotov had arrived Sunday in apparent good spirits, which he had maintained even after his Blair House talk with me, overnight the atmosphere had changed. At the evening meeting with Eden in the State Department great difficulties had developed over the Polish question. Moreover, a continuance of the foreign ministers' meeting this morning had produced no improvement. In fact, a complete deadlock had been reached on the subject of carrying out the Yalta agreement on Poland.

The Secretary pointed out once more that the Lublin, or Warsaw, government was not representative of the

Polish people and that it was now clear that the Russians intended to try to force this puppet government upon the United States and England. He added that it had been made plain to Molotov how seriously the United States regarded this matter and how much public confidence would be shaken by failure to carry out the Crimea decision.

It was now obvious, I said, that our agreements with the Soviet Union had so far been a one-way street and that this could not continue. I told my advisers that we intended to go on with the plans for San Francisco, and if the Russians did not wish to join us, that would be too bad. Then, one by one, I asked each of those present to state his views.

Secretary Stimson said that this whole difficulty with the Russians over Poland was new to him, and he felt it was important to find out what the Russians were driving at. In the big military matters, he told us, the Soviet government had kept its word and the military authorities of the United States had come to count on it. In fact, he said they had often done better than they had promised. On that account he felt that it was important to find out what motives they had in connection with these border countries and what their ideas of independence and democracy were in areas they regarded as vital to the Soviet Union.

Mr. Stimson remarked that the Russians had made a good deal of trouble on minor military matters and it had sometimes been necessary in these cases to teach them manners. In this greater matter, however, it was his belief that without fully understanding how seriously the Russians took this Polish question we might be heading into very dangerous waters, and that their viewpoint was undoubtedly influenced by the fact that before World War I most of Poland had been controlled by Russia.

Secretary Forrestal expressed the view that this difficulty over Poland could not be treated as an isolated incident — that there had been many evidences of the Soviet desire to dominate adjacent countries and to disregard the wishes of her allies. It was his belief that for some time the Russians had been under the impression that we would not object if they took over all of Eastern Europe, and he said it was his profound conviction that if the Russians were to be rigid in their attitude we had better have a showdown with them now rather than later.

Ambassador Harriman, in replying to Mr. Stimson's question about issues and motives, said he felt that when Stalin and Molotov had returned to Moscow after Yalta they had learned more of the situation in Poland and had realized how shaky the provisional government was. On that account they had come to realize that the introduction of any genuine Polish leader such as Mikolajczyk would probably mean the elimination of the Soviet handpicked crop of leaders. It was his belief, therefore, that the real issue was whether we were to be a party to a program of Soviet domination of Poland. He said obviously we were faced with the possibility of a break with the Russians, but he felt that, properly handled, it might still be avoided.

At this point I explained that I had no intention of delivering an ultimatum to Mr. Molotov — that my purpose was merely to make clear the position of this government.

Mr. Stimson then said he would like to know how far the Russian reaction to a strong position on Poland would go. He said he thought that the Russians perhaps were being more realistic than we were in regard to their own security.

Admiral Leahy, in response to a question from me, observed that he had left Yalta with the impression that the Soviet government had no intention of permitting a free government to operate in Poland and that he would have been surprised had the Russians behaved any differently. In his opinion, the Yalta agreement was susceptible of two interpretations. He added that he felt it was a serious matter to break with the Russians but that he believed we should tell them that we stood for a free and independent Poland.

Stettinius then read the part of the Yalta decision relating to the formation of the new government and the holding of free elections and said he felt that this was susceptible of only one interpretation.

General Marshall said he was not familiar with the political aspects of the Polish issues. He said from the military point of view the situation in Europe was secure but that we hoped for Soviet participation in the war against Japan at a time when it would be useful to us. The Russians had it within their power to delay their entry into the Far Eastern war until we had done all the dirty work. He was inclined to agree with Mr. Stimson that the possibility of a break with Russia was very serious.

Mr. Stimson observed that he agreed with General Marshall and that he felt the Russians would not yield on the Polish question. He said we had to understand that outside the United States, with the exception of Great Britain, there were few countries that understood free elections; that the party in power always ran the elections, as he well knew from his experience in Nicaragua.

Admiral King inquired whether the issue was the invitation to the Lublin government to San Francisco.

I answered that that was a settled matter and not the issue. The issue was the execution of agreements entered into between this government and the Soviet Union. I said that I intended to tell Mr. Molotov that we expected Russia to carry out the Yalta decision as we were prepared to do for our part.

Ambassador Harriman then remarked that while it was true that the Soviet Union had kept its big agreements on military matters, those were decisions it had already reached by itself, but on other military matters it was impossible to say they had lived up to their commitments. For example, over a year ago they had agreed to start on preparations for collaboration in the Far Eastern war, but none of these had been carried out.

General Deane said he felt that the Soviet Union would enter the Pacific war as soon as it was able, regardless of what happened in other fields. He felt that the Russians had to do this because they could not afford too long a period of letdown for their people, who were tired. He said he was convinced after his experience in Moscow that if we were afraid of the Russians we would get nowhere, and he felt that we should be firm when we were right.

I thanked the military leaders and said I had their points of view well in mind. Then I asked Stettinius, Harriman, Dunn and Bohlen to stay behind to work out subjects for my next talk with Molotov, which was scheduled for five-thirty.

When Molotov arrived, Secretary Stettinius, Ambassador Harriman, Mr. Bohlen, and Admiral Leahy were with me in my office. Molotov was accompanied by Ambassador Gromyko and interpreter Pavlov.

Unlike the evening before, there was little protocol, and after greeting the Russian Foreign Minister and his associates, I went straight to the point. I was sorry to learn, I said, that no progress had been made in solving the Polish problem.

Mr. Molotov responded that he also regretted that fact.

I told him that the proposals which were contained in the joint message from Churchill and me and which had been transmitted to Moscow on April 16 were eminently fair and reasonable. We had gone as far as we could to meet the proposals of the Soviet government as expressed in the message from Marshal Stalin on April 7. The United States Government, I pointed out, could not agree to be a party to the formation of a Polish government, which was not representative of all Polish democratic elements. I said bluntly that I was deeply disappointed that the Soviet government had not held consultations with representatives of the Polish government other than the officials of the Warsaw regime.

I told Molotov that the United States was determined, together with other members of the United Nations, to go ahead with plans for the world organization, no matter what difficulties or differences might arise with regard to other matters. I pointed out that the failure of the three principal allies who had borne the brunt of the war to carry out the Crimea decision with regard to Poland would cast serious doubt upon their unity of purpose in postwar collaboration.

I explained to Molotov that in Roosevelt's last message to Marshal Stalin on April 1 the late President had made it plain that no policy in the United States, whether foreign or domestic, could succeed unless it had public confidence and support. This, I pointed out, applied in the field of economic as well as political collaboration. In this country, I said, legislative appropriations were required for any economic measures in the foreign field, and I had no hope of getting such measures through Congress unless there was public support for them. I expressed the hope that the Soviet government would keep these factors in mind in considering the request that joint British and American proposals be accepted, and that Mr. Molotov would be authorized to continue the discussions in San Francisco on that basis.

I then handed him a message which I asked him to transmit to Marshal Stalin immediately.

"There was an agreement at Yalta," this communication read, "in which President Roosevelt participated for the United States Government, to reorganize the Provisional Government now functioning in Warsaw in order to establish a new government of National Unity in Poland by means of previous consultation between representatives of the provisional Polish Government of Warsaw and other Polish democratic leaders from Poland and from abroad.

"In the opinion of the United States Government the Crimean decision on Poland can only be carried out if a group of genuinely representative democratic Polish leaders are invited to Moscow for consultation. The United States Government cannot be party to any method of consultation with Polish leaders which would not result in the establishment of a new Provisional Government of National Unity genuinely representative of the democratic elements of the Polish people. The United States and British Governments have gone as far as they can to meet the situation and carry out the intent of the Crimean decisions in their joint message delivered to Marshal Stalin on April 8th.

"The United States Government earnestly requests that the Soviet Government accept the proposals set forth in the joint message of the President and Prime Minister to Marshal Stalin, and that Mr. Molotov continue the conversations with the Secretary of State and Mr. Eden in San Francisco on that basis.

"The Soviet Government must realize that the failure to go forward at this time with the implementation of the Crimean decision on Poland would seriously shake confidence in the unity of the three governments and their determination to continue the collaboration in the future as they have in the past."

Molotov asked if he could make a few observations. It was his hope, he said, that he expressed the views of the Soviet government in stating that they wished to cooperate with the United States and Great Britain as before.

I answered that I agreed, otherwise there would be no sense in the talk we then were having.

Molotov went on to say that he had been authorized to set forth the following point of view of the Soviet government:

1. The basis of collaboration had been established, and although inevitable difficulties had arisen, the three governments had been able to find a common language and that on this basis they had been settling these differences.
2. The three governments had dealt as equal parties, and there had been no case where one or two of the three had attempted to impose their will on another and that as a basis of co-operation this was the only one acceptable to the Soviet government.

I told him that all we were asking was that the Soviet government carry out the Crimea decision on Poland.

Mr. Molotov answered that as an advocate of the Crimea decisions his government stood by them and that it was a matter of honor for them. His government felt that the good basis which existed was the result of former work and that it offered even brighter prospects for the future. The Soviet government, he added, was convinced that all difficulties could be overcome.

I replied sharply that an agreement had been reached on Poland and that there was only one thing to do, and that was for Marshal Stalin to carry out that agreement in accordance with his word.

Molotov said that Marshal Stalin, in his message of April 7, had given his views on the agreement, and added that he personally could not understand why, if the three governments could reach an agreement on the question of the composition of the Yugoslav government, the same formula could not be applied in the case of Poland.

Replying sharply again, I said that an agreement had been reached on Poland and that it only required to be carried out by the Soviet government.

Mr. Molotov repeated that his government supported the Crimea decisions but that he could not agree that an abrogation of those decisions by others could be considered a violation by the Soviet government. He added that surely the Polish question, involving as it did a neighboring country, was of very great interest to the Soviet government.

Since Molotov insisted on avoiding the main issue, I said what I had said before — that the United States Government was prepared to carry out loyally all the agreements reached at Yalta and asked only that the Soviet government do the same. I expressed once more the desire of the United States for friendship with Russia, but I wanted it clearly understood that this could be only on a basis of the mutual observation of agreements and not on the basis of a one-way street.

"I have never been talked to like that in my life," Molotov said.

I told him, "Carry out your agreements and you won't get talked to like that."

# Atomic Diplomacy

### *Document 17*

On September 11, 1945, Secretary of War Henry Stimson sent a memo to Truman discussing the effect of the atomic bomb on relations with the Soviet Union. He argued that the bomb could be used as a diplomatic tool to encourage the Soviets to cooperate with the United States.

## 17 LETTER TO PRESIDENT TRUMAN
## Henry Stimson, Secretary of War
## September 11, 1945

Dear Mr. President:

In handing you today my memorandum about our relations with Russia in respect to the atomic bomb, I am not unmindful of the fact that when in Potsdam I talked with you about the question whether we could be safe in sharing the atomic bomb with Russia while she was still a police state and before she put into effect provisions assuring personal rights of liberty to the individual citizen.

I still recognize the difficulty and am still convinced of the ultimate importance of a change in Russian attitude toward individual liberty but I have come to the conclusion that it would not be possible to use our possession of the atomic bomb as a direct lever to produce the change. I have become convinced that any demand by us for an internal change in Russia as a condition of sharing in the atomic weapon would be so resented that it would make the objective we have in view less probable.

I believe that the change in attitude toward the individual in Russia will come slowly and gradually and I am satisfied that we should not delay our approach to Russia in the matter of the atomic bomb until that process has been completed. My reasons are set forth in the memorandum I am handing you today. Furthermore, I believe that this long process of change in Russia is more likely to be expedited by the closer relationship in the matter of the atomic bomb which I suggest and the trust and confidence that I believe would be inspired by the method of approach which I have outlined.

Faithfully yours,
Henry L. Stimson
Secretary of War

The President,
The White House

***Memorandum for the President***

*Subject:* The advent of the atomic bomb has stimulated great military and probably even greater political interest throughout the civilized world. In a world atmosphere already extremely sensitive to power, the introduction of this weapon has profoundly affected political considerations in all sections of the globe.

In many quarters it has been interpreted as a substantial offset to the growth of Russian influence on the continent. We can be certain that the Soviet Government has sensed this tendency and the temptation will be strong for the Soviet political and military leaders to acquire this weapon in the shortest possible time. Britain in effect already has the status of a partner with us in the development of this weapon. Accordingly, unless the Soviets are voluntarily invited into the partnership upon a basis of cooperation and trust, we are going to maintain the Anglo-Saxon bloc over against the Soviet in the possession of this weapon. Such a condition will almost certainly stimulate feverish activity on the part of the Soviet toward the development of this bomb in what will in effect be a secret armament race of a rather desperate character. There is evidence to indicate that such activity may have already commenced.

If we feel, as I assume we must, that civilization demands that some day we shall arrive at a satisfactory international arrangement respecting the control of this new force, the question then is how long we can afford to enjoy our momentary superiority in the hope of achieving our immediate peace council objectives.

Whether Russia gets control of the necessary secrets of production in a minimum of say four years or a maximum of twenty years is not nearly as important to the world and civilization as to make sure that when they do get it they are willing and cooperative partners among the peace-loving nations of the world. It is true if we approach them now, as I would propose, we may be gambling on their good faith and risk their getting into production of bombs a little sooner than they would otherwise.

To put the matter concisely, I consider the problem of our satisfactory relations with Russia as not merely connected with but as virtually dominated by the problem of the atomic bomb. Except for the problem of the control of the bomb, those relations, while vitally important, might not be immediately pressing. The establishment of relations of mutual confidence between her and us could afford to wait the slow progress of time. But with the discovery of the bomb they became immediately emergent. Those relations may be perhaps irretrievably embittered by the way in which we approach the solution of the bomb with Russia. For if we fail to approach them now and merely continue to negotiate with them, having this weapon rather ostentatiously on our hip, their suspicions and their distrust of our purposes and motives will increase. It will inspire them to greater efforts in an all-out effort to solve the problem. If the solution is achieved in that spirit, it is much less likely that we will ever get the kind of covenant we may desperately need in the future. This risk, is, I believe, greater than the other, inasmuch as our objective must be to get the best kind of international bargain we can — one that has some chance of being kept and saving civilization not for five or for twenty years, but forever.

The chief lesson I have learned in a long life is that the only way you can make a man trustworthy is to trust him; and the surest way to make him untrustworthy is to distrust him and show your distrust.

If the atomic bomb were merely another though more devastating military weapon to be assimilated into our pattern of international relations, it would be one thing. We could then follow the old custom of secrecy and nationalistic military superiority relying on international caution to prescribe the future use of the weapon as we did with gas. But I think the bomb instead constitutes merely a first step in a new control by man over the forces of nature too revolutionary and dangerous to fit into the old concepts. I think it really caps the climax of the age between man's growing technical power for destructiveness and his psychological power of self-control and group control — his moral power. If so, our method of approach to the Russians is a question of the most vital importance in the evolution of human progress.

Since the crux of the problem is Russia, any contemplated action leading to the control of this weapon should be primarily directed *to* Russia. It is my judgment that the Soviet would be more apt to respond sincerely to a direct and forthright approach made by the United States on the subject than would be the case if the approach were made as a part of a general international scheme, or if the approach were made after a succession of express or implied threats or near threats in our peace negotiations.

My idea of an approach to the Soviets would be a direct proposal after discussion with the British that we would be prepared in effect to enter an arrangement with the Russians, the general purpose of which would be to control and limit the use of the atomic bomb as an instrument of war and so far as possible to direct and encourage the development of atomic power for peaceful and humanitarian purposes. Such an approach might more specifically lead to the proposal that we would stop work on the further improvement in, or manufacture of, the bomb as a military weapon, provided the Russians and the British would agree to do likewise. It might also provide that we would be willing to impound what bombs we now have in the United States provided the Russians and the British would agree with us that in no event will they or we use a bomb as an instrument of war unless all three Governments agree to that use. We might also consider including in the arrangement a covenant with the U.K. and the Soviets providing for the exchange of benefits of future development whereby atomic energy may be applied on a mutually satisfactory basis for commercial or humanitarian purposes.

I would make such an approach just as soon as our immediate political considerations make it appropriate.

I emphasize perhaps beyond all other considerations the importance of taking this action with Russia as a proposal of the United States — backed by Great Britain but peculiarly the proposal of the United States. Action of any international group of nations, including many small nations who have not demonstrated their potential power or responsibility in this war would not, in my opinion, be taken seriously by the Soviets. The loose debates which would surround such proposal, if put before a conference of nations, would provoke but scant favor from the Soviet. As I say, I think this is the most important point in the program.

After the nations which have won this war have agreed to it, there will be ample time to introduce France and China into the covenants and finally to incorporate the agreement into the scheme of the United Nations. The use of this bomb has been accepted by the world as the result of the initiative and productive capacity of the United States, and I think this factor is a most potent lever toward having our proposals accepted by the Soviets, whereas I am most skeptical of obtaining any tangible results by way of any international debate. I urge this method as the most realistic means of accomplishing this vitally important step in the history of the world.

Henry L. Stimson
Secretary of War

## Cold War Declared

### *Document 18*

During a tour of the United States in 1946, Winston Churchill made a speech in which he announced that "from Stettin in the Baltic to Trieste in the Adriatic, an iron curtain has descended across the continent." Many historians cite this speech as the formal end of the Grand Alliance and the beginning of the cold war.

### 18 THE IRON CURTAIN SPEECH
### Winston Churchill
### Fulton, Missouri
### March 5, 1946

The United States stands at this time at the pinnacle of world power. It is a solemn moment for the American democracy. With primacy in power is also joined an awe-inspiring accountability to the future. As you look around you, you feel not only the sense of duty done but also feel anxiety lest you fall below the level of achievement. Opportunity is here now, clear and shining, for both our countries. To reject it or ignore it or fritter it away will bring upon us all the long reproaches of the after-time. It is necessary that constancy of mind, persistency of purpose, and the grand simplicity of decision shall guide and rule the conduct of the English-speaking peoples in peace as they did in war. We must and I believe we shall prove ourselves equal to this severe requirement. . . .

. . . Before we cast away the solid assurances of national armaments for self-preservation, we must be certain that our temple is built, not upon shifting sands or quagmires, but upon the rock. Anyone with his eyes open can see that our path will be difficult and also long, but if we persevere together as we did in the two World Wars — though not, alas, in the interval between them — I cannot doubt that we shall achieve our common purpose in the end.

I have, however, a definite and practical proposal to make for action. Courts and magistrates cannot function without sheriffs and constables. The United Nations Organization must immediately begin to be equipped with an international armed force. In such a matter we can only go step by step; but we must begin now. I propose that each of the powers and states should be invited to dedicate a certain number of air squadrons to the service of the world organization. These squadrons would be trained and prepared in their own countries but would move around in rotation from one country to another. They would wear the uniform of their own countries with different badges. They would not be required to act against their own nation but in other respects they would be directed by the world organization. This might be started on a modest scale and a grow [*sic* — Eds.] as confidence grew. I wished to see this done after the First World War and trust it may be done forthwith.

It would nevertheless be wrong and imprudent to entrust the secret knowledge or experience of the atomic bomb, which the United States, Great Britain, and Canada now share, to the world organization, while it is still in its infancy. It would be criminal madness to cast it adrift in this still agitated and ununited world. No one in any country has slept less well in their beds because this knowledge and the method and the raw materials to apply it are at present largely retained in American hands. I do not believe we should all have slept so soundly had the positions been reversed and some Communist or neo-Fascist state monopolized, for the time being, these dread agencies. The fear of them alone might easily have been used to enforce totalitarian systems upon the free democratic world, with consequences appalling to human imagination. . . .

. . . We cannot be blind to the fact that the liberties enjoyed by individual citizens throughout the United States and British Empire are not valid in a considerable number of countries, some of which are very powerful. In these states control is enforced upon the common people by various kinds of all-embracing police governments, to a degree which is overwhelming and contrary to every principle of democracy. The power of the state is exercised without restraint, either by dictators or by compact oligarchies operating through a privileged party and a political police. It is not our duty at this time, when difficulties are so numerous, to interfere forcibly in the internal affairs of countries whom we have not conquered in war, but we must never cease to proclaim in fearless tones the great principles of freedom and the rights of man, which are the joint inheritance of the English-speaking world and which, through Magna Carta, the Bill of Rights, the habeas corpus, trial by jury, and the English common law find their . . . expression in the Declaration of Independence. . . .

A shadow has fallen upon the scenes so lately lighted by the Allied victory. Nobody knows what Soviet Russia and its Communist international organization intends to do in the immediate future, or what are the limits, if any, to their expansive and proselytizing tendencies. I have a strong admiration and regard for the valiant Russian people and for my wartime comrade, Marshal Stalin. There is sympathy and good will in Britain — and I doubt not here also — toward the peoples of all the Russias and a resolve to persevere through many differences and rebuffs in establishing lasting friendships.

We understand the Russian need to be secure on her western frontiers from all renewal of German aggression. We welcome her to her rightful place among the leading nations of the world. Above all, we welcome constant, frequent, and growing contacts between the Russian people and our own people on both sides of the Atlantic. It is my duty, however, to place before you certain facts about the present position in Europe.

From Stettin in the Baltic to Trieste in the Adriatic, an iron curtain has descended across the continent. Behind that line lie all the capitals of the ancient states of central and eastern Europe. Warsaw, Berlin, Prague, Vienna, Budapest, Belgrade, Bucharest, and Sofia, all these famous cities and the populations around them lie in the Soviet sphere and all are subject, in one form or another, not only to Soviet influence but to a very high and increasing measure of control from Moscow. Athens alone, with its immortal glories, is free to decide its future at an election under British, American, and French observation.

The Russian-dominated Polish Government has been encouraged to make enormous and wrongful inroads upon Germany, and mass expulsions of millions of Germans on a scale grievous and undreamed of are now taking place. The Communist parties, which were very small in all these eastern states of Europe, have been raised to preeminence and power far beyond their numbers and are seeking everywhere to obtain totalitarian control. Police governments are prevailing in nearly every case, and so far, except in Czechoslovakia, there is not true democracy.

Turkey and Persia are both profoundly alarmed and disturbed at the claims which are made upon them and at the pressure being exerted by the Moscow government. An attempt is being made by the Russians in Berlin to build up a quasi-Communist party in their zone of occupied Germany by showing special favors to groups of left-wing German leaders. At the end of the fighting last June, the American and British Armies withdrew westward, in accordance with an earlier agreement, to a depth at some points of 150 miles on a front of nearly 400 miles, to allow the Russians to occupy this vast expanse of territory which the western democracies . . . conquered. . . .

In front of the iron curtain which lies across Europe are other causes for anxiety. In Italy the Communist Party is seriously hampered by having to support the Communist-trained Marshal Tito's claims to former Italian territory at the head of the Adriatic. Nevertheless, the future of Italy hangs in the balance. Again, one cannot imagine a regenerated Europe without a strong France. All my public life I have worked for a strong France and I never lost faith in her destiny, even in the darkest hours. I will not lose faith now.

However, in a great number of countries, far from the Russian frontiers and throughout the world, Communist fifth columns are established and work in complete unity and absolute obedience to the directions they receive from the Communist center. Except in the British Commonwealth, and in the United States, where communism is in its infancy, the Communist parties or fifth columns constitute a growing challenge and peril to Christian civilization. These are somber facts for anyone to have to recite on the morrow of a victory gained by so much splendid comradeship in arms and in the cause of freedom and democracy, and we should be most unwise not to face them squarely while time remains.

The outlook is also anxious in the Far East and especially in Manchuria. The agreement which was made at Yalta, to which I was a party, was extremely favorable to Soviet Russia, but it was made at a time when no one could say that the German war might not extend all through the summer and autumn of 1945 and when the Japanese war was expected to last for a further 18 months from the end of the German war. In this country you are all so well informed about the Far East and such devoted friends of China that I do not need to expatiate on the situation there.

On the other hand, I repulse the idea that a new war is inevitable, still more that it is imminent. It is because I am so sure that our fortunes are in our own hands and that we hold the power to save the future, that I feel the duty to speak out now that I have an occasion to do so. I do not believe that Soviet Russia desires war. What they desire is the fruits of war and the indefinite expansion of their power and doctrines. But what we have to consider here today while time remains, is the permanent prevention of war and the establishment of conditions of freedom and democracy as rapidly as possible in all countries.

Our difficulties and dangers will not be removed by closing our eyes to them; they will not be removed by mere waiting to see what happens; nor will they be relieved by a policy of appeasement. What is needed is a settlement, and the longer this is delayed, the more difficult it will be and the greater our dangers will become. From what I have seen of our Russian friends and allies during the war, I am convinced that there is nothing they admire so much as strength, and there is nothing for which they have less respect than for military weakness. For that reason the old doctrine of a balance of power is unsound. We cannot afford, if we can help it, to work on narrow margins, offering temptations to a trial of strength. If the western democracies stand together in strict adherence to the principles of the United Nations Charter, their influence for furthering these principles will be immense and no one is likely to molest them. If, however, they become divided or falter in their duty, and if these all-important years are allowed to slip away, then indeed catastrophe may overwhelm us all.

Last time I saw it all coming, and cried aloud to my own fellow countrymen and to the world, but no one paid any attention. Up till the year 1933 or even 1935, Germany might have been saved from the awful fate which has overtaken her and we might all have been spared the miseries Hitler let loose upon mankind.

There never was a war in all history easier to prevent by timely action than the one which has just desolated such great areas of the globe. It could have been prevented without the firing of a single shot, and Germany might be powerful, prosperous, and honored today, but no one would listen and one by one we were all sucked into the awful whirlpool.

We surely must not let that happen again. This can only be achieved by reaching now, in 1946, a good understanding on all points with Russia under the general authority of the United Nations and by the maintenance of that good understanding through many peaceful years, by the world instrument, supported by the whole strength of the English-speaking world and all its connections.

## A Plan for International Control of Atomic Weapons

### *Document 19*

In June 1946 the United States presented a plan, the Baruch Plan, to the United Nations for international control of atomic weapons. The plan called for the creation of a special international organization that would control all atomic weapons. All nations would promise not to produce atomic bombs. The new agency would inspect nations to ensure that they were not producing bombs and would enforce sanctions against those who tried to cheat. The United States would give up its atomic weapons to the new agency after it was set up and functioning.

### 19 THE BARUCH PLAN
### June 14, 1946

My Fellow Members of the United Nations Atomic Energy Commission, and My Fellow Citizens of the World:

We are here to make a choice between the quick and the dead.

That is our business.

Behind the black portent of the new atomic age lies a hope which, seized upon with faith, can work our salvation. If we fail, then we have damned every man to be the slave of Fear. Let us not deceive ourselves: We must elect World Peace or World Destruction.

Science has torn from nature a secret so vast in its potentialities that our minds cower from the terror it creates. Yet terror is not enough to inhibit the use of the atomic bomb. The terror created by weapons has never stopped man from employing them. For each new weapon a defense has been produced, in time. But now we face a condition in which adequate defense does not exist.

Science, which gave us this dread power, shows that it *can* be made a giant help to humanity, but science does *not* show us how to prevent its baleful use. So we have been appointed to obviate that peril by finding a meeting of the minds and the hearts of our people. Only in the will of mankind lies the answer. . . .

Through the historical approach I have outlined, we find ourselves here to test if man can produce, through his will and faith, the miracle of peace, just as he has, through science and skill, the miracle of the atom.

The United States proposes the creation of an International Atomic Development Authority, to which should be entrusted all phases of the development and use of atomic energy, starting with the raw material and including —

1. Managerial control or ownership of all atomic-energy activities potentially dangerous to world security.
2. Power to control, inspect, and license all other atomic activities.
3. The duty of fostering the beneficial uses of atomic energy.
4. Research and development responsibilities of an affirmative character intended to put the Authority in the forefront of atomic knowledge and thus to enable it to

comprehend, and therefor to detect, misuse of atomic energy. To be effective, the Authority must itself be the world's leader in the field of atomic knowledge and development and thus supplement its legal authority with the great power inherent in possession of leadership in knowledge.

I offer this as a basis for beginning our discussion.

But I think the peoples we serve would not believe — and without faith nothing counts — that a treaty, merely outlawing possession or use of the atomic bomb, constitutes effective fulfilment of the instructions to this Commission. Previous failures have been recorded in trying the method of simple renunciation, unsupported by effective guaranties of security and armament limitation. No one would have faith in that approach alone.

Now, if ever, is the time to act for the common good. Public opinion supports a world movement toward security. If I read the signs aright, the peoples want a program not composed merely of pious thoughts but of enforceable sanctions — an international law with teeth in it.

We of this nation, desirous of helping to bring peace to the world and realizing the heavy obligations upon us arising from our possession of the means of producing the bomb and from the fact that it is part of our armament, are prepared to make our full contribution toward effective control of atomic energy.

When an adequate system for control of atomic energy, including the renunciation of the bomb as a weapon, has been agreed upon and put into effective operation and condign punishments set up for violations of the rules of control which are to be stigmatized as international crimes, we propose that —

1. Manufacture of atomic bombs shall stop;
2. Existing bombs shall be disposed of pursuant to the terms of the treaty; and
3. The Authority shall be in possession of full information as to the know-how for the production of atomic energy.

Let me repeat, so as to avoid misunderstanding: My country is ready to make its full contribution toward the end we seek, subject of course to our constitutional processes and to an adequate system of control becoming fully effective, as we finally work it out.

Now as to violations: In the agreement, penalties of as serious a nature as the nations may wish and as immediate and certain in their execution as possible should be fixed for —

1. Illegal possession or use of an atomic bomb;
2. Illegal possession, or separation, of atomic material suitable for use in an atomic bomb;
3. Seizure of any plant or other property belonging to or licensed by the Authority;
4. Wilful interference with the activities of the Authority;
5. Creation or operation of dangerous projects in a manner contrary to, or in the absence of, a license granted by the international control body.

It would be a deception, to which I am unwilling to lend myself, were I not to say to you and to our peoples that the matter of punishment lies at the very heart of our present security system. It might as well be admitted, here and now, that the subject goes straight to the veto power contained in the Charter of the United Nations so far as it relates to the field of atomic energy. The Charter permits penalization only by concurrence of each of the five great powers — the Union of Soviet Socialist Republics, the United Kingdom, China, France, and the United States.

I want to make very plain that I am concerned here with the veto power only as it affects this particular problem. There must be no veto to protect those who violate their solemn agreements not to develop or use atomic energy for destructive purposes.

The bomb does not wait upon debate. To delay may be to die. The time between violation and preventive action or punishment would be all too short for extended discussion as to the course to be followed.

## The Soviet Plan

### *Document 20*

The Soviet Union rejected the Baruch Plan, claiming it was a trick by the United States to preserve its atomic monopoly. The Soviets also argued that the proposed inspection measures were an attempt by the West to learn Soviet military secrets. They proposed an alternative described here by Soviet Foreign Minister Andrei Gromyko. It would have required the United States to destroy its atomic weapons before the setting up of an international organization.

### 20 THE RUSSIAN PROPOSAL FOR INTERNATIONAL CONTROL
### Andrei Gromyko
### July 1, 1946

The proposals are as follows. The first one concerns the conclusion of an international agreement for the outlawing of the production and application of a weapon based upon the use of atomic energy for the purposes of mass destruction. The second concerns an organization of the work of the commission for the control of atomic energy. I will read the text of the first proposal.

Draft International Agreement to forbid the production and use of weapons based upon the use of atomic energy for the purposes of mass destruction. There follows after this a list of the signatory states, and the text continues: "Deeply aware of the extreme importance of the great scientific discoveries connected with the splitting of the atom and with a view to the use of atomic energy for the purposes of raising the welfare and standard of life of the peoples of the world, and also for the development of culture and science for the good of humanity; unanimously desiring universal cooperation as wide as possible for the use of all people of scientific discoveries in the field of atomic energy, for the improvement of the conditions of the life of the peoples of the whole world, the raising of their standard of welfare and further progress of human culture; taking account clearly of the fact that the great scientific discoveries in the field of atomic energy, contain a great danger first and foremost for the peaceful towns and civilian populations in case such a discovery were used as a means of applying an atomic weapon for the purposes of mass destruction; taking note also of the great importance of the fact that through international agreements, the use in time of war of suffocating, poisonous and other similar gases and also similar liquids, substances and processes, and also bacteriological methods have already been outlawed by common accord between the civilized peoples; and considering that the international outlawry of the use of the atomic weapon for mass destruction would correspond in still greater measure to the aspirations and the conscience of the peoples of the whole world; animated by an intense desire to remove the threat of the use of these scientific discoveries for the harm of humanity and against the interests of humanity; the high contracting parties decided to conclude an agreement to forbid the production and use of a weapon based upon the use of atomic energy, and for this purpose, appointed as their plenipotentiaries"—and here the list of plenipotentiaries will follow, whose credentials are found to be in due form—"agree as follows.

ARTICLE 1: The high contracting parties solemnly declare that they will forbid the production and use of a weapon based upon the use of atomic energy, and with this in view, take upon themselves the following obligations:

(a) Not to use, in any circumstances, an atomic weapon;

(b) To forbid the production and keeping of a weapon based upon the use of atomic energy;

(c) To destroy within a period of three months from the entry into force of this agreement all stocks of atomic energy weapons whether in a finished or semi-finished condition.

ARTICLE 2: The high contracting parties declare that any violation of Article 1 of this agreement shall constitute a serious crime against humanity.

ARTICLE 3: The high contracting parties, within six months of the entry into force of the present agreement, shall pass legislation providing severe punishment for the violation of the terms of this agreement.

ARTICLE 4: The present agreement shall be of indefinite duration.

ARTICLE 5: The present agreement is open for signature to all States whether or not they are Members of the United Nations.

ARTICLE 6: The present agreement shall come into force after approval by the Security Council, and after ratification by half the signature States, including all States Members of the United Nations, as under Article 23 of the Charter. The ratifications shall be placed for safe keeping in the hands of the Secretary-General of the United Nations.

ARTICLE 7: After the entry into force of the present agreement, it shall be an obligation upon all States whether Members or not of the United Nations.

ARTICLE 8: The present agreement of which the Russian, Chinese, French, English and Spanish texts shall be authentic, is drawn up in one copy and will be in the safe keeping of the Secretary-General of the United Nations. The Secretary-General shall communicate to all signatories a duly certified copy thereof."

I would like now to read the text of the second proposal. It concerns the organization of the work of the Commission for the control of atomic energy. Basing ourselves upon the decision of the General Assembly of the 24th of January, 1946, concerning the setting up of a Commission for the study of problems connected with the discovery of atomic energy and other related questions, and in particular upon Article 5 of this decision, stating the terms of reference of the Commission, the Soviet Delegation considers it necessary to make the following proposals concerning the plan of the organization of the work of the Commission for the initial period of its activity.

1. The setting up of committees of the Commission, pursuing the aims indicated in the decision of the General Assembly to "proceed with the utmost dispatch and inquire into all phases of the problem and make such recommendations from time to time with respect to that as it finds possible."

In connection with this item, it seems quite necessary to establish two committees which as auxiliary organs of the Commission would be responsible for a general study of the problem of atomic energy and the elaboration of recommendations which the Commission might make for the carrying out of the decision of the General Assembly and other organs of the United Nations.

It is proposed that there should be set up two committees, the first a committee for the exchange of scientific information. This committee would be set up for the purpose of studying point (a) of Article 5 of the decision of the General Assembly of the 24th of January,

1946. Among the tasks of this committee would be that of elaborating recommendations concerning practical measures for the organization of the exchange of information, (1) concerning the contents of scientific discoveries connected with the splitting of the atom and other discoveries connected with the obtaining and use of atomic energy, and (2) concerning the technology and the organization of technological processes for obtaining and using atomic energy. (3) Concerning the organization and method of industrial production of atomic energy and the use of such energy. (4) Concerning forms, sources, and the location of raw materials necessary for obtaining atomic energy.

I come now to the second proposed committee whose task would be to prevent the use of atomic energy for the harm of humanity. This committee should be set up in order to attain the aims set forth in points (b), (c), and (d) of Article 5 of the decision of the General Assembly. The task of this committee would be to prepare recommendations on the following subjects:

1. The preparation of a draft international agreement for the outlawing of weapons based upon the use of atomic energy and forbidding the production and use of such weapons and all similar forms of weapons destined for mass destruction.
2. The elaboration and creation of methods to forbid the production of weapons based upon the use of atomic energy and to prevent the use of atomic weapons and all other similar weapons of mass destruction.
3. Measures, systems and organizations, of control in the use of atomic energy to insure the observance of the conditions above-mentioned in the international agreement for the outlawing of atomic weapons.
4. The elaboration of a system of sanctions for application against the unlawful use of atomic energy.

## *Suggestions for Further Reading*

MIT Faculty, eds. *The Nuclear Almanac: Confronting the Atom in War and Peace* (Reading, MA: Addison-Wesley, 1984). A compilation of articles that includes good material on the Manhattan Project and the decision to build the H-bomb.

Rhodes, Richard. *The Making of the Atomic Bomb* (New York: Simon and Schuster, 1986). A comprehensive history.

Williams, Robert C., and Philip L. Cantelon, eds. *The American Atom: A Documentary History of Nuclear Policies from the Discovery of Fission to the Present, 1939–1984* (Philadelphia: U of Pennsylvania P, 1984). A compilation of very important official documents related to the development of the bomb and of nuclear doctrine.

*Two*

# THE WEAPON OF CHOICE

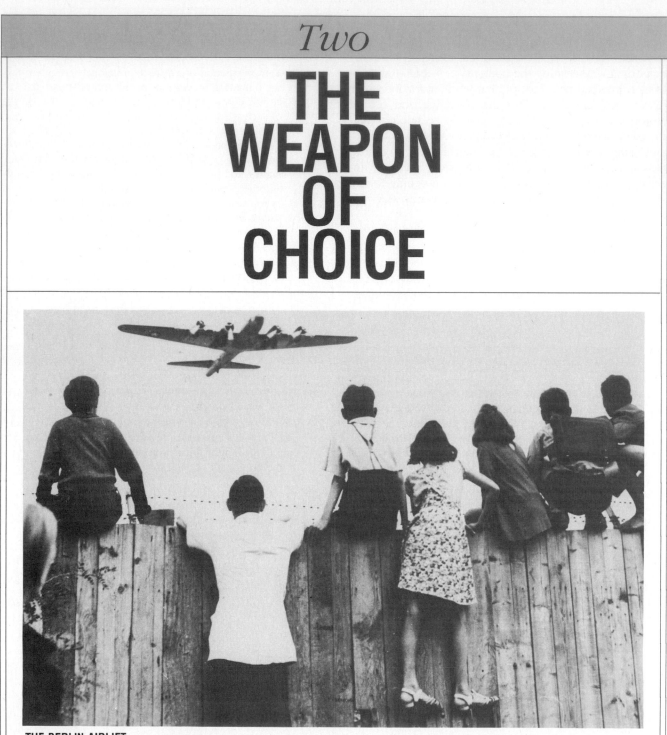

**THE BERLIN AIRLIFT**

West Berlin children watch as one of many U.S. airplanes delivers supplies of food and fuel to their city. The airlift was initiated in response to the Soviet Union's blockade of West Berlin, which began in the spring of 1948. AP/Wide World Photos

# INTRODUCTION

The period from 1947 to 1953 was in a number of respects the most formative in the postwar history of U.S. foreign and military policy. The United States emerged from World War II with many large questions about its international role and its military power unanswered. Would it play a substantial, even a leading, part in international diplomacy, or would it return to its long tradition of isolation in foreign policy? What would be the nature of its relations with the Soviet Union, and could the wartime cooperation with the world's greatest Communist power be continued in peacetime? What role, if any, would the United States play in structuring and preserving European security? And in the area of military policy: What threats would confront the United States now that Japanese and German military power had been defeated? How large should the peacetime military establishment be? And what role should the atomic bomb play in U.S. security policy? At war's end, the answers to these questions were neither obvious, inevitable, or predetermined, and considerable controversy and struggle accompanied the effort to define U.S. policy.

The years 1947–53, from the crisis in the Middle East that led to the Truman Doctrine to the end of the Korean War, were years of transition: the confusion and uncertainty about the United States' role and power were gradually but steadily replaced by a clear vision of the threats to U.S. security and of the requirements of U.S. diplomacy and military power. In this period U.S. leaders defined their answers to the basic questions about America's role in the nuclear age by the policy choices they made and the policy options they rejected and by their perceptions of the international environment and their interpretation of developments abroad. The answers that the Truman administration provided are extremely important because they have, in broad terms, governed U.S. security policy down to the present day.

The essential character of the transformation of U.S. policy in this period is captured in four major developments. First, the cold war had arrived. U.S. relations with the Soviet Union became deeply hostile, and opposition to Soviet power and influence became the central organizing principle of U.S. security policy. The core of this new "containment" approach was provided by prominent diplomat George Kennan in a famous article published in the July 1947 issue of *Foreign Affairs*.

There had been hopes that the two powers could work together to keep the peace and that the United Nations would serve as a cornerstone of security in the postwar era. But relations between the Soviet Union and the United States had been marked by suspicion and friction even during the war. Most American politicians and policy makers came to view the Soviet Union with growing fear and distaste.

These concerns were intensified by a series of developments in 1947 and 1948. The presence of Communists in the governments of France and Italy and the involvement of Communists in the Greek civil war led to worries that Soviet influence or domination might sweep across the rest of Europe. The coup in February 1948 that brought a Communist government to power in Czechoslovakia, the one country in Eastern Europe with a democratic tradition, had a dramatic impact on American opinion, causing a minor war scare and leading President Truman to call a special session of Congress to request additional defense appropriations. When, only several months later in June 1948, the Soviet Union imposed a blockade against West Berlin, it appeared to many that Stalin was testing the resolve of the democratic powers and was seeking to push U.S. power out of the center of Europe.

By the time the North Korean Communists invaded South Korea in June 1950, Stalin was viewed virtually as another Hitler, and the lesson of Hitler seemed to be that aggression unchecked whetted the appetite of the aggressor. By 1950, the United States was so convinced that the Soviet Union was an implacable ideological enemy bent on world domination that it was willing to fight a war to stop the spread of Communism.

The emergence of the cold war went hand in hand with the second major development of this period: the commitment of the United States to an internationalist foreign policy. This represented a dramatic departure in U.S. foreign policy. The United States possessed a long peacetime tradition, dating back to George Washington's injunction to "avoid entangling alliances," of isolationism, of remaining aloof from international diplomacy among major powers. As the Second World War ended, there was a widespread public feeling that U.S. troops should be brought home as quickly as possible, and U.S. policy makers hoped that the balance of power in Europe would be restored so that American involvement would be unnecessary.

Under the pressure of a rapidly growing sense of the Soviet threat, however, the United States soon began to feel it necessary to make overseas commitments. The first major step was the enunciation of the Truman Doctrine in March 1947, which proclaimed that the United States must support "free peoples" wherever they might be threatened. The Truman administration, fearing that the Soviet Union would exploit Western Europe's political and economic troubles to extend Communist influence, also offered in June 1947 to provide large amounts of economic assistance to help Europe back on its feet. This program, called the Marshall Plan because it was first outlined in a speech by Secretary of State George Marshall, was another step in the United States' growing involvement in Europe and in its struggle to contain Soviet influence.

By 1949 the U.S. government was prepared to offer a formal political guarantee of European security. It did so by signing the North Atlantic Treaty and by providing its new North Atlantic allies with military assistance. With the coming of the Korean War, this political commitment was transformed into a military commitment as well, and it became the agent for the permanent stationing of U.S. forces in Europe under a joint NATO command. In short, by 1950 it was clear that the United States would be deeply involved in Europe's security arrangements and that U.S. military power would be an integral part of the new balance of power.

U.S. involvement in the Korean War, which also led to a security treaty with Japan, brought Asia into the realm of formal U.S. security commitments. The United States had become a global power. This was an unprecedented development for U.S. diplomacy, but one that was a natural corollary of its mounting desire to contain the Soviet Union.

The third major development of this period is an obvious complement to the previous two: in order to resist Soviet power and to fulfill its international commitments, the United States had to become a larger military power than was its custom in peacetime. The effort to provide the United States with "adequate" military power had two dimensions. First, the United States rapidly increased and relied increasingly upon atomic weapons capability. In the first two years after the war, it appeared that atomic weapons might be scarce, very expensive, and hence not necessarily decisive in another war. Moreover, there were hopes that this terrible new weapon could be brought under international control. But these hopes were dashed by the emerging U.S.-Soviet rivalry. Atomic tests in 1947 and 1948, culminating in a series called Operation Sandstone demonstrated the feasibility of more efficient bomb designs and opened the way to the mass production of atomic weapons. The U.S. atomic arsenal, which numbered only fifty bombs in 1948, grew rapidly after 1949 and was composed of well over one thousand by the end of the Korean War. This growth in capability was accompanied by the increasing incorporation of these weapons into U.S. war plans. Atomic weapons came to occupy the prominent place in U.S. defense policy that they have never relinquished.

The Soviet nuclear test in the autumn of 1949 galvanized the United States to make another important nuclear weapons decision. Despite bitter divisions among his advisers, some of whom thought that the decision could be safely postponed in the hope that the Soviet Union would reciprocate this restraint, President Truman decided in January 1950 that the United States should move ahead with the development of thermonuclear weapons (also known as hydrogen or H-bombs), which had the potential to be many times more powerful than atomic weapons. This decision guaranteed that nuclear weapons would become weapons of annihilation and was the first large step in U.S.-Soviet nuclear competition.

Second, some of the president's advisers had by 1949 become concerned that the United States' conventional military power was insufficient and thought that a major buildup was necessary. In the fall of 1949 the president ordered a reappraisal of U.S. security policy. The resulting report, known as NSC 68, called for a substantial across-the-board buildup of both conventional and nuclear military power. NSC 68, which was presented to the president in April 1950, provided the rationale for a buildup; the Korean War made that buildup politically possible. In about two years, U.S. defense spending increased nearly fivefold, and it never returned to the previous low levels even when the war ended. Indeed, the Korean War buildup established the rough order of magnitude for U.S. defense spending for the next three decades. In another unprecedented development, the United States was to acquire an enormous peacetime military establishment.

A fourth important feature of this period has to do with the domestic turbulence caused by these dramatic transformations of U.S. foreign and military policy. As U.S. foreign policy became increasingly anti-Soviet, American society was caught up in anti-Communist hysteria. This was fueled in part by a series of spectacular spy cases, including those involving Klaus Fuchs, Ethel and Julius Rosenberg, and Alger Hiss, which involved the passing of U.S. military secrets to the Soviet Union. Fuchs, for example, had worked at Los Alamos on the Manhattan Project and had passed some of its secrets on to Soviet agents. Another symptom of the anti-Communist passion was the establishment of the House of Representatives Un-American Activities Committee (on which a young congressman named Richard Nixon first gained national prominence). This committee held widely publicized investigations of possible Communist infiltration of the movie industry, the universities, and other institutions. Those who were found or were suspected to have Communist affiliations or sympathies were commonly blacklisted, or they lost their jobs or had their careers if not their lives ruined. Very few of the victims of this zealous campaign were truly Soviet spies or real threats to security; their fates are signs of the frightened intolerance of the time.

The most malignant manifestation of the anti-Communist hysteria was the campaign of Sen. Joseph McCarthy, which has given us the term *McCarthyism*. Starting in February 1950, McCarthy turned himself into a powerful and feared national political figure by publicly alleging that the U.S. government was riddled with Communists and by claiming that he had lists of names to prove it. McCarthy said that U.S. foreign policy setbacks—the fall of China to the Communists in 1949, the stalemate in Korea, the rapid nuclear progress of the Soviet Union—were caused by the subversion of Soviet agents within the State Department. McCarthy's reign of terror lasted for several years, during which time he made dozens of damaging, if usually inaccurate, allegations not only against the State Department, but also against university professors, the U.S. Army, and even respected national figures such as Gen. George Marshall. Eventually, McCarthy was discredited, but the several years in which he flourished are evidence of the pervasive fear that was engendered by the United States' new contest with the Soviet Union.

In sum, by 1953 there were few unanswered questions. The Soviet Union was the powerful and much detested enemy. The United States was deeply and formally committed to the defense of Europe and to a global containment policy. It had invested in a very large military establishment that possessed a formidable nuclear capability. The U.S.-Soviet rivalry of the subsequent decades has been played out in the framework of the choices that were made in the formative years between 1947 and 1953.

## THE EMERGENCE OF THE COLD WAR

## Truman Calls for Aid to Oppose Communism

### *Document 1*

Early in 1947, the British government notified the Truman administration that it would cease to provide substantial assistance to Greece and Turkey as of March 31, 1947. The Greek government urgently requested aid from the United States. President Truman decided that the United States must face up to the threat of Communism in Europe by providing assistance to Greece and Turkey. On March 22, 1947, President Truman went before Congress and delivered probably his most famous speech, in which he requested authorization to send aid and advisers to these two countries. Truman also stated that in the growing confrontation with the Soviet Union (and Communism) "it must be the policy of the United States to support free peoples who are resisting attempted subjugation by armed minorities or by outside pressures." This signaled a willingness by the United States to assume the role of world leadership and to resist actively the spread of Communism.

### 1 THE TRUMAN DOCTRINE Speech to Congress March 12, 1947

The gravity of the situation which confronts the world today necessitates my appearance before a joint session of the Congress. The foreign policy and the national security of this country are involved.

One aspect of the present situation, which I wish to present to you at this time for your consideration and decision, concerns Greece and Turkey. The United States has received from the Greek government an urgent appeal for financial and economic assistance. . . .

The very existence of the Greek state is today threatened by the terrorist activities of several thousand armed men, led by communists, who defy the government's authority at a number of points, particularly along the northern boundaries. A commission appointed by the United Nations Security Council is at present investigating disturbed conditions in northern Greece and alleged border violations along the frontier between Greece on the one hand and Albania, Bulgaria, and Yugoslavia on the other. Meanwhile, the Greek government is unable to cope with the situation. The Greek army is small and poorly equipped. It needs supplies and equipment if it is to restore the authority of the government throughout Greek territory.

Greece must have assistance if it is to become a self-supporting and self-respecting democracy. The United States must supply that assistance. We have already extended to Greece certain types of relief and economic aid, but these are inadequate. There is no other country to which democratic Greece can turn. No other nation is willing and able to provide the necessary support for a democratic Greek government.

The British government, which has been helping Greece, can give no further financial or economic aid after March 31. Great Britain finds itself under the necessity of reducing or liquidating its commitments in several parts of the world, including Greece . . .

Greece's neighbor Turkey also deserves our attention . . . Since the war, Turkey has sought financial assistance from Great Britain and the United States for the purpose of effecting that modernization necessary for the maintenance of its national integrity. That integrity is essential to the preservation of order in the Middle East. The British Government has informed us that, owing to its own difficulties, it can no longer extend financial or economic aid to Turkey. As in the case of Greece, if Turkey is to have the assistance it needs, the United States must supply it. We are the only country able to provide that help.

I am fully aware of the broad implications involved if the United States extends assistance to Greece and Turkey, and I shall discuss these implications with you at this time . . .

To ensure the peaceful development of nations, free from coercion, the United States has taken a leading part in establishing the United Nations. The United Nations is designed to make possible lasting freedom and independence for all its members. We shall not realize our objectives, however, unless we are willing to help free people to maintain their free institutions and their national integrity against aggressive movements that seek to impose upon them totalitarian regimes. This is no more than a frank recognition that totalitarian regimes imposed on free peoples, by direct or indirect aggression, undermine the foundations of international peace and hence the security of the United States . . .

I believe that it must be the policy of the United States to support free peoples who are resisting attempted subjugation by armed minorities or by outside pressures. I believe that we must assist free peoples to work out their own destinies in their own way. I believe that our help should be primarily through economic and financial aid, which is essential in economic stability and orderly political processes . . .

Should we fail to aid Greece and Turkey in this fateful hour, the effect will be far-reaching to the West as well as to the East. We must take immediate and resolute action . . .

The seeds of totalitarian regimes are numbered by misery and want. They spread and grow in the evil soil of poverty and strife. They reach their full growth when the hope of a people for a better life has died. We must keep that hope alive. The free peoples of the world look to us for support in maintaining their freedoms. If we falter in our leadership, we may endanger the peace of the world — and we shall surely endanger the welfare of our nation.

Great responsibilities have been placed upon us by the swift movement of events. I am confident that the Congress will face these responsibilities squarely.

## The Marshall Plan and the Soviet Reaction

### *Documents 2 and 3*

By the spring of 1947, U.S. policy makers feared that Europe was on the verge of economic and political collapse. They were particularly worried that Communist parties would profit from Europe's deep economic difficulties. This worry was given credence by the burgeoning popular support for the Communist parties of Italy and France. Spurred by a sense of mounting crisis, Secretary of State George C. Marshall, in a commencement address at Harvard University on June 5, 1947, offered U.S. aid and cooperation in rebuilding Europe's shattered economy. In excerpts from the speech in document 2, Marshall argues that assistance would contribute greatly to the political stability of the nations of Europe and would thereby strengthen them against Communist subversion.

Marshall extended his offer of assistance to all Europe's war-ravaged nations, including the Soviet Union and its Eastern European satellites. As he had expected, the Soviet government quickly spurned his proposal. Deputy Foreign Minister Andrei Vyshinsky denounced it as an attack on Europe's sovereignty and a crude attempt to undermine the "People's Democracies" of Eastern Europe. This Soviet rejection (document 3) of Marshall's offer made complete the economic and political division of the Continent. The Marshall Plan provided large-scale economic assistance to the sixteen participating non-Communist nations. Ultimately, the Marshall Plan was judged one of the major successes of postwar U.S. diplomacy.

### 2 MARSHALL PLAN SPEECH
### George C. Marshall, Secretary of State
### Harvard Commencement Address
### June 5, 1947

In considering the requirements for the rehabilitation of Europe, the physical loss of life, the visible destruction of cities, factories, mines, and railroads was correctly estimated, but it has become obvious during recent months that this visible destruction was probably less serious than the dislocation of the entire fabric of European economy. For the past 10 years conditions have been highly abnormal. The feverish preparation for war and the more feverish maintenance of the war effort engulfed all aspects of national economies. . . . The breakdown of the business structure of Europe during the war was complete. Recovery has been seriously retarded by the fact that two years after the close of hostilities a peace settlement with Germany and Austria has not been agreed upon. But even given a more prompt solution of these difficult problems, the rehabilitation of the economic structure of Europe quite evidently will require a much longer time and greater effort than had been foreseen. . . .

The truth of the matter is that Europe's requirements for the next three or four years of foreign food and other essential products — principally from America — are so much greater than her present ability to pay that she must have substantial additional help or face economic, social, and political deterioration of a very grave character.

The remedy lies in breaking the vicious circle and restoring the confidence of the European people in the economic future of their own countries and of Europe as a whole. The manufacturer and the farmer throughout wide areas must be able and willing to exchange their products for currencies the continuing value of which is not open to question.

Aside from the demoralizing effect on the world at large and the possibilities of disturbances arising as a result of the desperation of the people concerned, the consequences to the economy of the United States should be apparent to all. It is logical that the United States should do whatever it is able to do to assist in the return of normal economic health in the world, without which there can be no political stability and no assured peace. Our policy is directed not against any country or doctrine but against hunger, poverty, desperation, and chaos. Its purpose should be the revival of a working economy in the world so as to permit the emergence of political and social conditions in which free institutions can exist. Such assistance, I am convinced, must not be on a piecemeal basis as various crises develop. Any assistance that this Government may render in the future should provide a cure rather than a mere palliative. Any government that is willing to assist in the task of recovery will find full cooperation, I am sure, on the part of the United States Government. Any government which maneuvers to block the recovery of other countries cannot expect help from us. Furthermore, governments, political parties, or groups which seek to perpetuate human misery in order to profit therefrom politically or otherwise will encounter the opposition of the United States.

It is already evident that, before the United States Government can proceed much further in its efforts to alleviate the situation and help start the European world on its way to recovery, there must be some agreement among the countries of Europe as to the requirements of the situation and the part those countries themselves will take in order to give proper effect to whatever action might be undertaken by this Government. It would be neither fitting nor efficacious for this Government to undertake to draw up unilaterally a program designed to place Europe on its feet economically. This is the business of the Europeans. The initiative, I think, must come from Europe. The role of this country should consist of friendly aid in the drafting of a European program and of later support of such a program so far as it may be practical for us to do so. The program should be a joint one, agreed to by a number, if not all, European nations.

An essential part of any successful action on the part of the United States is an understanding on the part of the people of America of the character of the problem and the remedies to be applied. Political passion and prejudice should have no part. With foresight, and a willingness on the part of our people to face up to the vast responsibility which history has clearly placed upon our country, the difficulties I have outlined can and will be overcome.

## 3 SOVIET INTERPRETATION OF THE MARSHALL PLAN
## Speech to the UN General Assembly
## Andrei Vyshinsky
## September 18, 1947

The so-called Truman Doctrine and the Marshall Plan are particularly glaring examples of the manner in which the principles of the United Nations are violated, of the way in which the Organization is ignored.

As the experience of the past few months has shown, the proclamation of this doctrine meant that the United States Government has moved towards a direct renunciation of the principles of international collaboration and concerted action by the great Powers and towards attempts to impose its will on other independent states, while at the same time obviously using the economic resources distributed as relief to individual needy nations as an instrument of political pressure. This is clearly proved by the measures taken by the United States Government with regard to Greece and Turkey which ignore and by-pass the United Nations as well as by the measures proposed under the so-called Marshall Plan in Europe. This policy conflicts sharply with the principle expressed by the General Assembly in its resolution of 11 December 1946, which declares that relief supplies to other countries "should . . . at no time be used as a political weapon."

As is now clear, the Marshall Plan constitutes in essence merely a variant of the Truman Doctrine adapted to the conditions of postwar Europe. In bringing forward this plan, the United States Government apparently counted on the cooperation of the Governments of the United Kingdom and France to confront the European countries in need of relief with the necessity of renouncing their inalienable right to dispose of their economic resources and to plan their national economy in their own way. The United States also counted on making all these countries directly dependent on the interests of American monopolies, which are striving to avert the approaching depression by an accelerated export of commodities and capital to Europe. . . .

It is becoming more and more evident to everyone that the implementation of the Marshall Plan will mean placing European countries under the economic and political control of the United States and direct interference by the latter in the internal affairs of those countries.

Moreover, this Plan is an attempt to split Europe into two camps and, with the help of the United Kingdom and France, to complete the formation of a *bloc* of several European countries hostile to the interests of the democratic countries of Eastern Europe and most particularly to the interests of the Soviet Union.

An important feature of this Plan is the attempt to confront the countries of Eastern Europe with a *bloc* of Western European States including Western Germany. The intention is to make use of Western Germany and German heavy industry (the Ruhr) as one of the most important economic bases for American expansion in Europe, in disregard of the national interests of the countries which suffered from German aggression.

I need only recall these facts to show the utter incompatibility of this policy of the United States, and of the British and French Governments which support it, with the fundamental principles of the United Nations.

## The Containment Strategy

### *Document 4*

After World War II, U.S.-Soviet relations deteriorated rapidly. Although the United States increasingly adhered to a policy of opposition to the spread of Soviet power, it lacked a central concept governing its behavior in the emerging cold war. In this setting an anonymous article (said to be written by "X," thus providing history with a convenient label for this essay) appeared in the July 1947 issue of the prominent quarterly, *Foreign Affairs*. Entitled "The Sources of Soviet Conduct," the article — whose author was soon revealed to be George Kennan — offers what was to become one of the fundamental concepts of U.S. policy toward the Soviet Union in the entire nuclear age: containment. In the excerpts here, Kennan urges that "the main element of any United States policy toward the Soviet Union must be that of a long-term, patient but firm and vigilant containment of Russian expansive tendencies."

### 4 THE SOURCES OF SOVIET CONDUCT (THE "X" ARTICLE)
### George Kennan, Senior State Department Official
### July 1947

The political personality of Soviet power as we know it today is the product of ideology and circumstances: ideology inherited by the present Soviet leaders from the movement in which they had their political origin, and circumstances of the power which they now have exercised for nearly three decades in Russia. . . .

Of the original ideology, nothing has been officially junked. Belief is maintained in the basic badness of capitalism, in the inevitability of its destruction, in the obligation of the proletariat to assist in that destruction and to take power into its own hands. But stress has come to be laid primarily on those concepts which relate most specifically to the Soviet régime itself: to its position as the sole truly Socialist régime in a dark and misguided world, and to the relationships of power within it.

The first of these concepts is that of the innate antagonism between capitalism and Socialism. We have seen how deeply that concept has become imbedded in foundations of Soviet power. It has profound implications for Russia's conduct as a member of international society. It means that there can never be on Moscow's side any sincere assumption of a community of aims between the Soviet Union and powers which are regarded as capitalist. It must invariably be assumed in Moscow that the aims of the capitalist world are antagonistic to the Soviet régime, and therefore to the interests of the peoples it controls. If the Soviet Government occasionally sets its signature to documents which would indicate the contrary, this is to be regarded as a tactical manœuvre permissible in dealing with the enemy (who is without honor) and should be taken in the spirit of *caveat emptor*. Basically, the antagonism remains. It is postulated. And from it flow many of the phenomena which we find disturbing in the Kremlin's conduct of foreign policy: the secretiveness, the lack of frankness, the duplicity, the wary suspiciousness, and the basic unfriendliness of purpose. These phenomena are there to stay, for the foreseeable future. There can be variations of degree and of emphasis. When there is something the Russians want from us, one or the other of these features of their policy may be thrust temporarily into the background; and when that happens there will always be Americans who will leap forward with gleeful announcements that "the Russians have changed," and some who will even try to take credit for having brought about such "changes." But we should not be misled by tactical manœuvres. These characteristics of Soviet policy, like the postulate from which they flow, are basic to the internal nature of Soviet power, and will be with us, whether in the foreground or the background, until the internal nature of Soviet power is changed.

This means that we are going to continue for a long time to find the Russians difficult to deal with. It does not mean that they should be considered as embarked upon a do-or-die program to overthrow our society by a given date. The theory of the inevitability of the eventual fall of capitalism has the fortunate connotation that there is no hurry about it. The forces of progress can take their time in preparing the final *coup de grâce.* Meanwhile, what is vital is that the "Socialist fatherland" — that oasis of power which has been already won for Socialism in the person of the Soviet Union — should be cherished and defended by all good Communists at home and abroad, its fortunes promoted, its enemies badgered and confounded. The promotion of premature, "adventuristic" revolutionary projects abroad which might embarrass Soviet power in any way would be an inexcusable, even a counter-revolutionary act. The cause of Socialism is the support and promotion of Soviet power, as defined in Moscow.

This brings us to the second of the concepts important to contemporary Soviet outlook. That is the infallibility of the Kremlin. The Soviet concept of power, which permits no focal points of organization outside the Party itself, requires that the Party leadership remain in theory the sole repository of truth. For if truth were to be found elsewhere, there would be justification for its expression in organized activity. But it is precisely that which the Kremlin cannot and will not permit.

The leadership of the Communist Party is therefore always right, and has been always right ever since in 1929 Stalin formalized his personal power by announcing that decisions of the Politburo were being taken unanimously.

On the principle of infallibility there rests the iron discipline of the Communist Party. In fact, the two concepts are mutually self-supporting. Perfect discipline requires recognition of infallibility. Infallibility requires the observance of discipline. And the two together go far to determine the behaviorism of the entire Soviet apparatus of power. But their effect cannot be understood unless a third factor be taken into account: namely, the fact that the leadership is at liberty to put forward for tactical purposes any particular thesis which it finds useful to the cause at any particular moment and to require the faithful and unquestioning acceptance of that thesis by the members of the movement as a whole. This means that truth is not a constant but is actually created, for all intents and purposes, by the Soviet leaders themselves. It may vary from week to week, from month to month. It is nothing absolute and immutable — nothing which flows from objective reality. It is only the most recent manifestation of the wisdom of those in whom the ultimate wisdom is supposed to reside, because they represent the logic of history. The accumulative effect of these factors is to give to the whole subordinate apparatus of Soviet power an unshakeable stubbornness and steadfastness in its orientation. This orientation can be changed at will by the Kremlin but by no other power. Once a given party line has been laid down on a given issue of current policy, the whole Soviet governmental machine, including the mechanism of diplomacy, moves inexorably along the prescribed path, like a persistent toy automobile wound up and headed in a given direction, stopping only when it meets with some unanswerable force. The individuals who are the components of this machine are unamenable to argument or reason which comes to them from outside sources.... Since there can be no appeal to common purposes, there can be no appeal to common mental approaches. For this reason, facts speak louder than words to the ears of the Kremlin; and words carry the greatest weight when they have the ring of reflecting, or being backed up by, facts of unchallengeable validity....

...Thus the Kremlin has no compunction about retreating in the face of superior force. And being under the compulsion of no timetable, it does not get panicky under the necessity for such retreat. Its political action is a fluid stream which moves constantly, wherever it is permitted to move, toward a given goal. Its main concern is to make sure that it has filled every nook and cranny available to it in the basin of world power. But if it finds unassailable barriers in its path, it accepts these philosophically and accommodates itself to them. The main thing is that there should always be pressure, unceasing constant pressure, toward the desired goal. There is no trace of any feeling in Soviet psychology that that goal must be reached at any given time.

These considerations make Soviet diplomacy at once easier and more difficult to deal with than the diplomacy of individual aggressive leaders like Napoleon and Hitler. On the one hand it is more sensitive to contrary force, more ready to yield on individual sectors of the diplomatic front when that force is felt to be too strong, and thus more rational in the logic and rhetoric of power. On the other hand it cannot be easily defeated or discouraged by a single victory on the part of its opponents. And the patient persistence by which it is animated means that it can be effectively countered not by sporadic acts which represent the momentary whims of democratic opinion but only by intelligent long-range policies on the part of Russia's adversaries — policies no less steady in their purpose, and no less variegated and resourceful in their application, than those of the Soviet Union itself.

In these circumstances it is clear that the main element of any United States policy toward the Soviet Union must be that of a long-term, patient but firm and vigilant containment of Russian expansive tendencies. It is important to note, however, that such a policy has nothing to do with outward histrionics: with threats or blustering or superfluous gestures of outward "toughness." While the Kremlin is basically flexible in its reaction to political realities, it is by no means unamenable to considerations of prestige. Like almost any other government, it can be placed by tactless and threatening gestures in a position where it cannot afford to yield even though this might be dictated by its sense of realism. The Russian leaders are keen judges of human psychology, and as such they are highly conscious that loss of temper and of self-control is never a source of strength in political affairs. They are quick to exploit such evidences of weakness. For these reasons, it is a *sine qua non* of successful dealing with Russia that the foreign government in question should remain at all times cool and collected and that its demands on Russian policy should be put forward in such a manner as to leave the way open for a compliance not too detrimental to Russian prestige.

In the light of the above, it will be clearly seen that the Soviet pressure against the free institutions of the western world is something that can be contained by the adroit and vigilant application of counter-force at a series of constantly shifting geographical and political points, corresponding to the shifts and manœuvres of Soviet policy, but which cannot be charmed or talked out of existence. The Russians look forward to a duel of infinite duration, and they see that already they have scored great successes. It must be borne in mind that there was a time when the Communist Party represented far more of a minority in the sphere of Russian national life than Soviet power today represents in the world community....

It is clear that the United States cannot expect in the foreseeable future to enjoy political intimacy with the Soviet régime. It must continue to regard the Soviet Union as a rival, not a partner, in the political arena. It must continue to expect that Soviet policies will reflect no abstract love of peace and stability, no real faith in the possibility of a permanent happy coexistence of the Socialist and capitalist worlds, but rather a cautious, persistent pressure toward the disruption and weakening of all rival influence and rival power.

Balanced against this are the facts that Russia, as opposed to the western world in general, is still by far the weaker party, that Soviet policy is highly flexible, and that Soviet society may well contain deficiencies which will eventually weaken its own total potential. This would of itself warrant the United States entering with reasonable confidence upon a policy of firm containment, designed to confront the Russians with unalterable counter-force at every point where they show signs of encroaching upon the interests of a peaceful and stable world.

But in actuality the possibilities for American policy are by no means limited to holding the line and hoping for the best. It is entirely possible for the United States to influence by its actions the internal developments, both within Russia and throughout the international Communist movement, by which Russian policy is largely determined. This is not only a question of the modest measure of informational activity which this government can conduct in the Soviet Union and elsewhere, although that, too, is important. It is rather a question of the degree to which the United States can create among the peoples of the world generally the impression of a country which knows what it wants, which is coping successfully with the problems of its internal life and with the responsibilities of a World Power, and which has a spiritual vitality capable of holding its own among the major ideological currents of the time. To the extent that such an impression can be created and maintained, the aims of Russian Communism must appear sterile and quixotic, the hopes and enthusiasm of Moscow's supporters must wane, and added strain must be imposed on the Kremlin's foreign policies. For the palsied decrepitude of the capitalist world is the keystone of Communist philosophy. Even the failure of the United States to experience the early economic depression which the ravens of the Red Square have been predicting with such complacent confidence since hostilities ceased would have deep and important repercussions throughout the Communist world.

By the same token, exhibitions of indecision, disunity and internal disintegration within this country have an exhilarating effect on the whole Communist movement. At each evidence of these tendencies, a thrill of hope and excitement goes through the Communist world; a new jauntiness can be noted in the Moscow tread; new groups of foreign supporters climb on to what they can only view as the band wagon of international politics; and Russian pressure increases all along the line in international affairs.

It would be an exaggeration to say that American behavior unassisted and alone could exercise a power of life and death over the Communist movement and bring about the early fall of Soviet power in Russia. But the United States has it in its power to increase enormously the strains under which Soviet policy must operate, to force upon the Kremlin a far greater degree of moderation and circumspection than it has had to observe in recent years, and in this way to promote tendencies which must eventually find their outlet in either the break-up or the gradual mellowing of Soviet power. For no mystical, Messianic movement — and particularly not that of the Kremlin — can face frustration indefinitely without eventually adjusting itself in one way or another to the logic of that state of affairs.

Thus the decision will really fall in large measure in this country itself. The issue of Soviet-American relations is in essence a test of the over-all worth of the United States as a nation among nations. To avoid destruction the United States need only measure up to its own best traditions and prove itself worthy of preservation as a great nation.

Surely, there was never a fairer test of national quality than this. In the light of these circumstances, the thoughtful observer of Russian-American relations will find no cause for complaint in the Kremlin's challenge to American society. He will rather experience a certain gratitude to a Providence which, by providing the American people with this implacable challenge, has made their entire security as a nation dependent on their pulling themselves together and accepting the responsibilities of moral and political leadership that history plainly intended them to bear.

## Soviet Call for Struggle with the West

### *Document 5*

George Kennan's "X" article seemed to signal U.S. determination to wage a protracted geopolitical struggle with the Soviet Union. For the Kremlin's part, a similar signal was given by Andrei Zhdanov, then Stalin's heir presumptive, at the founding conference of the Communist Information Bureau (Cominform) in Poland in September 1947. Zhdanov called upon the newly established Cominform to help consolidate the Soviet sphere in Eastern Europe. He also urged its French and Italian Communist party delegates to disrupt the national life of the "bourgeois democracies" in Western Europe. Thus, only two years after the Allies' hard-won victory over Hitler, the leadership of both blocs were describing the East–West contest in implacably hostile ideological terms that left little room for bargaining or compromise.

### 5 REPORT ON THE INTERNATIONAL SITUATION TO THE COMINFORM
### Andrei Zhdanov
### September 22, 1947

The fundamental changes caused by the war on the international scene and in the position of individual countries has entirely changed the political landscape of the world. A new alignment of political forces has arisen. The more the war recedes into the past, the more distinct become two major trends in post-war international policy, corresponding to the division of the political forces operating on the international arena into two major camps: the imperialist and anti-democratic camp, on the one hand, and the anti-imperialist and democratic camp, on the other. The principal driving force of the imperialist camp is the U.S.A. Allied with it are Great Britain and France. . . . The imperialist camp is also supported by colony-owning countries, such as Belgium and Holland, by countries with reactionary anti-democratic regimes, such as Turkey and Greece, and by countries politically and economically dependent upon the United States, such as the Near-Eastern and South-American countries and China.

The cardinal purpose of the imperialist camp is to strengthen imperialism, to hatch a new imperialist war, to combat socialism and democracy, and to support reactionary and anti-democratic profascist regimes and movements everywhere.

In the pursuit of these ends the imperialist camp is prepared to rely on reactionary and anti-democratic forces in all countries, and to support its former adversaries in the war against its wartime allies.

The anti-fascist forces comprise the second camp. This camp is based on the U.S.S.R. and the new democracies. It also includes countries that have broken with imperialism and have firmly set foot on the path of democratic development, such as Rumania, Hungary and Finland. Indonesia and Viet Nam are associated with it; it has the sympathy of India, Egypt and Syria. The anti-imperialist camp is backed by the labour and democratic movement and by the fraternal Communist parties in all countries, by the fighters for national liberation in the colonies and dependencies, by all progressive and democratic forces in every country. The purpose of this camp is to resist the threat of new wars and imperialist expansion, to strengthen democracy and to extirpate the vestiges of fascism.

The end of the Second World War confronted all the freedom-loving nations with the cardinal task of securing a lasting democratic peace sealing victory over fascism. In the accomplishment of this fundamental task of the post-war period the Soviet Union and its foreign policy are playing a leading role. This follows from the very nature of the Soviet socialist state, to which motives of aggression and exploitation are utterly alien, and which is interested in creating the most favourable conditions for the building of a Communist society. One of these conditions is external peace. As embodiment of a new and superior social system, the Soviet Union reflects in its foreign policy the aspirations of progressive mankind, which desires lasting peace and has nothing to gain from a new war hatched by capitalism. The Soviet Union is a staunch champion of the liberty and independence of all nations, and a foe of national and racial oppression and colonial exploitation in any shape or form. The change in the general alignment of forces between the capitalist world and the socialist world brought about by the war has still further enhanced the significance of the foreign policy of the Soviet state and enlarged the scope of its activity on the international arena.

The successes and the growing international prestige of the democratic camp were not to the liking of the imperialists. Even while World War II was still on, reactionary forces in Great Britain and the United States became increasingly active, striving to prevent concerted action by the Allied powers, to protract the war, to bleed the U.S.S.R., and to save the fascist aggressors from utter defeat. The sabotage of the Second Front by the Anglo-Saxon imperialists, headed by Churchill, was a clear reflection of this tendency, which was in point of fact a continuation of the Munich policy in the new and changed conditions. But while the war was still in progress British and American reactionary circles did not venture to come out openly against the Soviet Union and the democratic countries, realizing that they had the undivided sympathy of the masses all over the world. But in the concluding months of the war the situation began to change. The British and American imperialists already manifested their unwillingness to respect the legitimate interests of the Soviet Union and the democratic countries at the Potsdam tripartite conference, in July 1945.

The foreign policy of the Soviet Union and the democratic countries in these two past years has been a policy of consistently working for the observance of the democratic principles in the post-war settlement. The countries of the anti-imperialist camp have loyally and consistently striven for the implementation of these principles, without deviating from them one iota. Consequently, the major objective of the post-war foreign policy of the democratic states has been a democratic peace, the eradication of the vestiges of fascism and the prevention of a resurgence of fascist imperialist aggression, the recognition of the principle of the equality of nations and respect for their sovereignty, and general reduction of all armaments and the outlawing of the most destructive weapons, those designed for the mass slaughter of the civilian population. . . .

Of immense importance are the joint efforts of the diplomacy of the U.S.S.R. and that of the other democratic countries to secure a reduction of armaments and the outlawing of the most destructive of them — the atomic bomb.

Soviet foreign policy proceeds from the fact of the co-existence for a long period of the two systems — capitalism and socialism. From this it follows that co-operation between the U.S.S.R. and countries with other systems is possible, provided that the principle of reciprocity is observed and that obligations once assumed are honoured. Everyone knows that the U.S.S.R. has always honoured the obligations it has assumed. The Soviet Union has demonstrated its will and desire for co-operation.

## The Formation of NATO

### *Documents 6 and 7*

One of the most enduring and important actions taken in this period was the creation of the North Atlantic Pact, which soon grew into the North Atlantic Treaty Organization (NATO). Just as the Marshall Plan was designed to provide economic support and assistance, NATO was intended to provide political support and military assistance to Western Europe, threatened as it was by the proximity of Soviet power. Indeed, the two agreements were viewed as complementary efforts in the U.S. strategy of revitalizing Europe. In the North Atlantic Pact, the United States pledged itself to the defense of non-Communist Europe; in the treaty's famous Article 5, the signatories agreed that an attack on one is an attack on all.

Given the long U.S. tradition of remaining free of entangling alliances in peacetime, the North Atlantic Pact was sure to be controversial. As soon as its text was made public on March 18, 1949, Secretary of State Dean Acheson delivered a nationwide address, excerpted in document 6, describing and explaining the treaty; this marks the beginning of many months of deliberations on the ratification and implementation of the pact. Not surprisingly, the Soviet government vociferously denounced the proposed North Atlantic Treaty. Document 7 argues that the treaty's ostensible commitment to self-defense only thinly disguises its obviously aggressive intent and anti-Soviet character.

### 6 THE MEANING OF THE NORTH ATLANTIC PACT
### Address by Secretary of State Dean Acheson
### March 18, 1949

The text of the proposed North Atlantic pact was made public today. I welcome this opportunity to talk with my fellow citizens about it. . . .

I think the American people will want to know the answers to three principal questions about the pact: How did it come about and why is it necessary? What are its terms? Will it accomplish its purpose?

The paramount purposes of the pact are peace and security. If peace and security can be achieved in the North Atlantic area, we shall have gone a long way to assure peace and security in other areas as well. . . .

These are goals of our own foreign policy which President Truman has emphasized many times, most recently in his inaugural address when he spoke of the hope that we could help create "the conditions that will lead eventually to personal freedom and happiness for all mankind." These are also the purposes of the United Nations, whose members are pledged "to maintain international peace and security" and to promote "the economic and social advancement of all peoples." . . .

The Atlantic pact is a collective self-defense arrangement among the countries of the North Atlantic area. It is aimed at coordinating the exercise of the right of self-defense specifically recognized in article 51 of the United Nations Charter. It is designed to fit precisely into the framework of the United Nations and to assure practical measures for maintaining peace and security in harmony with the Charter. . . .

It is important to keep in mind that the really successful national and international institutions are those that recognize and express underlying realities. The North Atlantic community of nations is such a reality. It is based on the affinity and natural identity of interests of the North Atlantic powers. . . .

It is clear that the North Atlantic pact is not an improvisation. It is the statement of the facts and lessons of history. We have learned our history lesson from two world wars in less than half a century. That experience has taught us that the control of Europe by a single aggressive, unfriendly power would constitute an intolerable threat to the national security of the United States. We participated in those two great wars to preserve the integrity and independence of the European half of the Atlantic community in order to preserve the integrity and independence of the American half. It is a simple fact, proved by experience, that an outside attack on one member of this community is an attack upon all members.

We have also learned that if the free nations do not stand together, they will fall one by one. The stratagem of the aggressor is to keep his intended victims divided, or, better still, set them to quarreling among themselves. Then they can be picked off one by one without arousing unified resistance. We and the free nations of Europe are determined that history shall not repeat itself in that melancholy particular. . . .

What are the principal provisions of the North Atlantic pact? I should like to summarize them.

First, the pact is carefully and conscientiously designed to conform in every particular with the Charter of the United Nations. . . .

The second article is equally fundamental. The associated countries assert that they will preserve and strengthen their free institutions and will see to it that the fundamental principles upon which free institutions are founded are better understood everywhere. They also agree to eliminate conflicts in their economic life and to promote economic cooperation among themselves. Here is the ethical essence of the treaty — the common resolve to preserve, strengthen, and make understood the very basis of tolerance, restraint, and freedom — the really vital things with which we are concerned.

This purpose is extended further in article 3, in which the participating countries pledge themselves to self-help and mutual aid. In addition to strengthening their free institutions, they will take practical steps to maintain and develop their own capacity and that of their partners to resist aggression. They also agree to consult together when the integrity or security of any of them is threatened. The treaty sets up a council, consisting of all the members, and other machinery for consultation and for carrying out the provisions of the pact.

Successful resistance to aggression in the modern world requires modern arms and trained military forces. As a result of the recent war, the European countries joining in the pact are generally deficient in both requirements. The treaty does not bind the United States to any arms program. But we all know that the United States is now the only democratic nation with the resources and the productive capacity to help the free nations of Europe to recover their military strength.

Therefore, we expect to ask the Congress to supply our European partners some of the weapons and equipment they need to be able to resist aggression. We also expect to recommend military supplies for other free nations which will cooperate with us in safeguarding peace and security.

In the compact world of today, the security of the United States cannot be defined in terms of boundaries and frontiers. A serious threat to international peace and security anywhere in the world is of direct concern to this country. Therefore it is our policy to help free peoples to maintain their integrity and independence, not only in Western Europe or in the Americas, but wherever the aid we are able to provide can be effective. Our actions in supporting the integrity and independence of Greece, Turkey, and Iran are expressions of that determination. Our interest in the security of these countries has been made clear, and we shall continue to pursue that policy. . . .

But to return to the treaty, article 5 deals with the possibility, which unhappily cannot be excluded, that the nations joining together in the pact may have to face the eventuality of an armed attack. In this article, they agree that an armed attack on any of them, in Europe or North America, will be considered an attack on all of them. In the event of such an attack, each of them will take, individually and in concert with the other parties, whatever action it deems necessary to restore and maintain the security of the North Atlantic area, including the use of armed force.

This does not mean that the United States would be automatically at war if one of the nations covered by the pact is subjected to armed attack. Under our Constitution, the Congress alone has the power to declare war. We would be bound to take promptly the action which we deemed necessary to restore and maintain the security of the North Atlantic area. That decision would be taken in accordance with our constitutional procedures. The factors which would have to be considered would be, on the one side, the gravity of the armed attack, on the other, the action which we believed necessary to restore and maintain the security of the North Atlantic area. That is the end to be achieved. We are bound to do what in our honest judgment is necessary to reach that result. If we should be confronted again with a calculated armed attack such as we have twice seen in the twentieth century, I should not suppose that we would decide any action other than the use of armed force effective either as an exercise of the right of collective self-defense or as necessary to restore the peace and security of the

North Atlantic area. That decision will rest where the Constitution has placed it. . . .

The treaty has no time limit, but after it has been in effect 20 years any member can withdraw on 1 year's notice. It also provides that after it has been in existence 10 years, it will be reviewed in the circumstances prevailing at that time. Additional countries may be admitted to the pact by agreement of all the parties already signatories. . . .

To have this genuine peace we must constantly work for it. But we must do even more. We must make it clear that armed attack will be met by collective defense, prompt and effective.

That is the meaning of the North Atlantic pact.

## 7 MEMORANDUM OF THE SOVIET GOVERNMENT March 31, 1949

On March 18 the State Department of the United States published the text of the North Atlantic Treaty which the Governments of the United States of America, Great Britain, France, Belgium, the Netherlands, Luxemburg, and Canada intend to sign within the next few days.

The text of the North Atlantic Treaty fully confirms what was said in the declaration of the USSR Ministry of Foreign Affairs of January 29 this year, which is being attached hereto, both as regards the aggressive aims of this Treaty and the fact that the North Atlantic Treaty contradicts the principles and aims of the United Nations Organization and the commitments which the Governments of the United States of America, Great Britain, and France have assumed under other Treaties and Agreements. The statements contained in the North Atlantic Treaty, that it is designated for defense and that it recognizes the principles of the United Nations Organization, serve aims which have nothing in common either with the tasks of self-defense of the parties to the Treaty or with real recognition of the aims and principles of the United Nations Organization. Such great Powers as the United States, Great Britain, and France are parties to the North Atlantic Treaty. Thus the Treaty is not directed either against the United States of America, Great Britain, or France. Of the Great Powers only the Soviet Union is excluded from among the parties to this Treaty, which can be explained only by the fact that this Treaty is directed against the Soviet Union. The fact that the North Atlantic Treaty is directed against the USSR as well as against the countries of people's democracy was definitely pointed out also by official representatives of the United States of America, Great Britain, and France. . . .

. . . The North Atlantic Treaty is not a bilateral, but a multilateral treaty, which creates a closed grouping of states and, what is particularly important, absolutely ignores the possibility of a repetition of German aggression, consequently not having as its aim the prevention of a new German aggression. And inasmuch as of the Great Powers which comprised the anti-Hitlerite coalition only the USSR is not a party to this Treaty, the North Atlantic Treaty must be regarded as a Treaty directed against one of the chief allies of the United States, Great Britain, and France in the late war, against the USSR.

Participants in the North Atlantic Treaty are effecting extensive military measures which can in no way be justified by the interests of self-defense of these countries. The extensive military measures carried out by the United States in cooperation with Great Britain and France, under the present peacetime conditions, including the increase in all types of armed forces, the drafting of a plan for the utilization of the atomic weapon, the stock-piling of atom bombs, which are purely an offensive weapon, the building of a network of air and naval bases, etc. — bear a by no means defensive character. . . .

At the same time one cannot but see the groundlessness of the anti-Soviet motives of the North Atlantic Treaty, inasmuch as it is known to all that the Soviet Union does not intend to attack anyone and in no way threatens the United States of America, Great Britain, France, or the other parties to the Treaty. . . .

On the basis of all the above, the Soviet Government arrives at the following conclusions:

1. The North Atlantic Treaty has nothing in common with the aims of the self-defense of the states who are parties to the Treaty, who are threatened by no one, whom no one intends to attack. On the contrary, this Treaty has an obviously aggressive character and is aimed against the USSR, which fact is not concealed even by official representatives of the states who are parties to the Treaty in their public pronouncements.
2. The North Atlantic Treaty not only does not contribute to the consolidation of peace and international security, which is the duty of all members of the United Nations Organization, but runs directly counter to the principles and aims of the United Nations Charter and leads to undermining the United Nations Organization.
3. The North Atlantic Treaty runs counter to the treaty between Great Britain and the Soviet Union signed in 1942, under which both states assumed the obligation to cooperate in the maintenance of peace and international security and "not to conclude any alliances and not to participate in any coalitions directed against the other High Contracting Party."

# The U.S. Public Is Stunned

### *Document 8*

Political scientist Richard Smoke discusses the effect of two shocks to U.S. security that took place in the last half of 1949: the Communist takeover in China and the explosion of the first Soviet atomic bomb. Neither had been expected by top U.S. officials, and both stunned the U.S. public. The result was that President Truman decided to proceed with the development of the hydrogen bomb (or "Super") and ordered a high-level study to make changes in U.S. national security policy.

## 8 THE YEAR OF SHOCKS
## Richard Smoke

In the second half of 1949 occurred two events that severely shook Americans' sense of relative security. One was the final victory of the Communists in the Chinese civil war. For a dozen years starting in the 1920s, Mao Zedong and his Peoples' Liberation Army had fought the Nationalist government headed by Chiang Kai-shek. After the Japanese attacked in the 1930s, the two Chinese parties had made an alliance to fight the invader, each in the part of the country it controlled. But with the defeat of Japan in World War II, the civil war had erupted again more violently than ever, and the Communists began making rapid progress. By 1949 the Nationalists were evacuating their forces to the island of Taiwan, leaving Mao in possession of the mainland and its huge population.

Mao had briefly been interested in American assistance when the civil war had resumed; after being rebuffed he turned to the USSR. In exchange for increasingly close ties he received some aid, and after he formed a government the relationship was formalized in a treaty of friendship. The American people, who traditionally had felt a special, somewhat sentimental, attachment for China, were shocked when it was taken over by Communists and allies of the USSR. At one blow this doubled the territory and quadrupled the population controlled by Communism.

Even more stunning was the first atomic test explosion by the Soviet Union. American specialists had expected that this would not occur for several more years at the soonest; optimists had thought longer. Now, on September 23, the White House announced that it had already happened. Trying to forestall panic, it coupled the announcement with reassurances. Government spokesmen pointed out, for instance, that this explosion (like the first American test) was of a "device" too big to carry in an airplane, and that real bombs, even when designed, could not be manufactured rapidly. But people knew that they would be built as soon as they could be, and that before long America might become vulnerable to atomic attack. In the following years thousands of Americans would sign up for "Operation Skywatch," in which volunteers would scan the heavens with binoculars, looking for incoming Soviet bombers.

The "fall" of China and the Soviet atomic test, occurring back to back, shocked and worried Americans more than anything that had happened yet. Although the danger might not be immediate, the implications for the future were very ominous. The USSR and China together ruled over a quarter of the world's people, and controlled most of the world's greatest landmass, from the middle of Europe all the way around half the globe to the South China Sea. If the Communists had atomic bombs also, what might they try to take over next?

In response to this new and graver challenge, President Truman took two initiatives. One was to order a complete review and reanalysis of the world situation, with recommendations for new U.S. national security policies. (The results are discussed below.) The other was to proceed with a more terrible weapon that had now become possible.

Atomic bombs worked by the sudden fission of heavy uranium or plutonium atoms into smaller fragments. American scientists now knew that it would also be possible to set off even mightier explosions by the sudden fusion of lightweight hydrogen atoms into heavier elements. In a less explosive way this was the power that was keeping the sun bright and hot for untold ages. Plans had been drafted for developing a fusion bomb, initially called Super, and now the president ordered that Super be built.

There was little choice, Truman believed, because the Soviets would be working on a fusion bomb as well. He ordered that work on Super proceed as rapidly as possible, and the United States was the first to explode a hydrogen device, on a Pacific island in 1952. Even so it was the Soviet Union, not the United States, that was first to test a bomb, working partly on fusion, that was small enough to drop from an airplane. (This fact was not revealed to the American public for many years; and indeed it was not as significant as it would have seemed to the public at the time because the United States tested a fusion bomb soon after, and a better one.)

The U.S. and Soviet decisions to develop hydrogen bombs were of deep importance, because fusion weapons can be enormously more destructive than fission bombs. There is an inherent upper limit to the explosive power, called "yield," that a fission weapon can have, but there is none for fusion bombs. While the force of a fission bomb is awe-inspiring, that of a fusion bomb is almost incomprehensible. The yield of a fission weapon is measured by how many thousands of tons of the strongest chemical explosive, TNT, would be required to create a blast of equal size. The Hiroshima bomb, for instance, was the equivalent of about fifteen thousand tons of TNT, or fifteen "kilotons." But hydrogen weapons are measured in *millions* of tons of TNT, or "megatons."

The difference is more important than the average man on the street is likely to think offhand. A fission bomb of fifteen kilotons dropped on the Statue of Liberty in New York harbor would do little more than break windowpanes at the distance of Times Square (some seven miles away). But a ten-megaton hydrogen bomb dropped at the same place would utterly devastate all of Manhattan and, indeed, the entire New York City and harbor area. Although the public did not fully realize it when news of the hydrogen bomb was released, the step from fission to fusion bombs was at least as significant as the earlier step from the largest conventional bombs to fission. The wholesale death of most of a nation's people and the destruction of civilization — most peoples' image of "the end of the world" in atomic war — would actually be fairly difficult to accomplish with fission weapons only. With hydrogen weapons it becomes all too feasible.

Truman's other initiative, the reanalysis of the overall national security challenge, was carried out by a special task force drawn from several departments of government. The study it produced was to become a landmark in U.S. national security affairs.

## NSC-68

The study was submitted to the National Security Council in the spring of 1950, and became known as NSC-68 (that is, the 68th policy document prepared for the council). The task force had taken seriously Truman's request for a complete and general reassessment of the United States' overall position in the world. Drawing on all available intelligence, NSC-68 analyzed the American national security situation broadly and traced through the logic of existing and anticipated problems. In doing so it created something the United States had never had before: a comprehensive national security policy and strategy.

NSC-68 began with a review of the overall world situation. Stating that the USSR "seeks to impose its absolute authority over the rest of the world," and that Soviet political values are incompatible with those of a free society, the report identified the Soviet Union as a grave threat to American security. It reviewed the political and economic strengths and weaknesses of the two societies, and pointed out that the USSR devoted a "far greater proportion" of its total resources to military purposes than did the United States. It also concluded that international control over atomic weapons would remain impossible until such time as Soviet aggressive designs were so thoroughly frustrated that a drastic change in Soviet policy might follow.

NSC-68 then distinguished and analyzed four courses of possible American action: to continue present policies, to retreat into isolation and seek to defend only the Western Hemisphere, to launch a "preventive war," or to build up American power. It argued against the first three and strongly for the last. A substantial military buildup would be needed "to deter, if possible, Soviet expansion, and to defeat, if necessary, aggressive Soviet or Soviet-directed actions of a limited or total character."

The Soviet threat was now more urgent because the USSR possessed atomic bombs and could be presumed to be working on hydrogen bombs. NSC-68 estimated that by 1954 the Soviets could have 200 fission bombs and cautioned that its estimate might be low. Without an American buildup, the Soviets could then destroy enough of Western Europe to make any defense against the Red Army impossible, destroy Britain sufficiently to preclude its use in any subsequent effort to liberate Europe, and make devastating attacks on the United States.

Several things would have to be done. Clearly one was "to provide an adequate defense against air attack on the United States." Up to this time, the United States had never made any serious effort to protect its airspace. Now it must. This was one concrete recommendation of NSC-68 that was carried out. In the following years several lines of radar stations were erected across Canada, and extended out to sea on ships, to spot attacking Soviet bombers while they were still some distance away. A substantial force of fighter aircraft and of surface-to-air missiles (SAMs) was also deployed. Inevitably some Soviet bombers would get through, however.

NSC-68 also concluded that the United States must provide "an adequate defense against air and surface attack on the United Kingdom, Western Europe . . . and on the long lines of communication to these areas." This meant a large increase in U.S. *conventional* forces. Although the report did not point it out explicitly, defense against the enormous Red Army formations in Eastern Europe would mean a large commitment of American ground troops to Europe. An effort to defend Europe against the Soviet Air Force would also mean a significant USAF commitment. The NATO allies would not be able to carry this burden by 1954. In turn, American ground and air forces in Europe would have to have their supply lines across the Atlantic protected by adequate U.S. naval forces. Furthermore the United States should have conventional forces "in being and readily available to defeat local Soviet moves with local action," so that a limited attack did not become "the occasion for [all-out] war."

The conclusion that Europe would have to be defended represented a major departure in American thinking. Up to this time it had been assumed that the Red Army was deterred by SAC from marching into Western Europe. A Soviet invasion would mean all-out war, and all-out war would mean American atomic strikes on the USSR. Implicit in NSC-68 was a new logic. Soon the Soviets would also have the ability to make atomic strikes on an enemy's homeland. An American strike on the Soviet Union would presumably be answered in kind, by Soviet atomic attacks on America and Western Europe.

A new situation was developing in which each nuclear

power would know that striking the other side's cities would invite a counter-strike on one's own. In effect the two nuclear forces would balance and *mutually deter each other.* A nuclear stalemate would develop, in which neither side would dare launch an atomic attack on the other.

This meant, although NSC-68 did not develop the argument explicitly, that another way would have to be found to protect the European allies. SAC might *not* be unleashed if the Red Army invaded, or at any rate the Soviets might not think it would be. If they didn't think so they might not be deterred from invading. In a strategy of deterrence, what the enemy *thinks* is all important. If he does not believe your threat, he may attack and deterrence will have failed. It does not help then that you really did mean it.

So the United States would have to station conventional forces in Europe after all, and since they would hardly be sufficient by themselves, the NATO allies would have to contribute forces also, as their postwar recovery enabled them to. A combined force of American and West European armies, though probably not large enough to match the Red Army man for man, might be large enough to make an invasion too costly for the Soviets. Rather than a quick and predictable victory they would face a real European war, the results of which could not be foreseen. The risks to the Soviet empire in Eastern Europe, and even to the USSR itself, would be high in such a war. Hence the Soviets would be deterred from attacking. They would be deterred on the "level" of violence of a European war, just as they would be deterred at the level of war by long-range bombers by the mutual deterrence that would exist at that level.

By now deterrence was far from simple and far from effortless. The assumption of the first postwar years, that deterrence was almost automatic, had been blown up in the first Soviet nuclear test. Deterrence had now become an analytic problem and a vital policy objective — one that might be achieved only at considerable cost and trouble.

From an analytic point of view the first Soviet atomic explosion was more significant, in a sense, than the first American one. One nation that possessed nuclear weapons in quantity was, quite simply, supreme on the planet. What raised complicated and novel problems was the existence of *two* or more nuclear-weapon states. Implicit in NSC-68 was a grim logic of deterrence and counter-deterrence on multiple levels, a logic that was to become characteristic of national security problems in our era.

The report did not include estimates of how much it would cost to carry out its recommendations. State Department representatives on the team that wrote it guessed it might be $35 to $40 billion or more, in 1950 dollars. (This is roughly $130–$150 billion in 1983 dollars.) This amount was approximately triple what the defense budget had been over the immediately preceding years.

Through the spring of 1950, the paper was studied and debated in the upper circles of the government. Before a consensus could be reached or President Truman make a final decision, however, the Korean War broke upon the world. NSC-68 and the problems it raised were put aside while this newest emergency seized everyone's attention. The defense budget did go up to about $40 billion, but to meet the attack in Asia, not the demands of doctrine or a possible future attack in Europe. The approach to national security taken by NSC-68 was never finally approved by the president, and by the time the Korean War was over a new administration in Washington had decided on a different approach. Almost another decade would pass before the philosophy of NSC 68, under a different name, would finally triumph in American national security policy.

## Summary

The impossibility of creating a workable collective security system in the period just following World War II led the United States to fashion its own national security. Not surprisingly, organizational arrangements and a foreign policy goal, containment, came first. Next developed policies in support of containment, the Truman Doctrine and the Marshall Plan. Finally came a full-fledged national security analysis, NSC-68. In this sense, the step-by-step fashioning of American security followed a path of development that, in retrospect, seems almost predictable.

It did not seem so at the time, however. With the possible exception of Kennan's original cable, the direct cause of each of these steps was not any desire to sculpt a new American stance in the world, or to carry the development of American security to a new stage, but a pressing need to solve a specific, immediate problem. Until this operational need arose, the development did not occur. For example the full-fledged analysis was not operationally needed, and did not appear, until the American atomic monopoly was broken and the existence of two nuclear powers created novel analytical challenges.

The cumulative effect of these developments, though, was enormous, and from a security viewpoint the United States of early 1950 was very different from the United States of 1946. National security goals, concepts, institutions, policies, and programs were now in place that would have been almost inconceivable just after the war's end. Most of them would last a long time and prove successful. The central objectives of U.S. policy makers in that era, after all, were to forestall a third world war and to halt what they saw as a westward tide of Soviet power in Europe. Both of these objectives were accomplished fully.

At the same time the United States was becoming less

secure than before. The surprisingly early Soviet atomic test created a new situation in which all of America would be vulnerable within a short time to direct and devastating attack. No comparable threat had appeared before in American history, and absolutely nothing could be done to prevent its emergence. At best it could be hoped that a combination of offensive nuclear striking power and air defense could deter any actual attack, and limit the destruction if deterrence failed.*

*... The term "nuclear" will be used as a generic name to cover both fission and fusion weapons. This is consistent with common practice, although technically fusion processes (explosive or otherwise) are termed "thermonuclear." Most weapons now in the U.S. and Soviet arsenals are fusion weapons, but some are not, and yields of almost any size from very great down to quite small are available. Normally in wartime a military commander or civilian policy maker would want to know the approximate yield of weapons being used but would have little reason to be interested in whether they were fission or fusion.

The fundamental danger lay in the vast destructive power of nuclear weapons and the impossibility of maintaining the American monopoly for long. No complete defense was possible, because no air defense system could stop all incoming bombers and only a few atomic bombs dropped on American cities could wreak terrible destruction. By the time of NSC-68 it was becoming ever clearer that even increased defense expenditure could purchase only the uncertain kind of national security promised by deterrence. Future years would show that as nuclear weapons multiplied in numbers and variety, this approach to security would involve never-ending expenditures and hazards.

# THE GROWTH OF THE U.S. NUCLEAR ARSENAL

## A Plea for Universal Military Training

### *Document 9*

With the surrender of Japan in September 1945, the Truman administration began to demobilize rapidly the U.S. armed forces under pressure from a public weary of four years of wartime sacrifices. In doing so, however, President Truman and a number of his top military advisers worried that the country was myopically stripping itself of the military strength needed to deter Communist aggression. Accordingly, Truman delivered an urgent message to Congress in the fall of 1945 recommending that legislation be enacted that would require every qualified young man to participate in universal military training (UMT). Despite the urgency of Truman's plea, the proposal made little headway in an austerity-minded Congress eager to believe that the security of the United States was better guaranteed by its atomic arsenal than by a large, expensive conventional military.

### 9 SPEECH TO CONGRESS
### President Harry Truman
### October 22, 1945

For years to come the success of our efforts for a just and lasting peace will depend upon the strength of those who are determined to maintain the peace. We intend to use all our moral influence and all our physical strength to work for that kind of peace. We can insure such a peace only so long as we remain strong. We must face the fact that peace must be built upon power, as well as upon good will and good deeds. . . .

The surest guarantee that no nation will dare again to attack us is to remain strong in the only kind of strength an aggressor can understand — military power.

To preserve the strength of our nation the alternative before us is clear. We can maintain a large standing army, navy, and air force. Or we can rely on a comparatively small regular army, navy, and air force supported by well trained citizens who in time of emergency could be quickly mobilized.

I recommend the second course — that we depend for our security upon comparatively small professional armed forces, reinforced by a well trained and effectively organized citizen reserve. The backbone of our military force should be the trained citizen who is first and foremost a civilian, and who becomes a soldier or a sailor only in time of danger, and only when the Congress considers it necessary. This plan is obviously the more practical and economical. It conforms more closely to long-standing American tradition.

In such a system, however, the citizen reserve must be a trained reserve. We can meet the need for a trained reserve in only one way — by universal training. . . .

The sooner we can bring the maximum number of trained men into service, the sooner will be the victory and the less tragic the cost. Universal training is the only means by which we can be prepared right at the start to throw our great energy and our tremendous force into the battle. After two terrible experiences in one generation, we have learned that this is the way—the only way—to save human lives and material resources. . . .

In the present hour of triumph we must not forget our anguish during the days of Bataan. We must not forget the anxiety of the days of Guadalcanal. In our desire to leave the tragedy of war behind us we must not make the same mistake that we made after the First World War when we quickly sank back into helplessness.

I recommend that we create a postwar military organization which will contain the following basic elements:

First: A comparatively small regular Army, Navy, and Marine Corps;

Second: A greatly strengthened National Guard and organized reserve for the Army, Navy, and Marine Corps;

Third: A general reserve composed of all the male citizens of the United States who have received training. . . .

In order to provide this general reserve I recommend to the Congress the adoption of a plan for universal military training.

Universal military training is not conscription. The opponents of training have labeled it conscription and, by so doing, have confused the minds of some of our citizens. "Conscription" is compulsory service in the Army or Navy in time of peace or war. Trainees under this proposed legislation, however, would not be enrolled in any of the armed services. They would be civilians in training. They would be no closer to membership in the armed forces than if they had no training. Special rules and regulations would have to be adopted for their organization, discipline, and welfare.

Universal training is not intended to take the place of the present selective service system. The selective service system is now being used to furnish replacements in the armed forces for veterans of this war who are being discharged.

Only the Congress could ever draw trainees under a universal training program into the Army and Navy. And if that time ever came, these trainees could be inducted only by selective process, as they were inducted for World War I and World War II. The great difference between having universal training and no training, however, is that in time of emergency those who would be selected for actual military service would already have been basically trained.

That difference may be as much as a year's time. That difference may be the margin between the survival and the destruction of this great nation.

The emphasis in the training of our young men will not be on mere drilling. It will be on the use of all the instruments and weapons of modern warfare. The training will offer every qualified young man a chance to perfect himself for the service of his country in some military specialty.

## A Proposal to Accelerate the Atomic Energy Program

### *Document 10*

In the late 1940s, those responsible for U.S. security policy had to come to grips with the atomic bomb, a radically new factor in international politics.

The Soviet Union's detonation of its first atomic bomb in the summer of 1949 meant that the decision to use nuclear weapons in any future conflict was no longer one for Washington alone. In an October 1949 memo prepared for President Truman, a special committee of the National Security Council concluded that not only had it become technically feasible for the United States to accelerate its production and stockpiling of atomic weapons, but in light of the recent Soviet explosion it was militarily and politically advisable for it to do so as well. This decision began the growth of the U.S. atomic stockpile from a few tons of weapons in the late 1940s to more than one thousand A-bombs by the time that President Eisenhower took office. In addition, it laid the foundation for the subsequent enormous expansion in U.S. nuclear weapons capability in the 1950s. The United States might have lost its atomic monopoly, but it would seek to preserve its nuclear superiority.

### 10 TOP SECRET NSC MEMO TO TRUMAN October 10, 1949

#### The Problem

1. To prepare a recommendation to the President, as requested in letter dated 26 July 1949, on the proposal to expand the program of the Atomic Energy Commission along the lines recommended by the Joint Chiefs of Staff.

#### Analysis

*Considerations Presented by the Joint Chiefs of Staff in Support of Their Recommendation for an Acceleration of the Atomic Energy Program*

2. Since the detonation of the first atomic bomb, the Joint Chiefs of Staff have had the employment of atomic weapons under constant study, with a view to determining their optimum role in warfare. Certain developments and events, together with the results obtained from continuing studies under way, have led the Joint Chiefs of Staff to recommend, in June 1949, an additional acceleration of the atomic energy program. Among the developments, events, and considerations which led to this recommendation were the following:

a. The growing completeness of essential information on the effects and characteristics of atomic weapons which permitted a more realistic operational appraisal of atomic weapons. . . .

b. The completion of preliminary estimates which have indicated that it is probable that atomic bombs may be employed economically in lieu of conventional bombs against relatively small targets.

c. The realization that technical attainments in the plutonium separation process, waste recovery, and in the U-235 process probably will permit more efficient utilization of raw materials. This fact, together with the ability to foresee with greater assurance an adequate raw material supply, makes a limited degree of increased production feasible, in so far as raw materials are concerned.

d. Continued international tension, springing from the continuing refusal of the Soviet Union to become a cooperating member of the world community, the growing United States commitments on a world-wide scale, the growing realization of the necessity to defend Western Europe in the event of Soviet aggression; confirmation in detail of the full extent of the military prostration of our Western European allies as a result of facts developed in the course of negotiations for Western Union Planning, and the Military Aid Program. All these factors indicated that as soon as practicable the element of intrinsic scarcity must be eliminated as the predominant consideration of atomic weapon use in war in order to allow the JCS greater flexibility to plan as desirable the employment of atomic bombs for operations where they could be employed more economically than other military measures. While atomic weapons do not have universal application in war, they do provide swift and tremendous striking power for certain operations at a smaller over-all cost than other means. Accordingly, the JCS consider it in the national interest to have the capability for employing them for those tasks which can be accomplished more effectively and economically by atomic weapons.

e. The vital role of our atomic capability, which led to the conclusion that it would be unsound to rely on accelerating production in time of war. The increasing vulnerability of our plants with the advent of modern improved weapons; and the obvious high priority of their destruction or sabotage in the plans of an enemy; and the significant advantages accruing from large-scale use of atomic weapons early in the period of hostilities; led to the conclusion that it was in the national interest to possess on D-Day the fissionable material necessary to give us the desired flexibility to carry out our strategic plans. This consideration recommends production on a maximum basis for the clearly foreseeable future. Fortunately, fissionable material does not deteriorate or become obsolete with the passage of time, and can be stored indefinitely.

f. The failure of our proposals in the United Nations on the control of atomic energy, coupled with the fact that the time was approaching when the United States would lose its monopoly position in the atomic weapon field. By 1956, when it was estimated that the USSR probably would have achieved a significant stockpile of atomic weapons, the JCS consider it vital to the security of this nation that we possess an overwhelming superiority in these weapons for psychological and counter atomic offensive purposes, as well as for the achievement of our strategic objectives. As regards counter atomic offensive purposes, it is the view of the JCS that the U.S. can well afford to expend several times the number of bombs in the Soviet stockpile to counter atomic attacks against the United States if such targets present themselves.

g. The indication that the development of a smaller, lighter bomb may significantly improve the deliverability of these weapons and that military considerations may lay great emphasis on this development. However, it is to be noted that a smaller, lighter bomb and applications to guided missiles will be less efficient in the utilization of fissionable material. This fact, together with the increased flexibility of employment and new concepts for the use of smaller weapons, will tend to increase the requirements for fissionable material. . . .

4. The Joint Chiefs of Staff are of the opinion that the gain from the military standpoint of the proposed accelerated program over that which can be obtained from a continuation at the present level appears very significant in terms of lower unit cost of weapons; probable shortening of a war; increased military effectiveness; decreased logistical and manpower requirements for the prosecution of certain tasks in war; and increased flexibility in the conduct of the war, which is extremely important in view of the many imponderables now facing our planners. Furthermore, when the USSR attains a stockpile of atomic weapons, overwhelming superiority of our own stockpile and production rate will be necessary if our atomic weapon posture is to continue to act as a deterrent to war. Moreover, and from a military standpoint, the Joint Chiefs of Staff are of the opinion that the recent atomic explosion in the USSR underlines the military necessity of increased weapon production, and thus strongly reinforces and supports the justification and urgency of their previous recommendations.

*Feasibility of Meeting Proposed Increased Military Requirements as Assessed by the Atomic Energy Commission*

5. The Atomic Energy Commission has carefully studied the recommended program only from the viewpoint of its feasibility, and has concluded that the program is feasible. . . .

The estimated costs involved call for a capital cost of about $310 million and additional annual operating costs reaching about $54 million per year when the accelerated program attains equilibrium. . . .

*International Political Considerations as Assessed by the Department of State*

6. It may be assumed that some information concerning the expansion will become publicly known, particularly in the course of Congressional hearings thereon. The psychological effect at home and abroad of such knowledge is difficult to judge. On balance, however, the proposed expansion is not considered untimely from the point of view of possible international repercussions, particularly in view of the recent atomic explosion in the USSR, for the following reasons:

a. It is consistent with our announced determination to maintain our leadership in the field of atomic weapons in the absence of effective international control. This policy is well-known to the world, including the Soviet Union.

b. Other nations, in all probability, assume that we are producing atomic weapons to the full extent of our capabilities.

c. Recent construction activities at Hanford, representing a comparable visible increase of effort, did not produce any significant unfavorable domestic or international reaction.

d. In the light of the North Atlantic Pact and the Military Aid Program, it appears likely that Western Europe would consider an expansion of our program not only a desirable development but also positive evidence of our intent to increase our military strength for the security of all.

e. Approval of the proposed expansion would strengthen our position in the exploratory conversations with the United Kingdom and Canada, these conversations having as their objective the attaining of that allocation of effort which will bring about the most effective use of joint resources, specifically raw materials and effort. . . .

## A Recommendation for Military Buildup

### *Document 11*

After the traumatic autumn of 1949, which had been marked by the fall of China to the Communists and by the Soviet A-bomb test, President Truman ordered a comprehensive assessment of U.S. national security interests and capabilities. The result of this exercise was NSC 68, the single most famous national security document produced by the U.S. government in the nuclear age. NSC 68 was a lengthy, top-secret report that systematically examined the political, economic, psychological, and military components of the U.S. competition. The excerpts that follow focus primarily on the military dimension. NSC 68 argued that the Soviet threat was greater than previously recognized and that existing U.S. national security programs were woefully inadequate. Consequently, NSC 68 recommended a substantial, costly, across-the-board military buildup. It is unlikely that NSC 68 would have led to any large change in U.S. defense policy had the Korean War not broken out; President Truman was determined to balance the federal budget and did not want large additional expenditures on defense. But with the North Korean attack in June 1950, NSC 68's gloomy assessment of the intensifying Communist threat suddenly appeared very realistic, and large increases in defense spending became both necessary and politically feasible.

### 11 NSC 68
### April 14, 1950

**I. Backgrounds of the Present World Crisis**

Within the past thirty-five years the world has experienced two global wars of tremendous violence. It has witnessed two revolutions — the Russian and the Chinese — of extreme scope and intensity. It has also seen the collapse of five empires — the Ottoman, the Austro-Hungarian, German, Italian and Japanese — and the drastic decline of two major imperial systems, the British and the French. During the span of one generation, the international distribution of power has been fundamentally altered. For several centuries it had proved impossible for any one nation to gain such preponderant strength that a coalition of other nations could not in time face it with greater strength. The international scene was marked by recurring periods of violence and war, but a system of sovereign and independent states was maintained, over which no state was able to achieve hegemony.

Two complex sets of factors have now basically altered this historical distribution of power. First, the defeat of Germany and Japan and the decline of the British and French Empires have interacted with the development of the United States and the Soviet Union in such a way that power has increasingly gravitated to these two centers. Second, the Soviet Union, unlike previous aspirants to hegemony, is animated by a new fanatic faith, antithetical to our own, and seeks to impose its absolute authority over the rest of the world. Conflict has, therefore, become endemic and is waged, on the part of the Soviet Union, by violent or non-violent methods in accordance with the dictates of expediency. With the development of increasingly terrifying weapons of mass destruction, every individual faces the ever-present possibility of annihilation should the conflict enter the phase of total war.

On the one hand, the people of the world yearn for relief from the anxiety arising from the risk of atomic war. On the other hand, any substantial further extension of the area under the domination of the Kremlin would raise the possibility that no coalition adequate to confront the Kremlin with greater strength could be assembled. It is in this context that this Republic and its citizens in the ascendancy of their strength stand in their deepest peril.

The issues that face us are momentous, involving the fulfillment or destruction not only of this Republic but of civilization itself. They are issues which will not await our deliberations. With conscience and resolution this Government and the people it represents must now take new and fateful decisions. . . .

## III. Fundamental Design of the Kremlin

The fundamental design of those who control the Soviet Union and the international communist movement is to retain and solidify their absolute power, first in the Soviet Union and second in the areas now under their control. In the mind of the Soviet leaders, however, achievement of this design requires the dynamic extension of their authority and the ultimate elimination of any effective opposition to their authority.

The design, therefore, calls for the complete subversion or forcible destruction of the machinery of government and structure of society in the countries of the non-Soviet world and their replacement by an apparatus and structure subservient to and controlled from the Kremlin. To that end Soviet efforts are now directed toward the domination of the Eurasian land mass. The United States, as the principal center of power in the non-Soviet world and the bulwark of opposition to Soviet expansion, is the principal enemy whose integrity and vitality must be subverted or destroyed by one means or another if the Kremlin is to achieve its fundamental design. . . .

### *C. Military*

The Soviet Union is developing the military capacity to support its design for world domination. The Soviet Union actually possesses armed forces far in excess of those necessary to defend its national territory. These armed forces are probably not yet considered by the Soviet Union to be sufficient to initiate a war which would involve the United States. This excessive strength, coupled now with an atomic capability, provides the Soviet Union with great coercive power for use in time of peace in furtherance of its objectives and serves as a deterrent to the victims of its aggression from taking any action in opposition to its tactics which would risk war.

Should a major war occur in 1950 the Soviet Union and its satellites are considered by the Joint Chiefs of Staff to be in a sufficiently advanced state of preparation immediately to undertake and carry out the following campaigns.

a. To overrun Western Europe, with the possible exception of the Iberian and Scandinavian Peninsulas; to drive toward the oil-bearing areas of the Near and Middle East; and to consolidate Communist gains in the Far East;
b. To launch air attacks against the British Isles and air and sea attacks against the lines of communications of the Western Powers in the Atlantic and the Pacific;
c. To attack selected targets with atomic weapons, now including the likelihood of such attacks against targets in Alaska, Canada, and the United States. Alternatively, this capability, coupled with other actions open to the Soviet Union, might deny the United Kingdom as an effective base of operations for allied forces. It also should be possible for the Soviet Union to prevent any allied "Normandy" type amphibious operations intended to force a re-entry into the continent of Europe.

After the Soviet Union completed its initial campaigns and consolidated its positions in the Western European area, it could simultaneously conduct:

a. Full-scale air and limited sea operations against the British Isles;
b. Invasions of the Iberian and Scandinavian Peninsulas;
c. Further operations in the Near and Middle East, continued air operations against the North American continent, and air and sea operations against Atlantic and Pacific lines of communication; and
d. Diversionary attacks in other areas. . . .

. . . It is not possible at this time to assess accurately the finite disadvantages to the Soviet Union which may accrue through the implementation of the Economic Cooperation Act of 1948, as amended, and the Mutual Defense Assistance Act of 1949. It should be expected that, as this implementation progresses, the internal security situation of the recipient nations should improve concurrently. In addition, a strong United States military position, plus increases in the armaments of the nations of Western Europe, should strengthen the determination of the recipient nations to counter Soviet moves and in event of war could be considered as likely to delay operations and increase the time required for the Soviet Union to overrun Western Europe. In all probability, although United States backing will stiffen their determination, the armaments increase under the present aid programs will not be of any major consequence prior to 1952. Unless the military strength of the Western European nations is increased on a much larger scale than the current programs and at an accelerated rate, it is more likely that those nations will not be able to oppose even by 1960 the Soviet armed forces in war with any degree of effectiveness. Considering the Soviet Union military capability, the long-range allied military objective in Western Europe must envisage an increased military strength in that area sufficient possibly to deter the Soviet Union from a major war, or, in any event, to delay materially the overrunning of Western Europe and, if feasible, to hold a bridgehead on the continent against Soviet Union offensives.

We do not know accurately what the Soviet atomic capability is but the Central Intelligence Agency intelligence estimates, concurred in by State, Army, Navy, Air Force, and Atomic Energy Commission, assign to the Soviet Union a production capability giving it a fission bomb stockpile within the following ranges:

| | |
|---|---|
| By mid-1950 | 10– 20 |
| By mid-1951 | 25– 45 |
| By mid-1952 | 45– 90 |
| By mid-1953 | 70–135 |
| By mid 1954 | 200 |

This estimate is admittedly based on incomplete coverage of Soviet activities and represents the production capabilities of known or deducible Soviet plants. If others exist, as is possible, this estimate could lead us into a feeling of superiority in our atomic stockpile that might be dangerously misleading, particularly with regard to the timing of a possible Soviet offensive. On the other hand, if the Soviet Union experiences operating difficulties, this estimate would be reduced. There is some evidence that the Soviet Union is acquiring certain materials essential to research on and development of thermonuclear weapons.

The Soviet Union now has aircraft able to deliver the atomic bomb. Our intelligence estimates assign to the Soviet Union an atomic bomber capability already in excess of that needed to deliver available bombs. We have at present no evaluated estimate regarding the Soviet accuracy of delivery on target. It is believed that the Soviets cannot deliver their bombs on target with a degree of accuracy comparable to ours, but a planning estimate might well place it at 40–60 percent of bombs sortied. For planning purposes, therefore, the date the Soviets possess an atomic stockpile of 200 bombs would be a critical date for the United States for the delivery of 100 atomic bombs on targets in the United States would seriously damage this country.

At the time the Soviet Union has a substantial atomic stockpile and if it is assumed that it will strike a strong surprise blow and if it is assumed further that its atomic attacks will be met with no more effective defense opposition than the United States and its allies have programmed, results of those attacks could include:

a. Laying waste to the British Isles and thus depriving the Western Powers of their use as a base;
b. Destruction of the vital centers and of the communications of Western Europe, thus precluding effective defense by the Western Powers; and
c. Delivering devastating attacks on certain vital centers of the United States and Canada.

The possession by the Soviet Union of a thermonuclear capability in addition to this substantial atomic stockpile would result in tremendously increased damage. . . .

## VI. U.S. Intentions and Capabilities — Actual and Potential

### *C. Military*

The United States now possesses the greatest military potential of any single nation in the world. The military weaknesses of the United States vis-à-vis the Soviet Union, however, include its numerical inferiority in forces in being and in total manpower. Coupled with the inferiority of forces in being, the United States also lacks tenable positions from which to employ its forces in event of war and munitions power in being and readily available.

It is true that the United States armed forces are now stronger than ever before in other times of apparent peace; it is also true that there exists a sharp disparity between our actual military strength and our commitments. The relationship of our strength to our present commitments, however, is not alone the governing factor. The world situation, as well as commitments, should govern; hence, our military strength more properly should be related to the world situation confronting us. When our military strength is related to the world situation and balanced against the likely exigencies of such a situation, it is clear that our military strength is becoming dangerously inadequate.

If war should begin in 1950, the United States and its allies will have the military capability of conducting defensive operations to provide a reasonable measure of protection to the Western Hemisphere, bases in the Western Pacific, and essential military lines of communication; and an inadequate measure of protection to vital military bases in the United Kingdom and in the Near and Middle East. We will have the capability of conducting powerful offensive air operations against vital elements of the Soviet warmaking capacity.

If the potential military capabilities of the United States and its allies were rapidly and effectively developed, sufficient forces could be produced to deter war, or if the Soviet Union chooses war, to withstand the initial Soviet attacks, to stabilize supporting attacks, and to retaliate in turn with even greater impact on the Soviet capabilities. From the military point of view alone, however, this would require not only the generation of the necessary military forces but also the development and stockpiling of improved weapons of all types.

Under existing peacetime conditions, a period of

from two to three years is required to produce a material increase in military power. Such increased power could be provided in a somewhat shorter period in a declared period of emergency or in wartime through a full-out national effort. Any increase in military power in peacetime, however, should be related both to its probable military role in war, to the implementation of immediate and long-term United States foreign policy vis-à-vis the Soviet Union and to the realities of the existing situation. If such a course of increasing our military power is adopted now, the United States would have the capability of eliminating the disparity between its military strength and the exigencies of the situation we face; eventually of gaining the initiative in the "cold" war and of materially delaying if not stopping the Soviet offensives in war itself. . . .

## VIII. Atomic Armaments

### *A. Military Evaluation of U.S. and U.S.S.R. Atomic Capabilities*

1. The United States now has an atomic capability, including both numbers and deliverability, estimated to be adequate, if effectively utilized, to deliver a serious blow against the war-making capacity of the U.S.S.R. It is doubted whether such a blow, even if it resulted in the complete destruction of the contemplated target systems, would cause the U.S.S.R. to sue for terms or prevent Soviet forces from occupying Western Europe against such ground resistance as could presently be mobilized. A very serious initial blow could, however, so reduce the capabilities of the U.S.S.R. to supply and equip its military organization and its civilian population as to give the United States the prospect of developing a general military superiority in a war of long duration.

2. As the atomic capability of the U.S.S.R. increases, it will have an increased ability to hit at our atomic bases and installations and thus seriously hamper the ability of the United States to carry out an attack such as that outlined above. It is quite possible that in the near future the U.S.S.R. will have a sufficient number of atomic bombs and a sufficient deliverability to raise a question whether Britain with its present inadequate air defense could be relied upon as an advance base from which a major portion of the U.S. attack could be launched.

It is estimated that, within the next four years, the U.S.S.R. will attain the capability of seriously damaging vital centers of the United States, provided it strikes a surprise blow and provided further that the blow is opposed by no more effective opposition than we now have programmed. Such a blow could so seriously damage the United States as to greatly reduce its superiority in economic potential.

Effective opposition to this Soviet capability will require among other measures greatly increased air warning systems, air defenses, and vigorous development and implementation of a civilian defense program which has been thoroughly integrated with the military defense systems.

In time the atomic capability of the U.S.S.R. can be expected to grow to a point where, given surprise and no more effective opposition than we now have programmed, the possibility of a decisive initial attack cannot be excluded.

3. In the initial phases of an atomic war, the advantages of initiative and surprise would be very great. A police state living behind an iron curtain has an enormous advantage in maintaining the necessary security and centralization of decision required to capitalize on this advantage.

4. For the moment our atomic retaliatory capability is probably adequate to deter the Kremlin from a deliberate direct military attack against ourselves or other free peoples. However, when it calculates that it has a sufficient atomic capability to make a surprise attack on us, nullifying our atomic superiority and creating a military situation decisively in its favor, the Kremlin might be tempted to strike swiftly and with stealth. The existence of two large atomic capabilities in such a relationship might well act, therefore, not as a deterrent, but as an incitement to war.

5. A further increase in the number and power of our atomic weapons is necessary in order to assure the effectiveness of any U.S. retaliatory blow, but would not of itself seem to change the basic logic of the above points. Greatly increased general air, ground and sea strength, and increased air defense and civilian defense programs would also be necessary to provide reasonable assurance that the free world could survive an initial surprise atomic attack of the weight which it is estimated the U.S.S.R. will be capable of delivering by 1954 and still permit the free world to go on to the eventual attainment of its objectives. Furthermore, such a build-up of strength could safeguard and increase our retaliatory power, and thus might put off for some time the date when the Soviet Union could calculate that a surprise blow would be advantageous. This would provide additional time for the effects of our policies to produce a modification of the Soviet system.

6. If the U.S.S.R. develops a thermonuclear weapon ahead of the U.S., the risks of greatly increased Soviet pressure against all the free world, or an attack against the U.S., will be greatly increased.

7. If the U.S. develops a thermonuclear weapon ahead of the U.S.S.R., the U.S. should for the time being be able to bring increased pressure on the U.S.S.R.

### *B. Stockpiling and Use of Atomic Weapons*

1. From the foregoing analysis it appears that it would be to the long-term advantage of the United States if

atomic weapons were to be effectively eliminated from national peacetime armaments; the additional objectives which must be secured if there is to be a reasonable prospect of such effective elimination of atomic weapons are discussed in Chapter IX. In the absence of such elimination and the securing of these objectives, it would appear that we have no alternative but to increase our atomic capability as rapidly as other considerations make appropriate. In either case, it appears to be imperative to increase as rapidly as possible our general air, ground and sea strength and that of our allies to a point where we are militarily not so heavily dependent on atomic weapons. . . .

## Conclusions

The foregoing analysis indicates that the probable fission bomb capability and possible thermonuclear bomb capability of the Soviet Union have greatly intensified the Soviet threat to the security of the United States. This threat is of the same character as that described in NSC 20/4 (approved by the President on November 24, 1948) but is more immediate than had previously been estimated. In particular, the United States now faces the contingency that within the next four or five years the Soviet Union will possess the military capability of delivering a surprise atomic attack of such weight that the United States must have substantially increased general air, ground, and sea strength, atomic capabilities, and air and civilian defenses to deter war and to provide reasonable assurance, in the event of war, that it could survive the initial blow and go on to the eventual attainment of its objectives. In turn, this contingency requires the intensification of our efforts in the fields of intelligence and research and development. . . .

In the light of present and prospective Soviet atomic capabilities, the action which can be taken under present programs and plans, however, becomes dangerously inadequate, in both timing and scope, to accomplish the rapid progress toward the attainment of the United States political, economic, and military objectives which is now imperative.

A continuation of present trends would result in a serious decline in the strength of the free world relative to the Soviet Union and its satellites. This unfavorable trend arises from the inadequacy of current programs and plans rather than from any error in our objectives and aims. These trends lead in the direction of isolation not by deliberate decision but by lack of the necessary basis for a vigorous initiative in the conflict with the Soviet Union.

Our position as the center of power in the free world places a heavy responsibility upon the United States for leadership. We must organize and enlist the energies and resources of the free world in a positive program for peace which will frustrate the Kremlin design for world domination by creating a situation in the free world to which the Kremlin will be compelled to adjust. Without such a cooperative effort, led by the United States, we will have to make gradual withdrawals under pressure until we discover one day that we have sacrificed positions of vital interest.

It is imperative that this trend be reversed by a much more rapid and concerted build-up of the actual strength of both the United States and the other nations of the free world. The analysis shows that this will be costly and will involve significant domestic financial and economic adjustments.

The execution of such a build-up, however, requires that the United States have an affirmative program beyond the solely defensive one of countering the threat posed by the Soviet Union. This program must light the path to peace and order among nations in a system based on freedom and justice, as contemplated in the Charter of the United Nations. Further, it must envisage the political and economic measures with which and the military shield behind which the free world can work to frustrate the Kremlin design by the strategy of the cold war; for every consideration of devotion to our fundamental values and to our national security demands that we achieve our objectives by the strategy of the cold war, building up our military strength in order that it may not have to be used. The only sure victory lies in the frustration of the Kremlin design by the steady development of the moral and material strength of the free world and its projection into the Soviet world in such a way as to bring about an internal change in the Soviet system. Such a positive program — harmonious with our fundamental national purpose and our objectives — is necessary if we are to regain and retain the initiative and to win and hold the necessary popular support and cooperation in the United States and the rest of the free world.

This program should include a plan for negotiation with the Soviet Union, developed and agreed with our allies and which is consonant with our objectives. The United States and its allies, particularly the United Kingdom and France, should always be ready to negotiate with the Soviet Union on terms consistent with our objectives. The present world situation, however, is one which militates against successful negotiations with the Kremlin — for the terms of agreements on important pending issues would reflect present realities and would therefore be unacceptable, if not disastrous, to the United States and the rest of the free world. After a decision and a start on building up the strength of the free world has been made, it might then be desirable for the United States to take an initiative in seeking negotiations in the hope that it might facilitate the process of accommodation by the Kremlin to the new situation. Failing that, the unwillingness of the Kremlin to accept equitable terms or its bad faith in observing them would assist in consolidating popular opinion in the free world in support of the measures necessary to sustain the build-up.

In summary, we must, by means of a rapid and sustained build-up of the political, economic, and military strength of the free world, and by means of an affirmative program intended to wrest the initiative from the Soviet Union, confront it with convincing evidence of the determination and ability of the free world to frustrate the Kremlin design of a world dominated by its will. Such evidence is the only means short of war which eventually may force the Kremlin to abandon its present course of action and to negotiate acceptable agreements on issues of major importance.

The whole success of the proposed program hangs ultimately on recognition by this Government, the American people, and all free peoples, that the cold war is in fact a real war in which the survival of the free world is at stake. Essential prerequisites to success are consultations with Congressional leaders designed to make the program the object of non-partisan legislative support, and a presentation to the public of a full explanation of the facts and implications of the present international situation. The prosecution of the program will require of us all the ingenuity, sacrifice, and unity demanded by the vital importance of the issue and the tenacity to persevere until our national objectives have been attained.

# THE DEVELOPMENT OF THE HYDROGEN BOMB

## Opposition to the H-Bomb

### *Documents 12 and 13*

On September 23, 1949, President Truman announced that the Soviet Union had exploded an atomic bomb. This development added urgency to the question of whether the United States should vigorously pursue the hydrogen bomb (then also known as the "Super"). In theory, the H-bomb would be many times more powerful than the already enormously destructive atomic fission bomb; in 1949, however, it was not certain whether the H-bomb was technically feasible. The General Advisory Committee (GAC) of the Atomic Energy Commission, headed by J. Robert Oppenheimer, was asked to study this issue and offer a recommendation. In document 12, a statement that was appended to a substantial report on factors relating to the H-bomb, the members of the GAC weigh in strongly against proceeding with the "Super." Although the committee's recommendation not to build the H-bomb was ultimately overruled by Truman, Herbert York, a physicist who was intimately involved with the early U.S. atomic bomb program, argues in document 13 that from the perspective of a quarter-century later the GAC's unanimous opposition to the H-bomb appears largely justified.

### 12 TOP SECRET REPORT OF THE GENERAL ADVISORY COMMITTEE
### J. Robert Oppenheimer and Committee
### October 30, 1949

We have been asked by the Commission whether or not they should immediately initiate an "all-out" effort to develop a weapon whose energy release is 100 to 1000 times greater and whose destructive power in terms of area of damage is 20 to 100 times greater than those of the present atomic bomb. We recommend strongly against such action.

We base our recommendation on our belief that the extreme dangers to mankind inherent in the proposal wholly outweigh any military advantage that could come from this development. Let it be clearly realized that this is a super weapon; it is in a totally different category from an atomic bomb. The reason for developing such super bombs would be to have the capacity to devastate a vast area with a single bomb. Its use would involve a decision to slaughter a vast number of civilians. We are alarmed as to the possible global effects of the radioactivity generated by the explosion of a few super bombs of conceivable magnitude. If super bombs will work at all, there is no inherent limit in the destructive power that may be attained with them. Therefore, a super bomb might become a weapon of genocide.

The existence of such a weapon in our armory would have far-reaching effects on world opinion; reasonable people the world over would realize that the existence of a weapon of this type whose power of destruction is essentially unlimited represents a threat to the future of the human race which is intolerable. Thus we believe that the psychological effect of the weapon in our hands would be adverse to our interest.

We believe a super bomb should never be produced. Mankind would be far better off not to have a demonstration of the feasibility of such a weapon until the present climate of world opinion changes.

It is by no means certain that the weapon can be developed at all and by no means certain that the Russians will produce one within a decade. To the argument that the Russians may succeed in developing this weapon, we would reply that our undertaking it will not prove a deterrent to them. Should they use the weapon against us, reprisals by our large stock of atomic bombs would be comparably effective to the use of a super.

In determining not to proceed to develop the super bomb, we see a unique opportunity of providing by example some limitations on the totality of war and thus of limiting the fear and arousing the hope of mankind.

James B. Conant
Hartley Rowe
Cyril Stanley Smith
L[ee] A. DuBridge
Oliver E. Buckley
J. R[obert] Oppenheimer

## 13 THE DEBATE OVER THE HYDROGEN BOMB
**Herbert York**

In 1948 Czechoslovak Communists carried out a coup in the shadow of the Red Army and replaced the government of that country with one subservient to Moscow. Also in 1948 the Russians unsuccessfully attempted to force the Western allies out of Berlin by blockading all land transport routes to the city. In early 1949 the Communist People's Liberation Army captured Peking and soon afterward established the People's Republic of China. Taken together, these and similar but less dramatic events were generally perceived in the West as resulting in the creation of a monolithic and aggressive alliance stretching the full length of the Eurasian continent, encompassing almost half of the world's people and threatening much of the rest. Then in the fall of 1949 the Russians exploded their first atomic bomb and ended the brief American nuclear monopoly.

At the end of World War II most atomic scientists in the U.S. had estimated that the U.S.S.R. would need four or five years to make a bomb based on the nuclear-fission principle; the time interval from the first American test to the first Russian one turned out to be four years and six weeks. Even so, nearly everyone, including most U.S. Government officials and most members of Congress, reacted to the event as if it were a great surprise. Many of them had either forgotten or had never known the experts' original estimates, and in any case the accomplishment simply did not fit the almost universal view of the U.S.S.R. as a technologically backward nation.

Besides being a great surprise the Russian test explosion was a singularly unpleasant one. The U.S. nuclear monopoly had been seen by many as compensating for the difference between the hordes of conscripts supposedly available to the Communist bloc and the smaller armies available to the Western countries. Coming as it did at a time when virtually all Americans saw the cold war as rapidly going from bad to worse, the Russian test was seen as a challenge that demanded a reply. The immediate challenge being nuclear, a particularly intensive search for an appropriate response was conducted by those responsible for U.S. nuclear policy.

Most of the proposed responses involved substantial but evolutionary changes in the current U.S. nuclear programs: expand the search for additional supplies of fissionable material, step up the production of atomic weapons, adapt such weapons to a broader range of delivery vehicles and end uses, and the like. One proposal was radically different. It called for the fastest possible development of the hydrogen bomb, which was widely referred to at the time as the superbomb (or simply the Super). This weapon, based on the entirely new and as yet untested principle of thermonuclear fusion, was estimated to have the potential of being 1,000 or more times as powerful as the fission bombs that had marked the end of World War II. Work on the theory of the superbomb had already been going on for seven years, but it had never had a very high priority, and so far it had yielded no practical result. A number of scientists and politicians endorsed the proposal, but for years Edward Teller had been its leading advocate. The superbomb proposal led to a brief, intense and highly secret debate.

The opponents of the proposal argued that neither the possession of the new bomb nor the initiation of its development was necessary for maintaining the national security of the U.S., and that under such circumstances it would be morally wrong to initiate the development of such an enormously powerful and destructive weapon. In essence they contended that the world ought to avoid the development and stockpiling of the superbomb if it was at all possible, and that a U.S. decision to forgo it was a necessary precondition for persuading others to do likewise. Furthermore, they concluded that the dynamism and relative status of U.S. nuclear technology were such that the U.S. could safely run the risk that the U.S.S.R. might not practice similar restraint and would instead initiate a secret program of its own.

The advocates of the superbomb maintained that the successful achievement of such a bomb by the Russians was only a matter of time, and so at best our forgoing it would amount to a deliberate decision to become a second-class power, and at worst it would be equivalent to surrender. They added that undertaking the development of the superbomb was morally no different from developing any other weapon.

The secret debate about what the American response ought to be took place within the Government itself. Many organizations were involved, including the National Security Council, the Department of Defense, the Department of State and the Congressional Joint Committee on Atomic Energy, but the initial focus of the debate lay within the Atomic Energy Commission.

The early official reaction of the AEC's Los Alamos Scientific Laboratory to the Russian test was a proposal to step up the pace of the nuclear-weapons program in all areas. Among other measures, Norris E. Bradbury, the director, recommended that the laboratory go on a six-day work week and that they expand the staff, particularly in theoretical physics.

This acceleration was to include not only programs for improving fission weapons by conventional means but also tests of the booster principle. (In this context "booster" refers to a synergistic process in which the explosion of a comparatively large mass of fissionable fuel, say plutonium or uranium 235, causes a comparatively small mass of thermonuclear fuel, say deuterium and tritium, to burn violently. The high-energy neutrons produced in the thermonuclear process then react back on the fission explosion, boosting, or accelerating, it to a higher efficiency than would otherwise be the case.) The booster concept had been known for several years, and even before the Russian test it had been agreed to include a full-scale experimental test of the process in a 1951 nuclear-test series. The AEC's Director of Military Application, General James McCormack, Jr., received these proposals from the Los Alamos laboratory and sought the advice of the AEC's scientific experts on them. Other AEC division heads were similarly studying proposals for expanding the relevant programs within their jurisdiction.

At the same time Teller, then at Los Alamos, Ernest O. Lawrence, Luis W. Alvarez and Wendell M. Latimer at the University of California at Berkeley, Robert LeBaron at the Department of Defense, Senator Brien McMahon, Chairman of the Joint Committee on Atomic Energy, his staff chief William L. Borden and Commissioner Lewis L. Strauss of the AEC had all come to focus on the superbomb as the main element of the answer to the Russian atomic bomb, and they initiated a concerted effort to bring the entire Government around to their point of view as quickly as possible.

As a result of all this concern and activity the AEC called for a special meeting of its General Advisory Committee to be held as soon as possible. This committee was one of the special mechanisms established by the Atomic Energy Act of 1946 for the purpose of managing the postwar development of nuclear energy in the U.S. Its function was to provide the AEC with scientific and technical advice concerning its programs. The members of the committee were all men who had been scientific or technological leaders in major wartime projects. J. Robert Oppenheimer, who was elected chairman of the committee, had been director of the Los Alamos laboratory during the period when the first atomic bomb had been designed and built there. The other members, all scientists, were Oliver E. Buckley, James B. Conant, Lee A. DuBridge, Enrico Fermi, I. I. Rabi, Hartley Rowe, Glenn T. Seaborg and Cyril S. Smith. Many of the members of this committee and later General Advisory committees also served on other high-level standing committees and some key *ad hoc* committees, and so a rather complex web of interlocking advisory-committee memberships developed. As a result several of these men, including Oppenheimer, had much more influence than the simple sum of their various committee memberships would indicate.

Oppenheimer was not only the formal leader of the General Advisory Committee but also, by virtue of his personality and background, its natural leader. His views were therefore of special importance in setting the tone and determining the content of the committee's reports in this matter, as in most other matters.

Throughout Oppenheimer's service on the committee he generally supported the various programs designed to produce and improve nuclear weapons. At the same time he was deeply troubled by what he had wrought at Los Alamos, and he found the notion of bombs of unlimited power particularly repugnant. Ever since the end of the war he had devoted much of his attention to promoting the international control of atomic energy with the ultimate objective of achieving nuclear disarmament. He and Rabi had in effect been the originators of the plan for nuclear-arms control that later became known as the Baruch Plan. Oppenheimer's inner feelings about nuclear weapons were clearly revealed in an often quoted remark: "In some sort of crude sense which no vulgarity, no humor, no overstatement can quite extinguish, the physicists have known sin, and this is a knowledge which they cannot lose."

The call for the special meeting, in addition to raising the question of a high-priority program to develop the Super, also asked the committee to consider priorities in the broadest sense, including "whether the Commission is now doing things we ought to do to serve the paramount objectives of the common defense and security." As for the Super, the Commission wanted to know "whether the nation would use such a weapon if it could be built and what its military worth would be in relation to fission weapons." The meeting of the Oppenheimer committee was held on October 29 and 30, 1949; all members were present except Seaborg, who was in Europe. The committee in the course of its deliberations heard from many outside experts in various relevant fields, including George F. Kennan, the noted student of Russian affairs, General Omar Bradley, Chairman of the Joint Chiefs of Staff, and the physicists H. A. Bethe and Robert Serber. Toward the end of the two-day meeting the advisers had a long session with the Atomic Energy commissioners and with their intelligence staff. The next day the committee prepared its report.

The General Advisory Committee report consisted of three separate sections that were unanimously agreed on and two addenda giving certain specific minority views. In 1974 the report was almost entirely declassified, with only a very few purely technical details remaining secret.

Part I of the report dealt with all pertinent questions other than those directly involving the Super. The advisory committee in effect reacted favorably to the proposals of the various AEC division directors with regard to the expansion of the facilities for separating uranium isotopes, for producing plutonium and for increasing the supplies of uranium ore. These proposals and the committee's endorsement of them were followed eventually by a substantial increase in the rate of production of fissionable materials.

In Part I the committee also recommended the acceleration of research and development work on fission bombs, particularly for tactical purposes. Under the heading "Tactical Delivery" the report stated: "The General Advisory Committee recommends to the Commission an intensification of efforts to make atomic weapons available for tactical purposes, and to give attention to the problem of integration of bomb and carrier design in this field."

This quoted paragraph deserves special emphasis, since it has often been suggested that Oppenheimer, Conant and some of the others opposed nuclear weapons in general. They did apparently find them all repugnant, and they did try hard to create an international control organization that would ultimately lead to their universal abolition. In the absence of any international arms-limitation agreements with reliable control mechanisms, however, they explicitly recognized the need to possess nuclear weapons, particularly for tactical and defensive purposes, and they regularly promoted programs designed to increase their variety, flexibility, efficiency and numbers. For the next few years right up to the time Oppenheimer's security clearance was removed, he continued strongly to promote the idea of an expanded arsenal of tactical nuclear weapons. The only type of nuclear weapon the General Advisory Committee opposed—and it did so openly—was the Super.

Part I of the report further recommended that a project be initiated for the purpose of producing "freely absorbable neutrons" to be used for the production of uranium 233, tritium and other potentially useful nuclear materials. Perhaps most important of all in the present context, Part I also stated: "We strongly favor, subject to favorable outcome of the 1951 Eniwetok tests, the booster program." This short phrase makes it abundantly clear that the Oppenheimer committee favored conducting research fundamental to understanding the thermonuclear process, and that its grave reservations were specifically and solely focused on one particular application of the fusion process.

Part II discussed the Super. It outlined what was known about the hydrogen bomb, and it expanded on the unusual difficulties its development presented, but it concluded that the bomb could probably be built. In part it said: "It is notable that there appears to be no experimental approach short of actual test which will substantially add to our conviction that a given model will or will not work. Thus, we are faced with a development which cannot be carried to the point of conviction without the actual construction and demonstration of the essential elements of the weapon in question. A final point that needs to be stressed is that many tests may be required before a workable model has been evolved or before it has been established beyond reasonable doubt that no such model can be evolved. Although we are not able to give a specific probability rating for any given model, *we believe that an imaginative and concerted attack on the problem has a better than even chance of producing the weapon within five years.*"

That last sentence (the italics are added) deserves special emphasis. It has been suggested in the past that the General Advisory Committee in general and Oppenheimer in particular were deceptive in their analysis of the technological prospects of the Super; in other words, that they deliberately painted a falsely gloomy picture of its possibilities in order to reinforce their basically ethical opposition to its development. Given the technological circumstances then prevailing, this statement of the program's prospects could hardly have been more positive.

The report then discussed what might be called the "strategic economics" of the Super as they were then conceived: "A second characteristic of the super bomb is that once the problem of initiation has been solved, there is no limit to the explosive power of the bomb itself except that imposed by requirements of delivery. [In addition there will be] very grave contamination problems which can easily be made more acute, and may possibly be rendered less acute, by surrounding the deuterium with uranium or other material. . . . It is clearly impossible with the vagueness of design and the uncertainty as to performance as we have them at present to give anything like a cost estimate of the super. If one uses the strict criteria of damage area per dollar, it appears uncertain to us whether the super will be cheaper or more expensive than the fission bombs."

In Part III the committee members got to what to them was the heart of the matter, the question of whether or not the Super should be developed: "Although the members of the Advisory Committee are not unanimous in their proposals as to what should be done with regard to the super bomb, there are certain elements of unanimity among us. We all hope that by one means or another the development of these weapons can be avoided. We are all reluctant to see the United States take the initiative in precipitating this development. We are all agreed that it would be wrong at the present moment to commit ourselves to an all-out effort toward its development.

"We are somewhat divided as to the nature of the commitment not to develop the weapon. The majority feel that this should be an unqualified commitment. Others feel that it should be made conditional on the response of the Soviet government to a proposal to renounce such development. The Committee recommends that enough be declassified about the super bomb so that a public statement of policy can be made at this time."

In the two addenda those members of the committee who were present (that is, all except Seaborg) explained their reasons for their proposed "commitment not to develop the weapon." The first addendum was written by Conant and signed by Rowe, Smith, DuBridge, Buckley and Oppenheimer. In part it said: "We base our recommendation on our belief that the extreme dangers to mankind inherent in the proposal wholly outweigh any military advantage that could come from this development. Let it be clearly realized that this is a super weapon; it is in a totally different category from an atomic bomb. The reason for developing such super bombs would be to have the capacity to devastate a vast area with a single bomb. Its use would involve a decision to slaughter a vast number of civilians. We are alarmed as to the possible global effects of the radioactivity generated by the explosion of a few super bombs of conceivable magnitude. If super bombs will work at all, there is no inherent limit in the destructive power that may be attained with them. Therefore, a super bomb might become a weapon of genocide.

"We believe a super bomb should never be produced. Mankind would be far better off not to have a demonstration of the feasibility of such a weapon until the present climate of world opinion changes.

"In determining not to proceed to develop the super bomb, we see a unique opportunity of providing by example some limitations on the totality of war and thus of limiting the fear and arousing the hopes of mankind."

Contrary to a frequently suggested notion, the members of the Oppenheimer committee were not at all unmindful of the possibility that the U.S.S.R. might develop the Super no matter what the U.S. did. Indeed, they regarded it as entirely possible and explained why it would not be crucial: "To the argument that Russians may succeed in developing this weapon, we would reply that our undertaking it will not prove a deterrent to them. Should they use the weapon against us, reprisals by our large stock of atomic bombs would be comparably effective to the use of a 'Super.' "

The minority addendum, signed by Fermi and Rabi, expressed even stronger opposition to the Super but loosely coupled an American renunciation with a proposal for a worldwide pledge not to proceed: "It is clear that the use of such a weapon cannot be justified on any ethical ground which gives a human being a certain individuality and dignity even if he happens to be a resident of an enemy country.

"The fact that no limits exist to the destructiveness of this weapon makes its very existence and the knowledge of its construction a danger to humanity as a whole. It is necessarily an evil thing considered in any light.

"For these reasons we believe it important for the President of the United States to tell the American public, and the world, that we think it wrong on fundamental ethical principles to initiate a program of development of such a weapon. At the same time it would be appropriate to invite the nations of the world to join us in a solemn pledge not to proceed in the development of construction of weapons of this category."

As with the majority, Fermi and Rabi also explicitly took up the possibility that the Russians might proceed on their own, or even go back on a pledge not to: "If such a pledge were accepted even without control machinery, it appears highly probable that an advanced state of development leading to a test by another power could be detected by available physical means. Furthermore, we have in our possession, in our stockpile of atomic bombs, the means for adequate 'military' retaliation for the production or use of a 'Super.' "

On December 2 and 3, five weeks after the special meeting, the General Advisory Committee convened for one of its regularly scheduled meetings and carefully reviewed the question of the Super once again. According to Richard G. Hewlett, the AEC's official historian, Oppenheimer reported to the commissioners that no member wished to change the views expressed in the October 30 report.

For a time it appeared that the views of the Oppenheimer committee had a chance of being accepted. David E. Lilienthal, chairman of the AEC, was receptive to the committee's point of view. He similarly favored two parallel responses to the Russian test: (1) increasing the production of fission weapons and developing a greater variety of them, particularly for tactical situations, and (2) officially announcing our intention to refrain from proceeding with the Super while simultaneously reopening and intensifying the search for international control of all kinds of weapons of mass destruction. Lilienthal considered the complete reliance on weapons of mass destruction to be a fundamental weakness in U.S. policy, and he viewed a "crash" program on the hydrogen bomb as foreclosing what might be the last good opportunity to base U.S. foreign policy on "something better than a headlong rush into war with weapons of mass destruction." "We are," he said, "today relying on an asset that is readily depreciating for us, i.e., weapons of mass destruction. [A decision to go ahead with the Super] would tend to confuse and, unwittingly, hide that fact and make it more difficult to find some other course."

As we know now, the advice of the Oppenheimer committee was rejected. Early in 1950 President Truman, acting on the basis of his own political judgment and on the totality of the advice he had received on the matter, issued directives designed to set in motion a major U.S. program to develop the hydrogen bomb.

It is not possible here to give a full description of what happened next, but the following chronological outline of the Russian and American superbomb programs is designed to show how the "race" for the superbomb did in fact come out, and to facilitate making judgments about the General Advisory Committee's advice and about "what might have been."

First of all, it is now known that both countries initiated high-priority programs for the development of a hydrogen bomb at about the same time (late 1949–early 1950), and both had been seriously studying the subject for some years before that.

The first U.S. test series that included experiments designed to investigate thermonuclear explosions took place at Eniwetok in the spring of 1951. Known as Operation Greenhouse, the series included two thermonuclear experiments. One, with the code name Item, was a test of the booster principle. This experiment, it must be emphasized, was planned and programmed before the first Russian atomic-bomb test. The other (which actually took place first) was called George. It was a response to Joe 1, as the first Russian atomic-bomb test was called by the U.S. intelligence establishment. Reduced to its essentials, the purpose of the experiment was to show, as a minimum, that a thermonuclear reaction could under ideal conditions be made to proceed in an experimental device. This experiment came to play a key role in the Super program. As Teller later put it: "We needed a significant test. Without such a test no one of us could have had the confidence to proceed further along speculations, inventions and the difficult choice of the most promising possibility. This test was to play the role of a pilot plant in our development."

The George shot served its purpose well. During the final stages of calculations concerned with the expected performance of this device, Teller and Stanislaw Ulam came up with the climactic idea that made it possible to achieve the goal of the superbomb program: they invented a configuration that would make it possible for a small fission explosion to ignite an arbitrarily large fusion explosion.

The first test of a device designed to ignite a large thermonuclear explosion by means of a comparatively small quantity of fissionable material took place at Eniwetok on November 1, 1952 (local time). The device, known as Mike, produced a tremendous explosion, equivalent in its energy release to 10 megatons (10 million tons) of TNT. As had been repeatedly predicted since the early 1940's, the yield was roughly 1,000 times larger than the yield of the first atomic bombs. For certain practical reasons relating to the pioneering nature of the test, this first version of the Teller-Ulam configuration had liquid deuterium as its thermonuclear fuel. (The last point needs special emphasis. The Teller-Ulam invention, contrary to folklore, was not the notion of substituting easy-to-handle lithium deuteride for the hard-to-handle liquid deuterium. That possibility had been recognized several years earlier.)

Also in November, 1952, the U.S. tested a very powerful fission bomb, with the code name King, that had an explosive yield of 500 kilotons, or half a megaton. Its purpose was to provide the U.S. with an extraordinarily powerful bomb by means of a straightforward extension of fission-weapons technology, in case such large bombs should become necessary for any strategic or political reason. Originally proposed by Bethe as a substitute for the Super program, it became instead a backup for it.

The first Russian explosion involving fusion reactions took place on August 12, 1953. Russian descriptions of this test and later ones confirm that it was not a superbomb. It was only some tens of times as big as the standard atomic bombs of the day, about the same size as but probably smaller than King, the largest U.S. fission bomb. It evidently involved one of several possible straightforward configurations for igniting a fairly small amount of thermonuclear material with a comparatively large amount of fissionable material. It was the first device anywhere to use lithium deuteride as a fuel, and presumably it could have been readily converted into a practical weapon if there had been any point in doing so. It seems to have been a development step the U.S. bypassed in its successful search for a configuration that would make it possible to produce an arbitrarily large explosion with a relatively small quantity of fissionable material.

In the spring of 1954 the U.S. successfully exploded six more variants of the superbomb in Operation Castle. Their yields varied widely. The first and most famous of these tests, with the code name Bravo, was exploded on March 1, 1954, at Bikini. Its design, which was initiated before the Mike explosion, also incorporated the Teller-Ulam configuration, but it had the more practical lithium deuteride as its thermonuclear fuel. Bravo's yield was 15 megatons, even more than Mike's, and it was readily adaptable to delivery by aircraft.

On November 23, 1955, the U.S.S.R. exploded a bomb

that had a yield of a few megatons. According to a statement made by Secretary Khrushchev, this device involved an "important new achievement" that made it possible by "using a relatively small quantity of fissionable material . . . to produce an explosion of several megatons." Khrushchev's remark is generally taken as confirmation that the test was the first one in which the Russians incorporated the Teller-Ulam configuration or something like it. It also used lithium deuteride as a fuel and was therefore a true superbomb, comparable to the U.S. Bravo device exploded 20 months earlier, except for its yield, which was still probably only about a fifth the yield of Bravo.

With this chronology in mind, what can one say about what might have happened if the U.S. had followed the advice of Oppenheimer and the rest of the General Advisory Committee, backed by Lilienthal and the majority of the AEC commissioners, and had not initiated a program for the specific purpose of developing the Super in the spring of 1950?

At best the invention of very large, comparatively inexpensive bombs of the Super type would have been forestalled or substantially delayed. Very probably the work on the booster principle, which presumably would still have gone forward, would have led eventually to the ideas underlying the design of very big bombs, but those ideas might well have been delayed until both President Eisenhower and Secretary Khrushchev were in power. Those two leaders were both more seriously interested in arms-limitation agreements than their predecessors had been, and it is at least possible that they might have been able to deal successfully with the superbomb. To be sure, such a favorable result was not very probable (certainly it had much less than an even chance of coming about), but its achievement would have been so beneficial to mankind that at least some small risk was clearly worth running.

To evaluate just how much risk would have been involved let us next examine three other outcomes, which I have labeled the "actual world," the "most probable alternative world" and the "worst plausible alternative world"

In both of the hypothetical alternative worlds I assume that the U.S. would have forgone the development of the Super but that the Russians would have ignored this American restraint and would have proceeded at first just as they did in the actual world. I also assume that the U.S. would have vigorously followed the positive elements of the Oppenheimer committee's advice; thus the booster project and other ideas for improving fission bombs would have been accelerated. The difference between the most probable alternative world and the worst plausible alternative world and lies in the timing of the test of the first Russian superbomb. In the worst plausible world I assume that this test would have come on the same date that it did in the actual world. In the most probable alternative world, however, I assume that the test would have been substantially delayed.

In both of the two hypothetical alternative worlds, then, the Russians in August, 1953, would have exploded Joe 4, a large bomb deriving part of its explosive energy from a thermonuclear fuel and yielding a few hundred kilotons. Such a device, however, would have had no real effect on the "balance of terror." In both alternative worlds the U.S. would surely have already tested the 500-kiloton all-fission bomb in November, 1952 (or probably earlier, since the timing of Operation Ivy was determined by the availability of the much more complicated Mike device). Therefore the explosion of Joe 4 would have meant that the U.S.S.R. had caught up with but not surpassed the U.S. insofar as the capability of producing enormous damage in a single explosion was concerned.

Then what would have happened? From that point the Russians might conceivably still have gone on to produce their multimegaton explosion in November, 1955, but I think it is very probable that they would not have done so until much later. In the actual world they had the powerful stimulus of knowing from our November 1952 test that there was some much better, probably novel way of designing hydrogen bombs so as to produce much larger explosions than the one they demonstrated in their August 1953 experiment. A careful analysis of the radioactive fallout from the Mike explosion may well have provided them with useful information concerning how to go about it. In the hypothetical world where the U.S. would have followed the Oppenheimer-Lilienthal advice that stimulus and information would have been absent. Moreover, a comparison of the way nuclear-weapons technology advanced in the U.S. and the U.S.S.R. during that period makes it seem likely there would have been a much longer delay — probably some years — before they took that big and novel a step without such stimuli and information. Therefore in the most probable alternative world the first Russian superbomb test would have been delayed until well after the first American superbomb test (in other words, delayed until 1957 or 1958), whereas in the worst plausible alternative world it would have occurred just when it did in the actual world: in August, 1955.

What would the U.S. have done in the meantime?

It would have been known immediately that the Russian explosion of August, 1953, was partly thermonuclear and that this test was many times as big as the Russians' previous explosions. If one assumes that following this Russian test the American program in the worst plausible world would have gone along just as it did in the actual world following President Truman's 1950 decision, then the U.S. would have set off the Mike explosion in April,

1956. A simple duplication of those earlier events at this later time, however, would have been unlikely. Any analysis of U.S. reactions to technological advances by the U.S.S.R. shows that the detection of the August 1953 event would have resulted in the initiation of a very large, high-priority American program to produce a bigger and better thermonuclear device. Such a program would undoubtedly have had broader support than the one actually mounted in the spring of 1950. Moreover, the general scientific and technological situation in which a hydrogen-bomb program would have been embedded in 1953 would have been significantly different from the actual one in 1950. For one thing, the kind of theoretical work in progress on the Super before President Truman's decision would have continued and would have provided a solider base from which to launch a crash program. In addition the booster program would presumably have continued along the path already set for it in 1948 (which included a test of the principle in 1951), and therefore in 1953 there would have been available some real experimental information concerning thermonuclear reactions on a smaller scale.

Last but not least, there had been great progress in computer technology between 1950 and 1953. When the real Mike test was being planned, fast electronic computers such as MANIAC and the first UNIVAC either were not quite operating or were in the early stages of their operating career. By a year or so later they were in full running order and much experience had been gained in their utilization, so that they would have been much more effective in connection with any hypothetical post–Joe 4 American crash program. For all these reasons it is plausible to assume that the U.S. would have arrived at something like the Teller-Ulam design for a multi-megaton superbomb either in the same length of time or, even more likely, in a somewhat shorter period, say sometime between September, 1955, and April, 1956.

These dates bracket the actual date when the Russians arrived at roughly the same point in the actual world. A few months' difference either way at that stage of the program, however, would not have been meaningful. It takes quite a long time, typically several years, to go from the proof of a prototype to the deployment of a significantly large number of weapons based on it. Differences in production capacity would have played a much more important role than any small advantage in the date of the first experiment, and such differences as then existed surely favored the U.S. Hence even in the worst plausible alternative world the nuclear balance would not have been upset. Moreover, in the most probable alternative world the date the Russians would have arrived at that stage would have been delayed until well after the first large U.S. Mike-like explosion had showed them there was a better way; thus in this most probable case the U.S. would still have enjoyed a substantial lead.

In short, the common notion that has persisted since late 1949 that some sort of disaster would have resulted from following the Oppenheimer-Lilienthal advice is in retrospect almost surely wrong. Moreover, even if by some unlikely quirk of fate the Russians had achieved the Superbomb first, the large stock of fission bombs in the U.S. arsenal, together with the 500-kiloton all-fission bomb for those few cases where it would have been appropriate, would have adequately ensured the national security of the U.S.

This history and the conjectures about possible alternative pasts show that Oppenheimer, Conant, Fermi, Rabi and the others were right in their advice about the Super, and that they were right for the right reasons. They had correctly assessed the relative technological state of affairs, correctly judged the margin of safety inherent in the situation and correctly projected the ability of the U.S. to catch up rapidly if that should become necessary. The national security of the U.S. did not require the initiation of a high-priority program to develop the Super. It was therefore entirely appropriate to attempt to use the first Russian atomic explosion as a lever for reopening the entire question of nuclear-arms control.

The authors of the report could not, of course, predict the details of the alternative chronologies outlined above, and they did not try to do so, but they could and did correctly assess the general situation and the limits of the probable futures inherent in it. The large rate of production of fissionable material already in effect, the planned expansion in that rate, the resulting immense stock of fission weapons forecast for the early and middle 1950's and the existence of an entirely adequate means for delivering those weapons guaranteed that even the sudden surprise introduction of a few superbombs by the U.S.S.R. could not really upset the balance of power. The situation was reinforced by the projection, which proved to be correct in the King shot, that if need be the power of the World War II fission bombs could be multiplied up to the megaton range simply by more astutely employing the techniques and materials already known and available.

In the course of presenting its general admonition not to proceed with the crash development of the Super, the Oppenheimer committee made certain specific predictions about it. An examination of these predictions shows that they stood the test of time fairly well.

In their discussion of the superbomb the committee members said that "an imaginative and concerted attack on the problem has a better than even chance of producing the weapon within five years." Four years and four months later Bravo, the first practical American thermonuclear weapon, was tested at Bikini. Given the unknowns and uncertainties existing at the time, that is a remarkably accurate prediction. They went on to say that "once the problem of initiation has been solved, there is no upper limit . . . except that imposed by requirements of delivery." That also seems to be the case. The largest bomb exploded so far (by the Russians in 1961) is said to have been some 58 megatons, four times the size of Bravo, and there is every reason to believe bombs could indeed be made even larger than that.

The report also said that there "appears to be no experimental approach short of an actual test which will add to our conviction that a given model will or will not work" and that "many tests may be required before a workable model has been evolved." History has borne out the first part of the prediction. A quarter of a century had to pass and other inventions had to be made before thermonuclear explosions were produced on a laboratory scale by means of lasers, and even those are probably not closely relevant to the superbomb problem. The second part of the prediction turned out to be less precise. The number of U.S. tests needed to develop and check out a bomb was three: George, Mike and Bravo. The Russians needed only two tests, but they had an invaluable piece of information that was not available to the American workers: the sure knowledge that both small and large thermonuclear explosions were really possible. These numbers were very probably smaller than the "many" the Oppenheimer committee had in mind, but even so they were in each case sufficient to provide the other side with an adequate early warning that thermonuclear work was in progress.

Another interesting and perceptive technological prediction is contained in the report's statement about "very grave contamination problems which can easily be made more acute . . . by surrounding the deuterium with uranium." The very high levels of radioactive fallout associated with large hydrogen bombs do in fact result from such use of uranium. The very first test of a practical superbomb, Bravo, produced a blanket of fallout that evidently contributed to the death of one innocent bystander (the radioman of the *Fortunate Dragon*, a Japanese fishing ship) and came within a hair's breadth of killing hundreds of Marshall Islanders living on two nearby atolls. The fallout accident in turn provided the initial spark behind the movement to ban nuclear-weapons tests that ultimately led to the Partial Test-Ban Treaty in 1963.

The foregoing account is, I think, enough to show that the Oppenheimer committee's advice was sound, but it may not be enough to show unequivocally that President Truman should have taken this sound advice. The President, unlike the AEC commissioners and their advisers, had to take into account a broader array of information and political ideas than those discussed in detail here. The overall intensity of the cold war was increasing, Mao Tse-tung and Joseph Stalin had proclaimed the Sino-Soviet bloc and many important Republicans were withdrawing or modifying their support of the bipartisan foreign and military policies that had been in effect since the beginning of World War II. As the fall of 1949 wore on and the arguments about the Super began to leak out from behind the curtain of secrecy, those opinions favoring the Super were, in the overall context of the time, both simpler and more widely persuasive than those opposing it. There can be little doubt that Congressional and public opinion was beginning to come down heavily on the side of a strong response to the first Russian atomic-bomb test, and building the Super seemed to many to be just the kind of thing to keep the Russians in their place. President Truman, a professional politician, could therefore have concluded that rejecting the Super and running even a small risk of being second best was politically too difficult an alternative. Moreover, his decision to proceed with the Super, made on January 31, 1950, was based on the advice of the special committee of the National Security Council charged with studying the matter. Those committee members responsible for international relations (Secretary of State Dean Acheson) and national defense (Secretary of Defense Louis A. Johnson) strongly supported going ahead; the only reservations were expressed by the one committee member who was not responsible for those elements of national-security policy, namely Lilienthal, chairman of the AEC.

Nonetheless, it now seems clear to me in retrospect that President Truman should have taken the advice of the Oppenheimer committee; he should have held back on initiating the development of the Super while making another serious try to achieve international control over all nuclear arms, particularly the Super. The benefits that could have flowed from forestalling the Super altogether were incalculable; the chances of succeeding in doing so were small, but so were the risks in trying. It was certainly one of the few opportunities, and as Lilienthal said then, it may have been the last good opportunity to base American foreign policy on something better than reliance on weapons of mass destruction or, as it is now phrased, on the prospect of "mutual assured destruction."

## Proponents of the H-Bomb Win

### *Documents 14 and 15*

In document 14, a letter to President Truman in November 1949, Lewis Strauss of the Atomic Energy Commission responded to the General Advisory Committee's recommendation that the United States not proceed with the H-bomb. His letter offers a full survey of the arguments for building the "Super." He concludes with a warning that renunciation of the H-bomb by the United States could result in only the Soviet Union's having it. The view of Strauss and other hydrogen bomb proponents prevailed. In January 1950 (see document 15), Truman authorized the H-bomb program to move ahead as expeditiously as possible.

## 14 LETTER TO PRESIDENT TRUMAN
### Lewis Strauss
### November 25, 1949

Dear Mr. President:

As you know, the thermonuclear (super) bomb was suggested by scientists working at Los Alamos during the war. The current consideration of the super bomb was precipitated, I believe, by a memorandum which I addressed to my fellow Commissioners following your announcement on September 23rd of an atomic explosion in Russia. I participated in the discussions which were antecedent to the letter to you from the Commission on November 9th, but did not join in the preparation of the letter as I was then on the Pacific Coast. It was my belief that a comprehensive recommendation should be provided for you, embodying the judgement of the Commission (in the areas where it is competent), together with the views of the Departments of State and Defense. My colleagues, however, felt that you would prefer to obtain these views separately.

Differences on the broad question of policy between my associates as individuals were included in the Commission's letter to you, and it was correctly stated that the views of Commissioner Dean and mine were in substantial accord on the main issue. It is proper, I believe, that I should state them on my own responsibility and in my own words.

I believe that the United States must be as completely armed as any possible enemy. From this, it follows that I believe it unwise to renounce, unilaterally, any weapon which an enemy can reasonably be expected to possess. I recommend that the President direct the Atomic Energy Commission to proceed with the development of the thermonuclear bomb, at highest priority subject only to the judgment of the Department of Defense as to its value as a weapon, and of the advice of the Department of State as to the diplomatic consequences of its unilateral renunciation or its possession. In the event that you may be interested, my reasoning is appended in a memorandum.

/s/ Lewis L. Strauss

This is a memorandum to accompany a letter of even date to the President to supply the reasoning for my recommendation that he should direct the Atomic Energy Commission to proceed at highest priority with the development of the thermonuclear weapon.

***Premises***

1. The production of such a weapon appears to be feasible (i.e., better than a 50–50 chance).
2. Recent accomplishments by the Russians indicate that the production of a thermonuclear weapon is within their technical competence.
3. A government of atheists is not likely to be dissuaded from producing the weapon on "moral" grounds. ("Reason and experience both forbid us to expect that national morality can prevail in exclusion of religious principle." G. Washington, September 17, 1796.)
4. The possibility of producing the thermonuclear weapon was suggested more than six years ago, and considerable theoretical work has been done which may be known to the Soviets — the principle has certainly been known to them.
5. The time in which the development of this weapon can be perfected is perhaps of the order of two years, so that a Russian enterprise started some years ago may be well along to completion.
6. It is the historic policy of the United States not to have its forces less well armed than those of any other country (viz, the 5:5:3 naval ratio, etc. etc.).
7. Unlike the atomic bomb which has certain limitations, the proposed weapon may be tactically employed against a mobilized army over an area of the size ordinarily occupied by such a force.
8. The Commission's letter of November 9th to the President mentioned the "possibility that the radioactivity released by a small number (perhaps ten) of these bombs would pollute the earth's atmosphere to a dangerous extent." Studies requested by the Commission have since indicated that the number of such weapons necessary to pollute the earth's atmosphere would run into many hundreds. Atmospheric pollution is a consequence of present atomic bombs if used in quantity.

***Conclusions***

1. The danger in the weapon does not reside in its physical nature but in human behavior. Its unilateral renunciation by the United States could very easily result in its unilateral possession by the Soviet Government. I am unable to see any satisfaction in that prospect.
2. The Atomic Energy Commission is competent to advise the President with respect to the feasibility of making the weapon; its economy in fissionable material as compared with atomic bombs; the possible time factor involved; and a description of its characteristics compared to atomic bombs. Judgment, however, as to its strategic or tactical importance for the armed forces should be furnished by the Department of Defense, and views as to the effect on friendly nations or of unilateral renunciation of the weapon is a subject for the Department of State. My opinion as an individual, however, based upon discussion with military experts is to the effect that the weapon may be critically useful against a large enemy force both as a weapon of offense and as a defensive measure to prevent landings on our own shores.
3. I am impressed with the arguments which have been made to the effect that this is a weapon of mass destruction on an unprecedented scale. So, however, was

the atomic bomb when it was first envisaged and when the National Academy of Sciences in its report of November 6, 1941, referred to it as "of superlatively destructive power." Also on June 16, 1945, the Scientific Panel of the Interim Committee on Nuclear Power, comprising some of the present members of the General Advisory Committee, reported to the Secretary of War, "We believe the subject of thermonuclear reactions among light nuclei is one of the most important that needs study. There is a reasonable presumption that with skillful research and development, fission bombs can be used to initiate the reactions of deuterium, tritium, and possibly other light nuclei. If this can be accomplished, the energy release of explosive units can be increased by a factor of 1000 or more over that of presently contemplated fission bombs." This statement was preceded by the recommendation, "Certainly we would wish to see work carried out on the problems mentioned below."

The General Advisory Committee to the Atomic Energy Commission, in its recent communication to the Commission recommending against the development of the super bomb, noted that it "strongly favors" the booster program, which is a program to increase the explosive power and hence the damage area and deadliness of atomic bombs. These positions and those above appear not to be fully consistent and indicate that the scientific point of view is not unanimous.

4. Obviously the current atomic bomb as well as the proposed thermonuclear weapon are horrible to contemplate. All war is horrible. Until, however, some means is found of eliminating war, I cannot agree with those of my colleagues who feel that an announcement should be made by the President to the effect that the development of the thermonuclear weapon will not be undertaken by the United States at this time. This is because: (a) I do not think the statement will be credited in the Kremlin; (b) that when and if it should be decided subsequent to such a statement to proceed with the production of the thermonuclear bomb, it might in a delicate situation, be regarded as an affirmative statement of hostile intent; and (c) because primarily until disarmament is universal, our arsenal must be not less well equipped than with the most potent weapons that our technology can devise.

***Recommendation***

In sum, I believe that the president should direct the Atomic Energy Commission to proceed with all possible expedition to develop the thermonuclear weapon.

## 15 AUTHORIZATION OF H-BOMB
## President Harry Truman
## January 31, 1950

It is part of my responsibility as Commander in Chief of the Armed Forces to see to it that our country is able to defend itself against any possible aggressor. Accordingly, I have directed the Atomic Energy Commission to continue its work on all forms of atomic weapons, including the so-called hydrogen or superbomb. Like all other work in the field of atomic weapons, it is being and will be carried forward on a basis consistent with the overall objectives of our program for peace and security.

This we shall continue to do until a satisfactory plan for international control of atomic energy is achieved. We shall also continue to examine all those factors that affect our program for peace and this country's security.

# THE SIGNIFICANCE OF THE KOREAN WAR

## Aggression in Korea

### *Document 16*

Convinced that the Kremlin not only sought world domination but also controlled all major Communist bloc initiatives, U.S. policy makers assumed in June 1950 that Moscow had authorized and directed the North Korean attack against South Korea. Accordingly, the U.S. ambassador delivered a note demanding that the Soviet Union dissociate itself from North Korean aggression. In its reply, the Kremlin claimed that North Korea's military action had been provoked by border attacks from the South.

## 16 EXCHANGE OF VIEWS REGARDING INVASION OF SOUTH KOREA
## June 27-29, 1950

a) *Aide-Memoire from the United States Government Delivered to the Soviet Deputy Foreign Minister by the United States Ambassador, June 27, 1950:*

My Government has instructed me to call to your attention the fact that North Korean forces have crossed the 38th parallel and invaded the territory of the Republic of Korea in force at several points. The refusal of the Soviet Representative to attend the United Nations Security Council meeting on June 25, despite the clear threat to peace and the obligations of a Security Council member under the Charter, requires the Government of the United States to bring this matter directly to the attention of the Union of Soviet Socialist Republics. In view of the universally known fact of the close relations between the Union of Soviet Socialist Republics and the North Korean regime, the United States Government asks assurance that the Union of Soviet Socialist Republics disavows responsibility for this unprovoked and unwarranted attack, and that it will use its influence with the North Korean authorities to withdraw their invading forces immediately.

b) *The Soviet Reply, June 29, 1950.*

1. In accordance with facts verified by the Soviet Government, the events taking place in Korea were provoked by an attack by forces of the South Korean authorities on border regions of North Korea. Therefore the responsibility for these events rests upon the South Korean authorities and upon those who stand behind their back.

2. As is known, the Soviet Government withdrew its troops from Korea earlier than the Government of the United States and thereby confirmed its traditional principle of noninterference in the internal affairs of other states. And now as well the Soviet Government adheres to the principle of the impermissibility of interference by foreign powers in the internal affairs of Korea.

3. It is not true that the Soviet Government refused to participate in meetings of the Security Council. In spite of its full willingness, the Soviet Government has not been able to take part in the meetings of the Security Council inasmuch as, because of the position of the Government of the United States, China, a permanent member of the Security Council, has not been admitted to the Council, which has made it impossible for the Security Council to take decisions having legal force.

## MacArthur's Proposal to End the War

### *Document 17*

By October 1950 the United Nations forces under Gen. Douglas MacArthur had pushed the North Koreans back across the 38th parallel and were pursuing them toward the Yalu River bordering Manchuria. The UN advance seemed on the verge of forging a unified Korea under non-Communist control and U.S. influence. The Chinese Communists, however, were alarmed by the prospect of having a hostile new state lodged at a vital section of their border and repeatedly warned the United States that a UN drive further northward would bring China into the war. MacArthur continued his advance. By the end of October, U.S. troops first began to encounter Chinese "volunteers." By late November, the Chinese Army was pouring into the fighting en masse on the side of the North Koreans. The war settled into a bloody stalemate that stabilized roughly along the 38th parallel.

### 17 COMMUNIQUÉ ON CHINESE INTERVENTION
### Gen. Douglas MacArthur
### November 28, 1950

Enemy reactions developed in the course of our assault operations of the past four days disclose that a major segment of the Chinese continental armed forces in army, corps and divisional organization of an aggregate strength of over 200,000 men is now arrayed against the United Nations forces in North Korea.

There exists the obvious intent and preparation for support of these forces by heavy reinforcements now concentrated within the privileged sanctuary north of the international boundary and constantly moving forward.

Consequently, we face an entirely new war. This has shattered the high hopes we entertained that the intervention of the Chinese was only of a token nature on a volunteer and individual basis as publicly announced, and that therefore the war in Korea could be brought to a rapid close by our movement to the international boundary and the prompt withdrawal thereafter of United Nations forces, leaving Korean problems for settlement by the Koreans themselves.

It now appears to have been the enemy's intent, in breaking off contact with our forces some two weeks ago, to secure the time necessary surreptitiously to build up for a later surprise assault upon our lines in overwhelming force, taking advantage of the freezing of all rivers and roadbeds which would have materially reduced the effectiveness of our air interdiction and permitted a greatly accelerated forward movement of enemy reinforcements and supplies. This plan has been disrupted by our own offensive action, which forced upon the enemy a premature engagement.

*General MacArthur later issued this additional paragraph to the communiqué.*

This situation, repugnant as it may be, poses issues beyond the authority of the United Nations military council — issues which must find their solution within the councils of the United Nations and chancelleries of the world.

## Truman Justifies the Korean War

### *Document 18*

As the Korean War dragged on with no decisive result, it became increasingly unpopular. Truman decided to fire, for insubordination, Gen. Douglas MacArthur, the popular national hero whose exploits in World War II had brought him wide fame and acclaim. MacArthur had repeatedly been publicly critical of Truman's conduct of the war. In this excerpt from a radio address to the nation reporting on the war and explaining his decision to fire Gen. MacArthur, Truman makes a brief but powerful and eloquent statement about why the United States was fighting in Korea.

### 18 SPEECH TO THE NATION President Harry Truman April 10, 1951

My fellow Americans:

I want to talk to you tonight about what we are doing in Korea and about our policy in the Far East.

In the simplest terms what we are doing in Korea is this: We are trying to prevent a third world war.

I think most people in this country recognized that fact last June. And they warmly supported the decision of the government to help the Republic of Korea against the communist aggressors. Now many persons, even some who applauded our decision to defend Korea, have forgotten the basic reason for our action.

It is right for us to be in Korea now. It was right last June. It is right today.

I want to remind you why this is true.

The communists in the Kremlin are engaged in a monstrous conspiracy to stamp out freedom all over the world. If they were to succeed, the United States would be numbered among their principal victims. It must be clear to everyone that the United States cannot and will not sit idly by and await foreign conquest. The only question is: When is the best time to meet the threat and how?

The best time to meet the threat is in the beginning. It is easier to put out a fire in the beginning when it is small than after it has become a roaring blaze.

And the best way to meet the threat of aggression is for the peace-loving nations to act together. If they don't act together, they are likely to be picked off one by one.

If they had followed the right policies in the 1930's — if the free countries had acted together to crush the aggression of the dictators, and if they had acted in the beginning, when the aggression was small — there probably would have been no World War II.

## Commuting Soldiers

### *Document 19*

This 1950 article from the *Saturday Evening Post* paints an interesting picture of one aspect of the human side of the Korean war. The wives of the title see their husbands off every day to bomb and strafe the Chinese and North Koreans, then wait for them to return home. Home is just forty-five minutes from the battlefield.

### 19 THE WIVES WAIT OUT THE WAR September 30, 1950

It's hard to picture war as something a man can commute to, kissing his wife good-by in the morning and coming back home when the day's work is done, but in some ways our air war on Korea is like that. This doesn't mean that our pilots lead exactly the life of the civilian suburbanite who catches the 8:15 train every morning and the 5:15 every night, with two days off each week in which to recover from the wounds of the paper battle fought in his air-conditioned office. On the contrary, our combat fliers, from bases in Japan, are flying missions right around the clock, as many as three a day, seven days a week. But some of the pilots do have their families with them at the air bases, and when they're lucky they get to sleep at home. They don't see much of their children, though; they leave the house before dawn and don't come back until after the youngsters are in bed.

Before June twenty-fifth, life went on at a very pleasant clip at the air base I visited in Southern Japan, where one Fighter-Bomber Wing has its headquarters. More than 170 officers — fifty of them fighter pilots — and about the same number of airmen had their families with them, quartered in pleasant houses about five miles from the airstrip. Clubs at the base and at the nearby town were well patronized every night and jammed on week ends.

Those who had cars took off for the week end to some place where a pleasant glow, developed at the bar of a good hotel, would dull the senses to the smells of Japan. Others took their children to the beaches, to relax in the sun and surf. They had to admit to themselves that they never had it so good.

Suddenly, on June twenty-fifth, everything changed. Fighters from this Fighter-Bomber Wing were ordered to protect the evacuation of Americans from Seoul. To Col. Jack Price, the husky West Pointer in command of the wing, that meant shooting down communist airplanes. Two Yaks went down the following day, and the kills of succeeding days put the North Korean air force out of business.

The base became a madhouse of activity. Transport planes were loaded with ground troops at the airstrip. American refugees were arriving with just the clothes they had on, correspondents were hammering at operations officers for air transportation to Korea. For days no one got much sleep.

And during that first hectic interval most people were a little scared. They were uncomfortably aware of their closeness to Korea, and, with the Red Army plowing down the peninsula, the butterfly squadron made sorties in many assorted stomachs. Some wives became panicky when the siren signals were posted for alerts, air raids and attacks by air-borne troops. The parties stopped. No one left the base over the week end, and the officers'-club bar was strangely quiet, with just a handful of tired men downing a nightcap before hitting the sack. Rumors flew thick and fast, and no one was quite sure what would happen next.

The shock of the first casualties sobered the entire community. And the pilots and their wives, who made up a particularly close-knit group, took these first deaths hard.

Colonel Price has the unpleasant job of breaking the news personally to the widows of his downed fliers, and nowadays he hates to set foot into the dependent housing area, for he knows that every wife within visual range is wondering whether or not he is going to call on her. The colonel is a huge man, six feet four, who was an All-American tackle at West Point in 1930 and '31, but his manner is awkward and almost shy when he has to face one of these girls and tell her she's a widow. And the fact that she already knows the reason for his visit, just because he's there at all, doesn't make things any easier for him.

Two months of war have tested the wives of the fighter pilots. Those who thought at first that they wanted to go home are now more than ever anxious to stay. Their attitude has won the admiration of everyone, from the commanding officer down. Although throats still tighten and hearts do flip-flops when Colonel Price appears or when they see three jets returning from a mission instead of four — a mission that they knew their man was flying — there are no tears and no crackups.

Alper Munkres lost her husband, Lt. John Neil Munkres, twenty-five, of Weeping Water, Nebraska, when his flaming F-51 plunged into the sea off Ashiya on August fifteenth. They were married here at the Air Force Chapel on September 17, 1949. She is the daughter of Maj. and Mrs. Van Rensselaer Vestal, of Washington, D. C., and was with her family in a nearby city, where her father was provost judge, when she met young Munkres, a West Point graduate of 1946. Munk, as she called him, was lost on his sixty-second mission, sixty of which he had flown in F-80's.

Alper never worried about Munk's flying; she had supreme confidence in him and she knew that he had the same kind of confidence in his airplane. She always felt a little tugging fear that he might have to bail out over enemy territory, but she never let it bother her too much. She bore up well even under the shock of his death. She was dry-eyed and quiet, although she said that "something just dried up within me." Wives of other fighter pilots surrounded her, spending most of the day with her, eating meals with her and keeping her busy in the evenings with inconsequential things. They talked about the accident freely, speculating on what could have happened to set the engine ablaze.

The twenty-three-year-old widow is glad that she was here when it happened — here with her Air Force friends. "Air Force people understand each other," she said. "They speak a language of their own, and they think differently than people do back home. Besides, I was able to talk with those who last saw him and the man who last heard from him over the radio. All he said was: 'Having engine trouble.' I'm not morbid, but there was a certain comfort in seeing those people.

"Since I've experienced this terrible grief and loneliness, I've started to worry about the other wives. I find myself wondering which one will be the next. Before Munk's death such thoughts never crossed my mind. I know *they* are not thinking in that channel; they are just like I was: 'it can't happen to me.'

"I'm going home to Washington in about a week, flying home. I'd like to get a job as an airline hostess, preferably an overseas line, but flying to the other side of the world, Europe. I don't think I'll ever want to come out this way again."

The other wives continue their normal way of living, shopping at the base commissary, buying materials at the PX for their Japanese maids to sew into good-looking dresses. Most of the entertaining is now done in the home — bridge parties or a shower for a wife soon to have a baby. And most of the parties, even in the evenings, are hen parties. The husbands, if they're not flying night missions, are in the sack, catching up on the countless hours of sleep they've lost.

Every one of the wives can face a visit from Colonel Price bravely. None of them wants to go home, and they won't unless the Air Force throws them out or until that long-awaited rotation system goes into effect, which will take their men home with them. One squadron, at this writing, has an average of seventy missions per man.

There are some officers who would like to see the dependents sent home immediately. They point out that, with new men pouring in, billeting is becoming overcrowded, and that the food required to feed dependents in Japan takes up sizable ship space. As far as the Air Force is concerned, a rotation system will automatically send the pilot and his dependents home, which will solve their housing and feeding problems very neatly. And replacements will not be allowed to bring out their families.

This Fighter-Bomber Wing has maintained a terrific tempo. In two months of warfare its planes have flown 7200 sorties, a feat made possible by the fact that targets within enemy lines are only 180 air miles from the base. Fast-flying jets can attack these targets with several strafing and rocketing passes and be back on the runway in an hour and a half.

Returning pilots find a huge cake, baked by one of the wives, in the squadron lounge, where a Japanese boy serves hot coffee or soft drinks. The husbands make a beeline for the telephone to check in with their wives. Others, joining the men on stand-by alert, gripe about the scarcity of targets, although there have been some startling surprises on that score.

One mission, for instance, was sent out to attack an orchard. The flight leader located his target and wondered why they had been assigned to blow hell out of a group of trees lined up in the precise pattern of an orchard. The first rocket blast answered his question. The North Koreans had cut down all the trees in the orchard and had stuck them on top of tanks, weapons carriers and ammo trucks, carefully maintaining the original pattern.

On August twenty-second an F-80 mission went out to strafe and rocket the municipal building in Kosong. I flew with the four-plane group in a T-33 piloted by Lt. Clifford Singley, of Montgomery, Alabama. As our jets swooped into Kosong, Singley pointed out the target, a long low building with the name of the town painted on the roof. I wondered why this was a military objective.

Our flight leader, Capt. Warren Bennett, of Fargo, North Dakota, put his first rocket smack in the middle of one side of the building. We roared over the target, pulling about five G's in our climbing turn for a second pass. As we dived down again, we saw that the rockets fired by the planes following us had set a terrific blaze. Rivers of burning gasoline were running from the base of the building and spilling out into the big yard which fronted it. Before leaving, we made six passes at another building in the compound, strafing and rocketing; it, too, immediately burst into flames. There was no opposition.

As we pulled away from the burning buildings and climbed for the return flight home, smoke was rising to 3000 feet. On the intercom Singley said, "Now you know that wasn't just office furniture burning down there."

# The Legacy of the Korean War

## *Document 20*

The Korean War cost fifty-eight thousand American casualties and led to a bitter domestic debate over the wisdom of "limited" war. Despite the "never again" consensus reigning in the Pentagon, however, U.S. civilian policy makers came to view the outcome in Korea as a cold war victory, one that bolstered their willingness to combat Communist influence wherever it appeared. In addition, the war also resulted in a vast and permanent expansion of the U.S. defense establishment to a hitherto unprecedented peacetime size.

## 20 THE LESSONS OF THE WAR
## Samuel F. Wells, Jr.

For most Americans over 40, the bitter conflict on the Korean peninsula from 1950 to 1953 evokes memories and lessons that differ from those of other wars. The Korean War had special, ironic qualities from the start. American intervention had little to do with prior U.S. plans or interests in northeast Asia; the future development of Korea itself was largely irrelevant to many of Washington's critical war decisions; the clash of conventional armies ended amid secret U.S. threats of atomic holocaust. The accepted "lessons of Korea" have changed with each new generation of statesmen and scholars, but Korea is still recognized as a major turning point in the evolution of America's approach to peace and war in the nuclear age.

During the winter of 1949–50, responding to the recent Communist victory in China and the Soviet detonation of an atomic device several years earlier than predicted, President Harry S Truman and his principal advisers developed a set of austere, clearly defined international policies.

They assumed that the United States would face a protracted but peaceful war of nerves with the Soviet Union and its satellites. They saw the major dangers to the Republic as those of losing our sense of purpose, allowing our economy to stagnate, and accepting Communist penetration of Western Europe. The administration decided to step up the development of a hydrogen bomb to maintain our lead in technology, and it relied on air power to deter Soviet aggression. Added emphasis was put on the new NATO alliance in order to stem Communist political, not military, challenges in France and Italy.

### At the Bottom of the List

One broad review of national security policy produced the now-famous NSC-68 memorandum, which called for vastly increased U.S. military preparedness and more aggressive action to break up the Communist bloc. But Truman refused to approve the extra spending required;

he ordered his Secretary of Defense, Louis Johnson, to keep the defense budget under a low $13.5 billion ceiling for the 1951 fiscal year.

In East Asia, the Truman administration decided to encourage the tensions already evident between Moscow and the newly victorious Chinese Communists in Peking. Seeing American interests in the Korean peninsula as minimal, Washington decided to avoid any significant support for the one-man regime of Syngman Rhee in the South. The United States had already pulled its troops out of South Korea by the autumn of 1949. Only an advisory group remained behind. With regard to Soviet intentions, Major General W. E. Todd, director of the Joint Intelligence Group of the Joint Chiefs of Staff, told the Senate Foreign Relations Committee that in any ranking of Soviet targets for aggression "Korea would be at the bottom of that list. . . ."

## The Acheson Speech

To make all this clear to both friends and adversaries, Secretary of State Dean Acheson spelled out the administration's Asian policy before the National Press Club on January 12, 1950. He defined the United States defensive perimeter as running from the Aleutians through American-occupied Japan and the Ryukyu Islands to the Philippines — a line which, significantly, excluded Taiwan, Indochina, and South Korea.

In an often neglected section of his speech, Acheson emphasized that the recent dominance of the Soviet Union in absorbing large sections of the four northern provinces of China was "the single most significant, most important fact, in the relation of any foreign power with Asia."* He then warned: "We must not undertake to deflect from the Russians to ourselves the righteous anger, and the wrath, and the hatred of the Chinese people which must develop. It would be folly to deflect it to ourselves."

With the North Korean invasion of June 25, 1950 (Washington time), the Truman administration quickly reversed itself. The President committed first air power, then United States troops to help defend South Korea. The American decision to intervene rested on certain assumptions. Despite their awareness of Sino-Soviet friction, Truman, Acheson, and other Washington officials believed that Joseph Stalin and the Politburo not only sought world domination but controlled all major initiatives by Communist bloc governments, including China and North Korea. Thus, virtually all the American policymakers assumed in June 1950 that the Kremlin had approved and directed the North Korean invasion.

Today, significant evidence from Soviet and North Korean sources indicates that Stalin had endorsed a limited North Korean military push across the 38th Parallel, but had urged that it come not before November 1950. There is good reason to think that Kim Il-sung, North Korea's strong-minded dictator, launched a larger invasion than Stalin authorized and on his own initiative advanced the schedule. But it is now apparent that Truman and his senior advisers, with a Cold War mindset shared by most Americans, did not perceive such possibilities or seek to exploit any potential differences between Moscow and Pyongyang.

Convinced that the North Korean attack represented a coordinated Communist test of American will, Truman saw little alternative to intervention. In his memoirs, the President recalled his thoughts of how Nazi aggression, unchallenged in the 1930s, had led to World War II. "I felt certain that if South Korea was allowed to fall," he said, "Communist leaders would be emboldened to override nations closer to our own shores." Despite his inappropriate analogy to the Nazis and his simplistic view of the Communist bloc, Truman's instinctive decision to intervene was sound.

Responding quickly during a Soviet absence, the United Nations Security Council endorsed a resolution condemning the North Korean action as "a breach of peace" and on June 27 called upon all UN members to assist Syngman Rhee's Republic of Korea in repelling the invasion.

## Turning the Tide

The big question for the United States, given the weak state of its military forces, was how to help. With North Korean troops advancing rapidly down the peninsula, Truman directed General Douglas MacArthur in Tokyo to provide air and naval support to the South on June 27. Two days later, acting without formal congressional authorization and expecting the conflict to be brief, the President ordered American ground forces to join this UN-sponsored "police action."

Under MacArthur's leadership, American troops turned the tide. Starting from a small, hard-pressed defensive perimeter around the port of Pusan, the general executed a classic envelopment of the North Korean forces with a daring amphibious landing at Inchon — near Seoul, the capital — on September 15. Within two weeks the Communist armies had been decimated and driven from South Korean territory.

The euphoria of victory then led MacArthur into a fateful miscalculation. Disregarding a warning from Pe-

*Acheson mentioned Outer Mongolia, Inner Mongolia, Sinkiang, and Manchuria. Outer Mongolia had been Soviet-dominated since 1921 and declared its independence from China in 1945. In Manchuria, Acheson cited the Soviet-administered Far Eastern Railway. (He cited no specifics regarding Soviet behavior in Sinkiang and Inner Mongolia.) At the time Acheson spoke, Sino-Soviet negotiations were underway which resulted in the Russians relinquishing control of the Far Eastern Railway, and in a Soviet commitment to evacuate Port Arthur in Manchuria.

king that an American advance across the 38th Parallel would bring China into the war, the five-star UN commander stretched his instructions from the Joint Chiefs of Staff, who set as his military objective "the destruction of the North Korean Armed Forces." To General George C. Marshall, who had become Secretary of Defense on September 21, MacArthur declared: "Unless and until the enemy capitulates, I regard all of Korea open for our military operations."

## Truman vs. MacArthur

Against only slight resistance, widely-separated American and South Korean columns drove northward toward the Yalu River during October. Despite new reports of massed Chinese troops poised across the border in Manchuria, MacArthur pushed ahead, and the Joint Chiefs in Washington did not order him to stop. In the last week of October, American troops first encountered Chinese "volunteers." By late November, overwhelming Chinese armies had turned the UN advance into a costly retreat that shocked Washington and led to a major domestic debate over the wisdom of "limited" wars.

The Chinese intervention changed everything. It prevented a UN victory; a costly seesaw struggle led to a military stalemate that stabilized roughly along the 38th Parallel by late 1951.* The common desire of Peking and Moscow to sustain the North Koreans postponed for several years an open Sino-Soviet split. And intense hostility between the United States and the People's Republic of China endured until shortly before President Richard Nixon's dramatic visit to Peking in 1972. The Chinese intervention also led MacArthur, in an effort to restore his military reputation, to challenge both the limited war strategy and the authority of his Commander in Chief. But President Truman, convinced that America's principal danger came in Europe from the Soviet Union, refused to adopt MacArthur's proposals to take the war into Chinese territory. In April 1951, he brusquely fired the great hero of the Pacific war and, in the face of a popular uproar, made it stick.

The Korean War spurred a massive U.S. rearmament effort and a major shift in defense policy. Consistent with its assumptions about the war's origins, the Truman administration put the lion's share of its increased defense outlays into programs directed against the Soviet Union. The budget for defense and international affairs climbed from $17.7 billion in fiscal 1950 to $52.6 billion in fiscal 1953. The new departures included the development of tactical nuclear weapons, the rushed construction of numerous air bases at home and overseas, the dispatch of four additional Army divisions to Europe, the rearmament of West Germany within an integrated NATO force, expanded military help for other allies, and the inauguration of a more ambitious economic aid program. A new venture into psychological warfare was launched with the creation of the interagency Psychological Strategy Board in 1951. Covert operations increased, including the recently disclosed CIA mail surveillance (begun in 1952) and the American-supported coups in Iran in 1953 and Guatemala the following year. Additional U.S. commitments in Asia, aimed at containing China, included a pledge to defend Taiwan and sharply increased military aid to the French fighting Ho Chi Minh in Indochina.

* See David Douglas Duncan's photo-narrative *This Is War!* (1951) and combat historian S. L. A. Marshall's *The River and the Gauntlet* (1953) and *Pork Chop Hill* (1956).

## An End to Relaxation

As Americans have had further opportunity to learn in recent years, it is much easier to intervene in a small distant country than to withdraw. After the Chinese indicated (via the Soviets) a willingness to discuss terms, truce talks began in July 1951. But peace did not come easily. The Chinese proved to be as uncompromising at the negotiating table as on the battlefield. Differences arose over the withdrawal of all foreign troops from Korea, the compulsory repatriation of prisoners, and Syngman Rhee's efforts to prevent the signing of any agreement. As casualties continued to mount, American opinion turned increasingly against this limited war. Truman's popularity plummeted; the Republicans shrewdly chose Dwight D. Eisenhower, the hero of the European war, as their 1952 presidential candidate and ran him on a platform dedicated, in part, to ending the fighting in Korea. Early in his administration Eisenhower indicated the seriousness of his purpose by conveying through the Indian government a message to Peking: Continued deadlock at the truce talks could lead to American use of atomic weapons against China. With this incentive — possibly enhanced by the death of Stalin in March — negotiations at Panmunjom moved to the signing of an armistice in July 1953.

The most significant immediate results of the Korean War were a vast increase in American defenses against the Soviet Union and a marked improvement in the power and morale of the NATO alliance. American leaders took a number of lessons from the war. Despite the "no more Koreas" consensus in Washington, Congress demonstrated a new willingness to combat Communist influence wherever it appeared. Under the Eisenhower administration, United States security interests were to be maintained by increased use of covert operations, by a "New Look" military establishment with a much smaller Army, and by greater reliance ("More Bang for the Buck") on the deterrent effect of nuclear weapons within a strategy of Massive Retaliation. Never again were U.S. defenses to be reduced to the low pre-Korea level.

The Korean experience also served to bolster the authority of the President in foreign affairs and to increase the weight of national security arguments in public debate. In dealing with a Communist opponent who disregarded the established rules of international conduct, so the thinking went, the President had to have the authority to respond quickly and in kind to undeclared wars and covert operations. Since the Communists would exploit any weakness and would seldom negotiate in good faith, the United States must remain powerful and should never negotiate except from a position of strength. The MacArthur imbroglio showed that civilian authority must (and could) be maintained over the military. The North Korean attack and the Chinese intervention showed the importance of demonstrating the American will to resist Communist aggression. And most citizens agreed that the United States had to pursue a bipartisan approach to vital questions of national security.

### History Misread

By 1960, the policy implications of the Korean War had changed significantly. The outcome came to be viewed as a Cold War victory, and American leaders — including the "defense intellectuals" in academe — concluded that limited war could be successfully pursued by a democracy. Democratic politicians noted that Truman had demonstrated the resolve to meet force with force under adverse circumstances; many believed that any successful future president would have to adopt the same firm posture. Generals Maxwell Taylor and James Gavin persuaded President John F. Kennedy that the United States could avoid political difficulties by training Special Forces units for guerrilla warfare and by devoting greater effort to winning and maintaining popular support at home.

But the energetic leaders of the New Frontier, along with the press, Congress, and most of the public, ignored the crucial differences between Vietnam and Korea. "Controlled escalation" theories so popular in universities could not be applied successfully in Southeast Asia, for the circumstances were strikingly divergent. The Vietnam War in 1961–65 was not a formal military confrontation launched by an invasion across a recognized border, confined to a peninsula, fought by organized armies, and supported by coherent populations on two clearly distinguishable sides. In Korea, a limited military success was possible. In Vietnam, it was not.

## *Suggestions for Further Reading*

Gaddis, John Lewis. *The United States and the Origins of the Cold War, 1941–1947* (New York: Columbia UP, 1972). Sets the origins of postwar U.S.-Soviet hostility in the context of events before development of the atomic bomb.

Herken, Gregg. *The Winning Weapon: The Atomic Bomb in the Cold War, 1945–1950* (New York: Vintage Books, 1982). A history of nuclear diplomacy and policy based on declassified archival material.

Lieberman, Joseph J. *The Scorpion and the Tarantula: The Struggle to Control Atomic Weapons, 1945–1949* (Boston: Houghton Mifflin, 1970). Traces the failure of early efforts at nuclear arms control.

Sherwin, Martin J. *A World Destroyed: The Atomic Bomb and the Grand Alliance* (New York: Vintage Books, 1977). An earlier work based similarly on archival materials.

*Three*

# A BIGGER BANG FOR THE BUCK

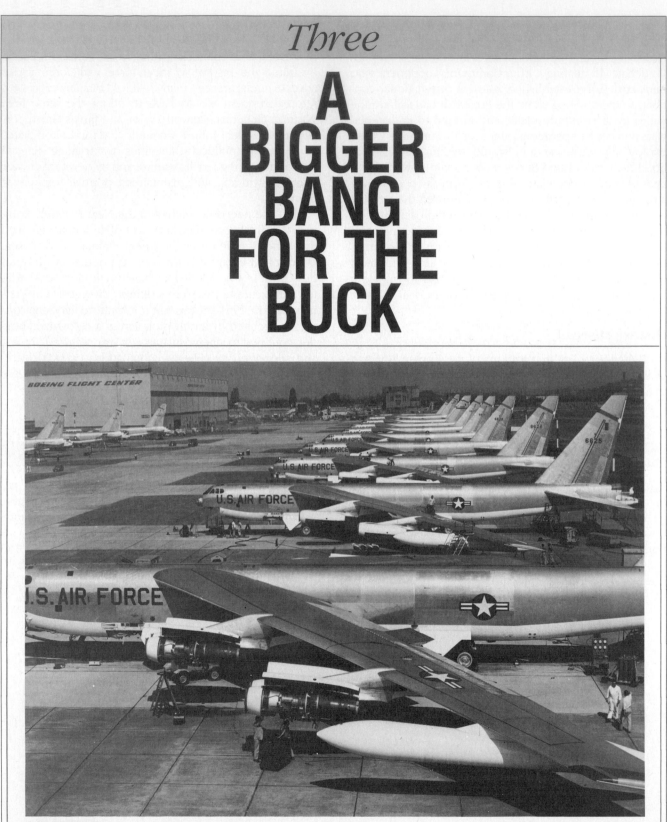

**B-52 BOMBERS**

The Strategic Air Command's Boeing B-52 bombers are lined up for test flights. American fears of a rapidly growing Soviet bomber force sped up production of this long-range bomber, which could fly at speeds exceeding 600 mph, at altitudes of 50,000 feet, and at ranges of 6,000 miles. The B-52 was first deployed in June 1955. The Bettmann Archive, Inc.

# INTRODUCTION

When Dwight D. Eisenhower became president in 1953, the basic features of U.S. foreign policy in the nuclear era had been set: containment of Soviet power, the expansion of U.S. alliance commitments, and an increase in U.S. military power, especially nuclear weapons. Eisenhower's policies fit within this general framework but with some special features. Perhaps most important, while the Truman administration had relied on both nuclear and conventional weapons to contain the Soviets, the Eisenhower administration strongly emphasized nuclear weapons.

Eisenhower was very much influenced by the standard Republican party view of government spending—that it was bad for the economy. As a result, he made a serious effort to control all federal spending including that for defense. The Eisenhower defense budget held constant throughout both his terms at about $145 billion (in 1983 dollars), less than half what it is today. At the same time, the administration was very aware that it would have to deal with the Soviet threat. In an attempt to do so while controlling the defense budget, the administration adopted the "New Look" defense policy that emphasized nuclear weapons and deemphasized conventional weapons and manpower.

In practice, this meant that each of the armed services was given nuclear weapons, while funds for personnel, tanks, artillery, aircraft, ships, and so forth were limited. For example, the Army was held to a small number of divisions, but it received nuclear artillery shells and mines. Short- and medium-range aircraft of the Navy and Air Force were armed with nuclear bombs. The Air Force gained the most, however, from the New Look. Nearly half of the defense budget went to the Strategic Air Command (SAC), whose mission in war was to destroy the Soviet Union's ability to fight.

A critical aspect of the Eisenhower administration's reliance on nuclear weapons to prevent Soviet gains was the doctrine of massive retaliation. On January 12, 1954, Secretary of State John Foster Dulles made a speech in which he threatened to launch a massive nuclear strike against the Soviet Union in the case of another attack against Western interests like that in Korea. The clear hope was that the U.S. threat would deter another such Korea-type conflict. In its later statements and actions, the Eisenhower administration made clear that the massive retaliation doctrine did not mean that each and every expansion of Communist power would be answered by a nuclear attack. For example, the United States considered using nuclear weapons to save French forces in Vietnam after the collapse of Dien Bien Phu but decided not to. Nevertheless, the threat of using nuclear weapons was an important part of the Eisenhower administration's foreign policy.

The United States believed that the Soviet Union would take this threat seriously because at the time it was made the United States had a huge advantage over the Soviet Union in nuclear weapons. Indeed, the United States had a significant advantage over the Soviet Union throughout the Eisenhower years. In numbers of nuclear weapons, for example, the United States had a better than ten-to-one advantage in 1960. Nevertheless, on several occasions U.S. leaders and the public feared that the Soviets had the advantage or were about to gain it. In the middle 1950s, the big worry was a "bomber gap." In 1957, the Gaither Report raised fears that U.S. nuclear forces were becoming vulnerable. As the Eisenhower administration came to a close in 1960 the Soviet "advantage" became an effective political issue for John Kennedy, who charged the administration with tolerating a "missile gap."

In part this perception of U.S. weakness was brought about through the relatively poor intelligence-gathering methods of the 1950s. In the absence of reliable information, U.S. agencies tended to favor worst-case analysis. In addition, the Soviets were not about to publicize their weakness. Indeed, they tried to bluff the United States into thinking Soviet nuclear forces were large, and Soviet leader Nikita Khrushchev rattled the nuclear sword in several crises. Finally, the Soviets did achieve some spectacular gains in space that caught the public imagination. It seemed logical that if the Soviets were better than the United States in building rockets for satellites, they would be better at building rockets to carry nuclear weapons.

Although Soviet nuclear forces were inferior to U.S. forces throughout the Eisenhower administration, the Soviet Union did make some important improvements during those years. In 1953, the Soviet Union had no nuclear forces that could reach the United States. By 1955 the Soviets had deployed a few intercontinental bombers, but they concentrated their efforts on developing ICBMs. Despite Khrushchev's boasts about Soviet rocket power, the Soviet Union managed to deploy only a handful of ICBMs by 1960. During the 1950s then, the Soviet Union went from having almost no capability to attack the United States with nuclear weapons to having a very modest capability to do so.

In addition to increasing the role played by nuclear weapons in the U.S. defense effort, the Eisenhower administration tried to make more organized and systematic the planning and method for their use in war. At first, however, nuclear planning was chaotic. Once the armed services realized that the defense budget was limited and that nuclear weapons were to play a dominant role, each of them tried to get a piece of the nuclear action. The Army, Navy, and Air Force each began their own missile programs. The Army tried to get more nuclear weapons for its own use on the battlefield. The Navy wanted nuclear bombs for its planes and — later — nuclear-armed missiles for its submarines. The Air Force wanted bombs and missiles. Although the Air Force (SAC) emerged with the most important nuclear mission, there was very little coordination among the services and much duplication of effort.

In August 1960, the Eisenhower administration attempted to organize nuclear war planning by creating a single nuclear command and setting up one coordinated planning document — the Single Integrated Operational Plan (SIOP) — for nuclear weapons. The first SIOP was based mainly on SAC's views of how to fight a nuclear war. These in turn were an updated version of the strategic bombing strategy that the Air Force had used in World War II — that is, bombing attacks against the means the enemy uses to make war. In general, this meant an all-out attack on the military forces, economic infrastructure, and population of the Soviet Union.

In addition to organizing nuclear war plans, the Eisenhower administration took the first steps toward creating the kinds of nuclear forces the United States deploys today. First, as might be expected given its emphasis on nuclear weapons, the Eisenhower administration dramatically increased the size of the U.S. nuclear stockpile. For most of its eight years, the Eisenhower administration relied on bombers to deliver nuclear weapons. In addition, the Eisenhower administration began to develop and deploy two new weapons that were to become the backbone of U.S. nuclear forces: land-based intercontinental ballistic missiles (ICBMs) and submarine-launched ballistic missiles (SLBMs).

To sum up, the Eisenhower administration dramatically increased the role played by nuclear weapons in U.S. defense policy. The numbers of weapons were greatly expanded, and the massive retaliation policy made the threat of nuclear war a key diplomatic tool.

## THE NEW LOOK AND MASSIVE RETALIATION

## The Eisenhower Administration Adopts a New Defense Policy

### *Document 1*

In this excerpt from his book, *The Cold War as History*, political scientist Louis J. Halle examines the reasons why the Eisenhower administration adopted the New Look and announced the policy of massive retaliation. Halle emphasizes the importance to Eisenhower of the need to control military spending in the interests of a balanced budget. Halle also points out that the Eisenhower administration began to back away from the more extreme implications of the massive retaliation policy soon after Secretary of Defense Dulles announced it.

### 1 THE NEW ADMINISTRATION AND THE PROBLEMS OF MILITARY POLICY
### Louis J. Halle

Ever since the great depression at the beginning of the 1930's there had been a basic difference between dominant opinion in the Republican and Democratic Parties, respectively, over what the nation could afford in the way of public expenditures. The thinking of the Democrats had been associated with academic economists, notably John Maynard Keynes, who minimized the importance of savings, who were not alarmed by a large and continuing public debt, who emphasized the point that nations cannot go bankrupt by borrowing from themselves, and who believed that any modern government has an overriding obligation to spend as heavily as need be for the maintenance of full employment and the stability of the national economy. Republican thinking, on the other hand, had been associated with business-men who were disposed to equate the soundness of a nation's economy with balanced budgets at a level of taxation low enough to give full play to the profit motive as an indispensable incentive of free productive enterprise. These businessmen had been alarmed at the vast expenditures, the high taxes, the unbalanced budgets, and the mounting public debt under twenty years of Democratic rule. They felt that continuing on this course was bound to lead to some kind of economic disaster, and that it was, in any case, destructive of the free-enterprise system.

The Republicans, more than the Democrats, thought in terms of a norm represented by the period (remembered from childhood) before the successive emergencies of World War I, the great depression, and World War II. These emergencies had perhaps required an abandonment of what they regarded as sound fiscal practices, just as an emergency in the career of an individual may require him temporarily to live beyond his income by borrowing or drawing on his savings. Such lapses, however, must not be continued as a normal practice, and the dominant elements in the Republican Party were alarmed at the failure, so many years after World War II, to return to what President Harding, after World War I, had called "normalcy."

The national budget, which had fallen to $32,289 million in Fiscal Year 1946–1947 (leaving a surplus of $754 million), had again risen, under the Truman Administration, to $73,982 million in 1952–1953 (leaving a deficit of over $900 million). For 1953–1954 the Truman Administration, before leaving office, had drawn up a budget of $78,587 million, and anticipated a deficit of $9,992 million. This sharp rise in expenditures and deficits represented, simply, the cost of containing Communism, of waging the Cold War. (Some three-quarters of President Truman's proposed budget for 1953–1954 was for expenditures on what were called 'national security programs,' about 60% going directly to the armed services.)

The dilemma that confronted the new Republican Administration was clear. The only way it could move toward a balanced budget and, at the same time, lower taxes was by a substantial reduction in military and related expenditures. (This was the more true because the preponderance of the other expenditures represented fixed charges for interest on the national debt and for veterans' programs.) It had, however, promised that it would adopt a much more aggressive and dynamic Cold War policy, by which it would put Russia on the defensive. How, its opponents asked, could it risk doing this at the same time that it was reducing the military strength of the United States?

The answer, at least in principle, was to be found in the abandonment of a conception of containment that, by implication, imposed unlimited expense on the United States. In his *Foreign Affairs* article Kennan had written: "Soviet pressure against the free institutions of the Western world is something that can be contained by the adroit and vigilant application of counter-force at a series of constantly shifting geographical and political points. . . ." Taken literally, this meant that the United States had to have "counter-force" available for immediate application at any point along the frontiers of the Russian empire, from Kamchatka to the mouth of the Elbe, at which Moscow, having the unchallenged initiative, chose to apply pressure.[1] Russia had the interior position and could strike without notice in any direction she wished, while the United States had to be prepared to counter her at whatever point, around an outer line of many thousands of miles, she might choose to strike. Such preparation, if actually made, would be immense in its requirements for all sorts of fighting forces and their transport. Taken literally, it would have implied a budget many times larger than any that even the Democratic Administration had proposed. Although no one in the Government ever had taken it literally, there can be no doubt that this conception was genuinely vulnerable to the kind of attack the Republicans had made on it in the campaign of 1952. The weakness they alleged was a genuine weakness.

At this point we may note that one main issue, cropping up always in new guises, dominates the Western debate on political–military strategy at every stage of the Cold War. The issue, put crudely, is whether the West should depend entirely on the strategic nuclear power of the United States, its ability to destroy the Russian (or Chinese) society by nuclear explosives delivered across thousands of miles, or whether it should furnish itself with other kinds of military force as well, in order to have alternatives, where military action is called for, to such a drastic move as that of initiating all-out nuclear war. If the West, in the face of aggression, found itself without any choices between the two extremes of all-out nuclear war, on the one hand, and the abandonment of containment (in effect, surrender), on the other, prudence would presumably constrain it to adopt the latter choice wherever the aggression was not, in itself, of such importance as to warrant recourse to universal destruction. On the other hand, it was argued, if the West provided itself with alternatives to strategic nuclear retaliation, then the potential aggressor would be less likely to be deterred from any sufficiently limited aggression because he would know that the West had prepared itself to respond to such an aggression with other means than those afforded by its strategic nuclear force, that it therefore did not intend to use that force. He would, according to either of these opposed arguments, be able to realize his supposed objective of world conquest by the simple strategy of undertaking a succession of aggressions, each one of which was so limited that it would not, in itself, justify the unlimited destruction involved in a strategic nuclear response. The free world, in the witty phrase of the time, would be nibbled to death.

In sum — according to one view, the aggressor might commit limited aggressions if the United States had, as its only means of responding, a strategic nuclear armament that it would presumably be unwilling to use to meet any small aggression; according to the other view, the aggressor might feel encouraged to commit limited aggressions if, by providing itself with limited means to deal with such aggressions, the United States showed that it did not intend to respond to them with its strategic nuclear armament.

What is clear is that the provision of alternatives to the strategic nuclear response was far more expensive than dependence on it alone. Therefore, those who attached a high enough value to budgetary economy were bound to end up in favor of an approach, at least, to exclusive dependence upon it.

In the new Republican Administration, which was so largely dominated by business-men, a drastic limitation in Government spending took priority over the demands of military defense. At least initially, the Administration took the position that national security depended, in the first instance, on a sound economy, which in turn depended on fiscal policies that limited expenditures to a level substantially lower than those that the Democratic Administrations had accepted. The purpose of the Communists, it was maintained, was to induce the United States to bankrupt itself by its military expenditures, whereupon they would be free to take over the world. The conclusion was that one had to decide in advance how large a defense-budget the country could afford, and then design its defense accordingly. The Democrats, on the other hand, insisted that one had first to decide what the requirements of defense were, and then meet those requirements at whatever cost. There was, here, a clear issue in which the prevailing opinion in the Republican Party differed from the prevailing opinion in the Democratic Party.

After the new Administration took office a complete review of American strategy was undertaken by the National Security Council. The product of this review was one of those documents that reconcile conflicting views by ambiguity. Anyone who read it would find that its language lent itself to a variety of interpretations.[2]

Throughout 1953 there had been constant speculation, fed by hints from members of the Administration, that a new and better strategy, a "new look" in defense policy, was being prepared. There was no doubt that such a new strategy, if only for reasons of economy, would involve a more complete dependence on strategic nuclear power, thereby decreasing the requirements for American ground and naval forces.[3] The anticipated "new look" aroused anxiety in Europe, where it was feared that the United States would drastically reduce its ground forces, if it did not withdraw them altogether.

Finally, on January 12, 1954, in an address delivered at the Council on Foreign Relations in New York, Secretary Dulles ostensibly presented, what had been awaited so long, the new policy of the Administration. He began by observing that American policy hitherto had represented nothing more than a succession of responses to emergencies created by Russian initiative, and he implied that long-range planning had been neglected.

> The Soviet Communists [he said] are planning for what they call "an entire historical era," and we should do the same. They seek . . . gradually to divide and weaken the free nations by overextending them in efforts which, as Lenin put it, are "beyond their strength, so that they come to practical bankruptcy." Then, said Lenin, "our victory is assured." Then, said Stalin, will be "the moment for the decisive blow."[4]

He referred to the need to avoid "military expenditures so vast that they lead to 'practical bankruptcy,' " and added: "This can be done by placing more reliance on deterrent power and less dependence on local defensive power."

Referring to the previous inadequacy of policy and planning, he said that the new Administration had had to take "some basic policy decisions." "This," he added, "has been done. The basic decision was to depend primarily upon a great capacity to retaliate, instantly, by means and at places of our choosing."

This last was the key sentence of an address that immediately aroused a storm of alarm and indignation throughout the Atlantic world. It was taken to mean that the United States was prepared to turn every local conflict into a worldwide nuclear war in which its allies, if not it as well, would be destroyed. The use of the word "instantly" was interpreted as meaning that the United States would not take the time to consult its allies before acting to transform a local conflict into Armageddon. Within hours of delivering the address the Secretary of State was a severely embarrassed man. President Eisenhower felt compelled to deny, at his press-conference the next day, that any new "basic decision" on defense policy had been taken at all; and on March 17 he would deny that the so-called "new look" defense policy (a phrase which he said he deplored) was either new or revolutionary. Dulles, as was clear to anyone who knew the National Security Council document on which his address was based, had interpreted it to suit his own mind.

Ordinarily, when an important statement of policy is made on behalf of the Government of the United States, its text is prepared and checked in every phrase and nuance with the assistance of a corps of advisors. A fault of the Truman Administration, as we have seen, was to carry this procedure of corporate drafting too far, to the point where such statements lost the integrity and authority that depend on a single hand holding the pen. Dulles, up to January 12, 1954, had gone to the other extreme. Uncomfortable as he always was with the bureaucratic organization he had inherited, he had not known how to use it effectively. The "massive retaliation" speech, as it came to be known, was written entirely by him, and apparently with only one exception even the members of his immediate professional staff in the State Department did not know about it until it was delivered and published.[5]

To this day, the "massive retaliation" speech is a poignant document purely as an expression of Dulles's personal character. There was always in him something of the little boy who, in his day-dreams, is the master-strategist, outmaneuvering and foiling his dastardly opponents at every turn by his boldness and craft. All his life he had cultivated a legend of himself based on this youthful day-dream, and now for the first time, at sixty-five years of age, he was in a position to realize it before the eyes of the whole world. More than once it happened that he was unable to resist the temptation to strike public attitudes in fulfillment of this dream, attitudes that, by their sheer exaggeration, provoked immediate public reactions highly embarrassing to him. One such occasion was when he briefed a reporter who wanted material for an article about him for *Life* magazine. He told the reporter, in the informal privacy of their meeting, and the reporter duly reported it in the issue of January 11, 1956, that "the ability to get to the verge without getting into the war is the necessary art," whereupon he proceeded to illustrate the practice of this art by showing how the United States, since he had assumed his position as master mind in the conduct of its foreign relations, had done precisely this with brilliant effect on three separate occasions. Published as an interview, the public impression that the Secretary of State's boasting gave was of an immaturity and recklessness in the United States, under the Eisenhower–Dulles Administration, that aroused wide-spread alarm throughout the alliance, just as the "massive retaliation" speech had two years earlier.[6]

One may suppose that, as was the habit of his mind, Dulles was not thinking of the impact of his speech abroad when he wrote it. To some extent he was still fighting the electoral campaign of 1952 by contrasting, for the benefit of the American public, the weakness and confusion of the previous Administration with the strength, the long-range vision, the daring, and the command of events that distinguished its successor. He was cultivating the legend, he was realizing the dream on the world's great stage. At the same time, he was showing how the Republican Party was honoring its electoral promise to strengthen the position of the United States in the world while reducing expenditures, how it was foiling international Communism both in its designs for aggression and in its plot to reduce the United States to "practical bankruptcy."

The speech aroused such immediate and incisive criticism (much of it misrepresenting what he had actually said), and had such an effect on confidence abroad in the maturity and sense of international responsibility represented by the American leadership, that remedial action had to be undertaken at once. For this purpose a shaken Secretary of State turned, the next day, to his professional staff to assist him in preparing a statement, which ultimately appeared as an article under his name in the April 1954 issue of *Foreign Affairs* ("Policy for Security and Peace"). In this article he expounded the strategy of the United States in terms that reduced the more extreme implications of what he had seemed to be saying in his "massive retaliation" speech.

## Notes

1. Kennan had referred to pressure against "the free institutions of the Western world," but the Truman Doctrine had virtually eliminated this qualification, which, in any case, had not been clearly made in the article, and after 1949 Americans had assumed that Communism must be contained no less in Asia then in "the Western world."
2. The contents of this document have been discussed in books on American strategy by writers who have never seen it, since it had remained a secret document. Their sources have been private reports of its general tenor by Government officials, or Secretary Dulles's address of January 12, 1954, which was based on what was, at least, his own interpretation of it. When one writer purports to reveal the contents of a secret document like this, other writers after him take him, and each other, as their authority, a process by which all doubt quickly disappears. What everyone says becomes what everyone knows, and what everyone knows is true.
3. The chief instrument of American strategic nuclear power was the Strategic Air Command (SAC) with its intercontinental bombers based in the United States and its overseas air bases. The Navy had at least a secondary role in the delivery of nuclear weapons (from aircraft carriers). The Army, however, had no strategic role at all.
4. In an article written immediately after this address, Dulles put this differently. ". . . The Soviet rulers," he wrote, "seek gradually to divide and weaken the free nations and to *make their policies appear as bankrupt* [my italics] by overextending them in efforts which, as Lenin put it, are 'beyond their strength.' Then, said Lenin, 'our victory is assured.' Then, said Stalin, will be the 'moment for the decisive blow.' " What Lenin actually said, or what Stalin actually said, if anything, is not known to me.
5. The exception was an able lawyer, brought into the Department from the outside and still new to foreign affairs, to whom the Secretary showed the text in advance, but who did not feel himself in a position to deal with it critically.
6. Important parts of this interview are given in Coral Bell, *Survey of International Affairs* (London, 1957), p. 24, fn. 4. The contents should be read, not as history, but for their revelation of a romantic imagination.

## Massive Retaliation

### *Document 2*

Secretary of State John Foster Dulles set out the policy of massive retaliation in a speech to the Council on Foreign Relations in January 1954. In these excerpts, Dulles says the United States has decided "to depend primarily upon the great capacity to retaliate, instantly, by means and at places of our choosing." He goes on to justify the strategy as a way to meet the Communist challenge without bankrupting the United States. "As a result," he says, "it is now possible to get and share more basic security at less cost." Dulles also implies that a nuclear threat helped to end the Korean War on "honorable terms."

## 2 SPEECH ON MASSIVE RETALIATION John Foster Dulles January 12, 1945

We live in a world where emergencies are always possible, and our survival may depend upon our capacity to meet emergencies. Let us pray that we shall always have that capacity. But, having said that, it is necessary also to say that emergency measures — however good for the emergency — do not necessarily make good permanent policies. Emergency measures are costly; they are superficial; and they imply that the enemy has the initiative. They cannot be depended on to serve our long-time interests.

### The Need for Long-Range Policies

This "long time" factor is of critical importance.

The Soviet Communists are planning for what they call "an entire historical era," and we should do the same. They seek, through many types of maneuvers, gradually to divide and weaken the free nations by overextending them in efforts which, as Lenin put it, are "beyond their strength, so that they come to practical bankruptcy." Then, said Lenin, "our victory is assured." Then, said Stalin, will be "the moment for the decisive blow."

In the face of this strategy, measures cannot be judged adequate merely because they ward off an immediate danger. It is essential to do this, but it is also essential to do so without exhausting ourselves.

When the Eisenhower administration applied this test, we felt that some transformations were needed.

It is not sound military strategy permanently to commit U.S. land forces to Asia to a degree that leaves us no strategic reserves.

It is not sound economics, or good foreign policy, to support permanently other countries; for in the long run, that creates as much ill will as good will.

Also, it is not sound to become permanently committed to military expenditures so vast that they lead to "practical bankruptcy."

Change was imperative to assure the stamina needed for permanent security. But it was equally imperative that change should be accompanied by understanding of our true purposes. Sudden and spectacular change had to be avoided. Otherwise, there might have been a panic among our friends and miscalculated aggression by our enemies. We can, I believe, make a good report in these respects.

We need allies and collective security. Our purpose is to make these relations more effective, less costly. This can be done by placing more reliance on deterrent power and less dependence on local defensive power.

This is accepted practice so far as local communities are concerned. We keep locks on our doors, but we do not have an armed guard in every home. We rely principally on a community security system so well equipped to punish any who break in and steal that, in fact, would-be aggressors are generally deterred. That is the modern way of getting maximum protection at a bearable cost.

What the Eisenhower administration seeks is a similar international security system. We want, for ourselves and the other free nations, a maximum deterrent at a bearable cost.

Local defense will always be important. But there is no local defense which alone will contain the mighty landpower of the Communist world. Local defenses must be reinforced by the further deterrent of massive retaliatory power. A potential aggressor must know that he cannot always prescribe battle conditions that suit him. Otherwise, for example, a potential aggressor, who is glutted with manpower, might be tempted to attack in confidence that resistance would be confined to manpower. He might be tempted to attack in places where his superiority was decisive.

The way to deter aggression is for the free community to be willing and able to respond vigorously at places and with means of its own choosing.

So long as our basic policy concepts were unclear, our military leaders could not be selective in building our military power. If an enemy could pick his time and place and method of warfare — and if our policy was to remain the traditional one of meeting aggression by direct and local opposition — then we needed to be ready to fight in the Arctic and in the Tropics; in Asia, the Near East, and in Europe; by sea, by land, and by air; with old weapons and with new weapons.

The total cost of our security efforts, at home and abroad, was over $50 billion per annum, and involved, for 1953, a projected budgetary deficit of $9 billion; and $11 billion for 1954. This was on top of taxes comparable to wartime taxes; and the dollar was depreciating in effective value. Our allies were similarly weighed down.

This could not be continued for long without grave budgetary, economic, and social consequences.

But before military planning could be changed, the President and his advisers, as represented by the National Security Council, had to take some basic policy decisions. This has been done. The basic decision was to depend primarily upon a great capacity to retaliate, instantly, by means and at places of our choosing. Now the Department of Defense and the Joint Chiefs of Staff can shape our military establishment to fit what is *our* policy, instead of having to try to be ready to meet the enemy's many choices. That permits of a selection of military means instead of a multiplication of means. As a result, it is now possible to get, and share, more basic security at less cost.

## The Far East

Let us now see how this concept has been applied to foreign policy, taking first the Far East.

In Korea this administration effected a major transformation. The fighting has been stopped on honorable terms. That was possible because the aggressor, already thrown back to and behind his place of beginning, was faced with the possibility that the fighting might, to his own great peril, soon spread beyond the limits and methods which he had selected.

The cruel toll of American youth and the nonproductive expenditure of many billions have been stopped. Also our armed forces are no longer largely committed to the Asian mainland. We can begin to create a strategic reserve which greatly improves our defensive posture.

This change gives added authority to the warning of the members of the United Nations which fought in Korea that, if the Communists renewed the aggression, the United Nations response would not necessarily be confined to Korea.

I have said in relation to Indochina that, if there were open Red Chinese army aggression there, that would have "grave consequences which might not be confined to Indochina."

I expressed last month the intention of the United States to maintain its position in Okinawa.[7] This is needed to insure adequate striking power to implement the collective security concept which I describe.

All of this is summed up in President Eisenhower's important statement of December 26.[8] He announced the progressive reduction of the U.S. ground forces in Korea. He pointed out that U.S. military forces in the Far East will now feature "highly mobile naval, air and amphibious units"; and he said in this way, despite some withdrawal of land forces, the United States will have a capacity to oppose aggression "with even greater effect than heretofore."

The bringing home of some of our land forces also provides a most eloquent rebuttal to the Communist charge of "imperialism."

## NATO

If we turn to Europe, we see readjustments in the NATO collective security effort. Senator Vandenberg called the North Atlantic Treaty pledges "the most practical deterrent and discouragement to war which the wit of man has yet devised." But he said also that "if the concept and objective are to build sufficient forces in being to hold the Russian line . . . it presents ruinous corollaries both at home and abroad."

In the first years of the North Atlantic Treaty Organization, after the aggression in Korea, its members made an emergency buildup of military strength. I do not question the judgment of that time. The strength thus built has served well the cause of peace. But the pace originally set could not be maintained indefinitely.

At the April meeting of the NATO Council, the United States put forward a new concept, now known as that of the "long haul."[9] That meant a steady development of defensive strength at a rate which will preserve and not exhaust the economic strength of our allies and ourselves. This would be reinforced by the striking power of a strategic air force based on internationally agreed positions.

We found, at the Council of last December, that there was general acceptance of the "long haul" concept and recognition that it better served the probable needs than an effort to create full defensive land strength at a ruinous price.[10]

## Notes

7. Bulletin of Jan. 4, 1954, p. 17.
8. *Ibid.*, p. 14.
9. For a report on the April meeting of the NATO Council, see *Ibid.,* May 11, 1953, p. 673.
10. For a report on the December meeting of the NATO Council, see *Ibid.,* Jan. 4, 1954, p. 3.

## Admiral Radford Spells Out Dulles's Ideas

### *Document 3*

Document 3 is a draft of a speech by Admiral Radford, the highest uniformed head of the U.S. armed forces. In the speech, Radford spells out some of the ideas implied by the Dulles speech. In particular, Radford makes reference to a decision by the National Security Council that "in the event of hostilities, the United States will consider nuclear weapons to be as available for use as other munitions." Radford also expresses the fear that civilian authorities are not taking this idea seriously enough. He worries that in an actual crisis the United States might not prove willing to use nuclear weapons.

### 3 TOP-SECRET MEMORANDUM Admiral Radford, Chairman of the Joint Chiefs of Staff September 11, 1954

In the summer of 1953 the present Joint Chiefs of Staff were directed by the President to review the overall military position of the United States in the world environment as it then existed and as it could be projected into the future, and to make recommendations as to the strategic concepts which should guide our national military policy. This study convinced *each member* of the new Joint Chiefs team that one of the cornerstones of our strength lay in our ability to employ nuclear weapons whenever and wherever it was to our military advantage to do so. Accordingly one of the conclusions in which the new Chiefs unanimously concurred was to the effect that we should "place in first priority the essential military protection of our continental U.S. vitals and the capability for delivering swift and powerful retaliatory blows."

In October of 1953 the National Security Council recommended and the President approved NSC 162/2 as the basic policy of the United States. This policy states in part:

> In the face of the Soviet threat, the security of the United States requires:
> a. Development and maintenance of:
> (1) A strong military posture, with emphasis on the capability of inflicting massive retaliatory damage by offensive striking power;
>
> In the event of hostilities, the United States will consider nuclear weapons to be as available for use as other munitions.

Thus, a fundamental of our national security policy in this atomic age is that we will use nuclear weapons whenever it is to our national advantage to do so. By adopting this policy, we gave as our answer to the massive military power generated by the Communist bloc a free world alliance under U.S. leadership capable and ready to use its nuclear strength to counter Communist aggression. This policy recognized and acknowledged that the free world was unwilling to drain its economies and prostitute its way of life by attempting to match man for man and rifle for rifle the regimented conventional military power of the Communist bloc. As General Gruenther said recently in a speech in London:

> We feel that if you ban those types of weapons (atomic and thermonuclear), you require our forces to adopt a wall-of-flesh type of strategy. . . . If, however, a decision is made that atomic weapons are not to be used, we at our headquarters will point out to our political superiors that our defensive posture can only be maintained successfully at the expense of increased manpower. When we consider the low value placed on human life by the Soviets, we, in our humble opinion, believe it would be a major mistake for the West to adopt a type of strategy which substitutes human beings for atomic weapons.

Since the time when NSC 162/2 was approved, certain changes in the international picture have occurred which highlight the importance of nuclear weapons as part of our national military power and emphasize the necessity of a policy which stands ready to use this part of our power should it be necessary. Our research and development program has already produced weapons ranging from low-yield atomic bombs to thermonuclear weapons with yields far beyond our estimates of several years ago. Our stockpile of fissile material is growing by geometric bounds and is rapidly approaching the point beyond which weapon availability will no longer constitute a bottleneck in military planning. On the other side of the coin, available evidence is convincing in support of the fact that the Communists are achieving a parallel development which, even though now trailing our own, will still reach the same goal in due time. Thus both sides in this world struggle will possess in increasing numbers nuclear weapons of devastating power. While this development has been underway, changes have also occurred in the relative conventional strengths of the two sides. On the Soviet side, there has been no indication of a diminution of its massive conventional power; on the contrary, it would seem that the increasing military strength of Communist China alone is sufficient to provide a marked increase in total Communist conventional capability. On the free world's side, our system of collective strength is currently undergoing a series of setbacks which retards our build-up of adequate forces and places parts of our collective system in the doubtful column. On balance, it can be reasonably said that, since the time the Joint Chiefs made their review in the summer of 1953, our reliance on nuclear weapons as a mainstay of our military strength has not decreased but, instead, has increased markedly.

With this background in mind, it would seem that the basic national policy set forth in NSC 162/2 was inescapably the only right national policy we could have and would, equally inescapably, commend the whole-hearted support of all of us. The past year has convinced me, however, that our basic national policy as regards nuclear weapons is not supported by important segments of our government, both on the military and on the civilian side.

The issue has been raised that we might, because of moral reasons or by virtue of a "gentlemen's agreement," fight a war against the Soviet Union without the use of nuclear weapons by either side. The morality which would throw a free world "wall-of-flesh" against a more massive Communist "wall-of-flesh" rather than use atomic weapons escapes me. Equally elusive to me is the system whereby we build this "wall-of-flesh" and still remain, in fact, a viable free world. A "gentlemen's agreement" requires "gentlemen" on both sides. I, for one, cannot visualize the Communist bloc losing a conventional war with unused nuclear weapons in its arsenal. Nor can I visualize our profit in planning and building to fight such a war if the Communists will allow it, while simultaneously planning and building for an atomic war should that be their choice. The possibility of atomic disarmament without conventional disarmament has been rejected by the United States as unworkable and unrealistic from our point of view. We stand ready to support any disarmament plan which would truly protect the security of the United States and of the free world, but, to this moment, no such plan is in sight.

Meanwhile we face the task of planning and building realistically for the security of the United States. "Realistically" means that we plan and build for emergencies under the conditions most likely to obtain. It means that we plan so that the United States can carry the financial and manpower burden for the long pull without wrecking either our economy or the essentials of our way of life. In short, it means that we support and carry out the basic national policy in NSC 162/2; it means that until and unless that policy is changed we implement it rather than debate it with each step of its implementation.

The necessity for planning and thinking at the national military level in terms of one basic policy holds true whether the project at hand is planning for an all-out world war or planning to combat a particular local Communist aggression. In the case of an all-out world war, the logic of the situation supports the fact that we will not, in the long run, have the choice of fighting such a war without nuclear weapons and that military strength built around nuclear weapons constitutes our most effective protection against the massive military power of the Communist bloc. In the case of local Communist aggression, a policy of furnishing to indigenous friendly forces U.S. naval and air support, including the use of atomic weapons if necessary, offers a possibility of countering such aggression without involving U.S. ground forces in endless and bloody wars of attrition with Soviet satellites.

I believe firmly that the elements of our national policy discussed in this memorandum need to be reemphasized to the National Security Council and to those key military and civilian officials who have important responsibilities in the implementation of our national policies. I feel particularly that the present trend toward devisive ineffectiveness in our military planning can best be checked by a reemphasis of these elements on the highest level.

## The Army Tests Troops with Nuclear Weapons

### *Document 4*

One aspect of the New Look was that each of the armed services would rely more heavily on nuclear weapons. In the early 1950s the Army began to develop and deploy nuclear weapons that could be used on the battlefield. The Army also began to test and train troops in a nuclear environment. This excerpt from *Atomic Soldiers* describes some of these early exercises and the effects on soldiers involved.

### 4 ATOMIC SOLDIERS
### Howard Rosenberg

Corporal Russell Jack Dann felt an uneasiness rumble up from the pit of his stomach as he settled back into a canvas sling along the plane's bulkhead and waited quietly for the pilots to lift C–124 Globemaster's lumbering body skyward. It wasn't the usual anxiety that all paratroopers feel before a jump that had the 20-year-old soldier's guts tied in knots but rather the uncertainty of what to expect when he finally faced the atomic bomb he knew was waiting for him on a desolate strip of Nevada desert. . . .

The roar of the Globemaster's four engines drowned out the chatter in the cabin as the plane taxied along the tarmac and Dann was left to mull over the events of the past few days which had led him to his present set of circumstances.

"You want to go to Camp Desert Rock?" the company clerk asked, stepping through the door of the communications shack where Dann was monotonously inventorying his unit's supply of wire after a recent field exercise. . . .

"How long will I be gone?" Dann asked.

"Only a few days."

"What are we going to do out there?"

"Ask Captain Hill. You wanna go?"

"You betcha. Anything to get out of this como [communications] shack."

"Great. Come on across the hall and talk to the captain." . . .

On Monday, the troops attended an indoctrination lecture on atomic effects at a nearby Quonset hut that had been converted into a classroom. The steel folding chairs were uncomfortable, but a few of the soldiers still managed to drift off to sleep. The most memorable detail of the nondescript classroom was a large sign hanging above the blackboard at the front of the hut. It read: "Anything you hear here while you are here, leave here when you leave here."

The indoctrination, which had been carefully coordinated by the HumRRO* team so material in their questionnaire would be covered, began with a film. Dann remembers the film opening with a scene on a street corner. One old codger, sitting under a nearby awning, turned to another and said, "This weather is all screwed up on account of those damn bombs." "Then the narrator would come on," said Dann, "and tell how foolish those people were. They don't understand what the bomb is, the narrator would say, and that there should be no fear at all."

The film was followed by a two-hour lecture on the bomb. The men were told what to expect and briefed on the nature of radiation. . . .

"The first thing you'll see when this bomb goes off is an intense light. Six miles away, the flash will be 100 times as bright as the sun. The blast itself will vaporize the material the bomb is made of and the firing platform or tower will become part of the fireball. As the fireball cools, the mushroom cloud you've heard or read about starts forming. This happens within a couple of seconds after the detonation. Within 10 seconds, the light will have subsided and the shock wave will have passed your position.

"The cloud, containing the fission products, the remnants of the firing platform and dirt and debris, rises high into the air. The heaviest particles and debris will drop right back down on the ground. Beyond about 7,000 feet, the immediate nuclear radiation is virtually harmless.

"As an observer during an atomic test, the position assigned you by the Nevada Test Organization will be one determined to be absolutely safe — even if you should be standing erect at the time the shock wave passes. This distance has also been calculated to be sufficient to protect you from the nuclear radiation. However, the flash of light might be dangerous. Exposure of the unprotected eye could result in a blind spot which might be permanent. This is why you must face away from the flash at the moment of detonation.

"No test is ever held when the weather indicates that there is any possibility of the radioactive 'stem' of the cloud settling back towards the observation area. You will be permitted to go forward into target and fallout areas, but only after monitoring teams have checked the areas and declared them safe.

"If highly radioactive fallout particles are deposited on or near the surface of your skin, like on your clothes or hair, and stay there for any long period of time, the beta radiation can cause you to lose your hair, discolor your skin or even burn you. This isn't likely to happen, but just in case, you should know about it.

"Beta burns look similar to burns from any other kind of heat, except they usually don't appear until about two weeks later and they take longer to heal. You can reduce the possibility of burns with simple decontamination measures, like bathing and changing clothes.

"Now, I want to debunk some of those horror stories I'm sure you guys have been told," the lecturer continued reassuringly. "It's true you can't see, feel, smell, taste or hear nuclear radiation. But that doesn't mean you have to fear it. Not too many of you can explain electricity I'll bet. But you've all learned to live with it and use it. It's the same with radiation."

After the indoctrination, the HumRRO psychologists handed out their questionnaires once again and asked the soldiers to fill them out. Many of the troopers had slept soundly throughout the lecture. They knew they were being propagandized, or as one soldier put it later, "the Army was just trying to blow smoke up our butts. I wondered if they actually think people are that dumb. Sure they said we'd be completely monitored at all times, but hell, nobody believed them. Nine chances out of ten the monitor was just some PFC assigned to the detail who didn't give a damn. Just a detail, just a job." . . .

The Smoky test repeated many of the previous exercises. Its primary purpose was to "indoctrinate selected individuals in the effects of atomic weapons and to conduct certain specified troop and material tests of doctrine, tactics, techniques and equipment related to atomic weapons." Yet the Smoky test had another objective, one that ultimately took precedence: the Army was especially interested in actually demonstrating how effective battle groups and pentomic warfare tactics could be. That made public relations equally as important as indoctrination and training.

More reporters, cameramen and television crews were invited to watch the Smoky shot than any other test. Military photographers and combat artists abounded. A film crew was even dispatched to record the event for

* Human Resources Research Office — formed in 1951 to investigate psychological and military effects of atomic blasts on soldiers.

the Army's "Big Picture," a television series then enjoying wide popularity on the airwaves. And the newsmen were treated royally.

In an after-action report compiled by the Army months after the exercise, the brass hats candidly admitted that the real purpose of Smoky was "to portray to the public the Army at its best employing pentomic organization in operations under atomic warfare conditions." In their zeal to impress the press corps, the Army commanders may have carried their mission a bit too far. . . .

## The Eisenhower Administration's Arms Control Efforts

### *Documents 5 and 6*

Although the 1950s were for the most part characterized by poor relations between the United States and the Soviet Union, Eisenhower made several efforts to control nuclear weapons. The two most important were the "Open Skies" proposal and some steps toward a ban on all nuclear testing. In 1955 at a conference of the "Big Four" (the United States, the Soviet Union, Britain, and France) in Geneva, President Eisenhower proposed Open Skies. He called on the United States and the Soviet Union to exchange blueprints of their respective military establishments and proposed that each nation provide facilities for aerial inspection to the other. By doing so, Eisenhower hoped to reduce fears of surprise attack and also to make other controls on nuclear weapons easier. Document 5 contains Eisenhower's formal proposal at Geneva. The Soviets rejected the idea.

The United States and the Soviet Union took some steps toward a ban on all nuclear tests but ultimately were unsuccessful in reaching an agreement. Document 6 reviews the U.S.-Soviet moves. By the mid-1950s nuclear testing had become quite controversial because of the health effects of nuclear fallout. The Soviets seized the political initiative first by announcing a unilateral test moratorium in 1958. The United States followed suit later that year, and the mutual moratorium lasted until 1961. The two sides could not reach agreement on a treaty, however, both for technical reasons and because U.S.-Soviet relations fell to a low point in 1960 after the Soviets shot down a U.S. spy plane, the U-2.

## 5 EISENHOWER'S "OPEN SKIES" PROPOSAL "Big Four" Conference, Geneva July 21, 1955

Disarmament is one of the most important subjects on our agenda. It is also extremely difficult. In recent years the scientists have discovered methods of making weapons many, many times more destructive — not only of opposing armed forces but also of homes, and industries and lives — than ever known or even imagined before. These same scientific discoveries have made much more complex the problems of limitation and control and reduction of armament.

After our victory as Allies in World War II, my country rapidly disarmed. Within a few years our armament was at a very low level. Then events occurred beyond our borders which caused us to realize that we had disarmed too much. For our own security and to safeguard peace we needed greater strength. Therefore we proceeded to rearm and to associate with others in a partnership for peace and for mutual security.

The American people are determined to maintain and if necessary increase this armed strength for as long a period as is necessary to safeguard peace and to maintain our security.

But we know that a mutually dependable system for less armament on the part of all nations would be a better way to safeguard peace and to maintain our security.

It would ease the fears of war in the anxious hearts of people everywhere. It would lighten the burdens upon the backs of the people. It would make it possible for every nation, great and small, developed and less developed, to advance the standards of living of its people, to attain better food, and clothing, and shelter, more of education and larger enjoyment of life.

Therefore the United States government is prepared to enter into a sound and reliable agreement making possible the reduction of armament. I have directed that an intensive and thorough study of this subject be made within our own government. From these studies, which are continuing, a very important principle is emerging to which I referred in my opening statement on Monday.

No sound and reliable agreement can be made unless it is completely covered by an inspection and reporting system adequate to support every portion of the agreement.

The lessons of history teach us that disarmament agreements without adequate reciprocal inspection increase the dangers of war and do not brighten the prospects of peace.

Thus it is my view that the priority attention of our combined study of disarmament should be upon the subject of inspection and reporting.

Questions themselves:

How effective an inspection system can be designed which would be mutually and reciprocally acceptable within our countries and the other nations of the world? How would such a system operate? What could it accomplish?

Is certainty against surprise aggression attainable by inspection? Could violations be discovered promptly and effectively counteracted?

We have not as yet been able to discover any scientific

or other inspection method which would make certain of the elimination of nuclear weapons. So far as we are aware no other nation has made such a discovery. Our study of this problem is continuing. We have not as yet been able to discover any accounting or other inspection method of being certain of the true budgetary facts of total expenditures for armament. Our study of this problem is continuing. We by no means exclude the possibility of finding useful checks in these fields.

As you can see from these statements, it is our impression that many past proposals of disarmament are more sweeping than can be ensured by effective inspection.

Gentlemen, since I have been working on this memorandum to present to this conference, I have been searching my heart and mind for something that I could say here that could convince everyone of the great sincerity of the United States in approaching this problem of disarmament.

I should address myself for a moment principally to the delegates from the Soviet Union, because our two great countries admittedly possess new and terrible weapons in quantities which do give rise in other parts of the world, or reciprocally, to the fears and dangers of surprise attack.

I propose, therefore, that we take a practical step, that we begin an arrangement, very quickly, as between ourselves — immediately. These steps would include:

To give to each other a complete blueprint of our military establishments, from beginning to end, from one end of our countries to the other, lay out the establishments and provide the blueprints to each other.

Next, to provide within our countries facilities for aerial photography to the other country — we to provide you the facilities within our country, ample facilities for aerial reconnaissance, where you can make all the pictures you choose and take them to your own country to study, you to provide exactly the same facilities for us and we to make these examinations, and by this step to convince the world that we are providing as between ourselves against the possibility of great surprise attack, thus lessening danger and relaxing tension.

Likewise, we will make more easily attainable a comprehensive and effective system of inspection and disarmament, because what I propose, I assure you, would be but a beginning.

Now from my statements I believe you will anticipate my suggestion. It is that we instruct our representatives in the Subcommittee on Disarmament in discharge of their mandate from the United Nations to give priority effort to the study of inspection and reporting. Such a study could well include a step-by-step testing of inspection and reporting methods.

The United States is ready to proceed in the study and testing of a reliable system of inspections and reporting, and when that system is proved, then to reduce armaments with all other to the extent that the system will provide assured results.

The successful working out of such a system would do much to develop the mutual confidence which will open wide the avenues of progress for all our peoples.

The quest for peace is the statesman's most exacting duty. Security of the nation entrusted to his care is his greatest responsibility. Practical progress to lasting peace is his fondest hope. Yet in pursuit of his hope he must not betray the trust placed in him as guardian of the people's security. A sound peace — with security, justice, well-being, and freedom for the people of the world — can be achieved, but only by patiently and thoughtfully following a hard and sure and tested road.

## 6 NUCLEAR TEST BANS Committee on International Security and Arms Control

### Introduction

The banning of nuclear testing has been a central and continuing objective of arms control since the mid-1950s. At the end of the Eisenhower and beginning of the Kennedy administrations, the United States and the United Kingdom made a major effort to negotiate a comprehensive test ban (CTB) treaty with the Soviet Union. Although these trilateral negotiations failed to produce a comprehensive test ban, agreement was finally reached in 1963 on the Limited Test Ban (LTB) Treaty (Appendix D), which banned all nuclear tests except those conducted underground. In 1974 the Nixon Administration negotiated the Threshold Test Ban (TTB) Treaty (Appendix E), which banned underground tests above 150 kt; and in 1976 the Ford Administration negotiated the companion Peaceful Nuclear Explosions (PNE) Treaty (Appendix F), which provided for the special handling of peaceful explosions under the threshold. The Carter Administration renewed the effort to negotiate a comprehensive test ban treaty but failed to produce an agreement. The Reagan Administration has taken the position that, while a comprehensive test ban remains a long-term U.S. goal, such a treaty would not be in the security interests of the United States at the present time.

### Background

#### *The Eisenhower Administration*

By the mid-1950s, public opposition to nuclear testing had become a significant domestic and international political force. The recurring U.S. and Soviet nuclear test series, involving growing numbers of explosions with rapidly increasing yields, were a constant reminder of the threat and consequences of nuclear war. With the unexpected discovery of the extent of the danger of fallout during the U.S. test series in 1954, nuclear testing was also widely seen as a direct threat to public health and safety. Early proposals to stop testing were opposed within the U.S. government by both military and civilian officials on the grounds that the requirements for more advanced nuclear weapons were so urgent as to far outweigh any immediate health dangers that might be associated with nuclear tests. Questions were also raised about the ability to verify a ban on nuclear tests. In early 1958, following a major Soviet test series, the Soviet Union seized the political initiative by announcing that it would stop testing unilaterally if the United States would do likewise.

In a major policy shift in the spring of 1958, President Dwight Eisenhower proposed to Soviet Secretary Nikita Khrushchev that scientists from the two sides meet to assess the verifiability of a ban on nuclear tests and to recommend a possible control system. In addition to political concern about the mounting international opposition to testing, President Eisenhower's decision reflected the advice of the newly formed President's Science Advisory Committee under James Killian. Challenging the positions of the Department of Defense and the Atomic Energy Commission, the committee advised the President that a test ban could be monitored and would be in the security interests of the United States given the relative status of the nuclear weapons programs of the two sides.

The Conference of Experts, which was held in Geneva, Switzerland, during the summer of 1958, brought together a remarkable group of outstanding scientists and specialists on nuclear test detection from the West (the United States, the United Kingdom, France, and Canada) and the East (the Soviet Union, Poland, Czechoslovakia, and Romania). The conference, which was conducted as a technical study and not as a political negotiation, examined the technical problems of monitoring nuclear tests in the atmosphere, in the oceans, and underground. The report of the conference found that an international control system, using available techniques and on-site inspection, would "make it possible to detect and identify nuclear explosions, including low-yield explosions (1-5 kt)." The proposed system would have been a worldwide network made up of some 160 to 170 land-based manned control posts and ten ships with appropriate instrumentation. Subsequently, it was agreed in a separate technical working group that the control system could also be applied to tests in space if satellite-borne detectors were incorporated into it.

On the basis of the findings of the Conference of Experts, President Eisenhower called for formal negotiations on a comprehensive test ban. At the same time he announced a one-year moratorium on all testing provided the Soviet Union did the same. This moratorium was subsequently extended to the end of 1959 and testing was not resumed until 1961. On October 31, 1958, the United States, the Soviet Union, and the United Kingdom, then the only nuclear powers, opened the Conference on the Discontinuance of Nuclear Tests in Geneva, Switzerland. Despite the technical agreement at the Conference of Experts, the political negotiators quickly found that the sides were far apart in defining how the control system would actually operate and how on-site inspections, which were supposed to resolve questions regarding unidentified events, would be conducted. The United States and the United Kingdom envisaged a system administered by international personnel and operating by a majority vote, while the Soviet Union insisted on a system that it could control within its own borders.

The United States soon complicated the negotiations further by introducing new technical data and new technical problems that brought into question the findings of the Conference of Experts. The U.S. delegation first reported that analyses of new data from U.S. underground tests conducted after the Conference of Experts indicated that the lowest seismic yield that could be identified as an earthquake was about twice as high as that originally estimated. More significantly, the U.S. delegation then reported that new studies revealed a number of techniques that could permit a violator to conduct relatively large-yield underground tests so that they would not be identified or even detected by the proposed control system.

The most striking of the clandestine testing techniques was the concept of testing in huge underground cavities. Such cavities were calculated to be capable of decoupling the seismic signal from a nuclear explosion by a factor of 100 or more. The United States also suggested the possibility of conducting tests during very large earthquakes to bury the seismic signal from the test in the much greater signal from the earthquake. The Soviet delegation rejected these technical developments as simply efforts to prevent agreement. In the United States, opponents of the test ban in the executive branch and Congress seized upon the technical developments as conclusive proof that a comprehensive ban could not be verified. The U.S. government initiated an extensive research and development program (Project Vela) directed at improving seismic monitoring and other verification capabilities.

In an attempt to bypass the increasing controversy over the verification of underground tests, the Eisenhower Administration proposed to ban only those tests that could be verified by the control system devised by the Conference of Experts. Early in 1960 the United States introduced a draft threshold treaty that would have banned all atmospheric and underwater tests, underground tests above magnitude 4.75 on the Richter scale, and tests in space to a distance (unspecified) at which detection was feasible. By defining the threshold in terms of seismic magnitude rather than yield, the proposal sought to avoid the problem of the substantially different coupling factors of explosions in different types of rock and in large cavities. This proposal established criteria that would have called for an estimated average of some 20 on-site inspections per year instead of the open-ended number of the previous proposal. The United States also proposed that a joint U.S.-Soviet seismic research program develop techniques to lower the threshold. In response, the Soviet Union called for a ban on all space tests, a five-year moratorium on underground tests below magnitude 4.75 while the joint seismic research program was under way, and a political decision on a specific number of on-site inspections.

After meeting with British Prime Minister Harold Macmillan, President Eisenhower agreed to the concept of a moratorium on tests below the magnitude 4.75 threshold, but only after a threshold treaty with an agreed quota of on-site inspections had been signed and a joint research program agreed upon. (The 1958-59 moratorium was no longer formally in effect, though neither side had conducted any tests since that time.) The Soviet Union accepted this approach, and arrangements were made for a Seismic Research Program Advisory Group to meet in Geneva to develop the joint program. The questions of the length of the moratorium and the quota of on-site inspections remained. There were also unresolved political problems relating to the organization and operation of the control system.

Whatever prospects the threshold approach might have had ended when a U.S. U-2 reconnaissance aircraft was shot down near Sverdlovsk on May 2, 1960. This led to a crisis in U.S.-Soviet relations and the cancellation of the Paris summit at which it had been planned to seek agreement on the duration of the moratorium and the quota of on-site inspections. The meetings in Geneva on the joint seismic research program adjourned at the end of May without filing a report when the Soviet delegation indicated there was no point in continuing. The formal treaty negotiations in Geneva continued but made no further progress during the remaining months of the Eisenhower Administration.

# THE BOMBER AND MISSILE GAPS

## Soviet Version of the New Look

### *Document 7*

In this excerpt from *Security in the Nuclear Age,* national security specialist Jerome Kahan discusses Soviet policies during the Eisenhower administration. Kahan points out that Khrushchev pursued a Soviet version of the New Look, limiting funds to conventional forces while trying to build up a nuclear force that could strike the United States. The Soviets made some gains and improved their nuclear forces vis-à-vis the United States by 1960 but still lagged far behind. Nevertheless, Khrushchev tried "*Sputnik* diplomacy" using Soviet scientific success to bluff the West into thinking Soviet power was greater than it was. One result was that Khrushchev took a number of seemingly aggressive actions and backed them up with nuclear threats.

### 7 SOVIET STRATEGIC POLICIES
**Jerome H. Kahan**

The Eisenhower administration's nuclear policies were devised to counter what was believed to be the Soviet strategic threat. But early U.S. force and policy decisions had an important effect on the evolution of Soviet strategic policies that, in turn, influenced later U.S. decisions and the prospects for curbing the emerging nuclear arms competition.

There is little doubt that Soviet leaders were fearful of the Eisenhower administration's massive retaliation policy, which threatened a nuclear first strike against the USSR in the event of serious Soviet aggression against the United States or its allies. Pronouncements of U.S. counterforce first-strike aims by American military leaders fueled Soviet fears still further. During 1954, for example, Defense Minister Nikolai Bulganin warned against the danger of a surprise nuclear attack by the United States in a series of public statements.[11] Looking back on the 1953–60 period, Khrushchev later remarked that Secretary Dulles's policy amounted to "barefaced atomic blackmail."[12]

The actual state of the U.S.-Soviet strategic balance in the early and mid-1950s contributed to the Soviet Union's alarm. In 1953, it should be recalled, the USSR possessed only small numbers of medium-range propeller-driven bombers, while the growing U.S. B-47 bomber force deployed overseas and U.S. carrier-based aircraft posed threats to the Soviet homeland. By 1955, the Soviet Union had acquired a small intercontinental bomber force and was introducing medium-range jet bombers into its fleet. These weapons gave Kremlin leaders the capability of inflicting damage against the U.S. homeland in addition to holding Western Europe hostage with shorter-range systems. But the United States had also begun to deploy the intercontinental B-52 bomber and, equally important from the Soviet standpoint, was continuing to expand its B-47 force. America's overseas basing facilities and aerial refueling techniques enabled the use of the U.S. medium-range bomber force for strategic missions, thus giving the nation an overwhelming strategic advantage over the USSR — even though the numerical balance of bomber forces on both sides was approximately equal and despite a large-scale air-defense network throughout the Soviet Union.

Although President Eisenhower and other officials came to accept the proposition that it was impossible to prevent the Soviet Union from inflicting severe damage on the United States or its Western European allies, it is possible to argue that the United States could have launched a first strike against the USSR in the mid-1950s and sustained only minimal damage from a retaliatory attack. Whatever the actual conditions, Kremlin leaders at that time seemed to believe that this was the situation, and Khrushchev himself acknowledged that during this period the USSR "did not possess sufficient means of retaliation."[13]

To be sure, Soviet leaders apparently believed that the United States would be extremely reluctant to deliberately initiate a nuclear attack against the USSR. The atomic bomb was not used against the Soviet Union when the United States had a monopoly, and President Eisenhower had publicly eschewed preventive war. But Moscow could not trust America's good intentions, and uncertainties over future U.S. strategic deployments seemed to trigger "worst-case" interpretations by Soviet officials. Kremlin leaders heard a chorus of mixed voices in the United States commenting on our strategic doctrine, making it difficult for the USSR to dismiss the possibility that the United States might seek overwhelming superiority, or perhaps a first-strike capability designed to destroy Soviet forces, in order to support the massive retaliation policy. At a minimum, the Kremlin feared that the United States might use its strategic power inadvertently or accidentally in a crisis. Finally, Soviet leaders must have realized that the USSR not only was inferior on the strategic level but also lacked a counter to the expanding U.S. tactical nuclear weapons arsenal that threatened to negate Soviet conventional superiority in the European theater.

Moscow's strategic policies in the 1950s were shaped by the internal debates over defense strategy and the role of nuclear weapons that erupted after Stalin's death. In early 1954, Premier Georgi Malenkov, echoing President Eisenhower, stated publicly that the availability of thermonuclear weapons on both sides meant that a world war would lead to "the destruction of world civilization.[14] Khrushchev and Bulganin, on the other hand, initially expressed the traditional Soviet view that only the West would be destroyed in a major conflict, but they soon came to accept Malenkov's concept as a reality of the nuclear age. Primarily for this reason, Khrushchev abandoned the idea that war between Communist and capitalist nations was inevitable and in 1956 set forth the principle of peaceful coexistence.[15]

For the reasons suggested above, however, neither Khrushchev nor Bulganin were prepared to assume that nuclear deterrence would operate automatically or to trust the United States to refrain from using its strategic power for purposes detrimental to Soviet security. The Kremlin leadership therefore faced the issue of how to respond to the Eisenhower administration's defense program — more specifically, how to avoid nuclear inferiority, gain a credible deterrent, and blunt U.S. military and political threats. The ensuing Soviet strategic policy was constrained by the state of technology and by bureaucratic pressures. Nevertheless, motivated by a strong personal conviction that defense spending should not be permitted to interfere with necessary domestic economic needs, Khrushchev managed to forge a strategy that seemed to follow a logic based on three principles.

First, rather than compete against SAC's B-52 force and the U.S. lead in bombers, Khrushchev decided to offset U.S. strategic superiority by emphasizing Russia's lead in missilery. Long-range bombers were expensive to build and operate, and the lack of overseas bases denied the USSR the option of using medium-range bombers for strategic purposes. Moreover, many Soviet officials were rapidly recognizing that ballistic missiles could make bombers obsolete; consequently, they saw substantial economic and security advantages to be gained by forgoing major investments in bombers and moving immediately to acquire a strategic missile force. Thus, while Kremlin leaders sought to create the opposite impression, and even as bomber gap fears were raised, the USSR did not produce the large fleet of intercontinental bombers predicted by the West. But the Soviet Union continued to enlarge its air-defense network in an attempt to diminish the U.S. bomber threat and to maintain the traditional Soviet emphasis on defense.

A second element in Khrushchev's strategy initially was to develop a powerful nuclear capability against Western Europe and then to acquire a substantial long-range capability against the United States. This was reflected in the decision to build a sizable medium-range bomber force rather than a long-range fleet and by the emphasis placed on the deployment of MR/IRBMs during the second half of the decade. Despite the obvious interest of Soviet leaders in attaining the capacity to extend the reach of Soviet nuclear forces to intercontinental distances, a temporary regional priority could be justified. For one thing, medium-range systems were less costly and difficult to produce than longer-range systems, and technical experience could be gained from constructing such systems. In addition, Soviet medium-range systems would not only provide an effective deterrent to the United States through the threat posed to its West European allies but would also enable the USSR to target the large network of U.S. overseas SAC bases. Finally, the deployment of nuclear systems aimed at Western Europe represented a military counter to NATO's tactical atomic forces and could serve the USSR's political objective of disrupting relations between the United States and its European allies.

The third and most distinctive dimension of Khrushchev's strategy was the use of rhetoric to create a false impression of Soviet strategic capabilities — the "Sputnick diplomacy" policy. This policy was foreshadowed soon after the USSR deployed MRBMs when Khrushchev directed threats against Western Europe, particularly during the Suez crisis in 1956. But the detection by the United States of Soviet long-range missile tests in the summer of 1957, followed by the Sputnik launchings later that year, provided Khrushchev with a unique opportunity to dramatize the power of Soviet ICBM forces through a series of claims and threats.[16]

The basic Soviet approach was to avoid specifics and to play on the uncertainties in U.S. intelligence estimates as USSR capabilities became exaggerated during the course of the missile gap debate. Accordingly, Khrushchev and other Soviet officials spoke only in vague terms of their ability to deliver "crushing blows" against the United States when alluding to "shifts" in the balance of power. Kremlin leaders issued general statements to the effect that any western use of nuclear weapons would be countered in kind, dropped hints that the USSR might initiate a nuclear exchange under certain circumstances, made broad assertions that neither the United States nor NATO could escape destruction in the event of a nuclear war, and reiterated amorphous demands for the West to cease provocative acts. Soviet missile claims were equally vague. After the Sputnik launch, Khrushchev first asserted that the USSR had successfully developed long-range missiles, then announced in November 1958 that "serial production" of ICBMs had been initiated, and finally claimed one year later, without citing facts or figures, that the USSR possessed a substantial operational capability of intercontinental missiles.

Once the United States and its allies showed evidence of fear that the strategic balance might begin to favor the USSR, Khrushchev, as noted, tried to exploit the West's concern by attempting to exert influence during the offshore islands crisis in 1958, putting pressure on Berlin, and generally seeking to intimidate the United States and its allies. On the other hand, most experts agree that Khrushchev throughout this period sought to extract maximum political and psychological benefits *without* running unnecessary risks of nuclear conflict with the United States — risks that Soviet leaders were clearly not prepared to take, given their actual position of strategic inferiority.

In retrospect, it is unclear whether Khrushchev's strategy was deliberately designed for aggressive purposes or whether it reflected a desire to neutralize U.S. superiority.[17] One line of reasoning suggests that the unexpectedly intense U.S. reactions to Sputnik provided Khrushchev with the opportunity to avoid the appearance of inferiority without investing resources in a major effort to deploy the costly and cumbersome first-generation ICBMs that had been developed. According to this theory, only then did Khrushchev decide that a continued fueling of missile gap fears might permit the USSR to defuse the U.S. nuclear threat while concealing the modest scope of its existing missile programs and gaining time to redress the strategic balance more efficiently with improved ICBM systems. An opposite view holds that the entire Soviet effort — from the earlier bomber gap to the missile gap — represented a systematic plan on the part of Khrushchev to exploit Soviet power by creating uncertainty in the West. The actual justifications for Khrushchev's policy obviously contained elements of both interpretations — as well as other domestic and international political factors. But whatever the mixture of motivations, Sputnik diplomacy influenced U.S.-Soviet relations, played a role in the crises of the late 1950s, and exerted an important effect on U.S. strategic policies and perceptions for almost three years.

Toward the end of 1960 — after the U-2 incident — Khrushchev's claims diminished. The Kremlin had been aware of the U-2 flights, and, as the Berlin crisis developed during 1959 and early 1960, Khrushchev probably suspected that President Eisenhower was beginning to regard the missile gap as a myth. Projections of Soviet missile strength were dropping, and American missile programs were proceeding on schedule. But the public exposure of the U-2 program in May 1960 finally undermined the military credibility and political value of Soviet missile claims. In dealing with the West and in maintaining a worldwide image, the USSR could no longer be confident of relying on deception to mask its lack of ICBM deployments.

While possibly gaining some political benefits, Khrushchev failed in his attempts to use the apparent shift in the nuclear balance to extract major concessions from the West. In one sense, however, his strategy could be considered a success, since it helped counter the perceived threat of the massive retaliation policy by placing the Eisenhower administration on the defensive and diminishing the intensity of America's claims of strategic superiority. But this short-term gain was offset by the fact that Khrushchev's policies had the effect of stimulating U.S. missile programs and ultimately leading to a *wid-*

*ening* of America's strategic advantage. Ironically, Sputnik diplomacy had backfired, and the USSR faced an extremely disadvantageous and potentially dangerous situation as the United States moved toward a position of clear strategic superiority in the 1960s.

It is interesting to note that in many respects Khrushchev shared President Eisenhower's military objectives and, during the latter part of the 1950s, pursued a defense policy somewhat similar to that of the Eisenhower administration.[18] Khrushchev recognized that a nuclear exchange would be catastrophic for both sides; for this very reason he came to believe, as did President Eisenhower, that a general war was unlikely and that the prospect of nuclear escalation would deter a lower-scale conflict. Therefore, in seeking to keep military spending in check, Khrushchev, like President Eisenhower, began to look to strategic power to provide a substitute for further expansions of conventional forces. Yet budget concerns also led Khrushchev to find a second-best position acceptable and to reject the goal of nuclear superiority for the USSR, much as President Eisenhower turned to the concept of adequacy. Finally, to the extent that it emphasized bluff and rhetoric, Khrushchev's Sputnik diplomacy resembled Dulles's strategy of brinkmanship. While the USSR may not have responded to U.S. strategic programs by building large-scale forces of its own, Soviet leaders seemed to have responded in kind to U.S. policy pronouncements.

## Notes

11. *Izvestiya,* July 22, 1954, cited in Horelick and Rush, *Strategic Power and Soviet Foreign Policy,* p. 22. For background on Soviet reactions to massive retaliation and on Soviet strategic policies in the 1950s, see V. D. Sokolovskii, *Soviet Military Strategy* (Prentice-Hall, 1966).
12. Cited in Chalmers Roberts, *The Nuclear Years: The Arms Race and Arms Control 1945–70* (Praeger, 1970), p. 41.
13. *ibid.*
14. *Pravda,* March 13, 1954, cited in Horelick and Rush, *Strategic Power and Soviet Foreign Policy,* p. 19.
15. Khrushchev did this at the Twentieth Communist Party Congress, February 1956. For background, see Thomas W. Wolfe, *Soviet Power and Europe 1945–70* (Johns Hopkins Press, 1970), pp. 128–59.
16. For a systematic discussion of Soviet threats and claims during the years 1956–60, see Horelick and Rush, *Strategic Power and Soviet Foreign Policy,* pp. 42–102.
17. See Wolfe, *Soviet Power and Europe,* pp. 84–89.
18. This point is discussed in Roman Kolkowitz and others, *The Soviet Union and Arms Control: A Superpower Dilemma* (Johns Hopkins Press, 1970), pp. 27–29.

# American Public Reacts to Soviet Union's Launch of Sputnik

### *Document 8*

This editorial from *Air Force Magazine* gives a sense of the shock, bordering on panic, that the American public felt after the Soviet Union launched the first orbiting satellite. The title alone is a good indication, and the article worries about the loss of world leadership in science and wonders when the Soviets will be ready to launch ICBMs (intercontinental ballistic missiles) in pursuit of world domination. The editorial calls for an acceleration of the U.S. ICBM program.

## 8 THE SPUTNIK PEARL HARBOR
### Peter J. Schenk

As Sputnik I orbited the earth, each radioed beep from outer space announced the Pearl Harbor of the Technological War.

When war in technological terms was introduced to our readers six years ago (AIR FORCE, *November 1951*) there were few to listen and believe. But, as reaction to Sputnik continues to spill over the front pages, there is evidence of a break-through against the destructive complacency which has long drugged this nation.

There is solace in this new awareness, but we can only hope that constructive reaction has not come too late.

How soon the men who launched Sputnik I in pursuit of knowledge will be ready to launch ICBMs (intercontinental ballistic missiles) in pursuit of world domination, one can only guess (along with our intelligence agencies).

But that these men are prepared to do so, if it suits their master plan, is beyond speculation. For surely the Soviet leaders who directed the killing of thousands of unarmed Hungarians would not hesitate to kill millions of Americans, equally unarmed in World War III terms.

Actually, we should be grateful that the modern Pearl Harbor has come in the form of a man-made moon, and that Russia has not introduced us to space flight with thermonuclear warheads.

Against such a grim background, the nation feels a desperate need for strong and enlightened leadership.

The first great opportunity for such leadership came the morning of October 9 [1957], a few days after the advent of Sputnik I, when Washington news correspondents crowded the White House press chamber.

Sputnik I signaled the need for a dynamic change in both the course and tempo of national policy. It gave the President an unequaled opportunity to shrug off political pressures and come to grips with the full meaning of Technological War. History was waiting to be made in the President's press conference of October 9.

What might he have said at that time? The New York *Herald Tribune,* in a searching editorial which appeared the same day, summed it up in this manner:

"If we learn the lesson that Sputnik has to teach us, here is what America, under the kind of leadership it is entitled to expect, will do:

"Launch a huge national program of basic research and development...."

"Break down the senseless walls of super-secrecy which are keeping nothing from the Soviets, but preventing our own scientists from cross-fertilizing each others' ideas....

"End the disgraceful interservice bickering over scientific development....

"Tackle the whole national educational crisis in a way a mighty and responsible nation ought to tackle it...."

Certainly nothing short of such heroic measures could meet the challenge of the hour. But our leadership was not equal to the crisis. As the Republican *Herald Tribune* commented sorrowfully the followoing day:

"What the nation expected yesterday from the President of the United States was leadership. It did not get it."

Instead, the nation received excuses and evasive maneuvers; a weak attempt to minimize, if not confuse, the true significance of the Soviet achievement.

Thus, the first "battle" following the Sputnik Pearl Harbor ended in a defeat for the American people.

Knowing how easy it is to criticize from the sidelines one is reluctant to place the blame squarely in the lap of the President. Yet, there is no other choice.

For several years a great group of men might logically have shared in the blame. Many men of influence, in and out of government, including leaders of science, had failed to grasp what Dr. Edward Teller told an Air Force Association conference last February.

"Within ten years" he said, "the Soviets will have the best scientists in the world. I am not saying this will happen unless we do this or that. I am simply saying it is going to happen. The time now has come to talk about the United States *recapturing* the world lead in science *not* how to keep that lead."

That conclusion, in all its ramifications, is not easy to accept. However, an increasing number of official and unofficial advisors to the White House have come to realize the appalling lack of leadership being applied to the problems of national survival.

On the other hand, the few really close advisors to the President have either failed to comprehend Russia's growing dominance in the Technological War or have chosen not to present the bad news to him.

Yet, in the last analysis, the finger must be pointed at this one man — who alone has the responsibility and power to turn the tide.

Presumably, the Commander in Chief has seriously believed that our position of dominance in the air and space above has not been in jeopardy. Even that reaction might have been understood, knowing the information pitfalls of Washington, until Sputnik I came along to open the eyes of all who would see. That is why the performance of the President at his Sputnik press conference was so depressing.

It is unfortunate that the scientists upon whom he admittedly depended for his reaction to Sputnik I, although capable men in their fields, are far removed from the technological issues at hand. This would suggest that the President merely has been inadequately advised on the scientific issues of the day. But that is far too pat an answer.

It is the President's responsibility to utilize the best scientific advice the nation has to offer. Why, then, has he permitted so few knowledgeable scientists to come before him? How could he tolerate a Secretary of Defense who couldn't understand that what man eventually discovers on the other side of the moon might drastically alter the nature of life on this planet? How could the President let the shortage of scientific brainpower be "solved" by reducing the demand for it through research budget reductions, at the very time that the Soviets were stepping up their scientific manpower programs? How could he allow the aviation industry, upon which the nation must depend for its new weapons, to be undermined by a rash of directives compromising efficient and economic performance?

Indeed, does the President really believe the nation has a dynamic research and development program, equal to the threat, when in fact that program has never in recent years been more sluggish, or at a lower ebb? Does he, in fact, truly see the greatest national problem as one of survival in an age of technological competition? In short, when will the President lead the way so we can again become a nation of explorers and pioneers?

Such a nation, for example, should not now be tempted by lost pride to merely duplicate the Soviet satellite too little and too late. Rather, we should accelerate and exploit our ICBM program with giant strides toward the conquest of space.

In this age of giant strides, the military background of the President, when measured against the nation's decreasing military stature, presents an enigma to many who serve him at close range as well as to those who judge him from afar. And yet, the record is there for all to see. Sputnik I merely has served as a catalyst to bring that record into focus.

We do not underestimate the burden carried by the President. However, we are reminded that Winston Churchill, at about the same age, came forth to rescue from incipient oblivion a once-powerful nation that had scorned him for his courage and vision.

Churchill's own words, describing an earlier crisis in his own nation, are pertinent today. He spoke of a time when, "short-sighted opinions, agreeable to the party spirit, pernicious to national interests, banished all purpose from the state."

As Sputnik I circles the heavens, an omen of disaster, only inspired leadership in the Churchill tradition can preserve the Free World.

## The Increasing Soviet Threat

### *Document 9*

These excerpts from a top-secret report to the National Security Council from a high-level advisory group warn of "an increasing threat which may become critical in 1959 or early 1960." The report called for major buildup of U.S. IRBMs (intermediate-range ballistic missiles) and ICBMs. It also called for a major program to reduce the vulnerability of U.S. bombers, which would be threatened by Soviet ICBMs. Much of the report was leaked to the public and helped create an atmosphere of concern about U.S. nuclear strength.

### 9 THE GAITHER REPORT
### Security Resources Panel of the Science Advisory Committee
### November 7, 1957

### Deterrence and Survival in the Nuclear Age

### I. Assignment

The Security Resources Panel was asked to study and form a broad-brush opinion of the relative value of various active and passive measures to protect the civil population in case of nuclear attack and its aftermath, taking into account probable new weapon systems; and to suggest which of the various active and passive measures are likely to be most effective, in relation to their costs. While fulfilling its assignment, the Panel was also asked to study the deterrent value of our retaliatory forces, and the economic and political consequences of any significant shift of emphasis or direction in defense programs.

The Panel has therefore examined active and passive defense measures from two standpoints: their contribution to deterrence; and their protection to the civil population if war should come by accident or design.

We have found no evidence in Russian foreign and military policy since 1945 to refute the conclusion that USSR intentions are expansionist, and that her great efforts to build military power go beyond any concepts of Soviet defense. We have, therefore, weighed the relative military and economic capabilities of the United States and the USSR in formulating our broad-brush opinions, basing our findings on estimates of present and future Russian capabilities furnished by the Intelligence community.

**Past and Projected Relationship Between U.S. and U.S.S.R. Military Effort**

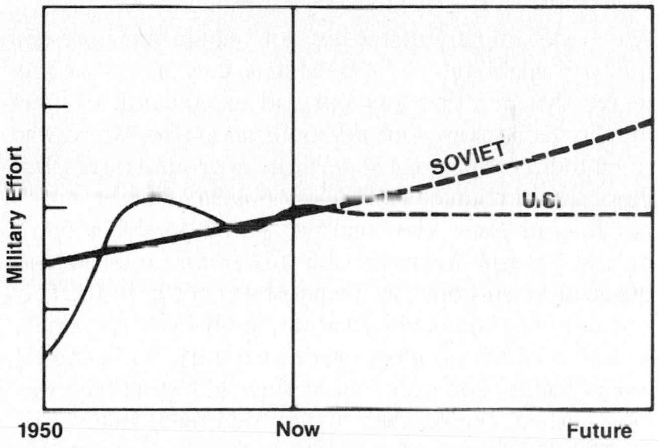


The evidence clearly indicates an increasing threat which may become critical in 1959 or early 1960. The evidence further suggests the urgency of proper time phasing of needed improvements in our military position vis-a-vis Russia. . . .

### II. Nature of the Threat

*A. Economic*

The Gross National Product (GNP) of the USSR is now more than one-third that of the United States and is increasing half again as fast. Even if the Russian rate of growth should decline, because of increasing difficulties in management and shortage of raw materials and should drop by 1960 to half its present rate, its GNP would be more than half of ours as of that date. This growing Russian economic strength is concentrated on the armed forces and on investment in heavy industry, which this year account for the equivalent of roughly $40 billion and $17 billion, respectively, in 1955 dollars. Adding these two figures, we get an allocation of $57 billion per annum, which is roughly equal to the combined figure for these two items in our country's current effort. If the USSR continues to expand its military expenditures throughout the next decade, as it has during the 1950's, and ours remains constant, its annual military expenditures may be double ours, even allowing for a gradual improvement of the low living standards of the Russian peoples.

This extraordinary concentration of the Soviet economy on military power and heavy industry, which is permitted, or perhaps forced, by their peculiar political structure, makes available economic resources sufficient to finance both the rapid expansion of their impressive military capability and their politico-economic offensive by which, through diplomacy, propaganda and subversion, they seek to extend the Soviet orbit.

### *B. Military*

The Soviet military threat lies not only in their present military capabilities — formidable as they are — but also in the dynamic development and exploitation of their military technology. Our demobilization after World War II left them with a great superiority in ground forces, but they had no counter in 1946 for our Strategic Air Force nor for our Navy. They had no atomic bombs, no productive capacity for fissionable materials, no jet engine production, and only an infant electronics industry. This situation was compatible with a then-backward country, so much of whose most productive areas had suffered military attack and occupation. Their industrial base was then perhaps one-seventh that of the United States.

The singleness of purpose with which they have pressed their military-centered industrial development has led to spectacular progress. They have developed a spectrum of A- and H-bombs and produced fissionable material sufficient for at least 1500 nuclear weapons. They created from scratch a long-range air force with 1500 B-29 type bombers; they then substantially re-equipped it with jet aircraft, while developing a short-range air force of 3000 jet bombers. In the field of ballistic missiles they have weapons of 700 n.m. range, in production for at least a year; successfully tested a number of 950 n.m. missiles; and probably surpassed us in ICBM development. They have developed air-to-surface and probably submarine-launched cruise missiles; built 250 to 300 new long-range submarines and partially modernized 200 others. They have created an air defense system composed of 1500 all-weather and 850 day jet fighters; equipped at least 60 sites, each with 60 launchers, for a total of over 3600 launching pads for surface-to-air missiles provided with a sophisticated and original guidance system and a ground environment of 4000 radars. At the same time, they have maintained and largely re-equipped their army of 175 line divisions, while furnishing large quantities of military equipment to their satellites and Red China.*

## III. Broad-Brush Opinions

The Panel has arrived at the following broad-brush opinions as to the present situation:

A. In case of a nuclear attack against the continental United States:

1. Active defense programs now in being and programmed for the future will not give adequate assurance of protection to the civil population. If the attack were at low altitude, or at high altitude with electronic countermeasures (jamming), little protection would be afforded. If the attack should come at moderately high altitude and without electronic countermeasures, some considerable protection will be afforded the civil population.
2. Passive defense programs now in being and programmed for the future will afford no significant protection to the civil population.

B. The protection of the United States and its population rests, therefore, primarily upon the deterrence provided by SAC. The current vulnerability of SAC to surprise attack during a period of lessened world tension (i.e., a time when SAC is not on a SAC "alert" status), and the threat posed to SAC by the prospects of an early Russian ICBM capability, call for prompt remedial action.

The Panel has arrived at the following conclusions as to the value, relative to cost, of various measures for protecting the civil population.

### *A. Measures to Secure and Augment Our Deterrent Power*

Since the prevention of war would best protect our urban population, we assign the highest relative value to the following measures to secure and augment our deterrent power. These would protect our manned bombers from surprise attack, increase our forces available for limited military operations, and give us an earlier and stronger initial operational capability (IOC) with intermediate-range and intercontinental ballistic missiles. Basic elements in this program are:

1. To lessen SAC vulnerability to a Russian surprise bomber attack in a period of low tension (a present threat):
   a. Reduce reaction time so an adequate number (possibly 500) of SAC planes can get off, weapons aboard, on way to target, within the tactical warning

*By the very nature of the sources of intelligence information, none of the specific numbers cited above can be precisely known. The approximate size of each number, however, and more importantly the overall order of accomplishment, are well established by the available data.

time available. This can be done by promptly implementing SAC's "alert" concept.

b. Improve and insure tactical warning. Radars in the seaward extensions need to be modernized to assure tactical warning at high and low altitude, and the extensions need to be lengthened to prevent "end runs."

c. Provide an active missile defense for SAC bases (Nike-Hercules or Talos) against bombers.

2. To lessen SAC vulnerability to an attack by Russian ICBMs (a late 1959 threat):
   a. Develop, to an operational status, a radar early-warning system for an ICBM attack.
   b. Further improve SAC's reaction time to an "alert" status of 7 to 22 minutes, depending on location of bases.
   c. Disperse SAC aircraft, to the widest extent practical, to SAC and non-SAC military bases in the ZI and possibly also to commercial airfields in the ZI.
   d. Protect a large part of SAC's planes by providing 100 to 200 psi shelters, and equivalent protection for weapons, personnel, and other needed supplies and facilities.
   e. Provide SAC bases with an active missile defense against ICBMs, using available weapons such as Nike-Hercules or Talos and the improved long-range tracking radars now existing in prototype.
3. To increase SAC's strategic offensive power (to match Russia's expected early ICBM capability):
   a. Increase the initial operational capability of our IRBMs (Thor and/or Jupiter) from 60 to 240.
   b. Increase the IOC of our ICBMs (Atlas and Titan) from 80 to 600.
   c. Accelerate the IOC of the Polaris submarine IRBM system, which offers the advantages of mobility and greatly reduced vulnerability.
   d. Every effort should be made to have a significant number of IRBMs operational overseas by late 1958, and ICBMs operational in the ZI by late 1959.
   e. Hardened bases for the ICBMs should be phased in as rapidly as possible.
4. Augment our and Allied forces for limited military operations, and provide greater mobility, to enable us to deter or promptly suppress small wars which must not be allowed to grow into big ones. The Panel suggests that a study be undertaken, at the national rather than at a Service level, to develop current doctrine on when and how nuclear weapons can contribute to limited operations.

### *B. Measures to Reduce Vulnerability of Our People and Cities*

The main protection of our civil population against a Soviet nuclear attack has been and will continue to be the deterrent power of our armed forces, to whose strengthening and securing we have accorded the highest relative value. But this is not sufficient unless it is coupled with measures to reduce the extreme vulnerability of our people and our cities. As long as the U.S. population is wide open to Soviet attack, both the Russians and our allies may believe that we shall feel increasing reluctance to employ SAC in any circumstance other than when the United States is directly attacked. To prevent such an impairment of our deterrent power and to ensure our survival if nuclear war occurs through miscalculation or design, we assign a somewhat lower than highest value, in relation to cost, to a mixed program of active and passive defenses to protect our civil population.

1. A massive development program to eliminate two major weaknesses in our present active defenses:
   a. The vulnerability of the radars in our ground environment and in our weapons control to "blinding" by enemy electronic countermeasures (ECM).
   b. The small probability of kills against a low-level attack.
2. Further strengthening of our active defenses as soon as their vulnerability to ECM and low-level attack is removed. Current research affords hope that at least our weapons-control radars can be made proof against ECM. Radars can be located at high points to guard against low-level attacks, and a barrage-type defense against low-level attacks from the sea might prove a stopgap. An effective air defense system is so important to ensure continuity of government, and to protect our civil population, our enormously valuable civil property and military installations, that these development programs we suggest should be pushed with all possible speed.
3. A nationwide fallout shelter program to protect the civil population. This seems the only feasible protection for millions of people who will be increasingly exposed to the hazards of radiation. The Panel has been unable to identify any other type of defense likely to save more lives for the same money in the event of a nuclear attack.

   The construction and use of such shelters must be tied into a broad pattern of organization for the emergency and its aftermath. We are convinced that with proper planning the post-attack environment can permit people to come out of the shelters and survive. It is important to remember that those who survive the effects of the blast will have adequate time (one to five hours) to get into fallout shelters. This is not true of blast shelters which, to be effective, must be entered prior to the attack.

   We do not recommend major construction of blast shelters at this time. If, as appears quite likely, an effective air defense system can be obtained, this will probably be a better investment than blast shelters. However, because of present uncertainties, on both active and passive fronts, it appears prudent to carry out promptly a research and development program for such blast shelters since we must be in a position to move rapidly into construction should the need for them become evident. . . .
4. A program to develop and install an area defense against ICBMs at the earliest possible date.

5. Increased emphasis on the R&D program to improve the Navy's anti-submarine effort, including defense against submarine-launched missiles. The principal protection against these latter may have to be provided by air and ballistic missile defense systems.

## The Missile Gap Becomes an Important Defense Issue

### *Documents 10, 11, and 12*

These documents give a sense of how the alleged "missile gap" became a political issue in the 1960 presidential campaign. Document 10, a *New York Times* story, reports testimony from President Eisenhower's Secretary of Defense Thomas Gates that reports of a "missile gap" were wrong. Gates claimed that the balance of military power remained "heavily in our favor." But document 11, a story in the *Times* a week later, indicates that the Democrats were not convinced. Democratic senator Stuart Symington is quoted as saying recent intelligence information confirms his view that the Soviet Union will have a three-to-one advantage in missiles in about two years. In document 12, Sen. John Kennedy attacks the Eisenhower administration for neglecting U.S. defenses and calls for a massive U.S. buildup to prevent a Soviet advantage. This was to become a major theme in his presidential campaign.

### 10 THE "MISSILE GAP"–I
### Hanson W. Baldwin

Moscow's claim yesterday of a one-and-a-quarter-mile circular error in a 7,762-mile rocket flight caused raised eyebrows but no excitement in the Pentagon.

The first of a number of Russian missile shots into a new impact area in the Central Pacific, whether or not it was as accurate and as successful as the Russians asserted, is unlikely to influence materially the vigorous and aggressive presentation of the Administration's defense policies just initiated.

Secretary of Defense Thomas S. Gates Jr.; Gen. Nathan F. Twining, chairman of the Joint Chiefs of Staff, and Under Secretary of State Livingston T. Merchant tipped the Administration's hand in their opening testimony in Congress this week.

Their composite testimony totaled, in the opinion of some Congressmen, the rosiest picture of the United States defense posture presented to Congress for a long time. The balance of military power is still "heavily in our favor," Secretary Gates said. Even a Soviet surprise attack with all available missiles could not eliminate our nuclear retaliatory capability.

#### The "Missile Gap"

Mr. Gates even cast considerable doubt on what has come by dint of constant repetition to be accepted as a fact by many in the nation: a "missile gap" between the United States and the Soviet Union in the next few years. He indicated that if the Russians produced intercontinental ballistic missiles at our present maximum estimate of their potential capabilities they might have a "moderate numerical superiority" in the next three years. But the United States has many other nuclear weapons systems, which, collectively, tip the balance of deterrent power "heavily in our favor."

This is an election year. The Democratic opposition is already attempting to make a campaign issue out of the deficiencies in our military posture and is emphasizing particularly the alleged "missile gap." The Republican Administration, on the other hand, has been aroused and stung by the opposition attacks. The President, in particular, is known to have been greatly angered by the criticisms voiced in "The Uncertain Trumpet," a book recently published by Gen. Maxwell D. Taylor, United States Army, retired, who completed four years as Army Chief of Staff last June. The President's mood, particularly about defense matters, is typified by his recent heated response to a somewhat pointed news conference question about defense:

"I've spent my life in this, and I know more about it than almost anybody I think in the country."

Is, then, Mr. Gates's testimony rhetoric, the opening guns of the defense in an election year; or is it solidly based on factual appraisal?

#### A Compound Answer

The answer to this question is almost certainly compound. Mr. Gates has too much integrity — he is a public servant who is no politician and owes no man anything — to give other than his honest opinion. But he is aware, as is the White House, that the Pentagon case has not been put skillfully or forcefully in the past.

The Administration feels that the public image of relative American weakness that has been created — partly by Communist propaganda, partly by undoubted Communist achievements, partly by the special pleading of the individual services, partly by opposition criticism, partly by inept Administration presentations of our strength — is grossly exaggerated. Mr. Gates, therefore, is certainly determined to put his best foot forward, not only for domestic political reasons but also because he is keenly aware that a strategic deterrent is no stronger than the enemy thinks it is.

But at the same time his optimistic statements are based on hard-headed comparative appraisals of our own and of Soviet strength. The Secretary spoke of new intelligence estimates of Soviet missile strength, which he described as "very significant."

These estimates were not made public, but in an explanatory conference later, the Secretary got on to slippery ground when he admitted that the new estimates took into account what the Russians intended to do in missile production, rather than, as in the past, merely estimating their capabilities.

In the intelligence field this issue of intentions versus capabilities is one of the oldest of pitfalls, and many experts have come a cropper by trying, in effect, to read the enemy's mind.

Nevertheless, the new intelligence reports do include an estimate of current Soviet long-range missile strength and of current Soviet missile production that, in comparison with our own current status, is by no means discouraging.

## 11 DEMOCRATS SAY C.I.A. MISSILE DATA JUSTIFY CONCERN
## Jack Raymond

WASHINGTON, Jan. 29 — Democratic Senators cited a secret intelligence briefing today to support their forecast of growing Soviet missile power.

The briefing was given by Allen W. Dulles, director of the Central Intelligence Agency, at a closed session of the Senate Preparedness subcommittee and the Aeronautical and Space Sciences Committee.

Lyndon B. Johnson, of Texas, the Democratic leader and chairman of both committees, said the Dulles testimony had made clear that the Soviet Union would have an "enormous advantage in missile striking power."

Senator Henry M. Jackson, Democrat of Washington, commented that Mr. Dulles had given a grimmer interpretation of this country's intelligence estimates than had Secretary of Defense Thomas S. Gates Jr.

"Some of the rosy color that Mr. Gates had in his presentation has been taken out," the Senator said.

### Symington Concurs

Senator Stuart Symington of Missouri said the testimony "completely confirms my position" that in about two years the Soviet Union will have a 3-to-1 advantage in missiles over the United States.

The Senate Republican leader, meanwhile, assailed the Democrats for their "nibbling, sniping and disparaging" statements about the Administration's defense policies.

In a speech on the floor, the leader, Everett McKinley Dirksen of Illinois, derided Democratic critics who set themselves up as "military experts" to criticize President Eisenhower — "the grand captain of the greatest military effort the world has ever seen." Senator Dirksen continued:

"Maybe we ought to set up a committee on the conduct of the cold and/or hot war. We might even put on it an artillery captain who later became Commander in Chief."

### "Picture Not Rosy"

This was an allusion to former President Harry S. Truman, who served as a battery commander in World War I.

Attention was focused on Mr. Dulles's testimony today because of a dispute last week. Secretary Gates had said that the latest intelligence estimates downgraded the Soviet missile threat and had been prepared according to a "new formula."

In a luncheon break during the day-long closed hearing, Senator Johnson said: 'Certainly the picture is not rosy."

Senator Jackson, another longtime Democratic critic of defense policies, said Mr. Dulles had testified that the Russians now had and would continue to have a "quantitative and qualitative lead in intercontinental ballistic missiles."

## 12 SENATE SPEECH ON INCREASING U.S. MILITARY DEFENSES
## Sen. John Kennedy
## February 29, 1950

Mr. John Kennedy (Dem., Mass.):

I thank the Senator from Florida for his courtesy and understanding.

Mr. President, Winston Churchill said: "We arm — to parley." We prepare for war — in order to deter war. We depend on the strength of armaments, to enable us to bargain for disarmament. It is my intention, later this week, to make a second address on what positive preparations for disarmament we can make now. We compare our military strength with the Soviets, not to determine whether we should use it, but to determine whether we can persuade them that to use theirs would be futile and disastrous, and to determine whether we can back up our own pledges in Berlin, Formosa, and around the world.

In short, peace, not politics, is at the heart of the current debate — peace, not war, is the objective of our military policy. But peace would have no meaning if the time ever came when the deterrent ratio shifted so heavily in favor of the Soviet Union that they could destroy most of our retaliatory capacity in a single blow. It would then be irrelevant as to whether the Soviets achieved our demise through massive attack, through the threat of such attack, or through nibbling away gradually at our security.

Will such a time come?

The current debate has too often centered on how our retaliatory capacity compares today with that of the Soviets. Our striking force, the President said one week ago Sunday night, is "ample for today — far superior to any other" and large enough to deter any aggressor. But the real issue is not how we stand today but tomorrow — not in 1960 but in 1961, 1962 and particularly 1963 and thereafter. Nineteen hundred and sixty is critical because this is the year that the money must be appropriated — by this session of this Congress — if we are to obtain initial results in subsequent years.

This year, our "mix" of forces undoubtedly is "far superior." But it is indisputable that we are today deficient in several areas — and that in one of those areas, ballistic missiles, our deficiency is likely to take on critical dimensions in the near future.

Those who uphold the administration defense budget are right on one count: We cannot be certain that the Soviets will have, during the term of the next administration, the tremendous lead in missile striking power which they give every evidence of building — and we cannot be certain that they will use that lead to threaten or launch an attack upon the United States. Consequently those of us who call for a higher defense budget are taking a chance on spending money unnecessarily. But those who oppose these expenditures are taking a chance on our very survival as a nation.

The ironic fact of the matter is that, despite all the debates, predictions, claims and counterclaims, the electorate will never be able to credit properly whichever side is right. For if we are successful in boosting our defenses, and no Soviet attack is ever launched or threatened, we shall never know with certainty whether our improved forces deterred that attack, or whether the Soviets would never have attacked us anyway. But, on the other hand, if the deterrent gap continues to go against us and invites a Soviet strike sometime after the maximum danger period begins, a large part of our population will have less than 24 hours of life in which to reflect that the critics of this administration were right all along.

The only real question is, Which chance, which gamble, do we take — our money or our survival? The money must be appropriated now — the survival will not, we hope, be at stake for a few more years.

It is easier therefore to gamble with our survival: it saves money now. It balances the budget now. It reassures the voters now. And now, 1960, is an election year. If a future administration or Congress is confronted with peril — if they lack the means in early 1963, for example, to back up our commitments around the world — that will be their problem. Let them worry about how to get by then; as we are getting by now. We can honestly say our striking force is second to none now — what happens then is their responsibility.

That is the easier alternative — to gamble with our survival. But I would prefer that we gamble with our money — that we increase our defense budget this year — even though we have no absolute knowledge that we shall ever need it — and even though we would prefer to spend the money on other critical needs in more constructive ways.

That is the harder alternative. It is less convenient in an election year. It makes us pay now, with our cash — instead of putting it off, in the hope that we will not have to pay later, with our lives. It exposes us to voter retaliation at the polls now, while the alternative course — if proven wrong — might well leave no voters able to retaliate.

But I am convinced that every American who can be fully informed as to the facts today would agree to an additional investment in our national security now rather than risk his survival, and his children's survival, in the years ahead — in particular, an investment effort designed, first, to make possible an emergency stopgap air alert program, to deter an attack before the missile gap is closed; second, to step up our ultimate missile program that will close the gap when completed: Polaris, Minuteman and long-range air-to-ground missiles — meanwhile stepping up our production of Atlas missiles to cover the current gap as best we can; and third; to rebuild and modernize our Army and Marine Corps conventional forces, to prevent the brush-fire wars that our capacity for nuclear retaliation is unable to deter.

These additional efforts do not involve a small sum, to be spent carelessly. There are other uses — schools, hospitals, parks and dams — to which we would rather devote it. But the total amount, I am convinced, would be less than 1 percent of our gross national product. It would be less than the estimated budget surplus.

It is, I am convinced, an investment in peace that we can afford — and cannot avoid.

I should think that anyone who heard tonight's news to the effect that Mr. Khrushchev said if he could not get an agreement on Berlin, he would sign a peace treaty with East Germany, in which event West Berlin would be a part of East Germany, will consider that to be a crisis which the Soviet Union might not postpone so long.

We cannot avoid taking these measures any more than the average American can avoid taking out fire insurance on his home. We cannot be absolutely certain of the danger. But neither can we risk our future on our estimates of a hostile power's strength and intentions, particularly when secrecy is that power's dominant characteristic — and particularly in the light of our consistent history of underestimating Soviet strength and scientific progress. The chance that our military improvidence will invite a national catastrophe is substantially greater — many, many times greater if you work out the odds on an actuarial basis — than the chance that your house or my house will burn down this year or next. But as individuals we are willing to pay for fire insurance — and, although we hope we never need it, we are surely equally prepared as a nation to pay every dollar necessary to take out this kind of additional insurance against a national catastrophe.

I am calling, in short, for an investment in peace. And my purpose today is to set forth the facts that every American should have to back up this investment.

To the extent possible, I want to avoid the conflicting claims and confusion over dates and numbers. These largely involve differences of degree. I say only that the evidence is strong enough to indicate that we cannot be certain of our security in the future, any more than we can be certain of disaster — and if we are to err in an age of uncertainty, I want us to err on the side of security.

Whether the missile gap — that everyone agrees now exists — will become critical in 1961, 1962, or 1963 — whether during the critical years of the gap the Russian lead will be 2 to 1, 3 to 1, or 5 to 1 — whether the gap can be brought to a close — by the availability in quantity of Polaris and Minuteman missiles — in 1964 or in 1965 or ever — on all these questions experts may sincerely differ. I do not challenge the accuracy of our intelligence reports — I do not charge anyone with intentionally misleading the public for purposes of deception. For whichever figures are accurate, the point is that we are facing a gap on which we are gambling with our survival — and this year's defense budget is our last real chance to do something about it. . . .

Unless immediate steps are taken, failure to maintain our relative power of retaliation may in the near future expose the United States to a nuclear missile attack. Until our own mobile solid-fuel missiles are available in sufficient quantities to make it unwise for any enemy to consider an attack we must scrape through with what we can most quickly make available. At the present time there are no Polaris submarines on station ready for an emergency. There are no hardened missile bases. There is no adequate air defense. There is no capacity for an airborne alert in anything like the numbers admittedly needed. Our missile early warning system — BMEWS — is not yet completed. Our IRBM bases — "soft," immobile, and undispersed — invite surprise attack. And our capability for conventional war is insufficient to avoid the hopeless dilemma of choosing between launching a nuclear attack and watching aggressors make piecemeal conquests.

Time is short. This situation should never have been permitted to arise. But if we move now, if we are willing to gamble with our money instead of our survival, we have, I am sure, the wit and resource to maintain the minimum conditions for our survival, for our alliances, and for the active pursuit of peace.

This is not a call of despair. It is a call for action — a call based upon the belief that at this moment in history our security transcends normal budgetary considerations.

But merely calling for more funds is not enough. Money spent on the wrong systems would not only be wasteful, it could slow us down. Merely to criticize is not enough, without stating clearly and candidly that to correct the situation will cost money. That money is not either mysteriously or easily made available. But I have indicated that I think the money must and can be made available, from elsewhere in the Pentagon, elsewhere in the budget, and elsewhere in the economy — including, if necessary, from additional tax revenues.

I am suggesting, therefore, three major changes in the pending defense budget:

First. We must provide funds to protect our investment in SAC, as long as it is our chief deterrent, primarily by making possible an airborne alert keeping 25 percent of our nuclear striking force in the air at all times, to prevent them from being destroyed along with their bases in the event of a sudden attack. . . .

Second. We must provide funds to step up our Polaris, Minuteman and air-to-ground missile development program, in order to hasten the day when a full, mobile missile force becomes our chief deterrent and closes any gap between ourselves and the Russians. . . .

Third. We must provide funds to augment, modernize and provide increased mobility and versatility for the conventional forces and weapons of the Army and Marine Corps. The more difficult a decisive nuclear war becomes the more important will be the forces designed to oppose nonnuclear aggression.

There are other essential needs requiring additional funds in this budget as well: to complete and improve our continental defense and warning systems and to disperse our bases, as already mentioned; to equip us for anti-submarine warfare; to restore our merchant marine; to expand our space and military research; and to initiate a realistic fallout shelter program.

## THE CONSOLIDATION OF U.S. NUCLEAR PLANNING

# The Head of the Strategic Air Command (SAC) Discusses Nuclear Strategy

### *Document 13*

This brief report on a March 1954 meeting between Gen. Curtis LeMay and representatives of the other armed services gives a picture of some of the Air Force's views. LeMay sees SAC as an elite corps that can crush the Soviet Union quickly and completely by massive atomic bombing attacks. LeMay makes the startling admission that the United States might go first if "pushed in the corner far enough." He also believes that SAC will get to use the lion's share of the strategic stockpile. LeMay's confidence reflects the fact that the United States enjoyed a tremendous superiority over the Soviet Union in the early 1950s.

## 13 QUESTION AND ANSWER SESSION ON STRATEGIC AIR WARFARE
## Gen. Curtis LeMay
## March 1954

Some of the interesting questions asked [of] General LeMay included:

Q. What period of time do you consider we should plan for to fight a "short war"? (Asked by a Navy Captain.)

A. About 30 days. SAC has been compiling continuous data on critical parts required to keep the planes operational. These parts are kept in "flying kits," one for each plane which are taken with the plane when it departs for a mission. I consider these critical parts so important that I have never allowed them to be taken out of flying kits for local use. Necessary parts have to be gotten from somewhere else other than the flying kits or else the plane stays on the ground until the part is obtained. (Note: It is understood that General LeMay has in the past indicated a 60-day period, later dropped to 45 days, and still later to 30 days. This question was apparently an effort to see if he had reached any lower estimate by now. It seemed apparent from General LeMay's answer that he is firmly convinced that 30 days is long enough to conclude World War III.)

Q. Is SAC prepared to conduct strategic air warfare in case the use of atomic weapons is outlawed? (Asked by a Navy Captain.)

A. You "sailor boys" are always asking this foolish question (or words to that effect). It is inconceivable to me that this situation will ever arise.

Q. How do SAC's plans fit in with the stated national policy that the U.S. will never strike the first blow?

A. I have heard this thought stated many times and it sounds very fine. However, it is not in keeping with United States history. Just look back and note who started the Revolutionary War, the War of 1812, the Indian Wars, and the Spanish–American War. I want to make it clear that I am not advocating a preventive war; however, I believe that if the U.S. is pushed in the corner far enough we would not hesitate to strike first (or words to this effect).

Q. Could you say a few words as to your thoughts on how to fight a war in Indo-China?

A. I could talk for 2 or 3 weeks on this. In fact, I wouldn't fight a war in Indo-China because this is a squabble that could be settled by political action. This may necessitate offering independence to those people ultimately.

Q. What would you advocate in case hostilities are renewed in Korea?

A. There are no suitable strategic air targets in Korea. However, I would drop a few bombs in proper places in China, Manchuria and Southeastern Russia. In those "poker games," such as Korea and Indo-China, we (U.N., I presume) have never raised the ante — we have always just called the bet. We ought to try raising sometime.

Q. We have heard a lot of optimistic statements today about SAC's capabilities. Do you have any reservations about these capabilities? (Asked by a Navy Captain.)

A. No, I would like to have a few more bases, however.

### Additional Interesting Statements Made by General LeMay

SAC's mission is to conduct strategic air warfare against the targets "assigned by the JCS." I hope that someday all the atomic weapon targets in the Soviet complex will be listed in a complete order of priority and that someone will be designated to drop bombs on every one of them. Anyone who has the capability to do this should be considered, including the "Beaver Patrol" if they have this ability.

We have a boss just like all other commanders and our bosses are the JCS. This is not always clearly understood even by members of the JCS themselves. Recently, when I was in Washington one of the JCS expressed apprehension to me that I would go off on my own dropping bombs wherever I please. He did not even realize that I work for him.

If any of you have any doubts about any parts of our program which can be demonstrated we will be glad to take you out and *show* you.

SAC's ultimate goal is to develop a true inter-continental bombing capability so that overseas bases and support will be unnecessary.

### General Impressions Received as a Result of This Briefing

SAC is, in effect, a sort of "elite corps" dominated by a forceful and dedicated commander, who has complete confidence in SAC's ability to crush Russia quickly by massive atomic bombing attacks. No aspect of the morals or long-range effect of such attacks were discussed, and no questions on it were asked.

SAC has planned a thorough and exacting training program — and is carrying it out. Accordingly, SAC is probably in a higher state of combat readiness today than any other U.S. military command.

SAC now must rely heavily on much in-flight refueling to carry out his strike plans.

SAC is confident that when the bell rings they will get the lion's share of the stockpile no matter what the JCS "allocations" are at the moment.

SAC purposely gives the impression at such briefings that they consider themselves a "delivery service" to attack whatever targets the JCS tell them to attack — and, in effect, do not *originate* strategic air targets directly or indirectly.

— W. B. Moore
Capt, USN

## The Navy's View of Nuclear Weapons

### *Document 14*

This excerpt from a 1959 article in *Fortune* outlines the Navy's view of nuclear weapons. Not surprisingly, the Navy assigns a great deal of importance to nuclear weapons launched from the Navy's new strategic submarines. The Navy also criticizes the Eisenhower administration's reliance on SAC, claiming that it leads strategy to a dead end. Adm. Arleigh Burke, Chief of Naval Operations, calls for more mobile-based nuclear weapons — for example, submarines. The article also points out how important it was for each branch of the armed forces to have a nuclear role. When the Army lost out on its bid for its own ICBM, its share of the defense budget fell.

## 14 THE NEW MIX
## Charles J.V. Murphy

### At Flank Speed

There can be little question about what the U.S. Navy expects of Captain Gayler in the Pacific. What can the U.S. expect of the Navy? How effective can a navy be in this nuclear age?

The U.S. Navy's response to these questions now comes with a confidence inspired by a revolutionary technology that it has fostered during the last few years. This technology, as we shall see, has provided the Navy with an extraordinary new weapon "mix," the Polaris-armed submarine, and, equally important in the Navy's view, a great new class of carriers. The Navy has already won some important battles in Washington, and it is strenuously and confidently pressing the strategic doctrine it has built around its weapon mix. It fought hard for the $11.6 billion in new money that it was allotted in the fiscal 1960 budget. It has served notice that it intends to push even harder for more in the fiscal 1961 budget, now in preparation in the Pentagon. The Navy is driving at flank speed toward four targets: a tremendous expansion of the nuclear-submarine fleet; a huge increment of nuclear-powered carriers; a brand-new system of highly functionalized, highly technical apparatus for dealing with the threat presented by the Soviet submarine flotillas; and finally, a general program for replacing all its World War II vessels (81 per cent of its 870 ships) before "block" obsolescence overtakes the fleet between 1962 and 1965.

What the Navy is asking for involves tremendous expenditures of money that many Congressmen believe can be better spent on other weapons. The Navy, too, is troubled by the costs of its weapons. When it sought another big carrier, its eighth, in the new budget, it stipulated one of the oil-burning *Forrestal* class, costing about $280 million, although two years ago Congress gave it the nuclear *Enterprise*. The reason for the Navy's strange stepback, after presenting a convincing case for the nuclear carrier, was that the cost of *Enterprise*'s propulsion unit had soared to $120 million, from an original estimate of $70 million, bringing her total cost to about $380 million (not counting her aircraft). Several months ago the House turned the Navy down, but the Senate Appropriations Subcommittee early in July restored the carrier, stipulating, however, that it be nuclear, and of the *Enterprise* class. The Navy's earlier argument for nuclear carriers had been more persuasive than the Navy itself dared hope.

The Navy's case is based on certain fundamental convictions the Navy has arrived at about national strategy. In recent months Admiral Arleigh A. Burke, Chief of Naval Operations, has suggested in public statements that the current trend of U.S. military investment, with its preponderant emphasis on heavy nuclear weapons for massive retaliation, and by implication its emphasis on the Strategic Air Command, is leading our strategy to a dead end. The U.S. delivery systems and the nuclear stockpiles now in hand, Burke argues, are sufficient to destroy our likely adversaries several times over. Among military planners, the term for this excess capacity is overkill. In the judgment of Burke and his Navy planners, the apparatus now in place or near prospect for massive retaliation is adequate to deter a general war. Burke goes a step beyond. He has concluded that, for the time being,

"Russia and the U.S. have reached a state of mutual intimidation" with their nuclear weapons; but it is likely to remain so only for *the time being*, because SAC's major delivery systems, bomber fleets as well as ICBM's, are all, in Burke's nomenclature, "fixed-based" systems. By this he means that they are tied to the land. Because their positions are certain to become known to our adversaries, their vulnerability to surprise attack is bound to increase dangerously as the Soviet Union's ICBM capability rises; hence an urgent need for a *mobile* general-war deterrent. The only system now in view which fits that definition is the Navy's Polaris-armed submarine, which will take the nuclear deterrent down into the ocean deep and keep it there in silent, hidden motion.

Burke's case for a new approach to nuclear strategy includes a corollary proposition. As the U.S. deterrent to general war is once again stabilized, the greater will be the possibilities of peripheral or limited wars. Hence a continuing requirement for big carriers. Burke's case for them rests on their mobility, and on naval aviation's competence in precision bombing with "iron" bombs (TNT) and missiles and its well-developed teamwork with the Marine Corps — factors that make the carriers a unique shield behind which the nation's capability for limited war can be maintained and projected.

Yet, in another context, the Navy sometimes justifies the carriers on the ground that they will broaden the nation's general-war or nuclear capability, since they can be used to launch nuclear-armed planes. And at the same time it is promoting the revolutionary and costly Polaris program as a general-war system. From this somewhat contradictory logic, the landlubber might suspect that the Navy, at this stage of its postwar evolution, hasn't quite made up its mind whether the theory of massive retaliation has indeed reached a dead end. The truth is that the Navy, like the Army, is struggling to hold on to its position in the strategic present while it maneuvers for a more promising position in the strategic future. Nuclear weaponry is where the big money is going now. When the Army lost out in its bid for the ICBM, its share of the national military budget began to decrease — from nearly 37 per cent in fiscal 1953 to not quite 23 per cent in fiscal 1960. Meanwhile the Air Force's share rose from 34 per cent to nearly 46 per cent. The Navy has stubbornly held its own. In fact, its share has slightly improved, from slightly less than 27 per cent in 1953 to better than 28 per cent in fiscal 1960. . . .

The Navy's shrewdness and foresight are reflected in several major items in the budget for fiscal 1960. The Navy has asked for $611 million, about 5.4 per cent of the total Navy budget, for the Polaris program. There is a $971-million item for research and development. During the past ten years the Navy has been acutely solicitious about research, even more so than the Air Force. And finally, there is a composite item of about $2.1 billion for new air power, in which are intermixed the current requirements for the new carrier and new aircraft. Thus the Navy is spreading itself across a broad range of nuclear and air technologies, all fitted to the sea.

## The Strange Fleet

The Navy, however, has retained a stable proportion of the military budget only by unabashedly discarding certain cherished dogmas. The turning point came when it discovered that a strategic-range solid-fuel missile was feasible, and that it could be fitted, without too much trouble, to the high-speed, nuclear-powered submarines that were being independently developed. Four years ago the Navy appeared to be frozen out of the IRBM and ICBM technology. It had an understanding with the Army that it would try to adapt the Army's IRBM Jupiter for launching from the deck of a converted merchantman or battleship, but few naval officers were attracted by the idea. The Jupiter weighs about fifty-five tons loaded for flight; it stands sixty feet high. Launching so cumbersome a vehicle from a deck in any sort of sea would be tricky business at best; and the fire hazard of its huge cargo of liquid oxygen was hardly appealing to a sailor. In the fall of 1955 the Navy began to experiment with solid propellants for ship-launched missiles. To its astonishment, it quickly found that a reliable fuel could be developed for a missile of 1,500-mile range. Not many months later, the Atomic Energy Commission learned that the weight of the thermonuclear warhead could be drastically reduced. These discoveries were at once put together by the Navy in the Polaris — a missile weighing about fifteen tons and only twenty-eight feet tall, small enough to go in a submarine. . . .

These ballistic submarines are among the strangest craft ever to take to the sea. Submerged, they displace 6,700 tons, are more than one-third as long (about 400 feet) as a *Forrestal* carrier, carry a crew of about 100 men, and will have a battery of sixteen missiles equipped in later versions with a warhead of near-megaton power. Being nuclear driven, they can cruise for weeks at depths of hundreds of feet, and so lie pretty much out of reach of all but the most esoteric tracking techniques. They will fire their missiles while submerged, using compressed air to shoot them just above the surface where the engines will ignite. On the basis of the Navy's already extensive experience with nuclear submarines, the expectation is that these craft will remain submerged on station, for months at a time, and that each will be manned by two full crews, who will relieve each other between patrols.

The submarine by itself costs about $100 million. To build the kind of fleet the Navy wants, with supporting tenders and shore facilities, would mean a capital outlay approaching $9 billion; the annual operating cost is estimated at about $300 million. The same capital investment would produce upwards of eleven wings of B-52 bombers, which would, of course, carry many more weapons of much greater power. The Navy's counter to the unfavorable cost factor is that SAC is becoming vulnerable on its bases to Soviet ICBM's, while the Polaris-armed submarines will be relatively immune to surprise or discovery in their deep, ever shifting ocean stations.

The logic underlying the request for a fleet of forty to fifty derives from two assumptions. Even with the two-crew conception, a nuclear submarine must return periodically to port to refit; the current assumption, for planning purposes, is that three Polaris submarines will be needed in order to keep two constantly at sea. The other assumption, which is not endorsed by Air Force planners, is that only about 150 to 175 target complexes in the U.S.S.R. are worth considering in a deterrent-retaliatory strategy. Although the Navy has not yet come right out and said the U.S. could get along without SAC, it does claim that twenty Polaris submarines on station, within range of the Soviet hinterland, would mean 320 Navy missiles in readiness, enough to deal with a decisive share of the targets, after allowing for 75 per cent reliability.

What is wryly interesting to those who remember the Navy's attack on the Air Force's nuclear doctrine during the B-36 hearings is that the sailors, in the process of inventing a weapon system that would retain for them a powerful role in a general-war strategy, have embraced a system possessed of the same moral and military blemishes they had earlier found in Air Force doctrine. This point doesn't appear to have embarrassed the Navy, now that it is having such success in adapting a revolutionary technology to the tactics and strategy of the sea. Nor does the Navy recognize institutionally the apparent inconsistency between its pressure for more Polarises and its "overkill" argument. Here its logic rests on the straightforward argument that SAC is too vulnerable to be trusted. Touching on this aspect of the debate in his testimony in March before the Senate Preparedness Subcommittee, Burke went so far as to theorize that, forty-eight hours after the outbreak of a general war, "it [might] well be that we will have the [only] power that is left . . . The Navy power at sea."

## Eisenhower Develops Single Integrated Operational Plan (SIOP) for Nuclear War

### *Document 15*

In this excerpt from a long article on the history of U.S. nuclear strategy, David Alan Rosenberg describes the intense interservice rivalry over nuclear weapons and nuclear war plans. President Eisenhower was greatly angered by this rivalry and made a major effort to overcome it. Rosenberg also describes how this rivalry helped generate a huge list of targets to be hit in the Soviet Union, numbering more than two thousand. Eisenhower found the overkill in such plans distressing. He finally succeeded in creating an integrated nuclear planning structure, the Joint Strategic Target Planning Staff, and an integrated plan for nuclear war, the Single Integrated Operational Plan, in 1960. This article is taken from a paper presented at a conference, "The Theory and Practice of American National Security, 1945–1960," held April 21–23, 1982, at the United States Military Academy, West Point, New York.

### 15 THE ORIGINS OF OVERKILL
### David Alan Rosenberg

On the morning of August 11, 1960, Secretary of Defense Thomas Gates met at the White House with President Dwight Eisenhower and top defense officials to present his proposal for coordinating planning for the use of strategic nuclear forces in the massive, simultaneous strike against the "Sino-Soviet bloc" planned for the first twenty-four hours of a war. Gates proposed that the commander in chief of the Strategic Air Command (SAC) be designated as "Director of Strategic Target Planning" with authority to develop, on behalf of the Joint Chiefs of Staff (JCS), a National Strategic Target List (NSTL) and a Single Integrated Operational Plan (SIOP). The defense secretary stopped short of endorsing the Air Force position that SAC should be given operational command of all U.S. nuclear forces. Gates argued, however, that the advent of operational ballistic missile forces, particularly Polaris missile submarines, created an urgent need for an integrated target and attack plan to replace the current system of joint target guidance, separate command operational plans, and periodic coordinating conferences. His proposal would also eliminate duplication of effort, estimated at 200 to 300 targets, thereby reducing weapons requirements.[19]

A heated two-hour discussion ensued. Admiral Arleigh Burke, the Chief of Naval Operations, told the President:

> This is not a compromise. . . . This proposal is a radical departure from previous practice. I am fearful that if the responsibility and authority for making a single operation plan is delegated to a single commander [then] the JCS will have lost control over operations at the beginning of a general war.

Burke argued that the JCS should retain "not only basic responsibility for directing effort in general war, but the means for generating the basic plans and for controlling the development of these plans."[20] Putting the NSTL and SIOP under SAC would undermine JCS authority, restrict the military options available to U.S. unified theater commanders, alarm NATO allies, and give SAC excessive influence in determining atomic weapons requirements and allocations, force levels and deployments, and military budgets. Coordination should be achieved by assigning retaliatory tasks — "not in specific detail" — to the unified commanders, including SAC, with the JCS directing implementation. Burke recommended that no final decision be made until the procedure had been tested and the Joint Chiefs had thoroughly evaluated the product.

Air Force General Nathan Twining, the chairman of the JCS, bristled at Burke's presentation. For ten years, he stated, the JCS had tried and failed to improve coordination in nuclear planning. The major stumbling block was always the Navy, whose leaders adamantly refused to adapt their carrier task forces or attack plans to unified command. Now Burke wanted the first NSTL and SIOP developed on an experimental basis only, in hopes that the process could be sabotaged.

The President rebuked Twining for this accusation, "a little bit gently," Burke thought, and commented that "too much emotion was being displayed over this question." This was not, Eisenhower said, "a good way to respond to serious military problems, nor did it speak too well of the ability of good men to get together and work out solutions in the nation's interest." There must be agreement that "rigid planning" was needed, and that it would not be "sufficient to assign retaliatory missions from the JCS to the different commanders." "This whole thing," he stressed, "has to be on a completely integrated basis. It must be firmly laid on. The initial strike must be simultaneous," and must utilize both Navy and Air Force nuclear capability, for "if we put large forces outside of the plan, we defeat the whole concept of retaliatory effort, which takes priority over everything else." The only question, as the President saw it, was who should develop the plan. He was inclined to agree with Gates that SAC was the logical choice. He approved preparation of an initial NSTL and SIOP as proposed, but agreed with Burke that the JCS should review the completed plans and recommend whether to continue the procedure. A final decision would be made by December 1960, so that Eisenhower would not "leave his successor with the monstrosity" of uncoordinated, unintegrated forces now in prospect.[21]

Within two weeks, the new Joint Strategic Target Planning Staff (JSTPS) headed by General Thomas S. Power, the SAC commander, was at work in Omaha, manned by 219 SAC personnel (who also retained their SAC staff jobs), 29 Navy, 10 Army, 3 Marine, and 8 additional non-SAC Air Force officers. Their efforts were guided by a National Strategic Targeting and Attack Policy (NSTAP) previously prepared by the JCS and approved by Gates.[22] Still classified, it appears to have called for a plan "which will provide for the optimum integration of committed forces for the attack of a minimum list of targets." Soviet strategic nuclear capability received first priority, followed by "primary military and government control centers of major importance." The NSTAP also called for a 90 percent probability of severe damage to at least 50 percent of industrial floor space in urban-industrial targets. The assurance of delivery factor in each case was to be at least 75 percent.[23]

By November, the JSTPS had produced the first NSTL and SIOP. Recently declassified Navy papers outline their grim parameters.[24] The JSTPS selected 2600 separate installations for attack, out of a target data base of 4100. This translated into an NSTL of approximately 1050 Designated Ground Zeros (DGZs) for nuclear weapons, including 151 urban-industrial targets. Given sufficient warning, the United States would launch its entire strategic force carrying 3500 nuclear weapons against the Soviet Union, Communist China, and the satellite nations. At the very least, an "alert force" composed of 880 bombers and missiles would attack some 650 DGZs (including 170 defense suppression targets) with over 1400 weapons having a total yield of 2100 megatons.[25]

The SIOP aimed for an assurance of delivery factor of 97 percent for the first 200 DGZs, and 93 percent for the next 400, well above the goals established by the NSTAP.[26] To achieve such levels, multiple strikes with high yield weapons were laid on against many individual targets. Little effort was made to develop an objectives plan based on what targets would have to be destroyed to achieve U.S. war aims. Instead the SIOP was a *capabilities plan*, aimed at utilizing all available forces to achieve maximum destruction.[27] As a result, although it eliminated duplication in targeting, it did not reduce the size of the target list. The plan made no distinction among different target systems, but called for simultaneous attacks on nuclear delivery forces, governmental control centers, and the urban-industrial base.

Navy leaders were quick to criticize the completed SIOP. They pointed out that the JSTPS had failed to determine the minimum force necessary to achieve military objectives, and had failed to leave an adequate reserve for follow-up strikes. They strongly objected to the excessively high damage and assurance criteria, and to SAC's failure to consider the secondary effects of blast, fire, and radiation in projecting damage. One Navy estimate noted that according to SAC's criteria, the damage caused by a 13 kiloton bomb on Hiroshima could only be assured by assigning 300 to 500 kilotons of weapons to a similar target.[28] Such inefficient, redundant targeting would also cause unmanageable levels of radioactive fallout. Admiral Harry Felt worried that if the whole SIOP were executed, his Pacific Command might have to be "more concerned about residual radiation damage resulting from our own weapons than from those of the enemy."[29] Another Navy message noted that executing just the alert force portion of the SIOP, "and assuming only one weapon delivered to each DGZ, the fallout already exceeds JCS limits for points such as Helsinki, Berlin, Budapest, Northern Japan, and Seoul."[30]

Even more important, the SIOP was not tailored to either retaliation or preemption. As Burke observed: "counterforce receives higher precedence than is warranted for a retaliatory plan, the less precedence than is warranted for an initiative plan."[31] He thought that plans should be made for each option under consideration, as well as for discriminating between Soviet targets and those in satellite nations.[32]

Burke communicated Navy concern through various channels to Eisenhower, who in early November dispatched his science adviser, Harvard professor George B. Kistiakowsky, to Omaha. Kistiakowsky came away convinced that the SAC/JSTPS "damage criteria and the directives to the planners are such as to lead to unnecessary and undesirable overkill."[33] He found that many judgments made in preparing the plans were arbitrary, and the SAC's vaunted computer procedures were in some cases "sheer bull." The SIOP itself, made up from a "background of plenty" in weapons and delivery systems, made a virtue of excess: "I believe that the alert force is probably all right, but not the follow-on forces which carry megatons to kill 4 and 5 times over somebody who is already dead."[34]

Kistiakowsky presented his evaluation to the President on the morning of November 25. The presentation, Eisenhower confided to his naval aide, Captain E.P. "Pete" Aurand, "frighten[ed] the devil out of me." The sheer numbers of targets, the redundant targeting, and the enormous overkill surprised and horrified him. Kistiakowsky, a scientist who represented no parochial service interest, had made the President realize that the SIOP might not be a rational instrument for controlling nuclear planning, but rather an engine generating escalating force requirements. He wondered whether a better strategy might be to reserve the Polaris force as a backup, and allow SAC "to have just one whack — not ten whacks" at each target, relying on Polaris "to clean up what isn't done," with the aid of reconnaissance satellites. We have got to set limits, he told Aurand, "We've got to get this thing right down to the deterrence."[35] . . .

## Coordinating Nuclear Targeting Strategy

By 1959, the sheer number of forces involved in atomic operations was creating serious command, control, and communication problems, even without the added complications of a Polaris fleet. JCS Chairman Twining was convinced that the "atomic coordination machinery" needed a major overhaul, but that the JCS were too divided to come up with any workable proposals. What was required was a "command decision." In August 1959, Twining sent Secretary of Defense McElroy his assessment of "Target Coordination and Associated Problems," and his proposed solutions. While not producing immediate action, this memo laid the groundwork for the establishment of the Joint Strategic Target Planning Staff the following year.

As early as 1952, Joint Coordination Centers had been established in Great Britain and Hawaii to help coordinate the operations of all U.S. atomic capable forces in war. To supplement this wartime coordination structure, in 1955, the unified and specified commanders began to meet annually at the Pentagon for "Worldwide Coordination Conferences," to review each others' target lists and war plans for inconsistencies and duplication before submitting them to the JCS for approval. Recent war games had indicated, however, that out of about 2,400 current targets, there were still some 300 duplications. These could result in "fratricidal" kills of friendly aircraft under chaotic wartime conditions. It was apparent, Twining wrote, that "atomic operations must be pre-planned for automatic execution to the maximum extent possible and with the minimum reliance on post-H-hour communications."[36]

The solution, Twining believed, would be to establish a clear national targeting policy, presumably based on the forthcoming recommendations of the Hickey committee study, and then to prepare a "national strategic target system" and a "single integrated operational plan," which could be objectively war gamed to identify areas of weakness or excess. Since SAC had the most experience in nuclear war planning, the best computer resources, and the bulk of the nuclear delivery forces, SAC should be responsible for preparing the target list and operational plan, under JCS control. To integrate Polaris into this arrangement, an "appropriate nucleus of Naval officers" could be assigned to the SAC staff, until such time as it was deemed desirable to create a Unified Strategic Command. This approach, Twining believed, would establish a clear framework, subject to objective analysis, within which target and coordination conflicts could be readily resolved.[37]

Twining's own preference was for the "optimum mix" targeting strategy, which combined counterforce targets with control centers, war-sustaining resources, and population centers. The Hickey committee endorsed this concept. This February 1960 report recommended a target list for Fiscal Year 1962 consisting of 2,021 targets, including 121 ICBM sites, 140 air defense bases, 200 bomber bases, 218 military and governmental control centers, and 124 other military targets, such as naval bases and nuclear weapons facilities, with the remaining targets apparently located primarily within 131 urban centers.[38] The list had been developed based on SAC methods of analysis, and clearly endorsed SAC's basic strategy.[39] The committee had implicitly rejected both no-cities counterforce and finite deterrence, and had opted for combining a decisive blow against Soviet will and capability to make war with a blunting attack on Soviet nuclear delivery capability. The Hickey target list was similar in composition to the list for 1960 prepared by the Air Intelligence Directorate in support of force level objectives, but, consistent with the President's desire to place limits on the offensive, it was fully 43 percent shorter. With Twining's enthusiastic support, Eisenhower approved the Hickey committee recommendation as the "point of departure" for all future JCS planning.[40]

By late 1959, Eisenhower's concept of massive retaliation appears to have been reduced to a strategy of desperate resolve. Appalled by the unimaginable destruction the United States might inflict or suffer in general war, he could no longer see beyond the first disastrous nuclear exchange. "All we really have that is meaningful is a deterrent," he repeatedly told his advisers.[41] "The central question is whether or not we have the ability to destroy anyone who attacks us, because the biggest thing today is to provide a deterrent to war."[42]

Eisenhower could not conceive of second strike counterforce as a feasible option, and turned aside the Air Force plea for the B-70 on these grounds. It was "crazy" to think that a manned bomber could "search out and knock out mobile ICBMs on railroads" after a Soviet strike. "We are not going to be searching out mobile bases for ICBMs, we are going to be hitting the big industrial and control complexes."[43] He similarly dismissed Navy arguments for using Polaris to provide a controlled, deliberate, and selective response to surprise attack. Polaris would be useful primarily "to disrupt and knock out organized defenses" in order to clear the way for SAC bombers, he stated in the spring of 1960.[44] He ruled against making "a full commitment" to the Polaris program until it was further tested and modified.[45]

Although Eisenhower had largely abandoned hope of disarming the Soviet Union, and increasingly favored targeting Soviet cities, he continued to emphasize the importance of rapid response. In May 1960, the President was briefed on the programming requirements for the solid-fueled, silo-based Minuteman ICBM, scheduled to be deployed in three squadrons of fifty missiles each in 1963. Current guidance, he was told, would permit only "volley" or "ripple" firing of an entire squadron, and did not provide for alternative target tapes to permit retargeting. In addition, the necessity of keeping the gyros in the inertial guidance system in constant operation in order to meet the requirement of firing within thirty seconds posed certain technical difficulties. These could be resolved by relaxing the requirement to about ten minutes. Eisenhower expressed support for exploring ways to make the Minuteman system more flexible, especially since the thirty-second rule "would allow no margin for error, and raise the chances of starting a war no one wanted." It might be better "to take a few extra minutes, to give someone high up in authority the decision." Any longer delay, even with hardened silos, might spell disaster.[46]

The Eisenhower Administration's top secret review of "U.S. Policy in the Event of War," approved by the NSC in March 1959, appears to have kept open the option of preemptive response to an impending Soviet strike, without specifically endorsing it. NSC-5904/1 was considered so sensitive that even its title was classified. In December 1959, reflecting ambiguity in high policy, as well as increasing doubts as to the feasibility of preemption, the JCS split over whether JSCP guidance should provide for "the possibility of obtaining strategic warning of sufficient precision to impel the President to direct the initiation of operations by United States forces."[47] The following month, in connection with targeting strategy, Twining raised with the President "certain questions relating to pre-emptive attack under conditions of conclusive advanced warning."[48] Although Eisenhower may have been less secure in his determination to launch SAC immediately in response to Soviet aggression, there is no indication that his basic position had shifted.

On July 6, 1960, Secretary of Defense Gates reported to the President that in fifteen meetings with the JCS since taking office in January he had been unable to resolve the basic splits over targeting and coordination. Gates did not believe that SAC and Polaris should be placed under a single operational command, but, like JCS Chairman Twining, felt strongly that an integrated target list and operational plan must be prepared for the nuclear striking force. Since the Joint Staff did not have the necessary computer capability, these plans should be prepared by SAC as an agent of the JCS. The Army and Navy viewed this proposal as a power play by the Air Force, Gates reported, and were firmly resisting it.

Eisenhower expressed disgust at the inability of the services, especially the Navy, to cooperate with each other. The "original mistake in this whole business," he remarked, "was our failure to create one single Service in 1947." Perhaps the JCS should be ordered to work together, and told "that if they fail to come up with an integrated plan within six months they will all be replaced." He agreed that a single plan was needed, and had no objection to assigning the task to SAC as agents of the JCS, as long as SAC planners were "augmented with personnel from the other Services." Gates agreed to work out a solution along these lines. "If SAC takes over the functions of the Joint Chiefs," he told the President, "it is the fault of the Chiefs themselves."[49]

### *The First SIOP: Institutionalization of Overkill*

On August 11, President Eisenhower formally approved Gates's proposal for the creation of the JSTPS, under SAC domination, to prepare the National Strategic Target List and Single Integrated Operational Plan. Accepting the finality of the President's ruling, Arleigh Burke left the meeting prepared to put his weight behind an effort to produce "the best possible NSTL and SIOP."[50] He sent a strong group of officers to Omaha, and urged Army Chief of Staff George Decker to do the same. Decker, however, considered the SIOP less relevant to Army concerns than the problem of limited war, and did not believe that his planners could influence its development in the limited time allowed.[51] Lacking effective Army support, and greatly outnumbered within the JSTPS, the Navy planners could do little to curb what they perceived to be excesses in the plan. In late November, Burke prepared an analysis of potential problems in the SIOP for General Lemnitzer, who had replaced Twining as Chairman of the JCS in September. Although the plan was basically acceptable, Burke wrote, there were problem areas which needed attention, including the high assurance of delivery and damage criteria, and anticipated excessive fallout.[52]

Burke's memorandum was passed on to Eisenhower on November 27, two days after Kistiakowsky's briefing. Shocked and angered by the level of overkill envisioned in the SIOP, the President realized that his attempt to set limits had failed. The NSTL was 29 percent longer than the approved Hickey committee list, and whatever restraints had been imposed on target selection had been negated by increased overlapping of weapons to achieve the high assurance criteria. By this time, however, it was too late for reconsideration. Even Burke, despite his reservations about the SIOP, did not consider withholding approval, although he hoped the JCS might express qualified endorsement and subject the completed plan to rigorous war gaming.[53] On December 2, the JCS approved SIOP-62, apparently without reservations, and Eisenhower passed on to his successor both the completed plan, as the nation's operational nuclear war plan for Fiscal Year 1962, and the criticisms which had been made of it.[54]

Although SAC's commitment to maximizing the impact of available forces accounted for the level of overkill institutionalized in the SIOP, it was the "background of plenty" in nuclear weapons and delivery vehicles which made it possible. Both the Truman and Eisenhower administrations had consciously promoted expansion of the strategic striking force. The overlapping and duplication which accompanied the shift from bombers to missiles toward the end of the Eisenhower years exacerbated the tendency toward excess. When Eisenhower left office, SAC had 538 B-52, 1,292 B-47, and 19 B-58 bombers, plus 1,094 tankers. Twelve Atlas ICBMs had been deployed in the United States; there were 60 Thor IRBMs in Britain; 30 Jupiter IRBMs were being deployed to Italy, and agreements had been signed to deploy them to Turkey as well. Construction of over 650 additional Atlas, Titan, and Minuteman missiles had been authorized, in addition to fourteen Polaris submarines, each of which was armed with sixteen missiles. The first Polaris submarine, U.S.S. George Washington, departed on deterrent patrol in November 1960.[55]

Expansion of the nuclear weapons stockpile was even more rapid. Eisenhower never took action to cut back the produciton of weapons designated for the strategic air offensive, despite his growing convinction that the nation already had more than adequate striking power. He also remained committed to using tactical nuclear weapons in limited conflict situations whenever militarily appropriate, and did not want to see their "possibilities" neglected, despite increasing doubts about whether it would be possible to "contain any limited war or keep it from spreading into general war" if such weapons were employed.[56] As a result, tactical nuclear weapons, like bullets, were stockpiled against a time of need, as were large numbers of air defense warheads. All were widely dispersed to prevent their destruction. From 1958 to 1960, the U.S. stockpile tripled in size, apparently growing from 6,000 to 18,000 weapons in only two years.[57]

The growth of U.S. nuclear capability was largely justified in terms of the need to counter a growing Soviet nuclear threat. The commitment to counterforce established under Truman and reinforced by Eisenhower was clearly a response to the unprecedented perils of the 1950s, as the nation suddenly found itself facing for the first time the possibility of physical annihilation. The President and his military advisers, particularly the Air Force high command, understandably perceived that their most urgent duty was to defend against that threat. By the time Eisenhower left office, the Strategic Air Command had been preparing and training for nearly a decade not only for massive retaliation, but for massive preemption. U.S. forces were routinely sized toward the objective of neutralizing Soviet nuclear forces, which were often grossly overestimated as a result of inadequate intelligence.

Despite growth of the planned U.S. nuclear offensive from a few dozen targets in 1948 to more than 2,500 in 1960, however, the secure achievement of the ability to disarm the Soviet Union appeared to remain just beyond reach. In the late 1950s, WSEG and the Air Force both produced pessimistic assessments of present and future U.S. capability to successfully locate, target, and destroy Soviet nuclear delivery forces, including mobile and concealed missiles.[58] Because counterforce was considered critical, but possibly infeasible, the Air Force held to the concept of striking Soviet war-making capacity as a crucial backup strategy. The atomic offensive against the urban-industrial base had initially been conceived as a means of maximizing the impact of scarce nuclear resources, but, with the advent of thermonuclear weapons, had appeared to promise in addition the possibility of successfully carrying out a single war-winning strike, thus avoiding a costly protracted struggle. General Thomas Power, conscious of SAC's limitations in both target intelligence and capability for repeated, sustained high and low level bomber operations in hostile Soviet air space, was particularly adamant in his commitment to the "optimum mix" strategy. When RAND strategist William Kaufmann visited SAC headquarters in the winter of 1961 to present a briefing on his ongoing study of counterforce, Power reacted with an angry cable to Chief of Staff White. The SAC commander wanted it made perfectly clear that Kaufmann's arguments did not reflect the current or future thrust of Air Force thinking.[59]

The RAND strategists, however, found a receptive audience in the incoming Kennedy Administration, and especially in Secretary of Defense Robert McNamara. When McNamara was briefed on SIOP-62 on February 4, 1961, he was disturbed by the rigidity of the plan, the "fantastic" fallout and destruction it would produce, and the absence of a clear strategic rationale for the counterforce/urban-industrial target mix.[60] The following month, he initiated an intensive reevaluation of U.S. strategic posture, including a review of basic national security policy with regard to nuclear weapons and "assumptions relating to 'counterforce' strikes," and an assessment by the JCS of the feasibility of planning for "controlled response and negotiating pauses" in the midst of a thermonuclear war. He also reconvened the Hickey committee to study quantitative requirements for deterrence through 1967, utilizing new intelligence data. This report, which contained updates of the target list developed in 1959–1960, was completed in June 1961.[61]

## Notes

19. This meeting is described in two documents: Andrew Goodpaster, Memorandum of Conference with the President (hereafter cited as MCP), August 11, 1960, dated August 13, 1960, in Staff Notes, August 1960 — 3 Folder, Box 51, DDE Diary, Ann C. Whitman File, Dwight D. Eisenhower Papers as President (hereafter ACWF, EPP), Dwight D. Eisenhower Library, Abilene, Kansas (hereafter DDEL); and Admiral Arleigh Burke, rough draft Memorandum for the Record, Subject: Meeting with the President on SecDef's Proposal to turn Targetting [*sic*] and the Preparation of Single Integrated Operational Plan over to SAC, 11 August 1960, in NSTL/SIOP Briefing Folder, Papers of Admiral Arleigh A. Burke (hereafter cited as AAB), Operation Archives, Naval Historical Center, Washington, D.C. (hereafter NHC).
20. Untitled memorandum, dated August 11, 1960, appended to MCP, August 13, 1960. This was a typed, unsigned version of Admiral Burke's arguments. The original handwritten and first typed drafts of this memo are contained in NSTL/SIOP Briefing Folder, AAB, NHC.
21. MCP, August 13, 1960.
22. History and Research Division, Headquarters, Strategic Air Command, *History of the Joint Strategic Target Planning Staff, Background and Preparation of SIOP-62* (partially declassified history released by the declassification branch, Joint Secretariat, Joint Chiefs of Staff, in April 1980), p. 14. Seventy-nine airmen and civilians were among the 219 SAC personnel assigned to JSTPS.
23. Portions of the NSTAP are quoted or described in Message, CNO to CINCLANTFLT, CINCPACFLT, CINCUSNAVEUR, R201933Z November 1960, NSTL/SIOP Messages, Exclusives and Personals, AAB, NHC; Memo, Op-06C to Op-00, Subject: CNO Discussions regarding NSTL/SIOP with Generals Lemnitzer, Decker, and Spivy on 9 Nov., with Enclosure, Precis re Army participation in the NSTL/SIOP dated 1 November 1960, BM00211-60, 8 November 1960; Special Edition, Flag Officers Dope, 4 December 1960; and Memo for the Record, by Rear Admiral Paul Blackburn, Subject: "Comments on the Questions," no serial, 12 October 1960, all in Memos and Letters (NSTL) Folder, AAB, NHC; and letter, Thomas Gates to Brigadier General A.J. Goodpaster, 10 August 1960, with draft memo to the JCS and TABS B and C, in Department of Defense Vol. IV-7, August 1960 Folder, Box 2, Department of Defense Subseries, Subject Series, White House Office, Staff Secretary (hereafter WHO-SS), DDEL.
24. In the summer of 1981, the Department of the Navy Declassification Team conducted two separate declassification reviews of five folders in the Arleigh Burke papers, NHC: the NSTL/SIOP Briefing Folder, the Memos & Letters (NSTL) Folder, the NSTL/SIOP Messages Folder, the Transcripts & Phone Cons (NSTL) Folder, and the NSTL/SIOP Messages-Exclusives & Personals Folder. A substantial portion of each of these folders was declassified. The information and statistics on the NSTAP, NSTL, and SIOP in this paper are based on information contained in those folders, particularly the periodic reports sent to Admiral Burke by Navy representatives in Omaha, and internal Office of the Chief of Naval Operations memoranda discussing Navy courses of action to deal with the evolving planning effort. Since JCS papers remain classified, it is not possible to confirm the accuracy and completeness of this information.
25. This information is derived from material contained in Special Edition, Flag Officers Dope, 4 December 1960; Memo, Rear Admiral C.V. Ricketts (Op-60) to Op-00, Op-60 BM-0001028-60, Subject: JCS 2056/189, The Initial NSTL & SIOP, 22 November 1960; Memo, Arleigh Burke for General Lemnitzer, Op-00 Memo 000683-60, Subject: NSTL/SIOP, 22 November 1960; Memo, Rear Admiral Paul Blackburn, Op-60C, to Op-00, BM-000222-60, Subject: Message Traffic Between CINCs and CNO, comments concerning, with Enclosures 1 and 2 summarizing messages; Resume of NSTL-SIOP Briefing, Offutt AFB, 28 September 1960, Attached to Op-06C to Op-00, BM-000167-60, 29 September; and Joint Strategic Target Planning Agency, Memo for the Record, Subject: Minutes of 1st Meeting of the Policy Committee, B-76824, 14 September 1960, all in Memos and Letters

(NSTL) Folder, AAB, NHC; and Message, to RBEP with JCS, Report of Preliminary Review of SIOP-62, 182250Z January 1961; Message, CNO to CINCPAC, CINCPACFLT, CINCLANTFLT, CINCUSNAVEUR, 241843Z November 1960; Cable, Brigadier General J.A. Spivy, USA, JCS Liaison Group Offutt, to JCS for Director, Joint Staff, Subject: 11th Weekly Activity Report–14th Meeting of Policy Committee, November 15–16, 19 November 1960; Message, CNO to CINCPACFLT, CINCLANTFLT, CINCUSNAVEUR, 0051/06 November 1960; and Message, CINCLANT to CNO, From Vice Admiral Fitzhugh Lee for Rear Admiral Blackburn, Subject: JSTPS Progress, 2031Z/22 October 1960; all in NSTL/SIOP Messages Folder, AAB, NHC. Five hundred ninety-nine DGZs covered nuclear delivery capability and government and military control centers; 151 convered the urban industrial base. This comprised the "Minimum NSTL." There were also 227 defensive DGZs, and 65 "other" DGZs, for a total NSTL of 1042. Cable, Spivy to JCS, 19 November 1960.

26. Memo, Burke to Lemnitzer, 22 November 1960; Message, CINCLANT to CNO, Subject: JSTPS Progress, 2031Z/22 October 1960.
27. Message, CNO to CINCPACFLT, CINCLANTFLT, CINCUSNAVEUR, 0051/06 November 1960; and Special Edition, Flag Officers Dope, 4 December 1960.
28. Precis appended to Memo, Op-06C to Op 00, BM-00211-60, 8 November 1960.
29. Message, CINCPAC to RBEP with JCS, Report of Preliminary Review of SIOP-62, 182250Z January 1961, NSTL-SIOP Messages Folder, AAB, NHC.
30. Message, CINCLANT to CNO, Subject: JSTPS Progress, 2031Z/22 October 1960.
31. Message, CNO to CINCLANTFLT, CINCPACFLT, CINCUSNAVEUR, R 201933Z November 1960.
32. Memo, Arleigh Burke to Rear Admiral Blackburn, Subject: Political Aspects of the SIOP, Serial 0653-60, 9 November 1960, in Originator's File, AAB, NHC.
33. George B. Kistiakowsky, *A Scientist at the White House* (Cambridge: Harvard University Press, 1976), pp. 396, 399–400, 405–407, 413–416; Transcript, Tel Con, Admiral Burke and Dr. Kistiakowsky, October 24, 1960, Transcripts & Phone Cons (NSTL) Folder, AAB, NHC.
34. Kistiakowsky, quoted in Transcript, Admiral Burke's conversation with Admiral [James] Russell, November 11, 1960, in Transcripts & Phone Cons (NSTL) Folder, AAB, NHC.
35. Transcript, Admiral Burke's Conversation with Captain Aurand, 25 November 1960, in Transcripts & Phone Cons (NSTL) Folder, AAB, NHC.
36. JCS 2056/131, 20 August 1959, declassified with deletions, 1980, CCS 3205 Target Systems (17 August 1959), JCS.
37. Ibid. See also *JSTPS History, SIOP-62*, pp. 6–11.
38. Brief Summary of Comparative Data, NESC 2009 and NTSDBs, dated 29 August and 7 September 1960, Memos and Letters (NSTL), AAB, NHC.
39. Transcript, Admiral Burke's Conversation with Admiral Russell, November 11, 1960.
40. A.J. Goodpaster, MCP, February 12, 1960, dated February 18, 1960, Staff Notes, February 1960, Folder 1, DDE Diary, Box 47, ACWF-EPP, DDEL; Tab B to Thomas Gates, draft memo to the JCS, appended to letter, Gates to Goodpaster, 10 August 1960.
41. A.J. Goodpaster, MCP, November 21, 1959, dated January 2, 1960, Defense Department, Vol. IV, Folder 1, January 1960, Subject Series, Defense Department Subseries, Box 2, WHO-SS, DDEL. See also A.J. Goodpaster, MCP, November 5, 1959, dated November 6, 1959, Staff Notes, November 1959, Folder 3, DDE Diary, Box 45, ACWF-EPP, DDEL.
42. A.J. Goodpaster, MCP, January 25, 1960, dated January 26, 1960, Staff Notes, January 1960, Folder 1, DDE Diary, Box 47, ACWF-EPP, DDEL.
43. A.J. Goodpaster, MCP, 16 November 1959, dated December 2, 1959, Budget, Military, FY 62, Folder 2, Subject Series, Defense Department Subseries, Box 3, WHO-SS, DDEL. This comment was repeated five days later. See MCP, November 21, 1959.
44. A.J. Goodpaster, MCP, May 5, 1960, dated May 7, 1960, Joint Chiefs of Staff, Folder 8, September 1959–May 1960, Subject Series, Defense Department Subseries, Box 4, WHO-SS, DDEL.
45. A.J. Goodpaster, MCP, April 6, 1960, Defense Department, Vol. IV, Folder 3, March–April 1960, Subject Series, Defense Department Subseries, Box 2, WHO-SS, DDEL. See also the President's comments on Polaris in A.J. Goodpaster, MCP, March 18, 1960, dated March 26, 1960, ibid.
46. A.J. Goodpaster, MCP, May 4, 1960, dated May 7, 1960, Dr. Kistiakowsky, Folder 3, April–June 1960, Subject Series, Alphabetical Subseries, Box 16, WHO-SS, DDEL.
47. Briefing Sheet for the Chairman, JCS, 7 December 1959, Subject: Joint Strategic Objectives Plan for 1 July 1963, with Enclosure, CCS 3130, JSOP (25 November 1959), JCS. NSC 5904/1, 17 March 1959, is listed without title in Annotated List of Serially Numbered NSC Documents, February 17, 1959 (updated to December 1960), but its title is listed in Memorandum by Chief of Staff of the Air Force on JSCP Definitions, CSAFM 84–60, 29 February 1960, CCS 3120, JSCP (24 August 1959), JCS. Questions on U.S. War Objectives are contained in James S. Lay, Jr., Memorandum for the NSC, January 7, 1959, Subject: Review of NSC 5410/1, with discussion paper enclosed. Folder NSC 5410/1, U.S. War Objectives, NSC Series, Policy Papers Subseries, Box 9, WHO-SANSA, DDEL.
48. A.J. Goodpaster, MCP, January 25, 1960.
49. A.J. Goodpaster, MCP, July 6, 1960, Staff Notes, July 1960 Folder, DDE Diaries, Box 51, ACWF-EPP, DDEL.
50. Message, CNO to CINCPACFLT, CINCLANTFLT, CINCUSNAVEUR, 0051/06 November 1960; Arleigh Burke, Memorandum for the Record, Subject: Conversation with Mr. Gates on the Preparation of the NSTL and SIOP, 15 August 1960, Op-00 Memo Serial 000469-60, 15 August 1960; and Arleigh Burke, Memo for the Record, Subject: Preparation of Basic National Target List and a Single Integrated Operational Plan, 15 August 1960, both in NSTL/SIOP Briefing Folder, AAB, NHC.
51. The Navy plans for dealing with the SIOP are laid out in Transcript, Admiral Burke's Conversation with Captain [F.A.] Bardshar, 22 August 1960, Transcripts & Phone Cons Folder, AAB, NHC; and in Rear Admiral Paul Blackburn, Memo for the Record, Subject: Comments on the Questions, 12 October 1960. Navy frustrations with the Army are indicated in Arleigh Burke, Memorandum for Op-06C, Subject: Army Participation in the NSTL/SIOP, Op-00 Memo 00638-60, 3

November 1960, Memos & Letters Folder (NSTL), AAB, NHC.
52. Memo, Burke to Lemnitzer, 22 November 1960.
53. L.R. Geis, Memo for the Record, Subject: NSTL/SIOP, Op-00 Memo, 000691-60, 28 November 1960, discussing Admiral Burke's conversations with Captain Aurand, Memos & Letters (NSTL) Folder, AAB, NHC; Special Edition, Flag Officers Dope, 4 December 1960, discusses Burke's doubts and pressures for approval.
54. Special Edition, Flag Officers Dope, 4 December 1960; A.J. Goodpaster, Memorandum for the Secretary of Defense, January 12, 1961, Department of Defense, Vol. IV, Folder 10, December 1960–January 1961, Subject Series, Department of Defense Subseries, Box 2, WHO-SS, DDEL; Kistiakowsky, *A Scientist at the White House*, p. 421.
55. *Development of Strategic Air Command*, pp. 79–81; Ball, *Politics and Force Levels*, pp. 43–53, 116–117; Lemmer, *The Air Force and Strategic Deterrence*, p. 44; Futrell, *Ideas, Concepts, Doctrine,* pp. 576–582.
56. Gordon Gray, Memorandum of Meeting with the President, Wednesday, August 24, 1960, dated August 25, 1960, Subject: Report of Panel of President's Science Advisory Committee on Weapons Technology for Limited Warfare, Staff Notes, August 1960, Folder 1, DDE Diary, Box 51, ACWF-EPP, DDEL. See also Eisenhower's comments in MCP, November 21, 1959.
57. Arkin, Cochran, and Hoenig, "The U.S. Nuclear Stockpile," pp. 1–2.
58. WSEG Report No. 50, Evaluation of Strategic Offensive Weapons Systems, 27 December 1960, Appendix E to Enclosure A, The Feasibility of Achievement of Counterforce Objectives, OSDFOI, pp. 64–81; John K. Gerhart, Memo to AFCCS, Subject: Analysis of the Problem of Finding and Striking Soviet Mobile Missiles, 7 November 1960, Folder 4–5, Missiles/Space/Nuclear, Box 36, White Papers, LC.
59. Air Staff Summary Sheet, Major General David A. Burchinal to General White, Subject: Reply to CINCSAC Message on RAND "Counterforce" Briefing, 1 March 1961, with message for General Power from General White, 7 March 1961, appended, Top Secret 1961 Folder, Box 48, White Papers, LC.
60. Message, Vice Admiral E.B. Parker to Admiral Burke, 052100Z February 1961, NSTL/SIOP Messages, AAB, NHC; Ball, *Politics and Force Levels*, pp. 119–120.
61. Message, CNO to CINCPACFLT, CINCLANTFLT, CINCUSNAVEUR, 191635Z May 1961, NSTL/SIOP Messages, AAB, NHC; Ball, *Politics and Force Levels*, pp. 186–190; Draft, Appendix 1 to The Memorandum for the President, September 23, 1961, Subject: Recommended Long Range Nuclear Delivery Forces, OSDFOI. The new Hickey study estimated 1,200 to 1,700 "aim points" for 1965, and 1,350 to 2,200 for 1967.

## Eisenhower on the "Military-Industrial Complex"

### *Documents 16 and 17*

President Eisenhower decided to go back to a little-used tradition and give a farewell address to the American people. The speech became famous for discussing a "military-industrial complex." In the excerpts in document 16, Eisenhower describes this complex as the "conjunction of an immense military establishment and a large arms industry which is new in the American experience." He warns against letting this complex gain too much power over government decisions. In document 17, Herbert F. York, a scientist who became a high official in the Pentagon, discusses Eisenhower's warning. He describes "hard-sell technologists" who try to use fears of Soviet breakthroughs to push forward their own favored programs.

### 16 FAREWELL RADIO AND TELEVISION ADDRESS TO THE AMERICAN PEOPLE
### President Dwight D. Eisenhower
### January 17, 1961

*My Fellow Americans:*

Three days from now, after half a century in the service of our country, I shall lay down the responsibilities of office as, in traditional and solemn ceremony, the authority of the Presidency is vested in my successor.

This evening I come to you with a message of leave-taking and farewell, and to share a few final thoughts with you, my countrymen.

Like every other citizen, I wish the new President, and all who will labor with him, Godspeed. I pray that the coming years will be blessed with peace and prosperity for all.

Our people expect their President and the Congress to find essential agreement on issues of great moment, the wise resolution of which will better shape the future of the Nation.

My own relations with the Congress, which began on a remote and tenuous basis when, long ago, a member of the Senate appointed me to West Point, have since ranged to the intimate during the war and immediate post-war period, and, finally, to the mutually interdependent during these past eight years.

In this final relationship, the Congress and the Administration have, on most vital issues, cooperated well, to serve the national good rather than mere partisanship, and so have assured that the business of the Nation should go forward. So, my official relationship with the Congress ends in a feeling, on my part, of gratitude that we have been able to do so much together. . . .

IV

A vital element in keeping the peace is our military establishment. Our arms must be mighty, ready for instant action, so that no potential aggressor may be tempted to risk his own destruction.

Our military organization today bears little relation to that known by any of my predecessors in peacetime, or indeed by the fighting men of World War II or Korea.

Until the latest of our world conflicts, the United States had no armaments industry. American makers of plowshares could, with time and as required, make swords as well. But now we can no longer risk emergency improvisation of national defense; we have been compelled to create a permanent armaments industry of vast proportions. Added to this, three and a half million men and women are directly engaged in the defense establishment. We annually spend on military security more than the net income of all United States corporations.

This conjunction of an immense military establishment and a large arms industry is new in the American experience. The total influence — economic, political, even spiritual — is felt in every city, every State house, every office of the Federal government. We recognize the imperative need for this development. Yet we must not fail to comprehend its grave implications. Our toil, resources and livelihood are all involved; so is the very structure of our society.

In the councils of government, we must guard against the acquisition of unwarranted influence, whether sought or unsought, by the military-industrial complex. The potential for the disastrous rise of misplaced power exists and will persist.

We must never let the weight of this combination endanger our liberties or democratic processes. We should take nothing for granted. Only an alert and knowledgeable citizenry can compel the proper meshing of the huge industrial and military machinery of defense with our peaceful methods and goals, so that security and liberty may prosper together.

Akin to, and largely responsible for the sweeping changes in our industrial-military posture, has been the technological revolution during recent decades.

In this revolution, research has become central; it also becomes more formalized, complex, and costly. A steadily increasing share is conducted for, by, or at the direction of, the Federal government.

Today, the solitary inventor, tinkering in his shop, has been overshadowed by task forces of scientists in laboratories and testing fields. In the same fashion, the free university, historically the fountainhead of free ideas and scientific discovery, has experienced a revolution in the conduct of research. Partly because of the huge costs involved, a government contract becomes virtually a substitute for intellectual curiosity. For every old blackboard there are now hundreds of new electronic computers.

The prospect of domination of the nation's scholars by Federal employment, project allocations, and the power of money is ever present — and is gravely to be regarded.

Yet, in holding scientific research and discovery in respect, as we should, we must also be alert to the equal and opposite danger that public policy could itself become the captive of a scientific-technological elite.

It is the task of statesmanship to mold, to balance, and to integrate these and other forces, new and old, within the principles of our democratic system — ever aiming toward the supreme goals of our free society. . . .

VI

Down the long lane of the history yet to be written America knows that this world of ours, ever growing smaller, must avoid becoming a community of dreadful fear and hate, and be, instead, a proud confederation of mutual trust and respect.

Such a confederation must be one of equals. The weakest must come to the conference table with the same confidence as do we, protected as we are by our moral, economic, and military strength. That table, though scarred by many past frustrations, cannot be abandoned for the certain agony of the battlefield.

Disarmament, with mutual honor and confidence, is a continuing imperative. Together we must learn how to compose differences, not with arms, but with intellect and decent purpose. Because this need is so sharp and apparent I confess that I lay down my official responsibilities in this field with a definite sense of disappointment. At one who has witnessed the horror and the lingering sadness of war — as one who knows that another war could utterly destroy this civilization which has been so slowly and painfully built over thousands of years — I wish I could say tonight that a lasting peace is in sight.

Happily, I can say that war has been avoided. Steady progress toward our ultimate goal has been made. But, so much remains to be done. As a private citizen, I shall never cease to do what little I can to help the world advance along that road.

## 17 COMMENT ON EISENHOWER'S ADDRESS
## Herbert York

I worked fairly closely with Dwight D. Eisenhower during the last three years of his Presidency, first as a member of the Science Advisory Committee he set up immediately after Sputnik under the chairmanship of James R. Killian, Jr., and second as the first Director of Defense Research and Engineering, a new position created by the Defense

Reorganization Act of 1958. In these jobs, I was directly concerned with precisely those scientific and technological programs in which the President himself was most involved, and I think, therefore, I have a good feeling for the context in which his thinking on the subject took place.

It also happened that after leaving the Presidency Eisenhower spent his winters in Palm Desert, California, a town less than one hundred miles from my home, and I called on him there on several occasions to pay my respects. Much of our conversation on those visits was devoted to the two warnings. He told me quite specifically that he had just two purposes in mind in making his farewell address. One was to say goodbye to the American people, whom he deeply loved. The other was to bring before the people precisely these warnings. The rest of the speech, he said, perhaps with some exaggeration, was there simply to fill it out and make the whole thing the appropriate length for a farewell address. I asked him to explain more fully what he meant by the warnings, but he declined to do so, saying he didn't mean anything more detailed than what he said at the time. I knew him well enough to understand what he meant: these warnings were not the result of a careful, methodical analysis; rather, they were the product of a remarkable intuition whose power has generally been underestimated.

What, then, was the context of these remarks? What annoyed and irritated him? Just whom are we to be wary of?

The context spanned the forty months from the launching of Sputnik to the end of his administration. The people who irritated him were the hard-sell technologists who tried to exploit Sputnik and the missile-gap psychosis it engendered. We were to be wary of accepting their claims, believing their analyses, and buying their wares.

The hard-sell technologist and their sycophants invented the term "missile gap," and they embellished that simple phrase with ornate horror stories about imminent threats to our very existence as a nation. They then promptly offered a thousand and one technical delights for remedying the situation. Most were expensive, most were complicated and baroque, and most were loaded more with engineering virtuosity than with good sense. Anyone who did not immediately agree with their assessments of the situation and who failed to recognize the necessity of proceeding forthwith on the development and production of their solutions was said to be unable to understand the situation, technically backward, and trying to put the budget ahead of survival.

The claims of such people that they could solve the problem if only someone would unleash them carried a lot of weight with the public and with some segments of the Congress and the press. Other scientists and technologists had performed seeming miracles in the recent past, and it was not unnatural to suppose that they could do it again. It seemed that radar had saved Britain, that the A-bomb had ended the war, and that the H-bomb had come along in the nick of time to save us from the Russian A-bomb. On the home front, antibiotics had saved our children from the scourges of earlier times, machines had uplifted us from drudgery, airplanes and electronics could carry us and our words great distances in short times. Scientists and technologists had acquired the reputation of being magicians who were privy to some special source of information and wisdom out of reach of the rest of mankind. A large part of the public was therefore more than ready to accept the hard-sell technologist's view of the world and to urge that the government support him in the manner to which he wanted to become accustomed. It seemed as if the pursuit of expensive and complicated technology as an end in itself might very well become an accepted part of America's way of life.

But it was not only the general public that believed the technologists understood something the rest of the world could not. Many of the technologists themselves believed that only they understood the problem. As a consequence, many of them believed it was their patriotic duty to save the rest of us whether or not we wanted them to. They looked at what the Soviets had done. They used their own narrow way of viewing things to figure out what the Russians ought to have done next. They decided then that since the Russians were rational (about these things anyway), what they ought to have done next was what they must now be doing, and they then determined to save us from the consequences of this next Russian technological threat. The Eisenhower Administration was able to deal successfully and sensibly with most of the resulting rush of wild ideas, phony intelligence, and hard sell. But some of these ideas did get through, at least for a while. Beyond that, dealing with self-righteous extremists who have all the answers — and there were many among the aerospace scientists and technologists at the time — is always annoying and irritating.

As we now know, the Byzantine technological ideas urged on us in those years were in fact a portent of things to come. Weapons systems have become still more complex in the years since Eisenhower's farewell address. And this complexity is creating new and serious problems of the general kind that Eisenhower warned us about.

## *Suggestions for Further Reading*


Betts, Richard K. "A Nuclear Golden Age? The Balance before Parity." *International Security* 11:3 (Winter 1986–87): 3-32. Betts discourages nostalgia for the 1950s by viewing the period through the perceptual lenses of the time. The United States did not feel secure; it felt beseiged.

Freedman, Lawrence. *The Evolution of Nuclear Strategy* (New York: St. Martin's, 1983). A thorough explication of the subject that treats all sides in the debate even-handedly.

— — —. *U.S. Intelligence and the Soviet Strategic Threat.* 2d ed. (Princeton, NJ: Princeton UP, 1986). An important and detailed treatment of U.S. estimates of Soviet military capabilities and their evolution from the 1950s through the 1970s.

Huntington, Samuel P. *The Common Defense: Strategic Programs in National Politics* (New York: Columbia UP, 1961). The classic study of the Eisenhower defense program.

Kaplan, Fred. *The Wizards of Armageddon* (New York: Simon and Schuster, 1983). A highly readable account of the civilian strategists and theorists who have influenced U.S. nuclear doctrine and force planning.

Four

# EUROPE GOES NUCLEAR

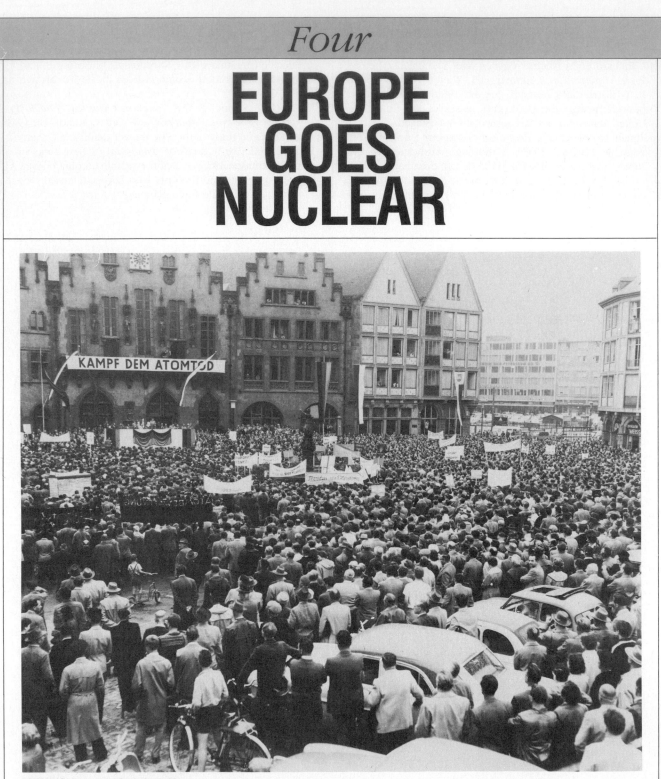

**ANTINUCLEAR DEMONSTRATION**

In June 1958, more than ten thousand West German citizens took part in the *Kampf dem Atomtod* (struggle against atomic death) demonstration in Frankfurt, West Germany. The marchers protested the stockpiling of U.S. tactical nuclear weapons on West German soil. AP/Wide World Photos

# INTRODUCTION

The United States decided to deploy nuclear weapons in Europe in the early 1950s because of Western Europe's conventional weakness and U.S. nuclear strength. Conventionally, in 1950 NATO's 12 divisions faced an estimated 175 Soviet divisions. Moreover, it was clear that the European members of NATO would not be willing to provide the troops necessary to balance Soviet conventional strength.

The U.S.-Soviet nuclear balance was quite different. During NATO's early years, the United States had more than a thousand bombers that could reach the Soviet Union (most from bases in Western Europe). But Soviet nuclear weapons could not reach the United States. The United States, in consultation with its NATO partners, decided to use its nuclear strength to offset NATO's conventional weakness. "Tactical" nuclear weapons were deployed with U.S. troops in Western Europe beginning in 1953. (Tactical nuclear weapons have shorter ranges than strategic weapons, but their destructive power is very high. Many tactical weapons are much more powerful than the Hiroshima and Nagasaki bombs.) Tactical weapons were to blunt the force of a Soviet conventional attack and buy time until the Strategic Air Command came into play. The number of tactical nuclear weapons deployed in NATO Europe reached about 4,000 by the late 1950s.

This strategy was accepted without much controversy by NATO's European members until the late 1950s when the Soviets made advances in missile technology and deployed a long-range bomber force that could reach the United States. At the time the Europeans began to ask a question that has been a source of controversy for NATO ever since: How realistic was it to expect the United States to use nuclear forces based in the United States to respond to a Soviet attack in Europe, since the use of U.S. nuclear forces might cause the Soviets to destroy U.S. cities? This European concern intensified when the Soviet Union began to deploy large numbers of SS-4 and SS-5 medium-range ballistic missiles targeted on Europe.

In an effort to respond to the European worries and to match Soviet forces, the NATO Council decided in 1957 to deploy 105 U.S. Thor and Jupiter medium-range missiles in Europe. These were deployed in England and Turkey in 1959 under NATO command but with the warheads in U.S. custody. The effectiveness of the missiles was limited by their vulnerability, and they were removed in 1963. Western European doubts about the U.S. nuclear guarantee did not go away, however. In fact, they in creased in the 1960s.

When the Kennedy administration came into office in 1961, it took a new, close look at the Soviet threat to NATO. It found that about half of the Soviet divisions facing NATO were in effect low-readiness reserves that in peacetime had only 10 percent of the manpower NATO had estimated. Other Soviet divisions were also not as strong as had been thought. This 1961 review convinced the Kennedy administration that a conventional defense of Western Europe was possible and that NATO therefore need not rely so heavily on U.S. nuclear weapons. The administration pressed for a buildup of NATO's conventional strength and a change in NATO strategy. The United States wanted the alliance to follow "flexible response," a doctrine that meant relying less on U.S. nuclear forces and more on conventional strength to defeat a Soviet attack.

To the Europeans, U.S. support for flexible response seemed to indicate that the United States was trying to back away from its promise to defend NATO with strategic nuclear weapons. In West European eyes, this posed two related dangers. First, the likelihood of a Soviet attack would increase, since the Soviets might not have to fear all-out retaliation from the United States. Second, if the Soviets did attack, U.S. reluctance to use its nuclear arsenal could mean that the next major war, whether nuclear or conventional, might be confined to European soil.

The French in particular concluded that the only way to be sure nuclear weapons would be used to protect their interests was to create an independent nuclear force. The British had already deployed nuclear weapons of their own, and the United States worried that other nations (especially West Germany) might also be tempted.

In an effort to resolve Western Europe's doubts and to head off French and other independent nuclear forces, the United States proposed the ill-fated Multilateral Force (MLF). The MLF was to have been composed of twenty-five surface ships, each carrying eight Polaris missiles and manned by multinational crews. The MLF fleet would have been assigned to NATO's military command. But the MLF never generated significant support in Europe and was abandoned in 1964. The French under Charles de Gaulle went forward with their plans for a nuclear force and eventually deployed an arsenal of bombers, land-based missiles, and nuclear missile–carrying submarines. France also withdrew from NATO's integrated military command in 1966, while remaining a member of the alliance.

In its effort to lessen NATO's reliance on nuclear weapons, the United States continued to push the alliance to accept the flexible response doctrine. NATO finally agreed to do so in 1967. This seemed to be a victory for the U.S. point of view, because NATO formally agreed to meet Soviet aggression on whatever level it occurred. In fact, the 1967 decision was a classic political compromise.

The West Europeans got what they wanted: as part of the 1967 decision, the United States reaffirmed that it would be willing to use its nuclear weapons to defend NATO. Flexible response also declared that the United States might use nuclear weapons first. The United States got what it wanted: the Europeans agreed that a Soviet attack might be met with a conventional response, at least at first. But the key questions — how nuclear weapons would be used against a Soviet attack, which nuclear weapons would be used, and when they would be used — were left open. European doubts about the U.S. nuclear guarantee remained and continued to cause the alliance serious problems (see chap. 10).

The United States tried to cope with these doubts by giving its NATO allies at least a limited role in nuclear decision making. In the late 1950s, the United States signed bilateral dual key agreements with several NATO allies, including West Germany, giving them access to nuclear weapons in wartime. This may well have been no more than a symbolic arrangement since it would be very cumbersome in an emergency. A more important step for NATO was the formation of the Nuclear Planning Group (NPG) in 1967 in the aftermath of the adoption of flexible response. The NPG encouraged discussion and study by NATO members of the alliance's nuclear posture.

Well before the 1960s drew to a close, the nuclearization of Europe was an accomplished fact. The Soviets deployed large numbers of MRBMs (medium-range ballistic missiles) and bombers targeted on Europe in the 1950s and 1960s. NATO had seven thousand U.S. tactical nuclear weapons by the mid-1960s, France and Great Britain had independent nuclear forces. The nuclearization of NATO did not occur without public protest. In the late 1950s there were significant disarmament movements in Great Britain and Germany. But these dwindled when the superpowers signed a treaty limiting nuclear testing in 1963. Significant antinuclear protest did not occur again for more than fifteen years.

# THE NUCLEARIZATION OF NATO

## Nuclear Weapons and the Defense of Europe

### *Documents 1 and 2*

In the early 1950s the newly formed NATO alliance believed it had to depend on nuclear weapons because its member nations, still recovering from World War II, could not hope to deploy conventional forces to match Soviet power. In document 1, a selection from *The Cold War as History,* analyst and historian Louis Halle describes how NATO thought of conventional forces not as a means to defeat the Soviet Army but as a way to make clear that a Soviet attack would cause a U.S. nuclear response. In document 2, a brief selection from *Strategies of Containment,* John Lewis Gaddis describes how the United States planned to use tactical nuclear weapons, not conventional forces, to defeat a Soviet attack. This meant that the United States was willing to be the first to use nuclear weapons.

### 1 THE COLD WAR AS HISTORY
### Louis J. Halle

The Americans who sponsored the North Atlantic Treaty in 1948 and 1949 did not see any immediate prospect that a barrier of ground forces on a scale to be effective in itself could be erected in the path of Russia's westward expansion. It was thought, rather, that without the American guaranty contained in the Treaty, with the atomic bomb behind it, the Europeans would feel so hopeless about their future, faced as they were by the unmatchable Russian might, that they would hardly have the heart for the effort that their own rehabilitation required. The American guaranty, rather than an actual build-up of forces, was the point of the Treaty — and its purpose was largely psychological. The strategic concept on which the common defense was now based did not vary essentially from the American recommendations as set forth by General Omar Bradley in a statement before the House Foreign Affairs Committee in July 1949.

> First, [he said] the United States will be charged with the strategic bombing. We have repeatedly recognized in this country that the first priority of the joint defense is our ability to deliver the atomic bomb.
>
> Second, the United States Navy and the Western Union naval powers will conduct essential naval operations, including keeping the sea lanes clear. The Western Union and other nations will maintain their own harbor and coastal defense.

> Third, we recognize that the hard core of the ground power in being will come from Europe, aided by other nations as they can mobilize.
>
> Fourth, England, France, and the closer countries will have the bulk of the short-range attack bombardment, and air defense. We, of course, will maintain the tactical air force for our own ground and naval forces, and United States defense.

This strategic concept made good sense in purely military terms, having regard for the resources and capabilities of the various countries concerned. Crudely stated, however, what it meant was that the United States, which would enjoy the commanding position in the organization of the common defense, would wear on its own shoulders the wings that would bear it into battle, if the occasion arose, while its European allies would provide the infantry that crawled over the ground or, in battle, was pounded into the mud. This would in time, although not immediately, cause many Europeans to look on it unfavorably.

In 1949 and 1950 a major concern of the European governments, still, was whether the United States would commit itself fully and permanently, and the terms on which it might so commit itself. The atom bomb, most authorities agreed, was all that deterred the Red Army from moving on to the Channel, and this would continue exclusively in American hands. What would make its use sure, and known to Moscow to be sure, in the event of Russian aggression against West Europe?

The discrepancy between the number of divisions facing each other at the Iron Curtain was understood to be of the order of 125 to 14 in favor of the Russians. Later estimates of total Communist divisions would range up to 263, the number facing the West being commonly given as 175.[1] It was evident that, without the atomic armament, the conventional forces of the Atlantic Treaty countries would hardly suffice even to delay the Red Army, should it march. Nor was it believed practicable for the West to build conventional forces of a magnitude remotely approaching that of the forces at Moscow's disposal.

A conception tailored to these harsh circumstances was now developed. It was represented by the analogy of the plate-glass window in a jeweler's shop: the window is easily broken, but from a thief's point of view there is a world of difference between seizing articles of display for which he has only to reach out his hand, and having first to smash a sheet of glass interposed between him and them. He may be deterred by the presence of the glass simply because, in smashing it, he would raise an alarm that might produce the most drastic consequences. The fragility of the glass, therefore, does not make it useless as a deterrent, even though it would be better if unbreakable.

The purpose of NATO's conventional forces could hardly be to frustrate and repel a Communist aggression by themselves.[2] As a minimum, their purpose must be to make it certain that the Red Army could not advance, as Hitler's Army had advanced into the Rhineland in 1936, without fighting. The minimum purpose must be to make it clear to Moscow that it could not order the Red Army forward without starting a real war. There would be a window to smash. Presumably the American divisions in Germany, of which there were two in 1949, would be in the path of the Red Army, thus assuring the immediate involvement of the United States, with its atomic armament, in such a war. The smashing of the window might detonate the atomic bomb.

By another metaphoric analogy this conception came to be known as that of the shield and the sword. The West's conventional forces constituted the shield that would receive the first impact of a Russian armed attack; the American atomic armament was the sword with which the return stroke would then be delivered. Without the shield, there might not be a chance to use the sword.

## Notes

1. Sources that should be authoritative are not in agreement on the size of the forces that faced each other across the Iron Curtain. On the Western side, a distinction has to be made between divisions in readiness and divisions that could be put into the field after a period of time. Russian divisions were generally smaller in manpower than Western divisions. See Stebbins, 1950, p. 145; Stebbins, 1951, p. 121; Calvocoressi 1953; p. 87, fn. 10; U.S. Senate Armed Forces Committee hearings, February 19, 1951; Gen. Eisenhower's report to NATO Planning Committee, October 10, 1951; etc. In the 1960's it began to be understood in Washington that the estimate of 175 Russian divisions had been greatly exaggerated, that 75 to 85 would have been nearer the mark.
2. NATO (the North Atlantic Treaty Organization) was established in late 1949 to plan and direct the common defense provided for by the Treaty.

## 2 IMPLEMENTING THE NEW LOOK
## John Lewis Gaddis

There would appear, at first glance, to have been a circularity in this reasoning: the United States would rely on nuclear weapons as an alternative to overseas ground force deployments, but in so doing would risk the very kind of confrontation that had made those deployments seem impracticable in the first place. But Eisenhower and Dulles calculated that a convincing demonstration of willingness to use nuclear weapons would make aggression unlikely; should deterrence nonetheless fail, the limited employment of those weapons still would not invariably lead, the President thought, to all-out war: "[T]he tactical use of atomic weapons against military targets would be no more likely to trigger off a big war than the use of twenty-ton 'block busters,'" he commented in 1956. It is significant that the following year Eisenhower found much that was "interesting and worth reading" in Henry Kissinger's "very provocative book," *Nuclear Weapons and Foreign Policy,* which argued that nuclear war could be kept limited and might even, under certain circumstances, produce less devastation than a conventional war.[3]*

The most important application of the principle that nuclear weapons could deter and, if necessary, repel conventional aggression took place in Western Europe, where the administration as early as 1953 had begun to deploy tactical nuclear weapons to bolster NATO defenses. Although progress had been made in building up the alliance's ground forces, there were limits to how much more could be done without imposing intolerable strains on West European economies. Even the addition of West German manpower through the European Defense Community would not, the administration thought, put NATO in a condition to resist a full-scale Soviet invasion. "The major deterrent to aggression against Western Europe," NCS 162/2 noted in October 1953, "is the manifest determination of the United States to use its atomic capability and massive retaliatory striking power if the area is attacked." American ground forces would be kept in Western Europe as a contribution "to the strength and cohesion of the free world coalition," but if a Soviet attack came primary reliance would be on the use of nuclear weapons to repel it. Asked if this meant that the United States was taking upon itself the responsibility for starting a nuclear war, NATO Supreme Commander General Alfred Gruenther replied: "That is right. The West is taking the responsibility of defending itself, because we do not have the capability to defend ourselves . . . by purely conventional means."[4]

From this point on, U.S. strategy — and NATO strategy as well — was to compensate for manpower deficiencies vis-à-vis the Soviet Union by making credible the prospect of escalation to nuclear war in case of attack. This required a delicate balancing act, because what had to be deterred was not only a Soviet invasion but also fears on the part of the West Europeans that the U.S. might abandon them, together with any temptations to deal with those fears either by attempting to appease the Russians, or by developing nuclear weapons of their own.* The retention of American ground forces in Europe, came to be seen, in time, as serving all of those functions: they provided a tangible sign of commitment — a "trip-wire" as the parlance of the day had it — to the Russians; they were also "hostages" to the West Europeans, since the U.S. could never evacuate them without at the same time defending Western Europe; and their access to nuclear weapons at the strategic and tactical levels could serve as a substitute for the national nuclear forces whose development Washington wished to avoid. It should be stressed, though, that the Eisenhower administration never intended to use these forces to fight a conventional war in Europe. As Eisenhower later commented with reference to the 1958–59 Berlin crisis: "If resort to arms should become necessary, our troops in Berlin would be quickly overrun, and the conflict would almost inevitably be global war. For this type of war our nuclear forces were more than adequate."[5]

*Eisenhower did object to the size of the military forces Kissinger wanted to maintain: "This would undoubtedly be a more expensive operation than we are carrying on at this time." (Eisenhower to Herter, July 31, 1957, Eisenhower Papers, Whitman File: DDE Diary, Box 14, "July 57 DDE Dictation.")

*The British had tested an atomic bomb in 1952, but the French did not until 1960.

## Notes

3. Goodpaster memorandum, Eisenhower conversation with Maxwell Taylor, May 24, 1956, Eisenhower Papers, Whitman File: DDE Diary, Box 8, "May 56 Goodpaster"; Eisenhower to Christian A. Herter, July 31, 1957, *ibid.,* Box 14, "July 57 DDE Dictation." See also Kissinger, *Nuclear Weapons and Foreign Policy,* pp. 183–89.
4. NCS 162/2, October 30, 1953, p. 11; Gruenther quotation in Richard P. Stebbins, *The United States in World Affairs: 1956*

(New York: 1957), pp. 370–71. See also Gruenther's speech to the National Security Industrial Association, New York City, September 29, 1954, DSB, XXXI (October 18, 1954), 564; and George H. Quester, *Nuclear Diplomacy: The First Twenty-Five Years,* second edition (New York; 1973), p. 111.

5. Eisenhower, *The White House Years: Waging Peace,* 1956–1961 (Garden City, N.Y.: 1965). p. 336n.

## Dulles on Nuclear Weapons in Europe

### *Document 3*

In this speech given to a meeting of NATO foreign ministers in April 1954, Secretary of State John Foster Dulles makes very clear the role of tactical nuclear weapons deployed in Europe. "We and our allies have placed great reliance upon new weapons to compensate in part for the numerical disparity between NATO and Soviet forces," he says. He adds that NATO's policy should be to meet a Soviet attack by using atomic weapons as if they were conventional weapons.

### 3 STATEMENT TO THE NORTH ATLANTIC COUNCIL
**John Foster Dulles**
**Paris**
**April 23, 1954**

I welcome this opportunity to contribute to a clearer understanding of the US official thinking regarding nuclear weapons, including both atomic and hydrogen weapons of all descriptions. Our attitude can best be explained in terms of the relation of these weapons to the free world system of defense against the Soviet threat.

The primary purpose of the United States, like the rest of the free world, is to deter aggression and prevent the outbreak of war. In our opinion, nuclear weapons have a vital role to play in achieving this purpose. . . .

III

Current NATO force programs fall short of providing the conventional forces estimated to be required to defend the NATO area against a full scale Soviet Bloc attack. In reaching the decision to level off force build-ups, and to concentrate on qualitative improvements, we and our Allies have placed great reliance upon new weapons to compensate in part for the numerical disparity between NATO and Soviet forces.[6] Current NATO military planning presupposes freedom to use atomic weapons in the defense of the NATO area in the event of Soviet Bloc aggression. The United States has accepted the current force programs and the NATO emergency plans as compromise measures on the premise that atomic weapons in substantial quantities would be available for the support of its presently programmed forces. Without the availability for[7] use of atomic weapons, the security of all NATO forces in Europe would be in grave jeopardy in the event of a surprise Soviet attack. The United States considers that the ability to use atomic weapons as conventional weapons is essential for the defense of the NATO area in the face of the present threat.[8]

In short, such weapons must now be treated as in fact having become "conventional." As I have said, these weapons are vital to the common defense of us all. Our main effort must be to see that our military capability is used to achieve the greatest deterrent effect. In order to achieve this, it should be our agreed policy, in case of [either general war or local] war, to use atomic weapons as conventional weapons against the military assets of the enemy whenever and wherever it would be of advantage to do so, taking account of all relevant factors. These include non-military, as well as military, considerations. . . .

VI

For the foregoing reasons, the United States believes that in any war forced upon us by the Soviet Bloc, we and our Allies must be free to use atomic weapons against appropriate elements of the enemy's military power where it is to our military advantage to do so.[9] We must be enabled to strike an aggressor where it hurts. And this by no means involves exclusively the use of atomic power.

This is the only formula which gives good assurances against aggression, because it means that an aggressor cannot calculate to gain by his aggression more than he could lose. Indeed, if an aggressor is allowed in advance to limit his losses by gaining for his most valued assets a sanctuary status, then aggression would be encouraged.[10] An aggressor glutted with manpower and occupying a central position would always be able to calculate on gaining from each local aggression more than he would lose. He would be relieved of the economic burden of defensive measures to protect his sources of power. He could concentrate on offensive means.

To deny these privileges to an aggressor does not however mean that every local war must automatically be turned into a general war. Nor does this mean that because atomic weapons are used locally they would be used indiscriminately for the bombing of civilian populations. The United States has never entertained such concepts.

As we all agree, our primary goal is to deter aggression and prevent war. To achieve this, the Soviet Union must recognize that the free world is able and ready to use its full power to defeat any such aggression if it should occur. In our judgment, this is the surest way to prevent the outbreak of a general war, which would be a disaster for all if it occurred. The deterrent will be effective, however, only so long as the free world maintains its strength and its determination and courage to use that strength effectively. The possession of a will, if need arises, to use strength is as important as possession of strength.[11]

If we can meet these tests, and I am convinced that we can, then mankind has good hope of escaping general war with all its attendant consequences.

## Notes

6. Original text contained the further phrase "thereby materially reducing the risk".
7. Original text contains word "and" in place of "for."
8. The following two paragraphs regarding the conventionality of nuclear weapons and consultation regarding their use were substantially revised from the original text, which reads as follows:

   "Accordingly, the United States has concluded that such weapons must be treated as in fact having become 'conventional'. If, unhappily, war should not be deterred but should actually occur, either in terms of general war or a local war, then it should be our collective policy to use atomic weapons as conventional weapons against the military assets of the enemy whenever and wherever it would be of military advantage to do so.

   "This policy contemplates prior consultation with our Allies in regard to all military emergencies whenever time permits. Certainly the United States intends to act in full and intimate cooperation with its Allies whenever possible. This is the essence of collective security. However, it must be recognized that any nation, even though a member of a collective security organization, might be forced by circumstances affecting its survival to take immediate independent action."
9. Original text continued to end of this paragraph as follows: "and that we must be enabled to strike an aggressor where it hurts."
10. From this point to the end of the following paragraph concluding with the sentence "The United States has never entertained such concepts," the original text reads: "for an aggressor glutted with manpower and occupying a central position would always be able to calculate on gaining from each local aggressor more than he would lose. To deny this privilege to an aggressor does not however mean that every local war must automatically be turned into a general war, or that because atomic weapons are used locally they would be used indiscriminately for the bombing of civilian populations. The United States has never entertained this concept."
11. This sentence is not in original text.

# A European View of Nuclear Weapons in Europe

### Document 4

**In this 1956 letter to President Eisenhower, British Prime Minister Anthony Eden discusses the role of nuclear weapons in the defense of Western Europe. He notes that a conventional forces "shield" is "still required; but it is no longer our principal military protection." Instead, NATO should rely more heavily on nuclear weapons. This could mean a reduction of conventional forces stationed in West Germany.**

## 17 LETTER TO PRESIDENT EISENHOWER
**British Prime Minister Anthony Eden**
**London**
**July 18, 1956**

Dear Friend:

I am so happy to hear that you are back at the White House again.[12] This tempts me to sent you some thoughts on the future of NATO which have been in my mind for some time.

2. I am fully in sympathy with the current project for improving the political cohesion of the Organisation,[13] but I am sure that this alone will not suffice. It was on the military aspects of the alliance that the strength of the Organisation was founded; and its military policy must command public confidence if its authority is to be maintained.

3. As it seems to me the strategic situation has been evolving since the development of the thermo-nuclear weapon. Two new factors have now been introduced. First, both sides now stand possessed of this weapon, and each now realises the devastation which its use would involve. Second, and perhaps as important, public opinion throughout the democracies has begun to realise that the danger of major war has for this reason receded and that the nature of such a war, if it came, would be very different from anything we have known hitherto. As this understanding deepens there is bound to be a growing reluctance, among the peoples of the free world, to accept the social and human sacrifices required for the maintenance of large forces of the conventional pattern.

4. It can be argued that even the Russians are adjusting the balance of their resources. They are certainly doing everything they can to develop the most up-to-date weapons and the means of delivering them. From this it is pretty clear that they believe in the power of the deterrent. Having taken that decision they have decided, it seems to me, to increase their labour force for industrial expansion and correspondingly to reduce their conventional military forces. They are skillfully making the maximum propaganda use of this decision.

5. We have surely to take account of these new elements in the situation. Some no doubt will say that these considerations lead to the logical conclusion that you, at any rate, and perhaps we, should fall back on a peripheral defense. This is not my view. I feel sure it would not be yours. The maintenance of independence and freedom in Western Europe is essential to any policy designed to preserve our free way of life in the world. You know, better than anyone, how the increasing military strength of the North Atlantic Alliance helped to build up political stability in Western Europe, for you did it. It was the forces in being under NATO Command, and particularly the presence of the United States and British forces in Europe, that gave confidence and courage to those who were ready to resist political encroachment by Communism in Europe. Or to put it another way: the political cohesion of the Western European countries in resisting the internal threat of Communism was inspired by growing confidence in the military side of the Alliance. The political need to maintain the solidarity of the European countries is as strong as ever. For this purpose, even if for no other, it would still be important that some United States and British forces should remain on the ground in Europe under NATO Command.

6. The military purposes for which these forces are now required are, however, different from those on which the military policy of NATO was first framed. It was originally designed to meet the threat of a Soviet land invasion, and its pattern was established before the advent of the nuclear weapon. Today, the situation is changing. It is on the thermo-nuclear bomb and atomic weapons that we now rely, not only to deter aggression, but to deal with aggression if it should be launched. A "shield" of conventional forces is still required; but it is no longer our prinicpal military protection. Need it be capable of fighting a major land battle? Its primary military function seems now to be to deal with any local infiltration, to prevent external intimidation and to enable aggression to be identified as such. It may be that it should also be capable of imposing some delay on the progress of a Soviet land invasion until the full impact is felt of the thermo-nuclear retaliation which would be launched against the Soviet Union.

7. The application of this concept would, I think, involve significant changes in the shape and size of the NATO forces, and possibly in their deployment. It would certainly have a profound effect on existing plans for reserve forces and for logistic support. I believe that it could lead to a reduction in the numbers of conventional forces stationed in Germany — though I should not wish such a reduction to be carried below the levels necessary to serve the political objectives outlined in paragraph 5 above. A reappraisal of the military policy of NATO along these lines is, I believe, necessary and urgent. It is necessary on its merits. It is urgent because we believe that NATO will not continue to command public confidence unless it shows its ability to adjust its policies to accord with changing circumstances and, as I have said, I doubt whether the peoples of the free world will be willing to go on bearing the heavy burden of defense programmes unless they are satisfied that these are directed realistically towards the new situation.

8. Much of this, as you know, was put by Roger Makins to Foster last month.[14] His reaction was most helpful. Since then we have had useful and encouraging conversations here in London with Al Gruenther.[15] But above all I have now been greatly heartened to hear that you are yourself proposing to take a hand in all this next month. Big decisions will be called for and maybe we shall have to take some risks if we are to carry our people with us and maintain public confidence in the Alliance. However, I am quite sure that this can be done and that we shall go forward together to shape the future as we have done the past. We have had many more difficult problems than this and as long as we are in step I have no doubt that we can handle this one without causing disarray. It is for this reason that I am writing to you now to let you know how my mind is working. I should be much encouraged if I could hear that you were in general agreement with this broad approach.

9. I hope that you will enjoy your trip to Panama.[16] Do not let any other kinds of Americans tire you too much.

Yours ever,

Anthony[17]

## Notes

12. Reference is to the President's absence from the White House while recuperating from surgery performed on June 10.

13. Reference is to the Committee of Three Ministers appointed at the NAC Ministerial meeting on May 5 to study ways to increase unity and nonmilitary cooperation with

the Atlantic community. See Documents 27–29. Regarding the final report of the committee, see Documents 47 and 48.
14. See Document 32
15. Gruenther reported on this meeting, July 4, in telegram 58 from Paris, July 5. (Department of State, Central Files, 740.5/7–556)
16. The President visited Panama to attend the commemorative meeting of the Presidents of the American Republics, July 20–24, 1956.
17. In his July 27 reply to Eden, Eisenhower said he appreciated knowing the Prime Minister's thoughts on this matter in which he had the deepest personal interest. He wrote:

"I know that you are aware of the profound and far-reaching political and military implications of the question of NATO defense policy, which must be considered most carefully in terms of their effect on the continuing unity and strength of our NATO alliance. We have to think about the effect on Germany and on our friend Adenauer.

"As Foster has told Roger Makins, we are giving our urgent attention to these matters and we hope to be ready about the middle of August to give you our views. I am confident that our exchange of views will help us to find the right solution." (Telegram 547 to London, July 27; Department of State, Central Files, 740.5/7–2756; Eisenhower Library, Whitman File, International File)

## Public Protest

### *Documents 5 and 6*

The nuclearization of Western Europe sparked public protest in the late 1950s and early 1960s. Document 5, a 1958 editorial in *The New Statesman,* a left-wing British newspaper, describes some of the actions and program of the Campaign for Nuclear Disarmament. It notes the CND plans for mass marches and its calls for Great Britain to renounce nuclear weapons unilaterally. Document 6 is a brief excerpt from a 1958 manifesto of *Kampf dem Atomtod* (Struggle Against Atomic Death), a West German protest group. It calls for Germany to refuse atomic weapons as a first step to a nuclear-free zone in Europe.

### 5 THE REVOLT OF COMMON SENSE May 10, 1958

Official circles are confused and alarmed about the Campaign for Nuclear Disarmament because it is a movement of a new pattern. It is unprecedented because it has no political group behind it; no showman's drum beats it up; it has no leaders serving personal ambitions; it is not inspired or indeed supported by the Communist Party, which is embarrassed by the obvious retort that the Soviet Union should also abandon nuclear weapons. The Establishment's alarm is illustrated by the grotesque waffling of ministers when they are asked if they are really prepared to press the button for total destruction, and by the refusal of the BBC to give publicity, even in the ordinary way of news, to Albert Schweitzer's lectures at Oslo, on the strange ground that they were "political." In an obviously inspired article *The Times* political correspondent even tried to support an argument that the Campaign is no longer watched "warily, even nervously" by the government; he implied that Bertrand Russell was somehow disingenuous in stating his personal belief in unilateral action — and stressing that he was speaking only for himself — when he forwarded the appeal of 618 British scientists that nuclear tests should be stopped by international agreement.

The complaint that the Campaign is inconsistent shows how far the authorities are from understanding its nature. The Committee for Nuclear Disarmament provides speakers for meetings and publishes leaflets in an endeavor to satisfy an insatiable demand. The speakers talk from different angles; some are pacifists; some are people who are now converted to a pacifist position because nuclear war is suicidal and indiscriminate. Some want to leave NATO; some want to retain defensive but not nuclear weapons. The one thing that differentiates them all from Conservative, and even from Labour, official policy is that they believe that Britain should no longer attempt to be a great power ensuring its own destruction by contributing a trivial quota towards the preparations for suicide. The movement is inspired by nothing more subversive than an elementary instinct of self-preservation.

The Aldermaston March was not arranged by politicians; it was supported, after it was planned, by the Campaign for Nuclear Disarmament. This Committee will have its work cut out to co-ordinate the manifold manifestations of the nuclear protest. The "Mass Lobby" of 20 May looks like being a large affair — far larger than its sponsors expected. Originally planned as a lobby of London MPs, it has now been spontaneously reinforced by coach-loads of supporters from Yorkshire, Scotland, Devon, Lancashire, Cornwall, Wales, and other parts of the country. No one has any axe to grind; the object is merely to impress on MPs that the thoughtful public of England does not intend passively to be murdered. An independent committee against nuclear war has also arranged a mass march on London from various points outside it, and the same committee is making preparations for a continuous vigil outside the US Embassy in protest against the arrest of the *Golden Rule,* the American ketch, which was sailing in protest to the Eniwetok test area. On 26 May Oxford has organised a march to the RAF base at Brize Norton to protest against patrols by aircraft carrying H-bombs.

Most of these demonstrators are people who in the normal course of events support the Labour Party. They are sharply aware of the difference between the chief parties on this issue. Labour stands for the unilateral ending of tests. But those who demonstrate are not convinced by the official Labour campaign. Aneurin Bevan was their obvious political leader, and they understand that, as a possible future foreign secretary, he may have reservations when making detailed promises about a situation that cannot be accurately foreseen. If the Labour Party were determined to abandon the H-bomb, but intended only to use its interim retention as a lever to stop Germany and France having nuclear weapons, many of the attacks on official Labour would evaporate. But its leaders have not convinced the world that they differ fundamentally about the use of nuclear weapons from Mr. Macmillan or General Norstad. When the demonstrators are sure that the Labour leadership really means to eliminate nuclear weapons from our armoury, they will again be its enthusiastic supporters.

### 6 MANIFESTO KAMPF DEM ATOMTOD (STRUGGLE AGAINST ATOMIC DEATH) 1950

The German people on both sides of the zonal frontier is delivered up to certain atomic death in the case of a thermonuclear war. There is no protection.

Participation in the atomic arms race and the use of German territory for atomic bases could only heighten this danger.

The goal of German policy must be relaxation of tension between East and West. Only such a policy serves the security of the German people and the national existence of a freely democratic Germany.

We call on the Bundestag and the Government not to take part in the atomic arms race, but as a contribution to relaxation to make every effort to support a nuclear-free zone in Europe.[18]

### *Note*

18. "Manifesto of the Campaign Against Atomic Death," *Die Welt*, March 11, 1958. Author's translation.

## REARMED ALLIES: GREAT BRITAIN, FRANCE, AND WEST GERMANY

## The British Bomb

### *Documents 7 and 8*

In the early years of research on atomic weapons, British and American scientists had cooperated a great deal. This cooperation ceased in 1946 when the U.S. Congress passed the McMahon Act, which greatly restricted the sharing of "atomic secrets" with any foreign power. In document 7, a 1946 telegram to President Truman, British Prime Minister Clement Attlee complains about the U.S. decision to stop cooperating with Great Britain on atomic weapons research. Document 8, two articles from *Scientific American* (April and December 1952), describes the British determination to develop atomic weapons despite the lack of U.S. cooperation.

### 7 TELEGRAM TO PRESIDENT TRUMAN British Prime Minister Clement Attlee June 6, 1946

Your telegram of the 20th April about the exchange of information on atomic energy.

I have held back my reply until I had been able to disucss the matter with Halifax and with Mackenzie King. . . .

. . . President Roosevelt had become interested in the idea of an atomic weapon and had decided to engage upon it all the vast resources of the United States. In October 1941 he wrote to Mr. Churchill and proposed that any extended efforts in this field should be coordinated or even jointly conducted. It was thus possible for us to decide that we would concentrate on assisting to the best of our ability the developing of the enterprise in the United States. It is not for me to try to assess what that assistance was worth, but we gave it in the confident belief that the experience and knowledge gained in America would be made freely available to us, just as we made freely available to you the results of research in other fields such as radar and jet propulsion, on which, as a result of this decision, we were able to concentrate. It was part of that wise division of effort and pooling of resources which was made possible by the system of reciprocal aid which, without attempting to compare and measure the aggregate contribution on each side, enabled both countries to concentrate their efforts on those fields where they seemed likely to be most productive. I must repeat that but for that system, we should have been forced to adopt a different distribution of our resources in this country, which would not have been so advantageous to the common interest.

As I said, we entered on these arrangements in a spirit of partnership and in the belief that both countries would pool the experience which they gained. It was, in fact, later expressly provided in the Quebec Agreement that there should be complete interchange of ideas and information on all sections of the project between members of the Policy Committee and their immediate technical advisers, and, at the lower level, interchange of information in the field of design and construction of large-scale plants was not ruled out but was made subject to *ad hoc* arrangements to be approved by the Combined Policy Committee. At the same time it was left to the President of the United States to specify the terms on which any post-war advantages of an industrial or a commercial character should be dealt with as between the United States and Great Britain....

Almost immediately the war came to an end, and we were told that until new arrangements could be concluded the supply of information must be stopped. When I visited Washington, therefore, in November, it was an important part of my purpose to secure that, as President Roosevelt had promised Mr. Churchill at Hyde Park in September 1944, the co-operation which had existed during the war should be continued and that it should be full and effective....

... It came as a surprise to us to find that your Government was not prepared to enter into any agreement, nor to proceed on the basis of the agreements previously reached between us, nor yet to agree that co-operation should, in fact, continue by administrative action. The clause of our Agreement, signed in November, by which the Combined Policy Committee was to recommend the arrangements required for continued co-operation has thus remained a dead letter.

I cannot agree with the argument that to continue such co-operation would be inconsistent with the public declaration on the control of atomic energy which you and Mackenzie King and I issued in November. That our three Governments stand in a special relationship to one another in this field is a matter of record and was, in fact, the reason why we took the initiative in issuing the declaration. It is surely not inconsistent with its purpose that the co-operation begun during the war should continue during the peace unless and until it can be replaced by a wider system. And until recently, at any rate, I think it is fair to say that it was generally assumed in both our countries that this co-operation was continuing. And, indeed, in one important part of the field it is: I am referring to our joint control of raw materials. We have not thought it necessary to abandon that—in my opinion, quite rightly. Why then should we abandon all further pooling of information?...

I have set out the position fully and frankly as I am sure you would have wished me to do. I realise that an additional complication may arise from the fact that the McMahon Bill containing stringent provisions about the disclosure of information has within the last few days been passed by the Senate.

I would nevertheless most strongly urge that for the reasons I have given our continuing co-operation over raw materials shall be balanced by an exchange of information which will give us, with all proper precautions in regard to security, that full information to which we believe that we are entitled, both by the documents and by the history of our common efforts in the past.

## 8 BRITAIN'S ATOMIC BOMB PROGRAM 1952

### Britain's Bomb

When Prime Minister Churchill visited the U.S. in January, his advisers sounded out U.S. authorities again on the delicate and painful question of a resumption of U.S.-British cooperation in atomic research. They got nowhere, as the present Atomic Energy Act in the U.S. forbids exchange of atomic energy information with other countries. During the following month hints began to appear in the press that Britain was producing an atomic bomb of her own and was ahead of the U.S. in theoretical work on atomic artillery and guided missiles. Mr. Churchill finally capped the hints with a formal announcement that his Government would test a British-made "atomic weapon" in Australia sometime during 1952.

Mr. Churchill informed the House of Commons that the British bomb was produced some months ago, during the Labor administration. He said he was astonished to learn when he took office "that not only had the Socialist Government made the atomic bomb as a matter of research, but that they had created ... important plant necessary for its regular production." He upbraided ex-Prime Minister Clement Attlee for having hidden Britain's light under a Socialist bushel. Mr. Attlee replied that the work was no secret within the Government and that Mr. Churchill's adviser, Lord Cherwell, should have kept the Conservative leader informed. He added that the U.S. Government had been "told about everything in order to get their cooperation."

In the U.S. officials were disappointed that Britain was making an independent test of its bomb in Australia. Senator Brien McMahon, chairman of the Joint Committee on Atomic Energy, remarked: "I might have wished that the British had seen fit to take advantage of our offer to make available a test site, subject to conditions which our law lays down."

**British Bomb**

Prime Minister Winston Churchill last month announced a few details of the first British atomic bomb test, made in the Monte Bello Islands off the Australian coast in October. The bomb was exploded inside a small frigate in a harbor. The ship, said Churchill, was completely vaporized, except for some red hot fragments that scattered over one of the islands. Measurements of the radiation energy as the blast broke out of the hull showed that the temperature at the hull was almost one million degrees.

Observers from the mainland reported that the cloud thrown up by the bomb, unlike the mushroom clouds characteristic of U.S. bombs, had the shape of a ragged "Z." Churchill said that "thousands of tons of water and of mud and rock from the sea bottom were thrown many thousands of feet into the air and a tidal wave was caused." He added that damage effects were tested in specimen structures erected at various distances from the explosion.

The bomb project cost the British well over $280 million. It was directed by W. G. Penney, a physicist who had worked at Los Alamos during World War II. Churchill said he hoped the successful test would lead to "a much closer American interchange of information" with Britain about atomic energy.

## The British Nuclear Force

### *Document 9*

The British developed an independent nuclear force. In the 1950s it consisted mainly of bombers. After the Nassau Agreement in 1962 (see document 16) the British shifted to a submarine-based force. Today the British deploy four nuclear missile carrying submarines, each with sixteen Polaris sea-launched ballistic missiles (SLBMs). In document 9, Lawrence Freedman, one of Great Britain's most important defense analysts, discusses the changing rationales for Britain's nuclear force. Freedman notes the close connection between the British force and the U.S. nuclear forces and argues that a nuclear deterrent has been seen by Britain as its "ticket of admission" to great power status.

### 9 THE BRITISH NUCLEAR FORCE
### Lawrence Freedman

The supporters of the British nuclear force did not present their case as an exercise in strategic logic. The framework was that of the need for deterrence, but within that framework a variety of purposes were, at different times, discerned for the British force. It was, if anything, subject to a law of diminishing rationales. In terms of deterring the Soviet Union, it was felt in the late 1940s that a British force might be necessary to make up the numbers in a Western retaliatory force against the East. By the early 1950s, when it was recognized that the United States could provide an imposing threat without Britain's help, it was argued that there might be targets of particular interest to Britain that might be neglected if the responsibility for the retaliatory strike was solely in American hands. By the early 1960s, with America having sufficient warheads to cover the whole of the Warsaw Pact target structure, the British were reduced to making a marginal European contribution to the retaliatory forces.

In 1957 the Government had reaffirmed its commitment to a policy of massive retaliation in uncompromising terms at the same time that the US Administration was beginning to have doubts. The critique of massive retaliation, however, had been developed in Britain at the same time as in the United States and, led by Liddell Hart and Blackett, evolved during the 1950s towards the view that the balance in NATO's force structure ought to be redressed in favour of conventional defence. Labour Party defence specialists encouraged this trend. One chapter in a book written by John Strachey was entitled "A reversal of NATO's strategy," and argued for more conventional forces.[19]

The debate over nuclear strategy was thus couched in NATO terms. As some sort of "great power" status could still be taken for granted, there was no need (yet) for symbols that might proclaim the nation's significance to doubting foreigners. More important, the British had always viewed nuclear issues as an Anglo-American matter, seeking to gain access to US nuclear secrets as a matter of right, a proper return on Britain's own wartime investment in atom bomb research. Diplomatic effort had been devoted to encouraging interdependence with the Americans in nuclear matters rather than striving for independence. The 1958 amendments to the US McMahon Act made greater Anglo-American co-operation possible. This, plus the rhetoric of the "special relationship," actively discouraged any interest in either an independent force or a strategic doctrine to support one.

The developing dependence of Britain on the US was most evident in the area of delivery vehicles. After plans for a British ballistic missile, *Blue Streak*, had been aborted, President Eisenhower agreed in 1960 to sell Britain the *Skybolt* air-launched missile, then under development. In return the British agreed to make available a base for US nuclear submarines at Holy Loch in Scotland. Unfortunately the *Skybolt* programme was beset with difficulties and these led to its cancellation in November 1962. The British affected surprise though they had been warned of the programme's problems.[20] The abrupt cancellation undermined Britain's nuclear programme and underlined the extent to which nuclear weapons were creating a form of dependence on the United States rather than becoming a source of influence. Britain's limited influence was clearly indicated by the minimal consultation Britain enjoyed during the Cuban Missile Crisis that had taken place two months before. To salvage Anglo-American relations, a hastily arranged summit conference was convened at Nassau between Prime Minister Macmillan and President Kennedy. This resulted in a deal by which Britain was allowed to purchase *Polaris* submarine-launched missiles.

This put the British force on a much sounder basis, given the reduced vulnerability of a submarine-based force. The option had been available in 1960 and it had been foolishly rejected by the British in favour of *Skybolt*. The agreement at Nassau stipulated that the UK *Polaris* submarines would be used "for the purpose of international defense of the Western Alliance in all circumstances." In this way the proposals could be a compromise between Alliance integration and national independence. However the agreement was unclear as to whether the Alliance nuclear force to which Britain was contributing was to be constructed as a multilateral or multinational force. Moreover, the final decision on use was with the British, based on their own understanding of whether "supreme national interests" were "at stake." It is, of course, only where supreme national interests are at stake that the question of whether or not to use nuclear weapons arises at all. Nevertheless, the underlying loyalty to the Alliance forced the British to pull their punches when explaining the need for their own forces.

The rationales used to justify this "independent" force were as much political as strategic, stressing the opportunities for the exercise of benign influence when all nuclear issues, from disarmament to NATO planning, were discussed. The argument had never been far below the surface. Prime Minister Harold Macmillan spoke in 1958 of how:

> The independent contribution . . . gives us a better position in the world, it gives us a better position with respect to the United States. It puts us where we ought to be, in the position of a Great Power. The fact that we have it makes the United States pay a greater regard to our point of view, and that is of great importance.[21]

After 1962 this argument was emphasized. Macmillan's successor, Alec Douglas-Home, spoke of the bomb as a "ticket of admission," providing "a place at the peace table as of right."[22]

The second argument, which became more prominent in the 1960s and which came to constitute the strongest popular rationale for the force, was based on the unreliability of the Alliance. It was often presented as a simple assertion that in a cruel and uncertain world, where others may get nuclear weapons and the United States' own willingness to engage in nuclear war on Europe's behalf was open to doubt, an independent British force was a necessary form of insurance. Without actually going so far as to directly question the US guarantee, the 1964 Statement on Defense diplomatically raised this point: "[I]f there were no power in Europe capable of inflicting unacceptable damage on a potential enemy he might be tempted . . . to attack in the mistaken belief that the United States would not act unless America herself were attacked.[23] This theory of a "second decision-centre," has been adhered to consistently because it provides little challenge to NATO orthodoxy.

There were problems in constructing plausible scenarios in which Britain "stood alone" yet still had the US furnishing the necessary support to keep the *Polaris* fleet operational, or in which the USSR picked Britain out for special treatment in a crisis, or in which there was any particular point in Britain rattling its nuclear weapons while the Soviet Army made its way across Europe. However, the main difficulty in dwelling on the possibility of acting independently of an alliance was that NATO remained in existence and that its preservation, backed by a forceful US nuclear commitment, was a prime objective of British policy. Excessive speculation on how it might be possible to do without the US could provide Washington with the necessary excuse. Hence the need to argue that the danger was not of the US reneging on its nuclear guarantee but of a mistaken Soviet belief that this might happen, to be corrected by forcing it to worry about another centre of nuclear decision.

The British Government was pleased to stress Britain's force as a contribution to NATO. No attempt was made to keep up with American ideas on flexible options; the theory behind them was either ignored or dismissed as American faint-heartedness about the awfulness of the capability they had created. As the *Polaris* programme turned out to be remarkably inexpensive, only modest justification to the British public for it was deemed necessary.

In 1980, contemplating the obsolescence of *Polaris* in the 1990s, there seemed to be no better successor than the same type of submarine force, this time equipped with US *Trident* missiles.* It was justified within exactly the same strategic and political framework as before. The only doubt was whether the economically weak British could afford the new system without damaging the over-stretched conventional forces. As the American connection made the force possible, the British were happy to suppress doubts as to US intentions towards NATO in order to stay in the nuclear business. The intellectual satisfaction, but financial burdens, of devising arguments for completely self-sufficient forces was left to France.

* Lawrence Freedman, *Britain and Nuclear Weapons* (London: Macmillan, 1980).

## Notes

19. John Strachey, *The Prevention of War* (London: Macmillan, 1962).
20. The problems of miscommunication in this affair are examined in Richard Neustadt, *Alliance Politics* (New York: Columbia University Press, 1970).
21. Television interview of February 1958. Andrew Pierre, *Nuclear Politics: The British Experience with an Independent Strategic Force, 1939–1970,* (London: Oxford University Press, 1972), P. 178.
22. *Ibid.*
23. *Statement on Defence 1964*, Cmnd 2270 (London: HMSO, 1964), p. 6.

# Conventional Defense Is Not Enough — A French View

### *Document 10*

After the Kennedy administration came into office, it took a new look at the conventional balance in Europe. U.S. defense officials urged NATO to improve its conventional forces as a way to reduce its reliance on nuclear weapons. Many Western European leaders, especially the French, worried that this proposed change in NATO strategy meant that the United States was backing away from its nuclear guarantee to Europe. In Document 10, Pierre Gallois, an influential French Air Force general, articulates these worries and rejects the rationale for the U.S. strategy. He concludes that if the United States weakens its nuclear guarantee it must accept the fact that other nations will develop independent nuclear forces.

## 10 A CONVENTIONAL OR NUCLEAR DEFENSE Gen. Pierre Gallois

The recapitulation of these complex diplomatic manipulations shows, once more, that the Western peoples still have much to learn about the characteristics of the nuclear era in which they must live and in which some of them must answer for the security of the world. Clearly, the responsibility for keeping a nuclear arsenal cannot be shared. The United States would be better advised to accept national deterrent forces instead of straining its diplomatic ingenuity to inhibit their creation. The present United States administration, had it better understood the problems of defending a European continent menaced by an adversary brandishing thousands of deadly weapons, would not have inaugurated its reign by asking for an increase in conventional forces.

Let us summarize the argument for more and better conventional forces: President Kennedy, like his predecessor, does not wish to be confronted in Europe with the dilemma of nuclear war or surrender. Understandably, he wishes to have the time to ponder the appropriate response to whatever might be the challenge. Yet, military specialists have known for years that it is impossible to switch suddenly from one strategy to another when one has to deal with arms as different as conventional and nuclear weapons. Two years ago, Henry Kissinger made it clear that once committed to a conventional defense system, the country that decided to switch to nuclear weapons would be lost.[24] Besides, there is no reason why a country should not resort from the start to nuclear weapons if it knew that it could thus gain a complete and immediate victory. . . .

In a lecture to the French Military Staff College in the fall of 1954, the then Colonel Ailleret stated:

> The extreme vulnerability to nuclear weapons of military personnel and vehicles in movement, of the means of communication, and of the strategic routes and port equipment will probably paralyze armies. Armed forces will have to spread out on very large areas and limit their actions to numerous infiltrations carried out by small units, for concentrations will be no longer possible. . . .
>
> Concentration of large infantry and artillery units gathered around centers of resistance are now out of the question. They would be easily destroyed or neutralized. Large units now must be abandoned, just as close order formation had to be when the automatic rifle was adopted.

It is likely that, after many years spent on study and experiment, the U.S. Joint Chiefs of Staff have come to the same conclusion as the present French Commander-in-Chief. Hence the contradiction between the views of the American Supreme Commanders-in-Chief in Europe, who insisted unwaveringly that Europe cannot be defended without resorting to nuclear weapons, and the arguments advanced by the U.S. government in favor of an increase in conventional forces.

It is easy to demonstrate that the two systems — the conventional one and the nuclear one — have hardly anything in common, and that, in a future contest, the latter must inevitably triumph over the former. . . .

To make European countries believe that they must increase their conventional forces, and that only upon the defeat of these forces should recourse be had to nuclear weapons, is a fanciful endeavor. Great Britain understood long ago the uselessness of conventional armament in Europe. The more the European nations on the Continent equip themselves conventionally, the more vulnerable they will be to nuclear attack and therefore the stronger will be the temptation for the opponent to use nuclear weapons. Thus, the promoters of conventional rearmament in Europe are defeating their own aims. They strengthen the potential power of the adversary, who knows that he has no reason to fear a nuclear response. They offer to his nuclear cudgel unprotected and tempting targets, and thus encourage him to take the initiative.

The likely explanation for such dangerous advice must be sought elsewhere than in the canons of strategic logic. Is it given with an eye to preparing the way for Western Europe's "denuclearization?" By substituting for the nuclear system an enlarged conventional system, backed up by a dubious threat of strategic nuclear action, the lower rungs of the nuclear ladder on which many Europeans think that their safety hinges would be removed — and "escalation" would, hopefully, be halted at the bottom.

Many decisions taken unilaterally by Washington convey the idea that this, indeed, is the policy of the United States. Thus, we have gone a long way from the solutions put forward by the United States in 1957, when it proposed to extend nuclear weaponry to all NATO theaters and to make available to the Supreme Commander in Europe IRBM squadrons that would be manned by European personnel. The nuclear tide of the late 1950's is now receding. Reliance on conventional means, though diminishing the direct risks of the Americans, certainly increases those incurred by the Europeans. . . .

The reason for the long-standing crisis of NATO is simple: the leader of the Western coalition tries to reconcile the irreconcilable. He refuses to accept for his country the formidable risks now inherent in all alliances. But, at the same time, he dares not face up to the logical consequences of the new situations, and proposes alternative solutions which are inadequate and dangerous as well as unacceptable to any country other than the U.S.

If it is not too late, it might be better to return to the policy of the previous Administration, namely the unconditional guarantee of the security of Western Europe. Today, Khrushchev is not afraid to run the very same risks in Cuba which Kennedy would like to avoid in Western Europe. But if the United States deems it imprudent to go back to Dulles' forthright pledge, then it must accept a measure of proliferation of nuclear weapons, a proliferations which it cannot prevent — no more in Western Europe than it has been able to do in China. The United States, by coming to terms with the necessities of the age, might find a way out of the deadlock in which it has become entangled.

## Note

24. Henry Kissinger, "Limited War: Conventional or Nuclear," *The Fifteen Nations*, March 1961.

# An Independent Nuclear Force for France

### *Documents 11 and 12*

In 1964, Premier Georges Pompidou justified France's decision to develop its own nuclear force. In document 11, Pompidou echoes General Gallois's concerns about the U.S. nuclear guarantee. He says France needs nuclear weapons to ensure that an aggressor knows an attack on Western Europe would receive a nuclear response. He also raises the fear that without a French nuclear force, a nuclear war might be confined to the territory of Western Europe. In document 12, French Army Chief of Staff Ailleret takes the argument one step further: that the world is no longer simply divided into two alliance groupings. Threats to French security could come from anywhere, so France cannot be locked into an alliance. France needs completely independent nuclear force and foreign policy.

## 11 ADDRESS TO THE NATIONAL ASSEMBLY French Premier Georges Pompidou December 2, 1964

France wants peace. France has no demands to make. France is not threatening anyone and has no expansionist aims anywhere. France is ready to disarm if those who are overarmed set the example. But in the present situation France is compelled to prepare to defend itself. Actually, defense today is impossible without nuclear force.

(1) The atomic bomb has changed everything. It is not only the most modern weapon, just as tanks, planes, or heavy artillery or machine guns were in the past. It is the weapon the possession of which gives certainty of victory — immediate and unchallengeable victory — over an adversary who does not have it.

One cannot, therefore, resign oneself to not having it, unless one resigns oneself either to being a protectorate, pure and simple, or to relying on the wisdom of all the nations and of all their leaders. The latter assumption is such a dangerous gamble that as soon as one has the means to possess the atomic weapon one has the obligation to do so. In any case it is a gamble that no great power seems willing to take since — and this is no accident — the five great powers at San Francisco, which became the permanent members of the Security Council, are today nuclear powers in varying degrees and everyone is talking about the desire of the others to get closer to the atomic weapon.

(2) The destructiveness of the atomic weapon is such

that war can only be envisaged as total catastrophe. Hence it is no longer a question of "preparing for victory" but of safeguarding the peace. In the words of a military writer, "the role of the nuclear weapon is not to make war but to prevent it." This is what is called deterrence, which means "to be in possession of a destruction capability, as compared with a possible enemy, which is such that the latter will realize that he will be able to gain the victory only at the cost of unbearable sacrifices."

For this it is desirable, but it is not essential, to be the equal of the enemy. It suffices if the blows that one has the capability to deal him are sufficiently heavy to remove temptation.

## Deterrence Rests Essentially on This Psychological Element

(3) But in order for it to count, it is necessary that the enemy be convinced that he cannot escape the impact of atomic weapons on his own soil. Otherwise, he might hope to win, either in a conventional war or in an atomic war waged beyond his own borders without great harm to him, particularly if he has sufficient mass potential and a territory protected by remoteness or by its vastness.

(4) This is what explains our attitude toward NATO, that is, toward American protection. As long as the United States had an actual monopoly on the nuclear weapon we were certain of victory, to be sure, but also of deterrence.

(5) Today the American Alliance still provides the certainty of final victory, but it no longer gives assurance of not being attacked, because the United States is henceforth within range of the nuclear weapons of its possible enemy. Hence the latter might hope to limit the theater of operations to Western Europe, conquer it by using its conventional or even its atomic means, and then see the United States draw back from the decision to destroy itself which an attack with all its nuclear weapons against the territory of the U.S.S.R. itself would involve. The risk is real. The past proves it since at a time when war was infinitely less terrible Wilhelm II could believe that Great Britain would not intervene and Hitler could believe that Great Britain and *a fortiori* the United States would accept the defeat of France and would halt the war or would not declare war. The risk lies not so much in our uncertainty regarding the decision of the United States as in the error in evaluation that the enemy might make. Was it not an analogous error in evaluation that Soviet Russia made just recently in the Cuban affair?

(6) It is necessary, therefore, that France, in order to be protected from the risk of war, should possess nuclear weapons such that the aggressor would know with certainty that he cannot hope to attack and win without inevitably suffering destruction such that he could not bear it, or at least such as to remove all attraction from the hypothesis of victory. Hence our program, which is giving us a destruction capability that is adequate because it is equivalent to the stake which our country can represent.

(7) By adopting this attitude we are at the same time amply helping to protect Europe. It goes without saying that if Great Britain had chosen to link itself closely to Western Europe, the addition of its nuclear power to ours would have increased the value of the deterrent considerably, but it did not choose to do so. We sincerely hope that some day it will change its policy. Meanwhile the only systems which have been suggested consist more or less of integrating the forces belonging to European nations with a portion of the American forces, creating a joint power of decision. This is a double-veto system. Such a system gives Europe no guarantee. In the first place, Europe is no longer sure of its defense in the sense that I meant it above since the enemy may at any moment doubt that the U.S.A. would decide to intervene all-out for the benefit of a European state.

Moreover, Europe would not find in such a system any real capability, either of blocking the launching of an atomic war or, on the other hand, of being free to launch one in its own defense. . . .

(9) It has been maintained that it would be better if this nuclear force did not remain exclusively French but were integrated in a European force. Theoretically, this would make it possible for the force to become stronger and thus be a more effective deterrent. However, it should be noted that because of the very fact that France is in Europe its force operates fully and automatically to the advantage of Europe, whose defense is inseparable from its own — which is not the case with forces, even allied forces, which are outside the European Continent.

Furthermore, the creation of a European nuclear force raises a number of questions for which there is no solution under the present circumstances.

In the first place, the question of Germany's participation. Arming Germany with nuclear weapons would, in the eyes of the U.S.S.R., constitute a grave act the consequences of which could not be measured. The U.S.S.R. has not yet forgotten what the last war was like, with Hitler's armies at the gates of Leningrad, Moscow and Sebastopol. Nor have Poland, Czechoslovakia, or Rumania, for their part, forgotten it. There is here a need for caution, which the Federal Republic itself has recognized.

Furthermore, an integrated European defense can be conceived of only if there is first a political Europe that has its own policy and consequently its own defense. That is an ideal we not only contemplate but hope for. . . .

Such is our national defense policy. It is none the less European, and we are not responsible for seeing that it becomes more so. National or European, it in no wise deviates from the Atlantic Alliance, which we know to be necessary for the final victory and extremely useful as a deterrent. In arming ourselves, not to prepare for war but to render war impossible because it would be tragic for the aggressor, however powerful he might be, we are discharging an essential duty to the country, the most important one of all, for on it depends the very survival of France and its people — and we are also discharging that duty to Europe. . . .

## 12 DIRECTED DEFENSE
## Général d'Armée Ailleret
## December 1967

For a long time now, we in France have been accustomed to having a favourite possible enemy, and sometimes even such a favourite as to be, in fact, the only one. Having been England for many years, this enemy was more recently the German Reich.

Thus in 1912 and 1913, when General Joffre was Chief of the General Staff and Commander in Chief designate of our forces, there was for him only one main enemy against whom he had to prepare: Germany. Although she might be assisted by Austria-Hungary, Joffre knew that it was against Germany that he would have to conduct operations with our forces. In the 1930s, too, it was still the same for the unfortunate General Gamelin, who knew that if he had to fight against anyone, it would be the armies of Hitler.

In these circumstances, with the passage of time it had become a sort of necessity for us to have a single, well-defined, possible enemy, against and in terms of whom it was expedient to prepare our plans and our forces. After World War II our main former enemy, Germany, had disappeared. That country, crushed and occupied, would need a long time to repair the extensive destruction which it had brought down upon itself as well as upon others. For the moment at least, it was no longer the dangerous enemy which it had been.

But exactly at that time another, equally dangerous, threat seemed to appear on the horizon, to the East of Europe, with the rise of Stalin's imperialism. Having already swallowed up half of the continent, it seemed ready to conquer the rest, and it certainly had the means to do so, even with conventional armaments only. Faced with this visible danger, our country again found one of those favourite enemies, of a special kind, against whom her defences had to be organized.

This was done; and, as was only natural in view of the disproportion between our forces and those of the possible aggressor, it was done within the framework of an alliance of a certain number of countries all concerned about the same threat: the Atlantic Alliance.

But since in those days the only threat to its members seemed to be that of the Soviet bloc, this alliance soon came to endow itself with a military organization whose aim was to concentrate all the defence efforts of the member countries in a single system, adapted to that threat; and it seemed reasonable to assume that the maximum output and efficiency would be obtained from the resources of the various allied countries.

A chain of integrated allied operational Commands was formed in peacetime, and a common infrastructure, jointly financed and spread over the territory of the various members, was launched. In these circumstances, it was not illogical from the point of view of the Alliance to wish to determine the amounts and types of forces which each country should put at the disposal of the Alliance in the event of a crisis, in terms of the single criterion of the output which it was possible to obtain from the global resources of the Alliance. NATO was continually trying to fix the possible national contributions. Since the United States' atomic "umbrella" furnished the destructive power with intercontinental range — which was also an effective deterrent — the other countries would be obliged to supply certain quantities of conventional forces, whose modern armaments would as far as possible, and preferably, be manufactured in the United States of America, "the arsenal of democracies."

According to this conception, it would have been quite useless, and even regrettable, that France should make the effort to manufacture her own nuclear armament, since there already was one in the USA, and since the effort would use up resources which, in the opinion of NATO, would be better employed in creating conventional units capable of reinforcing the famous 'shield', to use the terminology of that time.

Even in the case of a single danger in the present and in the future, that of Soviet aggression, this system would have had the serious disadvantage for us of basing our safety strictly on our membership of the Alliance, of making it depend entirely on the Alliance and in fact on the United States, since nuclear arms would henceforth be playing the vital role in world strategy.

The defence of France would therefore have been entrusted entirely to the United States of America, and French forces would, if the necessity arose, have been engaged by the decisions of American generals and not of French leaders acting upon the instructions of our Government. Our forces would thus have become a species of French sharp-shooters in the American armies, integrated into a system of which we would have formed one of the primitive parts; the sophisticated parts, powerful by nature and consequently considered noble, being American. France would thus have lost, together with her autonomy in defence, her actual independence.

There would, of course, have been the fiction of the collective management of the Alliance in which our country would have had a voice. But what could that one voice have been, compared with that of the most powerful (and by how much) member of the Alliance. France would only have been able, at the cost of much energy and thanks to the system of unanimity required for any "decision" to be adopted, to block the publication of certain "papers" without being in the least able to modify or even bend the policy of the predominant member. French forces and our whole country could thus have become engaged in a strategy which would have had the approval neither of our Government nor of our Command.

Thus, in the case of a threat of Soviet aggression, which was assumed to be the only threat now and for the future, France would no longer have had any role to play in her own defence, within the NATO system, except that of providing the Alliance's military organization with conventional facilities which would be at the disposal of an integrated Command, i.e., in practice, of an American Command. . . .

Yet another danger seemed, during the 1950s, to reduce the menace of Soviet aggression: the integrated military organization of the North Atlantic Treaty, an organization which was essentially defensive should it need to face external aggression, necessarily involved a mixture of the military systems of the member countries. There were many bases functioning on our territory. And, starting from those bases — especially air bases — which in theory had no other purpose than to meet aggression, our allies could operate freely with their resources, to support their policies of the time, which, unless we became protectorates, could be different from ours, or could even be opposed to ours.

Moreover, the dispositions of our forces, as well as our support organizations, were closely enmeshed with those of the allied forces. If then one of our allies came to be involved in a war which was not a result of Soviet aggression, and therefore in a situation which did not conform to the basic presumption of the Treaty, it was possible, if not probable, that he might or might not operate from bases situated on our territory, that these bases might be attacked by his enemy, which would involve our territory being attacked, and that his forces might also be attacked wherever they were, and consequently our forces, which were integrated with his, would also be attacked.

We thus ran the risk of being involved, without being able to decide upon our attitude, in a conflict which might not concern France. NATO thus presented a great danger for us in that it could draw our forces into military operations for the sole reason that certain of our allies, and in particular the leading allies, were involved in them.

But an even greater danger would have been that of continuing the French military effort in one direction only, namely against the threat which the Atlantic Alliance was designed to meet. For unrestricted participation in NATO would necessarily lead us to that situation. Already dependent upon the United States for our defence against a hypothetical Soviet attack, we should also have been dependent upon her in any other danger, whatever it was, which might threaten us. But could we then be certain that the Alliance, or its most powerful member, would always agree to defend us, especially in a situation which did not conform to the presumption of the Treaty?

This risk had not escaped those in our armies who from 1950 onwards, while proving that it was feasible, had begun to urge that France should form her own atomic armament, which would enable her to meet those threats not covered by NATO and, consequently, to recover a certain amount of national independence.

However, at the time when Stalin's imperialism was reaching its apogee and also had the nuclear weapon, one could reasonably have asked whether, apart from a few decolonization military operations, France would have to face any serious threats other than that of the possible Soviet aggression anticipated by the Atlantic Alliance.

Today an analysis of the world situation shows that we should not allow ourselves to be obsessed by the contemplation of this one danger. First, that danger, in its original form, seems to be considerably reduced. The Soviets appear at the moment to have no wish to launch a war. Busy as they are in rapidly developing their economy, in striving to raise the people's standard of living, they realize that to do this they need peace and also a certain amount of technical co-operation with the West. Moreover, the balance of terror between the Soviet and the American thermonuclear forces inevitably leads both parties to renounce war — at least large-scale war, if not war in its disguised, localized and proxy forms — in order to promote their policies.

On the whole, it does not seem that the great fear of Soviet aggression, so logical and explicable a few years after World War II, is justified today. Although the hypothesis of such aggression is still clearly a theoretical hypothesis which cannot be completely excluded for an indefinite future, it is certainly not to be considered the only or even the primary hypothesis.

The world situation offers us, on the contrary, a spectacle of such disorder, such agitation, such development, that while it is hardly possible to identify anywhere precisely the potential threats to our country, it is also impossible to rely on the present balances of power in order to forecast the future. These balances of power are, more often than not, so unstable that they may be replaced at any moment by completely different situations.

It should be noted here that one does not produce a defence and the means of defence (which are both, especially armies, their armaments and their doctrines, the result of a long process of continuous creation) shortly after setting to work. They are organized at the same time for the immediate future and for a more distant future; this gives rise to particularly difficult problems of selection when the world is developing as fast as it is today. If we plan the setting up of a defence today, it will not be completed for twenty years. What will the world situation be at that time? Who can say? . . .

. . . A major war of the future, other than those phoney wars which are the present-day local and limited conflicts, could henceforth originate anywhere and could immediately, or at least very quickly, set the whole world ablaze.

Our country, although it is utterly peaceful and has no intention of attacking anyone or interfering in the affairs of anyone, could thus be involved in a conflict of unforeseen origin, whether we were attacked by one of the adversaries who wanted to use our territory or our facilities in his struggle, or whether we were attacked or destroyed from a distance by one of the belligerents who wanted to prevent his enemy from using our land or our resources.

How can our country escape this threat since it would no longer be protected by distance or time? An *a priori* alliance could not give us a general guarantee of safety, since it is almost impossible to foresee what could one day be the cause of a serious conflict, and what would be the distribution of the powers between the various sides, or what hold, even unauthorized, any power would have over the territory of any other power.

It seems that, in order to be able to meet such situations, our country must have the maximum possible capacity to dissuade, by its possible actions, those who might be induced to seize our territory or destroy it with bombs. Our country must, therefore, be as strong as possible by itself, with due regard to its resources and the philosophy of life of its people. Now, in the arsenal of modern armaments, those which have the best output, that is the most efficiency for a given cost, are, by a long way, nuclear armaments. These are, moreover, those weapons which are capable, by their long distance action, by the threat of their terrible effects, of dissuading possible attacks by making them quite disproportionate to the benefits to be obtained.

If France wishes to escape the dangers which could threaten her, she must, therefore, possess a significant quantity — which does not need to be large by reason of their unit power — of megaton ballistic missiles, with a world-wide range, whose action could deter those who, from whatever part of the world they might be operating, might wish to exploit or destroy us in order to achieve their war aims.

To be as strong as possible, autonomously and individually, and to possess our own very long-range armament with very great power, capable of dissuading any aggressor, whatever his starting point, is clearly a completely different formula from that which would consist of forming, for the same expenditure, a force supplementary to that of the main member of an *a priori* alliance.

# European Worries About a Rearmed Germany

## *Document 13*

**When North Korea invaded South Korea in 1950, most Western leaders believed that this might be a prelude to a Soviet attack in Western Europe. Key U.S. leaders became convinced that West Germany should be allowed to join NATO and rearm. However, the French and other Europeans were not so enthusiastic about the idea. In document 13, a 1951 internal State Department memorandum, Secretary of State Dean Acheson argues that the German participation in West Europe's defense is needed. However, he argues that the French are sure to object because of their historical fears of a rearmed Germany.**

## 13 SECRET INTERNAL STATE DEPARTMENT MEMORANDUM
## Dean Acheson, Secretary of State
## July 6, 1951

There are several groups of problems which present obstacles — and indeed serious threats — to the creation of an adequate defense for Europe. This memorandum deals with two or three of these groups of problems.

I

The first group of problems relates to the question of German participation. These may be stated in several ways. One way is to separate them, for purposes of identification, into the problems of the United States, the French (and to some extent the European), and the German points of view.

### A. The United States Point of View

I doubt whether it will be possible to provide the steady and sustained United States effort which is necessary to solve the European defense problem unless the question of German participation is settled in the not too distant future. This flows from the strong American characteristic of wanting to see a practicable program for the solution of a problem before whole-hearted and sustained American effort can be evoked.

To us it seems that, without enthusiastic German participation, the problem is pretty hopeless. In the first place, when we look at the map of Europe, it seems clear that the area to be defended must include Germany in order that there can be a practicable military operation. In the second place, it seems to us that, if the decision is made to abandon Germany, that country and its people will fall to the other side and that will make the whole problem unmanageable. In the third place, Americans are not going to work wholeheartedly for the defense of a country, the people of which are not sharing in the burden of their own defense.

For all of these reasons, from the American point of view, the solution of the question of German participation cannot be long delayed.

### B. The French Point of View

To the French the creation of the German army presents the gravest fears and dangers. They believe that this would raise the historical dangers of German military aggression; that it might lead to the involvement of Western Europe in a German crusade to recover Eastern Germany and the lost provinces; and that it would certainly involve putting Germany in the position of holding the balance of power and asking for bids from East and West for German favor. The French, I believe, will not cooperate in a program of German rearmament which does not give what they regard as adequate safeguards.

Furthermore, France will not cooperate in the essential program of progressive restoration of sovereignty to Germany until the military question is settled. Failure to get on with this program will raise the gravest questions of German adherence to the West.

It is for these reasons that the French have put forward the idea of a European Army which would include German units in such form and under such controls that, should British and American troops be withdrawn from Europe, the German contingents could not become disentangled from an abiding European defense structure.

We find many of the French proposals are impracticable from a military point of view. Furthermore the desire to establish economic and political institutions, which would support and control the Army, in complete and final form, raises such difficult problems as to promise a very long delay.

### C. The German Point of View

While it is hard to state this accurately, it seems true that the Germans would accept rearmament in a European setting in which they had a position of equality. They fear, as do the French, the re-establishment of the old military organizations, because they would carry the serious risk of increasing political control in Germany by the General Staff and the Officer Corps.

To them, the heart of the matter is the restoration of a large degree of sovereignty and a position of equality or lack of discrimination. This is just what the French will not accord until the military question is settled.

These three attitudes are producing stalemate. We Americans are impatient and wish to get on with German participation. The Germans and the French will not move — the French, because the military question must be settled before the question of German sovereignty can be attacked; the Germans, because the question of sovereignty and equality must be settled before they will move on the military matter.

It seems to me that two conclusions emerge from this analysis.

The first is that progress requires meeting all these points of view simultaneously and not picking one out for priority of treatment.

The second is that all the questions involved in meeting these points of view cannot be settled finally and completely before any practical, forward steps are taken — if these steps are to be taken in time.

## The Soviets and Germans Disagree About German Rearmament

### *Documents 14 and 15*

The United States continued to press for German rearmament as a way to strengthen NATO. It was not easy. In 1954, after France blocked a proposal for an integrated European army with German participation, Secretary of State Dulles threatened to make an "agonizing reappraisal" of U.S. commitments to NATO unless some way were found to rearm Germany and integrate it into NATO. West Germany was finally admitted to NATO in 1955. and a program of rapid rearmament began. The Germans were forbidden to acquire long-range missiles or an independent nuclear weapons capability. Nuclear weapons under U.S. control were stationed and stored in West Germany (as they are today). German rearmament and especially the presence of nuclear weapons on German soil sparked angry criticism and threats from the Soviet Union.

In document 14, the West German government responds to some of the Soviet charges, arguing that its rearmament poses no threat to peace.

The Soviet reaction to German rearmament was not just verbal. In 1955 it set up the Warsaw Treaty Organization, a military alliance of the Soviet Union and its East European satellites. As document 15 indicates, it justified the new organization as a response to "the revival of German militarism and the integration of Western Germany into the aggressive North Atlantic bloc."

### 14 MEMORANDUM FROM WEST GERMANY TO THE SOVIET UNION
**Chancellor Konrad Adenauer**
**September 2, 1956**

(5) It cannot be accepted that the setting up by the Federal Republic of her own Armed Forces creates any

serious apprehension on the part of the Soviet Government with regard to their own security or the security of Germany's Eastern neighbours. It is one of the incontestable prerogatives of every sovereign State to exercise the right of individual and collective self-defence, a right accorded to every State in Article 51 of the Charter of the United Nations of which the Soviet Union is a member. Furthermore, the Soviet Government themselves proposed on the 10th of March, 1952 in their draft peace treaty for Germany that a reunited Germany should be allowed to have her own national armed forces (land, sea, and air) necessary for the defence of the country. The strength of the forces which the Federal Republic is planning to set up is, in proportion to the population of the Federal Republic, far below the level of armaments maintained by most of the other States in Europe, and in particular in Eastern Europe. The general compulsory military service introduced by the Federal Republic is the same form of military service as is usual in the Soviet Union. The Federal Republic was the only country in the world solemnly to forego the production not only of all weapons of mass destruction (atomic, biological, and chemical weapons) but, over and above this, of numerous kinds of heavy weapons. This fact alone clearly demonstrates the defensive nature of her military measures.

(7) Nor does the fact that the Armed Forces are being set up in connexion with the Federal Republic's membership of the North Atlantic Treaty Organisation and Western European Union change anything in this evaluation. If this is what is causing the Soviet Union apprehension, then it must be stated first of all that the concern expressed by the Soviet side with regard to the Federal Republic's membership of these organisations is based on erroneous assumptions as to their nature. Both the North Atlantic Treaty Organisation and Western European Union are associations which exclusively serve the purpose of individual and collective self-defence. In addition, Western European Union at the same time constitutes an effective system for limiting and controlling the armaments of member States. It is an example of what can be achieved in the field of limitation and control of armaments, if nations co-operate for the purpose of promoting peace and easing tension.

The members of the Atlantic and Western European defense organisations are in complete agreement as regards the defensive nature of their purpose. Each of them has the greatest interest in seeing that no member country in pursuing its national political aims takes any step which might lead to military entanglements. Membership of these organisations must therefore have a moderating effect on the policy of every member State. A member State may count on the help of its Allies only if it is found to have been attacked.

Here it must be repeated that, after the wars and catastrophes of recent decades, the craving of every people, and in particular, of the two peoples of Germany and the Soviet Union, so hard hit in two world wars, for an international order offering security and peace to all is profoundly understandable. The Federal Government are determined to achieve the reunification of the separated parts of Germany exclusively by peaceful means. They are ready at any time to repeat in binding form vis-à-vis the Soviet Union and other neighbouring Eastern States their renunciation of force declared to the Western peoples, a renunciation which holds good for their relationship with all peoples.

## 15 SOVIET REACTIONS TO THE WARSAW TREATY Moscow May 21, 1955

The Warsaw Treaty is a defensive treaty. The parties to it undertake, in the event of any of them being attacked, to exercise their right under Article 51 of the U. N. Charter and come to the immediate assistance of the state or states attacked with all the means they may deem necessary, including armed force. They have agreed to set up a joint command of the armed forces which they

"MAY I CARRY IT WHILE WE PASS THE BIG BOYS?"

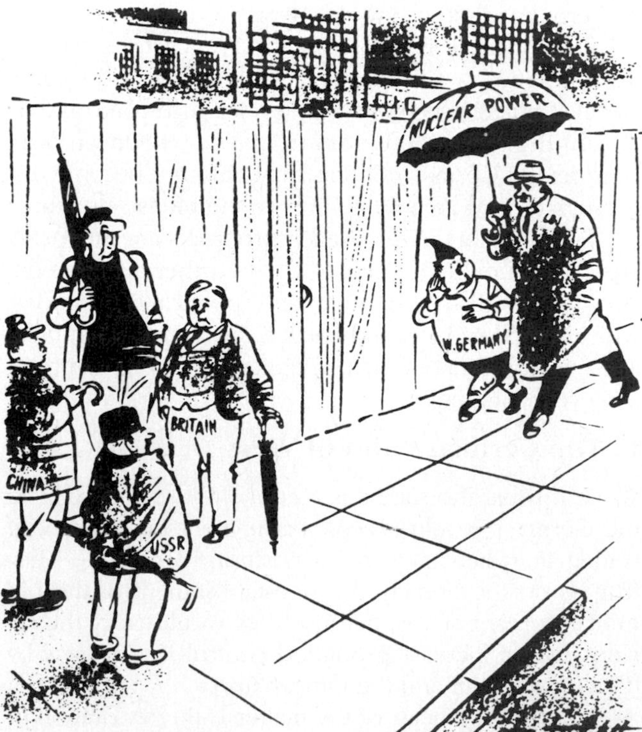


Pratt in *The Sacramento Bee*

The United States in World Affairs, 1965, published by the Council on Foreign Relations.

will by agreement assign to it. The aggressive blocs formed by the imperialist powers will henceforth be confronted with the combined might of the peaceable European states. The solid front of peace is further fortified by the unreserved support accorded to the Warsaw decisions by the 600 million people of China.

This fact upsets the equanimity of those who are planning to accomplish their aims by engineering and unloosing aggression in Europe. Their irritation is reflected in the columns of the reactionary press which, as usual, at first endeavoured to keep the substance of the Warsaw Treaty from the knowledge of the public. But realizing that this was futile, it has changed its tactics and is now trying to misrepresent the Warsaw decisions, to create a false impression of their nature and purpose.

First of all, it is insistently suggested that the Warsaw Treaty of Friendship, Cooperation and Mutual Assistance resembles the North-Atlantic pact, that its effect will be to "finalize" the division of Europe into two mutually-opposed military alignments. There is not an atom of truth in this claim.

The fact is that the Warsaw Treaty and such aggressive imperialist blocs as the North-Atlantic alliance are worlds apart. Whereas blocs formed by imperialist powers are based on the domination of some states and the subordination of others, the Warsaw Treaty is founded on the principle of respect for the sovereignty of states and non-interference in their internal affairs. A distinctive feature of aggressive blocs, directed against non-participating countries, is that they deny other states free accession to them. In contrast, the Warsaw Treaty is open to all countries that may wish to join it, regardless of their social and political systems. More, Article 11 of the Treaty states specifically that in the event of the establishment of a system of collective security in Europe, and of the conclusion of a general European treaty of collective security to this end the eight-nations Treaty will cease to be operative from the day the general European treaty enters into force.

Thus the assertion that the Warsaw Treaty countries are out to "finalize" the division of Europe is entirely without foundation. In fact, it is the other way round: the Warsaw Treaty opens up a real possibility of establishing an effective system of *all-European* security.

# MANAGING THE NATO DETERRENT

## The Birth of the British Sea-Based Deterrent

### *Document 16*

One of the United States' major problems in NATO in the late 1950s and 1960s was how to deal with independent nuclear forces in Great Britain and France. Through the 1962 Nassau Agreement, the United States developed a good working relationship with Great Britain.

In the 1950s Great Britain's nuclear deterrent consisted of V-bombers. In 1960 the United States agreed to sell the British Skybolt air-launched ballistic missiles to augment that force. But in 1962, the United States decided to cancel the Skybolt program. At a meeting between President Kennedy and British Prime Minister Harold Macmillan in late 1962, the United States offered Polaris submarine-launched missiles as a substitute. The British agreed. The Nassau Agreement, excerpted in document 16, marked the birth of the British sea-based deterrent, which remains the principal British nuclear force. Today, all British nuclear forces are assigned to NATO, although the British have the right to withdraw them from NATO control in times of national emergency.

### 16 THE NASSAU AGREEMENT 1962

(1) The President and the Prime Minister reviewed the development program for the Skybolt missile. The President explained that it was no longer expected that this very complex weapons system would be completed within the cost estimate or the time scale which were projected when the program was begun.

(2) The President informed the Prime Minister that for this reason and because of the availability to the United States of alternative weapons systems, he had decided to cancel plans for the production of Skybolt for use by the United States. Nevertheless, recognizing the importance of the Skybolt program for the United Kingdom, and recalling that the purpose of the offer of Skybolt to the United Kingdom in 1960 had been to assist in improving and extending the effective life of the British V-bombers, the President expressed his readiness to continue the development of the missile as a joint enterprise between the United States and the United Kingdom, with each country bearing equal shares of the future cost of completing development, after which the United Kingdom would be able to place a production order to meet its requirements.

(3) While recognizing the value of this offer, the Prime Minister decided, after full consideration, not to avail himself of it because of doubts that had been expressed about the prospects of success for this weapons system and because of uncertainty regarding date of completion and final cost of the program.

(4) As a possible alternative the President suggested that the Royal Air Force might use the Hound Dog mis-

sile. The Prime Minister responded that in the light of the technical difficulties he was unable to accept this suggestion.

(5) The Prime Minister then turned to the possibility of provision of the Polaris missile to the United Kingdom by the United States. After careful review, the President and the Prime Minister agreed that a decision on Polaris must be considered in the widest context both of the future defense of the Atlantic Alliance and of the safety of the whole Free World. They reached the conclusion that this issue created an opportunity for the development of new and closer arrangements for the organization and control of strategic Western defense and that such arrangements in turn could make a major contribution to political cohesion among the nations of the Alliance.

(6) The Prime Minister suggested and the President agreed, that for the immediate future a start could be made by subscribing to NATO some part of the forces already in existence. This could include allocations from United States Strategic Forces, from United Kingdom Bomber Command, and from tactical nuclear forces now held in Europe. Such forces would be assigned as part of a NATO nuclear force and targeted in accordance with NATO plans.

(7) Returning to Polaris the President and the Prime Minister agreed that the purpose of their two governments with respect to the provision of the Polaris missile must be the development of a multilateral NATO nuclear force in the closest consultation with other NATO allies. They use their best endeavours to this end.

(8) Accordingly, the President and the Prime Minister agreed that the U.S. will make available on a continuing basis Polaris missiles (less warheads) for British submarines. The U.S. will also study the feasibility of making available certain support facilities for such submarines. The U.K. Government will construct the submarines in which these weapons will be placed and they will also provide the nuclear warheads for the Polaris missiles. British forces developed under this plan will be assigned and targeted in the same way as the forces described in paragraph 6.

These forces, and at least equal U.S. forces, would be made available for inclusion in a NATO multilateral nuclear force. The Prime Minister made it clear that except where Her Majesty's Government may decide that supreme national interests are at stake, these British forces will be used for the purposes of international defense of the Western Alliance in all circumstances.

(9) The President and the Prime Minister are convinced that this new plan will strengthen the nuclear defense of the Western Alliance. In strategic terms this defense is indivisible, and it is their conviction that in all ordinary circumstances of crisis or danger, it is this very unit which is the best protection of the West.

(10) The President and the Prime Minister agreed that in addition to having a nuclear shield it is important to have a non-nuclear sword. For this purpose they agreed on the importance of increasing the effectiveness of their conventional forces on a worldwide basis.

## De Gaulle and the Nassau Agreement

### *Document 17*

The United States offered France the same deal it had reached with Great Britain at Nassau in the hopes of developing a similar close working arrangement that would prevent the creation of an independent French deterrent. In document 17, excerpts from a 1963 news conference, French President Charles de Gaulle rejects the U.S. offer and makes clear that he wants no part of an integrated NATO nuclear force.

### 17 NEWS CONFERENCE REMARKS
### President Charles de Gaulle
### January 14, 1963

*Question:* What is France's position concerning the Kennedy multilateral formula, that is to say, concerning the Nassau agreements? . . .

*Answer:* . . . We are in the atomic age and we are a country that can be destroyed at any moment unless the aggressor is deterred from the undertaking by the certainty that he too will suffer frightful destruction. This justifies both alliance and independence. The Americans, our allies and our friends, have for a long time, alone, possessed a nuclear arsenal. So long as they alone had such an arsenal and so long as they showed their will to use it immediately if Europe were attacked — for at that time Europe alone could be attacked — the Americans acted in such a way that for France the question of an invasion hardly arose, since an attack was beyond all probability. It was then a matter for the Atlantic Alliance, that is to say, for the American command, of having in Europe and America a tactical and strategic air force capable of using atomic weapons — for at that time only airplanes could do that — and thus capable of protecting Europe. It was also a matter of lining up in Europe itself conventional land, naval and air forces which could ensure the deployment and use of atomic weapons. It can be said that, during that period, the deterrent worked and that there existed a practically insuperable obstacle to an invasion of Europe. It is impossible to overestimate the extent of the service, most fortunately passive, that the Americans at that time, in that way, rendered to the freedom of the world.

Since then, the Soviets have also acquired a nuclear arsenal, and that arsenal is powerful enough to endanger the very life of America. Naturally, I am not making an evaluation — if indeed it is possible to find a relation between the degree of one death and the degree of another — but the new and gigantic fact is there. From then on, the Americans found and are finding themselves confronted with the possibility of direct destruction.Thus the immediate defense, and one can say privileged defense of Europe, and the military participation of the Europeans, which were once basic factors of their strategy, moved by the force of circumstances into second place. We have just witnessed this during the Cuban affair. . . .

Thus principles and realities combine to lead France to equip itself with an atomic force of its own. This does not all exclude, of course, the combination of the action of this force with the action of the similar forces of its allies. But, for us, in this specific case, integration is something that is unimaginable. Indeed, as you know, we have begun with our own and only means to invent, test and construct atomic bombs and the vehicles for launching them.

It is completely understandable that this French undertaking does not appear to be highly satisfactory to certain American circles. In politics and in strategy, as in the economy, monopoly quite naturally appears to the person who holds it to be the best possible system. . . .

. . . I only want to say that the French atomic force, from the very beginning of its establishment, will have the sombre and terrible capability of destroying in a few seconds millions and millions of men. This fact cannot fail to have at least some bearing on the intents of any possible aggressor.

Then, in the Bahamas, America and Britain concluded an agreement and we were asked to subscribe to it ourselves. Of course, I am only speaking of this proposal and agreement because they have been published and because their content is known. It is a question of constituting a so-called multilateral atomic force, in which Britain would turn over the weapons it has and will have and in which the Americans would place a few of their own. This multilateral force is assigned to the defense of Europe and is under the American NATO command. It is nevertheless understood that the British retain the possibility of withdrawing their atomic weapons for their own use should supreme national interest seem to them to demand it.

As for the bulk of American nuclear weapons, it remains outside the multilateral force and under the direct orders of the President of the United States. Furthermore and in a way by compensation, Britain may purchase from America, if it so desires, Polaris missiles which are, as you know, launched from submarines specially built for that purpose and which carry the thermonuclear warheads adapted to them for a distance of 1,100–2,000 miles. To build these submarines and warheads, the British receive privileged assistance from the Americans. You know — I say this in passing — that this assistance was never offered to us and you should know, despite what some report, that we have never asked for it.

"IF YOU NEED TO ASK WHAT IT COSTS, YOU CAN'T AFFORD IT."

By permission of Bill Mauldin and Wil-Jo Associates, Inc.

France has taken note of the Anglo American Nassau agreement. As it was conceived, undoubtedly no one will be surprised that we cannot subscribe to it. It truly would not be useful for us to buy Polaris missiles when we have neither the submarines to launch them nor the thermonuclear warheads to arm them. Doubtless the day will come when we will have these submarines and these warheads. But that day will be long in coming. For the World War, the invasion and their consequences have slowed us down a great deal in our atomic development. When we will one day have these submarines and these warheads, what will the Polaris missiles then be worth? At that time we will probably have missiles of our own invention. In other words, for us, in terms of technology, this affair is not the question of the moment.

But also, it does not meet with the principle about which I just spoke and which consists of disposing in our own right of our deterrent force. To turn over our weapons to a multilateral force, under a foreign command, would be to act contrary to that principle of our defense and our policy. It is true that we too can theoretically retain the ability to take back in our hands, in the supreme hypothesis, our atomic weapons incorporated in the multilateral force. But how could we do it in practice during the unheard of moments of the atomic apocalypse? And then, this multilateral force necessarily entails a web of liaisons, transmissions and interferences within itself, and on the outside a ring of obligations such that, if an integral part were suddenly snatched from it, there would be a strong risk of paralyzing it just at the moment, perhaps, when it should act.

In sum, we will adhere to the decision we have made: to construct and, if necessary, to employ our atomic force ourselves. And that without refusing, of course, cooperation, be it technological or strategic, if this cooperation is, on the other hand, desired by our allies.

## Failure of the Multilateral Force

### *Document 18*

In 1961 the Kennedy administration proposed the Multilateral Force (MLF), a fleet of twenty-five surface ships, each armed with eight nuclear-tipped Polaris missiles and staffed by sailors drawn from several NATO nations. The administration hoped the MLF would solve several problems. It would reassure NATO about the U.S. nuclear guarantee; it would satisfy the desire of some NATO nations for more say in nuclear planning and strategy; and it would head off the creation of an independent French nuclear force and lessen the danger that the West Germans might seek nuclear weapons.

In document 18, Josef Joffe, a West German political analyst, reviews the reasons why the MLF proved a failure. The MLF lacked a meaningful strategic role, and it tried to satisfy too many conflicting political interests. The MLF proposal was formally withdrawn by President Johnson in 1964.

### 18 ALLIES, ANGST, AND ARMS CONTROL: NEW TROUBLE FOR AN OLD PARTNERSHIP Josef Jaffe

#### From MLF to INF

Transatlantic doubts and debates about nuclear strategy have always been about politics. This is the central paradox of the postwar-security relationship between the United States and Europe. As we look at the widening fissures engendered by international-nuclear force (INF) modernization and arms control, fissures that have opened within societies as well as between allies, we might do well to recall the events of almost twenty years ago when the last attempt at countering the Soviet missile threat against Europe was launched and finally scuttled.

Twenty years ago, the Multilateral Force (MLF) raised a good many of the painful issues unsettling the alliance today. Although the MLF was ostensibly designed to address a strategic problem (Soviet medium-range ballistic missiles [MRBMs] deployed against Western Europe), it was at heart a political instrument of American diplomacy. Set in motion to allay European security concerns regarding the Soviet bloc, the missile-bearing fleet ended up provoking the most fearful disputes about power and paramountcy in the Western camp. In the process, the MLF provided an instructive case study in irony: solutions dramatized dilemmas; unifying moves deepened dissension; American accommodation to presumed European wishes spawned resentment and hostility among America's allies.

Reading an early postmortem of the MLF impresses the present-day reader with a haunting sense of deja vu. "The original proposal for a NATO multilateral force," wrote Henry Kissinger, a prominent student of the project, in 1965, grew out of a military "requirement" which had been generated in accordance with the NATO doctrine prevalent in the late fifties. According to this concept, SACEUR was to have the capability to destroy all weapons aimed at Europe. Thus when the Soviet Union began to deploy large numbers of medium-range ballistic missiles in western Russia, two NATO requirements emerged: a modernization program to replace vulnerable tactical aircraft with missiles and an interdiction mission giving NATO the capability to destroy the Soviet MRBMs.[25]

When a partial plan was first put forward by the Kennedy administration, "it did not elicit a significant European response." Nor was it, at this point "a high priority goal of American foreign policy."[26] The project assumed urgency only after French President de Gaulle, in his notorious press conference of January 14, 1963, vetoed Britain's application to the European Economic Community while heaping scorn on the very idea of nuclear integration. The MLF was infused with new vigor, but not because the strategic facts had suddenly changed. Ironically, "until six weeks before it emerged as a principal objective of American NATO policy, our highest officials had declared the MLF militarily necessary."[27] The MLF was activated because de Gaulle had issued his strongest-ever challenge to American hegemony at the same time that he was multiplying his efforts in the transatlantic tug-of-war for Germany's allegiance.

"If de Gaulle meant to make West Germany choose between France and the United States," an inside chronicler of the Kennedy administration noted, "the MLF, in Washington's view, was the way to make it clear that Bonn would find greater security in the Atlantic relationship."[28] The many-flagged fleet was thus set on a strictly political course, turning into a multipurpose diplomatic instrument. It was designed to harness Germany's presumed nuclear ambitions to a collective enterprise (under American control). It was to discourage the allies from following England's and France's lead into their own quest for a national deterrent. It was supposed to bridge the status gap between the alliance's nuclear haves and have-nots. In short, the MLF was to enhance centralized American control over nuclear weapons under the guise of sharing them, since Washington's veto on the actual use of the seaborne missiles was to be retained under all circumstances.

Given its political thrust, the MLF's strategic rationale remained in the dark — and mercifully so. The project raised many more problems than it could possibly solve. If the MLF's Polaris missiles were to generate a counterforce capability, why were only 200 projected? At this point, the Soviets had already deployed some 600 MRBMs against Western Europe; they could hardly be eliminated with a puny missile force a third as large. Yet if the MLF projectiles could achieve this task only in conjunction with the U.S. Strategic Air Command (SAC), why have two nuclear strike forces in the alliance — especially if both would remain under American control? If the new missiles were to lighten the burden of deterrence then carried by vulnerable strike aircraft, why put them on vulnerable surface ships? And if the MLF were to increase the credibility of extended deterrence by somehow integrating the European allies, why the insistence on an undiluted American veto? If the American president remained in charge, it was by no means self-evident that he would more readily launch a Polaris located on an MLF freighter off the European coast than the same missile located on an American submarine somewhere in the oceans. And if Washington were ever to relinquish its veto as some American officials were then hinting — the prospect was clearly absurd. It would have meant that the United States would either go to war with a very small portion of its nuclear arsenal (while holding back its SAC forces) or conversely throw everything into the battle, yet neither as result of a national decision, but rather in response to an Allied majority vote.

Luckily, these questions were never debated, luckily the MLF sank in the crossfire of political dissension before it could dramatize all the irreducible dilemmas embodied in a strategic doctrine erected on the uncertain premise of extended deterrence. The British remained politely indifferent. The French escalated their hostility as the Americans increased their pressure, and the smaller allies dropped out one by one. It was only in Germany that lukewarm interest changed into avid support. The transformation was preceded by a fierce domestic battle between Atlanticists and Gaullists (within the ruling CDU/CSU Party alignment). The day was carried by the Atlanticists around Chancellor Ludwig Erhard, yet the victory proved an empty one.

In the first place, Bonn's mounting attachment to the MLF (in the end only the Germans and the Americans were still committed to the project) was almost identical with its death knell. Among Bonn's allies this turn of events raised the specter of too much of a German say in matters nuclear (in a German-American axis) when most of them had warily gone along in order to prevent such increase. Secondly, once the Atlanticists had proved victorious at home (summer 1964) and once the Federal Republic loosened de Gaulle's embrace and returned to the American fold, the MLF was no longer necessary. Finally, American global interests began to shift — toward limited collaboration with the Soviet Union as exemplified by the Non-Proliferation Treaty (NPT) and toward escalation in Vietnam. By early 1965, the MLF was effectively scuttled.

## Notes

25. Henry A. Kissinger, *The Troubled Partnership* (New York: McGraw-Hill, 1965), p. 128.
26. *Ibid.,* pp. 130–31.
27. *Ibid.,* p. 141.
28. Arthur Schlesinger, *A Thousand Days* (New York: Fawcett Crest, 1967) pp. 744–5.

## Suggestions for Further Reading

Beer, Francis A. *Integration and Disintegration in NATO* (Columbus, O: Ohio State UP, 1969). A classic study of NATO's stresses and strains in its first two decades.

Kelleher, Catherine M. *Germany and the Politics of Nuclear Weapons* (New York: Columbia UP, 1975). A detailed and scholarly treatment of one of the core issues of European security.

Meyer, Stephen M. "Soviet Theater Nuclear Forces," *Adelphi Paper* Nos. 187 and 188 (London: International Institute for Strategic Studies, 1983). A comprehensive treatment of the development of Soviet doctrine, objectives, and forces for theater nuclear operations.

Schwartz, David. *NATO's Nuclear Dilemma* (Washington, D.C.: Brookings Institution, 1983). A study of the history of NATO's nuclear policy, focusing on the debate on the relative importance of nuclear and conventional forces in NATO's defense.

# Five

# AT THE BRINK

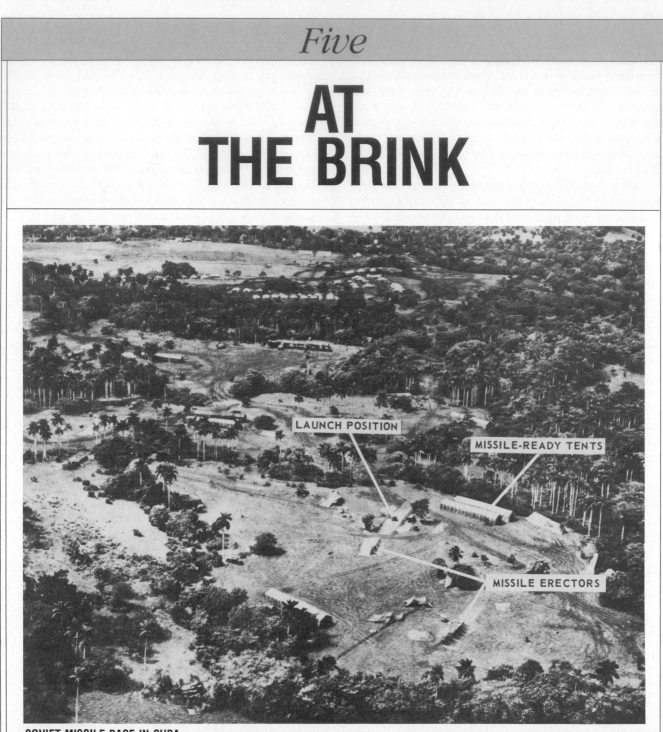

**SOVIET MISSILE BASE IN CUBA**

Although Soviet leaders denied the existence of Soviet missile bases in San Cristóbal, Cuba, this and other U.S. reconnaissance photographs provided evidence that such bases did indeed exist, setting off the Cuban missile crisis. The superpowers came frighteningly close to a nuclear war during this thirteen-day crisis in October 1962. AP/Wide World Photos

# INTRODUCTION

Although it is impossible to know exactly why the Soviets decided to deploy missiles in Cuba in 1962, it appears that they had several goals in mind. They surely wanted to protect their new ally, as Nikita Khrushchev stated in his memoirs. But it is unlikely that they would have taken such a huge gamble just to support Fidel Castro.

By 1962 Khrushchev's policy of nuclear bluff was clearly failing. His nuclear threats and boasts in the late 1950s had so alarmed the United States that the Kennedy administration launched a major buildup of nuclear weapons that extended the already significant U.S. lead. The new U.S. weapons and the U.S. counterforce doctrine appeared to pose a major threat to Soviet nuclear forces. In addition, improved U.S. intelligence-gathering methods had revealed the true size of the Soviet arsenal, so a bluff was no longer possible. Indeed, a Soviet effort to dislodge the West from Berlin had failed in 1961. Finally, Khrushchev probably realized that it would take a long time for the Soviet Union to catch up with the United States and that such an effort would use up scarce economic resources.

Deploying missiles in Cuba seemed to be a quick, cheap way to restore the balance. At a minimum it would be a political and propaganda triumph that would strengthen the Soviet's deterrent capability while solidifying Castro's position. Soviet leaders probably hoped that at worst the installation of missiles in Cuba would cause one more cold war diplomatic crisis. They also probably realized that a serious military confrontation might occur, but the high stakes made it worth the gamble.

Most experts agree, therefore, that the U.S. nuclear superiority was a major factor in the Soviet gamble that set off the crisis. But experts disagree on how great a role nuclear superiority played in the resolution of the crisis.

According to one view, the Cuban missile crisis proves how important nuclear superiority is and now dangerous it would be if the Soviets gained it. Analysts who hold this view argue that the United States was able to get the Soviets to withdraw their missiles because the Soviets knew the United States would come out well ahead in any nuclear exchange. Because of this U.S. superiority, the Soviets did not want to begin any chain of events that might lead to a nuclear exchange. The lesson of the missile crisis, these experts say, is that nuclear superiority does count.

Other experts disagree. They argue that the United States forced the Soviets to back down for two reasons. First, the United States had complete local conventional superiority. Cuba was only ninety miles from Florida, thousands of miles from the Soviet Union. Second, the United States triumphed because it convinced the Soviets that getting the missiles out was a vital interest that the United States would be willing to fight for. Although Cuba was important to the Soviets, in the end it was not a vital interest for them.

Those who hold this latter point of view argue that U.S. leaders did not behave as if they could be confident about the outcome of a nuclear war. Indeed, fear of nuclear escalation and the devastation it would bring to the United States was always on their minds.

Other "lessons" of the Cuban missile crisis are controversial. In 1972, a Soviet deputy foreign minister discussed the crisis, saying, "You Americans will never be able to do this to us again." It seems clear the Soviets decided they could never allow themselves to be in such a position of nuclear inferiority again. The Soviets embarked on a major strategic buildup in the mid-1960s that brought them parity less than a decade later.

In the first few years after the crisis, both superpowers concluded that they had to do more to reduce the danger of nuclear war. The first result was an agreement to set up the hot line. This was followed in 1963 with the Limited Test Ban Treaty and the start of negotiations on the Nonproliferation Treaty.

The crisis also provided lessons in crisis management in the nuclear age. The most dangerous situation is one in which one of the superpowers is faced with a choice between humiliation or surrender. President Kennedy and the Excom worked hard to leave the Soviets a graceful way out of the crisis by giving a public pledge not to invade Cuba and secret assurances that missiles in Turkey would be removed. Communication with the other side is critical. Much of the crisis focused on each side's communicating its demands and intentions to the other side.

Finally, although twenty-five years have passed, the leaders have changed, and the nuclear balance is very different, the crisis underlines certain continuing characteristics of the nuclear age. Each international crisis is played against the background of the possibility of nuclear war. The U.S.-Soviet competition for influence means that areas of the world with seemingly limited innate importance can lead to major crisis. In such a crisis, neither superpower can be completely confident that events can be controlled.

# BACKGROUND TO THE CUBAN MISSILE CRISIS

## Kennedy on the Threat from Cuba

### *Document 1*

The months following the abortive invasion attempt at the Bay of Pigs saw rising frustration among many Americans. Calls for a U.S. invasion or blockade of Castro's Cuba increased throughout the summer of 1962, particularly after Moscow began a massive military buildup on the island in late July. Upcoming congressional elections intensified criticism of Kennedy's handling of the Cuban situation.

In these excerpts from a September 1962 statement on his administration's policy toward Cuba, Kennedy forthrightly asserts that U.S. military intervention is neither required nor justified. He repeats his earlier warning that the United States would carefully monitor developments in the Caribbean and would do "whatever must be done to protect its own security and that of its allies" should Cuba attempt to export its revolution or become an offensive military base for the Soviet Union.

### 1 STATEMENT OF U.S. POLICY TOWARD CUBA
### President John F. Kennedy
### September 1962

There has been a great deal of talk on the situation in Cuba in recent days both in the Communist camp and in our own, and I would like to take this opportunity to set the matter in perspective. . . .

Ever since communism moved into Cuba in 1958, Soviet technical and military personnel have moved steadily onto the island in increasing numbers at the invitation of the Cuban government. Now that movement has been increased. It is under our most careful surveillance. But I will repeat the conclusion that I reported last week,[1] that these new shipments do not constitute a serious threat to any other part of this hemisphere.

If the United States ever should find it necessary to take military action against communism in Cuba, all of Castro's Communist-supplied weapons and technicians would not change the result or significantly extend the time required to achieve that result.

However, unilateral military intervention on the part of the United States cannot currently be either required or justified, and it is regrettable that loose talk about such action in this country might serve to give a thin color of legitimacy to the Communist pretense that such a threat exists. But let me make this clear once again: If at any time the Communist buildup in Cuba were to endanger or interfere with our security in any way, including our base at Guantanamo, our passage to the Panama Canal, our missile and space activities at Cape Canaveral, or the lives of American citizens in this country, or if Cuba should ever attempt to export its aggressive purposes by force or the threat of force against any nation in this hemisphere, or become an offensive military base of significant capacity for the Soviet Union, then this country will do whatever must be done to protect its own security and that of its allies.

We shall be alert to, and fully capable of dealing swiftly with, any such development. As President and Commander in Chief I have full authority now to take such action, and I have asked the Congress to authorize me to call up reserve forces should this or any other crisis make it necessary.

In the meantime we intend to do everything within our power to prevent such a threat from coming into existence. Our friends in Latin America must realize the consequences such developments hold out for their own peace and freedom, and we shall be making further proposals to them. Our friends in NATO must realize the implications of their ships' engaging in the Cuban trade.

We shall continue to work with Cuban refugee leaders who are dedicated as we are to that nation's future return to freedom. We shall continue to keep the American people and the Congress fully informed. We shall increase our surveillance of the whole Caribbean area. We shall neither initiate nor permit aggression in this hemisphere.

With this in mind, while I recognize that rash talk is cheap, particularly on the part of those who did not have the responsibility, I would hope that the future record will show that the only people talking about a war and invasion at this time are the Communist spokesmen in Moscow and Habana, and that the American people, defending as we do so much of the free world, will in this nuclear age, as they have in the past, keep both their nerve and their head.

### *Note*

1. *Department of State Bulletin,* Sept. 29, 1962, p. 450.

## Time for Action

### *Document 2*

Kennedy's Cuban policy was vigorously attacked by the Republicans as the fall 1962 congressional elections approached. Here, Republican Sen. Homer Capehart calls on Kennedy to stop "examining the situation" and take action against the Soviet threat.

### 2 SPEECH
### Sen. Homer L. Capehart (R-Ind.)
### August 27, 1962

How long will the President "examine the situation," as he has told a press conference he is doing? Until the hundreds of Russian troops grow into hundreds of thousands? Until the little Cuban military force grows into a big Russian force?

Whatever happened to the Monroe Doctrine? What the Russians are doing now and have been doing for months, with full knowledge of the White House, has been in violation of that same Monroe Doctrine adopted in 1823. Never before have we allowed it to be violated.

A lot of people in Washington have known for weeks that the so-called technicians, or at least a good part of them, are actually Communist military personnel. The facts are that there were about 400 agricultural experts and technicians in the Soviet ships which arrived and the rest of the 3,000 to 5,000 total were Communist military personnel.

Let me give you the facts as I know them:

Between 3,000 and 5,000 Soviet personnel arrived in Cuba in five Soviet passenger ships between July 27 and July 31.

Eleven cargo ships arrived in the same period.

Soviet personnel unloaded them.

Trucks were lowered into the holds of these ships, loaded and covered with tarpaulin.

Eyewitnesses reported seeing tanks, communications trucks and large truck-trailers carrying crates 40 feet long.

At least 15 more ships from Communist countries are on the way carrying the same kind of cargo and personnel.

Is Khrushchev testing the United States to see whether it is soft enough for him to continue such infiltration of other Latin-American countries?

It is time the American people demanded that President Kennedy quit "examining the situation" and start protecting the interests of the United States.

The law which permits him to do it is plain. From the standpoint of international law the United States has every right to land troops, take possession of Havana, and occupy the country, unless the Cuban Government answers satisfactorily the request of the U.S. Government that all Soviet military personnel be sent home and that no further shipments of military supplies be sanctioned by the Havana authorities.

## Khrushchev's Memoirs

### *Document 3*

In this excerpt from his memoirs, *Khrushchev Remembers,* Soviet leader Nikita Khrushchev emphasizes that he ordered nuclear-tipped missiles installed in Cuba as a tangible deterrent to another U.S.-sponsored invasion. He candidly admits, however, that he also desired to "equalize the balance of power" by increasing the military threat to the United States; intermediate-range missiles, once operational in Cuba, would become "ersatz ICBMs." Moreover, he notes, the deployment of Soviet missiles would enhance the Soviet Union's prestige in the Western Hemisphere and give the Americans a "little of their own medicine."

### 3 FIDEL CASTRO AND THE CARIBBEAN CRISIS
### Nikita Khrushchev

. . . Everyone agreed that America would not leave Cuba alone unless we did something. We had an obligation to do everything in our power to protect Cuba's existence as a Socialist country and as a working example to the other countries of Latin America. It was clear to me that we might very well lose Cuba if we didn't take some decisive steps in her defense.

The fate of Cuba and the maintenance of Soviet prestige in that part of the world preoccupied me even when I was busy conducting the affairs of state in Moscow and traveling to the other fraternal countries. While I was on an official visit to Bulgaria, for instance, one thought kept hammering away at my brain: what will happen if we lose Cuba? I knew it would have been a terrible blow to Marxism-Leninism. It would gravely diminish our stature throughout the world, but especially in Latin America. If Cuba fell, other Latin American countries would reject us, claiming that for all our might the Soviet Union hadn't been able to do anything for Cuba except to make empty protests to the United Nations. We had to think up some way of confronting America with more than words. We had to establish a tangible and effective deterrent to American interference in the Caribbean. But what exactly? The logical answer was missiles. The United States had already surrounded the Soviet Union with its own bomber bases and missiles. We knew that American missiles were aimed against us in Turkey and Italy, to say nothing of West Germany. Our vital industrial centers were directly threatened by planes armed with atomic bombs and guided missiles tipped with nuclear warheads. As Chairman of the Council of Ministers, I found myself in the difficult position of having to decide on a course of action which would answer the American threat but which would also avoid war. Any fool can start a war, and once he's done so, even the wisest of men are helpless to stop it — especially if it's a nuclear war.

It was during my visit to Bulgaria that I had the idea of installing missiles with nuclear warheads in Cuba without letting the United States find out they were there until it was too late to do anything about them. I knew that first we'd have to talk to Castro and explain our strategy to him in order to get the agreement of the Cuban government. My thinking went like this: if we installed the missiles secretly and then if the United States discovered the missiles were there after they were already poised and ready to strike, the Americans would think twice before trying to liquidate our installations by military means. I knew that the United States could knock out some of our installations, but not all of them. If a quarter or even a tenth of our missiles survived — even if only one or two big ones were left — we could still hit New York, and there wouldn't be much of New York left. I don't mean to say that everyone in New York would be killed — not everyone, of course, but an awful lot of people would be wiped out. I don't know how many: that's a matter for our scientists and military personnel to work out. They specialize in nuclear warfare and know how to calculate the consequences of a missile strike against a city the size of New York. But that's all beside the point. The main thing was that the installation of our missiles in Cuba would, I thought, restrain the United States from precipitous military action against Castro's government. In addition to protecting Cuba, our missiles would have equalized what the West likes to call "the balance of power." The Americans had surrounded our country with military bases and threatened us with nuclear weapons, and now they would learn just what it feels like to have enemy missiles pointing at you; we'd be doing nothing more than giving them a little of their own medicine. And it was high time America learned what it feels like to have her own land and her own people threatened. We Russians have suffered three wars over the last half century: World War I, the Civil War, and World War II. America has never had to fight a war on her own soil, at least not in the past fifty years. She's sent troops abroad to fight in the two World Wars — and made a fortune as a result. America has shed a few drops of her own blood while making billions by bleeding the rest of the world dry. . . .

**'I've Changed My Mind, Let's Argue on the Bench'**

LePelley in The Christian Science Monitor (c) 1962 TCSPS

I want to make one thing absolutely clear: when we put our ballistic missiles in Cuba, we had no desire to start a war. On the contrary, our principal aim was only to deter America from starting a war. We were well aware that a war which started over Cuba would quickly expand into a world war. Any idiot could have started a war between America and Cuba. Cuba was eleven thousand kilometers away from us. Only a fool would think that we wanted to invade the American continent from Cuba. Our goal was precisely the opposite: we wanted to keep the Americans from invading Cuba, and, to that end, we wanted to make them think twice by confronting them with our missiles. This goal we achieved — but not without undergoing a period of perilous tension.

# THE THIRTEEN DAYS

## How Should the United States Respond?

### *Document 4*

On the afternoon of October 14, 1962, a U.S. Air Force U-2 reconnaissance plane photographed Soviet intermediate-range ballistic missiles at launch sites under construction in Cuba. Disturbing rumors had been circulating for some months regarding the deployment of Soviet troops and offensive missiles on the Caribbean island; nevertheless, according to the president's brother, Attorney General Robert Kennedy, the discovery of Moscow's bold gambit left U.S. policy makers with a sense of "stunned surprise." In his memoir of the Cuban missile crisis, *Thirteen Days*, Kennedy chronicles the tension-filled discussions held by the president and his top advisers on how to respond.

## 4 "THE PRESIDENT . . . KNEW HE WOULD HAVE TO ACT." Robert Kennedy

After the meeting in the Cabinet Room, I walked back to the Mansion with the President. It would be difficult; the stakes were high — of the highest and most substantial kind — but he knew he would have to act. The U.S. could not accept what the Russians had done. What that action would be was still to be determined. But he was convinced from the beginning that he would have to do something. To keep the discussions from being inhibited and because he did not want to arouse attention, he decided not to attend all the meetings of our committee. This was wise. Personalities change when the President is present, and frequently even strong men make recommendations on the basis of what they believe the President wishes to hear. He instructed our group to come forward with recommendations for one course or possibly several alternative courses of action.

It was during the afternoon and evening of that first day, Tuesday, that we began to discuss the idea of a quarantine or blockade. Secretary McNamara, by Wednesday, became the blockade's strongest advocate. He argued that it was limited pressure, which could be increased as the circumstances warranted. Further, it was dramatic and forceful pressure, which would be understood yet, most importantly, still leave us in control of events. Later he reinforced his position by reporting that a surprise air strike against the missile bases alone — a surgical air strike, as it came to be called — was militarily impractical in the view of the Joint Chiefs of Staff, that any such military action would have to include all military installations in Cuba, eventually leading to an invasion. Perhaps we would come to that, he argued. Perhaps that course of action would turn out to be inevitable. "But let's not start with that course," if by chance that kind of confrontation with Cuba, and of necessity with the Soviet Union, could be avoided.

Those who argued for the military strike instead of a blockade pointed out that a blockade would not in fact remove the missiles and would not even stop the work from going ahead on the missile sites themselves. The missiles were already in Cuba, and all we would be doing with a blockade would be "closing the door after the horse had left the barn." Further, they argued, we would be bringing about a confrontation with the Soviet Union by stopping their ships, when we should be concentrating on Cuba and Castro.

Their most forceful argument was that our installation of a blockade around Cuba invited the Russians to do the same to Berlin. If we demanded the removal of missiles from Cuba as the price of lifting our blockade, they would demand the removal of missiles surrounding the Soviet Union as the reciprocal act.

And so we argued, and so we disagreed — all dedicated, intelligent men, disagreeing and fighting about the future of their country, and of mankind. Meanwhile, time was slowly running out.

An examination of photography taken on Wednesday, the 17th of October, showed several other installations, with at least sixteen and possibly thirty-two missiles of over a thousand-mile range. Our military experts advised that these missiles could be in operation within a week. The next day, Thursday, estimates by our Intelligence Community placed in Cuba missiles with an atomic-warhead potential of about one half the current ICBM capacity of the entire Soviet Union. The photography having indicated that the missiles were being directed at certain American cities, the estimate was that within a few minutes of their being fired eighty million Americans would be dead.

The members of the Joint Chiefs of Staff were unanimous in calling for immediate military action. They forcefully presented their view that the blockade would not be effective. General Curtis LeMay, Air Force Chief of Staff, argued strongly with the President that a military attack was essential. When the President questioned what the response of the Russians might be, General LeMay assured him there would be no reaction. President Kennedy was skeptical. "They, no more than we, can let these things go by without doing something. They can't, after all their statements, permit us to take out their missiles, kill a lot of Russians, and then do nothing. If they don't take action in Cuba, they certainly will in Berlin."

The President went on to say that he recognized the validity of the arguments made by the Joint Chiefs, the danger that more and more missiles would be placed in Cuba, and the likelihood, if we did nothing, that the Russians would move on Berlin and in other areas of the world, feeling the U.S. was completely impotent. Then it would be too late to do anything in Cuba, for by that time all their missiles would be operational.

General David M. Shoup, Commander of the Marine Corps, summed up everyone's feelings: "You are in a pretty bad fix, Mr. President." The President answered quickly, "You are in it with me." Everyone laughed, and, with no final decision, the meeting adjourned.

Later, Secretary McNamara, although he told the President he disagreed with the Joint Chiefs and favored a blockade rather than an attack, informed him that the necessary planes, men, and ammunition were being deployed and that we could be ready to move with the necessary air bombardments on Tuesday, October 23, if that was to be the decision. The plans called for an initial attack, consisting of five hundred sorties, striking all military targets, including the missile sites, airfields, ports, and gun emplacements.

I supported McNamara's position in favor of a blockade. This was not from a deep conviction that it would be a successful course of action, but a feeling that it had more flexibility and fewer liabilities than a military attack. Most importantly, like others, I could not accept the idea that the United States would rain bombs on Cuba, killing thousands and thousands of civilians in a surprise attack. Maybe the alternatives were not very palatable, but I simply did not see how we could accept that course of action for our country.

Former Secretary of State Dean Acheson began attending our meetings, and he was strongly in favor of an air attack. . . . He said that the President of the United States had the responsibility for the security of the people of the United States and of the whole free world, that it was his obligation to take the only action which could protect that security, and that that meant destroying the missiles.

With some trepidation, I argued that, whatever validity the military and political arguments were for an attack in preference to a blockade, America's traditions and history would not permit such a course of action. Whatever military reasons he and others could marshal, they were nevertheless, in the last analysis, advocating a surprise attack by a very large nation against a very small one. This, I said, could not be undertaken by the U.S. if we were to maintain our moral position at home and around the globe. Our struggle against Communism throughout the world was far more than physical survival—it had as its essence our heritage and our ideals, and these we must not destroy.

We spent more time on this moral question during the first five days than on any other single matter. At various times, it was proposed that we send a letter to Khrushchev twenty-four hours before the bombardment was to begin, that we send a letter to Castro, that leaflets and pamphlets listing the targets be dropped over Cuba before the attack—all these ideas and more were abandoned for military or other reasons. We struggled and fought with one another and with our consciences, for it was a question that deeply troubled us all.

## President Kennedy Announces a "Quarantine" of Cuba

### *Document 5*

On October 22, 1962, President Kennedy made a televised address in which he informed the American people and the world of the evidence of Soviet missile construction in Cuba. He declared that the United States would consider an attack from Cuba as the equivalent of an attack from the Soviet Union and announced a naval "quarantine" to halt further shipments of missiles to Cuba. With Soviet cargo ships on their way to Cuba and work on the missile installations proceeding apace, the stage was set for the most dangerous confrontation of the nuclear age.

### 5 RADIO AND TELEVISION ADDRESS
### President John F. Kennedy
### October 22, 1962

*Good Evening, My Fellow Citizens:*

This Government, as promised, has maintained the closest surveillance of the Soviet military buildup on the island of Cuba. Within the past week, unmistakable evidence has established the fact that a series of offensive missile sites is now in preparation on that imprisoned island. The purpose of these bases can be none other than to provide a nuclear strike capability against the Western Hemisphere.

Upon receiving the first preliminary hard information of this nature last Tuesday morning at 9 a.m., I directed that our surveillance be stepped up. And having now confirmed and completed our evaluation of the evidence and our decision on a course of action, this Government feels obliged to report this new crisis to you in fullest detail.

The characteristics of these new missile sites indicate two distinct types of installations. Several of them include medium range ballistic missiles, capable of carrying a nuclear warhead for a distance of more than 1,000 nautical miles. Each of these missiles, in short, is capable of striking Washington, D.C., the Panama Canal, Cape Canaveral, Mexico City, or any other city in the southeastern part of the United States, in Central America, or in the Caribbean area.

Additional sites not yet completed appear to be designed for intermediate range ballistic missiles — capable of traveling more than twice as far — and thus capable of striking most of the major cities in the Western Hemisphere, ranging as far north as Hudson Bay, Canada, and as far south as Lima, Peru. In addition, jet bombers, capable of carrying nuclear weapons, are now being uncrated and assembled in Cuba, while the necessary air bases are being prepared.

This urgent transformation of Cuba into an important strategic base — by the presence of these large, long-range, and clearly offensive weapons of sudden mass destruction — constitutes an explicit threat to the peace and security of all the Americas, in flagrant and deliberate defiance of the Rio Pact of 1947, the traditions of this Nation and hemisphere, the joint resolution of the 87th Congress, the Charter of the United Nations, and my own public warnings to the Soviets on September 4 and 13. This action also contradicts the repeated assurances of Soviet spokesmen, both publicly and privately delivered, that the arms buildup in Cuba would retain its original defensive character, and that the Soviet Union had no need or desire to station strategic missiles on the territory of any other nation. . . .

But this secret, swift, and extraordinary buildup of Communist missiles — in an area well known to have a special and historical relationship to the United States and the nations of the Western Hemisphere, in violation of Soviet assurances, and in defiance of American and hemispheric policy — this sudden, clandestine decision to station strategic weapons for the first time outside of Soviet soil — is a deliberately provocative and unjustified change in the status quo which cannot be accepted by this country, if our courage and our commitments are ever to be trusted again by either friend or foe. . . .

Acting, therefore, in the defense of our own security and of the entire Western Hemisphere, and under the authority entrusted to me by the Constitution as endorsed by the resolution of the Congress, I have directed that the following *initial* steps be taken immediately:

*First:* To halt this offensive buildup, a strict quarantine on all offensive military equipment under shipment to Cuba is being initiated. All ships of any kind bound for Cuba from whatever nation or port will, if found to contain cargoes of offensive weapons, be turned back. This quarantine will be extended, if needed, to other types of cargo and carriers. We are not at this time, however, denying the necessities of life as the Soviets attempted to do in their Berlin blockade of 1948.

*Second:* I have directed the continued and increased close surveillance of Cuba and its military buildup. The foreign ministers of the OAS, in their communique of October 6, rejected secrecy on such matters in this hemisphere. Should these offensive military preparations continue, thus increasing the threat to the hemisphere, further action will be justified. I have directed the Armed Forces to prepare for any eventualities; and I trust that in the interest of both the Cuban people and the Soviet technicians at the sites, the hazards to all concerned of continuing this threat will be recognized.

*Third:* It shall be the policy of this Nation to regard any nuclear missile launched from Cuba against any nation in the Western Hemisphere as an attack by the Soviet Union on the United States, requiring a full retaliatory response upon the Soviet Union.

*Fourth:* As a necessary military precaution, I have reinforced our base at Guantanamo, evacuated today the dependents of our personnel there, and ordered additional military units to be on a standby alert basis.

*Fifth:* We are calling tonight for an immediate meeting of the Organ of Consultation under the Organization of American States, to consider this threat to hemispheric security and to invoke articles 6 and 8 of the Rio Treaty in support of all necessary action. The United Nations Charter allows for regional security arrangements — and the nations of this hemisphere decided long ago against the military presence of outside powers. Our other allies around the world have also been alerted.

*Sixth:* Under the Charter of the United Nations, we are asking tonight that an emergency meeting of the Security Council be convoked without delay to take action against this latest Soviet threat to world peace. Our resolution will call for the prompt dismantling and withdrawal of all offensive weapons in Cuba, under the supervision of U.N. observers, before the quarantine can be lifted.

*Seventh and finally:* I call upon Chairman Khrushchev to halt and eliminate this clandestine, reckless, and provocative threat to world peace and to stable relations between our two nations. I call upon him further to abandon this course of world domination, and to join in an historic effort to end the perilous arms race and to transform the history of man. He has an opportunity now to move the world back from the abyss of destruction — by returning to his government's own words that it had no need to station missiles outside its own territory, and withdrawing these weapons from Cuba — by refraining from any action which will widen or deepen the present crisis — and then by participating in a search for peaceful and permanent solutions. . . .

My fellow citizens: let no one doubt that this is a difficult and dangerous effort on which we have set out. No one can foresee precisely what course it will take or what costs or casualties will be incurred. Many months of sacrifice and self-discipline lie ahead — months in which both our patience and our will will be tested — months in which many threats and denunciations will keep us aware of our dangers. But the greatest danger of all would be to do nothing. . . .

Our goal is not the victory of might, but the vindication of right — not peace at the expense of freedom, but both peace *and* freedom, here in this hemisphere, and, we hope, around the world. God willing, that goal will be achieved.

Thank you and good night.

## The Blockade Begins — An Eyewitness Account

### *Document 6*

In this November 1962 article from *U.S. News and World Report,* an American journalist offers an eyewitness account of the U.S. Navy's implementation of the presidential order to blockade Cuba. He concludes that the U.S. strength was "more than enough" to carry out an effective blockade.

### 6 HOW THE BLOCKADE BEGAN November 5, 1962

The blockade, as it got under way in the Caribbean, was something to watch.

At 10 a.m. on October 24, when the big "quarantine" of Cuba officially began, I was flying in a U.S. Navy plane over the blockade area. During the next four hours, we flew a course parallel to the north coast of Cuba — crossing all of the shipping lanes that Soviet vessels would have to use to reach Cuban ports.

The American blockade force was now spread out below, over thousands of square miles of blue Caribbean. From 10,000 feet in the air, the altitude maintained by our two-engine Navy transport, it was an impressive sight.

As we flew west from Puerto Rico, the first vessels we spotted were three fast-moving U.S. warships, apparently headed for the much-traveled Windward Passage between Cuba and Haiti. One of the gray vessels looked like a cruiser, the others like destroyer escorts.

Then a group of four relatively slow freighters appeared. Their nationality was unknown. Although well within the blockade area, they were not headed for Cuba and were not stopped.

By now, we were over Grand Turk Island, where the big U.S. missile-tracking station was helping to keep tabs on Cuba-bound shipping.

Pointing at the big radar installations on Grand Turk, a naval officer on the plane commented: "With those radars, a mosquito couldn't get through without its position being marked up by somebody's grease pencil."

#### Checking Channels

Flying a course that stayed roughly 150 miles from the Cuban coast, we soon could see how this blockade would be operated. We flew over a long series of islands that both screened Cuba from the open Atlantic and also channeled all ships from Europe through the passages between islands.

Russia's supply ships, in other words, had to pass through one of only half a dozen channels between the little tropical islands we were flying over — Caicos, Mayaguana, Long Island, Great Guana Cay, Andros.

We now began to spot U.S. destroyers below, all traveling at apparent high speed and operating singly, each evidently covering a channel between islands. There were no aircraft carriers this close in. These and other larger craft were reported forming a reserve force behind the blockade screen.

With clear weather and few clouds, you could see for great distances at this altitude. But there was little civilian shipping in sight, much less than I had seen over the same area just a few days before. There were a few sailboats, but no fishing boats or cruise ships, and as yet no Havana-bound freighters.

Finally, near Andros — the biggest of the Bahama Islands — we spotted what we had been especially watching for. This was a ship resembling an oil tanker with its superstructure in the rear. It could be the Soviet ship, equipped with an outsized hold, that was reported to be conveying big missiles from Russia to Havana.

This big ship was headed due west. It could be bound for the Florida Straits and New Orleans, or for the western tip of Cuba which includes Havana.

A closer look confirmed that it was merely a tanker. The blockade forces apparently had checked it out, as well. A destroyer, you could see, was not far away.

Just a few ships, thus, could effectively cover the approaches to Cuba, and were on station, at work.

#### A Rendezvous

A far larger force — sea and air — had been assembled by this time, however. The nucleus of this blockade fleet was the force of 40 warships that had been scheduled to conduct maneuvers off Puerto Rico. Most of these sailed out secretly on October 21. By October 24 they had been joined by more warships from several East Coast ports. Norfolk, Va., and the big base at Mayport, Fla., near Jacksonville, contributed the biggest number.

Involved, by this time, were several carriers, some cruisers, dozens of destroyers, even some submarines.

Aircraft were involved as well, but not in great numbers. We saw none in a four-hour flight across the blockade area. The big function of the blockade planes, at this stage, was to spot by their high-altitude radar all ships coming into the Caribbean, then to make a quick check on each one to find its nationality, type and course. It was the warships that were actively carrying out the blockade — and prepared to use force if necessary. Nonetheless, hundreds of planes had been assembled.

You could see that the U.S. this time appeared to have more than enough strength on hand, in position to carry out an effective blockade.

## Support and Worry from the Public

### *Document 7*

This article from the *New York Times* gives a sense of the public mood during the crisis. The public overwhelmingly supported the president's actions, but worries about nuclear war set off panic buying.

### 7 STORES IN CAPITAL FIND NO PANIC October 25, 1962

Water-buying housewives, tired-eyed Government officials and a big demand for transistor radios were the chief signs of crisis in Washington today.

All over town, the standard greeting was not "How are you?" but "What did you hear?" It was not hard to tell what was on people's minds.

Radio stations were giving out instructions for stocking fallout shelters and basements, and a lot of people were responding. But stores reported no real panic buying in response to the Cuban crisis.

The most sought-after item in town was bottled water, which was on the list of purchases urged by civil defense authorities. Several stores reported being sold out of one-gallon containers, retailing at 49 cents with a 25-cent deposit on the bottle.

Another fast-selling item, as reported by the Surplus Sales Company on Pennsylvania Avenue, was pemmican, a raisin-and-nut food concentrate with 400 calories to a pocket size can. In two days the store sold about 900 cans at 27 cents each.

#### Food Rations Sell Quickly

Si Amanuel, the store manager, said he had cleared his shelves of 400 cans of a five-day ration that he had on hand Monday. Other items in unusual demand were five-gallon water cans, mess kits, halazone tablets for sterilizing water, 25-cent cans of rust-proof water, K rations, and small alcohol stoves.

"You'd be surprised at how many people are buying the stuff," Mr. Amanuel said.

Not far away, at Dalmo's Discount House, a clerk said there had been "a tremendous buy" in progress on transistor radios, especially models costing from $25 to $35. He was not sure whether the women who were the chief customers were buying radios to get news, or whether they were planning ahead for a possible loss of electric power.

An electronics shop reported the sale of six "family radiation kits" but a drug company said it had had no increase in sales of tranquilizers.

In most ways, the mood of Washington appeared to be not far from business as usual.

At the Capitol, where painters and plasterers have taken over in the absence of Congress, a guide said there had been no increase or decrease in tourists.

Yesterday, 1,053 adults and 173 children toured the building, about normal for late October, the guide said. He added that many of them had asked the guides to keep them posted on news developments.

#### Town Full of Gossip

The Statler-Hilton, a downtown hotel, reported no cancellations.

Washington, once described as "instant rumor," was full of information, misinformation, gossip and hot tips.

A good source of rumors on troop and ship movements was the capital's secretaries and stenographers, who were suffering an unusual run of broken dates with soldiers, sailors, and marines.

Schools were another source of rumors. A father of two reported his seventh-grader had been told by her teacher that the "invasion has started," and his ninth-grader in the same school had been informed by another teacher that the whole crisis was "just politics."

#### Skeptical of Photograph

One woman emerged from a bus near the Soviet embassy, noticed a policeman guarding it and complained: "They can get protection, but the streets aren't safe for us."

And at a downtown lunch counter, a skeptic put his finger on a blurred newspaper photograph purporting to show a missile installation in Cuba.

"It'll be embarrassing if we get over there and find out it's an orphanage," he said.

A real estate woman reported that a client had refused to go through with buying a house, pending settlement of the crisis.

Recruiting offices said that there had been no rush of youths to enlist in the armed forces. There were a number of calls from veterans offering to re-enlist.

## The Soviet Media and Public React

### *Documents 8 and 9*

Document 8, an excerpt from the Soviet newspaper *Izvestia,* is typical of the vitriolic Soviet press coverage of the U.S. blockade. Document 9, an article from the *New York Times,* describes the reaction of citizens of Moscow. They argue that the Soviet missiles in Cuba are defensive and that the United States is increasing the chances of war.

### 8 HANDS OFF CUBA!
### N. Drachinsky and S. Kondrashov
### October 24, 1962

*New York, Oct. 23*

President Kennedy's radio and television address aroused profound concern for the fate of the world among the participants in the session of the U.N. General Assembly. All objective observers assess the U.S. government's actions as an inadmissible challenge to all peoples. Still fresh in the memory of the delegates are the statements of Stevenson, the American delegate, who insolently lied from the Assembly's rostrum that the U.S.A. has no aggressive intentions against Cuba. Today's actions by the American government expose this lie by its representative in the international organization, whose flowery words were nothing but a mask for the preparation of unprovoked aggression against the freedom-loving Cuban people.

The President announced a military blockade of Cuba. Flouting all the norms of international law, the U.S. government ordered its armed forces to intercept and search the vessels of all countries in international water. The U.S.A. threatens that vessels that disobey this order will be sunk. This is an act of aggression not against Cuba alone but also against other countries of the globe. It has just been reported that 40 American warships with 20,000 servicemen aboard have sailed for the Caribbean Sea for purposes of brigandage. Squadrons of planes have taken off on piratical missions. Military units are being feverishly transferred to Florida. The families of servicemen are being evacuated from Guantanamo, the American military base in Cuba.

The American press itself calls these outrageous actions of the U.S.A. steps toward war. "President Kennedy stressed that the extraordinary steps he has undertaken are 'initial ones.' This in itself was ominous, since the steps that have already been taken lead to the abyss of war," the New York Herald Tribune writes.

All Sunday long there were endless conferences in Washington. The President dispatched military jet planes on urgent missions to fly the congressional leaders of both parties to the White House. The Vice President interrupted his pre-election trip and rushed home from the Hawaiian Islands. In addition to high military and diplomatic officials, Dean Acheson, an ardent proponent of war, was invited to confer with the President. It is probably no accident that the President sent him, of all people, to Paris to brief the NATO Council on the U.S. government's military measures.

Thus the ruling circles of the U.S.A. have thrown off the mask and appeared openly before the whole world as military adventurists. The Messrs. Imperialists apparently cannot get used to the idea that in the second half of the 20th century you can no longer swing Theodore Roosevelt's "big stick" and hope for complete immunity. By raising international brigandage to the level of official policy, Washington has cast an insolent challenge before all peace-loving peoples.

### 9 WHY A BLOCKADE? MUSCOVITES ASK
### Theodore Shabad
### October 28, 1962

*Moscow, Oct. 27*

The Soviet man-in-the-street spoke out this afternoon in front of the United States Embassy and his mood foreshadowed in part Premier Khrushchev's offer of a deal on Cuban and Turkish bases.

While the front ranks of about 2,000 demonstrators chanted slogans, shook raised fists and planted posters on the embassy fence, bystanders in the rear bombarded an American in their midst with questions about the current impasse in Soviet-United States relations.

It was not an aggressive crowd, but some questions were tinged with belligerency as people pressed around to hear a United States view and give vent to their feelings.

"What is all this blockade about? Why don't you leave Cuba alone? Who gives you the right to stop ships on the high seas?" The questions came quick and sharp.

The Russians were told, in explanation, that the Soviet Union had installed offensive missile bases in Cuba and the United States had photographs to prove it.

#### Disbelief Expressed

Many listeners shook their heads in disbelief. After all, only this morning Viktor Mayevsky, an authoritative columnist in Pravda, the Communist party newspaper, had spoken in a dispatch from New York of "mythical offensive weapons allegedly found in Cuba."

Others in the crowd who appeared more knowledgeable conceded that there might be Soviet-manned bases in Cuba, though they affirmed that the intent was only defensive.

"Anyway," they said, "just suppose there are a few Soviet bases off the United States. Look at all the United States bases that ring the Soviet Union. Are we not justified in starting a blockade of our own?"

A recitation of United States defense commitments around the world made little impression on the crowd. Nor did the contention that United States bases had been in existence through most of the post-World War II period while Cuban missile sites changed the status quo to an extent that the United States found intolerable.

"Did you mean," one man retorted, "that the Soviet Union has had time to get used to the presence of hostile bases on its frontiers though this is still a fresh experience for the United States?"

"Why don't you agree to give up your bases and we'll give up ours, and we'll be friends as we were in the war," interjected another man, who said he had fought side by side with Americans in World War II.

The conversation shifted to the economic burden of armaments.

"We cannot afford the luxury of a heavy arms program," a poorly dressed man said in an insistent tone.

### Heavy Cost of Arms Cited

"Why do you force us into such heavy expenditures? We want to spend our money on improving our life and getting better clothes for ourselves," he added, fingering his frayed jacket.

A woman with a drawn face said bitterly. "Americans don't know what war is."

"If you had experienced war the way we did," she added, tears glistening in her eyes, "you would not always threaten us with war."

The Communist-controlled press here in the past has prominently reported statements made in the United States calling for military action to counter Soviet political and economic inroads.

For two hours the crowd pressed around the American in what was generally a good-natured debate.

"You are not afraid to stand here among us," one man said with a sly smile. "You don't think we'll tear you apart?"

It was only after the demonstrators had dispersed and the police tried to clear the ten-lane boulevard for traffic that the Russians reluctantly ended the conversation with the American, who was somewhat dazed but also buoyed by the experience.

### Stones Hurled at Embassy

*Moscow, Oct 27 (Reuters)*

Russian demonstrators hurled stones and bottles at the United States Embassy today in protest against the United States blockade of Cuba.

The demonstrators, many of whom seemed to be workmen, placed about 100 signs on the railing in front of the embassy demanding: "Hands Off Cuba" and "Away With the Blockade."

Other demonstrators, some of them young girls in aprons, used pocket mirrors in an attempt to divert the sun's rays and temporarily blind embassy employes looking from the windows of the building.

An embassy official said about three windows were broken by the bottles and stones.

The police disbanded the crowd after about four hours. The demonstrators whistled and shouted slogans outside the railing until the police herded them into the street.

Water-spraying trucks cleaned the road after the crowd left and embassy officials set to work taking down the banners.

## Khrushchev's Two Letters

### *Document 10*

With the danger of a military clash growing, on October 26 Khrushchev sent Kennedy a lengthy and intensely personal letter (not reprinted here) that contained the outline of a solution to the crisis. The letter, according to White House aide Arthur Schlesinger, "pulsated with a passion to avoid nuclear war and gave the impression of having been written in deep emotion." In it, Khrushchev admitted the presence of Soviet missiles in Cuba but torturously sought to portray them as purely defensive. Concluding the letter, he subtly proposed a bargain: if the United States lifted its blockade and publicly pledged not to invade Cuba, the need for Soviet missiles on the island would disappear. Earlier that day, a Soviet embassy official in Washington had met informally with an American television reporter, John Scali, and had outlined to him essentially the same proposal.

The following day, October 27, the White House received a second letter signed by Khrushchev that was strikingly different in tone and substance from the first. As the excerpts here indicate, this letter fails to mention the previous day's offer; instead, it proposes in vaguely threatening terms that Soviet missiles in Cuba be removed in return for the removal of U.S. missiles in Turkey, with the UN Security Council verifying each side of the deal. Apparently reflecting a split among the Kremlin leadership, the dispatch of this "harder" letter greatly complicated the diplomatic situation and heightened U.S. uncertainties about Soviet intentions.

### 10 LETTER TO PRESIDENT KENNEDY
### Chairman Nikita Khrushchev
### October 27, 1962

Dear Mr. President:

It is with great satisfaction that I studied your reply to Mr. U Thant on the adoption of measures in order to avoid contact by our ships and thus avoid irreparable fatal consequences. This reasonable step on your part persuades me that you are showing solicitude for the preservation of peace, and I note this with satisfaction. . . .

I understand your concern for the security of the United States, Mr. President, because this is the first duty of the president. However, these questions are also uppermost in our minds. The same duties rest with me as chairman of the USSR Council of Ministers. You have been worried over our assisting Cuba with arms designed to strengthen its defensive potential — precisely defensive potential — because Cuba, no matter what weapons it had, could not compare with you since these are different dimensions, the more so given up-to-date means of extermination.

Our purpose has been and is to help Cuba, and no one can challenge the humanity of our motives aimed at allowing Cuba to live peacefully and develop as its people desire. You want to relieve your country from danger and this is understandable. However, Cuba also wants this. All countries want to relieve themselves from danger. But how can we, the Soviet Union and our government, assess your actions which, in effect, mean that you have surrounded the Soviet Union with military bases, surrounded our allies with military bases, set up military bases literally around our country, and stationed your rocket weapons at them? This is no secret. High-placed American officials demonstratively declare this. Your rockets are stationed in Britain and in Italy and pointed at us. Your rockets are stationed in Turkey.

You are worried over Cuba. You say that it worries you because it lies at a distance of 90 miles across the sea from the shores of the United States. However, Turkey lies next to us. Our sentinels are pacing up and down and watching each other. Do you believe that you have the right to demand security for your country and the removal of such weapons that you qualify as offensive, while not recognizing this right for us? . . .

I think that one could rapidly eliminate the conflict and normalize the situation. Then people would heave a sigh of relief, considering that the statesmen who bear the responsibility have sober minds, an awareness of their responsibility, and an ability to solve complicated problems and not allow matters to slide to the disaster of war.

This is why I make this proposal: We agree to remove those weapons from Cuba which you regard as offensive weapons. We agree to do this and to state this commitment in the United Nations. Your representatives will make a statement to the effect that the United States, on its part, bearing in mind the anxiety and concern of the Soviet state, will evacuate its analogous weapons from Turkey. Let us reach an understanding on what time you and we need to put this into effect.

After this, representatives of the U.N. Security Council could control on-the-spot the fulfillment of these commitments. Of course, it is necessary that the Governments of Cuba and Turkey would allow these representatives to come to their countries and check fulfillment of this commitment, which each side undertakes. Apparently, it would be better if these representatives enjoyed the trust of the Security Council and ours — the United States and the Soviet Union — as well as of Turkey and Cuba. I think that it will not be difficult to find such people who enjoy the trust and respect of all interested sides.

We, having assumed this commitment in order to give satisfaction and hope to the peoples of Cuba and Turkey and to increase their confidence in their security, will make a statement in the Security Council to the effect that the Soviet Government gives a solemn pledge to respect the integrity of the frontiers and the sovereignty of Turkey, not to intervene in its domestic affairs, not to invade Turkey, not to make available its territory as a place d'armes for such invasion, and also will restrain those who would think of launching an aggression against Turkey either from Soviet territory or from the territory of other states bordering on Turkey.

The U.S. Government will make the same statement in the Security Council with regard to Cuba. It will declare that the United States will respect the integrity of the frontiers of Cuba, its sovereignty, undertakes not to intervene in its domestic affairs, not to invade and not to make its territory available as place d'armes for the invasion of Cuba, and also will restrain those who would think of launching an aggression against Cuba either from U.S. territory or from the territory of other states bordering on Cuba.

Of course, for this we would have to reach agreement with you and to arrange for some deadline. Let us agree to give some time, but not to delay, two or three weeks, not more than a month. . . .

All this, possibly, would serve as a good impetus to searching for mutually acceptable agreements on other disputed issues, too, on which there is an exchange of opinion between us. These problems have not yet been solved but they wait for an urgent solution which would clear the international atmosphere. We are ready for this.

These are my proposals, Mr. President.

Respectfully yours,

Nikita Khrushchev
*October 27, 1962*

## Kennedy Accepts Khrushchev's Offer

### *Document 11*

The Excom held a tension-filled meeting on October 27 to draft a reply to Khrushchev's perplexing dispatches. Following the suggestion made by his brother, Robert, President Kennedy decided simply to ignore the second letter. Accepting the Soviet leader's first, more conciliatory letter as the official Kremlin proposal for ending the crisis, Kennedy pronounced Khrushchev's offer to be a "generally acceptable" basis for a negotiated settlement. Kennedy's reply, however, continued to insist upon the dismantling of Soviet missiles in Cuba as a prelude to any diplomatic agreement.

### 11 LETTER TO CHAIRMAN KHRUSHCHEV
### President John F. Kennedy
### October 27, 1962

Dear Mr. Chairman:

I have read your letter of October 26th with great care and welcomed the statement of your desire to seek a prompt solution to the problem. The first thing that needs to be done, however, is for work to cease on offensive missile bases in Cuba and for all weapons systems in Cuba capable of offensive use to be rendered inoperable, under effective United Nations arrangements.

Assuming this is done promptly, I have given my representatives in New York instructions that will permit them to work out this weekend — in cooperation with the Acting Secretary General and your representative — an arrangement for a permanent solution to the Cuban problem along the lines suggested in your letter of October 26th. As I read your letter, the key elements of your proposals — which seem generally acceptable as I understand them — are as follows.

1) You would agree to remove these weapons systems from Cuba under appropriate United Nations observation and supervision; and undertake, with suitable safeguards, to halt the further introduction of such weapons systems into Cuba.

2) We, on our part, would agree — upon the establishment of adequate arrangements through the United Nations to ensure the carrying out and continuation of these commitments — (a) to remove promptly the quarantine measures now in effect and (b) to give assurances against an invasion of Cuba. I am confident that other nations of the Western Hemisphere would be prepared to do likewise.

If you will give your representative similar instructions, there is no reason why we should not be able to complete these arrangements and announce them to the world within a couple of days. The effect of such a settlement on easing world tensions would enable us to work toward a more general arrangement regarding "other armaments", as proposed in your second letter which you made public. I would like to say again that the United States is very much interested in reducing tensions and halting the arms race; and if your letter signifies that you are prepared to discuss a detente affecting NATO and the Warsaw Pact, we are quite prepared to consider with our allies any useful proposals.

But the first ingredient, let me emphasize, is the cessation of work on missile sites in Cuba and measures to render such weapons inoperable, under effective international guarantees. The continuation of this threat, or a prolonging of this discussion concerning Cuba by linking these problems to the broader questions of European and world security, would surely lead to an intensification of the Cuban crisis and a grave risk to the peace of the world. For this reason I hope we can quickly agree along the lines outlined in this letter and in your letter of October 26th.

John F. Kennedy

## The Crisis Resolved

### *Documents 12 and 13*

Early in the morning of October 28, General Secretary Khrushchev read over Radio Moscow a letter that he was sending to the White House. In document 12, he reiterates his claim that the installation of Soviet missiles in Cuba is a purely defensive measure. He adds, however, that he understands the president's strong feelings about the presence of nuclear-tipped missiles so close to the U.S. homeland and is therefore ordering them to be dismantled. In return, Khrushchev trusted Kennedy's assurance that there would be no invasion of Cuba.

In document 13, a hastily composed reply to Khrushchev's broadcast, President Kennedy announces that the U.S. quarantine would be lifted as soon as the UN has taken the "necessary measures," and further that the United States would not attack Cuba. Careful not to exult over the Kremlin's retreat, Kennedy welcomes the Soviet premier's "statesmanlike decision" in ending the crisis, particularly since "developments were approaching a point where events could have become unmanageable." It later became known that the Excom had planned to order an air strike against the missile sites in less than forty-eight hours.

### 12 MESSAGE TO PRESIDENT KENNEDY
### Chairman Khrushchev
### October 28, 1962

Dear Mr. President:

I have received your message of 27 October. I express my satisfaction and thank you for the sense of proportion you have displayed and for realization of the responsibility which now devolves on you for the preservation of the peace of the world.

I regard with great understanding your concern and the concern of the United States people in connection with the fact that the weapons you describe as offensive are formidable weapons indeed. Both you and we understand what kind of weapons these are.

In order to eliminate as rapidly as possible the conflict which endangers the cause of peace, to give an assurance to all people who crave peace, and to reassure the American people, who, I am certain, also want peace, as do the people of the Soviet Union, the Soviet Government, in addition to earlier instructions on the discontinuation of further work on weapons constructions sites, has given a new order to dismantle the arms which you describe as offensive, and to crate and return them to the Soviet Union.

Mr. President, I should like to repeat what I had already written to you in my earlier messages — that the Soviet Government has given economic assistance to the Republic of Cuba, as well as arms, because Cuba and the Cuban people were constantly under the continuous threat of an invasion of Cuba.

A piratic vessel had shelled Havana. They say that this shelling was done by irresponsible Cuban emigrees. Perhaps so. However, the question is from where did they shoot. It is a fact that these Cubans have no territory, they are fugitives from their country, and they have no means to conduct military operations.

This means that someone put into their hands these weapons for shelling Havana and for piracy in the Caribbean in Cuban territorial waters. It is impossible in our time not to notice a piratic ship, considering the concentration in the Caribbean of American ships from which everything can be seen and observed.

In these conditions, pirate ships freely roam around and shell Cuba and make piratic attacks on peaceful cargo ships. It is known that they even shelled a British cargo ship. In a word, Cuba was under the continuous threat of aggressive forces, which did not conceal their intention to invade its territory.

The Cuban people want to build their life in their own interests without external interference. This is their right, and they cannot be blamed for wanting to be masters of their own country and disposing of the fruits of their own labor. The threat of invasion of Cuba and all other schemes for creating tension over China are designed to strike the Cuban people with a sense of insecurity, intimidate them, and prevent them from peacefully building their new life.

Mr. President, I should like to say clearly once more that we could not remain indifferent to this. The Soviet Government decided to render assistance to Cuba with means of defense against aggression — only with means for defense purposes. We have supplied the defense means which you describe as offensive means. We have supplied them to prevent an attack on Cuba — to prevent rash acts.

I regard with respect and trust the statement you made in your message of 27 October 1962 that there would be no attack, no invasion of Cuba, and not only on the part of the United States, but also on the part of other nations of the Western Hemisphere, as you said in your same message. Then the motives which induced us to render assistance of such a kind to Cuba disappear.

It is for this reason that we instructed our officers — these means as I had already informed you earlier are in the hands of the Soviet officers — to take appropriate measures to discontinue construction of the aforementioned facilities, to dismantle them, and to return them to the Soviet Union. As I had informed you in the letter of 27 October, we are prepared to reach agreement to enable U.N. representatives to verify the dismantling of these means. Thus in view of the assurances you have given and our instructions on dismantling, there is every condition for eliminating the present conflict.

I note with satisfaction that you have responded to the desire I expressed with regard to elimination of the aforementioned dangerous situation, as well as with regard to providing conditions for a more thoughtful appraisal of the international situation, fraught as it is with great dangers in our age of thermonuclear weapons, rocketry, spaceships, global rockets, and other deadly weapons. All people are interested in insuring peace.

Therefore, vested with trust and great responsibility, we must not allow the situation to become aggravated and must stamp out the centers where a dangerous situation fraught with grave consequences to the cause of peace has arisen. If we, together with you, and with the assistance of other people of good will, succeed in eliminating this tense atmosphere, we should also make certain that no other dangerous conflicts, which could lead to a world nuclear catastrophe, would arise.

In conclusion, I should like to say something about a detente between NATO and the Warsaw Treaty countries that you have mentioned. We have spoken about this long since and are prepared to continue to exchange views on this question with you and to find a reasonable solution.

We should like to continue the exchange of views on the prohibition of atomic and thermonuclear weapons, general disarmament, and other problems relating to the relaxation of international tension.

Although I trust your statement, Mr. President, there are irresponsible people who would like to invade Cuba now and thus touch off a war. If we do take practical steps and proclaim the dismantling and evacuation of the means in question from Cuba, in so doing we, at the same time, want the Cuban people to be certain that we are with them and are not absolving ourselves of responsibility for rendering assistance to the Cuban people.

We are confident that the people of all countries, like you, Mr. President, will understand me correctly. We are not threatening. We want nothing but peace. Our country is now on the upsurge. Our people are enjoying the fruits of their peaceful labor. They have achieved tremendous successes since the October Revolution, and created the greatest material, spiritual, and cultural values. Our people are enjoying these values; they want to continue developing their achievements and insure their further development on the way to peace and social progress by their persistent labor.

I should like to remind you, Mr. President, that military reconnaissance planes have violated the borders of the Soviet Union. In connection with this there have been conflicts between us and notes exchanged. In 1960 we shot down your U-2 plane, whose reconnaissance flight over the USSR wrecked the summit meeting in Paris. At that time, you took a correct position and denounced that criminal act of the former U.S. administration.

But during your term of office as president another violation of our border has occurred, by an American U-2 plane in the Sakhalin area.[2] We wrote you about that violation on 30 August. At that time you replied that that violation had occurred as a result of poor weather, and gave assurances that this would not be repeated. We trusted your assurance, because the weather was indeed poor in that area at that time.

But had not your plane been ordered to fly about our territory, even poor weather could not have brought an American plane into our airspace, hence, the conclusion that this is being done with the knowledge of the Pentagon, which tramples on international norms and violates the borders of other states.

A still more dangerous case occurred on 28 October, when one of your reconnaissance planes intruded over Soviet borders in the Chukotka Peninsula in the north and flew over our territory. The question is, Mr. President: How should we regard this? What is this, a provocation? One of your planes violates our frontier during this anxious time we are both experiencing, when everything has been put into combat readiness. Is it not a fact that an intruding American plane could be easily taken for a nuclear bomber, which might push us to a fateful step; and all the more so since the U.S. Government and Pentagon long ago declared that you are maintaining a continuous nuclear bomber patrol?

Therefore, you can imagine the responsibility you are assuming; especially now, when we are living through such anxious times.

I should also like to express the following wish; it concerns the Cuban people. You do not have diplomatic relations. But through my officers in Cuba, I have reports that American planes are making flights over Cuba.

We are interested that there should be no war in the world, and that the Cuban people should live in peace. And besides, Mr. President, it is no secret that we have our people on Cuba. Under a treaty with the Cuban Government we have sent there officers, instructors, mostly plain people: specialists, agronomists, zootechnicians, irrigators, land reclamation specialists, plain workers, tractor drivers, and others. We are concerned about them.

I should like you to consider, Mr. President, that violation of Cuban airspace by American planes could also lead to dangerous consequences. And if you do not want this to happen, it would be better if no cause is given for a dangerous situation to arise. We must be careful now and refrain from any steps which would not be useful to the defense of the states involved in the conflict, which could only cause irritation and even serve as a provocation for a fateful step. Therefore, we must display sanity, reason, and refrain from such steps.

We value peace perhaps even more than other peoples because we went through a terrible war with Hitler. But our people will not falter in the face of any test. Our people trust their government, and we assure our people and world public opinion that the Soviet Government will not allow itself to be provoked. But if the provocateurs unleash a war, they will not evade responsibility and the grave consequences a war would bring them. But we are confident that reason will triumph, that war will not be unleashed, and peace and the security of the peoples will be insured.

In connection with the current negotiations between Acting Secretary General U Thant and representatives of the Soviet Union, the United States, and the Republic of Cuba, the Soviet Government has sent First Deputy Foreign Minister V. V. Kuznetsov to New York to help U Thant in his noble efforts aimed at eliminating the present dangerous situation.

Respectfully yours,

N. Khrushchev
*28 October 1962*

## Note

2. For background, see *Department of State Bulletin* of May 30, 1960, pp. 851 and 852; June 6, 1960, p. 809; June 13, 1960, pp. 947 and 955; and Sept. 24, 1962, p. 449.

## 13 REPLY TO CHAIRMAN KHRUSHCHEV
### President John F. Kennedy
### October 28, 1962

Dear Mr. Chairman:

I am replying at once to your broadcast message of October twenty-eight, even though the official text has not yet reached me, because of the great importance I attach to moving forward promptly to the settlement of the Cuban crisis. I think that you and I, with our heavy responsibilities for the maintenance of peace, were aware that developments were approaching a point where events could have become unmanageable. So I welcome this message and consider it an important contribution to peace.

The distinguished efforts of Acting Secretary General U Thant have greatly facilitated both our tasks. I consider my letter to you of October twenty-seventh and your reply of today as firm undertakings on the part of both our governments which should be promptly carried out. I hope that the necessary measures can at once be taken through the United Nations, as your message says, so that the United States in turn will be able to remove the quarantine measures now in effect. I have already made arrangements to report all these matters to the Organization of American States, whose members share a deep interest in a genuine peace in the Caribbean area.

You referred in your letter to a violation of your frontier by an American aircraft in the area of the Chukotskiy Peninsula. I have learned that this plane, without arms or photographic equipment, was engaged in an air sampling mission in connection with your nuclear tests. Its course was direct from Eielson Air Force Base in Alaska to the North Pole and return. In turning south, the pilot made a serious navigational error which carried him over Soviet territory. He immediately made an emergency call on open radio for navigational assistance and was guided back to his home base by the most direct route. I regret this incident and will see to it that every precaution is taken to prevent recurrence.

Mr. Chairman, both of our countries have great unfinished tasks and I know that your people as well as those of the United States can ask for nothing better than to pursue them free from the fear of war. Modern science and technology have given us the possibility of making labor fruitful beyond anything that could have been dreamed of a few decades ago.

I agree with you that we must devote urgent attention to the problem of disarmament, as it relates to the whole world and also to critical areas. Perhaps now, as we step back from danger, we can together make real progress in this vital field. I think we should give priority to questions relating to the proliferation of nuclear weapons, on earth and in outer space, and to the great effort for a nuclear test ban. But we should also work hard to see if wider measures of disarmament can be agreed and put into operation at an early date. The United States Government will be prepared to discuss these questions urgently, and in a constructive spirit, at Geneva or elsewhere.

John F. Kennedy

# The Last Days of the Crisis

### *Document 14*

**Recounting his role in the diplomatic negotiations between Washington and Moscow, Robert Kennedy describes the perilous final days of the crisis. Although White House officials later adamantly denied having struck a secret deal with the Kremlin to end the confrontation, Kennedy's account suggests that the United States tacitly agreed to trade NATO missile bases in Turkey for Soviet missiles in Cuba.**

## 14 "THE PRESIDENT ORDERED THE EX COMM . . ."
### Robert Kennedy

I telephoned Ambassador Dobrynin about 7:15 P.M. and asked him to come to the Department of Justice. We met in my office at 7:45. I told him first that we knew that work was continuing on the missile bases in Cuba and that in the last few days it had been expedited. I said that in the last few hours we had learned that our reconnaissance planes flying over Cuba had been fired upon and that one of our U-2s had been shot down and the pilot killed. That for us was a most serious turn of events.

President Kennedy did not want a military conflict. He had done everything possible to avoid a military engagement with Cuba and with the Soviet Union, but now they had forced our hand. Because of the deception of the Soviet Union, our photographic reconnaissance planes would have to continue to fly over Cuba, and if the Cubans or Soviets shot at these planes, then we would have to shoot back. This would inevitably lead to further incidents and to escalation of the conflict, the implications of which were very grave indeed.

He said the Cubans resented the fact that we were violating Cuban air space. I replied that if we had not violated Cuban air space, we would still be believing what Khrushchev had said — that there would be no missiles placed in Cuba. In any case, I said, this matter was far more serious than the air space of Cuba — it involved the peoples of both of our countries and, in fact, people all over the globe.

The Soviet Union had secretly established missile

bases in Cuba while at the same time proclaiming privately and publicly that this would never be done. We had to have a commitment by tomorrow that those bases would be removed. I was not giving them an ultimatum but a statement of fact. He should understand that if they did not remove those bases, we would remove them. President Kennedy had great respect for the Ambassador's country and the courage of its people. Perhaps his country might feel it necessary to take retaliatory action; but before that was over, there would be not only dead Americans but dead Russians as well.

He asked me what offer the United States was making, and I told him of the letter that President Kennedy had just transmitted to Khrushchev. He raised the question of our removing the missiles from Turkey. I said that there could be no quid pro quo or any arrangement made under this kind of threat or pressure, and that in the last analysis this was a decision that would have to be made by NATO. However, I said, President Kennedy had been anxious to remove those missiles from Turkey and Italy for a long period of time. He had ordered their removal some time ago, and it was our judgment that, within a short time after this crisis was over, those missiles would be gone.

I said President Kennedy wished to have peaceful relations between our two countries. He wished to resolve the problems that confronted us in Europe and Southeast Asia. He wished to move forward on the control of nuclear weapons. However, we could make progress on these matters only when the crisis was behind us. Time was running out. We had only a few more hours—we needed an answer immediately from the Soviet Union. I said we must have it the next day.

I returned to the White House. The President was not optimistic, nor was I. He ordered twenty-four troop-carrier squadrons of the Air Force Reserve to active duty. They would be necessary for an invasion. He had not abandoned hope, but what hope there was now rested with Khrushchev's revising his course within the next few hours. It was a hope, not an expectation. The expectation was a military confrontation by Tuesday and possibly tomorrow. . . .

I had promised my daughters for a long time that I would take them to the Horse Show, and early Sunday morning I went to the Washington Armory to watch the horses jump. In any case, there was nothing I could do but wait. Around 10:00 o'clock, I received a call at the Horse Show. It was Secretary Rusk. He said he had just received word from the Russians that they had agreed to withdraw the missiles from Cuba.

I went immediately to the White House, and there I received a call from Ambassador Dobrynin, saying he would like to visit with me. I met him in my office at 11:00 A.M.

He told me that the message was coming through that Khrushchev had agreed to dismantle and withdraw the missiles under adequate supervision and inspection; that everything was going to work out satisfactorily; and that Mr. Khrushchev wanted to send his best wishes to the President and to me.

## Khrushchev's Version

### *Document 15*

In this selection from his memoirs, Khrushchev offers his version of how the Cuban crisis was peacefully resolved. His accounts suggests that it was Kennedy, facing a possible military coup, who had been in need of assistance in a time of grave political challenge. Although effusive in his praise for the president's sober-minded handling of the crisis, Khrushchev claims that the solution to the confrontation in the Caribbean had been a gracious act on his part—a "triumph of common sense" as well as a "personal triumph" that had forced the Americans to "call off" their military and promise never to invade Cuba.

### 15 FIDEL CASTRO AND THE CARIBBEAN CRISIS
**Nikita Khrushchev**

I remember a period of six or seven days when the danger was particularly acute. Seeking to take the heat off the situation somehow, I suggested to the other members of the government: "Comrades, let's go to the Bolshoi Theater this evening. Our own people as well as foreign eyes will notice, and perhaps it will calm them down. They'll say to themselves, 'If Khrushchev and our other leaders are able to go to the opera at a time like this, then at least tonight we can sleep peacefully.' " We were trying to disguise our own anxiety, which was intense.[3]

Then the exchange of notes began. I dictated the messages and conducted the exchange from our side. I spent one of the most dangerous nights at the Council of Ministers office in the Kremlin. I slept on a couch in my office—and I kept my clothes on. I didn't want to be like that Western minister who was caught literally with his pants down by the Suez events of 1956 and who had to run around in his shorts until the emergency was over. I was ready for alarming news to come any moment, and I wanted to be ready to react immediately.

President Kennedy issued an ultimatum, demanding that we remove our missiles and bombers from Cuba. I remember those days vividly. I remember the exchange with President Kennedy especially well because I initiated it and was at the center of the action on our end of the correspondence. I take complete responsibility for the fact that the President and I entered into direct contact at the most crucial and dangerous stage of the crisis.

The climax came after five or six days, when our ambassador to Washington, Anatoly Dobrynin, reported that the President's brother, Robert Kennedy, had come to see him on an unofficial visit. Dobrynin's report went something like this:

"Robert Kennedy looked exhausted. One could see from his eyes that he had not slept for days. He himself said that he had not been home for six days and nights. 'The President is in a grave situation,' Robert Kennedy said, 'and he does not know how to get out of it. We are under very severe stress. In fact we are under pressure from our military to use force against Cuba. Probably at this very moment the President is sitting down to write a message to Chairman Khrushchev. We want to ask you, Mr. Dobrynin, to pass President Kennedy's message to Chairman Khrushchev through unofficial channels. President Kennedy implores Chairman Khrushchev to accept his offer and to take into consideration the peculiarities of the American system. Even though the President himself is very much against starting a war over Cuba, an irreversible chain of events could occur against his will. That is why the President is appealing directly to Chairman Khrushchev for his help in liquidating this conflict. If the situation continues much longer, the President is not sure that the military will not overthrow him and seize power. The American army could get out of control.' "[4]

I hadn't overlooked this possibility. We knew that Kennedy was a young President and that the security of the United States was indeed threatened. For some time we had felt there was a danger that the President would lose control of his military, and now he was admitting this to us himself. Kennedy's message urgently repeated the Americans' demand that we remove the missiles and bombers from Cuba. We could sense from the tone of the message that tension in the United States was indeed reaching a critical point.

We wrote a reply to Kennedy in which we said that we had installed the missiles with the goal of defending Cuba and that we were not pursuing any other aims except to deter an invasion of Cuba and to guarantee that Cuba could follow a course determined by its own people rather than one dictated by some third party.

While we conducted some of this exchange through official diplomatic channels, the more confidential letters were relayed to us through the president's brother. He gave Dobrynin his telephone number and asked him to call at any time. Once, when Robert Kennedy talked with Dobrynin, he was almost crying. "I haven't seen my children for days now," Robert Kennedy said, "and the President hasn't seen his either. We're spending all day and night at the White House; I don't know how much longer we can hold out against our generals."

We could see that we had to reorient our position swiftly. "Comrades," I said, "we have to look for a dignified way out of this conflict. At the same time, of course, we must make sure that we do not compromise Cuba." We sent the Americans a note saying that we agreed to remove our missiles and bombers on the condition that the President give us his assurance that there would be no invasion of Cuba by the forces of the United States or anybody else. Finally Kennedy gave in and agreed to make a statement giving us such an assurance....

As soon as we announced publicly that we were ready to remove our missiles from Cuba, the Americans became arrogant and insisted on sending an inspection team to the island. We answered that they'd have to get the Cuban government's permission to do that. Then the Chinese and American press started hooting and shouting about how Khrushchev had turned coward and backed down. I won't deny that we were obliged to make some big concessions in the interests of peace. We even consented to the inspection of our ships — but only from the air. We never let the Americans actually set foot on our decks, though we did let them satisfy themselves that we were really removing our missiles.

Once the evacuation was begun, there was some question in our minds whether the Americans would pull back their naval forces which surrounded the island. We were worried that as soon as we retreated the Americans might move in on the offensive. But no, good sense prevailed. Their ships started to leave Cuba's territorial waters, but their planes continued to circle the island. Castro gave an order to open fire, and the Cubans shot down an American U-2 reconnaissance plane. Thus another American spy, just like Gary Powers, was downed by one of our missiles.[5] The incident caused an uproar. At first we were concerned that President Kennedy wouldn't be able to stomach the humiliation. Fortunately, however, nothing happened except that the Americans became more brazen than ever in their propaganda. They did everything they could to wound our pride and to make Kennedy look good. But that didn't matter as long as they pulled back their troops and called off their air force.

The situation was stabilizing. Almost immediately after the President and I had exchanged notes at the peak of the crisis, our relations with the United States started to return to normal. Our relations with Cuba, on the other hand, took a sudden turn for the worse. Castro even stopped receiving our ambassador. It seemed that by removing our missiles we had suffered a moral defeat in the eyes of the Cubans. Our shares in Cuba instead of going up, went down....

In our negotiations with the Americans during the crisis, they had, on the whole, been open and candid with us, especially Robert Kennedy. The Americans knew that if Russian blood were shed in Cuba, American blood would surely be shed in Germany. The American government was anxious to avoid such a development. It had been, to say the least, an interesting and challenging situation. The two most powerful nations of the world had been squared off against each other, each with its finger on the button. You'd have thought that war was inevitable. But both sides showed that if the desire to avoid war is strong enough, even the most pressing dispute can be solved by compromise. And a compromise over Cuba was indeed found. The episode ended in a triumph of common sense. I'll always remember the late President with deep respect because, in the final analysis, he showed himself to be sober-minded and determined to avoid war. He didn't let himself become frightened, nor did he become reckless. He didn't overestimate America's might, and he left himself a way out of the crisis. He showed real wisdom and statesmanship when he turned his back on right-wing forces in the United States who were trying to goad him into taking military action against Cuba. It was a great victory for us, though, that we had been able to extract from Kennedy a promise that neither America nor any of her allies would invade Cuba.

## *Notes*

3. When the top men in the Kremlin turn up at the Bolshoi Theater in a body, all smiles, it frequently (though not infallibly) means that a crisis of some kind is brewing. One of the best remembered of such occasions was the evening before Beria's arrest. Beria himself, of course, was included in the party.
4. Obviously, this is Khrushchev's own version of what was reported to him. There is no evidence that the President was acting out of fear of a military take-over.
5. Major Rudolf Anderson, Jr., the pilot of the U-2, was in fact killed when his plane was shot down on October 27, 1962.

# LESSONS OF THE CUBAN MISSILE CRISIS

## The Hot Line and the Limited Test Ban

### *Documents 16 and 17*

The Cuban missile crisis brought home to both superpowers the dangers of nuclear confrontation. Both turned their attention to reducing the tensions that had led to the crisis. In June 1963, the two nations signed an agreement, excerpted here in document 16, that established a direct communications link, the hot line, between the two capitals. The missile crisis also gave new impetus to negotiations on limiting nuclear testing. Document 17 describes how the pace of negotiations picked up after October 1962 and eventually led to the Limited Test Ban Treaty (LTBT). The LTBT banned all nuclear testing in the atmosphere and space, and under the sea.

### 16 MEMORANDUM OF UNDERSTANDING BETWEEN U.S. AND U.S.S.R. Geneva June 20, 1963

For use in time of emergency the Government of the United States of America and the Government of the Union of Soviet Socialist Republics have agreed to establish as soon as technically feasible a direct communications link between the two Governments.

Each Government shall be responsible for the arrangements for the link in its own territory. Each Government shall take the necessary steps to ensure continuous functioning of the link and prompt delivery to its head of government of any communications received by means of the link from the head of government of the other party.

Arrangements for establishing and operating the link are set forth in the Annex which is attached hereto and forms an integral part hereof.

Done in duplicate in the English and Russian languages at Geneva, Switzerland, this 20th day of June, 1963.

### 17 NUCLEAR TEST BANS National Academy of Sciences

Although the trilateral negotiations on the test ban were adjourned indefinitely in January 1962, world opinion would not permit the negotiations to die. Negotiations were resumed in the spring of 1962 in the Eighteen Nation Disarmament Conference (ENDC), the multilateral forum for arms control negotiations. The United States began to relax its verification demands, but this did not narrow the gap with the Soviet position because the Soviet Union hardened its position, proposing a test ban verified only by national means of detection. In the late summer of 1962 the United States and the United

Kingdom proposed two alternative approaches. One was a treaty banning all nuclear tests without a threshold on underground tests. The provisions of this comprehensive test ban were essentially those of the previous threshold test ban, although it was suggested that the number of inspections would be reduced. The other approach was a treaty banning tests in or above the atmosphere and in the sea. The Soviet delegation rejected both approaches, the first because it required inspections and the second because it permitted testing to continue.

In mid-October 1962 the Cuban missile crisis suddenly brought home to leaders and ordinary citizens everywhere the stark realization that nuclear war could happen. President Kennedy and his advisers were clearly deeply moved by their close involvement in the events. Secretary Khrushchev and his advisors also appeared to be sobered by the experience. Following the intense and continuing U.S. and Soviet atmospheric test series, the missile crisis intensified world pressure for progress in the nuclear test negotiations, which were then the only serious, well-advanced arms control negotiations in progress. Significantly, the UN General Assembly passed two resolutions in the immediate aftermath of the Cuban missile crisis, one calling for a cessation of nuclear testing and another calling for either a comprehensive test ban or a limited ban coupled with a moratorium on underground testing.

Despite these strong pressures for an early agreement and intensive efforts over the next six months to negotiate formally at the ENDC and informally on a personal basis at various levels, the two sides were unable to resolve the remaining differences in their positions. The quota on inspections remained the major, but not the only, issue. Khrushchev reinstated his earlier offer of two or three annual inspections, reportedly in the mistaken belief that this would be acceptable to the United States. Kennedy eventually agreed to reduce the quota to seven annual inspections. Neither Kennedy nor Khrushchev apparently considered themselves sufficiently secure politically to propose a final compromise of five inspections, which appeared to some participants to be a logical outcome of the negotiating process. Kennedy was concerned over the strong opposition to further compromise from the military, the weapons laboratories, and influential members of Congress. Khrushchev told Western visitors that he had used up his political credit with his colleagues by agreeing to permit three inspections.

The number of on-site inspections was not the only difference. There was a similar impasse over the number of unmanned automatic seismic stations, or "black boxes," to be located in each country. The United States had accepted the Soviet proposal that these black boxes, which could be safeguarded to ensure the authenticity of their seismic data, should be used in place of manned control posts to eliminate the issue of the nationality of the staff at the posts. The Soviet Union had offered to locate three black boxes in the Soviet Union, and the United States had insisted on eight to ten. The gap was not narrowed. In addition to these quantitative differences that dominated the negotiations on the test ban, the two sides were far from agreement on the so-called modalities governing the conduct of individual on-site inspections and the installation and operation of the black boxes. Whether these detailed procedural issues, which were critical to the satisfactory operation of the control system whatever the quotas might be, could have been resolved if a political decision had been reached is difficult to judge. Certainly, the United States would have had to back off from the very elaborate inspection procedures it envisaged, and the Soviet Union would have had to grant considerably more access than it had yet shown signs of accepting.

The treatment of peaceful nuclear explosions was an issue that had not been resolved within the U.S. government and would eventually have to be faced with the Soviet Union. Within the Atomic Energy Commission and among influential members of Congress, there was strong support for a program of peaceful nuclear explosions, called Project Plowshare, for which great economic claims were being made. But it was also recognized within the government that continuation of Project Plowshare was inherently incompatible with a comprehensive test ban. The two sides had earlier tried to finesse the issue by permitting explosions for peaceful purposes provided the other side could inspect the internal design of the device to assure that it was not a weapon development test. Advocates of Project Plowshare, who recognized that such a provision was tantamount to stopping the program since it was most unlikely that either side would agree to it in practice, proposed instead that each side be given a quota for peaceful tests or projects. Such a proposal was recognized as being inherently contradictory to the goal of a comprehensive test ban.

At the urging of Prime Minister Macmillan, President Kennedy decided in the spring of 1963 to attempt to break out of the deadlocked ENDC negotiating framework by sending Averell Harriman to Moscow as a special personal representative to see if some resolution of the test ban issue was possible. In an exchange of personal letters, Khrushchev agreed to receive the Harrriman mission. On June 10, 1963, Kennedy announced in his famous American University speech that agreement had been reached to hold high-level discussions in Moscow on the test ban. In the speech, which examined the issues of war and peace and U.S.-Soviet relations in a nuclear world, Kennedy also declared a unilateral moratorium on atmospheric nuclear tests for as long as other states did likewise.

Averell Harriman's instructions were to seek a comprehensive treaty and, if this appeared unattainable, a limited agreement along the lines of the draft treaty the United States had originally submitted to the ENDC the previous year. The impasse on the comprehensive treaty and developments immediately prior to the meeting made it clear that a limited agreement was the hoped-for outcome on both sides. On July 2, Khrushchev announced that the Soviet Union was withdrawing its offer of three on-site inspections, claiming that the West would exploit them for espionage. He also stated that the Soviet Union was prepared to conclude an agreement banning testing in the atmosphere, in outer space, and underwater. The Soviet Union had previously rejected the possibility of such a limited treaty. In the United States there was growing support in Congress for this approach, which the military strongly preferred over a comprehensive test ban.

The negotiations began on July 15, and ten days later the Treaty Banning Nuclear Weapons Tests in the Atmosphere, in Outer Space and Under Water, or simply the Limited Test Ban Treaty (Appendix D), was initialed. There was essentially no discussion of a comprehensive ban, which was clearly out of reach for quick resolution, and the negotiations proceeded directly to the text of the limited treaty. Both sides clearly wanted an agreement, and the few matters of substance and drafting problems were quickly resolved and cleared directly with President Kennedy and Secretary Khrushchev. The Soviet delegation objected to a proposed U.S. provision permitting atmospheric tests for peaceful purposes if unanimously approved. The U.S. delegation withdrew this proposal when agreement was reached on a provision permitting treaty amendment by a majority of the parties, including the three original nuclear weapon parties, and on a U.S. provision explicitly permitting withdrawal from the treaty.

The Limited Test Ban Treaty, which was of unlimited duration, banned nuclear tests in all environments except for underground tests that contained the resulting radioactive debris so that it would not be present outside the territory of the country conducting the test. The treaty was to enter into force when ratified by the United States, the United Kingdom, and the Soviet Union and was open to signature by all countries. The treaty, which was considered verifiable by the National Technical Means (NTM) of the two sides, contained no special verification provisions.

After extensive hearings the Senate advised ratification of the treaty by a vote of 80 to 19. Support for the treaty in the hearings was not universal, with representatives of the weapons laboratories emphasizing the technological limits imposed by confining testing to underground shots. An important factor was the support of the Joint Chiefs of Staff, whose position was uncertain until the administration formally agreed to four safeguards that the chiefs proposed. These safeguards involved presidential commitments to conduct a comprehensive and continuing underground test program, to maintain the vitality of the weapons laboratories, to maintain the resources necessary for the prompt resumption of atmospheric testing, and to improve verification capabilities. The treaty was ratified by President Kennedy on October 7, 1963, and entered into force three days later.

In general, the treaty was very well received in the United States and throughout the world despite its failure to stop all testing. After the extreme tensions of the Cuban missile crisis, the first major arms control agreement between the United States and the Soviet Union came as a welcome relief. The termination of atmospheric testing also relieved widespread anxiety about immediate health effects. A large number of countries moved promptly to sign the treaty, and others have joined over the years. As of September 1984, 111 countries had signed the treaty, and all but 15 had ratified it. France and the People's Republic of China have not signed the treaty. Initially, both countries continued to test in the atmosphere, but since 1974 France has not conducted any atmospheric tests.

Although the preamble to the Limited Test Ban Treaty proclaimed the objective of "the discontinuance of all test explosions of nuclear weapons for all times," the treaty, by stopping atmospheric testing by the United States and the Soviet Union, had the effect of reducing domestic and international pressure for a comprehensive test ban. As a result, there was little serious effort to achieve a comprehensive test ban until trilateral negotiations were resumed 14 years later in the Carter Administration. Arms control activities shifted to other fields.

During the Johnson Administration the focus of arms control was on the negotiation of the Non-Proliferation Treaty (NPT) (Chapter 8). The Non-Proliferation Treaty was inherently discriminatory, since it divided the world into nuclear weapon states and non nuclear weapon states. To balance the commitment of the non-nuclear weapon states not to obtain nuclear weapons or any other nuclear explosive device, the nuclear weapons states agreed to share the benefits of the peaceful uses of atomic energy and to negotiate an end to the nuclear arms race. Article VI of the NPT specifically committed all parties to the treaty "to pursue negotiations in good faith on effective measures relating to cessation of the nuclear arms race at an early date." Moreover, the preamble to the treaty recalled the determination expressed in the preamble of the Limited Test Ban Treaty "to achieve the discontinuance of all test explosions of nuclear weapons for all time and to continue negotiations to this end."

In the eyes of most non-nuclear weapon states, nuclear testing, even though it was underground, remained the symbol of a continuing policy of active discrimination under the Non-Proliferation Treaty. Many states considered the failure to pursue serious efforts to achieve a comprehensive test ban to be a violation of the obligation to pursue this agreement "in good faith." This dissatisfaction continued even after the United States and the Soviet Union began the SALT process and achieved significant agreements. At the NPT review conferences in 1975 and 1980, key non-nuclear weapon states strongly criticized the United States and the Soviet Union for failing to make further progress on a comprehensive test ban.

## Did Nuclear Superiority Matter?

### *Document 18*

On the twentieth anniversary of the Cuban missile crisis, six of President Kennedy's key advisers, including Secretary of State Dean Rusk and Secretary of Defense Robert McNamara, coauthored an article in *Time* on the lessons of the crisis. They stress the importance of accurate information, effective communication, and options. In addition, they conclude that the crisis illustrates the "insignificance of nuclear superiority in the face of survivable thermonuclear forces."

Some defense analysts, however, argue that the lesson of the Cuban missile crisis is just the opposite. They claim that U.S. nuclear superiority at the time of the crisis allowed the United States to force the Soviets to withdraw. These analysts warn that the loss of U.S. nuclear superiority could make another crisis much more dangerous.

### 18 THE LESSONS OF THE CUBAN MISSILE CRISIS
### Dean Rusk, Robert McNamara, and Other Key Advisers
### September 27, 1982

For 13 chilling days in October 1962, it seemed that John F. Kennedy and Nikita S. Khrushchev might be playing out the opening scenes of World War III. The Cuban missile crisis was a uniquely compact moment of history. For the first time in the nuclear age, the two superpowers found themselves in a sort of moral road test of their apocalyptic powers.

The crisis blew up suddenly. The U.S. discovered that the Soviet Union, despite repeated and solemn denials, was installing nuclear missiles in Cuba. An American U-2 spy plane came back with photographs of the bases and their support facilities under construction: clear, irrefutable evidence. Kennedy assembled a task force of advisers. Some of them wanted to invade Cuba. In the end, Kennedy chose a course of artful restraint; he laid down a naval quarantine. After six days, Khrushchev announced that the Soviet missiles would be dismantled.

The crisis served some purposes. The U.S. and the Soviet Union have had no comparable collision since then. On the other hand, the humiliation that Khrushchev suffered may have hastened his fall. The experience may be partly responsible for both the Soviet military buildup in the past two decades and whatever enthusiasm the Soviets have displayed for nuclear disarmament.

Now, on the 20th anniversary of the crisis, six of Kennedy's men have collaborated on a remarkable joint statement on the lessons of that October. It contains some new information, particularly in Point Eight, and at least one of their conclusions is startling and controversial: their thought that, contrary to the wisespread assumption of the past two decades, the American nuclear superiority over the Soviets in 1962 had no crucial influence with Washington or Moscow at the time—and that in general, nuclear superiority is insignificant.

The authors are Dean Rusk, then Secretary of State, Robert McNamara, Secretary of Defense, George W. Ball, Under Secretary of State, Roswell L. Gilpatric, Deputy Secretary of Defense, Theodore Sorensen, special counsel to the President, and McGeorge Bundy, special assistant to the President for national security affairs. Their analysis:

In the years since the Cuban missile crisis, many commentators have examined the affair and offered a wide variety of conclusions. It seems fitting now that some of us who worked particularly closely with President Kennedy during that crisis should offer a few comments, with the advantages both of participation and of hindsight.

FIRST: The crisis could and should have been avoided. If we had done an earlier, stronger and clearer job of explaining our position on Soviet nuclear weapons in the Western Hemisphere, or if the Soviet government had more carefully assessed the evidence that did exist on this point, it is likely that the missiles would never have been sent to Cuba. *The importance of accurate mutual assessment of interests between the two superpowers is evident and continuous.*

SECOND: Reliable intelligence permitting an effective choice of response was obtained only just in time. It was primarily a mistake by policymakers, not by professionals, that made such intelligence unavailable sooner. But it was also a timely recognition of the need for thorough overflight, not without its hazards, that produced the decisive photographs. The usefulness and scope of inspection from above, also employed in monitoring the Soviet missile withdrawal, should never be underestimated. *When the importance of accurate information for a crucial policy decision is high enough, risks not otherwise acceptable in collecting intelligence can become profoundly prudent.*

THIRD: The President wisely took his time in choosing a course of action. A quick decision would certainly have been less carefully designed and could well have produced a much higher risk of catastrophe. The fact that the crisis did not become public in its first week obviously made it easier for President Kennedy to consider his options with a maximum of care and a minimum of outside pressure. Not every future crisis will be so quiet in its first phase, but *Americans should always respect the need for a period of confidential and careful deliberation in dealing with a major international crisis.*

FOURTH: The decisive military element in the resolution of the crisis was our clearly available and applicable superiority in conventional weapons within the area of the crisis. U.S. naval forces, quickly deployable for the blockade of offensive weapons that was sensibly termed a quarantine, and the availability of U.S. ground and air forces sufficient to execute an invasion if necessary, made the difference. American nuclear superiority was not in our view a critical factor, for the fundamental and controlling reason that nuclear war, already in 1962, would have been an unexampled catastrophe for both sides; the balance of terror so eloquently described by Winston Churchill seven years earlier was in full operation. No one of us ever reviewed the nuclear balance for comfort in those hard weeks. *The Cuban missile crisis illustrates not the significance but the insignificance of nuclear superiority in the face of survivable thermonuclear retaliatory forces. It also shows the crucial role of rapidly available conventional strength.*

FIFTH: The political and military pressure created by the quarantine was matched by a diplomatic effort that ignored no relevant means of communication with both our friends and our adversary. Communication to and from our allies in Europe was intense, and their support sturdy. The Organization of American States gave the moral and legal authority of its regional backing to the quarantine, making it plain that Soviet nuclear weapons were profoundly unwelcome in the Americas. In the U.N., Ambassador Adlai Stevenson drove home with angry eloquence and unanswerable photographic evidence the facts of the Soviet deployment and deception.

Still more important, communication was established and maintained, once our basic course was set, with the government of the Soviet Union. If the crisis itself showed the cost of mutual incomprehension, its resolution showed the value of serious and sustained communication, and in particular of direct exchanges between the two heads of government.

When great states come anywhere near the brink in the nuclear age, there is no room for games of blindman's buff. Nor can friends be led by silence. They must know what we are doing and why. *Effective communication is never more important than when there is a military confrontation.*

SIXTH: This diplomatic effort and indeed our whole course of action were greatly reinforced by the fact that our position was squarely based on irrefutable evidence that the Soviet government was doing exactly what it had repeatedly denied that it would do. The support of our allies and the readiness of the Soviet government to draw back were heavily affected by the public demonstration of a Soviet course of conduct that simply could not be defended. In this demonstration no evidence less explicit and authoritative than that of photography would have been sufficient, and it was one of President Kennedy's best decisions that the ordinary requirements of secrecy in such matters should be brushed aside in the interest of persuasive exposition. *There are times when a display of hard evidence is more valuable than protection of intelligence techniques.*

SEVENTH: In the successful resolution of the crisis, restraint was as important as strength. In particular, we avoided any early initiation of battle by American forces, and indeed we took no action of any kind that would have forced an instant and possibly ill-considered response. Moreover, we limited our demands to the restoration of the *status quo ante,* that is, the removal of any Soviet nuclear capability from Cuba. There was no demand for "total victory" or "unconditional surrender." These choices gave the Soviet government both time and opportunity to respond with equal restraint. *It is wrong, in relations between the superpowers, for either side to leave the other with no way out but war or humiliation.*

EIGHTH: On two points of particular interest to the Soviet government, we made sure that it had the benefit of knowing the independently reached positions of President Kennedy. One assurance was public and the other private.

Publicly we made it clear that the U.S. would not invade Cuba if the Soviet missiles were withdrawn. The President never shared the view that the missile crisis should be "used" to pick a fight to the finish with Castro; he correctly insisted that the real issue in the crisis was with the Soviet government, and that the one vital bone of contention was the secret and deceit-covered movement of Soviet missiles into Cuba. He recognized that an invasion by U.S. forces would be bitter and bloody, and that it would leave festering wounds in the body politic of the Western Hemisphere. The no-invasion assurance was not a concession, but a statement of our own clear preference—once the missiles were withdrawn.

The second and private assurance—communicated on the President's instructions by Robert Kennedy to Soviet Ambassador Anatoli Dobrynin on the evening of Oct. 27—was that the President had determined that once the crisis was resolved, the American missiles then in Turkey would be removed. (The essence of this secret assurance was revealed by Robert Kennedy in his 1969 book *Thirteen Days,* and a more detailed account, drawn from many sources but not from discussion with any of us, was published by Arthur M. Schlesinger Jr. in *Robert Kennedy and His Times* in 1978. In these circumstances, we think it is now proper for those of us privy to that decision to discuss the matter.) This could not be a "deal"—our missiles in Turkey for theirs in Cuba—as the Soviet government had just proposed. The matter involved the concerns of our allies, and we could not put ourselves in the position of appearing to trade their protection for our own. But in fact President Kennedy had long since reached the conclusion that the outmoded and vulnerable missiles in Turkey should be withdrawn. In the spring of 1961 Secretary Rusk had begun the necessary discussions with high Turkish officials. These officials asked for delay, at least until Polaris submarines could be deployed in the Mediterranean. While the matter was not pressed to a conclusion in the following year and a half, the missile crisis itself reinforced the President's convictions. It was entirely right that the Soviet government should understand this reality.

This second assurance was kept secret because the few who knew about it at the time were in unanimous agreement that any other course would have had explosive and destructive effects on the security of the U.S. and its allies. If made public in the context of the Soviet proposal to make a "deal," the unilateral decision reached by the President would have been misread as an unwilling concession granted in fear at the expense of an ally. It seemed better to tell the Soviets the real position in private, and in a way that would prevent any such misunderstanding. Robert Kennedy made it plain to Ambassador Dobrynin that any attempt to treat the President's unilateral assurance as part of a deal would simply make that assurance inoperative.

Although for separate reasons neither the public nor the private assurance ever became a formal commitment of the U.S. Government, the validity of both was demonstrated by our later actions; there was no invasion of Cuba, and the vulnerable missiles in Turkey (and Italy) were withdrawn, with allied concurrence, to be replaced by invulnerable Polaris submarines. Both results were in our own clear interest, and both assurances were helpful in making it easier for the Soviet government to decide to withdraw its missiles.

In part this was secret diplomacy, including a secret assurance. Any failure to make good on that assurance would obviously have had damaging effects on Soviet-American relations. But it is of critical importance here that the President gave no assurance that went beyond his own presidential powers; in particular he made no commitment that required congressional approval or even support. The decision that the missiles in Turkey should be removed was one that the President had full and unquestioned authority to make and execute.

*When it will help your own country for your adversary to know your settled intentions, you should find effective ways of making sure that he does, and a secret assurance is justified when a) you can keep your word, and b) no other course can avoid grave damage to your country's legitimate interests.*

NINTH: The gravest risk in this crisis was not that either head of government desired to initiate a major escalation but that events would produce actions, reactions or miscalculations carrying the conflict beyond the control of one or the other or both. In retrospect we are inclined to think that both men would have taken every possible step to prevent such a result, but at the time no one near the top of either government could have that certainty about the other side. *In any crisis involving the superpowers, firm control by the heads of both governments is essential to the avoidance of an unpredictably escalating conflict.*

TENTH: The successful resolution of the Cuban missile crisis was fundamentally the achievement of two men, John F. Kennedy and Nikita S. Khrushchev. We know that in this anniversary year John Kennedy would wish to emphasize the contribution of Khrushchev; the fact that an earlier and less prudent decision by the Soviet leader made the crisis inevitable does not detract from the statesmanship of his change of course. We may be forgiven, however, if we give the last and highest word of honor to our own President, whose cautious determination, steady composure, deep-seated compassion and, above all, continuously attentive control of our options and actions brilliantly served his country and all mankind.

## Managing Acute International Crises

### *Document 19*

Looking back on the president's handling of the U.S.-Soviet showdown over the "missiles of October," Robert Kennedy stresses that for government leaders to be able to manage acute international crises successfully they must effectively communicate their intentions to their counterparts and, above all, place themselves "in the other country's shoes."

## 19 "PLACING OURSELVES IN THE OTHER COUNTRY'S SHOES." Robert Kennedy

The final lesson of the Cuban missile crisis is the importance of placing ourselves in the other country's shoes. During the crisis, President Kennedy spent more time trying to determine the effect of a particular course of action on Khrushchev or the Russians than on any other phase of what he was doing. What guided all his deliberations was an effort not to disgrace Khrushchev, not to humiliate the Soviet Union, not to have them feel they would have to escalate their response because their national security or national interests so committed them.

This was why he was so reluctant to stop and search a Russian ship; this was why he was so opposed to attacking the missile sites. The Russians, he felt, would have to react militarily to such actions on our part.

Thus the initial decision to impose a quarantine

rather than to attack; our decision to permit the *Bucharest* to pass; our decision to board a non-Russian vessel first; all these and many more were taken with a view to putting pressure on the Soviet Union but not causing a public humiliation.

Miscalculation and misunderstanding and escalation on one side bring a counterresponse. No action is taken against a powerful adversary in a vacuum. A government or people will fail to understand this only at their great peril. For that is how wars begin — wars that no one wants, no one intends, and no one wins.

Each decision that President Kennedy made kept this in mind. Always he asked himself: Can we be sure that Khrushchev understands what we feel to be our vital national interest? Has the Soviet Union had sufficient time to react soberly to a particular step we have taken? All action was judged against that standard — stopping a particular ship, sending low-flying planes, making a public statement.

President Kennedy understood that the Soviet Union did not want war, and they understood that we wished to avoid armed conflict. Thus, if hostilities were to come, it would be either because our national interests collided — which, because of their limited interests and our purposely limited objectives, seemed unlikely — or because of our failure or their failure to understand the other's objectives.

President Kennedy dedicated himself to making it clear to Khrushchev by word and deed — for both are important — that the U.S. had limited objectives and that we had no interest in accomplishing those objectives by adversely affecting the national security of the Soviet Union or by humiliating her.

Later, he was to say in his speech at American University in June of 1963: "Above all, while defending our own vital interests, nuclear powers must avert those confrontations which bring an adversary to the choice of either a humiliating defeat or a nuclear war."

During our crisis talks, he kept stressing the fact that we would indeed have war if we placed the Soviet Union in a position she believed would adversely affect her national security or such public humiliation that she lost the respect of her own people and countries around the globe. The missiles in Cuba, we felt, vitally concerned our national security, but not that of the Soviet Union.

This fact was ultimately recognized by Khrushchev, and this recognition, I believe, brought about his change in what, up to that time, had been a very adamant position. The President believed from the start that the Soviet Chairman was a rational, intelligent man who, if given sufficient time and shown our determination, would alter his position. But there was always the chance of error, of mistake, miscalculation, or misunderstanding, and President Kennedy was committed to doing everything possible to lessen that chance on our side.

The possibility of the destruction of mankind was always in his mind. Someone once said that World War Three would be fought with atomic weapons and the next war with sticks and stones.

As mentioned before, Barbara Tuchman's *The Guns of August* had made a great impression on the President. "I am not going to follow a course which will allow anyone to write a comparable book about this time, *The Missiles of October*," he said to me that Saturday night, October 26. "If anybody is around to write after this, they are going to understand that we made every effort to find peace and every effort to give our adversary room to move. I am not going to push the Russians an inch beyond what is necessary."

After it was finished, he made no statement attempting to take credit for himself or for the Administration for what had occurred. He instructed all members of the Ex Comm and government that no interview should be given, no statement made, which would claim any kind of victory. He respected Khrushchev for properly determining what was in his own country's interest and what was in the interest of mankind. If it was a triumph, it was a triumph for the next generation and not for any particular goverment or people.

At the outbreak of the First World War the ex-Chancellor of Germany, Prince von Bülow, said to his successor, "How did it all happen?" "Ah, if only we knew," was the reply.

## Suggestions for Further Reading

Abel, Ellie. *The Missile Crisis* (Philadelphia: Lippincott, 1966). A journalist's classic contemporary account of the crisis.

Allison, Graham T. *Essence of Decision: Explaining the Cuban Missile Crisis* (Boston: Little, Brown, 1971). An exploration of the crisis from the standpoint of the rational decision maker, bureaucratic politics, and organizational behavior. A standard work on the crisis.

Trachtenberg, Marc. "White House Tapes and Minutes of the Cuban Missile Crisis: Introduction to Documents," *International Security* 10:1 (Summer 1985: 164–70; transcripts, pp. 170–203).

*Six*

# THE EDUCATION OF ROBERT McNAMARA

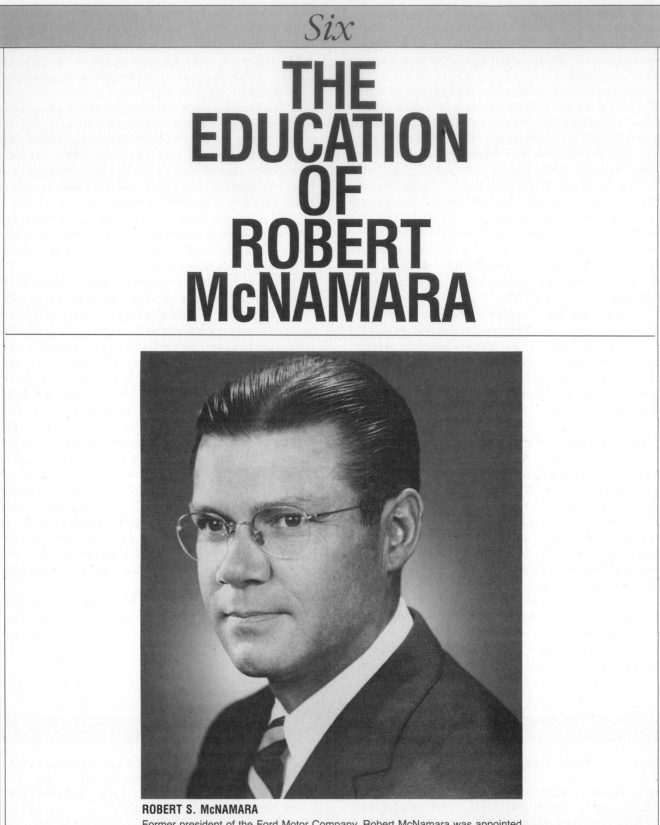

**ROBERT S. McNAMARA**

Former president of the Ford Motor Company, Robert McNamara was appointed U.S. secretary of defense by President John F. Kennedy. McNamara served from 1961 to 1968 and was largely responsible for reshaping U.S. nuclear forces and strategy. The Bettmann Archive, Inc.

# INTRODUCTION

During his tenure as secretary of defense, Robert McNamara made decisions that are largely responsible for the current structure of U.S. strategic nuclear forces. He also helped set the stage for two debates that continue to dominate discussions of U.S. nuclear strategy: the debate on counterforce and the debate on missile defense.

Although the Kennedy administration came into office convinced of a missile gap in the Soviets' favor, it soon learned that the gap was a myth. U.S. nuclear forces were numerically superior to the Soviet Union's. However, McNamara and his new team of systems analysts at the Pentagon believed that U.S. nuclear forces had two serious problems: survivability and doctrine.

In the early 1960s the U.S. nuclear forces were composed mostly of bombers, many of them stationed at bases very close to the Soviet Union. McNamara worried that a surprise Soviet missile attack might be able to destroy most of the bombers before they could get off the ground. The early intercontinental ballistic missiles (ICBMs) deployed by the Eisenhower administration were also vulnerable because they were liquid-fueled, and some were in above-ground launchers.

The Kennedy administration made a major effort to change the structure of U.S. forces to make them less vulnerable. McNamara stepped up the deployment of the Polaris submarine-launched ballistic missiles (SLBMs) and the Minuteman ICBM. Both were solid-fueled missiles. The Polaris' mobility aboard submarines made it invulnerable. The Minuteman was protected by its deployment in hardened silos. (This was to change — see chapter 11.) In 1960, the United States had most of its nuclear eggs in one basket: potentially vulnerable bombers. By 1968, when McNamara left office, the United States had a much more survivable triad of nuclear forces: bombers, ICBMs, and SLBMs. The basic triad structure is the one U.S. forces still have today.

McNamara and the people he brought with him to the Pentagon were also dissatisfied with the Eisenhower administration's nuclear strategy. Because the Soviets had nuclear forces that could reach the United States, by 1961, it did not seem credible to threaten massive retaliation as a deterrent to limited war. An all-out attack on Soviet cities and industry, of the kind the Eisenhower administration planned, would only encourage the Soviet Union to attack U.S. cities.

McNamara wanted a U.S. president to have more flexibility in responding to a Soviet attack, and he wanted to avoid setting off mutual attacks on cities. In 1962, McNamara announced a "no-cities" nuclear strategy. The United States, he said, would refrain from attacking cities early in a nuclear war (a countervalue attack) and concentrate on attacking Soviet military assets, especially the nuclear forces (a counterforce attack). The United States would also keep in reserve forces that could attack Soviet cities. Such a strategy would have at least two beneficial effects, McNamara believed. First, it would limit the damage the Soviets could do to the United States in a nuclear war, because Soviet nuclear forces would be destroyed. Second, this strategy would give the Soviets a powerful incentive to avoid attacks on U.S. cities.

The strategy was also based on the fact that, although Soviet nuclear forces could reach the United States, U.S. nuclear forces were still significantly superior. This meant that U.S. forces could limit in a real way the Soviet Union's ability to do damage. However, U.S. superiority did not last long. The Soviets began a major strategic buildup in 1964 that brought them to rough parity with the United States by the end of the decade. As this buildup progressed, McNamara came to believe that U.S. forces could not "contain" or "limit" damage in any meaningful way. Shortly after Lyndon Johnson was elected president in 1964, McNamara announced a change in U.S. strategy to shift it away from counterforce and damage limiting toward assured destruction.

In the late 1960s, McNamara argued that the United States could deter the Soviets by "maintaining a clear and convincing capability to inflict unacceptable damage on an attacker." This meant the United States had to have survivable retaliatory forces to "assure destruction." As long as U.S. nuclear forces had such an assured destruction capability, the Soviets would not be tempted to attack. The assured destruction mission also required fewer nuclear weapons than did damage limiting. The strategy helped McNamara resist some of the armed forces' requests for still larger nuclear forces.

McNamara began to argue that it would be expensive and ultimately futile for the United States to attempt to go beyond assured destruction and regain the superiority it had once had over the Soviet Union. The Soviets were clearly willing to match U.S. forces. In fact, both sides could be secure and the danger of nuclear war would recede if both followed an assured destruction policy. Mutual assured destruction (MAD) was the phrase that came to be used to describe such a stable situation.

Although McNamara moved away from no-cities counterforce, his arguments in favor of it were resurrected by later administrations (see chapters 7, 9, and 12).

McNamara also was very influential in the first debate on strategic defense. In the 1950s, both the superpowers deployed extensive air defense systems to knock out attacking bombers. In the 1960s both also moved forward with antiballistic missile (ABM) systems. By the mid-1960s, the Army was proposing deployment of a new ABM system called Nike-X to protect the U.S. population. McNamara and his staff concluded that such a system would not be effective. It could be fooled by Soviet decoys. Its components, especially radar, could be easily destroyed. In addition, McNamara believed that it would also be cheaper for the Soviets to build more missiles and decoys than it would be for the United States to beef up the ABM system.

McNamara fought against the ABM system inside the Pentagon. His position was weakened when the Soviets began work on an ABM system and the fears of a Chinese missile program grew. In the end, McNamara gave in to pressure from Congress and the armed services. He opted for a "thin" ABM system dubbed *Sentinel.* But the debate on strategic defense was far from over.

Most of the key debates on strategic policy of the 1970s and 1980s flowed directly from decisions McNamara helped to make in the 1960s.

# REDUCING U.S. VULNERABILITY

## U.S. Vulnerability

### *Document 1*

Late in the Eisenhower administration, Albert Wohlstetter, a noted strategic analyst at the RAND Corporation, published an article that argued that U.S. nuclear forces were dangerously vulnerable to attack. In these excerpts, he points out that the critical requirement for deterring the Soviet Union is the ability of U.S. forces to survive a Soviet nuclear attack and retaliate with a devastating counterblow. The growth of the Soviet nuclear threat, Wohlstetter says, especially the increase in the numbers of Soviet ICBMs, has made U.S. bombers very vulnerable.

Robert McNamara's drive to lessen the vulnerability of U.S. nuclear forces was greatly influenced by the views of Wohlstetter and others at RAND.

### 1 THE DELICATE BALANCE OF TERROR
### Albert Wohlstetter

I emphasize that requirements for deterrence are stringent. We have heard so much about the atomic stalemate and the receding probability of war which it has produced that this may strike the reader as something of an exaggeration. Is deterrence a necessary consequence of both sides having a nuclear delivery capability, and is all-out war nearly obsolete? Is mutual extinction the only outcome of a general war? This belief, frequently expressed by references to Mr. Oppenheimer's simile of the two scorpions in a bottle, is perhaps the prevalent one. . . . If peace were founded firmly on mutual terror, and mutual terror on symmetrical nuclear capabilities, this would be, as Churchill has said, "a melancholy paradox;" none the less a most comforting one.

Deterrence, however, is not automatic. While feasible, it will be much harder to achieve in the 1960s than is generally believed. One of the most disturbing features of current opinion is the underestimation of this difficulty. This is due partly to a misconstruction of the technological race as a problem in matching striking forces, partly to a wishful analysis of the Soviet ability to strike first.

Since Sputnik, the United States has made several moves to assure the world (that is, the enemy, but more especially our allies and ourselves) that we will match or overmatch Soviet technology and, specifically, Soviet offense technology. We have, for example, accelerated the bomber and ballistic missile programs, in particular the intermediate-range ballistic missiles. The problem has been conceived as more or better bombers — or rockets; or sputniks; or engineers. This has meant confusing deterrence with matching or exceeding the enemy's ability to strike first. Matching weapons, however, misconstrues the nature of the technological race. Not, as is frequently said, because only a few bombs owned by the defender can make aggression fruitless, but because even many might not. One outmoded A-bomb dropped from an obsolete bomber might destroy a great many supersonic jets and ballistic missiles. To deter an attack means being able to strike back in spite of it. It means, in other words, a capability to strike second. In the last year or two there has been a growing awareness of the importance of the distinction between a "strike-first" and a "strike-second" capability, but little, if any, recognition of the implications of this distinction for the balance of terror theory. . . .

Perhaps the first step in dispelling the nearly universal optimism about the stability of deterrence would be to recognize the difficulties in analyzing the uncertainties and interactions between our own wide range of choices and the moves open to the Soviets. On our side we must consider an enormous variety of strategic weapons which might compose our force, and for each of these several alternative methods of basing and operation. These are the choices that determine whether a weapons system will have any genuine capability in the realistic circumstances of a war. . . .

Some of the complexities can be suggested by referring to the successive obstacles to be hurdled by any system providing a capability to strike second, that is, to strike back. Such deterrent systems must have (a) a stable, "steady-state" peacetime operation within feasible budgets (besides the logistic and operational costs there are, for example, problems of false alarms and accidents). They must have also the ability (b) to survive enemy attacks, (c) to make and communicate the decision to retaliate, (d) to reach enemy territory with fuel enough to complete their mission, (e) to penetrate enemy active defenses, that is, fighters and surface-to-air missiles, and (f) to destroy the target in spite of any "passive" civil defense in the form of dispersal or protective construction or evacuation of the target itself.

Within limits the enemy is free to use his offensive and defensive forces so as to exploit the weaknesses of each of our systems. He will also be free, within limits, in the 1960s to choose that composition of forces which will make life as difficult as possible for the various systems we might select. It would be quite wrong to assume that we have the same degree of flexibility or that the uncertainties I have described affect a totalitarian aggressor and the party attacked equally. A totalitarian country can preserve secrecy about the capabilities and disposition of his forces very much better than a Western democracy. And the aggressor has, among other enormous advantages of the first strike, the ability to weigh continually our performance at each of the six barriers and to choose that precise time and circumstance for attack which will reduce uncertainty. It is important not to confuse our uncertainty with his. Strangely enough, some military commentators have not made this distinction and have founded their certainty of deterrence on the fact simply that there are uncertainties. . . .

In counteracting the general optimism as to the ease and, in fact, the inevitability of deterrence, I should like to avoid creating the extreme opposite impression. Deterrence demands hard, continuing, intelligent work, but it can be achieved. The job of deterring rational attack by guaranteeing great damage to an aggressor is, for example, very much less difficult than erecting a nearly airtight defense of cities in the face of full-scale thermonuclear surprise attack. Protecting manned bombers and missiles is much easier because they may be dispersed, sheltered or kept mobile, and they can respond to warning with greater speed. Mixtures of these and other defenses with complementary strengths can preserve a powerful remainder after attack. Obviously not all our bombers and missiles need to survive in order to fulfill their mission. To preserve the majority of our cities intact in the face of surprise attack is immensely more difficult, if not impossible. (This does not mean that the aggressor has the same problem in preserving his cities from retaliation by a poorly protected, badly-damaged force. And it does not mean that *we* should not do more to limit the extent of the catastrophe to our cities in case deterrence fails. I believe we should.) Deterrence, however, provided we work at it, is feasible, and, what is more, it is a crucial objective of national policy.

## Kennedy's Views on the Defense Budget

### *Document 2*

The Kennedy administration's concern about the vulnerability of U.S. strategic forces is evident in these selections from the president's special message to Congress on the defense budget. Kennedy recommends speeding up a number of new systems, including the Polaris SLBM and the Minuteman ICBM.

### 2 SPECIAL MESSAGE TO CONGRESS
**President Kennedy**
**March 8, 1961**

*To the Congress of the United States:*

In my role as Commander-in-Chief of the American Armed Forces, and with my concern over the security of this nation now and in the future, no single question of policy has concerned me more since entering upon these responsibilities than the adequacy of our present and planned military forces to accomplish our major national security objectives.

In January, while ordering certain immediately needed changes, I instructed the Secretary of Defense to reappraise our entire defense strategy, capacity, commitments and needs in the light of present and future dangers. The Secretary of State and others have been consulted in this reappraisal, and I have myself carefully reviewed their reports and advice.

Such a review is obviously a tremendous task and it still continues. But circumstances do not permit a postponement of all further action during the many additional months that a full reappraisal will require. Consequently we are now able to present the most urgent and obvious recommendations for inclusion in the fiscal 1962 Budget. . . .

5. Our strategic arms and defense must be adequate to deter any deliberate nuclear attack on the United States or our allies — by making clear to any potential aggres-

sor that sufficient retaliatory forces will be able to survive a first strike and penetrate his defenses in order to inflict unacceptable losses upon him. As I indicated in an address to the Senate some 31 months ago, this deterrence does not depend upon a simple comparison of missiles on hand before an attack. It has been publicly acknowledged for several years that this nation has not led the world in missile strength. Moreover, we will not strike first in any conflict. But what we have and must continue to have is the ability to survive a first blow and respond with devastating power. This deterrent power depends not only on the number of our missiles and bombers, but on their state of readiness, their ability to survive attack, and the flexibility and sureness with which we can control them to achieve our national purpose and strategic objectives.

6. The strength and deployment of our forces in combination with those of our allies should be sufficiently powerful and mobile to prevent the steady erosion of the Free World through limited wars; and it is this role that should constitute the primary mission of our overseas forces. Non-nuclear wars, and sub-limited or guerrilla warfare, have since 1945 constituted the most active and constant threat to Free World security. Those units of our forces which are stationed overseas, or designed to fight overseas, can be most usefully oriented toward deterring or confining those conflicts which do not justify and must not lead to a general nuclear attack. In the event of a major aggression that could not be repulsed by conventional forces, we must be prepared to take whatever action with whatever weapons are appropriate. But our objective now is to increase our ability to confine our response to non-nuclear weapons, and to lessen the incentive for any limited aggression by making clear what our response will accomplish. In most areas of the world, the main burden of local defense against overt attack, subversion and guerrilla warfare must rest on local populations and forces. But given the great likelihood and seriousness of this threat, we must be prepared to make a substantial contribution in the form of strong, highly mobile forces trained in this type of warfare, some of which must be deployed in forward areas, with a substantial airlift and sealift capacity and prestocked overseas bases. . . .

## II. Strengthening and Protecting Our Strategic Deterrent and Defenses

### *A. Improving Our Missile Deterrent*

As a power which will never strike first, our hopes for anything close to an absolute deterrent must rest on weapons which come from hidden, moving, or invulnerable bases which will not be wiped out by a surprise attack. A retaliatory capacity based on adequate numbers of these weapons would deter any aggressor from launching or even threatening an attack — an attack he knew could not find or destroy enough of our force to prevent his own destruction.

1. *Polaris* — The ability of the nuclear-powered Polaris submarine to operate deep below the surface of the seas for long periods and to launch its ballistic, solid fuel nuclear-armed missiles while submerged gives this weapons system a very high degree of mobility and concealment, making it virtually immune to ballistic missile attack.

In the light of the high degree of success attained to date in its development, production and operation, I strongly recommend that the Polaris program be greatly expanded, and accelerated. I have earlier directed the Department of Defense, as stated in my State of the Union Message, to increase the fiscal year 1961 program from 5 submarine starts to 10, and to accelerate the delivery of these and other Polaris submarines still under construction. This action will provide 5 more operational submarines about nine months earlier than previously planned.

For fiscal year 1962, I recommend the construction of 10 more Polaris submarines, making a total of 29, plus one additional tender. These 10 submarines, together with the 10 programmed for fiscal year 1961, are scheduled to be delivered at the rate of one a month or twelve a year, beginning in June 1963, compared with the previous rate of 5 a year. Under this schedule, a force of 29 Polaris submarines can be completed and at sea two months before the present program which called for 19 boats, and two years earlier than would be possible under the old 5-a-year rate. These 29 submarines, each with a full complement of missiles, will be a formidable deterrent force. The sooner they are on station, the safer we will be. And our emphasis upon a weapon distinguished primarily for its invulnerability is another demonstration of the fact that our posture as a nation is defensive and not aggressive.

I also recommend that the development of the long-range Polaris A-3 be accelerated in order to become available a year earlier at an eventual savings in the procurement of the A-2 system.

This longer range missile with improved penetration capability will greatly enhance the operational flexibility of the Polaris force and reduce its exposure to shore-based anti-submarine warfare measures. Finally, we must increase the allowance of Polaris missiles for practice firing to provide systematic "proving ground" data for determining and improving operational reliability.

The increases in this program, including $15 million in new obligational authority for additional crews, constitute the bulk of the budget increases — $1.34 billion in new obligational authority on a full funded basis, over a 4 year period though only $270 million in expenditures in fiscal 1962. I consider this a wise investment in our future.

2. *Minuteman*—another strategic missile system which will play a major role in our deterrent force, with a high degree of survivability under ballistic missile attack, is the solid fuel Minuteman. This system is planned to be deployed in well-dispersed, hardened sites and, eventually, in a mobile mode on railroad cars. . . .

(4) Minuteman capacity production should be doubled to enable us to move to still higher levels of strength more swiftly should future conditions warrant doubling our production. . . .

3. *Skybolt*—another type of missile less likely to be completely eliminated by enemy attack is the air-to-ground missile carried by a plane that can be off the ground before an attack commences. Skybolt is a long-range (1000 mile) air-launched, solid-fuel nuclear-warhead ballistic missile designed to be carried by the B–52 and the British V bombers. Its successful development and production may extend the useful life of our bombers into the missile age—and its range is far superior to the present Hound Dog missiles.

I recommend that an additional $50 million in new obligational authority be added to the 1962 budget to enable this program to go forward at an orderly rate.

### *B. Protecting Our Bomber Deterrent*

The considerably more rapid growth projected for our ballistic missile force does not eliminate the need for manned bombers—although no funds were included in the January budget for the further procurement of B–52 heavy bombers and B–58 medium bombers, and I do not propose any. Our existing bomber forces constitute our chief hope for deterring attack during this period prior to the completion of our missile expansion. However, only those planes that would not be destroyed on the ground in the event of a surprise attack striking their base can be considered sufficiently invulnerable to deter an aggressor.

I therefore recommend the following steps to protect our bomber deterrent:

1. *Airborne alert capacity.* That portion of our force which is constantly in the air is clearly the least vulnerable portion. I am asking for the funds to continue the present level of indoctrination training flights, and to complete the stand-by capacity and materials needed to place one-eighth of our entire heavy bomber force on airborne alert at any time. . . .

2. *Increased ground alert force and bomb alarms.* Strategic bombers standing by on a ground alert of 15 minutes can also have a high degree of survivability provided adequate and timely warning is available. I therefore recommended that the proportion of our B–52 and B–47 forces on ground alert should be increased until about half of our total force is on alert. . . .

### *C. Improving Our Continental Defense and Warning Systems*

Because of the speed and destructiveness of the intercontinental ballistic missile and the secrecy with which it can be launched, timely warning of any potential attack is of crucial importance not only for preserving our population but also for preserving a sufficient portion of our military forces—thus deterring such an attack before it is launched. . . . We must assure ourselves, therefore, that every feasible action is being taken to provide such warning.

To supplement the Ballistic Missile Early Warning System (BMEWS), on which construction is now proceeding as fast as is practical, the satellite-borne Midas system, now under development, is designed to provide about 30 minutes of warning by detecting missiles immediately after launching. Together with BMEWS, Midas would greatly increase the assurance and reliability of timely warning. I recommend that an additional $60 million in new obligational authority be added to the 1962 budget to accelerate completion of the development phase of the Midas program, with the goal of achieving an operational system at an earlier date. . . .

### *D. Improving the Command and Control of Our Strategic Deterrent*

The basic policies stated at the beginning of this message lay new emphasis on improved command and control—more flexible, more selective, more deliberate, better protected and under ultimate civilian authority at all times. This requires not only the development and installation of new equipment and facilities, but, even more importantly, increased attention to all organizational and procedural arrangements for the President and others. The invulnerable and continuous command posts and communications centers provided in these recommendations (requiring an additional $16 million in new obligational authority) are only the beginning of a major but absolutely vital effort to achieve a truly unified, nationwide, indestructible system to insure high-level command, communication and control and a properly authorized response under any conditions. . . .

## Conclusion

Our military position today is strong. But positive action must be taken now if we are to have the kind of forces we will need for our security in the future. Our preparation against danger is our hope of safety. The changes in the Defense program which I have recommended will greatly enhance the security of this Nation in the perilous years which lie ahead. It is not pleasant to request additional funds at this time for national security. Our interest, as I have emphasized, lies in peaceful solutions, in reducing tension, in settling disputes at the conference table and not on the battlefield. I am hopeful that these policies will help secure these ends. I commend them to the Congress and to the Nation.

John F. Kennedy

## The Whiz Kids

### *Document 3*

McNamara brought with him to Washington a group of young, mathematically oriented civilian analysts, recruited largely from Eastern universities and the RAND Corporation, who were soon dubbed the "Whiz Kids." Determined to coordinate and rationalize a defense policy-making process dominated by interservice rivalry, McNamara and his defense intellectuals quickly began to centralize in the Office of the Secretary of Defense many of the functions previously relegated to the armed services. In particular, they took over the services' dominant role in weapons procurement decisions. The young civilians made procurement and other budgetary choices based on cost-benefit analyses that often ignored the military's advice, experience, and traditions. This caused resentment among the professional military and its supporters in Congress. But McNamara and his Whiz Kids, described in these *Time* articles, caused a "managerial revolution" that for a time transformed the vocabulary and procedural practices of the Pentagon.

### 3 THOSE YOUNG MEN IN MUFTI
### August 3, 1962

Early one morning last week, Defense Secretary Robert McNamara and other top Pentagon officials flew out of Washington in two separate planes for a quick unannounced trip to North Carolina's Fort Bragg. Their mission: to get a close-up view of Army aircraft going through their paces and confer with members of a special Army panel that is taking a new, hard look at the problem of moving troops fast in battle. Among the men with stars on their shoulders and scrambled eggs on their hats flew young men in mufti whose schooling in warfare took place not on the beachheads of Normandy or Inchon but on the blackboards of universities and Government-contract think factories. The men in mufti exert a powerful and controversial influence in the Pentagon these days—and they often have more to say about cold war military planning than the generals.

#### Second Generation

They are known—sometimes disparagingly—as "the Whiz Kids," the tag originally hung on McNamara and nine fellow Army Air Forces officers who sold themselves to Ford as a team after World War II. Today's second-generation Whiz Kids share many of the qualities of the old McNamara group. They are young (mostly in their 30s), intellectual, aggressive, forever questioning. They bring to the Defense establishment, along with their slide rules, a fresh, imaginative approach to the increasingly intricate problem of turning dollars into deterrence: just how much should go for M-14 rifles, how much for ICBMs. Before McNamara, the Joint Chiefs of Staff were accustomed—as one New Frontiersman puts it—to "render advice as though it were engraved on stone." Today, the Whiz Kids assemble the facts and the alternatives—including unorthodox possibilities—so that the Secretary of Defense can grasp the whole problem and make up his mind for himself.

#### Computers v. Clausewitz

This unusual new breed of analysts and planners, more learned in computers than in Clausewitz, is dedicated to the belief that the demands of defense in the thermonuclear age have outdated the methods as well as the armor that served in past wars. Says Dr. Alain C. Enthoven, 31, a key man in pulling together and evaluating military information: "There are many things that simply cannot be calculated—the reliability of an ally, or the psychological and political consequences of a military operation. But there are also many things that cannot be done intuitively or based entirely on experience. Intuition and experience unaided by calculations will not tell us how many ICBMs are needed to destroy a target system, or how many C-141 transports are required to move a division."

Free of ingrained military prejudices—as well as lacking in military experience—the Whiz Kids delight in finding new and often totally unexpected solutions even to conventional military problems. While working on guerrilla warfare, one of them remembered reading books by British-born Author John Masters, whose *The Road Past Mandalay* described his World War II experiences with Orde Wingate's Chindits behind the Japanese lines in Burma, got Masters to write several valuable reports on guerrilla warfare. Enthoven calculated that one Chinook helicopter could do the job—at less expense in men and money—now performed by 15 to 20 of the Army's workhorse "deuce and a half" (2½-ton) trucks. And Dr. Merton Joseph Peck helped design the celebrated McNamara blueprint for reorganizing the Army National Guard and reserves.

#### Waffled Disagreements

While the Whiz Kids acknowledge in principle the usefulness of long experience in uniform, they give the professional soldiers poor marks at paperwork. Says one: "The military too often are inarticulate. In papers, they resort to the all-purpose sentence that doesn't recommend anything, but merely waffles over disagreements within their ranks." They think that the military too often fall back on tradition and intuition rather than clear-headed analysis. After Whiz Kids studies, the RS-70 bomber program was curtailed, though Air Force Chief of Staff Curtis LeMay is thoroughly convinced that the bomber's promised ability to fly farther and faster will be an essential ingredient in future U.S. aerial superiority.

As a result, the Whiz Kids are often disliked and distrusted both in the Pentagon and on Capitol Hill. One Air Force officer complained that their computers, rather than common sense, cut back the RS-70. Complains another: "These guys have never fired a shot in anger. And yet they try to come in here and suggest what experienced military men should do."

There is no open warfare in the Pentagon, but among the uniformed ranks there is a resentment based not only on the fact that the Whiz Kids are not members of the club (West Point or Annapolis); the military men feel that they are being passed over and disdained, that their hard-won knowledge is dismissed as obsolete and service pride taken for sentimental partisanship, that their inability to talk the new Whiz Kid lingo is taken as stupidity. The best of the old soldiers long ago tried to get sophisticated themselves in developing and using the advanced weapons, and planning the strategy and tactics of modern warfare. These men think that they will be the ones who, even in a pushbutton war, will have to do the fighting, and that the military tradition they are imbued with — of courage, stubbornness, independence, imagination, and self-respect — will be required of them and those who serve under them. All this, they believe, the new young men regard too lightly.

As for the Whiz Kids, they take pains to insist that they make only analyses and never policy, but their influence is wide if only because they work in terms that McNamara understands. The military are getting the message. Says one Army planner: "It's an entirely different way of doing business. But we've just had to adjust to it. No longer can you prove a point with civilian defense leaders by saying it's so because you know as a professional military man that it's just so. You've got to prove it now." To help prove it, the military are belatedly paying the Whiz Kids the most familiar form of flattery: they themselves are now bringing in younger, university-trained soldier-scientists to act as the military equivalent of the Whiz Kids.

*Though the ranks of the Whiz Kids in the Defense Department are proliferating, five stand out for the scope and strength of their influence [only three are listed here]:*

*Alain C. Enthoven,* 31, intense and dark-suited, looks more like a young college professor than a weapons analyst. Yet, as deputy comptroller for systems analysis, this young economist must lay bare the calculations on which many defense decisions are made. After graduating from Stanford with honors in economics, spending two years at Oxford as a Rhodes scholar and getting his Ph.D. from M.I.T., he joined the Rand Corp. think factory, where he helped direct a major study of Strategic Air Command operations and strategy that later became part of the Kennedy Administration's defense policy. Deeply concerned by the problems of defense ("The survival of the country seemed to be at stake"), he took a leave from Rand to work in the Defense Department two years ago, decided to stay on. Though he at first worked 70 to 80 hours a week, he is now in his office only from 8 a.m. to 7 p.m. Says he: "I can't increase output by working longer."

*Harold Brown,* 34, unlike most of the Whiz Kids, occupies a position of direct power as director of defense research and engineering. A forceful advocate of U.S. nuclear testing, Physicist Brown is Secretary McNamara's principal technical adviser, and is probably the scientist to whom President Kennedy now pays closest heed. Complains an Air Force officer who tangled with him over the derailed RS-70 bomber program: "He's awfully cocky and sure of himself." A Columbia Ph.D. at 21, he worked throughout the 1950s with the University of California's Radiation Laboratory, where he did research in the design and application of nuclear explosives, the detection of nuclear blasts, and the controlled release of thermonuclear energy.

*Henry S. Rowen,* 36, Deputy Assistant Secretary of Defense for policy planning and national security affairs, also came to Defense through the Rand Corp. after graduating from M.I.T. and studying at Oxford. Planner Rowen concentrates on strategic questions for the future rather than day-to-day defense programs, originated major elements in the "no-city" strategy outlined by McNamara in Ann Arbor, Mich., last month; under it, U.S. retaliation to surprise attack would concentrate on Soviet military objectives and avoid destruction of cities. Articulate and wide-ranging in his interests — which may be NATO or guerrilla warfare — he worked at Rand on a broad study of overseas bases that turned into a full-dress comparative review of U.S. *v.* Soviet strategic airpower. "As soon as he touches a sensitive nerve," says an Air Force planner, "the military begin to yell. But he always knows what he's talking about." . . .

## The Kennedy Buildup

### Document 4

In this description of the Kennedy administration's nuclear weapons policy, political analyst Richard Smoke points out how the administration added new, more survivable weapons such as the Polaris and Minuteman while dismantling more vulnerable systems. This buildup was in anticipation of a Soviet threat that did not develop. Thus by the middle 1960s the United States once again had a tremendous lead over the Soviet Union in nuclear forces.

## 4 THE AMERICAN STRATEGIC BUILDUP
**Richard Smoke**

When the Kennedy administration entered office determined to improve the American strategic posture, it took several steps at once. The ground alert that SAC had already begun was upgraded, to the point where almost half the bomber force was constantly ready to take off on about fifteen minutes notice. The administration pushed deployment of the first-generation Atlas and Titan ICBMs, the first of which were now beginning to enter the strategic force. The ICBMs had to be deployed at launch sites above ground, however, because the technology of constructing hardened underground silos for missiles had not yet been perfected. These early ICBM sites were every bit as vulnerable to Soviet attack as bomber bases, and hence contributed little to a secure second-strike force, although they did multiply the Soviet targeting problem. Of greater long-term significance than these developments was the administration's acceleration and expansion of U.S. programs for second-generation missiles.

Work had begun in the late 1950s on these missiles, which were improvements over their predecessors in many ways, but one above all — they used solid rather than liquid fuel. The Atlas and Titan missiles could not be kept fueled at all times; they had to be filled with liquid fuel after the command to be ready for launch. This was a time-consuming and somewhat difficult procedure. Solid-fuel missiles, on the other hand, have their fuel prepacked, in a stable form that lasts a long time. They are always ready and can be launched on very short notice. Though perfecting the solid-fuel technology was more difficult, the decision (made by the Eisenhower administration) to shift to solid fuel in the next generation of missiles was to give the United States a considerable advantage over the Soviet Union, which developed this technology much more slowly, and indeed still does not use it in many missiles.

Two solid-fueled missile programs had begun in the 1950s. One was America's second-generation ICBM, called the Minuteman. So named because it could be fired on about one minute's warning, the Minuteman was procured in large numbers by the Kennedy and Johnson administrations. It was designed from the outset to be launched from hardened underground silos, and after it became available in quantity the Atlas and most of the Titan missiles were gradually retired from the ICBM force. A few Titans were retained, however, and put in underground silos, because the Titan can carry a heavier warhead than any other American missile. In the jargon of the trade, the Titan has a larger "throw weight," and for this reason fifty-four of these missiles were kept in the American arsenal for a long time. Only in 1981 was it announced that they would be phased out.

The other solid-fueled missile was the Polaris, designed to be carried in submarines. Launching missiles from below the ocean's surface was a concept developed in the 1950s (and never yet improved upon) as a solution to the challenge of making strategic forces secure. Submarines are difficult to locate if they cruise submerged and if they do not have to come to the surface to fire their missiles. Officials and analysts both inside and outside the Eisenhower administration agreed that if all the necessary technologies could be developed, "submarine launched ballistic missiles," or SLBMs, could give the United States a highly secure second-strike capability, and the attempt was pursued with a high priority.

The development of the Polaris SLBM and of the submarine (also called Polaris) to carry it, proved to be one of the most successful research and development programs in postwar American history. With relatively few setbacks, the complicated technical problems involved were solved one by one, and the first Polaris submarines came "on station" in 1961, a remarkably rapid schedule. The first Polaris missiles had only an "intermediate" range of 1,500 miles or so; they were later replaced with improved models having a longer range. In the 1970s, these were replaced again with a new SLBM called Poseidon that had an intercontinental range. Each enlargement in range meant that more targets could be reached, and more importantly, that the submarines would have a much larger ocean area in which to hide. Since a rotating portion of the submarine fleet must be in port at any one time, longer range also meant that in a crisis, the submarines in port could be sent to sea and reach their cruising areas quickly.

By now, the strategic forces deployed by the United States, followed later by the Soviet Union, had become so diverse that it is useful to display information in the form of tables. Table 1 indicates the two sides' strategic forces as of October 1962. Similar tables later in the book give parallel data for other times.

When McNamara became secretary of defense he used some of the supplementary funds requested from Congress to accelerate the Minuteman and Polaris programs. The Kennedy administration was also faced with choices about how many of these missiles to deploy and was inclined, now and over the next several years, to create a comparatively large force. Ultimately one thousand Minutemen would be deployed, and forty-one Polaris submarines carrying sixteen missiles each, or a total of 656 Polaris missiles. With the fifty-four Titans, this added up to a strategic missile force of 1,710 ICBMs and

**Table 1. American and Soviet Strategic Forces as of October 1962**

| | Soviet Union | United States |
|---|---|---|
| ICBMs | 75 (approx.) | 100 Minuteman I (approx.)<br>90 Atlas<br>36 Titan<br>226 |
| SLBMs | 0 | 144 Polaris missiles carried by nine Polaris submarines |
| Long-range bombers | 70 Bears<br>120 Bisons<br>190 | 600 B-52s (approx.)<br>750 B-47s (approx.)<br>1350 |

*Notes:* Bear and Bison are NATO code names. The Bear was a propeller-driven heavy bomber; the Bison was a lighter bomber with four jets, somewhat less capable than the B-47. The B-47s were being rapidly phased out at this time.

All Soviet ICBMs were at very vulnerable above-ground launch sites. So were the U.S. Titans and most of the Atlases. The Minuteman I missiles were in hardened underground silos. The Minuteman I force was being rapidly expanded at this time; eight months later, in July 1963, about 450 were deployed.

*Source:* Institute of Strategic Studies, London: The Communist Bloc and the Western Alliance: The Military Balance 1962–63.

SLBMs, although this total was not reached until the second half of the 1960s. This number, approximately decided upon while Kennedy was still president, was to remain the same well into the 1970s, although the quality of the forces (in reliability, accuracy, range, payload, and other factors) was improved steadily.

Decisions about the numbers of missiles to build had to be made relatively early since years would pass between the time of decision and the actual entry of many of these missiles into the operating forces. When this magnitude was decided upon, analysts still were expecting a large Soviet deployment to show up on spy satellite photographs before long, and the decision was guided by a desire to at least equal the reasonable maximum that the USSR was likely to deploy. The years of inflated propaganda claims, and the more aggressive turn in Soviet foreign policy that had accompanied them, suggested that it would be unwise to allow the USSR again to achieve even an appearance of superiority.

Through approximately the first half of the 1960s, however, the Soviets did *not* deploy many ICBMs. Apparently they experienced technical difficulties in perfecting their second-generation missiles; by the beginning of 1965, for instance, they still had only about 200 ICBMs.* At this time, too, the Soviets had not yet developed any SLBM forces; nor did they have a jet bomber of intercontinental range. Though later in the decade Soviet forces were to expand markedly (and continue to thereafter), in the early to mid-1960s American analysts remained pleasantly surprised by a continuing low level of Soviet intercontinental striking power, compared to U.S. power. (The USSR did build up its intermediate range forces aimed at Europe.)

This meant that the current U.S. strategic program was creating, rather unexpectedly, a growing *American* numerical superiority in the strategic competition. The Soviet Union's missile bluff earlier, the strong American reaction, and the Soviets continuing into the 1960s to deploy only a few ICBMs, all combined to create a situation that neither Washington nor, probably, Moscow had anticipated. Numerical strategic superiority was passing back to the United States. Even though the U.S. buildup was cut back slightly from what had been planned at one time, and the United States later withdrew some intermediate-range missiles that had been stationed at vulnerable, above-ground sites overseas, the balance in missile forces began to run heavily in America's favor. And this did not count the huge U.S. advantage in strategic bombers, nor the "tactical" aircraft carrying nuclear bombs stationed overseas and on aircraft carriers.

The first half of the 1960s was also the time when the United States was beefing up its conventional power, as Flexible Response counseled. Improvements in airlift, sealift, and communications, upgrading of the combat effectiveness of army and marine corps divisions, and expansion of these "general purpose forces," as they now came to be called, were creating a range of conventional options that the country had never previously possessed. The total surge in American military power, including general purpose as well as nuclear forces, in the early 1960s added up to the greatest peacetime military buildup that any nation had undertaken in a short period anytime in the twentieth century.

At this time, too, the United States was still ahead of the USSR in the numbers and kinds of nuclear weapons for tactical use; and contributions of various kinds of forces from the NATO allies were increasing. Although on paper NATO was still unequal to the Warsaw Pact in total number of troops, the Kennedy administration became confident that even in Europe the real balance of power was not disadvantageous to the West. In short, the return of strategic superiority was being accompanied by an increasingly favorable position over the military spectrum as a whole.

In this partly accidental, partly deliberate fashion, the period of the early to mid-1960s became a second era of American military superiority. The Kennedy administration, at first concerned that a missile gap might be appearing or about to appear, and later believing quite reasonably that the Soviets would begin a large missile deployment soon, took steps to increase American strategic power greatly. When the expected Soviet missiles did not materialize for some years, these steps proved

* The reader should recall that while this number was small compared to the American ICBM arsenal of the day, it represented tremendous destructive power if used in a first strike. Just ten percent of the force could have wiped out twenty American cities if all missiles reached their targets. All 200 could have almost annihilated the United States.

to be considerably more than had been necessary at the time. There was a missile gap in reverse. For the second time in the history of the cold war, American officials found that they were coming to possess marked strategic superiority. Also for the second time, this was less planned or intended than it was a reaction to fears about sudden advances in Soviet power.

## The Soviets Close the Nuclear Gap

### *Document 5*

In this review of Soviet strategic policies in the 1960s, Jerome Kahan, a strategic analyst, notes that by the end of 1961, the United States knew that Soviet claims to have a large missile force were a bluff. In Soviet eyes, this enabled the West to act boldly in the 1961 Berlin crisis and in the Cuban missile crisis a year later. After Khrushchev was ousted, the Soviets began a major expansion of their nuclear forces.

## 5 SOVIET STRATEGIC POLICIES
## Jerome H. Kahan

As noted earlier, the USSR found itself in an extremely unfavorable strategic position in the early 1960s. The lack of large-scale Soviet ICBM deployments and the sizable and expanding U.S. strategic arsenal had led to a reversal of the missile gap. Moreover, the dramatic disclosure in mid-1961 that the United States was able not only to count but to locate and target the USSR's small missile force and its bomber bases caused some Kremlin leaders to fear, as in 1954, that the United States was moving toward a first-strike doctrine. Public pronouncements of American superiority added to Soviet concern. Defense Minister Rodion Malinovsky, for example, reacting to Gilpatric's speech in late 1961, accused the United States of preparing a surprise nuclear attack, and a statement attributed to President Kennedy in early 1962, suggesting that the United States would be prepared to use nuclear weapons first in certain circumstances, was apparently interpreted by Khrushchev as an effort to intimidate the Soviet Union. Finally, when Secretary McNamara articulated the no-cities doctrine in June 1962, Soviet fears that the United States was pursuing a counterforce strategy were exacerbated.[1]

### Redressing the Strategic Imbalance

Most Kremlinologists claim that, aside from the potential threat to Soviet deterrent forces, the nature of the nuclear balance raised serious foreign policy problems for Moscow. The crisis over Berlin in late 1961, which coincided with U.S. exposure of the missile gap myth, seemed to demonstrate to many Soviet officials that it was no longer possible to sustain the image of superiority and underscored the danger as well as the futility of attempting to obtain political benefits through Sputnik diplomacy. The Kennedy administration's behavior during the Berlin crisis and the accelerated U.S. strategic buildup may have been viewed by the Kremlin as a systematic strategy to use nuclear power for diplomatic purposes. With the strategic balance shifted against them, Soviet leaders apparently feared that they might be unable to protect their vital interests in diplomatic dealings with the West and to maintain their image as leader of the Communist bloc. In addition, planned improvements in U.S. *nonnuclear* capabilities threatened to deprive the Soviet Union of its conventional superiority in Europe and thus negate what the Kremlin considered to be a crucial counterweight to Washington's nuclear advantage.

By mid-1962, therefore, the prospect of overwhelming U.S. military superiority gave the Soviet Union a strong political as well as military incentive to redress the balance of intercontinental strategic forces. It was not enough for the USSR to rely on its large medium-range missile and bomber capability targeted against Western Europe, since long-range strategic missiles had become the most relevant measure of nuclear strength. Ironically, Khrushchev's "rocket-rattling" policy of the late 1950s had actually enhanced the value of these systems as political currency. But attempts to overtake the United States in number of intercontinental systems would have entailed a massive Soviet effort, for the United States had a considerable lead in ICBMs and SLBMs — apart from its established superiority in long-range bombers. Furthermore, the existing Soviet technology of soft and slow-reacting missiles would have made a crash ICBM program particularly costly while yielding marginal security benefits. In any event, the Soviet leader remained unwilling to commit his nation to an enormously expensive strategic program that would detract from his ability to meet domestic requirements. Thus, Khrushchev was faced with the need to increase the USSR's strategic strength rapidly while holding expenditures in check. . . .

#### *Strategic Arms Expansion*

After Khrushchev's departure in late 1964, the Soviet Union launched a major effort to redress the nuclear balance. Evidence suggests that Leonid Brezhnev and Alexei Kosygin were more motivated than Khrushchev to accomplish this objective and were willing to allocate greater resources to improve the Soviet Union's defense posture. In early 1965, drawing on the research and development programs initiated under Khrushchev, the new Kremlin leaders decided to substantially upgrade and enlarge the Soviet Union's strategic force. The decisions to deploy the SS-9 and SS-11 ICBMs were apparently made at that time, as well as the commitment to acquire a Polaris-type system to supplement the small and relatively ineffective Soviet missile-firing submarine fleet. The Soviet force increased from a level of about 200 ICBMs in late 1964 — which represented a four-to-one inferiority in this category alone — to 340 in 1966 and to 730 in 1967. By the end of 1968, the USSR was approaching parity with the United States in number of hardened ICBMs and had begun to deploy operational missile-firing submarines. As it turned out, the USSR built a substantially larger strategic force during the years 1966–69 than even worst-case U.S. estimates had predicted.

Soviet decisions to pass the United States in number of ICBMs, develop simple multiple warheads, and construct a large SLBM fleet were obviously influenced by a variety of factors. Some USSR officials may have seen these programs as an opportunity to gain numerical superiority and an eventual counterforce capability against U.S. ICBMs; and bureaucratic considerations, technological momentum, and the desire to negotiate from strength undoubtedly contributed to the Soviet arms buildup. Nevertheless, one of the most important reasons for the sustained Soviet buildup may have been the USSR's basic need to maintain a confident deterrent posture — for, as the Soviet Union began to close the gap in the late 1960s, the United States had moved the arms competition into a new phase. Although the number of U.S. strategic missiles and bombers had remained constant, a conservative Soviet analyst projecting ahead to the early 1970s could easily have demonstrated that the combination of accurate U.S. MIRVs and the completed Sentinel ABM deployment would endanger the USSR's nuclear retaliatory capability, unless additional systems, particularly sea-based forces, were produced.

## Note

1. For a discussion of Soviet reactions to early Kennedy administration strategic policies, see Horelick and Rush, *Strategic Power*, pp. 85–105; and Thomas W. Wolfe, *Soviet Power and Europe, 1945–1970* (Johns Hopkins Press, 1970), pp. 85–95.

# The Berlin Crisis

### *Document 6*

As the newly inaugurated Kennedy administration settled into office, the divided city of Berlin once again became the center of an intense East–West crisis. West Berlin had served for many years as an escape valve for East Germans dissatisfied with Communist rule; by 1961 this steady stream of refugees had swollen into a flood that undermined the stability of the East German regime. Cold war tensions, already running high over Soviet leader Nikita Khrushchev's saber-rattling efforts to dislodge the Western powers from the city, were further heightened in August 1961 by the Soviet-inspired barrier across the divided city. Berlin became the focus of a war of nerves between Washington and Moscow that threatened to erupt into a shooting war. Only after several tense months did the crisis finally begin to abate, as Khrushchev withdrew his demands and tacitly accepted the "abnormal" situation in the city.

## 6 BERLIN FLARE-UP
## September 3, 1962

Once again, after weeks of relative quiet, Berlin has flared up into the world's No. 1 crisis area.

For three days and nights, dangerous rioting raged along the western side of the Communist Wall across Berlin.

No sooner had that outburst been brought under control than Russia abruptly announced, on August 22, that it was pulling its military command out of East Berlin. On August 23, an officer of the East German Army took over.

Thus, Nikita Khrushchev applied one more squeeze to try to force the Western Allies out of the city and pressure the U.S. into dealing with the East German Communists.

Within hours of Moscow's decision, President Kennedy told his news conference in Washington that the Russians would not be allowed to let their action jeopardize U.S. rights in Berlin. The three Western Allies — U.S., Britain and France — notified Moscow that the Russians, not the East German Communists, are responsible for events in the city.

In the midst of all this, on August 23, the Communists for the second time in a week shot and killed an East German boy as he fled to the sanctuary of West Berlin.

### Power Facing Power

The combination of developments confronted the U.S. and its allies with a dilemma that has haunted them since the Communists walled off the eastern half of this city on Aug. 13, 1962. The dilemma is this:

What happens if Berlin really explodes and circumstances force a showdown between the U.S. and the Soviet Union?

The danger, widely recognized, lies in the fact that divided Germany is the only place in the world where

U.S. and Russian armies — combat trained and fully armed — confront each other across a border.

The U.S. has 250,000 soldiers in Europe. Most of them are in West Germany, including 5,000 in West Berlin. Russia has an estimated 400,000 Soviet soldiers in East Germany.

It was the outbreak of rioting in West Berlin that touched off the renewed crisis — and West German authorities have evidence that Communist infiltrators had a hand in stirring up the trouble. What happened was this:

On August 17, an 18-year-old East German named Peter Fechter tried to scale the Communist barricade and escape to the West. Communist guards shot him at the barrier, in plain sight of West Berlin police and U.S. troops. The Communists left him to bleed to death. Nobody on either side of the Wall made a move to aid him as he cried for help. Only after he died, an hour later, did the Communists remove the body.

The West Berliners, who have lived in an atmosphere of nervous peace on their side of the Wall, erupted in violence. For the next three days, they rioted at the Wall against the Communist guards who had killed young Fechter, and against the West Berlin police and American soldiers on this side who were holding them back. They stoned Soviet military cars carrying Russian troops to the Soviet Army Memorial in West Berlin. There were angry shouts of "Americans, go home!"

On August 21, the U.S. stationed ambulances along the Wall, with the announced intention of going to the aid of victims of the Communist guns hereafter. But the whole episode served as a measure of the explosiveness of Berlin.

Since the Communist Wall went up a year ago, more than 12,000 East Germans have escaped to the West. But 50 or so have been killed trying — a fact that brought this comment from London's "Times":

"To a great extent, the whole Berlin crisis is a probing operation to test the will of the West. The Wall was accepted because the West as a whole didn't realize its implications, and the dangers of knocking it down didn't seem justified. To stand back and watch the murder of refugees is somewhat different, and involves very strong human emotions which cannot be wholly suppressed."

### West German Worries

What gave the riotous reaction to the killing of Peter Fechter added significance was the fact that, for months now, there have been signs of increasing difference between the U.S. and the West German Government. One diplomat was quoted as saying:

"There has never been such distrust between the United States and the West German Government as is being expressed at this time."

The West Berliners are distrustful of negotiations between the U.S. and Russia, trying to reach a settlement of differences over the future of this city. They fear any agreement will be a victory for Moscow, at their expense.

In Bonn, the Adenauer Government fears the U.S. is shifting its defense policy in Europe to give primary importance to conventional forces at the expense of nuclear defense of the Continent. The United States has denied such a plan.

### Letter from Kennedy

The worry in Germany reached the point where, on August 22, President Kennedy announced in Washington that he had written Chancellor Adenauer a personal letter to try to calm nerves in Germany.

Then came the Russians' announcement that they were removing their military commander from Berlin and turning the job over to an East German. This could leave the U.S., British, and French commanders with nobody to talk to in Berlin except the East German Communists — something they refuse to do.

The Western Allies, under the occupation agreement made with the Soviet Union at the end of World War II, hold the Russians responsible for maintaining Western access to the city and for everything else that happens in Berlin.

Khrushchev, however, has insisted for years that Western troops get out of West Berlin. Repeatedly, he has threatened to sign a peace treaty with East Germany and give the East Germans power to say who can and cannot cross their territory in the Berlin corridors.

British officials believe that, despite the atmosphere of crisis, Khrushchev now is following a cautious, step-by-step campaign aimed at weakening the Western military position in the city, but without risking war with the U.S.

### New Try at "Free City?"

Some authorities feel that closing of the Soviet command headquarters may be setting the stage for more important moves in the future — such as a Russian proposal to make West Berlin a "free city" under control of the United Nations. Khrushchev already has proposed that a U.N. force replace Allied garrisons here.

The Soviet dictator is expected to renew that argument if he attends the U.N. General Assembly session coming soon in New York. If Khrushchev does attend, President Kennedy has said he would plan to meet with him.

But, among Western Allies, there is some disagreement over the wisdom of U.S.-Russian conversations on Berlin — talks that have gone on for months.

Although the British officially support the talks, some

in London suggest privately that they should be broken off.

In France, President de Gaulle has opposed the U.S.-Russian contacts from the very beginning. He feels that the Allies are in Berlin as a matter of right, and there is nothing to discuss with Khrushchev — that it's none of his business.

Whatever happens in the period just ahead, it is clear now that Berlin has moved back into position as the No. 1 crisis zone of the cold war. And it can be expected to remain there — a potential explosion point — for months to come.

## Fallout Shelters

### *Document 7*

**As part of its campaign to reduce the vulnerability of the United States to a nuclear attack, the Kennedy administration in 1961 launched an expanded program to encourage the building of fallout shelters. Articles like the one excerpted here from a 1961 issue of *Life* helped set off a wave of "shelter mania" that lasted about a year. The shelter program was deemphasized as McNamara moved to an assured destruction policy.**

### 7 A NEW URGENCY, BIG THINGS TO DO — AND WHAT YOU MUST LEARN
### September 15, 1961

The White House
September 7, 1961

*My Fellow Americans:*

Nuclear weapons and the possibility of nuclear war are facts of life we cannot ignore today. I do not believe that war can solve any of the problems facing the world today. But the decision is not ours alone.

The government is moving to improve the protection afforded you in your communities through civil defense. We have begun, and will be continuing throughout the next year and a half, a survey of all public buildings with fallout shelter potential, and the marking of those with adequate shelter for 50 persons or more. We are providing fallout shelters in new and in some existing federal buildings. We are stocking these shelters with one week's food and medical supplies and two weeks' water supply for the shelter occupants. In addition, I have recommended to the Congress the establishment of food reserves in centers around the country where they might be needed following an attack. Finally, we are developing improved warning systems which will make it possible to sound attack warning on buzzers right in your homes and places of business.

More comprehensive measures then these lie ahead, but they cannot be brought to completion in the immediate future. In the meantime there is much that you can do to protect yourself — and in doing so strengthen your nation.

I urge you to read and consider seriously the contents of this issue of *Life*. The security of our country and the peace of the world are the objectives of our policy. But in these dangerous days when both these objectives are threatened we must prepare for all eventualities. The ability to survive coupled with the will to do so therefore are essential to our country.

John F. Kennedy

The President's letter to all Americans . . . emphasizes the urgency which could be felt across the nation last week. As the warlike rattle rolled out of Moscow and as small amounts of fallout from the daily successions of Soviet nuclear tests floated over the U.S., the people woke up to the fact that they ought to be doing something to protect themselves.

This was a new idea. For years, most people have had the fatalistic idea that it was no use trying to do anything about protection against a nuclear bomb. If the blast did not kill them, they felt, radiation certainly would. The man down the street with a backyard shelter was considered odd. But he is actually a solid, sensible man — and a responsible citizen.

If the enemy attacks, he will probably aim first at military targets like missile and SAC bases. Large cities and industrial centers, which do not have the capacity to strike back, will be secondary targets. If a military-objective attack should come now to an unprepared nation, 45 million Americans — a fourth of the population — would die. Some would die in the blast. But the greatest danger to by far the greatest number would come from fallout, the deadly cloud of radioactive dust and debris which would blow across the land.

Hundreds of miles from the target, people would come into contact with destructive fallout, which they could not necessarily see, touch or smell. They could get enough on their skin to cause burns and sickness. Fallout might also contaminate their food and water and damage their vital organs.

But if Americans took precautions against fallout the mortality could drop sharply. About five million people, less than 3% of the population, would die. This in itself is a ghastly number. But you have to look at it coldly. Unprepared, there is one chance in four that you and your family will die. Prepared, you and your family could have 97 chances out of 100 to survive.

Basically, fallout protection consists of covering your body, food and water so the radioactive particles cannot contaminate them. If you have sufficient shielding between you and the fallout you are safe. You should be prepared to take cover for at least two weeks.

Obviously, this will not always be easy to do. What if you are in a city like New York? Though some notable steps have been taken, most cities are far behind in their preparations for fallout protection. People must know instantly where to go. But your chances of surviving fallout in a big city would be good. If you are in a large apartment house or office building you could either go to the basement or stay in an inner corridor on one of the middle floors.

A subway system or any city tunnels offer an excellent shelter. Wherever you live or work, you should try to keep a potable supply of water ready. You can live for several weeks without food, but not without water.

It is likely that any attack will come at night while you are at home — so the enemy will have daylight to prepare for the retaliation. (When it is midnight in New York, it is 8 a.m. in Moscow.) If you own a home, you can build a family shelter there. No civilian shelter will stand up against a direct or nearby blast. And the 97% survival figure is the optimum, based on good protection and some warning. There is no guarantee that any of your defenses — or even the nation's defenses — will be adequate if the enemy attacks all-out with complete surprise. But they will increase your odds. And every family shelter will contribute to the nation's total deterrent. For if the U.S. is so well prepared that it cannot be knocked out, the enemy may never attack.

Fallout preparation will take effort, money — and time. On these pages, LIFE shows practical ways in which you can protect yourself and your family and a rundown on what to do in an attack. If you want a rudimentary shelter, you can dig a cave in a hillside or build wooden double walls in your basement, filling them with earth. But good shelters can be built at modest expense. . . .

The standard Civil Defense signal for an alert is a steady 3- to 5-minute blast of a siren or whistle. The warning to take cover is a 3-minute period of short blasts or a wailing siren. If an attack should come, however, the first warning you may get could be the flash itself. Your first move should be to close your eyes and bury your head in your arms or clothing to block out the light. The flash may last for several seconds, so keep covered until it begins to dim.

The shockwave will come next. Take cover so you will not be knocked down. If you are in a car, roll down windows to avoid flying glass and lie on the floor. Try to count the seconds between the flash and shockwave. This will help you estimate how far away the bomb has hit and how long you have to find better cover before the fallout can reach you. To get the distance of the blast in miles count the seconds and divide them by five. The fallout would travel at a minimum speed of a mile in three minutes.

Wherever you are, try to reach a radio — preferably a battery radio since the electricity may be out — and tune it to 640 or 1240 on your dial, which are the Conelrad frequencies for emergency instructions. If you have a shelter, go to it immediately. If there seems to be time, you should turn off all electrical appliances so they will not start a fire if subsequent blasts damage your home. Close windows and doors. Shut off your furnace or heaters and gas lines. Close your chimney dampers to keep out dust. Turn off the inlet valve to your water heater so that the water supply will be cut off before it becomes contaminated. Fill available tubs and utensils with water. Water from underground reservoirs and deep wells will be safe, uncontaminated by fallout. Remember that water will probably be needed not just for drinking but for washing off fallout dust.

Rogers Cannell, civil defense expert at Stanford Research Institute, emphasizes the importance of having you and your family ready with a rehearsed plan for survival so that each member knows exactly what to do. Unless advised to do so you should not try to evacuate, for you may only move from a relatively safe area to one where fallout is greater. Your children should remain at school — unless they are advised to the contrary — and comply with the school survival plan rather than risk exposure by heading for home.

If you have no shelter and there is an hour or so left before the fallout is due to reach your area, you can block up the windows of your basement with one foot of earth, and take shelter there under tables on which you have piled books and magazines for extra shielding. You should also get together a supply of food and water and take it to the basement with you.

If you think you have been contaminated by fallout, remove all your clothing as soon as possible and wash off your skin and especially your hair. You may eat canned or packaged food (after washing off the container) and even fresh fruits and vegetables, provided you peel them first. The best first aid for radiation sickness — whose symptoms are nausea, fatigue and fever — is to take hot tea or a solution of baking soda to combat the nausea and aspirin for the fever. You can recover from a mild case of radiation sickness just as you recover from a cold. It is not contagious.

Radiation loses its deadliness rapidly. It is only 1/10th of its original strength seven hours after an attack. After several days you may be able to leave your shelter to pick up extra supplies of food and water. In any event, before your family leaves the shelter you should wait for official instructions over the two Conelrad frequencies.

# THE EVOLUTION OF U.S. STRATEGIC DOCTRINE

## Flexible Response

### Document 8

The Kennedy administration wasted little time in reducing the previous administration's reliance on using nuclear weapons to deter limited aggression. The new administration sought to minimize risks by giving the United States options beyond escalating to nuclear war or not acting at all in responding to a provocation. Such flexibility required an ability to take coordinated and controlled action appropriate to the situation at hand. In this account of McNamara's early tenure in office, William Kaufmann, a former RAND Corporation analyst and a consultant to the new secretary of defense, highlights the theoretical assumptions underlying the administration's "flexible response" strategy.

### 8 THE SEARCH FOR OPTIONS
### William Kaufmann

The strategy of the flexible response rested upon several premises. The first was that there were circumstances in which deterrence might not work. The second was that the number of lives lost in a thermonuclear war would vary significantly, depending, among other factors, on the types of targets attacked by the belligerents. The third was that limiting damage to the United States and its allies would constitute a major wartime objective, and that it could best be done by attacking the enemy's bombers and missiles, and providing active and civil defenses for American and allied populations. The fourth and related premise was that the combination of avoiding enemy cities and holding forces in reserve would provide the enemy with incentives to confine his own attacks to American and allied military targets and thus contribute further to the limitation of damage. Whether or not the incentives would prove powerful enough, it would be foolish, according to this argument, automatically to destroy cities at the outset of the war when they could always be taken under attack by reserve forces at some later stage, if that should seem necessary. Finally, there was the premise that even a thermonuclear conflict would not totally erase the interest of the United States in the postwar world; hence, sufficient forces should be available to eliminate or neutralize residual enemy capabilities, bring the war to a conclusion, and provide a measure of protection thereafter. Proponents of the flexible response answered the argument that a shift in strategy would weaken deterrence by asking whether the enemy would be any more willing to go to strategic nuclear war if he faced the prospect of being thwarted in his objectives and suffering substantial damage than if the outcome was likely to be mutual civil devastation. As for the arms race, they questioned whether unilateral American restraint would really slow it down, and pointed out that under the concept of the flexible response there were limits to the numbers of offensive forces that it would be necessary to procure, owing simply to the combination of high costs and the law of diminishing returns.

## The No-Cities Doctrine

### Document 9

Profoundly dissatisfied with the Eisenhower administration's unrestrained, highly rigid war plans that would kill an estimated 400 million Communist-bloc civilians in a matter of hours, McNamara and his staff began to develop a nuclear strategy that emphasized greater flexibility and discrimination in targeting options. In June 1962, McNamara publicly unveiled this strategy in a commencement address delivered at the University of Michigan at Ann Arbor. Outlining the new U.S. policy, he argues that the "principal objectives, in the event of a nuclear war . . . should be the destruction of the enemy's military forces, not of his civilian population." The incorporation of more flexible and controlled targeting options into the SIOP, McNamara asserts, would enable the United States to refrain from automatically destroying enemy cities in the event of nuclear war. Moreover, it would allow the United States to hold in reserve a large, invulnerable strategic nuclear force, whose devastating retaliatory potential would give an adversary "the strongest possible incentive to refrain from striking American cities" and to reach rapidly a negotiated end to the war. Fundamentally, McNamara's "no-cities" doctrine represented an attempt both to avert ultimate disaster should a nuclear war break out and to preserve the credibility of the U.S. retaliatory threat, particularly in Europe, in the face of the impressive growth of the Soviet atomic arsenal. It moved U.S. declaratory policy distinctly away from the doctrine of massive retaliation.

### 9 COMMENCEMENT ADDRESS
### Robert McNamara
### University of Michigan, Ann Arbor
### June 1962

I am glad to be home, and I am particularly glad to be here for a university occasion. For this University gives meaning and focus to life in Ann Arbor — even for those who are not privileged to be associated with it directly — as the academic community serves to clarify the objectives and focus the energies of the Free World. . . .

What I want to talk to you about here today are some of the concrete problems of maintaining a free community in the world today. I want to talk to you particularly about the problems of the community that bind together the United States and the countries of Western Europe. . . .

The North Atlantic Alliance is a unique alignment of governments. The provision for the common defense of the members has led to a remarkable degree of military collaboration and diplomatic consultation for a peacetime coalition. The growth of the alliance organization has accelerated as the task of defending the treaty area has increased in scope, size and complexity. NATO has had its stresses and strains, but it has weathered them all.

Today, NATO is involved in a number of controversies, which must be resolved by achieving a consensus within the organization in order to preserve its strength and unity. The question has arisen whether Senator Vandenberg's assertion is as true today as it was when he made it 13 years ago. Three arguments have raised this question most sharply:

It has been argued that the very success of Western European economic development reduces Europe's need to rely on the U. S. to share in its defenses.

It has been argued that the increasing vulnerability of the U. S. to nuclear attack makes us less willing as a partner in the defense of Europe, and hence less effective in deterring such an attack.

It has been argued that nuclear capabilities are alone relevant in the face of the growing nuclear threat, and that independent national nuclear forces are sufficient to protect the nations of Europe.

I believe that all of these arguments are mistaken. I think it is worthwhile to expose the U. S. views on these issues as we have presented them to our allies. In our view, the effect of the new factors in the situation, both economic and military, has been to increase the interdependence of national security interests on both sides of the Atlantic, and to enhance the need for the closest coordination of our efforts.

A central military issue facing NATO today is the role of nuclear strategy. Four facts seem to us to dominate consideration of that role. All of them point in the direction of increased integration to achieve our common defense. First, the Alliance has over-all nuclear strength adequate to any challenge confronting it. Second, this strength not only minimizes the likelihood of major nuclear war, but it makes possible a strategy designed to preserve the fabric of our societies if war should occur. Third, damage to the civil societies of the Alliance resulting from nuclear warfare could be very grave. Fourth, improved non-nuclear forces, well within Alliance resources, could enhance deterrence of any aggressive moves short of direct, all-out attack on Western Europe.

Let us look at the situation today. First, given the current balance of nuclear power, which we confidently expect to maintain in the years ahead, a surprise nuclear attack is simply not a rational act for any enemy. Nor would it be rational for an enemy to take the initiative in the use of nuclear weapons as an outgrowth of a limited engagement in Europe or elsewhere. I think we are entitled to conclude that either of these actions has been made highly unlikely.

Second, and equally important, the mere fact that no nation could rationally take steps leading to a nuclear war does not guarantee that a nuclear war cannot take place. Not only do nations sometimes act in ways that are hard to explain on a rational basis, but even when acting in a "rational" way they sometimes, indeed disturbingly often, act on the basis of misunderstandings of the true facts of a situation. They misjudge the way others will react, and the way others will interpret what they are doing. We must hope, indeed I think we have good reason to hope, that all sides will understand this danger, and will refrain from steps that even raise the possibility of such a mutually disastrous misunderstanding. We have taken unilateral steps to reduce the likelihood of such an occurrence. We look forward to the prospect that through arms control, the actual use of these terrible weapons may be completely avoided. It is a problem not just for us in the West, but for all nations that are involved in this struggle we call the Cold War.

For our part, we feel and our NATO allies must frame our strategy with this terrible contingency, however remote, in mind. Simply ignoring the problem is not going to make it go away.

The U. S. has come to the conclusion that to the extent feasible, basic military strategy in a possible general nuclear war should be approached in much the same way that more conventional military operations have been regarded in the past. That is to say, principal military objectives, in the event of a nuclear war stemming from a major attack on the Alliance, should be the destruction of the enemy's military forces, not of his civilian population.

The very strength and nature of the Alliance forces make it possible for us to retain, even in the face of a massive surprise attack, sufficient reserve striking power to destroy an enemy society if driven to it. In other words, we are giving a possible opponent the strongest imaginable incentive to refrain from striking our own cities. . . .

In particular, relatively weak national nuclear forces with enemy cities as their targets are not likely to be sufficient to perform even the function of deterrence. If they are small, and perhaps vulnerable on the ground or in the air, or inaccurate, a major antagonist can take a variety of measures to counter them. Indeed, if a major antagonist came to believe there was a substantial likelihood of it being used independently, this force would be inviting a pre-emptive first strike against it. In the event of war, the use of such a force against the cities of a major nuclear power would be tantamount to suicide, whereas its employment against significant military targets would have a negligible effect on the outcome of the conflict. Meanwhile, the creation of a single additional national nuclear force encourages the proliferation of nuclear power with all of its attendant dangers.

In short, then, limited nuclear capabilities, operating independently, are dangerous, expensive, prone to obsolescence, and lacking in credibility as a deterrent. Clearly, the United States nuclear contribution to the Alliance is neither obsolete nor dispensable.

At the same time, the general strategy I have summarized magnifies the importance of unity of planning, concentration of executive authority, and central direction. There must not be competing and conflicting strategies to meet the contingency of nuclear war. We are convinced that a general nuclear war target system is indivisible, and if, despite all our efforts, nuclear war should occur, our best hope lies in conducting a centrally controlled campaign against all of the enemy's vital nuclear capabilities, while retaining reserve forces, all centrally controlled.

We know that the same forces which are targeted on ourselves are also targeted on our allies. Our own strategic retaliatory forces are prepared to respond against these forces, wherever they are and whatever their targets. This mission is assigned not only in fulfillment of our treaty commitments but also because the character of nuclear war compels it. More specifically, the U. S. is as much concerned with that portion of Soviet nuclear striking power that can reach Western Europe as with that portion that also can reach the United States. In short, we have undertaken the nuclear defense of NATO on a global basis. This will continue to be our objective. In the execution of this mission, the weapons in the European theater are only one resource among many.

There is, for example, the POLARIS force, which we have been substantially increasing, and which, because of its specially invulnerable nature, is peculiarly well suited to serve as a strategic reserve force. We have already announced the commitment of five of these ships, fully operational, to the NATO Command.

This sort of commitment has a corollary for the Alliance as a whole. We want and need a greater degree of Alliance participation in formulating nuclear weapons policy to the greatest extent possible. We would all find it intolerable to contemplate having only a part of the strategic force launched in isolation from our main striking power.

We shall continue to maintain powerful nuclear forces for the Alliance as a whole. As the President has said, "Only through such strength can we be certain of deterring a nuclear strike, or an overwhelming ground attack, on our forces and allies."

But let us be quite clear about what we are saying and what we would have to face if the deterrent should fail. This is the almost certain prospect that, despite our nuclear strength, all of us would suffer deeply in the event of major nuclear war.

We accept our share of this responsibility within the Alliance. And we believe that the combination of our nuclear strength and a strategy of controlled response gives us some hope of minimizing damage in the event that we have to fulfill our pledge. But I must point out that we do not regard this as a desirable prospect, nor do we believe that the Alliance should depend solely on our nuclear power to deter actions not involving a massive commitment of any hostile force. Surely an Alliance with the wealth, talent, and experience that we possess can find a better way than extreme reliance on nuclear weapons to meet our common threat. We do not believe that if the formula, $e = mc^2$, had not been discovered, we should all be Communist slaves. On this question, I can see no valid reason for a fundamental difference of view on the two sides of the Atlantic.

With the Alliance possessing the strength and the strategy I have described, it is most unlikely that any power will launch a nuclear attack on NATO. For the kinds of conflicts, both political and military, most likely to arise in the NATO area, our capabilities for response must not be limited to nuclear weapons alone. The Soviets have superiority in non-nuclear forces in Europe today. But that superiority is by no means overwhelming. Collectively, the Alliance has the potential for a successful defense against such forces. In manpower alone, NATO has more men under arms than the Soviet Union and its European satellites. We have already shown our willingness to contribute through our divisions now in place on European soil. In order to defend the populations of the NATO countries and to meet our treaty obligations, we have put in hand a series of measures to strengthen our non-nuclear power. . . .

We expect that our allies will also undertake to strengthen further their non-nuclear forces, and to improve the quality and staying power of these forces. These achievements will complement our deterrent strength. With improvements in Alliance ground force strength and staying power, improved non-nuclear air capabilities, and better equipped and trained reserve forces, we can be assured that no deficiency exists in the NATO defense of this vital region, and that no aggression, small or large can succeed.

I have described very briefly the United States' views on the role of nuclear forces in the strategy of the Alliance. I have pointed out that the Alliance necessarily depends, for the deterrence of general nuclear war, on the powerful and well protected nuclear forces of the United States, which are necessarily committed to respond to enemy nuclear strikes wherever they may be made. At the same time, I have indicated the need for substantial non-nuclear forces within the Alliance to deal with situations where a nuclear response may be inappropriate or simply not believable. Throughout I have emphasized that we in the Alliance all need each other.

I want to remind you also that the security provided by military strength is a necessary, but not sufficient, condition for the achievement of our foreign policy goals, including our goals in the field of arms control and disarmament. Military security provides a base on which we can build Free World strength through the economic advances and political reforms which are the object of the President's programs, like the Alliance for Progress and the Trade Expansion legislation. Only in a peaceful world can we give full scope to the individual potential, which is for us the ultimate value.

## Soviet Reaction to the No-Cities Doctrine

### *Document 10*

The city-avoidance doctrine outlined in McNamara's Ann Arbor speech was greeted with hostility in Moscow. Soviet strategists rejected the logic of the new U.S. counterforce policy. Highly suspicious of McNamara's declarations that the United States would never initiate strategic nuclear war, the Soviets charged that the U.S. counterforce strategy made sense only for a disarming first strike. Furthermore, Kremlin planners dismissed the underlying premise that a nuclear war could be fought in a limited or controlled way. Soviet doctrinal writings, such as Marshall V. D. Sokolovskiy's highly authoritative work, *Soviet Military Strategy*, excerpted here, continued to emphasize the horrific nature of nuclear war.

### 10 MILITARY STRATEGY OF IMPERIALIST COUNTRIES
### Marshall V.D. Sokolovskiy

There has been created, as they say in the West, "a nuclear stalemate": on the one hand a tremendous increase in the number of nuclear rocket weapons and on the other, the incredible danger in their use. Under these conditions, according to the political and military evaluations of the USA and NATO, both sides had attained the position of so-called "mutual deterrence."

All this led to the conclusion that the strategy of "massive retaliation" proved to be inflexible and could no longer guarantee the achievement of the political aims of the American imperialists. While previously the United States could, with almost complete immunity, threaten the unrestrained use of nuclear weapons in any incident, even in local military conflicts which might possibly arise, the changed balance of power has made it dangerous to engage in "nuclear blackmail" and to risk the security of the country.

These circumstances had an especially strong effect on the European satellites of the USA. In particular, even by the end of 1959, it was noted directly in the decisions of the Western European alliance that the European countries can no longer rely exclusively on the strategic nuclear forces of the United States, as was previously the case, since there are no grounds for assuming that the Americans will be automatically involved in war in the case of any military conflict springing up in Europe, not wishing to risk nuclear attacks from the Soviet Union.

From an evaluation of the new conditions, the political and military leadership of the United States began to recognize the strategy of so-called "flexible response" as the most acceptable and expedient one. This, in their opinion, makes it possible, if necessary, to conduct either a general nuclear war or a limited war with or without the use of tactical nuclear weapons. . . .

Thus, the strategy of "massive retaliation," which existed for the USA and NATO until 1961, and provided only for the preparation and waging of a nuclear war against the Soviet Union and other countries of the socialist camp, had outlived its time and has been replaced by the strategy of "flexible response" which provides for preparation and conduct against the socialist countries both of a general nuclear war and limited wars with or without the use of nuclear weapons.

It is characteristic that the strategy of "flexible response" which is suitable for general nuclear war is now being further developed. On June 16, 1962, the American Secretary of Defense, McNamara, defined the essence of the strategy of "counterforce" (or "exclusion of cities"). Fearing a retaliatory nuclear strike against military-economic and military-political centers of the United States, he announced: "The United States came to the conclusion that we should approach the basic military strategy in a possible general nuclear war to a considerable extent just as we approach more conventional operations in the past. This means that the main military task in the event of nuclear war . . . should be the destruction of the enemy's armed forces, and not the civilian population."

The American military clique came to such a conclusion as a result of a lengthy study of how to conduct nuclear war as a whole. It was necessary to determine the destruction of which objectives could lead to the rapid defeat of the enemy.

Various points of view were expressed on this score. Some recommended concentrating the main efforts on inflicting strikes on the most important military objectives, in the first place, on the locations of strategic weapons; others recommended strikes against large populated places. In the opinion of the American military command, the solution of this problem was of basic significance.

The launching of nuclear strikes against enemy strategic weapons is a more difficult task in comparison with the launching of strikes against large cities. These difficulties are caused primarily by the fact that, first of all, there are significant numbers of such weapons and, secondly, by the fact that the majority of them, especially rocket weapons, in modern conditions are an absolute weapon, located in underground bases of low vulnerability, on submarines, etc. In this connection, there is a growing tendency toward the increase of their invulnerability.

The decision as to which objectives should be the ones against which nuclear strikes are launched—against strategic weapons or cities—depends to a considerable degree on the weapons system on hand and on its quantity. If the weapon is so inaccurate that it cannot be used to destroy small-dimension targets such as ballistic missile launching pads or airports, and there are not enough of them, it can only be used against large objectives, for example, cities.

According to press reports, over a number of years the American command conducted war games with the use of computer machines, during which computations were performed of the different variations for launching strikes with strategic weapons against the Soviet Union and other countries of the socialist camp. These calculations led the military leaders of the United States to come to the following conclusion: the launching of strikes against cities does not remove the threats of powerful retaliatory strikes by the enemy because in this case his strategic weapons remain practically untouched, and strikes against cities may lead to the destruction of a tremendous number of people and to the destruction, not only of the cities, but of the country as a whole. With the launching of strikes against enemy strategic weapons, its possibilities for destroying American cities and the population are reduced considerably.

On the basis of these very calculations, the command of the USA came to a final conclusion concerning the necessity to destroy the enemy's armed forces, first of all his strategic weapons, about which the Secretary of Defense spoke in his speech.

The American press notes that the strategy of "counterforce" has been approved by the Joint Chiefs of Staff and the White House and interprets it as some kind of recommendation to the Soviet Union concerning "rules" for the conduct of nuclear war.

The political implication of this strategy is that by conducting a so-called "controlled" nuclear war, the destruction of the capitalist system can be prevented. However, the illusory nature of these hopes is too obvious. If nuclear war is unleashed by the militarists, then no strategy, however it may be called, will save imperialism from destruction.

As a matter of fact, how can everyone be "convinced" of the necessity to adhere to the "new rules" that nuclear strikes should be launched only against military objectives and not against cities, when the majority of such objectives are located in large or smaller cities and populated places? If these "rules" are followed then, as noted in the press, the United States and her European allies must carry out an extremely expensive shifting of all military objectives from the large cities. This task is considered as unrealistic; however, the press stresses that if the United States and her allies set about moving military objectives from the cities, the USSR will draw the conclusion that the United States is preparing for an attack.

Moreover, in the opinion of the American press, the strategy of "counterforce" assumes the necessity for construction of a wide network of shelters for the population, the role and significance of which are extremely problematical for a future war.

## McNamara's Doubts About the No-Cities Doctrine

### *Document 11*

Turning away from his widely misinterpreted and much-criticized "no-cities" policy, McNamara became increasingly concerned with the stability of deterrence in a world of growing atomic arsenals. In this December 1962 interview with journalist Stewart Alsop of the *Saturday Evening Post*, he contends that the "balance of terror" would be more stable if both sides developed a secure second-strike capability. He suggests that the Soviet Union's push to enhance the survivability of its strategic nuclear forces should be tacitly encouraged, because it reduces destabilizing preemptive fears and incentives.

### 11 McNAMARA THINKS ABOUT THE UNTHINKABLE
### Robert McNamara and Stewart Alsop
### December 2, 1962

ALSOP: It seems to me interesting to compare what you said at Ann Arbor about the strategic balance of forces and what was being said only a few years ago by responsible people about the prospect of great Soviet superiority in missiles. How do you explain the difference?

MCNAMARA: This nation created a myth of its own weakness. That is the main reason. The myth was the result of incomplete intelligence; although it was created by intelligence analysts acting in good faith, it was a myth all the same.

ALSOP: How confident are you that the myth of the missile gap was and is a myth?

MCNAMARA: Absolutely confident. Of course there is a margin of error. There always is. But the margin of error is much less than the margin of our superiority. And the ending of the myth has made it possible to take a firm line with our adversaries and at the same time to reassure our friends that we are strong and determined to use our strength if we have to.

ALSOP: What do you think about the proposition that the price of any kind of nuclear war is so high that the nuclear weapon is not a rational instrument of national policy?

MCNAMARA: Your question suggests the reason why we have made a great effort to achieve nonnuclear options, so that we cannot have nuclear war forced upon us because we have no other choice. Suppose you were to start from the premise that nuclear war is unthinkable and that you are not capable of fighting a nonnuclear war. If that is true, then you have no military foundation at all for your policy.

No sane man wants nuclear war, or any kind of war. But war *has* to be conceivable in support of vital national interests. Otherwise you have no real national power. You have to meet three tests. First, you have to have the power to support your policy. Second, you have to know you have that power. Third, he — the other side — has to know you have that power, and he has to believe that you will use it if your vital interests are threatened.

We have today sufficient nuclear power so that we could take a full surprise attack and respond in such a way that we would literally destroy the aggressor. We also have sufficient nuclear power so that we could respond by hitting only military targets.

### Option of No-Cities Response?

ALSOP: In other words, you have the option of adopting the so-called no-cities, or counterforce, response, which you discussed in your Ann Arbor speech.

MCNAMARA: Yes, we would have that option. I think in some ways the press overplayed that part of the speech. I carefully qualified what I said, and I made it clear that this was only one of a series of options. I would want to be absolutely certain that we had the other options.

ALSOP: Surely we must assume that the time will come when the other side will have a sure second-strike capability — solid-fuel missiles, hardened bases and all the rest of it.

MCNAMARA: Yes, and that raises an interesting point. I believe myself that a counterforce strategy is most likely to apply in circumstances in which *both* sides have the capability of surviving a first strike and retaliating selectively. This is a highly unpredictable business, of course. But today, following a surprise attack on us, we would still have the power to respond with overwhelming force, and they would not then have the capability of a further strike. In this situation, given the highly irrational act of an attempted first strike against us, such a strike seems most likely to take the form of an all-out attack on both military targets and population centers. This is why a nuclear exchange confined to military targets seems more possible, not less, when *both* sides have a sure second-strike capability. Then you might have a more stable "balance of terror." This may seem a rather subtle point, but from where I'm sitting it seems a point worth thinking about.

### "No Pressure on Us to Preempt"

ALSOP: As you know, some writers here and abroad have interpreted what you said in your Ann Arbor speech as implying the possibility of the United States' adopting a first-strike strategy — a strategy of hitting first.

MCNAMARA: What I said meant exactly the opposite. Because we have a sure second-strike capability, there is no pressure on us whatsoever to preempt. I assure you that we really never think in those terms. Under any circumstances, even if we had the military advantage of striking first, the price of any nuclear war would be terribly high. One point I was making in the Ann Arbor speech is that our second-strike capability is so sure that there would be no rational basis on which to launch a preemptive strike.

ALSOP: It seems to me that a no-cities doctrine only makes sense if it is married to a serious fallout-shelter program. Otherwise, even if the cities were left standing, the fatalities from fallout would be astronomical.

MCNAMARA: Yes. Some people seem to feel that even to think about the fatalities which might result from a nuclear war is immoral. But you have to think about it. You have to ask yourself whether there are *no* situations in which one side or the other might use nuclear weapons. Your answer has to be that there are such situations. Then you have to recognize that there is a tremendous difference, a vital difference, between, say, thirty percent fatalities and sixty percent. A serious national fallout-shelter program could make that sort of difference.

ALSOP: When you think in terms of fatalities in the tens of millions, aren't you forced to ask yourself, again, whether the nuclear weapon is in fact a rational instrument of national policy?

MCNAMARA: In a sense, nuclear war is certainly irrational — all war is irrational. But being irrational doesn't make it inconceivable. You might be forced into nuclear war as a result of an irrational act on the other side, for example, or of a misjudgment of our response to an attack on our vital interests. And given a nuclear capability on the other side, you *must* have a credible deterrent on your side. And you can't create a credible deterrent by threatening an incredible action. For example, the use of nuclear weapons would be an incredible response to the building of the Wall, or to certain kinds of political-military pressure on the periphery. You can't fashion a deterrent by threatening to take action which no one in fact believes you will take.

The nuclear weapon, for example, becomes a rational weapon only in relation to situations in which the weapon might credibly be used — those situations in which the alternative might be even worse than the risk of nuclear war — for example, a surrender by stages to Communist aggression. There are certain circumstances in which the other side is dead sure we will use the nuclear weapon — an attack on the United States or on our NATO allies, for example. But there is always the danger of miscalculation. This is why it was important to make clear in a public statement that we mean to defend Berlin and that, if necessary, all weapons will be used for that purpose.

ALSOP: Berlin seems to me to symbolize our great central weakness. We're in far better shape to fight another limited conventional war like Korea than we were. But we still do not really have the "conventional option" in Europe.

MCNAMARA: I don't maintain that the balance of conventional forces in Europe is all we would like it to be. But the NATO forces have been made much stronger — General Norstad quantifies the increment at twenty-five percent. Our own conventional forces have been increased by forty-five percent — from eleven to sixteen combat-ready divisions in the Army, for example. What is more, all sixteen divisions are better combat divisions, with more mobility, more airlift and more tactical air support. So the true increment is greater than forty five percent.

We have stockpiled equipment for two divisions in Europe, and exercises prove that the men for these divisions could be airlifted to Europe in a matter of a week or so. We have a strategic reserve in this country of eight divisions as against three a couple of years ago. Our air power in Europe is at least equal to theirs, and there is on the central front about an equal number of men on both sides of the line.

### "NATO a Match for Communist Side"

ALSOP: Yes, but they have much greater reserve power, don't they? Isn't the real difference that the threshold is higher — that they would have to mobilize and bring up their reserves to gain conventional superiority in Europe?

MCNAMARA: Yes, they would have to bring up their reserves. But can they? We have a lot of air power in Europe. And we have reserves, too, don't forget. We spend two billion dollars a year on the reserves and the National Guard. I'm not saying that we wouldn't all be a lot happier if we had more conventional power in Europe. But conventional power is only part of the equation, and as I've said, if necessary we would use all weapons. But if we say that the Western powers are hopelessly inferior, then we're creating another myth of weakness. By any sensible standards — wealth, manpower, resources — NATO is, or can be, more than a match for the Communist side.

## Assured Destruction

### Document 12

Although McNamara never formally retreated from his insistence that U.S. nuclear war plans include counterforce targeting options, by the mid-1960s he had supplanted the "no-cities" strategy outlined in his Ann Arbor speech with "assured destruction." This new declaratory policy emphasized the requirements for deterring, rather than for fighting, a nuclear war. It set as the preeminent goal of U.S. strategic nuclear force planning the maintenance of an "assured-destruction" capability — that is, the capability of U.S. forces to destroy the Soviet Union as a viable society even after absorbing a well-executed Soviet surprise attack. Pentagon planners concluded that Moscow would be sufficiently deterred from attacking if the surviving U.S. retaliatory forces could destroy at least 30 percent of the Soviet Union's population and 50 percent of its industry — levels of destruction that they calculated could be achieved by delivering 400 megatons of explosive power. These were already well within U.S. capabilities in the mid-1960s. Although these requirements reflected abstract calculations of diminishing marginal returns rather than determinations of what Soviet leaders would consider to be "unacceptable" damage, they established guidelines for answering the Whiz Kids' often asked question: How much is enough? As a criterion of nuclear sufficiency, McNamara's assured destruction doctrine offers an upper limit to the rapid growth of the U.S. strategic nuclear arsenal.

## 12 MUTUAL DETERRENCE
## Robert S. McNamara

In a complex and uncertain world, the gravest problem that an American Secretary of Defense must face is that of planning, preparation and policy against the possibility of thermonuclear war. It is a prospect that most of mankind understandably would prefer not to contemplate, for technology has now circumscribed us all with a horizon of horror that could dwarf any catastrophe that has befallen man in his more than a million years on earth.

Man has lived now for more than twenty years in what we have come to call the Atomic Age. What we sometimes overlook is that every future age of man will be an atomic age, and if man is to have a future at all, it will have to be one overshadowed with the permanent possibility of thermonuclear holocaust. About that fact there is no longer any doubt. Our freedom in this question consists only in facing the matter rationally and realistically and discussing actions to minimize the danger.

No sane citizen, political leader or nation wants thermonuclear war. But merely not wanting it is not enough. We must understand the differences among actions which increase its risks, those which reduce them and those which, while costly, have little influence one way or another. But there is a great difficulty in the way of constructive and profitable debate over the issues, and that is the exceptional complexity of nuclear strategy. Unless these complexities are well understood, rational discussion and decision-making are impossible.

One must begin with precise definitions. The cornerstone of our strategic policy continues to be to deter deliberate nuclear attack upon the United States or its allies. We do this by maintaining a highly reliable ability to inflict unacceptable damage upon any single aggressor or combination of aggressors at any time during the course of a strategic nuclear exchange, even after absorbing a surprise first strike. This can be defined as our *assured-destruction capability*.

It is important to understand that assured destruction is the very essence of the whole deterrence concept. We must possess an actual assured-destruction capability, and that capability also must be credible. The point is that a potential aggressor must believe that our assured-destruction capability is in fact actual, and that our will to use it in retaliation to an attack is in fact unwavering. The conclusion, then, is clear: if the United States is to deter a nuclear attack on itself or its allies, it must possess an actual and a credible assured-destruction capability.

When calculating the force required, we must be conservative in all our estimates of both a potential aggressor's capabilities and his intentions. Security depends upon assuming a worst plausible case, and having the ability to cope with it. In that eventuality we must be able to absorb the total weight of nuclear attack on our country — on our retaliatory forces, on our command and control apparatus, on our industrial capacity, on our cities, and on our population — and still be capable of damaging the aggressor to the point that his society would be simply no longer viable in twentieth-century terms. That is what deterrence of nuclear aggression means. It means the certainty of suicide to the aggressor, not merely to his military forces, but to his society as a whole.

Let us consider another term: *first-strike capability*. This is a somewhat ambiguous term, since it could mean simply the ability of one nation to attack another nation with nuclear forces first. But as it is normally used, it connotes much more: the elimination of the attacked nation's retaliatory second-strike forces. This is the sense in which it should be understood.

Clearly, first-strike capability is an important strategic concept. The United States must not and will not permit itself ever to get into a position in which another nation, or combination of nations, would possess a first-strike capability against it. Such a position not only would constitute an intolerable threat to our security, but it obviously would remove our ability to deter nuclear aggression.

We are not in that position today, and there is no foreseeable danger of our ever getting into that position. Our strategic offensive forces are immense: 1,000 Minuteman missile launchers, carefully protected belowground; 41 Polaris submarines, carrying 656 missile launchers, with the majority hidden beneath the seas at all times; and about 600 long-range bombers, approximately 40 percent of which are kept always in a high state of alert.

Our alert forces alone carry more than 2,200 weapons, each averaging more than the explosive equivalent of one megaton of TNT. Four hundred of these delivered on the Soviet Union would be sufficient to destroy over one-third of her population and one-half of her industry. All these flexible and highly reliable forces are equipped with devices that ensure their penetration of Soviet defenses.

Now what about the Soviet Union? Does it today possess a powerful nuclear arsenal? The answer is that it does. Does it possess a first-strike capability against the United States? The answer is that it does not. Can the Soviet Union in the foreseeable future acquire such a first-strike capability against the United States? The answer is that it cannot. It cannot because we are determined to remain fully alert and we will never permit our own assured-destruction capability to drop to a point at which a Soviet first-strike capability is even remotely feasible.

Is the Soviet Union seriously attempting to acquire a first-strike capability against the United States? Although this is a question we cannot answer with absolute certainty, we believe the answer is no. In any event, the question itself is — in a sense — irrelevant; for the United States will maintain and, where necessary, strengthen its retaliatory forces so that, whatever the Soviet Union's intentions or actions, we will continue to have an assured-destruction capability vis-à-vis their society.

# THE ABM DEBATE

## McNamara and ABM

### *Document 13*

This review of McNamara's decisions on the development of an antiballistic missile (ABM) system highlights the secretary of defense's struggles with the Army and the Joint Chiefs of Staff. (An ABM system is also often called a ballistic missile defense [BMD] system.)

The military services favored going forward with the Nike-X ABM system, later renamed Sentinel. McNamara fought hard against ABM, first on cost-effectiveness grounds and later because he was worried that an ABM deployment might set off a new arms race. When the Soviets began to deploy an ABM system and refused to enter arms control negotiations, McNamara felt he had no choice but to go forward with a "thin" ABM system. Within a year after McNamara had left office, the ABM had become the subject of public debate.

## 13 PAST AND PRESENT: THE HISTORICAL LEGACY
## David N. Schwartz

The Pentagon under the stewardship of Robert McNamara took a similarly jaundiced view of the operational capabilities of Nike-Zeus, even after the army had conducted a series of tests at the Kwajalein missile range that indicated that Nike-Zeus could be used to shoot down incoming RVs from first-generation U.S. intercontinental ballistic missiles (ICBMs).[2] Of particular concern, initially, to McNamara and his staff was the army's tendency to argue Nike-Zeus's effectiveness against *current* Soviet technology; the new civilian planners insisted on measuring the system's effectivenss against the likely *future* Soviet ICBM threat, which might include sophisticated penetration aids and decoys. Against such a threat Nike-Zeus could not measure up.

But the technical issues were only some of the concerns of the new staff at the Pentagon. Among the new strategic concepts brought in by the Kennedy administration was the objective of damage limitation. In assessing the value of various defensive efforts in limiting damage to U.S. society and weighing the value against the relative costs, the Pentagon concluded that passive defensive measures — particularly an enhanced civil defense-shelter program — were far more cost effective than BMD. As a result of analyses conducted by the Pentagon's Weapon System Evaluation Group, McNamara concluded that production of Nike-Zeus would make no sense if the United States had already invested in an effective shelter program.[3]

In the fiscal 1962 and fiscal 1963 budget cycles McNamara was able to resist army pressures to authorize Nike-Zeus production, for the reasons cited above. In the fiscal 1963 budget cycle, however, he chose a new tactic, which redirected the army program and virtually eliminated pressure for Nike-Zeus production. On the basis of an ongoing BMD study, Project Defender, ARPA had concluded that emerging technologies in radar, data processing, and rocket propulsion could be put to use in a new ABM system. ARPA Director Jack Ruina had been asked by Director of Defense Research and Engineering Harold Brown to consider possible alternatives for continued BMD development programs. Ruina outlined four options: NZ-0, which was the current Nike-Zeus system under development in the army; NZ-1, which was similar to NZ-0 except that it would use a much higher velocity interceptor missile, allowing for endoatmospheric target discrimination and intercept; NZ-2, another spinoff of NZ-0, which would use the faster interceptor missile and a phased-array radar to locate and track multiple targets in a short period of time; and NX, which would not rely on NZ-0 as a basis but would use the faster interceptor, phased-array radars, and new computers, integrated into a totally new system. Thus was born "Nike-X."[4]

Because Nike-X was conceived as an endoatmospheric system — its objective would be to destroy RVs after they had entered the atmosphere — its tracking radars could use the differing effect of atmospheric drag on RVs and decoys to help solve the problem of discriminating between the two. However, waiting this long for initiating interception would allow the RV to approach very near the target — at very high speed — before it could be destroyed. This imposed a requirement for an interceptor capable of extremely high acceleration to reach altitudes of several miles in several seconds. The technology needed to develop such a missile (which was the forerunner of Sprint) and to guide this missile to its target was on the horizon. Phased-array radars, the feasibility of which had been demonstrated by ARPA studies in 1963, would enable Nike-X to handle large numbers of incoming targets. With such technology, the saturation problem would be less a result of slow radar acquisition and tracking than it would be a function of RVs in excess of interceptors.

Defense scientists believed the Nike-X concept was feasible. In fiscal 1963, McNamara authorized a dramatic shift in R&D resources to the Nike-X program, and the army — under General Austin Betts — spent the next eighteen months developing Nike-X to the point where a production decision looked reasonable.

The army, convinced that Nike-Zeus should be produced and deployed against the current threat, resisted this development. Nonetheless, the shift to Nike-X was a significant improvement in the prospects for BMD. McNamara had not relinquished his position that investment in ABM production would only make sense after the nation had invested in a civil defense program. But he had acknowledged that the technical and operational questions regarding Nike-Zeus were in principle rectifiable. More important, he was persuaded to fund research and development if only to keep open future options, and had authorized $350 million in 1963 to do just that.

But the battle for BMD was not over. While the army was developing Nike-X, McNamara became concerned about yet another aspect of BMD — its potential for stimulating an arms race. The logic of this concern, articulated in the civilian policy offices of the Pentagon beginning as early as 1962, was simple but compelling.[5] If the Soviet Union were intent upon maintaining a capability to inflict a given degree of damage on the United States, an ABM system that degraded that capability would stimulate growth in Soviet offensive capabilities to offset that degradation in capability. This would bring the offensive threat to the United States back to its pre-ABM levels; the United States would then respond by increasing its defensive systems to compensate for the growth in Soviet offensive capabilities. Such a ratcheting up of the arms race was considered to be a serious, almost decisive argument against BMD programs that were technically feasible.

Against such a critique, few ABM systems — not even the Nike-X, far superior from a technical standpoint to the Nike-Zeus — could meet the criterion of arms race stability imposed by McNamara. Nevertheless, General Betts was successful in gaining full support from the Joint Chiefs of Staff for the program. In 1966, the army and the Joint Chiefs made a concerted effort to gain production authority from the president.

By this time many of the arguments McNamara had used to postpone Nike-Zeus production could no longer be used against Nike-X. Because of the development of phased-array radars, high acceleration rockets, and advanced data processing, the arguments regarding Nike-Zeus's inability to discriminate RVs from decoys in time to destroy the RVs and defend targets of value were not valid for Nike-X. Furthermore, although it could still be saturated, Nike-X was better able than Nike-Zeus to deal with RVs arriving at close intervals. Although the United States had not invested a substantial sum in civil defense preparations, McNamara had little hope of or inclination for getting more resources devoted to this area. Soviet improvements in strategic offensive forces, not evident in 1961, also argued for taking the BMD mission more seriously. Finally, there was evidence that the Soviet Union was proceeding with an intensive BMD effort of its own.

In sum, time had forced McNamara into a corner. As the debate over Nike-X moved into 1966 — the fiscal 1968 budget cycle — McNamara was forced to rely less on his previous arguments against deployment and more on the implications of the action-reaction phenomenon. Analyses done in the Pentagon examined how two specific ABM postures, based on the Nike-X system, would affect the Soviet "assured destruction" capability, and how various Soviet responses would degrade the performance of these two postures.[6]

Posture A consisted of an area defense system of the United States, and a local defense of twenty-five cities. This was the posture advocated by the Joint Chiefs as an initial step. Posture B was more extensive, involving defense of some fifty-two cities, and probably reflected the ultimate goal of the services. (In addition, because of demographics, defense of more than fifty cities showed greatly diminishing marginal returns.) It was clear from Pentagon analyses that even posture A could result in a 90 percent degradation of Soviet assured destruction capabilities. Posture B would degrade these capabilities still further. Civilian analysts, supported by McNamara, argued that such degradation would not be tolerated by Soviet military planners, who would seek various means to offset it. If the Soviet Union invested in multiple independently targetable reentry vehicle (MIRV) technology and penetration aids and moved to a force that included 100 mobile ICBMs, it could regain 90 percent of its capability against posture A. Posture B might provoke the Soviet Union to increase investment in mobile ICBMs to some 500 systems; such a response, combined with MIRV and penetration aid technology, would regain 80 percent of its capability. Looked at in this light, either BMD posture being analyzed by systems analysts in the Pentagon stood a good chance of stimulating a destabilizing arms race with no foreseeable termination.

These conclusions were not shared by the armed services. Having spent several billion dollars in R&D money to develop an ABM system that looked as though it would actually work against Soviet offensive forces in being at the time, the armed services were reluctant to forgo the program on strategic grounds. They argued variously that there was little evidence that the Soviet Union sized its forces according to the assured destruction criteria that guided the civilian analysts; that the Soviet Union would not be able to afford a response of the type foreseen by these analysts; and that even if it could, it would be doomed to an unending game of catch-up with the United States that would be politically damaging and extremely costly. Thus, they pressed for an anti-Soviet ABM program along the lines of posture A, described above.

These arguments came before the president in a series of meetings on the 1968 defense budget in late 1966.[7] Both positions were argued forcefully, in particular at a December 6 meeting in Austin, Texas, where

McNamara and his deputy Cyrus Vance put forward the case against Nike-X, and General Earle G. Wheeler and other service chiefs put the case in favor of posture A as an interim step toward eventual adoption of posture B. When President Lyndon Johnson indicated his decision to move ahead with deployment, McNamara offered a compromise that the president accepted. The 1968 budget would contain several hundred million dollars for production and procurement of long-lead items for Nike-X, but this money would be withheld pending efforts to explore bilateral, negotiated ABM limitations with the Soviet Union.

Many observers have remarked on the way in which this turn of events, however spontaneous, reflected McNamara's deep and growing concern about the U.S.-Soviet nuclear arms race. There can be little doubt on this score. Nevertheless, the proposal *was* spontaneous and conditioned in large part by the secretary's perception that he could no longer postpone production as he had during the previous five years. Time had run out for McNamara; in recognizing this, he was committed to keeping deployments as low as possible and to engaging Soviet cooperation toward this end.

Diplomatically, the six-month period between the Austin meeting and the June 1967 U.S.-Soviet summit at Glassboro, New Jersey, was a period of intensive activity, as the United States tried to engage the Soviet Union in arms control talks on ABM.[8] High level, secret contacts in Washington and Moscow indicated that the Kremlin was interested in talking, although it insisted that talks include offensive weapons as well as ABM. In March, however, it was announced that the two governments had agreed in principle to begin discussions on both offensive and defensive systems, but no date was set. Work on the U.S. negotiating position, begun in January in a small working group of the State and Defense departments, continued, as did contacts in Washington and Moscow. But when the June 1967 Glassboro summit arrived, Johnson was unable to gain Soviet Premier Aleksei Kosygin's agreement on a timetable for talks. Indeed, Kosygin still seemed skeptical regarding the urgency of constraints on defensive systems, even after hearing the U.S. secretary of defense expound on the matter over a luncheon meeting.

Faced with Soviet unreadiness to proceed promptly with strategic nuclear arms control, Johnson saw no choice but to move ahead with funding for Nike-X, which had been renamed Sentinel. Johnson had been willing to postpone while McNamara sounded out the Soviet representatives. In January Johnson had also been treated to an extraordinary White House meeting, orchestrated by McNamara, to which were invited all past and present presidential science advisers and directors of defense research and engineering — in effect the leaders of the defense science establishment.[9] Their unanimous recommendation had been against deployment of a major anti-Soviet ABM deployment and only marginally more supportive of a smaller anti-China deployment. Still, that month Johnson had earmarked $375 million for Sentinel production in fiscal 1968 pending contacts with the Soviet Union, in accordance with his decision of December 1966. Now that the contacts had failed to produce prompt agreement that talks should begin, McNamara's problem became how to justify the $366 million expenditure that Congress had agreed to in July.

The problem was difficult. Persuaded that expansion of a "thin" ABM system into a large anti-Soviet system would represent a tragedy of major proportions, McNamara was determined to find a rationale that was not keyed to an anti-Soviet deployment and that effectively precluded the later expansion of the system into an anti-Soviet one. Several such rationales had existed for years in the U.S. defense bureacracy; McNamara had suggested some of these in previous annual reports to Congress. In intensive debates within Pentagon staffs, and supported by some within the State Department, he eventually fixed on one of them — a system to defend in the medium term against the nascent Chinese nuclear threat.[10] In June 1967 China had detonated its first thermonuclear device; U.S. intelligence considered Chinese ICBMs to be inevitable, if several years away. Using work that had been previously done by the systems analysis staff, and updating it somewhat, the civilian Pentagon leadership fashioned an anti-Chinese rationale to fit McNamara's bill.

But more was needed. McNamara felt he needed something to constrain the enthusiasm of the Joint Chiefs. He had no doubts that, once construction had been authorized, the Joint Chiefs would continue to press for expansion of the system into one that could handle the Soviet ICBM threat as well. Determined to prevent this, he marshaled all the arguments he could find against a Soviet-oriented system, relying heavily on the action-reaction phenomenon that continued to trouble him.

The result of this intensive search for the safest rationale, the one that held the least danger in the future, was a remarkable speech McNamara delivered before the Press Club in San Francisco on September 18, 1967. In it he pleaded passionately against the feasibility, utility, and wisdom of an anti-Soviet Sentinel system, alluding at one point to the "mad momentum" of the arms race. Toward the end of the speech, however, he turned his attention toward China and announced the administration's plan to deploy a "thin" Sentinel system to defend against the predicted small Chinese ICBM threat and accidental launches.

This speech marked a turning point in the history of the ABM issue. Over the next four years, until the U.S.-Soviet ABM Treaty was signed in May 1972, the ABM issue became the focus of intense public debate and equally intense diplomatic maneuvers between the United States and the Soviet Union.

The public debate found its locus in the U.S. Senate, where interest in ABM had been sporadic over the past decade. A small but influential group of senators on the Armed Services Committee, friendly to the services and fearful of the Soviet ABM effort to protect Moscow, had unsuccessfully but regularly pressed the administration to fund ABM production ever since the early 1960s. This group, led by Strom Thurmond, John Stennis, Richard Russell, and Henry Jackson, maintained a strong interest throughout the 1968–72 period in promoting Sentinel and its revised version after 1969, Safeguard.[11]

Opposition to ABM in the Senate was confined in these early years to a small group of liberal senators, such as J. William Fulbright, Albert Gore, and Edward Kennedy, who brought a general skepticism about defense spending, stimulated by opposition to the Vietnam War, to the particular issue of Sentinel and Safeguard.[12] In April 1968, however, they were joined by the powerful Republican senator from Kentucky, John Sherman Cooper, who began to organize opposition to Sentinel deployment in the summer of 1968.[13] The coalition he developed in mid-1968 attempted three times — in June, August, and October — to delay or cut funding of Sentinel production, relying on a set of arguments that included the action-reaction phenomenon, the danger of defense in a world of arms race instability, technical deficiencies in the system, and financial considerations. Each time it failed, but it was surprisingly strong; the first vote in June found thirty-four senators voting in favor of postponing Sentinel deployment for one year while renewed efforts could be mounted to reach agreement on strategic arms limitations.

The administration fought these efforts to delay or cut Sentinel and was generally successful. In addition, in the summer of 1968 the Soviet Union had agreed on holding arms control talks. Plans for a summit meeting and the opening of the strategic arms limitation talks (SALT) were scuttled, however, when the Soviet Union invaded Czechosolvakia in August, and the Democrats had lost the 1968 election before they were able to put the talks back on the agenda.[14]

Public concern, quiescent until 1968, became widespread as it was revealed that the first phase of Sentinel — a population defense system — would involve missile deployments north of several major cities, including Chicago and Boston. When the full fiscal 1969 ABM funding of $1.2 billion was approved in October 1968,[15] the public took to the streets in these cities, and the major demonstrations of this period persuaded even sympathetic senators, such as Everett Dirksen, that Sentinel could become a serious political liability.[16]

## Notes

2. Benson D. Adams, "McNamara's ABM Policy, 1961–1967," *Orbis,* vol. 12 (Spring 1968), p. 211.
3. *Ibid.,* pp. 213, 218–219; see also Edward Randolph Jayne II, "The ABM Debate: Strategic Defense and National Security" (Ph.D. Dissertation, Massachusetts Institute of Technology, 1969), pp. 183–84.
4. Interview with Jack Ruina, May 2, 1982.
5. An early, comprehensive statement of this view was provided by Jack Ruina and Murray Gell-Mann in "Ballistic Missile Defense and the Arms Race," a paper prepared for the Twelfth Pugwash Conference on Science and World Affairs, Udaipur, January 27–February 1, 1964.
6. The following summary of Pentagon analyses is drawn from Alain C. Enthoven and K. Wayne Smith, *How Much Is Enough? Shaping the Defense Program, 1961–69* (Harper and Row, 1971), pp. 184–94.
7. Several useful summaries of these crucial meetings exist. See Jayne, "The ABM Debate," pp. 333–43; and John Newhouse, *Cold Dawn: The Story of SALT* (Holt, Rinehart and Winston, 1973), p. 86.
8. Newhouse, *Cold Dawn*, pp. 87–89.
9. *Ibid.*, p. 89. See also Ernest J. Yanarella, *The Missile Defense Controversy: Strategy, Technology and Politics, 1955–1972* (University Press of Kentucky, 1977); p. 124.
10. Newhouse, *Cold Dawn*, pp. 95–96.
11. Yanarella, *Missile Defense Controversy*, p. 125; Jayne, "The ABM Debate," pp. 126, 184–91.
12. Yanarella, *Missile Defense Controversy*, pp. 145–57.
13. *Ibid.*, pp. 149–52.
14. Newhouse, *Cold Dawn*, pp. 131–32.
15. "Numerous Moves Fail to Kill Plans for ABM System," *Congressional Quarterly Almanac*, 90 Cong. 2 sess., vol. 24 (Washington, D.C.: Congressional Quarterly Service, 1968), p. 95.
16. Yanarella, *Missile Defense Controversy*, p. 152.

## McNamara Decides in Favor of the Sentinel ABM

### *Document 14*

In a speech delivered in San Francisco in September 1967, McNamara partially acceded to pressure from Congress and the military. He reluctantly announced that the United States would begin production of a scaled-down ABM system designed to protect American cities against an incipient Chinese missile threat. He made this announcement, however, at the end of an address in which he presented a dispassionate analysis of the dynamics of U.S.-Soviet military competition. Reviewing the recent history of the superpower nuclear rivalry, McNamara concluded that the "action-reaction phenomenon" underlying the arms race made it futile for the United States to spend billions of dollars on a massive ABM system because the Soviet Union would counter any such system — at considerably less expense — with an increased offensive missile program. McNamara's widely noted speech expanded the scope of the debate emerging in U.S. defense circles over the feasibility and desirability of ballistic missile defense.

### 14 SPEECH BEFORE EDITORS OF UNITED PRESS INTERNATIONAL
### Robert S. McNamara
### September 18, 1967

The cornerstone of our strategic policy continues to be to deter deliberate nuclear attack upon the United States, or its allies, by maintaining a highly reliable ability to inflict an unacceptable degree of damage upon any single aggressor, or combination of aggressors, at any time during the course of a strategic nuclear exchange — even after our absorbing a surprise first strike.

This can be defined as our "assured destruction capability."

Now it is imperative to understand that assured destruction is the very essence of the whole deterrence concept.

We must possess an actual assured destruction capability. And that actual assured destruction capability must also be credible. Conceivably, our assured destruction capability could be actual, without being credible — in which case, it might fail to deter an aggressor.

The point is that a potential aggressor must himself believe that our assured destruction capability is in fact actual, and that our will to use it in retaliation to an attack is in fact unwavering.

The conclusion, then, is clear: If the United States is to deter a nuclear attack on itself or on our allies, it must possess an actual and a credible assured destruction capability.

When calculating the force we require, we must be "conservative" in all our estimates of both a potential aggressor's capabilities, and his intentions. Security depends upon taking a "worst plausible case" — and having the ability to cope with that eventuality.

In that eventuality, we must be able to absorb the total weight of nuclear attack on our country — on our strike-back forces; on our command and control apparatus; on our industrial capacity; on our cities; and on our population — and still be fully capable of destroying the aggressor to the point that his society is simply no longer viable in any meaningful, twentieth century sense.

That is what deterrence to nuclear aggression means. It means the certainty of suicide to the aggressor — not merely to his military forces, but to his society as a whole.

Now let us consider another term: "First-strike capability." This, in itself, is an ambiguous term, since it could mean simply the ability of one nation to attack another nation with nuclear forces first. But as it is normally used, it connotes much more: The substantial elimination of the attacked nation's retaliatory second-strike forces.

This is the sense in which "first-strike capability" should be understood.

Now, clearly, such a first-strike capability is an important strategic concept. The United States cannot — and will not — ever permit itself to get into the position in which another nation, or combination of nations, would possess such a first-strike capability, which could be effectively used against it.

To get into such a position vis-à-vis any other nation or nations would not only constitute an intolerable threat to our security, but it would obviously remove our ability to deter nuclear aggression — both against ourselves and against our allies.

Now, we are not in that position today — and there is no foreseeable danger of our ever getting into that position.

Our strategic offensive forces are immense: 1,000 Minutemen missile launchers, carefully protected below ground; 41 Polaris submarines, carrying 656 missile launchers — with the majority of these hidden beneath the seas at all times; and about 600 long-range bombers, approximately 40 per cent of which are kept always in a high state of alert.

Our alert forces alone carry more than 2,200 weapons, averaging more than one megaton each. A mere 400 one-megaton weapons, if delivered on the Soviet Union, would be sufficient to destroy over one-third of her population, and one-half of her industry.

And all of these flexible and highly reliable forces are equipped with devices that insure their penetration of Soviet defenses.

Now what about the Soviet Union?

Does it today possess a powerful nuclear arsenal?

The answer is that it does.

Does it possess a first-strike capability against the United States?

The answer is that it does not.

Can the Soviet Union, in the foreseeable future, acquire such a first-strike capability against the United States?

The answer is that it cannot.

It cannot because we are determined to remain fully alert, and we will never permit our own assured destruction capability to be at a point where a Soviet first-strike capability is even remotely feasible.

Is the Soviet Union seriously attempting to acquire a first-strike capability against the United States?

Although this is a question we cannot answer with absolute certainty, we believe the answer is no. In any event, the question itself is — in a sense — irrelevant. It is irrelevant since the United States will so continue to maintain — and where necessary strengthen — our retaliatory forces, that whatever the Soviet Union's intentions or actions, we will continue to have an assured destruction capability vis-à-vis their society in which we are completely confident. . . .

The Soviets are now deploying an antiballistic missile system. If we react to this deployment intelligently, we have no reason for alarm.

The system does not impose any threat to our ability to penetrate and inflict massive and unacceptable damage on the Soviet Union. In other words, it does not presently affect in any significant manner our assured destruction capability.

It does not impose such a threat because we have already taken the steps necessary to assure that our land-based Minuteman missiles, our nuclear submarine-launched new Poseidon missiles, and our strategic bomber forces have the requisite penetration aids — and in the sum, constitute a force of such magnitude, that they guarantee us a force strong enough to survive a Soviet attack and penetrate the Soviet A.B.M. deployment.

Now let me come to the issue that has received so much attention recently: The question of whether or not we should deploy an A.B.M. system against the Soviet nuclear threat.

To begin with, this is not in any sense a new issue. We have had both the technical possibility and the strategic desirability of an American A.B.M. deployment under constant review since the late 1950s.

While we have substantially improved our technology in the field, it is important to understand that none of the systems at the present or foreseeable state of the art would provide an impenetrable shield over the United States. Were such a shield possible, we would certainly want it — and we would certainly build it.

And at this point, let me dispose of an objection that is totally irrelevant to this issue.

It has been alleged that we are opposed to deploying a large-scale A.B.M. system because it would carry the heavy price tag of $40-billion.

Let me make very clear that the $40-billion is not the issue.

If we could build and deploy a genuinely impenetrable shield over the United States, we would be willing to spend not $40-billion, but any reasonable multiple of that amount that was necessary.

The money in itself is not the problem: The penetrability of the proposed shield is the problem.

There is clearly no point, however, in spending $40-billion if it is not going to buy us a significant improvement in our security. If it is not, then we should use the substantial resources it represents on something that will.

Every A.B.M. system that is now feasible involves firing defensive missiles at incoming offensive warheads in an effort to destroy them.

But what many commentators on this issue overlook is that any such system can rather obviously be defeated by an enemy simply sending more offensive warheads, or dummy warheads, than there are defensive missiles capable of disposing of them.

And this is the whole crux of the nuclear action-reaction phenomenon.

Were we to deploy a heavy A.B.M. system throughout the United States, the Soviets would clearly be strongly motivated to so increase their offensive capability as to cancel out our defensive advantage.

It is futile for each of us to spend $4-billion, $40-billion, or $400-billion — and at the end of all the spending, and at the end of all the deployment, and at the end of all the effort, to be relatively at the same point of balance on the security scale that we are now.

In point of fact, we have already initiated offensive weapons programs costing several billions in order to offset the small present Soviet A.B.M. deployment, and the possibly more extensive future Soviet A.B.M. deployments.

That is money well spent; and it is necessary.

But we should bear in mind that it is money spent because of the action-reaction phenomenon.

If we in turn opt for heavy A.B.M. deployment — at whatever price — we can be certain that the Soviets will react to offset the advantage we would hope to gain.

It is precisely because of this certainty of a corresponding Soviet reaction that the four prominent scientists — men who have served with distinction as the science advisers to Presidents Eisenhower, Kennedy and Johnson, and the three outstanding men who have served as directors of research and engineering to three Secretaries of Defense — have unanimously recommended against the deployment of an A.B.M. system designed to protect our population against a Soviet attack.

These men are Doctors Killian, Kistiakowsky, Wiesner,

Hornig, York, Brown and Foster.

The plain fact of the matter is that we are now facing a situation analogous to the one we faced in 1961; we are uncertain of the Soviets' intentions.

At that time we were concerned about their potential offensive capabilities; now we are concerned about their potential defensive capabilities.

But the dynamics of the concern are the same.

We must continue to be cautious and conservative in our estimates — leaving no room in our calculations for unnecessary talk. And at the same time, we must measure our own response in such a manner that it does not trigger a senseless spiral upward of nuclear arms.

Now, as I have emphasized, we have already taken the necessary steps to guarantee that our offensive strategic weapons will be able to penetrate future, more advanced, Soviet defenses.

Keeping in mind the careful clockwork of lead-time, we will be forced to continue that effort over the next few years if the evidence is that the Soviets intend to turn what is now a light and modest A.B.M. deployment into a massive one.

Should they elect to do so, we have both the lead time and the technology available to so increase both the quality and quantity of our offensive strategic forces — with particular attention to highly reliable penetration aids — that their expensive defensive efforts will give them no edge in the nuclear balance whatever.

But we would prefer not to have to do that. For it is a profitless waste of resources, provided we and the Soviets can come to a realistic strategic arms-limitation agreement.

As you know, we have proposed U.S.-Soviet talks on this matter. Should these talks fail, we are fully prepared to take the appropriate measures that such a failure would make necessary.

The point for us to keep in mind is that should the talks fail — and the Soviets decide to expand their present modest A.B.M. deployment into a massive one — our response must be realistic. There is no point whatever in our responding by going to a massive A.B.M. deployment to protect our population, when such a system would be ineffective against a sophisticated Soviet offense.

Instead, realism dictates that if the Soviets elect to deploy a heavy A.B.M. system, we must further expand our sophisticated offensive forces, and thus preserve our overwhelming assured destruction capability.

But the intractable fact is that should the talks fail, both the Soviets and ourselves would be forced to continue on a foolish and reckless course.

It would be foolish and reckless because — in the end — it would provide neither the Soviets nor us with any greater relative nuclear capability.

The time has come for us both to realize that, and to act reasonably. It is clearly in our own mutual interest to do so.

Having said that, it is important to distinguish between an A.B.M. system designed to protect against a Soviet attack on our cities, and A.B.M. systems which have other objectives.

One of the other uses of an A.B.M. system which we should seriously consider is the greater protection of our strategic offensive forces.

Another is in relation to the emerging nuclear capability of Communist China. . . .

Up to now, the lead-time factor has allowed us to postpone a decision on whether or not a light A.B.M. deployment might be advantageous as a countermeasure to Communist China's nuclear development.

But the time will shortly be right for us to initiate production if we desire such a system. . . .

President Johnson has made it clear that the United States will oppose any efforts of China to employ nuclear blackmail against her neighbors.

We possess now, and will continue to possess or as far ahead as we can foresee, an overwhelming first-strike capability with respect to China. And despite the shrill and raucous propaganda directed at her own people that "the atomic bomb is a paper tiger," there is ample evidence that China well appreciates the destructive power of nuclear weapons.

China has been cautious to avoid any action that might end in a nuclear clash with the United States — however wild her words — and understandably so. We have the power not only to destroy completely her entire nuclear offensive forces, but to devastate her society as well.

Is there any possibility, then, that by the mid-1970s China might become so incautious as to attempt a nuclear attack on the United States or our allies?

It would be insane and suicidal for her to do so, but one can conceive conditions under which China might miscalculate. We wish to reduce such possibilities to a minimum.

And since, as I have noted, our strategic planning must always be conservative, and take into consideration even the possible irrational behavior of potential adversaries, there are marginal grounds for concluding that a light deployment of U. S. A.B.M.s against this possibility is prudent.

The system would be relatively inexpensive — preliminary estimates place the cost at about $5-billion — and would have a much higher degree of reliability against a Chinese attack than the much more massive and complicated system that some have recommended against a possible Soviet attack.

Moreover, such an A.B.M. deployment designed against a possible Chinese attack would have a number of other advantages. It would provide an additional indication to Asians that we intend to deter China from nuclear blackmail, and thus would contribute toward our goal of discouraging nuclear weapon proliferation among the present non-nuclear countries.

Further, the Chinese-oriented A.B.M. deployment would enable us to add—as a concurrent benefit—a further defense of our Minuteman sites against Soviet attack, which means that at modest cost we would in fact be adding even greater effectiveness to our offensive missile force and avoiding a much more costly expansion of that force.

Finally, such a reasonably reliable A.B.M. system would add protection of our population against the improbable but possible accidental launch of an intercontinental missile by any of the nuclear powers.

After a detailed review of all these considerations, we have decided to go forward with this Chinese-oriented A.B.M. deployment, and we will begin actual production of such a system at the end of this year. . . .

The danger in deploying this relatively light and reliable Chinese-oriented A.B.M. system is going to be that pressures will develop to expand it into a heavy Soviet-oriented A.B.M. system.

We must resist that temptation firmly—not because we can for a moment afford to relax our vigilance against a possible Soviet first strike—but precisely because our greatest deterrent against such a strike is not a massive, costly, but highly penetrable A.B.M. shield, but rather a fully credible offensive assured destruction capability.

The so-called heavy A.B.M. shield—at the present state of technology—would in effect be no adequate shield at all against a Soviet attack, but rather a strong inducement for the Soviets to vastly increase their own offensive forces. That, as I have pointed out, would make it necessary for us to respond in turn—and so the arms race would rush hopelessly on to no sensible purpose on either side.

Let me emphasize—and I cannot do so too strongly—that our decision to go ahead with *limited* A.B.M. deployment in no way indicates that we feel an agreement with the Soviet Union on the limitation of strategic nuclear offensive and defensive forces is any the less urgent or desirable.

## A Soviet View of ABM

### *Document 15*

In the 1960s, the Soviets favored ballistic missile defenses. Reflexively hostile to the concept of mutually assured destruction, Kremlin officials resolutely insisted that no nation in the long run could trust its survival to the benevolence of another. They asserted that ultimate security rested on defenses that they portrayed as having a stabilizing influence on international relations in the nuclear age. Maj. Gen. N. Talensky's 1964 article in *International Affairs* is symptomatic of Soviet attitudes. While acknowledging the uncertain hazards associated with antiballistic missile efforts, Talensky argues that they are far outweighed by the fragility of deterrence and its vulnerability to human folly. He concludes that ABM systems are a stabilizing, desirable development and not something to be banned.

### 15 THE WESTERN ATTITUDE
### Maj. Gen. N. Talensky
### October 1964

As soon as there was convincing evidence that the problem of anti-missile defence was being successfully solved in the Soviet Union, many official and unofficial statements were made in the West concerning the possible consequences of the creation of an effective anti-missile defence system. A number of proposals were put forward with a view to eliminating these consequences which were almost all qualified as "dangerous".

Let us look into the chief arguments of Western spokesmen.

The main objection to anti-missile systems, as seen by Western politicians and public figures, is that they tend to upset the nuclear balance thereby undermining the system of mutual deterrence through nuclear rockets, that is, the system of "deterrence through fear". To prove their point they ignore the obvious facts and resort to verbal tricks instead of convincing arguments.

Take the official statements by Western spokesmen in the 18-Nation Committee at Geneva. U.S. delegate Fisher, for instance, flatly declared that "anti-ballistic systems are no longer purely defensive; they become part of the balance on which our stability and peace now depend". This argument was taken up by the British delegate Mason. He said: "If one or other side were to possess a really effective anti-ballistic missile defence system, that—ironic though it may seem—would be extremely dangerous, because it would upset the stability of the nuclear balance. It would be extremely dangerous because it would make one side or other think that it was immune from potential nuclear retaliation. Any side which thought this would obviously not be deterred in its actions."

In other words, anti-missile systems are defensive but, as the West insists, they upset the mutual deterrence based on the threat of a nuclear strike. This gives rise to the question: who stands to gain and who is faced with "serious difficulties"? Let us take two countries, one peaceable and concerned with maintaining peace and security, and the other inclined to an aggressive policy and not at all loath to resort to nuclear rockets for its aggressive ends, but with a minimum of losses.

It is obvious that the creation of an effective anti-missile defence merely serves to build up the security of the peaceable, non-aggressive state; the fact that it is in possession of a combination of anti-missile means and effective nuclear-rocket forces serves to promote the task of deterring a potential aggressor, ensuring its own security and maintaining the stability of world peace. A country not willing to abandon its aggressive policy will naturally not be too happy about such a state of affairs.

Upon the other hand, if the effective anti-missile system is built by the side which adheres to an aggressive policy, a policy from positions of strength, this may well intensify the danger of an outbreak of war, but such a danger may also arise quite apart from the creation of any anti-missile defence, for it may be brought about by other factors of technical progress or may spring from political causes, which, I think, would be the more correct assumption. But the creation of an effective anti-missile defence system by a country which is a potential target for aggression merely serves to increase the deterrent effect and so helps to avert aggression.

It is said that the international strategic situation cannot be stable where both sides simultaneously strive towards deterrence through nuclear-rocket power and the creation of defensive anti-missile systems.

I cannot agree with this view either. From the standpoint of strategy, powerful deterrent forces and an effective anti-missile defence system, when taken together, substantially increase the stability of mutual deterrence, for any partial shifts in the qualitative and quantitative balance of these two component elements of mutual deterrence tend to be correspondingly compensated and equalised.

In that case, the danger lurks in politics. An aggressive policy and a course set for nuclear attack with "acceptable" losses for oneself as a result of a counter strike create the danger of an outbreak of thermo-nuclear war, whether or not anti-missile defence systems are to hand. But these systems considerably enhance the security of peace-loving states.

There are other big advantages as well in the creation of an effective anti-missile defence system. After all, when the security of a state is based only on mutual deterrence with the aid of powerful nuclear rockets it is directly dependent on the goodwill and designs of the other side, which is a highly subjective and indefinite factor.

"The main thing in the policy of maintaining the *status quo* by means of a threat," says the French General Gallois, "is of course awareness on the part of both adversaries of the risk they take in resorting to the use of force. . . . The more powerful the adversary's counter-strike forces appear to each side, the more stable the peace. It would be an excellent thing if the aggressive bloc in general overrated the enemy's forces."[17]

But what if the aggressive bloc happens to underrate the deterrent and overrate its own forces of attack? There is a great deal of history to show that political and military leaders on the aggressive side are more apt to underrate the enemy's strength. The Government and the Grand General Staff of Kaiser Germany miscalculated in assessing the enemy and clearly underestimated his strength. History has clearly demonstrated that great revolutions cannot be crushed with armed force, but that did not prevent the Governments of the capitalist states from launching their armed intervention against Soviet Russia between 1918 and 1920. . . .

If that is so, can we afford to rely only on deterrence through the threat of a nuclear-rocket force? . . .

In such conditions, *the creation of an effective anti-missile system enables the state to make its defences dependent chiefly on its own possibilities, and not only on mutual deterrence, that is, on the goodwill of the other side.* And since the peace-loving states are concerned with maximum deterrence, in its full and direct sense, it would be illogical to be suspicious of such a state when it creates an anti-missile defence system on the ground that it wants to make it easier for itself to resort to aggression with impunity.

Some say the construction of anti-missile defence systems may accelerate the arms race, and that the side lagging in such systems may build up its nuclear-rocket attack weapons. That is one of the arguments against defensive systems.

Such a development is not at all ruled out, in much the same way as the possibility that the nuclear-rocket race may be stepped up quantitatively and qualitatively even without any anti-missile systems. In any case, there is this question: what is more preferable for security as a result of the arms race, a harmonious combination of active means of deterrence and defence systems, or the means of attack alone? An exhaustive analysis of this can be made only on the basis of highly concrete military and technical data, but at any rate the side which makes a spurt in the means of attack will instantly expose its aggressive intentions, and stand condemned as the aggressor with all the negative political consequences that this entails.

Another argument is that it is not in the Soviet Union's interest to spend large sums of money and resources to build anti-missile defences for cities and economic areas because the West has adopted the "counter-force" strategy and will not use nuclear weapons against non-military objectives. This argument will hardly convince anyone. History has taught the Soviet Union to depend mainly on itself in ensuring its security and that of its friends. The Soviet people will hardly believe that a potential aggressor will use humane methods of warfare, and will strike only at military objectives, etc. The experience of the last war, especially its aerial bombardments and in particular the combat use of the first atomic bombs, is all proof to the contrary. That is why the Soviet

Union attaches importance to making as invulnerable as possible not only its nuclear-rocket deterrent but also its cities and vital centres, that is, creating a reliable defence system for the greatest number of people.

## Note

17. Pierre Gallois, *Stratégie de l'âge nucléaire.* Paris, 1960, p. 150.

# The ABM Debate Begins

### *Documents 16 and 17*

By 1968, a major debate had erupted over McNamara's plans to deploy an ABM system. The debate was not confined to the small group of defense experts who were usually interested in such matters. It soon involved key civilian scientists and eventually the public. In document 16, an influential 1968 article in *Scientific American,* distinguished physicists Richard Garwin and Hans Bethe argue that the proposed defensive system is technologically inadequate and could be easily neutralized by cheaper countermeasures. In document 17, Donald Brennan, an ABM advocate, claims that even a technologically imperfect ballistic missile defense offers important benefits, in particular that it could save American lives.

## 16 ANTI-BALLISTIC-MISSILE SYSTEMS Richard Garwin and Hans Bethe

Last September, Secretary of Defense McNamara announced that the U.S. would build a "relatively light and reliable Chinese-oriented ABM system." With this statement he apparently ended a long and complex debate on the merits of any kind of anti-ballistic-missile system in an age of intercontinental ballistic missiles carrying multi-megaton thermonuclear warheads. Secretary McNamara added that the U.S. would "begin actual production of such a system at the end of this year," meaning the end of 1967.

As two physicists who have been concerned for many years with the development and deployment of modern nuclear weapons we wish to offer some comments on this important matter. On examining the capabilities of ABM systems of various types, and on considering the stratagems available to a determined enemy who sought to nullify the effectiveness of such a system, we have come to the conclusion that the "light" system described by Secretary McNamara will add little, if anything, to the influences that should restrain China indefinitely from an attack on the U.S. First among these factors is China's certain knowledge that, in McNamara's words, "we have the power not only to destroy completely her entire nuclear offensive forces but to devastate her society as well."

An even more pertinent argument against the proposed ABM system, in our view, is that it will nourish the illusion that an effective defense against ballistic missiles is possible and will lead almost inevitably to demands that the light system, the estimated cost of which exceeds $5 billion, be expanded into a heavy system that could cost upward of $40 billion. The folly of undertaking to build such a system was vigorously stated by Secretary McNamara. "It is important to understand," he said, "that none of the [ABM] systems at the present or foreseeable state of the art would provide an impenetrable shield over the United States. . . . Let me make it very clear that the [cost] in itself is not the problem: the penetrability of the proposed shield is the problem."

In our view the penetrability of the light, Chinese-oriented shield is also a problem. It does not seem credible to us that, even if the Chinese succumbed to the "insane and suicidal" impulse to launch a nuclear attack on the U.S. within the next decade, they would also be foolish enough to have built complex and expensive missiles and nuclear warheads peculiarly vulnerable to the light ABM system now presumably under construction (a system whose characteristics and capabilities have been well publicized). In the area of strategic weapons a common understanding of the major elements and technical possibilities is essential to an informed and reasoned choice by the people, through their government, of a proper course of action. In this article we shall outline in general terms, using nonsecret information, the techniques an enemy could employ at no great cost to reduce the effectiveness of an ABM system even more elaborate than the one the Chinese will face. First, however, let us describe that system.

Known as the Sentinel system, it will provide for long-range interception by Spartan antimissile missiles and short-range interception by Sprint antimissile missiles. Both types of missile will be armed with thermonuclear warheads for the purpose of destroying or inactivating the attacker's thermonuclear weapons, which will be borne through the atmosphere and to their targets by reentry vehicles (RV's). The Spartan missiles, whose range is a few hundred kilometers, will be fired when an attacker's reentry vehicles are first detected rising above the horizon by perimeter acquisition radar (PAR).

If the attacker is using his available propulsion to

deliver maximum payload, his reentry vehicles will follow a normal minimum-energy trajectory, and they will first be sighted by one of the PAR's when they are about 4,000 kilometers, or about 10 minutes, away. If the attacker chooses to launch his rockets with less than maximum payload, he can put them either in a lofted trajectory or in a depressed one. The lofted trajectory has certain advantages against a terminal defense system. The most extreme example of a depressed trajectory is the path followed by a low-orbit satellite. On such a trajectory a reentry vehicle could remain below an altitude of 160 kilometers and would not be visible to the horizon-search radar until it was some 1,400 kilometers, or about three minutes, away. This is FOBS: the fractional-orbit bombardment system, which allows intercontinental ballistic missiles to deliver perhaps 50 to 75 percent of their normal payload.

In the Sentinel system Spartans will be launched when PAR has sighted an incoming missile; they will be capable of intercepting the missile at a distance of several hundred kilometers. To provide a light shield for the entire U.S. about half a dozen PAR units will be deployed along the northern border of the country to detect missiles approaching from the general direction of the North Pole. Each PAR will be linked to several "farms" of long-range Spartan missiles, which can be hundreds of kilometers away. Next to each Spartan farm will be a farm of Sprint missiles together with missile-site radar (MSR), whose function is to help guide both the Spartans and the shorter-range Sprints to their targets. The task of the Sprints is to provide terminal protection for the important Spartans and MSR's. The PAR's will also be protected by Sprints and thus will require MSR's nearby.

Whereas the Spartans are expected to intercept an enemy missile well above the upper atmosphere, the Sprints are designed to be effective within the atmosphere, at altitudes below 35 kilometers. The explosion of an ABM missile's thermonuclear warhead will produce a huge flux of X rays, neutrons and other particles, and within the atmosphere a powerful blast wave as well. We shall describe later how X rays, particles and blast can incapacitate a reentry vehicle.

Before we consider in detail the capabilities and limitations of ABM systems, one of us (Garwin) will briefly summarize the present strategic position of the U.S. The primary fact is that the U.S. and the U.S.S.R. can annihilate each other as viable civilizations within a day and perhaps within an hour. Each can at will inflict on the other more than 120 million immediate deaths, to which must be added deaths that will be caused by fire, fallout, disease and starvation. In addition more than 75 percent of the productive capacity of each country would be destroyed, regardless of who strikes first. At present, therefore, each of the two countries has an assured destruction capability with respect to the other. It is usually assumed that a nation faced with the assured destruction of 30 percent of its population and productive capacity will be deterred from destroying another nation, no matter how serious the grievance. Assured destruction is therefore not a very flexible political or military tool. It serves only to preserve a nation from complete destruction. More conventional military forces are needed to fill the more conventional military role.

Assured destruction was not possible until the advent of thermonuclear weapons in the middle 1950's. At first, when one had to depend on aircraft to deliver such weapons, destruction was not really assured because a strategic air force is subject to surprise attack, to problems of command and control and to attrition by the air defenses of the other side. All of this was changed by the development of the intercontinental ballistic missile and also, although to a lesser extent, by modifications of our B-52 force that would enable it to penetrate enemy defenses at low altitude. There is no doubt today that the U.S.S.R. and the U.S. have achieved mutual assured destruction.

The U.S. has 1,000 Minuteman missiles in hardened "silos" and 54 much larger Titan II missiles. In addition we have 656 Polaris missiles in 41 submarines and nearly 700 long-range bombers. The Minutemen alone could survive a surprise attack and achieve assured destruction of the attacker. In his recent annual report the Secretary of Defense estimated that as of October, 1967, the U.S.S.R. had some 720 intercontinental ballistic missiles, about 30 submarine-launched ballistic missiles (excluding many that are airborne rather than ballistic) and about 155 long-range bombers. This force provides assured destruction of the U.S.

Secretary McNamara has also stated that U.S. forces can deliver more than 2,000 thermonuclear weapons with an average yield of one megaton, and that fewer than 400 such weapons would be needed for assured destruction of a third of the U.S.S.R.'s population and three-fourths of its industry. The U.S.S.R. would need somewhat fewer weapons to achieve the same results against the U.S.

It is worth remembering that intercontinental missiles and nuclear weapons are not the only means of mass destruction. They are, however, among the most reliable, as they were even when they were first made in the 1940's and 1950's. One might build a strategic force somewhat differently today, but the U.S. and the U.S.S.R. have no incentive for doing so. In fact, the chief virtue of assured destruction may be that it removes the need to race — there is no reward for getting ahead. One really should not worry too much about new means for delivering nuclear weapons (such as bombs in orbit or fractional-orbit systems) or about advances in chemical or biological warfare. A single thermonuclear assured-destruction force can deter such novel kinds of attack as well.

Now, as Secretary McNamara stated in his September speech, our defense experts reckoned conservatively six to 10 years ago, when our present strategic-force levels were planned. The result is that we have right now many more missiles than we need for assured destruction of the U.S.S.R. If war comes, therefore, the U.S. will use the excess force in a "damage-limiting" role, which means firing the excess at those elements of the Russian strategic force that would do the most damage to the U.S. Inasmuch as the U.S.S.R. has achieved the level of assured destruction, this action will not preserve the U.S., but it should reduce the damage, perhaps sparing a small city here or there or reducing somewhat the forces the U.S.S.R. can use against our allies. To the extent that this damage-limiting use of our forces reduces the damage done to the U.S.S.R. it may slightly reduce the deterrent effect resulting from assured destruction. It must be clear that only surplus forces will be used in this way. It should be said, however, that the exact level of casualties and industrial damage required to destroy a nation as a viable society has been the subject of surprisingly little research or even argument.

One can conceive of three threats to the present rather comforting situation of mutual assured destruction. The first would be an effective counterforce system: a system that would enable the U.S. (or the U.S.S.R.) to incapacitate the other side's strategic forces before they could be used. The second would be an effective ballistic-missile defense combined with an effective antiaircraft system. The third would be a transition from a bipolar world, in which the U.S. and the U.S.S.R. alone possess overwhelming power, to a multipolar world including, for instance, China. Such threats are of course more worrisome in combination than individually.

American and Russian defense planners are constantly evaluating less-than-perfect intelligence to see if any or all of these threats are developing. For purposes of discussion let us ask what responses a White side might make to various moves made by a Black side. Assume that Black has threatened to negate White's capability of assured destruction by doing one of the following things: (1) it has procured more intercontinental missiles, (2) it has installed some missile defense or (3) it has built up a large operational force of missiles each of which can attack several targets, using "multiple independently targetable reentry vehicles" (MIRV's).

White's goal is to maintain assured destruction. He is now worried that Black may be able to reduce to a dangerous level the number of White warheads that will reach their target. White's simplest response to all three threats — but not necessarily the most effective or the cheapest — is to provide himself with more launch vehicles. In addition, in order to meet the first and third threats White will try to make his launchers more difficult to destroy by one or more of the following means: by making them mobile (for example by placing them in submarines or on railroad cars), by further hardening their permanent sites or by defending them with an ABM system.

Another possibility that is less often discussed would be for White to arrange to fire the bulk of his warheads on "evaluation of threat." In other words, White could fire his land-based ballistic missiles when some fraction of them had already been destroyed by enemy warheads, or when an overwhelming attack is about to destroy them. To implement such a capability responsibly requires excellent communications, and the decision to fire would have to be made within minutes, leading to the execution of a prearranged firing plan. As a complete alternative to hardening and mobility, this fire-now-or-never capability would lead to tension and even, in the event of an accident, to catastrophe. Still, as a supplemental capability to ease fears of effective counterforce action, it may have some merit.

White's response to the second threat — an increase in Black's ABM defenses — might be limited to deploying more launchers, with the simple goal of saturating and exhausting Black's defenses. But White would also want to consider the cost and effectiveness of the following: penetration aids, concentrating on undefended or lightly defended targets, maneuvering reentry vehicles or multiple reentry vehicles. The last refers to several reentry vehicles carried by the same missile; the defense would have to destroy all of them to avoid damage. Finally, White could reopen the question of whether he should seek assured destruction solely by means of missiles. For example, he might reexamine the effectiveness of low-altitude bombers or he might turn his attention to chemical or biological weapons. It does not much matter how assured destruction is achieved. The important thing, as Secretary McNamara has emphasized, is that the other side find it credible. ("The point is that a potential aggressor must himself believe that our assured destruction capability is in fact actual, and that our will to use it in retaliation to an attack is in fact unwavering.")

It is clear that White has many options, and that he will choose those that are most reliable or those that are cheapest for a given level of assured destruction. Although relative costs do depend on the level of destruction required, the important technical conclusion is that for conventional levels of assured destruction it is considerably cheaper for White to provide more offensive capability than it is for Black to defend his people and industry against a concerted strike.

As an aside, it might be mentioned that scientists newly engaged in the evaluation of military systems often have trouble grasping that large systems of the type created by or for the military are divided quite rigidly into several chronological stages, namely, in reverse order: operation, deployment, development and research. An operational system is not threatened by a system that is still in development; the threat is not real until the new system is in fact deployed, shaken down and fully operative. This is particularly true for an ABM system, which is obliged to operate against large numbers of relatively independent intercontinental ballistic missiles. It is equally true, however, for counterforce reentry vehicles, which can be ignored unless they are built by the hundreds or thousands. The same goes for MIRV's, a development of the multiple reentry vehicle in which each reentry vehicle is independently directed to a separate target. One must distinguish clearly between the *possibility* of development and the development itself, and similarly between development and actual operation. One must refrain from attributing to a specific defense system, such as Sentinel, those capabilities that *might* be obtained by further development of a different system.

It follows that the Sentinel light ABM system, to be built now and to be operational in the early 1970's against a possible Chinese intercontinental ballistic missile threat, will have to reckon with a missile force unlike either the Russian or the American force, both of which were, after all, built when there was no ballistic-missile defense. The Chinese will probably build even their first operational intercontinental ballistic missiles so that they will have a chance to penetrate. Moreover, we believe it is well within China's capabilities to do a good job at this without intensive testing or tremendous sacrifice in payload.

Temporarily leaving aside penetration aids, there are two pure strategies for attack against a ballistic-missile defense. The first is an all-warhead attack in which one uses large booster rockets to transport many small (that is, fractional-megaton) warheads. These warheads are separated at some instant between the time the missile leaves the atmosphere and the time of reentry. The warheads from one missile can all be directed against the same large target (such as a city); these multiple reentry vehicles (MRV's) are purely a penetration aid. Alternatively each of the reentry vehicles can be given an independent boost to a different target, thus making them into MIRV's. MIRV is not a penetration aid but is rather a counterforce weapon: if each of the reentry vehicles has very high accuracy, then it is conceivable that each of them may destroy an enemy missile silo. The Titan II liquid-fuel rocket, designed more than 10 years ago, could carry 20 or more thermonuclear weapons. If these were employed simply as MRV's, the 54 Titans could provide more than 1,000 reentry vehicles for the defense to deal with.

Since the Spartan interceptors will each cost $1 million to $2 million, including their thermonuclear warheads, it is reasonable to believe thermonuclear warheads can be delivered for less than it will cost the defender to intercept them. The attacker can make a further relative saving by concentrating his strike so that most of the interceptors, all bought and paid for, have nothing to shoot at. This is a high-reliability penetration strategy open to any country that can afford to spend a reasonable fraction of the amount its opponent can spend for defense.

The second pure strategy for attack against an ABM defense is to precede the actual attack with an all-decoy attack or to mix real warheads with decoys. This can be achieved rather cheaply by firing large rockets from unhardened sites to send light, unguided decoys more or less in the direction of plausible city targets. If the ABM defense is an area defense like the Sentinel system, it must fire against these threatening objects at very long range before they reenter the atmosphere, where because of their lightness they would behave differently from real warheads. Several hundred to several thousand such decoys launched by a few large vehicles could readily exhaust a Sentinel-like system. The attack with real warheads would then follow.

The key point is that since the putative Chinese intercontinental-ballistic-missile force is still in the early research and development stage, it can and will be designed to deal with the Sentinel system, whose interceptors and sensors are nearing production and are rather well publicized. It is much easier to design a missile force to counter a defense that is already being deployed than to design one for any of the possible defense systems that might or might not be deployed sometime in the future.

One of us (Bethe) will now describe (1) the physical mechanisms by which an ABM missile can destroy or damage an incoming warhead and (2) some of the penetration aids available to an attacker who is determined to have his warheads reach their targets.

Much study has been given to the possibility of using conventional explosives rather than a thermonuclear explosive in the warhead of a defensive missile. The answer is that the "kill" radius of a conventional explosive is much too small to be practical in a likely tactical engagement. We shall consider here only the more important effects of the defensive thermonuclear weapon: the emission of neutrons, the emission of X rays and, when the weapon is exploded in the atmosphere, blast.

Neutrons have the ability to penetrate matter of any kind. Those released by defensive weapons could penetrate the heat shield and outer jacket of an offensive warhead and enter the fissile material itself, causing the atoms to fission and generating large amounts of heat. If sufficient heat is generated, the fissile material will melt and lose its carefully designed shape. Thereafter it can no longer be detonated.

The kill radius for neutrons depends on the design of the offensive weapon and the yield, or energy release, of the defensive weapon. The miss distance, or distance of closest approach between the defensive and the offensive missiles, can be made small enough to achieve a kill by the neutron mechanism. This is particularly true if the the defensive missile and radar have high performance and the interception is made no more than a few tens of kilometers from the ABM launch site. The neutron-kill mechanism is therefore practical for the short-range defense of a city or other important target. It is highly desirable that the yield of the defensive warhead be kept low to minimize the effects of blast and heat on the city being defended.

The attacker can, of course, attempt to shield the fissile material in the offensive warhead from neutron damage, but the mass of shielding needed is substantial. Witness the massive shield required to keep neutrons from escaping from nuclear reactors. The size of the reentry vehicle will enable the defense to make a rough estimate of the amount of shielding that can be carried and thus to estimate the intensity of neutrons required to melt the warhead's fissile material.

Let us consider next the effect of X rays. These rays carry off most of the energy emitted by nuclear weapons, especially those in the megaton range. If sufficient X-ray energy falls on a reentry vehicle, it will cause the surface layer of the vehicle's heat shield to evaporate. This in itself may not be too damaging, but the vapor leaves the surface at high velocity in a very brief time and the recoil sets up a powerful shock wave in the heat shield. The shock may destroy the heat shield material or the underlying structure.

X rays are particularly effective above the upper atmosphere, where they can travel to their target without being absorbed by air molecules. The defense can therefore use megaton weapons without endangering the population below; it is protected by the intervening atmosphere. The kill radius can then be many kilometers. This reduces the accuracy required of the defensive missile and allows successful interception at ranges of hundreds of kilometers from the ABM launch site. Thus X rays make possible an area defense and provide the key to the Sentinel system.

On the other hand, the reentry vehicle can be hardened against X-ray damage to a considerable extent. And in general the defender will not know if the vehicle has been damaged until it reenters the atmosphere. If it has been severely damaged, it may break up or burn up. If this does not happen, however, the defender is helpless unless he has also constructed an effective terminal, or short-range, defense system.

The third kill mechanism — blast — can operate only in the atmosphere and requires little comment. Ordinarily when an offensive warhead reenters the atmosphere it is decelerated by a force that, at maximum, is on the order of 100 *g*. (One *g* is the acceleration due to the earth's gravity.) The increased atmospheric density reached within a shock wave from a nuclear explosion in air can produce a deceleration several times greater. But just as one can shield against neutrons and X rays one can shield against blast by designing the reentry vehicle to have great structural strength. Moreover, the defense, not knowing the detailed design of the reentry vehicle, has little way of knowing if it has destroyed a given vehicle by blast until the warhead either goes off or fails to do so.

The main difficulty for the defense is the fact that in all probability the offensive reentry vehicle will not arrive as a single object that can be tracked and fired on but will be accompanied by many other objects deliberately placed there by the offense. These objects come under the heading of penetration aids. We shall discuss only a few of the many types of such aids. They include fragments of the booster rocket, decoys, fine metal wires called chaff, electronic countermeasures and blackout mechanisms of several kinds.

The last stage of the booster that has propelled the offensive missile may disintegrate into fragments or it can be fragmented deliberately. Some of the pieces will have a radar cross section comparable to or larger than the cross section of the reentry vehicle itself. The defensive radar therefore has the task of discriminating between a mass of debris and the warhead. Although various means of discrimination are effective to some extent, radar and data processing must be specifically set up for this purpose. In any case the radar must deal with tens of objects for each genuine target, and this imposes considerable complexity on the system.

There is, of course, an easy way to discriminate among such objects: let the whole swarm reenter the atmosphere. The lighter booster fragments will soon be slowed down, whereas the heavier reentry vehicle will continue to fall with essentially undiminished speed. If a swarm of objects is allowed to reenter, however, one must abandon the concept of area defense and construct a terminal defense system. If a nation insists on retaining a pure area defense, it must be prepared to shoot at every threatening object. Not only is this extremely costly but also it can quickly exhaust the supply of antimissile missiles.

Instead of relying on the accidental targets provided by booster fragments, the offense will almost certainly want to employ decoys that closely imitate the radar reflectivity of the reentry vehicle. One cheap and simple decoy is a balloon with the same shape as the reentry vehicle. It can be made of thin plastic covered with metal in the form of foil, strips or wire mesh. A considerable number of such balloons can be carried uninflated by a single offensive missile and released when the missile has risen above the atmosphere.

The chief difficulty with balloons is putting them on a "credible" trajectory, that is, a trajectory aimed at a city or some other plausible target. Nonetheless, if the defending force employs an area defense and really seeks to protect the entire country, it must try to intercept every suspicious object, including balloon decoys. The defense may, however, decide not to shoot at incoming objects that seem to be directed against nonvital targets; thus it may choose to limit possible damage to the country rather than to avoid all damage. The offense could then take the option of directing live warheads against points on the outskirts of cities, where a nuclear explosion would still produce radioactivity and possibly severe fallout over densely populated regions. Worse, the possibility that reentry vehicles can be built to maneuver makes it dangerous to ignore objects even 100 kilometers off target.

Balloon decoys, even more than booster fragments, will be rapidly slowed by the atmosphere and will tend to burn up when they reenter it. Here again a terminal ABM system has a far better chance than an area defense system to discriminate between decoys and warheads. One possibility for an area system is "active" discrimination. If a defensive nuclear missile is exploded somewhere in the cloud of balloon decoys traveling with a reentry vehicle, the balloons will either be destroyed by radiation from the explosion or will be blown far off course. The reentry vehicle presumably will survive. If the remaining set of objects is examined by radar, the reentry vehicle may stand out clearly. It can then be killed by a second interceptor shot. Such a shoot-look-shoot tactic may be effective, but it obviously places severe demands on the ABM missiles and the radar tracking system. Moreover, it can be countered by the use of small, dense decoys within the balloon swarms.

Moreover, it may be possible to develop decoys that are as resistant to X rays as the reentry vehicle and also are simple and compact. Their radar reflectivity could be made to simulate that of a reentry vehicle over a wide range of frequencies. The decoys could also be made to reenter the atmosphere — at least down to a fairly low altitude — in a way that closely mimicked an actual reentry vehicle. The design of such decoys, however, would require considerable experimentation and development.

Another way to confuse the defensive radar is to scatter the fine metal wires of chaff. If such wires are cut to about half the wavelength of the defensive radar, each wire will act as a reflecting dipole with a radar cross section approximately equal to the wavelength squared divided by $2\pi$. The actual length of the wires is not critical; a wire of a given length is also effective against radar of shorter wavelength. Assuming that the radar wavelength is one meter and that one-mil copper wire is cut to half-meter lengths, one can easily calculate that 100 million chaff wires will weigh only 200 kilograms (440 pounds).

The chaff wires could be dispersed over a large volume of space; the chaff could be so dense and provide such large radar reflection that the reentry vehicle could not be seen against the background noise. The defense would then not know where in the large reflecting cloud the reentry vehicle is concealed. The defense would be induced to spend several interceptors to cover the entire cloud, with no certainty, even so, that the hidden reentry vehicle will be killed. How much of the chaff would survive the defensive nuclear explosion is another difficult question. The main problem for the attacker is to develop a way to disperse chaff more or less uniformly.

An active alternative to the use of chaff is to equip some decoys with electronic devices that generate radio noise at frequencies selected to jam the defensive radar. There are many variations on such electronic countermeasures, among them the use of jammers on the reentry vehicles themselves.

The last of the penetration aids that will be mentioned here is the radar blackout caused by the large number of free electrons released by a nuclear explosion. These electrons, except for a few, are removed from atoms or molecules of air, which thereby become ions. There are two main causes for the formation of ions: the fireball of the explosion, which produces ions because of its high temperature, and the radioactive debris of the explosion, which releases beta rays (high-energy electrons) that ionize the air they traverse. The second mechanism is important only at high altitude.

The electrons in an ionized cloud of gas have the property of bending and absorbing electromagnetic waves, particularly those of low frequency. Attenuation can reach such high values that the defensive radar is prevented from seeing any object behind the ionized cloud (unlike chaff, which confuses the radar only at the chaff range and not beyond).

Blackout is a severe problem for an area defense designed to intercept missiles above the upper atmosphere. The problem is aggravated because area-defense radar is likely to employ low-frequency (long) waves, which are the most suitable for detecting enemy missiles at long range. In some recent popular articles long-wave radar has been hailed as the cure for the problems of the ABM missile. It is not. Even though it increases the capability of the radar in some ways, it makes the system more vulnerable to blackout.

Blackout can be caused in two ways: by the defensive nuclear explosions themselves and by deliberate explosions set off at high altitude by the attacker. Although the former are unavoidable, the defense has the choice of setting them off at altitudes and in locations that will cause the minimum blackout of its radar. The offense can sacrifice a few early missiles to cause blackout at strategic locations. In what follows we shall assume for purposes of discussion that the radar wavelength is one meter. Translation to other wavelengths is not difficult.

In order to totally reflect the one-meter waves from our hypothetical radar it is necessary for the attacker to create an ionized cloud containing $10^9$ electrons per cubic centimeter. Much smaller electron densities, however, will suffice for considerable attenuation. For the benefit of technically minded readers, the equation for attenuation in decibels per kilometer is

$$\alpha = \frac{4.34}{3 \times 10^5} \frac{\omega_p{}^2}{\omega^2 + \gamma_e{}^2} \gamma_e.$$

Here $\omega_p$ is the plasma frequency for the given electron density, $\omega$ is the radar frequency in radians per second and $\gamma_e$ is the frequency of collisons of an electron with atoms of air. At normal temperature this frequency $\gamma_e$ is the number $2 \times 10^{11}$ multiplied by the density of the air ($\rho$) compared with sea-level density ($\rho_0$), or $\gamma_e = 2 \times 10^{11}\ \rho/\rho_0$. At altitudes above 30 kilometers, where an area-defense system will have to make most of its interceptions, the density of air is less than .01 of the density at sea level. Under these conditions the electron collision frequency $\gamma_e$ is less than the value of $\omega = (2\pi \times 3 \times 10^8)$ and therefore can be neglected in the denominator of the equation. Using that equation, we can then specify the number of electrons. $N_e$, needed to attenuate one-meter radar waves by a factor of more than one decibel per kilometer: $N_e > 350\rho_0/\rho$. At an altitude of 30 kilometers, where $\rho_0/\rho$ is about 100, $N_e$ is about $3 \times 10^4$, and at 60 kilometers $N_e$ is still only about $3 \times 10^6$. Thus the electron densities needed for the substantial attenuation of a radar signal are well under the $10^9$ electrons per cubic centimeter required for total reflection. The ionized cloud created by the fireball of a nuclear explosion is typically 10 kilometers thick; if the attenuation is one decibel per kilometer, such a cloud would produce a total attenuation of 10 decibels. This implies a tenfold reduction of the outgoing radar signal and another tenfold reduction of the reflected signal, which amounts to effective blackout.

The temperature of the fireball created by a nuclear explosion in the atmosphere is initially hundreds of thousands of degrees centigrade. It quickly cools by radiation to about 5,000 degrees C. Thereafter cooling is produced primarily by the cold air entrained by the fireball as it rises slowly through the atmosphere, a process that takes several minutes.

When air is heated to 5,000 degrees C., it is strongly ionized. To produce a radar attenuation of one decibel per kilometer at an altitude of 90 kilometers the fireball temperature need be only 3,000 degrees, and at 50 kilometers a temperature of 2,000 degrees will suffice. Ionization may be enhanced by the presence in the fireball of iron, uranium and other metals, which are normally present in the debris of nuclear explosion.

The size of the fireball can easily be estimated. Its diameter is about one kilometer for a one-megaton explosion at sea level. For other altitudes and yields there is a simple scaling law: the fireball diameter is equal to $(Y\rho_0/\rho)^{1/3}$, where Y is the yield in megatons. Thus a fireball one kilometer in diameter can be produced at an altitude of 30 kilometers (where $\rho_0/\rho = 100$) by an explosion of only 10 kilotons. At an altitude of 50 kilometers (where $\rho_0/\rho = 1{,}000$), a one-megaton explosion will produce a fireball 10 kilometers in diameter. At still higher altitudes matters become complicated because the density of the atmosphere falls off so sharply and the mechanism of heating the atmosphere changes. Nevertheless, fireballs of very large diameter can be expected when megaton weapons are exploded above 100 kilometers. These could well black out areas of the sky measured in thousands of square kilometers.

For explosions at very high altitudes (between 100 and 200 kilometers) other phenomena become significant. Collisions between electrons and air molecules are now unimportant. The condition for blackout is simply that there be more than $10^9$ electrons per cubic centimeter.

At the same time very little mass of air is available to cool the fireball. If the air is at first fully ionized by the explosion, the air molecules will be dissociated into atoms. The atomic ions combine very slowly with electrons. When the density is low enough, as it is at high altitude, the recombination can take place only by radiation. The radiative recombination constant (call it $C_R$) is about $10^{-12}$ cubic centimeter per second. When the initial electron density is well above $10^9$ per cubic centimeter, the number of electrons remaining after time $t$ is roughly equal to $1/C_R t$. Thus if the initial electron density is $10^{12}$ per cubic centimeter, the density will remain above $10^9$ for 1,000 seconds, or some 17 minutes. The conclusion is that nuclear explosions at very high altitude can produce long-lasting blackouts over large areas.

The second of the two mechanisms for producing an ionized cloud, the beta rays issuing from the radioactive debris of a nuclear explosion, can be even more effective than the fireball mechanism. If the debris is at high altitude, the beta rays will follow the lines of force in the earth's magnetic field, with about half of the beta rays going immediately down into the atmosphere and the other half traveling out into space before returning earthward. These beta rays have an average energy of about 500,000 electron volts, and when they strike the atmosphere, they ionize air molecules. Beta rays of average energy penetrate to an altitude of about 60 kilometers; some of the more energetic rays go down to about 50 kilometers. At these levels, then, a high-altitude explosion will give rise to sustained ionization as long as the debris of explosion stays in the vicinity.

One can show that blackout will occur if $y \times t^{-1.2} > 10^{-2}$, where $t$ is the time after the explosion in seconds and $y$ is the fission yield deposited per unit horizontal area of the debris cloud, measured in tons of TNT equivalent per square kilometer. The factor $t^{-1.2}$ expresses the rate of decay of the radio-active debris. If the attacker wishes to cause a blackout lasting five minutes ($t = 300$), he can achieve it with a debris level $y$ equal to 10 tons of fission yield per square kilometer. This could be attained by spreading one megaton of fission products over a circular area about 400 kilometers in diameter at an altitude of, say, 60 kilometers. Very little could be seen by an area-defense radar attempting to look out from under such a blackout disk. Whether or not such a disk could actually be produced is another question. Terminal defense would not, of course, be greatly disturbed by a beta ray blackout.

The foregoing discussion has concentrated mainly on the penetration aids that can be devised against an area-defense system. By this we do not mean to suggest that a terminal-defense system can be effective, and we certainly do not wish to imply that we favor the development and deployment of such a system.

Terminal defense has a vulnerability all its own. Since it defends only a small area, it can easily be bypassed. Suppose that the 20 largest American cities were provided with terminal defense. It would be easy for an enemy to attack the 21st largest city and as many other undefended cities as he chose. Although the population per target would be less than if the largest cities were attacked, casualties would still be heavy. Alternatively the offense could concentrate on just a few of the 20 largest cities and exhaust their supply of antimissile missiles, which could readily be done by the use of multiple warheads even without decoys.

It was pointed out by Charles M. Herzfeld in *The Bulletin of the Atomic Scientists* a few years ago that a judicious employment of ABM defenses could equalize the risks of living in cities of various sizes. Suppose New York, with a population of about 10 million, were defended well enough to require 50 enemy warheads to penetrate the defenses, plus a few more to destroy the city. If cities of 200,000 inhabitants were left undefended, it would be equally "attractive" for an enemy to attack New York and penetrate its defenses as to attack an undefended city.

Even if such a "logical" pattern of ABM defense were to be seriously proposed, it is hard to believe that people in the undefended cities would accept their statistical security. To satisfy everyone would require a terminal system of enormous extent. The highest cost estimate made in public discussions, $50 billion, cannot be far wrong.

Although such a massive system would afford some protection against the U.S.S.R.'s present armament, it is virtually certain that the Russians would react to the deployment of the system. It would be easy for them to increase the number of their offensive warheads and thereby raise the level of expected damage back to the one now estimated. In his recent forecast of defense needs for the next five years, Secretary McNamara estimated the relative cost of ABM defenses and the cost of countermeasures that the offense can take. He finds invariably that the offense, by spending considerably less money than the defense, can restore casualties and destruction to the original level before defenses were installed. Since the offense is likely to be "conservative," it is our belief that the actual casualty figures in a nuclear exchange, after both sides had deployed ABM systems and simultaneously increased offensive forces, would be worse than these estimates suggest.

Any such massive escalation of offensive and defensive armaments could hardly be accomplished in a democracy without strong social and psychological effects. The nation would think more of war, prepare more for war, hate the potential enemy and thereby make war more likely. The policy of both the U.S. and the U.S.S.R. in the past decade has been to reduce tensions to provide more understanding, and to devise weapon systems that make war less likely. It seems to us that this should remain our policy.

## 17 THE CASE FOR MISSILE DEFENSE
## Donald G. Brennan

In an important sense, the key issues in the debate about BMD are not technical. Within the community of people who have carried out the BMD development, certain estimates have been made as to the plausible range of technical and economic effectiveness of systems that can be achieved in the near future. These estimates are subject to some controversy, yet even if the uncertainty and controversy concerning these estimates were wholly removed, most of the articulate critics of BMD would remain critical: their objections are rooted in other concerns. Nevertheless, technical issues are vital to the debate, since most of the support for BMD deployment depends on the fact that a defense of substantial effectiveness is judged to be feasible.

The most common way of characterizing the effect of a BMD system is to estimate the number of lives it might save in various specified circumstances. In a table of such estimates given in McNamara's 1968 posture statement,[18] it was indicated that there could be 120 million American fatalities in certain possible wars of the mid-1970s if no significant BMD were deployed. Assuming opposing forces and attacks of the same strength, it was indicated that BMD systems costing from $10 to $20 billion could reduce American fatalities to between 10 and 40 million, depending on the level of the defense and the details of the war. Damage to production and transportation resources would, of course, be similarly reduced, a result that could not be achieved with economically feasible civil-defense shelter programs. Thus, such a defense might change the postwar situation from one in which over half the U.S. population was gone, and recovery in any time period would be problematical, to one in which perhaps 90 percent survived and economic recovery might be achieved within five to ten years. This difference would be enormous.

It is this possible difference that constitutes the major reason for deploying heavy defenses. In effect, procuring such defenses is like buying "insurance" that would limit the consequences of a war; the outcome would still be a disaster, but probably one of a very different order than would result from having the same offensive forces expended in a war with no missile defense.

It is possible that a BMD system might perform in an actual war much less well than expected, because of some unforeseen technical failure; it is, however, about equally likely that the opposing offensive forces will perform much less well than expected, which is to say that the defenses may perform much better than expected. (Critics of BMD are prone to emphasize the first of these points much more than the second.) . . .

It is worth noting that a BMD system may possibly have important effects even if it later failed to perform as expected in a war. If the Soviets were to react to a U.S. defense by fitting their existing missile force with decoys and other penetration aids, without a major increase in the number of rockets, they would reduce the total payload available for warheads, and thereby reduce the potential damage the U.S. might incur in a war even if the defense failed utterly. This effect, which is known in the trade as "virtual attrition" and is often encountered in defensive systems of other kinds, is likely to be quite modest. A more important possibility is that a U.S. defense would induce the Soviets to re-target their offensive force; they might concentrate most or all of their offensive missiles (apart from those used for missile bases or other military targets) on the largest cities to be sure of destroying them, and leave unattacked many medium and small cities. Or they might attack only undefended areas, and leave aside most or all of the largest (defended) cities. In either case, the mere presence of the defense could result in saving many millions of lives whether it "worked" or not.

There are three other positive reasons for favoring BMD deployment. First, the time may soon arrive, if it is not already here, when there will be some possibility of attacks of anonymous or disguised origin. Since these would not be subject to standard threats of deterrence, active defenses may be the primary protection against them. Second, the possibility of a purely accidental launch of some part of the Soviet force is probably very remote, but the possibility of an unauthorized launch, especially during an intense crisis, may not be so remote and should be protected against. Even a modest defense might be very effective against such an attack; this has been one of the arguments used — rightly, I believe — in support of the current Sentinel program. Third, missile defenses (even light defenses) would considerably complicate the planning of an attacker who hoped to penetrate them; this phenomenon seems likely to serve as an additional "firebreak" to the initiation of a strategic nuclear war.

III

One of the main areas of concern to critics of missile defense has to do with its impact on fundamentals of deterrence. The problem has often been related to what McNamara termed "Assured Destruction," defined by him in his 1968 posture statement as "an ability to inflict at all times and under all foreseeable conditions an unacceptable degree of damage upon any single aggressor, or combination of aggressors — even after absorbing a surprise attack." McNamara recognized that what constituted "an unacceptable degree of damage" was not subject to precise specification, and in spelling out this requirement, he said: "In the case of the Soviet Union, I would judge that a capability on our part to destroy, say, one-fifth to one-fourth of her population [*i.e.* about 50 million Russians] and one-half of her industrial capacity would serve as an effective deterrent."

Because McNamara came to regard the ability to destroy 50 million Russians as the keystone of Western security, he viewed Soviet deployment of BMD as a potential threat to that security, and intended to nullify any Soviet defenses with added U.S. offensive forces. He also appeared to believe, and frequently asserted, that the Soviets had a similar requirement for an Assured Destruction capacity, and that any U.S. interference with this requirement would in all likelihood only cause the Soviets to increase their offensive forces. It appears that this perception was at the core of McNamara's opposition to BMD deployment, as it was for many other opponents of missile defenses. The U.S. strategic posture that has evolved from this perception in recent years has been aptly dubbed "Assured Vulnerability" by Steuart Pittman.[19] . . .

It is clear from the origin of this perfectly reasonable logic that, to the extent the maximum possible Soviet motivation for such an attack might have been reduced, or to the extent the U.S. motivation to deter it might have been reduced, the scale of the retaliatory threat might have been reduced in some corresponding degree. It is this linkage that appears to have been wholly overlooked. Instead, we preferred to fix once and for all some intended level of Assured Destruction believed capable of deterring the Soviets from any actions whatever. There are a number of problems resulting from such a posture, of which the most immediate for our purposes is that it tends to make it difficult for us to limit damage to *ourselves*—*i.e.* it tends to force *us* into a posture of Assured Vulnerability.

In particular, a determination to maintain a strong capability for Assured Destruction led McNamara in 1967–68 to respond to incipient Soviet missile defenses by scheduling an increase in our offensive forces, and the theory that the Soviets would do likewise led him to oppose American deployment of an anti-Soviet BMD system. In view of the effectiveness of modern defense, we might better use the U.S. resources committed to increasing our offensive forces to increase our defenses instead. By thus reducing the Soviet threat, rather than increasing our own, we could reduce both the extent to which the Soviets might gain by attacking us, and the extent to which we are intensely motivated to deter the attack.

Consider a situation in which Soviet and American offensive forces are fixed at similar unchanging levels on each side, and in which both the United States and the Soviet Union are building comparable levels of defenses. If the American and Soviet defenses are both "light," then our BMD would not much diminish Soviet ability to destroy us, but then Soviet BMD would not much reduce the effectiveness of our assured-destruction forces either; if both American and Soviet defenses are "heavy," then our assured-destruction forces would be significantly degraded, but so too would the capability of the Soviets to eliminate the United States as a fighting society.

This points to the following formulation of a reasonable requirement for a conservative American strategic posture: Following any plausibly feasible strategic attack by the Soviet Union, the United States should have the capacity to inflict as much or more total damage (of similar kind) on the Soviet Union as the Soviets had inflicted and could still inflict on the United States. (This principle implies that the strategic offensive forces must be quite well protected, which appears to be feasible.) In short, we should have a reliable capability to do at least as badly unto the Soviets as they had done or could do unto us. The Soviets could not achieve a significant military advantage by a strategic attack, and an irrational, coercive or punitive attack—whether large or small—would risk bringing as much or more destruction on the Soviets as they could or did bring on us. This would make the initiation of nuclear blackmail unattractive to any reasonable decision-maker at any effective level of strategic forces. . . .

From the mid-1950s to the mid 1960s, the strategic postures of the superpowers were dominated by the logic that, since we could not defend, we had to deter. This position, for which there was originally ample justification, now seems to be interpreted in some minds—chiefly certain American ones to mean that, since we must deter, we cannot defend. This should count as the non sequitur of the decade.

## Notes

18. The main published sources of information for use in considering the prevailing technical estimates are the unclassified "posture statements" issued annually in recent years by the Secretary of Defense, especially those issued by McNamara in 1967 and 1968, although some supplementary information has been contained in Government hearings and speeches.

19. Steuart Pittman, former Assistant Secretary of Defense for Civil Defense, "Government and Civil Defense," in E.P. Wigner, ed., "Who Speaks for Civil Defense?" (New York: Scribners, 1968), p. 95.

## Suggestions for Further Reading

Ball, Desmond. *Politics and Force Levels: The Strategic Missile Program of the Kennedy Administration* (Berkeley, CA: U of California P, 1980). Examines the background of the Kennedy buildup.

Enthoven, Alain, and K. Wayne Smith. *How Much Is Enough? Shaping the Defense Program, 1961–1969* (New York: Harper Colophon, 1971). An account of the McNamara revolution in Pentagon planning and procurement by two of the main protagonists.

Greenwood, Ted. *Making the MIRV* (Cambridge, MA: Ballinger, 1975). The definitive treatment of the origins of this key weapon technology.

Kaufmann, William W. *The McNamara Strategy* (New York: Harper & Row, 1964). A highly readable account of Robert McNamara's early tenure as secretary of defense and of the man himself.

Schelling, Thomas C. *Arms and Influence* (New Haven, CT: Yale UP, 1966). Seminal work on nuclear deterrence, diplomacy, and arms race.

Seven

# ONE STEP FORWARD . . .

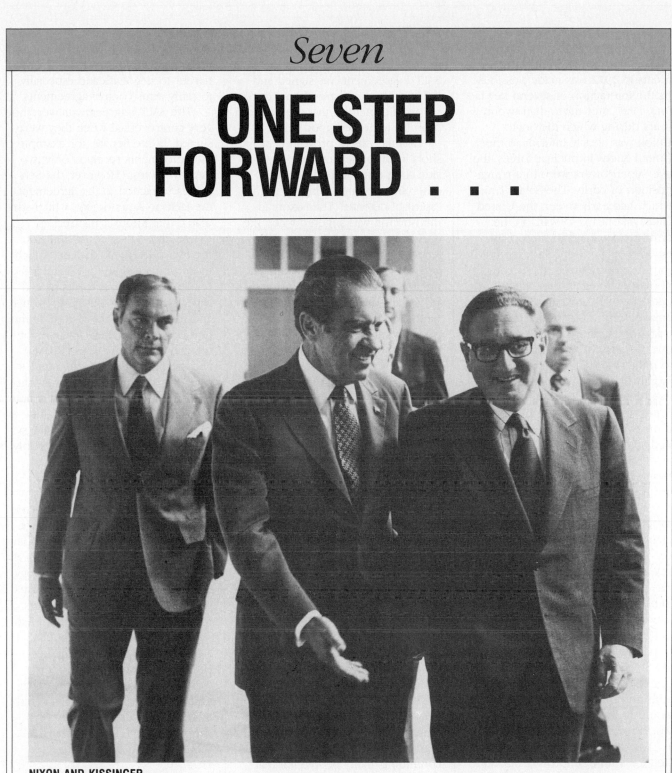

**NIXON AND KISSINGER**

U.S. President Richard Nixon talks with his national security adviser, Henry Kissinger. The Nixon administration (1969–1974) ushered in the "era of détente" and began major arms control negotiations with the Soviets, resulting in the first strategic arms limitation treaty. AP/Wide World Photos

# INTRODUCTION

The signing of the SALT I agreements in 1972 was made possible by the interaction of several key factors. First, after more than twenty years during which the Soviet Union was clearly inferior to the United States in nuclear forces, the two superpowers were in a rough position of parity. The Soviet Union, which had earlier seen the United States take leaps forward in the arms race, wanted to protect its newly won position. The Nixon administration realized that it could not hope to regain the strategic superiority that the United States had enjoyed in the past. On the contrary, the administration worried that, because of the public hostility to military spending stemming largely from the Vietnam War, it would be difficult for the United States to stay even with the Soviets if the Soviet buildup was not limited somehow.

In addition, Secretary of State Henry Kissinger, the dominant figure in the foreign policy of the Nixon and Ford administrations, adopted a new, less ideological foreign policy toward the Soviet Union. It culminated in détente. A key aspect of Kissinger's approach was to encourage the Soviet Union to become a part of a stable international system, instead of seeking to destabilize international affairs. In particular, Kissinger hoped that the Soviet Union would join the United States in limiting nuclear arms and that the Soviet Union would reduce its support for Third World revolutionary struggles.

The détente policy worked quite well for a time. Improved U.S.-Soviet relations made it easier for the two superpowers to negotiate arms control agreements and made it easier for the Nixon administration to win popular support for the agreements. The high point for détente and the high point for arms control in the Nixon-Ford administrations came in 1972 when the SALT I agreement was signed and the superpowers agreed on a declaration of principles that seemed to promise improved good relations.

Détente was to prove relatively short-lived for several reasons. Each side soon came to feel that the other side was not living up to the "spirit of détente." The Nixon administration was angered when the Soviets continued to oppose U.S. interests in the Third World. (Kissinger was especially upset with Soviet meddling in the Mideast during the 1973 war between Egypt and Israel.) The Soviet Union was angered when the U.S. Congress made improved economic relations dependent on greater freedom of emigration from the Soviet Union.

The most important reason for the decline of détente was that, although both sides shared certain common interests — most importantly arms control — other interests continued to be very different. The United States thought détente meant the Soviets would curb their activities in the Third World. The Soviet Union believed that having stabilized the strategic arms competition and secured formal recognition of its superpower status, it could now be even more active in the Third World.

As these conflicts of interest became clear, détente suffered. In the United States, détente had raised expectations very high. The statement "the cold war is over" appeared in many newspapers and journal articles. When it turned out that the U.S.-Soviet competition was continuing, many people felt that the Kissinger policy had turned out to be a one-way street, and there was a backlash against détente. For example, Ronald Reagan came very close to winning the Republican nomination for president in 1976 largely on the strength of antidétente feeling. The result of the détente backlash was to make it much harder to negotiate and especially to ratify arms control agreements.

The SALT I agreements were not very controversial when they were signed. In the Senate, for example, the agreements received only two negative votes. (However, the Senate also attached to the agreements the Jackson Amendment, which stipulated that future arms treaties would have to set equal limits on the two sides.) SALT II had a much more difficult time (see chapter 9).

The SALT I agreements placed severe restrictions on ABM systems and technology. They also froze the numbers of launchers for intercontinental ballistic missiles (ICBMs) and sea-launched ballistic missiles (SLBMs). The agreements were thus not disarmament treaties but arms control treaties. The most significant controls were on defensive systems, and the agreements probably prevented a defensive arms race. The limits on offensive systems were modest.

In fact, a key aspect of the offensive limits were what they did not cover — multiple independently targetable reentry vehicles (MIRVs). By failing to limit this new technology, SALT I allowed a new kind of arms race to go forward. The numbers of missiles, submarines, and bombers changed very little after SALT I. However, because each missile could be MIRVed, enabling it to carry more than one warhead, the number of nuclear weapons could increase. And that is exactly what happened. Each side deployed thousands of new weapons after 1972.

Critics of SALT I have based much of their hostility to the agreements on this fact. Conservative critics argue that SALT I did not stop the Soviet buildup. Liberal critics argue that SALT I did not stop the arms race because each side continued to add weapons. Defenders of

SALT I point out that the treaty was never meant to be a disarmament measure; it was an exercise in arms control. Defenders of SALT I argue that the arms race would have been much worse without the agreements. Both sides would have been competing in antiballistic missile (ABM) systems, and both sides would have had no limits on offensive weapons. (Defenders of SALT I note that U.S. military leaders were convinced that Soviet forces would have grown much more without SALT I than they did with the agreements.)

Finally, the two key systems associated with SALT I — MIRV, which SALT I did not limit, and ABM, which SALT I did — continued to play important roles in the nuclear age. Although the United States was ahead of the Soviet Union in MIRV technology, the Soviets eventually caught up. When they did they made their ICBMs powerful enough to threaten the survivability of U.S. ICBMs. This created a "window of vulnerability" which was to pose a major problem for the Carter and Reagan administrations. The ABM controversy lay dormant for a decade. It came back to life when President Reagan launched the Strategic Defense Initiative (SDI) in 1983.

# ARMS CONTROL AND DÉTENTE

## Military Cooperation Between Potential Enemies

### *Document 1*

Modern theories of arms control date from the early 1960s, when several key books on the subject appeared. One of the most influential of these was *Strategy and Arms Control* by defense analysts Thomas Schelling and Morton Halperin. In this selection from a new edition of the classic work, Schelling and Halperin present what has become the standard definition of arms control: "forms of military cooperation between potential enemies in the interest of reducing the likelihood of war, its scope and violence if it occurs, and the political and economic costs of being prepared for it." They also point out that arms control is based on potential enemies' common interest in avoiding war.

### 1 STRATEGY AND ARMS CONTROL
### Thomas Schelling and Morton Halperin

This study is an attempt to identify the meaning of arms control in the era of modern weapons, and its role in the pursuit of national and international security. It is not an advertisement for arms control; it is as concerned with problems and difficulties, qualifications and limitations, as it is with opportunities and promises. It is an effort to fit arms control into our foreign and military policy, and to demonstrate how naturally it fits rather than how novel it is.

This is, however, a sympathetic exploration of arms control. We believe that arms control is a promising, but still only dimly perceived, enlargement of the scope of our military strategy. It rests essentially on the recognition that our military relation with potential enemies is not one of pure conflict and opposition, but involves strong elements of mutual interest in the avoidance of a war that neither side wants, in minimizing the costs and risks of the arms competition, and in curtailing the scope and violence of war in the event it occurs.

Particularly in the modern era, the purpose of military force is not simply to win wars. It is the responsibility of military force to deter aggression, while avoiding the kind of threat that may provoke desperate, preventive, or irrational military action on the part of other countries. It is the responsibility of military policies and postures to avoid the false alarms and misunderstandings that might lead to a war that both sides would deplore.

In short, while a nation's military force opposes the military force of potentially hostile nations, it also must collaborate, implicitly if not explicitly, in avoiding the kinds of crises in which withdrawal is intolerable for both sides, in avoiding false alarms and mistaken intentions, and in providing — along with its deterrent threat of resistance or retaliation in the event of unacceptable challenges — reassurance that restraint on the part of potential enemies will be matched by restraint on our own. It is the responsibility of military policy to recognize that, just as our own military establishment is largely a response to the military force that confronts us, foreign military establishments are to some extent a response to our own, and there can be a mutual interest in inducing and reciprocating arms restraint.

We use the term "arms control" rather than "disarmament." Our intention is simply to broaden the term. We mean to include all the forms of military cooperation between potential enemies in the interest of reducing the likelihood of war, its scope and violence if it occurs, and the political and economic costs of being prepared for it. The essential feature of arms control is the recognition of the common interest, of the possibility of reciprocation and cooperation even between potential enemies with respect to their military establishments. Whether the most promising areas of arms control involve reductions in certain kinds of military force, increases in certain kinds of military force, qualitative changes in weaponry, different modes of deployment, or arrangements superimposed on existing military systems, we prefer to treat as an open question.

If both sides can profit from improved military communications, from more expensive military forces that are less prone to accident, from expensive redeployments that minimize the danger of misinterpretation and false alarm, arms control may cost more not less. It may by some criteria seem to involve more armament not less. If we succeed in reducing the danger of certain kinds of war, and reciprocally deny ourselves certain apparent military advantages (of the kind that cancel out for the most part if both sides take advantage of them), and if in so doing we increase our military requirements for other dangers of warfare, the matter must be judged on its merits and not simply according to whether the sizes of armies go up or down. If it appears that the danger of accidental war can be reduced by improved intelligence about each other's military doctrines and modes of deployment, or by the provision of superior communication between governments in the event of military crisis, these may have value independently of whether military forces increase, decrease, or are unaffected.

This approach is not in opposition to "disarmament" in the more literal sense, involving the straightforward notion of simple reductions in military force, military manpower, military budgets, aggregate explosive power, and so forth. It is intended rather to include such disarmament in a broader concept. We do not, however, share the notion, implicit in many pleas for disarmament, that a reduction in the level of military forces is necessarily desirable if only it is "inspectable" and that it necessarily makes war less likely. The reader will find that most of the present study is concerned less with reducing national *capabilities* for destruction in the event of war than in reducing the *incentives* that may lead to war or that may cause war to be the more destructive in the event it occurs. We are particularly concerned with those incentives that arise from the character of modern weapons and the expectations they create.

An important premise underlying the point of view of this study is that a main determinant of the likelihood of war is the nature of present military technology and present military expectations. We and the Soviets are to some extent trapped by our military technology. Weapon developments of the last fifteen years, especially of the last seven or eight, have themselves been responsible for some of the most alarming aspects of the present strategic situation. They have enhanced the advantage, in the event war should come, of being the one to start it, or of responding instantly and vigorously to evidence that war may have started. They have inhumanly compressed the time available to make the most terrible decisions. They have almost eliminated the expectation that a general war either could be or should be limited in scope or brought to a close by any process other than the sheer exhaustion of weapons on both sides. They have greatly reduced the confidence of either side that it can predict the weapons its enemy has or will have in the future. In these and other ways the evolution of military technology has exacerbated whatever propensities towards war are inherent in the political conflict between us and our potential enemies. And the greatly increased destructive power of weapons, while it may make both sides more cautious, may make the failure to control these propensities extremely costly.

Arms control can be thought of as an effort, by some kind of reciprocity or cooperation with our potential enemies, to minimize, to offset, to compensate or to deflate some of these characteristics of modern weapons and military expectations. In addition to what we can do unilaterally to improve our warning, to maintain close control over our forces, to make our forces more secure against attack, to avoid the need for precipitant decisions, to avoid accidents or the mistaken decisions that they might cause and to contain conflict once it starts, there may be opportunities to exchange facilities or understandings with our enemies, or to design and deploy our forces differently by agreement with our enemies who do likewise, in a way that enhances those aspects of technology that we like and that helps to nullify those that we do not.

We say this to anticipate the objection that armaments are only a reflection of existing conflicts and not a cause of them. It is true that modern armaments and military plans are a response to basic international conflicts. It is also true that the size and character of military forces are an important determinant of national fears and anxieties, and of the military incentives of our potential enemies. There is a feedback between our military forces and the conflicts that they simultaneously reflect and influence. We have no expectation that by working on weaponry alone, or military deployments or expectations, we can eliminate the political, economic and ideological differences that genuinely underlie present international antagonisms. We do believe that much can be done through careful design of our military strategy, or weaponry, our military deployments and doctrines, to reduce the military danger of those hostilities to our security. We believe that, in addition to what can be accomplished unilaterally in this regard, there are actions and restraints for which the inducements are greater on each side if the other side reciprocates or leads the way. And we believe that something in the way of rules, traditions, and clearer expectations about each other's reactions and modes of behavior may reduce the likelihood of military action based on mistake or misunderstanding.

What is striking is not how novel the methods and purposes of arms control are, and how different from the methods and purposes of national military policy; what is striking is how much overlap there is, There is hardly an objective of arms control to be described in this study that is not equally a continuing urgent objective of national military strategy — of our unilateral military plans and policies. What this study tries to do is to suggest those points at which these unilateral actions can be extended or supplemented through joint understandings with our potential enemies. In some cases the scope for such reciprocal action seems substantial, in other cases very modest; but in all cases it seems worth taking into consideration. Since this dimension of military policy has traditionally been so little appreciated, we have felt it worth while to indicate many areas in which arms control may possibly prove helpful, even if we cannot yet perceive just where the promise lies.

We have also considered arms control to include the less formal, less institutionalized, less "negotiated" understandings and agreements. Some may object that there is no "control" when both sides simply abstain from an action which, if done by one party, yields an advantage but if done by both parties cancels out the advantages and raises risks all around. Our resolution of this semantic problem is to interpret "control" to mean induced or reciprocated "self-control," whether the inducements include negotiated treaties or just informal understandings and reciprocated restraints.

In surveying the possible areas in which arms control may play a role, we have tried to err on the generous side, doubting whether we can yet perceive all of the forms that arms control may take and the areas in which it may occur. In our discussion of the negotiation and administration of concrete agreements, we have been concerned to identify the difficulties, in the belief that these must be anticipated if experiments at arms control are to avoid unnecessary disappointment or disaster.

We have not stated what we believe to be the "ultimate goal" of arms control — whether it be a world disarmed, a world policed by a single benevolent military force or a world in which some military "balance of prudence" has taken the fear out of the "balance of fear." We should, however, acknowledge that we do not believe the problems of war and peace and international conflict are susceptible of any once-for-all solution. Something like eternal vigilance and determination would be required to keep peace in the world at any stage of disarmament, even total disarmament. International conflict, and the military forces that are their reflection, are not in our judgment simply unnatural growths in human society which, once removed, need never recur. Conflict of interest is a social phenomenon unlikely to disappear, and potential recourse to violence and damage will always suggest itself if the conflict gets out of hand. Man's capability for self-destruction cannot be eradicated — he knows too much! Keeping that capability under control — providing incentives to minimize recourse to violence — is the eternal challenge.

This is the objective of responsible military policy. And a conscious adjustment of our military forces and policies to take account of those of our potential enemies, in the common interest of restraining violence, is what we mean by arms control.

In the study that follows we are concerned mainly with the direct relation of arms control to the military environment. Arms control can also affect, for good or ill, our political relations with allies, neutrals and potential enemies. It can reduce tension or hostilities; it can reduce vigilance. It can strengthen alliances, collapse them, or make them unnecessary. It can create confidence and trust or create suspicion and irritation. It can lead to greater world organization and the rule of law or discredit them. And it evidently lends itself to the short-run competiton in propaganda.

In focusing this book on the military environment we have not meant to depreciate the more purely political and psychological consequences. We have just not covered the whole subject. We do, however, incline to the view that the political and psychological benefits that may stem from arms control will be the more genuine, the more genuine is the direct contribution to international security. We doubt therefore whether the approach of this book is wholly inconsistent with an approach that emphasizes the political environment more and the military environment less.

## Modern Arms Control — A Brief History

### *Document 2*

Political scientist Donald Snow discusses the types of arms control agreements: arms freezes, arms reductions, and disarmament. He then reviews briefly the record of U.S.-Soviet arms control up to SALT I. Before 1963, most arms control proposals were little more than propaganda exercises designed by one superpower to make the other look bad. Serious arms control began in the 1960s and entered its golden age in the 1970s when détente was at its height.

## 2 ARMS CONTROL AND THE BALANCE

Donald M. Snow

### Types of Arms Control Agreements

There are basically three forms that agreements regulating levels of strategic arms may take. These are arms freezes, arms reductions, and disarmament. They vary greatly in terms of the severity of the consequences they impose on arsenal sizes and even characteristics; an arms freeze, for instance, does not alter arsenals much, if at all, whereas total disarmament does. At the same time, these agreements may vary inversely in terms of the incentives that states entering into them have to violate them, and thus in the burdens placed upon verification.

This latter point requires some explanation before we look at the individual types of agreement. One must start from the realization that no verification scheme is completely comprehensive and reliable. There will always be some at least incremental ability to cheat if the will and incentive to do so are present. This is partly true because of the vast areas the United States and Soviet Union occupy that must be monitored, and it is also true because the eighth corollary to Murphy's Law has truth: "Nothing is foolproof because fools are so ingenious."

If some cheating is always possible, then the question is: When does it make sense to cheat? There are, after all, two possible outcomes when one cheats: one can get caught or one can get away with it. Since the possibility of being caught and exposed is always possible, then it only makes sense to take the risk if there is some real gain to be accrued. That incentive varies considerably depending on the kind of agreement reached.

The simplest and most straightforward form of arms control agreement is an *arms freeze.* Under this kind of arrangement, both parties agree to halt (or freeze) the growth of their arsenals now or at some future time, normally in a manner that results in some sort of parity with which each feels comfortable.

This is the least difficult kind of agreement to reach (no arms control agreement is reached easily). There are two reasons for this comparative facility. The first is that a freeze does not require either side to give up anything, thereby making the agreement less threatening to supporters of particular systems and to those somewhat suspicious of arms control in the first place. The second is that verification requirements under a freeze are likely to be less stringent than under other forms. With arsenals at the size they currently are, a marginal ability to cheat and to accumulate an increment of weapons in excess of the agreed limits is hardly likely to provide much advantage to the violator. Hence, the incentives to cheat are at a comparative minimum.

The second form of agreement is *arms reduction.* Under this sort of scheme, the parties agree not only to quit building additional weapons, but to eliminate part of the arsenals they already possess. In general terms, there are two forms of arms reduction: "shallow cut" and "deep cut" reductions. As the names suggest, these vary in the proportions of the arsenals to be eliminated. A shallow cut calls for comparatively mild reductions, while deep cutting entails substantial reductions. There is no particular agreement about when a shallow cut becomes deep. An arsenal reduction in the order of 50 percent, such as was called for in the rough proposal by Gorbachev and counterproposal by Reagan on the eve of the 1985 summit, probably represents a reasonable dividing line.

Arms reductions are more difficult to negotiate than arms freezes, and deep-cut reductions are tougher to gain agreement on than shallow-cut arrangements. This is so because the relationships between arsenal sizes, cheating incentives, and verification requirements become an issue as one begins to envisage reducing arsenals. The bureaucratic problem that reduction requires giving up things one may not want to relinquish also becomes more important as the cuts become deeper. There is also the question whether cuts threaten real security.

As arsenal sizes are decreased, cheating incentives may increase, because the ability to calculate advantage from cheating rises. Say, for illustrative if arbitrary purposes, that it is always possible to hide 200 nuclear weapons launchers within any verification scheme. When arsenal sizes are around 2200–2400 launchers, as they would be under a freeze of current arsenals, such cheating would represent less than a 10 percent increment in capability and would hardly be worth the effort. In a shallow-cut arrangement such as SALT II, which proposed reductions to 2250 launchers apiece, or even in President Carter's 1977 proposal to reduce to 1800 apiece, the incentive is not that great.

A deep-cut reduction might alter that perception. If arsenals were drawn down by 60 percent, remaining forces would be in the range of 1000 launchers, in which case the ability to hide 200 would represent a 20 percent increase in capability; this might afford advantage.

As reductions occur, there are also bureaucratic difficulties. Those who have built arsenals and their components presumably have done so because they believed their actions enhanced the national defense. When one begins eliminating weapons, and especially if those reductions are profound, traumatic changes in arsenal sizes and characteristics will be resisted.

There is also the question whether arms reductions enhance security. Proponents of deep arsenal cuts generally base their arguments in the horrible destructive capacities of current arsenals and the need to reduce that destructive ability in case deterrence should fail. They are, in other words, attempting to reduce the deadliness of a potential nuclear war. But a question raised earlier must be answered: In the process, is the danger of war increased by this action? This question is particularly relevant in assessing the most stringent form of arms control, *nuclear disarmament.*

Disarmament, of course, refers to the total elimination of all nuclear weapons and is the most radical form of regulation (some would argue it is not even a form of arms control, since that term connotes some arms to be controlled). It is advocated on the basis that the only way to be truly free from the possibility of nuclear holocaust is by doing away entirely with this awful form of weaponry, whose very existence threatens man's survival.

Disarmament also faces the strongest opposition. One objection arises from the possibilities for cheating. In a world of no nuclear weapons (assuming disarmament could be adequately monitored), the ability to cheat at the level of our hypothetical 200 launchers could provide great advantage. Even if they could all be eliminated, the knowledge of how to build them could not, meaning that arsenals could always be reconstructed if the need seemed to arise.

One must also ask if security is enhanced by disarmament. At one level, the answer is clearly that it would, in that the danger of nuclear war would be eliminated. War should then be a considerably less deadly prospect.

But would nuclear disarmament make the world safe from conventional war instead? Would the danger of war in, say, Europe increase as its consequences diminished? This is an open question that cannot be answered definitively, because we lack direct evidence about the answer. It is, however, asked often by those who oppose disarmament, and proponents have not completely addressed it.

## The Evolution of Arms Control

Efforts to limit strategic nuclear armaments can usefully be divided into three periods. The first spans the period from the first American test and use of a nuclear device to the signing of the Limited Test Ban Treaty (LTBT) on August 5, 1963; it was a time when arms-control efforts were generally quite unsuccessful. The second period encompasses the afterglow of the LTBT up to the failure of the U.S. Senate to ratify the SALT II agreement and was a period when a fairly substantial number of agreements were concluded. The third period, beginning with the inauguration of Ronald Reagan and continuing to the present, has been marked by sporadic arms control activity and the absence of substantive agreements, at least to date.

### *The Early Period, 1945–1963*

The failure of arms control in the earliest period is attributable to several factors. It began with an American proposal, known as the Baruch plan — after its proposer, Bernard Baruch — to internationalize all atomic research and to place all atomic matters under an international agency. This proposal was rejected by the Soviet Union during the period of deteriorating Soviet-American relations in the late 1940s as a thinly veiled American attempt to impede Soviet research efforts to produce a nuclear bomb while the United States retained the expertise in that area. The period ended with the LTBT, the first major U.S.-USSR agreement on nuclear weapons. What changes occurred in the interim?

The first problem early on was that arms control was deemed to be antithetical to national security. On the one hand, atomic weapons were to play a major role in American defense against the Soviet menace, and anything that might interrupt the dynamic research effort in this direction met with great opposition in both the scientific and policy communities. On the other hand, many of the early arms control efforts called for disarmament rather than simple limitation, and the proponents of such schemes were looked upon as utopian dreamers by national security planners.

A second problem was that a large portion of the relevant scientific community was engaged in atomic research and did not want to see its efforts shackled. Certainly there were those who opposed the entire enterprise or parts of it. Development of the Super (the hydrogen bomb), for instance, met with considerable opposition on both scientific and policy grounds from prominent scientists such as Robert Oppenheimer and David Lilienthal, but a coalition of policymakers and atomic scientists (aided in their arguments by the success of Soviet atomic bomb research) was powerful enough to overcome such objections.

There was also a verification problem. In an era before the first manmade satellites had been lofted into orbit, the ability to monitor compliance was very limited. The only available means were espionage (so-called human intelligence), remote sensing (which by contemporary standards was very primitive), and overflight. As mentioned earlier, President Eisenhower proposed his "open skies" idea to allow overflight as a means of monitoring in 1955, and it was rejected out of hand by the Soviet Union. Some aerial reconnaissance was conducted by high-flying U-2 aircraft in the late 1950s, but that practice came to a screeching halt when the Soviets shot down and captured U-2 pilot Francis Gary Powers early in 1960.

A fourth and related problem was the general tenor of U.S.-Soviet relations during this period. Especially in the 1940s and well into the 1950s, the Cold War was at its peak. The competition between the superpowers was viewed as increasingly intractable and pervasive, with no room for compromise or cooperation. In that atmosphere, breaking out of the prisoner's dilemma on the basis of trust was simply impossible.

By the end of the period, things had changed substantially enough to allow an agreement. Although it was not universally embraced, the Limited Test Ban Treaty, which banned the testing of nuclear weapons in the atmosphere, was not viewed as a major threat to national security. It was not a disarmament scheme, and thus did not meet that form of objection. Instead, it was argued that it would enhance security by making it more difficult for countries that did not already possess the bomb to conduct the testing necessary to develop nuclear capability. This argument appealed to both the United States and the Soviet Union.

The balance of opinion within the scholarly and military policy community was also not in great opposition. By 1963, a great deal more was known about the harmful effects of radiation than had earlier been the case (as a gruesome example, the way radiation levels after tests were measured in the early 1950s was to send unprotected soldiers with Geiger counters into the blast zone). Public opinion in the United States and abroad (especially in Japan, which was downwind from Soviet tests) was turning solidly against atmospheric testing, making the ban quite popular. As an indication of public concern, weather reports regularly carried radiation levels, in much the same way that the air quality index is reported now.

The policy-making and atomic science community were also much less opposed than had previously been the case. During the intervening period, the atomic scientists had learned a great deal more from above-ground testing, so that both the Soviets and Americans could conduct future tests underground without much loss of knowledge. (In a bit of irony, one thing about which not much had been learned was the climatological effects of detonations — the basis of the nuclear winter. No one thought to keep such records at the time.)

The treaty was also easily verifiable. The first satellites with photographic capability had been launched in 1961, allowing verification by national-technical means. In addition, changes in local or global radiation levels would reveal if anyone was testing in the atmosphere and who the culprit might be. The treaty was thus verifiable by nonintrusive means, so that the Soviets could not object and the Americans could feel confident of compliance.

Finally, Soviet-American relations had changed. They began to improve during the Eisenhower administration, which witnessed the beginnings of "summit diplomacy" (meetings between the president and the Soviet leader), the visit of Nikita Khrushchev to the United States, and cultural and athletic exchanges.

From the standpoint of arms control, the most important change in atmosphere was the result of a traumatic event, the Cuban missile crisis. While that confrontation was important for a variety of reasons, it had special significance in the area of strategic arms. During the nuclear missile-rattling that went on over the removal of Soviet offensive missiles from Cuba, the United States and the USSR came closer to nuclear war than they ever had before (and some would argue since), and the experience was profoundly sobering. One particularly important realization was the horrible prospect of possible nuclear war, and hence that the two superpowers had a common and compelling interest in its avoidance. At least in this one area, American and Soviet interests coincided, and the result was a period of cooperation in strategic arms limitation.

### *The "Golden Age" (1963–1979)*

The second period of arms control followed from the success of the LTBT. It was a period of improved U.S.-Soviet relations generally, in which arms control served as the centerpiece of the phenomenon known in the United States as detente. The heart of the process became the Strategic Arms Limitation Talks (SALT), which occupied center stage for nearly a decade.

Buoyed by the realization that cooperation in avoiding nuclear confrontation was both possible and certainly in the national interests of both countries, a number of agreements supplementing the LTBT were quickly negotiated. As a British commentator said with typical understatement, "There followed a spate of agreements not to do things that nobody would want to do anyhow; not to plant nuclear weapons on the seabed, not to use nuclear weapons in an accidental or unauthorized way, not to militarize the moon, not to put nuclear weapons into orbit round the earth, not to introduce nuclear weapons into Latin America." Of these, the one with the most enduring interest is the Outer Space Treaty of 1967, because its prohibition against stationing "nuclear or other weapons of mass destruction" in space is a point of contention with regard to the Strategic Defense Initiative.

There were two initiatives of major significance during the period. One, of course, was SALT, which will be discussed below. The other was the negotiation leading to the Nuclear Nonproliferation Treaty (NPT). This is significant because it shows how and when the Soviets and Americans can agree on things — but also for its singular ineffectiveness.

The dynamic underlying NPT was the desire to avoid the spread of nuclear weapons to states that did not already possess them. This is an aim shared by the superpowers and everyone else who already has these weapons. The logic in this desire is that no state that does not have nuclear weapons can use them; but the more states that have the bomb, the more likely nuclear war is to occur.

Given this interest, the U.S. and the USSR jointly

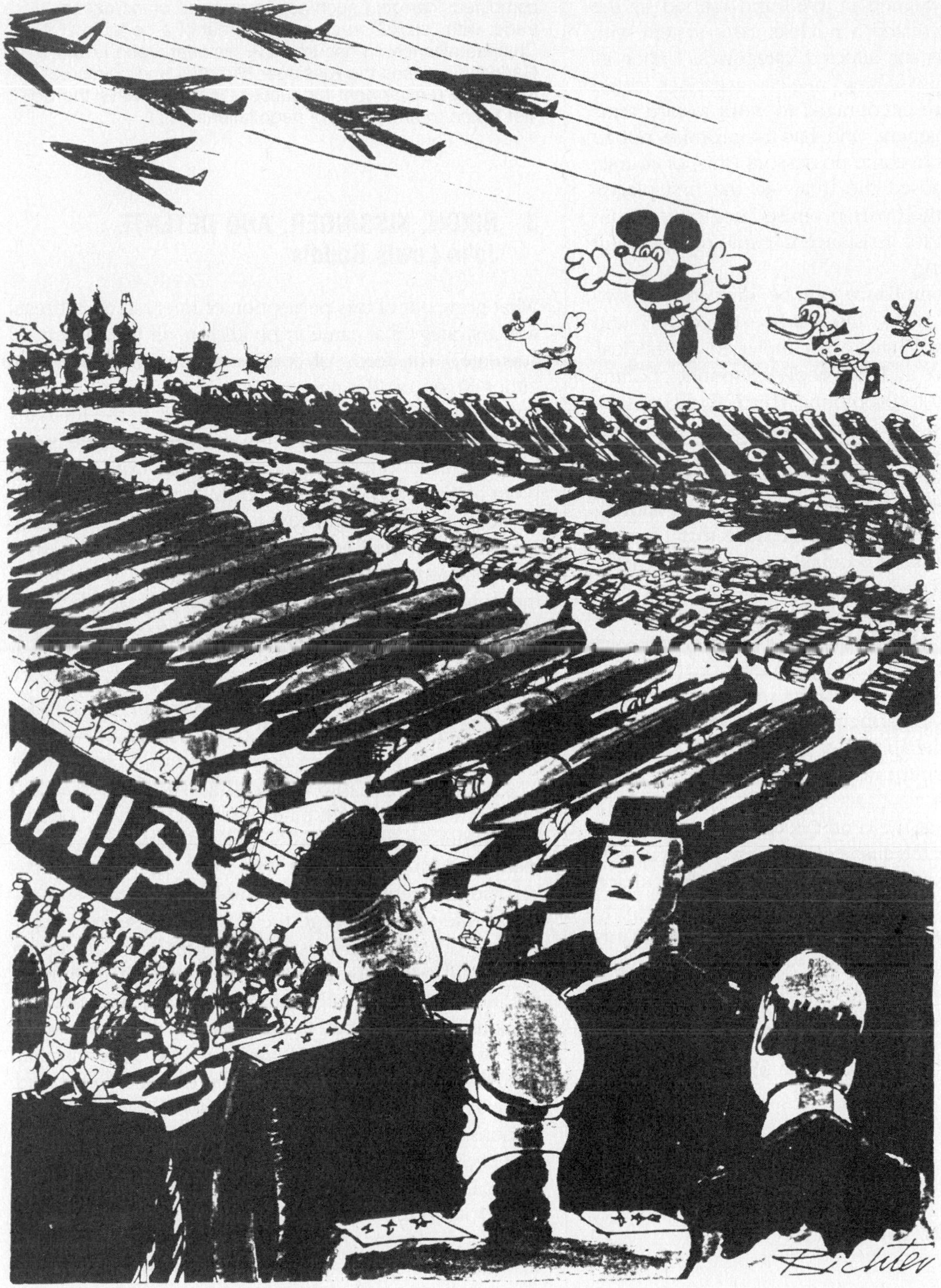


"Détente."

Drawing by Richter, © 1974 The New Yorker Magazine

proposed the NPT. Signed in 1968 and ratified by the Senate in 1970, it created a nuclear caste system with different obligations for affected categories. Under its provisions, states possessing nuclear weapons could keep them, but were encouraged to work toward arms control and disarmament, and had to promise not to help nonpossessors become possessors (this, of course, was why they proposed the treaty in the first place). Nonpossessors, for their part, promised not to try to gain the bomb, in return for assistance in exploiting peaceful uses of nuclear energy.

Reaction and compliance can be divided into two basic categories of states, those who signed NPT and those who declined. Signatories included all nuclear powers except France and the People's Republic of China (at the time wedded to promoting Third World causes), the states that could physically build nuclear weapons but that had decided not to (e.g., Japan, West Germany, Sweden), and those who had no earthly prospect of ever being able to build them (e.g., Mali). The more troubling category was the nonsignatories, because that list contained almost all the states normally designated as prime candidates to produce nuclear weapons (e.g., India, Pakistan, South Africa, Israel, Argentina, Brazil).

The NPT, in effect, bound all those who did not need binding and placed no shackles whatsoever on those who needed restraining. That was not its intent, of course; it had been designed to further joint American-Soviet interests in avoiding the spread of weapons that might be used to draw the superpowers inexorably if reluctantly into a war.

SALT, however, was the centerpiece. The negotiations began in 1969 under the auspices of a newly inaugurated President Richard Nixon (they were supposed to have begun in 1968 as the capstone of Lyndon Johnson's presidency, but were postponed because of the Soviet invasion of Czechoslovakia). In 1972, the discussions produced a series of agreements cumulatively known as SALT I, followed by an interim second step signed by Brezhnev and President Ford at Vladivostok in 1974, and culminating in the ill-fated SALT II in 1979.

## The Kissinger Blueprint

### *Document 3*

Henry Kissinger, the dominant figure in creating the foreign policy of the Nixon and Ford administrations, wanted to move U.S.-Soviet relations beyond the cold war. He hoped to change the Soviet concept of international relations so that the Soviets would join the United States in promoting a stable world order. To do so, he followed a policy that combined "carrots," such as the promise of increased trade, with "sticks," such as the threat of a de facto U.S.-Chinese alliance. In document 3, historian John Lewis Gaddis discusses the Kissinger blueprint and points out that a key requirement for success was to involve the Soviet Union in arms control negotiations.

### 3 NIXON, KISSINGER, AND DÉTENTE
### John Lewis Gaddis

What grew out of this perception of interests and threats was a strategy that came to be known, all too loosely, as "détente." The term, of course, did not originate with either Nixon or Kissinger — Kennedy had used it to describe the process of relaxing tensions with the Russians as early as 1963.[1] Nor did the word convey the same meaning in all quarters — it was French, critics liked to point out, and had no precise equivalent in either English or Russian.* Nixon and Kissinger were clear about the meaning they attached to "détente," though: they viewed it as yet another in a long series of attempts to "contain" the power and influence of the Soviet Union,[2] but one based on a new combination of pressures and inducements that would, if successful, convince the Russians that it was in their own best interests to be "contained." The goal, as had been the case with Kennan two decades earlier, was nothing less than to change the Soviet Union's concept of international relations, to integrate it as a stable element into the existing world order, and to build on the resulting equilibrium a "structure of peace" that would end once and for all that persistent abnormality known as the "Cold War."

The first requirement for implementing the strategy of détente was to engage the Russians in serious negotiations on substantive issues. Negotiations had always been held out as the ultimate objective of containment: the idea since 1950 had been that once the West reached a "situation of strength" with respect to the Russians, they would be willing to talk, and the crisis that had produced the Cold War would have come to an end. Kissinger thought this reasoning specious for several reasons. First, he had long insisted that no nation could be expected to accommodate itself willingly to an international order that left it in a permanent position of inferiority. The Russians had no business demanding absolute security for themselves at the price of absolute insecurity for everyone else, but the West had no right to do that either: "stability depends on the relative satisfaction and therefore also the relative dissatisfaction of

* "Détente" in French means "calm, relaxation, easing," but it can also mean the trigger of a gun. The closest Russian equivalent is "razriadka," which means a "lessening," or "reduction," or "relaxation," but also "discharging" or "unloading."

the various states."[3]* Second, the West in fact had never been more powerful vis-a-vis the Russians than in the early days of the Cold War: postponing negotiations until some mythical position of "strength" had been reached had only allowed Moscow the opportunity to build actual strength — as it had now done. Finally, negotiations were not, in themselves, a sign of weakness. Properly managed, with a view to the identification of common interests as well as the frank recognition of irreconcilable antagonisms, they could become the primary means of *building* a stable world order, not simply a luxury to be enjoyed once stability had been achieved.[4]

These negotiations should be conducted, Kissinger insisted, without illusions. "We will deal with the Communist countries on the basis of a precise understanding of what they are about in the world, and then of what we can reasonably expect of them and ourselves." Ideological differences should not be obscured for the purpose of reaching superficial agreements, but neither should negotiations become a forum for Cold War invective. Nor should the course of negotiations be dictated by the pressures for "success" that had so often, in the past, raised and then dashed Western expectations regarding "summitry." Careful and deliberate preparation was vital: "we will not become psychologically dependent on rapid or extravagant progress." Above all, negotiations, and the agreements they produced, would have to offer solid mutual benefits if they were to have lasting effects: "We must be mature enough to recognize that to be stable a relationship must provide advantages to both sides, and that the most constructive international relationships are those in which both parties perceive an element of gain. . . . The balance cannot be struck on each issue every day, but only over the whole range of relations and over a period of time."[5]

But what prospect was there that the Russians would be willing to negotiate on this basis? The Soviet Union, Kissinger argued, had reached a crucial turning point in its own affairs: there were "ambiguous tendencies" that could lead Moscow into either cooperation or further confrontation with the West. These included: (1) rivalries within the international communist movement that intensified pressures to compete for the "mantle of militancy" in Asia, but at the same time relaxed inhibitions about dealing with the United States and forced the Soviet Union to reassess its own security concerns; (2) the achievement of Soviet strategic parity, which doubtless tempted Kremlin leaders to press on for superiority but at the same time freed them from their fear of inferiority and thus made possible, for the first time, serious negotiations on arms control; (3) the expansion of Soviet military and economic power into the Third World, which meant a growth of Moscow's influence but at the same time a new interest in controlling crises there; and (4) the emergence, inside the Soviet Union, of a mature industrial economy, which could serve as the base for a major arms buildup but at the same time might make feasible a consumer-oriented society, integrated with and to an extent dependent on the industrialized West. American objectives in these circumstances were simple, Kissinger argued: to try to reinforce those "tendencies" inclined in the direction of accommodation, and to discourage those that were not.[6]

Kissinger's approach here resembled, as did so many other elements of his strategy, what Kennan had been trying to do in the late 1940's. Kennan, it will be recalled, had compared Soviet power to a growing tree: it was possible to channel its energies in certain directions, but only by a combination of external pressures and inducements, steadily but selectively applied. Abrupt or extreme constraints would not work. The idea had been to convince the Russians that their own best interests lay in exhibiting restraint: "If . . . situations can be created in which it is clearly not to the advantage of their power to emphasize the elements of conflict in their relations with the outside world, then their actions, and even the tenor of their propaganda to their own people, *can* be modified."[7] Kissinger's technique of identifying "ambiguous tendencies" within the Soviet system, and then attempting to strengthen those that were positive and deter those that were not, was very much in the same tradition: it was, like Kennan's, an exercise in behavior modification, based on the application of appropriate punishments and rewards, designed, simultaneously, to prod and cajole a heretofore "revolutionary" state into accepting the "legitimacy" of the existing international order.*

* "Could a power achieve all its wishes," Kissinger had written in 1957, "it would strive for absolute security, a world-order free from the consciousness of foreign danger and where all problems have the manageability of domestic issues. But since absolute security for one power means absolute insecurity for all others, it is never obtainable as a part of a legitimate settlement, and can be achieved only through conquest.

"For this reason an international settlement which is accepted and not imposed will always appear *somewhat* unjust to any one of its components. Paradoxically, the generality of this dissatisfaction is a condition of stability, because were any one power *totally* satisfied, all others would have to be *totally* dissatisfied and a revolutionary situation would ensue. The foundation of a stable order is the *relative* security — and therefore the *relative* insecurity — of its members." (*A World Restored,* pp. 144–45.)

* " 'Legitimacy' as here used should not be confused with justice. It means no more than an international agreement about the nature of workable arrangements and about the permissible aims and methods of foreign policy. It implies the acceptance of the framework of the international order by all major powers, at least to the extent that no state is so dissatisfied that, like Germany after the Treaty of Versailles, it expresses its dissatisfaction in a revolutionary foreign policy. . . . [T]he distinguishing feature of a revolutionary power is not that it feels threatened — such feeling is inherent in the nature of international relations based on sovereign states — but that nothing can reassure it. Only absolute security — the neutralization of the opponent — is considered a sufficient guarantee, and thus the desire of one power for absolute security means absolute insecurity for all the others." (Kissinger, *A World Restored,* pp. 1–2.)

Success in this endeavor did not, anymore for Kissinger than for Kennan, require changing the internal nature of the Soviet regime. Encrustations of history and ideology were too deep: "we cannot demand," Kissinger argued, "that the Soviet Union, in effect, suddenly reverse five decades of Soviet, and centuries of Russian, history." Efforts should go, rather, toward changing Moscow's approach to the outside world, toward convincing Soviet leaders that it was in their own interest to stress cooperation over confrontation in their dealings with the West. At the same time, though, the U.S.S.R. was not immune to internal pressures for change: "Changes in Soviet society have already occurred, and more will come." Such trends would be more likely to develop, Kissinger pointed out, in an atmosphere of détente: "A renewal of the Cold War will hardly encourage the Soviet Union to . . . adopt a more benevolent attitude toward dissent."[8] Internal change, then, should not be made a condition for negotiations, but it was itself a condition that might well evolve from them.

A second and related element in the strategy of détente was the concept of "linkage." Attempts to modify Soviet behavior would not succeed, Kissinger believed, if negotiations were allowed to proceed in separate compartments, with progress in one unaffected by difficulties in another. "I am convinced that the great issues are fundamentally inter-related," he wrote, in a letter prepared for Nixon's signature in February 1969:

> I recognize that the previous Administration took the view that when we perceive a mutual interest on an issue with the USSR, we should pursue agreement and attempt to insulate it as much as possible from the ups and downs of conflicts elsewhere. This may well be sound on numerous bilateral and practical matters such as cultural or scientific exchanges. But, on the crucial issues of our day, I believe we must seek to advance on a front at least broad enough to make clear that we see some relationship between political and military issues. I believe that the Soviet leaders should be brought to understand that they cannot expect to reap the benefits of cooperation in one area while seeking to take advantage of tension or confrontation elsewhere.

The Russians themselves saw "ambiguous tendencies" in American policy, Kissinger reminded Nixon: they were unsure whether "reasonable" or "adventurous" forces would prevail within the new administration, and were seeking to use the prospect of negotiations to encourage the former and discourage the latter. What the United States had to do was to "utilize this Soviet interest, stemming as I think it does from anxiety, to induce them to come to grips with the real sources of tension, notably in the Middle East, but also in Vietnam." The basic issue, as Kissinger later put it, was "whether we will use them or they will use us."[9]

The trick was to seize the initiative, and this Nixon and Kissinger quickly sought to do. They began with an estimate of Russian priorities: a strategic arms agreement that would freeze Western but not Soviet weapons systems at existing levels; a relaxation of trade barriers that would permit badly needed imports of Western food and technology, together with the credits to pay for them; the stability, even respectability, that would come from Western recognition, once and for all, of the post-World War II boundaries in Eastern Europe; and opportunities to advance Soviet interests in the Third World without risking war. Against these, they balanced American priorities: a negotiated settlement of the Vietnam War that would not result in humiliation; an acknowledgment by the Russians of permanent Western rights in Berlin; a strategic arms agreement that would limit the continuing Soviet military buildup; and some means of managing Third World crises so that they would neither get out of hand nor further Moscow's designs. They then made it clear that negotiations were interlocked: progress toward satisfying Soviet priorities could not come without equivalent progress, across the board, in satisfying those set by the United States.[10]

The Russians did not take easily to this procedure. Their preferred approach was compartmentalization: issues should be treated as discrete units, with cooperation in one field taking place independently of such competition as might exist in others.[11] To get them to accept the concept of "linkage." Nixon and Kissinger had to feign relative disinterest in reaching agreements: they sought constantly to convince Kremlin leaders that they needed negotiations more than the United States did. Nixon thus delayed, for several months, beginning strategic arms talks the Johnson administration had already agreed to in principle. There was, again in contrast to Johnson, no rush to the summit; instead the administration insisted on detailed and deliberate preparation, with virtual guarantees of success assured in advance. Nixon and Kissinger were not above even holding the summit "hostage" to the satisfaction of other priorities. In December 1971, for example, Kissinger openly threatened to cancel it unless the Russians prevailed on their ally, India, not to invade West Pakistan. And in May 1972, two weeks before he was to meet with Brezhnev for the first time, Nixon in response to a North Vietnamese offensive ordered the mining of Haiphong harbor, despite the incorrect expectation of most of his advisers, Kissinger included, that such a move would kill the summit.[12]

"Linkage" could work in several different ways. It could be used as a tool of crisis management, as in the India-Pakistan War or during the hectic month of September 1970, when the administration headed off both a Soviet attempt to build a submarine base in Cuba and a Syrian invasion of Jordan by warning Moscow that such actions could torpedo détente. It could be used to create bargaining chips in direct talks with the Russians: there would be no strategic arms agreement or recognition of boundaries in Eastern Europe, Kissinger made it clear, without a permanent settlement of the Berlin issue. It could be used to induce third parties to negotiate: a major function of "linkage" was to secure Soviet cooperation in ending the Vietnam War by holding back on SALT and the relaxation of trade barriers until Moscow had put pressure on Hanoi to moderate its requirements for a cease-fire. It could even be used, more subtly, to make the U.S.S.R. economically dependent on the West: "Over time," Kissinger suggested, "trade and investment may leaven the autarkic tendencies of the Soviet system, invite gradual association of the Soviet economy with the world economy, and foster a degree of interdependence that adds an element of stability to the political equation."[13]

All of this tied in with Kissinger's "behavior modification" strategy: "linkage" provided the means by which both positive and negative reinforcement would take place. But "linkage" was, for Kissinger, more than just a negotiating instrument. It reflected as well the reality that, however diffuse and multidimensional power had become in the more relaxed international environment of the 1970's, its elements still affected one another; interests and threats, however capable of differentiation or specification, still did not exist in discrete vacuums.

> Displays of American impotence in one part of the world would inevitably erode our credibility in other parts of the world. . . . Our posture in arms control negotiations could not be separated from the resulting military balance, nor from our responsibilities as the major military power of a global system of alliances. By the same token, arms limitation could almost certainly not survive in a period of growing international tensions. We saw linkage, in short, as synonymous with an overall strategic and geopolitical view.

There was little recognition of this within the bureaucracy, which, compartmentalized itself, tended to look at the world in compartmentalized terms. "Linkage" served, then, as a means of imposing conceptual order on American policy as well as a device for moving Soviet policy in desirable directions. It was, Kissinger recalled, "another of the attempts of the new Administration to free our foreign policy from oscillations between overextension and isolation and to ground it in a firm conception of the national interest."[14]

There was yet another form of "linkage," one important enough to merit consideration as a third distinctive element in the Nixon-Kissinger strategy: this was the effort to establish links between the United States and the Soviet Union's chief rival in the communist world, as a means of putting further pressure on Moscow. The idea, in principle, was not new: Kennan had advocated exploiting fissures within the communist bloc as early as 1948, and that had been consistently done in relations with Yugoslavia ever since. But the main rivalry within the communist world, that between the Soviet Union and the People's Republic of China, had flourished openly for more than a decade without any significant American attempt to take advantage of it. The problem had been that relations with Peking were, if anything, worse than with Moscow: bitterness over China's role in the Korean War still rankled, as did Peking's sympathy for, and aid to, North Vietnam. Considerations of domestic politics made any thought of withdrawing support from Nationalist China imprudent, if not unthinkable; furthermore, China during the mid-1960's seemed determined to cut itself off from the rest of the world as a by-product of Mao Tse-Tung's quixotic quest for an institutionalized revolution. Accordingly, little had been done to exploit the Sino-Soviet split at the time the Nixon administration took office.

During the late 1960s, both Nixon and Kissinger had reached the conclusion that it would not be wise to leave China permanently isolated. "Taking the long view," Nixon had written in 1967, "we simply cannot afford to leave China forever outside the family of nations, there to nurture its fantasies, cherish its hates and threaten its neighbors." But before the world could change its attitude toward China, that country would have to change its attitude toward the world: China could be pulled back into the international community only "as a great and progressing nation, not as the epicenter of world revolution." Kissinger, writing a year earlier, had argued that such a change might in fact be possible: despite China's ostentatious ideological militancy, its leaders had not yet become dependent on their own bureaucracies, and hence might have greater flexibility in changing their policies than their counterparts in the Soviet Union.[15] In a speech written for Nelson Rockefeller during the 1968 campaign, Kissinger had advocated learning "to deal imaginatively with several competing centers of Communist power. . . . In a subtle triangle of relations between Washington, Peking, and Moscow, we improve the possibilities of accommodations with each as we increase our options with both." Still, the Nixon administration did not have, upon taking power, any specific plan for a reconciliation with Peking, or any indication that such an initiative, if offered, would be reciprocated.[16]*

What focused attention on the problem was the outbreak of fighting between Russian and Chinese forces along the Ussuri River in March 1969, followed by dis-

*Nixon did authorize Kissinger, on February 1, 1969, to "plant" the idea with East European sources that the United States was "exploring" a rapprochement with China. "The maneuver," Kissinger recalls," was intended to disquiet the Soviets, and almost certainly — given Nixon's preoccupations — to provide an incentive for them to help us end the war in Vietnam." (*White House Years,* p. 169.)

creet Soviet inquiries as to what the American response would be if the Kremlin should authorize a pre-emptive attack against Chinese nuclear facilities.[17] Only five years before, on the eve of China's first nuclear test, the Johnson administration had considered the possibility of joint Soviet-American military action against that country,[18] but now the Nixon administration took a wholly different tack. Acting in line with Kissinger's theory that it was better in a triangular relationship to side with the weaker instead of the stronger antagonist, Nixon told an incredulous cabinet on August 14 that the United States could not allow China to be defeated in a Sino-Soviet war. "The worst thing that could happen for us would be for the Soviet Union to gobble up Red China," he explained several days later. "We can't let it happen. . . . We're not doing this because we love the Chinese. We just have to see to it that the U.S. plays both sides."[19]

This was a remarkable position to take, well before diplomatic contacts of consequence had begun with the Chinese, well before Washington knew how Peking would react. It reflected the assumption, consistent with the Nixon administration's revised assessment of interests and threats, that American security required maintenance of a world balance of power, that China was a crucial element in that balance, and that therefore the United States had a stake in China's survival, regardless of what kind of regime was in charge there. The point was as much to make Moscow *think* that a Sino-American rapprochement was underway as to achieve one: as Kissinger wrote Nixon after a conversation with a worried Soviet Ambassador Anatolii Dobrynin, "there is no advantage in giving the Soviets excessive reassurance."[20]

In fact, though, the Chinese — themselves adept at triangular politics — did respond, and two-and-a-half years later, Nixon found himself reciting Mao Tse-tung's poetry in the Great Hall of the People in Peking. Kissinger repeatedly insisted that the new Sino-American relationship was in no way directed against Moscow: this, he later acknowledged, was "the conventional pacifier of diplomacy by which the target of a maneuver is given a formal reassurance intended to unnerve as much as to calm, and which would defeat its purpose if it were actually believed." At the same time, though, he stressed with equal fervor the need to avoid giving the Chinese a veto over American relations with the Soviet Union: "we were not willing to foreclose the option of a genuine easing of tensions with Moscow if that in time could be achieved." The idea was to walk a fine line: to refrain from tempting either side into retaliation or blackmail by giving it the impression that the United States was "using" it against the other. "The hostility between China and the Soviet Union served our purposes best if we maintained closer relations with each side than they did with each other. The rest could be left to the dynamic of events."[21]

It is difficult to think of anything the Nixon administration could have done that would have produced a more dramatic shift in world power relationships of greater benefit to the United States at less cost. For the first time since the Korean War, it was Russians, and not Americans, who faced rivals more determined to contain them than to contain each other. As a consequence, Nixon and Kissinger had been able, even before formally consummating the new Sino-American relationship, to abandon the old "two-and-a-half war" standard used since the Kennedy administration to calculate conventional force requirements.* "I believe that a simultaneous Warsaw Pact attack in Europe and a Chinese conventional attack in Asia is unlikely," Kissinger had written to Nixon as early as October 1969. "In any event, I do not believe such a simultaneous attack could or should be met with ground forces." Accordingly, he recommended, and Nixon accepted, reliance henceforth on a "one-and-a-half war" standard — conventional forces capable of meeting major aggression in Europe or Asia, but not in both at the same time.[22] Triangular politics had made possible progress toward John Foster Dulles's old goal of maximum deterrence at minimum cost — not by threatening escalation, though, but through the simple approach, made feasible by the triumph of geopolitics over ideology, of reducing the number of adversaries to be deterred.

This reduction in adversaries, in turn, made possible a fourth key element in the Nixon-Kissinger strategy: a phasing down of American commitments in the world, formally expressed in what came to be known as the Nixon Doctrine.† Delivered first to an informal press briefing on Guam in July 1969, the Nixon Doctrine, as later refined by the White House, consisted of three propositions:

> First, the United States will keep all of its treaty commitments.
>
> Second, we shall provide a shield if a nuclear power threatens the freedom of a nation allied with us or of a nation whose survival we consider vital to our security.
>
> Third, in cases involving other types of aggression, we shall furnish military and economic assistance when requested in accordance with our treaty commitments. But we shall look to the nation directly threatened to assume the primary responsibility of providing the manpower for its defense.

* Public announcement of the "one-and-a-half war" standard apparently played a major role, in turn, in convincing Peking that the Nixon administration was serious about wanting an improvement in relations with China. (See Kissinger, *White House Years,* pp. 221–22.)

† The press initially labeled Nixon's pronouncement the "Guam doctrine," much to the discomfort of its author, who, as Kissinger later wrote, thought that the phrase should commemorate "the person rather than the place." (Kissinger, *White House Years,* p. 224.)

Kissinger later further generalized the doctrine into an assertion "that the United States will participate in the defense and development of allies and friends, but that America cannot — and will not — conceive *all* the plans, design *all* the programs, execute *all* the decisions and undertake *all* the defense of the free nations of the world." The United States would give first priority to its own interests: "Our interests must shape our commitments, rather than the other way around."[23]

Since it provided for honoring existing obligations, the Nixon Doctrine changed little immediately with respect to Asia, the part of the world to which the President had originally applied it. But as an indication of shifts in long-term global strategy, it was significant. It constituted the first official acknowledgment of what Johnson had tacitly recognized early in 1968 when he turned down Westmoreland's request for an additional 206,000 troops to be sent to Vietnam — that the United States could not afford indefinitely to proliferate foreign commitments, and then undertake to honor them on a timetable and in a manner set by its adversaries.[24] Resources — economic and human — were not inexhaustible: like Eisenhower and Dulles after the Korean War, Nixon and Kissinger were now, in the wake of Vietnam, proclaiming their own "New Look" in the form of a determination to regain the initiative by shifting the arena of competition onto terrain more favorable to the United States.

## Notes

1. See Kennedy's speech at the University of Maine, October 19, 1963, *KPP: 1986,* p. 795.
2. See, on this point, Bell, *The Diplomacy of Detente,* p. 1.
3. Kissinger address to Pacem in Terris III Conference, Washington, October 8, 1973, in *American Foreign Policy,* p. 121. See also *ibid.,* p. 35; and Nixon's annual foreign policy report, February 18, 1970, NPP: 1970, p. 122.
4. Kissinger, *White House Years,* pp. 61–62, 1302.
5. Annual foreign policy report, February 18, 1970, NPP: 1970, pp. 178–79; Kissinger statement to the Senate Foreign Relations committee, September 19, 1974, in *American Foreign Policy,* p. 145.
6. Annual foreign policy report, February 9, 1972, NPP: 1972, pp. 206–7. See also Kissinger's statement to the Senate Foreign Relations Committee, September 19, 1974, in *American Foreign Policy,* pp. 148–49; also *ibid.,* p. 88; and Kissinger, *White House Years,* p. 128.
7. NSC 20/1, August 18, 1948, in Etzold and Gaddis, eds., *Containment,* p. 187.
8. Kissinger statement to Senate Foreign Relations Committee, September 19, 1974, in *American Foreign Policy,* pp. 173–83. See also *ibid.,* pp. 124–26, 145, and 157; also Nixon's annual foreign policy report, February 18, 1970, NPP: 1970, p. 178.
9. Nixon to Rogers, Laird, and Helms (drafted by Kissinger), February 4, 1969, quoted in Kissinger, *White House Years.* p. 136; Kissinger to Nixon, February 18, 1969, *ibid.,* pp. 143–44. See also *ibid.,* p. 1134.
10. Kissinger, *White House Years,* pp. 127–30, 265–69; Nixon, RN. p. 346.
11. Edmonds, *Soviet Foreign Policy,* 1962–1973, p. 3.
12. Kissinger, *White House Years,* pp. 130–38, 903–18, 1174–94.
13. Kissinger statement to the Senate Foreign Relations Committee, September 19, 1974, in *American Foreign Policy,* pp. 158–59. See also Kissinger, *White House Years,* pp. 127–30, 265–69, 619, 627–31, 639–52.
14. *Ibid.,* pp. 129–30.
15. Nixon, "Asia After Viet Nam," pp. 121–23: Kissinger, "Domestic Structures," *American Foreign Policy,* pp. 38–39.
16. Kissinger, *White House Years,* pp. 165–70.
17. *Ibid,* pp. 183–85. See also p. 548.
18. See above, pp. 210–11.
19. Quoted in William Safire, *Before the Fall: An Inside View of the Pre-Watergate White House* (New York: 1975), p. 370. See also Kissinger, *White House Years,* pp. 178–82, 185–86.
20. Kissinger, *White House Years,* p. 187. See also *ibid.,* pp. 764–65.
21. *Ibid.,* pp. 712, 836–37, 1076.
22. Kissinger, *White House Years,* pp. 220–21.
23. Nixon radio-television address, November 3, 1969, NPP: 1969, pp. 905–6; Annual foreign policy report, February 18, 1970, NPP: 1970, pp. 118–19. For Nixon's initial informal enunciation of the Nixon Doctrine, see his press briefing on Guam, July 25, 1969, NPP: 1969, pp. 544–55.
24. See, on this point, Kissinger, *White House Years,* p. 232.

# Détente's High Point—Nixon Goes to Moscow

### *Document 4*

In May of 1972, President Nixon journeyed to Moscow to sign the SALT I agreements and, in the spirit of détente, to continue discussions on other areas of conflict between the two superpowers. Max Frankel's report in the *New York Times* from the Moscow summit places the arms negotiations in the larger context of the evolving relations between the two countries. Frankel explores the underlying reasons on both sides for venturing into a new sort of relationship. Among other important issues, Frankel's analysis briefly considers the Soviet desire to acquire foreign technology and trade with the West, the effect of China's emergence from isolation and receptivity to U.S. diplomatic initiatives, and the Nixon administration's desire for Soviet help in extricating the United States from the Vietnam War.

## 4 SUMMIT REALISM
## Max Frankel

*Moscow — May 22*

President Nixon was given a correct dose of pomp today and was put up in the imperial quarters of the Kremlin.

This was doubly sweet in view of all the snubs he had suffered from some of the Soviet leaders on a private visit five years ago. And it was generous enough for a leadership that had written off Richard M. Nixon as hostile and beyond redemption when he first walked these streets as Vice President 13 years ago.

The lyric for the harmony today was "realism." President Nixon sang it in his opening toast, offering to proceed "on the basis of equality" and renouncing his once-favored theme of "relative positions of strength." President Nikolai V. Podgorny responded in kind by defining peaceful coexistence as something more than the absence of war and by going to great lengths to justify this week's wheeling and dealing to some restive Communists both here and abroad.

In the spirit of the new realism, the Soviet and American Governments had paved the road to this summit with the building blocks of big and little agreements on arms control. Berlin, trade, space, health, maritime courtesies and communications and by setting aside the awkward boulders of Vietnam and the Middle East.

The agreements are virtually ready for signature, thus guaranteeing at least a formal sense of success in the Moscow talks. But it turns out now, from all accounts, that it is the discussions of the troublesome hot spots that really interest the two parties the most.

President Nixon is pleading at every turn for Soviet "restraint," by which he does not mean restraint in the formal bargaining that is producing the series of accords, but restraint in the supply of weapons to Syria or Egypt or India or North Vietnam without satisfactory limitations on how they are to be used.

And the Russians, without accepting the blame in those situations, at least agree that whenever Moscow and Washington can jointly balance their interests and those of other countries, then acute conflicts do have a way of dissolving.

### Attractions of Collaboration

Indeed, the President and his hosts are plainly tempted by the thought that their collaboration could dampen most of the world's crises and help preserve peace throughout the globe. This is the kind of "duopoly" that escaped the leaders of the two countries a decade ago, when they were still obsessed by their own power competition.

The irony is that, a summit meeting made possible by the diffusion of power to China, to North and South Vietnam, to West Germany and Japan and other nations, is tending beneath the surface toward the kind of compact that is sure to be questioned and even challenged in other capitals. Not only with their words of assurance to allies, but also with their restrained deportment here, the leaders of the two superpowers have shown themselves extremely sensitive to this problem.

There is irony also in the American demands for restraint at a time when the Russians felt challenged, almost unbearably, by Mr. Nixon's escalation of force in and around North Vietnam.

And eager as they were to demonstrate in Moscow this week an ability to do real business with the President, in contrast with the simple exchanges of toasts and expressions of good intentions during his visit to Peking in February, the Russians are plainly nervous about the possibility that the fighting in Asia and the bargaining here is all part of an elaborate American election-year extravaganza.

### Russians Feared Ultimatums

But the biggest irony of all turns on the forbidden word of this meeting: "Linkage." This concept, first floated by Mr. Nixon and his policy adviser, Henry A. Kissinger, in the first weeks of their Administration, holds that progress in one sphere will invariably lead to progress on other subjects, whereas tension in one area is bound to cause friction across the board.

The Russians saw conditions and ultimatums written all over that concept and managed to banish it quickly from the American vocabulary. But the Moscow meetings, even now, are testimony to the success of several artful link-ups in policy bargaining, and the hopes of the two sides for a new and enduring collaboration depend upon even firmer links of concepts in the future.

When they started the climb to the summit two years ago, Mr. Nixon and Mr. Kissinger let it be known that the questions of arms control and trade concessions should move in tandem, and they asked also for help from Moscow in negotiating an end of the war in Vietnam, in reducing the tension in the Middle East and, above all, in putting an end to the periodic flare-ups over Berlin.

When Soviet weapons helped Syria to attack Jordan last year while Soviet engineers began work on a submarine base in Cuba, the White House protested that this was precisely the kind of marginal bid for short-term advantage that would destroy all chances of long-term cooperation.

Privately, Americans put it more colorfully, saying that even when they dropped a nickel during a million-dollar negotiation, the Russians somehow could not resist lunging violently for the trifling coin.

But when those tensions were overcome, the preparations for the summit meeting resumed, including many private exchanges between Mr. Nixon and his principal partner here this week, Leonid I. Brezhnev, the Communist party's General Secretary.

The Russians insisted, as they still do, that peace with Hanoi had to be obtained from Hanoi, but they agreed to put pressure on the East Germans for progress on Berlin and to put pressure on their own military for real advances toward an agreement to freeze the number of nuclear missiles.

In return, President Nixon held out the bait of American technology and credit to an increasingly production-minded and consumption-minded leadership here. Not only were these subjects unmistakably linked to each other, but the bargains that have now been struck require continuing goodwill and performance on various timetables, so that real crisis would become increasingly costly to both sides.

And in this lies the ultimate "linkage." As Mr. Kissinger has remarked, the great power and the giant bureaucracies of the Soviet Union and the United States have invariably encouraged competition and strife, often out of sheer habit and momentum.

The link-up here this week, Mr. Nixon hopes, will finally divert many of those energies and give great numbers of officials, economic planners, businessmen, artists and scientists in both countries a vast new stake in better relations, so that when the temptations of crisis appear — as they did in Vietnam last month — there will be enough important men on both sides to demand that nothing be allowed to sever the new relationship.

## Brezhnev's View of Détente

### *Documents 5 and 6*

Soviet leader Leonid Brezhnev's view of the U.S. motivations for seeking bilateral arms control is presented in these two speeches from the early 1970s. U.S. economic difficulties and mass protests against U.S. foreign policy — both undeniable realities in the United States at the time — are cited. But Brezhnev's principal explanation is that East–West détente followed from an increase in Soviet power. The Soviet Union's successful effort to catch up to the United States in nuclear weaponry prevented the United States from negotiating from a point of strength and encouraged more "realistic" policies. The Soviet Union's own agenda for the arms negotiations, suggested by these speeches, is to manage the state of "strategic parity" (or "equal security") and to restrain any attempt by the United States to regain superiority. The first speech was made in 1971 shortly after the twenty-fourth Congress of the Communist Party of the Soviet Union (CPSU), at which Brezhnev spelled out a "peace program" signaling the Soviet Union's interest in wide-ranging international negotiations. By 1973, with two important arms control agreements behind him, Brezhnev took a slightly different tack in his foreign policy speeches. In this speech made in 1973, wariness has given way to conciliation and an emphasis on the importance of détente.

### 5 SPEECH ON THE STABILIZATION OF INTERNATIONAL PEACE
**Leonid Brezhnev**
**June 11, 1971**

It goes without saying that the struggle for disarmament is a difficult matter. Here, just as in many other problems of foreign policy, one comes up against the stubborn resistance of the imperialist forces. Nevertheless, we regard the slogans put forward by the 24th Congress of the CPSU, not as propaganda slogans, but as slogans for action reflecting political goals which are becoming increasingly attainable in our epoch.

What precisely permits us to present the matter in this way? First and foremost, the changed balance of forces in the world — both sociopolitical and military. Even a few years ago, the imperialists, and above all the U.S. imperialists, really hoped to strengthen their positions on the world arena with the help of the arms race and hoped, at the same time, to weaken the economy of the USSR and other socialist countries and frustrate our plans for peaceful construction. Now, the failure of such schemes of those who wish us ill has become perfectly obvious. Now everyone sees that socialism is sufficiently strong to ensure both reliable defenses and economic development, although it is true that without the great expenditure on defense we would have ensured a much faster advance of our economy. On the other hand, the imperialists, including those of the richest capitalist country — the United States of America — increasingly sense the negative economic and political consequences of an unrestrained arms race. The tremendous military expenditures give rise to chronic inflation in the capitalist countries, cause systematic monetary and financial crises and prevent the solution of worsening domestic problems. At the same time, the working peoples' indignation over the militarist and aggressive policy is growing. In the United States the anti-war movement is assuming an increasingly mass scale and is bringing strong pressure to bear on the government. Resistance to the increase in military spending is growing in other NATO countries, too. As a result, even some members of the ruling circles of the western states are ceasing to regard the arms race as an undoubted blessing. All this, of course, facilitates, to a certain extent, the struggle of the socialist and other peace-loving countries against the arms race. That struggle is becoming a more realistic proposition than it was in the past.

In this situation, growing importance is undoubtedly acquired by the Soviet-American strategic arms limitation talks, a favorable outcome for which would, in our opinion, accord with the interests of the peoples of both countries and with the task of strengthening world peace. *I have already said that the decisive factor for the success of these talks is strict observance of the principle of equal security for both sides, renunciation of attempts to secure any unilateral advantages at the expense of the other side.** It is to be hoped, therefore, that the United States administration will also take a constructive stand.

The principle of equal security is recognized in words by Washington, too. In actual fact, however, the American side simply cannot bring itself to carry this out consistently in practice. In the United States, time and time again, for instance, a hue and cry is raised about the Soviet defense programs — particularly on the eve of adopting a new military budget in Washington. The measures we take to strengthen our defenses are presented at the same time as something well nigh amounting to "treachery," as a direct threat to the success of the talks. But what grounds, we are entitled to ask, has Washington for expecting us to abandon programs that have already been adopted† if the U.S. administration itself, during the period of the talks, has taken a number of very important decisions on building up its strategic forces?‡ It is high time to get rid of this double yardstick, this double standard in assessing one's own actions and the actions of the other side.

And this does not only apply to missiles. The U.S. propaganda machine has launched an extensive campaign concerning the Soviet Navy. Washington, if you please, sees a threat in the fact that our warships appear in the Mediterranean, the Indian Ocean, and other seas. But at the same time, U.S. politicians regard it as normal and natural for their Sixth Fleet to be constantly present in the Mediterranean, hard by the side of the Soviet Union, as it were, and for the Seventh Fleet to be stationed off the coasts of China and IndoChina. . . .

## 6 SPEECH TO THE INDIAN PARLIAMENT
## Leonid Brezhnev
## November 29, 1973

International *détente* is opening favourable conditions for progress all along the front of struggle for stopping the arms race, for disarmament. The Soviet Union has been waging this struggle for many decades. Our efforts, the efforts of the other socialist states and of all peace-loving countries are already yielding fruit. But the main thing still lies ahead. The arms race still continues, which is fraught with serious danger for mankind. And this comes in ever greater conflict with the general trend in the development of international relations towards *détente* and the consolidation of peaceful coexistence.

The partial steps taken in the field of disarmament, such as a ban on some kinds of weapons, an end to all nuclear tests by everybody and everywhere, reduction of military budgets along with further measures for the limitation of strategic arms of the states most powerful in military respect will bring the world closer to achieving the final goal in this field, that is general and complete disarmament. The Soviet state has been struggling for this great goal since the first years of its existence. It has already made a considerable contribution to this cause. And I wish to assure the Parliament of friendly India that the Land of the Soviets will do its utmost to bring closer the day when the centuries-old dream of mankind's greatest minds to destroy the means of mutual extermination will come true.

Esteemed Members of the Parliament!

The changes for the better which have taken place in the relations between the Soviet Union and the United States of America in the last 2 years are undoubtedly of great importance for a stable change in the entire international situation — towards a more durable peace and security. Speaking of what is of primary importance for other countries, the essence of these changes consists in the fact that the two strongest powers — one socialist and one capitalist — have recognised mutually and in a binding legal form the principle of peaceful coexistence to be the basis of their relations. Moreover, they have pledged to pursue their foreign policy in a way as to prevent the eruption of a nuclear war.

I think there is no need to prove that all the peoples of the world interested in the prevention of a new world war stand to gain from such agreement. Taking these steps to improve relations with the USA, the Soviet Union acted in compliance with the well-known principles of its peaceable socialist foreign policy. We duly appreciate the fact that the leaders of the United States of America have shown in this case political realism, foresight and understanding of the requirements of the times.

Like all the significant changes in historical development, this change in the relations between the USSR and the USA is not proceeding smoothly; it is proceeding amid the struggle of different forces, with some zigzags and hitches. We clearly see that certain circles in the military-political bloc of Western powers, and also within the United States itself, are against the establishment of relations of lasting peace and mutually advantageous co-operation between the Soviet Union and the United States and are doing their best to prevent it. It is also known how active such circles are in the United States, although this activity, as we are deeply convinced, has

* [Author's italics. — Ed.]
† [In particular, an ABM system around key cities in the USSR. — Ed.]
‡ [President Nixon's decision to build an ABM system protecting U.S. underground missile sites. — Ed.]

By permission of Bill Mauldin and Wil-Jo Associates, Inc.

nothing in common with the interests of the American people.

However, what has been achieved as a result of the Soviet-American summit talks in 1972 and 1973 as regards directing relations between the Soviet Union and the United States into a healthy normal course undoubtedly accords with the basic, long-term interests of both the Soviet and the American peoples and the interests of universal peace. And here, if I may, dear friends, I will be quite plain: we in the Soviet Union are convinced that nobody will be able to cancel out the peaceful gain of this constructive policy!

The Soviet Union firmly intends to continue to ad vance along the same road of *détente* and peaceful cooperation. We, of course, proceed from the assumption that the American side will act accordingly.

## SALT I: THE ABM TREATY AND THE INTERIM AGREEMENT

## Why Negotiate Limits on Nuclear Weapons?

### *Document 7*

Why did the superpowers decide to negotiate limits on nuclear weapons in SALT I? In this selection from *Cold Dawn — The Story of SALT*, John Newhouse, who has written on diplomacy and who once served in the Arms Control and Disarmament Agency and on the staff of the Senate Foreign Relations Committee, attempts an answer. He observes that most experts believe that once parity had been achieved both superpowers wanted to stabilize the arms race, not end it. Each hoped to limit the other in SALT I.

### 7 PIERCING THE VEIL
### John Newhouse

Thus, even though progress may be slow, the affair prone to bog down occasionally, SALT could develop a cumulative impact on the world system comparable to that of the Congress of Vienna whose achievement was to spare Europe any major bloodletting for 100 years. Such is the hope.

Piercing the veil of SALT to a point where the fascination begins means acquiring three insights: why the United States and the Soviet Union are engaged in this wholly unique enterprise; why SALT is opaque; what the essence of SALT really is.

The immediate question turns on why Washington and Moscow are even negotiating on strategic arms. The answer, as yet unclear and incomplete, will determine whether SALT will produce further agreement and, if so, whether it will actually stabilize the power balance — that is, blunt each side's incentive to seek strategic advantage.

"The Congress of Vienna," Castlereagh told the British House of Commons, "was not assembled for the discussion of moral principles, but for great practical purposes, to establish effectual provisions for the general security." Castlereagh's stricture could apply as well to SALT. Yet such is the complexity of SALT that few senior officials involved in the process — or middle-level bureaucrats for that matter — appear to agree on why the superpowers opted for SALT; indeed, opinions clash on whether SALT is even desirable. Of course, governments, like people, rarely take their major decisions for a single obvious reason. Then, too, the motives animating official actions may be easily obscured by the actions themselves, or by the rhetoric clothing the actions. SALT, like most actions of consequence, illustrates this tendency.

Still, there is a kind of agreed-upon rationale for SALT. The senior official finding himself before a seminar on arms control and asked why bother with SALT might answer something like this:

The talks were launched, not from a common impulse to reduce armaments, but from a mutual need to solemnize the parity principle — or, put differently, to establish an acceptance by each side of the other's ability to inflict unacceptable retribution in response to a nuclear attack. (The assumption here is that neither side will initiate a first strike if the other's retaliatory capability is strong enough to survive its impact. Mutual deterrence, then, rests on the awareness by each side of the other's retaliatory — or second-strike — capacity.) Thus, each *may* recognize that an unlimited arms race would undermine deterrence — and, hence, stability — conceivably by allowing one side or the other to acquire a margin of superiority that in turn would create risks of a first strike. But additionally, a failure to set limits could mean sustaining indefinitely the push for more and better nuclear arms, with costs driven constantly upward — possibly at the expense of other priorities. Here, too, stability, the equivalent in the nuclear age of Castlereagh's "general security," could be degraded.

For all kinds of reasons traceable to internal politics, foreign policy, and competing defense priorities, both great powers want to stabilize spending on arms. Each is obliged to maintain large general-purpose (as distinct from strategic) defense forces. Each confronts internal pressure to reorient priorities. If the entire U.S. defense budget were stabilized, or even modestly cut, the resources liberated for other purposes over the next few years would be negligible; it follows that any rise in the proportion of resources earmarked for defense would retard some programs aimed at improving society and preclude others.

Each side, our senior official might continue, makes coldly analytical assumptions about the other's purposes and goals. Each assumes the other is negotiating because parity has been achieved. Each also suspects the other may be engaged in a "hold-and-explore" gambit — trying to buy time in order to catch up or jump ahead, either "quantitatively" (in number of weapons) or "qualitatively" (in destructive potential of existing and follow-on systems).

The Russians, he would add, are in the talks partly because they have caught up with the United States in strategic weapons. Their efforts, after the Cuban missile trauma, to match the Americans by achieving a balanced second-strike force have succeeded. Now, the Soviet leaders, like America's, hope to head off another major offensive weapons cycle. They know that to succeed they must inhibit ballistic-missile defense, an insight acquired from the Americans. Baldly, this means that defending people is the most troublesome of all strategic options, for stability demands that each of the two societies stand wholly exposed to the destructive power of the other. Acceptance of this severe and novel doctrine illustrates the growing sophistication of Soviet thinking and some willingness to break with fixed attitudes, including the old Russian habit of equating security with territorial defense. And it points up the American interest in raising the Russian learning curve — in creating a dialogue that will encourage, however gradually, a convergence of American and Russian thinking about stable deterrence. Thinking about deterrence is mind bending even for initiates. It takes time and some knowledge of the weapons as well as the issues.

The gap in such thinking is not just between the U.S. strategic community and the Russians, whose concern with these concepts is more recent. It is also between the Americans and their European allies, and between those Americans directly involved ("in house") and those observing from the sidelines of academia.

Both sides are at the negotiating table at least in part to get a better grip on their own internal policy issues. SALT forces decisions through the two bureaucracies (if not in the same way for each); within the U.S. system, it obliges competing elements to settle differences and take what might become self-limiting steps. Briefly, SALT offers a way for both sides to do some thing that each may want to do anyway. Doing some of them as part of a bilateral agreement is easier than trying to do them from within, unilaterally. In the bureaucratic idiom, it is a "high-confidence" way of taking various steps because the other party—the adversary—"signs off" on the same piece of paper and because both sides are agreed on what they are talking about. That alone is novel, as well as crucial.

Our senior official, especially if he were representing the State Department or the Arms Control and Disarmament Agency (ACDA), might conclude his answer to the question—why SALT?—with a word on parity. The alternative to parity, he would say is a quest for superiority, a goal robbed of its strategic value by the undoubted continuing ability of each side to destroy most of the other's society. Parity, as such, may have even more significance for the Russians. It represents a cherished objective—the claim to power the equal of America's, and with this power, expanding political horizons; Europeans worry that the United States is even less likely to use its nuclear weapons to defend them against Soviet force should the need arise. Europe and other parts of the world are thus put on notice that Soviet nonnuclear forces, also growing, can back a venturesome, possibly aggressive, diplomacy with minimal risk of a nuclear confrontation with Washington. Parity, then, is as much a political as a strategic value.

Just as governments rarely do anything for one reason, different parts of the official apparatus will agree to take an action often for quite different reasons. At least some part of the Soviet system is thought to have favored a leisurely SALT negotiation as a means of sniffing out the anxieties of European NATO governments about the talks and, if possible, of maneuvering these anxieties into open slits between the United States and its allies. This is just one of the numerous collateral motives of which each side, rightly or wrongly, suspects the other.

The pace and style of the Congress of Vienna eventually taxed Talleyrand's patience with what Harold Nicolson, in his fine portrait of the Congress, characterized as "Castlereagh's caution and Metternich's unbearable habit of twisting the issues into small cat's-cradles of string."[25]

"Prince Metternich," wrote Talleyrand himself, "has shown at this sitting the full extent of his mediocrity, of his taste for petty intrigues and an uncertain and tortuous course, as also of his marvelous command of words that are vague and void of meaning."[26]

One wonders how Europe's consummate diplomat would have reacted to SALT. Like the Congress of Vienna, SALT is a political negotiation concerned with finding an equilibrium in which the great powers feel secure. Unlike the Congress, whose pivotal issue was purely political (the control of Poland and Saxony), SALT is an anarchy of technical issues and asymmetries, frequently so complex as to frustrate efforts to agree on common definitions and terms of reference. The essence of SALT is political, but technical issues are used on all sides to shore up political and strategic biases.

Understanding SALT means getting behind this and other veils: the secrecy of the process; the theological approach that has overtaken the Americans, or many of them; the mythology of SALT; the ambiguities arising from the savagely conflicting attitudes within what might be called the defense and arms-control communities in the U.S. as well as the deeper ambiguities emerging from the Soviet performance on SALT-related matters.

## Notes

25. Harold Nicholson, *The Congress of Vienna* (New York: Harcourt, Brace and Co., 1946), p. 187.

26. *Ibid.*, p. 176.

## The ABM Controversy

### *Documents 8 and 9*

The Nixon administration decided to deploy an antiballistic missile system, though it modified the system it had inherited from the Johnson administration. Nevertheless, the Nixon ABM decision sparked protests, both from defense specialists and from the public. In document 8, an excerpt from a *New Yorker* article, author Calvin Trillin describes the concerns of the public in the early days of the Nixon administration when it appeared that the ABM system would be deployed in cities. In document 9, defense analyst David Schwartz describes the opposition to the ABM among scientists and from Congress. In 1969, the administration won a key Senate vote on ABM funding only after Vice President Agnew broke a 50–50 tie. This weak support for an ABM system probably contributed to the administration's willingness to agree to an ABM ban in SALT I.

## 8 TARGETS
### Calvin Trillin

During a year I once spent in Atlanta, those permanent residents who enjoyed entertaining me with lists of civic attributes always seemed to include the boast that Atlanta was "the fourth target on the Kremlin's map of nuclear destruction." Exactly the same phrase was used every time—"the fourth target on the Kremlin's map of nuclear destruction"—and it was always expressed in a prideful tone, the same tone used to tell me the number of national firms that were represented in Atlanta, or to inform me that Atlanta was the second-highest major city in the United States. I was always at a loss for a decently appreciative reply. "I see" or "That's interesting" seemed a pedestrian way to respond to the possibility of a nationally ranked apocalypse. Once, in a confused effort to be a good guest, I burst out with "I think it ought to be *first!*" My informant for a moment looked gratified—then uncertain, and then offended. The Bomb, which has been blamed for juvenile delinquency and for an increase in tornadoes and for a decrease in humorists and for general despair, has even made civic pride confusing.

The citizens who live around Chicago were informed last fall that the Sentinel Anti-Ballistic Missile System would include a site in the area, because Chicago was such an eminent target for nuclear destruction. Practically none of the citizens took the selection as a point of pride. In fact, some of them objected to having the site on the theory that it might *make* Chicago an eminent target. Chicago is presumably important enough to be a target already (of just what rank I don't know; the people in Atlanta knew only which city was No. 4), and it might be thought that having some defense against nuclear destruction would make everyone feel more secure. But the only known defense against a nuclear missile is another nuclear missile, in this case a Spartan missile with a multi-megaton warhead, and a lot of people in Chicago, musing on the multi-megaton warheads that a Spartan site would have to keep at the ready, have come to believe that the possibility of their own defense accidentally destroying them is no more remote than the possibility of an enemy nuclear power maliciously attacking them—and is much harder to put out of their thoughts. Chicagoans tend to believe that if Chicago has to be defended it could be defended very nicely from South Dakota, although they also speak highly of northern Iowa.

The Chicago *Sun-Times* phoned a few Dakota mayors to ask, more or less, how they would feel about the gift of a Spartan-missile site from the people of Chicago. The mayors said they would be delighted. From my experience in Atlanta, I would guess that some cities in the United States might welcome a site as a way to assure themselves of the importance that is implied by a place in the hypothetical holocaust. Also, there are some areas so poor or so obsessed with economic development that they would probably welcome the Federal Typhoid and Scrofula Center if the government guaranteed a large payroll and promised to contract for the construction locally. Fifteen cities have been chosen for Sentinel sites, and practically no protest has been heard from the smaller ones (or from New York—raising the possibility that New Yorkers have resigned themselves to living in a state of permanent disaster that could not be affected by an accidental nuclear blast or two). The Defense Department's announcement on February 6th that the Sentinel program would be held up until it had been reviewed—an announcement celebrated by Chicago anti-ABM protesters as a Pentagon retreat brought about partly by their efforts—presumably threw such proposed Sentinel hosts as Great Falls, Montana, and Grand Forks, North Dakota, into civic gloom. "They love us in Albany, Georgia," the Army colonel in charge of Sentinel "site activation" told me.

The colonel has had less than romantic experiences with citizens in Seattle, Boston, Detroit, Los Angeles, and, particularly, Chicago. In Glenview, one of five suburbs that were under consideration for the Chicago site, the village board passed a resolution against having a site anywhere near Chicago and sent the resolution to eighty other towns and villages in the area, suggesting that they pass it as well. After the Army announced that it had decided on an abandoned Nike base in Lake County, four miles south of Libertyville and about thirty miles north of the Loop, some people from a group called Northern Illinois Citizens Against ABM obtained a court order temporarily blocking any construction. At public meetings, the Army has shown Lake County citizens color slides of the computer-operated nuclear-defense system designed to protect them and their loved ones from what are commonly referred to as "primitive Chinese missiles" (conjuring up visions of thousands of Chinese peasants laboriously carting the mud of the Yangtze to crude molds, creating out of the baked earth something that roughly resembles an intercontinental ballistic missile, straining together to pull it back on some enormous catapult, and launching it seven thousand miles over the Pole in an attempt to obliterate Chicago). But the same meetings have almost always included a scientist from the Argonne National Laboratory, a center for non-military nuclear research just west of Chicago; explaining that he is speaking not as an official representative of the laboratory but as a private citizen who happens to be a nuclear physicist, he reminds everyone that an unauthorized explosion is possible, even though extremely unlikely, and that such an explosion would destroy from a hundred and fifty thousand to two million citizens, "depending on which way the wind is blowing."

A citizen who looks into the abstract arguments about

the wisdom of a defensive-missile system is likely to find them confusing enough to encourage his retreat to the sports pages. Sentinel is, among other things, an anti-ballistic-missile shield that everyone agrees could not stop a concentrated missile attack, a strickly defensive system that its critics consider more belligerent than our current policy of keeping enough offensive missiles to make any attack suicidal, a five- or ten-billion-dollar "thin" shield against the Chinese (who have no missiles) which many people believe will grow into a fifty- or hundred-billion-dollar "thick" shield against the Russians (who have too many to be affected by a thick shield), a boondoggle according to Dwight Eisenhower, a sensible compromise according to Robert McNamara, a "pile of junk" according to the prevailing view among scientists, and a functioning national program by act of Congress. Although the protest movement in Chicago has had the effect of providing a constituency for anti-ABM senators who may be interested in the abstract arguments about the wisdom of defensive-missile systems, it has made its appeal to people interested mainly in not being blown up. The diagram most often used by ABM opponents for posters and leaflets demonstrates the consequences of a nuclear explosion near Libertyville by superimposing a series of concentric circles on a map of the Chicago suburbs — showing which towns would be in the Blast Area, which in the Fire Area, which in the Body Burn Area, and which would be far enough away to permit some hope that the wind would not carry too much fallout in their direction. There has been no attempt to compose a battle cry about how Sentinel could hinder efforts to control nuclear arms; the poster announcing the first meeting in the suburbs north of Chicago to protest the selection of Libertyville was headlined "A Bomb in Your Backyard?"

A way to misunderstand the problems of local protest in the United States is to assume that if Karl Marx were reincarnated in, say, Muncie, Indiana, as a decently dressed jobholder with revolutionary ideas he would be barred from speaking at the luncheons of the local Lions Club and Rotary Club and Kiwanis Club. Service-club program chairmen fear the absence of a speaker more than they fear the revolution. Chances are he would be invited to speak, he would call for the workers of the world to throw off their chains, he would be asked three or four courteous questions from the floor (none of them dealing precisely with workers' throwing off their chains), and then the chairman would glance at his watch, remind the membership of the rule about breaking up at one-fifteen sharp, and say, "Karl, it was real nice of you to come, and I'm sure you've given us all a lot to think about." Although the Argonne nuclear physicists who began the anti-ABM protest in Chicago last fall have, strictly speaking, been criticizing one of the government's attempts to defend its people from the Communist threat, the emphasis on safety has avoided identification with appeasement, and they have remained well within the political tolerance of local service clubs. In the evenings, the scientists have often appeared with Army spokesmen at public meetings held in high-school auditoriums — the soldiers and the scientists travelling around Lake County like old prizefighters staging exhibitions, or like William F. Buckley, Jr., and Arthur Schlesinger, Jr., touring the Ivy League debating circuit. The Army team ordinarily consists of two full colonels (one of whom introduces the other), a lieutenant colonel working the slide projector, and a civilian public-relations man with a pipe, a Sentinel tie clasp, and an elaborate tape recorder. One of the colonels, using a retractable pointer to gesture at the slides, carefully goes through the components of the Sentinel system — the long-range Spartan, the shorter-range Sprint, to catch those missiles that manage to elude the Spartan, the two types of radar — and assures everyone that chances of an accident are "essentially nil." Then the Argonne scientist explains what an accident could mean, and argues that if the Army is planning only the thin area-defense system approved by Congress there is no reason to build Spartan sites within a hundred miles of heavily populated areas. One evening, somebody asked one of the colonels why a missile designed to intercept the enemy hundreds of miles away had to be so close to the city. The colonel mentioned something about an increasing Chinese threat and the parameters that had been calculated, and finally said, "It just does." The Army spokesmen have been accused of using security restrictions to avoid answering legitimate questions — or to hide the fact that their answers might not be particularly persuasive. The colonels usually manage to give the impression that they could demolish the opposition's argument if only they were the type of men who were willing to break their sworn oath of secrecy instead of exerting the awesome will power necessary to restrain themselves. Sometimes when a citizen asks a question the colonel will start to form the words, pause, and then say, "I'm sorry, I just can't tell you that." Then the physicist, announcing first that he is privy to no confidential information, will answer the question from what he has read in the newspapers.

When a garbage dump in a suburb west of Chicago was being considered for the Spartan site, the Argonne scientists found themselves allied with residents who were concerned that a military takeover of the dump would mean increased garbage-hauling charges. But, for the most part, the leaders of the protest against the Libertyville site — including the physicists themselves — oppose the entire ABM system and see the argument about where the site should be mainly as a way to dramatize the issue of whether Sentinel should exist at all.

## 9 PAST AND PRESENT: THE HISTORICAL LEGACY
### David N. Schwartz

These events, combined with the Nixon administration's desire to undertake a comprehensive review of U.S. strategic policy when it came into office in January 1969, made it relatively easy for the new secretary of defense, Melvin Laird, to suspend the Sentinel program in early February 1969, pending a full review. In mid-March President Richard M. Nixon made public his revised ABM program, Safeguard.[27] Using much the same technology as Sentinel, Safeguard would be reoriented away from population defense to a greater emphasis on point defense of ICBMs. At the same time, it would retain an area-defense mission, although no interceptors would be based near major cities. The system would be directed against the Soviet ICBM threat — the Chinese threat had failed to materialize at the pace predicted in 1967 — and would be designed to take into account new offensive technologies, including MIRV.

This new proposal prompted a strong public reaction. The Senate Foreign Relations Committee held a series of intensive hearings on the subject and brought an array of nongovernmental expert witnesses to testify on the technical and political implications of ABM.[28] A broad spectrum of the U.S. scientific community now became embroiled in the controversy, and major figures carried on bitter debates before Senators in these hearings and in parallel ones held by friends of Safeguard in the Armed Services Committee.[29] The Cooper coalition reformed to do battle with the new proposal, but in the end — by a vote of 51–50, with Vice-President Spiro T. Agnew casting the tie-breaking vote — the Senate approved funding of the first phase of Safeguard.[30]

Throughout this debate and a similar one in 1970 over funding for expanding phase I of the Safeguard program, the administration used Soviet development of the Galosh ABM system around Moscow and the growth of the Soviet strategic offensive arsenal to justify deployment of the system. Another justification used was related to SALT, which began in November 1969. The administration argued that only by continuing to fund Safeguard would there be any incentive for the Soviet Union to agree to negotiated ABM limitations. This rationale became increasingly important as the negotiations dragged on. By May 1971 the United States and the Soviet Union publicly announced that an agreement on defensive systems, separate but loosely linked to one on offensive systems, would be in the interests of both sides.[31] By May 1972 the two governments had agreed on a treaty that put a cap — at a very low level — on the ABM capabilities of the superpowers.

Some have read into this treaty an endorsement by the superpowers of the strategic doctrine of mutual assured destruction, articulated by Secretary of Defense McNamara in the 1960s principally as a means of capping offensive arms expenditures. According to this doctrine, stability and deterrence are enhanced if the two superpowers leave their societies exposed to second-strike retaliation by each other and avoid posing a first-strike offensive threat to those retaliatory forces. Both sides seemed to understand that defensive preparations could inject an element of instability into the superpower relationship. If effective, a defense system could deny the enemy the capacity to retaliate after a nuclear attack and could conceivably increase the incentives of either side to preempt in a time of crisis, though obviously for different reasons. More likely, since the systems developed in the 1960s could be offset with a relatively marginal increase in offensive forces by the other side, deployment of an ABM system could stimulate long-term pressures for an arms race — the action-reaction phenomenon McNamara had articulated in his various reports to Congress and in his September 1967 Sentinel speech.

At the same time, the actual behavior of the superpowers since 1972 leads to some serious questions as to how deeply the mutual assured destruction doctrine was adopted by either side. In offensive programs both sides pursued, within the limits of the offensive force constraints imposed by SALT, vigorous programs to multiply the numbers of RVs on ICBMs and submarine-launched ballistic missiles (SLBMs) and to increase the accuracy of these RVs to the point where today each side could do substantial damage in a first strike against the other's strategic retaliatory forces. Nor has either side foresworn ABM. As table 9-1 shows, the United States has maintained an impressive level of funding for basic research and development since 1972. Many concepts have been examined on the blackboards of defense scientists. But since 1972 no operational prototypes of new systems have been built, in accordance with the treaty. . . .

## Notes

27. Yanarella, *Missile Defense Controversy*, pp. 143–86.
28. *Strategic and Foreign Policy Implications of ABM Systems.* Hearings before the Subcommittee on International Organization and Disarmament Affairs of the Senate Committee on Foreign Relations, 91 Cong. 1 sess. (Government Printing Office, 1969), 3 pts.

29. See, in particular, Anne Hessing Cahn, "American Scientists and the ABM: A Case Study in Controversy," in Albert H. Teich, ed., *Scientists and Public Affairs* (MIT Press, 1974), pp. 41–120.
30. "Nixon Missile Plan Wins in Senate by a 51–50 Vote; House Approval Likely," *New York Times*, August 7, 1969.
31. Newhouse, *Cold Dawn*, p. 217.

## Henry Kissinger and Gerard Smith Describe the Agreements

### *Document 10*

In these excerpts from a press conference held shortly after the signing of the SALT I agreements, Henry Kissinger and Gerard Smith, the head of the U.S. SALT I delegation, briefly describe the SALT I agreements. They note that SALT I included two agreements: The ABM Treaty, of unlimited duration, limiting each side to no more than two (later reduced by mutual agreement to one) ABM installations and restricting ABM technology; and the Interim Agreement on Strategic Offensive Arms, a five-year agreement that froze the numbers of launchers of ICBMs and SLBMs on both sides.

### 10 PRESS CONFERENCE
### Henry Kissinger and Gerard Smith
### Moscow
### May 26, 1972

DR. KISSINGER. Gentlemen, I thought that the most useful thing I could do was to give you a general background on these negotiations and of the President's view of the treaty, and Ambassador Smith, of course, who has conducted the negotiations and brought them to this conclusion, is in the best position to go through the details of the agreement. . . .

Nothing that this administration has done has seemed to it more important for the future of the world than to make an important first step in the limitation of strategic arms. All of us have been profoundly convinced that to arrest the arms race is one of the overriding concerns of this period. Now it is a subject of enormous technical complexity, and for the two great nuclear powers to make a beginning in putting their armaments under some restraint required political decisions and an enormous amount of technical work.

It is a process that has continued for many years. It started with extensive technical studies in Washington. It went through two and a half years of negotiations alternating between Helsinki and Vienna. It has been brought to a conclusion because both governments decided that in an agreement of this kind the stakes were larger than the simple technical issues; that what was at stake was a major step toward international stability, confidence among nations, and a turn in the pattern of postwar relationships.

This is why at various crucial moments in these negotiations there had been direct contacts between the President and Soviet leaders, which led by mutual agreement to breakthroughs — the first on May 20 of 1971, in which there was an agreement that broke the deadlock that had developed between the Soviet insistence that an agreement cover antiballistic missile systems only and our view that an agreement involved as well the offensive weapons. The compromise was that the initial treaty would deal with ABMs and that this would be accompanied by a freeze on certain categories of offensive weapons.

The next deadlock developed over the issue of what offensive weapons should be included, whether it should be confined to intercontinental ballistic missiles or whether submarine-launched ballistic missile systems should also be involved. The answer — this deadlock was broken at the end of April and in large part by direct contact between the Soviet leaders and the President — has finally resulted in the present agreement which Ambassador Smith has just brought back from Helsinki and which will be signed at eleven o'clock. Ambassador Smith is in the best position to explain the provisions of this agreement, but I wanted to make a few general observations about its significance and how it should be looked at.

The first point to make is that in an agreement that involves the central armaments on both sides it is foolish or shortsighted to approach the negotiations from the point of view of gaining a unilateral advantage. Neither nation will possibly put its security and its survival at the hazard of its opponent, and no agreement that brings disadvantage to either side can possibly last and can possibly bring about anything other than a new circle of insecurity. Therefore, the temptation that is ever present when agreements of this kind are analyzed as to who won is exceptionally inappropriate. We have approached these negotiations from the very beginning with the attitude that a wise proposal is one that is conceived by each side to be in the mutual interest, and we believe that if this agreement does what we hope it will, that the future will record that both sides won.

Secondly, let me make a few observations with respect to the freeze of offensive weapons, which has perhaps some of the more complicated provisions and the anticipation of which has aroused some comments in the United States.

First, the freeze concerns only two categories of offensive weapons; that is to say, intercontinental ballistic missiles and submarine-launched ballistic missiles. It does not include the number of warheads, nor does it include bombers, nor does it include, obviously, other systems based elsewhere than at sea or in the territory of each country.

Secondly, in assessing the significance of the freeze, it is not useful to analyze whether the freeze reflects a gap between the forces that are being frozen. In the two categories that are being frozen, that is to say, ICBMs and submarine-launched ballistic missiles, the facts are these: The Soviet Union has more intercontinental ballistic missiles than the United States. The Soviet Union has been building intercontinental ballistic missiles; the United States has not and has no such program at the moment. The Soviet Union has been building submarine-launched ballistic missiles at the rate of eight submarines a year. The United States has at this moment no submarines under construction.

Therefore, the question to ask in assessing the freeze is not what situation it perpetuates but what situation it prevents. The question is where we would be without the freeze. And if you project the existing building programs of the Soviet Union into the future, as against the absence of building programs over the period of the freeze in either of the categories that are being frozen, you will get a more correct clue to why we believe that there is a good agreement and why we believe that it has made a significant contribution to arresting the arms race.

The weapons are frozen, as we pointed out, in categories in which we have no ongoing programs. Now, having said this, however, I am not implying that we gained a unilateral advantage, because it is perhaps true that in the ABM field we had the more dynamic program, which is being arrested as a result of these developments.

AMBASSADOR [Gerald C.] SMITH . . . First, let me say perhaps the obvious, that these documents are the product of long, careful, complex, and exhaustive negotiations. As a matter of fact, we were not finished with the last detail after we got on the airplane this evening in Helsinki. . . . I invited some of the Soviet delegation, including the chief of the delegation, Minister Semenov, to join us, and we continued to work on our way here to Moscow. So, this is about the freshest treaty that I have ever talked about.

I think that in sum these documents, when you look at them carefully, will demonstrate a solid, concrete, yet first step in the problem of controlling strategic arms. They are not the end of the road by any means, but I think that they are a very solid step forward.

You know, we have an obligation that sometimes people forget under the Nonproliferation Treaty of some years ago to get on with trying to limit strategic arms and get on with disarmament. I think as a general proposition these documents will show that we are not lax in that respect. We are conscious of our responsibilities.

Now, as Henry said, there are two basic documents here, the ABM treaty and the interim agreement, which, in effect, is a negotiating freeze arrangement to hold the situation to permit us to, hopefully, negotiate a treaty to match in the offensive field the treaty that we have succeeded in negotiating in the defensive field.

In the defensive field, I would urge you to look very carefully at the language of Article I, which looks very general but to my mind is a most significant step forward in relations between two great powers. In effect, it says that neither side is going to try to defend its nationwide territory. This is an admission of tremendous psychological significance, I believe — recognition that the deterrent forces of both sides are not going to be challenged.

When you think of the concerns that we have had for the last twenty-five years about first strike and counterforce, it seems to me a general recognition by both countries that they are not going to field a nationwide system is of first importance, politically, psychologically, and militarily.

In addition to that, the countries are going to agree not to lay the base for such a nationwide system. That got us into all sorts of radar problems which some of you people perhaps felt we took too long in solving, but much of the time we have spent was in trying to wrestle with this radar problem to prevent the possibility of a nationwide system arising.

In addition to that, the two nations have made commitments not to even try for a thick or regional defense in one part of the country except as specifically permitted under the agreement; that is, to defend one's capital or to defend a relatively small number of ICBM silos. So, although Article I looks like sort of a general statement, to my mind it is one of the most significant articles in the whole agreement.

Now, Article II defines what we are talking about and has a very important bearing on the whole question of what we call future ABM systems. This treaty has as a most significant aspect that it not only limits the present situation but has a choking-off effect on future systems which, under the terms of the treaty as we have reached understandings, will not be deployable unless this treaty is amended.

Article III is the heart of the treaty and deserves a great deal of study. I think we spent more time trying to wrestle with Article III than any other part of the treaty. I will go into details later if you like, but it says both sides can have two sites with no more than 100 launchers at each site, with radar sharply limited; one site for the defensive capital and one for the ICBMs. The Soviets will agree to deploy the ICBM site well away from the capital site, so the possibility for a base of a nationwide system is very poor.

In addition to the numbers, we have had to work out problems involving test ranges, numbers of test launchers, the question of modernization, the question of how you verify this treaty, and one of the significant conclusions that we have reached is that this treaty can safely be verified by national means of verification; that is, without onsite inspection. This is largely a limitation on numbers of relatively large objects which we are confident can be monitored, if you will, without onsite inspection. As a matter of fact, if I had my druthers and could have onsite inspection instead of our present national means, there would be no question in my mind that we would be much better off with national means of verification.

In addition to that, we will have commitments from the Soviets not to interfere with those national means of verification and not to take measures to conceal their operation so as to prevent the workings of national means of verification. . . .

We are going to set up a Joint Consultative Commission which will, in effect, act as a surveying agent that will watch over the operation of the agreement, to which ambiguous situations can be referred, which will be a forum for further discussion of the possible amendments to see how this treaty is working, and to make sure that it stays viable over the years.

This treaty will have indefinite duration, but if it doesn't work, if our supreme interests are jeopardized, there is a provision that on short notice either side can escape from the binding obligations under the treaty.

Turn, now, for a minute to the offensive side. As Henry said, what we are trying to do is to set up a useful device that will hold the situation while we negotiate, hopefully, a matching treaty; that is, to match the treaty in the ABM defense field. I think that the measures that we have succeeded in spelling out in this interim agreement with the Russians will do just that. There will be a commitment on their part not to build any more of these ICBMs that have concerned us over the years. That commitment will extend to not building such things as SS-9s, and there will be provisions that if the sides want to increase their submarine missiles — which, if you can say so, are a more benign form of weapons system than ICBMs — they may do so, but only at the price of a substantial reduction program in other weapons systems.

Keep this in mind when you think about the possibility of increasing SLBMs: it is not for free. It is at a very substantial price in terms of reductions of other weapons systems. Reductions have never before been successfully negotiated, so I think this ought to be considered a great accomplishment.

I think I had better stop at that, since I am going to have a chance to go into specifics. I understand that there are to be some questions at this point.

Q. Mr. Smith, could you answer just a couple of basic things? On the question of the radar, could you give us an estimate of what percentage of the national territory will be protected by the ABM radar on each side? Secondly, on the offensive side, the submarines, there are no figures in the Fact Sheet, and the phrasing there seems to be a little ambiguous. Could you give us what you consider to be, in terms of numbers, the current levels of submarines on each side?

AMBASSADOR SMITH. On the question of radar, I cannot give you a precise percentage. The radar coverage, of course, is not the essential consideration. No reentry vehicle was ever killed by a radar. It takes a lot of interceptors, in addition to radar, to do a defensive job. The radar coverage, however, will be minute, and especially in the case of radar around ICBM fields, where there will be quantitative limitations as well as qualitative limitations, so only a relatively few radars will be permitted in these ICBM fields. We are quite confident that a radar base for a nationwide or thick regional defense is not possible under the terms of this treaty.

Now, in terms of numbers of submarines, I would like to reserve that until I can go into it more specifically.

Q. Do the Russians complete their construction of submarines presently under construction? They have seventeen operational and twenty-five presumably at some stage of construction. Will they be allowed to complete those before the freeze becomes effective?

AMBASSADOR SMITH. Under the interim arrangement, they will be permitted to finish construction of submarines, yes. . . .

Q. Would you clear up the withdrawal rights from the treaty "if supreme interests are jeopardized and on six months' notice"? Is that "and/or" or must both conditions be prevalent, a supreme interest endangered; does this then require six month's notice of withdrawal?

AMBASSADOR SMITH. That is correct. That is the same condition as in previous arms control treaties, such as the Nonproliferation Treaty.

Q. Does this Commission decide whether or not supreme interests are involved?

AMBASSADOR SMITH. No. That is a unilateral decision for both countries.

Q. Doesn't this allow them to protect all of their ICBMs while we protect some of ours?

AMBASSADOR SMITH. No. This will permit them to protect a smaller percentage of their ICBMs than ours, since they have substantially more than we have.

Q. If after five years there is no comprehensive offensive agreement, does the interim agreement lapse?

AMBASSADOR SMITH. If the five years is past and the negotiations look fruitless, I would think we would not want to continue it. If the negotiations look as if they might still bear fruit, if both sides agree to extend the five-year arrangement, that is certainly in our field of vision.

## Senator's Jackson's Concern About "Inequalities"

### *Documents 11 and 12*

Although the SALT I agreements passed by huge margins, some key members of the Senate were concerned about what they thought were "inequalities" in the treaty. Sen. Henry Jackson in particular pointed out that the Interim Agreement allowed the Soviets to have more ICBMs and SLBMs than the United States. SALT I defenders responded that the agreements said nothing about bombers, a category of weapons in which the United States had a significant lead. This did not satisfy Jackson, who pushed for an amendment to SALT I that committed the United States in future negotiations to seek agreements that "would not limit the United States to levels of intercontinental strategic forces inferior to the limits provided for the Soviet Union." Jackson's amendment also committed the United States to "a vigorous research and development and modernization program." Documents 11 and 12 include the Jackson Amendment and some of Senator Jackson's arguments in favor of its passage. The Nixon administration reluctantly agreed to the amendment, and it became law. It was to play a role in the battle over the ratification of SALT II.

## 11 THE JACKSON AMENDMENT 1950

SEC. 3

The Government and the people of the United States ardently desire a stable international strategic balance that maintains peace and deters aggression. The Congress supports the stated policy of the United States that, were a more complete strategic offensive arms agreement not achieved within the five years of the interim agreement, and were the survivability of the strategic deterrent forces of the United States to be threatened as a result of such failure, this could jeopardize the supreme national interests of the United States; the Congress recognizes the difficulty of maintaining a stable strategic balance in a period of rapidly developing technology; the Congress recognizes the principle of United States-Soviet Union equality reflected in the antiballistic missile treaty, and urges and requests the President to seek a future treaty that, inter alia, would not limit the United States to levels of intercontinental strategic forces inferior to the limits provided for the Soviet Union; and the Congress considers that the success of these agreements and the attainment of more permanent and comprehensive agreements are dependent upon the maintenance under present world conditions of a vigorous research and development and modernization program as required by a prudent strategic posture.

## 12 SENATE DEBATE ON THE JACKSON AMENDMENT Senator Jackson August 14, 1972

MR. JACKSON. Mr. President, senators who share my view that the Senate ought to go on record in support of the policy of the United States to seek a follow-on agreement that limits the threat to the survivability of our deterrent forces will welcome my amendment. The first part does precisely that. It urges restraint on the part of the Soviet Union by indicating that a failure to achieve a threat-limiting agreement could jeopardize the supreme national interests of the United States. In so doing, the amendment takes account of the fact that while the interim agreement may have some slight effect on the rate of growth of the Soviet threat to the survivability of our deterrent, it does not halt it. Therefore, should the threat overtake the negotiation of a follow-on agreement at any time within the next five years, our supreme national interests could be jeopardized. I will be surprised, Mr. President, to learn that there is any substantial opposition to this view within the Senate.

Mr. President, I have elsewhere described the present agreement as providing the United States with "interim subparity." The agreement confers on the Soviets a 50 percent advantage in numbers of land- and sea-based launchers and a 400 percent advantage in throw-weight. Now, the argument is made that this enormous disparity in numbers of launchers and throw-weight is offset by superior technology and numbers of warheads on our side. There is a certain limited truth to this claim. It is not an enduring truth: for while numbers are limited under the agreement, technology is not. It stands to reason, therefore, that in the long run "superior" technology cannot be relied upon to offset inferior numbers.

The inability of technology to compensate for numbers is not only true in general but is, in the present case, true for specific reasons as well. The greatest part of our presumed technological advantage lies in our lead over the Soviets in the development and deployment of MIRV warheads on our missile forces.

This lead is not one that can be maintained at anything approaching our current margin. On the contrary, when the Soviets develop a MIRV capability—and they are expected to do so at "any moment"—the combination of that capability and their vastly superior throw-weight will give them, given time and effort on their part, superiority in numbers of warheads.

There is an enormous volume of misinformation on the subject of alleged U.S. advantages arising from technology and geography. There is no doubt that in the long run, technology will tend toward equalization. How well I remember those who argued that the Soviets would require a decade or more to catch up with the United States in developing hydrogen weapons. The same sort of scientists who today argue that we can rest comfortably with inferior numbers of launchers because of an unbridgeable advantage in technology miscalculated by about nine and a half out of ten years back in 1947. The Russians, of course, were only months behind us, and our scientists were behind the eight ball.

As to geography, I have heard it argued — the chairman of the Foreign Relations Committee made the case himself last week — that owing to our possession of forward bases for our submarine fleet we need fewer submarines than the Soviets in order to maintain on-station times equal to theirs. Now, sea-based strategic forces are assuming increasing importance; so it is essential that we be correct on this point. Despite some statements to the contrary, the geographical asymmetries favor the Soviet submarine fleet and not our own. With the increased range such as that of the Soviet SS-NX-8 submarine-launched missile, the importance of forward bases is greatly diminished. Russian submarines will be on station with respect to a large number of U.S. targets within one day's travel time from Murmansk or Petropavlovsk. This is not substantially different from the situation of our submarines operating out of their forward bases. What is more important, however, is that the Russians have a very large land mass between our submarines and their vulnerable points while we do not. Most of the U.S. points that are targets for Soviet submarine-launched missiles are coastal or near-coastal.

So there is little substance to the claim that we are in a favorable geographical situation.

The point I wish to make, Mr. President, is that, over the long run, there is no substitute for equal numbers of launchers, taking account of throw-weight differentials. I believe that the Senate should join with our negotiators and administration spokesmen in rejecting, for the future, the sort of disparities that we have agreed to, on an interim basis, in the present agreement. And in so doing I believe that we ought to insist that the principle that was applied in the case of the ABM treaty — the principle of equality on which the Russians insisted — ought to be applied to a treaty on offensive weapons.

I was concerned, Mr. President, that our consent to the interim agreement, containing, as it does, the wide disparities to which I have referred, might be misunderstood as reflecting on the acceptability of such disparities in a follow-on treaty. In order to make the record clear I asked a number of witnesses before the Armed Services Committee to comment on this issue.

On 18 July, I asked Ambassador Gerard Smith, the director of the Arms Control and Disarmament Agency and head of our SALT delegation, "Would the present interim agreement be acceptable as a permanent agreement?"

Ambassador Smith replied, "Not to me."

I then directed the same question to other members of the SALT delegation. The former deputy secretary of defense and now assistant to the secretary of defense for SALT, Mr. Paul Nitze, said "No." General Royal Allison, a member of the delegation and assistant to the chairman of the joint chiefs of staff for strategic arms negotiations, also said "No."

On 24 July, I directed a similar question to Secretary Laird, with respect to whether a SALT II agreement should continue the numerical relationships established in the interim agreement. Secretary Laird, speaking for the administration, said:

> I would hope that in these negotiations we could move in the direction of equality as far as numbers and also as far as some of the other important areas dealing with offensive strategic weapon systems. I feel that this should be a very important thrust of our negotiations because this is very basic to the continued support of the obligations that we have undertaken with our friends and allies throughout the world in order to prevent the possibility of a nuclear exchange in the future.

The chief of naval operations, Admiral Zumwalt, testified:

> It is my view that in SALT II, we must achieve an equality of numbers. Just as the Soviets insisted on symmetry with regard to the ABM treaty, if we are going to go into a permanent treaty on the strategic side, I think we absolutely must insist on symmetry.

I know of no one in a responsible position in the administration who is in disagreement with this widely expressed view.

My amendment provides the Senate with an opportunity to declare itself in favor of equality in a follow-on agreement; and I am certain that in view of the basic good sense of that position and the overwhelming testimony before us, we will act to affirm it.

Mr. President, the question of what is to be included in the computation of equal forces in a follow-on agreement is related to the difficult issue of our forward deployments in Europe which are dedicated to the defense of our European allies and which are at sea.

The intent of my amendment as it bears on this matter is, I believe, perfectly clear and straightforward. In stating that "the Congress recognizes the principle of United States–Soviet Union equality reflected in the antiballistic missile treaty" and that accordingly "the Congress requests the President to seek a future treaty that, *inter alia,* would not limit the United States to levels of intercontinental strategic forces inferior to the limits provided for the Soviet Union," it is unmistakably clear that so-called forward-based systems, which are not intercontinental, should not be included in that calculation of equality. It is my view, and the intent of the pending amendment, that any eventual treaty must recognize the necessity that the intercontinental strategic forces of the U.S. and the U.S.S.R. — by which I mean to include ICBMs, submarine-launched nuclear missiles, and intercontinental-range bombers of the two powers — should bear an equal relationship to one another. This says nothing about the eventual role of or disposition of the issue of forward-based systems.

With regard to the question of forward-based systems it has been my understanding, as clearly set forth by representatives of the administration in testimony before the Senate, that the United States has refused to negotiate the issue of forward-based systems in a bilateral U.S.–U.S.S.R. negotiation. I understand that this position was based on the entirely justifiable view that such systems are part and parcel of our alliance defense commitment and could not appropriately be considered without satisfactory alliance participation. I fully support the administration's view on this matter and there is nothing in my amendment which in any way contradicts that position.

My amendment, in its final sentences, simply points to the need for a vigorous program of research, development, and modernization leading to a prudent strategic posture. I wish to emphasize that adoption of this language is not intended to bear upon the wisdom of any particular procurement item. Decisions on procurement ought to be taken on a case-by-case basis. So while it is useful for the Senate to go on record to the effect that we must continue our efforts in the research, development, and modernization area, senators can rest assured that this does not constitute an endorsement of any particular weapons system or any particular research and development effort. I emphasize this, Mr. President, because I would not wish senators to gain the impression that in voting for my amendment they are committing themselves to any future action on procurement items.

## SALT I: Guaranteeing Soviet Strategic Superiority

### *Document 13*

Most of the criticism of SALT I came from conservatives, who echoed Jackson's argument that the treaty was not equitable. In these excerpts from a 1972 article in the conservative *National Review,* Donald Brennan argues that the Interim Agreement "guarantees" Soviet strategic superiority. He adds that SALT I is based on the naive American belief that the Soviets view nuclear war in the same way we do — that is, they believe in mutually assured destruction.

At the same time this article was written, strategic analyst Brennan's views on SALT and nuclear strategy were not shared by much of the public or by key opinion makers. During the middle and late 1970s, however, they found a wider and wider audience.

### 13 WHEN THE SALT HIT THE FAN
### Donald G. Brennan

On Friday, May 26, 1972, Richard Nixon and Leonid Brezhnev signed what will doubtless prove to be the most important arms-control agreements negotiated in the nuclear era — or, it may be, in any era. But their indubitable importance does not, unfortunately, automatically make them a cause for rejoicing; the San Francisco earthquake, for instance, was important too. It remains to be seen whether the agreements of May 26 will prove to be more or less of a disaster than the earthquake. There is some possibility, not as large as we should wish, that the agreements will not be a disaster at all, and a remote chance, which neither the American public nor the Administration bureaucracy deserves, that they will prove a resounding success.

Whatever their chance of success, they are profoundly unwise. And the unwisdom is not confined to the United States alone; it is certainly shared by some of our allies, and may well be shared, though in reduced degree, by the Soviet Union. This is a particular disappointment to those of us who have been hoping and working for a strategic arms-control agreement that would make a genuine contribution to American security.

The agreements are two: 1) A proposed treaty limiting the deployment of defenses against ballistic missiles, called the Treaty on ABMs, and 2) a proposed "Interim Agreement" limiting certain kinds of strategic offensive forces, namely ICBMs and SLBMs (Intercontinental and Submarine-Launched Ballistic Missiles, respectively). The problems of these two are very different.

The Interim Agreement guarantees not merely Soviet parity with, but Soviet strategic superiority over the United States, to a potentially substantial degree. The unwisdom of this agreement lies in the dramatic announcement it makes that the United States has not only become, but apparently is willing to remain, the second nuclear power. This foolishness is, of course, in no way shared by the Soviets; indeed, as one prominent American strategist put it, the Soviets must be pinching themselves to make sure they are not dreaming.

The ABM Treaty is more symmetric in its immediate effects; in contrast to the Interim Agreement, it does not allow the Soviets four times as much as we are allowed. Apart from a limited (but potentially significant) defense of national capitals, and a limited (and strategically insignificant) defense of missile fields, we and the Soviets have agreed not to defend ourselves — not only against each other, but, interestingly, against anyone else either.

On the American side, this agreement stems purely from a sophomoric ideology and fashion, and is pure foolishness; on the Soviet side, the politburo may have accepted the same ideology, in which case they share equally in the foolishness. It is as if we and the Soviets had become seized with a theory that motor vehicles were bad for us, and, proceeding from that theory, both agreed to destroy all the motor vehicles of all kinds we produced in the future. In other words, that we and the Soviets might agree on some completely symmetric arrangement would not of itself prove that the arrangement was in our interest. In my view, the ABM Treaty provides an equally good illustration.

In my initial analysis of the Interim Agreement and the ABM Treaty, I shall concentrate on their shortcomings. I shall return later to the circumstances and forces that led to these agreements.

## The Interim Agreement

The basic provisions of the Interim Agreement are as follows. First, we and the Soviets undertake not to start construction of additional fixed land-based ICBM launchers after July 1, 1972. Second, we both agree not to convert land-based launchers for "light" ICBMs into launchers for "heavy" ICBMs. Third, we agree to limit SLBM launchers and the submarines that carry them to the numbers operational and under construction as of the date of signature (May 26), except that additional launchers (and appropriate numbers of submarines) may be constructed as replacements for an equal number of obsolete ICBM launchers or for launchers on older submarines. In a protocol appended to the Interim Agreement, this is spelled out: The U.S. may have no more than 710 SLBM launchers, and no more than 44 submarines; of those, launchers above 656 and submarines above 41 (the current numbers) must be replacements for equal numbers of obsolete ICBM launchers (in our case, the Titan II). The Soviet Union may have no more than 950 SLBM launchers and no more than 62 "modern" submarines; of those, launchers over 740 (the presumptive current number) must similarly be replacements for older ICBM launchers and SLBM launchers. Fourth, subject to the foregoing restrictions, modernization and replacement of strategic offensive ballistic missiles and launchers is permitted. Fifth, compliance with the agreement shall be monitored with "national technical means of verification," meaning such things as reconnaissance satellites, and it is also agreed not to interfere with each other's means of observation or to use deliberate concealment measures that could impede that verification.

The intended immediate purpose of this Agreement is to freeze strategic offensive forces where they now stand, understanding that whatever is under construction at the prescribed date is to be included as if finished. Such an objective is not fundamentally irrational; I have myself urged consideration of a different freeze in other times and circumstances. The difficulties stem largely from the fact that the United States strategic forces have not changed very much in basic capacity for the past eight years, while the Soviet payload capacity — the amount of weight their missile force could deliver on targets, sometimes called the "throw weight" — has increased enormously since 1966, and it now stands around four times the payload capacity of the American force. A secondary problem resides in the extraordinarily generous terms given the Soviets for converting some obsolete missiles into additional modern SLBMs and submarines.

Supporters of the Agreement will point out, and correctly, that, while the Soviet Union has more launchers than the United States, we have — we believe — many more warheads deployed *on* those launchers. The estimate is based on the belief that the American technology for MIRV (Multiple Individually-targeted Re-entry Vehicles) is much further advanced than the Soviet technology, and that we have deployed MIRV warheads on a substantial fraction of our strategic force while the Soviets have scarcely started (if they have begun at all). However, if the Soviets wish to achieve large numbers of warheads by deploying lighter MIRV warheads within their existing payload capacity, the technology for doing so is within their reach; we, on the other hand, are precluded from achieving the payload capacity of the Soviets by the Interim Agreement.

The throw weight of a strategic force is unquestionably the most important single parameter for characterizing the potential of that force, even though other parameters — notably the number, yield and accuracy of warheads that can be delivered — are of more immediate importance. Some examples of how payload capacity can be used may be instructive. For example, the maximum capacity of a Poseidon launcher is perhaps in the area of three thousand pounds or less. A Poseidon missile, it is said, can accommodate from ten to fourteen MIRV warheads, which must therefore weigh no more than three hundred pounds each. These warheads would be relatively "small" weapons of perhaps fifty kilotons each, but one missile could attack ten separate targets. Some models of the Soviet SS-9 missile have a single large warhead, and some people might think that, at least for many purposes, a single Poseidon missile is therefore worth ten SS-9s. In fact, however, that single SS-9 warhead is often estimated to be perhaps 25 megatons, which would suggest that the missile payload capability is around twelve thousand pounds, or at least four times the payload capacity of a Poseidon missile. Therefore, if a Poseidon booster could launch ten MIRV warheads, an SS-9 could launch forty of the same kind.

The SS-9 probably has from five to ten times the

payload capacity of our various Minuteman missiles, and therefore the Soviet force of approximately three hundred SS-9s by itself probably has two to three times the payload capability of our entire Minuteman force of one thousand. However, the Soviets have perhaps another 1,300 ICBMs in addition to their SS-9s, most of which are also larger than our Minutemen.

Considering both SLBM and ICBM payloads, it is probable that the Interim Agreement will allow the Soviets a throw weight roughly four times ours, with present booster technology. (Either side is at liberty to improve its booster technology; in fact, the Soviets have recently given evidence of a new model of SS-9 with perhaps twice the payload capability of earlier models.)

Some Administration analysts argue that the Soviets do not now have MIRV technology and could not deploy significant numbers of MIRV warheads within the five-year lifetime of the Interim Agreement. In evaluating this position, three points should be borne in mind. First, if no better agreement is negotiated before this one expires, there will be intense pressures to renew it. Second, the estimates that the Soviets could not get substantial MIRV capability come from the same community of intelligence analysts who led former Defense Secretary Robert McNamara to announce in the mid-1960s that the Soviets had accepted permanent strategic inferiority, and who were confident in advance of the first Chinese nuclear explosion in October 1964 that that bomb would be a plutonium device. It proved to be a uranium bomb; and it is an easy point that an operating diffusion plant for separating U-235 is very much harder to conceal than a MIRV test.

Most important, we developed MIRV from scratch in about six years, and the system development for the advanced specific systems probably did not take more than three or four years.

Since our own MIRV programs have been noisily advertised to the Soviets since early 1968 (and public mention of the idea can be found as far back as 1963), it would be surprising indeed if the Soviets did not by now have some very advanced ideas on how to do MIRV. Some analysts do, in fact, believe that the Soviets could achieve substantial MIRV capability within the lifetime of the Interim Agreement. Admiral Thomas Moorer, Chairman of the Joint Chiefs of Staff, said in his statement before the Senate Armed Services Committee on February 15: "... our intelligence specialists believe that by the mid or late 1970s the Soviets could have MIRVed SLBMs in their operational forces."

Published comparisons of Soviet and American missile forces showing a substantial American lead in warheads, as for instance in a chart on the front page of the *New York Times,* May 27, showing 5,700 warheads for the U.S. and 2,500 for the Soviet Union, should be understood as having, in all probability, a highly limited lifetime of validity. Even today, the Soviet warheads are much larger and more destructive than ours.

(The estimates that are given for the Soviet ICBM force, incidentally, such as the number 1,618, are all derived from American intelligence; the Soviets have refused to say how many missiles they have. Thus, our estimates of the Soviet strategic forces are presumably lower bounds. The limitation in the Interim Agreement is stated as a prohibition on new silo starts, not as an absolute ceiling on numbers. If we later discover a whole field of ICBMs, which I am told has happened in the past, there may be some controversy over just when it was started. There is also room for controversy over what constitutes "light" or "heavy" ICBMs.)

If the Soviets have paid any significant attention to MIRV technology in the past, as is very likely, it would be well within their capability to deploy ten thousand or more MIRV warheads on their allowed booster force within the lifetime of this Agreement. They could do this with sufficient yield in warheads, combined with sufficiently upgraded guidance in their missiles, so that they could wipe out virtually all of our Minuteman force with less than half of their missile force.

This is not to say that launching such an attack would be attractive to the Soviets under ordinary circumstances; the United States has important offensive forces other than Minuteman, and these other forces retain considerable deterrent persuasiveness. Even the Minuteman force by itself would still provide some deterrence; a calculation that it could be substantially eliminated would be only a calculation and not likely to be appealing to political leaders except under desperate circumstances. But the lopsided nature of the situation will likely have important adverse consequences, as discussed below.

The Administration's justification for not only accepting this embarrassing posture but engraving it in a formal agreement, is that Congress will not in any event provide money for the forces needed to equalize the Soviet strategic force. Indeed, the Administration believes, and sincerely, that if it were not for this Agreement the Soviets would increase their margin of superiority to some even larger extent. For example, the current rate of construction of Soviet ballistic-missile submarines is nine or ten per year; if that rate were continued, in five years the Soviets could have not 62, but perhaps ninety modern missile-launching submarines. Therefore, instead of having the 50 per cent superiority in submarines the Agreement will potentially give them, they could have a 2 to 1 margin (assuming that Congress would not provide the several billion dollars necessary for us to keep pace, an assumption that has not been seriously tested, and may well be false.)

Some Administration analysts argue that the degree of strategic superiority given the Soviets by the Interim Agreement, while admittedly large, is nevertheless less than suggested above. The chief arguments they advance are: a) the Agreement does not include bombers, in which we have substantial superiority; b) the Agreement omits what are called "Forward Based Systems," i.e., our nuclear delivery systems based in Europe; and c) the apparent Soviet superiority in submarines (62 Soviet *v.* 44 American) is not real, since the Soviets do not or cannot operate their submarines as efficiently as we can with our bases (at Rota and Holy Loch) closer to the Soviet Union. These arguments are more cosmetic than tenable. As for a), it is possible to believe in the superiority of American bomber forces only so long as Soviet medium bombers are not counted; they have some seven hundred of these, which could attack targets in the United States and continue on to airfields in Cuba and Mexico.

As for b), the Soviets have some seven hundred intermediate- or medium-range ballistic missiles that can attack European targets, to which our Forward Based Systems are mainly in response. These Soviet missiles are in no way affected by the Agreement; they can build as many more as they please. As for c), there is nothing to prevent the Soviets from adopting more efficient means of using their submarines. They could, for instance, resupply the submarines and change their crews from ocean-going tenders, so that a larger fraction of the submarines would be on station. Of course, the Soviets *may* not do this, but it would certainly not be difficult to do so and there is nothing in the proposed Agreement to prevent them.

The real Administration argument for the Interim Agreement is that it will limit the extent to which the Soviets will achieve strategic-force lead more reliably than any other approach in sight. But that Soviet advantage, by any reasonable assessment, is already real, and may well become greater as the Soviets deploy MIRVs and otherwise upgrade their permitted force in the coming years. The political consequences of this superiority, or more precisely of the general public recognition of it, are several, and all bad.

First, it will reinforce and confirm previously established Soviet images and expectations of a declining American role in world affairs. Within the past two years, Soviet commentators on the American scene have exhibited increasing contempt for the United States, its power and its role in international affairs. For instance, Soviet analysts often make such remarks as: "The United States must be adjusting itself, in the manner of the United Kingdom at the end of World War II, to its loss of power and influence in the world." The Soviets correspondingly think of themselves as very much in the ascendant. These Soviet attitudes and expectations will be reflected in their peacetime bargaining and will increase their aggressiveness in possible crisis confrontations.

Second, the Agreement and the Soviet lead it establishes will do much to establish an image of American inferiority in American government circles. The effects of this, of course, will be the obverse of those to be expected from the attitudes in the Soviet bureaucracy, though probably less marked in degree.

Third, the new imbalance of power will become firmly established in the minds of our allies, which will ultimately lead them to be more responsive, perhaps unduly responsive, to Soviet diplomatic pressures and initiatives. To use the current jargon, the Interim Agreement will contribute to "Finlandizing" tendencies in the policies of our allies.

Fourth, enshrining this degree of Soviet superiority as a substantially permanent thing will almost certainly have adverse consequences in any serious crises that may develop. For instance, we could not reasonably expect as favorable an outcome in a replay of the Cuban missile crisis. (The success of that outcome did not reside so much in the immediate outcome in Cuba as that the Soviets were deterred from counter-escalating in Turkey, or, especially, in Berlin, a fact that apostles of parity find convenient to ignore.)

It is in a certain sense true that different degrees of superiority can in the last analysis be translated only into different degrees of "victory" that would in any event be altogether Pyrrhic. However, this often-repeated observation conveniently ignores the fact that most political leaders and many military leaders are not academic strategists: These leaders not only count weapons, they tend to think in terms of who will come out "ahead," and their (perhaps simplistic) attitudes about these matters will influence their expectations, demands and flexibility in a crisis (other things — such as the guts and the political support of the leaders on the scene — being equal). Therefore, a commitment to a position of strategic disadvantage is, at least in some statistical sense, an invitation to be pushed around in the next crisis.

## The ABM Treaty

The key terms of the Treaty on ABMs are as follows: First, "Each party undertakes not to deploy ABM systems for a defense of the territory of its country and not to provide a base for such a defense, and not to deploy ABM systems for defense of an individual region except as provided for in Article III of this treaty." The basic philosophy is clear: Apart from the exceptions indicated, we may not defend our homeland against missile attack.

Second, Article III provides for a limited defense by one hundred interceptors of Moscow and Washington, and another defense system, similarly limited to one hundred interceptors, of ICBM silos in some area remote from the national capital.

Third, both we and the Soviets undertake not to develop, test or deploy ABM systems or components which are sea-based, air-based, space-based or mobile land-based.

Fourth, it is prohibited to transfer ABM systems or their components to other states or to deploy them outside Soviet and American national territory.

Fifth, compliance with the provisions of the Treaty shall be monitored by "national technical means of verification," as in the Interim Agreement, and (also similarly) there are obligations not to interfere with such means or to attempt deliberate concealment.

American strategic nuclear policy has been dominated in recent years by the concept of "assured destruction," according to which the chief task of the U.S. strategic forces is to be able to mount a nuclear attack that will be sure to destroy a substantial fraction of Soviet society, even after a major Soviet strike on American forces. (Recent statements by the Nixon Administration have emphasized a doctrine called "strategic sufficiency," but it is clear that something like the concept of "assured destruction" still dominates American strategic policy.)

This domination extends to strategic arms-control matters. It is argued that the most stable, secure, cheap and generally desirable arrangement is one in which we and the Soviets maintain a "mutual assured destruction" posture, in which no serious effort is made by either side to limit the civilian damage that could be inflicted by the other. Most of the opposition in the West to substantial systems of missile defense for cities, including the opposition embodied in this proposed ABM Treaty, derives from the alleged benefits of such a posture. And much of the opposition to the Safeguard ABM system, which was not intended to provide a substantial defense of cities, stemmed from a concern that it might expand to provide such a defense.

The concept of mutual assured destruction provides one of the few instances in which the obvious acronym for something yields at once the appropriate description; for it, that is, a Mutual Assured Destruction posture as a goal is, almost literally, mad. MAD. If technology and international politics provided absolutely no alternative, one might reluctantly accept a MAD posture. But to think of it as desirable — for instance, as a clearly preferred goal of our arms-control negotiations, as the proposed ABM treaty automatically assumes — is bizarre. Let us consider the simplest and most effective means of realizing it.

At present, we and the Soviets achieve a MAD posture by means of long-range missiles and bombers armed with thermonuclear weapons. There are, however, many problems associated with these forces. Missiles and bombers may be attacked before they are launched; they may fail to perform properly; they may fail to penetrate enemy defenses. Concern about such vulnerabilities helps fuel the arms race. These forces are also expensive; the U.S. alone spends about $8 billion a year on them.

Now, if it were genuinely desirable to have a MAD posture, we could achieve it effectively, reliably and cheaply. We could have an arms-control agreement to mine each other's cities: We could install very large thermonuclear weapons with secure firing arrangements in, say, Moscow, Leningrad and Kiev, etc. while the Soviets could install similar weapons and arrangements in New York, Chicago and Los Angeles, etc. It is technically feasible to make such a system quite secure; with the vulnerabilities mentioned above eliminated, arms-race pressures would be reduced. While such a system would have its own technical problems, analysis indicates they would be far simpler to solve than those of the current system; it could save billions. Yet almost everyone will dismiss it as being merely absurd. If a mined-city system is the best way of realizing a MAD posture, it follows that posture as a goal is itself fundamentally absurd.

There are three fundamental problems here: The first is that, in spite of our best efforts, a major nuclear war could happen. An institutionalized MAD posture is a way of insuring, now and forever, that the outcome of such a war would be nearly unlimited disaster for everybody. While technology and politics may conspire to leave us temporarily in such a posture, we should not welcome it — we should rather look for ways out of it.

The second fundamental difficulty is essentially political: We do not have a Department of Defense for the purpose of deliberately making us all hostages to enemy weapons. The government is supposed, according to the Constitution, to "provide for the common defense," and plainly most Americans would revolt at the idea of a mined-city system as a sensible way to do this. The Defense Department should be more concerned with assuring live Americans than dead Russians.

The third fundamental difficulty is moral: We should not deliberately create a system in which millions of innocent civilians would be exterminated should the system fail. The system is not *that* reliable. Again, if we accept a MAD posture as an interim solution, we should be looking for ways out of it, not ways to enshrine it.

Why, then, do some advocate a MAD posture? The advocates are, in the main, technically oriented people accustomed to theoretical models, and the arguments involve appeals to "stability' of various kinds and reference to other sophisticated jargon — jargon that I understand very well, having helped to articulate it a decade or more ago. For instance, one argument sometimes heard — it is, e.g., reflected in the preamble to the proposed ABM Treaty — is that this posture will best protect against nuclear war altogether, but this proposition is very dubious indeed.

While these MADvocates are undoubtedly sincere, and many of them intelligent, I believe they have been bemused by theoretical models of strategic interactions, models which seem sophisticated and intellectually appealing but which are in fact much oversimplified descriptions of reality. Some few technical people have been so bemused by the models that they seriously advocate deployment of a mined-city system.

If an institutionalized MAD posture is not desirable as a permanent way of life, and it is not, what alternative is available? The answer is to put increasing emphasis on defense, with a corresponding reduction in the effort devoted to strategic offensive forces.

There is much controversy about just how effective any defense (such as ABM) can be made against existing or further enlarged offensive forces. I cannot discuss this controversy here. However, there is very little controversy over the fact that defense can be made quite effective if the opposing offense is suitably reduced, while allowed defense is built up. This is precisely the direction that the Strategic Arms Limitation Talks should have taken, but did not.

Even if it were agreed that currently achievable defense is too ineffective to be useful against even a suitably reduced offensive threat (a position that few informed persons would take), it makes little sense to preclude the possibility of a more effective defense being found in the future. The proposed treaty does exactly that.

It might be possible to achieve similar effects simply by sharply reducing offensive forces, without any defense, if it were not for two factors: a) there are other countries in the world besides the United States and the Soviet Union, and b) perfect inspection of sharply reduced offensive forces probably cannot be achieved, and defense can provide protection against clandestine weapons.

The MAD philosophy originally took hold in the American arms-control community about 1960. This might have been ultimately unimportant but for the fact that Robert S. McNamara became a determined believer in the concept, and imposed the "Assured Destruction" philosophy on the civilian staffs in the Pentagon with the full force of his personality. This was in a sense a *tour de force,* because at the time, the Soviets conspicuously did not share this philosophy (although he often asserted that they did). The evidence is overwhelming that, at least up until the late 1960s, the Soviets did not consider a MAD posture desirable. For instance, Premier Kosygin, asked about a moratorium on missile defenses at a press conference in London on February 9, 1967, replied, in part: "I believe that defensive systems, which prevent attack, are not the cause of the arms race, but constitute a factor preventing the death of people. Some argue like this: What is cheaper, to have offensive weapons which can destroy towns and whole states or to have defensive weapons which can prevent this destruction? At present the theory is current somewhere that the system which is cheaper should be developed. Such so-called theoreticians argue as to the costs of killing a man — $500,000 or $100,000. Maybe an antimissile system is more expensive than an offensive system, but it is designed not to kill people but to preserve human lives. I understand that I do not reply to the question I was asked, but you can draw yourselves the appropriate conclusions." This is not the comment of a man who was friendly to a moratorium on missile defense.

Many other Soviet pronouncements, public and private, official and unofficial, left no doubt that the Soviets favored heavy emphasis on active defense, at least up through 1968 and early 1969. But beginning in 1969 or 1970, the Soviet government leaders either began to change their views, or else decided to make us *think* they had changed their views. Thus the overt indications in the SALT negotiations for the past two years have suggested whole-hearted Soviet acceptance, at least at the top of the hierarchy, of the MAD philosophy.

If the Soviets have indeed come to this position, they have had a good deal of American help in getting there. Almost every American who argued with almost any Russian about arms-control matters in the 1960s tried to make the point that missile defenses were wicked. This stemmed, of course, from the commitment in certain American quarters to the MAD philosophy. Up until 1968, the universal Soviet reaction to this argument was a polite raspberry. But some U.S. spokesmen could not be easily ignored. In particular, McNamara himself did his best to convert the Soviets to his philosophy, both in public statements and in private meetings (notably at the Glassboro Conference in June 1967, when he forcefully presented the case for MAD directly to Kosygin, who did not go for the idea, at least at that time). Another forceful input to the Soviets came from President Lyndon B. Johnson, who, according to his memoirs, sent Premier Kosygin a secret letter in January 1967 warning him that the incipient deployment of Soviet missile defenses had put him under pressure to "increase greatly our capabilities to penetrate any defensive systems which you might establish." Johnson continued: "If we should feel compelled to make such major increases in our strategic weapons capabilities, I have no doubt that you would in turn feel under compulsion to do likewise." It seems likely that this letter was stimulated by Secretary McNamara.

Perhaps the most persuasive pressure on the Soviets was not an argument per se, but the American decision of late 1967 and early 1968 to proceed with a major MIRV program for the American strategic offensive force, leading to the deployment of Minuteman III and Poseidon. This program was intended to add something like five thousand additional warheads to the American offensive force. The almost theological, not to say fanatic, faith McNamara had in the MAD philosophy is reflected in the fact that, while he viewed the beginning of a Soviet system for defense of the homeland as highly provocative, he apparently saw nothing provocative in spending many billion dollars to add several thousand additional warheads to the American force, especially at a time and under circumstances that would have made it impossible for the Soviets to know what accuracy these weapons might achieve.

For whatever combinations of reasons, the Soviets have now either accepted the MAD philosophy or are pretending to. It should be noted that, up to the time of writing, one cannot detect many hints of this philosophy in the papers of Soviet colonels writing for each other in *Red Star*; however, this may indicate merely that the message has not yet come down from the top. (Some well-placed Soviet officials have in fact indicated to Americans, very privately, that the ABM Treaty will mean a major doctrinal overhaul in the Soviet military establishment, and may well require a considerable shuffling of senior personnel. It will be interesting to see if this in fact comes to pass.)

# AFTER SALT I: MIRVs, STRATEGIC PARITY, AND THE DECLINE OF DÉTENTE

## The Decline of Détente

### *Document 14*

In the Nixon administration, the SALT process was closely linked to détente. However, after reaching its high point in 1972 and 1973, détente began to unravel under the strains of U.S. domestic politics, Soviet assertiveness in the Third World, and increasing U.S.-Soviet disagreements. Harvard political scientist and former National Security Council staff member Samuel Huntington reviews the events that strained détente in the late 1970s. The decline of détente meant that future arms control would face serious obstacles.

## 14 RENEWED HOSTILITY
## Samuel P. Huntington

### The Cresting of Détente: 1972–1973

Nixon's visit to Moscow in May 1972 marked the cresting of the détente wave. Its momentum continued through the first part of 1973. Congress overwhelmingly approved the SALT accords in the late summer of 1972. Agreements concerning trade, credits, and the still outstanding lend-lease debts were signed in the early fall. In November the SALT II talks got underway in Geneva, and a month later the Standing Consultative Committee authorized by the SALT I agreement was established. In January 1973 the Vietnam cease-fire agreement was signed, and the MBFR talks began in Vienna. In the late spring and early summer, Brezhnev first visited Bonn, where he signed an economic cooperation agreement, and then Washington, where he signed the Agreement on the Prevention of Nuclear War. The first round of the CSCE talks got under way in Helsinki during the summer. U.S.-Soviet trade shot up from $106.6 million in 1971 to $702.6 million two years later. All in all, the relaxation of tensions, the multiplication of contacts and exchanges, the signing of agreements, and the proliferation of negotiating arenas were the order of the day.

The core of détente was the perceived mutual interests of the two sides in trade and arms control. The Soviets needed trade with the West, particularly the United States, to promote economic development and to avoid economic reform. Elements of U.S. business saw substantial Soviet trade opportunities, and the U.S. administration saw increased trade as a means of enhancing the Soviet stake in international stability. Both sides would gain from arms-control agreements regularizing and limiting the competition, with an additional benefit to the Soviets from the formal U.S. recognition of their equality as a superpower. The overall military balance of the early 1970s was not markedly unfavorable to either side and thus seemed to provide a secure underpinning for arms-limitations agreements. In fact, however, the trends in the military balance during the years of détente overwhelmingly favored the Soviet Union. This was one major weakness in détente, for Americans seemed to assume that détente meant the continuation of the existing military balance, while the Soviets seemed to assume that it meant the continuation of the prevailing trends in that balance. Despite Soviet declarations of their intention of continuing ideological and political competition within the détente framework, Americans also assumed that they would not use détente "as a cover to exacerbate conflicts in international trouble spots," as Henry Kissinger put it during the October War.[32] In a similar vein, but in reverse, the Soviets undoubtedly assumed that détente was incompatible with Western "interference" in internal matters such as treatment of dissidents, Jewish emigration, and their relations with their satellites. Détente was thus strongest in the core areas of negotiated mutual benefits — trade and arms control. It was weakest where the interests were too sensitive, asymmetrical, and diffuse to be negotiated: Soviet involvement with the Third World and Western involvement with human rights.

## The Recession of Détente, Fall 1973–Winter 1977

Détente did not end in the fall of 1973. The October War was, however, the first major event to highlight its weaknesses and its fragility. During the following three years, American and Soviet statesmen committed to détente — Brezhnev, Nixon, Kissinger — tried to maintain its momentum, particularly in the central areas of trade and arms control. In both areas, however, the hoped-for achievements failed to materialize, in large part because of the antagonisms and concerns that blossomed forth in the other three major areas of Soviet-American relations. The Soviets became increasingly concerned with U.S. and, to a lesser extent, European pressure with respect to human rights, particularly Jewish emigration. Americans were aroused by apparent Soviet complicity in the launching of the October War, the extensive Soviet efforts to encourage and support the Arab states in that conflict, and the Soviet threat to introduce its troops into the Middle East. Two years later Soviet support for Cuban intervention in Angola refueled these concerns. In addition, American leaders, both within and outside the government, became increasingly alarmed by the Soviet military buildup and the virtually across-the-board relative decline in U.S. military capabilities vis-à-vis those of the Soviets. By 1976 roughly three-quarters of the American public still favored détente, but it had also become a concept that American politicians either rejected or avoided.

During the years 1973–76 the two administrations under the foreign policy guidance of Henry Kissinger made serious efforts to negotiate arms-control and trade agreements with the Soviet Union. Until 1975, however, they remained relatively indifferent to the changing military balance and to human rights issues. They also adamantly opposed Soviet efforts to extend their military presence and influence in the Third World. In Kissinger's view, such efforts were to be stopped by local counteraction — diplomatic, covert, or military if need be. It was useless and self-defeating to attempt to prevent Soviet Third World expansion by attempting to link it to either SALT or trade. "[E]xpansion can be checked only where there is a local balance of forces; indirect means can succeed only if rapid local victories are foreclosed."[33] The administration had acted along these lines during the imbroglio over Soviet expansion of their base facilities in Cuba in 1970. It acted along similar lines when it altered U.S. military forces in response to possible Soviet deployments to the Middle East. It was prepared to take action to prevent the North Vietnamese conquest of South Vietnam in 1974 and 1975. It attempted to take what it considered to be appropriate counteraction against Soviet-Cuban intervention in Angola in 1975–76.

These latter two cases indicate the extent to which the administration's view of the forceful actions needed to sustain détente lacked a solid base in U.S. public opinion. The early and mid-1970s were the years when the proportion of the American public that identified itself as isolationist increased dramatically (from 8 percent in 1964 to 23 percent in 1974), when Americans were generally unwilling to use American troops to defend other countries, including close allies, and when elites in the media and Congress were even more suspicious of and opposed to anything that smacked of potential military involvement or covert action. Reflecting these sentiments, Congress in 1973 sealed the ultimate fate of Indochina by prohibiting future American military action there, and then, in 1975, prevented the administration from providing financial and material support to the anti-Soviet forces in Angola.

At the same time that public and congressional opinion obstructed the administration's efforts to counter Soviet military expansion, it also obstructed the administration's efforts to promote the expansion of Soviet trade. Senator Henry Jackson first raised the issue of Jewish emigration with respect to the trade reform bill in 1972. In 1973 provisions were added to the bill linking U.S. granting of most-favored-nation (MFN) status and Export-Import Bank credits to the Soviets' allowing free emigration from their country. President Nixon vetoed the bill. A year later, after complex negotiations in which the secretary of state mediated between Soviets and senators, a revised bill was passed. The Soviets, however, denounced the bill and rejected the earlier-negotiated trade agreement. The ceiling had been reached on U.S.-Soviet economic relations.

In the course of one year, Congress had thus twice defeated administration initiatives in Soviet-American relations: it had prevented both the extension of credits and most favored nation status, on the one hand, and anti-Cuban covert action in Angola, on the other. In terms of defining the limits of détente, the Congress wanted to promote human rights in the Soviet Union, while the administration wanted to stop Soviet expansion in the Third World. The result, from the viewpoint of the leading American détente-ist, was the worst of all possible worlds: "constant pinpricks of the Soviet bear (denial of MFN status, for example), but not coupled with a readiness on our part to run the risks that alone could produce Soviet caution (in Angola, for example)."[34]

Throughout 1973–76, U.S. public opinion was overwhelmingly unsympathetic to the strengthening of U.S. military forces. So were the dominant groups in Congress. During this period, however, officials in the executive branch gradually became more concerned with what appeared to be continuing unfavorable trends in the military — particularly the strategic — balance. This concern was fueled both by new Soviet programs and by the reevaluation of past and continuing Soviet programs. Soviet military spending was increasing at a rate of 3–4 percent a year; Soviet conventional forces were being strengthened and modernized; the Soviet navy had acquired the capabilities to maintain significant forces in the Indian Ocean, the Mediterranean, and elsewhere; the Soviets were beginning deployment of a new generation of intercontinental missiles. Most alarming from the American viewpoint was the Soviet progress in MIRVs. The Soviets flight-tested a new generation of ICBMs that could carry MIRVs in the winter of 1975.

In addition, the United States began to reexamine its earlier appraisals of the Soviet military effort and to focus on the extent to which that effort had been underestimated. In 1974 Albert Wohlstetter published his analysis of the failure of U.S. intelligence to predict the rate and size of the Soviet ICBM buildup in the 1960s.[35] In 1975–76 the CIA revised upward its estimates of the percentage of the Soviet GNP going for defense from 6–8 percent to 10–15 percent and also increased its estimate of the extent to which Soviet military spending (in dollars) exceeded U.S. military spending from 20 to 40 percent.[36] Coincidentally, various presumably well-informed people, such as former chief of naval operations Admiral Zumwalt, alleged that the Soviets had been engaged in "massive violations" of the SALT I agreements.[37] This combination of events led to a more general concern with the extent to which U.S. policymakers were getting a comprehensive and accurate picture of Soviet intentions and capabilities, leading, in turn, to CIA director George Bush's appointing the "B team" of outsiders to make an independent assessment of what the Soviet Union was up to.

The administration was generally sensitive to the need to halt and to reverse, if possible, what by 1975 was the seven-year decline in U.S. defense spending. The question was how ready it should be to sacrifice what was left of détente in order to achieve this goal. Secretary of State Kissinger grimly stuck with both the concept of détente and the desirability of working out compromises to remove the obstacles to a strategic weapons agreement. Secretary of Defense Schlesinger, on the other hand, was much more willing to highlight the Soviet threat in order to strengthen American defenses. This difference was one factor, albeit perhaps not the principal one, leading to Schlesinger's departure from the administration in the fall of 1975 and his joining the growing circle of critics urging the administration to take a tougher stand regarding the Soviets.

As we have indicated, mass public opinion generally remained pro-détente, anti-defense spending, and anti-foreign involvement down through 1976. At the same time, however, the traditional liberal public philosophy was losing its intellectual vitality. This manifested itself first with respect to domestic issues and the reaction against Lyndon Johnson's Great Society programs and the expectations they had generated. The final defeat in Vietnam in April 1975, however, also cleared the way for a conservative, nationalistic reaction in foreign affairs. Conservatism was on the march intellectually and politically in the middle and late 1970s. Presidential politics in 1976 was distinguished by Jimmy Carter's defeat of the more traditional liberals in the contest for the Democratic nomination and by the extent to which Ronald Reagan came close to defeating President Ford in the Republican contest.

In its annual *Strategic Survey* for 1972, the International Institute for Strategic Studies announced that the cold war had been "buried." In its survey for 1973, however, it spoke of "Tensing the Détente." By 1975, it reported that a "general 'détente fatigue'" was pervading the West.[38] It seems likely that a parallel and perhaps comparable process had been under way on the Soviet side. The widening of economic détente, at least with the United States, ceased at the end of 1975. The rising concern in the U.S. with what might be negotiated in the SALT II talks certainly must have reinforced Soviet doubts as to whether a treaty could be arrived at that would be satisfactory from their point of view. The weakening of the American presidency during and after Watergate had caused Nixon to embrace détente as his unique contribution to world peace and then caused Ford to carry it forward in order to demonstrate just the opposite. By 1976, however, détente and its architect in both administrations, Henry Kissinger, were under serious fire from major elements in the Republican party, and Ford, who had embraced détente in order to demonstrate that he was president, now had to back away from it in order to remain president. In the end, the increasing suspicions among Republicans concerning détente, and particularly the SALT II negotiations, forced the administration to accept language in its foreign policy plank that virtually disassociated itself from the policies it had been following vis-à-vis the Soviets.

## Notes

32. See his speech at the Pacem in Terris Conference, Washington, D.C., October 8, 1973, quoted in Henry Kissinger, *Years of Upheaval* (Boston: Little, Brown, 1982), p. 239.

33. Henry A. Kissinger, "The Permanent Challenge of Peace: U.S. Policy toward the Soviet Union," address, Commonwealth Club and World Affairs Council of Northern Califor-

nia, San Francisco, Calif., February 3, 1976 (Washington, D.C.: Department of State, Bureau of Public Affairs, Office of Media Services, 1976).

34. Henry A. Kissinger, *White House Years* (Boston: Little, Brown, 1979), p. 1143.

35. Albert Wohlstetter, "Is There a Strategic Arms Race?" *Foreign Policy*, no. 15 (Summer 1974), pp. 3–20, and "Rivals But No 'Race,'" *Foreign Policy*, no. 16 (Fall 1974), pp. 48–81.

36. *The New York Times*, October 23, 1975, p. 29; February 28, 1976, p. 12.

37. International Institute of Strategic Studies (IISS), *Strategic Survey 1975* (London: IISS, 1976), p. 53.

38. International Institute of Strategic Studies (IISS), *Strategic Survey 1972* (London: IISS, 1973), p. 1; *Strategic Survey 1973* (London: IISS, 1974), p. 2; *Strategic Survey 1975* (London: IISS, 1976), p. 5.

## The Failure to Ban MIRV

### *Document 15*

As the SALT negotiations started, the United States was at work on a new technological development that would allow a missile to carry two or more warheads aimed at different targets. Originally, each ballistic missile carried only one warhead and one reentry vehicle. (The reentry vehicle is a container that protects and carries the warhead through its journey.) A missile that had multiple independently targetable reentry vehicles — in strategic terminology, a MIRVed missile — was capable of delivering accurately each of several warheads along separate trajectories. (For example, today's MX missile carries ten warheads.) Consequently, a MIRVed missile increased by severalfold the destructiveness and capability of the missile. By the time the SALT I agreement had concluded, the United States had already started deploying MIRVs. The Soviets, many years behind, were still in the testing phase.

Some government officials and analysts in the United States, such as chief U.S. SALT negotiator Gerard Smith, argued that the SALT negotiations should try for a ban on MIRVs before the new technology was fully developed. The Nixon administration rejected this view. In the following excerpt from his book on his experience as a SALT I negotiator, Ambassador Smith argues that the United States should have tried to ban MIRVs and offers some reasons why it didn't.

### 15 THE GREAT MIRV MYSTERY
### Gerard Smith

In retrospect, the weak effort to ban MIRVs was a key aspect of SALT. It was considered by some knowledgeable people as the leading lost opportunity of the negotiation. While the United States and the Soviet Union negotiated to limit the numbers of their strategic launchers they were increasing or preparing to increase their warheads manyfold. It is far from sure that even if we had made a more reasonable offer on MIRVs the Soviets would have accepted it. It seems somewhat doubtful that they would have locked themselves into a MIRVless condition, and it is most unlikely that the United States would, while stopping U.S. MIRV deployments, have permitted the Soviets to develop them through the testing stage. While there may have been an opportunity missed, it was not a clear one.

MIRVs were originally designed in the United States as a hedge. Their purpose was to assure that, even if attacked, the United States missile retaliatory forces would be able to penetrate a Soviet dense ABM defensive screen which it was assumed would exist by the late 1970s. With their striking power thus MIRV-multiplied, the potential of American missiles surviving any attack would be seen by the U.S.S.R. to be so great as to make such attack irrational. The integrity of our retaliatory forces would thus be preserved even if the Soviets deployed major ABM defenses. The SALT ABM Treaty of 1972 sharply reduced the likelihood that such ABM systems would ever be built. But MIRV programs persist.

Some MIRVed missiles can have more than a dozen nuclear warheads. MIRV multiplication of nuclear destruction is enormous. Without MIRVs, one United States strategic submarine could deliver warheads to 16 targets. With MIRVs, assuming only 10 warheads per missile, that submarine could launch attacks against 160 targets — more than all German and Japanese urban industrial areas bombed by the Allies in World War II. Small wonder that MIRVs were a key issue in any effort to control strategic arms. Great wonder that the issue was treated so cavalierly.

The major difficulty in trying to structure American and Soviet offensive strategic forces by international agreement rather than by unilateral decisions of each nation lies in the differing composition of the two forces, owing to historical, geographical and technological developments. In 1969 when SALT started, the Soviets were rapidly increasing the number of their missile launchers. The United States was not. The United States had a much larger and better intercontinental bomber force. In SALT the U.S.S.R. was to claim that the United States had a substantial advantage in fighter bombers forward based in Europe and the Far East and in the strategic submarine forces of its allies, England and France.

But the most important asymmetry of this period was in MIRVs. The MIRV capability to have a large number of warheads independently guided to separate targets was the most significant nuclear weapons development since the ballistic missile itself. It may well be that, although the Soviet position on American FBS was the ostensible cause of the failure to reach a treaty limiting offensive arms in SALT I, the real reason was that the United States was years ahead of the U.S.S.R. in MIRV technology. We were actually deploying MIRVed missiles during the negotiation. The Soviet Union had not even started to test them.

To many American officials, it was a very unattractive proposition to give up this great advantage, no matter what counter-concessions the Soviets might make. It was equally unappetizing to the U.S.S.R. to consider locking itself into an international commitment banning a fundamental new weapons system whose technology it had not yet mastered. Planners for a nation's security have to consider what the strategic balance would be if an arms limitation arrangement collapses. It is one thing to agree to stop construction of ICBM silos which could be resumed without much delay if the agreement was terminated. It is quite another to give up development of a major system which one's rival already has in stock. That is what the MIRV ban proposed by the United States in April 1970 would have required of the U.S.S.R.

One of our main purposes was to stop Soviet ICBM and SLBM launcher construction programs. The Soviets must have asked themselves what weapons programs the United States was proposing to stop in return. None. MIRVs were the only programs that the United States had to bargain with for Soviet stoppage of launcher construction programs. When it became clear that the United States was not willing to trade with them, the prospect of treaty restraints on Soviet offensive launchers dimmed. In a June 1969 letter to Secretary of State Rogers, I had written:

> It may be that our giving up MIRVs would be the only quid pro quo that the Soviets would be interested in for their halting deployment of ICBMs, SLBMs, ABMs. I believe that a strong case can also be made that in the long run it is not in U.S. interests to see MIRVs enter U.S. and Soviet arsenals. Certainly it will bring increased instability.

The failure to reach a MIRV ban foreshadowed the slushiness of the interim freeze on Soviet ICBM and SLBM launchers finally reached in May 1972. Although cast in terms of mutual obligations, the freeze (which left out MIRVs) did not constrain any United States programs. As Henry Kissinger said to the press at Moscow after the freeze agreement was signed, we were not in "the most brilliant bargaining position I would recommend people to find themselves in." That was because we had not been willing seriously to negotiate for a MIRV ban. MIRV was the decisive asymmetry which ultimately prevented reaching meaningful controls over offensive forces in SALT I. Seven years after SALT's start, when the U.S.S.R. had mastered MIRV technology and was deploying MIRVed missiles, it agreed in SALT II to a limit on offensive strategic launchers including those for MIRVed missiles at equal though high levels. But SALT II remains in unratified limbo in 1980.

The United States military had no interest in giving up MIRV programs in any SALT I settlement. They saw them as America's alternative to building more launchers and as a great boost to the effectiveness of ICBMs and SLBMs. They had worried for some time about the so-called SAM-upgrade problem. In a MIRVless world with many fewer American warheads for the Soviets to cope with, this problem could become much more serious. Their Soviet counterparts apparently also had little interest in blocking themselves off from this most fruitful weapons development. The Soviet military perhaps saw the U. S. MIRV programs as provocative after the U.S.S.R. would have stopped its ABM program at the unfinished Moscow defense. In both capitals, political authorities would have to take and sustain extremely difficult positions vis-à-vis their military if MIRVs were to be controlled, positions which could undermine crucial military support for the entire SALT effort. This common military interest in letting MIRV run free went a long way to spoil chances for a MIRV ban.

Given this state of affairs, how did the two nations handle the issue? At best only halfhearted efforts were made. Both said they favored a MIRV ban. Neither expressed disappointment when no ban was agreed upon.

The case for banning MIRVs was strong. They would increase the threat to both sides' fixed-based ICBMs. They would unnecessarily expand the cost of weaponry. United States MIRV programs cost about $14 billion. There is no reason to think the Soviet MIRV programs are much cheaper. MIRV would vastly expand the destructiveness of a general nuclear war. MIRV multiplication of destructive nuclear power would be enormous, from around 2,000 to perhaps 10,000 nuclear warheads on each side, all substantially more powerful than the atomic bombs used in August 1945.

The prime need for MIRV control was reflected in the United States SALT objective of minimizing the prospective vulnerability of its ICBMs. Soviet MIRVs would increase the threat from their large ICBMs to American ICBMs especially as large missiles became more accurate and able to deliver many and large-yield warheads. Dr. Harold Brown, a principal SALT delegate, wrote in 1969: "Accurate MIRVs would tend to lessen the chance of land-based missiles surviving an attack since one first-strike missile with accurate MIRVs would destroy several deterrent missiles in their silos. . . . Clearly an agreement to ban the deployment of MIRVs would be desirable in order to forestall erosion of the capability to deter." Because of failure to ban MIRV, the threat to our ICBMs has not been significantly reduced in SALT. The United States for some years sublimated this danger, learned to live with it. But it won't go away. The SALT II agreed ceilings on MIRVed missile launchers are so high as to give only modest relief in the view of those analysts who project a high degree of ICBM vulnerability.

The Johnson Administration left an important arms control legacy to President Nixon. Had it not been for the invasion of Czechoslovakia in August 1968, SALT would have already started when President Nixon took office in January 1969. United States SALT positions prepared for that expected start in 1968 called for control of ABM systems and land- and submarine-based offensive missile launchers, the three systems which ultimately were included in the 1972 SALT agreements. But no ban on MIRVs was then included. The 1968 Pentagon had been opposed and proponents of a MIRV ban didn't want to take on the Department of Defense in a MIRV fight right at the start. They feared that the Pentagon could have stopped SALT cold before it even started. They hoped that the dynamics of the negotiation would gradually bring the two governments to realize the advantages of MIRV control and the weakness of an agreement that did not ban them.

If there was a possibility of MIRV control, the asymmetries in the sides' programs suggested that it would have to be agreed early in a negotiation before U.S. deployment programs were far along. I believed that the United States should take the lead in proposing a ban. We were testing MIRVs as the Nixon Administration's SALT preparations got under way. In order to verify a MIRV deployment ban adequately, it was thought that MIRV testing would also have to be banned. In the absence of intrusive on-site inspection, it was thought to be impossible to determine with high confidence whether or not a deployed missile contained MIRV warheads. Some felt that even with on-site inspection this would not be possible. MIRV flight tests, on the other hand, would be observable by national means. If the sophisticated MIRV hardware could not be developed through flight testing, the chance that MIRVs would be produced and deployed on a large scale was small. Still, some U.S. officials argued that a MIRV test ban alone would not be adequate assurance. Even to its advocates a MIRV ban looked practical only if agreed on before a significant amount of testing had been done. Strategic analysis based on computer runs had shown that suspension by the United States of MIRV testing for as long as one year would not prejudice U.S. retaliatory capabilities during the mid-1970s.

Although there had been proposals for deferral of U. S. MIRV testing, it does not seem that serious consideration had been given to them during the Johnson Administration. By the winter of 1969 an early decision about stopping or continuing MIRV testing was clearly needed. Should it be suspended for a time to permit efforts to ban MIRVs before either side was in a position to deploy them? Unless something was done soon after the Nixon Administration took office, the option to pursue a MIRV ban could be closed out. During the winter and spring of 1969, I argued the need for a ban and emphasized the relationship between U.S. testing and the likely timing of SALT. I tried to capitalize on the President's known aversion to having his options closed out by actions of the bureaucracy, as in a memorandum I wrote him on May 22, 1969, which appears in Appendix 2.

I repeated my concern to Secretary Rogers on June 6:

> Your press conference statement that continuation of MIRV testing would not prevent a successful SALT negotiation is, I understand, the "party line." In fact, at some point in the MIRV testing, the development of this new weapons system will be sufficiently advanced as to make a verification of its non-deployment an impossibility without on-site inspection of such an intrusive nature that we, let alone the Soviets, would probably not be willing to accept it. That will mean the most we can expect is a SALT agreement which permits the deployment of the many thousands of new warheads which a MIRV deployment would produce. What is involved here is for the United States, for example, an increase in nuclear warheads from 2,600 to between 7,000 and 9,500 by 1977. This is hardly a way to limit strategic arms.

My MIRV ban proposals soon merged into a broader position called SWWA, "Stop Where We Are," which involved not only stopping MIRV testing but cessation of Soviet ICBM and SLBM launcher construction programs. This proposal stemmed from a suggestion made by an Arms Control Agency official, Sidney Graybeal, who was a member of the SALT delegation and later the U.S. commissioner on the Soviet-American Standing Consultative Commission set up by the 1972 agreements. SWWA was based on a simple concept that the way to stop arms competition was to stop strategic construction programs on both sides. Both now had sufficient strategic forces to deter nuclear war. Instead of trying to elaborate agreed levels for strategic forces and other complex arrangements, why not just freeze things at the 1969 level? At the suggestion of Henry Owen, a former colleague on the Policy Planning Staff of the State Department and later its director, I recalled for the President the worldwide support which the United States received when Charles Evans Hughes proposed such a plan for strategic naval forces at the Washington Naval Conference in 1921. It was not at all clear that the U.S.S.R. would accept such a proposal, but by proposing it we could take the "high ground" psychologically and, if necessary later, move to something more modest if that was the most the Soviets would accept. I considered SWWA the best way to start the negotiation.

During a number of NSC meetings in the spring of 1969, I made the SWWA case for a moratorium on construction starts on all strategic systems, emphasizing the need to preserve the President's option to try to negotiate a MIRV ban. At this time Secretary of Defense Laird was publicly stressing the growing vulnerability of American ICBMs in the face of the threat posed by large Soviet missiles, especially as they came to be MIRVed. Owing in good part to his concerns, the Administration seemed unclear as to whether the Soviets were much further along on MIRVs than the intelligence community thought. The U.S.S.R. was testing multiple warheads, called multiple re-entry vehicles or MRVs, which were not capable of being independently targetable as are MIRVs. Laird said on a number of occasions, "I don't make the distinction between MRVs and MIRVs." All other U.S. military and intelligence officials did. In fact, MIRVed Poseidon missiles to be fitted into launchers on U.S. strategic submarines were to replace Polaris missiles with three warheads (MRVs). It was surprising to me that Secretary Laird was not more of a proponent of a MIRV ban, which would have moderated the prospective Soviet threat to American ICBMs. Laird used this threat to point up the dynamics of the Soviet missile programs and generate support for U.S. strategic programs but did not advocate the best way to avoid that threat — a MIRV ban.

The Joint Chiefs of Staff under Nixon were as adamantly opposed to a MIRV ban as under Johnson. Their SALT representative, General Allison, argued that the United States should not and in fact could not stop the march of technology. A first SALT agreement, he said, should be simple, easy to fulfill and to monitor, limited to quantitative ceilings and not affecting modernization programs such as MIRV. America's greatest military advantage was its technological superiority. That advantage could be maintained. Yes, the U.S.S.R. would someday deploy MIRVs, but who could tell when? Even if ABMs were to be limited or banned, MIRVs would still be needed for greater target coverage capability and as insurance against a sudden ending of an ABM treaty. It was a strong case, but not as convincing, I thought, as the argument that a MIRV ban was of central importance if the strategic arms competition was to be significantly curbed.

In June, I was encouraged by Secretary Laird's statement before the Senate Foreign Relations Committee that "MIRV is certainly something that is negotiable as far as any arms limitation talks are concerned." But civilian officials in his department then joined with some military analysts to elaborate rather obscure techniques which they said the Soviets could use to develop and deploy MIRVs without full-range testing. By 1970, Laird had lost his stomach for a MIRV ban if he ever had one. Kissinger advised me that Laird was now opposed.

## The Technological Arms Race Continues

### *Document 16*

The "doomsday clock" of the *Bulletin of the Atomic Scientists* was moved back to stand at twelve minutes before midnight following the SALT I agreements. (The clock dates back to December 1947 when it was devised by a group of scientists involved in making the first atomic bomb to symbolize mankind's approach to nuclear catastrophe. It was originally set at seven minutes and has moved as close as two minutes to midnight.) This editorial by Bernard Feld, one of the Manhattan Project scientists, explains why the clock was moved back and why it was not moved back more. In particular, Feld is critical of the failure of SALT I to constrain the development of MIRVs and other qualitative developments in the arms race.

## 16 LOOKING TO SALT II
## Bernard Feld

The only surprise about the Russian-American SALT agreements, signed by Brezhnev and Nixon in Moscow on May 26, is that the summit meeting came off at all. But once the Russians decided to carry on as hosts to the man whom they had reviled as the architect of Vietnamization and the perpetrator of the renewed and intensified bombing of North Vietnam and the mining of its harbors, the rest was as predictable as a grade-B television western, including the irreconcilable differences that could be resolved only by the last-minute intervention of the two great statesmen-leaders.

Now we have been presented with the greatest step towards world peace since the Sermon on the Mount, and we are torn between the impulse to cry "bravo" and the desire to shout "fraud."

Despite all the careful orchestration, it is impossible to hide the fact that this agreement could have been had anytime during the past two years. By drawing out the negotiations, the audience has become more desperate and, correspondingly, less demanding; so we can expect less opposition, both from the skeptics and from the peaceniks. But it is also true that both we and the Russians have accumulated lots of new arms and some dangerous new systems during these years.

Still, the accomplishments are very real and important: We have succeeded in avoiding a costly and futile race in the deployment of antiballistic missile systems; we have halted the upward spiral in the numbers of long-range nuclear-tipped missiles, both land and submarine based. That is an accomplishment whose importance can only be measured against the numbers that would probably be emplaced if the missile race were permitted to continue unabated. These are clear and direct gains; the indirect ones are even more important.

We have accepted the principle of *parity*, and agreed to define it loosely enough so as not to preclude small and irrelevant imbalances in one or another particular subsystem. We have agreed that verification through mutual inspection by national satellite systems is not only possible, but also important enough for the stability of the agreement that we must both eschew actions that would threaten to impair these verification capabilities. This represents the beginnings of sophistication. We have also acknowledged that mutual deterrence is vitally dependent on a continuing understanding and appreciation by both sides of the actions and intentions of the other, and we have set up a regular mechanism for trying to insure this mutual understanding through a continuing interchange of views. And we have promised one another and the world that this SALT-I agreement is only the first step.

Bravo — all that warrants setting back the clock!

But our frustration — and it is a large one — comes from the more that might easily have been, and from all the obvious, and some not so obvious, pitfalls and obstacles that have been set along the route to SALT-II.

We could have had a total ban on ABMs, if either we or the Russians had insisted on it. Instead, they are now committed to a missile-site deployment in which they don't believe and we to a national command post (Washington) site that we don't want, both in addition to the useless systems we already have. Not only are these a waste of money and resources, but such arbitrarily limited systems are an invitation to a technological race to see how far it may be possible to stretch their effectiveness. Chalk one up for the Generals on both sides.

## No MIRV Ban

With no serious ABM, there is no rationale for MIRV (multiple independently targetable reentry vehicles). Yet there is no MIRV-ban in the agreements, because we are too far along with our deployment and the Russians too far behind — an asymmetry that we do not want to give up and they do not want to freeze. So we have accepted that we will both go to MIRV, after which it will be too late to avoid MIRV without unacceptably intrusive inspection. Chalk another one up for the Generals.

With MIRV in the offing, the vulnerability to a first strike of both their and our systems of fixed land-based missiles is greatly increased — especially if we both continue to improve missile guidance accuracy. Any chance of putting some kind of a lid on improved accuracy? Not a word in the agreements.

In any case, we've both still got our nuclear missile-firing submarines — Polaris-Poseidon for us and Yankee for them, with their possible successors (improvements and replacements are allowed by the SALT-I agreements). In fact, one of the encouraging features of SALT-I is its recognition of the growing importance of the submarine-based deterrent for maintaining an invulnerable second-strike retaliatory force on both sides; for there is no foreseeable means whereby either side could eliminate any substantial portion of the other's submarine fleet in a surprise attack. But both we and the Russians are spending vast sums on anti-submarine warfare (ASW) research and development, much of it aimed at undermining the invulnerability of the nuclear submarine — a self-defeating effort as dangerous in the long run as ABM. To insure the continuing invulnerability of the nuclear submarine, and to avoid an ASW race, it is important to place limits on or to ban certain types of ASW activities. The agreements say nothing on this issue.

Nor is there any mention of the one qualitative limitation that could be immediately agreed upon and implemented — the Comprehensive Nuclear Test Ban, extending the 1963 Treaty to include underground testing. An opportunity missed.

All these missed opportunities point up the major flaw in SALT-I. Not only does it fail to address itself to the problem of controlling new and destabilizing *qualitative* developments, but, by its overemphasis on numbers and by its omissions, it may actually encourage a shifting of the arms race from the quantitative to the qualitative. As a result, if this shift actually occurs, the danger of a nuclear war could be increased as a result of SALT-I, despite the fact that both the ABM limitation and the missile freeze are good things in themselves. But our overkill capabilities are already so great — we are already so close to saturation in this respect — that more missiles do not represent the most serious danger. Rather, it is qualitative changes, changes that could undermine the stability of the present balance of terror and render it much more likely of breaking down in a time of crisis, that are much more to be feared. SALT-I does not touch at all on these problems.

## Forego ABM Options

Maybe we should not move that clock back quite so far.

There are at least two directions in which we must move to rectify these differences in SALT-I. First, their correction must be put at the top of the agenda for SALT-II; and we must not tolerate any unnecessary delays in getting on with the job. The freeze agreement gives us five years, but it would be a fatal miscalculation to think that we have anything like that length of time to halt the technological dangers now on the horizon. Meanwhile, we must establish an atmosphere that will encourage both the U.S. and the Soviet governments to exhibit the utmost restraints in the development, testing, and most especially the deployment of new or improved systems that, although permitted by the letter of SALT-I, would violate its spirit by tending to destabilize the deterrent, make the achievement of SALT-II more difficult, and delay or impede the substantial reduction in current missile and weapons numbers that must remain the long-range aim of SALT.

A good beginning, in this regard, would be for the United States to forego its option of an ABM around Washington and for the Soviet Union, reciprocally, to forego its right to a missile-site ABM deployment, at least as long as no better cases are made for these deployments than have been made until now.

As has so often been the case in recent years, further successes in limiting nuclear arms will be determined more by internal "hawk-dove" battles in each country than by the international negotiating process. In particular, we are already seeing the beginnings of a vociferous campaign, on the part of military-industrial hawks and their Senatorial spokesmen, to make Senate ratification of the SALT-I Treaty contingent on a commitment from the Administration to pursue vigorously all permitted research and development activities and deployments; nor if the past is any guide, can we expect the present Administration to provide much leadership for resisting such pressures. What needs to be avoided at almost any cost is a replay of what happened to President Kennedy on his way to ratification of the Test Ban Treaty in 1963; in that case, the "Jackson safeguards," extracted as the price of ratification, have made a travesty of the arms control aspects of that agreement. We must not permit SALT-I to go the way of the Test Ban.

We can prevent this only, I believe, by turning the tables on the hard-liners. This is an election year, and Mr. Nixon is running on a platform promising "a generation of peace." The success of SALT is essential for the fulfillment of that promise. There are enough clear-thinking liberals in the Senate to be able to block ratification of SALT-I, or to threaten to do so, unless it is accompanied by a firm commitment to hold down the lid on the testing and deployment of new systems while we pursue serious negotiations aimed at further stabilization and arms reduction in SALT-II.

Until now, we arms control advocates have been so desperate for progress that we have been willing to accept crumbs. But this is, I believe, a case where half a loaf may be worse than none. Then let us for once be as tough as our opponents in insisting that ratification of the SALT-I treaty with reservations that nullify its intent is simply not acceptable.

## Coping with Parity

### *Document 17*

The SALT I agreements codified U.S.–Soviet strategic parity. In document 17, Benjamin Lambeth, an expert on the Soviet military, examines the effect of strategic parity on Soviet behavior. He concludes that the Soviets believe parity has given them a new freedom of action vis-à-vis the United States. Although Lambeth is uncertain whether the Soviets will settle for sufficiency or will pursue superiority, he says it is clear that they will never again allow themselves to be less than equal to the United States in nuclear forces.

### 17 THE POLITICAL POTENTIAL OF SOVIET EQUIVALENCE
**Benjamin Lambeth**

What all of this means for the purposes of this discussion is that we cannot examine Soviet perceptions of strategic adequacy using the frame of reference typically employed in Western strategic analysis. For Soviet planners, strategic power is partly a function of the physical makeup, numerical size, and operational versatility of deployed forces, but it also depends heavily on other inputs into the correlation of forces, such as external political trends and the advantages they provide Soviet diplomacy, the momentum of Soviet foreign policy and the ability of the leadership to sustain and exploit it, and so on. Moreover, a specific level of arms accumulation that Soviet planners might regard as sufficient for underwriting certain peacetime political objectives (such as enforcing global recognition of the USSR as an equal to the United States) may well be deemed inadequate for bearing the more demanding burdens that could be imposed on Soviet leaders in a severe test of military strength (such as providing the means for successfully implementing Soviet military doctrine should a major nuclear catastrophe appear unavoidable).

#### Soviet Assessments of the Strategic Balance

From an overall political perspective, the Soviet leadership has every reason to be warmly pleased with the force posture it has acquired as a result of its military modernization efforts of the past decade. The rhetoric of contemporary Soviet diplomacy, in due obeisance to the spirit of detente, has been notably muted in comparison to the stridency that characterized Soviet pronouncements during the Khrushchev era. Yet the Soviets have studiously reminded their Western audiences that this image of confidence and composure is amply supported by the major shift in the East-West relationship that has occurred as a direct result of the post-Khrushchev Soviet strategic buildup. One rarely encounters a Soviet utterance on the state of the global scene any more that fails to include at least perfunctory reference to this changed strategic relationship. It is now a ritual Soviet argument that SALT, detente, and the general resurgence of the socialist community in international affairs have all been exclusively rendered possible by the newly emergent Soviet posture of strategic equality with the United States.

As an adjunct of their peacetime diplomacy, there is no doubt in the minds of the Soviet leaders that their investment in strategic force expansion has yielded handsome political dividends. Among other things, it has forced the United States to abandon its commitment to strategic superiority and obliged it to accept the Soviet Union as a full-fledged strategic equal. It has further driven the United States to settle for detente as the best framework for bilateral superpower relations it can realistically aspire to and has stimulated it to seek a regulation of the arms competition through SALT, thereby providing the Soviet Union considerable *de facto* control over the character and pace of U.S. weapons programs. Finally, coupled with the parallel growth in Soviet capabilities for remote area intervention, the Soviet buildup has played a major part in emboldening the leadership toward vigorous efforts to project its presence and influence in contested third world areas with little fear of serious U.S. opposition. References to "the unalterable truth that the balance of forces . . . has changed radically and continues to change to the detriment of imperialism" are now the stock-in-trade of Soviet declaratory commentary.[39] They seem to reflect an increasingly entrenched Soviet conviction that the momentum of history has decisively swung to their side.

This mood of sublime self-assurance inspired by the growth of Soviet strategic power has perhaps been most confidently expressed in the widely-cited proclamation of Foreign Minister Gromyko that "the present marked preponderance of the forces of peace and progress gives them the opportunity to lay down the direction of international politics."[40] It has also been conducive to more than occasional hints of outright arrogance in recent Soviet pronouncements, indicating that for at least some Soviet observers, life in the world of equivalence has become a decidedly heady experience. The Soviet assumption of license to meddle in such troubled third world areas as Angola, the Horn of Africa, and Southeast Asia has been typically explained by the glib assertion that "the struggle for military detente should in no way be taken as a refusal to support wars of liberation on the part of . . . the socialist nations."[41] Yet Soviet spokesmen waste few opportunities to lecture the United States for "importunately attempting to disseminate its own ideological principles and thrust them on other nations in the name of the struggle for human rights."[42] This double standard is scarcely novel to Soviet declaratory rhetoric, but it has assumed heightened significance in that the Soviets now speak as though they genuinely believe their position in the global strategic balance has bestowed upon them the natural right to insist on it and the capabilities to enforce it. In the current Soviet idiom, "the idea that detente can 'withstand' a burden made up of steps aimed at interfering in [Soviet] internal affairs and of attempts to insure one-sided advantages for the United States" falls in the category of what, in more polite language, the Soviets label "incorrect notions.."[43] Yet it is evidently quite acceptable, in the Soviet view, that detente should be expected to "withstand" Soviet imperial adventures abroad, unimpeded conventional force enhancement opposite NATO, continued strategic force diversification, and obdurate indifference to legitimate U.S. concerns with regard to SALT. In all events, both their rhetoric and their diplomatic comportment radiate strong Soviet convictions that the strategic balance is tilting in their favor and that their attainment of equivalence has brought them manifold political returns that would otherwise not have been forthcoming. In terms of its symbolic value and demonstrated capacity to affect the perceptions and peacetime behavior of the United States and other countries, the current Soviet strategic posture appears to have handily met the expectations of its architects.

As for the extent to which the Soviets believe their force improvements have provided useable resources for exerting leverage on the United States during crises, there is obviously much less that can be said with confidence. The Soviets have no published analytical literature on the role of strategic power in crisis diplomacy in any way comparable to ours, and we have thus far avoided a head-on collision analogous to the Cuban showdown of 1962 that might provide unambiguous insight into Soviet views on the blackmail potential of strategic forces under conditions of parity. Whatever the content of private Soviet thinking on this score may be, Soviet spokesmen have conspicuously refrained from telegraphing indications of it in open discourse and have generally restricted themselves to attacking American academic and governmental perspectives on the matter.

Indeed, it may be that by attempting to divine explicit Soviet concepts for employing strategic threats for political gain, we may be looking for a philosophy that simply does not exist in any systematic form. Throughout the past decade, Soviet military theorists have incessantly assailed U.S. concepts of strategic bargaining and coercive diplomacy as bankrupt notions that are provocative, have never worked, and would dangerously threaten international security if invoked in future superpower conflicts. While much of this commentary has been blatantly propagandistic, there is no reason automatically to dismiss it as having no practical meaning for Soviet planners. One of the principal hallmarks of Soviet military thought is its unadorned simplicity, dominated by a belief that the purpose of strategic power is neither more nor less than to deter enemies in peacetime and defeat them in war. This doctrinal focus is the product of a distinctive strategic culture that knows no counterpart in our own civilian defense intelligentsia, which has been largely responsible for promulgating such sophisticated (and, to the Soviet mind, misguided) concepts as "compellence," intracrisis bargaining, and the like.[44]

To most Soviet military writers, these concepts come across as distinctly bourgeois notions more appropriate to the marketplace than the battlefield. The insistent Soviet disavowal of such Western strategic ideas as demonstration attacks, limited nuclear operations, and slow-motion counterforce duels could, in one interpretation, be read as a subtle indication of genuine Soviet conviction that war is a serious business not to be played at with less than total determination. In peacetime and during crises, according to this view, the daring political utility of strategic power inheres simply in the tacit threat potential projected by visible Soviet forces in being, rather than in any carefully concocted bag of tricks for the application of that potential in selective or incremental half-measures. Indeed, the more forthcoming Soviet commentators on strategic matters have occasionally voiced explicit doubts regarding the utility of strategic forces for bringing their influence directly to bear in what Herman Kahn has labeled "Type II Deterrence" situations, namely, intense crises where core superpower values short of national survival lie at stake.

In this spirit, Colonel Kulish observes that while "the ability of the USSR to deliver nuclear-missile weapons to any point on the earth's surface . . . is extremely important from the standpoint of preventing all-out nuclear war . . . this form will not always be effective in those situations that could develop into limited wars, even though the interests of the Soviet Union and other socialist countries might be directly involved." For these situations, Kulish notes, "the Soviet Union may require mobile and well-trained and well-equipped [conventional] forces." In such circumstances, he adds, "the very knowledge of a Soviet military presence in an area in which a conflict situation is developing may serve to restrain the imperialists and local reaction."[45] In this unusual public foray by a Soviet spokesman into the realm of Soviet force requirements for crisis diplomacy, Kulish seems to be arguing that in less than apocalyptic situations, what deters the adversary is not any specific set of threats levied by central nuclear forces, but simply the specter of direct superpower conflict involving untold escalatory potential. In this situation, what will largely swing the political-military course of events at the point of engagement will be the local correlation of forces, influenced only indirectly by the backdrop of intercontinental nuclear weaponry.

If the Soviets have little to say about their thinking on the active uses of strategic forces in crisis confrontations short of war, however, they have revealed a great deal — both in their statements and weapons deployment activities — regarding their attitudes toward the passive value of such forces and the negative political consequences that can accrue from being grossly underequipped. Whether or not the Soviets perceived themselves as having been expressly "manipulated" by U.S. strategic superiority during the Cuban missile crisis, they almost certainly felt constrained in their freedom of action by the combined U.S. local preponderance of forces and the manifest imbalance of power at the strategic level which together allowed the United States to control the flow of events. In the aftermath of the crisis, Soviet U.N. representative Kuznetsov soberly remarked to a U.S. diplomat that the USSR would never again allow such a humiliating disaster to occur due to perceived Soviet weakness, and there is every reason to believe that the principal motivation behind the initial post-Khrushchev Soviet buildup was a collective determination on the part of the new leadership to correct once and for all the gross disparity between U.S. and Soviet nuclear forces which, in the Soviet view, allowed the United States to get away with its brazen conduct in the Cuban affair. From their experience gained during the Cuban episode, the principal lesson drawn by the Soviets was probably less that strategic superiority offers predictable payoffs in crisis diplomacy than the notion that it definitely costs to be on the inferior side in any major confrontation of countervailing resolve. By closing the gap with the United States through their concerted pursuit of offensive force equality, the Soviets probably feel that they have now acquired options for initiative and control that formerly were only available to the United States. They also doubtless draw considerable satisfaction from having knowingly forced a shift in the burdens of anxiety onto the United States in any superpower crisis that may occur in the future.

Where the Soviets almost surely harbor the gravest doubts about the adequacy of their strategic force improvement efforts to date, lies in the capacity of those efforts to underwrite the probable wartime demands of Soviet military doctrine, namely, seizing the initiative decisively at the brink of a major nuclear calamity, controlling events throughout the period of hostilities, minimizing damage to Soviet society, and ultimately laying the groundwork for a recognizable and politically meaningful Soviet victory. Because these obligations place open-ended demands on Soviet force availability, performance, and durability, the Soviet leaders can never feel so complacent about the adequacy of their preparedness efforts as to permit any prolonged resting on their strategic oars. If the Soviet Union shared our belief in the sufficiency of assured destruction capabilities and endorsed the Western willingness to settle for an international status quo based on an equitable division of spheres of influence, then we might conceivably enjoy a situation in which the historic competition between the social systems could be waged on exclusively political and economic rather than military grounds. Because the

Soviet leadership remains steadfastly unpersuaded by Western strategic logic, and because the requirements of Soviet doctrine place such immoderate demands on Soviet weapons acquisition, however, we are likely to remain consigned to a future of continued offsetting measures, within the constraints of detente and mutually accepted SALT agreements, in order to avoid a position of gross inequality in the superpower balance.

This is not to suggest, of course, that the Soviet Union is inexorably committed to the permanent achievement of strategic superiority whatever the costs. There is ample cause to doubt whether the Soviets believe such a goal lies within their grasp, given the considerable economic resources, technological capabilities, and political determination possessed by the United States to neutralize any Soviet effort to acquire a posture of manifest strategic advantage. It might be argued that Soviet leaders may see tangible benefits to be garnered from less grandiose variants of strategic advantage (such as a credible disarming capability against U.S. ICBMs), on the grounds that such a capability, joined to an imaginative counterforce strategy in the event of war, could significantly deplete U.S. combat resources while preserving a large residual Soviet force, even though portions of the U.S. SSBN and bomber fleets would remain survivable. Soviet decisionmakers might also be able to persuade themselves in a crisis that the U.S. leadership, faced with such an unprecedented stressful situation, would be driven by the shock effect of the initial Soviet offensive into autohypnosis and immobilism, either physically incapable of retaliating with its surviving nuclear forces or unwilling to endure the urban-industrial losses that such a retaliation would inevitably trigger.

## Conclusions

It has been the implicit argument of the foregoing discussion that the Soviet leadership employs multiple criteria for assessing the adequacy of its strategic inventory. In normal peacetime relations, strategic equivalence is probably deemed wholly sufficient — if not optimal — for supporting Soviet participation in global diplomacy. It provides the basis for enforcing Western acceptance of the USSR as a strategic equal and assures that the Soviet Union will be accorded its due deference as a militarily mature superpower. It further guarantees that the Soviet leaders will at least enjoy the privilege of an equal voice to the United States in the resolution of major international conflicts, whether or not it will fully support their indulging in "laying down the direction of international politics," in Foreign Minister Gromyko's extravagant formulation.

For crisis diplomacy, it is harder to assess how much confidence the Soviets have in the sufficiency of their forces for successfully coercing the United States, and it is almost impossible to isolate any systematic Soviet "theory" concerning the political exploitability of strategic muscle. The best that can be said here is that the Soviet leaders harbor unforgettable memories of what it means to be on the short end of the stick in superpower showdowns and have every intention of maintaining a force at least equal to that of the United States in appearance and versatility so as to deny Washington the certainty of escalation control in future confrontations. On this count, equivalence may or may not be regarded by the Soviets as an acceptable measure of sufficiency, but it clearly constitutes a *sine qua non* beneath which the Soviet leaders will not sit still and beyond which they will accumulate as much as they reasonably can.

It is in the domain of war-fighting capabilities that any potential Soviet consensus with the West on the adequacy of equivalence ultimately collapses and becomes supplanted by a compulsion to push Soviet force improvement to the limits drawn by Soviet resources and U.S. forbearance. In this domain, the Soviet incentive is not unlike that felt by many American military men. It rests squarely on the belief that however satisfactory equivalence may be for fair-weather diplomatic tests, the ultimate guarantee of Soviet survival lies in a force providing reasonable prospect for fighting and winning a war in the event that the rationality and good judgment of political leaders should become strained to the breaking point by uncontrolled events. The difference lies in the discrepancy between the officially-approved defense policies of the two superpowers. The United States has expressly committed itself to essential equivalence as an accepted goal of its strategic planning. The Soviet Union has, as yet, appeared uninterested in doing likewise. So long as this fundamental conceptual and policy discrepancy persists, we can expect a detente relationship in which both superpowers continue to pay formal obeisance to the ambiguous norm of "equal security" at the political level, while each strives in its unilateral R&D and deployment activities to press at the margins of feasibility — the Soviet Union in order to serve the edicts of its military doctrine within the limits of practicality, and the United States, for its part, simply in order to stay abreast.

## Notes

39. A. Migolat'ev, "Who Is Forcing the Arms Race and Why?" *Mezhdunarodnaia Zhizn',* No. 10, October 1977, p. 87.
40. Foreign Minister A. A. Gromyko, "The Peace Program in Action," *Kommunist,* No. 14, September 1975, p. 5.
41. Lieutenant General P. Zhilin, "The Great October and the Defense of the Socialist Homeland," *Voenno-Istoricheskii Zhurnal,* No. 10, October 1977, p. 18.
42. G. Sviatov, "United States Policy Regarding Armed Forces Construction and Arms Limitation," *Voprosy Istorii,* No. 2, February 1978, p. 90.
43. Yu. Oleshuk, "The Bankrupt Arguments of the Opponents of Detente," SShA: *Ekonomika, Politika, Ideologiia,* No. 10, October 1977, p. 44.
44. For further discussion, see Jack L. Snyder, *The Soviet Strategic Culture: Implications for Limited Nuclear Operations* (The Rand Corporation R-2154-AF, September 1977).
45. Kulish, *Military Force and International Relations,* p. 103.

## Suggestions for Further Reading

Blacker, Coit D., and Gloria Duffy. *International Arms Control: Issues and Agreements,* 2d ed. (Palo Alto, CA: Stanford UP, 1984). Standard text that reviews the history of arms control efforts since World War II. Chapter 11 is devoted to SALT I.

Kissinger, Henry. *White House Years* (Boston: Little, Brown, 1979). Memoirs of the president's national security adviser, giving his version of the SALT story.

Wolfe, Thomas. *The SALT Experience* (Cambridge, MA: Ballinger, 1979). An analytical account of SALT I by a senior analyst and Soviet scholar at the RAND Corporation.

*Eight*

# HAVES AND HAVE-NOTS

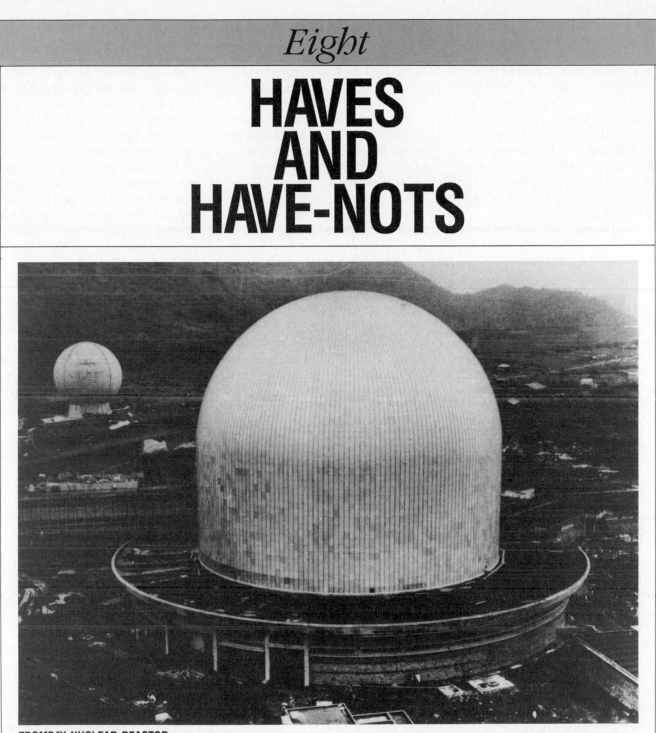

**TROMBAY NUCLEAR REACTOR**

The nuclear research reactor at the Trombay site, fifteen miles east of Bombay, India, began operating in 1960. While this and other nuclear research facilities are intended for "peaceful" purposes, there is a danger that such facilities may aid the development of nuclear weapons. AP/Wide World Photos

# INTRODUCTION

So far, this book has focused on nuclear energy as it is used to produce weapons. But the energy released by nuclear reactions can also be used for peaceful purposes, such as to produce electric power. The peaceful and weapons uses of nuclear energy combine to pose a major problem in the nuclear age: the proliferation of nuclear weapons to additional states.

The United States and the Soviet Union share a common interest in preventing the emergence of additional nuclear-armed states. Such an increase raises the number of nuclear threats each superpower must deal with. Proliferation also increases the chance that nuclear weapons might be used by accident or miscalculation or that nuclear weapons might come under the control of irresponsible leaders. Not surprisingly, both superpowers have worked hard to prevent the spread of nuclear weapons.

But the superpowers' attempts to prevent proliferation have been complicated by peaceful nuclear power. Since 1953, when President Eisenhower inaugurated the Atoms for Peace program, the United States and other Western nations have promoted the use of nuclear energy for peaceful purposes by supplying a large number of nations with the materials and expertise necessary to build nuclear power plants. The U.S. effort to encourage peaceful uses of the atom, for example, included cooperation agreements with more than thirty nations, liberal grants to make it easier to purchase research reactors, training programs, and technology transfer. The problem is that the technologies needed to develop nuclear weapons overlap with those needed for peaceful nuclear power.

This is not to say that building nuclear weapons is easy. Acquiring the capability to do so often takes decades, starting with training programs and research centers. Obtaining nuclear explosive material either by enriching uranium or reprocessing plutonium has proved a considerable technical challenge. As a result, the nuclear club has not grown as fast or as large as some experts predicted in the 1960s. China exploded a nuclear weapon almost twenty-five years ago. India conducted a nuclear test, which it labeled a "peaceful nuclear explosion," in 1974.

Nevertheless, nuclear proliferation is a major problem. The number of states able to build nuclear weapons has grown. Most experts believe that Israel has nuclear weapons and that South Africa has the capability to build them. In addition, Pakistan stands at the threshold of becoming a nuclear state, and several other states have taken steps toward manufacturing nuclear weapons.

The superpowers have tried to prevent proliferation in a number of ways. Perhaps the most cooperative action they have taken is the Nonproliferation Treaty (NPT). After the 1962 Cuban missile crisis, the United States and the Soviet Union took a number of measures designed to decrease the likelihood of nuclear war, including the agreement setting up the hot line and the 1963 Limited Test Ban Treaty. The superpowers next turned to the proliferation problem, starting a complex negotiation process that eventually took four years. The NPT was signed in 1968 and came into force two years later.

The negotiations were complicated for several reasons. First, the Soviets tried to use the NPT to prevent the United States from sharing nuclear weapons with its NATO allies. In addition, not all states shared the U.S.-Soviet view that proliferation was a bad thing. China and France wanted nuclear weapons and developed them in the mid-1960s. Other states argued that it was hypocritical for the superpowers to say that the spread of nuclear weapons was dangerous, while the number of U.S. and Soviet weapons continued to grow. Still other states worried that controls on the spread of nuclear weapons would prevent them from obtaining peaceful nuclear power. Finally, India and other countries argued that a treaty that allowed some states to have nuclear weapons and forbade others from obtaining them was discriminatory and infringed on national sovereignty.

In the end agreement was reached. The NPT is interesting because it is one of the few international treaties that does not treat all the signers equally. States with nuclear weapons have different rights and responsibilities than do those without. In essence, the nuclear states pledge not to give nuclear weapons capabilities to the non-nuclear states, and the non-nuclear states pledge not to develop nuclear weapons. In addition, the treaty tries to meet some of the concerns of non-nuclear states: it guarantees the "inalienable right" of all parties to develop peaceful nuclear energy and pledges the signers to cooperate to secure that right; it pledges all parties to seek to negotiate an end to the arms race. To execute the NPT, all signers pledge to accept international atomic energy safeguards on their nuclear installations and to accept safeguards on nuclear exports.

The NPT has been fairly successful. The United States, the Soviet Union, and Great Britain have signed, along with more than 125 non-nuclear states. But there are some very important non-signers. The declared nuclear weapons states China and France have not signed. Other key holdouts are Argentina, Brazil, Cuba, India, Israel, Pakistan, and South Africa.

The reasons for not signing are different in each case, but in general each of the latter group of countries faces a regional security situation that each believes requires leaving open the nuclear weapons option. Israel is surrounded by hostile neighbors. So is South Africa. India and Pakistan have fought several wars and engaged in arms races. Cuba feels threatened by the United States. Although Latin America is not nearly as volatile as other regions, Argentina and Brazil are regional rivals for whom nuclear weapons would be an important symbol of national power.

The United States, the Soviet Union, and the other nations that export nuclear materials have cooperated rather well in preventing the export of knowledge or material that could be used for nuclear weapons. However, several nations on the threshold of developing nuclear weapons have recently been gaining what they need by subterfuge or by threat. This nuclear "gray market" is difficult to control. In the future, it may not be possible to slow the spread of nuclear weapons by controlling the technology and the fuel. The focus on nonproliferation efforts in the future will probably center on resolving the security concerns of those near-nuclear nations that feel themselves threatened.

# NUCLEAR WEAPONS AND NUCLEAR POWER

## Producing Nuclear Weapons Material — A Primer

### *Document 1*

In this selection from his book *The New Nuclear Nations,* proliferation expert Leonard Spector describes how states can obtain the material needed for nuclear weapons. Spector notes that the major technical barrier to making a nuclear device is "obtaining the nuclear material for its core." The two sources of this material are enriched uranium or reprocessed plutonium. Both of these can be produced from the fuel used in the nuclear reactors that generate electricity. Although producing nuclear weapons material is a challenging technical task requiring large, sophisticated facilities, the technical capability to do so is within reach of several nations currently outside the nuclear club.

### 1 THE NEW NUCLEAR NATIONS
### Leonard Spector

It is generally accepted today that designing an atomic bomb — drawing the blueprint — is within the capabilities of most nations. Indeed, a number of American college students have come up with workable designs based on unclassified sources.

The major technical barrier to making a nuclear device is obtaining the nuclear material for its core. Twenty-five kilograms (fifty-five pounds) of highly enriched uranium, or eight kilograms (about eighteen pounds) of plutonium are generally considered the necessary minimum, although in both cases more sophisticated designs relying on high compression of the core material, neutron reflecting "tampers," or both, enable a bomb to be built with considerably less material — perhaps 15 kilograms of highly enriched uranium and 5 kilograms of plutonium, and even smaller amounts can apparently be used. Neither of these materials occurs in nature, however, and highly complex and expensive facilities must be built and operated in order to make them — an undertaking of considerable difficulty for developing nations without assistance from more advanced nuclear supplier countries.

#### Highly Enriched Uranium

To make a weapon from uranium, the unstable 'isotope" of uranium having a total of 235 protons and neutrons in its nucleus ($U^{235}$) is used. Since natural uranium consists of less than one percent $U^{235}$, while nuclear weapons use material that is made up of 90 percent or more $U^{235}$, natural uranium must be upgraded at an enrichment plant to achieve this concentration. Uranium enrichment is an extremely complex process and requires considerable investment. For this reason, the uranium enrichment route is generally considered a less likely path to proliferation than the plutonium option. However, South Africa, Argentina, and (with extensive outside aid obtained mostly by clandestine means) Pakistan have all developed independent uranium enrichment capabilities, and Israel, Brazil, and India are known to be conducting research in the field.

Enriched uranium can also be used as a fuel in nuclear power or research reactors. The power reactors used in the United States and most other countries (called "light water reactors") use *low-enriched uranium* fuel, i.e., uranium that has been enriched to 3 percent $U^{235}$. Thus a country can have entirely legitimate, non-weapons-related reasons for developing uranium enrichment technology even though the same technology can be used to upgrade uranium to the high enrichment level useful for nuclear weapons. On the other hand, developing a sizable independent uranium enrichment capability is economically justifiable only for nations with large domestic nuclear power programs or significant potential export markets.

Because highly enriched uranium is sometimes used to fuel research reactors, a nation can have legitimate reasons for obtaining small quantities of this material, depsite its usefulness in nuclear explosives. In recent years the United States and France have developed lower-enriched uranium fuels that can be used in lieu of highly enriched material in most of these reactors, however, considerably reducing the proliferation risks they pose.

Producing highly enriched uranium entails many steps apart from the enrichment process itself, and many other installations and capabilities are necessary. For nations wishing to obtain highly enriched uranium without international restrictions prohibiting its use for nuclear explosives, all of these would have to be developed independently, or obtained illegally, since virtually all nuclear exporter states are unwilling to sell nuclear equipment and materials unless recipients pledge not to use them for nuclear explosives purposes and place them under the inspection system of the International Atomic Energy Agency. For illustrative purposes the basic nuclear resources and facilities that would be needed include

- uranium deposits;
- a uranium mine;
- a uranium mill (for processing uranium ore containing less than 1 percent uranium into uranium oxide concentrate, or yellowcake);
- a conversion plant (for purifying yellowcake and converting it into uranium hexaflouride, the material processed in the enrichment plant);
- an enrichment plant (for enriching the uranium hexafluoride gas in the isotope $U^{235}$); and
- a capability for converting the enriched uranium hexafluoride gas into solid uranium oxide or metal (usually associated with a yellowcake-to-hexafluoride conversion plant).

## Plutonium

To obtain plutonium a country needs a *nuclear reactor.* This can be one designed specifically to maximize plutonium production (a "production reactor"), a large research reactor, or a power reactor for producing electricity. *Uranium fuel,* usually in the form of uranium-filled tubes (fuel rods) made of zirconium alloy (zircaloy), is placed in the reactor. For most production, power, and for a number of large research reactors, the fuel itself is either natural or low-enriched uranium, which is not usable for nuclear weapons at this point. As the reactor operates, the uranium fuel is partly transformed into plutonium. This is amalgamated in the fuel rods with unused uranium and highly radioactive waste products, however, and must then be extracted. To do this, "spent" fuel rods are taken to a *reprocessing plant* where they are dissolved in nitric acid and the plutonium is separated from the solution in a series of chemical processing steps. Since the spent fuel rods are highly radioactive, heavy lead casks must be used to transport them, and the rooms at the reprocessing plant where the chemical extraction of the plutonium occurs must have thick walls, lead shielding, and special ventilation to prevent radiation hazards.

Although detailed information about reprocessing was declassified by the United States and France in the 1950s and is generally available, it is still a complex procedure from an engineering point of view, and virtually every nation at the nuclear-weapons threshold that has attempted it has sought outside help from the advanced nuclear supplier countries.

Like enrichment facilities, however, reprocessing plants can also be used for legitimate civilian purposes, because plutonium can be used as fuel in nuclear power reactors. Indeed, through the 1970s it was generally assumed that as the use of nuclear power grew, worldwide uranium resources would be depleted and plutonium extracted from spent fuel would have to be "recycled" as a substitute fuel in conventional power reactors.

In addition, research and development is underway in many advanced nations on a new generation of reactors known as breeder reactors. These use plutonium as fuel surrounded with a "blanket" of natural uranium; as the reactor operates, slightly more plutonium is created in the blanket than is consumed in the core, thereby "breeding" new fuel.

Like plutonium recycle, the economic advantage of breeders depends on natural uranium becoming scarce and expensive. But over the past decade new uranium reserves have been discovered, nuclear power has reached only a fraction of its expected growth levels, and reprocessing spent fuel to extract plutonium (a critical step in both cases) has proven far more expensive and complex than anticipated. Moreover, concern over the proliferation risks of widescale use of plutonium as a fuel has grown. These factors have led one advanced nation, the United States, to abandon its plans to use plutonium fuel, although Japan, France, Britain, and West Germany are continuing to develop this technology actively. Nevertheless, the advanced nuclear-supplier countries are strongly discouraging plutonium use in nations of proliferation concern.

The long-standing view that plutonium is a legitimate and anticipated part of civilian nuclear programs, however, has allowed India, Pakistan, Argentina, and Brazil, to justify their reprocessing programs — even though they currently provide these nations with a nuclear-weapons capability, or may soon do so.

Like the production of enriched uranium, the production of plutonium entails many steps and many installations and capabilities apart from the reactor and reprocessing plant are needed. For illustrative purposes, the following facilities and resources would be required for an independent plutonium production capability assuming a heavy-water research or power reactor is used:

- uranium deposits;
- a uranium mine;
- a uranium mill (for processing uranium ore containing less than one percent uranium into uranium oxide concentrate, or yellowcake);
- a uranium purification plant (to further improve the yellowcake into reactor grade uranium dioxide);
- a fuel fabrication plant (to manufacture the fuel elements placed in the reactor), including a capability to fabricate zircaloy tubing;
- a heavy-water research or power reactor,
- a heavy water production plant; and
- a reprocessing plant.

If the option of building a natural-uranium/graphite reactor is used, the needs would be the same although reactor-grade graphite would have to be produced instead of heavy water. A light water reactor would necessitate use of low-enriched uranium, implying an enrichment capability was available; if so, highly enriched uranium could be produced, obviating the need for plutonium as a weapons material.

## Typical Nuclear Material Requirements and Production Rates

*Nuclear Weapons*

Amounts of highly enriched uranium or plutonium needed for core of multi-kiloton atomic bomb.*

Plutonium
5 to 8 kilograms (11 to 17.6 pounds)

Highly Enriched Uranium
15 to 25 kilograms (33 to 55 pounds)

*Note: Rough estimates; no allowance made for losses in fabrication. Smaller quantities can apparently be used if more sophisticated designs are employed. Eight kilograms of plutonium and 25 kilograms of highly enriched uranium are used by the IAEA as the minimum amounts of material necessary for nuclear weapons. The smaller figures, however, appear to be conservative, widely accepted benchmarks. See Thomas B. Cochran, et al., *U.S. Nuclear Forces and Capabilities* (Cambridge, MA: Ballinger, 1984), pp. 24–25; U.S. Congress, Office of Technology Assessment, *Nuclear Proliferation and Safeguards* (Washington, D.C.: Office of Technology Assessment, 1977), pp. 154–158; John Kerry King, ed., *International Political Effects of the Spread of Nuclear Weapons* (Washington, D.C.: U.S. Central Intelligence Agency, 1979), p. 7.

*Nuclear Power Plants*

*1,000 MW low-enriched-uranium/light-water reactor (PWR type)*[a]

Fueled by uranium enriched to about 3%, requires:

| | Start-up | Annual | 30-year life |
|---|---|---|---|
| $U_3O_8$[b] | 324 tons | 140 tons | 4,350 tons (approx.) |
| SWUs[c] | 227,000 | 110,000 | 3,500,000 (approx.) |

Produces about 168 kg fissile plutonium per year

*1,000 $MW_e$ natural uranium/heavy-water (CANDU) reactor*[a]

Fueled by natural uranium moderated by heavy water ($D_2O$), requires:

| | Start-up | Annual[d] | 30-year life |
|---|---|---|---|
| $U_3O_8$[b] | 130 tons | 120 tons | 3,600 tons |
| $D_2O$ | 800 tons | 10-20 tons | 1,200 tons |

Produces about 300 kg fissile plutonium per year

[a] Data on $U_3O_8$ and SWUs derived from International Nuclear Fuel Cycle Evaluation, Report of Working Group 8 (1980); data on $D_2O$ from Non-Proliferation Alternative Systems Assessment Program, Vol. 3 (Department of Energy, 1980).
[b] Uranium oxide. Yellowcake (uranium concentrate) is about 80% $U_3O_8$. Uranium ore when mined typically contains about .1% $U_3O_8$, though both lower and higher concentrations occur.
[c] Separative work units (a measure of enrichment effort), in kilograms. South Africa's semi-commercial enrichment plant at Valindaba, for example, is expected to have a capacity of about 300,000 SWU's, enough for annual reloads for the two 922-megawatt Koeberg reactors.
[d] CANDU reactors are continuously refueled, but this is the approximate aggregate of fresh fuel required per year.

# Atoms for Peace

## Document 2

In December 1953, President Eisenhower made his Atoms for Peace proposal to the United Nations General Assembly. In these excerpts from his speech, Eisenhower proposes the setting up of an International Atomic Energy Agency (IAEA) that would devise ways so that "fissionable material would be allocated to serve the peaceful pursuits of mankind, especially the production of electric energy." Although an IAEA was not set up until 1957, the United States made a major effort to share knowledge with non-nuclear countries and to help them set up nuclear power reactors. Cooperation agreements were signed with more than thirty nations that received U.S. aid in exchange for pledges not to use nuclear power for military uses. The recipient nations also agreed to let their facilities be inspected to ensure that safeguards were being carried out.

## 2 SPEECH TO UNITED NATIONS GENERAL ASSEMBLY
## President Eisenhower
## December 1953

### For the Benefit of Mankind

But I do not wish to rest either upon the reiteration of past proposals or the restatement of past deeds. The gravity of the time is such that every new avenue of peace, no matter how dimly discernible, should be explored.

There is at least one new avenue of peace which has not yet been well explored — an avenue now laid out by the General Assembly of the United Nations.

In its resolution of November 18th [*28*], 1953, this General Assembly suggested — and I quote — "that the Disarmament Commission study the desirability of establishing a sub-committee consisting of representatives of the Powers principally involved, which should seek in private an acceptable solution . . . and report on such a solution to the General Assembly and to the Security Council not later than 1 September 1954."[1]

The United States, heeding the suggestion of the General Assembly of the United Nations, is instantly prepared to meet privately with such other countries as may be "principally involved", to seek "an acceptable solution" to the atomic armaments race which overshadows not only the peace, but the very life, of the world.

We shall carry into these private or diplomatic talks a new conception.

The United States would seek more than the mere reduction or elimination of atomic materials for military purposes.

It is not enough to take this weapon out of the hands of the soldiers. It must be put into the hands of those who will know how to strip its military casing and adapt it to the arts of peace.

The United States knows that if the fearful trend of atomic military buildup can be reversed, this greatest of destructive forces can be developed into a great boon, for the benefit of all mankind.

The United States knows that peaceful power from atomic energy is no dream of the future. That capability, already proved, is here — now — today. Who can doubt, if the entire body of the world's scientists and engineers had adequate amounts of fissionable material with which to test and develop their ideas, that this capability would rapidly be transformed into universal, efficient, and economic usage.

To hasten the day when fear of the atom will begin to disappear from the minds of people, and the governments of the East and West, there are certain steps that can be taken now.

### Proposal for Joint Atomic Contributions

I therefore make the following proposals:

The Governments principally involved, to the extent permitted by elementary prudence, to begin now and continue to make joint contributions from their stockpiles of normal uranium and fissionable materials to an International Atomic Energy Agency. We would expect that such an agency would be set up under the aegis of the United Nations.

The ratios of contributions, the procedures and other details would properly be within the scope of the "private conversations" I have referred to earlier.

The United States is prepared to undertake these explorations in good faith. Any partner of the United States acting in the same good faith will find the United States a not unreasonable or ungenerous associate.

Undoubtedly initial and early contributions to this plan would be small in quantity. However, the proposal has the great virtue that it can be undertaken without the irritations and mutual suspicions incident to any attempt to set up a completely acceptable system of world-wide inspection and control.

The Atomic Energy Agency could be made responsible for the impounding, storage, and protection of the contributed fissionable and other materials. The ingenuity of our scientists will provide special safe conditions under which such a bank of fissionable material can be made essentially immune to surprise seizure.

The more important responsibility of this Atomic Energy Agency would be to devise methods whereby this fissionable material would be allocated to serve the peaceful pursuits of mankind. Experts would be mobilized to apply atomic energy to the needs of agriculture, medicine, and other peaceful activities. A special purpose would be to provide abundant electrical energy in the power-starved areas of the world. Thus the contributing powers would be dedicating some of their strength to serve the needs rather than the fears of mankind.

The United States would be more than willing — it would be proud to take up with others "principally involved" the development of plans whereby such peaceful use of atomic energy would be expedited.

Of those "principally involved" the Soviet Union must, of course, be one.

### Out of Fear and into Peace

I would be prepared to submit to the Congress of the United States, and with every expectation of approval, any such plan that would:

First — encourage world-wide investigation into the most effective peacetime uses of fissionable material, and with the certainty that they had all the material needed for the conduct of all experiments that were appropriate;

Second — begin to diminish the potential destructive power of the world's atomic stockpiles;

Third — allow all peoples of all nations to see that, in this enlightened age, the great powers of the earth, both of the East and of the West, are interested in human aspirations first, rather than in building up the armaments of war;

Fourth — open up a new channel for peaceful discussion, and initiate at least a new approach to the many difficult problems that must be solved in both private and public conversations, if the world is to shake off the inertia imposed by fear, and is to make positive progress toward peace.

Against the dark background of the atomic bomb, the United States does not wish merely to present strength, but also the desire and the hope for peace.

The coming months will be fraught with fateful decisions. In this Assembly; in the capitals and military headquarters of the world; in the hearts of men everywhere, be they governors or governed, may they be the decisions which will lead this world out of fear and into peace.

To the making of these fateful decisions, the United States pledges before you — and therefore before the world — its determination to help solve the fearful atomic dilemma — to devote its entire heart and mind to find the way by which the miraculous inventiveness of man shall not be dedicated to his death, but consecrated to his life.

I again thank the delegates for the great honor they have done me, in inviting me to appear before them, and in listening to me so courteously. Thank you.

## *Note*

1. "General Assembly Resolution 715 (VIII): Regulation, Limitation, and Balanced Resolution of All Armed Forces and All Armaments: Report of the Disarmament Commission, Nov 28, 1953," reprinted in *Documents on Disarmament*, 1954-1960, volume 1, Washington: 1961.

# Nonproliferation and the U.S. Nuclear Power Industry

### *Document 3*

**As it faced the energy crisis in 1977, the newly elected Carter administration made a major review of the connections between nuclear power and the proliferation problem. The administration decided not to pursue nuclear power technologies that would have produced large quantities of plutonium, a nuclear material that can be used for nuclear weapons production. In particular, as document 3 indicates, the Carter administration decided to deemphasize plutonium reprocessing and the plutonium breeder reactor.**

## 3 CARTER ADMINISTRATION'S NUCLEAR POWER POLICY April 1977

There is no dilemma today more difficult to resolve than that connected with the use of nuclear power. Many countries see nuclear power as the only real opportunity, at least in this century, to reduce the dependence of their economic well-being on foreign oil — an energy source of uncertain availability, growing price, and ultimate exhaustion. The U.S., by contrast, has a major domestic energy source — coal — but its use is not without penalties, and our plans also call for the use of nuclear power as a share in our energy production.

The benefits of nuclear power are thus very real and practical. But a serious risk accompanies worldwide use of nuclear power — the risk that components of the nuclear power process will be turned to providing atomic weapons.

We took an important step in reducing the risk of expanding possession of atomic weapons through the nonproliferation treaty, whereby more than 100 nations have agreed not to develop such explosives. But we must go further. The U.S. is deeply concerned about the consequences for all nations of a further spread of nuclear weapons or explosive capabilities. We believe that these risks would be vastly increased by the further spread of sensitive technologies which entail direct access to plutonium, highly enriched uranium, or other weapons usable material. The question I have had under review from my first day in office is how can that be accomplished without forgoing the tangible benefits of nuclear power.

We are now completing an extremely thorough review of all the issues that bear on the use of nuclear power. We have concluded that the serious consequences of proliferation and direct implications for peace and security — as well as strong scientific and economic evidence — require:

— a major change in U.S. domestic nuclear energy policies and programs; and
— a concerted effort among all nations to find better answers to the problems and risks accompanying the increased use of nuclear power.

I am announcing today some of my decisions resulting from that review.

*First,* we will defer indefinitely the commercial reprocessing and recycling of the plutonium produced in the U.S. nuclear power programs. From our own experience, we have concluded that a viable and economic nuclear power program can be sustained without such reprocessing and recycling. The plant at Barnwell, South Carolina, will receive neither Federal encouragement nor funding for its completion as a reprocessing facility.

*Second*, we will restructure the U.S. breeder reactor program to give greater priority to alternative designs of the breeder and to defer the date when breeder reactors would be put into commercial use.

*Third*, we will redirect funding of U.S. nuclear research and development programs to accelerate our research into alternative nuclear fuel cycles which do not involve direct access to materials usable in nuclear weapons.

*Fourth*, we will increase U.S. production capacity for enriched uranium to provide adequate and timely supply of nuclear fuels for domestic and foreign needs.

*Fifth*, we will propose the necessary legislative steps to permit the U.S. to offer nuclear fuel supply contracts and guarantee delivery of such nuclear fuel to other countries.

*Sixth*, we will continue to embargo the export of equipment or technology that would permit uranium enrichment and chemical reprocessing.

*Seventh*, we will continue discussions with supplying and recipient countries alike, of a wide range of international approaches and frameworks that will permit all nations to achieve their energy objectives while reducing the spread of nuclear explosive capability. Among other things, we will explore the establishment of an international nuclear fuel cycle evaluation program aimed at developing alternative fuel cycles and a variety of international and U.S. measures to assure access to nuclear fuel supplies and spent fuel storage for nations sharing common nonproliferation objectives.

We will continue to consult very closely with a number of governments regarding the most desirable multilateral and bilateral arrangements for assuring that nuclear energy is creatively harnessed for peaceful economic purposes. Our intent is to develop wider international cooperation in regard to this vital issue through systematic and thorough international consultations.

## ATTEMPTS TO CONTROL PROLIFERATION

## Proliferation — A Nuclear Nightmare?

### *Document 4*

These excerpts from an article by Lewis Dunn, who worked on the proliferation problem in the State Department during the Reagan administration, summarize many of the reasons why the superpowers worry about proliferation. Dunn warns about regional nuclear balances of terror, the increased likelihood of nuclear war, and spreading nuclear terrorism.

### 4 NUCLEAR PROLIFERATION AND WORLD POLITICS
### Lewis A. Dunn

Within the coming decades, a growing number of countries could decide to acquire nuclear weapons.[2] Should such a second wave of proliferation occur, among its distinguishing features would be the spread of nuclear weapons to less developed, politically unstable Third World countries, the nuclearization of existing regional confrontations, and eventual access to nuclear weapons by subnational groups. Some observers regard the possibility of more widespread nuclear proliferation with relative equanimity. They argue either that present Western fears of proliferation are based upon an erroneous, if not racist, charge of Third World irresponsibility[3] or that the diffusion of nuclear weapons would contribute in some cases to increased regional stability.[4] Several of these persons go so far as to contend that widespread proliferation could result in the outlawing of large-scale violence.[5] On the contrary, a proliferated world is likely to be a nasty and dangerous place, entailing threats to the security and domestic well-being of virtually all nations and posing a serious possibility of a longer-term decay of global political order. To see why this may be so, it is necessary first to consider briefly the varied meanings of "going nuclear."

## Going Nuclear

The often-used characterization "going nuclear" telescopes a range of important proliferation choices and outcomes. But depending upon the specific characteristics of possible future Nth country nuclear weapon programs and postures, the distinguishing features and risks of a proliferated world would vary. For our present purposes, it suffices to note the following probable critical characteristics.[6]

### *"In the Business" v. "Serious but Technically Deficient" Programs*

At least initially, some future proliferators are likely to seek only "in the business" nuclear-weapon capabilities, that is, their purpose would be to demonstrate that they, too, could detonate a nuclear explosive device. Perhaps motivated by prestige considerations, or at a latter stage of proliferation by fashion, these countries would not seek a militarily operational nuclear force.

A greater number of prospective proliferators, however, could be expected to do otherwise. They are likely instead to attempt to develop serious nuclear forces, combining a growing stockpile of nuclear weapons; delivery systems; command, control, and communication procedures; protection against surprise attack; and strategic doctrine. In many of these cases, the resultant nuclear force may be characterized by significant technical deficiencies.

Although development of relatively well-packaged fission weapons, deliverable by a range of readily accessible weapon systems, should not pose a major problem for nearly all potential proliferators, their early-generation nuclear warheads might lack adequate safety design mechanisms. Moreover, if insufficient attention is paid to the risk of a nuclear-weapon accident, even later-generation weapons could be accident prone.[7]

Comparable concern about possibly inadequate provisions for control against unauthorized seizure and use of nuclear weapons by a dissident domestic group, a cabal of officers, or even an isolated military man also is warranted. Within existing nuclear-weapon states, such as the United States and the Soviet Union, development of sophisticated electronic permissive action link (PAL) systems has permitted them to purchase tight control without sacrificing operational readiness or accepting an increased vulnerability to surprise attack. Conversely, taken together, fear of surprise attack by a local nuclear rival and limited technological sophistication could force even such coup-vulnerable prospective proliferators as, for example, Iraq, Egypt, Syria, South Korea, Pakistan, Argentina, and Brazil *not* to follow their likely initial preference for tight control of their nuclear arsenal. More generally, development of a reliable and survivable command, control, and communication network may exceed the capabilities of the many low-to-medium technology prospective proliferators.

As for protection against an opponent's surprise disarming attack, crude mutual survivability should not be presumed to be the expected outcome of nuclearizing regional confrontations. Depending upon the specific opponents, the stage of proliferation, and their prior technical choices, reciprocal vulnerability, survivability against each other but not against a superpower, or unilateral vulnerability are as likely to be the resultant strategic balances. Moreover, in some cases whatever survivability does exist is likely to have been purchased by reliance upon a hair trigger, launch-on-warning (LOW) mode of protecting the nuclear force. These are yet additional reasons for skepticism about the technical characteristics of many new nuclear forces, for believing that not infrequently such forces probably would be characterized by what once was termed a high "propensity for war."[8]

### *Doctrinal Perceptions of Nuclear Weapons Utility*

The mainstream of Western strategic studies increasingly has argued that the sole purpose of nuclear weapons should be to deter the use or threatened use of other nuclear weapons. It would be false to presume, however, that the initial strategic thinking of all future proliferators would honor this conception of nuclear weapons' purposes and utility. On the contrary, some possible proliferators, especially where geography serves to provide natural invasion corridors, as in the case of Taiwan, South Korea, and perhaps Iran, appear more likely to look upon nuclear weapons as potentially useful battlefield weapons. Others must be expected to consider seriously these weapons' possible limited and coercive use or threatened use, either within a war-fighting defensive strategy or in support of expansionist, non-status quo oriented objectives. An Israel contemplating responses to a breakdown of its conventional defenses in a sixth Arab-Israeli war could contemplate the former; a nuclear-armed Iran seeking hegemony in the Persian Gulf in the early 1990s the latter.

Longer-term doctrinal development and perceptions of nuclear weapons' utility probably would be influenced heavily by the specific characteristics and consequences of the first use of nuclear weapons since Nagasaki. Successful use or threatened use by a new proliferator would erode the nuclear taboo and encourage others to reappraise upward their assessment of the military utility of nuclear weapons. Conversely, unsuccessful use, accidental use, or unauthorized use — perhaps during an internal political struggle — would have the opposite effect. Thus, the first nuclear use clearly would be a proliferation turning point. And, as the next section indicates, the probability that that will occur has to be evaluated as high.

## Regional Interaction in a Proliferated World

If efforts to control proliferation prove inadequate, a world of 30 or more nuclear-weapon states, many locked in hostile confrontations, could emerge by the late 1980s–early 1990s. Even though in isolated cases such nuclearization of regional confrontations could prove locally stabilizing,[9] most frequently the outcome would be increased political and military competitiveness, confrontation, and probably conflict. Moreover, the destructiveness of future small-power nuclear wars would be significantly greater than that of either past local wars or manmade or natural disasters.

### *Patterns of Regional Nuclear Arms Racing*

Nuclear proliferation is likely to be accompanied frequently, at least initially, by fairly intense qualitative and quantitative nuclear arms races. There is no reason to believe that the major countries in the Middle East, South Asia, and the Persian Gulf, for example, would acquiesce readily to second-class non-nuclear status or to a position of marked nuclear inferiority vis-à-vis their regional opponents.

Such regional nuclear arms racing would be fueled by several factors. Regional insecurity, competition for regional status, and traditional hostility all would play a part. In addition, in those arms races where each side's decisions were highly sensitive to estimates of the opponent's capabilities and intentions, for example, in the Middle East and South Asia, limited intelligence on those factors might intensify initial arms "spurts." Fears, and in some cases the reality, of the opponent acquiring a first-strike capability also would exacerbate arms race pressures. Finally, if nuclear weapons were used successfully in any region, that too would stimulate arms race efforts.

Nonetheless, it must be added that in some regional strategic situations, resource availability could become a serious constraint once such arms racing began. In South Asia, for example, Pakistan without outside assistance might find itself unable to keep up with India in a nuclear arms race. Thus, some regional nuclear arms races might begin, spurt, and then end with the weaker side reluctantly accepting an inferior position. In fact, where prior recent history of intense political and military conflict is absent, a combination of resource-constraint and a limited sense of threat could foster at the outset a more leisurely arms-race pattern. A possible future Argentinian-Brazilian nuclear arms race could be a case in point, although even here competition for regional influence and mutual uncertainty might result in more active arms racing.

Thus, a mixture of arms racing effects, skewed at least initially toward more intense regional competition, should be expected. Such nuclear arms racing would entail a costly diversion of scarce technical, economic, and organizational resources. Moreover, in regions that already are or could become arenas of politico-military conflict, existing hostility probably would be exacerbated and efforts to achieve a regional modus vivendi hindered. Further, in the ensuing political climate, the risk of inadvertent nuclear war, as discussed next, would be magnified commensurately.

### *Small Power Nuclear Wars*

Inherent to the nuclearization of existing confrontations in the Middle East, South Asia, and the Persian Gulf in all probability would be a high risk of inadvertent or calculated nuclear weapon use. Either or both governmental or nongovernmental action might be involved.[10]

To begin, given the likely technical deficiencies of many Nth country nuclear forces, discussed earlier, unintended nuclear exchanges erupting out of an intense crisis or low-level conventional conflict could occur. For example, if reciprocal vulnerability to surprise nuclear attack characterizes, as it may, the initial stages of nuclear strategic interaction between India and Pakistan and Israel and Egypt, strong preemptive pressures and growing reciprocal fears of surprise attack can be expected. Moreover, within such a strategic situation, the occurrence of a nuclear weapon accident, an unauthorized launch by a cabal of lower-level officers, anonymous nuclear detonation by a PLO-type group, or a warning system malfunction — any of which, for reasons already noted, would be possible — might trigger that inadvertent nuclear exchange.

However, concern about the outbreak of small-power nuclear wars is not based solely on an assessment of the potential propensity to war of particular Nth country nuclear forces. Some countries, to repeat, are likely to be attracted to nuclear weapons because of their possible military uses and consciously could decide to escalate to the employment of nuclear weapons rather than accept a conventional military defeat. Pakistani tactical use of nuclear weapons against invading Indian military formations in a hypothetical late-1980s conflict would be one possibility; Israeli coercive nuclear attacks against Arab military targets and high-value Egyptian targets such as the Aswan Dam, in response to an Arab breakthrough on the battlefield, would be another.

Another case of a conscious and calculated use of nuclear weapons would be an attempt by one new proliferator — or, following their unauthorized access to nuclear weapons, by members of its military — to trigger a nuclear exchange between two other hostile Nth countries. The risk of such a catalytic nuclear war erupting out of an intense crisis or low-level conflict in the early stages of Middle East nuclearization has to be taken seriously.

Nor can the risk of local anonymous use of nuclear

weapons be dismissed. To illustrate, again with reference to a nuclearized Middle East, a more radical Arab government might conclude that a successful anonymous attack against Israel in the midst of serious peace negotiations was the only way to ensure those negotiations' collapse. It probably would succeed, if only because Israeli public opinion could be expected to preclude the government making any political-military concessions in the wake of such an Arab action. And, given the prospect of unauthorized access to nuclear weapons, the perpetrators here, too, could be a cabal of middle-ranking, fanatic officers.

The danger of preemptive nuclear wars also exists. Should proliferation occur, some countries are likely already to have deployed rudimentary nuclear forces by the time their opponents begin to do so, for example, Iran versus Iraq or Saudi Arabia or India versus Pakistan. To these earlier entrants, a preemptive attack against a potentially dangerous budding rival may not be unattractive. Or, assuming that nuclear use were thought too dangerous — perhaps for fear of a superpower response — a preemptive attack against the opponent's nuclear facilities using precision-guided conventional weapons still might be contemplated.

Even though the level of destruction in such small-power nuclear wars would vary with the specific case, the spread of nuclear weapons would bring an upward leap in the expected consequences of regional military conflicts. To illustrate, detonation of a single nominal yield nuclear weapon in a Middle Eastern city might kill upwards of 100,000 people, while a counter-city exchange between small Indian and Pakistani nuclear forces could cause 10 million fatalities on each side. In contrast, the death toll in past Arab-Israeli wars has been counted in the thousands, while approximately 1 million persons, virtually all civilians, lost their lives in the 1971 Pakistani civil war. As for natural disasters, their death toll has only rarely been counted in the hundreds of thousands, let alone the potential millions of a local nuclear war.[11]

### *The Regional Consequences of Nuclear Coups d'État*

Widespread nuclear proliferation is likely to be accompanied not only by increased competitiveness and more destructive regional clashes, but also by intensified domestic political conflict. In the many politically unstable future proliferators with their previous histories of military intervention in domestic politics, nuclear coups d'état may occur. Two aspects of this phenomenon, as well as its implications for regional stability, warrant brief attention.[12]

On the one hand, just as denying the government access to the radio station and neutralizing pro-government military formations outside of the capital have been critical elements of successful past coups, future Nth-country coup-makers may have to deny the government access to its nuclear force. Failure to do so might permit a leader who had survived the initial assault to use his access to nuclear weapons to rally his supporters and demoralize his opponents and their potential civilian allies; to threaten civil war; and, in essence, to change the situation from a military clash to a confrontation marked by coercive bargaining.

On the other hand, efforts by military factions within future coup-vulnerable proliferators to seize control of nuclear weapons also can be expected. By doing so, such a faction could hope to trigger a more widespread uprising, to force a loyal military leadership to meet its demands, to deter the use of force against them, or otherwise to use the threat of nuclear conflict to support their own coup. And, of greater significance, their access to nuclear weapons probably would make the difference between success and failure for some future factional coup-makers.

The implications for regional stability of such nuclear coups d'état should not be missed. Buttressed by their possession of nuclear weapons, more radical and romantic military men than might have been able previously to do so could gain power. And, once in full control of their country's nuclear arsenal, manifold opportunities for nuclear mischief would become evident to them. Alternatively, fearing that eventual control of nuclear weapons by more radical and romantic coup-makers, neighboring countries might intervene militarily. If time permitted, such intervention could involve support for the existing government. Or, to keep that country's nuclear weapons from falling into the "wrong hands," a disarming attack against its nuclear force and stockpile might be launched. For this reason, as well, continuing nuclear proliferation probably would result in increased and intensified local instability.

## Global Repercussions of Local Proliferation

The longer-run consequences for global political life of widespread proliferation could be equally serious. Local proliferation might contribute to the emergence of disruptive new transnational forces and set in motion long-term trends, both of which could culminate in a corrosion of domestic political authority and legitimacy and growing global anarchy.

### *An Erosion of Existing Alliances?*

If existing patterns of Soviet and American global involvement continue, most future confrontations between hostile proliferators would be characterized at least initially by some degree of superpower entanglement. Depending upon the specific situation, either superpower could be a reluctant guarantor, a committed ally, a partly disengaged ally, a patron, or an aspiring suitor of one of the hostile parties. More important, in many cases the two superpowers might find themselves involved on opposite sides of a hostile local confrontation. Inherent to that situation is the risk of a direct Soviet-American confrontation, high-level crisis, and even outright military conflict.

But, because of that risk of conflict, initial superpower entanglement gradually might give way to efforts to put political distance between themselves and at least some new nuclear-weapon states.[13] That is, both superpowers would be likely to reassess carefully their vital interests, those warranting continued acceptance of the risk of confrontation. In the United States, strong pressures to disengage might emerge, for example, if Taiwan and South Korea or perhaps even Israel and Iran overtly acquired nuclear weapons.[14] And, even where traditional vital American interests were seen to exist — as in the case of West Germany and Japan — if suffficient influence over these countries' nuclear postures were unobtainable, such pressures could grow.

An erosion or breakup of existing alliances, should it occur, would remove one important source of postwar order. To begin, in light of the earlier discussion of regional interaction, the stability of such a loosely structured global system may be questioned. Moreover, in some regions — both halves of Europe come to mind — superpower involvement may have served to prevent the recrudescence of past hostilities and tensions. And, at least in Western Europe, the American alliance structure by doing so has provided a necessary framework for regional political and economic cooperation. Further, dependence upon outside allied support has required at least some countries to moderate their regional behavior and could be expected to have a comparable future restraining impact.

Thus, local proliferation could trigger superpower disengagement and the partial erosion of existing alliances. That, in turn, would contribute to growing global disorder. Conversely, to the extent that present patterns of superpower entanglement remained unchanged, the risk of spreading conflict from small-power nuclear confrontations and wars cannot be discounted.

### *Nuclear "Black and Gray Marketeering"*

Much recent attention has focused upon the possible emergence of nuclear black marketeering, entailing the sale of stolen fissile material or nuclear weapons themselves.[15] An equally disruptive potential global repercussion of increasing local proliferation would be the growth of nuclear "gray marketeering." A spectrum of transactions and activities might be involved. These range from covert government to government transfer of critical technical assistance for a nuclear weapon program to the actual sale or barter of nuclear weapons or their critical components. Also encompassed would be the ready availability of nuclear mercenaries willing to sell their knowledge and services to countries attempting to develop nuclear weapons.

Various economic, political, and ideological pressures might foster such gray marketeering. Selling technical assistance, or even the weapons themselves or their components, would be one way for a new nuclear-weapon state to reduce the financial burden of its own nuclear weapon program. Or, under certain conditions, a country might come to regard its nuclear weapon expertise as a service good to be bartered in exchange for needed vital raw materials or oil. Such economic motivations clearly would be an important factor in the hiring of nuclear mercenaries. As for ad hoc political pressures, to a possible future nuclear-armed Pakistan, provision of technical assistance or the transfer of special nuclear material and design information could appear an attractive way to acquire or solidify Arab or Iranian political support or at least to persuade them not to support its Indian opponent. Finally, broader ideological and political perspectives also might contribute to these activities' emergence. To illustrate, Israel, South Africa, and Taiwan are likely to be increasingly isolated in world politics as time passes. They might come to comprise a "pariah international," among whose activities could include nuclear weapon cooperation. An eventual Muslim nuclear weapon cooperative would be another, though less likely, example.

The growth of black and gray marketeering would change the characteristics of a future proliferated world. Not only would an expanding number of countries be able to develop nuclear weapons and to do so sooner; but, in particular, both very-low technology countries and nongovernmental organizations that otherwise would have been unable to do so increasingly would be able to acquire rudimentary nuclear-weapon capabilities.[16] Consequently, the problems of managing in a proliferated world would become more intractable, further heightening the risk of growing disorder.

### *Spreading Nuclear Terrorism*

Further contributing to the erosion of global order would be the spreading of nuclear terrorism. Not only would widespread local proliferation increase the likelihood of terrorist acquisition of nuclear weapons, but it cannot be assumed that future terrorists would have no rational motive for using or threatening to use nuclear weapons.

A terrorist group might obtain a nuclear weapon in several ways. If plutonium recycling is practiced widely in the 1980s, physical security measures might not suffice to prevent the theft of fissile material with which they might fabricate their own device. Alternatively, the opportunities for stealing a nuclear weapon would be increased by widespread local proliferation. Furthermore, a radical government or an alienated military faction might arrange for a terrorist group to steal one of its nuclear weapons, thinking that its own purposes would be served by resultant terrorist use with a lessened risk of suffering the consequences of that action. Finally, if a black market emerges, the sale of special nuclear materials or of the weapons themselves would provide an additional source.

Possession of one or more nuclear weapons could be especially valuable for a terrorist group. To illustrate, consider a future successor group to the Palestine Liberation Organization (PLO). Such a group might threaten local action as a means of deterring hostile military action against it and of establishing a protected sanctuary for its activities. Intranation deterrence could be pursued, that is, against future equivalents of "Black September" in Jordan and current Syrian intervention in Lebanon. Actual use of a nuclear weapon by such a hypothetical successor to the PLO also could occur. Assuming movement in the late 1980s toward an Arab-Israeli peace settlement damaging to Palestinian interests, anonymous detonation of a nuclear weapon in Israel might be regarded as the only way to block such a settlement.

Moreover, the target of future terrorist use need not be local. Such a prospective radical Arab terrorist group could threaten anonymously, for example, to detonate clandestinely-inserted nuclear devices within American cities unless the United States stopped shipping arms to Israel. If the United States failed to heed this warning, then a device could be exploded. Or the target could be a West European ally of the United States whose ports were being used to ship NATO military stocks to Israel during a sixth Arab-Israeli war. Alternatively, for a future terrorist group whose objective was bringing down Western bourgeois society — just as the Japanese Red Army and the Baader-Meinhof Gang now propose — use of an externally procured nuclear weapon might be regarded as an appropriate means.

This prospect of spreading nuclear terrorism is a cause for concern partly because of its direct consequences. To note one, a single terrorist nuclear detonation within a Middle Eastern, American, or West European city probably would kill upwards of 100,000 persons. However, of equal concern is the danger that spreading nuclear terrorism would contribute to that corrosion of governmental authority and legitimacy discussed next.[17]

### *Corrosion of Political Authority and Legitimacy*

The initial result of attempts to manage both the specific problems of a proliferated world and the pressures inherent in living in a world of 30 or more nuclear-weapon states could be a global authoritarian political shift. Two sources of that authoritarian shift should be noted.

On the one hand, controlling against nuclear theft, nuclear terrorism, and other proliferation threats could be seen within existing democratic societies to require and justify the adoption of measures inconsistent with liberal values and procedural norms. For example, restrictions over government power in such civil liberties areas as search and seizure, arrest and questioning of suspects, surveillance methods, individual privacy, and the collection and computer storage of dossiers all might be eroded. Similarly, restrictions on movement in and out of these countries as well as on internal movement could increase markedly. At the same time, the leadership within more authoritarian societies probably would find in these specific threats a useful pretext for even more extensive domestic repression and control. That is, just as President Park of South Korea has used the threat of a North Korean invasion to crack down on domestic dissidents, future leaders within similar countries could use similarly the threat of anonymous or terrorist nuclear attack.

On the other hand, the increased insecurity, hostility, and competitiveness of a world with upwards of 30 nuclear weapon states probably in itself would create pressures for increased political authoritarianism. A siege mentality, fueled by a perception of the world as a much more dangerous and inhospitable environment and by political leaders' efforts to cope as best as possible with the manifold threats of that world might emerge. That siege mentality could manifest itself in a growing insularity, an intolerance of others, and in a national paranoia, all of which probably would have domestic counterparts.

Such an intensification of political authoritarianism might be, however, only a temporary phenomenon. If governments, even after adopting more authoritarian measures, proved unable to ensure national security, they might lose their authority and legitimacy. Popular and elite opinion, believing that governments were not meeting their obligations to "provide for the common defense," no longer would support them. Managing even domestic concerns could become increasingly difficult. Particularly in Western democracies, compromises, ambiguities, and partial solutions previously accepted as a matter of course in democratic political life might no longer be tolerated in the general climate of insecurity and reduced confidence in governmental capacity.

Moreover, even though such a loss of legitimacy and crisis of confidence might be more pronounced in industrialized countries, governmental legitimacy in the eyes of the elite probably would be eroded within less developed ones as well. In both cases, the outcome could be a growing inability to govern and perhaps the rise of new chiliastic mass movements within which individuals would seek a restored sense of security.

### *Growing Global Anarchy?*

A world of several dozen nuclear-weapon states, therefore, would in all probability be a nasty and dangerous place, variously threatening the national security and domestic political well-being of virtually all nations. Should it prove impossible to defuse these varied threats, the resultant regional and global disorder could lead to purposive national efforts on the part of the strong to pull inward, reducing contacts with an increasingly anarchic environment. Over the long-term, a renewed insularity and domestic authoritarianism partly could replace today's interdependence. However, many weaker, politically unstable less developed nations not only might be unable to seal themselves off from a hostile world, but are also likely to confront growing threats to their domestic political integrity. Their viability as sovereign political entities could become even more tenuous as subnational groups and military factions gained access to nuclear weapons.[18] Thus, increasingly isolated bastions of authoritarian stability might well exist in the midst of recurring small-power nuclear wars; terrorist threats; "local Munichs"; and nuclear coups d'état, separatist struggles, and civil wars.

## Notes

2. See Lewis A. Dunn and Herman Kahn, *Trends in Nuclear Proliferation*, Report prepared for the U.S. Arms Control and Disarmament Agency, HI–2336/3–RR (Croton-on-Hudson, N.Y.: Hudson Institute, May 15, 1976), pts. 1 and 2.
3. See K. Subrahmanyam, "India's Nuclear Policy," in *Nuclear Proliferation and the Near-Nuclear Countries*, ed. Onkar Marwah and Ann Schulz (Cambridge, Mass.: Ballinger Publishing Company, 1975), p. 131.
4. See, for example, Steven Rosen, "Nuclearization and Stability in the Middle East," in Marwah and Schulz, *Nuclear Proliferation*, p. 157; and Frederick C. Thayer, "Proliferation and the Future: Destruction or Transformation?" in *Annals of the American Academy of Political and Social Science* 430 (March 1977): 133–46.
5. See Pierre M. Gallois, *The Balance of Terror: Strategy for the Nuclear Age* (Boston: Houghton Mifflin Company, 1961), p. 113. For a more recent version, emphasizing proliferation of low-yield battlefield nuclear capabilities, see R. Robert Sandoval, "Consider the Porcupine: Another View of Nuclear Proliferation," *Bulletin of the Atomic Scientists*, May 1976, p. 19.
6. For elaboration, see Dunn and Kahn, *Trends in Nuclear Proliferation*, pt. 3.
7. Current American weapons can be dropped accidentally without producing a nuclear yield and can survive the heat and impact of air crashes. Achieving this degree of safety, however, necessitated a considerable expenditure of money and thought in the early to mid-1950s.
8. Thomas C. Schelling, *Arms and Influence* (New Haven: Yale University Press, 1966), p. 234.
9. Possible future Taiwanese acquisition might facilitate the emergence of more stable relations between Taiwan and the People's Republic of China by precluding invasion and strengthening domestic morale on Taiwan. Against that positive effect, nonetheless, would have to be balanced the adverse impact upon proliferation momentum and pressures for proliferation in Asia that probably would follow Taiwan's emergence as a nuclear-weapon state. Thus, it may not be possible to pick and choose which proliferation to oppose.
10. "Local Munichs" and nuclear blackmail, involving threatened use of nuclear weapons, also can be expected to occur.
11. This estimate assumes the use of relatively low-yield fission weapons; the advent of fusion weapons could result in an additional upward leap in expected destructiveness.
12. For elaboration, see Lewis A. Dunn, "Military Politics, Nuclear Proliferation, and the 'Nuclear Coup d'Etat,'" HI–2392/2–P (Croton-on-Hudson, N.Y.: Hudson Institute, Apr. 20, 1976).
13. The not necessarily negligible risk of nuclear attack or retaliation by a local proliferator also might increase pressures for reduced superpower involvement in unstable newly nuclearized regions.
14. Particularly in the cases of Taiwan and South Korea, partial American disengagement probably would have preceded these countries' decisions to acquire nuclear weapons. It would be a question, therefore, of undoing residual, though perhaps not insignificant, American ties.
15. See Mason Willrich and Theodore B. Taylor, *Nuclear Theft: Risks and Safeguards* (Cambridge, Mass.: Ballinger Publishing Company, 1974), pp. 107–20.
16. For elaboration, see Lewis A. Dunn, "Nuclear 'Gray Marketeering,'" *International Security* 1, no. 3 (Winter 1977).
17. For a more complete discussion of terrorism's other implications, see the paper by David Krieger, "What Happens If . . .? Terrorists, Revolutionaries and Nuclear Weapons," *Annals of the American Academy of Political and Social Science* 430 (March 1977): 44–57.
18. See also George H. Quester, "The Politics of Twenty Nuclear Powers," in *The Future of the International Strategic System*, ed. Richard Rosecrance (San Francisco: Chandler Publishing Company, 1972), pp. 67–70. Quester's analysis, however, underestimates the impact of widespread proliferation upon interstate, as opposed to intrastate, relations.

# The Nonproliferation Treaty

## *Document 5*

In 1984, after more than four years of complex negotiations, the Nonproliferation Treaty (NPT) was signed. This excerpt from a National Academy of Sciences review of arms control describes the treaty's terms. In essence, the superpowers got a pledge from non–nuclear weapons states not to acquire nuclear weapons. In exchange, the superpowers promised to assist the nonnuclears with their personal nuclear power programs.

## 5 NONPROLIFERATION
### Committee on International Security and Arms Control

The Treaty on the Non-Proliferation of Nuclear Weapons . . . which was originally signed on July 1, 1968, and has been in force since March 5, 1970, was designed to help stop the spread of nuclear weapons to additional states. The treaty, which divided the world into nuclear weapon states (the United States, the Soviet Union, the United Kingdom, France, and China) and non-nuclear weapon states (all other countries) places on all signatories the following basic obligations:

- Article I: "Each nuclear-weapon State Party to the Treaty undertakes not to transfer to any recipient whatsoever nuclear weapons or other nuclear explosive devices or control over such weapons or explosive devices directly or indirectly; and not in any way to assist, encourage, or induce any non-nuclear-weapon State to manufacture or otherwise acquire nuclear weapons or other nuclear explosive devices, or control over such weapons or explosive devices."
- Article II: "Each non-nuclear-weapon State Party to the Treaty undertakes not to receive the transfer from any transferor whatsoever of nuclear weapons or other nuclear explosive devices or of control over such weapons or explosive devices directly, or indirectly; not to manufacture or otherwise acquire nuclear weapons or other nuclear explosive devices; and not to seek or receive any assistance in the manufacture of nuclear weapons or other nuclear explosive devices."
- Article III calls on all parties not to export nuclear materials or equipment to any non-nuclear weapon state without international safeguards designed to verify that such exports are not diverted to nuclear explosive programs.

Despite ominous predictions that most states would not chose to adhere to the treaty, the NPT currently has 124 parties, including all members of NATO and the Euratom countries other than France, all members of the Warsaw Pact, and most of the other states in the world having nuclear programs. The parties to the NPT, together with France, which has made clear that it will act as if it were a party to the treaty, account for 98 percent of the world's installed nuclear power capacity, 95 percent of the nuclear power capacity under construction, and all of the world's exporters of enriched uranium. This means not only that the overwhelming majority of the world's civil nuclear activities are directly under the treaty's regime, but also that any nonparty seriously interested in developing nuclear power must rely at least in part on cooperation with parties to the treaty, whose exports are covered by international safeguards.

Despite these impressive statistics, not all relevant states have joined the treaty. In addition to France and China, which already have nuclear weapons, the most notable holdouts are Israel, India, Pakistan, South Africa, Argentina, Brazil, and Cuba. Each of these non-nuclear weapon states presents a special case (these cases are discussed in the final part of this chapter). The primary effect of the treaty for the nuclear weapon states is on their export policies. It is therefore important to note that France has voluntarily conformed its nuclear export policies to those called for by the treaty and that China has not yet become a significant nuclear exporter.

To make adherence to the treaty more attractive and to minimize charges of discrimination, three significant provisions (Articles IV, V, and VI) were added during the negotiation process. Article IV declares that nothing in the treaty should be interpreted as affecting "the inalienable right" of all parties to develop nuclear energy for peaceful purposes without discrimination. It also provides that all parties should facilitate, and have a right to participate in, the fullest possible exchange of equipment, materials, and scientific and technological information for the peaceful uses of nuclear energy.

Article V guarantees the sharing of any peaceful benefits from nuclear explosives. This was designed to prevent the nuclear weapon states from gaining special economic advantage from these developments, which they alone could pursue. During the 1960s the United States had promoted the potential of nuclear explosives for a variety of peaceful purposes. This led some non-nuclear weapon states to charge that the prohibition on the development of nuclear explosives in the treaty would inhibit their economic development. This was cited as a further example of the discriminatory nature of the NPT. Although some holdout states (including India, Argentina, and Brazil) still refer to this issue, the increasingly pessimistic assessments of the prospects for such peaceful applications have greatly reduced its appeal. Article VI contains a very important provision for all parties to "pursue negotiations in good faith on effective measures relating to cessation of the nuclear arms race at an early date and to nuclear disarmament."

## Soviet Worries over U.S. Transfers of Nuclear Weapons

### *Document 6*

During the negotiations on the NPT, the Soviets were concerned about U.S. efforts such as the Multilateral Force (MLF) (see chapter 4) to share nuclear weapons with NATO allies. As these excerpts show, the Soviets tried to restrict such transfers of nuclear weapons. This issue was resolved when the United States dropped the MLF idea for good toward the end of 1965.

### 6 STATEMENT BY SOVIET REPRESENTATIVE Eighteen-Nation Disarmament Committee July 21, 1966

With your permission, Mr. Chairman, I shall now go on to state our views on the question under consideration by the Committee. The debate in the Committee is revealing more and more clearly how the participants in the negotiations approach the problem of non-proliferation of nuclear weapons. Besides the nuances in the positions of this or that delegation, two concepts of non-proliferation can be seen. There is the broad concept which, as the representative of Mexico, Mr. Gomez Robledo, said at the last meeting, is gaining ground.[19] There is also the tendency to narrow the very concept of non-proliferation of nuclear weapons, and accordingly to restrict the range of measures which should be taken in order to prevent proliferation.

It could be stressed that measures to prevent proliferation of nuclear weapons, like measures to prevent the spread of an epidemic, cannot be half-measures, because in such a case they will not achieve their purpose. It could be pointed out that the effective solution of the problem of non-proliferation would create more favourable opportunities for the solution of other problems of disarmament. However, at the present stage of the negotiations it is hardly necessary to demonstrate the advantages of one approach over another. The Committee has before it two draft treaties on the non-proliferation of nuclear weapons, and a concrete comparison of the provisions of these drafts will perhaps help to elucidate the meaning of the differences in the positions of the socialist States on the one hand and of the Western States on the other.

The principal provisions of both the Soviet and the United States drafts are contained in the first two articles, which set out the obligations of nuclear and non-nuclear States respectively in regard to the non-proliferation of nuclear weapons. The United States now recognizes in its draft that certain prerogatives in respect of nuclear weapons must not be granted either to third States or associations of States or to units of the armed forces or military personnel of other States even if such units or personnel are under the command of a military alliance. But what precisely are the prerogatives that must not be granted? They are defined by the word "control", and the meaning which the United States side now gives to that word is specified in article IV of the United States draft, which stipulates in its sub-paragraph (c): " 'Control' means right or ability to fire nuclear weapons without the concurrent decision of an existing nuclear-weapon State".[20]

The Soviet delegation has already pointed out on a previous occasion that the United States gave a much broader meaning to the concept of "control" when, for example, twenty years ago the question of atomic weapons was being discussed at the United Nations. The members of the Committee are also aware that the General Assembly of the United Nations has always been guided in its approach to the problem of non-proliferation by a broader conception of what precisely proliferation is; but, however, that may be, we have to deal with that concept of the problem which is now put forward by the United States. What is to be prohibited and what is to be allowed under the United States draft treaty?

In the first place — and this is very important — the United States does not prohibit, and consequently it proposes to allow, the transfer of nuclear weapons for the armament of a non-nuclear State and its national forces. Nuclear weapons can be transferred to the command of a military alliance, to units of the armed forces and to individual military personnal. The recipients of the nuclear weapons have in this case to promise not to use these weapons of their own initiative. In the opinion of the United States side we should not regard such a transfer as proliferation of nuclear weapons. Thus, I repeat, the United States proposes that the transfer by nuclear Powers of nuclear bombs and warheads to non-nuclear States should not be considered and should not be called proliferation.

The United States delegation tries to justify such a narrow and qualified concept of non-proliferation by claiming that the nuclear weapons transferred would in any case be, as it were, a dead weight in the hands of other States and that they would not be able to use them. But that is not so at all. The States which received nuclear weapons would, of course, be able to use them, otherwise there would be no point in their receiving them. There are at least two ways in which the nuclear weapons received by them could be used.

One way which, as is evident from the explanations given by the United States delegation, the United States considers quite allowable is that some nuclear Power would give permission for the use of nuclear weapons. In other words, under the United States draft treaty it could turn out in the end that States which do not at present possess nuclear weapons would make war by means of those weapons. The United States solution of the problem of non-proliferation explicitly provides for such a possibility. This, of course, is not a solution of the problem of non-proliferation at all.

The other way is that a State which had received nuclear weapons would, in order to carry out its aggressive designs or revanchist policies, use those weapons without anyone's permission. Moreover, that could be done not only by a State but also by an individual military commander or group of military personnel, because the United States draft treaty allows the transfer of nuclear weapons directly to units of the armed forces or military personnel of other States on the same conditions: namely, with the obligation not to use those weapons without permission.

Such a concept of non-proliferation has, of course, nothing to do with the solution of the problem of genuine non-proliferation of nuclear weapons. States are being asked to make their security dependent upon whether a State or individual general or group of military personnel that has received nuclear weapons would keep its word in regard to their use. No responsible government could agree to such a step, which would mean agreeing to nuclear chaos.

## Notes

19. ENDC/PV 274, p. 10.

20. ANPF, p. 160.

# Chinese Objections to the Nonproliferation Treaty

### *Document 7*

**As this statement on the NPT demonstrates, the Chinese, who exploded a bomb in 1964, wanted no part of the new treaty. They denounced it as a trick designed to allow the superpowers a free hand to run the world as they liked.**

## 7 CHINESE COMMUNIST COMMENT ON DRAFT NONPROLIFERATION TREATY September 3, 1967

The so-called draft treaty on the "non-proliferation of nuclear weapons," concocted by Washington and Moscow, was finally served up at the disarmament conference in Geneva.[21] It is one of the concrete results of the secret talks in Glassboro between the chieftains of U.S. imperialism and Soviet modern revisionism. It is a major step in their counter-revolutionary collaboration on a world-wide scale and is another treacherous crime committed by the Brezhnev-Kosygin renegade clique in betraying the interests of the people of the world.

Because the international class struggle today is increasing in intensity and the people's revolutionary movement of the world is gaining ever greater momentum, the going grows tougher and tougher for the U.S. imperialists and Soviet revisionists. This prompted them to hurriedly put forward the draft treaty and play it up with much fanfare, in order to promote the atmosphere of U.S.-Soviet collaboration and facilitate their global collusion. Especially in the case of Vietnam, the U.S. imperialists and the Soviet revisionists are intensely working out new manoeuvres to force Vietnam to enter into "peace talks" by more extensive bombing, and trying to create conditions for a dirty deal over Vietnam as the next step. Obviously, Washington and Moscow are hoping to use the draft treaty as a means of pushing their criminal activity against communism, against the people, against revolution and against China, in an attempt to stem the revolutionary tide in the world.

The United States and the Soviet Union worked on the treaty for several years. Previously, they mainly wanted to bind China hand and foot and prevent it from possessing nuclear weapons. But atom bombs, guided missiles and hydrogen bombs were possessed by the Chinese people before their treaty was drawn up. This magnificent achievement of the Chinese people dealt a death-blow to the U.S.-Soviet policy of nuclear monopoly and nuclear blackmail and has encouraged the revolutionary people of the world tremendously. Thus, Washington and Moscow had to come up with the treaty in the hope of using it as a means of agitation against China and to contain socialist China's influence abroad.

The U.S.-Soviet draft treaty stipulates that non-nuclear countries should not develop and possess nuclear weapons, nor should they even develop nuclear explosion devices in the use of nuclear energy for peaceful purposes. Thus, the United States and the Soviet Union are to be given the privilege of carrying out nuclear blackmail for aggression, while the non-nuclear countries subjected to threats and aggression will not only be deprived of their right to develop nuclear weapons to resist U.S.-Soviet nuclear threats, but their development of nuclear industry for peaceful purposes will also be subjected to the insolent intervention and control by the United States and the Soviet Union. Obviously, the U.S. imperialists and Soviet revisionists concocted the treaty to put all non-nuclear countries in a subordinate position, that of being "protectorates," so that they may maintain their special status as big nuclear powers and remain "nuclear overlords."

Washington and Moscow loudly advertise that the conclusion of the "nuclear non-proliferation" treaty can bring about "nuclear disarmament" and will "contribute to preventing the threat of nuclear war." Is this really the case?

It is common knowledge that U.S.-led imperialism and its lackeys are the source of contemporary wars. The menace of nuclear war comes from U.S. imperialism and its accomplices. The so-called "nuclear non-proliferation" treaty cannot prevent the United States and the Soviet Union from manufacturing and stockpiling nuclear weapons, nor can it prevent them from using nuclear weapons in any war. Moreover, the United States long ago set up many nuclear bases all over the world; U.S. aircraft carrying nuclear warheads have been flying over various continents and U.S. submarines carrying nuclear warheads have been prowling the oceans. U.S. nuclear weapons have been proliferated all over the world. Nor does the draft treaty prevent the West German militarists from laying their hands on nuclear weapons through the NATO "Nuclear Defence" Committee. Is there any inkling of "nuclear disarmament" in the draft? What has it got to do with "preventing the threat of nuclear war"? If the U.S. imperialists and Soviet revisionists really want to prevent nuclear war, why then don't they propose the complete prohibition and total destruction of nuclear weapons?

The U.S.-Soviet treaty is an outright hoax. They want to use this scrap of paper to lull the people's vigilance so that under cover of this treaty they can have a free hand to vigorously carry out their nuclear blackmail and nuclear threat, control and bully other countries, sabotage the revolutionary movement of the people of the world and realize their fond hope of being the overlords of the world.

Our great leader Chairman Mao has pointed out: "Those who refuse to be enslaved will never be cowed by the atom bombs and hydrogen bombs in the hands of the U.S. imperialists."[22] The Soviet revisionist clique and the U.S. imperialists are today working hand in glove to try and salvage their already bankrupt nuclear monopoly positions through the "nuclear non-proliferaton" treaty and also to oppose the world's revolutionary people with their atom and hydrogen bombs. However, their nuclear hoax can no longer help them, and atom and hydrogen bombs cannot save them. Because they have made themselves the enemy of the world's people, they cannot escape their inevitable doom.

## Notes

21. "Draft Treaty on the Nonproliferation of Nuclear Weapons, August 24, 1967," *Documents on Disarmament 1967* (Washington: 1968), pp. 338–341.

22. *Peking Review*, Jan. 17, 1964, p. 5.

## Non-Nuclear States Criticize the Nonproliferation Treaty

### *Document 8*

This excerpt from a study by the Stockholm International Peace Research Institute summarizes the criticisms of the treaty made by India and others who thought the non-nuclear states had been unfairly treated. In sum, such critics believed that the nuclear states had far too few obligations and the non-nuclear states far too many.

### 8 CRITICISMS OF THE TREATY
**Stockholm International Peace Research Institute**

A number of countries are critical of the NPT. India, for example, has always been a major critic — voicing criticisms shared with varying emphasis by many of the others. The main objections to the NPT can be summarized as follows:

1. The Treaty does not ensure the non-proliferation of nuclear weapons but only stops their spread to non-nuclear-weapon states, without imposing any restraints on the continued manufacture, stockpiling and sophistication of nuclear weapons by the existing nuclear-weapon states.
2. The Treaty does nothing to remove the special status of superiority in power and prestige conferred by the possession of nuclear weapons.
3. The Treaty does not provide for a balance of obligations and responsibilities between the nuclear-weapon states and non-nuclear-weapon states. Most of the obligations are imposed on non-nuclear-weapon states, and the nuclear weapon states accept very few.
4. The Treaty is not a step towards nuclear disarmament.
5. The Treaty does not prohibit one nuclear-weapon state from assisting another nuclear-weapon state by providing technical assistance.
6. The Treaty endorses and legitimizes the present state of affairs and legalizes, if not encourages, an unrestrained vertical proliferation by the present nuclear-weapon powers.
7. The Treaty gives a false sense of security to the world.
8. The Treaty is discriminatory so far as the benefits of peaceful nuclear explosions are concerned.
9. The Treaty is discriminatory in regard to safeguards and controls which are all imposed on the non-nuclear-weapon states while none whatsoever are imposed on the nuclear-weapon states.

Few would deny that the NPT is a fragile document. The Treaty is weak because two nuclear-weapon powers (China and France) and many key states with ambitious nuclear plans (Argentina, Brazil, India, Israel, Pakistan and South Africa among them) have not associated themselves with it. But perhaps the greatest weakness of the Treaty is the imbalance between the obligations of, and benefits for, the non-nuclear-weapon parties — the "have-nots" — and those of, and for, the nuclear-weapon parties — the "haves". Moreover, the nuclear-weapon parties have failed to fulfill the few obligations under the Treaty which they do have.

Weak though it is, the NPT is our only barrier to proliferation. As such it is clearly a useful instrument. But can it be strengthened?

## President Johnson Urges Ratification of the Nonproliferation Treaty

### *Document 9*

In this message to the U.S. Senate, President Johnson urges ratification of the NPT, arguing that it is a contribution to peace. He also tries to respond to some of the criticism from non-nuclear states by emphasizing how the treaty will help expand the peaceful uses of nuclear energy

### 9 MESSAGE TO THE U.S. SENATE
**President Lyndon Johnson**
**July 9, 1968**

I am transmitting herewith, for the advice and consent of the Senate to ratification, the Treaty on the Non-Proliferation of Nuclear Weapons.[23]

This treaty was opened for signature on July 1, 1968 in Washington, London and Moscow. Ninety-five members of the United Nations had voted to commend it, and to request that it be opened for signature and ratification at the earliest possible date.

On July 1 it was signed in Washington by the United States of America, the United Kingdom of Great Britain and Northern Ireland, the Union of Soviet Socialist Republics and 53 other states. Many others have indicated their intention to sign it promptly.

I consider this treaty to be the most important international agreement limiting nuclear arms since the nuclear age began. It is a triumph of sanity and of man's will to survive.

The treaty takes a major step toward a goal the United States has been seeking for the past twenty-two years. Beginning with the McMahon Act in 1946,[24] our statutes have forbidden the transfer of our nuclear weapons to others.

In the Executive branch, efforts to prevent the spread of nuclear weapons have complemented those of the

Congress. Ever since the Baruch Plan of 1946,[25] we have sought to achieve an international consensus on this subject.

In making the first United States test ban proposal, President Eisenhower noted that his purpose was to curtail the uncontrolled spread of nuclear weapons.[26]

When President Kennedy announced the successful negotiation of the Nuclear Test Ban Treaty in 1963, he expressed the hope that it would be the opening wedge in a campaign to prevent the spread of nuclear weapons. He pointed out that a number of other nations could soon have the capacity to produce such weapons, and urged that we use whatever time remained to persuade such countries not to follow that course.[27]

In 1964, in the first message I submitted to the Geneva Disarmament Conference, I proposed an agreement that nuclear weapons not be transferred to non-nuclear countries, and that all transfers of nuclear materials for peaceful purposes take place under international safeguards.[28]

In 1966, the United States Senate clearly showed its support for negotiations toward a non-proliferation treaty. Ninety-nine Senators declared themselves in favor of the Pastore resolution (Senate Resolution 179).[29] It commended serious and urgent efforts to negotiate international agreements limiting the spread of nuclear weapons. It supported additional efforts by the President which were appropriate and necessary for the solution of nuclear proliferation problems.

The treaty I am submitting to you today is the product of these efforts by the legislative and executive branches. Its provisions are described in detail in the accompanying report of the Secretary of State.[30]

Its central purpose is to prevent the spread of nuclear weapons. Its basic undertaking was deliberately patterned after United States atomic energy legislation, which forbids transfers of our nuclear weapons to others. The treaty not only makes such a prohibition binding on all nuclear powers; it reinforces the prohibition by barring nonnuclear countries from receiving them from any source, from manufacturing or otherwise acquiring them, and from seeking or receiving any assistance in their manufacture.

The treaty, however, does more than just prohibit the spread of nuclear weapons. It would also promote the further development of nuclear energy for peaceful purposes under safeguards.

This is the goal of the International Atomic Eneregy Agency (IAEA), which resulted from President Eisenhower's "Atoms for Peace" plan.[31] The IAEA is charged with the primary responsibility for safeguards under the nonproliferation treaty. It already has considerable experience in applying safeguards under international agreements for cooperation in the civil uses of nuclear energy.

I believe that this treaty will greatly advance the goal of nuclear cooperation for peaceful purposes under international safeguards.

It will require that all parties which export nuclear materials and equipment to non-nuclear-weapon states for peaceful purposes make sure that such materials, and those used or produced in such equipment, are under international safeguards.

It will require all non-nuclear parties to accept international safeguards on *all* peaceful nuclear activities within their territories, under their jurisdiction, or carried out under their control anywhere.

It will help insure cooperation in the field of peaceful uses of nuclear energy, and the exchange of scientific and technological information on such peaceful applications.

It will enable all countries to assist non-nuclear parties to the treaty with their peaceful nuclear activities, confident that their assistance will not be diverted to the making of nuclear weapons.

It obligates the nuclear-weapon parties to make potential benefits from any peaceful applications of nuclear explosions available — on a non-discriminatory basis, and at the lowest possible cost — to parties to the treaty that are required to give up the right to have their own nuclear explosives.

By 1985 the world's peaceful nuclear power stations will probably be turning out enough by-product plutonium for the production of tens of nuclear bombs every day. This capability must not be allowed to result in the further spread of nuclear weapons. The consequences would be nuclear anarchy, and the energy designed to light the world could plunge it into darkness.

But the treaty has a significance that goes beyond its furtherance of these important aspects of United States nuclear policy. In the great tradition of the Nuclear Test Ban Treaty, it represents another step on the journey toward world peace. I believe that its very achievement, as well as its provisions, enhances the prospects of progress toward disarmament.

On Monday, July 1 — as this treaty was signed on behalf of the United States — I announced that agreement had been reached with the Soviet Union to enter into discussions in the nearest future on the limitation and reduction of both offensive nuclear weapons systems, and systems of defense against ballistic missiles. Thus there is hope that this treaty will mark the beginning of a new phase in the quest for order and moderation in international affairs.

I urgently recommended that the Senate move swiftly to enhance our security and that of the entire world by giving its consent to the ratification of this treaty.

## *Notes*

23. *Documents on Disarmament, 1968*, pp. 461–465.
24. *Documents on Disarmament, 1945–1959,* vol. I, pp. 45–52.
25. *Documents on Disarmament, 1945–1959,* vol. I, pp. 7–16.
26. *Public Papers of the Presidents of the United States: Dwight D. Eisenhower, 1960–61,* pp. 329–330.
27. *Documents on Disarmament, 1963,* pp. 254–255, 291–293.
28. *Ibid., 1964,* pp. 7–9.
29. *Ibid., 1966*, pp. 306–307.
30. *Ante,* pp. 470–478.
31. *Documents on Disarmament, 1945–1959,* vol. I, pp. 401–407.

# Who's Signed? Who Hasn't?

### *Documents 10 and 11*

Document 10 lists the signers of the NPT as of 1986. Document 11 is a brief 1987 review of nations that many experts believe are quite close to developing nuclear weapons.

## 10 SIGNERS OF THE NPT 1986

### A. Parties to the Non-Proliferation Treaty

| | |
|---|---|
| Afghanistan | 1970 |
| Antigua and Barbuda | 1985 |
| Australia | 1973 |
| Austria | 1969 |
| Bahamas, The | 1976 |
| Bangladesh | 1979 |
| Barbados | 1980 |
| Belgium | 1975 |
| Belize | 1985 |
| Benin | 1972 |
| Bhutan | 1985 |
| Bolivia | 1970 |
| Botswana | 1969 |
| Brunei | 1985 |
| Bulgaria | 1969 |
| Burkina Faso | 1970 |
| Burundi | 1971 |
| Cameroon | 1969 |
| Canada | 1969 |
| Cape Verde | 1979 |
| Central African Rep. | 1970 |
| Chad | 1971 |
| Colombia | 1986 |
| Congo | 1978 |
| Costa Rica | 1970 |
| Cyprus | 1970 |
| Czechoslovakia | 1969 |
| Denmark | 1969 |
| Dominica | 1968 |
| Dominican Republic | 1971 |
| Ecuador | 1969 |
| Egypt | 1981 |
| El Salvador | 1972 |
| Equatorial Guinea | 1984 |
| Ethiopia | 1970 |
| Fiji | 1972 |
| Finland | 1969 |
| Gabon | 1974 |
| Gambia, The | 1975 |
| Germany (East) | 1969 |
| Germany (West) | 1975 |
| Ghana | 1970 |
| Greece | 1970 |
| Grenada | 1975 |
| Guatemala | 1970 |
| Guinea | 1985 |
| Guinea-Bissau | 1976 |
| Haiti | 1970 |
| Holy See | 1971 |
| Honduras | 1973 |
| Hungary | 1969 |
| Iceland | 1969 |
| Indonesia | 1979 |
| Iran | 1970 |
| Iraq | 1969 |
| Ireland | 1968 |
| Italy | 1975 |
| Ivory Coast | 1973 |
| Jamaica | 1970 |
| Japan | 1976 |
| Jordan | 1970 |
| Kampuchea | 1972 |
| Kenya | 1970 |
| Kiribati | 1985 |
| Korea (South) | 1975 |
| Laos | 1970 |
| Lebanon | 1970 |
| Lesotho | 1970 |
| Liberia | 1970 |
| Libya | 1975 |
| Liechtenstein | 1978 |
| Luxembourg | 1975 |
| Madagascar | 1970 |
| Malawi | 1986 |
| Malaysia | 1970 |
| Maldives | 1970 |
| Mali | 1970 |
| Malta | 1970 |
| Mauritius | 1969 |
| Mexico | 1969 |
| Mongolia | 1969 |
| Morocco | 1970 |
| Nauru | 1982 |
| Nepal | 1970 |
| Netherlands | 1975 |
| New Zealand | 1969 |
| Nicaragua | 1973 |
| Nigeria | 1968 |
| N. Korea | 1985 |
| Norway | 1969 |
| Panama | 1977 |
| Papua New Guinea | 1982 |
| Paraguay | 1970 |
| Peru | 1970 |
| Philippines | 1972 |
| Poland | 1969 |
| Portugal | 1977 |
| Romania | 1970 |
| Rwanda | 1975 |
| San Marino | 1970 |
| Sao Tome & Principe | 1983 |
| St. Lucia | 1979 |
| St. Kitts & Nevis | 1983 |
| St. Vincent & The Grenadines | 1984 |
| Senegal | 1970 |
| Seychelles | 1985 |
| Sierra Leone | 1975 |
| Singapore | 1976 |
| Solomon Islands | 1981 |
| Somalia | 1970 |
| Sri Lanka | 1979 |
| Sudan | 1973 |
| Suriname | 1976 |
| Swaziland | 1969 |
| Sweden | 1970 |
| Switzerland | 1977 |
| Syrian Arab Republic | 1969 |
| Taiwan | 1970 |
| Thailand | 1972 |
| Togo | 1970 |
| Tonga | 1971 |
| Tunisia | 1970 |
| Turkey | 1980 |
| Tuvalu | 1979 |
| Uganda | 1982 |
| USSR* | 1970 |
| United Kingdom* | 1968 |
| United States* | 1970 |
| Uruguay | 1970 |
| Venezuela | 1975 |
| Vietnam | 1982 |
| Western Samoa | 1975 |
| Yemen, (Aden) | 1979 |
| Yemen, (Sana) | 1986 |
| Yugoslavia | 1970 |
| Zaire | 1970 |

### B. Countries That Have Signed but Not Ratified the Treaty

Kuwait
Trinidad & Tobago

### C. Countries That Have Neither Signed Nor Ratified the Treaty

| | | |
|---|---|---|
| Albania | Djibouti | Portugal |
| Algeria | France* | Qatar |
| Angola | Guyana | Saudi Arabia |
| Argentina | India** | South Africa |
| Bahrain | Israel | Spain |
| Brazil | Mauritania | Tanzania |
| Burma | Monaco | United Arab Emirates |
| Chile | Mozambique | Vanuatu |
| Comoros | Niger | Zambia |
| China* | Oman | Zimbabwe |
| Cuba | Pakistan | |

*Nuclear weapon state
**India has detonated a "peaceful nuclear device."

## 11 EMERGING NUCLEAR WEAPONS NATIONS 1986-1987

The following list of nations whose nuclear capability bears watching was compiled by the Carnegie Endowment for International Peace.

*Argentina*

- Negotiating nuclear restraints with Brazil.
- Civilian government opposed to nuclear arming.
- Building facilities necessary for nuclear weapons capability as part of nuclear energy program, but not subject to international inspection.
- Not party to Non-Proliferation Treaty (NPT).

*Brazil*

- Negotiating nuclear restraints with Argentina.
- Civilian government opposed to nuclear arming, but military would keep option.
- Building facilities necessary for nuclear weapons capability as part of nuclear energy program, but not under international inspection.
- Not party to NPT.

*India*

- Tested nuclear device in 1974.
- May have small number of undeclared atomic bombs.
- Has greatly expanded nuclear weapons production capability in recent years.
- Pursuing space program with ballistic missile potential.
- Not party to NPT.

*Iran*

- Years away from possibly building nuclear weapons indigenously.
- Some nuclear installations and weapons research inherited from Shah.
- Party to NPT.

*Iraq*

- Many years away from possibly building nuclear weapons indigenously.
- Thought to have been developing nuclear weapons capability until Israel destroyed Osiraq reactor in 1981.
- Party to NPT.

*Israel*

- Thought to have obtained the first nuclear weapons in late 1960s.
- May have 100-200 atomic bombs.
- Since 1982 allegedly built "boosted" weapons that rely on hydrogen bomb principle.
- Thought to have deployed short-range nuclear-capable missiles in early 1980s.
- Not party to NPT.

*Libya*

- Many years away from possibly building nuclear weapons indigenously.
- Attempted to purchase atomic bomb in early 1970s, 1981.
- Party to NPT.

*North Korea*

- Many years away from possibly building nuclear weapons indigenously.
- Building suspiciously large research reactor, but joined NPT in 1986, which will put plant under international inspection.

*Pakistan*

- During 1986 apparently manufactured all components for first atomic weapon; weapons production thought to be continuing.
- Not party to NPT.

*South Africa*

- Able to build nuclear weapons since 1980-1981.
- Possible arsenal of 10-15 weapons.
- Not party to NPT.

## WHO'S NEXT?

First we got the bomb, and that was good,
'Cause we love peace and motherhood.
Then Russia got the bomb, but that's okay,
'Cause the balance of power's maintained that way.
Who's next?

Then France got the bomb, but don't you grieve,
'Cause they're on our side (I believe).
China got the bomb, but have no fears,
'Cause they can't wipe us out for at least five years.
Who's next?

Japan will have its own device,
Transistorized at half the price.
South Africa wants two, that's right:
One for the black and one for the white.
Who's next?

Egypt's gonna get one too,
Just to use on you know who.
So Israel's getting tense,
Wants one in self defense.
"The Lord's our shepherd," says the psalm,
But just in case we better get a bomb.
Who's next?

Luxembourg is next to go,
And (who knows?) maybe Monaco.
We'll try to stay serene and calm
When Alabama gets the bomb.
Who's next?
Who's next?
Who's next?
Who's next?

From *Too Many Songs by Tom Lehrer* 1981

# THE SPREAD OF NUCLEAR WEAPONS CAPABILITY

## The Chinese Explode Atomic and Hydrogen Bombs

### *Documents 12 and 13*

**China joined the nuclear club on October 16, 1964, when it exploded an atomic bomb. Less than three years later, China exploded a much more powerful hydrogen bomb. In these two official statements, Chinese officials justify their new weapons as necessary to protect them from the United States and the Soviet Union.**

## 12 CHINESE STATEMENT ON NUCLEAR WEAPONS October 16, 1964

China exploded an atom bomb at 1500 hours on 16 October 1964, and thereby conducted successfully its first nuclear test. This is a major achievement of the Chinese people in their struggle to increase their national defense capability and oppose the U.S. imperialist policy of nuclear blackmail and nuclear threats.

To defend oneself is the inalienable right of every sovereign state, and to safeguard world peace is the common task of all peace-loving countries. China cannot remain idle and do nothing in the face of the ever-increasing nuclear threat posed by the United States. China is forced to conduct nuclear tests and develop nuclear weapons.

The Chinese Government has consistently advocated the complete prohibition and thorough destruction of nuclear weapons. Should this have been realized, China need not have developed the nuclear weapon, but this position of ours met the stubborn resistance of the U.S. imperialists.

The Chinese Government pointed out long ago that the treaty on the partial halting of nuclear tests signed by the United States, Britain, and the Soviet Union in Moscow in July 1963 was a big fraud to fool the people of the world, that it tried to consolidate the nuclear monopoly held by the three nuclear powers and tie the hands and feet of all peace-loving countries, and that it not only did not decrease but increased the nuclear threat of U.S. imperialism against the people of China and the whole world.[32]

During the past year and more, the United States has not stopped manufacturing various nuclear weapons on the basis of the nuclear tests which it had already conducted. Furthermore, seeking for ever greater perfection, the United States has during this same period conducted several dozen underground nuclear tests and thereby perfecting even more the nuclear weapons it manufactures.

In stationing nuclear submarines in Japan, the United States is posing a direct threat to the Japanese people, the Chinese people and the peoples of all other Asian countries. The United States is now putting nuclear weapons into the hands of the West German revanchists through the so-called multilateral nuclear force and thereby threatening the security of the German Democratic Republic and the other East European socialist countries. U.S. submarines carrying Polaris missiles with nuclear warheads are prowling the Taiwan Straits, the Tonkin Gulf, the Mediterranean Sea, the Pacific Ocean, the Indian Ocean, and the Atlantic Ocean, threatening everywhere peace-loving countries and all peoples who are fighting against imperialism, colonialism, and neocolonialism.

Under such circumstances, how can it be considered that the U.S. nuclear blackmail and nuclear threat against the people of the world no longer exist just because of the false impression created by the temporary halting of atmospheric tests by the United States?

The atom bomb is a paper tiger. This famous saying by Chairman Mao Tse-tung is known to all.[33] This was our view in the past and this is still our view at present. China is developing nuclear weapons not because we believe in the omnipotence of nuclear weapons and that China plans to use nuclear weapons. The truth is exactly to the contrary. In developing nuclear weapons, China's aim is to break the nuclear monopoly of the nuclear powers and to eliminate nuclear weapons.

The Chinese Government is loyal to Marxism-Leninism and proletarian internationalism. We believe in the people. It is the people who decide the outcome of a war, and not any weapon. The destiny of China is decided by the Chinese people, and the destiny of the world by the peoples of the world, and not by the nuclear weapon. The development of nuclear weapons by China is for defense and for protecting the Chinese people from the danger of the United States launching a nuclear war.

The Chinese Government hereby solemnly declares that China will never at any time and under any circumstances be the first to use nuclear weapons.

## Notes

32. The test ban treaty appears in *Documents on Disarmament, 1963,* pp. 291–293.

33. See Mao Tse-tung, *Talks with the American Correspondent Anna Louise Strong* (Peiping, 1961), p. 6.

# 13 CHINESE COMMUNIQUÉ ON FIRST HYDROGEN BOMB TEST June 17, 1967

Chairman Mao Tse-tung pointed out as far back as June 1958: I think it is entirely possible for some atom bombs and hydrogen bombs to be made in ten years' time.

Amidst the song of decisive victory of the great proletarian cultural revolution of our country, we solemnly announce to the people of China and the whole world that this brilliant prediction, this great call, of Chairman Mao's has been realized. Today, on June 17, 1967, after the five nuclear tests in two years and eight months, China successfully exploded her first hydrogen bomb over the western region of the country.

The success of this hydrogen bomb test represents another leap in the development of China's nuclear weapons. It marks the entry of the development of China's nuclear weapons into an entirely new stage. The Chinese people are proud of this, and the revolutionary people the world over will also take it as a matter of pride. With happiness and elation, we hail this fresh great victory of Mao Tse-tung's thought, this fresh splendid achievement of the great proletarian cultural revolution.

The Central Committee of the Communist Party of China, the State Council, the Military Commission of the Central Committee of the Party and the Cultural Revolution Group Under the Central Committee extend the warmest congratulations to all the commanders and fighters of the Chinese People's Liberation Army, the workers, engineers, technicians and scientists and the other personnel who have been engaged in the research, manufacture and testing of the nuclear weapons. Under the correct leadership of the Party's Central Committee, Chairman Mao and his close comrade-in-arms Comrade Lin Piao, they have held high the great red banner of Mao Tse-tung's thought, kept proletarian politics in the fore, creatively studied and applied Chairman Mao's works, firmly upheld the proletarian revolutionary line represented by Chairman Mao, resolutely opposed the revisionist line of the handful of top Party persons in authority taking the capitalist road, grasped revolution and promoted production, given play to their collective wisdom and strength, co-operated closely with each other, surmounted all difficulties in the revolutionary spirit of "seize the day, seize the hour" and, opening up a path of their own, have ensured the smooth success of this hydrogen bomb test.

Chairman Mao has said: "In the fields of the struggle for production and scientific experiment, mankind makes constant progress and nature undergoes constant change; they never remain at the same level. Therefore, man has constantly to sum up experience and go on discovering, inventing, creating and advancing."[34] It is hoped that the Chinese People's Liberation Army and the broad masses of the revolutionary workers and staff and the scientific and technical personnel — following these teachings of Chairman Mao and responding to the call of Comrade Lin Piao to "strengthen the revolutionary spirit, scientific approach and sense of organization and discipline" — will guard against conceit and impetuosity, continue to exert themselves and win new and still greater merit in accelerating the development of our country's national defence science and technology and the modernization of our national defence.

China has got atom bombs and guided missiles, and she now has the hydrogen bomb. This greatly heightens the morale of the revolutionary people throughout the world and greatly deflates the arrogance of imperialism, modern revisionism and all reactionaries. The success of China's hydrogen bomb test has further broken the nuclear monopoly of U.S. imperialism and Soviet revisionism and dealt a telling blow at their policy of nuclear blackmail. It is a very great encouragement and support to the Vietnamese people in their heroic war against U.S. aggression and for national salvation, to the Arab people in their resistance to aggression by the U.S. and British imperialists and their tool Israel and to the revolutionary people of the whole world.

Man is the factor that decides victory or defeat in war. The conducting of necessary and limited nuclear tests and the development of nuclear weapons by China are entirely for the purpose of defence, with the ultimate aim of abolishing nuclear weapons. We solemnly delcare once again that at no time and in no circumstances will China be the first to use nuclear weapons. We always mean what we say. As in the past, the Chinese people and Government will continue to make common efforts and carry on an unswerving struggle together with all the other peace-loving people and countries of the world for the noble aim of completely prohibiting and thoroughly destroying nuclear weapons.

## Note

34. *Quotations from Chairman Mao Tse-tung* (Peking: Foreign Language Press, 1966), pp. 203–204.

## India Joins the Nuclear Club

### *Documents 14 and 15*

**When India exploded a nuclear device on May 18, 1974, the Indian government declared that it was not a nuclear weapon but a peaceful nuclear device. Document 14 makes clear that Pakistan thought otherwise. As India's longtime rival and opponent in armed conflicts, Pakistan saw the bomb as a threat to its security. In document 15, India tries to reassure its neighbor and the world of its peaceful intentions. The Indian nuclear explosion was denounced by most of the key adherents of the NPT, who tended to agree with Pakistan that there was no difference between a peaceful nuclear test and a nuclear weapons test.**

### 14 STATEMENT BY GOVERNMENT OF PAKISTAN May 19, 1974

This does not come as a surprise to us. We have been repeatedly warning the United Nations, particularly the nuclear weapon powers and the International Community, for a decade that India's ambitious nuclear programme aimed at equipping itself with a nuclear option was being undertaken to carry out a nuclear weapon explosion and stake a claim to the status of a nuclear weapon power.

It must be stated that the news of the underground nuclear explosion by India is a development which cannot but be viewed with the degree of concern matching its magnitude by the whole world and more especially, by India's immediate neighbours. This concern can in no way be alleviated by India's contentions that the test has been carried out for peaceful purposes. It is an incontrovertible fact, stressed by the super powers themselves, that there is no difference between explosion of a so-called peaceful nuclear device and the detonation of a nuclear weapon. Therefore, any state which explodes a so-called peaceful nuclear device stands as much in violation of the Non-Proliferation Treaty[35] as the one which tests it for military purposes. Hence, India's disavowal of intention to produce nuclear weapons is lacking in credibility.

The principal aim of the Non-Proliferation Treaty which was concluded in 1968 under sponsorship and aegis of the United States and the Union of Soviet Socialist Republics was to prevent the further spread of nuclear weapons among states other than the then five nuclear weapon powers, namely, themselves and France, Britain and the People's Republic of China. Now that India has taken the fateful step, throwing restraint to the winds and in contradiction to its earlier disavowal of designs to carry out a nuclear explosion, efforts of the United Nations and the International Community since the Moscow Partial Test Ban Treaty of 1963[36] to curb the nuclear arms race have been rendered futile. The Non-Proliferation Treaty has been dealt a death blow.

## Notes

35. *Documents on Disarmament, 1968,* pp. 461–65.

36. *Documents on Disarmament, 1963–64,* pp. 120–22.

## 15 STATEMENT BY THE INDIAN EXTERNAL AFFAIRS MINISTER May 21, 1974

We are very happy to note that the peaceful nuclear experiment which took place on 18 May 1974 represents a step forward on the road to peaceful uses of nuclear energy for the welfare of our people. I would like to congratulate our scientists and others who have made possible this achievement by our country. This experiment is an important landmark in the development of nuclear technology for peaceful and economic uses. We have no intention of developing nuclear weapons.

Indian scientists and technologists have been active in this field for two decades; and it is well-known that already two atomic power plants are supplying nuclear energy into our national power grid for the use of our people. The present experiment is important because it represents our resolve to develop our indigenous resources of energy for the benefit of our people through our own efforts. In performing this scientific test, India has not violated any of her international obligations. We are heartened by the enthusiastic support which we have received in this endeavour from countries of the developing world.

It is singularly unfortunate that the peaceful nature of this nuclear experiment of ours should be misconstrued and misread in Pakistan. Apprehensions aroused in Pakistan are unfounded. We value our commitment under the Simla Agreement to settle all our differences with Pakistan by peaceful and bilateral means. Moreover, both countries have resolved that past policies of confrontation and conflict are banished forever.

We hope therefore that whatever misconception has arisen in Pakistan about this experiment will be replaced after cool reflection by more objective and realistic assessment. India has always supported development of co-operation amongst countries of this region on the basis of sovereign equality. Pakistan's allegations of hegemonistic designs have no basis at all and are, to say the least, uncharitable.

# Pakistan Develops Nuclear Weapons

### *Document 16*

Not surprisingly, the Indian nuclear explosion helped push Pakistan toward developing nuclear weapons. This article from the London *Observer* details how Pakistan used deception and clandestine methods to obtain materials critical to atomic weapons.

## 16 STEALING THE BOMB FOR PAKISTAN December 9, 1980

Islamabad, Pakistan's capital, has little in common with the rest of the country. Below the pretty Margalla Hills, the leafy avenues where the diplomats and civil servants live are laid out in a grid pattern, American style. On the outskirts is a new block where Dr. Abel Qader Khan lives. He is the most successful nuclear spy since Klaus Fuchs and Alan Nunn May took their secrets to the Kremlin. His house is guarded by young thugs who have no compunction about beating up inquisitive journalists and diplomats who stray into the area.

Dr. Khan is now working on the trigger device that will enable Pakistan to explode a nuclear bomb within the next two years. That one of the world's poorest and least stable countries will soon become a nuclear power is largely due to Khan's former Dutch employers. They took four years to warn their British and German partners in Urenco, an international corporation engaged in nuclear research, that Kahn, a metallurgist in a subcontracting research laboratory in Amsterdam called FDO, had been allowed to study classified documents not directly concerned with his work.

Before he announced that he was leaving Amsterdam for "an offer I can't refuse in Pakistan," he even managed to spend some time in the consortium's secret uranium enrichment plant at Almelo near the Dutch-German border. Then, while the Dutch remained silent about the breach in security, the Pakistanis set up dummy companies to import the components needed to build an enrichment plant under the pretext that they were needed for a new textile mill.

It was a considerable espionage coup. A country with a tiny industrial base had acquired advanced nuclear technology by stealing a process that took decades to develop. Whereas Fuchs and May supplied the Russians with missing pieces of the jigsaw for an atomic bomb, Khan stole the secrets of an entire multistage process for enriching uranium.

The Khan affair has been the subject of a Government inquiry in Holland, and a secret report is now being studied by officials of Urenco in Britain and Germany. The enormity of the leak has caused considerable bitterness between the Dutch and their partners, who are furious at the sloppiness of Dutch security.

Urenco says that Khan was not employed by it, but by FDO. Holland's Department of Economic Affairs, which is responsible for screening people who work in security areas, blames Urenco's security man at Almelo for failing to tell the Dutch security service of Khan's visit there. The security service, in turn, blames Dutch overseas intelligence for not telling it how desperate the Pakistanis were to achieve nuclear parity with India.

Khan's activities might not have been revealed had not other countries been following Pakistan's nuclear progress. Last July in London, Frank Allaun, a member of Parliament, asked the Government why Emerson Industrial Controls, the Swindon-based British subsidiary of an American company, was about to ship a consignment of high-frequency inverters to Pakistan. He told us that "a friend of a friend" would not disclose his source of information about the inverters, but it is likely that the tipoff came from Israel.

The Israelis have been watching Pakistan's nuclear program closely. They suspect Libyan financial backing and are fully aware, from their own experience, of the sort of trading you can do when you are in a hurry to make a nuclear bomb. Israel is now believed to have stockpiled enough nuclear bombs to wipe out every Arab capital.

Despite military links with Libya — the Pakistanis train much of the Libyan Air Force — President Zia ul-Haq has always denied there is a Libyan connection. But there is strong evidence pointing to Libya's backing. Pakistan cannot afford guns before butter, and Libya is willing to pay anything for nuclear knowhow.

There is another indication of Libyan involvement in Pakistan's nuclear program. Pakistan is short of uranium ore. Libya shares a border with Niger, a country with some of the world's most promising uranium deposits. A truck carrying twenty tons of the orange powder known as di-uranate — uranium ore which has been milled to remove some impurities — was hijacked near the mining town of Arlit in Niger, and later found overturned and empty near the Libyan border. Indian scientists are convinced that this di-uranate has been delivered to Pakistan.

Frank Allaun's question eventually led Britain's Department of Trade to put an export control order on the inverters. People began asking where the Pakistanis had acquired such a detailed knowledge of the centrifuge technique that they were able to circumvent restrictions imposed by the London Group (an organization of industrialized nations including Britain) on exports that might encourage nuclear proliferation.

The trail led inexorably to Khan, but when the matter was first raised in the Dutch Parliament early in 1979, the Government asserted that he had no access to nuclear secrets. It was not until June, when the Middle East magazine *8 Days* broke the story and the Israeli Government protested to The Netherlands, that the Dutch Foreign Minister announced there would be an inquiry. Since then the Dutch have conveyed the impression that Khan was caught with evidence of his spying, and was quietly allowed to leave to avoid a scandal. This never happened.

A spokesman for Urenco in The Hague reports that Khan was a "trouble-shooter." Anything he asked for he was given, and he asked for a lot. The puzzle is why the Dutch employed a Pakistani in a highly sensitive area when they had experts from three closely linked Western European countries to choose from.

Before he left for Pakistan late in 1975, Khan had been a student and postgraduate researcher in Belgium and Holland for more than ten years. A former colleague in Amsterdam described him as reserved. He had a Dutch wife, who was born in Rhodesia and carried a British passport, but he did not socialize much with his Western colleagues and rarely invited them to his home. It was believed this was partly because he was a Moslem and did not drink.

As a scientist he was regarded as "good" but by no means "exceptional." Nobody remembers any signs of fervent nationalism, or any discussion that could be remotely termed political.

Khan is not, as he is sometimes described, a physicist. He is a metallurgist. This takes him to the heart of ultra-high-speed centrifuge technology, where the main problem has been to find a metal strong enough to resist disintegration at 100,000 revolutions per minute.

Long before 1974, when the Indians had their "peaceful nuclear explosion" in the Rajasthan Desert, Prime Minister Zulfikar Ali Bhutto had decided that Pakistan should have a nuclear capability. There was, he said, "a Christian bomb, a Jewish bomb, and now a Hindu bomb. Why not an Islamic bomb?"

But after the Indian test, the world's major nuclear exporting countries formed the London Group to restrict the export of nuclear technology. One of its first acts was to identify a fuel reprocessing plant as one of the key preliminaries to a country's acquisition of the bomb-making process. France was about to furnish Pakistan with such a plant. Under American pressure, France reluctantly — for it was a major export order — cancelled the deal. This is where Dr. Khan came in.

Because of his employers' work for Urenco, he had to be screened by the Dutch security service. His wife's Dutch origins, and a declaration that he also intended to acquire Dutch nationality, quelled suspicions about his background.

The most likely date for his decision to start spying for his country is Spring, 1974, when the Indian explosion upset many Pakistanis still stung by their defeat in the 1971 war. The FDO laboratories have since maintained that Khan did many other things beside work on projects connected with Urenco. But FDO's main customer is Urenco, and its brochures make much of the fact that it has been involved with the centrifuge technique since 1955.

One thing Khan managed, according to former colleagues in Belgium, was to get involved in procuring materials for FDO's work on behalf of Urenco. In this way he could compile a list of suppliers. But his highest accomplishment, toward the end of his time in Holland, was to get inside the secret plant at Almelo.

Anthony Kuys, a director at the FDO laboratories, insists that this came about quite accidentally. "It was pure chance," he said. "He was a specialist in hydrogen corrosion, and he happened to be the best man for the job."

Khan completed the first part of his task in November, 1975, when he left FDO and returned to Pakistan. If Urenco officials felt any disquiet about this change of mind by the man who had said he might become a Dutch citizen, they never said so. At their offices in The Hague, an official told us that it would have been normal for the FDO laboratory to notify Urenco of Khan's departure. If this had happened, all three member nations would have been aware that a top scientist had left them to conduct his work in another country.

Much thought and ingenuity went into the next stage of the Pakistani operation — the clandestine purchase of parts. The quantities of money and material involved were so vast, and the sources of supply were so varied, that Khan, while still employed in Holland, must certainly have sat down with Pakistani advisers and worked out the priorities.

Once in Pakistan, he worked in liaison with the Special Works Organization, an authority created to buy centrifuge components from Europe. Some parts, such as lathes, could be openly bought and exported to Pakistan directly. But we know from SWO activities in Britain that the Pakistanis thought the purchase of more sensitive equipment might arouse suspicion if it was sent directly for export.

Dummy companies were set up to buy the most strategic units, the ones most carefully watched by the London Group. One such company was Weargate, Ltd., of Swansea in Wales. It bought inverters, a vital link in the assembly of centrifuges, from Emerson Electrical Controls in Swindon. Emerson sent the inverters to Swansea, and from there they found their way to Pakistan.

After Allaun had asked his Parliamentary question about the sale of inverters to Pakistan, it was discovered that Weargate was two-thirds owned by a Pakistani couple, Mr. and Mrs. Abdul Salaam, who have yet to be traced. Elsewhere in Europe, similarly ephemeral ventures were buying up fiberglass rotors and high vacuum valves.

Recently the British Government finally banned the export of other items concerned with centrifuge technology such as hexafluoride gas, pressure gauges and various alloys. The U.S. also is concerned about the imminent prospect of Pakistan acquiring a bomb and then selling the knowhow, perhaps to the Palestinians.

Even if he wanted to do so, it would be political suicide for Gen. Zia to abandon the nuclear program he inherited from Bhutto. So while he blandly insists, to general disbelief, that his nuclear program is entirely peaceful, Dr. Khan and his team continue with their research.

## Israel's Nuclear Weapons Capability

### *Document 17*

Most experts assume that the Israelis have a nuclear weapons capability. This article from *Time* magazine discusses how Israel obtained the expertise, facilities, and nuclear material necessary for nuclear weapons. It also describes how the United States became convinced that the Israelis have nuclear weapons.

## 17 HOW ISRAEL GOT THE BOMB April 12, 1974

For years there has been widespread speculation about Israel's nuclear potential — speculation that has now been confirmed. At a briefing for a group of American space experts in Washington recently, an official of the Central Intelligence Agency estimated that Israel had between ten and 20 nuclear weapons "available for use." In fact, TIME has learned, Israel possesses a nuclear arsenal of 13 atomic bombs, assembled, stored and ready to be dropped on enemy forces from specially equipped Kfir and Phantom fighters or Jericho missiles. These weapons have a 20-kiloton yield, roughly as powerful as those that obliterated Hiroshima and Nagasaki.

Israel has thus joined a nuclear club that includes, of course, the U.S. and Soviet Union, both of which have so much megatonnage that it is difficult to measure. France and Britain have several hundred nuclear warheads; India and China are estimated to be in Israel's class as fledgling atomic powers.

Israel's 13 bombs, TIME has also learned, were hastily assembled at a secret underground tunnel during a 78-hr. period at the start of the 1973 October War. At that time, the Egyptians had repulsed the first Israeli counterattacks along the Suez Canal, causing heavy casualties, and Israeli forces on the Golan Heights were retreating in the face of a massive Syrian tank assault. At 10 p.m. on Oct. 8, the Israeli Commander on the northern front, Major General Yitzhak Hoffi, told his superior. "I am not sure that we can hold out much longer." After midnight, Defense Minister Moshe Dayan solemnly warned Premier Golda Meir: "This is the end of the third temple."* Mrs. Meir thereupon gave Dayan permission to activate Israel's Doomsday weapons. As each bomb was assembled, it was rushed off to waiting air force units. Before any triggers were set, however, the battle on both fronts turned in Israel's favor. The 13 bombs were sent to desert arsenals, where they remain today, still ready for use.

Did Israel's nuclear capability play a part in the U.S. global military alert of Oct. 25, 1973? According to TIME's sources, the Israelis were convinced that the Russians had learned of the newly acquired nuclear potential, possibly through a Soviet Cosmos spy satellite over the Middle East. What is certain is that on Oct. 13, the Russians dispatched nuclear warheads from Nikolaev — the naval base at Odessa — to Alexandria, to be fitted on Russian Scud missiles already based in Egypt. The U.S., in turn, detected the Soviet warheads as the ship carrying them passed through the Bosphorous on Oct. 15 and issued a warning to Moscow by means of a world military alert.

TIME's sources further believe that the U.S. learned about the bombs as a result of a reconnaissance sweep of the Middle East by a spy plane. Some high officials in Washington insist that the U.S. had no knowledge of the bombs and deny that they were a factor in the alert. The plane was spotted by Israeli air defenses and two Phantom jets scrambled to intercept it. "I have it on my radar," the Israeli pilot radioed. "It is an [SR-71] American Blackbird." Back to him came a direct order from a high-ranking Israeli Air Force commander: "Down it." The SR-71, flying effortlessly at 85,000 ft., easily outclimbed and outdistanced the Israelis and returned to its base with significant readings.

*A symbolic reference to the state of Israel. The first two temples were destroyed by invading Babylonians around 586 B.C. and by the Romans in A.D. 70.

The origins of the nuclear bomb project date back to Israel's birth. Atomic scientists were encouraged by Chaim Weizmann, Israel's first President and a chemist of international repute. Israeli nuclear experts produced low-grade uranium from phosphate in the Negev and developed an efficient technique for producing heavy water. In 1953, Israel, in exchange for these processes, was allowed to study France's nuclear program and participate in its Sahara tests. Four years later, France gave Israel its first nuclear reactor. Later, the French also helped with the design of Israel's Dimona Atomic Research Community in the Negev, which Premier David Ben-Gurion called nothing but a "textile factory."

The Dimona nuclear reactor went into operation in 1964. Meanwhile, an intense secret debate had begun within Israel, about whether the government should also build a separation plant to produce the fissionable material necessary for an A-bomb. Ben-Gurion and Shimon Peres, then Deputy Defense Minister and currently Israel's Defense Minister, favored doing so. Others, including Mrs. Meir and Yigal Allon, now Israel's Foreign Minister, initially opposed the project. So did Ben-Gurion's successor as Premier, Levi Eshkol. The Israeli equivalent of the U.S. National Security Council vetoed the separation-plant project in early 1960. Shortly afterward, Eshkol discovered that Dayan — in the wake of the 1967 Six-Day War — had secretly ordered the start of construction on an S.P. Eshkol and his advisers felt that they could only rubberstamp a project already under way.

Dayan believes that a nuclear capability is essential to Israel. "Israel has no choice," he recently told TIME Correspondent Marlin Levin. "With our manpower we cannot physically, financially or economically go on acquiring more and more tanks and more and more planes. Before long you will have all of us maintaining and oiling the tanks."

Some Western intelligence experts believe that Israel conducted an underground nuclear test in the Negev in 1963, and that preparation of nuclear material for assembly into A-bombs began soon thereafter. The S.P. was completed in 1969, but Israel did not immediately begin manufacturing bombs. Instead, Israeli scientists concentrated on developing new methods for shortening the time necessary to produce nuclear weapons.

The Dimona research facility and the separation plant are protected not only by Israeli troops but by highly sophisticated electronic systems and radar screens that operate around the clock. All aircraft — including Israeli military planes — are barred from flying over the areas where the nuclear plants are located. During the Six-Day War, in fact, an Israeli Mirage III — either out of control or with its communications gear inoperative — inadvertently flew over Dimona. Israeli defenders shot it down with a ground-to-air missile. In 1973 a Libyan airliner flying from Benghazi to Cairo lost its way because of a navigational error and flew toward a forbidden area. Israeli fighters tried to turn it back. Then, for security reasons, they shot it down, causing the death of 108 of the 113 people aboard.

## Prospects for Further Proliferation of Nuclear Weapons

### Document 18

Leonard Spector prepares an annual report on the spread of nuclear weapons for the Carnegie Endowment for International Peace. In these excerpts from his report, Spector briefly reviews the prospects for further proliferation. While noting that some of the impediments to proliferation have been strengthened, he warns about a new "nuclear netherworld" of clandestine dealings by states that want nuclear weapons. He also points to danger signs in Argentina, Brazil, Iran, Iraq, North Korea, and South Africa.

### 18 GOING NUCLEAR
### Leonard Spector

Like the buildup of the superpowers' nuclear arsenals, the continuing spread of nuclear weapons to additional nations poses incalculable risks to the world community. Many believe that a nuclear confrontation involving one of the emerging nuclear nations is the most likely catalyst of a future nuclear holocaust. Indeed, few would predict the outcome of a nuclear crisis initiated by a regional power in the Middle East or South Asia, where the United States and the Soviet Union are now so vitally engaged.

Even a nuclear war that remained confined to a particular region could cause extraordinary devastation. If new estimates of Israel's nuclear might are accurate, it now has the weaponry to level every urban center in the Middle East with a population of over 100,000. South Africa could theoretically do the same in Southern Africa. India will shortly have enough nuclear-weapons material unrestricted by external non-proliferation controls to cause untold destruction in all of Pakistan's principal cities, and it appears that it will not be long before Pakistan will be able to wreak comparable havoc throughout northwestern India.

Since the People's Republic of China conducted its first nuclear test over two decades ago in 1964, no country has officially joined the nuclear-weapons club, whose other declared members today are the United States, the Soviet Union, Great Britain, and France. Nevertheless, the number of countries able to manufacture nuclear weapons and apparently ready to do so in response to regional pressures has mounted steadily.

Israel apparently achieved this status in the late 1960s. India did so by 1974 when it conducted its first and only nuclear test — something no other nation beyond the five declared nuclear powers has done — which it termed a "peaceful nuclear explosion." South Africa became a de facto nuclear state in 1980 or 1981, as it gained the capability to produce nuclear-weapons material. Pakistan stands at this threshold today. Argentina, Brazil, Iran, Iraq, and Libya, although they lack the ability to manufacture nuclear explosives, have all taken steps in this direction in the past decade.

While relatively stable nuclear relationships have emerged among the five declared nuclear powers, the spread of nuclear arms to the new nuclear nations presents a host of unpredictable dangers. Many of these states are located in highly volatile regions and a significant number have engaged in armed conflicts in recent years. The Iran-Iraq war, Israel's invasion of Lebanon, Argentina's occupation of the Falklands, and South Africa's incursions into Angola and other nearby countries are but some examples of the uncertainties of military decision making in the emerging nuclear states that may some day lead to nuclear confrontation.

The spread of nuclear weapons also increases the danger that nuclear arms may fall into the hands of radical, anti-status quo forces as the result of war, revolution or coup d'état. This danger afflicted two of the declared nuclear powers during the early stages of their nuclear-weapons programs, France and China. It is a particular concern in countries experiencing internal instability today, such as South Africa and, to a lesser extent, Pakistan. . . .

With the proliferation of nuclear capabilities, the threat of nuclear terrorism also grows. Indeed, according to a major international study released in 1986, the probability of nuclear terrorism, though low, is increasing today because of a confluence of factors, including "the growing incidence, sophistication, and lethality of conventional terrorism," the "apparent evidence of state support, even sponsorship, of terrorist groups," and growing world-wide stocks of nuclear-weapons material.*

The spread of nuclear weapons is also increasing the likelihood of conventional war, as governments have been tempted to strike preemptively against the nuclear installations of potential adversaries. Israel, Iraq, and Iran have already carried out raids against foreign nuclear plants, and there is evidence that Libya and India have contemplated similar action.

For these reasons the international community has struggled to contain the spread of nuclear arms. This book describes the progress and the setbacks of the past year.

*"Report of the International Task Force on Prevention of Nuclear Terrorism" (Washington, D.C.: Nuclear Control Institute, June 25, 1986), p.1.

## Slowing the Spread

Acquiring the capability to produce nuclear arms often takes decades, starting with training programs and the establishment of nuclear research centers. The most difficult obstacle is obtaining nuclear explosive material, either highly enriched uranium or plutonium. To obtain the former material, natural uranium must be improved to weapons grade in a highly complex enrichment plant. Plutonium is produced in uranium fuel when this is used in a nuclear reactor. The used fuel must then be transferred to a reprocessing plant where plutonium is extracted from other fuel constituents. For nuclear threshold countries, building the facilities for either process has proved a considerable technological challenge, requiring many years' effort even with active foreign assistance.

With the exception of India's 1974 detonation, none of the emerging nuclear countries is known to have conducted a nuclear test and most, if not all, appear unlikely to do so for the foreseeable future. This has served as a valuable constraint on proliferation by reducing the risk of wide-open escalation of nuclear weaponry akin to that of the nuclear-weapon states. The absence of testing has also dampened pressures on neighboring states to develop their own nuclear capabilities.

Reliable early generation atomic weapons, however, can be developed without testing; indeed, the type of bomb dropped on Hiroshima had never been tested. Moreover, as discussed later in this book in greater detail, new evidence concerning the Israeli nuclear program suggests that advanced atomic weapons, employing some concepts of the hydrogen bomb, and nuclear weapons small enough to serve as ballistic missile warheads can be developed without testing, at least by scientifically advanced nations. Developing true hydrogen bombs, weapons hundreds of times as powerful as the atom bombs used in World War II, still apparently remains out of reach without nuclear-weapons testing, however.

The international non-proliferation regime places additional constraints on the manufacture of nuclear arms. Its linchpin is the safeguards system of the International Atomic Energy Agency (IAEA), a Vienna-based international organization founded in 1957 and comprising more than 100 member states. The Agency's safeguards consist of reporting requirements, audits, and on-site inspections, which it applies to the vast majority of nuclear installations in non-nuclear-weapon countries to verify that these facilities are not used to support nuclear-weapons programs. Despite certain shortcomings, these safeguards can probably detect most illegal uses of these plants and therefore pose a significant deterrent to proliferation. But safeguards are less effective against the misuse of highly enriched uranium or plutonium, both directly usable for nuclear weapons. If it had made the necessary preparations, a country possessing either substance could abrogate safeguards and build weapons before the international community could intervene.

The 1968 Treaty on the Non-Proliferation of Nuclear Weapons (NPT), now ratified by over 130 non-nuclear-weapon states, is a second key element of the regime. Non-weapon-state NPT signatories pledge not to manufacture nuclear arms and agree to accept IAEA safeguards on all of their nuclear installations, while all parties agree to require safeguards on all of their nuclear exports. Argentina, Brazil, India, Israel, Pakistan, and South Africa have not ratified the treaty, however, and each possesses unsafeguarded nuclear facilities. Moreover, although Iran, Iraq, and Libya are parties to the pact, their lack of respect for other norms of international behavior has called into question their commitment to the accord.

The Nuclear Suppliers Group, formed in 1974, at a time when several exporting states had not ratified the NPT, has also required IAEA safeguards on all of its participants' nuclear exports. Its most prominent members are Belgium, Canada, France (the only non-NPT participant today), Great Britain, Italy, Japan, the Netherlands, the Soviet Union, Sweden, Switzerland, the United States, and West Germany. The People's Republic of China is not a member, but it has pledged that it will require safeguards on its future exports. Since the mid-1970s the nuclear suppliers, largely at U.S. urging, have also greatly restricted exports of enrichment and reprocessing technology. (Before it unilaterally adopted more restrictive policies on nuclear transfers in 1984 and 1985, China, which is not a party to these understandings, is believed to have helped Pakistan to develop its uranium enrichment capability — and to design nuclear arms themselves.)

Several individual supplier nations have adopted export policies that go beyond those adopted by the suppliers as a group. The 1978 U.S. Nuclear Non-Proliferation Act, for example, prohibits the sale of nuclear reactors and fuel to nations that have not placed *all* of their nuclear installations under IAEA safeguards.

Despite the intensity of their own nuclear rivalry, the United States and the Soviet Union have cooperated actively to strengthen the non-proliferation regime. U.S.-Soviet tensions in the Middle East and other troubled areas, however, have often impeded their respective efforts to arrest proliferation by their regional allies. Moreover, many fear that it will only be a matter of time until the unwillingness of the superpowers to restrain their own nuclear arsenals begins to undermine the non-proliferation system.

In some respects, international efforts to curb proliferation are gaining strength. The renunciation of nuclear weapons is slowly becoming a norm of international conduct, as demonstrated by the increasing number of parties to the Non-Proliferation Treaty and the slow rate at which new nations are crossing the nuclear-weapons threshold. The recent decisions of China, Argentina, South Africa and, apparently, Brazil to require IAEA safeguards on their exports also indicate the vitality of this control. Moreover, the nuclear-supplier nations appear to be exercising greater care than ever before in restricting exports that could aid additional nations to develop nuclear capabilities, although their controls remain imperfect.

International pressure aside, self-interest has also played a significant role in retarding proliferation. The nuclear threshold nations have avoided overt nuclear arming, for example, partly for fear that this might stimulate rival powers to do the same or to enlarge preexisting nuclear capabilities; concerns over possible preemptive action, noted above, have also been a restraining influence. In addition, military considerations dictate that along with nuclear weapons themselves, costly delivery systems must be acquired, customized, and maintained, all of which can impose a heavy burden on a developing economy. National leaders in states with deep ethnic or regional divisions must also consider domestic security, including whether the development of specialized nuclear forces will allow one or another group to gain unacceptable political leverage as the appointed guardian of the nation's nuclear arms and whether such arms might fall into the hands of the regime's domestic adversaries.

These various factors have not yet arrested the trend toward further proliferation, but they appear to have reduced the attractiveness to emerging nuclear powers of outright development of nuclear weapons — the model followed by the five declared nuclear-weapon states. Instead, Pakistan seems likely to continue following the more ambiguous approach of Israel, South Africa, and (since 1974) India of acquiring a nuclear capability without overtly manufacturing weapons or conducting nuclear tests. Argentina, Brazil, Iran, and Iraq also appear to have followed this model.

While such indeterminate nuclear-weapons capabilities may well present fewer overall risks than full-fledged programs under which nuclear arms are integrated into national military forces and can be used almost instantaneously, a world with six, possibly more, de facto nuclear-weapon states, which could count on having such arms in any protracted conflict, still poses serious dangers. Nor is there any guarantee that as more nations reach this level of nuclearization, they will remain at this plateau or that still others will not be encouraged to follow their example. For these reasons, international efforts to curb the spread of nuclear weapons continue to aim at preventing nations from reaching even this ambiguous stage of nuclear arming. As the events of the past year indicate, these efforts have met with only limited success.

## Nuclear Proliferation Today

The developments from mid-1985 to the fall of 1986 chronicled in this book are profoundly troubling. New information on the Israeli nuclear program reveals that the scale of proliferation in that country has been far greater than previously recognized. Details, published here for the first time, concerning Libya's attempt to purchase nuclear weapons in 1981 and newly unearthed evidence that the Shah of Iran had launched a nuclear-weapons research program — which presumably has been inherited by the Khomeini government — underscore the risk of proliferation by these nations. The threat of a nuclear arms race between India and Pakistan has also intensified, amidst increasing evidence that Pakistan has manufactured all of the components necessary to produce nuclear weapons for the first time. Worsening racial strife in South Africa, meanwhile, may lead Pretoria to reconsider its policy against nuclear testing and raises the fearful possibility that its nuclear-weapons capability might fall into the hands of extremists — of the right or the left. Only in Latin America are trends more favorable, as Argentina and Brazil took steps to dampen their long-standing nuclear rivalry.*

### *The Nuclear Inheritors*

With two nuclear-threshold nations, South Africa and Pakistan, now experiencing serious domestic unrest that could lead to the collapse of internal order or to the advent of anti-status quo governments, there is a growing risk that radical forces may gain control of nuclear weapons or the ability to manufacture them — a possibility that may pose one of the gravest dangers of the next decade. Although radicals have never acquired lasting control over such nuclear assets as the result of war, revolution, or coup d'état, there is historical precedent for the key elements of this scenario. In 1961, a group of right-wing French generals based in Algeria appears to have briefly taken control of a nuclear device at France's Sahara nuclear test site during an unsuccessful coup attempt, and an insubordinate province chief in the People's Republic of China, until he was ousted in 1968, similarly threatened to take over China's Lop Nor nuclear-weapons assembly and testing site during China's Cultural Revolution. In Iran in 1979, on the other hand, a radical, anti-status quo government took power and gained permanent control over an extensive nuclear infrastructure, although this did not include nuclear arms or the ability to produce them. Finally, the United States

*The developments summarized here are discussed in detail in the respective sections dealing with particular countries, along with detailed citations that will not be repeated.

was able to prevent, by means of a last-minute rescue mission, a modest quantity of non-weapons-usable reactor fuel from falling into the hands of North Vietnamese forces when they overran South Vietnam in 1975; preventing radicals from inheriting far more sensitive nuclear assets in South Africa or Pakistan, however, would pose a daunting, and possibly insurmountable, challenge.

### *Asia*

Despite an auspicious December 1985 agreement between India and Pakistan not to attack each other's nuclear installations, a subsequent chilling of Indo-Pakistani relations and unsettling domestic political developments in each nation dimmed prospects for a further easing of regional nuclear tensions. Meanwhile, both nations continued to advance their nuclear-weapons capabilities. India obtained for the first time weapons-usable plutonium unencumbered by any non-proliferation controls, while Pakistan, where senior political figures have now begun openly advocating the development of a nuclear deterrent, may have acquired its first stocks of highly enriched uranium (the alternative nuclear-weapons material), which it would be similarly free to use for nuclear arms. If Pakistan has in fact crossed this threshold and if both nations have taken steps to prepare other needed components, as some reports suggest, it is possible that they could assemble a number of aircraft-deliverable atomic bombs within a matter of months. For the time being, however, it appears that neither is likely to conduct a nuclear test or openly declare its possession of nuclear arms.

An important positive development in Asia was North Korea's adherence to the Non Proliferation Treaty, which will go far toward alleviating concerns that a large, indigenous nuclear-research reactor, now under construction there, might be used for the development of a nuclear-weapons capability.

### *The Middle East*

A detailed exposé of Israel's nuclear program published in October 1986 indicates that it is far more advanced than previously recognized and, accordingly, that the pace of proliferation in the region has been more rapid in recent years than generally acknowledged. The exposé, based on information and photos supplied by a technician formerly employed at Israel's classified Dimona nuclear complex, indicates that Israel may now possess between 100 and 200 nuclear weapons—not the 20 to 25 previously estimated—and that some of them may employ nuclear fusion, the principle of the H-bomb, which would make them tens of times more powerful than the atom bombs used in World War II. New evidence also appears to confirm that Israel deployed the short-range (400-mile) Jericho II missile, capable of carrying a nuclear warhead, in the early 1980s. If these various reports are accurate, Israel has vastly increased its nuclear might since 1980.

Libya, Iraq, and Iran are not known to have taken specific steps towards nuclear arming during the period covered by this volume. There has been evidence in past years of Libyan and Iraqi interest in acquiring such arms, however, and Iranian nuclear activities (included in this survey for the first time) also merit attention, given that nation's radical foreign policy and its inherited nuclear infrastructure. Iraq's continued violation of international arms control norms by repeatedly using chemical weapons against Iran and Syria's possession of advanced Soviet surface-to-surface missiles, reported development of an indigenous chemical-weapons capability, and possible Soviet nuclear guarantees are additional factors that could increase the risk of escalation to the nuclear level in any future Middle East conflict.

### *Latin America*

The advent of civilian governments in Argentina and Brazil in late 1983 and early 1985, respectively, along with a series of subsequent bilateral initiatives aimed at easing the countries' long-simmering nuclear rivalry, promise to reduce substantially the threat that either will build nuclear weapons. Elements in both nations supportive of more open-ended nuclear development continue to wield significant power, however, and have retarded the adoption of more far-reaching non-proliferation restraints, while obtaining continued support for previously initiated projects that may ultimately permit the production of unrestricted nuclear-weapons material.

The relevation in August 1986 that the Brazilian military may have taken steps to build a nuclear test site at a remote army reservation raised additional questions about the direction of the Brazilian program. Argentina, however, accepted the assurances of Brazil's civilian leaders that the site was not intended for this purpose, and bilateral non-proliferation discussions do not appear to have been affected. (Brazil is not expected to possess unrestricted nuclear-weapons material for a number of years, so the development of a test site would have been quite premature, in any event).

### *South Africa*

South Africa has had the capability to produce nuclear weapons since 1980 or 1981. Given its past activities indicating an intent to develop such arms, there is reason for concern that since 1985 it has slowly added to its stocks of nuclear-weapons material or, if it has indeed decided to build nuclear arms, added several weapons to an undeclared nuclear arsenal of perhaps a dozen atomic bombs.

It has been widely assumed that South Africa will not conduct a nuclear test for fear of complicating relations with the West. With these ties already under increasing stress during 1986 because of Pretoria's racial policies, however, the added diplomatic costs of a test — which would give a major boost to white morale — may not loom as large in Pretoria's calculations as they once did. Another danger inherent in South Africa's nuclear capability is the risk, noted earlier, that a radical faction within the country may gain control over nuclear weapons or nuclear-weapons material and blackmail other elements in the nation or outside states to advance its political goals.

### *Controls and Safeguards*

The International Atomic Energy Agency demonstrated its vitality by serving as the forum for the drafting of two major international conventions on nuclear accidents in the aftermath of the April 1986 disaster at the Soviet Chernobyl reactor. Similarly, at the IAEA General Conference in late September, a bid by several Arab states to impose sanctions against Israel was withdrawn for lack of support, seeming to end years of turmoil in the Agency that had led to repeated threats by the United States to withdraw from the organization. The matter was laid to rest only days before the revelations about Israel's nuclear program were published, however, raising the possibility that the sanctions issue will lead to renewed controversy at the 1987 General Conference.

With respect to controls over nuclear transfers, finally, a number of episodes of clandestine trade in nuclear-related equipment and materials were reported. These include Pakistan's acquisition of specially hardened steel from West Germany; Pakistani and Indian efforts to obtain Swedish flash X-ray machines, used for testing nuclear-weapons components; and India's unannounced importation of heavy water (used in its nuclear reactors).

## *Suggestions for Further Reading*

Dunn, Lewis A. *Controlling the Bomb: Nuclear Proliferation in the 1980s* (New Haven, CT: Yale University Press, 1982). Short, very good overview of the technical and political origins of nuclear proliferation for the nontechnical reader.

Greenwood, Ted, George Rathjens, and Jack Ruina. "Nuclear Power and Weapons Proliferation," *Adelphi Paper* No. 130 (London: International Institute for Strategic Studies, 1976). Comprehensive summary of nuclear weapons technology, nuclear fuel cycles, and nuclear power technology that is accessible to nontechnical readers.

Meyer, Stephen M. *The Dynamics of Nuclear Proliferation* (Chicago: U of Chicago P, 1984). Assesses states' incentives to acquire nuclear weapons, using analytical models.

Yager, Joseph A. *Nonproliferation and U.S. Foreign Policy* (Washington, D.C.: Brookings Institution, 1980). Good treatment of U.S. policy through the Carter administration.

# Nine

# CARTER'S NEW WORLD

**SALT II**

After the ceremonious signing of the SALT II Treaty on June 18, 1979, U.S. President Jimmy Carter and Soviet President and Party Chief Leonid Brezhnev exchange SALT documents in the Vienna Imperial Hofburg Palace, Austria. AP/Wide World Photos

# INTRODUCTION

Early in the Carter administration, key foreign policy officials made clear that the United States would not become as preoccupied with the Soviet Union as it had been during the Nixon-Ford administrations. In his first major speech on foreign policy, President Jimmy Carter announced that it was time to move beyond the "inordinate fear of Communism." During the 1976 campaign, Carter also had promised a major cut in the defense budget. In his inaugural address he spoke about a world free of nuclear weapons.

Less than three years later, Carter described U.S.-Soviet relations as "the most critical factor in determining whether the world will live in peace or be engulfed in global conflict." He announced the Carter Doctrine, threatening military force if the Soviets attempted to move into the Persian Gulf; he increased the defense budget and took steps toward reinstituting the draft; and he withdrew the SALT II Treaty from Senate consideration to protest the Soviet invasion of Afghanistan.

Although other administrations have reversed themselves on key aspects of foreign policy, the Carter administration seemed to follow contradictory national security policies throughout its tenure. As historian John Lewis Gaddis has said, the administration seemed to lack a "coherent and discernible conception of American interests in the world, potential threats to them and feasible responses." The reasons for this incoherence seem to stem from what Gaddis calls "an unusual interaction of politics, personalities, and circumstances."

By the time the Carter administration came to office, many of the policies of Henry Kissinger had become politically unpopular. Détente had lost popularity because many believed that the United States had gained relatively little from it. Watergate and the Vietnam War had increased cynicism about government in general and about government secrecy in particular.

President Carter wanted his administration to appear to be quite different from that of its predecessors. Therefore he launched a number of initiatives designed to highlight the differences between his approach and Henry Kissinger's. The most important of these were the human rights campaign and a new approach to the SALT II negotiations, the March 1977 proposal.

However, although the Carter administration wanted for political reasons to *appear* different, in fact it also wanted to preserve most of the major accomplishments of the Nixon-Ford administration: the ongoing SALT negotiations, improved relations with the Soviet Union, acceptance of the Sino-Soviet split, and so forth. In short, the Carter administration wanted to be both "tough" and "conciliatory."

These conflicting tendencies were intensified by conflicts of personalities. Secretary of State Cyrus Vance tended to favor a conciliatory approach, while National Security Adviser Zbigniew Brzezinski tended to be more hawkish, especially later in the administration. Instead of complementing each other, the two key figures pulled the administration in opposite directions and helped make the administration policies incoherent.

Finally, and perhaps most importantly, the Carter administration faced a new phenomenon: the Soviet Union, having reached strategic parity with the United States, had begun to play a much more assertive role. The Soviets continued their efforts to expand their influence in the Third World, which culminated in the occupation of Afghanistan by Soviet troops.

The new Soviet challenge and the conflicting tendencies within the administration made arms control policy especially difficult. The United States and the Soviet Union had been negotiating on the SALT II Treaty for five years when Carter became president. In the third month of his term, Carter presented the Soviets with a brand new comprehensive proposal on SALT II. Secretary of State Vance took the proposal to Moscow with great fanfare. To the Soviets, the proposal seemed to be an attempt to undo all the progress that had been made on SALT II to that point. The U.S. proposal also seemed, in Soviet eyes, very one-sided. When the Soviets rejected the proposal, it set back the SALT II negotiations many months.

The two sides did finally manage to get down to serious negotiating, and they did sign a treaty in 1979. However, during the negotiations, the administration was far from united. Conflicts among various branches and personalities in the administration led to leaks to Congress and the press, which hampered the negotiations. The internal conflicts would have made ratification a difficult task, even in the absence of the Afghanistan situation.

In the SALT II negotiations, a key U.S. goal was to achieve equal ceilings, because the Nixon administration had been criticized for agreeing to "unequal" limits on SALT I. This was made difficult because the U.S. and Soviet arsenals are structured so differently. In addition, new weapons and technologies posed problems for SALT II. In the end, the two sides agreed on ceilings that were somewhat lower than those agreed to in SALT I. They also, for the first time, agreed on some significant qualitative limits (controls on technology) for offensive systems, and they strengthened measures designed to promote verification of the treaties.

The SALT II Treaty was signed in June 1979. But U.S.-Soviet conflicts over the Third World and Cuba made it hard for the Carter administration to win public support for arms control measures. Finally, when the Soviet Union invaded Afghanistan, President Carter realized that SALT II had no chance of ratification. He asked the Senate not to bring the treaty to a vote.

By 1980, President Carter had also long since abandoned his rhetoric about eliminating nuclear weapons. Although he canceled the B–1 bomber, Carter decided to go ahead with the MX missile (see chap. 11) and adopted the counter-vailing strategy, which required a large number of nuclear weapons.

# A TROUBLED ADMINISTRATION

## The Kissinger Legacy

### *Document 1*

In document 1, historian John Lewis Gaddis discusses the growing public dissatisfaction with Henry Kissinger's policies, policies from which Jimmy Carter benefited during the 1976 election. Critics argued that Kissinger's foreign policy was "amoral" because it neglected human rights, used covert means against democratically elected governments, and seemed willing to sacrifice human lives in support of a vague notion of "honor." Carter promised to restore the "moral authority" of the presidency.

### 1 IMPLEMENTING DÉTENTE
### John Lewis Gaddis

Centralization had another unfortunate effect as well in the eyes of Kissinger's critics: it eroded the foundation of moral principle upon which American foreign policy had to rest if it was to reflect the nation's most fundamental aspirations. As presidential candidate Jimmy Carter put it during the 1976 campaign:

> Our foreign policy is being evolved in secret, and in its full details and nuances, it is probably known to one man only. . . . Because we have let our foreign policy be made for us, we have lost something crucial in the way we talk and the way we act toward other peoples of the world. . . . [I]t must be the responsibility of the President to restore the moral authority of this country in its conduct of foreign policy.

For too long, Carter charged, foreign policy had consisted "almost entirely of maneuver and manipulation, based on the assumption that the world is a jungle of competing national antagonisms, where military supremacy and economic muscle are the only things that work and where rival powers are balanced against each other to keep the peace." That approach might have been appropriate in 1815, or even 1945, but not in the 1970's. Kissinger's "Lone Ranger" foreign policy "inherently has had to be closely guarded and amoral, and we have had to forego openness, consultation and a constant adherence to fundamental principles and high moral standards."[1]

Whatever one thinks of Carter's assumption that democratic decision-making produces moral diplomacy, there was a widespread sense, by the end of the Ford administration, that Kissinger and the presidents he served had neglected the proper alignment between policy and principle that any nation must have in order to maintain self-confidence. At its most extreme, this argument could lead to charges of complicity in nothing less than genocide. Thus, it has been suggested, Nixon and Kissinger carefully looked the other way while Nigeria in 1969–1970 starved out the Biafran rebels. They insisted on supporting Pakistan in 1971, despite that government's slaughter of its own citizens in its rebellious eastern provinces. They only temporarily suspended aid to Burundi, despite evidence between 1972 and 1974 of officially sanctioned mass murders carried out against the numerically dominant but politically powerless Hutu population there. And, through their casual expansion of the Vietnam War into Cambodia, they set in motion the chain of events that would lead after 1975 to the depredations of Pol Pot and the Khmer Rouge, and to the near-extermination of an entire people. "Cambodia," one critic has asserted, "was not a mistake; it was a crime."[2]

The assumption here is that statesmen must be judged by the consequences of their actions, whatever their intent.[3] That standard would be fair enough if it could be demonstrated that a direct relationship exists between actions taken and effects produced, but that demonstration is difficult to make in the four cases cited. The extent of Nigerian and Pakistani atrocities was not at first clearly understood in Washington, nor is there evidence that even if it had been, it would have been within the administration's power to stop them. The same was true of Burundi, which rated so low in the White House scale of priorities that Kissinger took the unaccustomed step of delegating key decisions regarding that country to subordinates.[4] In the case of Cambodia, it was North

Vietnamese forces, not Americans, who first violated neutrality there; the advent of Pol Pot was less a function of the 1970 U.S. military "incursion" than of Hanoi's final victory over South Vietnam in 1975. To blame Washington for the horrors that occurred in these situations is not only to give undue weight to single elements in complex causal chains; the argument suggests as well a certain backhanded chauvinism, assuming as it seems to that violence and terror have no independent existence in the world, and that they appear only as the result of action (or inaction) by the United States.

A more convincing version of the "amorality" critique is that Kissinger was too prone to let ends justify means: that in his haste to accomplish specific objectives, he employed methods inappropriate to, and at times destructive of, the larger goals he was trying to achieve.[5] The argument could be applied to the events just described; its more obvious application, though, can be found in the administration's policies regarding the democratically elected Marxist government of Salvadore Allende in Chile, and the de-escalation of the Vietnam War.

Throughout the Cold War, the United States had claimed to oppose communism, not because it was revolutionary, but because it denied freedom of choice. Should a people ever freely elect a government of that persuasion, the argument ran, Washington would respect that judgment.[6] Thus, Nixon acknowledged early in 1971 that although Allende's election was "not something that we welcomed, . . . that was the decision of the people of Chile, and . . . therefore we accepted that decision. . . . [F]or the United States to have intervened — intervened in a free election and to have turned it around, I think, would have had repercussions all over Latin America that would have been far worse than what has happened in Chile." Later that year, in a section of the administration's annual foreign policy report headed "A Community of Diversity," Kissinger noted: "We hope that governments will evolve toward constitutional procedures. But it is not our mission to try to provide — except by example — the answers to such questions for other sovereign states. . . . [W]e are prepared to have the kind of relationship with the Chilean government that it is prepared to have with us."[7]

And yet, it is now clear that the White House, long before the Chilean elections took place, had authorized covert action designed to swing them to Allende's opponents; that it sought by means that included consideration of a military coup to keep him from taking power; and that, once he was installed in office, it pursued a vigorous policy of economic and political pressure aimed at "destabilizing" his regime. It did all this on the basis of vague fears that Chile under Allende would become a communist dictatorship, along the lines of Castro's Cuba. "I don't see why we have to let a country go Marxist just because its people are irresponsible," Kissinger is said to have commented, in an Orwellian remark that seemed to suggest a willingness to subvert democracy in order to preserve democracy. Whether Allende would in fact have gone the way of Castro is impossible to know: he was overthrown and assassinated in 1973, to the unconcealed glee — though apparently without the direct involvement — of the Nixon administration. What is clear is, first, that the White House lied about its activities in Chile; second, that its actions confirmed the view of Marxism's more militant exponents that that ideology could succeed in Latin America only by violent means and only over the opposition of the United States; and third, that Washington failed its own test of tolerating distasteful but democratic regimes.[8]

Kissinger's position on Chile, as on Eurocommunism in Western Europe, was that the United States could accept only a certain range of political outcomes, even if produced by democratic means. The American commitment to diversity did not extend to the acceptance of governments that might in some way upset the balance of power. As Kissinger acknowledged to his staff at one point: "We set the limits of diversity."[9] But the costs of limiting diversity could be high, as Kissinger found out when information on the Chilean affair became public late in 1974, setting off a protracted (and highly public) Congressional investigation into this and other covert activities. Moreover, the dangers that had justified this departure from principle could never be proven, since the actions involved had been intended to prevent hypothetical threats from becoming real ones. Nixon may well have been more prophetic than he knew when he said, for public consumption in 1971, that the repercussions of intervention in Chile would be worse than the provocations that might cause it in the first place.

A similar resort to means inconsistent with ends shaped the Nixon administration's de-escalation of the war in Vietnam. The chief rationale for remaining in that country until an acceptable peace settlement had been worked out had been to preserve self-confidence at home and respect abroad. "A nation cannot remain great if it betrays its allies and lets down its friends," Nixon had told the nation in his first major address on Vietnam in late 1969. "Our defeat and humiliation in South Vietnam without question would promote recklessness in the councils of those great powers who have not yet abandoned their goals of world conquest." Kissinger made the same point in emotional terms in his memoirs, a decade later:

> I believed in the moral significance of my adopted country. America, alone of the free countries, was strong enough to assure global security against the forces of tyranny. Only America had both the power and the decency to inspire other peoples who struggled for identity, for

> progress and dignity. . . . There was no one now to come to America's rescue if we abandoned our international responsibilities or if we succumbed to self-hatred.

The prerequisites for an acceptable settlement were simple; the return of American prisoners-of-war, and the survival of South Vietnam as an independent state. Within these narrow limits, the administration was successful: Hanoi after four years came around to Washington's position on the prisoners-of-war and the continuation of the Thieu regime in Saigon, so that, by its own standards, the White House could claim upon conclusion of the Paris peace agreements in January 1973 to have achieved "an honorable ending to a long and costly effort."[10]

But were the means chosen appropriate to the ends sought — self-assurance at home and respect abroad? Measurements of such intangibles will always be imprecise; still there is reason to question whether the methods Nixon and Kissinger used to ward off defeat and humiliation in Vietnam did not bring about some of the very consequences they had sought to prevent. Despite evidence of the obviously corrosive effect it had had on government credibility during the Johnson years, the White House continued to resort to, and even expanded, the use of official deception to increase freedom of action. Hence, Nixon could publicly claim, in March 1970, that "we respect Cambodia's neutrality," when in fact he had a year earlier ordered the secret bombing of that country, and the falsification of military records to cover up the fact.[11] Later that year, he dispatched American ground troops into Cambodia to demonstrate, as he put it, that the United States was not a "pitiful helpless giant," but in the process set off not only unprecedented domestic disorders but also the first serious Congressional efforts to limit the president's war-making authority. Concern over the resulting challenge to presidential power provoked Nixon into sanctioning the wire-taps and break-ins that led to Watergate;* that event in turn produced an erosion of presidential power that not only made it difficult to implement "linkage" or to rearm in the face of the Soviet military buildup, but also made it impossible for the Ford Administration to honor Nixon's pledge to save South Vietnam if the cease-fire broke down, as it did in 1975.

One might well wonder whether all of this — not to mention the additional 20,553 American and unknown number of Vietnamese lives lost between 1969 and 1973[12] — was worth it to defend a concept of American "honor" thought to require the survival of a government in Saigon incapable of standing on its own, even after years of support. To be sure, that government's collapse in 1975 set off surprisingly little recrimination within the United States; there was no replay of the "who lost China" debates of a quarter century earlier, or alarm among American allies. This fact has been taken as a retrospective justification for the strategy of protracted withdrawal.[13] Still, one has the impression that those Nixon and Kissinger were trying to impress by remaining in Vietnam — the American public, allies overseas, certainly the Chinese, possibly even the Russians — would have reacted more with relief than chagrin had the official perception of "honor" permitted withdrawal at an earlier date, and at less expense. For "honor" must also be tempered, at least in the affairs of nations, by common sense: that aspiration is rarely served, even in the eyes of sympathetic observers, by the passionate pursuit of untenable objectives at exorbitant costs.

Yet another dimension of the "amorality" argument was the charge that Nixon and Kissinger attached greater importance to stability and order in international relations than to the cause of "human rights." Curiously, this position found support on both the right and left wings of the American political spectrum.[14] Liberals could criticize the administration's close ties with authoritarian regimes in South Korea, the Philippines, Pakistan, Iran, Greece, Portugal, and, after 1973, Chile: it had acquiesced in the suppression of democratic procedures in those countries, it was argued, because the United States needed their help to maintain the world balance of power against communism. Conservatives, conversely, could complain about the administration's reluctance to protest violations of human rights in the Soviet Union, Eastern Europe, and Communist China: the cause of dissent in those countries, it was asserted, had been sacrificed on the altar of détente.

There were elements of truth in both of these arguments. The Nixon administration — like all of its postwar predecessors — was clearly more tolerant of authoritarianism on the right than on the left. Such regimes ran no risks of becoming Soviet satellites; moreover, there persisted in Washington the belief that right-wing dictatorships were more likely to be reversible than those on the left.[15] As a consequence, the White House tended not to make an issue of the suppression of human rights in countries otherwise on the "right" side in the Cold War. Nor was there an inclination to hold détente hostage to improvements in Moscow's treatment of its own people or its satellites, as was apparent in the administration's hostility to the Jackson amendment, its support through

* "In hindsight I can see that, once I realized the Vietnam war could not be ended quickly or easily and that I was going to be up against an anti-war movement that was able to dominate the media with its attitudes and values, I was sometimes drawn into the very frame of mind I so despised in the leaders of that movement. They increasingly came to justify almost anything in the name of forcing an immediate end to a war they considered unjustified and immoral. I was similarly driven to preserve the government's ability to conduct foreign policy and to conduct it in the way that I felt would best bring peace. I believed that national security was involved. I still believe it today, and in the same circumstances, I would act now as I did then. History will make the final judgment on the actions, reactions, and excesses of both sides; it is a judgment I do not fear." (Nixon, *RN,* pp. 514–15.)

the inadvertently publicized "Sonnenfeldt doctrine"* of a more "organic" relationship between Eastern Europe and the Soviet Union, and Kissinger's recommendation to Ford not to receive the exiled Aleksandr Solzhenitsyn at the White House.[16] These were positions consistent with the administration's determination to stress interests over ideology in its diplomacy: "Our objective," Kissinger later recalled, "was to purge our foreign policy of all sentimentality."[17]

But an unsentimental foreign policy did not, in Kissinger's mind, necessarily imply an amoral one. There was in his thinking a surprisingly strong concern with the moral dimensions of world politics: his speeches on the subject as Secretary of State may well represent the most sustained official attempt since Woodrow Wilson to reconcile the competing claims of power and ideals.[18] Kissinger resolved the dilemma in a classic Niebuhrian sense (much as Kennan also had done years earlier): balance of power politics, he argued, were not inconsistent with moral principles, because ideals could hardly flourish under conditions of perpetual war or anarchy. Some minimal standard of order, achieved by manipulating power, was necessary before justice could be attained. "The true task of statesmanship," he suggested in 1975, "is to draw from the balance of power a more positive capacity to better the human condition — to turn stability into creativity, to transform the relaxation of tensions into a strengthening of freedom, to turn man's preoccupations from self-defense to human progress." Or, as he put it in his memoirs: "If history teaches anything it is that there can be no peace without equilibrium and no justice without restraint. But I believed equally that no nation could face or even define its choices without a moral compass that set a course through the ambiguities of reality and thus made sacrifices meaningful."[19]

There has been a perennial and probably unresolvable debate over the extent to which foreign policy should reflect moral principles.[20] On the one hand, it has been argued, it is important for a nation to "stand" for something: an ideology based on shared aspirations can generate self-confidence, a sense of momentum, the conviction that "history" is on one's side. But ideologies, as Kissinger liked to warn, can also be dangerous: excessive preoccupation with them can lead to misperceptions of one's own or an adversary's power; it can also preclude agreements that might otherwise be in the mutual interests of both. There is little reason to doubt that the Nixon-Kissinger effort to "purge" foreign policy of "sentimentality" was carried out in the sincere belief that only on such a basis could agreements be reached that would make possible a reduction in Cold War tensions. The issue, though — and the point upon which the "amorality" of Kissinger's diplomacy hinges — is this: did he carry that process so far as to undermine the ideological foundation necessary for the conduct of a self-confident and popularly supported foreign policy?

* So called for Helmut Sonnenfeldt, counselor to the State Department and a close Kissinger adviser, who told a group of American ambassadors on an off-the-record basis in London in December 1975 that "it must be our policy to strive for an evolution that makes the relationship between the Eastern Europeans and the Soviet Union an organic one. . . . [O]ur policy must be a policy of responding to the clearly visible aspirations in Eastern Europe for a more autonomous existence within the context of a strong Soviet geopolitical influence." (Summary of remarks, *New York Times,* April 6, 1976.)

## Notes


1. Carter speech to the Chicago Council on Foreign Relations, March 15, 1976, and to the Foreign Policy Association, New York, June 23, 1976, *The Presidential Campaign, 1976,* volume I, part 1, pp. 110–13, 266.
2. William Shawcross, *Sideshow: Kissinger, Nixon and the Destruction of Cambodia* (New York: 1979), p. 396. See also Morris, *Uncertain Greatness,* pp. 120–30, 213–30, 265–68.
3. Shawcross, *Sideshow,* p. 396.
4. Morris, *Uncertain Greatness,* p. 268.
5. See, on this point, Shawcross, *Sideshow,* p. 396.
6. See Chapters Two, Three, and Seven.
7. Nixon radio-television interview, January 4, 1971, NPP; 1971, p. 12. Annual foreign policy report, February 25, 1971, *ibid.,* pp. 246–47.
8. Morris, *Uncertain Greatness,* pp. 240–41; Szule, *The Illusion of Peace,* pp. 720–25. Kissinger's defense of his Chilean policy is in *White House Years,* pp. 653–83. See also U.S. Congress, Senate, Select Committee to Study Government Operations with Respect to Intelligence Activities, *Covert Action in Chile.* 1963–1973 (Washington: 1975).
9. Quoted in Morris, *Uncertain Greatness,* p. 241.
10. Nixon radio-television address, November 3, 1969, NPP: 1969, p. 903: Kissinger, *White House Years,* p. 229; Annual foreign policy report, May 3, 1973, NPP: 1973, p. 376. See also Nixon, *RN,* p. 348.
11. Nixon press conference, March 21, 1970, NPP; 1970, p. 292. See also Shawcross, *Sideshow,* pp. 19–35.
12. Herring, *America's Longest War,* p. 250.
13. Bell, *The Diplomacy of Détente,* pp. 127–29, 224; Brown, *The Crises of Power,* p. 52.
14. Elizabeth Drew, "A Reporter at Large: Human Rights," *New Yorker,* LIII (July 18, 1977), 36; Bell, *The Diplomacy of Détente,* pp. 31–32.
15. See, on this point, Richard H. Ullman, "Washington, Wilson, and the Democrat's Dilemma," *Foreign Policy,* #21 (Winter, 1975–76), 108–9; and Stoessinger, *Kissinger,* p. 218.

16. Ford, *A Time to Heal,* pp. 297–98.
17. Kissinger, *White House Years,* p. 191.
18. See, especially, Kissinger's speeches at Minneapolis, July 15, 1975, and Montreal, August 11, 1975, also his 1968 essay, "Central Issues of American Foreign Policy," all printed in Kissinger, *American Foreign Policy,* pp. 91–97, 195–236.
19. *Ibid.,* pp. 218–19; Kissinger, *White House Years,* p. 55.
20. For a recent account, see Arthur M. Schlesinger, Jr. "Human Rights and the American Tradition," *Foreign Affairs,* LVII ("America and the World: 1978"), 503–26; and for some of the strikingly comparable dilemmas of British foreign policy in the nineteenth century, David Fromkin, "The Great Gain in Asia," *ibid.,* LVIII (Spring, 1980), especially 941–45.

# The New Soviet Threat

## *Documents 2 and 3*

In document 2, Soviet expert David Holloway discusses a key problem that President Carter inherited: the increasingly active role taken by the Soviet Union in the late 1970s. Holloway traces this new assertiveness to the Soviet Union's achievement of strategic parity with the United States, the U.S. defeat in Vietnam, and the opportunities presented by the decline of Western colonial empires. He also argues that Soviet concern about a possible U.S.-Chinese alliance played a role. In document 3, Richard Smoke discusses the Soviet nuclear buildup in the late 1970s. He notes that this buildup was of concern to all defense analysts, but "hawks" believed the United States had to launch a major buildup in response. In the late 1970s, the hawks were especially effective in getting their message to the U.S. public.

## 2 MILITARY POWER AND FOREIGN POLICY
## David Holloway

### Expansion and Encirclement

The Soviet intervention in Angola was the first sign of a more active Soviet policy in the Third World in the late 1970s. Several different factors combined to encourage the Soviet leaders to take a greater interest in the use of military power in Africa and Asia. First, they may well have felt that the Soviet status of political equality with the United States gave them (in the words of one Soviet official) an "equal right to meddle in Third Areas."[21] As the Defence Minister, Marshal Grechko, put it — less succinctly — in 1974:

> at the present stage the historic function of the Soviet Armed Forces is not restricted to their function in defending our Motherland and the other socialist countries. In its foreign policy activity the Soviet state purposefully opposes the export of counter-revolution and the policy of oppression, supports the struggle for national liberation, and resolutely resists imperialist aggression in whatever distant region of our planet it may appear.[22]

The Soviet leaders now claimed full equality with the United States and evidently felt that it was their right to exercise their power on a global scale.

Second, the North Vietnamese victory over the United States showed that small states could defeat the largest Western power. Shavrov claimed in 1975 that the Western "strategy of local wars" was going through a crisis. The Soviet leaders may have felt that a more active military policy on their part could further weaken Western positions in the Third World, for, as Shavrov had argued, Soviet aid could be a most important factor in determining the outcome of a local war.[23] The Soviet Union's ocean-going navy and growing airlift capability could be used increasingly to support Soviet allies and inhibit Western intervention in local conflicts.

Third, the setbacks to Soviet-American detente in 1974 and 1975 may well have encouraged the Soviet leadership to pursue a more active policy in the Third World. There was now less to be gained from restraint. In any event, Brezhnev told the 25th Party Congress in February 1976 that "detente does not in the slightest abolish and cannot abolish or alter the laws of the class struggle. Some bourgeois leaders affect surprise over the solidarity of Soviet Communists, of the Soviet people, with the struggle of other people for freedom and progress. This is either outright naivete or more likely a deliberate befuddling of minds."[24] It was clear that Soviet and American conceptions of detente were different. The United States had hoped to restrain Soviet expansion by offering the Soviet Union cooperation in areas of mutual interest. The Soviet leaders, on the other hand, saw detente as a relationship of both cooperation and conflict. They rejected the American concept of linkage, arguing that cooperation in such areas as arms control and trade was mutually beneficial, and that therefore the Soviet Union should not be expected to pay an extra price by changing its political system or modifying its foreign policy to conform to American ideas about the norms of international behaviour. Moreover, whatever prospects may have existed in 1972 and 1973 that the Soviet Union would modify its foreign policy in order to improve relations with the United States had diminished by 1976, for most of the incentives for such modification had vanished.

The Soviet leaders were encouraged to pursue a

more active policy in the Third World by the feeling that they had attained a new international status, and a new ability to influence events around the world. They have used arms transfers, military advisers and Cuban troops to help governments and movements that they supported; only in Afghanistan have Soviet combat troops been used on a large scale. But Soviet actions should not be seen merely as the result of a single policy decision, for contingent factors have played an important role. The collapse of three empires — the Portuguese (1974), Ethiopian (1974) and Iranian (1979) — created opportunities the Soviet Union felt able to exploit. Moreover, Soviet policy has been guided not only by the desire to assert Soviet status as a global power, but also by more specific objectives: the security of its own frontiers, the containment of China, the restriction of Western power and influence. Soviet policy has to be interpreted not merely in terms of Soviet ambitions, but in the context of the regions where it intervenes. The Soviet Union is indeed an important actor on the international stage, but it does not devise the plot, write the script, set the scene and direct the play as well.

In 1977 the Soviet Union airlifted arms and sent military advisers to help the revolutionary government in Ethiopia. Ethiopia had been invaded by Somalia, which was trying to seize the province of Ogaden, and faced rebellion in other parts of the country, notably in Eritrea. The Soviet intervention included the airlift of Cuban troops, who fought under Soviet command to push the Somalis out of the Ogaden. As in Angola, the intervention by the Soviet Union and Cuba was decisive in ensuring the victory of the forces they supported.[25]

Both of these interventions stimulated pressure in the United States for a tougher foreign policy. The Soviet Union was increasingly seen as a global power, willing and able to use military force around the world to further its political ambitions. Since it was a major aim of American policy to restrain Soviet expansion by linking cooperation in arms control and trade to Soviet behaviour abroad, Soviet activities in Africa inevitably undermined American faith in cooperation. Carter's national security adviser Zbigniew Brzezinski later noted that the SALT II Treaty lay "buried in the sands of the Ogaden."[26]

As Soviet relations with the United States deteriorated, so American ties with China grew stronger. After Mao's death in 1976 the Soviet Union put out feelers to see whether the new leadership was ready for an improvement in relations. But it was soon clear that, in spite of major changes in domestic affairs, hostility towards the Soviet Union would remain a feature of Chinese policy. The new Chinese leaders were determined to make China a modern industrial state by the year 2000 and sought closer contact with the United States, Western Europe and Japan.

In August 1978 China and Japan signed a Treaty of Peace and Friendship, which included an "anti-hegemony" clause that, in spite of disavowals, was clearly directed against the Soviet Union. The Soviet government denounced the Treaty as "a threat to stability in Asia."[27] In November of the same year Vietnam (within weeks of signing a Treaty of Friendship and Cooperation with the Soviet Union) invaded Kampuchea, which was allied to China, and installed a pro-Vietnamese government there. In December the United States and China announced that they had reached agreement on the position of Taiwan and would now proceed to establish normal diplomatic relations. In February 1979 China invaded Vietnam in order to "teach it a lesson" for its invasion of Kampuchea, but withdrew its forces within a month. The Soviet Union both gained and lost from this flurry of invasions and Friendship Treaties. Vietnam and the Vietnamese-backed government in Kampuchea were now firmly allied with the Soviet Union against China. But in June 1978 Brezhnev had warned the United States not to play the "China card" against the Soviet Union, declaring that this was a "short-sighted and dangerous policy" which its architects might bitterly regret.[28] Six months later Japan, China and the United States had drawn much closer together.

## Notes

21. Quoted in Alexander Dallin, "The Road to Kabul: Soviet Perceptions of World Affairs and the Afghan Crisis," in *The Soviet Invasion of Afghanistan,* ACIS Working Paper No. 27, Center for International and Strategic Affairs, UCLA, September 1980, p. 57.
22. Marshal A. A. Grechko, "Rukovodyashchaya rol' KPSS v stroitel'stve armii razvitogo sotsialisticheskogo obshchestva," *Voprosy istorii KPSS,* May 1974, p. 39.
23. Shavrov, *loc. cit.,* April 1975, p. 96.
24. *Pravda,* 25 February 1976.
25. Colin Legum, "Angola and the Horn of Africa," in Kaplan (ed.), *op. cit.,* pp. 605–37.
26. *New York Times,* 18 January 1981.
27. *Pravda,* 13 August 1978.
28. *Pravda,* 26 June 1978.

## 3 THE SOVIET BUILDUP
## Richard Smoke

### The Soviet Strategic Buildup

During the 1970s the USSR produced four new ICBM models. One was not a success and was never deployed in quantity. The other three missiles are all much larger than any American missile. In NATO terminology they are called the SS-17, SS-18 and SS-19. The SS-18 in particular is huge. Its throw weight is seven times that of the most powerful American missile, the Minuteman III. Where the latter carries three MIRVs, the SS-18 carries eight, every one of which has a much larger yield than the Minuteman MIRVs. (More data are given on the accompanying table.)

Technically, the Soviet decision to build very big new ICBMs was more a confession of weakness than a statement of strength, though psychologically and politically the effect was the opposite. The Soviets had to build large missiles, and new ones, because the older ones were too small to carry the large MIRV vehicles the Soviets were obliged to design. They had not mastered the technology of miniaturization, so both their warheads and their bus for carrying them were necessarily larger. This in turn required a much larger missile to carry the size and weight.

By contrast the Americans had succeeded in designing, from the beginning, a much smaller bus and warhead. The MIRV package for ICBMs fit onto the existing American ICBM, the Minuteman; the MIRV package for SLBMs fit onto the Poseidon missile, which in turn fit inside the same submarine tubes as the old Polaris missile. But this early U.S. technical triumph later came to seem almost a liability, when some Americans were frightened by the sheer size of the Soviet missiles and the fact that they were new.

At sea there were comparable Soviet improvements. At the beginning of the 1970s the Soviet Navy was still deploying a fairly primitive SLBM, roughly comparable to America's first Polaris missile, with a range of only about 1,750 miles. By mid-decade a new fleet of submarines, called Deltas in the West, were carrying a new, much-improved SLBM with a range of almost 5,000 miles. The table gives additional data.

By the end of the 1970s yet another SLBM was entering the Soviet forces. This one had about the same 5,000-mile range but carried MIRVs. And a colossal new model of missile-carrying submarine, called the Typhoon in the West, was under construction. The largest submarine ever built, the Typhoon apparently is intended to be able to remain at sea for long periods of time.

During the decade of the 1970s the USSR also began deploying the Backfire bomber in quantity, as discussed in the previous chapter. Although the Backfire is not, on balance, as capable a bomber as the United States' B-52 or FB-111 bombers, improved with advanced electronics and standoff missiles, the Backfire also does not have to face nearly as difficult an air defense system as American bombers must face.

**Table 6. American and Soviet strategic forces as of mid-1975**

| | *Soviet Union* | *United States* |
|---|---|---|
| ICBMs | 1,618 (includes about 70 new SS-17, SS-18, SS-19 missiles) | 1,054 (includes 550 Minuteman III missiles |
| SLBMs | 784 in 75 submarines | 656 (includes 400 Poseidon missiles) in 41 submarines |
| Long-range bombers | 135 Bears and Bisons | 463 B-52s and FB-111s |

*Notes:* Data for Soviet long-range bombers do not include about 25 Backfire bombers deployed as of this time. The American FB-111 is technically a medium-range bomber, but acquires long range with aerial refueling, a technique long practiced and perfected with FB-111s.

*Source:* International Institute of Strategic Studies, London: The Military Balance, 1975–76.

There were other improvements in the Soviet strategic posture as well. Some of the ICBM silos were "superhardened," making them invulnerable to anything but an almost direct hit. The USSR also continued work on a civil defense system. While programs for creating shelters and stocking them with provisions had been abandoned in the West by the mid-1960s, the Soviets chose to continue and improve their similar program, and their plans for evacuation of Soviet cities in a crisis. Exactly how effective this civil defense program would prove in a real war is a matter of debate among Western analysts.

Much of this strategic buildup was predictable and in that sense undisturbing. But the number of models of missiles, their size, and the pace of their development and deployment exceeded Western expectations. Western leaders naturally were disturbed when the Soviet strategic effort proved to be greater than Western intelligence had anticipated. Toward the end of the 1970s the Carter administration revealed that Moscow had begun work on a group of four more strategic missiles — the fifth generation — and a new long-range strategic bomber. Later the new bomber was given the name "Blackjack" in the West.

Once the MIRV era was launched it also became predictable that both superpowers would end up deploying large numbers of warheads. But some American officials had believed in the late 1960s and early 1970s that it would take the USSR longer to develop and deploy MIRVs than it actually did. Here too the Soviet strategic drive exceeded expectations. And the large size of Soviet missiles meant that, if and when the Soviets mastered the miniaturization technology, the USSR could deploy many more MIRVs than the United States could, on the same number of launch vehicles. Barring a long-lasting negotiated limit on total numbers of warheads, the United States could eventually face a tremendous disadvantage, missile for missile. . . .

## The American Reaction to the Soviet Buildup

At all times there is a spectrum of opinion, corresponding vaguely to the left-right dimension of political attitudes, among American national security and arms control specialists regarding the best policy options for the United States. To describe this spectrum fairly is not easy. The "dove" versus "hawk" terminology so popular during the Vietnam era has often been resisted by specialists, who see their policy positions and rationales as containing too many offsetting ingredients for such simple descriptions. Nor does the difference always come down to a choice between more arms control or more weapons. For instance, many of those who usually favor larger defense expenditures also favor arms control, given the right conditions. Perhaps the best way to characterize the spectrum of opinion is in terms of *which risks* a particular analyst or group emphasizes in any given situation: the risks that may be posed by adversaries enhancing their power, or the risks (and costs) posed by continuing and perhaps accelerating the arms race. Thus nearly all specialists may favor negotiating some kind of new strategic arms control treaty, for instance, but some will emphasize the risks in failing to find strict treaty conditions that constrain the USSR, and some will emphasize the risks of delaying or losing the treaty out of a search for stricter conditions.

During the 1970s almost the entire spectrum of U.S. national security and arms control specialists became concerned about the buildup in Soviet military power, but it was viewed with more alarm by some than by others. Toward one side of the spectrum, analysts tended to find explanations for it that emphasized Soviet motives other than aggressive ones. Possible motives included Moscow's fear of China or other possible enemies, Soviet reaction to American choices (such as MIRV), the great influence of Soviet generals and heavy-industry bureaucrats in Kremlin decision making, and the sheer exploitation of technical possibilities. Toward the other side analysts stressed the increasing dangers the USSR could, in fact, pose to the United States even if the military expansion might indeed result partly from other motives. As the momentum of the Soviet arms drive continued, some of these specialists became increasingly vocal and organized.

Best known was a group called the Committee on the Present Danger, formed in 1976 to promote popular support for an answering increase in American military power. The committee was headed by Paul Nitze, who had been a principal member of the U.S. negotiating team for SALT I and, many years earlier, one of the principal architects of NSC-68. Later Nitze and the committee assumed the leadership of those opposed to the SALT II agreement, both during its final stages of negotiation when its main outlines were known, and afterwards when the Carter administration submitted it to the Senate.

Also in 1976, considerable publicity was generated for the so-called "Team B Report," which expressed alarm about the Soviet buildup. Team B was a group of national security specialists, some of them shortly to be leaders of the committee, and all sharing its viewpoint. George Bush, then director of the CIA, formed the team and invited it to challenge the regular annual CIA estimate of Soviet capabilities.

This annual review and certain other major intelligence reviews are known as "National Intelligence Estimates," or NIEs. They form the basis for much official national security planning. Previously the CIA had come under some criticism for underestimating the USSR's power and it decided to respond by opening its data, and the regular, "Team A," interpretation thereof, on a highly classified basis to a group of critics who could form their own judgment.

The Team B Report was itself classified but its main conclusions were leaked to the press. The Kremlin leaders do believe a nuclear war could be fought and won by the USSR under advantageous circumstances, said Team B, and are driving toward the advantage necessary either to defeat the United States or force it to back down in crises. These conclusions (and the team's assessment that the Soviet Union had already achieved a significant degree of superiority) were later reviewed by the CIA's own analysts and rejected, at least so far as that time period was concerned. But in the following years the exact extent and character of the Soviet buildup remained a subject of intense discussion among U.S. national security specialists.

Much of the debate revolved around differing estimates of Soviet military expenditures. The official defense budget published by the USSR is a fiction; in actuality expenditures are considerably higher, exactly how much being a matter of estimate. A CIA figure commonly cited holds that over the ten-year period of the 1970s the Soviet Union spent on its military forces about $300 billion *more* than the United States spent. Analysts of the "present danger" viewpoint have suggested that the difference may be even greater, and strongly advocate that the United States close the gap.

Specialists taking the opposing point of view argue that some of the Soviet expenditure represents money wasted — on an air defense system, for instance, that the United States can penetrate — and some of the expenditure goes to forces deployed against China. For these and other reasons these analysts reject the idea that the United States should have to match Soviet expenditures. The United States, they argue, is in a quite different position from the USSR and should plan its forces on the basis of its own needs and goals.

These analysts also challenge the validity of the estimates themselves. Normally the figures are derived by calculating how much it would cost the United States to develop the same forces. This is misleading, they argue, because many of the components cost more in America than in the Soviet Union. This is especially true of manpower: American military personnel are much better paid than their Soviet counterparts, and *American* pay scales are used in calculating what it would cost to reproduce the USSR's forces in America. These analysts argue that if one examines what personnel and other components actually cost the Kremlin, the real difference between Soviet and American military expenditures is much less, though still not negligible. Specialists on the opposing side reply that other inaccuracies creep into any effort to calculate the Kremlin's "actual" costs, and pricing Soviet forces in terms of what they would cost in America is really the fairest method. The debate is unresolved and, due to the differences in the structure of the American and Soviet economies, may be unresolvable.

## A New Foreign Policy

### *Document 4*

Early in his administration, Jimmy Carter laid out the fundamental principles of his foreign policy in a speech at the University of Notre Dame. The excerpts here make clear that Carter wanted to differentiate his foreign policy from Kissinger's. He discusses the importance of human rights, the need for a democratic foreign policy "based on fundamental values," and openness. He also says the United States is free of the "inordinate fear of Communism."

### 4 COMMENCEMENT ADDRESS
### President Jimmy Carter
### University of Notre Dame
### May 22, 1977

Last week, I spoke in California about the domestic agenda for our Nation: to provide more efficiently for the needs of our people, to demonstrate — against the dark faith of our times — that our Government can be both competent and more humane.

But I want to speak to you today about the strands that connect our actions overseas with our essential character as a nation. I believe we can have a foreign policy that is democratic, that is based on fundamental values, and that uses power and influence, which we have, for humane purposes. We can also have a foreign policy that the American people both support and, for a change, know about and understand.

I have a quiet confidence in our own political system. Because we know that democracy works, we can reject the arguments of those rulers who deny human rights to their people.

We are confident that democracy's example will be compelling, and so we seek to bring that example closer to those from whom in the past few years we have been separated and who are not yet convinced about the advantages of our kind of life.

We are confident that the democratic methods are the most effective, and so we are not tempted to employ improper tactics here at home or abroad.

We are confident of our own strength, so we can seek substantial mutual reductions in the nuclear arms race.

And we are confident of the good sense of American people, and so we let them share in the process of making foreign policy decisions. We can thus speak with the voices of 215 million, and not just of an isolated handful.

Democracy's great recent successes — in India, Portugal, Spain, Greece — show that our confidence in this system is not misplaced. Being confident of our own future, we are now free of that inordinate fear of communism which once led us to embrace any dictator who joined us in that fear. I'm glad that that's being changed.

For too many years, we've been willing to adopt the flawed and erroneous principles and tactics of our adversaries, sometimes abandoning our own values for theirs. We've fought fire with fire, never thinking that fire is better quenched with water. This approach failed, with Vietnam the best example of its intellectual and moral poverty. But through failure we have now found our way back to our own principles and values, and we have regained our lost confidence.

By the measure of history, our Nation's 200 years are very brief, and our rise to world eminence is briefer still. It dates from 1945, when Europe and the old international order lay in ruins. Before then, America was largely on the periphery of world affairs. But since then, we have inescapably been at the center of world affairs.

Our policy during this period was guided by two principles: a belief that Soviet expansion was almost inevitable but that it must be contained, and the corresponding belief in the importance of an almost exclusive alliance among non-Communist nations on both sides of the Atlantic. That system could not last forever unchanged. Historical trends have weakened its foundation. The unifying threat of conflict with the Soviet Union has become less intensive, even though the competition has become more extensive.

The Vietnamese war produced a profound moral crisis, sapping worldwide faith in our own policy and our system of life, a crisis of confidence made even more grave by the covert pessimism of some of our leaders.

In less than a generation, we've seen the world change dramatically. The daily lives and aspirations of most human beings have been transformed. Colonialism is nearly gone. A new sense of national identity now exists in almost 100 new countries that have been formed in the last generation. Knowledge has become more widespread. Aspirations are higher. As more people have been freed from traditional constraints, more have been determined to achieve, for the first time in their lives, social justice.

The world is still divided by ideological disputes, dominated by regional conflicts, and threatened by danger that we will not resolve the differences of race and wealth without violence or without drawing into combat the major military powers. We can no longer separate the traditional issues of war and peace from the new global questions of justice, equity, and human rights.

It is a new world, but America should not fear it. It is a new world, and we should help to shape it. It is a new world that calls for a new American foreign policy — a policy based on constant decency in its values and on optimism in our historical vision.

We can no longer have a policy solely for the industrial nations as the foundation of global stability, but we must respond to the new reality of a politically awakening world.

We can no longer expect that the other 150 nations will follow the dictates of the powerful, but we must continue — confidently — our efforts to inspire, to persuade, and to lead.

Our policy must reflect our belief that the world can hope for more than simple survival and our belief that dignity and freedom are fundamental spiritual requirements. Our policy must shape an international system that will last longer than secret deals.

We cannot make this kind of policy by manipulation. Our policy must be open; it must be candid; it must be one of constructive global involvement, resting on five cardinal principles.

I've tried to make these premises clear to the American people since last January. Let me review what we have been doing and discuss what we intend to do.

First, we have reaffirmed America's commitment to human rights as a fundamental tenet of our foreign policy. In ancestry, religion, color, place of origin, and cultural background, we Americans are as diverse a nation as the world has even seen. No common mystique of blood or soil unites us. What draws us together, perhaps more than anything else, is a belief in human freedom. We want the world to know that our Nation stands for more than financial prosperity.

This does not mean that we can conduct our foreign policy by rigid moral maxims. We live in a world that is imperfect and which will always be imperfect — a world that is complex and confused and which will always be complex and confused.

I understand fully the limits of moral suasion. We have no illusion that changes will come easily or soon. But I also believe that it is a mistake to undervalue the power of words and of the ideas that words embody. In our own history, that power has ranged from Thomas Paine's "Common Sense" to Martin Luther King, Jr.'s "I Have a Dream." . . .

Second, we've moved deliberately to reinforce the bonds among our democracies. In our recent meetings in London, we agreed to widen our economic cooperation, to promote free trade, to strengthen the world's monetary system, to seek ways of avoiding nuclear proliferation. We prepared constructive proposals for the forthcoming meetings on North-South problems of poverty, development, and global well-being. And we agreed on joint efforts to reinforce and to modernize our common defense. . . .

Third, we've moved to engage the Soviet Union in a joint effort to halt the strategic arms race. This race is not only dangerous, it's morally deplorable. We must put an end to it.

I know it will not be easy to reach agreements. Our goal is to be fair to both sides, to produce reciprocal stability, parity, and security. We desire a freeze on further modernization and production of weapons and a continuing, substantial reduction of strategic nuclear weapons as well. We want a comprehensive ban on all nuclear testing, a prohibition against all chemical warfare, no attack capability against space satellites, and arms limitations in the Indian Ocean.

We hope that we can take joint steps with all nations toward a final agreement eliminating nuclear weapons completely from our arsenals of death. We will persist in this effort.

Now, I believe in détente with the Soviet Union. To me it means progress toward peace. But the effects of détente should not be limited to our own two countries alone. We hope to persuade the Soviet Union that one country cannot impose its system of society upon another, either through direct military intervention or through the use of a client state's military force, as was the case with Cuban intervention in Angola.

Cooperation also implies obligation. We hope that the Soviet Union will join with us and other nations in playing a larger role in aiding the developing world, for common aid efforts will help us build a bridge of mutual confidence in one another. . . .

Let me conclude by summarizing: Our policy is based on an historical vision of America's role. Our policy is derived from a larger view of global change. Our policy is rooted in our moral values, which never change. Our policy is reinforced by our material wealth and by our military power. Our policy is designed to serve mankind. And it is a policy that I hope will make you proud to be Americans.

Thank you.

## Carter's New Proposal to the Soviets

### *Documents 5 and 6*

In an effort to make a break with past approaches to arms control, the Carter administration made a new comprehensive proposal on SALT II to the Soviets in March 1977. It added major new numerical reductions and qualitative constraints to what had been agreed upon at Vladivostok during the Ford administration.

In document 5, Dennis Ross, a specialist on the Soviet Union and the Middle East who has worked in the Defense Department and on the National Security Council, describes how the Carter administration believed this was a fair package that would help prevent either side from developing a first-strike capability. Ross also points out that, to the Soviets, the proposal seemed like a one-sided measure designed to protect U.S. advantages. In document 6, a selection from a speech given after the Soviets rejected the March proposal, Foreign Minister Andrei Gromyko attacks the United States for trying to undo the progress already accomplished in the *SALT II talks.*

### 5 THE IDEAS OF MARCH
### Dennis Ross

The historical record reminds us that arms control negotiations neither induce countries to relax their perceived security requirements significantly nor make them any more likely or willing to surrender their military advantages. On the contrary, because technological, geographical and political asymmetries make it difficult to determine equal balances, arms control negotiations have traditionally been used by the parties to cement their military advantages and thus further ensure their security. While pursuit of these objectives within the context of arms control negotiations is understandable and probably also unavoidable, particularly given impulses to err on the safe side, it need not rule out arms control agreements. Rather, it rules out the belief that comprehensive solutions to arms race problems can be discovered. It rules in the understanding that incremental improvements or agreements that result from hard bargaining are probably the most that are achievable.

While this line of reasoning seems commonsensical, it apparently did not prevail initially in the Carter Administration. In March, 1977, the Administration offered a plan for "deep cuts" in the strategic forces of both sides, which was summarily rejected by the Soviets. The March, 1977 episode raises two important issues: Why was such a proposal made, and why was it so unacceptable to the Soviets? A review of the March plan indicates that the Soviet rejection reflected a belief that the proposal was unfair to them and evidently it was rejected for that reason and not because the Soviets have no interest in arms control. The interaction over the proposal also highlights crucial asymmetries between the two sides and, thus, serves to illustrate what kind of SALT agreements are possible.

#### Comprehensive Proposal

The comprehensive proposal made in March of 1977, if accepted, clearly would have imposed significant quantitative and qualitative controls on Soviet and U.S. strategic arsenals. Its most important provisions might be summarized as follows:

(1) Reduction of the Vladivostok ceilings on strategic delivery vehicles from 2,400 to between 1,800 and 2,000.

(2) Reduction of the ceiling on total MIRVable launchers from 1,320 to between 1,100 and 1,200; limiting the number of ICBMs that could be MIRVed to 550.

(3) Reduction of the number of heavy missiles to 150.

(4) Banning the deployment of cruise missiles of greater than 2,500 km range, while allowing unlimited deployment beneath this range.

(5) Banning modifications of existing ICBMs, and prohibiting any new ICBMs. To enforce this qualitative provision, ICBM test-firings were to be limited to six a year. In addition to making modification or future development difficult, the planned limits would have made reliability testing difficult. The net effect would have been to make both sides increasingly less confident in their missiles and therefore less inclined to strike first in a crisis.

Why did the Administration make this kind of proposal?

From what can be pieced together from the public record, the following picture emerges. The Carter Administration came onto the scene believing that SALT had amounted to very little. They apparently perceived that neither side had been interested in serious arms control and, instead, had used SALT as a forum for legalizing increased competition.

Believing that it was about time for SALT to amount to much more — indeed to be a forum for real arms control and reduction — the Carter White House understood that SALT would have to be premised on a drastic reduction in counterforce capabilities and systems with counterforce potential. Since the structure of Soviet forces concentrates nuclear firepower in ICBMs, the burden of reduction would fall on the U.S.S.R. The Soviets would have to cut the number of their heavy or modern large ballistic missiles (MLBMs) significantly and they would have to curtail the planned MIRVing of their ICBMs sharply.

For its part, the U.S. was prepared to forego the retrofitting of the MK-12A warhead on the Minuteman III and the deployment of the next generation ICBM, the MX. If the Soviets were not prepared to accept this approach to SALT then, so it was believed, they were going to have to be prepared to be relatively worse off in the resulting military competition.

The administration believed not only that a change in approach was necessary, but also that the time—particularly in light of the U.S. strategic position—was propitious for such a change. The Administration apparently believed that the U.S. technological lead and planned systems (cruise missiles, MX, Trident II) gave it a strategic cushion that allowed the U.S. to drive a hard bargain with the Russians that would force them to make the fundamental changes in their nuclear arsenal necessary for long-range stability.

## Domestic Concerns

While the U.S. proposal was shaped largely by strategic considerations, it was also designed to respond to domestic political realities and concerns. The criticism that the previous administration had suffered on SALT and the substantial senatorial opposition to the February 1977 nomination of Paul Warnke to be head of the Arms Control and Disarmament Agency, convinced the Carter White House that a broad consensus needed to be achieved on arms control. To achieve such a consensus, both the Jackson opposition and the professional arms control community had to be satisfied. The March proposal contained elements important to both. On the one hand, the Jackson constituency was pleased with the provisions that would have reduced Soviet heavy missile and throwweight advantages. On the other hand, the "arms controllers" were especially attracted to the provisions that would have imposed the first significant qualitative constraints on Soviet-American strategic arms development. In addition to believing that an arms control consensus had to be forged, the Administration also felt that domestic politics required that a clear-cut difference in the style of diplomacy from the previous administration (open vs. secretive) be established. In administration eyes, this was necessary not only to overcome the suspicion that Kissingerian diplomacy had allowed the Russians to get the better of the U.S., but also to redeem campaign pledges and help restore the faith of the American people in their government and its purposes.

## Public Style

The very public style in which the proposal was proffered—the President was discussing the proposal publicly almost at the same time as the Soviet leadership was seeing it—had a lot to do with the *style* of the Soviet rejection. The forceful, peremptory, and angry Soviet rejection was largely a response to the public way in which the proposal was made. In Soviet eyes, the style of presentation indicated that the proposal was probably designed more to make them look bad than for serious negotiation.

Nevertheless, the Soviets didn't reject the proposal because of the public manner in which it was made or even because of the impact that the human rights campaign had had on Soviet-American relations. The Soviets rejected the proposal because they quite genuinely found it unequal and threatening. On philosophical grounds, the Soviets will traditionally refuse a proposal requiring them to make the bulk of the concessions. In Soviet eyes, having to make the lion's share of the concessions, and presumably doing so, in the words of Soviet commentator George Arbatov, "under the threat of U.S. deployment of new arms systems," would reflect basic Soviet weakness, and would thus amount to admitting that the Soviet Union needed SALT more than the United States. Besides being an unacceptable and indeed impossible admission of weakness, conveying this impression would violate the objectives that have long driven Soviet SALT policy: codifying the U.S. recognition of the U.S.S.R. as an equal superpower with all the appropriate global rights and privileges; formalizing the U.S. acceptance of "parity," while officially rejecting the possibility or feasibility of trying to achieve superiority over the Soviet Union; and acknowledging that Soviet power precludes dealing with the Soviet Union from "positions of strength."

## Cuts Must Be Mutual

In pursuit of these broad objectives, with the more specific goal of constraining the U.S. so it can not again surge ahead strategically, the Soviets will make concessions only on a strictly mutual basis. Given this general orientation, the Soviets judge any SALT proposal not in terms of U.S. abstract principles such as whether the agreement serves strategic stability but rather in terms of what they have to give up in comparison to what the United States will have to surrender. While the Administration's proposal reflected its recognition that far-reaching arms control required strategic convergence, its proposal also represented a position that was not really negotiable.

One might argue that making this kind of proposal could just have been a good bargaining ploy. The fact that it was made public and also highly touted by the administration suggests that it wasn't. Because any final agreement would necessarily be far more limited, it would appear as if the U.S. had made all the concessions.

For an administration that had obviously considered domestic political factors in shaping the proposal, it would have been strange, indeed, for them consciously to create political problems for themselves when the time came to sell a far more limited agreement.

That it wasn't negotiable becomes even more clear when one looks at the specific provisions of the proposal that the Soviets found so objectionable and one-sided. The Soviets perceived the restriction on testing as a device to freeze them in a position of technological inferiority. Aside from rejecting this position in principle, the Soviets saw a more immediate threat in this provision. Where the United States had already been able to refine its MIRV technology, the limits on testing would apparently prevent the Soviets from doing likewise, a condition of perceived inequality that by Soviet definition was unacceptable and a condition that they had, in fact, already pledged to reject.

In addition to the restriction on testing, the Soviets saw the provisions on cruise missiles, MIRV ceilings, and heavy ICBMs as also designed to give the United States important qualitative as well as quantitative advantages. The Soviets had several basic objections to the cruise missile proposals. The Carter proposal, allowing unlimited deployment of cruise missiles up to 2,500 km range, not only retreated from what the previous administration had agreed to, but, in Soviet eyes, seemed to provide no constraint on the development of this new system. The cruise missile is a system that the United States had and the Soviets didn't and, therefore, a system that if not checked in some way would defeat a central Soviet purpose for being in SALT.

## Cruise Worried Soviets

The possibility that the cruise missile provision would provide the U.S. but not the U.S.S.R. with means to compensate for any arms reduction at the strategic level was even more objectionable to the Soviets. By allowing unlimited deployment of air, sea and ground launched cruise missiles with ranges up to 2,500 km, U.S. deployment of cruises in forward areas could enable the United States to maintain and perhaps increase its target coverage in the Soviet Union, while also building a large strategic reserve despite SALT-imposed reductions in strategic delivery vehicles. Indeed, the larger the strategic reductions, the more significant forward based systems and forward based cruise missiles would become and the more significant would be the disparities between the U.S. and Soviet capabilities to strike each other's homelands. That Soviet thinking ran along these lines is indicated by the following Soviet comment on the U.S. proposal: "... all these numerous nuclear means [forward based nuclear systems-cruise missiles, carrier based aircraft, etc.] would not be affected under the American plan and consequently their role and significance would grow to the detriment of the security of the U.S.S.R. in case of the proposed reduction of intercontinental ballistic missiles, submarine-launched missiles and heavy bombers."

The perceived implications of the cruise provision highlighted the geographical asymmetries that favored the United States, and that, from the Soviet perspective, required compensating advantages for the U.S.S.R. Without such tradeoffs, any proposal would, in Soviet words, "violate the principle of equality and equal security of the sides" and would be "prejudicial to Soviet security." Indeed, without such tradeoffs the Soviets believed that they would be doing all the giving, while the United States wouldn't be surrendering anything.

This particular Soviet concern seemed to be borne out not only by the cruise missile provision but also by the ICBM MIRV ceiling that was called for in the U.S. plan. The U.S. proposal called for a ceiling of 550 on the number of ICBMs that could be MIRVed, the exact number the U.S. had programmed and deployed, but a number considerably below what the Soviets had apparently planned for themselves.

## Missile Cuts Feared

Additionally, the U.S. call for a reduction of heavy missiles or MLBMs from 308 to 150 affected only the Soviets. The U.S. didn't have any missiles in this category. Beyond being self-serving, the Soviets saw a far more threatening U.S. motive behind this part of the proposal. In combination with the U.S. call for a ban on modifying existing ICBMs or introducing new ones, this provision convinced the Soviets that the U.S. proposal was designed to weaken Soviet strength by seeking a reduction precisely in the area where the Soviets believed they competed most effectively with the U.S. Not surprisingly, the Soviets reacted vigorously to this part of the proposal, saying that they would neither accept such reductions nor alter their programs just "because some quarters in the USA do not like some of our missiles," or because they believe Soviet missiles are " 'too heavy' or 'too effective.' "

In short, since the Soviets consider their large ICBMs to constitute the backbone of their strategic arsenal, they naturally tended to interpret this part of the Carter proposal as another attempt by the United States to get Moscow to play the strategic game according to Washington's rules. In Soviet eyes, these rules meant giving up what they do best and adopting a configuration of forces that served U.S. interests and exploited U.S. advantages. Soviet commentator G. A. Trofimenko observed, "American 'advantages' can become real advantages only under conditions of using American rules—hence the constant striving to impose these rules on the other side." Given this kind of Soviet view, it is not too surprising that the Soviets would strongly resist having U.S. rules stressing reduced number of heavy missiles, reduced throwweight levels, and acceptance of Mutual Assured Destruction serve as the basis for SALT.

### Different Rules

The differing American and Soviet "rules" grow not just out of differing purposes, but more fundamentally out of a basic conceptual asymmetry between the two sides. Their attitudes about how to achieve deterrence, and therefore security, have been and remain different. Throughout SALT, perhaps most directly embodied in the comprehensive proposal, the American conception of strategic deterrence has been essentially one of deterrence through punishment — based on assured destruction. The Soviet conception has been primarily one of deterrence through denial, based on damage limitation.

The Soviet approach to deterrence is premised on the belief that being able to limit or deny their adversary a military gain or a successful military outcome is a more certain way to achieve deterrence than is their ability to threaten to inflict punishment upon him. Put simply, the Soviet conception amounts to believing that the best way to ensure that their adversary will not attack them is to convince him that they have the will to and can prevail in any conflict. Under these circumstances, so their thinking goes, their enemy will be denied any incentive for initiating a war. The Soviet attitude toward deterrence is suggested by Major General V. Larionov's comment on his country's military doctrine and strategy:

> [They] are consistent in setting and resolving the *tasks of averting war,* containing the aggressor and preparing to repulse it in the event of war. The Soviet Armed Forces' readiness to rout an aggressor is a visible material factor, which is meant to *dispel any illusions* about an act of aggression going unpunished. Precisely in this sense the USSR Armed forces serve as the bulwark of peace and international security. (Emphasis added)

The Soviet approach to deterrence reflects the standard military way to think about the problem. The Soviets draw no distinction between deterrence and defense, and believe that the more credible the war-fighting capability, the more certain the deterrent. That the Soviet approach to deterrence takes this form should not be surprising. After all, military men, not civilian strategists, have been responsible for formulating Soviet ideas on the subject. Moreover, because Soviet ideology suggests that war or at least a kind of intractable struggle with the United States remains possible, the political leadership has little reason to question a strategic military approach that emphasizes war fighting and war survival capabilities. In addition to an ideology which gives them a more expectant view of war, Soviet historical experience also inclines the political leadership to favor a war fighting/survival strategic posture. The devastating traumas of the civil war, the purges, and World War II have probably convinced the current generation of political leaders that they must always hedge against or be prepared for the next possible disaster. Where a deterrence through punishment strategy would provide no hedge if deterrence failed, a deterrence through denial approach would provide what little insurance might be possible in the event of a nuclear disaster.

Finally, a denial, unlike a punishment approach, is without any obvious limit or endpoint. One always requires more to achieve war fighting/survival objectives in a nuclear context. Thus the doctrine serves the interest of important segments in the Soviet hierarchy, the military, the defense industries, and the ideological high priests of the system. All of these factors combine to make the Soviet approach to deterrence a deeply rooted one that can't be expected to change in the near future.

As a result, attempts by the U.S. to use far-reaching arms control proposals to change or frontally challenge the Soviet approach are probably doomed to failure. More gradualistic proposals that don't so directly challenge Soviet doctrine, strategic approaches or the institutional arrangements at the apex of the Soviet regime are far more likely to meet with success. In this sense, the most achievable in SALT are essentially limited agreements of the SALT I, Vladivostok and SALT II kind.

## 6 REMARKS TO THE PRESS
## Foreign Minister Andrei Gromyko
## Moscow
## March 31, 1977

Way back in Vladivostok an accord was reached that the Soviet Union and the United States will each have 2,400 strategic arms carriers, including 1,320 MIRVs. This is the main content of the Vladivostok accord.

You know that there were many reports — both official and semiofficial — saying that there was progress after Vladivostok. There were also more moderate reports. But, in general, it is true that quite a few steps forward have been made. There were opportunities to bring things to completion. This, however, did not happen. Then all of a sudden the question arose of the so-called cruise missiles. What does this mean? There is hardly need to dwell on the technical aspect of the matter. They tried to prove that the Vladivostok accord did not refer to the cruise missiles, that these missiles . . . are generally not subject to any limitations and that the Vladivostok accord concerns ballistic missiles only. We resolutely objected to this attempt. At Vladivostok the question was posed differently. No green light was given there to the cruise missiles. The question was posed thus: to achieve such an agreement that would shut off all channels of the strategic arms race and reduce the threat of nuclear war.

The United States of America and the Soviet Union exchanged relevant official documents which sealed the Vladivostok accords. Everything, it seemed, was clear, and it remained to carry the matter forward to the signing of an agreement. Working on some of the questions, including the juridical wording of the agreement, were the delegations of the U.S.S.R. and the U.S.A. at Geneva. At first, things were moving. But all of a sudden, a wall had risen and everything was frozen. Apparently somebody, some influential forces in the U.S., found all this not to their liking. And you know that great difficulties arose and these difficulties have not been removed. If one is to speak frankly, of late these difficulties have increased. What should we call this situation and this kind of position, which certain people in the United States began taking after Vladivostok? This is the line of revision, a line of revising the commitments taken in Vladivostok.

We are categorically opposed to this. We are all for the edifice that was built by such hard work in Vladivostok — an edifice on which such intellectual and other resources were spent — not only to be preserved, but that things should be brought to a conclusion and a new agreement on limiting strategic arms should be concluded between the U.S.S.R. and the U.S.A.

We were told, and it was said to us even in the last days when the talks were on in Moscow, that one of the obstacles is the Soviet Union's possession of a certain type of bomber (it is called Backfire in the United States), which, it was said, can be used as a strategic weapon, and that this plane absolutely must be taken into consideration in the agreement. We categorically rejected it and continue rejecting such attempts. Time and again, Leonid Brezhnev personally explained to President Ford, specifically during the meeting in Helsinki [during the European Security Conference, 30 July to 1 August 1975], and later to President Carter, that it concerns a medium range bomber and not a strategic bomber. Nevertheless, this question was tossed at us once again. Somebody evidently needs to artificially create this additional obstacle. It is better known to the Americans at what level these obstacles are being created. We note that this question is being artificially introduced to complicate the situation along the road of concluding an agreement. . . .

Throughout the talks here in Moscow, our side emphasized the main idea that the foundation for a new agreement that has been built up should not be destroyed, but that it should be preserved at all cost. And truly, what will happen if the arrival of a new leadership in some country will scrap all the constructive things that were achieved in relations with other countries? What stability in relations with other countries can be talked about in such a case? What stability can be talked about in relations between the U.S.A. and the U.S.S.R. in this case? We, our side, would like to see precisely stability in our relations, and that these relations should be as good as possible and based on the principles of peaceful coexistence and, even better, that they should be friendly. This is our stand and we would like to see similar actions in reply from the other side, that is, the United States of America.

A version is now being circulated in the U.S.A. alleging that the U.S. representatives at the Moscow talks proposed some broad program for disarmament, but that the Soviet leadership did not accept this program. I must say that this version does not accord with reality. This version is essentially false. Nobody proposed such a program to us.

I am dwelling on some facts from which you, certainly, will draw for yourselves some conclusions. For example, it is proposed to us now to reduce the total number of strategic arms carriers to 2,000 or even to 1,800 units, and MIRVs to 1,200–1,100. What is more, it is simultaneously proposed to liquidate half of those rockets in our possession which are simply disliked by somebody in the United States. They are described differently: sometimes "too heavy" or "excessively effective." They dislike these rockets and that is why the Soviet Union must be deprived of half of these weapons. So the question is whether such a unilateral way of putting the question is a way to agreement. No; it only damages the Vladivostok accord, breaks the balance of limitations concerning which agreement was reached in Vladivostok. What changed after Vladivostok? Nothing; absolutely nothing changed. Call this as you like, but this is no way of solving problems.

Next, in the talks with Cyrus Vance it was suggested that we revise the right of the two sides to modernize existing missiles as laid down in the present agreement, just as in the Vladivostok accord. This was taken for granted. No problems arose here. But no, it is now proposed to break up the agreement also in this respect, and to do so in a way that would give advantages to the United States, with the Soviet Union finding itself in a worse position. Clearly, we shall not depart from the principle of equality also in this respect. And to put forward such demands is a dubious if not a cheap move.

One more fact. It was proposed to us to include in the agreement a clause prohibiting the development of new types of weapons. At a first glance, it would seem that there is nothing wrong with this. But I would like to recall that the Soviet Union itself has long ago made the proposal on banning the manufacture of new types and new systems of weapons of mass extermination. Moreover, we have submitted to the United Nations a draft of the relevant international treaty. And what was the response? Maybe the U.S. government supported this treaty? No, it did not say a single word in support of this treaty.

Indeed, at the Moscow talks too, only the most general words were uttered to the effect that such a clause should be included into the agreement, in a "package" at that, or geared to other obviously unacceptable proposals. All this made a very dubious impression. If there is a serious intention in this matter then, as I have already said, there is a concrete proposal. . . .

It seems to us that in international affairs in general, including relations between the U.S.A. and the Soviet Union, it would be better to examine relevant problems on a more realistic, on an honest basis. The more attempts there are to play a game in this matter, to tread on the foot of the partner, the more difficulties there will be. This will not promote an improvement in Soviet-American relations, the cause of détente, consolidation of peace. This should be said especially in connection with recent statements appearing in the United States in newspapers and, unfortunately, not only in newspapers.

I should like to add a few more words. If the U.S.A. is prepared to ban new types of weapons, why then is the need to produce the B-1 strategic bomber, so beloved by some people in the U.S.A., defended all that much? The same is true of the manufacture of the Trident atomic submarine. Leonid Brezhnev spoke of these new American weapons systems both in his public speeches and in his remarks during the official negotiations with the American side, and did so repeatedly. So what we have is that certain declarations by the American side do not tally with the actual readiness to ban new types of weapons of mass extermination.

One would rather not speak on this theme, but one has to. In his last statement, the President of the United States used the word "sincerity" when referring to the Soviet leadership's attitude to questions of strategic arms limitation. I would like to say: We do not lack sincerity. We have plenty of it. It is on this basis that we are building all our policy and would want all to build their policies on the same basis, so that the deeds would not differ from the words.

U.S. representative Cyrus Vance described his proposals as the basis for a broad and all-encompassing agreement. But it is easy, after an objective study of these proposals, to draw the conclusion that they pursue the aim of getting unilateral advantages for the U.S.A. to the detriment of the Soviet Union, its security and the security of its friends and allies. The Soviet Union will never be able to agree to this. This was openly said by Leonid Brezhnev to the U.S. Secretary of State during the first talk. He said the same during the last talk which was held yesterday.

Reading some of the statements made in the U.S.A. you probably noticed that not only what some people call all-encompassing proposals, but also an alternative "narrow proposal" has been made to us. But what is the essence of this "narrow proposal?" Here it is: we are simply told, let us conclude an agreement that will concern ballistic missiles and strategic bombers. At the same time, it is proposed to leave aside the cruise missiles and the Soviet bomber referred to as Backfire which, as I have already mentioned, is not strategic at all. It looks as if a concession is being made to us, but this is an extremely strange concession. We are offered what does not belong to the United States. A nonstrategic aircraft was named a strategic one, and then they say: We are ready not to include this bomber in the agreement now, if the Soviet Union consents to give a green light for the manufacture and deployment of the U.S. cruise missiles. So according to this narrower agreement, the cruise missiles would be totally excluded from an agreement. Such a decision would mean that, while plugging one gap — the ballistic missiles — a new gap, maybe an even wider and deeper one, would be simultaneously opening — nuclear weapons carriers.

I stress nuclear weapons carriers. But it is our objective to prevent an outbreak of a nuclear war, to deliver mankind from nuclear war. Is it not the same for a human being to die of a weapon from a cruise missile, as from a weapon from a ballistic missile? The result is the same. Apart from it, the manufacture of cruise missiles will swallow up no less funds, dollars, pounds sterling, rubles, francs, lire, et cetera. Do people stand to gain from it? One cannot help asking what such an agreement will give for security. And is it going to be security in general? No, it will not be security, which peoples sincerely want. It will not even be a semblance of security. That is why we rejected, frankly speaking, this so-called narrow agreement too. We declared that it does not present a solution to the problem and does not even come close to solving this problem. This is what the U.S. Secretary of State took back when he left Moscow.

We do not know how all this will be presented to public opinion in the U.S.A. Judging by the first symptoms, the actual state of things is distorted. The results of the exchange of opinions and the statements that were made to the U.S. Secretary of State were also distorted. Leonid Brezhnev's statements were distorted too.

All this does not help towards a productive solution of problems, though we would sincerely wish so. But we are ready to continue talks on all these problems. The Soviet leaders have enough patience. We would like the discussions, regardless of where they are held — here in Moscow, in Washington or in other places — to finally come to a favorable conclusion.

Leonid Brezhnev strongly emphasized: We firmly stand for good relations with the United States just as with other countries in the world. We stand for relations based on the principles of peaceful coexistence, for friendly relations. And the possibilities for it are far from having been exhausted. They have not been exhausted because the point at issue is the United States and the Soviet Union.

We do not intend to belittle the substantial differences that now exist between the stands of the U.S.A. and the Soviet Union. The Secretary of State was told about it frankly. But does this mean that there are insurmountable obstacles? No, it does not. We would like to express the hope that the leadership of the United States will take up a more realistic stand, that it will give greater consideration to the interests of the security of the Soviet Union and its allies and will not strive for unilateral advantages. . . .

## A Difference of Opinion

### *Document 7*

This 1978 article in the *New York Times* describes a key characteristic of the Carter administration's foreign policy: the split between Secretary of State Cyrus Vance and National Security Adviser Zbigniew Brzezinski. The split made it very difficult for the United States to have a coherent national security policy.

### 7 TENSION GROWS BETWEEN BRZEZINSKI AND STATE DEPARTMENT
**Richard Burt**

*Washington — April 16*

On the long flight home from Africa on Air Force One earlier this month, Zbigniew Brzezinski, the President's national security adviser, finally got the opportunity to corner Hodding Carter 3d, the State Department spokesman, and ask him a question that had been troubling him for months:

Why couldn't Mr. Carter keep State Department officials from leaking stories critical of the White House adviser?

Mr. Carter's reply, officials on the Presidential plane report, was that 7,000 people worked at the State Department and that it was impossible to keep an eye on all of them.

"I don't think reporters are getting their stories from the janitors there," Mr. Brzezinski is said to have retorted.

#### A New Coolness

According to several officials who were interviewed last week, this exchange is typical of the new coolness that has crept into relations between the State Department and the White House's National Security Council during recent weeks.

In part, officials attribute the tension to "bureaucratic misunderstandings" and pressures created by recent criticism at home and abroad of the Administration's foreign policy performance. But some officials argue that at the core of the disagreement is the question of how best to insure smooth relations with Moscow and, particularly, how to achieve a new arms agreement that would win the approval of Congress.

A high-ranking State Department official described the basic disagreement this way: "Zbig believes that only by displaying backbone can the Administration achieve its goals with Moscow. But most people around here think that tough talk and a threatening posture could ruin the chances for working out a more stable relationship."

The disagreements within the Administration first became evident early in March, when Secretary of State Cyrus R. Vance and Mr. Brzezinski seemed to differ over the consequences for arms negotiations of the continued Soviet military involvement in Africa. Since then, there have been disputes over a Presidential address on defense policy and over the handling of the neutron weapon issue.

#### Differences Come to Surface

The differences became more visible in recent days as Mr. Vance prepared for his visit to Moscow this week for talks on a new strategic arms agreement. At the White House, officials indicated that they did not expect the mission to accomplish much and some questioned whether Mr. Vance and his advisers would take a firm enough line in discussions with the Kremlin. A high State Department official called the White House concerns "absurd."

Many officials contend that the disputes between the State Department and White House were inevitable, in spite of the special care that top aides have taken during the last year to avoid the bickering that characterized the making of foreign policy during the Nixon-Ford period. However, they stress that so far the feuding has not injured relations between Mr. Vance and Mr. Brzezinski.

In an interview, Mr. Brzezinski emphasized that he remained on good terms with Mr. Vance and denied that they were at odds over policy toward Moscow. "Both on the fundamentals of American-Soviet relations as well as the tactics, there is no disagreement between Cy and myself," he said.

However, he was angry about reports in the press quoting unnamed State Department officials as criticizing his judgment and he indicated that he was unhappy about recent actions of some of Mr. Vance's advisers.

#### "Second Echelon" Blamed

Some White House officials express this view more forcefully, arguing that "second echelon" officials at the State

Department have "undercut" policies worked out by Mr. Brzezinski and approved by President Carter.

White House officials appear particularly upset over State Department actions surrounding a speech on defense delivered by Mr. Carter at Wake Forest University on March 17. The speech, written by a Brzezinski aide, Samuel Huntington, was meant, officials said, to provide a clear signal to Moscow that its continued military buildup could jeopardize future Soviet-American economic and technical cooperation.

However, they said that the effect of the speech might have been diluted when Marshall D. Shulman, a State Department adviser on Soviet Affairs, received Mr. Vance's permission to telephone an official in the Soviet Embassy and urge that the complete text of the speech be transmitted to Moscow so that Soviet leaders could read the conciliatory positions.

"How do you think the Soviets interpreted the call?" said a White House official. "I'm sure they took it to mean that they didn't take the President's statements seriously."

### "A State Department Interpreter"

Another official said, "The Soviets don't need a State Department interpreter to read a speech by Mr. Carter."

Following this episode and press reports saying Mr. Carter's speech was essentially designed for domestic consumption, White House officials said that Soviet diplomats had to be called in and told that the firm language contained in the address was meant to be taken seriously.

For their part, State Department officials expressed annoyance that they had not been given advance copies of the speech. But White House officials insist that Mr. Vance was given an early draft of the speech as well as a final version before it was made.

Mr. Shulman figured in another dispute early last week, when State Department officials suggested that Moscow be informed of Mr. Carter's decision not to begin production of the neutron weapon. A draft letter to the Soviet leader, Leonid L. Brezhnev, was cabled to Air Force One to receive Presidential approval. But Mr. Brzezinski immediately quashed the idea. "Zbig was just furious that Shulman and others at State wanted to tell the Soviets about the neutron bomb decison before we told the allies in Europe," a White House aide said.

At the State Department, officials including Mr. Shulman deny any effort to undermine White House policy. One official, in an effort to explain the White House complaints, said "with things not going too smoothly with Moscow, or foreign policy generally, Brzezinski and his people are looking for scapegoats."

A close aide to Mr. Vance suggested that the tension could be the product of an honest misunderstanding. He suggested that Mr. Brzezinski's unhappiness with second-level State Department officials resulted from "a lack of clear policy direction from the top down."

"We don't have a consistent policy toward Moscow," he said, "and when this is the case people get into trouble. It's not that the State Department is trying to undercut policy, we are only trying to carry out what we think the policy is."

## Doctrines at Odds

### *Document 8*

These excerpts from a 1977 article by Soviet specialist Richard Pipes present an argument that became more and more influential during the 1970s, especially as the Soviet buildup continued: that the Soviets had a fundamentally different approach to nuclear war that made them willing to take dangerous risks. Such arguments were used to criticize the Carter arms control policy and the SALT II Treaty.

## 8 WHY THE SOVIET UNION THINKS IT COULD FIGHT AND WIN A NUCLEAR WAR
### Richard Pipes

American and Soviet nuclear doctrines, it needs stating at the outset, are starkly at odds. The prevalent U.S. doctrine holds that an all-out war between countries in possession of sizable nuclear arsenals would be so destructive as to leave no winner; thus resort to arms has ceased to represent a rational policy option for the leaders of such countries vis-à-vis one another. The classic dictum of Clausewitz, that war is politics pursued by other means, is widely believed in the United States to have lost its validity after Hiroshima and Nagasaki. Soviet doctrine, by contrast, emphatically asserts that while an all-out nuclear war would indeed prove extremely destructive to both parties, its outcome would not be mutual suicide: the country better prepared for it and in possession of a superior strategy could win and emerge a viable society. "There is profound erroneousness and harm in the disorienting claims of bourgeois ideologies that there will be no victor in a thermonuclear world war," thunders an authoritative Soviet publication.[29] The theme is mandatory in the current Soviet military literature. Clausewitz, buried in the United States, seems to be alive and prospering in the Soviet Union.

The predisposition of the American strategic community is to shrug off this fundamental doctrinal discrepancy. American doctrine has been and continues to be formulated and implemented by and large without reference to its Soviet counterpart. It is assumed here that there exists one and only one "rational" strategy appropriate to the age of thermonuclear weapons, and that this strategy rests on the principle of "mutual deterrence" developed in the United States some two decades ago. Evidence that the Russians do not share this doctrine which, as its name indicates, postulates reciprocal attitudes, is usually dismissed with the explanation that they are clearly lagging behind us: given time and patient "education," they will surely come around.

It is my contention that this attitude rests on a combination of arrogance and ignorance; that it is dangerous; and that it is high time to start paying heed to Soviet strategic doctrine, lest we end up deterring no one but ourselves. There is ample evidence that the Soviet military say what they mean, and usually mean what they say. When the recently deceased Soviet Minister of Defense, Marshal Grechko, assures us: "We have never concealed, and do not conceal, the fundamental, principal tenets of our military doctrine,"[30] he deserves a hearing. This is especially true in view of the fact that Soviet military deployments over the past twenty years make far better sense in the light of Soviet doctrine, "primitive" and "unrealistic" as the latter may appear, than when reflected in the mirror of our own doctrinal assumptions. . . .

The strategic doctrine adopted by the USSR over the past two decades calls for a policy diametrically opposite to that adopted in the United States by the predominant community of civilian strategists: not deterrence but victory, not sufficiency in weapons but superiority, not retaliation but offenseve action. The doctrine has five related elements; (1) preemption (first strike), (2) quantitative superiority in arms, (3) counterforce targeting, (4) combined-arms operations, and (5) defense. We shall take up each of these elements in turn.

## Preemption

The costliest lesson which the Soviet military learned in World War II was the importance of surprise. Because Stalin thought he had an understanding with Hitler, and because he was afraid to provoke his Nazi ally, he forbade the Red Army to mobilize for the German attack of which he had had ample warning. As a result of this strategy of "passive defense," Soviet forces suffered frightful losses and were nearly defeated. This experience etched itself very deeply on the minds of the Soviet commanders: in their theoretical writings no point is emhasized more consistently than the need never again to allow themselves to be caught in a surprise attack. Nuclear weapons make this requirement especially urgent because, according to Soviet theorists, the decision in a nuclear conflict in all probability will be arrived at in the initial hours. In a nuclear war the Soviet Union, therefore, would not again have at its disposal the time which it enjoyed in 1941–42 to mobilize reserves for a victorious counteroffensive after absorbing devastating setbacks.

Given the rapidity of modern warfare (an ICBM can traverse the distance between the USSR and the United States in thirty minutes), not to be surprised by the enemy means, in effect, to inflict surprise on him. Once the latter's ICBM's have left their silos, once his bombers have taken to the air and his submarines to sea, a counterattack is greatly reduced in effectiveness. These considerations call for a preemptive strike. Soviet theorists draw an insistent, though to an outside observer very fuzzy, distinction between "preventive" and "preemptive" attacks. They claim that the Soviet Union will never start a war — i.e., it will never launch a preventive attack — but once it had concluded that an attack upon it was imminent, it would not hesitate to preempt. They argue that historical experience indicates outbreaks of hostilities are generally preceded by prolonged diplomatic crises and military preparations which signal to an alert command an imminent threat and the need to act. . . .

## Quantitative Superiority

There is no indication that the Soviet military share the view prevalent in the U.S. that in the nuclear age numbers of weapons do not matter once a certain quantity had been attained. They do like to pile up all sorts of weapons, new on top of old, throwing away nothing that might come in handy. This propensity to accumulate hardware is usually dismissed by Western observers with contemptuous references to a Russian habit dating back to Czarist days. It is not, however, as mindless as it may appear. For although Soviet strategists believe that the ultimate outcome in a nuclear war will be decided in the initial hours of conflict, they also believe that a nuclear war will be of long duration: to consummate victory — that is, to destroy the enemy — may take months or even longer. Under these conditions, the possession of a large arsenal of nuclear delivery systems, as well as of other types of weapons, may well prove to be of critical importance. . . .

## Counterforce

Two terms commonly used in the jargon of modern strategy are "counterforce' and "countervalue." Both terms refer to the nature of the target of a strategic nuclear weapon. Counterforce means that the principal objective of one's nuclear missiles are the enemy's forces — i.e., his launchers as well as the related command and communication facilities. Countervalue means that one's principal targets are objects of national "value," namely the enemy's population and industrial centers. . . .

Soviet nuclear strategy is counter*force* oriented. It targets for destruction — at any rate, in the initial strike — not the enemy's cities but his military forces and their command and communication facilities. Its primary aim is to destroy not civilians but soldiers and their leaders, and to undermine not so much the will to resist as the capability to do so. In the words of Grechko:

> The Strategic Rocket Forces, which constitute the basis of the military might of our armed forces, are designed to annihilate the means of the enemy's nuclear attack, large groupings of his armies, and his military bases; to destroy his military industries; [and] to disorganize the political and military administration of the aggressor as well as his rear and transport.[31]

Any evidence that the United States may contemplate switching to a counterforce strategy, such as occasionally crops up, throws Soviet generals into a tizzy of excitement. It clearly frightens them far more than the threat to Soviet cities posed by the countervalue strategic doctrine.

## Combined-Arms Operations

Soviet theorists regard strategic nuclear forces (organized since 1960 into a separate arm, the Strategic Rocket Forces) to be the decisive branch of the armed services, in the sense that the ultimate outcome of modern war would be settled by nuclear exchanges. But since nuclear war, in their view, must lead not only to the enemy's defeat but also to his destruction (i.e., his incapacity to offer further resistance) they consider it necessary to make preparations for the follow-up phase, which may entail a prolonged war of attrition. At this stage of the conflict, armies will be needed to occupy the enemy's territory, and navies to interdict his lanes of communications. "In the course of operations [battles], armies will basically complete the final destruction of the enemy brought about by strikes of nuclear rocket weapons."[32] Soviet theoretical writings unequivocally reject reliance on any one strategy (such as the *Blitzkrieg*) or on any one weapon, to win wars. They believe that a nuclear war will require the employment of all arms to attain final victory.

The large troop concentrations of Warsaw Pact forces in Eastern Europe — well in excess of reasonable defense requirements — make sense if viewed in the light of Soviet combined-arms doctrine. They are there not only to have the capacity to launch a surprise land attack against NATO, but also to attack and seize Western Europe with a minimum of damage to its cities and industries *after* the initial strategic nuclear exchanges have taken place, partly to keep Europe hostage, partly to exploit European productivity as a replacement for that of which the Soviet Union would have been deprived by an American second strike. . . .

## Defense

As noted, the U.S. theory of mutual deterrence postulates that no effective defense can be devised against an all-out nuclear attack: it is this postulate that makes such a war appear totally irrational. In order to make this premise valid, American civilian strategists have argued against a civil-defense program, against the ABM, and against air defenses.

Nothing illustrates better the fundamental differences between the two strategic doctrines than their attitudes to defense against a nuclear attack. The Russians agreed to certain imprecisely defined limitations on ABM after they had initiated a program in this direction, apparently because they were unable to solve the technical problems involved and feared the United States would forge ahead in this field. However, they then proceeded to build a tight ring of anti-aircraft defenses around the country while also developing a serious program of civil defense.

Before dismissing Soviet civil-defense efforts as wishful thinking, as is customary in Western circles, two facts must be emphasized.

One is that the Soviet Union does not regard civil defense to be exclusively for the protection of ordinary civilians. Its chief function seems to be to protect what in Russia are known as the "cadres," that is, the political and military leaders as well as industrial managers and skilled workers — those who could reestablish the political and economic system once the war was over. . . .

In World War II, the Soviet Union lost 20 million inhabitants out of a population of 170 million — i.e., 12 per cent; yet the country not only survived but emerged stronger politically and militarily than it had ever been. Allowing for the population growth which has occurred since then, this experience suggests that as of today the USSR could absorb the loss of 30 million of its people and be no worse off, in terms of human casualties, than it had been at the conclusion of World War II. In other words, all of the USSR's multimillion cities could be destroyed without trace or survivors, and, provided that its essential cadres had been saved, it would emerge less hurt in terms of casualties than it was in 1945.

Such figures are beyond the comprehension of most Americans. But clearly a country that since 1914 has lost, as a result of two world wars, a civil war, famine, and various "purges," perhaps up to 60 million citizens, must define "unacceptable damage" differently from the United States which has known no famines or purges, and whose deaths from all the wars waged since 1775 are estimated at 650,000 — fewer casualties than Russia suffered in the 900-day siege of Leningrad in World War II alone. Such a country tends also to assess the rewards of defense in much more realistic terms.

How significant are these recondite doctrinal differences? It has been my invariable experience when lecturing on these matters that during the question period someone in the audience will get up and ask: "But is it not true that we and the Russians already possess enough nuclear weapons to destroy each other ten times over" (or fifty, or a hundred — the figures vary)? My temptation is to reply: "Certainly. But we also have enough bullets to shoot every man, woman, and child, and enough matches to set the whole world on fire. The point lies not in our ability to wreak total destruction: it lies in intent." And insofar as military doctrine is indicative of intent, what the Russians think to do with their nuclear arsenal is a matter of utmost importance that calls for close scrutiny.

Enough has already been said to indicate the disparities between American and Soviet strategic doctrines of the nuclear age. These differences may be most pithily summarized by stating that whereas we view nuclear weapons as a deterrent, the Russians see them as a "compellant" — with all the consequences that follow. Now it must be granted that the actual, operative differences between the two doctrines may not be quite as sharp as they appear in the public literature: it is true that our deterrence doctrine leaves room for some limited offensive action, just as the Russians include elements of deterrence in their "war-fighting" and "war-winning" doctrine. Admittedly, too, a country's military doctrine never fully reveals how it would behave under actual combat conditions. And yet the differences here are sharp and fundamental enough, and the relationship of Soviet doctrine to Soviet deployments sufficiently close, to suggest that ignoring or not taking seriously Soviet military doctrine may have very detrimental effects on U.S. security. There is something innately destabilizing in the very fact that we consider nuclear war unfeasible and suicidal for both, and our chief adversary views it as feasible and winnable for himself.

SALT misses the point at issue so long as it addresses itself mainly to the question of numbers of strategic weapons: equally important are qualitative improvements within the existing quotas, and the size of regular land and sea forces. Above all, however, looms the question of intent: as long as the Soviet persist in adhering to the Clausewitzian maxim on the function of war, mutual deterrence does not really exist. And unilateral deterrence is feasible only if we understand the Soviet war-winning strategy and make it impossible for them to succeed.

## Notes

29. N.V. Karabanov in N.V. Karabanov, et al., *Filosofskoe nasledie V. I. Lenina i problemy sovremennoi voiny* ("The Philosophical Heritage of V. I. Lenin and the Problems of Contemporary War") (Moscow, 1972), pp. 18–19, cited in Leon Gouré, Foy D. Kohler, and Mose L. Harvey, eds., *The Role of Nuclear Forces in Current Soviet Strategy* (1974), p. 60.
30. A. A. Grechko, *Vooruzhonnye sily sovetskogo gosudarstva* ("The Armed Forces of the Soviet State") (Moscow, 1975), p. 345.
31. A. A. Grechko, *Na strazhe mira i stroitel'stva Kommunizma,* ("Guarding Peace and the Construction of Communism") (Moscow, 1971), p. 41.
32. *Metodologicheskie problemy,* p. 288.

# GEOPOLITICS AND ARMS CONTROL: THE QUESTION OF LINKAGE

## The U.S. and Soviet Views of Third World Intervention

### *Document 9*

The Carter administration's efforts to negotiate arms control agreements with the Soviet Union were made difficult by the problem of linkage. That is, U.S.-Soviet disagreements or conflicts not directly related to arms control were nevertheless linked to arms control because they soured superpower relations. Poor U.S.-Soviet relations made it difficult for the American public to support arms control treaties with the Soviet Union. In the 1970s, many U.S.-Soviet disagreements were over intervention in the Third World. In this excerpt from his *Détente and Confrontation,* Soviet specialist Raymond Garthoff explores the different views of the superpowers on the Third World. Each tended to believe that the other's interventions were unwarranted and aggressive.

## 9 COMPETITION IN THE THIRD WORLD
## Raymond Garthoff

The Soviet leaders' perceptions of the events of this period were quite different from those of the U.S. leaders. These differences in perspective and perceptions of the two sides are important to a better understanding of the reasons for the deterioration of relations in the 1970s, and to a more sound understanding in the future. Such an understanding does not necessarily eliminate differences or obviate conflicts. But recognizing the elements of validity of the contradictory perceptions of the two sides, which neither has really done, may lead to a modification of views and to a clarification of how the two adversaries can better deal with their competition.

Many in the United States saw Angola, and even the October War of 1973, as being Soviet attempts to gain influence. While the United States had faced down the challenge in 1973, it did not succeed in doing so in Angola in 1975–76. And from 1977 on it seemed that the Soviet Union and its Cuban and Vietnamese "proxies" were ever more on the march, particularly in Ethiopia in 1977–78 and Indochina in 1978, in the Shaba incursions in 1977 and 1978, in the coups in South Yemen and Afghanistan in 1978, in the occupation of Kampuchea in 1978–79, and finally in the occupation of Afghanistan in December 1979.

Initiative has usually been ascribed to the Soviets, sometimes in terms of seizing opportunities, but sometimes as involving a more deliberate plan for geopolitical envelopment of the oil of the Persian Gulf, or as twin pincers in Southwest and Southeast Asia. While local events have sometimes been recognized as contributing to those opportunities, there was growing concern and unease in the late 1970s that the Soviet advance was being facilitated by increasing signs of weakness in American military power, resolve, or both.

In the Soviet view the United States had been aggressively pursuing policies under détente to reduce Soviet influence and to gain advantage for itself throughout the third world. It had, from the very outset of détente in 1972, worked to exclude the Soviet Union from the Middle East — a key area adjoining the Soviet Union itself. The Soviets noted with suspicion and foreboding the decision in Presidential Directive (PD)–18 as early as August 1977 to establish a greater rapid deployment capability for distant military intervention, even though the United States did not move actively on that stated policy until 1979. They noted that the United States had, especially after 1978, developed collaborative relations with China on an anti-Soviet basis. Even in the third world, particularly in the volatile arc of crisis, Moscow saw the United States or its allies and associates as having almost invariably taken the first steps in external intervention or involvement.

Thus Moscow's perception is that the United States (and the West generally) has been taking the initiative and aggressively seeking ways to stem the tide of indigenous progressive change and national liberation. (China, too, has been seen as taking a parallel road in some cases in pursuit of its own hegemonistic aims.) This point is important, as Moscow views normalcy, or the status quo, not as a static condition but as a flow of progressive historical change. While peaceful coexistence between established states characterizes détente, détente does not preclude revolutionary change within states; in fact, détente should abet it. . . .

Earlier conflicts in Asia, from the Korean War to the Vietnam War, had involved extensive American intervention and use of proxy forces. In Korea the United States had the mantle of the United Nations and contingents of armed forces from a dozen countries. In Vietnam it brought in a larger number of South Korean military forces than the Cubans had introduced in Angola or Ethiopia, as well as Australian, New Zealand, and Philippine contingents. While the United States and these countries did not view these forces as proxies, from the Soviet viewpoint they certainly were.

American allies, protégés, or protectorates continued to resort to military interventions. Israel is the notable case, with its repeated operations in Lebanon in the late 1970s and early 1980s (and other actions from Entebbe in 1976 to the bombing of the Iraqi reactor in 1981). There were also the examples in western and southern Africa cited earlier. Again, while the United States and the countries involved did not regard these as proxy actions, from the Soviet standpoint they were activities by local paladins serving the interests of the imperialists.

Finally, the Soviets interpreted the overall pattern of these actions to mean that the United States did not *in practice* see détente in the 1970s as marking any radical departure from the tradition of direct, proxy, and allied intervention of the 1950s and 1960s. What was new was the possibility that the Soviet Union could play a somewhat more active (if still carefully selective) role in countering, or emulating, such activities in the third world.[33] There were ample precedents and parallels for its doing so. Even the introduction of Cuban proxies into Africa in Angola (apart from its being, in important part, an initiative of Castro's initially) followed an American precedent — it was the United States that had brought its own Cuban proxies — anti-Castro Cuban mercenaries — into the Congo (Zaire) in 1964 to help Mobutu establish control.[34]

This quick review of the record as seen from the perspective of the Soviet leaders makes clear, on the basis of just the decade of the 1970s, the decade of détente, that while the Soviet leaders pursued their own interests vigorously, in doing so they were less influenced by Kissinger's (and later Brzezinski's) lectures on a code of conduct and reciprocal restraint than by U.S. actions as they perceived them.* To paraphrase another member of the Nixon administration, Attorney General John N. Mitchell, the Soviet leaders looked at what the United States did, not what it said.

This brief review also makes clear the great difference in Soviet and American perspectives. Each, of course, has a basis in reality, but perceived by each side through distorting filters of selectivity, emphasis, and preconception. While American attention focused on Cuban troops in Angola and Ethiopia, and Soviet use of naval facilities in Ethiopia and South Yemen, Soviet attention focused on French troops in Djibouti, the Central African Republic, Chad, Senegal, Gabon, and the Ivory Coast, and on American use of military facilities in Morocco, Kenya, Somalia, Oman, Bahrein, and Egypt. Both sets of facts are real, but neither is *the* facts.

As noted earlier, the American reaction to events in Southwest Asia such as the Iranian revolution has been to fear Soviet intervention, while the Soviet reaction has been to fear American intervention in this area adjoining the Soviet Union. Thus as the regime of the shah was falling, the Soviets warned that American military intervention in Iran would be a matter affecting its security interests.[35] Similarly, the Soviets were highly suspicious of the longer-term purposes of the American buildup of a major fleet in the Indian Ocean in 1979–80.

The Soviets see active and purposeful actions by the imperialists, especially the United States, and their minions, protectorates, and proxies, to maintain and where possible expand their sway in the third world. They see a Western propensity to use force, including military force, to prevent a natural, progressive, political and economic revolutionary advance of society. This picture contrasts with what they had expected to see in the 1970s — a lessening of American and in general Western resort to force. The reason was basically the overall change in the correlation of forces in the world, and also a more sober and realistic recognition of the changing structure of global power by American and Western leaders. The growth of Soviet military power and the approach to military parity with the United States were seen as elements affecting the global balance and the calculations of Western leaders, although not as the central factor. The changing economic structure (especially within the Western world and between the Western and third worlds) was seen as another important factor — one of particular importance in Marxist analysis. So, too, the American experience in Vietnam and more generally in the 1960s, as reflected in American changes in policy such as the Nixon Doctrine, led to expectations of a lessened — but by no means abandoned — dependence on military means to deal with political and economic challenges.

The American tendency has been to see new challenges as arising from situations either instigated or at least exploited by a Soviet Union feeling its oats as a new global power. The fear has been that Soviet military parity with the United States would lead the Soviets to be bolder in expanding their power and influence, although by means other than military. Détente, the United States believed, could give the Soviet leaders a stake in not upsetting the status quo and thus restrain its impulses to exploit expansionist opportunities. But then the course of events from Angola through Afghanistan was seen as a successful Soviet pursuit of expansion overriding any restraint from détente.

The United States on the whole has tended even more than the Soviet Union to underrecognize the independent roles and initiatives of third world countries and third parties (although in some cases the Soviet leaders also have erred grossly). Paradoxically, the United States, with an ideology championing pluralism and pragmatism in the conduct of foreign relations, has tended in recent decades to view the world in excessively oversimplified terms — all other political realities are subordinated to a conflict between a "Free World" and a "Communist World," headed respectively by the United States and the Soviet Union. While this view had become attenuated by the 1970s and was partially submerged under détente, its rebirth by the early 1980s showed it deep roots. The lack of a comprehensive American worldview meant that superpower rivalry loomed as the overarching political reality, and it was then given an ideological rationale.

The Soviet leaders, on the other hand, while originally proceeding from a stereotyped ideological view that defined world politics in terms of two antagonistic classes, had learned from more than sixty-five years of experience that reality is far more complex. Without abandoning their central ideological worldview, they see a great variety of political entities, including friendly capitalist states and hostile communist ones, from the standpoint of Soviet interests.

Thus the Soviet leaders are only too ready to see interimperialist rivalries, especially in terms of competition for economic resources, that lead to diverging and conflicting policies within the West. The Soviets have learned as well that the third world has given birth to a variety of socialisms and political systems. The Soviet

* This account has been limited to developments grounded in actual historical fact and presumably available to the Soviet leaders, even though perceived through the bias of preconceptions. Soviet propaganda includes many other examples of alleged American and other Western intervention, either distorted or imagined, some of which the Soviet leaders may also believe.

For another analysis making this point, see Robert Legvold, "The Super Rivals: Conflict in the Third World," *Foreign Affairs,* vol. 57 (Spring 1979), pp. 755–78.

For a conveniently available, articulate Soviet view of this general issue, prepared for an American readership, see Henry Trofimenko, "America, Russia and the Third World," *Foreign Affairs,* vol. 59 (Summer 1981), pp. 1021–40.

Union was, for example, keenly aware of and concerned over Chinese actions in Africa and in the arc of crisis, while the United States was scarcely aware of Chinese activities in Angola, Mozambique, the Horn, South Yemen, and other places, and failed to recognize Soviet-Chinese rivalry as a factor in a number of these situations, in some cases a factor affecting Soviet decisions. . . .

Geopolitical considerations certainly figure in Soviet and American decisionmaking on third world interventions, but it has been the dynamics of local situations rather than geopolitical ambitions that have been responsible for the agenda of crises. The Carter administration, and in particular Brzezinski, saw a pattern of Soviet initiative in Africa, then in surrounding Saudi Arabia,[36] and finally in a massive pincers in Southwest and Southeast Asia. In fact these actions were not part of a grand design but were several separate mosaics — the Vietnamese-Kampuchean-Chinese-Soviet parallelogram bore no intrinsic relationship to the separate courses of events in the Horn of Africa, the Yemens, the Middle East, and Afghanistan. Similarly, while the Soviets saw American interest from 1977 on in building a rapid deployment force for the Middle Eastern–Indian Ocean area, they failed to appreciate the extent to which their own actions (and some other developments, notably the collapse of the rule of the shah of Iran and the subsequent hostage crisis) contributed to the American decisions to build a permanent military presence in the area.

The purpose of this review of the different perspectives on superpower interventions in the third world is not to weigh and judge them, but to point out their pervasiveness, salience, and consequences. The review in some detail of the crises and conflicts in the Middle East in 1973 (chapter 11), Angola (chapter 15), and Zaire, the Horn of Africa, and the Yemens shows the misperceptions and, even more, distorted imbalance in the views of the events and of their significance by leaders in both Washington and Moscow. These divergent perceptions reflect in part conflicting ambitions and reciprocal fears, as well as different expectations based on differing worldviews and conceptions of détente.

In reviewing the differing perspectives on third world conflicts, and especially on superpower involvement in them, the emphasis has been on American views of *Soviet* intervention, and Soviet views of *American* and other Western intervention. These views are an important part of reality, one not given due weight on either side. The real situation is not, however, limited to reactive (or defensive) moves by the two sides, even allowing for self-convincing arguments that justify offensive thrusts as defensive or reactive actions.

The United States has sometimes seen itself as required, even destined, by its predominant power to restore the peace and defend the status quo. (Usually it describes this role as assuming a burden, although elsewhere in the world it is often seen to be a self-appointed role nominally as the world's policeman while really serving U.S. interests.) In practice the United States has, for whatever blend of motivations, and for what its leadership and people have almost always perceived as acting for defensive purposes, frequently turned to the threat or use of force.[37] And even apart from occasional resort to force, the United States has played a far more active, not merely reactive, role in world politics than most Americans realize.

On the other hand, the Soviet leaders, with the bias of their ideological beliefs and from the vantage point of their perspective, have overstated the extent of active and offensive U.S. initiative. They also see their experience with the United States as validating their ideologically conditioned expectations that the leaders of the imperialist powers will use any opportunity to exert leverage and pressure on them and others when circumstances allow. The Soviets are not merely projecting their own intentions, although they too seek to take advantage of opportunities to pursue their own interests. While the Soviets may, as noted, overestimate American offensive initiative, friends of America in the world also see it as playing a much more activist role than most Americans do, including most American leaders (with Nixon, Kissinger, and Brzezinski as notable exceptions to a significant degree). . . .

Direct use by the superpowers of their own military forces to support other countries has been much more limited. The United States made massive commitments of American troops in the Korean War and the Vietnam War and provided military forces in a number of other cases, such as in Lebanon in 1958 and again (under different circumstances) in 1983. The Soviet Union has done so in providing air defense to Egypt (1970–72) and Syria (1982–present) and supporting Cuban forces in defending Ethiopia from Somali attack (1977–78). All of these were, it will be noted, protective situations.

All the cases of direct coercive use of Soviet military power have occurred in its directly adjacent national security zone — Hungary (1956), Czechoslovakia (1968), and Afghanistan (December 1979–present). Each case was unquestionably perceived by the Soviet leaders as strategically defensive and protective against counterrevolutionary challenges, although objectively and analytically the actions were coercive. While the defensive nature of the Soviet action may not be accepted, the significance of the subjective perception of a defensive purpose should not be neglected in evaluating the Soviet propensity to use force and in predicting whether, where, and when the Soviet Union might do so again.

On the whole the United States has used its own military forces coercively more frequently: carrying the Korean War north of the thirty-eighth parallel (1950), occupying the Dominican Republic (1965), bombing

North Vietnam (1964 and 1965–72), bombing and then invading Cambodia (1970), bombing Kampuchea in the *Mayaguez* incident (1975), setting up and shooting down Libyan fighters over the Gulf of Sidra (1981), and invading Grenada (1983). All these instances had declared defensive purposes and were perceived in Washington as defensive, but whatever the justification they, too, were coercive uses of military force.

Both powers also use their military power coercively through threats of use more frequently than actual use. For example, Soviet troop concentrations near Poland in 1980 and 1981 served to influence Polish behavior. Similarly, American military concentrations near Nicaragua from 1981 to the present (1985) have been intended to influence Nicaraguan behavior.

Both American and Soviet leaders have exaggerated the propensity of the other to resort to military force. The record actually shows discrimination and caution, particularly by the Soviet Union. For example, the Soviet-supported Cubans in Angola since 1976 have been held back to protect the regime in Luanda rather than sent out to repulse South African forays and even most assaults by UNITA guerrillas. The Soviets kept the Ethiopians from invading Somalia after defeating the Somali army and forcing its withdrawal from Ethiopia in 1978. Nor did the Soviets use their forces in Syria to prevent the Israeli defeats of Syrian forces in Lebanon. They have exercised restraint in not attacking the Afghan insurgents in their sanctuaries in Pakistan and Iran (beyond a few signals to remind of that capability). The question is not one of who was right or wrong in any given instance, or whether particular actions by either side were justified, or whether they were wise (a separate question). There is a record of use of force by both powers that helps illuminate the circumstances under which, and the ways in which, each uses or chooses not to use military force.

## Notes

33. This brief recital of Western intervention also serves as a reminder of the very large number of crises and political upheavals in which the Soviet Union has refrained from intervening. In these cases it deemed such a move to be inappropriate because of insufficient local opportunity, excessive requirements for commitment of Soviet resources or prestige, high risks or costs, or for other reasons.
34. Victor Marchetti and John Marks, *The CIA and the Cult of Intelligence* (Knopf, 1974), pp. 31, 117; this information was confirmed by official sources.
35. Brezhnev himself delivered a clear warning in November 1978, stating, "Any interference, especially military intervention, in the internal affairs of Iran — a state bordering on the Soviet Union — would be regarded by the USSR as a matter affecting the interests of its security." See "L. I. Brezhnev's Reply to the Question of a Pravda Correspondent," *Pravda,* November 19, 1978.
36. *Ibid.,* pp. 181, 196. Time and again in his memoir Brzezinski stresses his concern in early 1978 over what he describes as "Moscow's misuse of detente to improve the Soviet geopolitical and strategic position around Saudi Arabia," especially through its Cuban proxy in Ethiopia and South Yemen. *Ibid.,* p. 203.
37. For a useful overall survey, see Barry M. Blechman and Stephen S. Kaplan, eds., *Force without War: U.S. Armed Forces as a Political Instrument* (Brookings Institution, 1978).

## Soviet Views on U.S. Policy

### *Document 10*

This article from the official organ of the Soviet Union's Communist party gives the official Soviet version of why détente was in trouble. Not surprisingly, *Pravda* blames aggressive U.S. actions.

### 10 PRAVDA EXAMINES AMERICAN POLICY June 17, 1978

Recent facts indicate that changes dangerous to the cause of peace are taking place in the policy of the USA. An acute struggle has been going on for quite some time now in the ruling circles of that country over questions of détente and relations with the Soviet Union and other socialist countries. And as times goes on, there are more and more signs that the representatives of groupings that would like to undermine détente and return the world to the cold war, to new confrontations and unrestrained military rivalry, are beginning to take the upper hand. This is testified to not only by speeches coming from the President and a number of other high-ranking U.S. officials, but also by Washington's concrete deeds.

Contrary to the aspirations of the peoples to put an end to the arms race, the U.S. is taking the course of whipping it up, is adopting new vast plans for building up its military power, even for decades ahead. At the same time, negotiations with the Soviet Union on strategic arms limitation are being deliberately slowed down.

The U.S. Government is also undertaking actions the purpose of which are difficult to evaluate in any other way than as the deliberate worsening of bilateral relations with the U.S.S.R. There is no end to attempts at interfering in our country's internal affairs. The ties and contacts between the two countries are being restricted by U.S. unilateral actions.

The opponents of good USA-U.S.S.R. relations are seeking a common language with the aggressive anti-Sovietism of the Chinese rulers who loudly proclaim détente and peace to be a fraud, and war the only real prospect.

The USA, lastly, has become the main inspirer of a new colonialism in Africa — of a policy of armed interventions and open interference in the affairs of African states, of suppressing the national liberation movements. . . .

Implementing a turn-about in politics on such a broad front is, of course, no simple matter. It has to be somehow "justified." For these purposes, attempts are being made again to blame the Soviet Union and other socialist countries for the worsening of the international situation. The makers of Washington's "new" policy are trying to put it on some "theoretical" base, exaggerating in every way the elements of rivalry and belittling the importance of cooperation in U.S.S.R.-USA relations. Some members of the administration, for example, the presidential assistant, Zbigniew Brzezinski, did this so grossly and clumsily that they gave rise to a lot of confusion in the minds of both U.S. allies and their own compatriots.

An attempt to clarify things was made in President Jimmy Carter's recent speech at Annapolis. However the U.S. President obviously failed to introduce clarity into American policy, above all, into its policy in regard to the U.S.S.R. He failed for the simple reason that his speech was an attempt to reconcile the irreconcilable: assurances of loyalty to the ideas of détente and of improving Soviet-American relations, with unconcealed attacks addressed at the Soviet Union; expressions of respect for the peaceableness and staunchness of the Soviet people, who lost 20 million of their sons and daughters in the war against Hitler's aggression, with so preconceived and distorted a description of Soviet realities as one has not encountered even in the most ill-wishing American papers since the times of the cold war. . . .

. . . Let us now turn to the Strategic Arms Limitation Talks. These talks, aimed at working out a new agreement on limiting strategic arms, have been going on, as is known, for many years, and agreement has already been reached on an overwhelming majority of questions. The Soviet Union is doing everything in its power for the successful finalization of the remaining questions on a reciprocally acceptable basis and for the earliest conclusion of the preparations for the agreement. For this purpose, it is constantly submitting concrete and constructive proposals.

Such proposals were submitted during the recent talks of Andrei Gromyko, the Foreign Minister of the U.S.S.R., with President Carter and Secretary of State Cyrus Vance. However, while verbally recognizing the importance of concluding an agreement, the American leadership did not actually display readiness to discuss concretely the still unresolved issues. In general, it did not submit any proposals of its own. Moreover, absurd statements were made which the American press, too, could not assess otherwise than unacceptable to the Soviet Union. The United States, you see, would wait until the U.S.S.R. accepted the American proposals.

Noteworthy also is another point. Much is being said now in the United States, in official circles among others, about the difficulties with which the ratification of a future agreement could meet in the Senate. But the government itself, obviously, does not hasten to assume a definite stand, to start upholding the agreement in Congress and before public opinion by denying the various falsehoods to which the arms limitation opponents resort in respect to the future agreement. On the contrary, in this complicated situation many government leaders are busy stirring up mistrust toward the Soviet Union, spreading lies about the "Soviet military threat." Is there anything surprising, therefore, in the fact that the atmosphere around the future agreement is not clearing, but rather becoming even more complicated?

Artificial complications are also being created in the other negotiations on disarmament. Despite official denials, a line is actually being pursued to link the disarmament negotiations with other absolutely unrelated questions. . . .

What grounds, in the light of all these facts, does the United States have to sound the alarm about the Soviet Union's desire to achieve "military superiority?" What grounds? No, it is not these concocted dangers that the U.S. fears in reality, but equality, parity; it does not want its preservation, expecting to establish its own military superiority by means of new lunges ahead in the arms race and by putting a brake on the negotiations. It goes without saying that this runs counter to the initial principle of equality and equal security of sides agreed upon by the U.S.S.R. and the United States. The U.S.S.R. does not intend to violate it, but it will not allow this principle to be violated by others. Yes, it will not allow this to happen.

Along with stepped-up military preparations, the changes in the U.S. course find expression also in the transition to an openly interventionist, neocolonialist policy vis-à-vis the countries of Africa. This is borne out by the events in Zaire, the armed interference in the internal affairs of this country by several Western states under the political and military leadership of Washington, plans to include these or other African states in the sphere of NATO activities and attempts to knock together imperialist collective armed forces to suppress the liberation struggle on that continent. And, here again, concoctions about the "Soviet threat" to Africa, about "Soviet-Cuban interference" in its affairs, are resorted to as a diverting maneuver. Even the already refuted inventions on this score are being upheld as before without any shame.

In the meantime, Moscow learned about the events in Zaire from reports of Western news services. There are, in general, no Soviets or Cubans in any capacity whatsoever in Shaba. Just as there are no copper, cobalt or uranium mines belonging to the U.S.S.R. in that land. They are at the disposal of the Western nations, primarily the United States.

Particularly disastrous for mutual confidence are the attempts to interfere in the internal affairs of the other side. And such attempts have now been elevated in the United States to the level of state policy. Seemingly nice-sounding motives are being chosen for them. "human rights," "humanism," "defense of freedom." But actually we have here the same designs to undermine the socialist system that our people have had to encounter in this or that form since 1917. ... Such actions engender new doubts about the true intentions of the leaders of the United States and certain nations allied to it, poison the political atmosphere, and complicate cooperation.

The latest intrigues — to be more exact, the "petty intrigues" — of Washington around China in no way serve to strengthen confidence. The desire in itself to use the "Chinese card" in the global game is not at all new for American politicians. However, up until now the U.S. leaders, it appeared, realized that this card could not be used without creating dangers to the cause of peace and to themselves, for that matter, to the national interests of the United States.

However, certain leaders who hold high posts in Washington are so overwhelmed by anti-Soviet emotions that, judging by everything, they are now dismissing these dangers. Such leaders close their eyes to the fact that alignment with China on an anti-Soviet basis would rule out the possibility of cooperation with the Soviet Union in the matter of reducing the danger of a nuclear war and, of course, of limiting armaments. They forget also that the Chinese leaders are playing here a game of their own. If the United States and the NATO countries are not loathe to exploit in their own interests the difficulties which have arisen in Soviet-Chinese relations, the Peking leaders, for their part, have something quite different on their mind — namely, to aggravate to the limit the relations between the U.S.S.R. and the United States and to exploit this aggravation by no means in American, but in their own interests. Soviet-American confrontation and, still better, war — this is the cherished dream of Peking. Maybe Washington will give a thought to this matter without rashness, coolly. ...

... The world public is concerned also by the following question: How will the Soviet Union respond to the toughening of the American policy? This question acquires the greater topicality the more obvious the insufficiently considered and, at times, openly provocative nature of many actions undertaken by the United States becomes. ...

The Soviet Union is not intending to assist the authors of such plans. Our people have seen too much and experienced too much to give in to pressure, to retreat before saber-rattling. We chose the road of peace and will not allow anyone to push us off this road. We are not accepting the invitation to join the funeral of détente and of the hopes of millions of people for a peaceful future, for a possibility of a life worthy of man and his children.

Détente and the struggle for peace and disarmament have proved their great vital force and have the broadest support of the peoples. The Soviet Union and the other countries of socialism are fully resolved to conduct a consistent and stubborn struggle for them along all directions and, first of all, along such a direction as the limitation and reduction of armaments. ... In the situation complicated by the policy of the United States, the Soviet Union confirms again its course aimed at the relaxation of international tension and the development of good, mutually advantageous relations with the United States, given that the United States also wants this. ...

It is impossible to press for such aims proclaimed by the United States President as strengthening peace, limiting armaments, and normal relations with the Soviet Union, and at the same time to whip up an anti-Soviet hysteria, to try by means of attacks on the U.S.S.R. to solve one's problems — both external, domestic, and even personal ones. The present course of the United States is fraught with serious dangers — dangers for the United States, for all countries interested in peace, and for the entire course of international relations. We hope for the speediest realization of this truth in Washington.

## Soviet Dissident on Human Rights

### *Document 11*

Human rights was also a part of the linkage problem. By making the promotion of human rights a key theme in his foreign policy, President Carter left himself open to the question of how the United States can negotiate with the Soviet Union while it is violating the rights of its citizens. In document 11, a prominent Soviet dissident argues that the campaign for human rights should not slow progress on arms control. Other dissidents argued the opposite, however, and the human rights campaign hampered Carter's efforts to ratify SALT II.

## 11 THE HUMAN RIGHTS MOVEMENTS IN THE U.S.S.R. AND EASTERN EUROPE
### Andrei Sakharov

What do I expect from people in the West who sympathize with the human rights struggle? It is true beyond a doubt that their help is very important. And in this connection I should like to focus my attention on a few questions which are now being debated. The great deal of attention directed toward human rights problems in the USSR and the countries of Eastern Europe, especially following the period of trials in the spring and summer of 1978, is an extremely important factor on which I place much hope. But expanded possibilities also demand extreme accuracy and judiciousness in action, keeping all the possible consequences fully in mind.

In the Western press the thought has sometimes been expressed that the strategic arms limitations talks, in whose success the Soviet Union is interested, as is the entire world, have opened up possibilities of applying pressure on the USSR on the question of human rights. In my opinion, such a viewpoint is not correct. I believe that the problem of lessening the danger of annihilating humanity in a nuclear war carries an absolute priority over all other considerations. I believe that the principle of practicably separating the question of disarmament from other problems, as formulated by the United States Administration, is completely correct. Consequently, the strategic arms limitation talks must be considered separately; and considered separately, we must ask ourselves whether it will lessen the danger and destructive power of a nuclear war, strangthen international stability, or prevent a one-sided advantage for the USSR or a consolidation of its already existing advantages. Such a separate, practical approach does not negate, of course, the doubtless fact that a durable international security and international trust are impossible without the observance of the basic rights of man, specifically, political and civil rights. It should also be pointed out that the West should not consider the cutting of military expenditures as the main goal of arms limitation. The basic goals can only be international stability and the elimination of the possibility of a nuclear war. . . .

# The Cuban Brigade

## *Document 12*

As the Senate hearings on the SALT II agreements were drawing to a close, the chairman of the Foreign Relations Committee, Frank Church, disclosed that U.S. intelligence agencies had discovered a brigade of Soviet military advisers in Cuba. As these excerpts from a story in *Aviation Week and Space Technology* make clear, the disclosure of the brigade's presence set off a major controversy that hurt the prospects for SALT II ratification.

The existence of the brigade was nothing new and represented no threat to the United States. Its role in the SALT ratification process illustrates how the U.S.-Soviet arms control process can be disrupted by events not directly related to arms control.

## 12 U.S.S.R. CUBA FORCE CLOUDS DEBATE
### Clarence A. Robinson, Jr.

*Washington —*

Public reaction to the presence of a brigade-size Soviet force — including satellite communications experts — based in Cuba is becoming a significant new element in Senate debate on whether Strategic Arms Limitation Treaty 2 should be ratified.

The fate of the strategic arms agreements may hinge on the success of the Carter Administration in forcing the USSR to withdraw its troops from the island.

U.S. officials said last week that the Russian forces in Cuba are positioned there for several reasons, but that none of them are believed for offensive excursions in the Western Hemisphere because the Russian brigade is at the end of the Soviet supply line. . . .

. . . U.S. officials are blaming President Carter for the inability of the intelligence agencies to pinpoint the location of the Soviet ground combat brigade in Cuba until late August. They said Carter personally ordered a halt to all USAF/Lockheed SR-71 reconnaissance flights over the island by the Strategic Air Command within 10 days after he took office in 1977. . . .

. . . Secretary of State Cyrus R. Vance reconfirmed last week earlier State Dept. announcements that a combat brigade from the Soviet Union is located in Cuba. That move by Vance closely followed the Senate Foreign Relations Committee's postponement early last week of hearings on ratification of SALT 2 until Administration officials appeared before the committee to testify on the Soviet brigade in Cuba.

### Soviet Presence Disclosure

Sen. Frank Church (D.-Idaho), chairman of the committee, who has been in favor of the SALT 2 ratification, revealed the presence of the Soviet brigade in Cuba while on a visit to his home state during the congressional recess.

The senator, who is considered a liberal based on his voting record, faces a conservative in his reelection bid next year. Sen. Church indirectly linked SALT 2 with the Russians in Cuba and scheduled the hearings on that subject. After hearing Administration witnesses last week, including Vance and Adm. Stansfield Turner, Central Intelligence Agency director, the committee decided to resume SALT 2 ratification hearings this week, with the markup on SALT 2 scheduled next week.

Sen. Church warned that the Senate may not accept Cuba being turned into a Russian base, and that SALT 2 could be rejected or modified unless Soviet troops are removed.

The State Dept. called in the Soviet charge d'affaires to express its concern over the Soviet ground force unit on Aug. 29.

Sen. Richard Stone (D.-Fla.) scored the Administration over the Soviet unit in Cuba. He said last week that the brigade must be removed or that his vote on SALT 2 may be against the ratification. He said he believes the Russians are testing U. S. resolve and have positioned troops in Cuba to apply pressure on El Salvador, Honduras and Guatemala, which the Soviets want to add as client states.

Sen. Howard Baker (R.-Tenn.), the Senate minority leader, said the existence of the Soviet unit in Cuba is Russian nose-thumbing at the U. S. Sen. Baker said the Soviets are really saying that the U. S. should ratify the treaty even though it gives the USSR a significant advantage in strategic weapons, and to cap it off the Soviets sent 3,000 combat troops to Cuba. "I find that astonishing," Sen. Baker said.

Former astronaut Sen. John Glenn (D.-Ohio), who has raised concerns over whether the SALT 2 agreement can be adequately verified, used the presence of Soviet troops in Cuba to question verification again and whether the Central Intelligence Agency can monitor Soviet actions under SALT 2. Sen. Glenn alluded to congressional CIA budget cuts and questioned not only the capability to monitor Soviet SALT compliance, but also U. S. intelligence gathering capabilities in Cuba and elsewhere in the world. Without adequate SALT verification, treaty ratification is unlikely, he believes.

White House officials maintained that the Soviet brigade poses no threat to the U. S., but they agreed that it could threaten the SALT 2 ratification process.

While the Soviet unit in Cuba does not appear to violate any formal agreement with the USSR, it is a public issue, one U. S. official said, "and politicians are sensitive to public reaction. Sen. Church has taken a turn to the right—at least for the next year. In fact, we are in the unusual position of finding the senator to the right of Cy Vance."

U. S. intelligence agencies came under harsh congressional criticism after Sen. Church revealed the Soviet brigade's location in Cuba. On July 17, Defense Secretary Harold Brown, in response to questions on the Soviet military personnel in Cuba during a closed session of the Foreign Relations Committee, said there is no evidence of a substantial increase in the size of Soviet forces there. "Apart from a military group that has been advising the Cuban armed forces for 15 years or more, our intelligence does not warrant the conclusion that there are any other significant Soviet military forces in Cuba," Brown told the committee. . . .

. . . "There is no evidence of any significant increase of Soviet presence in Cuba other than those forces generally associated with the defense of Soviet equipment, support and maintenance," one high-level Administration official said last week. He added that USSR equipment is positioned there as a reward for Cuba's surrogate role, and that Soviet aid to the island totals around $1 billion per year.

"This is no ominous new threat to the U. S. The USSR goes by the book when deploying forces, and this is the package set requirement for a unit sized to defend Soviet installations: artillery, armor and armored personnel carrier units along with air defense elements," the official added.

In comparison with the deployment of two squadrons of MiG-23s last year, the official considers the brigade presence in Cuba militarily "a tempest in a teapot."

Vance said last week the Carter Administration regards the presence of the Soviet brigade in Cuba as a very serious matter, "affecting our relations with the Soviet Union." He added that the presence of the unit runs counter to long-held U. S. policies.

The secretary of State said the presence of the unit had "recently been confirmed by our intelligence community." He added that U. S. intelligence had concluded that the unit has been in Cuba since the mid-1970s, and that older, fragmentary data in the light of new information suggest that elements of a Soviet brigade may have been there since the early 1970s.

Vance said the unit appears to consist of 2,000-3,000 personnel and includes motorized rifle battalions, tank and artillery battalions along with combat service units. He stressed that these figures are separate from an estimated 1,500-2,000 military advisors and technical personnel in Cuba.

Vance emphasized there is no air or sealift capacity associated with the brigade that would give it an assault role.

The Administration held a top-level meeting last week on the issue of the brigade.

The meeting was limited to cabinet-level officials including Brown, Vance, Turner and National Security Adviser Zbigniew Brzezinski in the form of a presidential review committee. Its decision, according to some White House officials, was to await the Soviet reaction to the U. S. protest.

## Soviet Gains and U.S. Losses

### *Document 13*

This selection from a 1979 article in *Business Week* gives a sense of the growing impression among the public that

U.S. power was declining during the Carter years. The article highlights Soviet gains and U.S. losses, and criticizes the administration for indecisiveness. This growing sense of U.S. weakness also made it difficult for the Carter administration to pursue arms control.

## 13 A CRISIS OF INDECISION GRIPS CARTER'S FOREIGN POLICY March 12, 1979

Washington is beginning to cry "enough" over President Carter's shaky handling of international affairs and a string of foreign policy reversals that have created an image of U. S. impotence abroad. As a result, Carter has become the target of growing criticism from a broad spectrum of Republicans and Democrats for his perceived failure to defend adequately vital U. S. interests abroad.

Carter, like many Presidents, had hoped for a series of foreign triumphs to offset his domestic frustrations. Instead, he finds himself besieged over his conduct in international political, military, and economic affairs. How Carter responds to these challenges could decide his political fate in 1980. But more important, decisions made at the White House in coming weeks will determine the role of the U. S. in the world for years to come.

Carter came into office committed to a foreign policy that sought to reassert American idealism by promoting self-determination, human rights, and the national interest in a delicate balance between "ideals and power." At the same time, Carter accepted the idea, advanced by former President Nixon and Secretary of State Henry A. Kissinger, that there are limits to the power of the U. S. to control events in all quarters of the globe. Carter defined these international objectives:

- Limiting the global arms race, both by negotiating a new strategic arms limitation treaty (SALT) with the Soviet Union and by curbing the sale of conventional arms to developing countries.
- Bringing peace to the battle-torn Middle East, first by pushing for a comprehensive settlement and later by personal involvement in the Israeli-Egyptian peace negotiations.
- Reducing U. S. dependence on foreign oil and assuring adequate supplies of oil at tolerable prices to industrial nations.
- Promoting stable international economic growth through concerted action by the U. S., Germany, and Japan.
- Supporting Third World calls for greater economic equality and black African aspirations for self-rule.
- Normalizing relations with the People's Republic of China to promote peace in East Asia and exert restraint upon Soviet actions.

Carter has had some successes. He coaxed the Egyptians and Israelis to the verge of a peace treaty. He won a tough fight for ratification of the Panama Canal treaties, removing the major irritant in U.S.-Latin American relations. He normalized relations with China. He strengthened the North Atlantic Treaty Organization by boosting the defense spending of the U. S., and he has virtually concluded a bruising, five-year round of negotiations on a new multilateral trade agreement.

But Carter's foreign policy reversals, culminating with the fall of the Shah of Iran and the outbreak of war between China and Vietnam in Southeast Asia, are overshadowing the successes. These two events alone are threatening the vital supply of oil to the West and the superpower balance upon which world peace depends. In addition, his human rights policy is decried both by conservatives and those upset by its negative impact on U.S.-Soviet relations. Conservatives charge that it is ineffectual and needlessly complicates the conduct of U. S. foreign policy. Many liberals complain that the policy is unevenly applied.

### Strategic Debate

Congress is taking the lead in putting pressure on Carter to both clarify and stiffen his foreign policy. The stormiest debate is raging over whether the U. S. is falling behind the Soviet Union in strategic might.

For most of the post-World War II period, the U. S. enjoyed clear strategic superiority over Russia, both in the quantity of nuclear weapons and in the quality of their delivery systems. By the mid-1970s, the Soviets had made great strides in matching U.S. capabilities — partly as a result of a deliberate policy to let the Soviets come close to parity in the hope this would improve the prospects for controlling strategic weapons. But now, serious questions are being raised as to whether U. S. nuclear strength is sufficient to deter a nuclear first strike by the Russians.

Critics charge that Carter's decisions to cancel production of the B-1 strategic bomber and to delay development of the new-generation MX mobile missile, which would be less vulnerable to Soviet attack, endanger the U. S. deterrent edge. "We are still stronger than the Soviet Union," says Senate Minority Leader Howard Baker (R-Tenn.). "But we are not going to be stronger for very much longer if we don't reverse some of Carter's decisions." Kissinger argues that the American failure to match Soviet development of an MX-type missile in the mid-1970s leaves the U. S. with only the "politically paralyzing" option of massive destruction of the Russian population.

This question will be the core of the SALT debate, which Republicans and conservative Democrats will broaden into a full-scale critique of U. S.-Soviet relations.

Administration officials insist that the silo-busting capability of existing U. S. land-based missiles, plus the city-killing capability of U. S. submarine-launched missiles, constitute a sufficient deterrent now. But they acknowledge that the land-based missiles are fast becoming vulnerable to a Soviet first-strike. The MX, which will be available by the mid-1980s, will improve on the power and accuracy of existing missiles, and even more important, will be far less vulnerable. In any event, says one White House international expert, "the notion that both sides will be playing nuclear weapons like pianos strikes me as inherently incredible. The Soviets cannot believe that they could destroy our land-based missiles, killing 20 million Americans, without starting general nuclear war."

### Cat on a Cold Stove

Vietnam caused a loss of confidence in the ability of the U. S. to defend nonCommunist regimes in Third World countries against subversion and military takeovers by Moscow's allies. This perception of paralysis was confirmed when the U. S. stood by helplessly as Russian-backed insurgents, aided by Cuban troops, took over Angola. And it was enhanced when the Soviet-aligned Ethiopian government crushed separatist movements in Eritrea and the Ogaden. The image of the U. S. as a "pitiful, helpless giant" was intensified when the nation could not respond effectively to the fall of the Shah and the sacking of its embassy in Tehran. To do nothing in the face of such events, Baker feels, "invites the interpretation that we do not have the will or the resolve to react under any circumstances." Baker, a potential 1980 Presidential candidate, has urged "Entebbe-style raids and economic sanctions" in response to violence against U. S. outposts.

"The lessons of Vietnam have been over-learned," concedes a White House planner. "The old saying is that the cat won't sit on a hot stove twice. But after he's burned, he won't sit on a cold stove either." But, adds another aide, "our response can't always be to launch a Mayaguez raid — in which more people are killed than saved." The Administration argues that intervention cannot permanently affect the course of revolutionary or nationalistic movements.

But there are fears in Congress that Carter's apparent willingness to turn the other cheek emboldens U.S. enemies. "I'd rather flex our muscles a little bit on a weekly basis than have to resort to a great display of force at some very high level of danger," says Senate Armed Services Committee member Sam Nunn (D-Ga.). To date, the Administration has rejected these calls. "You'll notice that none of our critics has had an answer for what we could have done differently in Iran or Afghanistan," says an Administration analyst.

A charge to which the White House has no ready rejoinder is that U. S. ability to anticipate and respond to explosive foreign developments has been undercut by the decline of U. S. intelligence capability. Carter, who campaigned heavily on Watergate-era abuses of power by the Central Intelligence Agency, leaned toward the view of liberals such as Senate Foreign Relations Committee Chairman Frank Church (D-Idaho), who told BUSINESS WEEK in 1976 that "the CIA should not carry out any covert activities." Since he took office, Carter has supported further moves to limit the CIA's operational authority and, as a result, has seriously undermined the agency's already plummeting morale. "Long after we examined allegations of CIA misconduct and proved some," says Baker, "we kept right on flogging the agency. It's time to stop." One immediate result of this attitude is that pending legislation to place further restrictions on the CIA is now considered dead.

## U. S. Loses Confidence in Carter?

***Document 14***

This column by Russell Baker, written shortly after President Carter had returned from Vienna with the SALT II Treaty, describes another kind of "linkage." Although humorous, the column makes the serious point that the American public did not have a great deal of confidence in Carter's leadership ability.

### 14 TO THE SEASHORE, JIMMY
**Russell Baker**
**June 23, 1979**

The trouble with the world as defined by this week's news is too many bombs and not enough gas.

To put it another way, you can now be destroyed between 30 and 40 times by nuclear blasting power but can't get a weekend at the seashore.

This is a silly pickle, since almost everybody would rather go to the seashore than be destroyed 30 or 40 times. Nevertheless, it is the kind of mess nations get themselves into when they move up from being great powers and become super.

In the old days when there were nothing but great powers, they were satisfied to destroy you once. They were economical and did a better job of balancing the budget than we do. Now we have the superpowers, and they have to destroy you over and over until it gets tiresome.

The President's Vienna trip was an attempt to do something about this excess. When he hurried home the other night to tell the Congress about it, however, a lot of Congressmen found it more urgent to be elsewhere.

Like a lot of us, I suppose, they were cruising the highways in search of a working gasoline pump. When the gas buggy's vital juices run low, it is hard to agitate the public's juices with news that the superpowers will only be able to destroy you 29 times over instead of 32, if everything goes according to plan.

When you have lived with the multimegaton megalopolis-buster for thirty years, your worry organs get callouses. Worrying about the supers' ability to give you the business 30 times over is more heavy-duty worrying than most people can manage after the first couple of years of working at it.

It's the futility of the exercise that grinds you down. No matter how much you worry about those megatons, there is almost nothing you can do about them unless you have a job in the Government so eminent that they don't send you to prision for looking at secret documents.

Even then it is not a sure thing, since the top men are always trying to reassure each other so there will not be any "miscalculation." In a "miscalculation," if I understand them clearly, it's goodbye, Mr. Chips, 30 or 40 times.

Finally you have to do your worrying about matters you can have some effect on, and gasoline is a good example. It's only natural that most Americans generate more heat about gasoline than about limitations on strategic arms.

It is possible, with sufficient cunning and stamina, to obtain enough gasoline to get to the seashore. And why not? If you have no say about whether you're going to be wiped out 30 or 40 times, you ought at least to have a little say about where the obliteration is going to take place.

Most people would rather undergo it in a refreshing sea breeze than in some steaming apartment with deodorant commercials flickering on a picture tube. When they are balked in this civilized preference, as they are by the current oil shortage, they naturally become churlish, particularly about the Government.

While Americans these days like to complain that there is too much government, they also enjoy abusing the Government for not stepping in when they are inconvenienced by something like the gasoline drought. In short, while there is too much government to suit the American worrier, neither is there enough government.

People like the President who get paid for looking at the big picture and taking the long view probably get impatient with this. It must be hard, when you are trying to reduce the megatonnage threat, to find that the people you are trying to save are more interested in going to the seashore.

It must be even harder to realize that if you somehow supply the gasoline to get them there, they will abuse you even worse, come winter, for having given them auto fuel last summer instead of laying in enough heating oil to keep them from freezing in January.

It must be hardest of all to know that the big-picture, long-view attempt to reduce their megatonnage burden will help you very little next Election Day unless you can also get the people to the seashore in the summer and keep them out of long johns in the winter.

From the small-picture, short-view side of the population, on the other hand, it is hard to understand what is so super about being a superpower when it may require you to be destroyed 30 times in return for the right to be limited to three gallons of gas on days you are wearing the right license plate during hours the gas pumper feels like working.

## SALT II: NEGOTIATIONS AND AGREEMENT

## The Case for Salt II

### *Documents 15 and 16*

In document 15, President Carter's secretary of defense, Harold Brown, reviews the provisions of the SALT II Treaty, arguing that the limits are equitable and will not prevent the United States from making needed improvements in its strategic forces. In document 16, David Jones, then chairman of the Joint Chiefs of Staff, supports the SALT II Treaty but notes the military's reservations. In urging ratification of the treaty, Jones calls attention to the limits it places on Soviet systems and argues that the treaty will allow the United States to modernize its forces.

### 15 TESTIMONY TO THE U.S. SENATE
### Harold Brown, Secretary of Defense
### July 9–11, 1979

. . . I have examined this treaty with care and in the light of what I know about the nuclear armaments that exist in the world today and are likely to exist in the future. My judgment is that this treaty will make the people of the United States more secure militarily than we would be without it. For that reason I recommend that the Senate give its approval. . . .

## Role of Arms Control

Turning first to arms control itself, I start with the proposition that we cannot be militarily secure unless our strategic military forces are at least in approximate balance with those of the Soviet Union. The forces of the two countries are in a position of essential equivalence today.

There are two ways to maintain that equivalence. One is for both sides to add to their nuclear arsenals in equivalent or offsetting ways. The other is for both sides to limit their arsenals or to reduce them on a comparable basis. We have the option to follow either course. Either can maintain our security.

The course of limiting arms is preferable, however, for a number of reasons. First, it tends to make the future balance more predictable and stable and less likely to become one sided. Second, it provides more certainty to each side about the current program of the other. Third, it is obviously less costly for both sides. Overall, it is less risky for both sides.

Neither the present balance, nor ongoing Soviet programs, nor the state of arms control agreements, are such that we can avoid substantial defense programs needed for our military security. In fact, we need to increase our present level of such programs overall, regardless of this treaty. But SALT II is a clear and valuable, though limited, step toward curtailing the numbers and types of weapons that can be added by either side, and even toward reducing — by some measures — the number of weapons systems that one side (the Soviet Union) already has on hand.

In short, our military security can be enhanced either by increasing our own defense programs or by limiting the forces of the Soviet Union. Arms control, carried out with balance and care, can add to our military security just as can added defense programs. SALT II takes that approach toward making this country safer. . . .

## Deterrence

Deterrence of nuclear war is our most fundamental defense objective. For us to achieve this, our potential adversaries must be convinced we possess sufficient military force that, whatever the circumstances, if they were to start a course of action that could lead to war, they would either (1) suffer unacceptable damage or (2) be frustrated in their effort to achieve their objective.

Our strategy requires us to be able to inflict such damage on a potential adversary — and for him to be convinced in advance of our ability — that, regardless of the circumstances, the prospect of that damage will preclude his attack on the United States or our vital interests. To achieve this we need, first of all, a survivable capability to devastate the industry and cities of the Soviet Union, even if the Soviets were to attack first, without warning. That capacity, called assured destruction capability, is the bedrock of nuclear deterrence. It is not, in my judgment, sufficient in itself as a strategic doctrine. Massive retaliation may not be appropriate — nor will its prospect always be sufficiently credible — to deter the full range of actions we seek to prevent. . . .

## SALT II Treaty

The treaty is to last through 1985. It does these things:

It limits each side by the end of 1981 to a total of 2,250 intercontinental ballistic missile (ICBM) launchers, submarine-launched ballistic missile (SLBM) launchers, and heavy bombers.

This will require the Soviets to reduce by approximately 250 these strategic nuclear delivery vehicles (called SNDVs). Without SALT II, if the present trend continued, as I believe it would, the Soviet Union would instead have about 3,000 such weapons by 1985, instead of 2,250. No operational U.S. system will have to be reduced.

Within the 2,250 overall limit, the treaty sets a lower limit of 1,200 for launchers of ballistic missiles that carry multiple warheads aimed at more than one target (these systems are called MIRVed). Also, the number of such launchers plus the number of heavy bombers carrying air-launched cruise missiles (ALCM) cannot exceed 1,320.

Again, these limits hold the Soviets down to a level well below what I believe they otherwise could be expected to reach. For example, without SALT II, I would expect them by 1985 to have 1,800 multiple-warhead missiles instead of 1,200.

The limits placed on heavy bombers with cruise missiles will permit us to build the heavy bomber forces we have planned by 1985. To the extent that we may be required to reduce multiple-warhead systems, they will be older ones (chiefly Minuteman III missiles of increasing vulnerability) whose place will be taken by heavy bombers with cruise missiles or Trident submarines, leaving us stronger.

The treaty also sets a sublimit of 820 on launchers for land-based missiles which have multiple warheads that can be aimed at more than one target (MIRVed ICBMs). Those are the most threatening part of the Soviet nuclear arsenal as far as we are concerned.

The 820 figure is at least 100 fewer than we expected a few years ago that the Soviets would reach even under the SALT II limits, and much lower than the number they could reach by 1985 without SALT given their current trend. The 820 figure, however, is well above the number we plan to deploy.

The treaty also contains qualitative limits. It limits each side to only one new type of land-based intercontinental ballistic missile, and it requires that any such new missile not carry more than 10 independently targeted warheads or reentry vehicles (RVs).

This limit permits us to build the only new land-based missile we have planned to develop through 1985, the MX. It permits us to place on it the maximum number of warheads we intended — 10.

The Soviets, on the other hand, have been developing several new land-based missiles, their fifth generation of them. The treaty limit means that now all but one of those new missiles will have to be restricted to quite limited modifications of their predecessors. It will also mean that instead of developing a separate specialized new missile for each of several missions, the Soviets will have to make some tough choices. For example, they will have to choose either a replacement for their existing single-warhead land-based missile (the SS-11) or another new missile with up to 10 warheads to replace their SS-17s (4 warheads) and SS-19s (6 warheads). They cannot, under SALT II, develop both of these, nor can they develop a new type missile to replace the SS-18.

The treaty also places a limit on what we call "fractionation." This means that the number of reentry vehicles on existing or modified ICBMs cannot be increased from what it is now and that the permitted new ICBM could not, if MIRVed, have more than 10 reentry vehicles.

We have no plans to increase the number of warheads on our principal land-based missile, the Minuteman III; doing so would not increase its military effectiveness. The Soviets, however, have much larger missiles that could be adapted to carry many more warheads. The treaty takes away the ability of the Soviets to exploit this. For example, except for this limit, the Soviet SS-18 missile could be equipped to carry 20 or even 30 independently targeted warheads in the 1980s. With SALT II, that will not happen.

The treaty also provides measures to permit unimpeded verification by national technical means.

### Protocol

The protocol covers a shorter period; it expires on December 31, 1981. It bars operational deployment of ground-launched and sea-launched cruise missiles (GLCMs and SLCMs) with ranges greater than 600 kilometers through 1981, but it permits unimpeded testing and development of such vehicles of any range. This limit will have no impact whatsoever on our present cruise missile testing and development schedule. I might add that the protocol provision was adjusted to our schedules and not vice versa. The protocol also bars deployment of mobile land-based or air-to-surface balistic missiles through 1981; again, this will not affect our MX development, which will not enter its flight-test phase until 1983.

### Statement of Principles

Finally, the agreement includes a statement of principles to guide SALT III, plus Soviet commitments not to produce more than 30 Backfire bombers per year and to limit increases in its capability. The Backfire production restriction means that the Soviets now will not be able to divert Backfires to a strategic role (where they would add only marginally anyway) without greatly reducing Soviet capability for the naval and regional missions to which Backfires are normally assigned. . . .

Without the SALT II agreement, the Soviet Union could have nearly one-third more strategic systems than with the agreement — instead of the 2,250 delivery vehicles of the treaty, they could have 3,000. And there would be corresponding effects on other measures — including overall throw-weight, megatonnage, weapons numbers, and the like. Naturally, we do not know what the Soviets would do in the absence of a treaty, but these higher strategic system levels are well within their capability. . . .

First, the simple addition of numbers would force us to increase our own programs still further to preserve essential equivalence, to maintain areas of U.S. advantage to offset Soviet leads in other areas. . . .

Second, while SALT II won't solve the Minuteman vulnerability problem, it will make the solution of the problem easier than without an agreement. . . .

Third, to the extent that, as seems to me extremely likely, the lack of SALT limits would result in greater Soviet programs, and larger U.S. responses, we would be diverting scarce defense resources. . . .

## 16 TESTIMONY TO THE U.S. SENATE
## David Jones, Chairman of the Joint Chiefs of Staff
## July 9–11, 1979

. . . We are unanimous in our view that, although each side retains military advantages, Soviet momentum has brought them from a position of clear inferiority to their present status of at least military equality with the United States. In some areas, they have already surpassed us and we are concerned because their momentum will allow them to gain an advantage over the United States in most of the major static indicators of strategic force by the early 1980s. There is room for reasoned debate about the practical implications of this prospect, but it is important that we face up to its reality as we consider our own strategic responses.

It is also important to realize that any impending changes in the strategic balance will be the consequence of more than 15 years of unequal rates of investment in force modernization — the product of unilateral choices rather than an outcome of negotiated arms control. Overall, the Soviets have been outinvesting us for 10 years and, for the past few years, their total military investment effort has been about 75% larger than our own. With respect to investments for strategic forces, the disparity has, for many years, been even larger, with the Soviets outspending the United States by a factor of nearly three to one. Moreover, because of lead times in modern weapons programs, this progressive shift in the military balance will continue into the mid-1980s with or without SALT. A major concern my colleagues and I share is how best to minimize the period, extent, and consequences of any Soviet advantages. . . .

## SALT's Contribution to U.S. Security

Having sketched the strategic framework as seen by the Joint Chiefs of Staff, I will now turn to the SALT II agreement itself, and provide an assessment of its contribution to our broader security aims. Such assessments should be based on realistic and reasonable criteria which avoid both unrealistic expectations and overgenerous appraisals. The criteria which my colleagues and I on the Joint Chiefs of Staff have endorsed are threefold.

- The agreement must stand on its own merits regarding equity and mutual interest, to include adequate verification.
- It must accommodate (in fact and in perception) our broader strategic interests, particularly our alliance relationships and the need to preserve our freedom of action in sharing appropriate technology.
- It must be a suitable framework for — and be accompanied by — the national commitment and strategic programs required to arrest the deteriorating state of the military balance. . . .

We should bear in mind that one of the objectives of SALT is to regulate, in a balanced fashion, aspects of two fundamentally dissimilar and asymmetrical force structures. Not only are the force structures different in their composition, but different features on each side's forces are viewed as more threatening by the other side. These different perspectives have produced a negotiating process marked by various compromises and tradeoffs as each side seeks to protect the essential character of its own forces while attempting to minimize the most threatening aspects of the other side's. The result is an agreement with some provisions clearly favoring one side and some clearly favoring the other. The question of equity, then, cannot adequately be addressed by a narrow and selective critique of portions of the SALT II agreement. Only a balanced appraisal of the total will yield an adequate evaluation.

Two issues of particular concern to us with regard to equity have been the Soviets' unilateral right to deploy 308 modern large ballistic missiles (MLBM), which was allowed in SALT I and carried forward to SALT II, and the exclusion of the Backfire from the aggregate totals of strategic nuclear delivery vehicles (SNDVs).

Clearly, the desired result would have been a major reduction in Soviet MLBMs in order to have reduced their very significant throw-weight capability and attendant potential to carry large numbers of warheads. Having failed to achieve that objective, we should accentuate our determination to obtain substantial reductions in future negotiations as a major objective. In the interim, limiting the SS-18 to 10 warheads achieves an important restraint on their MLBM potential.

The second major concern is the failure to count the Backfire bomber in the SNDV aggregate totals. While we are well aware of its employment capabilities in peripheral and maritime roles, the Joint Chiefs of Staff consistently recommended that the Backfire be included in the aggregate because it has an intercontinental range capability.

Nevertheless, the United States did obtain some constraints on the Backfire, the most important of which is a production limit not to exceed 30 per year. Furthermore, the United States retains the right to build and deploy an aircraft with equivalent capabilities. . . .

Among the most important provisions having an impact on Soviet plans for strategic forces are:

- Aggregate limits that will require the Soviets to dismantle (or convert to nonoffensive systems) 250-plus operational systems — these are older and less capable weapons but still a significant fraction of their total systems and megatonnage;
- The various limitations that will enhance the predictability of the range of Soviet force developments, thus assisting us in our force planning;
- The cap on RV fractionation that denies full exploitation of the major Soviet throw-weight advantage for the period of the treaty; and
- Testing, production, and deployment of the SS-16 banned.

On the other hand, the specific limits on the United States are quite nominal and provide the following options in planning our strategic forces.

- We can build an ICBM which fully meets our security requirements.
- We can continue with the modernization of our submarine-launched ballistic missile (SLBM) program at the pace we determine.
- We can continue to modernize our airbreathing systems, including the exploitation of our air-, ground-, and sea-launched cruise missiles. . . .

None of us is totally at ease with all the provisions of the agreement. I expressed our concerns on the Soviet MLBMs and Backfire earlier and we also have significant concerns with regard to our ability to monitor certain aspects of the agreement. We believe, though, that the risks in this area are acceptable provided we pursue vigorously challenges to questionable Soviet practices, improvements in the capability of our monitoring assets, and modernization of our strategic forces. In this context, the Joint Chiefs of Staff believe the agreement is adequately verifiable.

Also, despite differing degrees of concern on specific aspects of SALT II, all of us judge that the agreement which the President signed in Vienna is in the U.S. national interest and merits your support. We believe it is essential that the nation and its leadership view SALT II as a modest but useful step in a long-range process which must include the resolve to provide adequate capabilities to maintain strategic equivalence coupled with vigorous efforts to achieve further substantial reductions. . . .

## Criticism from the Left

### *Document 17*

Some supporters of disarmament believed the SALT II Treaty did not go nearly far enough in ending the arms race. In this selection from a 1978 article in *The Progressive,* Sidney Lens argues that the treaty's terms allow the superpowers to retain too many nuclear weapons and do nothing to stop new weapons. "No matter how one looks at it," Lens concludes, "SALT II does not deserve the support of the anti-war movement."

### 17 ON SALT II
### Sidney Lens

The imminent agreement — or, at least, potentially imminent agreement — between the United States and the Soviet Union in the Strategic Arms Limitation Talks poses a dilemma for the American anti-war movement: Should it support, with reservations, the SALT II agreement or oppose it? The question is beginning to generate serious controversy among peace activists.

When the first SALT agreements were signed in 1972, the peace movement was preoccupied with the Vietnam war, and was therefore virtually immobilized on the broader issue of disarmament. Today, an anti-war movement more actively involved in seeking nuclear disarmament generally views the SALT I agreements as a hoax. They did nothing to limit the arms race, either quantitatively or qualitatively, and certainly did nothing to reverse it. . . .

I know no one in today's anti-war movement who asserts support for SALT I, or says he or she would have helped mobilize public opinion in behalf of those agreements. In fact, recognition of the deceptive character of SALT I helped spur the emergence of such new anti-war forces as the Mobilization for Survival and the Coalition for a New Foreign and Military Policy.

But SALT II is generating a somewhat different reaction. There are several reasons:

*First,* there is a widespread assumption among peace activists that the Carter Administration, unlike the Nixon-Ford Administration, really wants "arms limitation," and that some in the Administration actually want to go beyond "limitation" to a substantial *reduction* in arms — disarmament. . . .

*Second,* the pending agreement — assuming it is pending — is expected to shave 200 delivery launchers from the 2,400-limit agreed to by the United States and the Soviet Union at Vladivostok in December 1974. . . .

*Third,* there is a disposition among some peace activists — including communists as well as non-communists who believe the Soviet Union is peace oriented — to accept any treaty to which the Kremlin agrees as implicitly progressive. If it suits Soviet purposes, they think, it must be directed toward reversing the arms race.

*Finally,* there is apprehension over the growing influence of the Committee on the Present Danger, the right-wing armaments lobby. Since the Committee will probably oppose the eight-year agreement now envisioned by the Carter Administration on the grounds that it "gives away too much," some peace activists are convinced the anti-war movement must close ranks behind SALT II to win ratification by the U.S. Senate. The rationale is that if the agreement is rejected, the arms race will escalate even more furiously, so we must give the treaty "critical" support, without compromising the ultimate objective of nuclear disarmament.

All of these are, of course, complex moral and political considerations. But they do not alter the central fact that SALT II, in its present form, will not freeze or reverse the arms race but will significantly escalate it. Both sides will have more deliverable nuclear warheads, more advanced weapons, and greater death-dealing capabilities than at present. In fact, the pact offers *incentives* for building up the arsenal as rapidly as possible.

The contemplated treaty will, for example, place an overall limit of 1,200 on missiles with multiple warheads (MIRVs). The Soviet Union now has only 250 MIRVed missiles, but when the pact is signed it will certainly equip 950 additional missiles with as many as four, ten, or fourteen warheads each — instead of the present single warhead.

Similarly, the United States will not be precluded from substituting ten new Trident submarines for ten of the old Polaris submarines first deployed in 1964. The Polaris fleet has 160 missiles, with only one warhead on each — 160 in all; the Trident fleet will carry 240 missiles, with eight warheads on each, for a total of 1,920. Thus, the number of missiles will be 50 per cent greater, the number of warheads 800 per cent greater.

After ratification of the SALT I pacts, the United States increased its strategic arsenal from 4,600 deliverable warheads (deliverable by land-based missiles, submarine-launched missiles, and bombers) to 9,000 today, and the Soviets increased their arsenal from 2,100 warheads to 4,000. Every indication is that there will be a similar jump under SALT II. A projection made by the Center for Defense Information shows that U.S. strategic weaponry would climb to 10,154, plus 2,000 cruise missiles — an increase of about 35 per cent — and the Soviet force would double to 8,124.

These figures do not take into account the fact that there are no restrictions in SALT II on *quality* improvements, especially in accuracy, which Dick Creecy, former executive secretary of the U.S. SALT negotiation team, calls a "far more significant factor." If the Mark-12A warhead, for example, is installed on Minutemen III ICBMs, as presently planned, it could land a 370-kiloton bomb within a tenth of a mile of its target and substantially increase what is called the "lethality factor." If the maneuverable re-entry vehicle (MARV) — as especially accurate weapon — is perfected and deployed, it will show even more impressive results. An increase in yield of 20 per cent — say from 200 kilotons to 240 kilotons — increases the "lethality factor" by only 12 per cent, but an increase in accuracy of 20 per cent boosts the "lethality factor" by 55 per cent. SALT II puts no limits on accuracy, and the Pentagon is making sensational progress in this field.

Clearly, SALT II will not reverse the arms race; like SALT I, it will propel it toward higher "peaks." The only aspect that had any promise originally was the "protocol." If the superpowers could have agreed to a total ban on research, testing, development, production, and deployment of all new weapons systems — even for three years, as the present protocol provides — that would have been an important breakthrough. But, though we do not yet know all the details, the protocol appears to have been diluted to the vanishing point. It would no longer slow the tempo of weapons development at all. The Trident and the new Soviet submarine missile, the Delta, both of which may be deployable within the next three years, have been excluded — they can and will be deployed. The prohibition on new land-based missiles will not affect the United States because the MX — the mobile missile that will carry ten to fourteen warheads and run on an underground track three to five miles long — will not be ready within three years anyway.

Furthermore, nothing in the protocol will prevent continued research and development. The Mark 12-A is not covered; the MARV may be, but, according to experts, it is not likely that a deployable MARV will be ready within three years either. The only important testing restriction will be a 360-mile limit on land or sea-launched cruise missiles. Beyond that, as Stefan Leader of the Center for Defense Information notes, "it is not exactly clear what will be classified a new weapon" or "how stringent the controls on new weapons will turn out." One thing Leader is certain of is that "the agreement will certainly not close up the research and development establishments in the Pentagon and in the Soviet Union."

No matter how one looks at it, SALT II does not deserve the support of the anti-war movement. The mere fact that the Committee on the Present Danger opposes the agreement does not make it palatable for those at the other end of the spectrum, any more than the opposition of hawks to Nixon's step-by-step withdrawal of troops from Vietnam made the Nixon policy palatable to the peace movement. . . .

. . . Pacifists are not purists. They sometimes work — critically — for partial objectives (such as a campaign against a single weapons system, or against a single company engaged in the arms race, or for a non-proliferation treaty or test ban that may have loopholes). In such instances they are, at least, moving in the right direction, toward a reduction in armaments. But pacifists are not opportunists who will work for a treaty that heads in the wrong direction, toward an *increase* in armaments, simply because it is accepted by old friends who are now in the Government — and in the process of being coopted. Furthermore, the doves in the Administration would be hindered by such support: It would reduce their leverage against the hawks they must contend with. On the other hand, their position would be strengthened if they could demonstrate that there is *less* support for the SALT II escalation than the hawks claim.

There is a historic parallel: The anti-war movement did not improve its position in 1964 when most of its adherents decided to go "part of the way with LBJ." Had the peace forces withheld support from President Johnson and reduced his margin of victory, he might have thought twice about sending half a million troops to Vietnam. "Part of the way with LBJ" did not destroy the anti-war movement, but it certainly slowed its development in that first period of escalation, and made it more difficult to rally an opposition.

"Part of the way" with SALT II may also be only a temporary setback for the anti-nuclear forces. But it will certainly not advance the campaign for disarmament.

## Criticism from the Right

### *Documents 18 and 19*

The most effective attacks on the SALT II Treaty came from the right. Document 18, a 1979 article from the *Wall*

*Street Journal,* describes the efforts of Paul Nitze to defeat the treaty. The article notes that Nitze was very effective in arguing that the treaty would lock the United States into a position of inferiority while allowing the Soviets to move forward. Nitze is especially concerned about the vulnerability of U.S. intercontinental ballistic missiles. In document 19, excerpts from testimony to the U.S. Senate, Nitze gives a more detailed summary of his arguments against the treaty, arguing especially that it would benefit the Soviet Union much more than it would the United States.

## 18 FIGHTING A TREATY
## Kenneth H. Bacon
## June 29, 1979

*Washington —*

While on a business trip to Louisiana in the summer of 1940, Paul Nitze, then a New York investment banker, got a telegram saying: "Be in Washington Monday morning. Forrestal."

Mr. Nitze went to the capital and took a job with James Forrestal, who had just left Wall Street to become an assistant to President Franklin Roosevelt. Mr. Nitze has been here ever since, holding a series of top government jobs, including Secretary of the Navy and Deputy Secretary of Defense. These posts have put him in the middle of many of the country's national security decisions over the past four decades.

But it is as an outsider — he calls himself "essentially a businessman" managing his extensive investments — that the 72-year-old Mr. Nitze hopes to have his biggest impact on the nation's security policies. He has become a leading critic of the new Strategic Arms Limitation Treaty that President Carter has just signed with the Soviet Union. Over the past two years, the white-haired Mr. Nitze has been crisscrossing the nation to oppose the arms control treaty as a threat to U.S. security.

"I believe SALT II doesn't reduce the risk of war; it can increase the risk of war," Mr. Nitze argues. He contends that the treaty will lock the U.S. into a position of military inferiority while allowing the Soviets to continue what he sees as a march toward world domination. The treaty, he argues, "could result in a forced accommodation to the Soviet Union," leading to "world retreat" by the U.S.

As a one-time SALT negotiator, Mr. Nitze's views carry weight in the debate over the treaty, which must be ratified by at least two-thirds of the Senate. In the past two years, "Paul has effectively defined the terms of the debate about SALT and a whole host of strategic issues," says a military expert on Capitol Hill. In the absence of substantial amendments to the treaty or an acceleration of U.S. weapons programs, Mr. Nitze plans to oppose ratification.

### SALT Backers' Stand

SALT supporters, led by President Carter, strongly challenge the criticism by treaty opponents. Administration officials say the new limits on nuclear weapons will reduce the uncertainties and the cost of military competition, between the U.S. and the Soviet Union, and thereby set the stage for increased world stability. And they contend that the treaty won't compromise U.S. security.

Both supporters and opponents say critics such as Mr. Nitze will play an important role in the SALT ratification fight. The Senate vote, after months of debate, is expected to be very close. If ratification fails, "I think it will be possible to look back and say it's because the administration didn't start early enough to counteract Paul Nitze and others," says William Kincade, executive director of the Arms Control Association, a private pro-SALT group.

Meantime, Mr. Nitze keeps attacking the treaty. He does so by issuing anti-SALT pamphlets on the U.S.-Soviet defense balance and on terms of the treaty. These are distributed by the Committee on the Present Danger, a pro-defense group of business men, labor leaders and former government officials, that Mr. Nitze helped organize in 1976. He also testifies frequently before congressional committees and gives two or three speeches a week to business and other groups.

### Personal Crusade

The anti-treaty fight has become a personal crusade for the septuagenarian. "Paul is really a compulsive man at this stage. It's very difficult for him to say that reasonable men can differ on issues of life-and-death importance," says an admirer on Capitol Hill. Mr. Nitze explains his dedication this way: "I've devoted my entire life to what happens to the world, to the United States."

Friends say he brings the same vigor to all his activities. An avid piano player, Mr. Nitze loves to discuss Bach. And every July 4th he throws a big party at his suburban Washington farm and shoots off thousands of dollars' worth of fireworks.

It's Mr. Nitze's tough-minded attention to detail, associates say, that makes him a formidable force in the SALT debate. Lt. Gen. Edward Rowny, the Joint Chiefs' of Staff representative to the SALT talks, recalls long, demanding study sessions with Mr. Nitze, then a treaty negotiator, in 1973 and 1974.

"Nitze would work his pipe with his finger and then stab me (with his finger) in the chest saying, 'Rowny, Rowny, consider this,' " the Army general says. "My wife used to judge my day by the number of nicotine stains on my shirt."

Currently, Mr. Nitze is trying to persuade former Secretary of State Henry Kissinger to oppose SALT II. Opposition from Mr. Kissinger, who helped negotiate the first SALT pact in 1972, would be a damaging blow to ratification of the new treaty. So far, Mr Kissinger hasn't taken a public stand.

The efforts by Mr. Nitze and his committee are modest compared with anti-SALT groups such as the American Conservative Union and the American Security Council, which are mounting costly televison campaigns to oppose the treaty. But the Nitze message has been broadly disseminated, partly because he deals skillfully and frequently with the press.

"He's done quite a job of getting anti-SALT facts into the hands of editorial writers and commentators," notes Thomas Halsted, a public affairs adviser at the State Department. "Every place I go to speak or meet with an editorial board, somebody has got Nitze's documents and starts asking me questions," Mr. Halsted says. 'He's perceived to have a high reputation for accuracy and patriotism, and he's generated a lot of skepticism."

SALT supporters don't question the sincerity of Mr. Nitze's strong views on defense, but they challenge his conclusions about the treaty. "His views have been absolutely consistent over the last 30 years," Mr. Kincade notes, "but I don't think anybody would argue that the world hasn't changed since 1949."

### Long Favored Controls

In Mr. Nitze's view, one central fact hasn't changed — the Soviet Union seeks to dominate the world, and the U.S. must maintain military superiority to frustrate that goal. What has changed, he says, is that successive American administrations have failed to match the growth of Soviet forces. He concedes that in the past he has predicted faster improvements in Soviet weaponry than actually have occurred, but he thinks the U.S. "edge has slipped away." He believes that the U.S. should strengthen its forces by increasing defense spending as much as $20 billion a year.

Part of Mr. Nitze's influence stems from his long record as an arms control advocate. Following World War II, he led a government study of the effect of the atomic bombs that the U.S. dropped on Japan. "Since that time," he says, "I've spent a large percentage of my time worrying about the posture the U.S. should take in light of this dreadful fact, the existence of nuclear weapons."

As Deputy Secretary of Defense in the Johnson administration, Mr. Nitze, a life-long Democrat, helped lay the ground work for the first round of arms control talks with the Soviets. From 1969 to 1974 — during the Nixon administration — he worked on the U.S. team that helped negotiate SALT I and began work on SALT II. He resigned in protest in 1974 because he thought President Nixon was conceding too much to the Soviets in a rush to reach a treaty that would divert attention from Watergate.

### Pentagon Data Cited

Mr. Nitze believes that "both sides in SALT want a pact, but for discrepant aims." The U.S. goal "is to arrange a standoff," he says, while the Soviets want "to nail down strategic primacy so as to be in a position to direct the course of international politics."

He contends that the treaty would allow the Soviets to gain an edge in nuclear fire-power. He adds that "over the past 15 years it couldn't have profited either side to attack first with nuclear weapons because the first strike would have used more weapons than it would have destroyed and thus left the victim with large forces for retaliation. But by the early 1980s, that situation will have changed in favor of the Soviets," Mr. Nitze says.

He cites Pentagon calculations that by 1982 the Soviet Union will have deployed enough highly accurate nuclear warheads to destroy most of America's land-based intercontinental ballistic missiles while retaining thousands of additional warheads with which to threaten U.S. cities and other military targets. This will put the U.S. at a strategic disadvantage that the Soviets could be tempted to exploit, he fears.

Administration officials say Mr. Nitze and other SALT critics focus too narrowly on the projected vulnerability of U.S. ICBMs, and slight the U.S. lead in nuclear weapons designed for launch from bombers or submarines. About 80% of the Pentagon's 9,550 strategic warheads are deployed on submarines and bombers. These weapons are less vulnerable, although they lack the combination of high accuracy and speed that gives land-based missiles the ability to destroy quickly certain military targets.

Administration officials say the idea that the U.S. should achieve nuclear superiority is unrealistic, despite its patriotic appeal. "Modern nuclear weapons technology is such that while equivalence is a realistic goal, superiority isn't, providing that the other side is determined to prevent it," Defense Secretary Harold Brown says. In the past 10 years, U.S. Presidents have spoken of the need to maintain strategic parity or equivalence with the Soviet Union but disclaimed the idea that the U.S. can or should maintain superior nuclear forces.

### Brown's Position

Secretary Brown, Mr. Nitze's old friend and former subordinate at the Pentagon, maintains that the U.S. deterrent against attack will remain strong during the life of the treaty. "Our capacity to make selective strikes at military and other targets, while maintaining a reserve, is large now and will grow in the future, despite ICBM vulnerability," Mr. Brown says.

The U.S. plans to make substantial improvements to its nuclear weapons deployed on bombers and submarines during the life of the treaty, the Defense Secretary notes; the agreement allows both the U.S. and the Soviet Union to add to their arsenals within certain limits. The 9,550 U.S. warheads compare with 4,950 for the Soviets, and the U.S. still will have a numerical advantage when the treaty expires at the end of 1985.

In addition, Mr. Brown says that U.S. plans to proceed with one of a number of options to make land-based missiles less vulnerable. But Mr. Nitze isn't reassured. "Due to 40 years of history and experience with assurances given by various executive branches," he says, "I've developed a certain amount of skepticism."

## 19 TESTIMONY TO THE U.S. SENATE
## Paul Nitze, Former Deputy Secretary of Defense, and Former Secretary of the Navy
## July 9-12, 1979

MR. NITZE. Thank you, Mr. Chairman, Senator Javits, and Senator Percy.

It is an honor to appear before your distinguished committee, Mr. Chairman.

The issue before the Senate is broader than merely whether or not to consent to the ratification of the SALT II agreement signed at Vienna on June 18. The Constitution also places on the Senate the responsibility to advise with respect to treaties brought up to it for consideration.

For some time, the SALT II proponents have been explaining the agreements in a manner intended to praise them. In so doing, they have given what I believe to be a one-sided and misleading picture. The Senate is entitled to a more critical and balanced analysis.

### Agreements Unequal in Legal, Practical Effect

Supporters of the agreements stress equality in the main provisions of the treaty. Despite the superficial appearance of equality, the agreements are unequal, both in their legal and in their practical effects.

The supporters assert that the agreements put a cap on the so-called arms race and initiate a process of reductions in offensive strategic nuclear armaments. On the contrary, the limits in the agreements are so designed and are so high that they put no effective limit on Soviet offensive strategic nuclear capabilities. Rather than forcing a reduction, there will be a continuous and large increase in Soviet capabilities during the term of the treaty. There will be some increase in our capabilities as well; but in net terms, the strategic balance will move from a position not far from parity to one of Soviet strategic nuclear superiority.

### SALT II Verifiability

The SALT II proponents assert that the agreements are adequately verifiable. Strict adherence to many of the provisions of the agreements cannot be confidently verified. But the agreements so one-sidedly favor the Soviet Union that verifiability, in my view, is not the major issue. What could be gained by cheating would be less significant than the shift in strategic capabilities permitted without the necessity for cheating.

### SALT II as Foundation for Future Agreements

It is also asserted that, despite their shortcomings, the agreements are a good and necessary foundation for the negotiation of better future agreements — SALT III, SALT IV, and so forth. To the contrary, there is no evidence whatever that, as the strategic nuclear balance shifts further in favor of the Soviet side, the Soviet leaders will become less resolute in pressing every possible advantage.

It is almost certain that, if SALT II is ratified as signed at Vienna, SALT III will be less favorable to the United States and more favorable to the U.S.S.R. than SALT II.

Further, there is the broader political question of how best to deal with the Soviet Union. Is unequal and one-sided accommodation by us the best way to assure the cooperation of the Soviet leadership toward world progress and toward peace?

Again, history gives no support to that hope. I believe we are headed for difficult times ahead in our relations with the world, and particularly with the Soviet Union, whether SALT II is ratified or not.

Finally, the Senate must resolve the question of whether, in times of increasing danger, including military danger, it is wise to let down our guard or whether it is time to pull the country together for the major effort that is required on many fronts.

### Nitze Papers Concerning SALT II

As many of you know, I have, over the last 3 years, revised and kept up to date a series of papers concerning SALT II. The first of these is a condensed summary of the status of the SALT negotiations. The second is an analysis, in words, of the 15 central issues raised by SALT II. The third is an analysis of the probable evolution of the strategic nuclear balance in numbers. The fourth is a set of charts which display those numbers graphically.

Using the State Department Selected Document 12A, which contains the full Vienna documentation, I have brought those four papers up to date and have attached them as annexes to this statement. The changes required from the earlier drafts were not substantial. I have also included as additional annexes two further papers. The first is entitled, "A Method for Dealing with Certain Fallout Questions." The second is a copy of my February 6 statement before the House Armed Services Committee addressed to the survivability and endurance of U.S. deterrent forces.

I have included the paper on fallout which, at the request of Secretary Brown, was reviewed and confirmed for accuracy by the Defense Nuclear Agency, because it demonstrates the incorrectness of the overkill argument which is so frequently relied upon by the more ardent wing of the arms control community.

### Agreements Are Unequal in Legal, Practical Effects

Annexes I, II, and III fully support the assertion that the agreements are unequal both in their legal and in their practical effects.

In legal terms, the Soviet side is permitted 308 modern, heavy ballistic missile launchers; we are permitted none. The destructiveness of those missiles alone is greater than the destructiveness of all our strategic missiles, both ICBM's and SLBM's combined. The Soviet side is permitted up to 10 reentry vehicles [RV] on their existing ICBM's. We are permitted no more than 3. . . .

. . . MR. NITZE. In practical terms, the Soviet side can be expected, by the expiration of the treaty in 1985, to have approximately the same number of launchers and warheads as we, but due to the greater size of their missiles and warheads coupled with their rapidly improving accuracy, they will exceed us in every other measure of strategic nuclear capability. They will have twice the area destructive capability, five times the ICBM plus SLBM hard-target kill capability, three times the megatonnage, and twice our throw weight.

If our obsolescent B-52's can get off their bases, arrive close enough to launch their cruise missiles, if those cruise missiles can penetrate to their targets through unconstrained Soviet air defenses, and if no allowance is made for the offsetting capabilities of the Backfire bombers, we will have a continuing, in fact growing, superiority in what is called delayed counter military potential, but this will not be sufficient to offset the other factors.

When one takes all factors into account, including the fact that the initiative is apt to be theirs, that their command control and wartime intelligence facilities are substantially harder and more diverse, that they have more and harder hard targets, that their active defenses and their civil defense preparations are substantially greater than ours, it is quite evident that strategic parity is slipping away from us and that the Soviets can be expected to achieve meaningful strategic superiority probably by 1982, and most certainly by 1985, unless we take the most urgent and prompt steps to reverse current trends.

### Soviet Threats Concerning SALT II Ratification

The Soviet leaders threaten us with dangers ahead if the Senate does not consent to the ratification of the SALT II terms exactly as signed at Vienna. No one can guarantee that their threat is a bluff. The point might be the core of a valid issue if one could truly say that acceptance of the treaty as drafted would bring us safety. That is not the case. We are not at a crossroads between safety and perplexity. There is no formula for salvation in making these inequitable provisions into the supreme law of the land.

However the Senate may vote, there is trouble in prospect. Amendment of the treaty does not assure Soviet acceptance of the amended terms, nor does failure of the treaty assure strategic balance, but neither will acceptance of the Vienna draft assure strategic balance; to the contrary, it will tend to nail down dangerous strategic imbalance.

### Redressing the Strategic Balance

That brings me to the heart of the problem posed by SALT II. To accept the case that is being made for the Vienna terms, with all its fallacies and implausibility, can only incapacitate our minds and wills for doing the things necessary to redress the strategic balance. The first step out of danger is to recognize danger.

We have to come to terms with the plight we are in before we can correct it. In Lincoln's words, "First, we must disenthrall ourselves, and then we shall save the country."

The executive branch has decided to proceed with the engineering development of the M-X missile. It has not decided on its deployment mode. I understand a decision on the deployment mode is expected by August 1. I should think your committee would wish to assure itself that that deployment mode is at least generally as effective as the multiple protective shelter system previously recommended by the Pentagon and is recognized by the Soviet Union as being permitted under the terms of the agreement.

I should think your committee would wish to assure itself that granting the Soviet Union the unilateral right to deploy modern heavy ballistic missiles is made equitable merely by our decision many years ago not to contribute to crisis instability by deploying such destabilizing weapons.

I should think your committee would wish to assure itself of the adequacy of the Soviet commitment not to increase to an intercontinental radius the capability of their Backfire bombers when none of the U.S. bombers have the capability to hit their targets in the Soviet Union and return to the bases from which they take off.

I should think your committee would also wish to inquire into the executive branch's plans to implement the U.S. commitment in the Vienna agreements promptly to resolve the issues left undecided by the protocol.

I should also think your committee would wish to consider whether the numerous shortcomings of the agreement signed at Vienna can be corrected merely by reservation or whether significant clarifications and improvements in the actual terms of the agreement are required. I frankly think they are required, but it is the Senate that must decide that.

Finally I should think the Senate as a whole would wish to assure itself of the adequacy of the U.S. strategic programs actually planned and budgeted by the executive branch and consistent with the terms of the agreement to deny the Soviet Union the hope of achieving strategic nuclear superiority.

I believe that those plans as described by Secretary Brown yesterday with direct costs of $12 billion a year are inadequate.

## A Soviet View: SALT — A Fair Bargain

### *Document 20*

In this 1979 article from the *Bulletin of the Atomic Scientists,* Henry Trofimenko, head of the foreign policy department of the Soviet Union's Institute of U.S. and Canadian Studies, argues that SALT II has benefits for both superpowers. He also criticized the argument that the Soviet Union is seeking superiority over the United States.

### 20 A FAIR BARGAIN
**Henry Trofimenko**
**Moscow**
**June 3, 1979**

What is better — to have a SALT II treaty or not to have it? To have it is the only right answer, no doubt about that. And it is not that the USSR wants this treaty because, as some American politicians claim, it gives more to the Soviet Union than to the United States. The point is that the treaty is a measure to limit arms, and, however imperfect, the limitations are better for both sides than none at all.

As all the experts admit, neither the USSR nor the United States will ever allow each other to obtain a substantial advantage in strategic armaments even if there were no SALT II in existence. But to keep this balance without a treaty would mean that one side would overdo things sometimes because of uncertainty about the rate and scale of the other side's strategic arms development. With a treaty in force both nations will know the "ceilings" to go by and, what is more, the ceilings to be lowered before the treaty expires. Isn't that a factor to promote stability and diminish the war danger?

Furthermore, the treaty will provide the framework and guidelines for drafting SALT III, as the basic principles of SALT II stipulate, and will extend the range and parameters of the arms to be limited.

It would be good, of course, for the security of both nations to rest, not on their mutual vulnerability or equal insecurity, so to speak, but on some sounder safeguards. The only way to do so, evidently, is through a more fundamental solution of disarmament issues. There have been far-reaching Soviet proposals to this effect: One was for nations with large military potentials to stop all numerical buildup and qualitative improvement of their armaments and armed forces. Another was for a total ban on the development of new types of mass destruction weapons and systems. These still stand. But pending such a solution, the SALT agreements will continue to be the most realistic way to follow in this direction. . . .

The Vladivostok accord underlies the SALT II Treaty, drafted at long last, which limits the strategic armaments of the parties concerned in an equal and fair measure. Further, it establishes strategic parity between the USSR and the United States until the mid-1980s. The very possibility of a SALT II agreement ever being reached arose only after the American side had desisted from its attempts at obtaining purely unilateral advantage through these negotiations and accepted an equal compromise arrangement. That did not happen overnight. For a few months after Carter took office, the Pentagon pressed the Administration to impose absolutely unacceptable terms on the USSR.[38]

The significance of the SALT II Treaty lies, above all, in its importance as a step toward disarmament. It is designed to maintain a parity between the strategic armaments of the two countries by common consent rather than by unilateral action to redress the balance. Had there been no other reason to warrant SALT II, the contractual quantifying of the arms in question is a solid achievement. The treaty gives each side a chance to judge the other's capabilities, enabling both to guide their military programs not by the "maximum expected threat" or even by the "greater than expected threat" principle behind U.S. military planning in the 1960s, but with a certain measure of restraint.

Furthermore, the treaty offers illuminating and conclusive evidence to other nations that the USSR and the United States mean business in declaring themselves determined to limit and stop the arms race between themselves. This will give greater weight to the two nations' efforts to oppose any further spread of nuclear weapons around the world, and the arms race in general. For it is all too obvious that the arms race in the rest of the world will, unless halted, strain bilateral Soviet-American relations still further. The very fact of renewed agreement between the two giants of the modern world in respect to the main dynamo of confrontation — the arms build-up contest — will, no doubt, contribute to strengthening mutual confidence and resolving a whole series of problems at issue between the two nations in other areas as well.

In some West European NATO countries the SALT II Treaty has been criticized because some of the limitations it will impose, for example, on the deployment of cruise missiles, will weaken NATO's military power in Europe. But it would be naive to think that, should the United States embark on a massive deployment of cruise missiles in Western Europe, the Soviet Union would fail to take countermeasures. And it is unlikely that the bulk of West Europeans would be keen on having the arms race in Europe escalate when there are certain prospects for slowing it down and for the power balance in Central Europe to be stabilized as a result of the Vienna talks.

Finally, in the so-called "gray weapons" area — nuclear arms designed for use primarily on the European continent — the very fact of a Soviet-American agreement to limit central weapons systems will provide an opportunity to discuss the European nuclear arms problem as well. As Warsaw Pact states stressed during the conference of their Political Consultative Committee in Moscow in November, 1978, there is no type of armaments they would not be prepared to see limited or reduced by mutual agreement, guided by the principle of undiminished security of all the parties concerned.

Of course, the SALT II Treaty will not, unfortunately, stop all the channels of the arms race. Moreover, to persuade the military to accept the SALT II Treaty, the Carter administration is offering in advance to give them a go-ahead for the development of entirely new strategic weapons systems and more money to fund them. This can only damage SALT II, since it makes the continued qualitative improvement of these systems an indispensable, if collateral, condition for SALT II itself.

Neither, of course, can such a stand please any openhearted partisans of disarmament. As The Washington Post, on Dec. 5, 1978, has rightly pointed out, "at some point in these domestic tradings, however, the lines may begin to cross; the price for approval of an agreement can get so high that it sharply diminishes the value of the agreement itself." The paper said this was "one of the traps" the President would do well to escape. . . .

One of the main arguments produced by those who seek to prove the SALT II Treaty "unacceptable" for the United States as it stands is that this treaty "does not ensure equality in second-strike capabilities," and that it will put the United States at a disadvantage. Their line of reasoning is that the greater throw-weight of Soviet ICBMs will enable the Soviet Union to acquire a capability for the first counter-force strike at American ICBMs toward the mid-1980s, to knock out this component of the American strategic forces and to win a "victory" over the United States in an exchange of nuclear strikes.

Under the Soviet military-political doctrine, missiles and nuclear weapons at the Soviet Union's disposal are designed, as Soviet leaders have repeatedly stressed, not for attack but for a devastating retaliatory blow at the aggressor who attacks the USSR or its allies. The Soviet Union does not subscribe to first-strike concepts, regarding them as rash. As Brezhnev has emphasized:

> The allegations that the Soviet Union is going beyond what it actually needs for its national defense, that it is trying to attain superiority in weapons in order to deal "the first blow," are absurd and totally unfounded. . . . The Soviet Union has always been and remains strongly opposed to such concepts. . . . Not superiority in weapons, but a course aimed at reducing armaments, at easing the military confrontation — such is our policy.

American hawks are likely to feign ignorance of these unequivocal statements by Soviet government leaders and juggle with all kinds of technical estimates in an effort to prove the "possibility," indeed "probability," of the USSR venturing upon such a strike at American ICBMs because it would mean an "easy victory." Yet the actual situation, even if seriously examined from the standpoint of military technology alone, will be found to be entirely different from the way it is depicted by those who would like to kill the SALT II agreement by rhetoric of this kind.

One can, of course, set out to "prove" anything by all manner of falsification. Specialized American literature has been trying for some time to sell the idea that the so-called counter-force megatonnage of a single Soviet ICBM is quite enough to knock out almost all of the 1,054 American ICBMs.[39]

The first puzzle to solve is what particular aim the USSR might have in attempting to destroy one of the three components of the American strategic triad. For in making such an attack, any country ought to realize that it will be launching not a "limited trial of strength," as American advocates of "limited war" argue, in an effort to prove that a Soviet strike at American ICBMs will cause no more than 800,000 casualties in the United States, but a full-scale third World War.[40] In such a context, the attacking side will have to think not of one component of the "triad," but of the other two as well, which could be applied in retaliation.

To follow the reasoning of such people as Paul Nitze, Eugene Rostow or Henry Jackson, who regard the throw-weight of the strategic systems as a critical parameter, it turns out that, judging by American estimates only, the throw-weight of American ICBMs make up a mere 8.5 percent of the combined throw-weight of all the U.S. strategic forces (two million out of the 23.7 million pounds).[41] What, one may wonder, would the USSR stand to gain from destroying 8.5 percent of the throw-weight of the U.S. strategic forces while leaving 91.5 percent intact? And this question arises from the utterly incredible assumption that the USSR is prepared to start a third World War. This calculation, as we see, shows that a preemptive strike at American ICBMs cannot deprive the United States of its retaliation capability.

But I am prepared to go further and to admit, following the argument of such a distinguished specialist as Albert Wohlstetter, that the throw-weight is not the parameter the Pentagon has considered to be supreme in the last few years.[42] Rather, the main parameter in which the United States has been trying to outstrip the USSR is the number of targetable strategic warheads. To take this parameter, one can see again that ICBMs account for less than a quarter of the total number of the nuclear warheads of the U.S. strategic forces.[43] This means that even the complete destruction of American ICBMs by a sudden attack would leave intact 75 percent of the nuclear warheads of the U.S. strategic forces which could be used for retaliation. Who, in these circumstances, can contemplate a strike at American ground-based ICBMs?

It is worth enlarging somewhat on this argument and applying it to the American possibilities and perhaps intentions. Consider, for one thing, that MIRV warheads (which U.S. experts call counter-silo kill devices) have long since been installed on American ground- and sea-based missiles[44] and, for another, that the strategic missile command is, indeed, the major component of Soviet armed forces. Isn't it likely for Soviet specialists to get the impression that it is the United States that is planning such a counterforce strike at Soviet ICBMs in the hope of being eventually able to "limit the damage" by a strike from Soviet submarines and bombers? (The latter, incidentally, the Pentagon does not fear at all, for it has seen no need for the U.S. mainland to have any ramified continental anti-aircraft defense system.)

Putting the matter this way and considering American press reports that the Carter administration's projected revision of U.S. strategy will mean enhancing the counterforce capabilities of the U.S. strategic forces — that is, their capabilities for hitting military targets "such as missile silos, airfields, war plants, troop and tank concentrations,"[45] — one can state that the Soviet side does have far more reason to fear such American tactics than the United States may have to fear those of the USSR.

Yet Soviet military specialists are not scaring their citizens with any prospect of a "pre-emptive American strike," nor do any Soviet daily newspapers or even specialized magazines, unlike those in the United States, carry alarming articles or venture any calculations of a possible or probable strategic U.S. attack on our country. The Soviet military and civilian leadership have a far more responsible attitude toward the problems of war and peace. Far from having any desire to alarm their citizens, they are unswerving in their policy to promote the relaxation of tensions and a lessening of mutual suspicion; in short, to achieve a more comprehensive détente.

At the same time not a day passes by without the American press frightening its readership with the "Soviet threat." Moreover, the Western, and especially the American press, can sometimes be seen to speculate on Soviet intentions in a way I can only describe as premeditated foul play. . . .

To call a spade a spade, all these attempts at hoodwinking Americans with the "growing military threat" of the Soviet Union (made by members of such organizations as the American Security Council, the Committee on the Present Danger or the Coalition for Peace through Strength) are seen in Moscow not as responsible warnings about a real threat, but as the hysterics of people reluctant to accept the principle of strategic parity between the United States and the USSR. Since World War II, the United States has been strategically invulnerable and many representatives of the Washington establishment have been for too many years looking down on the military and other potentials of foreign nations. This makes it very difficult for them to accept the principle of equality with a country they have traditionally regarded as inferior to the United States, militarily and technologically.

Why not spurt ahead once more, with no SALT in the way? That seems to be the overriding American ambition hidden behind all the pseudo-scientific theories of the alleged disproportions "damaging to U.S. interests" arising from the SALT II Treaty.

Suffice it to refer to Eugene Rostow's arguments against the SALT II Treaty. If, as he reasons, the United States is really behind the Soviet Union, "in almost every relevant category of military power — behind in production, behind in research and behind in programming,"[46] then it is plain common sense that even this is an argument in favor of SALT II rather than against it. If the United States is so terribly behind the USSR, then stabilizing the balance by fixing identical total ceilings and subceilings for strategic offensive systems will offer America the best possible opportunity to catch up with its opponent. There is nothing simpler than that!

But the chairman of the Committee on the Present Danger is by no means worried by a prospect of losing parity. He is nostalgic about the days of the "unchallengeable nuclear superiority" of the United States when, to quote him, the United States could back up its diplomatic moves by "veiled nuclear threats"[47] to compel solutions of world problems to America's liking. Now, whatever diplomatic action cannot be backed up by such a threat is, in Rostow's view, nothing short of "appeasement." That is the rub!

The days of American military superiority are gone, never to be brought back by any incantations or unilateral breakthroughs in arms programs. SALT or no SALT, the Soviet Union will never allow America to regain that kind of superiority in power which would encourage it to act from positions of strength, still less to have the assurance that its counterforce superiority is great enough for it to launch a nuclear war at a relatively low risk, or use the threat of such a war as a shield to cover up acts of armed aggression with conventional weapons.

We realize that the American leadership is determined, for its part, not to allow the Soviet Union to acquire any notable strategic superiority. This is precisely why the SALT II Treaty, by reducing the possibility of either side breaking free "on the sly," to reach a position of superiority, responds to the security interests of both nations — provided, of course, that this security is seen as a peaceful environment for a quiet life rather than as one enabling unchecked "shows of force" or pressure on other nations from positions of strength.

## *Notes*

38. In 1974, the Pentagon tried to get then President Nixon to pursue at the SALT II talks in Moscow what he said "amounted to an unyielding hard line against any SALT agreement that did not ensure an overwhelming American advantage. It was a proposal that the Soviets were sure to reject out of hand." Richard Nixon, *Memoirs* (New York: Grosset and Dunlap, 1978), p. 1024.
39. "It is possible to demonstrate mathematically that a country with one ICBM with a yield of 25 megatons and a CPE (circular probable error) of .01 would have a sufficient countersilo kill capability (KN) to destroy 97 percent of the U.S. ICBM force. $KN = NY^{2/3}/(CPE)^2 = (1)(25)^{2/3}/(.01)^2 \sim 90{,}000$ (whereas a KN of only 82,080 is required to achieve a 97 percent probability of destruction of the U.S. ICBM force)," American military writers say, criticizing this sort of "logic." See Robert Kennedy and James A. Kuhlman, *The Quantitative Balance: A Qualitative Assessment* (Carlisle Barracks, Penn.: Strategic Studies Institute, U.S. Army War College, May 20, 1978), p. 8.
40. "Several years ago, for example, the Pentagon floated a story that the Soviets could so confine an attack on our land-based missiles as to kill only 800,000 people. A follow-up study conducted at the request of the committee resulted in revised estimates showing that up to 22 million could be killed, even if the Soviets attacked our Minuteman bases alone." Senator Frank Church, chairman of the U.S. Senate Committee on Foreign Relations, in "Strategic Arms Limitation Talks and Comprehensive Test Ban Negotiations," report to Senate Committee on Foreign Relations (Washington, GPO, 1978), p. 11.
41. According to James Schlesinger at the time he was U.S. Defense Secretary, the throw-weight of American ICBMs totalled nearly two million pounds. "U.S.-U.S.S.R. Strategic Policies," hearing before Senate Subcommittee on Arms Control, International Law and Organization Committee on Foreign Relations, 93rd Cong., 2nd session — top secret hearing held on March 4, 1974; sanitized and made public on April 4, 1974 (Washington: GPO, 1974), p. 5. Such a reliable source as the Pentagon's Joint Strategic Bomber Study states that the throw-weight of the U.S. strategic air force amounted to 21 million pounds toward the mid-1970s. Cong. Record, May 20, 1976, p. S7709. The throw-weight of the American SBMs — 691,000 pounds — has been calculated from reports on the throw-weight of the Polaris A-3 and the Poseidon-borne SBMs, published by American magazines on many occasions. With Trident-1 SBMs in service along with a certain reduction of the bomber fleet, the share of the submarine throw-weight of the U.S. strategic forces will somewhat increase in the aggregate throw-weight of these forces.
42. According to Wohlstetter's estimates, the major trend in the development of American strategic systems has been a systematic reduction of the aggregate megatonnage of strategic forces and a reduction of the mean charge of offensive nuclear warheads, with a simultaneous increase in the number of warheads themselves, in enough delivery vehicles to carry them, and in their enhanced accuracy. *Foreign Policy,* Nos. 15 and 16, 1974.
43. Cong. Record, Aug. 5, 1977. p. S14074.
44. Besides, more powerful and more accurate Mark 12A warheads are now being installed on Minuteman-3 missiles, while nuclear submarines carrying Poseidon missiles are beginning to be equipped with even more powerful and better targetable warheads.
45. *International Herald Tribune,* Jan. 6–7, 1979.
46. E. V. Rostow, *Policy Review,* 6 (Fall 1978), p. 45.
47. Rostow, p. 47.

## *Suggestions for Further Reading*

Brzezinski, Zbigniew. *Power and Principle* (New York: Farrar Straus & Giroux, 1983). Memoirs of Carter's national security adviser, the most hawkish senior member of the Carter team.

Carter, Jimmy. *Keeping the Faith* (New York: Bantam Books, 1982). President Carter's memoirs of his years in office.

Smith, Gaddis. *Morality, Reason and Power: American Diplomacy in the Carter Years* (New York: Hill and Wang, 1986).

A concise but comprehensive look at the period, its competing personalities, and their policy perspectives.

Tyroler, Charles, ed. *Alerting America: The Papers of the Committee on the Present Danger* (Washington, D.C.: Pergamon-Brassey's, 1984). Compilation of the writings of SALT II's most aggressive critics.

Vance, Cyrus. *Hard Choices* (New York: Simon and Schuster, 1983). Memoirs of Carter's secretary of state.

*Ten*

# ZERO HOUR

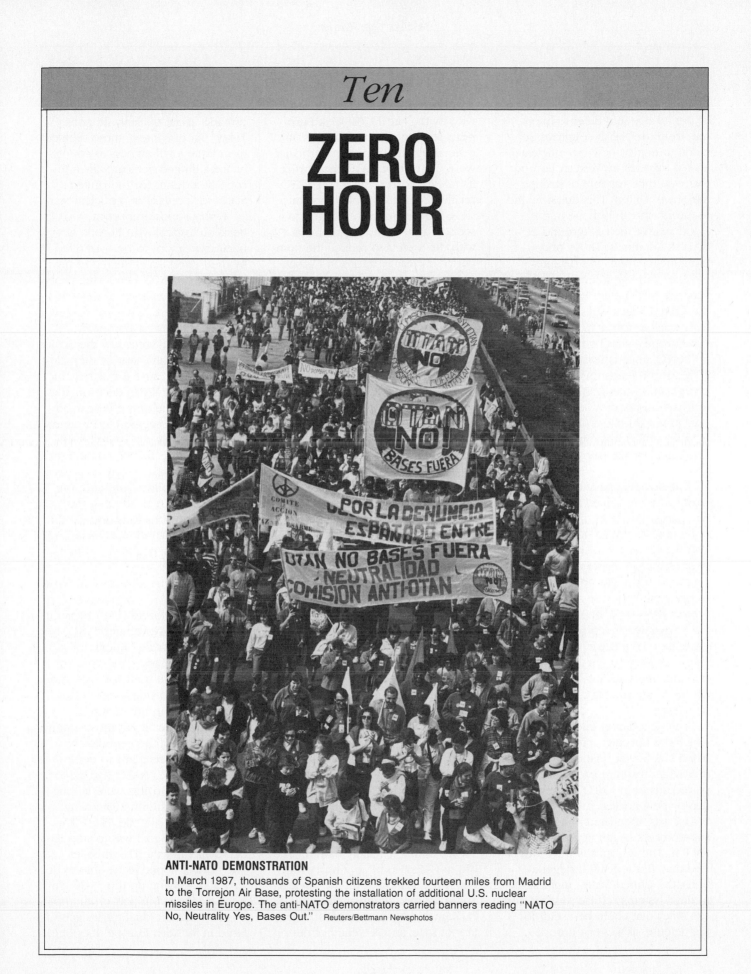

**ANTI-NATO DEMONSTRATION**

In March 1987, thousands of Spanish citizens trekked fourteen miles from Madrid to the Torrejon Air Base, protesting the installation of additional U.S. nuclear missiles in Europe. The anti-NATO demonstrators carried banners reading "NATO No, Neutrality Yes, Bases Out." Reuters/Bettmann Newsphotos

# INTRODUCTION

On December 12, 1979, a meeting of the foreign and defense ministers from the NATO countries decided to deploy new U.S. nuclear-armed missiles in Western Europe that would be capable of striking the Soviet Union. This decision and its aftermath can only be understood against the background of NATO's dilemmas: Those of coupling, negotiation, and détente.

The coupling dilemma — that of how the NATO allies can be sure the United States will use its strategic nuclear forces to defend Western Europe — has been a problem for NATO since at least the late 1950s. But it tends to fade into the background unless NATO is forced to focus attention on nuclear weapons. In the middle and late 1970s, a number of factors combined to bring nuclear weapons issues to the fore.

The Soviets had attained nuclear parity with the United States, and that parity had been officially sanctioned by the SALT I agreements. This increased the worries of some West European leaders that the United States might not be willing to risk New York City or Chicago to protect Paris or Bonn. Moreover, the Soviets were deploying a new generation of nuclear weapons targeted on Western Europe, most importantly the Backfire bomber and the SS-20 intermediate-range ballistic missile.

The negotiation dilemma — in which the Europeans feel at risk when U.S.-Soviet relations are good *and* when they are bad — also played a role in NATO's decision to deploy new nuclear missiles. After SALT I was negotiated in 1972, the superpowers began negotiations on SALT II. The Europeans were worried that, in the SALT II negotiations, the United States might agree to limit systems (cruise missiles, for example) that could be useful for the defense of Western Europe.

These were the main reasons why, by the late 1970s, West European leaders, West German Chancellor Helmut Schmidt in particular, were urging that NATO modernize its nuclear forces. But when NATO finally decided to deploy new missiles, the alliance also pledged to seek an arms control agreement with the Soviets to reduce the number of nuclear weapons in Europe. A major reason for this "negotiation track" of the dual track decision was the détente dilemma. Despite concerns about a Soviet nuclear buildup in Europe, the West Europeans wanted to do all they could to hold onto what they had gained from détente. Keeping the door open for negotiations seemed the best way to do so.

Despite NATO's efforts to balance modernization and negotiation, massive protests erupted in Western Europe after the dual decision. Why did this happen after more than fifteen years of almost no visible public concern about nuclear weapons? The simplest answer is that the West Europeans did not want nuclear weapons in their back yards. But the reality is more complicated. Until the dual track decision of 1979, concern about nuclear weapons had been largely limited to West European governments. During the era of détente, the European public had not focused on nuclear weapons or negotiations. They assumed that the balance of terror had been stabilized. The wide publicity received by the dual track decision brought home the European nuclear predicament once again.

In addition, the new Reagan administration alarmed many Europeans. It discarded the SALT II Treaty, calling it "fatally flawed," and did not seem to be in a hurry to begin negotiations with the Soviets. Some Reagan administration officials, including the president, secretary of state, and secretary of defense, made some less than careful remarks about nuclear weapons. Taken out of context, these seemed to indicate a willingness to countenance a limited nuclear war in Europe or a desire for the United States to "prevail" in a nuclear war.

Perhaps most important, NATO's decision to deploy in Europe new nuclear weapons to be controlled by the United States served to highlight one of NATO's enduring problems: the dependence of Western Europe on the U.S. nuclear forces. As long as the West Europeans felt that the United States saw the Soviet Union in the same way as they did, they had little cause for alarm. But because of the NATO decision and the new attitude of the Reagan administration, it seemed to the European public that the United States was taking risks for which the Europeans would have to pay. As a result of domestic political pressure on the missile issue, leaders of the West European nations pressed the Reagan administration to make progress in the negotiations with the Soviets.

U.S.-Soviet negotiations on what came to be called intermediate-range nuclear forces (INF) began in earnest in late November 1981. Progress was made difficult for a number of reasons. The most important was that until 1985 the motives of the two sides were so different that compromise was extremely difficult. Put most simply, the U.S. goal in the negotiations was to protect its plans to deploy the new missiles NATO had agreed to, unless the Soviets were willing to give up all intermediate-range missiles, especially the SS-20. The primary Soviet goal was to stop the deployment of the U.S. missiles. The Soviets hoped to be able to do so without giving up the SS-20. This hope was based in part on the opposition that the dual track decision faced in Western Europe. If political protest made it impossible for the new missiles to be deployed, the Soviets would not have to make concessions in the INF negotiations.

In early 1985, when the INF talks were resumed after an interruption of more than a year, there were finally some signs of movement. In particular, the Soviets seemed more willing to compromise than they were earlier. While it is impossible to know the exact reasons for this change, it appears to be due to several factors. Mikhail Gorbachev became the leader of the Soviet Union in early 1985, and he launched a number of initiatives in foreign policy. In addition, the Soviets probably wanted to use the INF talks as a carrot to encourage the Reagan administration to accept limits on the Strategic Defense Initiative (SDI). Finally, before 1983 the Soviets had a monopoly on INF missiles in Europe. By 1985 the Euromissiles were in place. The Soviets had failed to stop them. In addition, since the deployment had taken the momentum from the West European protest movement, it seemed unlikely that the missiles would be removed without the Soviet arms control concessions.

The new Soviet willingness to compromise helped move the negotiations forward. At a superpower summit in Washington, D.C., in December 1987, Reagan and Gorbachev signed an agreement eliminating intermediate-range and short-range missiles in Europe. The INF Treaty called for the United States to dismantle and destroy Pershing II and cruise missiles in Europe, and for the Soviet Union to dismantle and destroy the SS-20s deployed in Europe. The treaty closely resembled the zero option proposed by President Reagan at Western European urging in 1981. Interestingly, as the superpowers came close to agreement, NATO's dilemmas once again began to play a role. Some West European leaders, who in the early 1980s had worried that the Reagan administration was not doing enough to negotiate with the Soviets, in 1987 were worried that the United States was going too far in the negotiations. Ironically, a major task for the Reagan administration in 1987 was to convince the West Europeans that getting rid of nuclear missiles in Europe was a good idea.

# NATO'S DILEMMAS

## Europe Worries About NATO's Unevenness

### *Document 1*

Document 1, an article by Stanley Hoffman, professor of government and director of the Center for European Studies at Harvard University, reviews some of the enduring problems of the NATO alliance. Hoffman emphasizes NATO's "unevenness of political structure and organization," in particular that the Western Europeans are militarily dependent on U.S. nuclear forces for security. An important result of this unevenness is the European fear of being decoupled from the strategic balance — that is, the Europeans worry that the United States might not be willing to risk the survival of U.S. cities to protect Western Europe. Hoffman reviews the effects of these worries about coupling on alliance nuclear strategy and on arms control.

### 1 PERSISTENT PROBLEMS IN THE NATO ALLIANCE
### Stanley Hoffman

There are three Alliance continuities listed below, in order of decreasing importance: (1) a geopolitical unevenness in the Alliance, about which nothing can be done; (2) an unevenness of political structure and organization; and (3) a susceptibility of the Alliance to the environment.

The geographical unevenness is the most interesting. By unevenness, I mean that the two sides of the Atlantic experience in very different ways what political scientists call the "security dilemma." To put it bluntly, it is a problem of military dependency for the Europeans. Ever since the Alliance was established, the potential or real conventional imbalance between the Western Europeans and the forces on the other side (depending on one's estimates of Soviet strength) have been evident. This conventional imbalance is caused by two factors: first, the obvious factor of numbers — as much as the Europeans may try to mobilize by themselves, it is likely that the Russians could mobilize more. This problem is aggravated by geography. The Soviets, situated in the middle of Europe, are capable of hitting the vital centers of Western Europe, even with weapons of limited range. There is a vast glacis between the iron curtain and vital centers in the Soviet Union, whereas Western Europe begins right at the iron curtain. To correct this imbalance, the Europeans have depended on American nuclear forces for security.

Because of its geographic and demographic determinants, the imbalance cannot be reduced by rhetoric. Furthermore, it has a number of built-in effects, the most important being a fundamental lack of symmetry between U.S. and West European interests. The problem is one of defense versus deterrence. While Americans can coolly contemplate the defense of Europe, for most West

Europeans the defense of Europe means the destruction of Europe. The United States can envisage freely what it would do in Europe if deterrence fails. The Europeans, however, know that the failure of deterrence does not leave many happy alternatives. Thus, when de Gaulle expressed doubts in the early 1960s about the credibility of the American promise to consider Europe a part of the American turf, and when he refused to accept the notion of flexible response, he was — as often happened — merely expressing in extreme form the fears of most West Europeans.

Although the Europeans may have disagreed about the best deterrence strategy, there was general agreement about the need to place all possible eggs in the deterrence basket. Once one starts to talk about defense, one is talking about actual warfare; and actual warfare, even if it is merely a World War III version of World War II, is unacceptable for anyone living west of the iron curtain. This problem will remain unless (1) the geographical difference between Western Europe and the United States is annihilated in some way; (2) the United States could find a way to show not only the Russians (which, although difficult, is possibly the least complicated objective) but everyone else that Western Europe is exactly like Massachusetts, Montana, Kansas City, and Colorado; in other words, unless a way of treating the whole Atlantic Community as one block could be found.

The fundamental asymmetry in the way in which the two sides of the ocean view the possible failure of deterrence has generated a number of problematic effects. The first is the West Europeans' recurrent fear that the United States will drag them into military adventures for reasons that are not vital to Europe. . . .

The second fear is exactly the opposite, and the Europeans oscillate from one extreme to the other. When they are not afraid of being implicated by the Americans, they are afraid of being abandoned by them. These concerns have been evident in a number of ways. Sometimes they have appeared as an anguish that the French have been particularly good at stoking: e.g., the fear of a superpower duopoly, by which Western Europe would be left to the tender mercy of the two superpowers, with one power more present and pressing than the other. This fear was apparent during the end of the Pompidou years, when Mr. Kissinger and Mr. Brezhnev signed those many meaningless statements about mutual consultation should there be a threat of nuclear war, and about giving up the search for unilateral advantages. Another expression of the West European fear of abandonment was the great emotion that seized West Europeans during the years when Senator Mansfield was an amendment before he became an ambassador. Anxieties were caused by the possibility of a unilateral withdrawal of American forces from Europe.

There is a third fear that deserves to be examined separately — the fear of being "decoupled" from the central strategic balance. At first, it seems to be a milder variety of the fear of abandonment: it is the fear of not being seen as equivalent to Boston or Omaha. But in another sense the fear of being decoupled is different. To fear being treated separately from the way in which the Americans would treat an attack on American territory means to fear becoming a freefire zone. To tell the Soviets that the American strategic weapons will not, or not for a certain period of time, be used in the event of a war in Europe, seems to the West Europeans to weaken deterrence and to incite the Soviets to take greater risks. . . .

In contrast to the problem of a reticent Germany, there is the special problem of France, which has been anything but reticent. The French have, and are still developing, an atomic force of their own. This is indeed the logical conclusion to be deduced from the absolute priority that France gives to nuclear deterrence: if you are for nuclear deterrence, and if you doubt that the Americans will give that same priority to it or keep you under their strategic umbrella, then you create your own deterrent. This provides an insurance policy against the three fears I have mentioned. It is more difficult for Americans to decouple if your strategic nuclear force can try to oblige the Americans to recouple. You will feel less abandoned if you can believe in your capability to tear an arm off the Russian bear, as de Gaulle put it. And, finally, you have an independent insurance policy against being dragged into some affair you do not consider to be in your own interest.

In addition to this French atomic idiosyncrasy, there was another broader one, from which the French nuclear force actually derived: the French emphasis on an independent diplomacy and strategy. This is a legacy from the disastrous experiences of the interwar period, when France subordinated its foreign policy to that of England; when, in the war years, France submitted to the Nazis; and when de Gaulle fought against Anglo-Saxon predominance. Out of this French reassessment came the Fifth Republic's decision to withdraw from the integrated command structure of NATO and its refusal to put French tactical nuclear forces on German soil. These forces are considered an element in the nuclear deterrence of an attack on France, not as one ingredient in a flexible response to an attack on NATO (i.e., Germany) that might never reach the strategic nuclear level.

The third continuity is what I earlier called the susceptibility to the environment, or the hidden agendas (which have become quite public) of the Atlantic Alliance. The alliance did start primarily as a military pact, but soon everyone realized that military potential and military effectiveness depended on many other things as well. When Mr. Moynihan was (briefly) ambassador to NATO, he startled its members by explaining that priority should be given to the collective defense of the ecological environment, which was not exactly what the treaty of 1949 indicated.

In this realm, there have been a number of issues of lasting importance. The first one is the significance of the whole economic context since 1949. . . .

A final aspect of the environment with which the alliance has had to deal more and more openly, is the importance of internal political developments. From the beginning, the Atlantic Alliance was a vehicle by which the United States hoped to consolidate in the right direction the domestic political scene in Europe, by tying the countries of Western Europe to the American mast. The Alliance continues to play this role in France and Italy. In those countries and others like them, one of the yardsticks of Communist evolution is whether or not the Communists accept the maintenance of NATO, the maintenance of American bases, and the membership of their country in the Alliance. Conversely, the Alliance has always been susceptible to domestic crises; not only the crises in France in 1958 and the lingering Italian crisis in 1968, but also crises within the United States, which mark periods of uncertainty for the Alliance. . . .

A new and rather fierce debate has been generated by two questions. First, what are the effects or the potential effects on NATO of the vulnerability of Minuteman in the central strategic balance? We have all read assurances that the Soviet capacity to destroy Minuteman, which would leave us with the alternatives of either the destruction of Soviet cities (followed of course by the destruction of ours) or submission, will have a crippling effect on the U.S. position in the world. We have also read arguments that this scenario of Soviet triumph through nuclear blitz is a nightmarish fantasy. (I belong to this group.) There is a second question: What are the effects for the Europeans not only of Minuteman's approaching vulnerability but of the new special Soviet nuclear arsenal aimed specifically at Europe — the Backfire bomber and, of course, the SS-20? The Soviets now have the capability to use "Euro-specific" nuclear weapons, which gives what might be called limited strategic options to the Soviet Union. We do not possess such options because NATO's theater nuclear weapons cannot, on the whole, reach targets in the Soviet Union (only the British and French nuclear forces can). The Soviet Union's conventional superiority is no longer offset at either the central strategic level or the intermediate nuclear level. The Soviet Union always had short-range tactical nuclear options in Europe, as did the United States; and the Soviets always had the possibility of using intercontinental strategic missiles against the Europeans (as well as against the United States). The Soviets now have the possibility of using their new weapons for strategic options limited to Europe. This would not look as though they were beginning to resort to overall strategic nuclear war, as it might if they used some of their long-range ground- or submarine-launched missiles against Europe. (It is sometimes argued that the accuracy of the SS-20 allows the Soviets, for the first time, to launch a pure counterforce attack against weapons, forces, and other military targets in Western Europe. But the notion of pure counterforce in an area as densely populated as Europe makes very little sense. This is not where the innovative aspects of the SS-20 or the Backfire are.)

These new questions accentuate the rift between two camps within the Alliance. Some people still believe that any actual warfighting in Europe would be disastrous; they feel that for NATO to give itself a counterforce capability of its own in reply to the new Soviet capability would be a mistake, for if it signaled a willingess to fight a limited, progressive war of attrition over Europe with nuclear weapons, the continent would be destroyed. They believe that the best reply to the Soviet build-up is the reassertion of America's willingness to use its *strategic* forces for the protection of Europe against Soviet attacks, including attacks with nuclear weapons of a range that excludes the United States. On the other side are those who believe that it is necessary to provide NATO with the means to fight such a war — to plan, in effect, a flexible response that includes counterforce strikes against the other side. They believe in the necessity of planning such a war first because the Soviets may be planning to do so and second, because the old strategy of relying on mutual assured destruction is even less plausible now, both because of the new Soviet arsenal in Europe and because of the changes in the central strategic balance. In other words, there must be a possibility of a piecemeal war. What do you do, to use the old cliché, if the Soviets just grab Hamburg? (Why they would, I have never understood.) Do you reply by launching absolutely everything, or do you need a capability comparable to the adversary's to fight a limited war? . . .

. . . The Europeans are therefore faced with the following dilemma. If the Alliance's reply to the new Soviet arsenal and to Minuteman vulnerability is mere complacency, why should the Europeans need to worry, as long as the Americans still have a capability of inflicting tens of millions of casualities on the Russians? This would create, I think, a fear of being abandoned: the fear that the Americans might not resort to their strategic arsenal, and that the Europeans would be left with inferior means. On the other hand, if the Americans, in order to meet the fear of abandoment, start building up a new NATO-specific nuclear arsenal, there would arise again the fear of decoupling — the fear that the Americans would adopt these new weapons systems so as to be better able to fight a war limited to Europe only, sparing their own territory. And in addition to the possibility of decoupling, there would still be no guarantee that the Europeans would not be abandoned after all, since the resort to all these weapons would remain under American control. One rediscovers the MLF dilemmas at a higher level of anxiety, and with less ability to maintain ambiguity than in the 1960s.

The second new problem on the strategic scene is the interference of arms control with strategy....

The real problem is posed by the SALT process. Here there are two fears among the Europeans. First, the fear that has been forcibly expressed recently by Raymond Aron that the SALT process, by its very nature, leads or may lead to some kind of decoupling. The Americans and the Soviets discuss the strategic balance by themselves; they leave Europe out. This in itself is a form of decoupling. They make decisions that may be wise for the global balance but very unwise for the local one. And this is precisely the second fear: SALT may leave the Euro-strategic balance, not only separate from the central one, but worse off, by closing off certain options for NATO, while no ceilings are put on Soviet nuclear systems aimed specifically at Europe. This problem has been raised during the SALT II discussions of limits on cruise missiles.

## Nuclear Parity and Nuclear Coupling

### *Documents 2 and 3*

**In document 2, a selection from a 1979 speech by Henry Kissinger at the International Institute of Strategic Studies (IISS), the former national security adviser and secretary of state warns that NATO's strategic situation has been fundamentally changed because the Soviets have attained strategic parity. Kissinger implies that NATO can no longer be as sure of the U.S. nuclear guarantee as it once was. Kissinger also warns NATO not to make too many concessions to preserve détente with the Soviet Union. Document 3 is a speech given a week later by McGeorge Bundy, national security adviser to President Kennedy. Bundy says that the strategic guarantee is as strong as ever. It has not been weakened by parity and does not depend on the deployment of new nuclear weapons in Europe. Bundy says the guarantee depends on the visible presence of U.S. troops in Europe and on the risk that any war would become nuclear.**

### 2 SPEECH–IISS CONFERENCE Henry A. Kissinger September 1979

First, at the risk of repeating myself, let me state once again what I take to be the fundamental change in the strategic situation as far as the United States is concerned and then examine the implications for NATO. When NATO was created, the United States possessed an overwhelming strategic nuclear superiority. That is to say, for a long period of time we were likely to prevail in a nuclear war, certainly if we struck first and for a decade perhaps even if we struck second; we were in a position to wipe out the Soviet strategic forces and to reduce the counter-blow to us to an acceptable level. And that situation must have looked more ominous to the Soviet Union even than it looked favourable to us.

If we think back to the Cuban missile crisis of 1962 which all of the policy-makers of the time were viewing with a consciousness of an approaching Armageddon, one is almost seized with nostalgia for the ease of their decisions. At that time the Soviet Union had about seventy long-range missiles that took ten hours to fuel, which was a longer period of time than it would take our airplanes to get to the Soviet Union from forward bases.

Today, or even in the Middle East crisis of 1973, when we had a superiority of about eight to one in missile warheads, if one compares this with the current and foreseeable situation, we are approaching a point where it is difficult to assign a clear military objective to American strategic forces in a strategic nuclear exchange. In the 1950s, and for much of the 1960s, NATO was protected by a preponderance in American strategic striking power which was capable of disarming the Soviet Union, and by a vast American superiority in theatre nuclear forces, although, as I will discuss, we never had a comprehensive theory for using theatre nuclear forces. Since all intelligences services congenitally overestimate the rationality of the decision-making process which they are analysing, it is probable that the Soviet Union made more sense out of our nuclear deployment in Europe than we were able to make ourselves. In any event, it was numerically superior. And it was in that strategic framework that the allied ground forces on the continent were deployed.

No one disputes any longer that in the 1980s and perhaps even today, but surely in the 1980s — the United States will no longer be in a strategic position to reduce a Soviet counter-blow against the United States to tolerable levels. Indeed, one can argue that the United States will not be in a position in which attacking the Soviet strategic forces makes any military sense, because it may represent a marginal expenditure of our own strategic striking force without helping greatly in ensuring the safety of our forces....

...In the 1980s we will be in a position where (1) many of our own strategic forces, including all of our land-based ICBMs, will be vulnerable and (2) such an insignificant percentage of Soviet strategic forces will be vulnerable as not to represent a meaningful strategic attack option for the United States. Whether that means that the Soviet Union intends to attack the United States or not is certainly not my point. I am making two points.

First, that the change in the strategic situation that is produced by our limited vulnerability is more fundamental for the United States than even the total vulnerability would be for the Soviet Union because our strategic doctrine has relied extraordinarily, perhaps exclusively on our superior strategic power. The Soviet Union has never relied on its superior strategic power. It has always depended more on its local and regional superiority. Therefore, even an equivalence in destructive power, even assured destruction for both sides is a revolution in NATO doctrine as we have known it. It is a fact that must be faced....

...And therefore I would say, which I might not say in office, the European allies should not keep asking us to multiply strategic assurances that we cannot possibly mean, or if we do mean, we should not want to execute because if we execute, we risk the destruction of civilization. Our strategic dilemma isn't solved with reassurances. There is no point in complaining about declining American will or criticizing this or that American administration, for we are facing an objective crisis and it must be remedied....

...All Western governments must demonstrate and must conduct a serious effort to relax tensions and to negotiate outstanding differences. But there is something deeper involved in the West. There is, in the West, a tendency to treat detente quite theatrically; that is to say, not as a balancing of national interests and negotiations on the basis of strategic realities but rather as an exercise in strenuous goodwill in which one removes, by understanding, the suspiciousness of a nation that otherwise would have no motive to attack. This tendency to treat detente as an exercise in psychotherapy, or as an attempt in good personal relations, or as an effort in which individual leaders try to gain domestic support by proving that they have a special way in Moscow—this is disastrous for the West. And it is the corollary to the assured destruction theory, in the sense that it always provides an alibi for not doing what must be done. Against all evidence we were told that ABM would ruin the chances of arms control. The fact was that Kosygin in 1967 told President Johnson that the idea of not engaging in defence was one of the most ridiculous propositions that he had ever heard. By 1970, when he had an ABM programme, however inadequate, it was the only subject the Soviet Union was willing to discuss with us in SALT. When we gave up the B-1 we asked the Soviets to make a reciprocal gesture. We have yet to see it. When we gave up the neutron weapon, we were told that this position was correlation to the deployment of our SS-20. (If so it was an inverse correlation to the SS-20.) And now we are told that of course we are all for theatre nuclear forces. But first let us have another effort at negotiation. I saw a report about a distinguished American Senator returning from Moscow the other day who said: "It is virtually certain that cruise missiles will be deployed and that NATO will undertake a build-up of its own unless negotiations to a new Treaty are begun soon." If this is our position, all the Soviets have to do is to begin a negotiation to keep us from doing what they are already doing, negotiation or no negotiation.

Such a version of detente leads to unilateral disarmament for the West. I favour negotiation on theatre nuclear forces, but the talks will accelerate the more rapidly as we build such theatre nuclear forces. Then we can consider some numerical balance or some deployment pattern, but we cannot defer the strategic decisions we must make for the sake of initiating a negotiation. We must have a detente, but the detente must be on a broad front in the sense that all of the NATO nations must pursue comparable policies. The illusion that some countries can achieve a preferential position with the USSR is theoretically correct, but it is the best means of dividing the Alliance. The illusion that some subjects can be separated for individual treatment of detente while conflict goes on in all other areas, that turns detente into a safety valve for aggression.

## 3 KEYNOTE ADDRESS–IISS CONFERENCE McGeorge Bundy 1979

This is not the place to sort out the doctrines of NATO, nor the issues of nuclear modernization. They are not trivial. Even though there is an inherent tension between military desires and peace-time budgets, in all NATO countries, even though NATO has served its purpose without ever coming close to its own force goals, and even though there is inescapable unpredictability in planning for any kind of third European war, there is some threshold of strength and plausibility beneath which NATO forces should not fall. So I support the general effort of the last two years.

But as to the future of the strategic deterrent over Europe, I find myself both conservative and optimistic. In its essence it has never been a separate force. For many years NATO's most truly strategic weapons have been their assigned American submarines, and they in turn have always been only as reliable as the American guarantee. There is no way of changing this reality by new deployments of long-range weapons on land and no reason for Americans to press that mode on their allies. Nor is the basic guarantee best measured by comparing the numbers of long-range American-controlled weapons in NATO alone against SS-20s and *Backfires*. Remembering that this strategic world is ineluctably bipolar, we must recognize that in any moment of serious stress neither Washington nor Moscow is at all likely to regard such American weapons as a separately usable or clearly limited kind of force. Any American-controlled weapons that can reach the Soviet Union will almost surely be all alike to them both.

It follows that the strategic protection of Europe is as strong or as weak as the American strategic guarantee, no matter what American weapons are deployed under NATO. (I do not here exclude a useful contribution from the existence of British and French weapons, but that is not a major variable in the current debate, however one estimates it.) And I believe the effectiveness of this American guarantee is likely to be just as great in the future as in the past. It has worked, after all, through thirty years, and, as we have seen, twenty of those years have been a time of underlying parity in mutual destructive power.

The enduring effectiveness of the American guarantee has not depended on strategic superiority. It has depended instead on two great facts: the visible deployment of major American military forces in Europe, and the very evident risk that any large-scale engagement between Soviet and American forces would rapidly and uncontrollably become general, nuclear, and disastrous. The most serious assault on the strategic umbrella in those years was the campaign of Senator Mansfield for troop reduction, and I take it as a very good sign that with his retirement from the Senate the reduction of our military engagement in Europe has disappeared as a political issue.

Now of course no one *knows* that a major engagement in Europe would escalate to the strategic nuclear level. But the essential point is the opposite; no one can possibly know it would not. Precisely because these weapons are different, and precisely because the existing balance in Europe is endurable to both sides, even a small risk of a large nuclear exchange is much too much. I am a believer in what Michael Howard has called "Healey's Theorem," on the deterrent power of even an uncertain threat: "if there is one chance in a hundred of nuclear weapons being used, the odds would be enough to deter an aggressor even if they were not enough to reassure an ally."[1] And to reassure the ally I would point to the reality of my presence, the reality of my continuing attention to increased effort, and the reality of the strategic stability. I would also point out that there is in fact great deterrent strength in detente itself. Who among us really believes that the Soviet Union is eager to stir us all back to the levels of arms expenditure we reached after Korea and Sputnik? . . .

My conclusion, then, is that marginal changes in strategic numbers are no threat to the American strategic guarantee in NATO. That guarantee rests not on numbers of warheads but on an engagement that poses a wholly unacceptable and innately unpredictable risk to the other side. Nor do I think the real effectiveness of this deterrent is highly sensitive to the ebb and flow of European confidence in any particular American administration. Certainly two-way trust across the Atlantic is important, and certainly NATO has an unhappy history of recurrent misunderstanding. But the neutron bomb is not the shield of Europe. That shield is the *American* Triad believably engaged by 300,000 Americans in place. . . .

## Note

1. Michael Howard, "The Relevance of Traditional Strategy," *Foreign Affairs,* 51, 2, p. 262, Jan. 1973.

# NATO's Dilemmas and the Deployment Decision

### *Document 4*

**Strategic analyst Leon Sigal reviews the relationship between NATO's dilemmas and the decision to deploy Euromissiles. He notes that NATO has to balance its political and military missions. That is, NATO wants to be militarily strong enough to deter the Soviets from attacking; NATO also does not want to take actions that might greatly increase tensions with the Soviet Union. The NATO decision to deploy new missiles brought the inherent tension between NATO's military and political missions to the surface.**

## 4 A FAUSTIAN BARGAIN
## Leon V. Sigal

In December 1979 NATO foreign and defense ministers meeting in Brussels decided to deploy new American nuclear-armed cruise and ballistic missiles in Europe, missiles capable of striking deep into the USSR from bases in Great Britain, West Germany, Italy, Belgium, and the Netherlands. At the same time they decided to have the United States seek an arms control agreement with the Soviet Union on these and other nuclear weapons of less than intercontinental range.

The decision to tie nuclear deployments to arms control seemed a Faustian bargain to many observers. Those who saw peace in Europe threatened by growing Soviet military strength considered arms control an impediment to NATO's efforts to redress any perceived imbalance of forces. Others, who saw no basic shift in the military balance, regarded peace in Europe as jeopardized by political differences between East and West that deployment of the new missiles would exacerbate. They wanted to ameliorate if not resolve these differences through mutual accommodation, including negotiations of limits on the nuclear arsenals of both sides at the lowest possible levels. The December 1979 decision satisfied few in either group. Buffeted from both right and left, it seemed politically unstable from its inception.

Yet for NATO to have sought either nuclear buildup or arms control alone would have made little sense politically or militarily. Politically, either decision would have been unsustainable. Negotiations to limit Soviet theater nuclear forces would have had little chance of success without the leverage created by the prospect of at least some new NATO deployment, unless the United States were willing to reduce some of its strategic forces in return for reductions in Soviet theater nuclear forces. And deployment without a good-faith attempt at arms control would not have mustered even the tepid public and parliamentary support it now has.

Militarily, the proposed deployment of a modest number of U.S. missiles in Europe seemed to many to promise little improvement in the nuclear component of NATO's strategy of flexible response. For most Europeans the means at America's disposal were not in doubt, but some did question the willingness to use those means, especially strategic nuclear weapons based in the United States and at sea, in Europe's behalf. For the United States to threaten nuclear escalation in order to deter hostilities in Europe, as called for in NATO's strategy, no longer seemed wholly credible after the early 1960s when the United States became vulnerable to Soviet nuclear retaliation. Just how the deployment of new American missiles would restore that credibility — or what NATO experts call "coupling" American nuclear might to European security — was never quite clear. It was clear, however, that European anxiety would persist whether new U.S. nuclear weapons were not deployed at all or whether they were deployed and were followed by a Soviet counterdeployment that added to the number of missiles it had already fielded. For the United States then to deploy additional weapons would bring the size of its nuclear arsenal in Europe to a point at which doubt would only grow anew about its willingness to use strategic nuclear forces, as distinct from European-based nuclear forces. One way out for NATO, it seemed, was to achieve negotiated limits on the theater nuclear forces of both sides. Whether those limits were achievable was open to question.

Many of the expressed objections to the 1979 decision masked deeper reservations about the military and political wisdom of NATO's course. The decision underscored the assumption, as prevalent in official circles as in the public mind, that nuclear deterrence alone had preserved the peace in Europe for the past three decades. Because this assumption is not subject to disproof and because it diverts attention from contemplating the consequences of a failure of deterrence, it offers some comfort. Yet it is simplistic, perhaps dangerously so.

Another equally plausible explanation for the durability of the peace in Europe starts with the mutual pledge of the United States and fourteen European states to come to each other's defense and to prepare accordingly through an enduring, possibly permanent alliance. The symbol and embodiment of that mutual pledge are the standing armies — American, British, French, and German — on the central front. These armies are NATO's first line of defense, and it is just as plausible that they, not nuclear weapons, are its principal deterrent to aggression. Both by declared strategy and accepted practice, NATO depends upon initial use of conventional deterrence in the event of attack by Warsaw Pact countries. And even if conventional strength were insufficient by itself to disabuse a would-be aggressor, a robust conventional defense that would make war in Europe more deadly than any that has yet been fought lends the ultimate deterrent — the threat to initiate use of nuclear weapons — whatever credibility it may have.

Those armies and the alliance they defend create a bulwark against two historic sources of war in Europe: a Germany too weak to defend itself against depredation by its neighbors or a Germany too strong to be contained by them. NATO not only guards West Germany against external menace but also weaves it securely into a web of military relationships, giving it no reason and no capacity to act on its own militarily. The alliance thus removes a source of insecurity for all West Germany's neighbors, not the least of them the Soviet Union and its allies. For West Germany to acquire nuclear weapons of its own would revive fears of its strength and would unsettle European security. If it were to loosen its ties to the West, however, and to renounce basing nuclear weapons on its soil, West Germany would raise almost as fearful a prospect of weakness and uncertainty in central Europe. Yet the postwar political settlement, a divided Germany without all the means of securing its own future, remains a historical anomaly. West German security and European security are thereby entwined in the alliance with the United States.

The unity of that alliance, based on members' acceptance of shared risk, remains its fundamental source of strength. America's allies in Europe add formidable military, economic, and political resources to its capacity to secure the blessings of liberty. To be sure, providing for the common defense does bring with it recurrent irritations, but they are minor compared to the distress that would exist if that defense were not sought in common. Nothing so threatens the unity of the alliance, however, as the possibility of a decision to use nuclear weapons. Were those weapons — their stationing or their potential use — to disrupt that unity, their sheer destructive force could not offset the resulting loss of security. Worse yet, nothing so undermines public support for NATO as a strategy that contemplates relying on those weapons for security. Whenever they come to public attention, nuclear weapons are a source of friction in alliance politics and disaffection in domestic politics.

That disaffection is dangerous. Unless a nation's military strategy enjoys widespread public acceptance, its government may well lack the determination to provide the means to sustain it and the will to carry it out. Without political legitimacy, strategy itself collapses, especially in the nuclear era when the sacrifices demanded by what passes for strategy are potentially enormous. That relationship between public approval and military strategy holds as true for alliances as it does for individual nations.

Michael Howard, the distinguished military historian, has rightly called attention to the often neglected social dimensions of strategy. In an address to the 1982 conference of the International Institute for Strategic Studies in The Hague, he noted that "for an appreciable number of Europeans, what was once seen as the prime requirement of deterrence, that is, the commitment of American power to the defense of Western Europe, no longer provides the political reassurance that once it did; in some respects indeed the exact opposite."[2] There is now a rather sharp disjunction between what Howard calls deterrence and reassurance: "The object of deterrence is to persuade an adversary that the costs to him of seeking a military solution to his political problems will far outweigh the benefits. The object of reassurance is to persuade one's own people, and those of one's allies, that the benefits of military action, or preparation for it, will outweigh the costs."[3]

The source of the disjunction between deterrence and reassurance is the mutual vulnerability that nuclear weapons have imposed on the superpowers and their allies. The vulnerability causes enduring contradictions in NATO's military doctrine, its military posture and practices, and its military and political course, contradictions that are harder and harder to ignore. Mutual vulnerability calls into question the very notion of strategy, in Clausewitz's sense of the rational economy of force applied to political ends. Apart from deterring the use of nuclear weapons by NATO's adversary, what political ends could nuclear weapons serve for which their use and the resulting retaliation would not be grossly disproportionate? That question underlies the doubts about NATO's doctrine of first use of nuclear weapons — that NATO is prepared to respond to conventional attack by initiating nuclear war. And the greater the attention paid to the doctrine, the more profound the doubts. The very logic of the doctrine generates a series of dilemmas that the decision to deploy new American missiles, far from resolving, only makes more salient. The consequent tepid public acceptance of NATO doctrine has thus been far from reassuring.

The mutual vulnerability of East and West also has a critical bearing on NATO's military posture and practices. Deterrence alone no longer suffices as the sole criterion for procuring nuclear forces, putting them into the field, and planning for their potential use. An equally important consideration is military stability. NATO cannot amass weapons to deter the USSR and its allies from deliberately going to war without also considering whether the quality or quantity of those weapons might so threaten the Warsaw Pact as to appear provocative. In a crisis, that could give rise to a vicious circle in which both sides would feel compelled to use nuclear weapons before the other side does. NATO must therefore size and configure its forces so that neither side could calculate an advantage from going to war deliberately. At the same time it must avoid a force posture and war plans that would increase the risk of inadvertent war. Under conditions of mutual vulnerability, both deterrence and stability must be criteria for NATO's own security.

Stable deterrence poses no logical contradiction, but it does pose a practical one, a consequence of the forces NATO has chosen to deploy in the past and the way it has postured them. The new missile deployments may not bring NATO much closer to satisfying the requirements of stable deterrence because of the compulsion they exert on both sides to preempt in a crisis. Indeed, the perverse consequences for stability of putting missiles in Europe within range of the USSR have long been recognized by European statesmen. Helmut Schmidt, for one, noted that "everyone capable of objective reasoning must concede that the stationing of enemy I.R.B.M.s, so to speak, on its very threshold (Turkey), must produce the psychological effect of a provocation on any great power. One need only imagine how the Americans would react if the Soviets were to station I.R.B.M.s in Cuba."[4] Those words were published in early 1962, shortly before the missile crisis.

Mutual vulnerability also underscores what has long been a condition of international relations — that military stability, while necessary, is not sufficient for security. Political stability is also essential. The pressure for mutual political accommodation or détente is acknowledgment of states' interdependence for security and insecurity in the nuclear age. The concern that adding to armaments can only exacerbate political tensions is valid. Just as valid is the concern that too great a preoccupation with political accommodation can jeopardize popular support for the military preparations essential to secure the material basis for that accommodation, a military balance of power. Again the contradiction is not a logical but a practical one. What is the current state of the military balance and what is the proper mix of policy between deterrence and détente under those circumstances? Finding answers to these questions provides an enduring source of friction within the alliance.

The December 1979 decision forced all these military and political dilemmas to the surface. They are addressed in the chapters to come. . . .

More than a few participants and observers have wondered whether NATO could ever implement its December 1979 decision and whether the alliance could survive failure to do so. Others have questioned whether its implementation was worth the risk to alliance unity and have called for undoing the Faustian bargain. The decision to pursue both deployment and arms control was not the first occasion on which nuclear choices have opened profound divisions in the alliance, nor will it be the last.

## Notes

2. Michael Howard, "Reassurance and Deterrence. Western Defense in the 1980s," *Foreign Affairs,* vol. 61 (Winter 1982/83), p. 315.
3. *Ibid.,* p. 317.
4. Helmut Schmidt, *Defense or Retaliation: A German View* (Praeger, 1962), p. 27.

# NATO'S DECISION TO DEPLOY NEW NUCLEAR WEAPONS

## The Threat of the SS-20 and Backfire

### *Document 5*

**This excerpt from a 1981 article by Harvard policy analyst Gregory Treverton describes the changes in Soviet INF that worried many West Europeans. Treverton points out the improved capabilities of the SS-20 and Backfire. He also notes European worries about Soviet shorter-range nuclear systems.**

## 5 THE SOVIET THREAT TO EUROPE
## Gregory Treverton

There is more continuity to the Soviet continental threat than is implied by public discussion of the SS-20. What makes a difference now is the new Soviet continental capabilities in combination with changes in the strategic balance and developments at other levels of TNF. Unquestionably, the most important change is the emergence, and clear recognition, of something like strategic parity between the United States and the Soviet Union. Parity has raised starkly the credibility of the coupling of the American strategic deterrent to the defence of Europe.

The United States could be counted upon to fire missiles from her strategic arsenal — thereby putting her cities at some risk — in response to a Soviet nuclear strike on Western Europe so long as the United States possessed clear nuclear superiority. Now, it is argued, Europe cannot be sure of the American response. The fear is of long standing; parity has sharpened it, and ICBM vulnerability gives it additional analytic justification. SALT is less a cause of the current concern than a precipitant. It has directed attention to nuclear deterrence in general. By emphasizing what aspects of the nuclear balance are being negotiated, it also underscores what is being excluded, especially Soviet "medium" range weapons.

The second set of changes from the mid-1960s is the new continental weapons that the Soviet Union has now begun to deploy against Western Europe (and China), primarily but not exclusively the SS-20 mobile IRBM and the *Backfire* bomber. Militarily these weapons give the Soviet Union new kinds of options in attacking Western Europe. Each SS-20 has 3 MIRV, and is both mobile (and so less vulnerable) and more accurate than the SS-4s and SS-5s it supersedes: its accuracy has been reported to be as good as 440 feet over a 2,500 mile range, and its range is over 3,000 miles. This yield of an SS-20 warhead is still large — 150 KT, the same as *Minuteman* — but it is much lower than the megaton yield of the SS-4s and SS-5s. Hence it is somewhat more selective and so more credible as a theatre weapon for attacking military targets while reducing collateral damage. Some 220 were deployed in mid-1981; and the annual rate of increase is between 50 and 60. Two hundred would provide as many warheads as the existing force of SS-4s and SS-5s. With an allowance for new targets, and assuming the phasing out of the older missiles, that would suggest a force in the neighborhood of 300, a number the Soviet Union would reach by the end of 1982.

A third change — and one too little discussed in the current debate — is the modernization of Soviet shorter-range TNF. The Soviet Union has some 1,300 nuclear missile launchers among her forces in Eastern Europe, with ranges from 10-85 miles for the *FROG,* 50-185 miles for the *Scud,* to 500 miles for the *Scaleboard* (all the names are the NATO terms). None of those systems is of recent vintage; the first *Scud* were deployed in 1957, and the most recent, the *Scaleboard,* in 1969. The Soviet Union is developing and deploying successors for all three missiles — the SS-21 for *FROG,* the SS-22 for *Scaleboard* and the SS-23 for *Scud.* Moreover, the Soviet Union is now deploying nuclear-capable artillery, a NATO monopoly in the past, and has an impressive array of modern nuclear-capable strike fighters and medium bombers with range/payload characteristics to cover Western Europe, mostly at low level.

All these new Soviet shorter-range weapons are more accurate, more mobile and have a wider choice of range than their predecessors, and they are also likely to have lower yields. The problems this Soviet modernization poses for NATO are somewhat different to those raised by the SS-20, but the effect may be much the same; targets in Western Europe are now threatened by a whole series of Soviet nuclear systems, not just the SS-20, the *Backfire* and the older M/IRBM. That may give rise to the possibility that NATO would either be deterred from using nuclear weapons in a losing conventional conflict, or no less disturbing, that NATO's existing nuclear delivery systems would be destroyed before they could be used.

So long as NATO was clearly superior to the Soviet Union in shorter-range TNF, Soviet leaders could never be sure that NATO would not use tactical nuclear weapons first, almost irrespective of uncertainties about the balance of nuclear force at higher levels of escalation. Now, the prospective ability of the Soviet Union to respond effectively at shorter ranges in a nuclear war that might be limited to Europe may deter NATO from using nuclear weapons at all.

Geography imposes another asymmetry, to NATO's disadvantage: West Germany (or Holland or France) understandably may feel that any nuclear weapon that can strike them is "strategic," whether the weapon is an SS-20 fired from the Soviet Union or an SS-21 fired from a short distance inside the East German border. By contrast, none of NATO's current European inventory of land-based missiles can reach beyond Eastern Europe into the Soviet Union and few of NATO's nuclear-capable aircraft combine the necessary range with a sufficiently high assurance of penetration.

## West German Concerns About the Nuclear Balance

### *Document 6*

The most forceful and influential statement of European concerns about the growing arsenal of Soviet weapons targeted on Western Europe was this speech by then chancellor of West Germany Helmut Schmidt. Schmidt argued that because the SALT process had formalized strategic parity, SALT had neutralized the effect of strategic nuclear weapons. Therefore, the importance of shorter-range nuclear weapons (like the SS-20 and Backfire) had increased, and the Soviet advantage in these systems was especially dangerous. To deal with this problem, Schmidt argued, NATO might have to deploy new weapons of its own. Schmidt also called for negotiations with the Soviet Union to place limits on the numbers of such weapons.

### 6 SPEECH–IISS CONFERENCE Helmut Schmidt, Chancellor of West Germany October 1977

Most of us will agree that political and military balance is the prerequisite of our security, and I would warn against the illusion that there may be grounds for neglecting that balance. Indeed, it is not only the prerequisite for our security but also for fruitful progress in East-west détente.

In the first place we should recognize that — paradoxical as it may sound — there is a closer proximity between a hazardous arms race, on the one hand, and a successful control of arms, on the other, than even before. There is only a narrow divide between the hope for peace and the danger of war.

Second, changed strategic conditions confront us with new problems. SALT codifies the nuclear strategic balance between the Soviet Union and the United States. To put it another way: SALT neutralizes their strategic nuclear capabilities. In Europe this magnifies the significance of the disparities between East and West in nuclear tactical and conventional weapons.

Third, because of this we must press ahead with the Vienna negotiations on mutual balanced force reductions (MBFR) as an important step toward a better balance of military power in Europe.

No one can deny that the principle of parity is a sensible one. However, its fulfillment must be the aim of all arms-limitation and arms-control negotiation, and it must apply to all categories of weapons. Neither side can agree to diminish its security unilaterally.

It is of vital interest to us all that the negotiations between the two superpowers on the limitation and reduction of nuclear strategic weapons should continue and lead to a lasting agreement. The nuclear powers have a special, and overwhelming responsibility in this field. On the other hand, we in Europe must be particularly careful to insure that these negotiations do not neglect the components of NATO's deterrence strategy.

We are all faced with the dilemma of having to meet the moral and political demand for arms limitation while at the same time maintaining a fully effective deterrent to war. We are not unaware that both the United States and the Soviet Union must be anxious to remove threatening strategic developments from their relationship. But strategic arms limitations confined to the United States and the Soviet Union will inevitably impair the security of the West European members of the alliance vis-à-vis Soviet military superiority in Europe if we do not succeed in removing the disparities of military power in Europe parallel to the SALT negotiations. So long as this is not the case we must maintain the balance of the full range of deterrence strategy. The alliance must, therefore, be ready to make available the means to support its present strategy, which is still the right one, and to prevent any developments that could undermine the basis of this strategy.

At the meeting of Western heads of state and government in London last May I said that the more we stabilize strategic nuclear parity between East and West, which my Government has always advocated, the greater will be the necessity to achieve a conventional equilibrium as well.

Today, again in London, let me add that when the SALT negotiations opened we Europeans did not have a clear enough view of the close connection between parity of strategic nuclear weapons, on the one hand, and tactical nuclear and conventional weapons on the other, or if we did, we did not articulate it clearly enough. Today we need to recognize clearly the connection between SALT and MBFR and to draw the necessary practical conclusions.

At the same meeting in May I said that there were, in theory, two possible ways of establishing a conventional balance with the Warsaw Pact states. One would be for the Western Alliance to undertake a massive buildup of forces and weapons systems; the other for both NATO and the Warsaw Pact to reduce their force strength and achieve an overall balance at a lower level. I prefer the latter.

The Vienna negotiations have still not produced any concrete agreement. Since they began the Warsaw Pact has, if anything, increased the disparities in both conventional and tactical nuclear forces. Up to now the Soviet Union has given no clear indication that she is willing to accept the principle of parity for Europe, as she did for SALT, and thus make the principle of renunciation of force an element of the military balance as well.

Until we see real progress on MBFR, we shall have to rely on the effectiveness of deterrence. It is in this context and no other that the public discussion in all member states of the Western alliance about the "neutron weapon" has to be seen. We have to consider whether the "neutron weapon" is of value to the alliance as an additional element of the deterrence strategy, as a means of preventing war. But we should not limit ourselves to that examination. We should also examine what relevance and weight this weapon has in our efforts to achieve arms control.

For the first time in history, arms control negotiations are being conducted when there exists a weapon capable of destroying all living things. Failure of such negotiations can no longer be compensated for by banking on military victory. That is why it is of such crucial importance that all should realize the seriousness of the Vienna negotiations, and why results must be achieved there. I would like to list seven "musts" and "must nots" for these negotiations:

1. Both sides, all participants in the MBFR negotiations, must state their willingness to bring the negotiations to a positive conclusion and to be party to reductions on an equal basis.
2. Priority must be given to the aim — and it must be achieved without delay — of preventing any further increase in the military confrontation, and thus dispelling apprehensions.
3. The threat of a surprise attack must be eliminated.
4. The confidence building measures voluntarily agreed at the CSCE must be accepted with binding effect.
5. It must remain the principal objective of MBFR to achieve, by means of reductions, a balance of forces at a lower level.
6. Force reductions must be oriented to the principle of parity and must be verifiable. Parity and collectivity must be recognized as the fundamental and determining principles.
7. The capability of both alliance systems to organize their defense must not be impaired.

We should also consider whether it is necessary to extend the confidence-building measures beyond the agreed scope. Even if we should achieve conventional parity within the MBFR reduction area, this will still fall considerably short of parity of conventional forces in Europe as a whole. This is underlined by the fact that the Soviet Union has substantially increased her strategic reinforcement capabilities and could rapidly bring forward forces concentrated outside the reduction area whereas American forces, if reduced in MFBR, would be cut off from Europe by the Atlantic.

Since the West formulated its double strategy of deterrence and détente 10 years ago, progress along the road to détente has been respectable. The "Ostpolitik" of the Federal Republic of Germany, based firmly on the Alliance, has promoted and helped to shape this development. The Quadripartite Agreement on Berlin has been another step toward stability and security in Europe, Berlin, once a major source of crisis, is not the problem it was. Security in Europe has been reinforced by bilateral agreements in which the parties undertake not to resort to force.

The American commitment to Europe no longer stems solely from rights and obligations arising from World War II. Rather, that commitment rests on the security interests of the United States and Western Europe alike. The Soviet Union and her allies have explicitly *recognized* this fact by putting their signatures to the Final Act of the CSCE in Helsinki. For us in Germany, the German question remains open; we are called upon to achieve the reunification of Germany. But the German question cannot, and must not, have priority over peace. This is a contribution of the Federal Republic of Germany to stability in Europe. . . .

## The Dual Track Decision

### *Document 7*

NATO announced its dual track decision on December 12, 1979, at a special meeting in Brussels of NATO foreign and defense ministers. Document 7 is the joint communiqué from that conference. The first track of the decision was the announcement that NATO would modernize its nuclear forces by deploying 108 new Pershing II ballistic missiles and 462 new ground-launched cruise missiles (GLCMs). (It was later announced that the cruise missiles would be deployed in Great Britain, Italy, Belgium, and Holland. The Pershing IIs would be deployed in West Germany.) The second track of the decision was that NATO urged the Soviets to negotiate limits on nuclear weapons in Europe.

### 7 NATO COMMUNIQUÉ December 12, 1979

1. At a special meeting of Foreign and Defense Ministers in Brussels on December 12, 1979:

2. Ministers recalled the May 1978 Summit where governments expressed the political resolve to meet the challenges to their security posed by the continuing momentum of the Warsaw Pact military build-up.

3. The Warsaw Pact has over the years developed a large and growing capability in nuclear systems that directly threaten Western Europe and have a strategic significance for the Alliance in Europe. This situation has been especially aggravated over the last few years by Soviet decisions to implement programs modernizing and expanding their long-range nuclear capability substantially. In particular, they have deployed the SS–20 missile, which offers significant improvements over previous systems in providing greater accuracy, more mobility, and greater range, as well as having multiple warheads, and the Backfire bomber, which has a much better performance than other Soviet aircraft deployed hitherto in a theater role. During this period, while the Soviet Union has been reinforcing its superiority in Long-Range Theater Nuclear Forces (LRTNF) both quantitatively and qualitatively, Western LRTNF capabilities have remained static. Indeed these forces are increasing in age and vulnerability and do not include land-based, long-range theater nuclear missile systems.

4. At the same time, the Soviets have also undertaken a modernization and expansion of their shorter range TNF and greatly improved the overall quality of their conventional forces. These developments took place against the background of increasing Soviet intercontinental capabilities and achievement of parity in intercontinental capability with the United States.

5. These trends have prompted serious concern within the Alliance, because, if they were to continue, Soviet superiority in theater nuclear systems could undermine the stability achieved in intercontinental systems and cast doubt on the credibility of the Alliance's deterrent strategy by highlighting the gap in the spectrum of NATO's available nuclear response to aggression.

6. Ministers noted that these recent developments require concrete actions on the part of the Alliance if NATO's strategy of flexible response is to remain credible. After intensive consideration, including the merits of alternative approaches, and after taking note of the positions of certain members, Ministers concluded that the overall interest of the Alliance would best be served by pursuing two parallel and complementary approaches of TNF modernization and arms control.

7. Accordingly ministers have decided to modernize NATO's LRTNF by the deployment in Europe of U.S. ground-launched systems comprising 108 Pershing II launchers, which would replace existing U.S. Pershing I–A, and 464 ground-launched cruise missiles (GLCM), all with single warheads. All the nations currently participating in the integrated defence structure will participate in the program: the missiles will be stationed in selected countries and certain support costs will be met through NATO's existing common funding arrangements. The program will not increase NATO's reliance upon nuclear weapons. In this connection, ministers agreed that as an integral part of TNF modernization, 1,000 U.S. nuclear warheads will be withdrawn from Europe as soon as feasible. Further, ministers decided that the 572 LRTNF warheads should be accommodated within that reduced level, which necessarily implies a numerical shift of emphasis away from warheads for delivery systems of other types and shorter ranges. In addition they noted with satisfaction that the Nuclear Planning Group is undertaking an examination of the precise nature, scope and basis

of the adjustments resulting from the LRTNF deployment and their possible implications for the balance of roles and systems in NATO's nuclear armory as a whole. This examination will form the basis of a substantive report to NPG Ministers in the autumn of 1980.

8. Ministers attach great importance to the role of arms control in contributing to a more stable military relationship between East and West and in advancing the process of détente. This is reflected in a broad set of initiatives being examined within the Alliance to further the course of arms control and détente in the 1980's. Ministers regard arms control as an integral part of the Alliance's efforts to assure the undiminished security of its member States and to make the strategic situation between East and West more stable, more predictable, and more manageable at lower levels of armaments on both sides. In this regard they welcome the contribution which the SALT II Treaty makes toward achieving these objectives.

9. Ministers consider that building on this accomplishment and taking account of the expansion of Soviet LRTNF capabilities of concern to NATO, arms control efforts to achieve a more stable overall nuclear balance at lower levels of nuclear weapons on both sides should therefore now include certain United States and Soviet long-range theater nuclear systems.

This would reflect previous Western suggestions to include such Soviet and U.S. systems in arms control negotiations and more recent expressions by Soviet President Brezhnev of willingness to do so. Ministers fully support the decision taken by the United States following consultations within the Alliance to negotiate arms limitations on LRTNF and to propose to the U.S.S.R. to begin negotiations as soon as possible along the following lines which have been elaborated in intensive consultations within the Alliance:

A. Any future limitations on U.S. systems principally designed for theater missions should be accompanied by appropriate limitations on Soviet theater systems.
B. Limitations on United States and Soviet long-range theater nuclear systems should be negotiated bilaterally in the SALT II framework in a step-by-step approach.
C. The immediate objective of these negotiations should be the establishment of agreed limitations on United States and Soviet land-based long-range theater nuclear missile systems.
D. Any agreed limitations on these systems must be consistent with the principle of equality between the sides. Therefore, the limitations should take the form of de jure equality both in ceilings and in rights.
E. Any agreed limitations must be adequately verifiable.

10. Given the special importance of these negotiations for the overall security of the Alliance, a special consultative body at a high level will be constituted within the Alliance to support the U.S. negotiating effort. This body will follow the negotiations on a continuous basis and report to the Foreign and Defense Ministers who will examine developments in these negotiations as well as in other arms control negotiations at their semiannual meetings.

11. The Ministers have decided to pursue these two parallel and complementary approaches in order to avert an arms race in Europe caused by the Soviet TNF buildup, yet preserve the viability of NATO's strategy of deterrence and defense and thus maintain the security of its member States.

A. A modernization decision, including a commitment to deployments, is necessary to meet NATO's deterrence and defense needs, to provide a credible response to unilateral Soviet TNF deployments, and to provide the foundation for the pursuit of serious negotiations on TNF.
B. Success of arms control in constraining the Soviet buildup can enhance Alliance security, modify the scale of NATO's TNF requirements, and promote stability and détente in Europe in consonance with NATO's basic policy of deterrence, defense and détente as enunciated in the Harmel Report. NATO's TNF requirements will be examined in the light of concrete results reached through negotiations.

## The New Missiles

### *Document 8*

This selection from a congressional report on NATO's decision describes the missiles that were to be deployed — the Pershing II and the GLCM. The Pershing II is a very accurate ballistic missile with a range of about 1,000 miles. It is able to strike targets inside the Soviet Union from Western Europe but is not able to reach Moscow. The GLCM is like an unmanned jet aircraft. It flies in the atmosphere like a jet plane, is very accurate, and has a range of about 1,600 miles. Both the Pershing II and GLCM are mobile missiles.

## 8 CONGRESSIONAL REPORT ON NATO DECISION December 31, 1980

### A. Pershing II Extended Range (ER) Missile[5]

The Pershing II was originally planned as a replacement for the Pershing 1A (P–1A)[6] currently deployed with the United States and West German forces. 108 P–1A launchers are deployed with American Army units in the Federal Republic and 72 launchers with the Air Force of the Federal Republic.

Initially the Pershing modernization program had as its objective improved accuracy and lower yield in order to reduce collateral damage and provide a more credible theater nuclear interdiction capability. In 1977 following recommendations from the Secretary of Defense and SACEUR — then General Haig — the requirements for a substantial increase in range was generated. The range of the Pershing II ER will be close to 1,000 miles as opposed to 400 miles for the 1A.

The Pershing II ER will have a new two-stage missile and reentry vehicle (RV) and will use a modified version of the present erector/launcher and other ground support equipment. Following SACEUR's recommendation, the Pershing II will resemble the 1A as closely as possible. The main physical difference will be weight, the new missile being approximately 15,500 lbs as opposed to approximately 10,000 lbs for the 1A.

Unlike the Pershing 1A, which follows a ballistic trajectory from RV separation to the target, the P–II's RV will be terminally guided to the target by an onboard radar. The all-weather radar will be activated during the terminal phase of flight to correlate radar returns from the area surrounding the target with a prestored reference map of the target area. Success corrections during RV descent are expected to achieve accuracies of between 20 to 40 meters CEP compared with 400 meters CEP for the Pershing 1A.

The Pershing II will use either the W–85 or W–86 warheads either of which can employ selectable yields. The higher accuracy of the P–II will allow the use of lower yields for a given mission.

During peacetime, Pershing II's will be deployed in casernes at quick reaction alert (QRA) sites, and will disperse during crisis conditions to their firing positions. While the Pershing II continues to be support and manpower intensive, its reaction time and deployment time on the move has been considerably speeded up.

The basic Pershing II firing unit is a platoon consisting of three erector launchers with one missile per launcher and associated ground equipment. The Pershing II is still in the development stage and thus expected improvements remain to be achieved. The earliest initial operational capability (IOC) for the system is August 1983.

The United States is preserving a short-range version of the P–II to meet FRG or other NATO requirements. U.S. officials have indicated that while no formal demand has been made, they expect the FRG to buy the single-stage version of the P–II particularly as the FRG has bought all previous improvements to the Pershing and as the FRG has budgeted out-year funds to upgrade its Pershing force.[7]

## B. The Ground-Launched Cruise Missile (GLCM)

Many observers believe that the evolution of cruise missile technology in terms of accuracy, penetration, and survivability offers substantial potential for improving NATO's defense capabilities.[8] Having examined the air, ground, and sea-launched options for cruise missiles, the HLG decided that the ground-launched version offered the optimum solution.

The GLCM will be a version of the Tomahawk cruise missile adapted for launch from air transportable, ground mobile platforms. It is powered by a turbofan engine. Guidance is by inertial navigation with terrain contour matching (Tercom) updates at periodic intervals. Flying at a speed of around .8 mach at an altitude of below 100 meters, the GLCM's operational range will be approximately 2,500 kms with an anticipated terminal accuracy of less than 80 meters CEP.

GLCM's will be deployed with American Air Force units. The missiles will be transported four to a launch platform. Four transporter/erector/launchers (TEL) with 16 missiles controlled by two launch control centers will constitute a fire control unit or flight.

The GLCM will use the W–84 warhead which provides selectable yields.

Similar to the Pershing II, the prelaunch survivability of the GLCM derives from the system's mobility. Unlike the Pershing, the GLCM will be deployed during peacetime at permanent sites in hardened shelters capable of withstanding blast effects at up to 2,000 p.s.i. Given warning time, the GLCM could move from its main operating base to a field location.

As with Pershing, many of the performance objectives of the GLCM have still to be fulfilled in testing. Reports have suggested two particular problems regarding the Tercom guidance system: First, to date the cruise missile has not been tested over terrain representative of potential operational areas — much of the terrain which the missile would almost certainly traverse — western parts of the Soviet Union — are very flat and lack the distinctive contours for which Tercom is best suited; second, the provision of the maps necessary for Tercom may be a more difficult problem than previously assumed.

The IOC for the GLCM in Europe has been given as December 1983. However, Department of Defense officials have recently indicated a 6-month delay in the testing of GLCM due to technical difficulties in the computer and communications equipment. This raises the question of a slippage in the IOC.

## Notes

5. This study provides a general description of the technical characteristics of the LRTNF systems. A more detailed technical study is currently being prepared by the General Accounting Office for the Subcommittee on Europe and the Middle East.
6. The Pershing missile was first deployed in Europe in 1962 to provide medium range nuclear support to NATO forces. The original Pershing was a mobile system with a large 60–400KT warhead and a range of about 100–400 nm. Deployment of an improved system — the P–1A — was carried out from 1969 to 1971.
7. See the statement by Dr. Percy A. Pierre, Assistant Secretary of the Army, to the Subcommittee of the Committee on Appropriations. U.S. House of Representatives, Apr. 15, 1980.
8. For discussion of the potential application of cruise missiles within NATO, see the forthcoming Brookings Institution study on cruise missiles.

# The European Public Reaction

### *Documents 9 and 10*

Soon after the dual track decision was announced, public protests began. They reached their peak in 1982 and 1983 when huge demonstrations were held in almost all the capitals of the European members of NATO. Document 9, excerpts from a report from the Swedish International Peace Research Institute, reviews some of the public opinion research on the European protest movement. It shows the growing concern about nuclear war and the growing public opposition to the European missiles. Document 10, an article from *The Times* of London, describes one of the largest demonstrations.

## 9 NUCLEAR WEAPONS AND THE NEW PEACE MOVEMENT November 22, 1983

### I. Introduction

In 1982, over one million Europeans demonstrated in several large gatherings for peace and against nuclear weapons, and on 12 June over half a million people gathered in New York City in what was probably the largest peace demonstration ever held. Meanwhile, in the United Nations, government representatives achieved less at the Second Special Session on Disarmament than they had at the first in 1978. . . .

The growth in the past few years of the new popular movements for peace and disarmament is one of the political events of our time. Their influence has to be taken into account in any discussion of the success or failure of arms control negotiations. In some countries — the UK and the Netherlands — the policies put forward by these movements have, to a significant extent, been adopted by one of the major political parties. In the United States, nine states held a referendum — the largest of its kind in US history — on a nuclear "freeze" as advocated by an important sector of the US peace movement; a majority approved the freeze in eight of the nine states. More generally, governments now consider that they have to appeal to public opinion, on military matters, much more than they ever did before. For example, both the Pentagon and the Soviet Ministry of Defence have produced well-illustrated booklets to show that world peace is threatened by the military deployment of the Soviet Union and the United States, respectively.[9,10]

This chapter documents the public's increased fear of nuclear war, and provides some information on the rise of the new movements. It discusses what brought about these changes — showing, for instance, that there is no simple relationship with the increase in the world's nuclear stockpiles. It looks at the variety of movements that now exist in this area; and at the end of the chapter it considers some of the government responses, actual and potential, to these new movements.

### II. Public Fear of Nuclear War and Support for Nuclear Disarmament

Public opinion polls show that the fear of nuclear war has increased markedly in recent years. For example, in a Swedish poll in 1973, 55 per cent expressed fear of nuclear war, in 1982, the figure was 78 per cent.[11] In a 14-nation sample in another poll, estimates of the probability of a world war in the next 10 years ranged from 29 to 47 per cent. . . .[11]

In a recent eight-nation poll in Western Europe and the United States, the "Soviet military build-up" was considered "most responsible for international tension" in all countries except France and Spain. But US military policy or "US aggressive policies towards the Soviet Union" or "superpower activities in the Third World" were ranked as the second biggest worry in every country except the United States.[12] In general, the polls in Western Europe suggest a lack of confidence in the two great powers.

There continues to be considerable public support for arms control and disarmament. As early as 1950, a majority of US respondents in a poll supported arms control negotiations with the Soviet Union. They were asked the question: "Do you think we should try again to work out an agreement with Russia to control the atomic bomb before we try to make the hydrogen bomb?". Forty-eight per cent said Yes, 45 per cent No, and 7 per cent had no opinion.[13]

More recently, a summary of an international survey conducted on behalf of the Atlantic Institute and a number of major newspapers concluded:

> Americans who attach importance to dialogue with the Soviet Union and greater Western cooperation outnumber those who believe in greater emphasis on the military.
>
> Arms control is believed to be at least as important for security as the military balance with the Soviet Union in all countries, including the United States. "Productive arms control" was especially important to the Norwegians and Dutch, followed by the French and West Germans.
>
> In the United States, military balance with the Soviet Union, a Reagan administration priority, was ranked in the poll as a minor element in security.[12]

The summary concluded that, while the threat of war and nuclear weapons were major concerns, "inadequate defence emerged as the least important source of concern in every country".

A series of opinion polls in the United States on the issue of a nuclear freeze show overwhelming public support.[13] This is in spite of the fact that since the late 1970s Americans, as well as West Europeans, have tended to see the USA as lagging behind the USSR in the nuclear arms race.[13,14] Opinion polls in the countries affected by the NATO decision on new nuclear missiles indicate majorities of the public opposed to the stationing of the new missiles. In the UK, 50 per cent opposed the government's decision to "allow the American government to base cruise missiles on British soil" in an April 1981 survey, while 41 per cent supported the decision. In the previous September, 49 per cent had supported the decision while 43 per cent opposed it.[15]

In FR Germany, 39 per cent in May 1981 opposed the deployment of new intermediate-range missiles on West German soil, while 29 per cent supported the deployment. One-third were undecided. A question explicitly coupling deployment to the requirement to engage in disarmament talks with the Soviet Union produced 50 per cent in favour and 20 per cent against.[15]

In Belgium, in a September 1980 poll[15], 42 per cent opposed the installation of US missiles on Belgian territory while 26 per cent were in favour.

In the Netherlands, 68 per cent opposed and 28 per cent supported, in April 1981, the siting of cruise missiles in that country. A survey the previous autumn showed 53 per cent opposed to the presence of nuclear weapons on Dutch soil and 39 per cent in favour.[15]

From the Netherlands and the United Kingdom there is evidence of a substantial and perhaps growing minority supporting *unilateral* nuclear disarmament. In September 1980, two polls in the UK gave figures of 21 and 28 per cent supporting unilateral disarmament. In October and November, following a Labour Party Congress in which nuclear disarmament was a major issue, the polls showed a rise to 35 and 41 per cent. (In September 1982, the Labour Party Congress voted with a two-thirds majority in favour of unilateral British nuclear disarmament.) A poll in the Netherlands in April 1981 showed 38 per cent in favour of the West disarming unilaterally.[15]

It should be emphasized that these questions related specifically to the issue of nuclear weapons. All the poll evidence shows a majority of the population in favour of maintaining defence expenditures at approximately current levels (rather than either reducing or increasing them) and for remaining in NATO, even though there appears to be a significant minority, particularly amongst educated young people, favouring a more neutralist position and increased military expenditure.[15]

## Notes

9. US Department of Defense, *Soviet Military Power* (US Government Printing Office, Washington, D.C., 1981).
10. *Whence the Threat to Peace* (Military Publishing House, Moscow, 1982).
11. *SIFO Indikator* (Stockholm), Vol. 7, 18 May 1982.
12. Fitchett, J., "U.S. arms buildup worries Europeans," *International Herald Tribune,* 25 October 1982.
13. *Public Opinion,* August/September 1982, p. 35.
14. de Boer, C., "The polls: our commitment to World War III," *Public Opinion Quarterly,* Vol. 45, 1981, pp. 126–34.
15. Adler, K. and Wertman, D., "Is NATO in trouble? A survey of European attitudes," *Public Opinion,* August/September 1981, pp. 8–12, 50.

## 10 400,000 JOIN IN NETHERLANDS' BIGGEST PROTEST
### November 23, 1981

Some 400,000 demonstrators marched through Amsterdam yesterday to protest against the deployment of new nuclear missiles in Europe. It was the largest demonstration ever held in The Netherlands and the final and largest of the peace marches held in West European capitals, including Bonn, London, Brussels, Paris and Rome, this autumn.

Although the number of demonstrators taking part was twice that expected, there were no serious incidents. A 19-year-old man was killed, however, when one of more than 2,000 buses carrying the demonstrators overturned on the way home.

Amsterdam's main station had to be closed for an hour when about 15,000 demonstrators simultaneously tried to take one of the 22 extra trains home.

Apparently impressed by the demonstration, Mr. Andries van Agt, the Christian Democratic Prime Minister, told a meeting of his party yesterday that the Dutch Cabinet would actively follow a policy of peace aimed at the removal of nuclear weapons.

He called these weapons "a crime against God's creation." Referring to President Reagan's zero option proposal, Mr. van Agt said: "Our voice has been heard."

President Nikolai Ceausescu of Romania, in an interview on Dutch television last night, called Mr. Reagan's proposal "an important step towards negotiations aimed at averting the deployment of new missiles in Europe and the dismantling of existing systems."

Asked if this included the Soviet SS-20 systems, Mr. Ceausescu replied that Romania favoured the dismantling and destruction of all existing nuclear weapons systems. He added that this sentiment had been reflected in the peace march recently held in his country against all nuclear missiles. Romania is the only East Block country where such a demonstration has been held. President Ceausescu said Europe must play a more active role in the solution of problems concerning disarmament, peace and security.

Mr. van Agt's Christian Democratic Party was the only Government party not present at the Amsterdam demonstration.

The organizers of the Inter-Church Peace Council had refused a speaker for the Christian Democrats because the party did not fully support the demonstration's official slogans opposing new nuclear missiles in Europe, calling on the Dutch Government to rescind its approval of NATO's decision to modernize theatre nuclear weapons and calling on it to put pressure on its NATO allies to also rescind this decision.

The two other parties in the centre-left coalition, Labour and the Democrats' 66, both took part in the demonstration. Mr. Wim Meijer, the parliamentary leader of the Labour Party, told the rally that as long as his party was in power there would be no new American missiles on Dutch soil.

His speech, however, was rendered nearly inaudible by the crowd voicing its disapproval over the far milder way in which he had expressed himself on the issue during the four day debate in the Lower House of Parliament on the Cabinet's plans for the coming four years.

According to Mr. Mient Jan Faber, the Secretary of the Inter-Church Peace Council, which claims to have been the source of inspiration for the demonstrations in other European capitals, the demonstration was aimed both against the deployment of the new American missiles in Western Europe and against the systems already deployed by the Soviet Union.

About 500 members of the armed forces took part in the demonstration in uniform, despite orders forbidding them to do so.

# European Alternatives to the Euromissiles

### *Documents 11 and 12*

Although there was massive opposition to the Euromissiles, critics of the NATO decision were not united on what should be done instead. Some favored a denuclearization of Western Europe. In document 11, E. P. Thompson, British historian and antinuclear activist, argues that the zero option is a phony proposal designed to allow the United States to put new missiles in Europe. He calls for a European disarmament conference to remove all nuclear weapons in Western Europe. Others believed in the need for nuclear weapons in Western Europe but rejected specifics of the dual decision. In document 12, Klaas DeVries, a Labour party member of the Dutch parliament and chairman of its Defense Committee in the early 1980s, argues that the NATO decision was based on the wrong premises. He argues that the alliance's already existing INF forces, U.S. aircraft, British aircraft, and U.S. sea-launched ballistic missiles (SLBMs) are sufficient to meet the Soviet threat. He also argues that the allies should do more to negotiate INF before deploying the new missiles.

## 11 FOR DISARMING EUROPE
### E. P. Thompson

For three years, on both sides of the Atlantic, there have been conferences and church meetings and marches and agonizing over the fate of the Earth. Well, are we serious or not? Somewhere, at some time, some people have got to decide that they will say no. We in the European peace movement have decided that the place is Europe and the time is now and that the people will have to be us. Europe is the no-man's-land between the superpowers where at last the nuclear arms race might be stopped.

We are not interested in President Reagan's "zero option" — to forgo deployment of American intermediate-range nuclear missiles in exchange for a Soviet agreement to dismantle its intermediate-range missiles — or in his compromise "zero plus" proposal for limiting these missiles. The European peace movement decided long ago that the matter is not open to negotiation. Even one cruise missile on our territory, owned and operated by a foreign power, takes us across an unacceptable threshold.

Mr. Reagan is supposed to have made the "zero plus" proposal reluctantly in response to European pressure. Maybe we should examine the term "European pressure." In reality, European peace movements brought pressure on their governments, which in turn brought pressure on the United States. European leaders ran to Washington and pleaded with Mr. Reagan to get them off the hook of their own restive public opinion. The purpose of the "zero plus" proposal was less to achieve a settlement with Moscow than to aid leaders of the North Atlantic Treaty Organization countries to reassert control over their domestic constituencies.

After the demonstrations two weeks ago in Britain, the Netherlands and West Germany, it must be clear to the President that something has gone wrong. He, and the American public, should be warned that, just as they got into the present mess in part by listening too closely to Helmut Schmidt, the former Chancellor, and a narrow circle of Atlanticist "defense experts," so they are signing on for another period of purgatory by following the same kind of ill advice from the same political circles.

The President is badly briefed. In his calculation, the Soviet Union has a "monopoly" of missiles in Europe, at a ratio of some 1,000 warheads to nil. That depends on what categories you count and what you hold your hand over while counting. What was being hidden was all the tactical stuff and all the aircraft-launched stuff (on both sides), the American Poseidons under NATO command, the British Polaris submarine-launched missiles, the whole French armory and the multitude of American air-launched and sea-launched cruise missiles now on their way. All this can be added up and balanced in different ways, but the sum is never 1,000 to nil.

In any case, it is disputable whether the Pershing 2s and ground-launched cruise missiles can be properly described as "intermediate" missiles at all. They are forward-based American strategic missiles, to be owned and operated by American personnel on European territory, that can strike deeply into the Soviet Union — whereas the SS-20, nasty as it is, cannot cross the Atlantic.

Europeans who have been counting and recounting these beads for three years find the President's calculations only boring. The "zero plus" proposal was boring also, for it, too, offers to match missile numbers only in this one notional category, while ignoring all the rest. Besides, it would amount to only a small reduction in the missiles planned for Europe.

I doubt that the Russians are interested in the "zero plus" proposal, but it matters little, since there are three parties who must consent in this negotiation. And certainly the European peace movement will not be cosignatories. The missiles will have to be brought by helicopter into installations at Greenham Common and Comiso in the face of our refusal at the gates.

The only numbers game that would interest us would be a Dutch auction, downward. What we want is a freeze, of course. As for Euromissiles, we want no phony counting — and Poseidon submarines and Polaris missiles should be thrown into the calculus as sweeteners to bring Moscow to eliminate all SS-20s.

We propose also a European disarmament conference with this agenda: removing all nuclear weapons (including British and French) from Europe (measured from the eastern Atlantic waters to the Urals), mutual deep reductions in conventional forces, and guarantees of the human rights clauses of the Helsinki Final Act. Finally, we call for a summit meeting between the President and the leader of the Soviet Union to bring World War II to a final settlement, with the mutual withdrawal, by phases, of all American and Soviet forces in Europe.

It may seem to the superpower leaders that nuclear weapons are for security, stability, certainty. Their terminus is certain also: The stability of the tomb.

## 12 RESPONDING TO THE SS-20
## Klaas G. DeVries

In the coming months, the member states of the North Atlantic Alliance must decide whether, with the advent of US Soviet strategic parity and in the light of the current modernization and enhancement of Soviet capabilities, NATO should deploy additional long-range theatre nuclear forces (LRTNF) in Europe. Although the reports of the two NATO bodies examining this question, the High Level Group (HLG) and the Special Group, have not been released, it is evident that the Alliance will be asked to approve the deployment in Europe of a mixed force of several hundred ground-launched cruise missiles (GLCMs) and extended-range *Pershing* II ballistic missiles. In parallel with this modernization programme, NATO will attempt to engage the Soviet Union in substantive arms-control negotiations on theatre systems. A decision on this approach is expected to be taken at the December Ministerial meetings, a decision which then would be submitted to the respective parliaments for their consideration in 1980.

The ensuing debate can be expected to revive many of the arguments concerning the basic tenets of NATO strategy, particularly the role of nuclear weapons. It will re-emphasize differing perspectives within the Alliance as to what constitutes the most credible and effective policy of deterrence and underscore a problem central to the unity of the Alliance, that of allaying European fears of being decoupled from the US strategic nuclear guarantee. At the same time, the LRTNF decision will challenge Europeans to participate as full partners in an extended debate over deterrence theory. . . .

Some observers maintain that increased Soviet superiority in theatre systems presents a threat for which the Alliance has no counter. The Alliance has never possessed a fully-fledged, independent theatre nuclear capability, as it has always integrated its LRTNF in targeting with US central strategic systems. However, these observers believe that because of strategic parity this integration does not provide sufficient flexibility in planning credible LRTNF employment scenarios.

The Alliance does of course already possess substantial LRTNF assets in Europe, consisting principally of the two wings of United States F-111s stationed in Britain, a squadron of British *Vulcans*, and a number of *Poseidon* SLBMs dedicated to the European strike plan. However, current generation SLBMs are relatively inaccurate and are not thought by some to constitute a credible counter-force response to a counter-force strike, although accuracy improvements are planned. They also lack the visibility, which is now considered by some observers to be a prime requirement, to offset Soviet theatre forces. From the Soviet perspective, use of the *Poseidons* under SACEUR's strike plan might be indistinguishable from SLBM attacks conducted as part of a general strategic retaliation. Thus some observers believe that the NATO-dedicated *Poseidons* do not meet the criteria of providing a discreet, but lower, rung on the escalation ladder and hence do not afford NATO sufficient retaliatory flexibility.

The F-111 possesses excellent all-weather, day/night conventional strike capabilities that are in short supply in NATO, and thus during a conventional phase of a European war, NATO would have to decide whether to hold them back for possible longe-range nuclear attacks. The aircraft would also experience certain penetration problems against Soviet strategic air defences. Due to these factors, some US defence officials contend that new LRTNF deployments are dictated by straight-forward military considerations related to NATO's needs within its own doctrine (e.g., releasing dual-capable aircraft for nuclear roles), irrespective of developments on the Soviet side. Finally, it should be noted that both France and Britain possess independent strategic forces but neither of these possesses the accuracy necessary to provide a "selective" response. . . .

## Critique

In my opinion, the rationale behind current Western concern does not stand up to careful scrutiny. Firstly, I do not agree that strategic parity neutralizes the deterrent effect of the central nuclear systems for all situations except a direct attack on the homeland. The object of deterrence is to cause sufficient uncertainty in the mind of a likely aggressor concerning the potential risks and gains of an aggressive action. The current and projected capabilities of the United States plus its pronounced willingness to defend Western Europe are sufficient to deter any Soviet leader from a move that could result in the destruction of Soviet society. No potential gain could possibly be worth taking such a risk. As McGeorge Bundy recently stated, ". . . no one knows that a major engagement in Europe would escalate to the strategic nuclear level. But the esssential point is the opposite: no one can possibly know it would not."[16]

European confidence in the United States' strategic guarantee is, of course, the basis of current Western concern. Yet, it is difficult to see how the deployment of additional US systems in Europe would bolster that confidence. If Europeans already have no confidence that the American President would launch a retaliatory strike against the Soviet Union with existing LRTNF based in Europe, or with missiles from the United States or sea-based systems, why should the availability of an admittedly small increment of weapons employing new technologies suddenly erase such deep-rooted doubts. Indeed, if this were the case, it can be argued that rather than strengthening the escalation ladder, such deployments will weaken it by making possible the containment or limitation of a nuclear exchange in European territory. In short, the deployment of longe-range capabilities may *lessen* the American perception of the linkage between its strategic forces and its security interests in Western Europe, a development which would have profound implications.

Whereas some NATO officials see the *Poseidon* missiles dedicated to SACEUR as inhibiting NATO's escalation dominance, I believe that it is precisely because these weapons systems are so closely associated with central strategic systems that their threatened use so effectively underscores the linkage between the theatre and strategic echelons of the NATO deterrence Triad. The Soviet Union is not likely to make the same types of distinction between categories of NATO LRTNFs as some Western theorists are inclined to believe. As was forcefully argued by Mr. Bundy in his IISS speech, "Any American-controlled weapons that can reach the Soviet Union will almost surely be all alike to them both. It follows that the strategic protection of Europe is as strong or as weak as the American strategic guarantee, no matter what American weapons are deployed under NATO."[17]

Moreover, it is doubtful that any amount of juggling with the location of United States capabilities can ever satisfy the permanent doubters of the US guarantee. This doubt is inherent in the geo-strategic structure of the Alliance and the physical detachment of the chief guarantor from its Allies. The only satisfactory solution for these observers would be the creation of European-based, owned and operated nuclear forces, a development that is neither desirable nor possible within the foreseeable future, and a development which both the FRG and France have specifically rejected in recent months.

With regard to the more precise question of the increase in military potential represented by the SS-20, it has already been noted that the West has lived under the shadow of 600 MR and IRBMs and hundreds of medium-range bombers for the past 20 years. Thus the new threat currently comprises approximately 60–75 SS-20 launchers and approximately 40–60 *Backfire* bombers. Do the actual military characteristics of these systems represent a quantum jump in capability? It is not easy to appreciate the meaning of the term "selective capability" when it is used to describe the use of the SS-20 to deliver 150 KT warheads (each ten times the yield of the bomb used against Hiroshima) on a heavily urbanized and densely populated Europe.

In my opinion, the perception of weakness in NATO's theatre nuclear forces has regrettably been created by the combined effects of too much weight being given to the need for theatre nuclear parity on the part of some Europeans, an exaggerated public response to the military potential of the SS-20 and an excessive preoccupation with limited nuclear war scenarios. Nevertheless, whatever the reality of the Soviet theatre threat, it is undeniable that a perception of Western weakness has been created and popularized. The image of the "monster" SS-20 has been born and some Alliance reaction is necessary, if only for political reasons, in order for the West to reaffirm the credibility of its security policy. However, it is crucial to establish the precise criteria on which this reaction is to be based. Should a Western response be designed to satisfy military or political requirements? This distinction is crucial as the nature of the response and its potential cost in political terms will vary depending on the precise nature of these objectives.

It is interesting to note that at the recent Brussels conference on NATO, former SACEUR Alexander Haig characterized the HLG proposals as representing only "political expediency and tokenism."[18] If indeed neither the perception of weakness nor the proposed NATO response are supported by sound military logic, then the Alliance has other, politically less costly, solutions available than the somewhat dramatic development that the introduction of new capabilities in Europe to strike the Soviet Union would represent. In my opinion, a more adequate solution to the political problem that currently exists would include unequivocal reassurances of the American guarantee to Europe and the promotion of higher public awareness of the substantial capabilities of existing systems. In this regard the recent statement by US Secretary of State Cyrus Vance is a positive step. On 10 September 1979, the Secretary declared, "There should be no question about America's commitment to defend Europe with all the means necessary — nuclear and conventional. The substantial forces we have deployed to Europe are one concrete evidence of that commitment."[19]

Two key difficulties are associated with NATO's envisioned programme of proceeding with arms control in parallel with modernization. Firstly, the concept of developing systems as bargaining chips does not have a very convincing record in arms-control negotiations. The West German Foreign Minister Hans-Dietrich Genscher pointed to this danger when he warned that the Alliance should be wary of the theory that there is no point in negotiating with the Soviet Union on arms control as long as the Alliance has achieved no approximate parity with regard to these weapons, in other words, that we should not first arm in order to disarm.

Secondly, a decision to proceed with a technical solution presupposes a decision on basing. However, the basing question could arouse a degree of public opposition that would prevent a number of governments making public commitments to locate these new systems. Failure to obtain such commitments could undermine efforts to bargain with the Soviet Union, as it would almost certainly foreclose a number of options open to the Alliance. It could also have serious divisive consequences within the Alliance: firstly, in the sense of apportioning blame to certain countries for their failure to accept their responsibilities and secondly, in increasing American disillusionment over the inability of European governments to adopt measures deemed necessary for their own security.

## Conclusion

In my view, the arms-control option should be pursued before any decision is made concerning the deployment of new capabilities. I believe that the potential options are far enough advanced in their development phase to present a real and credible threat to the Soviet Union. If, as is reported, the Soviet Union is deeply and genuinely concerned over the potential introduction of cruise missiles into the European theatre, then she must realize that with the ALCM close to deployment, the deployment of SLCMs or GLCMs cannot be far behind. The existence and status of these programmes, and the capability of the Alliance to implement them if satisfactory results are not obtained through negotiations, should be sufficient to obtain satisfactory restraints on Soviet systems.

The most appropriate forum for such negotiations is SALT III, wherein the most likely and obtainable results would be achieved, in the form of bilateral packages between the United States and the USSR, e.g., restraint in developing GLCMs or SLCMs over a certain range for a satisfactory ceiling on SS-20s. US willingness to discuss an extension of those portions of the Protocol dealing with SLCMs and GLCMs would provide the Soviet Union with substantial incentive to negotiate limits on the SS-20, even without an Alliance decision on a final LRTNF package in December.

It should be noted that the West's current lead in the technology of the cruise missile cannot be expected to be retained indefinitely. The case of MIRVs provides an excellent example of how quickly a Western technological lead can disappear, and how adversely consequential it can be once the USSR attains such improved weapons technologies. In this respect, an agreement extending parts of the Protocol in exchange for SS-20 limitations could pay double dividends.

Given the 31 December 1981 expiration date of the Protocol, the Alliance would have to move quickly into SALT III in order to realize the leverage afforded it by the impending Protocol expiration. Once under way, however, SALT III should, within its first two years, provide sufficient time for the Soviet Union to agree to terms linking SS-20 and cruise missile restrictions. If successful in this first phase, SALT III could broaden the LRTNF portion of its agenda and pursue more comprehensive limitations, including prohibitions on new theatre ballistic missile and bomber types.

Finally, it must be noted that much of the current Western apprehension is based on the fear of an unrestrained expansion of Soviet theatre forces. Whatever the reality of the current threat, unrestrained development in this field by the Soviet Union could not go unchallenged by the West. It is important to convey to the Soviet leaders that their modernization and deployment plans will inevitably have an impact on Western policies. A Western perception that the Soviet Union is having a "free ride" in terms of theatre systems is unacceptable and would have adverse consequences for East-West relations.

Accordingly, if the Soviet Union did not agree to effective restraints on her theatre systems prior to the expiration date of the Protocol, the Alliance should allow the Protocol to lapse and decide on what new LRTNF deployments might be needed. Should arms control fail, this approach would entail at most a one or two year delay in the deployment of new NATO LRTNF. Yet unlike the emerging NATO programme of parallel arms-control and modernization efforts, this approach would permit the Alliance to confront the modernization decision with the confidence that public opinion in the various countries would appreciate that a legitimate effort had first been made to eliminate disparities at the theatre level via arms control.

## Notes

16. Address before the IISS 21st Annual Conference, Villars, Switzerland, 7 September 1979.
17. *Ibid.*
18. Atlantic News, No. 1149, 12 September 1979, p. 2.
19. *Ibid.*

# THE INF NEGOTIATIONS

## The Soviet View of INF

### *Document 13*

In these excerpts from his book, *The Soviet Union and the Arms Race,* Soviet expert David Holloway analyzes the Soviet view of INF. He points out that the Soviets have deployed nuclear weapons aimed at Western Europe almost from the time they began to acquire nuclear weapons. Holloway believes that the Soviets thought it was necessary to deploy the SS-20 and the Backfire because their older INF missiles were becoming obsolete and vulnerable. On the other hand, the Soviets saw the NATO decision to deploy new systems as an attempt by the United States to gain an advantage over the Soviet Union. The Soviets were particularly worried by the Pershing II, which they viewed as a potential first-strike weapon. Holloway also describes how the Soviet Union and the United States saw the nuclear balance in Europe very differently.

## 13 THE POLITICS OF ARMS CONTROL David Holloway

In April 1947, at a meeting in the Kremlin, Stalin pointed to the importance of intercontinental rockets: "Do you realize the tremendous strategic importance of machines of this sort? They could be an effective straitjacket for that noisy shopkeeper Harry Truman. We must go ahead with it, comrades. The problem of the creation of transatlantic rockets is of extreme importance to us."[20] Ten years later, in August 1957, the Soviet Union conducted the world's first successful flight test of an ICBM. . . .

The Soviet decision to give priority to the deployment of medium-range systems in the late 1950s and early 1960s appears to have been influenced by several different considerations. The first was technological. The early intercontinental bombers suffered from serious deficiencies: the *Bison,* which was a jet bomber, did not have a great enough range for two-way intercontinental missions, while the turboprop *Bear,* which had a greater range, had a lower speed and ceiling and was thus more vulnerable to air defences.[21] The ICBM was, from the Soviet point of view, a much better weapon because it did not require bases close to the United States (which the Soviet Union did not have) or inflight refuelling to be effective; nor could it be brought down by air defences. The first ICBM, however, was not suitable as a military missile because it used a highly unstable, nonstorable propellant and needed ground stations for guidance. These drawbacks did not prevent it from being used as one of the main launchers in the space program.[22]

The second consideration was that many of the nuclear forces that could threaten the Soviet Union were based close to the Soviet borders, particularly in and around Europe; other nuclear forces might be redeployed to those regions in the event of war.[23] Soviet military thinking assumed that a world war would inevitably be nuclear. If war came, the Soviet Union would try to destroy the enemy's forces and his capacity to wage war. The most important targets for nuclear strikes were thought to be the enemy's war industry, communications, command and control centres, and his strategic nuclear forces. These were the targets the Soviet Union would wish to strike with its medium-range forces.[24] (Short-range missiles were intended for use on the battlefield against enemy tactical nuclear weapons and troop formations.) It made sense, therefore, to give priority to those systems that could destroy the nuclear forces that posed the most direct threat to Soviet territory.

The third consideration was that the threat of nuclear destruction in Western Europe would help to deter an attack by the United States. In September 1961, during the Berlin crisis, *Izvestia* carried a report of an interview Khrushchev had given the *New York Times.* This said that "Khrushchev believes absolutely that when it comes to a showdown, Britain, France and Italy would refuse to join the United States in a war over Berlin for fear of their absolute destruction. Quite blandly he asserts that these countries are, figuratively speaking, hostages to the USSR and a guarantee against war."[25] Khrushchev is reported to have told the British Ambassador during the same Berlin crisis that all Western Europe was at his mercy: six hydrogen bombs would annihilate the British Isles, while nine others would take care of France.[26]

The aim of deterring an American attack by threatening Western Europe with destruction complemented rather than contradicted the interest in war-fighting. Even if the early medium-range systems were targeted against military installations alone (and the missiles were not accurate enough to be wholly suited to this mission) they could not have been used without immense destruction and loss of life. In November 1958 Khrushchev told students graduating from military academies that "now it is enough to press one button and not only airfields and the communications of various staffs, but whole cities too will be blown sky-high, whole countries can be destroyed."[27] In May of the following year he said, when speaking of American missiles based in Italy, that "if an attack is undertaken against us, we shall try above all to destroy the rocket bases directed against us. And what does it mean to destroy these bases? They are situated not on bare cliffs but there where people live."[28] Soviet military thought did not then and does not now draw a sharp distinction between weapons intended to strike military targets in the event of war and weapons designed to deter through the threat of destroying cities. The deterrent effect of these weapons was not seen as something separate from their utility in fighting a war.

Deployment of medium-range nuclear forces ended in the mid-1960s and did not begin again until the mid-1970s. In the intervening years these forces faced three major problems. The first was the growing vulnerability of the SS-4s and SS-5s to attack by enemy nuclear missiles. Although Soviet strategic thought at this period seems to have placed considerable importance on preemption, the Soviet leaders tried to ensure that their missile force would be able to retaliate even if attacked first. In January 1960 Khrushchev said that

> we deploy our missile complexes in such a way as to insure duplication and triplication. The territory of our country is vast; we are able to disperse our missile complexes, to camouflage them well. We are creating such a system that, if some means intended for a retaliatory blow were put out of commission, one could always send into action the means of duplicating them and hit the targets from reserve positions.[29]

This statement was made before reconnaissance satellites became operational. These soon made it possible to locate the SS-4 and SS-5 launch sites accurately. Only a small proportion of the missiles were placed in underground silos, and most were thus poorly protected against nuclear weapons blast. This vulnerability was increased by the concentration of the launchers, with three or four to each site.[30] The Soviet Union tried to solve this problem in the mid-1960s by developing new mobile land-based systems, the SS-14 MRBM and the SS-15 IRBM. These missiles were derived from the solid-fuel SS-13 ICBM, but — apparently for technical reasons — they were not deployed in any number.[31]

The second problem was that a discrepancy emerged between the operational characteristics of the SS-4s and SS-5s and Soviet thinking about the course a war might take in Europe. These missiles apparently take from eight to twenty-four hours to make ready for firing. This slow reaction time was a serious drawback, given the Soviet interest in preemption. It became more serious when Soviet ideas about a war in Europe began to change in the late 1960s as a result of NATO's shift towards a strategy of flexible response, which envisages the possibility that war in Europe may begin with a conventional phase. The Soviet Union did not wish to be tied into an inflexible one-variant strategy of its own, and accordingly adjusted its policy to prepare for non-nuclear as well as nuclear operations in Europe. Since a European conflict might go nuclear at any time, flexible weapons, which could be fired quickly, were required. The SS-4s and SS-5s did not meet this requirement.

The third problem was the transformation of the Sino-Soviet dispute into a military confrontation. In the mid-1960s the Soviet leaders decided that the state of their relations with China required a build-up of military forces along the Sino-Soviet border. As part of this build-up they redeployed some of their SS-4s and SS-5s to the Far East.[32] After 1969 they also deployed the new SS-12, an operational-tactical missile with a range of about 800 kilometres, in the area. The confrontation with China now meant that a new element had entered into Soviet calculations of the balance in medium-range nuclear forces.

The Soviet Union responded to these problems by adapting the variable-range SS-11 ICBM for use against targets in the European theatre. By the early 1970s some 120 of these missiles had been deployed in SS-4 and SS-5 missile fields in the western part of the country.[33] Some SLBMs (Submarine Launched Ballistic Missiles) appear to have been assigned to the European theatre too. But in the mid-1970s two new purpose-built systems began to enter service: the Tu-22M *Backfire* bomber and the SS-20 IRBM. Both of these systems are a considerable improvement, in operational terms, over their predecessors.

The *Backfire* can fly at very low altitudes and at very high speeds and thus has a greater capacity to penetrate enemy air defences. It has greater range and more modern armament than the *Badger* or *Blinder,* and would be more effective against mobile targets. The SS-20 is also a significant improvement over the SS-4 and SS-5. It is a solid-fuel missile, derived from the SS-16 ICBM. It is mobile and therefore less vulnerable to attack. It can deliver three warheads, and is more effective against military targets, and better suited for a preemptive strike. It takes an hour to make ready for firing, and is thus more flexible. It also has a greater range, which allows it to reach more targets in Europe and China. In the mid-1970s the SS-19 ICBM, which can carry multiple warheads, began to replace the SS-11s deployed in the SS-4 and SS-5 missile fields.[34]

Development of these systems must have begun in the 1960s, but the decision to deploy them was probably taken in the early 1970s. By that time it was clear that medium-range systems would not be covered by SALT I. The old systems were obsolescent. The case for deployment must have seemed overwhelming. . . .

. . . NATO claims that its December 1979 decision was necessary to restore the military balance in Europe.

The Soviet Union, however, claims that parity exists, and that the new missiles are part of an attempt by the United States to regain superiority. From the Soviet point of view, the new American systems are not so much an addition to NATO's theatre forces as an augmentation of American strategic power, and thus a means of upsetting the balance ratified by the SALT Treaties. In a speech to military leaders in June 1980, Marshal Ogarkov, Chief of the General Staff, said that the implementation of NATO's plan "would not only disrupt sharply the approximate balance of medium-range nuclear systems that has been created in Europe, but would also lead to sharp qualitative changes in the military political situation, since it would create the threat of a surprise suppression of the launches of our strategic nuclear forces."[35] The Pershing II missile is of special significance in this regard, because it is highly accurate and could reach targets in the Western part of the Soviet Union within four to six minutes of being launched from Western Europe. If the Soviet Union has adopted a launch-on-warning policy, Pershing II's short flight time poses a particular threat because the missile could strike command and control installations in the Western Soviet Union with very little warning. Some Soviet commentators also argue that the GLCM's great accuracy would make it an effective first-strike weapon against missile silos.[36]

Soviet leaders see further evidence of an effort to break out of the relationship of parity in the increasing attention American strategic thought has given to the selective and controlled use of nuclear weapons in war. Soviet commentators have interpreted the idea of selective nuclear strikes as springing from a desire to restore political and military utility to American strategic forces.[37] There is nothing in Soviet military thinking or weapons deployment to suggest that a nuclear war could be controlled, and much to suggest that it could not.[38] Party leaders have been at pains to stress that nuclear war could not be conducted in a limited and selective manner, and they have warned that such ideas increase the risk of war by making it more "thinkable." Brezhnev told the 26th Party Congress in February 1981 that "a 'limited' nuclear war, as conceived by the Americans in, say, Europe, would from the outset mean certain destruction of European civilization. And, of course, the United States too, would not be able to escape the flames of war."[39] It is ironic that while NATO has been worried that the Soviet leaders might doubt the American commitment to its allies, the Soviet leaders have professed anxiety that the United States might make the mistake of thinking that it could conduct a nuclear war in Europe without incurring a nuclear strike on its own territory.

What has been taking place between NATO and the Warsaw Pact is not only a competition in arms, but also — and perhaps more importantly — a competition in strategies. Each side believes that the other is attempting to make its strategy unworkable and thereby to undermine its security. NATO sees Soviet policy as an effort to destroy the credibility of the strategy of flexible response, and thus to give the Soviet Union a military and political advantage through its preponderance of conventional forces. The Soviet Union claims that NATO is attempting to achieve military superiority, in order to be able to deal with the Soviet Union from a position of strength.

**Table 4.1. Soviet and U.S. Views of the Balance of Medium-Range Nuclear Forces in Europe, November 1981**

**United States View: USSR leads by 6 to 1**

| | *USA* | *USSR* |
|---|---|---|
| *IRBM* | 0 | 250 SS-20 |
| | | 350 SS-4/5 |
| | | 100 SS-12/22 |
| *SLBM* | 0 | 30 SS-N-5 |
| *Bombers* | 164 F-111 in W. Europe | 45 *Backfire* |
| | 63 FB-111 in USA | 350 { *Blinder*, *Badger* } |
| | 265 F-4 | |
| | 68 A-6/7 | 2,700 { Su-17, Su-24, MiG-27 } |
| | 560 Total | 3,825 Total |

**Soviet View: USSR and NATO in balance**

| | *USA + NATO* | *USSR* |
|---|---|---|
| *IRBM* | 18 French | 243 SS-20 |
| | | 253 SS-4/5 |
| *SLBM* | 80 French | 18 SS-N-5 |
| | 64 British | |
| *Bombers* | 65 US FB-111 | 461 { *Backfire*, *Blinder*, *Badger* } |
| | 172 US F-111 | |
| | 246 US F-4 | |
| | 240 US A-6/7 | |
| | 46 French *Mirage* IVA | |
| | 55 British *Vulcan* | |
| | 986 Total | 975 Total |

## Conclusion

There are those in the West who think that the driving force of the arms race is the Soviet pursuit of superiority, and that if the Soviet Union would commit itself wholeheartedly to parity, the arms race could be brought to a halt. Similarly, the Soviet leaders have argued that it is the American striving after superiority that fuels the arms race, and that if the United States would abandon that ambition, the arms race could be ended. The United States and the Soviet Union see each other as accepting parity only under duress, and each fears that the other is seeking to gain superiority. The United States argues that the Soviet Union enjoys superiority in theatre nuclear forces in Europe. The Soviet Union, for its part, claims that parity exists in medium-range nuclear forces in Europe and that the United States is trying to break out of the relationship of parity by deploying the new systems in Europe.

The absence of an agreed standard of measurement for nuclear forces makes it difficult to define parity unambiguously. This has emerged clearly from the public arguments that preceded the opening of the Geneva negotiations. The Soviet Union and the United States have differed over the categories of weapons to be considered in the balance. They have stressed different units of measurement: the United States is concerned to limit warheads, while the Soviet Union has put more emphasis on launchers. The United States would like to see limitations on Soviet medium-range systems east of the Urals. The Soviet Union would like to confine agreement to Europe, so as not to restrict its military policy in the Far East.

The problems of measurement are compounded by the asymmetries between the two sides in terms of force of structure, geography, technology and military strategy. Soviet medium-range forces are very different in structure from those of NATO countries. Their development has been shaped by geography — the proximity of American bases in Western Europe, and the confrontation with China; by technology — in particular by the early successes of the rocket development program; and by military strategy — the stress on preparing to fight war. All these factors greatly complicate the problem of defining parity precisely in terms of the levels of arms on either side.

The dynamism of military technology makes it difficult to give a stable definition of parity. New weapons may upset the balance, and it is not always clear in advance what those will be. At SALT I the head of the Soviet delegation dismissed American proposals for the limitation of cruise missiles. The head of the American delegation, Gerard Smith, writes that

> Semenov analogized cruise missiles to prehistoric animals of the Triassic period. I recalled that a Soviet Ambassador

> Tsarapkin had argued at the Geneva Conference on disarmament as early as 1964 that all bombers were obsolete, but now the Soviets were placing great stress not only on heavy bombers but also on lighter delivery aircraft (FBS). If Semenov was right their FBS position was really an attempt to summon up ichthyosaurs. Semenov closed out the conversation by saying, "A nightingale to one is an owl to another." Now the Soviet owl has become a nightingale, and in the SALT II negotation they pressed very hard for limitations on cruise missiles.[40]

The modern cruise missile, with its greatly improved guidance system, now poses a threat to the Soviet Union, and will no doubt, once the Soviet Union has developed the technology, pose a similar threat to NATO. Moreover, the cruise missile presents formidable problems for arms control. Because it is small and mobile, limitations on deployment will be difficult to verify.

All these factors point towards the conclusion that defining parity in specific terms is not a technical, but a political problem. Where there are so many disagreements, and no agreed technique for resolving them, the only solution is a political one. Only negotiation — whether formal or informal — can provide an agreed definition of parity in terms of the numbers of arms on either side. The process of negotiation presents difficulties of its own, however, apart from those already discussed. Weapons may be developed and produced as bargaining chips, or agreements may direct interest towards technologies that are not limited. In this way arms control negotiations may actually stimulate competition. Moreover, tough negotiating (and what government wants to negotiate flabbily?) may draw out the process, to the point where the agreement is overtaken by the development of new weapons technologies.

Arms control is not isolated from politics, but is deeply rooted in the East–West political relationship. It is at once an arrangement for pursuing the cooperative objective of regulating the competition in arms, and an arena in which the two sides try to further their coempting interests. In the prelude to the Geneva negotiations both the Soviet Union and the United States declared their interest in controlling the arms race, and tried to present themselves as more armed against than arming. It is not clear whether, in view of the great differences that divide them, they can translate their professions of interest in arms limitation into an effective agreement.

## Notes

20. G. A. Tokaty, "Soviet Rocket Technology," in E. M. Emme (ed.), *The History of Rocket Technology,* Detroit. Wayne State U.P., 1964, p. 281.
21. Jean Alexander, *Russian Aircraft Since 1940,* London: Putnam, 1975, pp. 289–93, 384–7; A. N. Ponomaryvov, *Sovetskie aviatsionnye konstruktory,* Moscow: Voenizdat 1977, pp. 198–200; N. S. Khrushchev, *Khrushchev Remembers. The Last Testament,* London: Andre Deutsch, 1974, pp. 39–40.
22. David Holloway, "Military Technology," in R. Amann, J. Cooper, R. W. Davies (eds.), *The Technological Level of Soviet Industry,* New Haven and London: Yale U.P., 1977, pp. 458–9.
23. Robert Berman and John C. Baker, *Soviet Strategic Forces,* Washington, D.C.: The Brookings Institution, forthcoming.
24. Maj. Gen. M. Cherednichenko, "Ob osobennostyakh razvitiya voennogo iskusstva v poslevoennyi period," *Voennoistoricheskii zhurnal,* 1970, no. 6, p. 25; see also Raymond L. Garthoff, *Soviet Strategy in the Nuclear Age,* London: Stevens and Sons, 1958, pp. 221–2.
25. Quoted in Arnold L. Horelick and Myron Rush, *Strategic Power and Soviet Foreign Policy,* Chicago and London: The University of Chicago Press, 1966, p. 94.
26. Committee on Foreign Affairs, U.S. House of Representatives, Special Studies on Foreign Affairs Issues, vol. 1, *Soviet Diplomacy and Negotiating Behavior: Emerging New Context for U.S. Diplomacy,* by Joseph G. Whelan, Washington D.C.: USGPO, 1979, p. 283.
27. *Pravda,* 15 November 1958.
28. *Pravda,* 28 May 1959.
29. *Pravda,* 15 January 1960.
30. Berman and Baker, *op. cit.*
31. Edward I. Warner III, *The Military in Contemporary Soviet Politics. An Institutional Analysis,* New York: Praeger Special Studies, 1977, p. 195; Gregory Treverton, *Nuclear Weapons in Europe,* Adelphi Papers No. 168, London: International Institute for Strategic Studies, 1981, p. 6.
32. Warner, *op. cit.,* p. 195.
33. Warner, *op. cit.,* p. 194; Treverton, *op. cit.,* p. 6.
34. Berman and Baker, *op. cit.*
35. N. V. Ogarkov, "V interesakh povysheniya boevoi gotovnosti," *Kommunist Vooruzhennykh Sil,* 1980, no. 14, p. 26.
36. Raymond L. Garthoff, "The TNF Tangle," *Foreign Policy,* No. 41, Winter 1980–81, pp. 92–3; Raymond L. Garthoff, "Soviet Perspectives," in Richard K. Betts (ed.), *Cruise Missiles, Technology, Strategy, Politics,* Washington D.C.: The Brookings Institution, 1981, p. 345.
37. See, for example, M. A. Mil'shtein and L. S. Semeiko, "Problema nedopustimosti yadernogo konflikta (o novykh podkhodakh v SShA)," *SShA,* 1974, no. 11, pp. 2–13.
38. Desmond Ball, *Can Nuclear War Be Controlled?,* Adelphi Papers No. 169, London: International Institute for Strategic Studies, 1981, pp. 30–5.
39. *Pravda,* 24 February 1981.
40. Gerard Smith, *Doubletalk. The Story of the First Strategic Arms Limitations Talks,* New York: Doubleday, 1980, pp. 130–1.

## President Reagan's Zero Option

### *Document 14*

In November 1981 President Reagan made an opening INF arms control proposal to the Soviet Union. His proposal, the zero option, was an approach that European leaders had urged on him. Reagan proposed that the United States cancel its planned deployments of new missiles if the Soviet Union would dismantle all of its INF missiles — the new SS-20s, as well as the older SS-4s and SS-5s.

### 14 SPEECH
### President Ronald Reagan
### The National Press Club
### November 18, 1981

Now let me turn now to our hopes for arms control negotiations. There's a tendency to make this entire subject overly complex; I want to be clear and concise. I told you of the letter I wrote to President Brezhnev last April? Well, I've just sent another message to the Soviet leadership.

It's a simple, straightforward yet historic message. The United States proposes the mutual reduction of conventional, intermediate-range nuclear and strategic forces. Specifically, I have proposed a four-point agenda to achieve this objective in my letter to President Brezhnev.

The first and most important point concerns the Geneva negotiations. As part of the 1979 two-track decision, NATO made a commitment to seek arms control negotiations with the Soviet Union on intermediate-range nuclear forces. The United States has been preparing for these negotiations through close consultation with our NATO partners. We're now ready to set forth our proposal.

I have informed President Brezhnev that when our delegation travels to the negotiations on intermediate-range land-based nuclear missiles in Geneva on the 30th of this month, my representatives will present the following proposal:

The United States is prepared to cancel its deployment of Pershing 2 and ground-launched missiles if the Soviets will dismantle their SS-20, SS-4 and SS-5 missiles. This would be an historic step.

With Soviet agreement, we could together substantially reduce the dread threat of nuclear war which hangs over the people of Europe. This, like the first footstep on the moon, would be a giant step for mankind.

Now we intend to negotiate in good faith and go to Geneva willing to listen to and consider the proposals of our Soviet counterparts. But let me call to your attention the background against which our proposal is made. During the past six years, while the United States deployed no new intermediate-range missiles and withdrew 1,000 nuclear warheads from Europe, the Soviet Union deployed 750 warheads on mobile, accurate ballistic missiles. They now have 1,100 warheads on the SS-20's, SS-4's and 5's. And the United States has no comparable missiles. Indeed, the United States dismantled the last such missile in Europe over 15 years ago.

As we look to the future of the negotiations, it's also important to address certain Soviet claims which, left unrefuted, could become critical barriers to real progress in arms control. The Soviets assert that a balance of intermediate-range nuclear forces already exists; that assertion is wrong. By any objective measure, as this chart indicates, the Soviet Union has developed an increasing, overwhelming advantage. They now enjoy a superiority on the order of 6 to 1. The red is the Soviet buildup, the blue is our own. That is 1975, and that is 1981.

Now Soviet spokesmen have suggested that moving their SS-20's behind the Ural Mountains will remove the threat to Europe. Well, as this map demonstrates, the SS-20's, even if deployed behind the Urals, will have a range that puts almost all of Western Europe — the great cities, Rome, Athens, Paris, London, Brussels, Amsterdam, Berlin and so many more, all of Scandinavia, all of the middle East, all of Northern Africa — all within range of these missiles, which, incidentally, are mobile and can be moved on shorter notice. These little images mark the present location, which would give them a range clear out into the Atlantic.

## The Key Issues in the INF Negotiations

### *Document 15*

Document 15, part of a study by the National Academy of Sciences, summarizes the positions of the United States and the Soviet Union at the time the INF negotitions were broken off at the end of 1983. The main issues included: the systems to be covered, the geographic scope of the negotiations, whether French and British forces would be covered, and verification.

### 15 THE INF NEGOTIATIONS
### 1985

#### The European Nuclear Balance: Different U.S. and Soviet Perspectives

The underlying issue in the INF negotiations is the different assessments of the balance of nuclear forces in

Europe by the Unites States and the Soviet Union. These differing views determined each side's position on the scope of the negotiations. The United States and NATO believe that there is a significant imbalance favoring the Soviet Union, which was the main reason for NATO's 1979 decision to have the United States deploy 464 GLCMs and 108 Pershing IIs in Europe. The Soviet Union believes that there is presently a regional balance, which was the main Soviet rationale for opposing any U.S. deployments in Europe. Analysts have argued for years about the actual number of nuclear systems in Europe. The following sections describe the official U.S. and Soviet assessments of the balance of intermediate-range nuclear systems since the INF negotiations began in 1981.

### The U.S. View

The U.S. perspective, which its NATO allies share, is that since the mid-1970s there has been a growing disparity in the nuclear balance in Europe. The most important factor that has contributed to the growing threat to Western Europe and to the instability of the European military balance has been the continuing deployment of Soviet intermediate-range systems, in particular the new mobile solid-fueled SS-20 missile. Since 1977 the Soviet Union has deployed some 378 SS-20s, each with three accurate 150-kt MIRVed warheads. More than 240 of these SS-20s can be targeted on Western Europe. The United States and its NATO allies consider the SS-20 to be a new generation of longer-range, qualitatively improved intermediate-range missiles, not simply an improvement on the older, fixed Soviet SS-4 and SS-5 systems previously deployed in Europe. Also, unlike the SS-4s and SS-5s, the SS-20s can be reloaded, which further complicates the balance. The United States has estimated that as of January 1, 1984, Soviet warheads on all intermediate range missiles including those in the Far East totaled approximately 1,300, not including the SS-20's reload capacity.

In the U.S. view, until the deployment of the U.S. Pershing II and GLCM systems begin in the late fall of 1983, the United States and its NATO allies had no systems that posed a comparable threat and thus provided a deterrent against a Soviet threat of attack or actual attack on Western Europe. This situation led to NATO's 1979 dual-track decision to modernize its intermediate-range nuclear forces while pursuing arms control to reduce the threat posed by these Soviet systems. The United States and its allies were concerned that without the U.S. deployment in Europe or without an agreement that would decrease the Soviet threat, the NATO alliance would have to rely upon U.S. strategic forces to respond to a Soviet attack with intermediate-range missiles. The alliance would also have to rely solely on these U.S. strategic forces to deter a Soviet threat of attack to attain political goals. Under such circumstances the United States and its allies feared that deterrence would be undermined, since the Soviet Union might miscalculate in a crisis that an attack limited to Europe would not produce a strategic response from the United States.

Further disrupting the balance in Europe in the U.S. view was Soviet development and deployment of a new generation of shorter-range ballistic missiles (the SS-22s and SS-23s) with ranges from 500 to 1,000 km. Once the U.S. Pershing IA missiles are replaced by Pershing IIs, the United States will have only a small number of operational short-range (110 km) Lance missiles. In the U.S. view, the shorter-range Soviet missile systems pose an increasing threat to the survivability of NATO's air bases and seaports, command, control, and communications facilities, and key nuclear and conventional forces. In the mid-1970s the Soviet Union also markedly enhanced its theater nuclear aircraft capabilities when it started to deploy the Backfire bomber. In the U.S. view, all of these recent Soviet deployments have increased the gap between NATO's nuclear capabilities and those of the Soviet Union.

President Reagan countered the Soviet claim of approximate parity in the overall European balance, including missiles and aircraft, with the claim that the Soviet Union had an overwhelming six to one advantage. According to estimates provided by the U.S. State Department in 1981, total U.S. intermediate-range nuclear systems numbered about 560, compared with 3,825 Soviet systems. The U.S. estimate included 2,700 Soviet fighter-bombers that U.S. analysts believe can deliver nuclear weapons or can be readily converted to that status. The Soviet Union does not include these bombers in its estimates. The United States also pointed out that the Soviet Union claimed that parity existed in Europe from 1979 through 1982, during which time the number of Soviet missile warheads on land-based intermediate-range missiles increased from 800 to 1,300. The United States also criticized the Soviet calculations for including the independent British and French nuclear systems.

### The Soviet View

The Soviet Union has continued to insist that rough parity in intermediate-range weapons existed in Europe throughout the late 1970s and early 1980s until it was disrupted by the U.S. deployment of Pershing IIs and GLCMs. In 1979, according to Soviet calculations, the rough parity included approximately 1,000 systems apiece for the Soviet Union and the NATO countries. The Soviet estimates included on their side the SS-20, SS-4 and SS-5 missiles and intermediate-range bombers; on the NATO side the Soviet estimates included the U.S. forward-based nuclear force (FB-11) bombers, F-111 and F-4 fighter-bombers, A-6 and A-7 carrier-based aircraft, and the Pershing IA missiles, together with the nuclear forces of Britain and France (ground-based French S-2 and S-3 missiles, British Polaris and French M-20 submarine-based ballistic missiles, and Vulcan, Buccaneer, and Mirage bombers). At the end of 1983, then Soviet Chief of the General Staff Marshall Ogarkov presented slightly different estimates that included 938 Soviet launchers (465 bombers and 473 missiles) and 857 NATO launch vehicles (695 aircraft and 162 British and French missiles). Soviet spokesmen pointed out that NATO delivery systems have a range of 1,000 to 4,000 km and thus can reach targets within the Soviet Union, making them analogous in combat potential to Soviet SS-20 missiles.

The Soviet Union has argued that the SS-20 is simply a replacement on a one-for-one or one-for-two basis for the older SS-4 and SS-5 missiles, whose service lives have expired. To counter the arguments about the destabilizing nature of the upgraded SS-20s, Soviet spokesmen have noted that even though they carry three warheads, their combined yield (three times 150 kt) is less than that of one old SS-4 and SS-5 warhead (around 1 Mt). Consequently, Soviet spokesmen have repeatedly stated that the process of replacing obsolete missiles has decreased both the total number of Soviet "carriers" and the total yield of the warheads these systems could deliver. At the end of 1983 the Soviet Union stated that it had reduced its missile launchers from 600 to 473 and that the SS-5 missile had been totally withdrawn. President Andropov charged that U.S. assessments of an imbalance pretend that 1,000 medium-range U.S. and NATO nuclear systems in the European zone do not exist.

The Soviet government has argued that the deployment of new U.S. intermediate-range systems will disrupt the existing rough parity by giving NATO a major advantage in both the number of missile launchers and associated missile warheads. With these new deployments, according to the Soviet Union, the United States is starting another exceptionally dangerous round in the arms race.

The Soviet Union has also emphasized the charge that the new U.S. missiles dramatically change the nuclear balance since they can reach Soviet territory in a very short time whereas similar Soviet missiles cannot reach the United States at all. In the Soviet view, these new U.S. systems, particularly the Pershing IIs, undercut the foundation of strategic stability because they threaten the Soviet command and control systems. More generally, the Soviet Union has argued that these new U.S. deployments in Europe are part of a larger U.S. program designed to give the United States the capability to launch a preemptive attack against the Soviet Union. In the Soviet view, the Pershing II, in the context of the MX missile, the Trident II D-5 missile, anti-satellite weapons, the new command and control systems, and the new ballistic missile defense initiative, will produce a destabilizing shift toward U.S. preemptive superiority.

## The Main Differences Between the U.S. and Soviet INF Proposals

The main differences between the U.S. and Soviet proposals center on three main issues: (1) the systems to be included in the negotiations, (2) the geographic scope of the negotiations, and (3) the treatment of third-country nuclear forces.

## The U.S. Approach

The five criteria guiding the U.S. approach to the negotiations were that an agreement (1) must entail equal limits and rights for the United States and the Soviet Union, (2) should address only U.S. and Soviet systems, (3) should apply to INF missiles regardless of location and should not shift the security problem in Europe to the Far East, (4) should not weaken the U.S. contribution to NATO's conventional deterrence and defense, and (5) must be verifiable.

### *The U.S. View: Systems to Be Covered*

In the view of the United States and its NATO allies, the chief source of the destabilizing imbalance in Europe has been the new SS-20 missile. Therefore, the opening U.S. position, the zero option, sought to eliminate the entire class of intermediate-range land-based missiles, together with their launchers and certain support structures and equipment. It also banned testing and production of new intermediate-range missile systems. The practical implication of the zero option was that the United States, which had no system comparable with the SS-20, SS-4, or SS-5 missiles, was willing to forego the deployment of its Pershing IIs and GLCMs if the Soviet Union would eliminate its existing intermediate-range systems.

The U.S. interim proposal covered the same land-based missiles. Throughout the negotiations the United States insisted that it must have equal rights to deploy intermediate-range systems to offset any Soviet deployments if these systems were not to be eliminated. The informal walk-in-the-woods formula suggested that the United States might be prepared to forego deployment of the Pershing II missiles while proceeding with the deployments of the GLCMs in exchange for certain Soviet concessions, but the U.S. government officially rejected that approach and continued to argue that both systems were necessary to offset the Soviet advantage in this area. As long as the Soviet Union maintained an SS-20 force, the United States argued, the right to deploy a mix of Pershing IIs and GLCMs was essential to provide flexibility in delivery systems and to hedge against the possible loss of either system.

Even though the United States would not forego the right to deploy either Pershing IIs or GLCMs, it did modify its position, announcing that it was willing to negotiate the mix of the planned deployment level of the Pershing IIs and GLCMs. Toward the end of the negotiations the United States also acknowledged the Soviet concern about aircraft by indicating a readiness to explore limits on specific types of U.S. and Soviet aircraft. But the two sides continued to disagree over what aircraft should be counted and how aircraft should be included in the negotiations. The U.S. assessment gave the Soviet Union a five-to-one advantage in this area, whereas Soviet assessments gave NATO an advantage.

The U.S. approach on intermediate-range missiles also included collateral restraints on shorter-range nuclear missiles. The original U.S. position included limits on Soviet missiles with ranges between those of the Soviet SS-23 and SS-12/22 (500 to 1,000 km) at the levels deployed as of January 1, 1982. The net effect of the U.S. zero option proposal would have been to ban any ground-launched nuclear missiles with ranges greater than that of the Soviet SS-12/22. The United States did not include limits on the shorter-range U.S. Pershing IA missile (700 km), on the grounds that shorter-range Soviet systems could fulfill the missions of Soviet intermediate-range missiles to a much greater extent than the Pershing IA could fulfill the mission of U.S. intermediate-range systems. However, in June 1983, after the Soviet Union agreed to consider limitations on these shorter-range systems, the United States agreed to consider restraints on the Pershing IA.

### *The U.S. View: Geographic Scope*

The U.S. proposal called for worldwide limits on intermediate-range missiles because the range, mobility, and transportability of the SS-20s made these missiles a potential threat to the NATO allies even if deployed in the Far East. The U.S. zero option solved this problem by completely eliminating these systems. Under the interim proposal the main reason for global limits was to ensure that the security threat to Europe was not shifted to the Far East. In September 1983 the United States modified its position by stating that under an agreement providing for equal global ceilings, the United States was prepared not to match the entire worldwide deployment of Soviet intermediate-range missiles with U.S. missiles in Europe and offered to explore the level of these European deployments.

With regard to the Soviet proposal, the United States argued that, with the range of 5,000 km it calculated for the SS-20, the line behind which the Soviets proposed to deploy SS-20s would still have them within range of Western Europe. In addition, the Soviet offer to freeze intermediate-range systems in Asia was subject to a unilateral Soviet assessment of the strategic situation there and thus did not constitute a real limitation.

### *The U.S. View: Third-Country Forces*

The U.S. position dealt only with U.S. and Soviet systems. It excluded any limitation on or compensation for third-country forces. In response to the Soviet argument that British and French nuclear forces should be included, the United States maintained that these were independent forces of two sovereign nations that were not parties to the negotiations. The United States also argued that it does not determine or control the composition or employment of these forces, which are national minimum deterrents. They are for the most part submarine-based and differ in role and characteristics from the land-based intermediate-range missiles under discussion at Geneva. The U.S. negotiators argued that, unlike the U.S. systems, the British and French systems were not intended to deter attacks on other nonnuclear NATO countries. The U.S. negotiators also argued that the Soviet effort to include those forces violated the fundamental principle of equal rights and limits between the United States and the Soviet Union. Finally, top-level U.S. government officials noted that, while the Soviet Union had previously sought in other arms control negotiations to obtain compensation for British and French forces, it had in the past found it possible to enter into agreements with the United States even though its demands for compensation were rejected. . . .

## The Soviet Approach

The main thrust of the Soviet approach has been that there is a balance of medium-range missiles in Europe between NATO and the Soviet Union and that the subject of the negotiations should be limitations on the nuclear arms of the Soviet Union and all NATO forces threatening the Soviet Union. Only this approach will assure the Soviet Union equality and equal security in Europe. The Soviet Union argued that the SS-20 had not disrupted the balance and was in fact simply a modernized replacement of older systems whose service lives had come to an end. The deployment of new U.S. missiles, however, constituted a buildup of new nuclear weapons capabilities. This buildup therefore undermined the very purpose of the talks and made the negotiations meaningless in the Soviet view. The Soviet Union emphasized that no Soviet systems in Europe can target the United States, whereas the new U.S. systems can hit the Soviet Union in about ten minutes.

In the Soviet view, theater forces are directly related to the overall strategic balance that was implicitly agreed to in SALT I and SALT II. In these agreements, overall capabilities were pronounced equal. Soviet advantages in intercontinental ballistic missiles and theater forces offset U.S. advantages in strategic bombers, forward-based systems threatening the Soviet Union, allied forces, and the overall quality of U.S. forces, as exemplified by its submarine-launched ballistic missiles. Any revisions of the SALT approach would have to be reciprocal and equal. Present systems would be traded for present systems; future systems would be traded for future systems.

### *The Soviet View: Systems to Be Covered*

From the outset of the negotiations the Soviet Union maintained that if the sides did not agree to remove all nuclear weapons from Europe, then an agreement should provide for equal reduced levels of both missiles and aircraft between the Soviet Union and NATO, not just the United States. Since a balance of theater forces already existed in Europe, the Soviet Union called for a ban on the deployment of new U.S. intermediate-range missiles. The Soviet Union argued that both the Pershing IIs and the GLCMs would disrupt the existing balance, but it focused particular attention on the dangerous and destabilizing aspects of the Pershing IIs. Although in the walk-in-the-woods formula the Soviet negotiator appeared to be agreeing to allow the United States to deploy GLCMs in Europe within a larger set of trade-offs, the Soviet Union officially rejected this approach and reaffirmed its insistence on no U.S. deployments.

The Soviet Union argued that its proposals were seeking approximate parity at lower levels of medium-range systems. In the Soviet view, it is a false distinction to separate nuclear weapons on aircraft from those on missiles. The Soviet Union argued that it cannot ignore the thousands of nuclear weapons on U.S. aircraft in the European zone and on U.S. aircraft carriers, just as it cannot ignore the other nuclear weapons on NATO delivery systems.

Although toward the end of the negotiations the United States agreed to consider aircraft, the Soviet Union argued that U.S. accounting of aircraft turned the NATO's real 50 percent advantage over Soviet medium-range aircraft into a fivefold advantage for the Soviet Union. The Soviet Union insisted that the United States was counting, along with Soviet medium-range bombers, a large number of tactical fighter-bombers that have never carried and cannot, as now configured, carry nuclear weapons. At the same time, it asserted that the United States excluded whole categories of U.S. forward-based aircraft capable of striking the Soviet Union. Consequently, the initial Soviet approach in the negotiations was to call for a ban on new U.S. deployments and a reduction to equal levels of U.S. and Soviet medium-range missiles and aircraft in or intended for use in Europe, with British and French systems being counted under the U.S. totals. This position eventually evolved to include a subceiling for missiles and to allow warheads to be the unit of account to compare Soviet forces with existing British and French forces. The resulting warhead ceiling of 420 would have required reducing Soviet SS-20 launchers within range of Europe to 140.

### *The Soviet View: Geography*

The Soviet Union argued that the negotiations should not include missiles or aircraft out of range of European targets, since its missiles in the Far East pose no threat to Europe. These missiles are intended to protect Soviet security in the Far East. By the end of the negotiations, the Soviet Union proposed to freeze the number of its SS-20 missiles in Asia contingent on the "strategic situation." The Soviet Union stated that this geographic distinction would be assured by its proposed "zone of reduction and withdrawal" behind which, it asserted, the SS-20s could not hit European targets. In defining the zone the Soviet Union claimed that the SS-20 has a range of 4,000 km, while the United States claimed that it has a range of up to 5,000 km.

### *The Soviet View: Third-Country Forces*

By the end of the negotiations, the Soviet claims for compensation for British and French forces became the central issue of disagreement. The Soviet Union argued that it could not be expected to ignore more than 400 warheads on British and French sea- and land-based missiles that are aimed at the Soviet Union and its allies. Moreover, these warheads are likely to increase from the present level to 1,200 by 1990 and to 2,000 by the end of the century if planned programs are carried out. Under such circumstances, the Soviet Union argued that it was impossible to exclude these missiles from the count of NATO weapons in Europe threatening the Soviet Union. In addition, the Soviet Union claimed that its proposals addressed European concerns about the deployment of the SS-20s by reducing the warheads on Soviet intermediate-range systems to below the level that existed in 1976.

The Soviet Union has not accepted the rationale that the British and French systems are independent, given British participation in NATO and vigorous French support for the decision to deploy U.S. missiles. Soviet representatives also argued that it defies logic for the United States to present the modernization decision as a NATO mandate while claiming that NATO armaments should not be counted in the negotiations.

### *General Soviet Criticisms of the U.S. Proposals*

The Soviet Union criticized the U.S. proposals generally on the grounds that they called for inequitable and disproportionate reductions in Soviet forces. In the Soviet view, the zero option was, in effect, an attempt to impose unilateral disarmament on the Soviet Union, since it would have to scrap all of its medium-range missiles while the United States and its NATO allies would retain all of their nuclear weapons in this category.

The U.S. interim proposals, in the Soviet view, also ran counter to the principle of equal security. The interim proposal would allow the deployment of U.S. Pershing

IIs and GLCMs in Europe, which would pose a new strategic threat to the Soviet Union and disrupt the existing balance in Europe. Thus, by proposing a trade between future U.S. systems and present Soviet systems with no constraints on British and French forces, the U.S. proposals contradicted the principles of equality and equal security and the overall balance incorporated in SALT I and SALT II.

The Soviet Union also criticized the general U.S. approach to the negotiations, charging that the United States simply used the negotiations as a smokescreen for the U.S. missile deployments in Europe. In this context, Soviet spokesmen criticized the United States for revealing and distorting the private negotiations for propaganda purposes.

## The Soviets Move Toward the Zero Option

### *Document 16*

In January 1985 Mikhail Gorbachev, the new leader of the Soviet Union, made a major speech on arms control. In this analysis of the speech, Soviet specialist Raymond Garthoff points out that Gorbachev made a number of concessions that, in effect, accepted President Reagan's earlier zero option. Gorbachev for the first time separated the question of limits on British and French systems from the question of limits on U.S. and Soviet INF missiles. Gorbachev also seemed willing to eliminate all Soviet INF missiles, though some details of this were left unclear.

### 16 THE GORBACHEV PROPOSAL AND PROSPECTS FOR ARMS CONTROL
**Raymond Garthoff**

The comprehensive Soviet proposal was advanced in a major pronouncement as a "formal declaration" by General Secretary Gorbachev. . . .

The most dramatic new step was the proposal for elimination of all U.S. and Soviet intermediate-range missiles[41] in the European zone. This decoupling of Soviet INF missile levels from the existing British and French missile levels was new, and a major Soviet concession. It also implied possible equal U.S. and Soviet levels other than zero. The call for no "buildup" of British and French forces,[42] while reasonable, was clearly beyond U.S. negotiating competence and beyond what the United States could be expected to press from its allies. But reference in the plan itself to the first stage as involving only U.S. and Soviet forces may imply a readiness by the Soviet Union to fall back to a unilateral assertion (as in SALT I) of a right to compensation in its own forces for any future British and French buildup — a right that the United States and its allies would no doubt initially object to, but might acquiesce in.

The call for non-transfer of U.S. strategic and intermediate-range missiles to other countries was intended mainly to block a loophole that the Soviet Union could not afford to overlook. Soviet leaders have been wary of such loopholes, particularly after the SALT II obligation of noncircumvention of strategic force levels through third countries was followed by the NATO INF deployment decision. The planned United States sale of Trident II missiles to Britain is the only current transaction that would be affected. But the Soviets also want to foreclose the possibility of any U.S. transfer of Pershing II and GLCM systems to other NATO powers. Whether such a ban would raise a problem concerning NATO interest in non-nuclear cruise missile technology transfers is not clear.

The Soviet reference to eliminating intermediate-range missiles "in the European zone" has authoritatively been explained to include SS-20 deployments all the way to 80 degrees longitude east, between Omsk and Novosibirsk in central Siberia. The number of SS-20 launchers in this zone stands again today at 243, the same total (including those then under construction) as when the first Soviet moratorium was declared in March 1982. After U.S. INF deployments began in November 1983, the Soviet Union in response installed an additional 27 SS-20 launchers in this area in 1984–85. However, these launchers were removed and the facilities deactivated in the latter part of 1985 in an effort to influence the Dutch INF deployment decision. The Soviets are also gradually eliminating a small number of old SS–4 missile launchers in this zone.

## Notes

41. In Soviet terminology, "medium-range" systems is a category embracing all systems from 1,000 to 5,000 kilometers range. The formerly distinct Western categories of medium and intermediate-range systems have now generally come to be called "intermediate-range nuclear forces" (INF), and that term is used here.

42. The Gorbachev plan would not bar modernization of the British and French strategic forces, except for "building up" (presumably in numbers of launchers and warheads); in practice it would ban the planned large augmentation in numbers or warheads incident to MIRVing.

## Will NATO Accept Its Own Proposal?

### *Document 17*

At the Reykjavik summit, the Soviets made clear that they were serious about INF limits (see chap. 12). Soviet negotiators agreed to eliminate all INF missiles from Europe and to limit Soviet warheads in Asia to one hundred. After the summit, the Soviets also took steps to resolve some of NATO's other concerns on shorter-range missiles and verification. As the United States and the Soviet Union appeared to move close to an agreement that would eliminate most nuclear systems in Europe, an ironic development took place. European leaders began to worry that arms control was becoming too successful. They feared that if NATO gave up its new missiles and some shorter-range ones, Soviet conventional superiority would become more important. In this editorial in the *New York Times,* former chancellor of West Germany, Helmut Schmidt, notes the irony of the situation. He recommends that NATO now accept its own proposal.

## 17 IF MISSILES GO, PEACE MAY STAY
**Helmut Schmidt**
**April 29, 1987**

The rapid movement toward an arrangement that would remove both Soviet and Western intermediate-range missiles from the European theater has caused great concern — even among long-time advocates of arms control. As one who originally encouraged the "zero-zero option," and was forced from office partly for advocating the idea, I urge my nervous friends in Europe and America to embrace it. Their fears that the removal of these weapons will leave Europe vulnerable to Soviet attack are misplaced.

It is first necessary to understand some recent history. The problem was created by the Soviet Union's decision to deploy newly developed SS-20 rockets in the mid-1970's, which created a disparity of power in Europe. This fact was noted by President Gerald R. Ford and his Secretary of State, Henry A. Kissinger, during the Vladivostok summit meeting in 1974.

Mr. Ford, however, decided to solve the problem after his expected reelection in 1976 within the framework of the SALT II agreements, a course that I, as West German Chancellor, accepted. But Jimmy Carter, who became President, did not accept my opinion that the SS-20's posed a growing political and military threat to West Germany, and he decided not to tackle this problem within the framework of SALT II.

Annoyed, I went public with my concerns in a speech in London in the autumn of 1977, which prompted the White House to re-evaluate the matter the next year. Finally, in January 1979, in a meeting involving Mr. Carter, Prime Minister James Callaghan of Britain, Prime Minister Valéry Giscard d'Estaing of France and myself on Guadeloupe, Mr. Carter offered to balance off the SS-20's by deploying American intermediate-range missiles on West European soil, and West German soil in particular.

The three European leaders suggested a variation on this strategy, which became known as the dual-track approach. What it amounted to was that, if negotiations were fruitless, the North Atlantic Treaty Organization would deploy its own missiles in Europe to counter the Soviet buildup, but would push forward with further negotiations to limit the deployment of intermediate-range missiles on both sides. President Carter agreed to this idea and so did the Western European allies, despite heavy domestic opposition and demonstrations, particularly in the Netherlands, West Germany and Britain.

During the 1980's, I repeatedly pointed to a zero-zero solution, under which both sides would eliminate all intermediate-range missiles, as being the optimal outcome of the negotiations. Leonid I. Brezhnev, the Soviet leader, rejected this formula but agreed to negotiations, which began in the fall of 1981. In the meantime, President Reagan, at my suggestion, had publicly endorsed the zero-zero formula. In spite of great effort and skill applied by the American negotiator Paul H. Nitze, the negotiations failed and the deployment of Pershing 2's and ground-launched cruise missiles started at the end of 1983.

Given this history, it is ridiculous to claim that the zero-zero solution is a "Communist proposal," as some American public figures are quoted as having said. The truth is that it has been a Western proposal from the beginning. If in 1987, as I sincerely hope, the zero-zero formula is going to be agreed between East and West, it will be a concession by the East and not by the West.

Why does Mikhail S. Gorbachev make that concession? (Incidentally, I am inclined to think that not only Mr. Gorbachev but also his predecessor, Yuri V. Andropov, might have accepted the formula if only he had lived on a couple of more years.) The Kremlin has two main reasons:

First, it had hoped, with the help of the peace movements in Western countries and other protestors, to prevent the deployment of Western intermediate-range missiles. These missiles were deployed, and the Soviet leaders now realize that the Pershing 2's and ground-launched cruise missiles are a serious threat to targets on Soviet soil.

Second, Mr. Gorbachev must open a gateway toward further mutual arms reductions because he urgently needs, for economic reasons, to scale down his military expenditures, which amount to 12 to 14 percent of the Soviet gross national product. He cannot otherwise hope tangibly to improve the Soviet standard of living, an improvement he dearly desires.

The intra-Western debate about zero-zero is somewhat confused. Nevertheless, it has produced two arguments against striking the deal that deserve careful consideration:

1. Since 1983, the Soviet Union has deployed additional short-range nuclear weapons in forward areas close to West Germany, in Czechoslovakia and in East Germany in particular, thereby creating an additional disequilibrium in its favor. This disequilibrium has to be dealt with in the framework of negotiations on intermediate-range missiles, and Mr. Gorbachev has indicated his willingness to do so.

2. Some military thinkers in the West, especially the Supreme Allied Commander in Europe, Gen. Bernard D. Rogers, have stressed their belief that total abandonment of short-range missiles will deprive the West of the capacity to use nuclear weapons first in response to a Soviet conventional attack.

Pointing to the Soviet Union's numerical superiority in conventional weapons in Europe, General Rogers argues that the option to use short-range nuclear weapons first is vital to credible deterrence. Yet this numerical conventional superiority has always existed, although it is absurd to include in it the Polish, Czechoslovak and East German troops: In case of a Soviet attack, these troops would be very unreliable allies and would need Soviet guards to prevent them from following their own national instincts.

I am not really afraid of the remaining conventional disequilibrium because I strongly believe in the high capability and fighting spirit of the West German forces. There are 500,000 soldiers on the spot, and this number can grow quickly to 1.3 million in less than a week after mobilization. We Germans, like the French and all other continental Western European countries, have maintained the draft; we thus have at our disposal numerous fully trained reserves, whose deterrence value is high. It would be still higher if the French, the Benelux and the West German forces were integrated in the future.

In case of a zero-zero agreement, including short-range weapons, the West would still have enough nuclear artillery and nuclear-equipped fighter-bombers so that the famous "flexible response" strategy could still be applied. Nevertheless, I would like to restate my long-standing judgment that "flexible response" has never presupposed genuine flexibility. Instead, it has always implied a quick escalation toward very early first use of nuclear weapons by the West. But it is unrealistic to believe that West German soldiers would fight after the explosion of the first couple of nuclear weapons on West German soil; the West Germans would certainly not act any more fanatically or suicidally than the Japanese did in 1945 after Hiroshima and Nagasaki.

Western nuclear weapons are necessary and valuable only in order to deter the Eastern side from a first use of Soviet nuclear weapons. This also applies to nuclear weapons of so-called strategic ranges. Nuclear weapons must not be perceived as an instrument to deter limited war or even larger-scale conventional attack.

What we do need in order to discourage and deter an adversary from limited aggression, whether in Afghanistan, Europe or elsewhere, are credible conventional forces. Such forces exist in Western Europe in almost satisfactory numbers. To tell the West Germans that their territory could be defended effectively only if we in the West were willing to be the first ones to strike with nuclear weapons is a sure way of undermining West Germany's will to fight if the need to defend itself actually arose.

More broadly, West Germany would be deeply concerned if the zero-zero proposal, which it helped sponsor and encourage, were now to be abandoned by the West.

## *Suggestions for Further Reading*

Boutwell, Jeffrey. "NATO Theater Nuclear Forces: The Third Phase, 1977–85," in *The Nuclear Confrontation in Europe,* Jeffrey Boutwell, Paul Doty, Gregory Treverton, eds. (London: Croon, Helm, 1985). A brief article that discusses recent developments in the modernization of nuclear weapons in Europe, and analyzes the INF arms control talks.

Buteux, Paul. *Strategy, Doctrine, and the Politics of the Alliance: Theater Nuclear Force Modernization in NATO* (Boulder, CO: Westview Press, 1983). A review of NATO's theater nuclear force modernization and its effect on the alliance.

Clarke, Michael, and Marjorie Mowlam, eds. *Debate on Disarmament* (Boston: Routledge and Kegan Paul, 1982). A collection of articles by prominent members of the European disarmament movement.

Rush, Kenneth, Brent Scowcroft, and Joseph Wold, eds. *Strengthening Deterrence: NATO and the Credibility of Western Defense in the 1980s* (Cambridge, MA: Ballinger, 1982). Articles examining the need to upgrade NATO defenses, including conventional forces.

Thompson, E. P., and Dan Smith, eds. *Protest and Survive* (New York: Monthly Review Press, 1981). An influential collection of articles critical of U.S. nuclear policy in general and of the Euromissile decision in particular.

Treverton, Gregory F. *Making the Alliance Work: The United States and Western Europe* (Ithaca, NY: Cornell UP, 1985). A study of the issues that will face NATO in the future, with some suggested policies aimed to help the alliance continue.

*Eleven*

# MISSILE EXPERIMENTAL

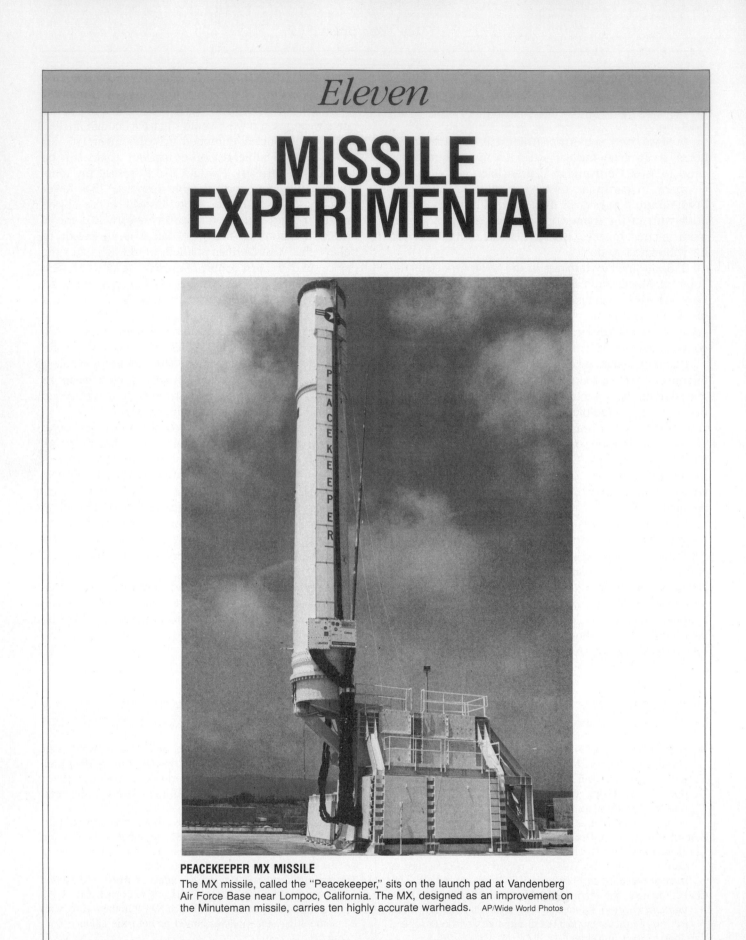

**PEACEKEEPER MX MISSILE**

The MX missile, called the "Peacekeeper," sits on the launch pad at Vandenberg Air Force Base near Lompoc, California. The MX, designed as an improvement on the Minuteman missile, carries ten highly accurate warheads. AP/Wide World Photos

# INTRODUCTION

For almost fifteen years, the United States has been trying to modernize its land-based nuclear forces by developing and deploying a new intercontinental ballistic missile (ICBM). For most of that time, the missile experimental (MX), also called Peacekeeper, has been the prime candidate. Recently, a new missile, the small ICBM, or Midgetman, has become a candidate. While most key decisions on nuclear weapons development are made without public involvement, the story of the MX and Midgetman has been well publicized, in large part because Congress has been very involved. As a result, outside observers have a rare chance to analyze how nuclear weapons are decided upon in the nuclear age. The story involves a complex interaction among technology, interservice rivalry, nuclear strategy, arms control, and domestic politics.

Turning first to technology, the MX was an attempt by the Air Force to develop a technologically more sophisticated successor to the Minuteman III. Thus, the MX missile was made larger, more powerful, and with more numerous and more accurate warheads than its predecessors. This meant that it had a significant hard-target kill capability. But technology also contributed to the problems that MX later faced with Congress and the public. As Soviet missile technology improved, it appeared that the Soviets were developing the capability to knock out U.S. missiles based in fixed silos. If the MX were to be survivable, therefore, it would have to be based in a way that would not allow the Soviets to know precisely where it is located. But finding such a basing mode was a major technical challenge (and a political one, as will be discussed shortly) that three administrations struggled with unsuccessfully. A major justification for the Midgetman was that, since it was a smaller missile, a survivable way to base it would be easier to find.

Nuclear strategy also played an important role in the development of the MX and Midgetman. In the Kennedy and Johnson administrations, Robert McNamara espoused an assured destruction policy that did not emphasize hard-target kill weapons. Key defense officials in the Nixon, Ford, Carter, and Reagan administrations, however, believed that assured destruction was not enough. The United States needed a wide range of nuclear options, including the ability to attack Soviet missile silos quickly. Without such options, they believed that the Soviets could have an advantage, defense officials said, and could in a crisis force the United States into a choice between suicide and surrender. A survivable MX fit this view of strategy perfectly.

During the same period, the Navy started replacing its Polaris submarines with the much larger, long-range Trident, which would be equipped with larger missiles capable of carrying eight highly accurate warheads. These had a counterforce capability similar to that of the MX, yet this program went forward with little controversy or public discussion. The question of whether *both* MX and Trident were needed was hardly discussed within the government; at least one reason was that the Air Force would have bitterly resisted allowing the most effective counterforce to move to the Navy.

Arms control was another critical factor. Each administration argued that the MX was needed as a bargaining chip in negotiations with the Soviets. In the case of Midgetman, one argument in favor of the new missile was that deploying a single-warhead missile could make it more likely that the Soviets would be sympathetic to deMIRVing through arms control.

Each of these factors was also linked directly to the most important influence on MX and Midgetman: domestic politics. The Carter administration supported the MX in part to woo conservative and moderate support for the SALT II Treaty. But the MX basing mode proposed by the Carter administration to solve the vulnerability problem proved politically unsound. The "race track" system aroused public opposition in Utah and Nevada.

When the Reagan administration proposed the Dense Pack basing mode, Congress rejected it out of hand. Protecting missiles by bringing them close together was just not credible after three administrations had spent ten years telling Congress the MX had to be hidden or moved around. In addition, lack of progress in arms control made it difficult for the Reagan administration to justify the MX to Congress as a bargaining chip. Indeed, by early 1983, the MX's political problems had placed the future of the missile in serious jeopardy.

The MX was saved, at least for the time being, by the Scowcroft Commission report, a document carefully crafted to win broad political support in Congress. The report appealed to conservatives because it recommended deployment of one hundred MX missiles. It appealed to moderates and liberals by strongly recommending an arms control approach that encouraged deMIRVing. Finally, it endorsed a weapon that some liberals and moderates were calling for: a small, single-warhead ICBM.

Midgetman, then, was the direct product of a political compromise with Congress. It is perhaps not surprising that Congress has been intimately involved with the development of Midgetman ever since. Congress has specified the number of missiles to be deployed and has even set limits on the weight of the missile.

The ultimate fate of both MX and Midgetman is still undecided. The Scowcroft Commission compromise shows some signs of unraveling. Fewer than fifty MX missiles, as of 1987, have been deployed in Minuteman silos, and the final number will almost certainly be far fewer than the two hundred originally planned. Questions are being raised in Congress about the cost of the Midgetman, and it is unclear how enthusiastic the executive branch really is about the missile. The problem of ICBM modernization will have to be resolved by the next administration.

# THE ORIGINS OF THE MX

## Early History

### *Document 1*

In this excerpt from a 1975 report to Congress, Secretary of Defense James Schlesinger describes the reasons for the Ford administration's decision to develop the MX. He notes that the Minuteman III is no match for the Soviet missiles, so a new U.S. ICBM is needed. He also discusses the need for mobility for the new missile and describes some of the early basing options being considered.

### 1 REPORT TO CONGRESS
### James Schlesinger

Last year we requested $37 million to continue the development of new technology leading to the development of an entirely new ICBM. We did so in order to ensure the availability of a realistic option for the modernization of our ICBM forces in the 1980s and beyond. I noted at the time that this effort would be focused primarily on three problem areas — the selection of the preferred basing mode, the unique guidance requirements for mobile missiles (both air-launched and ground-launched), and the technology required for more efficient rocket motors.

These three problem areas reflect our principal concerns with regard to the kind of an ICBM we ought to have available for deployment in the period beyond the early or mid-1980s. By that time, MINUTEMAN silos may become increasingly vulnerable to the Soviet ICBM forces; hence our interest in new basing modes. Airmobile ICBMs, utilizing unaided, all inertial guidance, are inherently less accurate than fixed-based ICBMs, hence our interest in more capable guidance systems which would be needed to maintain the desired degree of accuracy.

Furthermore, the MINUTEMAN III, as compared with the new family of Soviet ICBMs, has a relatively small throw-weight. If the Soviet Union decides to replace all of its existing ICBMs with this new family of ICBMs, it could acquire an ICBM throw-weight advantage of 5 or 6 to 1 — i.e., 10 to 12 million pounds for the Soviet Union versus 2 million pounds for the U.S. Such a great disparity in throw-weight, in my judgment, would be very destabilizing. It would give the USSR a distinct advantage in one of the basic parameters that shape the future effectiveness of the strategic offensive forces. Hence our interest in new rocket motor technology, which would give us a greater amount of throw-weight per pound of propellant.

By far the most difficult problem which must be resolved in this new ICBM program is the selection of the basing mode. Fixed silos may become vulnerable to a Soviet counterforce attack, but they have some very important advantages, namely, accuracy, good two-way communications up and down the chain of command, general responsiveness to control by the National Command Authorities, and low operating costs. These are very important considerations in context with our efforts to expand our range of response options (i.e., increase our targeting flexibility), and we want to preserve them to the greatest extent feasible should we find it necessary to shift to a new basing mode in the future.

A large part of the Advanced ICBM Technology Program investigations concern alternate basing modes. We have a great deal of experience in the operation of fixed-based ICBM systems but virtually no operational experience with air- and land-mobile systems and thus the reason for their emphasis.

There are several types of air- and land-mobile options under consideration. One of the leading land-based candidates is the so-called shelter system. This system depends for its survivability on deception, that is, the missile mounted on a transporter-launcher would move from one relatively hard shelter to another within a complex. The attacker would have to target all of the shelters, since he would not know in which shelter the missile was deployed. Thus, the cost to us per emergency shelter and the cost to him per reliable RV needed to destroy that shelter would be the critical factors driving the cost-exchange ratio of the shelter system. While this system would retain the accuracy of a silo-based system, its costs and operating problems are immediately apparent.

The air-mobile system would be the most expensive

to acquire and to operate. It would require the acquisition of a fleet of suitable aircraft which could be modified wide-bodied jets or new low cost aircraft. To ensure prelaunch survivability, aircraft with the missile aboard preferably would be kept on airborne alert, and this we know is a very expensive operation. Alternatively, the aircraft with the missile aboard could be kept on ground alert, but then it would have the same pre-launch vulnerabilities as the bomber/tanker force.

Finally, as previously mentioned, the air-mobile system with unaided navigation is inherently less accurate than any of the land systems since without navigation aids it is difficult to precisely determine aircraft velocity and heading. An in-flight position fixing system for the aircraft or a terminal homing system for the missile would help to alleviate this problem. We have the potential solution to the position fixing problem in a new high precision satellite navigation system now under development, called the NAVSTAR Global Positioning System. However, both NAVSTAR and the terminal homing system are still in early stages of development.

Given the many problems that still have to be resolved, we now propose advanced development of an ICBM that could be deployed interchangeably in the existing MINUTEMAN silos, in a land-based shelter or random deployment mode, or in an air-mobile mode. The new MX ICBM would have new, more efficient rocket motors and a new, more accurate guidance system. The MX could be designed to be cold-launched from a cannister in a silo or on a transporter-launcher. In the air-mobile system, the missile could be pulled out of the cannister by parachute and fired when vertical stability had been achieved.

The MX could be deployed in the existing MINUTEMAN silos, since that is the least expensive mode, until such time as the threat to those silos has been definitely ascertained. At that point, we could commence deployment of the missile in one of the mobile modes.

Meanwhile, we propose to continue advanced development of the key components of the mobile systems. A series of air drops has already been conducted from the C-5A, including three "Bathtub" drops (concrete slabs of increasing size and weight), three "mass simulation" drops (to investigate missile shape stability), one inert but instrumented MINUTEMAN I, one fueled but unfired MINUTEMAN I (the "dress rehearsal" test), and one "short burn" MINUTEMAN I (the final test of the series). These tests have proved the feasibility of air-dropping an ICBM, but many other problems remain to be solved before the technical feasibility of the air-mobile system as a whole can be demonstrated. The MINUTEMAN I, moreover, weighs about 75,000 pounds; the MX will weigh about 150,000 pounds.

Some work has also been done on the land-mobile systems. The problem here is not so much the technical feasibility of these systems as it is their operational feasibility. And the economic feasibility of all three mobile systems needs a great deal of additional study.

Accordingly, we are requesting for the Advanced ICBM technology program (i.e., MX and related projects) a total of $41 million in FY 1976, $15 million in the three month transition period, and $70 million for authorization only in FY 1977. Most of these funds would be devoted to guidance, control and propulsion. The cost to completion of the MX development is estimated at about $2.5 billion. . . .

## The MX Described

### *Document 2*

**This brief description of the MX — excerpted from a 1980 report by the Congressional Office of Technology Assessment, a think tank set up and funded by Congress — shows how the new missile is a significant technical improvement over its predecessors. It is larger, carries more warheads, and has more destructive power.**

### 2 MX MISSILE BASING May 1980

The MX missile is a four stage intercontinental ballistic missile (ICBM) presently in full-scale engineering development. Like its predecessor, the Minuteman III, the first

**Figure B–1 Missile Comparison**

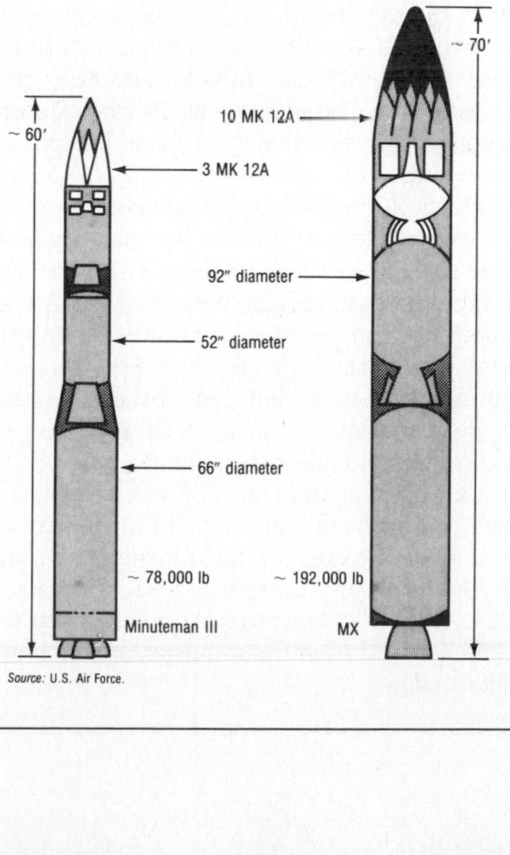


*Source:* U.S. Air Force.

**Figure B–2 MX Post Boost Vehicle**

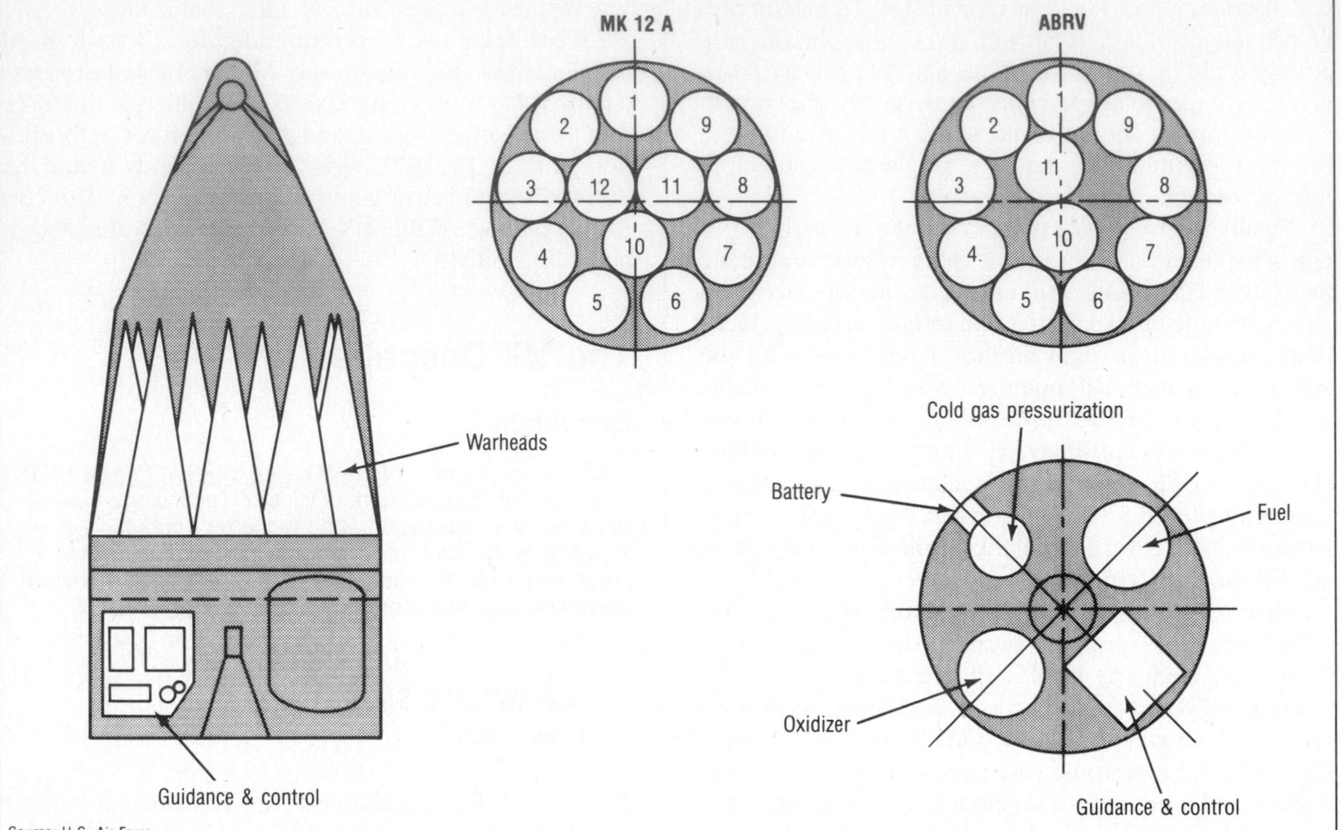


*Source:* U.S. Air Force.

three rocket stages are solid propellant, with a liquid-fueled fourth stage/post-boost vehicle. Weighing about 192,000 lb, the missile will be 70 ft long, with a 92 inch diameter. The MX is a MIRVed (multiple independently targetable reentry vehicle) missile, and will carry 10 MK 12A warheads. The Minuteman III carries three MK 12As. A comparison between the MX and the Minuteman is given in figure B-1.

A drawing of the MX fourth stage post-boost vehicle (PBV) is shown in figure B-2. We see that it is designed to be able to carry 12 MK 12A warheads, or alternatively, 11 advanced ballistic reentry vehicles (ABRV). SALT II would limit the number of reentry vehicles (RVs) to 10. The inertial measuring unit (IMU) of the MX's guidance and control system is a significant advance in guidance technology over Minuteman, and is designed to give the MX much greater accuracy on target.

Also unlike Minuteman, the MX missile will be "cannisterized," to facilitate handling and movement of the missile, and to provide for the missile's environment control. The MX is also designed to be "cold launched" from the cannister. This means that for launch, the missile is first gas-expelled from the cannister, at which point it fires its first stage.

The MX missile is scheduled to begin flight testing in January 1983, for a total of 20 tests before system is in initial operating capability. The last flight test is scheduled for April 1986. These tests will check for a wide variety of missile functions and of associated equipment, including rocket stage performance, guidance and control, reentry system performance, range and payload capability, retargetting, and many others.

## The Need for Counterforce

### *Document 3*

After James Schlesinger became secretary of defense early in President Nixon's second term, he made a concerted effort to move U.S. nuclear strategy away from assured destruction. In these excerpts from a 1973 speech, Schlesinger argues that the United States must have a range of nuclear options so that a president will not be faced with the choice between suicide and surrender. In particular, the United States must have the ability to destroy a wide range of Soviet targets in addition to cities. In short,

Schlesinger's strategy meant U.S. forces must have hard-target kill capability.

Although Schlesinger does not mention the MX here, the nuclear options strategy was one of the reasons the Ford administration decided to go forward with the new missile.

## 3 SPEECH James Schlesinger 1973

President Nixon underlined the drawbacks to sole reliance on assured destruction in 1970 when he asked:

> Should a President, in the event of a nuclear attack, be left with the single option of ordering the mass destruction of enemy civilians, in the face of the certainty that it would be followed by the mass slaughter of Americans? Should the concept of assured destruction be narrowly defined and should it be the only measure of our ability to deter the variety of threats we may face?

The questions are not new. They have arisen many times during the nuclear era, and a number of efforts have been made to answer them. We actually added several response options to our contingency plans in 1961 and undertook the retargeting necessary for them. However, they all involved large numbers of weapons. In addition, we publicly adopted to some degree the philosophies of counterforce and damage-limiting. Although differences existed between those two concepts as then formulated, particularly in their diverging assumptions about cities as likely targets of attack, both had a number of features in common.

- Each required the maintenance of a capability to destroy urban-industrial targets, but as a reserve to deter attacks on U.S. and allied cities rather than as the main instrument of retaliation.
- Both recognized that contingencies other than a massive surprise attack on the United States might arise and should be deterred; both argued that the ability and willingness to attack military targets were prerequisites to deterrence.
- Each stressed that a major objective, in the event that deterrence should fail, would be to avoid to the extent possible causing collateral damage in the USSR, and to limit damage to the societies of the United States and its allies.
- Neither contained a clear-cut vision of how a nuclear war might end, or what role the strategic forces would play in their termination.
- Both were considered by critics to be open ended in their requirement for forces, very threatening to the retaliatory capabilities of the USSR, and therefore dangerously stimulating to the arms race and the chances of pre-emptive war.
- The military tasks that each involved, whether offensive counterforce or defensive damage-limiting, became increasingly costly, complex, and difficult as Soviet strategic forces grew in size, diversity, and survivability.

Of the two concepts, damage-limiting was the more demanding and costly because it required both active and passive defenses as well as a counterforce capability to attack hard targets and other strategic delivery systems. Added to this was the assumption (at least for planning purposes) that an enemy would divide his initial attack between our cities and our retaliatory forces, or switch his fire to our cities at some later stage in the attack. Whatever the realism of that assumption, it placed an enormous burden on our active and passive defenses—and particularly on anti-ballistic missile (ABM) systems—for the limitation of damage.

With the ratification of the ABM treaty in 1972, and the limitations it imposes on both the United States and the Soviet Union to construct no more than two widely separated ABM sites (with no more than 100 interceptors at each), an essential building-block in the entire damage-limiting concept has now been removed. As I shall discuss later, the treaty has also brought into question the utility of large, dedicated anti-bomber defenses, since without a defense against missiles, it is clear that an active defense against bombers has little value in protecting our cities. The salient point, however, is that the ABM treaty has effectively removed the concept of defensive damage limitation (at least as it was defined in the 1960s) from the contention as a major strategic option.

Does all of this mean that we have no choice but to rely solely on the threat of destroying cities? Does it even matter if we do? What is wrong, in the final analysis, with staking everything on this massive deterrent and pressing ahead with a further limitation of these devastating arsenals?

No one who has thought much about these questions disagrees with the need, as a minimum, to maintain a conservatively designed reserve for the ultimate threat of large-scale destruction. Even more, if we could all be guaranteed that this threat would prove fully credible (to friend and foe alike) across the relevant range of contingencies—and that deterrence would never be severely tested or fail—we might also agree that nothing more in the way of options would ever be needed. The difficulty is that no such guarantee can be given. There are several reasons why assurance on this score is impossible.

Since we ourselves find it difficult to believe that we would actually implement the threat of assured destruction in response to a limited attack on military targets that caused relatively few civilian casualties, there can be no certainty that, in a crisis, prospective opponents would be deterred from testing our resolve. Allied concern about the credibility of this particular threat has been evident for more than a decade. In any event, the actuality of such a response would be utter folly except where our own or allied cities were attacked.

Today, such a massive retaliation against cities, in response to anything less than an all-out attack on the U.S. and its cities, appears less and less credible. Yet . . . deterrence can fail in many ways. What we need is a series of measured responses to aggression which bear some relation to the provocation, have prospects of terminating hostilities before general nuclear war breaks out, and leave some possibility for restoring deterrence. It has been this problem of not having sufficient options between massive response and doing nothing, as the Soviets built up their strategic forces, that has prompted the President's concerns and those of our Allies.

Threats against allied forces, to the extent that they could be deterred by the prospect of nuclear retaliation, demand both more limited responses than destroying cities, and advanced planning tailored to such lesser responses. Nuclear threats to our strategic forces, whether limited or large-scale, might well call for an option to respond in kind against the attacker's military forces. In other words, to be credible, and hence effective over the range of possible contingencies, deterrence must rest on many options and on a spectrum of capabilities (within the constraints of SALT) to support these options. Certainly such complex matters as response options cannot be left hanging until a crisis. They must be thought through beforehand. Moreover, appropriate sensors to assist in determining the nature of the attack, and adequately responsive command-control arrangements, must also be available. And a venturesome opponent must know that we have all of these capabilities.

Flexibility of response is also essential because, despite our best efforts, we cannot guarantee that deterrence will never fail; nor can we forecast the situations that would cause it to fail. Accidents and unauthorized acts could occur, especially if nuclear proliferation should increase. Conventional conflicts could escalate into nuclear exchanges; indeed, some observers believe that this is precisely what would happen should a major war break out in Europe. Ill-informed or cornered and desperate leaders might challenge us to a nuclear test of wills. We cannot even totally preclude the massive surprise attack on our forces which we use to test the design of our second-strike forces, although I regard the probability of such an attack as close to zero under existing conditions. To the extent that we have selective response options — smaller and more precisely focused than in the past — we should be able to deter such challenges. But if deterrence fails, we may be able to bring all but the largest nuclear conflicts to a rapid conclusion before cities are struck. Damage may thus be limited and further escalation avoided.

I should point out in this connection that the critics of options cannot have the argument both ways. If the nuclear balance is no longer delicate and if substantial force asymmetries are quite tolerable, then the kinds of changes I have been discussing here will neither perturb the balance nor stimulate an arms race. If, on the other hand, asymmetries do matter (despite the existence of some highly survivable forces), then the critics themselves should consider seriously what responses we should make to the major programs that the Soviets currently have underway to exploit their advantages in numbers of missiles and payload. Whichever argument the critics prefer, they should recognize that:

— inertia is hardly an appropriate policy for the United States in these vital areas;
— we have had some large-scale pre-planned options other than attacking cities for many years, despite the rhetoric of assured destruction;
— adding more selective, relatively small-scale options is not necessarily synonymous with adding forces, even though we may wish to change their mix and improve our command, control, and communications.

It is worth stressing at this point . . . that targets for nuclear weapons may include not only cities and silos, but also airfields, many other types of military installations, and a variety of other important assets that are not necessarily collocated with urban populations. We already have a long list of such possible targets; now we are grouping them into operational plans which would be more responsive to the range of challenges that might face us. To the extent necessary, we are retargeting our forces accordingly.

Which among these options we might choose in a crisis would depend on the nature of any enemy's attack and on his objectives. Many types of targets can be preprogrammed as options — cities, other targets of value, military installations of many different kinds, soft strategic targets, hard strategic targets. A number of so-called counterforce targets, such as airfields, are quite soft and can be destroyed without pinpoint accuracy. The fact that we are able to knock out these targets — counterforce though it may be — does not appear to be the subject of much concern.

In some circumstances, however, a set of hard targets might be the most appropriate objective for our retaliation, and this I realize is a subject fraught with great emotion. Even so, several points about it need to be made.

— The destruction of a hardened target is not simply a function of accuracy; it results from the combined effects of accuracy, nuclear yield, and the number of warheads applied to the target.

**March 22, 1981**

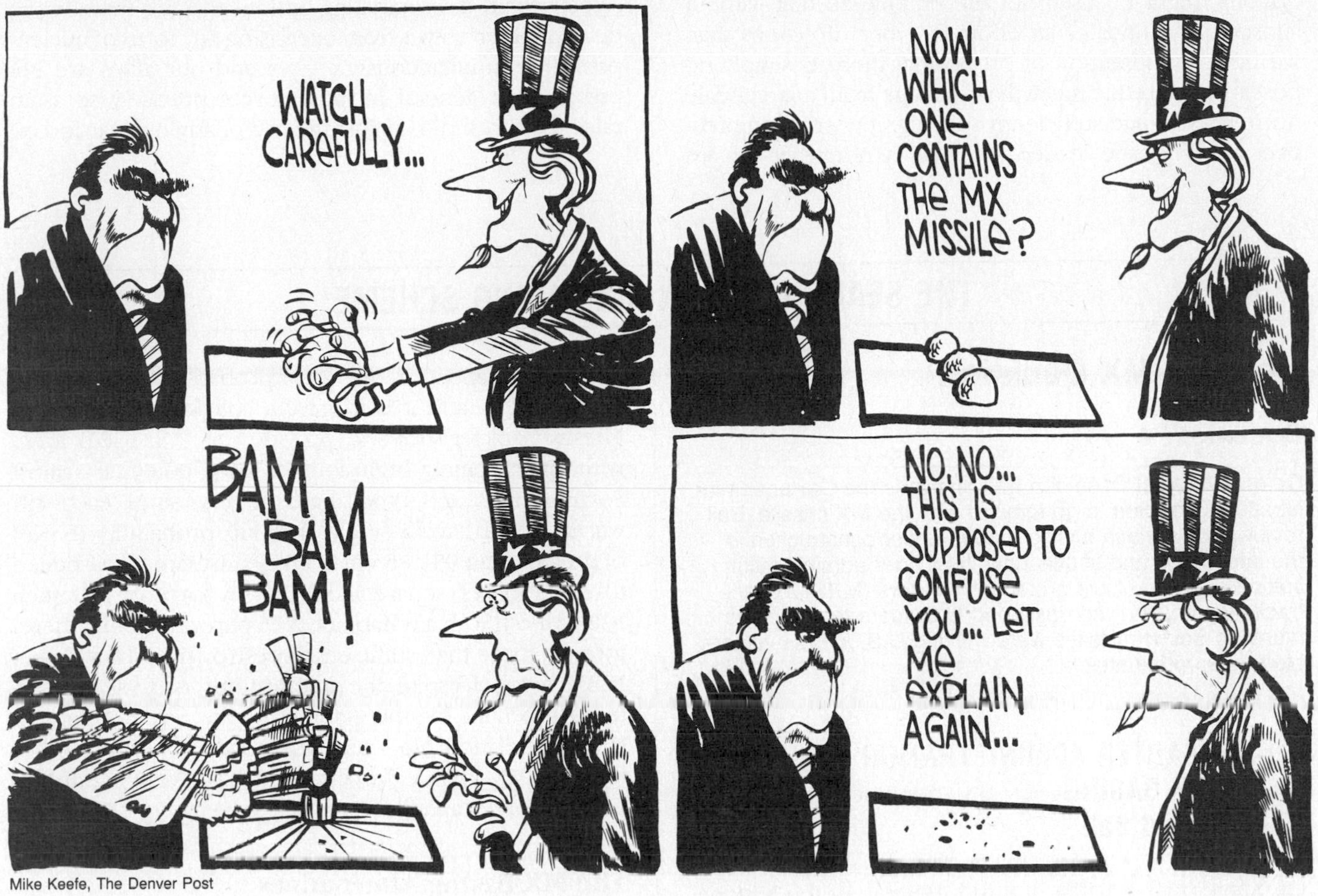


Mike Keefe, The Denver Post

— Both the United States and the Soviet Union already have the necessary combinations of accuracy, yield, and numbers in their missile forces to provide them with some hard-target-kill capability, but it is not a particularly efficient capability.

— Neither the United States nor the Soviet Union now has a disarming first strike capability, nor are they in any position to acquire such a capability in the foreseeable future, since each side has large numbers of strategic offensive systems that remain untargetable by the other side. Moreover, the ABM Treaty forecloses a defense against missiles. As I have already noted in public: "The Soviets, under the Interim Offensive Agreement, are allowed 62 submarines and 950 SLBM launchers. In addition, they have many other nuclear forces. Any reasonable calculation would demonstrate, I believe, that it is not possible for us even to begin to eliminate the city-destruction potential embodied in their ICBMs, let alone their SLBM force."

The moral of all this is that we should not single out accuracy as some sort of unilateral or key culprit in the hard-target-kill controversy. To the extent that we want to minimize unintended civilian damage from attacks on even soft targets, as I believe we should, we will want to emphasize high accuracy, low yields, and airburst weapons.

To enhance deterrence, we may also want a more efficient hard-target-kill capability than we now possess: both to threaten specialized sets of targets (possibly of concern to allies) with a greater economy of force, and to make it clear to a potential enemy that he cannot proceed with impunity to jeopardize our own system of hard targets.

Thus, the real issue is how much hard-target-kill capability we need, rather than the development of new combinations of accuracy and yield per se. Resolution of the quantitative issue, as I will discuss later, depends directly on the further evolution of the Soviet strategic offensive forces and on progress in the current phase of the Strategic Arms Limitation Talks. . . .

With a reserve capability for threatening urban-industrial targets, with offensive systems capable of increased flexibility and discrimination in targeting, and with concomitant improvements in sensors, surveillance, and command-control, we could implement response options that cause far less civilian damage than would now be the case. For those who consider such changes potentially destabilizing because of their fear that the options might be used, let me emphasize that without substantially more of an effort in other directions than we have any intention of proposing, there is simply no possibility of reducing civilian damage from a large-scale nuclear exchange sufficiently to make it a tempting prospect for any sane leader. But that is not what we are talking about here. At the present time, we are acquiring selective and discriminating options that are intended to deter another power from exercising any form of nuclear pressure. Simultaneously . . . we and our allies are improving our general purpose forces precisely so as to raise the threshold against the use of any nuclear forces.

# THE SEARCH FOR AN MX BASING SCHEME

## Carter's MX Decision

### *Document 4*

**Defense analyst Desmond Ball analyzes the Carter administration's decision to go forward with the MX missile. Ball reviews the various basing modes under construction in the late 1970s and shows how the Carter administration settled on the multiple protective shelters (MPS), or race track system. He also described U.S. fears that improvements in Soviet missiles were making U.S. ICBMs vulnerable to a surprise attack.**

## 4 THE CARTER ADMINISTRATION'S DECISION ON MX BASING
## Desmond Ball

On September 5, 1979, at a full meeting of the National Security Council (NSC) presided over by the President himself, the Carter Administration decided to begin full-scale engineering development of a system of multiple horizontal shelters for basing the MX inter-continental ballistic missiles (ICBMs) currently being developed as a successor to the Minuteman missile. This decision followed more than a deacde of official consideration. The time span did not, however, make it any easier, and many of the issues were no closer to resolution than they had been in the 1960s. Indeed, the particular basing configuration eventually chosen only emerged as a leading candidate at the end of spring 1979, and some of the critical parameters and operational details of the system were only agreed to immediately before the September 5 decision. That decision was very much a product of compromise.

Surprisingly, it proved much easier for the Administration to reach agreement on the characteristics of the MX missile itself, the full-scale development of which was approved in early June 1979. The MX ICBM is to be 92 in. in diameter and to weigh 190,000 lb (as compared with about 78,000 lb for the current Minuteman III); it is to carry 10 Mark 12A multiple independently targetable re-entry vehicle (MIRV) warheads, each with a yield of about 350 kt and a circular error probable (CEP) of about 300 to 400 ft, and it is to have a cold-launch capability. These characteristics will provide the U.S. ICBM force with an extremely high counter-force potential against Soviet ICBMs and other hard targets, since each MX warhead will have a single shot kill probability (SSKP) of greater than 95 percent even against targets hardened to 2,000 lb per square inch (psi). A force of 200 such ICBMs, each with a reliability of 75 percent, would, therefore, be more than sufficient to destroy the whole Soviet ICBM force. Despite the implications of this counter-force potential for the stability of the Soviet-American strategic relationship, there was never any question but that the MX missile force would have very significant counter-force capability.[1]

### The MX Basing Alternatives

More than a dozen alternative basing modes for the MX were formally considered in the decade or so before September 1979. Most of these involved some sort of mobile basing, such as moving the MX around by road, by rail, across the countryside, along canals, in lakes or pools, along tunnels and trenches, or within wide-bodied transport aircraft. The majority of these concepts were rejected before being subjected to detailed cost-effectiveness analysis. As General Stafford has testified:

> Many were rejected because they did not preserve the desired characteristics of the ICBM force. For example, most of the road mobile concepts were highly dependent on warning for acceptable survivability. Those mobile concepts that were not dependent on warning required continuous movement, and hence involved high operations and support costs with a high degree of public interface and security problems. Other concepts such as the buried arsenal were rejected because they presented operational problems (subterranean basing of crews and equipment) and high technical risks. In addition, this family of concepts did not preserve the rapid response-capability of the current ICBM force. For example, preparatory actions for launch readiness ranged anywhere from hours to days.[2]

By the late 1970s, the choice had narrowed to four principal modes — a buried trench system, an air-mobile system, a system of vertical multiple protective structures (MPS), and a system of horizontal MPS.

The trench system was the favorite of the U.S. Air Force in 1976–77. In this system, each MX missile would have been deployed in concrete-encased trenches some 10–12 miles long, buried beneath 5 ft of soil, along which it would move at random. Survivability was to be derived from the fact that with the trenches hardened to 600 psi, so that a 1-mt warhead could destroy slightly less than 4,000 ft, the Soviet Union would need to launch about 4,000 perfectly placed 1-mt warheads in order to destroy 200 MX missiles. Unfortunately, this would be well within the capacity of the Soviet ICBM force by the early 1980s. The construction of segments or spurs of greater hardness every half-mile would have increased the overall survivability, but the Have Host test blasts in 1977 were not encouraging. Moreover, the trenches would have cost some $1.3 million to $2 million per nautical mile to build, depending on the blast resistance (psi) sought. This scheme was dropped by the Air Force in November 1977.[3]

The Air Force now came to favor MPS basing systems, a concept previously known as Multiple Aim Point (MAP) basing. Studies conducted by the Air Force Space and Missile Systems Organization (SAMSO) and the MX Basing Ad Hoc Working Group of the Air Force Systems Command in 1978 estimated that 200 MX ICBMs could be deployed in a complex of 4,500 vertical shelters, each hardened to about 600 psi and spaced not more than 7,000 ft apart, for a cost of about $30 billion, some $2 billion less than a comparable system of horizontal shelters.[4] The shelters were to be sited in the Great Basin of Nevada and Utah; the Sonoran Desert, Arizona; and the highlands of Arizona and New Mexico.

Deployment of this system, with an initial operational capability (IOC) of FY 1986, was recommended by the Air Force to the Secretary of Defense through the Defense System Acquisition Review Council (DSARC) on December 5, 1978.[5]

However, the DSARC directed that the Air Force review a range of air-mobile concepts in addition to undertaking further refinement of the vertical MPS concept. The air-mobile concepts reviewed by the Air Force, and presented to the Secretary of Defense on March 31, 1979, involved the acquisition of from 210 to 290 wide-body (Boeing 747 and McDonnell Douglas DC-10) or STOL (YC-14 and YC-15) transport aircraft, each with a single MX ICBM, which would be deployed at five principal Air Force bases. On receipt of warning of a possible Soviet submarine-launched ballistic missile (SLBM) attack, these missile carriers would disperse to 31 "alert bases" in the central United States and then, as the attack appeared imminent, to some 115 "primary dispersal sites." Following the attack, the aircraft would proceed to some 2,340 "secondary dispersal sites," from which retaliatory missile launch could be undertaken. Assuming a day-to-day alert rate of 75 percent, a force of 210 aircraft would provide an alert force of just over 150 MX carriers. The total acquisition costs of the various air-mobile concepts considered ranged from $31.1 billion to $34.6 billion, with annual operating and support costs of $0.9 billion to $1.1 billion, depending on the type of carrier aircraft selected, the number of carriers held on alert, and the particular dispersal configuration.[6] Air mobility was pushed throughout the spring of 1979 by the President's Science Advisor and the Office of Science and Technology Policy within the White House but was eventually rejected because of its higher costs, as compared with the ground-mobile alternatives, as well as because of various technical and operational risks.

The fourth system, the horizontal MPS, although never as comprehensively analyzed as the alternative systems, nor having any comparable institutional support, was still the system eventually chosen. The extent to which it was a compromise choice is reflected directly in the particular parameters and operational characteristics of the selected configuration.

### The Horizontal MPS System

The horizontal MPS system involves the deployment of 200 MX ICBMs at random among 4,600 shelters. Each MX is to be carried on board a transporter-erector-launcher (TEL) vehicle among 23 shelters spaced about 7,000 ft apart on spurs along a road some 10–15 miles in length. The number of road lengths per complex ranges from 3 to 7 or 8, depending on the surrounding terrain, making for about 40 MX complexes. These are probably to be located in southern Utah and Nevada, although areas of New Mexico and Arizona are also being studied. Only about 25 square miles, made up of small enclosures around each shelter, is actually to be fenced off from the public.[7] The shelters are spaced so that they are "strike independent," i.e., no two shelters can be destroyed by a single Soviet warhead.[8] Indeed, the proposed spacing of 7,000 ft includes a very large safety margin.[9]

The TEL is a 6-axle, 24-wheel vehicle which weighs 670,000 lb. In addition to the MX missile canister (which is 120 ft long and 12 ft in diameter, or about the size of the fuselage of a Boeing 707), the TEL carries a 140,000-lb "modesty shield," designed to prevent satellite observation of the missile canister and its deportment in any particular shelter.

A number of peculiar operational features have been adopted to enhance Soviet technical means of monitoring U.S. compliance with the SALT agreement. The MX canister is loaded onto the TEL in a special missile assembly area, in full view of Soviet satellite surveillance. The TEL then enters the closed-loop road through a "choke point," which is immediately closed, and proceeds to visit each of the 23 shelters in turn. While the "modesty shield" prevents Soviet determination of the particular shelter at which the MX is unloaded (if, indeed, the decision is not to keep the missile aboard the TEL vehicle!), the Soviet Union can be assured that there is only one missile within each loop. The shelter roofs each have four "SALT verification removable closures," or "plugs," which are opened periodically or on challenge to verify that only one of the shelters actually contains a missile.

The Air Force had argued that the horizontal MPS system was less survivable than its preferred vertical MPS mode. The decision to act counter to this argument was taken in the light of two considerations. First, the NSC staff were concerned to ensure that there would be no infringement of the principles regarding either ICBM mobility or national technical means of verification (NTMV) that had been negotiated in SALT. There was some concern that Soviet reconnaissance satellites might have difficulty in seeing to the bottom of a vertical silo and hence in verifying that a particular one did not contain a missile. This argument was in fact rather specious, since there is no need to see the *bottom* of a silo to know that it is empty, but it did highlight the perceived necessity to effect a clear conceptual distinction between shelters and launchers — something that seemed more difficult in the case of silos as compared with horizontal shelters! [The SALT II Treaty placed limits on numbers of ICBM *launchers,* not on numbers of missiles or, in this case, shelters. — Ed.]

The second consideration was that the horizontal MPS system has far greater mobility than the vertical system. Given a "dash" speed of 15–20 mph, the TEL vehicle in the horizontal MPS basing mode can move from one shelter to another within the expected time from warning of a Soviet missile launch to warhead impact, giving the system some residual survivability in the eventuality that the Soviet Union determines the locations of the MX missiles in the shelter complexes. This capability was not possible with the vertical MPS system.

The Administration estimated the cost of the horizontal MPS shelter system, including that of the first 10 years of operation, at $33 billion (in 1980 dollars).[10] However, the Office of Management and Budget (OMB) estimated that it is more likely to be $37.7 billion,[11] and some critics charged that the final cost will be closer to $55 billion.[12]

The viability of the system is essentially dependent upon two principal factors — that it is possible to maintain Soviet uncertainty about the precise locations of the MX missiles within each group of shelters, and that Soviet strategic offensive missile capabilities will not exceed those projected in the 1977 National Intelligence Estimate (NIE).[13]

## Assumptions About the Soviet Threat

Although the parametric configuration of the horizontal MPS system has been widely described, the underlying assumptions have never been explicated by the Administration nor drawn out by the critics of the system. It turns out, however, that the viability of the system depends on some very specific assumptions about the character of the Soviet threat to the system; the degree of sensitivity is surprising for a system intended to provide survivability for the United States land-based ICBM force through to the twenty-first century.

The first assumption is that the United States needs some 1,000 ICBM warheads (i.e., 1,000 re-entry vehicles [RVs], each with significant hard-target capability) to survive a Soviet first-strike attack. This number of surviving warheads would provide the capability to destroy most industrial targets in the Soviet Union or, alternatively, to attack a large portion of Soviet military targets.[14] Administration officials have argued that if the Soviet Union wishes to deny this capability, she must fully disarm her own land-based ICBM forces, which re-defines the strategic balance in terms wholly of SLBMs and long-range bombers, where the United States has a clear advantage.

The second assumption is that only the MIRVed portion of the Soviet ICBM force (i.e., the SS-17, SS-18, and SS-19 missiles) would be used to attack U.S. ICBMs. Given that SALT II constrains both the United States and the Soviet Union to the deployment of no more than 820 MIRVed ICBMs, this limits the threat to the U.S. ICBM force to about 6,000 RVs, depending on the eventual mix of SS-17s, SS-18s, and SS-19s in the Soviet arsenal.[15] It is further assumed that a proportion of these re-entry vehicles would be held in reserve, at least some of which would be targeted on China.[16] Although this proportion has never been officially disclosed, it is understood that 15 percent is a reasonable assumption. This leaves approximately 5,100 RVs for use against U.S. counterforce targets.

Since there is no strategic rationale in strikes against the MX system without also attacking the other U.S. ICBMs, it is assumed by the Pentagon that the Soviet Union would allocate two RVs each against the 54 Titan II, 450 Minuteman II, and the remaining 350 Minuteman III ICBMs,[17] taking up slightly more than 1,700 RVs. It is also assumed that another 300 RVs would be allocated for use against some 150 other counter-force targets in the United States, including the 80 Minuteman launch control centers.

This leaves 3,100 RVs for possible use against the MX system. The next assumption is that Soviet ICBM reliability is only about 75 percent, which results in some

2,325 reliable RVs available for the attack. Assuming a CEP of 600 ft for Soviet RVs in the late 1980s, and an average yield of about 750 kt, each of these would have an SSKP of greater than 95 percent against shelters hardened to 600 psi. The number of shelters which would survive this postulated Soviet attack is therefore just slightly more than 2,300. Given that the proportion of surviving MX missiles is the same as that of the surviving shelters (i.e., that the Soviet attack is neither "unexpectedly lucky or unlucky"),[18] the number of MX missiles surviving is 100, with the magic number of 1,000 RVs.

These assumptions are extremely static. There is some degree of trade-off possible among some of the variables — for example, one can assume that the proportion of RVs held in reserve is 20 percent (1,200) rather than 15 percent (900) and, on the other hand, that there is no targeting of the ICBM command and control centers (since the probability of destroying all the ICBM silos is sufficiently high anyway). However, if any of the principal assumptions are relaxed, the whole basing system loses its viability. For example, the Soviet Union could choose to use her MIRVed SLBM force against the shelters; this is expected to consist of 380 SS N 18 SLBMs, which currently have three 1-2 mt warheads each but which have been tested with seven warheads. U.S. SLBMs already have a quite substantial counterforce capability, and the Soviet Union must be expected to have something similar by the late 1980s. She could also decide to allocate one rather than two re-entry vehicles to each of the 854 U.S. silo-based ICBMs. By the late 1980s, SSKPs will be sufficiently high even against the 2,000 psi of the Minuteman silos that the second RV would only be necessary as insurance against the possible in-flight failure of the first; however, most sources of missile unreliability become apparent very soon after launch, so a second wave of RVs can be quite specific and relatively small. In any case, if Soviet ICBM reliability were itself to improve from the assumed 75 percent up to 90 percent, then the number of surviving MX missiles would be almost halved. This would also happen if the USSR was to deploy, as her "one new type of ICBM" allowed under the SALT II Agreement, an ICBM with 10 MIRVs to replace the current generation SS-17s and SS-19s. The numbers of Soviet missiles in the Pentagon's analyses are based generally on the SALT II constraints, which in fact limit missile launchers, rather than the number of actual missiles and nuclear waheads, that may be produced and stockpiled. Both the United States and the Soviet Union routinely produce more missiles than they deploy in order to provide spares for maintenance and for missile testing and crew training.[19] According to one report, the Soviet Union currently possesses a stockpile of about 1,000 extra missiles not deployed in silos, consisting of a mix of older single-warhead SS-11 and SS-9 ICBMs and newer MIRVed ICBMs.[20] If only a quarter of these were MIRVed ICBMs, or if more such ICBMs are produced but not deployed in the next decade, the whole U.S. ICBM force (Minuteman, Titan II, and MX) would once again be totally vulnerable. The USSR would have to find some way to launch these extra missiles, but cold-launch canisters could undoubtedly be produced for some, and she may "already possess a potential ability to launch extra missiles from expedient above-ground launch pads."[21] Of course, if the Soviet Union were to abrogate the SALT Agreements and deploy more ICBMs, or place more than 10 RVs on her MIRVed ICBMs, then the U.S. ICBM force, including the MX system, would again be vulnerable to destruction by only a fraction of the Soviet ICBM force. . . .

## Conclusion

The basing system for the Minuteman ICBMs that the MX is to replace in the late 1980s was designed in the late 1950s and expected at the outset to provide survivability for those missiles through to the 1970s. That expectation proved quite pessimistic. Although substantial upgrading of the hardness of the Minuteman silos took place during the 1970s, the concept proved viable for some two and a half decades. The horizontal MPS system was intended to provide survivability of the MX ICBM force through to the 21st century. The belief that it would do so depended on certain assumptions about the size and character of the Soviet strategic ballistic missile threat and Soviet surveillance techniques. Any successor to the horizontal MPS system will be similarly dependent on a set of assumptions of this sort. It may be an open question, whether, given that threat and those techniques, the vulnerability of a land-based system of any sort can be reduced to a satisfactory level at a tolerable cost.

## Notes

1. By September 1978, the smallest missile under consideration for selection as the MX was one of 83 in. in diameter and a weight of 150,000 lb, with its first two stages identical to that of the US Navy's *Trident* II (D-5) SLBM; however, even this missile would have carried 10 Mark 12A warheads. *Aviation Week and Space Technology,* 2 October 1978, p. 13.
2. House Appropriations Committee, *Department of Defense Appropriations for 1980.* (Washington DC: USGPO, March 1979), Part 3, p. 277.

3. House Armed Services Committee, *Hearings on Military Posture and H.R. 10929,* (February–March 1978), Part 3, Book 2, pp. 892–907; and Senate Armed Services Committee, *Department of Defense Authorization for Appropriations for Fiscal Year 1980,* (March–April 1979), Part 6, pp. 3478–3480.
4. Senate Armed Services Committee, *Department of Defense Authorization for Appropriations for Fiscal Year 1979,* (April–May 1978), Part 9, pp. 6505–6509.
5. House Appropriations Committee, *op. cit.* in note 2, pp. 217–8.
6. Senate Armed Services Committee, *op. cit.* in note 4, pp. 3488–3501.
7. *New York Times,* 8 September 1979.
8. The calculus for determining "strike independence" is discussed in Desmond J. Ball and Edwin Coleman, "The Land-mobile ICBM System: a Proposal," *Survival,* vol. XIX, no. 4, July/August 1977, pp. 158–9.
9. According to testimony of General Hepfer, MX Program Manager, the 7,000 ft spacing is "very conservative . . . It has a safety factor of 4 in it." Senate Armed Services Committee, *op. cit.* in note 3, p. 3487. The lethal radius (LR) of a 1 MT warhead against a 600 psi structure is just under 2,000 ft.
10. *New York Times,* 8 September 1979.
11. *Defense/Space Daily,* 5 September 1979, p. 2.
12. *Aviation Week and Space Technology,* 12 November 1979, p. 19.
13. Senate Armed Services Committee, *op. cit.* in note 3, p. 3485. It should be noted that the 1977 NIE on Soviet offensive forces (NIE 11-8) was rather more sanguine in this respect than its 1976, 1978 or 1979 counterparts.
14. Congressional Budget Office, *The MX Missile and Multiple Protective Structure Basing: Long-Term Budgetory Implications.* (Washington, DC: USGPO, 1979), p. XVIII.
15. Under the SALT II Agreement, the Soviet Union can deploy 308 SS-18 "heavy" ICBMs each with 10 RVs. Assuming the balance of the Soviet MIRVed ICBM force is comprised of all SS-19s, each with six RVs, the total number of RVs on MIRVed ICBMs comes to 6,152. However, if she continues to deploy both SS-17s (with four RVs each) and SS-19s, in the ratio which she had in 1978 (approximately 3:10), then the total comes to only 5,928 (comprised of 3,080 RVs on the SS-18s, 2,400 RVs on 400 SS-19s and 448 RVs on 112 SS-17s).
16. Testimony of General Burke, House Appropriations Committee, *op. cit.* in note 2, p. 198.
17. It is assumed that one existing silo-based *Minuteman* III missile would be retired for each new missile deployed in the MPS basing system. See Congressional Budget Office. *op. cit.* in note 14, p. 25.
18. *Ibid.,* p. 27.
19. *Ibid.,* p. 59.
20. See Henry S. Bradsher, "New US Study Finds More Soviet Missiles," *Washington Star,* 12 April 1979, p. A–1. With respect to US missiles, General Slay stated in 1977 that there were "some 123 *Minuteman* III missiles that we could deploy if the occasion should arise." *International Herald Tribune,* 11 October 1977. Other sources credit the US with approximately 250 undeployed *Minuteman* II and III ICBMs. See William R. Graham and Paul H. Nitze, "Viable US Strategic Missile Forces for the Early 1980s," in William R. Van Cleave and W. Scott Thompson, (eds.), *Strategic Options for the Early Eighties: What Can Be Done?,* (New York: National Strategy Information Center, Inc., 1979), p. 138.
21. Congressional Budget Office, *op. cit.* in note 14, p. 66.


# The Countervailing Strategy

## *Document 5*

**One reason the Carter administration decided to go forward with the MX was its nuclear strategy. In this excerpt from a report to Congress, President Carter's secretary of defense, Harold Brown, describes the countervailing strategy. Brown argues that the best way to deter the Soviet Union is to follow a strategy that targets a wide range of Soviet assets, including hardened Soviet missile silos. This strategy requires a hard-target kill-capable missile such as the MX.**

## 5 REPORT TO CONGRESS
**Harold Brown**
**January 19, 1981**

A significant achievement in 1980 was the codification of our evolving strategic doctrine, in the form of Presidential Directive No. 59. In my Report last year, I discussed the objectives and the principal elements of this countervailing strategy, and in August 1980, after P.D. 59 had been signed by President Carter, I elaborated it in some detail in a major policy address. Because of its importance, however, the countervailing strategy warrants special attention in this Report as well.

Two basic points should underlie any discussion of the countervailing strategy. *The first is that, because it is a strategy of deterrence, the countervailing strategy is designed with the Soviets in mind.* Not only must we have the forces, doctrine, and will to retaliate if attacked, we must convince the Soviets, *in advance,* that we do. Because it is designed to deter the Soviets, our strategic doctrine must take account of what we know about Soviet perspectives on these issues, for, by definition, deterrence requires shaping Soviet assessments about the risks of war — assessments they will make using their models, not ours. We must confront these views and take them into account in our planning. We may, and we do, think our models are more accurate, but theirs are the reality deterrence drives us to consider.

Several Soviet perspectives are relevant to the formulation of our deterrent strategy. First, Soviet military doctrine appears to contemplate the possibility of a relatively prolonged nuclear war. Second, there is evidence that they regard military forces as the obvious first targets in a nuclear exchange, not general industrial and economic capacity. Third, the Soviet leadership clearly places a high value on preservation of the regime and on the survival and continued effectiveness of the instruments of state power and control — a value at least as high as that they place on any losses to the general population, short of those involved in a general nuclear war. Fourth, in some contexts, certain elements of Soviet leadership seem to consider Soviet victory in a nuclear war to be at least a theoretical possibility.

All this does not mean that the Soviets are unaware of the destruction a nuclear war would bring to the Soviet Union; in fact, they are explicit on that point. Nor does this mean that we cannot deter, for clearly we can and we do.

*The second basic point is that, because the world is constantly changing, our strategy evolves slowly, almost continually, over time to adapt to changes in U.S. technology and military capabilities, as well as Soviet technology, military capabilities, and strategic doctrine.* A strategic doctrine that served well when the United States had only a few dozen nuclear weapons and the Soviets none would hardly serve as well unchanged in a world in which we have about 9,000 strategic warheads and they have about 7,000. As the strategic balance has shifted from overwhelming U.S. superiority to essential equivalence, and as ICBM accuracies have steadily improved to the point that hard target kill probabilities are quite high, our doctrine must adapt itself to these new realities.

This does not mean that the objective of our doctrine changes; on the contrary, deterrence remains, as it always has been, our basic goal. Our countervailing strategy today is a natural evolution of the conceptual foundations built over a generation by men like Robert McNamara and James Schlesinger.

The United States has never — at least since nuclear weapons were available in significant numbers — had a strategic doctrine based simply and solely on reflexive, massive attacks on Soviet cities and populations. Previous administrations, going back almost 20 years, recognized the inadequacy as a deterrent of a targeting doctrine that would give us too narrow a range of options. Although for programming purposes, strategic forces were sometimes measured in terms of ability to strike a set of industrial targets, we have always planned both more selectively (for options limiting urban-industrial damage) and more comprehensively (for a wide range of civilian and military targets). The unquestioned Soviet attainment of strategic parity has put the final nail in the coffin of what we long knew was dead — the notion that we could adequately deter the Soviets solely by threatening massive retaliation against their cities....

Our countervailing strategy — designed to provide effective deterrence — tells the world that no potential adversary of the United States could ever conclude that the fruits of his aggression would be worth his own costs. This is true whatever the level of conflict contemplated. To the Soviet Union, our strategy makes clear that no course of aggression by them that led to use of nuclear weapons, on any scale of attack and at any stage of conflict, could lead to victory, however they may define victory. Besides our power to devastate the full target system of the USSR, the United States would have the option for more selective, lesser retaliatory attacks that would exact a prohibitively high price from the things the Soviet leadership prizes most — political and military control, nuclear and conventional military force, and the economic base needed to sustain a war.

Thus, the countervailing strategy is designed to be fully consistent with NATO's strategy of flexible response by providing options for appropriate response to aggression at whatever level it might occur. The essence of the countervailing strategy is to convince the Soviets that they will be successfully opposed at any level of aggression they choose, and that no plausible outcome at any level of conflict could represent "success" for them by any reasonable definition of success.

### A. Flexibility

Our planning must provide a continuum of options, ranging from use of small numbers of strategic and/or theater nuclear weapons aimed at narrowly defined targets, to employment of large portions of our nuclear forces against a broad spectrum of targets. In addition to pre-planned targeting options, we are developing an ability to design other employment plans — in particular, smaller scale plans — on short notice in response to changing circumstances.

In theory, such flexibility also enhances the possibility of being able to control escalation of what begins as a limited nuclear exchange. I want to emphasize once again two points I have made repeatedly and publicly. First, I remain highly skeptical that escalation of a limited nuclear exchange can be controlled, or that it can be stopped short of an all-out, massive exchange. Second, even given that belief, I am convinced that we must do everything we can to make such escalation control possible, that opting out of this effort and consciously resigning ourselves to the inevitability of such escalation is a serious abdication of the awesome responsibilities nuclear weapons, and the unbelievable damage their uncontrolled use would create, thrust upon us. Having said that, let me proceed to the second element, which is escalation control.

## B. Escalation Control

Plans for the controlled use of nuclear weapons, along with other appropriate military and political actions, should enable us to provide leverage for a negotiated termination of the fighting. At an early stage in the conflict, we must convince the enemy that further escalation will not result in achievement of his objectives, that it will not mean "success," but rather additional costs. To do this, we must leave the enemy with sufficient highly valued military, economic, and political resources still surviving but still clearly at risk, so that he has a strong incentive to seek an end to the conflict.

## C. Survivability and Endurance

The key to escalation control is the survivability and endurance of our nuclear forces and the supporting communications, command and control, and intelligence ($C^3I$) capabilities. The supporting $C^3I$ is critical to effective deterrence, and we have begun to pay considerably more attention to these issues than in the past. We must ensure that the United States is not placed in a "use or lose" situation, one that might lead to unwarranted escalation of the conflict. That is a central reason why, while the Soviets cannot ignore our *capability* to launch our retaliatory forces before an attack reaches its targets, we cannot affort to rely on "launch on warning" as the long-term solution to ICBM vulnerability. . . . Survivability and endurance are essential prerequisites to an ability to adapt the employment of nuclear forces to the entire range of potentially rapidly changing and perhaps unanticipated situations and to tailor them for the appropriate responses in those situations. And, without adequate survivability and endurance, it would be impossible for us to keep substantial forces in reserve.

## D. Targeting Objectives

In order to meet our requirements for flexibility and escalation control, we must have the ability to destroy elements of four general categories of Soviet targets.

### *1. Strategic Nuclear Forces*

The Soviet Union should entertain no illusion that by attacking our strategic nuclear forces, it could significantly reduce the damage it would suffer. Nonetheless, the state of the strategic balance after an initial exchange — measured both in absolute terms and in relation to the balance prior to the exchange — could be an important factor in the decision by one side to initiate a nuclear exchange. Thus, it is important — for the sake of deterrence — to be able to deny to the potential aggressor a fundamental and favorable shift in the strategic balance as a result of a nuclear exchange.

### *2. Other Military Forces*

"Counterforce" covers much more than central strategic systems. We have for many years planned options to destroy the full range of Soviet (and, as appropriate, non-Soviet Warsaw Pact) military power, conventional as well as nuclear. Because the Soviets may define victory in part in terms of the overall post-war military balance, we will give special attention, in implementing the countervailing strategy, to more effective and more flexible targeting of the full range of military capabilities, so as to strengthen deterrence.

### *3. Leadership and Control*

We must, and we do, include options to target organs of Soviet political and military leadership and control. As I indicated earlier, the regime constituted by these centers is valued highly by the Soviet leadership. A clear U.S. ability to destroy them poses a marked challenge to the essence of the Soviet system and thus contributes to deterrence. At the same time, of course, we recognize the role that a surviving supreme command could and would play in the termination of hostilities, and can envisage many scenarios in which destruction of them would be inadvisable and contrary to our own best interests. Perhaps the obvious is worth emphasizing: possession of a capability is not tantamount to exercising it.

### *4. Industrial and Economic Base*

The countervailing strategy by no means implies that we do not — or no longer — recognize the ultimate deterrent effect of being able to threaten the full Soviet target structure, including the industrial and economic base. These targets are highly valued by the Soviets, and we must ensure that the potential loss of them is an ever-present factor in the Soviet calculus regarding nuclear war. Let me also emphasize that while, as a matter of policy, we do not target civilian population *per se,* heavy civilian fatalities and other casualties would inevitably occur in attacking the Soviet industrial and economic base, which is collocated with the Soviet urban population. I should add that Soviet civilian casualties would also be large in more focused attacks (not unlike the U.S. civilian casualty estimates cited earlier for Soviet attacks on our ICBM silos); indeed, they could be described as limited only in the sense that they would be significantly less than those resulting from an all-out attack.

## E. Reserve Forces

Our planning must provide for the designation and employment of adequate, survivable, and enduring reserve forces and the supporting $C^3I$ systems both during and after a protracted conflict. At a minimum, we will preserve such a dedicated force of strategic weapon systems.

Because there has been considerable misunderstanding and misinterpretation of the countervailing strategy and of P.D. 59, it is worth restating what the countervailing strategy is *not*.

— It is *not* a new strategic doctrine; it is *not* a radical departure from U.S. strategic policy over the past decade or so. It *is* a refinement, a re-codification of previous statements of our strategic policy. It *is* the same essential strategic doctrine, restated more clearly and related more directly to current and prospective conditions and capabilities — U.S. and Soviet.

— It does *not* assume, or assert, that we can "win" a limited nuclear war, nor does it pretend or intend to enable us to do so. It *does* seek to convince the Soviets that they could not win such a war, and thus to deter them from starting one.

— It does *not* even assume, or assert, that a nuclear war could remain limited. I have made clear my view that such a prospect is highly unlikely. It *does,* however, prepare us to respond to a limited Soviet nuclear attack in ways other than automatic, immediate, massive retaliation.

— It does *not* assume that a nuclear war will in fact be protracted over many weeks or even months. It *does,* however, take into account evidence of Soviet thinking along those lines, in order to convince them that such a course, whatever its probability, could not lead to Soviet victory.

— It does *not* call for substituting primarily military for primarily civilian targets. It *does* recognize the importance of military and civilian targets. It *does* provide for increasing the number and variety of options available to the President, covering the full range of military and civilian targets, so that he can respond appropriately and effectively to any kind of an attack, at any level.

— It is *not* inconsistent with future progress in arms control. In fact, it *does* emphasize many features — survivability, crisis stability, deterrence — that are among the core objectives of arms control. It does *not* require larger strategic arsenals; it *does* demand more flexibility and better control over strategic nuclear forces, whatever their size.

— Lastly, it is *not* a first strike strategy. Nothing in the policy contemplates that nuclear war can be a deliberate instrument for achieving our national security goals, because it cannot be. The premise, the objective, the core of our strategic doctrine remains unchanged — deterrence. The countervailing strategy, by specifying what we would do in response to any level of Soviet attack, serves to deter any such attack in the first place.

## A Technical Evaluation of MX-Basing Modes

### *Document 6*

These excerpts from a 1980 report by the Congressional Office of Technology Assessment review some of the pluses and minuses of some of the MX schemes that had been suggested by the Pentagon over the years, including MPS, placing the missiles on aircraft, putting missiles on new small submarines, putting the missiles on trucks, and so on. The report finds that MPS could complicate arms control efforts and would "severely impact the socioeconomic and physical characteristics of the deployment region."

### 6 MX MISSILE BASING May 1980

The U.S. Air Force is developing a new intercontinental ballistic missile (ICBM) known as the MX. Because the hardened "silos" in which existing ICBMs are based are considered increasingly vulnerable to a Soviet attack as a result of the improving accuracy of Soviet missiles, Congress and the Department of Defense (DOD) have agreed that a more survivable mode than hardened silos should be found for basing any new missile. OTA has examined a variety of ways in which such a missile could be based.

The purpose of this study is to identify MX basing modes and to assess the major advantages, disadvantages, risks, and uncertainties of each. At the outset of this study, OTA reviewed all the basing modes that could be identified, including those addressed in past DOD studies. On the basis of criteria of technical feasibility and the likely ability of each basing mode to provide survivability against a range of plausible Soviet threats, the list was narrowed to 11 basing modes that were analyzed in detail. This report presents these analyses, and also states briefly why other possibilities were rejected. Detailed analyses narrowed the range to five possibilities:

1. multiple protective shelter (MPS) basing in several variants,
2. antiballistic missile (ABM) defense of MPS basing,
3. launch under attack,
4. basing on small submarines, and
5. basing on large aircraft.

There is a variety of criteria against which these basing modes can be evaluated, though there is no general agreement about their relative importance. Indeed, since no basing mode ranks highest against all the commonly used criteria, deciding how to choose and weigh the criteria of evaluation is the essence of choosing a basing mode. . . .

OTA does not have a recommendation as to which basing mode, or combination of basing modes, Congress should choose. OTA is therefore able to present the relevant technical information regarding each possibility without the need to make and defend a choice. This study provides data, analyses, and explanations that will assist Congress to understand and evaluate the forthcoming Reagan administration proposal, whether this proposal turns out to be a reaffirmation of the existing program as shaped by the Carter administration, a relatively minor modification, or a major change in direction.

## Principal Findings

1. There are five basing modes that appear feasible and offer reasonable prospects of providing survivability and meeting established performance criteria for ICBMs. They are: 1) MPS basing of the type now under development by the Air Force or in one of several variants. MPS basing involves hiding the missiles among a much larger number of shelters, so that the Soviets would have to target all the shelters in order to attack all the missiles. If there were more shelters than the Soviets could effectively target, then some of the missiles would survive. This approach was the choice of the Carter administration, and one variant of MPS is now under engineering development by the Air Force. 2) MPS basing defended by a low-altitude ABM system known as LoADS (Low Altitude Defense System); 3) reliance on launch under attack so that the missiles would be used before the Soviets could destroy them; 4) basing MX on small submarines; and 5) air-mobile basing in which missiles would be dropped from wide-bodied aircraft and launched while falling. As described below, each of these alternatives has serious risks and drawbacks, and it is believed that choosing which risks and drawbacks are most tolerable is a judgment that cannot be made on technical grounds alone.

2. No basing mode is likely to provide a substantial number of survivable MX missiles much before the end of this decade. While some basing modes would permit the first missiles to be operational as soon as 1986 or 1987, these missiles could not be considered more survivable than the existing Minuteman missiles until additional elements of the basing system were in place.

3. MPS basing would preserve the existing characteristics and improve the capabilities of land-based ICBMs, but has three principal drawbacks.

- MX missiles based in MPS would provide better accuracy and endurance, and comparable responsiveness, time-on-target control, and retargeting capability, when compared to other feasible basing modes.
- Survivability depends on what the Air Force calls "preservation of location uncertainty" (PLU), that is, preventing the Soviets from determining which shelters hold the actual missiles. PLU amounts to a new technology, and while it might well be carried out successfully, confidence in PLU will be limited until prototypes have been successfully tested. Even then lingering doubts might remain.
- MPS basing cannot ensure the survivability of the missiles unless the number of shelters is large enough relative to the size of the Soviet threat. The "baseline" system of 200 MX missiles and 4,600 shelters would not be large enough if the Soviets chose to continue to increase their inventory of warheads. If the trends shown in recent Soviet force modernization efforts continue into the future, an MPS deployment of about 350 missiles and 8,250 shelters would be needed by 1990 to provide survivability. Although the number of missiles and shelters needed depends on what the Soviets do, the leadtimes for construction are so long that decisions on size must be made before intelligence data on actual, as distinct from possible, Soviet programs are available.
- MPS would severely impact the socioeconomic and physical characteristics of the deployment region. At a minimum, the deployment area would suffer the impacts generally associated with very rapid population growth in rural communities; but larger urban areas would also be affected by economic uncertainties regarding the size of the MPS construction work force and its regional distribution. The physical impacts of MPS would be characteristic of the impacts of major construction projects in arid regions; but because the grid pattern of MPS would mean that a very large area would be close to construction activities, it is possible that thousands of square miles of rangeland could be rendered unproductive.

4. None of the variants of MPS would reduce the risks and uncertainties associated with PLU or significantly alter the number of shelters required. However, split basing or the selection of a different deployment area would mitigate the regional impacts. . . .

5. A LoADS ABM system could effectively double the number of shelters in an MPS deployment provided two conditions were met. . . .

6. Basing MX missiles in silos and relying on launching the missiles before a Soviet attack could destroy them (launch under attack, or LUA) would be technically feasible, but it would create extreme requirements for availability of, and rapid decisionmaking by, National Command Authorities. . . .

7. MX missiles based on small submarines would be highly survivable. Submarine-based MX would not be significantly less capable than land-based MX, but submarine-basing would involve a reorientation of U.S. strategic forces. . . .

8. An air-mobile MX — carried on wide-bodied aircraft and launched in midair — would be survivable provided the aircraft received timely warning and took off immediately. . . .

9. The problems associated with other basing modes studied by OTA appear more substantial.

# SALT II and MX

### *Document 7*

**The MX was influenced by arms control. One of the reasons President Carter decided to go forward with the MX**

was to attempt to defuse conservative criticism that he was too soft on the Soviets. Arms control influenced the MX in another way too. During the SALT II negotiations, it was very important to the Carter administration that the public see a SALT II agreement as treating both superpowers equally. Therefore, the U.S. negotiators pressed the Soviets to agree to have the treaty allow the MX ten warheads, the same number as the largest Soviet missile. This selection from the book *Endgame* by Strobe Talbott describes the U.S. push for a ten-warhead limit, even though the MX might have been more efficient with only six or eight warheads. (A "fractionation freeze" is a freeze on the number of warheads each type of missile would be allowed to carry.)

### 7 SOLUTIONS BEGET PROBLEMS
### Strobe Talbott

. . . But as was so often the case in SALT, the pursuit of a constraint on Soviet systems was complicated by the need to protect an American system at the same time — that is, to keep an option open. Just as the Carter administration had sought — and finally achieved — a new-types ban that left it free to proceed with the development of the MX, so it sought a fractionation freeze that left the U.S. free to arm the MX with ten warheads. The motivation here was largely political. Pentagon studies concluded that the MX might be most efficient with six to eight warheads. Some Pentagon officials even proposed at one point that the U.S. accept a six-warhead limit on the MX so that the Russians would be bound by the same limit on their new type of ICBM in case they decided to go with a MIRVed new type. But the administration decided that it would help the cause of ratification if the U.S. could reserve the right to put as many warheads on its new ICBM, the MX, as the Soviets had on their largest existing ICBM, the SS-18. As 1978 wore on and the battle in the Senate loomed closer, the policy-makers gave increasing weight to considerations of political appearance. How would the final treaty *look* with or without a particular provision? On the issue of MX fractionation, there was little interagency dispute. Leslie Gelb's Bureau of Politico-Military Affairs at the State Department, Walter Slocombe's SALT Task Force at the Pentagon, Paul Warnke and his colleagues in ACDA, David Aaron and Roger Molander at the National Security Council, all agreed that the treaty would look more equitable and would be easier to ratify if the U.S. could have ten MIRVs on the MX. The ability to match the SS-18 warhead for warhead was seen as a way of redressing the most blatant inequity in SALT — the holdover provision from the interim agreement that allowed the U.S.S.R. some 300 heavy missiles and the U.S. none. Thus, the American proposal on fractionation was to freeze the number of warheads on each side's existing types of ICBM but to allow as many warheads on the one allotted new type as on the largest existing type — i.e., ten.

The Soviets took the position that the U.S. was trying to have it both ways — minimum fractionation on Soviet existing types but maximum fractionation on the American new type — and they did not want the U.S. to have it either way. The Russians spun out an array of counterproposals, the purpose of which was to permit them to put additional warheads on their existing types of ICBMs while preventing the U.S. from putting ten on the MX. . . .

## Anti-MX Reaction

### *Document 8*

The Carter decision to base MX in a race track system sparked protests in Utah and Nevada, the states due to receive the new missile. Document 8, an article in *Newsweek* in February 1980, describes the Defense Department's efforts to sell the MX to people in the western states and the growing local resistance.

### 8 MX SPELLS TROUBLE OUT WEST
### February 11, 1980

Alamo, Nev., is barely a scattering of house trailers and cinder-block bungalows along a two-lane highway in the desert. The town's only gas station is also its only café and general store, a cozy place where you can get a quart of oil, hamburger, a box of shotgun shells, a saddle or some good conversation. These days, the talk runs to a threat to Alamo's rural isolation and quiet way of life — the coming of MX.

The people of Alamo are not alone in their concern about the proposed $33 billion MX mobile-missile system, one of the largest public-works projects in U.S. history. Last week, Air Force Brig. Gen. Forrest S. McCartney and a troop of military officers and civilian consultants finished a tour of a dozen towns and cities in Nevada and Utah. Their mission was to present the government's case for MX and invite questions about potential problems (as research for an environmental-impact statement the Air Force must submit in June). What they found at each stop was chronic anxiety about what MX would do to local water supplies, agriculture and the slow but sane pace of development in the area.

Shell Game: MX, in effect, is a vast nuclear shell game that would be played out across 47 desert valleys in the two states. It would consist of 200 loops of roadway, each 10 to 15 miles long and 4 to 6 miles wide. Each loop would have 23 hardened missile shelters and a transporter-erector-launcher to shuttle one MX missile between them. The mobile transporter would slowly tour the unpaved loop every few months and secretly deposit its missile in one of the 23 shelters. In all, there would

"IT'S THE NICE MAN FROM THE JOINT CHIEFS, HARVEY — HERE TO SEE ABOUT THE MX BASING MODE AGAIN!"



be 200 missiles concealed among 4,600 shelters. The system would require up to 250 square miles of land, although only the 2½ acres surrounding each shelter would be fenced off; the rest of the land would presumably be accessible for normal public use.

The people McCartney encountered in his series of "scoping" sessions doubted that things would ever be the same after MX. There was a litany of "Who will pay?"; there were questions about lost land and water and the burden of local services for an estimated 105,000 people who will move in to build and run the system. "We will certainly address that in the environmental-impact statement," McCartney often responded. He even had to deny a wild rumor that nerve gas would be used to protect the shelters.

Some of the concerns could not be so easily soothed. "Our Mormon way of life is important to us," said alfalfa farmer Robert Christiansen of Beaver, Utah. "We send our girls off to the picture show and they walk home at eleven at night. That would end if MX comes." Most of the small-town gatherings, however, yielded a sense of patriotic resignation. "I'd rather that the MX didn't come at all," sighed LeMoine Davis, proprietor of Alamo's general store. "But I'd rather that the Russians didn't come either."

Last week's meeting in Las Vegas was a different story — the most dramatic challenge yet to McCartney's traveling PR roadshow. It was organized by an unlikely grab bag of organizations — the Sierra Club, the antinuclear Sagebrush Alliance, the Southern Nevada Off Road Enthusiasts (SNORE) and others — all allied under an umbrella group called Nevadans Opposed to MX (NO MX). A cluster of college-age activists passed out pamphlets, bumper stickers and "NO MX" badges outside the city commission chambers. Inside, 50 people, many with prepared statements, signed up to speak. One issued a fourteen-point manifesto that included a demand for $2 million from Congress simply to help local governments plan for coping with MX. Another urged the Air Force to study alternatives to the MX system. And NO MX organizer Bob Maichle charged that the system was being "shoved down our throats" because "there are fewer people in Nevada and Utah to vote against it."

Grounded: McCartney's detachment also ran into some logistical problems. In Las Vegas, the crowd did not miss the irony of a lieutenant colonel searching desperately for a light bulb to replace one that blew out on the overhead projector during the presentation. Earlier in the tour, a military helicopter carrying Air Force Under Secretary Antonia Chayes was grounded on a highway by bad weather en route to a meeting in Delta, Utah. Chayes abandoned her MX mission and hitched a ride on a passing truck bound for Salt Lake City. The government is not likely to give up that easily.

## FROM MX TO MIDGETMAN

# A Comic Look at Proposed Basing Schemes

### *Document 9*

Early in the Reagan administration, columnist Russell Baker took a comic look at the many basing schemes that had been proposed for the MX. His column indicated that it was getting harder for the public to take the new MX basing schemes seriously.

## 9 UNIVERSAL MILITARY MOTION
**Russell Baker**
**April 4, 1981**

The idea behind the MX system is sound enough: Stack a supply of H-bombs on railroad trains and keep them moving constantly so enemy targeters will not know where to aim. To confuse things further, run decoy trains so the enemy cannot distinguish between false bomb carriers and the real thing.

The only flaw overlooked by MX designers is that Americans can't run a railroad. My own strategic thinkers did not make this mistake when they designed the MX Pentagon system. When approached by thermonuclear experts to solve the Pentagon problem, we immediately pointed out the error in relying on rail transport.

The problem they wanted solved was how to protect the Pentagon from incoming atomic artillery. It obviously makes no sense to have our H-bombs rattling around securely on confusing tangles of rail as long as our command center is anchored like a moose with four broken legs on the side of the Potomac River.

Please note that our first decision was not to put the Pentagon on a train. Dangerously low bridge clearances and excessively narrow rights of way argued persuasively against rail movement. In addition, generals and admirals could not be expected to generate enthusiasm for railroad vending-machine meals and would feel demeaned when shunted onto sidetracks while freight trains rumbled past them.

More important, however, we recognize that railroading is one thing Americans do abominably. Note that the Government implicity concedes the point by planning to do away with Amtrak.

Having conceded the nation's incompetence at railroading, why does the Government seriously consider building an entirely new rail system for H-bombs? Our own strategic thinkers avoided this logical inconsistency when they drew their blueprints for the MX Pentagon.

What does America do superbly? That was the first question we asked ourselves. The answers were: highways and fast-food restaurants. With these answers, the solution to the Pentagon problem began falling into place. Obviously, the Pentagon would have to move by highway.

We immediately realized, however, that placing the Pentagon on huge tractor-trailers and driving it endlessly along randomly selected roads would not provide sufficient protection against nuclear attack. The Pentagon is very big. On a clear day if it is being moved along a highway, it does not help to hold its speed down to 55 miles per hour to avoid attracting attention. People can see it coming from miles away. It is, in short, a fat, easy target.

As with the MX missile system, the solution here is to create decoys. This is why we propose building 250 moveable structures so precisely like the Pentagon that no one can tell the fake Pentagons from the real thing.

With 251 Pentagons constantly cruising the roads, enemy attackers will face the maddening problem of finding a needle in the haystack. Moreover, it will be much harder for spies to follow their movements.

Consider: With only one Pentagon on the highway, its movements would be constantly known to any enemy agent who bothered to read the headlines: "Pentagon Headed for Terre Haute," "Pentagon Trapped Two Hours In Denver Traffic Jam," "Pentagon Dented in Lincoln Tunnel Collison: Admiral Suffers Contusions."

With 251 Pentagons in circulation, however, the sight of a Pentagon on the highway will attract no more newspaper attention than a politician's indictment. But just to add another margin of security, we will confuse matters further by building 1,500 Pentagons disguised as fast-food restaurants along the nations' highways.

Each of these will be an exact replica of the genuine Pentagon, at least as seen from the outside. Inside, of course, they will be equipped to provide all the necessities of acute indigestion, thus providing the wherewithal of highway travel and, in the process, earning the Government a little income on its expenditures.

Occasionally, when generals and admirals tire of touring and yearn for a little stability, the real Pentagon will be parked alongside the road to masquerade as a fast-food Pentagon. The danger of highway travelers wandering in for a quick hot dog and making trouble while the authentic Pentagon is in the "parked" or "fast-food" mode has also been considered.

These interlopers will simply be told by receptionists that hot dogs are in the back of the building and directed to walk the long route around the Pentagon's outer ring. As they drop from exhaustion they will be removed by military police, carried to their cars, given free hot dogs and advised that next time they should enter their Pentagon fast-food dispensary through the rear door.

There are problems to be ironed out in the MX Pentagon, but we are too busy at the moment perfecting our MX Congress system to trifle with details. With 850 United States Capitols on the highway, we have an extremely touchy problem in deciding whether a Capitol or a Pentagon should have the right of way when they meet at an intersection.

## The Reagan Administration Grapples with MX: Dense Pack

### *Document 10*

Soon after coming to office, The Reagan administration abandoned as too unwieldy the Carter administration's planned race track system. But this left the MX once again without a basing mode. In October 1981, the Reagan administration announced that only one hundred missiles would be deployed, half the number the Carter administration had planned. But the administration still did not have a basing mode. Under pressure from Congress, the Reagan administration finally made a move. In a November 1982 speech excerpted here, President Reagan announced that the MX would be deployed on an Air Force base in Wyoming in closely spaced silos. This basing scheme was also called Dense Pack. It would have required much less land than MPS and would have avoided local political problems. But it did not win support in Congress.

### 10 SPEECH TO THE AMERICAN PEOPLE
### President Ronald Reagan
### November 22, 1982

Our deployed nuclear forces were built before the age of microcircuits. It is not right to ask our young men and women in uniform to maintain and operate such antiques. Many have already given their lives in missile explosions and aircraft accidents caused by the old age of their equipment. We must replace and modernize our forces. And that is why I decided to proceed with the production and deployment of the new ICBM known as the MX. Three earlier Presidents worked to develop this missile.

Based on the best advice that I could get I concluded that the MX is the right missile at the right time. On the other hand, when I arrived in office I felt the proposal on where and how to base the missile simply cost too much in terms of money and the impact on our citizens' lives. I have concluded, however, it is absolutely essential that we proceed to produce this missile and that we base it in a series of closely based silos at Warren Air Force Base near Cheyenne, Wyoming. This plan requires only half as many missiles as the earlier plan and will fit in an area of only twenty square miles. It is the product of around-the-clock research that has been underway since I directed a search for a better, cheaper way.

I urge the members of Congress who must pass this plan to listen and examine the facts before they come to their own conclusion. Some may question what modernizing our military has to do with peace. Well as I explained earlier, a secure force keeps others from threatening us and that keeps the peace. Just as important, it also increases the prospects of reaching significant arms reductions with the Soviets, and that is what we really want.

The United States wants deep cuts in the world's arsenal of weapons, but unless we demonstrate the will to rebuild our strength and restore the military balance, the Soviets, since they are so far ahead, have little incentive to negotiate with us. Let me repeat that point because it goes to the heart of our policies. Unless we demonstrate the will to rebuild our strength, the Soviets have little incentive to negotiate. If we had not begun to modernize, the Soviet negotiators would know we had nothing to bargain with except talk. They would know that we were bluffing without a good hand because they know what cards we hold just as we know what is in their hand. . . .

## The Move Away from MIRVed Missiles

### *Documents 11 and 12*

Congress would not support the new Dense Pack scheme. After ten years of being told the MX had to be hidden or made mobile, a sudden complete reversal was too much to accept. At the time MX was encountering trouble, some liberals and moderates were focusing on the need to de-MIRV ballistic missiles. They reasoned that since much of the worry about ICBM vulnerability was caused by the large numbers of MIRVed missiles each superpower had, something should be done to encourage the superpowers to abandon MIRVs and deploy small, single-warhead missiles. In documents 11 and 12, former Secretary of State Henry Kissinger and liberal Sen. Albert Gore present similar analyses of nuclear strategy and arms control. Both urge that the United States begin to move toward deploying single-warhead missiles.

### 11 A NEW APPROACH TO ARMS CONTROL
### Henry Kissinger
### March 21, 1983

#### The Present Dilemma

There is a "flaw" in SALT II, though not the one usually discussed. It is that SALT limitations were expressed in terms of numbers of delivery vehicles at the precise moment when the increase in the accuracy and number of warheads caused numerical "equivalence" to be more and more beside the point. With each side possessing the capability (the Soviets' actual, ours latent) of making its opponent vulnerable, arms control after a decade of negotiations had returned to its starting point.

This problem cannot be solved simply by deep reductions in delivery vehicles. Given the disproportion between warheads and launchers, reductions either are irrelevant to the danger of surprise attack or, perversely, *increase* it. With present weapons, the greater the reductions, the fewer would be the targets for a first strike and the greater would be its calculability.

This is well illustrated by President Reagan's Eureka College speech of May 9, 1982, which contains the basic American proposal for the Strategic Arms Reduction Talks (START). It was an advance over an uncontrolled arms race because it set a ceiling. It was an advance over SALT in relating the ceiling to warheads rather than launchers. And it stressed significant mutual reductions of strategic forces. It was a brave first attempt that unfortunately did not solve the root issue of multiple warheads. Even were the Soviets to accept our proposal, the Eureka scheme would at best maintain the existing balance; it would almost surely worsen rather than ease our dangers. A quick glance at the numbers involved illustrates the problem.

Under SALT II about 5,000 Soviet land-based warheads would be aimed at 1,054 American launchers — a ratio of less than 5 to 1. The Eureka proposal would reduce the permitted warheads to 2,500 on at most 400 launchers. Even were it technically feasible to distribute warheads in this manner (and the Soviets would have to redesign their entire strategic force to do so), this would give the side striking first an advantage in warheads to targets of better than 6 to 1. And at these lower numbers of launchers an attack would be far more calculable.

The Eureka proposal would also establish limits of 2,500 to 3,000 sea-based warheads. This would force a reduction of our submarine force from the 42 permitted under SALT to 15 or fewer (depending on the type). We could keep at most ten vessels at sea at one time, *vs.* the current 25 to 30. If there are any advances in antisubmarine warfare technology, as is probable, arms control will have increased the vulnerability of both our underwater *and* our land-based strategic forces — the supreme irony. The Soviet proposal of a flat 25% reduction in launchers, while simpler, suffers from the identical disability.

In short, a negotiation begun more than a decade ago to enhance stability and reduce vulnerability is in danger of achieving the opposite. Arms control is heading for an intellectual dead end.

## Where Do We Go from Here?

We face two related tasks. First, arms control requires not so much a new proposal as a fresh concept. Second, it must become an organic part of defense policy. This requires that we return to first principles. The principal cause of instability with current weapons systems is the disproportion between warheads and launchers. All the remedies that have been tried are vulnerable to technology: hardening to accuracy, sea-based systems to advances in antisubmarine technology. There is no effective or intellectually adequate solution to this problem except to seek to eliminate multiple warheads within a fixed time, say ten years.

Fortunately technology, which creates the problem, can offer a solution. According to published literature, it is possible to develop a mobile missile that could be protected in a heavily armored canister. Its mobility alone could complicate the task of the attacker. Moreover, the new missile could — and should — be equipped with a single warhead. With strategic forces of such design, numerical limits would be both simple to establish and far more significant than under SALT II or START.

Once we decided on such an approach, we could proceed with it either as part of an arms control agreement or unilaterally as part of our defense policy. For example, we could propose to reduce and transform the strategic arsenals of both sides to a low number of single-warhead missiles over a ten-year period. The totals should be set at the lowest number that could be monitored; that is, at a level where a violation significant enough to overturn it could not be hidden. The permitted number of missiles may be as low as 500; at any rate, the number of warheads in this scheme would be only a small fraction of current totals, probably 20% or less of the Eureka scheme. Each side would be free to choose whether the permitted missiles would be mobile or in silos. Mobility would reduce the incentive of surprise attack, but equivalence at low numbers of single-warhead missiles would, in any event, assure considerable stability.

This course does not depend on Soviet agreement. It should be pursued whatever the Soviet reaction. If they refused our proposal — this one or another embodying the same concept — the U.S. could announce that after a certain date, say 1990 (or before then if the new missile could be developed earlier), it would deploy no more MIRVed land-based intercontinental missiles but would emphasize single-warhead launchers, the majority mobile. The size of that force would be geared to the number of warheads deployed by the Soviets: we would reserve the right to match each Soviet warhead with single-warhead missiles of our own. In practice, we would almost certainly choose a lower number that we calculate could survive the maximum Soviet attack capable of being launched. The purpose would be to increase the number of targets the Soviets would have to hit but without increasing our capacity for surprise attack. We would gradually phase out our MIRVed missiles. If the Soviets agreed to a formal proposal, schedules for the mutual destruction of MIRVs would be negotiated. If they refused, we would build up single-warhead missiles to a level consonant with our security. The Soviets could always put a ceiling on our deployment by cutting the number of their warheads.

This scheme should pose no insurmountable verification problems. Fixed launchers can be detected through national technical means; existing Soviet MIRVed ICBMs could not be made mobile; development of a new mobile MIRVed ICBM would require extensive testing, which could be detected and would therefore be proscribed. Mobile single-warhead missiles would be more difficult to detect; this is why agreed numbers would have to be sufficient so that they could be exceeded only by a violation our means of detection would not miss. Obviously, the more airtight the inspection, the smaller can be the numbers. Only missiles tested *solely* with single warheads would be permitted; any tested with a MIRV warhead would be proscribed.

No one can predict how the rigid Soviet bureaucracy would react to this approach. It may upset too many vested interests. The new leadership may be too dependent on military support to challenge its military-industrial complex. Yet sometimes an impasse can be broken only by a daring departure; surely the nitpicking SALT negotiations offer little hope for the traditional approach. If the Soviets can ever be interested in stability and in easing the economic burden of the arms race, they should — probably only on second thought — study this scheme with care. Like the Eureka approach, it requires them to redesign their forces; unlike the Eureka approach, it reduces their vulnerability. And upon reflection, the Soviets must realize that, one way or another, we will cure the vulnerability of our forces and in the process will almost surely enhance the vulnerability of theirs.

If the Soviets refuse to discuss such a proposal, one of three conclusions is inescapable; a) their arms program aims for strategic superiority if not by design then by momentum; b) they believe strategic edges can be translated into political advantages; c) arms control to the Soviets is an aspect of political warfare whose aim is not reciprocal stability but unilateral advantage.

Where does this leave the MX? A presidential commission is studying that question. I will address one issue: Should we have a "counterforce" capability (an ability to strike accurately at Soviet missile silos or command centers), or should we continue to aim for "assured destruction" of civilian and industrial targets? Ever since the Soviets began to approach strategic parity, it should have been obvious that a strategy aiming at civilian destruction was an irrational, suicidal, indeed nihilistic course that no President could implement. Undiscriminating slaughter is not a defense policy but a prelude to unilateral disarmament.

Similarly, why should a Soviet counterforce capability — as now exists — be treated as consistent with strategic stability, while our attempt, represented by the MX, to provide a much smaller means to respond is considered as somehow destabilizing? If the U.S., by its abdication, guarantees the invulnerability of Soviet missile forces while the Soviets keep ours exposed, any Soviet incentive for serious negotiation will vanish. A secure Soviet first-strike capability poses an unprecedented danger — ultimately that it may some day be used, in the near term that it may increase Soviet willingness to run risks in regional crises.

Whatever level of MX deployment is recommended by the Scowcroft Commission should be strategically meaningful beyond a mere token deployment. At the same time, the MX, like the new single-warhead missile, should be an organic part of an arms-control strategy. To this end, we should offer to postpone MX deployment if the Soviets agree to destroy MIRVed SS-18s (their heavy missiles) over three years starting in 1986, and to abandon MX altogether once the SS-18s are dismantled.

This analysis has been confined to land-based missiles. Were the Soviets to show interest in the scheme outlined here, account would have to be taken of sea-based forces. Just as we cannot be asked to ratify our own vulnerability in land-based forces, the Soviets should not be expected to acquiesce in U.S. submarine-launched missiles capable of surprise attack. Specifically, as part of the agreement proposed here, we should be prepared to move to single warheads at sea as well, though over a longer period, say 15 years, because of the long lead times. In that case, the submarines would have to be made smaller and less expensive. It would be too risky to put so many eggs in one basket, as is the case with the current Trident submarines, each of which carries 24 missiles. A new regimen would be required as well for heavy bombers.

The deployment–arms control scheme would then look as follows:

A. The U.S. would make a fundamental decision to shift to single-warhead missiles as soon as possible. Ideally, this decision would be reflected in an agreed ceiling at a very low number — perhaps 500 — negotiated with the Soviets. An agreement should also limit throw weight to prevent development of huge single-warhead weapons.

B. If the Soviets refused such a scheme, we would proceed unilaterally toward our goal. The final size of a single-warhead force would depend on the number of warheads in the Soviet force and on what we need to assure our invulnerability.

C. The U.S. would begin deploying MXs starting in 1986. It would be prepared to postpone deployment if, before 1986, the Soviet Union agreed to a schedule by which its SS-18s would be destroyed over a three-year period starting in 1986.

D. Both sides would also agree to dismantle the remaining land-based MIRV forces starting in 1990.

E. In that case, both sides would agree not to increase the number of warheads on MIRVs while they remain in the force.

F. Other mixes are possible. For example, a small number of MIRVed missiles and bombers, no more than 200, could be joined with a reduced single-warhead deployment, say 300.

This approach would be a serious test of Soviet intentions. It would conclusively end the danger of a first strike. It would establish clear equivalence. It would transcend the SALT and START debate and put strategy and arms control in a coherent context. If refused, it would be a clear signal of a Soviet bid for superiority; we would draw the appropriate conclusions. If we proceeded unilaterally, nevertheless, it would be a major contribution to strategic stability and U.S. security.

Of course, even the achievement of strategic stability would open up areas of concern now dormant. It would bring to the fore the pressing need to build up conventional forces to deter nonnuclear challenges. That problem would be addressed in a new environment. For all parties would know that they have taken — at last — a big step toward avoiding nuclear catastrophe. This is an imperative that humanity demands and reality imposes.

## 12 THE FORK IN THE ROAD
## Albert Gore, Jr.
## May 5, 1982

. . . Advocates of a freeze and advocates of a massive nuclear force buildup have more in common than they may realize.

It is obvious that the counterforce weapons now in the hands of the Soviet Union constitute the greatest source of concern to Americans. President Reagan stated this concern succinctly in his March 31 press conference: "The Soviets' great edge is one in which they could absorb our retaliatory blow and hit us again." This reference to our "retaliatory blow" obviously presumes a first strike against us by the nuclear forces of the Soviet Union. . . .

. . . I have proposed a set of detailed guidelines for a new, comprehensive strategic arms agreement between the United States and the Soviet Union — a proposed agreement which selects counterforce weapons as its focus. The proposal has two phases. The first phase is a selective freeze on any additions to the counterforce inventory of either side and on any improvements to counterforce weapons currently deployed. This might also be described as a "negotiators' pause," designed to give breathing room to the negotiators by slowing the momentum of technical development at the cutting edge of the arms race. This selective moratorium would be followed immediately by negotiations for reductions, which would begin with the synchronized dismantling of the remaining counterforce weapons on both sides, starting with the MIRVed version of the Soviet SS18. In return for substantially larger reductions on the Soviet side, the U.S. would agree not to deploy the MX or the Trident D-5, although development and testing of both would be allowed to continue as a hedge against the breakdown of negotiations. To maintain mutual deterrence, the agreement would mandate replacement of MIRVed ICBMs with a new, less destabilizing type: an ICBM carrying just one warhead.

If both sides were to carry out this change, neither would ever be in a position to make the arithmetic of a first strike work. Although either side could attack the other's ICBMs, the attacker would have to use up his entire ICBM inventory and a very large proportion of his submarine-based missiles to do the job. Detailed calculations have convinced me that under these circumstances, the side that struck first would find itself at a disadvantage even against the residual forces of its enemy.

At the same time, in order to constrain the overall nuclear force available to each side, the totals of strategic launchers — ICBMs, SLBMs, and heavy bombers — should be limited, and reduced. It seems reasonable, as a first step, to take a number already familiar to both sides through SALT II: 2,250 systems. The Soviets have already accepted this ceiling, a number which would entail a 10-percent reduction of their currently deployed launchers.

Within the contours of this agreement, each side would retain great flexibility to redesign its remaining nuclear forces if it wished to do so, in order to protect against the reappearance of the vulnerability problem. The U.S. could either continue with existing programs, or make some changes. We could, for example, rethink our decision on B-1, and we could also have a second look at whether the entire submarine-launched missile force should be concentrated in a relatively small number of large Ohio-class submarines, as presently intended.

The essential point, however, is that once each side recalculated its land-based systems by getting rid of MIRVed ICBMs, both sides would be in a much better position to continue the arms control process in an atmosphere less fraught with mutual apprehension. Moreover, the process of moving into deep reductions would already be well underway. For example, as compared to SALT II, the number of nuclear warheads available to either side would be on the order of 50 percent less.

As an interesting consequence of the reductions, the Soviet advantage in throw-weight would be substantially narrowed, and, in fact, the United States would have the ability to achieve equal throw-weight if it chose to do so. Moreover, the number of ICBMs would turn out to be equal.

All elements of the proposal are verifiable with a high degree of certainty by using a variety of methods within the scope of "national technical means." (However, the Soviets could increase the chances for ratification of this or any other proposal by agreeing to additional means of verification.) . . .

The agreement I have proposed would undeniably reduce the likelihood of nuclear war by making a first strike against the ICBMs of the other once again "unthinkable." Surprisingly, there are some who believe that this might be unwise, for two reasons. First, they worry that if the Soviets think our nuclear forces are stalemated, then this perception might encourage them to press their luck, and that a miscalculation could then lead to nuclear war. Second, some worry that the U.S. would have no alternative in such a war but to carry out the doctrine of "Mutual Assured Destruction" by attacking Soviet cities.

It is precisely at this point that clear judgment is required to save our civilization. This is the fork in the road.

The arid language of "surgical first strikes" and "nuclear exchanges" can lull us into forgetting the devastation they would cause. Estimates of U.S. deaths resulting from strikes against missile silos alone range as high as 20 million. The number of casualties in case of a U.S. first strike against Soviet ICBM fields would also be very high. And an attack against missile silos is hardly the limit of what either side would have to do to carry out a full-scale counterforce strike. The list of priority targets would include bomber bases, submarine ports, command and control centers of both military and civil systems, and others. The civilian casualties resulting from an attack against this set of targets would add more scores of millions of deaths.

Do we really believe that the response from the victim of such an attack would be rational, measured, or constrained? That it would not be driven by rage, grief, and revenge to exact the highest possible penalties? The answer is clear. We must make nuclear war less likely, not more likely. If the Administration chooses wisely at this fork in the road, we will have a better opportunity to create a relationship with the Soviet Union which deters aggression — and which condemns war as "an old habit of thought that must now pass."

## A Classic Compromise

### *Document 13*

Congressional hostility toward Dense Pack placed the fate of the MX in doubt. Supporters of MX realized that something had to be done to win the support of moderates and liberals who favored deMIRVing. In January 1983, President Reagan appointed the President's Commission on Strategic Forces (the Scowcroft Commission, as it is often called) to study the MX problem and recommend solutions. The commission delivered its recommendations in April, and there was a serious attempt to achieve consensus. The commission effectively closed the window of vulnerability. It argued that the survivability of U.S. nuclear forces is provided by the strategic triad as a whole. Although it is desirable for each leg by itself to be survivable, this is not essential. The key is that the interaction of the three legs can provide survivability. The clear implication was that the MX basing mode did not have to guarantee the survivability of the MX.

Based on this reasoning, the commission recommended the deployment of one hundred MX missiles in existing Midgetman III silos, and gained the support of the MX partisans. To gain the support of the moderates, the commission strongly recommended the deployment of a mobile, single-warhead missile called the small ICBM and now popularly called Midgetman. Beyond calling for a single-warhead mobile missile, the Scowcroft Commission did not specify exactly what the Midgetman should look like nor precisely how it should be based.

## 13 THE SCOWCROFT COMMISSION REPORT April 6, 1983

### IV. U.S. Strategic Forces and Trends
### A. Strategic Forces as a Whole

The development of the components of our strategic forces — the multiplicity of intercontinental ballistic missiles (ICBMs), submarine-launched ballistic missiles (SLBMs), and bombers — was in part the result of an historical evolution. This triad of forces, however, serves several important purposes.

First, the existence of several strategic forces requires the Soviets to solve a number of different problems in their efforts to plan how they might try to overcome them. Our objective, after all, is to make their planning of any such attack as difficult as we can. If it were possible for the Soviets to concentrate their research and development efforts on putting only one or two components of U.S. strategic forces at risk — e.g., by an intensive effort at anti-submarine warfare to attempt to threaten our ballistic missile submarines — both their incentive to do so and their potential gains would be sharply increased. Thus the existence of several components of our strategic forces permits each to function as a hedge against possible Soviet successes in endangering any of the others.

For example, at earlier times uncertainties about the vulnerability of our bomber force were alleviated by our confidence in the survivability of our ICBMs. And although the survivability of our ICBMs is today a matter of concern (especially when that problem is viewed in isolation) it would be far more serious if we did not have a force of ballistic missile submarines at sea and a bomber force. By the same token, over the long run it would be unwise to rely so heavily on submarines as our only ballistic missile force that a Soviet breakthrough in anti-submarine warfare could not be offset by other strategic systems.

Second, the different components of our strategic forces would force the Soviets, if they were to contemplate an all-out attack, to make choices which would lead them to reduce significantly their effectiveness against one component in order to attack another. For example, if Soviet war planners should decide to attack our bomber and submarine bases and our ICBM silos with simultaneous detonations by delaying missile launches from close-in submarines so that such missiles would *arrive* at our bomber bases at the same time the Soviet ICBM warheads (with their longer time of flight) would arrive at our ICBM silos — then a very high proportion of our alert bombers would have escaped before their bases were struck. This is because we would have been able to, and would have, ordered our bombers to take off from their bases within moments after the launch of the first Soviet ICBMs. If the Soviets, on the other hand, chose rather to *launch* their ICBM and SLBM attacks at the same moment (hoping to destroy a higher proportion of our bombers with SLBMs having a short time of flight), there would be a period of over a quarter of an hour after nuclear detonations had occurred on U.S. bomber bases but before our ICBMs had been struck. In such a case the Soviets should have no confidence that we would refrain from launching our ICBMs during that interval after we had been hit. It is important to appreciate that this would not be a "launch-on-warning," or even a "launch under attack," but rather a launch *after* attack — after massive nuclear detonations had already occurred on U.S. soil.

Thus our bombers and ICBMs are more survivable together against Soviet attack than either would be alone. This illustrates that the different components of our strategic forces should be assessed collectively and not in isolation. It also suggests that whereas it is highly desirable that a component of the strategic forces be survivable when it is viewed separately, it makes a major contribution to deterrence even if its survivability depends in substantial measure on the existence of one of the other components of the force.

The third purpose served by having multiple components in our strategic forces is that each component has unique properties not present in the others. Nuclear submarines have the advantage of being able to stay submerged and hidden for months at a time, and thus the missiles they carry may reasonably be held in reserve rather than being used early in the event of attack. Bombers may be launched from their bases on warning without irretrievably committing them to an attack; also, their weapons, though they arrive in hours, not minutes, have excellent accuracy against a range of possible targets. ICBMs have advantages in command and control, in the ability to be retargeted readily, and in accuracy. This means that ICBMs are especially effective in deterring Soviet threats of massive conventional or limited nuclear attacks, because they could most credibly respond promptly and controllably against specific military targets and thereby promptly disrupt an attack on us or our allies. . . .

## E. ICBM Programs

The problem that led to the establishment of this Commission is the same one that has been at the heart of much of the controversy concerning strategic forces and arms control for over a decade — the future of our ICBM force. As described above (Section IV.A.) our ICBM force has three main strategic purposes: (1) serving as a hedge against possible vulnerabilities in our submarine force; (2) introducing complexity and uncertainty into any plan of Soviet attack, because of the different types of attacks that would have to be launched against our ICBMs and our bombers; and (3) helping to deter Soviet threats of massive conventional or limited nuclear attacks by the ability to respond promptly and controllably against hardened military targets.

ICBM modernization is also particularly important now in order to encourage the Soviets to reach stabilizing arms control agreements and to redress perceived U.S. disadvantages in strategic capability.

The Commission believes that, because of changing technology, arms control negotiations, and our own domestic political process, this issue — the future of our ICBM force — has come to be miscast in recent years.

To many the problem has become: "How can a force consisting of relatively large, accurate land-based ICBMs be deployed quickly and be made survivable, even when it is viewed in isolation from the rest of our strategic forces, in the face of increasingly accurate threatened attacks by large numbers of warheads — and how can this be done under arms control agreements that limit or reduce launcher numbers?" It is this complex problem that many, inside and outside the government, have sought to solve for a variety of reasons. These reasons fall into five main groups.

First, in order to serve one of the necessary purposes of a strategic force — namely to hedge against possible failure by the others, such as would be caused by a Soviet breakthrough in anti-submarine warfare — many have felt that any new ICBM deployment should be almost totally survivable even when viewed in isolation from our bomber force and the rest of our strategic forces. The threat now posed by accurate Soviet ICBMs to the Minuteman force, viewed in isolation, has also led many to argue that this particular survivability problem has to be solved quickly.

Second, the overall perception of strategic imbalance caused by the Soviets' ability to destroy hardened land-based targets — with more than 600 newly-deployed SS-18 and SS-19 ICBMs — while the U.S. is clearly not able to do so with its existing ballistic missile force, has been reasonably regarded as destabilizing and as a weakness in the overall fabric of deterrence. In particular, since the ICBM force helps to deter massive conventional or limited nuclear attack against us or our allies, this has led many to believe that the serious imbalance between U.S. and Soviet capabilities should be rectified quickly in the overall interest of the alliance.

Third, arms control agreements — in part to be verifiable without resort to the sorts of co-operative measures such as on-site inspection typically opposed by the Soviets — have concentrated to a significant degree on limiting or reducing strategic missile launchers rather than warheads. This is in some measure because launchers are more easily counted by satellite reconnaissance than are other ICBM characteristics and because launcher numbers provide relatively unambiguous terms for a treaty. Launcher or missile limits have the indirect effect, however, of encouraging both sides to build large ICBMs with many warheads.

Fourth, if one sets aside survivability, basing, and other cost considerations and looks solely at the cost of the missiles themselves, it is cheaper to deploy a given number of warheads in a few relatively large missiles than to deploy the same number of warheads on a larger number of smaller missiles. Fewer expensive guidance systems need to be purchased, for example.

Fifth, for almost two decades our minuteman ICBM force had virtually all of the positive characteristics desirable for any strategic system. It was survivable, even when an attack on it was viewed in isolation, because Soviet accuracies were not good enough to threaten silos. Command and control was comparatively easy. ICBMs were more accurate than submarine-based missiles and could reach their targets faster than bombers. And, when compared to either submarine-based missiles or bombers, silo-based ICBMs, once purchased, had strikingly low annual operating costs. This history has led many to continue to seek to replicate those two decades of Minuteman history, and in so doing to try not only to meet these objectives, but to do so with a single way of basing a single type of ICBM that would have all of these desirable characteristics.

These five sets of considerations, different ones of them of greater importance to different decision-makers at different times, have led us as a nation in recent years to try to re-create all of the desirable characteristics that Minuteman possessed during the sixties and much of the seventies. We have tried to do so by deploying a few relatively large missiles as quickly as possible, in a single basing mode, on land, under arms control agreements limiting or reducing launcher numbers, in the face of a threat of attack by increasingly accurate and numerous warheads — and to do so in a manner that seeks to preserve ICBM survivability for the long term, even when the ICBM force is viewed in isolation. But by trying to solve all ICBM tasks with a single weapon and a single basing mode in the face of the trends in technology, we have made the problem of modernizing the ICBM force so complex as to be virtually insoluble.

In arriving at its recommendations regarding ICBM programs, the Commission was mindful of the following criteria. For the near term, it would concentrate on possible deployments and basing modes that appeared to have straightforward and achievable technical and military value. For the long term, compatibility of ICBM programs with the need for flexibility and innovation in responding to possible Soviet actions would be of great importance. Economic cost would be considered carefully. The Commission would not insist on seeking a single solution to all the problems — near-term and long-term — with which the ICBM force must cope. Finally, and of great importance, our ICBM programs should support pursuit of a stable regime of arms control agreements.

The Commission has concluded that the preferred approach for modernizing our ICBM force seems to have three components: initiating engineering design of a single-warhead small ICBM, to reduce target value and permit flexibility in basing for better long-term survivability; seeking arms control agreements designed to enhance strategic stability; and deploying MX missiles in existing silos now to satisfy the immediate needs of our ICBM force and to aid that transition.

A more stable structure of ICBM deployments would exist if both sides moved toward more survivable methods of basing than is possible when there is primary dependence on large launchers and missiles. Thus from the point of view of enhancing such stability, the Commission believes that there is considerable merit in moving toward an ICBM force structure in which potential targets are of comparatively low value — missiles containing only one warhead. A single-warhead ICBM, suitably based, inherently denies an attacker the opportunity to destroy more than one warhead with one attacking warhead. The need to have basing flexibility, and particularly the need to keep open the option for different types of mobile basing, also suggests a missile of small size. If force survivability can be additionally increased by arms control agreements which lead both sides toward more survivable modes of basing than is possible with large launchers and missiles, the increase in stability would be further enhanced.

In the meantime, however, deployment of MX is essential in order to remove the Soviet advantage in ICBM capability and to help deter the threat of conventional or limited nuclear attacks on the alliance. Such deployment is also necessary to encourage the Soviets to move toward the more stable regime of deployments and arms control outlined above.

The Commission stresses that these two aspects of ICBM modernization and this approach toward arms control are integrally related. They point toward the same objective — permitting the U.S. and encouraging the Soviets to move toward more stable ICBM deployments over time in a way that is consistent with arms control agreements having the objective of reducing the risk of war. The Commission is unanimous that no one part of the proposed program can accomplish this alone.

### *1. ICBM Long-Term Survivability: Toward the Small, Single-Warhead ICBM*

The Commission believes that a single-warhead missile weighing about fifteen tons (rather than the nearly 100 tons of MX) may offer greater flexibility in the long-run effort to obtain an ICBM force that is highly survivable, even when viewed in isolation, and that can consequently serve as a hedge against potential threats to the submarine force.

The Commission thus recommends beginning engineering design of such an ICBM, leading to the initiation of full-scale development in 1987 and an initial operating capability in the early 1990s. The design of such a missile, hardened against nuclear effects, can be achieved with current technology. It should have sufficient accuracy and yield to put Soviet hardened military targets at risk. During that period an approach toward arms control, consistent with such deployments, should also seek to encourage the Soviets to move toward a more stable ICBM force structure at levels which would obviate the need to deploy very large numbers of such missiles. The development effort for such a missile need not and should not be burdened with the uncertainties accompanying a crash program; thus its timing can be such that competitive development is feasible. . . .

### *2. Immediate ICBM Modernization: Limited Deployment of the MX Missile*

#### A. THE MX IN MINUTEMAN SILOS

There are important needs on several grounds for ICBM modernization that cannot be met by the small, single-warhead ICBM.

First, arms control negotiations — in particular the Soviets' willingness to enter agreements that will enhance stability — are heavily influenced by ongoing programs. . . .

. . . Abandoning the MX at this time in search of a substitute would jeopardize, not enhance, the likelihood of reaching a stabilizing and equitable agreement. It would also undermine the incentives to the Soviets to change the nature of their own ICBM force and thus the environment most conducive to the deployment of a small missile.

Second, effective deterrence is in no small measure a question of the Soviets' perception of our national will and cohesion. Cancelling the MX, when it is ready for flight testing, when over $5 billion have already been spent on it, and when its importance has been stressed by the last four Presidents, does not communicate to the Soviets that we have the will essential to effective deterrence. Quite the opposite.

Third, the serious imbalance between the Soviets' massive ability to destroy hardened land-based military targets with their ballistic missile force and our lack of such a capability must be redressed promptly. . . .

Fourth, our current ICBM force is aging significantly. The Titan II force is being retired for this reason and extensive Minuteman rehabilitation programs are planned to keep those missiles operational. . . .

These objectives can all be accomplished, at reasonable cost, by deploying MX missiles in current Minuteman silos. . . .

A program of deploying on the order of 100 MX missiles in existing Minuteman silos would, on the other hand, accomplish the objectives set forth in this section and it would do so without threatening stability. The throw-weight and megatonnage carried by the 100 MX missiles is about the same as that of the 54 large Titan missiles now being retired plus that of the 100 Minuteman III missiles that the MXs would replace. Such a deployment would thus represent a replacement and modernization of part of our ICBM force. It would provide a means of controlled limited attack on hardened targets but not a sufficient number of warheads to be able to attack all hardened Soviet ICBMs, much less all of the many command posts and other hardened military targets in the Soviet Union. Thus it would not match the overall capability of the recent Soviet deployment of over 600 modern ICBMs of MX size or larger. But a large deployment of several hundred MX missiles should be unnecessary for the limited but very important purposes set forth above. Should the Soviets refuse to engage in stabilizing arms control and engage instead in major new deployments, reconsideration of this and other conclusions would be necessary. . . .

## What's Next for MX?

### *Documents 14 and 15*

The Scowcroft Commission seemed to have saved the MX and resolved the basing mode controversy. But the Scowcroft compromise was short-lived. The commission had strongly recommended that the Reagan administration make serious arms control efforts. Many liberals came to believe that the administration did not intend to live up to that part of the bargain. In addition, congressional doubts about the MX would not go away. As strategic analyst and MX supporter Colin Gray recounts in document 14, Congress cut the number of missiles to be deployed, thus breaking part of the Scowcroft bargain. Moreover, it remained uncertain exactly how the MX would be deployed. As indicated by the excerpts in document 15 from an article in *Aviation Week and Space Technology,* an authoritative defense magazine, by early 1987 the Reagan administration was thinking about putting the MX on rail cars on the nation's railroad system.

## 14 POLITICS, PROCUREMENT, AND STRATEGY Colin Gray

Because strategic forces have a very long lead time from drawing board to silo, launch tube, or runway and because Congress is not inclined to make truly definitive decisions concerning major weapons programs, a few strategic weapons issues tend to be a familiar fixture in U.S. political discourse. Once a weapon or program assumes controversial status, then political support in the Congress will ebb and flow in response to a wide range of environmental influences: hints of Soviet seriousness in Geneva, threats and bribes from party leaders in the legislative branch and from the White House, concerns about the economy, fears of electoral punishment, and the like. In general, one should think of strategic policy and the force posture that it guides (and to which it supposedly gives expression and meaning) as a never-ending story.

Defense preparation in peacetime is a tale of permanent becoming and profound indeterminacy. The quality of intended deterrent effect built into the scale and character of the U.S. strategic nuclear arsenal is keyed to the one hypothetical day in several decades, or longer, when a group of desperate and fearful Soviet leaders might be tempted to seek a military solution to an imperial political problem. Beyond the prudent maxim that the strategic forces should be large in number and diverse in character, there is a noticeable absence of authoritative strategic conclusions around which an enduring consensus could be built. Typically senior officials and legislators staple together projects that have been considered seriatim, more or less innocent of serious strategic justification, and dignify the result with the name *defense program.*[22]

Even if they were capable of doing otherwise, officials and legislators are discouraged by political realities from probing the strategic meaning of strategic forces. If political necessity requires one to reaffirm on all possible occasions some close facsimile of the uplifting formula that a "nuclear war cannot be won and must never be fought," it can be no easy matter to attempt to argue that 200, or 100, or 50 MX ICBMs is the right number.[23] When an administration, for thoroughly astrategic reasons, reduces by half the planned scale of MX procurement that it inherited from its predecessor and succumbs to the temptation to assert the need for the program almost exclusively with reference to its alleged value as leverage over Soviet minds in the arms control process, it is scarcely surprising that the Congress should feel at liberty to effect a further 50 percent cut.

The fundamental lack of seriousness about administration and congressional approaches to the ICBM force is pervasive in other areas of nuclear policy as well. That policy, as reflected in weapon programs and arms control proposals, is driven more by transitory judgments of what the domestic and allied political traffic will bear than by any serious examination of the need to support foreign policy commitments in the face of a dynamic threat.[24] This is not a naive plea to take politics out of defense but rather a claim that weapon system procurement can make no sense except in terms of a guiding strategy, which itself is meaningless if isolated from the political purposes for which military power is purchased.

If an administration does not have a strategic rationale for 2,000, as opposed to 1,000, MX warheads or for 572 as opposed to some lower number of warheads on intermediate-range nuclear systems, it is only to be expected that legislators will not heed a president when he insists on one magic number rather than any other. In fact, there is a distinct lack of magic about any number.

### MX Missile

The Scowcroft commission consensus was strained nearly to the breaking point early in 1985, while in the realm of MX missile numbers, it actually fractured in some important matters. The Scowcroft commission in April 1983 assembled a package of components of varying attractiveness to different constituencies, linked quite tightly with arguments of varying plausibility. . . .

Procurement funds for an additional twenty-one MX missiles were unfenced in the spring of 1985. This action, which brought to forty-two the total number of missiles authorized for procurement, came about because Congress was unwilling to deny the administration what it claimed to need for leverage in the renewed arms control negotiating process in Geneva. The importance of the Geneva process and the significance of MX for leverage in that process were both exaggerated unrealistically, if not shamelessly, by major figures in the ongoing debate over the MX.

Early in 1985 it was clear that the scale, and possibly even the fact, of MX missile deployment was still unsettled business in the eyes of the Congress. As a result of the Soviet decision to reenter the formal arena of strategic arms control negotiations, President Reagan achieved what had seemed impossible a few months earlier: the rescue of twenty-one MX ICBMs. (The tragic murder of Major Arthur Nicholson by Soviet soldiers in East Germany, which occurred during the House debate on the twenty-one missiles, undoubtedly hardened attitudes toward the Soviet Union and helped the president's cause.) However, the administration's hard-won victory on the FY 1985 MX funds' unfencing was more than a little Pyrrhic in character. Legislators who had virtuously, and with well-publicized misgivings, supported the president and his negotiating team on the fiscal year (FY) 1985 MX allotment, were not about to roll over on the FY 1986 request for production funding of forty-eight additional missiles.

In a speech on March 26, 1985, just days after the Senate vote to unfence the twenty-one FY 1985 MX missiles, Senator Sam Nunn (D-Ga.) announced in effect that it was open season yet again on the MX program.[25] The senator indicated that he saw the need for a warm MX production line as a political signal of national will. He also acknowledged that "the imbalance in hard-target kill capability must be readdressed."[26] But Nunn stated that he had never approved, or intended to imply approval, of the scheme to deploy as many as one hundred MX missiles in "vulnerable silos." Adroitly quoting a 1982 Air Force report that initial deployment of forty missiles would have considerable deterrent value without being destabilizing, Nunn proposed that legislation for FY 1986 and subsequent years authorize that no more than forty MX ICBMs be placed in Minuteman III silos. The administration succeeded in raising this figure to fifty but did not press the case for one hundred, recognizing that although the Soviet return to Geneva had yielded a political victory, the most likely alternative to reasonably graceful acquiescence in a legislated cap in the forty to fifty range for silo-deployed MX ICBMs was not a program steaming on course for one hundred deployed, but rather no missiles at all.

At the end of 1985, fifty-four MX missiles had been acquired or funded for production. This number included twelve of the forty-eight missiles requested in the FY 1986 budget. The Department of Defense (DOD), somewhat belatedly, recognized that the second fifty MX missiles it wished to deploy would be approved by Congress only if they were to be deployed in a basing mode that moderate critics of the silo-basing plan judged to provide adequate survivability. As a consequence, the administration agreed to devote the better part of eighteen months to preparation of its plans for basing the second fifty and to present those plans in the context of FY 1988 rather than FY 1987.

Thus on the MX front in 1985, the administration became somewhat overconfident concerning its seemingly perennial ability to snatch victory from the jaws of defeat for the MX program; in the past, something had always turned up. Officials were torn between anxiety over losing political momentum toward full-scale deployment and the attractions of a cap that, although unwanted, nonetheless served as a guarantee for half-scale deployment. In practice, the administration had no real choice. Once Senator Nunn articulated his determination to bound silo deployment at forty, victory with respect to FY 1986 would be legislative approval in the forty to fifty range.

The capping of MX silo deployment at fifty is a shrewd tactic intended to compel a truly serious official focus upon stand-alone survivability for the second fifty missiles and to help direct official and congressional attention toward the under-debated small intercontinental ballistic missile (SICBM) program. One can never forecast with confidence that a great debate will justify its advance billing, but one could discern the stage setting in 1985 for what could be a great debate in 1986 on U.S. strategic policy, keyed to the relatively novel budgetary issues of a SICBM program scheduled to receive a decision on full-scale development, and to SDI.

In 1986 officials and legislators may be obliged to discuss and explain the interrelationships among the MX program (with a new basing story in detailed preparation), SICBM, and the SDI. Moreover, given that a prominent thrust in the still-emerging critique of the SICBM concept pertains to the potential problem of penetration survivability versus a more heavily weaponized Soviet ballistic missile defense, 1986 may well see the beginning of debate over the implications of the new commitment to active defenses for the scale and quality of the offensive force modernization program.

Issues of strategic policy should not be debated in isolation. The outcome of the debate over SICBM that will occur in 1986 could have a major influence over the receptivity of the Congress to the administration's advocacy of the second fifty MX missiles — in a "new" survivable basing mode — early in 1987. Reciprocally, developments in the MX basing saga in 1986 could influence the outcome of the debate over SICBM. Overhanging both programs for ICBM modernization is what amounts to the wild card of possible new Soviet defensive deployments in the 1990s and beyond and therefore the possible consequences of the U.S. SDI.

At the end of 1985, the administration endeavored to be responsive to congressional insistence that it develop a basing scheme for the second fifty MX missiles, which would permit the force to ride out an attack. Senator

Nunn and others indicated unequivocally that superhard silos would not qualify as a new survivable basing scheme. They appeared to believe that superhardening would be both unduly costly and futile in the face of predictable improvements in Soviet missile accuracy.

The strength of this congressional prejudice against superhardening is unfortunate since it may be technically ill founded and since it has been the option most favored at higher levels in the DOD. Nonetheless, the administration has been advised that superhard basing of MX will not be considered seriously by the Congress for the second fifty. Given the transitory nature of strategic opinion in Congress (though not on the part of Senator Nunn), it is always possible that the program orphan of 1985 may be hailed as the savior of the strategic posture in 1987.

The basing modes currently under investigation for the second fifty MX missiles include several options: varieties of superhardening; varieties of closely spaced and possibly superhardened silos; mobility (above and below ground) with deceptive basing; and missile canister hardening for mobile and deceptive basing. Active missile defense is also being given modest consideration.

It is unlikely that any one of these options alone could pass the tests of political acceptability and military effectiveness. President Reagan and Secretary Caspar Weinberger will foreclose on anything that looks like the Carter MX multiple protective shelter scheme (4,600 hardened horizontal shelters) that was killed unceremoniously in 1981; the Congress will foreclose on any apparent reappearance of the closely spaced basing scheme that it rejected precipitately in December 1982. Congress has already denied the acceptability of superhard silos, and ballistic missile defense (BMD) options would have political ramifications that both the administration and the Congress would prefer not to face with narrow reference to what may be only a fraction of one leg of the triad. All of these points generally are quite aside from critical budgetary considerations.

Bearing in mind that the quality of the technical rationale may bear only slightly, if at all, on the official and the congressional view of the matter, a suitably robust MX basing mode would probably comprise a mix of some measure of silo superhardening, close spacing of silos, and active terminal defense. Such a technically mixed story would be military viable and sufficiently different from all previous schemes that it should receive as serious a political review by Congress as would be possible for any MX basing mode.[27]

## Notes

22. The thesis that U.S. defense policy is harmfully deficient in guidance by strategy is pervasive, and pervasively persuasive, throughout Edward N. Luttwak, *The Pentagon and the Art of War* (New York: Simon and Schuster, 1985).
23. See for one recent example, Caspar W. Weinberger, "What Is Our Defense Strategy?" (Remarks prepared for delivery to the National Press Club, Washington, D.C., October 9, 1985); Office of Assistant Secretary of Defense, Public Affairs, news release no. 606-85, October 9, 1985, p. 10.
24. The administration's hastily contrived counterproposal to the Gorbachev *demarche* on the eve of the November 1985 summit in Geneva is a case in point in which the public politics of arms control would seem to have dominated consideration of strategic stability. Reportedly the United States proposed that air-launched cruise missile numbers be restricted to 1,500, though any eventual agreement is near certain to place no constraints on Soviet air defenses. Furthermore, the U.S. proposal that a ceiling of 4,500 be set for ICBM and SLBM warheads would mean that some drastic surgery would have to be performed on current U.S. plans regarding its ICBM and SLBM forces for the late 1990s of a kind that might not contribute to stability. Absent depredations by arms control restrictions, radical action by the U.S. Congress, or major changes of policy course by the executive, the United States should or could have approximately 6,790 warheads on its ICBM and SLBM forces by 1999 (1,000 MX, 500 SICBM-Midgetman, 1,450 Minuteman III, and 3,840 Trident II D-5). The new U.S. proposal would compel a reduction in these plans by 2,290. Probably some fraction of the reduction would have to come from Trident deployment (which already is cause for some anxiety, with its planned D-5 deployment on a much lower number of platforms than has been the case since the birth of the operational SSBN force in 1960), in the face of a Soviet ASW capability totally untouched by arms control. For some of the details of the U.S. arms control offer, see Lou Cannon and David Hoffman, "Weinberger Opposed U.S. Arms Proposal," *Washington Post,* November 3, 1985, pp. A1, A26.
25. Senator Sam Nunn, "The MX" (remarks delivered at Institute for Foreign Policy Analysis breakfast, March 26, 1985).
26. *Ibid.,* p. 6. The senator qualified this point by adding, "*at least in part,* if the Soviets are to have incentives either to move towards mobility on their own or to do so under a negotiated arms control regime" (emphasis added).
27. This hybrid basing scheme is my personal preference. It is not a prediction of what the Reagan administration will choose to present in support of the FY 1988 budget request.

## 15 REAGAN WILL PURSUE RAIL-BASED MX
**John D. Morrocco**
**January 5, 1987**

*Washington —*

The Reagan Administration has decided to seek congressional approval to proceed with full-scale development of a 37,000-lb. small intercontinental ballistic missile with a single warhead, and to develop a rail garrison basing mode for the MX missile.

Under the rail garrison basing plan, MX missiles would be placed on railroad cars that would be housed at military installations around the country. In a national emergency, the cars would be dispersed at classified sites along the more than 200,000 mi. of track in the nation's rail system.

Gen. Charles M. May, Air Force special assistant for ICBM modernization, estimated it would cost $2.5 billion to develop the rail garrison basing system and another $4-5 billion to procure enough railroad cars and associated equipment to deploy 50 MXs.

Congress approved the deployment of the first 50 MXs in existing Minuteman silos, but has withheld funding for an additional 50 missiles the Air Force wants until a more survivable basing mode is adopted. The first 10 MX missiles deployed in refurbished Minuteman 3 silos at Warren AFB, Wyo., became operational on Dec. 22. The 50 MXs scheduled for deployment in existing Minuteman silos eventually could be deployed in the rail garrison mode, according to May.

The Air Force plans to ask Congress for "several hundred million dollars" in the Fiscal 1988 budget to begin developing the rail basing system, May said. The Air Force is seeking a December, 1991, initial operating capability date.

May estimated the total life cycle cost to deploy 50 MX missiles in the rail garrison mode would be less than $15 billion. But the Air Force will not request any funds to procure additional MXs in the Fiscal 1988–1989 two-year budget request. May said the earliest the Administration would ask for additional MX missiles for the rail garrison system would be in Fiscal 1990, although long-lead funding may be included in the Fiscal 1989 request.

May said the Air Force is optimistic that the rail garrison MX system and single-warhead SICBM strategic modernization package will be endorsed by Congress.

While lawmakers have been critical of the Administration's MX proposals, there has been strong support in Congress for the SICBM, or Midgetman. The single-warhead missiles would be deployed on hardened mobile launchers in two modes — at existing Minuteman facilities and at random movement sites across the western United States.

The Air Force has selected Boeing Aerospace Co. over Martin Marietta Aerospace to develop the mobile launchers for the small ICBM. Boeing received a $283.7-million contract on Dec. 23 from the Air Force Ballistic Missile Office to develop its launcher, which is a wheeled vehicle that runs on specially designed Goodyear steel-belted radial tires. Martin Marietta proposed a tracked vehicle using rubber treads designed by Caterpillar Tractor Co.

The Air Force also awarded a $121.7-million contract to Morton Thiokol's Wasatch Div. to develop the SICBM's first-stage booster. Aerojet Strategic Propulsion Co. won a $179-million contract to begin development of the missile's second-stage booster, and Hercules Aerospace Products was awarded a $169.5-million contract for work on the third-stage booster.

Hercules also had bid to develop the second-stage booster. United Technologies Corp.'s Chemical Systems Div. bid to develop the first and third-stage boosters but failed to win a contract.

The Air Force expects to make a final production decision on the SICBM in 1989 or 1990, allowing for an initial operational capability date of 1992. May estimated it would cost $40-50 billion to develop the SICBM and deploy a force of 500 of the single-warhead missiles.

The Air Force rejected recommendations to add additional warheads to the SICBM. An Air Force study begun last February found that a three-warhead version of the SICBM would not be sufficiently mobile.

A two-warhead version, which was considered nearly as mobile as a single-warhead missile, would have reduced the total life-cycle cost of the program by about 12% and saved an additional 25% in terms of manpower costs. But the option was rejected since it would have meant recompeting the propulsion contracts, which would have delayed the program for two years.

May said the single-warhead 37,000-lb. version will be capable of carrying penetration aids to help foil Soviet defenses.

The first SICBM is scheduled to be deployed at Minuteman facilities at Malstrom AFB, Mont. Succeeding missiles could be deployed at Warren AFB, Wyo., and Ellsworth AFB, S.D. Later SICBMs will be deployed on tracts of government land in the southwestern U.S. with Holloman AFB, N.M., and Yuma Proving Ground, Ariz., serving as the main operating bases.

Warren AFB also is set to be the main operating base for the MX rail garrison system. Additional garrisons will be located at defense installations across the continental U.S. Candidate locations include 10 Air Force bases, mainly Strategic Air Command bases, which could take advantage of existing nuclear weapons maintenance and security facilities.

Plans call for 25 trains carrying two MX missiles apiece, according to May, with as many as two to four trains stationed at each base. Each train will consist of six cars — a locomotive, two missile cars, two security cars and a launch command and control car. The missiles will be launched directly from the rail cars.

The Air Force intends to procure off-the-shelf railroad cars and equipment for the trains, since building special railroad cars hardened to protect against the effects of a nuclear blast would be extremely expensive and unnecessary, according to the Air Force.

The railroad cars will carry commercial markings to shield their identity. The Air Force also is considering building dummy garrison sites with decoy railroad sidings to further complicate the task of Soviet military planners. Other options include basing the missile trains on secret sidings instead of in the normal garrisons.

## How Should Midgetman Be Based?

### *Document 16*

Congress has been very involved in the development of Midgetman. Votes in Congress have specified the number of missiles to be deployed (five hundred) and even the weight of the missiles. But many questions about Midgetman remain unresolved. In document 16, Les Aspin, chairman of the House Armed Services Committee and a strong supporter of Midgetman, reviews the possible modes for the new missiles. These include continuous dispersal on government land, location on Minuteman sites, special garrisons for Midgetman launchers, and continuous wide-area peacetime dispersal. Aspin concludes that the first two options are the most promising.

### 16 MIDGETMAN: WHY WE NEED A SMALL MISSILE
### Les Aspin

. . . In theory, then, a mobile, hardened Midgetman seems a promising approach to improving the survivability of our ICBM force and thus to enhancing deterrence and stability. Nevertheless, important practical questions remain: Where should the Midgetman missiles be deployed? How should Midgetman be configured?

The Air Force is considering the following four main options for deploying the Midgetman:

1. *Continuous dispersal on government land.* Midgetman launchers would be dispersed in peacetime along roads on the periphery of some existing military bases (four to seven bases are being considered by the Air Force). This means that the Midgetman force would be dispersed over about 4,000 square miles in peacetime. In a crisis, though, the Midgetman launchers could move off the peripheral roads into the interior of these military reservations, thereby providing a total dispersal area of about 8,000 square miles. Upon warning of an enemy attack, the Midgetman launchers could disperse both toward the base and away from base. Using this government land deployment option, therefore, and given the warning time of 30 minutes we would probably have of a Soviet ICBM attack, the Midgetman launchers could be dispersed over approximately 18,000 square miles.

2. *Location at Minuteman sites.* Currently, there are 1,000 Minuteman silos dispersed throughout the central part of the United States. The Midgetman launchers would be parked on the same land now occupied by Minuteman silos, in a position that would not interfere with Minuteman operations. Upon a decision in a crisis to disperse, or upon warning of an incoming Soviet ICBM attack, the Midgetman launchers would travel from their peacetime Minuteman locations. Using this deployment option, Midgetman launchers could be dispersed over 30,000 square miles within the 30-minute warning period.

3. *Garrisons for Midgetman launchers.* The Midgetman launchers would be located at approximately 50 garrisons in peacetime. Upon a decision to disperse in crisis, or after warning of a Soviet ballistic missile attack, the launchers would move out of their peacetime garrisons and disperse throughout the region. Using this deployment option, the Midgetman launchers could be dispersed over 21,000 square miles within the 30-minute warning period.

4. *Continuous wide-area peacetime dispersal.* The Midgetman missiles would be loaded onto vehicles similar to commercial trucks and would travel the nation's public roads.

If each of these options is analyzed in terms of the three essential criteria of survivability, cost, and political feasibility, wide-area peacetime dispersal quickly drops out as a realistic alternative. Dispersal on public roads would require continuous contact between Midgetman and the general public. It seems highly unlikely that such an approach would be accepted by the public because of the widespread fear of nuclear accidents. Moreover, Midgetman missiles would be inviting targets for terrorists.

The other three basing options, which would isolate the Midgetman system from the general public in peacetime, would have a much better chance of gaining political support and would involve lower security costs.

It is useful to now look more closely at the costs and survivability of these three options. . . .

*Costs.* Deploying the Midgetman at Minuteman sites would be the cheapest of the three options to buy and to operate, mainly because it could use already existing support facilities at Minuteman bases. Its life cycle cost would be \$3.3 billion less than garrison basing and \$5.5 billion less than dispersal on government land. For a similar reason, deployment at Minuteman fields would require the smallest number of new staff.

Basing the Midgetman on government land or at 50 garrisons would require roughly equal numbers of personnel. Overall, garrison basing would be slightly cheaper than dispersal on government land because the garrison option would involve a slower pace of peacetime operations (the Midgetman launchers would not have to be continuously on the move) and would probably draw more heavily on already existing military support structures.

*Survivability.* For a hardened Midgetman force, the key to survivability would be the extent to which the missiles could be dispersed before a Soviet attack. In general, the more territory the force could cover, the better. To evaluate the relative survivability of the three politically feasible deployment options, it is necessary to examine the performance of the Midgetman under a number of scenarios.... It is evident that the most important survivability factor for all three basing options is warning time. In the case of a "bolt-out-of-the-blue" attack, in which there would be no warning time, none of the Midgetman missiles would survive under any of the options. This is because such a Soviet attack could cover 4,800 square miles, and under none of the basing options would missiles be dispersed beyond such an area. (The government-land-dispersal option would come fairly close, with the missiles being dispersed over 4,000 square miles in peacetime.) However, a bolt-out-of-the-blue attack is not a serious scenario. What is of greater concern is the possibility of an attack in time of crisis or war. As warning time increases, more and more Midgetman missiles would survive, although each deployment option performs slightly differently.

Using the government-land-dispersal option, significant numbers of Midgetman missiles would survive with only a few minutes of warning time; in fact, half the force would survive with as little as five minutes of warning time. This is because the Midgetman launchers would be widely dispersed to begin with under this option.

Using the Minuteman-site option, it would take ten minutes rather than five minutes for the Midgetman launchers to disperse enough to survive. However, once they started to disperse, their survivability would increase rapidly. Because the launchers would disperse from 500 different Minuteman sites, a lot of dispersal area would be covered quickly. At 15 minutes of warning time, though, the dispersal area of one Minuteman site would merge into the areas of adjacent sites. Past this point, therefore, dispersal area — and survivability — would grow at a slower rate.

Garrison basing would require more warning time than the other options to achieve any Midgetman survivability. Because dispersal would start from only 50 sites (versus 500 sites for Minuteman basing), it would take more time — at least 20 minutes — to get beyond the 4,800-square-mile area that would come under Soviet attack.

These differences in minutes are important because it is usually thought that the warning time will be 30 minutes for a Soviet ICBM attack and 15 minutes for a Soviet submarine-launched ballistic missile (SLBM) attack. Dispersal on government land could give good survivability in both cases. Minuteman-site basing would provide good survivability against an ICBM attack but would leave only a small margin for error for a SLBM attack. Garrison basing would do well for an ICBM attack but might not work if the Soviets used SLBMs instead of SS-18s.

...An all-out SS-18 attack would saturate 9,600 square miles. Using any of the three deployment options, it would take a while for the Midgetman launchers to disperse over an area larger than this threshold: 10 minutes for government-land dispersal, 15 minutes for Minuteman-site basing, and 25 minutes for garrison basing. As a result, the Midgetman force would have much more trouble surviving an all-out SS-18 attack than it would have with the 1,500-warhead attack discussed earlier. A number of factors should be kept in mind, however. In the most likely circumstances, the United States would have substantially more than 60 minutes of warning. In preparing for war, the Soviets would almost certainly improve the low peacetime readiness of their forces. Moving their strategic submarines out of port, putting their bombers on alert, and dispersing their mobile missiles would take hours if not days. These actions would give us warning time and would trigger dispersal of the Midgetman forces. In addition, the Soviets would not commit their entire SS-18 force just to attack a fraction of U.S. targets, especially because it would cost them at least six warheads to destroy one of our warheads.

To sum up, of the four main options under consideration for basing the Midgetman in peacetime, government-land dispersal and Minuteman-site basing are the leading candidates. Government-land dispersal has the advantage of continuous peacetime dispersal, thereby offering some hedge against short warning of a Soviet attack. The Minuteman-site option has a cost advantage, and it also makes public acceptance of Midgetman deployment easier. Garrison basing of the Midgetman seems less desirable because it is not as effective in providing survivability compared with the Minuteman-site or government-land-dispersal options; furthermore, it offers no appreciable cost savings over the other two options. Deployment on public roads seems out of the question because it is unlikely to be accepted by the U.S. public, which fears nuclear accidents and terrorist operations involving the Midgetman missile....

## Doubts About Midgetman

### *Documents 17, 18, and 19*

Although Midgetman continues to enjoy strong support in Congress, doubts have begun to arise, and the new missile has been criticized from both left and right. In document 17, Sen. Pete Wilson, a Republican member of the Senate Armed Services Committee, raises questions about the huge cost of Midgetman — $40–$60 billion for the system, $100 million per warhead. In document 18, arms control specialists John Baker and Joel Wit warn that Midgetman could pose serious difficulties for arms control. In document 19, Scott L. Berg, an engineer and former SAC aircrew commander, argues that Midgetman faces a number of difficult technical hurdles.

## 17 MIDGETMAN: SMALL AT ANY COST? Senator Pete Wilson (R-Calif.) 1986

This year Congress will decide whether or not to proceed with the development of one of the most expensive weapons systems in history: a small, single-warhead, mobile ICBM called the Midgetman. Estimates of the total cost of the Midgetman program range from $40 billion to $60 billion for the planned 500 missiles. This breaks down to almost $100 million for each Midgetman warhead, which is much higher than per-warhead costs for other new nuclear weapons systems. The per-warhead cost of the survivable Trident II submarine-launched ballistic missile (SLBM) system will be only $13 million, including the cost of the new Trident submarine. The cost per warhead of the B-1B strategic bomber is $16 million, and the next 50 MX Peacekeeper warheads will cost only about $4 million apiece.

At its currently planned size (30,000 pounds) and configuration (one warhead), the Midgetman missile — the "Congressman" as it might be more appropriately dubbed, given that its size has been legislated by Congress — will cost a fortune and still fail to achieve the strategic stability and enhanced deterrence claimed by its proponents. The Midgetman missile can and should be made much more cost-effective. I believe the way to do this is to enlarge the Midgetman so that it can carry penetration aids and more than one multiple independently targeted reentry vehicle (MIRV) warhead. If each Midgetman missile can carry three warheads, the estimated cost to deploy 500 warheads (on 166 mobile launchers) is about $22 billion — roughly half the cost of deploying 500 warheads on small, single-warhead mobile missiles.[28] Moreover, these warheads — as well as penetration aids — could be added without sacrificing the Midgetman missile's most essential characteristic — survivability.

We must continue to modernize our strategic forces, but we must also spend our scarce defense dollars wisely. The high cost of the Midgetman poses two threats. The first is that the new missile may be delayed or not built at all. Last year the small-ICBM program cost more than $600 million. This year the request is for $1.4 billion, and next year the costs of Midgetman will soar to more than $2.5 billion. These kinds of increases are simply out of line with Gramm-Rudman-Hollings budget constraints and the likely trends in defense expenditures.

The second threat is that the high cost of the Midgetman could jeopardize vital strategic weapons systems that cost much less, such as the advanced technology (Stealth) bomber, the advanced cruise missile, the Trident II D-5 missile, and even the MX Peacekeeper missile. These systems and the Strategic Defense Initiative receive the lion's share of spending for strategic weapons systems. A single-warhead Midgetman missile program costing $50 billion would mean there will not be enough money to go around. . . .

I believe that if Congress votes to go ahead with the too-small missile this year, the United States will be committing a monumental blunder. Our national security would be much better served if Congress waited a year before committing to full-scale development of the Midgetman missile. During that time the Air Force should be directed to analyse the costs and feasibility of Midgetman alternatives and report its findings to the Defense Department and Congress. This analysis should include an examination of an enlarged mobile missile deployed with three MIRV warheads and equipped with penetration aids. A one-year delay in the engineering and development of the Midgetman could save $22 billion — money that is essential for funding other defense systems needed to achieve our goal of strategic modernization.

Aspin and other small-Midgetman proponents have argued recently that such a delay, which might mean pushing back the Midgetman's initial operational capability (the date the missile is first deployed) one or two years, would be unacceptable. They have claimed that the delay would outweigh the benefits of a more cost-effective missile design, even if the savings were to total tens of billions of dollars. I reject this reasoning. The Midgetman should not be allowed to bankrupt the strategic budget. Moreover, a delay of one or two years in the initial operational capability of a new ICBM need not entail a delay for the more important milestone of *full* operational capability (when the last of the missiles would be deployed).

There may well be an important place in the U.S. strategic arsenal for the right mobile missile. But the single-warhead Midgetman missile — costing around $50 billion — is definitely the wrong one. For ICBMs to remain a vital part of our strategic triad, they must be made survivable, but at the same time they must be made practical and affordable. I am confident that ICBMs can be made survivable, practical, and affordable, and I am certain that they must be.

## Note

28. RAND Corporation, "Cost Reduction Options for the Small ICBM," unpublished paper, August 1985.

## 18 MOBILE MISSILES AND ARMS CONTROL

**John Baker and Joel Wit**

Despite years of study and debate, the impact of mobile missile deployments on military planning and arms control is still controversial. Indeed, just as the United States is faced with key arms control and funding decisions with regard to mobile missiles, there seems to be considerable confusion on the issue. For example, while mobile missiles are thought by many to enhance nuclear stability, the Reagan administration recently proposed banning mobile ICBMs altogether. Yet one point about mobile missiles remains clear: their future will be shaped in large part by the kind of strategic arms control agreement, if any, the United States negotiates with the Soviet Union. The objective of this article is to examine the opportunities and problems posed by these new weapons and to offer suggestions for coping with both. . . .

The development of Midgetman is just beginning. Problems that bedeviled previous U.S. mobile missile programs may eventually affect Midgetman. In the absence of an arms control agreement limiting the size of Soviet forces, Midgetman could be vulnerable to attack, regardless of countermeasures. The missile's mobility could raise environmental and other concerns among people living near proposed deployment areas. Also, several technical challenges in developing a small mobile ICBM must be resolved. For example, Midgetman is being designed to have a highly accurate guidance system that will enable it to strike hardened Soviet targets such as missile silos and $C^3$ installations. But the Air Force faces problems in building an affordable guidance and control system. [See Scott Berg article, page 416.] Finally, the cost of a 500 missile force, according to a General Accounting Office (GAO) report, could reach $44 billion, an exceedingly large amount of money for single-warhead missiles whose contribution to the overall U.S. force posture might be modest. For these reasons, Midgetman's eventual deployment is still in question. . . .

Mobile missiles pose a challenge for the dual goals of crisis stability and arms race stability. Like long-range cruise missiles, they highlight the fact that these two objectives are not always entirely compatible. Both weapons can enhance crisis stability but can also create new difficulties for negotiating verifiable arms agreements to control the arms race.

In theory, mobile missiles, by presenting undeniable uncertainties for the enemy's targeting efforts, can contribute to stability by improving survivability. However, what may be true as a general principle does not necessarily hold for specific mobile missile deployments. Each missile system must be evaluated according to its specific operational plans and its numerical relationship to the overall force posture. . . .

If mobile missiles offer some potential for improving stability, the price is likely to be in terms of further complicating the problem of reaching arms control agreements. Mobile missiles pose three particular problems for devising theater and strategic arms limitations agreements: 1) mobile launchers can be redeployed, 2) distinguishing between mobile theater and intercontinental missiles can be difficult, and 3) mobile systems create pressures to limit total missile inventories, both deployed and stored.

The first problem, that mobile missiles can be redeployed, and therefore transferred in and out of different theaters, has already complicated previous negotiations to reach an INF agreement. In the INF negotiations, the United States has argued that any Soviet SS-20s in the Far East could be redeployed westward to cover targets in Europe. Consequently, the United States has been unwilling to agree simply to freeze the level of SS-20 missile deployments at Far Eastern bases. Instead, the U.S. position is that both sides must accept global limits on their INF deployments.

Second, negotiating arms control limits on mobile missiles is complicated by the fact that different types of mobile systems often use the same basic components, such as rocket stages or missile launchers. Under the SALT II Treaty at U.S. insistence the Soviets agreed to ban any deployment of the SS-X-16 mobile ICBM because it has two rocket stages in common with the SS-20 IRBM, which was not being limited. This problem of "commonality" threatened to complicate future treaty verification by making it difficult to distinguish clearly between these two mobile missiles. It could reappear in the future with new generations of Soviet IRBMs and ICBMs.

The third problem is that mobile missiles, because of their unusual refire capability, create pressures to limit total inventories of missiles in addition to launchers. The SALT I and SALT II agreements focused heavily on limiting deployed launchers, not the total number of missiles on each side. When the SALT I agreement was signed in 1972, the limitation on missile launchers, which could be readily verified using national technical means (NTM), was an effective surrogate for limiting useable missiles, which could not be easily monitored by NTM. This was true as long as only one missile could be fired from one launcher.

Over the next decade, this association between one launcher and one missile began to break down as a result of technological developments. Certain Soviet ICBMs, such as the SS-18, could be 'cold launched' from their silos in a way that permitted them to be reused, albeit such a process would take days. Nevertheless, some U.S. experts worried that the Soviet Union might gain a strategic advantage over the U.S. by deploying these weapon systems, and the United States successfully insisted on provisions in SALT II designed to hinder reloading missile silos. Moreover, the dubious utility of possessing refire missiles for silos was highlighted in recent official testimony in which the U.S. Air Force explained its own lack of interest in procuring refires for the cold-launch MX/*Peacekeeper* ICBM because of the difficulty of trying to reload silos in wartime. Presumably, this problem applies to the Soviet Union as well.

The Soviet SS-20 IRBM highlighted a new, more difficult side of the question of whether treaty limits should be expanded to include missile inventories. The U.S. intelligence community credits the SS-20 with a 'refire' capability whereby extra missiles are maintained for each mobile launcher. Also, mobile missile launchers can be prepared to launch an additional missile in only a matter of hours, not days. Finally, some analysts argue that, unlike the reloading operation for a silo which occurs at a known target, mobile launchers are likely to prove more survivable throughout a conflict. In short, mobile missiles challenge the earlier arms limitation assumption that, in practical terms, only one missile can be fired from each launcher. As a result, there has been renewed American interest in limiting total missile inventories, both stored and deployed.

Yet, negotiating equal limits on total missile inventories in a future START or INF agreement would be a difficult task at best. One problem is where to begin counting missiles against treaty limits. Many solid-fuel ballistic missiles are not fully assembled until they arrive at their final deployment site. For example, the MX/*Peacekeeper* ICBM will remain in four separate stages until each is lowered into the underground missile silo. . . .

In sum, pursuit of limits on total missile inventories would be a complicated exercise that is probably not necessary for national security given the limited military significance of the excess missiles. Mobile missile reloads seem to raise more concerns than are probably warranted and their dangers should be kept in context. The above approach assumes that refires and stored mobile launchers have a potential for sudden 'breakout" from treaty limits to gain political advantage, as well as a utility in fighting a nuclear war. Yet, it remains unclear what sudden political advantages could be gained which would outweigh the risks of breakout. The feasibility of prolonged nuclear war-fighting and the utility of land-based mobiles in such scenarios is also open to debate. Storage and loading sites are likely to be destroyed in the earliest stage of a nuclear conflict and the missile would be difficult to load and transport in a nuclear war environment. . . .

Future U.S. policy must seek to maximize the potential benefits of mobile missiles, at the same time attempting to minimize potential problems. Such a policy can be ensured through certain unilateral and bilateral measures. First, U.S. decisions to proceed with the deployment of mobile missiles must be based on the judgement that these weapons make sense on their own merits. Second, the United States should seek negotiated arrangements with the Soviet Union designed to enhance the contributions of mobile missiles to stability, to minimize their political and economic costs, and to alleviate their potentially adverse impact on strategic arms control.

If the U.S. mobile missile effort is to stand on its own merits, it may require a thorough reexamination of the current Midgetman program. Already, questions are increasing as to the affordability and political acceptability of a single-warhead ICBM. The program may soon be derailed altogether. The United States should seriously consider redesigning Midgetman to carry a small number, perhaps two or three, of MIRV warheads. This approach could retain the stability benefits of Midgetman while modestly increasing the number of survivable warheads based on mobile missiles. At the same time, it could minimize objections to the system based on cost-effectiveness, and would be much preferable to the present force structure. . . .

Finally, efforts should begin now to encourage both sides to avoid deploying mobile missile systems in ways that seriously complicate the verification of treaty limits. While design practices can be altered to solve the problem of 'commonality' mentioned earlier, it might prove useful to build into future agreements Functionally Related Observable Differences (FRODs) to delineate between various mobile missile types that are similar in design. For example, mobile missile FRODs could be based on different characteristics of missile launchers or missile stages.

## 19 MIDGETMAN: THE TECHNICAL PROBLEMS
## Scott L. Berg

Three years ago, the President's Commission on Strategic Forces (the Scowcroft Commission) recommended developing a mobile, single-warhead, small, intercontinental ballistic missile (SICBM). That project, nicknamed "Midgetman," remains very popular with Congress, and many defense analysts see mobility as the only practical, cost-effective approach to assuring future ICBM survivability. However, in its recent strategic arms proposal in Geneva, the administration proposed banning mobile ICBMs. Serious questions are being raised by the program's critics and even by many of its supporters.

Many aspects of the Midgetman project are still undefined. Although mobile basing is considerd the most likely basing mode, silo basing, or a combination of mobile and silo basing modes are being studied. The Air Force must also choose between several Hard Mobile Launcher (HML) designs, and decide on the type of guidance and launch system.

One major area of concern is Midgetman's anticipated *cost*. Because many aspects of the project have not been determined, cost estimates are speculative. However, the requirements of mobility and survivability are driving costs upward. Using a 500 missile baseline, the General Accounting Office (GAO) reported in July 1985 that estimated Midgetman life-cycle costs (in 1982 dollars) for optimally spaced superhardened silos were $49 billion; for hard-mobile launchers $44 billion; and for soft-mobile launchers (SML) $43 billion. This translated to $86-$98 million per warhead. In comparison, the MX, the most expensive ICBM to date, will cost about $25 million per warhead if based in superhardened silos.

Personnel requirements are a critical factor driving overall lifecycle costs for a mobile system. The GAO estimates that 20,000 people will be required for a hard-mobile system, and 34,000 for a soft mobile. The Air Force is looking for novel ways to reduce manpower requirements, but the prospect for large reductions is poor.

Midgetman must also overcome a number of *technical* hurdles. A low missile launch weight is critical because increases in missile weight tend to diminish mobility (one of the system's strongest selling points). Meeting the congressionally mandated weight goal of 30,000 pounds will require innovations in missile casings, propellants, and exhaust nozzle technologies. The propellant technology is especially challenging. Midgetman might be exposed to wide ranges in humidity and temperature, and be subjected to more and greater impact shocks than any previous ICBM. Thus, the fuel must not only have a very high energy content per pound (to save weight), but must also be chemically and mechanically stable.

The missile's guidance system has always been considered a great technical challenge. The Air Force requires that Midgetman have a hard-target kill capability similar to that of the MX. Achieving high accuracy with a light, reliable guidance system that is not exorbitantly expensive is a difficult problem. Mobility makes the task even tougher because small position or orientation errors at launch can result in large errors at the impact point. One way around this problem is for the guidance system to update or correct itself in flight, but because of reliability, complexity, and vulnerability concerns the Air Force has been reluctant to accept any system that requires updating after launch.

For rapid missile response to a launch command, the guidance system should quickly align and calibrate from a dormant state. (Dormancy is desirable to reduce the missile's power requirements and improve its post-attack endurance.) However, current guidance systems that are quick to align and calibrate are not sufficiently accurate, and those that are sufficiently accurate fall far short of the Air Force's cold-start responsiveness goal.

Many consider the program's most difficult technical challenge to be developing the Hard Mobile Launcher. It must be as fast as possible, yet be able to carry its relatively fragile cargo off-road to evade Soviet tracking and targeting efforts.

But the greatest HML design challenge is "hardening" the vehicle. Although it must withstand a whole array of nuclear effects, discussion usually centers around the HML's resistance to blast overpressure. The oft-specified goal is 30 pounds per square inch. (The Army's new Abrams tank can only withstand about 10 psi overpressure.) The HML must also resist winds of several hundred miles per hour without overturning. Because the Limited Test Ban Treaty forbids atmospheric nuclear tests, the prospective designs can only be tested against simulated nuclear effects. Thus, some uncertainty about the HML's real survivability will always exist.

The task of command, control, and communication with the missiles is proving to be a major problem. A strength of fixed ICBM forces, opposed to other legs of the triad, is their comparatively reliable $C^3$ system. But for mobile missiles, new ground-mobile launch control centers will need to operate both during and long after an attack and must communicate with missiles deployed over a large area. According to the GAO, "This presents communication problems not previously faced by the Air Force's fixed ICBM forces."

Several silo basing modes are being considered, including superhardened silos and a "Carry Hard" system that encases the missile in a hardened canister moved among 10 to 20 silos. Superhardening would be very expensive and the missile would eventually be vulnerable to increasingly accurate warheads. The "Carry Hard" concept is new, under study, and therefore raises many unanswered questions.

Midgetman's *operational effectiveness* is also in question. Traditionally, ICBMs were valued for their accuracy and ability to respond quickly. As was explained earlier, mobility makes high accuracy difficult, and there are still questions about how quickly the selected guidance systems will calibrate and align. The GAO has serious reservations about the system's ability to fire at any time and operate reliably over a protracted period.

The Air Force's goal for a 6,000 nautical mile range is also in doubt. Midgetman may need to carry penetration aids to foil Soviet missile defenses. This additional payload would require either increasing the missile's weight by about 8,000 pounds or reducing the missile's range.

Midgetman's survivability may rely on a dependable attack warning system. Some basing options limit the deployment area during day-to-day operations. This technique saves money, but increases the system's reliance on a timely warning to disperse and survive. Furthermore, because public concerns or environmental considerations will likely limit permissible basing areas, a determined Soviet surprise attack could probably saturate those areas. Thus Midgetman's survival may depend on reaching an arms control agreement that precludes Soviet barrage capability, perhaps by reducing Soviet missile throw-weight or warhead levels.

Finally, a shortage of *suitable land* may leave Midgetman with no room to roam. The Air Force has narrowed its choices to 51 sites in 13 states. For a 500 missile system, they believe at least 4,000 square miles of land will be needed for daily operations. During periods of increased alert, that area will expand to 8,000 square miles, and if there is danger of imminent attack, the launchers would further disperse. The GAO warned that securing sufficient land for deploying a mobile system would be challenging and time consuming. In addition, it revived an important issue from the MX debate, saying, "Environmental concerns will have to be resolved before a hard-mobile ICBM can be deployed."

The Midgetman program faces many obstacles, but solutions or compromises can undoubtedly be found. However, solving the system's siting, technical, operational, and cost problems will likely delay the 1992 Initial Operational Capability date and further increase costs. Whether Congress, the Executive Branch, and the Defense Department will remain committed to this system in an era of tight budgets and large monetary expenditures for other strategic systems, such as the Stealth Bomber and the Trident sea-launched ballistic missile program, remains to be seen.

## *Suggestions for Further Reading*

Holland, Lauren H., and Robert A. Hoover. *The MX Decision: A New Direction in Weapons Procurement Policy* (Boulder, CO: Westview Press, 1985). A detailed discussion of the history of the MX.

Office of the Undersecretary of Defense for Research and Engineering, "Report of the Defense Science Board Task Force on Small Intercontinental Ballistic Missile Modernization" (Washington, DC: Defense Department, March 1986). An analysis of the basing alternatives, survivability, and stability of the small ICBM (Midgetman) which strongly recommends going ahead with a small missile.

Scoville, Herbert, Jr. *MX—Prescription for Disaster* (Cambridge, MA: MIT Press, 1981). Reviews the development of the MX and argues vigorously against it.

Utgoff, Victor. "In Defense of Counterforce," *International Security* 6:4 (Spring 1982). A strong argument in favor of counterforce by a former member of the Carter NSC.

Walker, Paul F., and John Wentworth. "Midgetman: Missile in Search of a Mission," *Bulletin of the Atomic Scientists* (November 1986). A generally critical review of the strategic rationale for a small ICBM (Midgetman).

*Twelve*

# REAGAN'S SHIELD

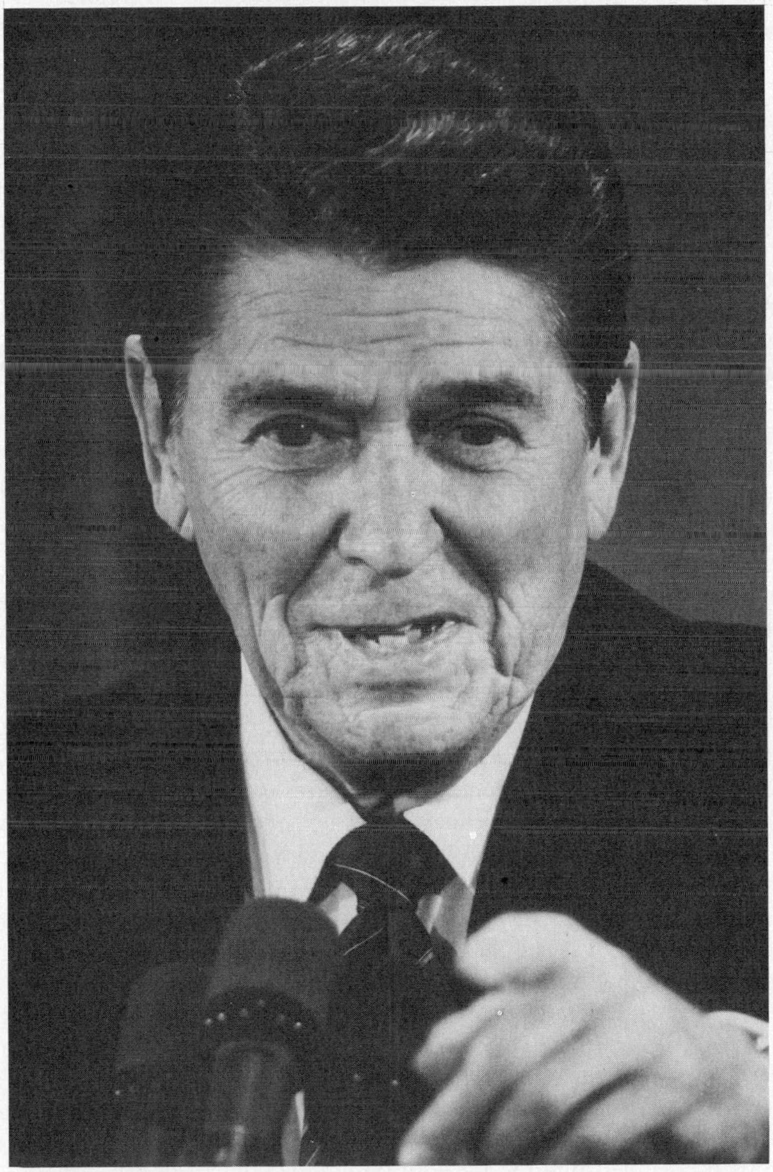

**RONALD REAGAN**

In March 1983, U.S. President Ronald Reagan proposed the Strategic Defense Initiative (SDI), also known as "Star Wars." The goal of SDI is a "near perfect" defense system, composed of weapons capable of intercepting and destroying Soviet ballistic missiles in flight. AP/Wide World Photos

# INTRODUCTION

In many ways, the Reagan administration's policies toward nuclear weapons can be understood as a reaction to the policies of the previous decade and a half. The key figures in the Reagan administration came into office convinced that the national security and arms control policies of previous Republican and Democratic administrations had been gravely flawed and that a real break with the past was necessary to set things right. In particular, since the late 1960s every administration had assumed that the nuclear forces of the United States were at least equal to those of the Soviet Union. Each administration improved U.S. nuclear forces and worried that the Soviets might pull ahead, but they believed Soviet superiority might occur only in the future and only if the United States let its guard down.

The Reagan administration came to office convinced that the Soviets were already clearly superior to the United States in nuclear forces. At a news conference in March 1982, President Reagan said, "The truth of the matter is that on balance the Soviet Union does have a definite margin of superiority." This view of the balance had several important implications, which also represented a clear break with past policy. In the Reagan view, the Soviets had overtaken the United States in part because past administrations had dangerously neglected U.S. military forces. This meant that a major defense buildup and a significant increase in the defense budget were necessary.

In addition, the Reagan administration believed that U.S. inferiority could be blamed on the arms control approach of the previous fifteen years. In Ronald Reagan's view, SALT I and SALT II were fatally flawed. They had failed to slow the growth of the Soviet strategic arsenal but had prevented the United States from improving its forces in needed ways. Moreover, such agreements had lulled the United States to sleep and helped blind the U.S. public to the danger of the Soviet threat.

Many of the Reagan administration's national security policies, especially in the first Reagan term, followed directly from this critique of U.S. actions. One major change was the rise in defense spending that increased the Defense Department's budget by 50 percent between 1981 and 1985 — the largest peacetime increase in U.S. history. In addition, since key Reagan defense officials believed that the Soviet Union was superior, the buildup of U.S. forces was given a much higher priority than reaching an arms control agreement. Perhaps the most dramatic break with the past, however, was President Reagan's decision to go forward with the Strategic Defense Initiative (SDI).

In the area of arms control, when the administration did finally begin to formulate proposals, these proposals were based on assumptions quite different from those that had guided previous administrations' arms control efforts. The first assumption was that the main goal of arms control negotiations was not to set equal aggregates of nuclear forces, as the SALT agreements had done. Because the administration believed that the Soviet Union was significantly ahead, the goal of arms control had to be to make the destructive power of U.S. and Soviet missile forces equal. In practical terms, this meant that the Soviets would have to cut drastically their most powerful weapons, while the United States could not afford to limit its forces.

Second, the Reagan administration believed that earlier administrations had been much too willing to make concessions to the Soviets. The better way to proceed was for the U.S. side to lay out its positions and stick to them until the Soviets agreed. If the Soviets did not agree, there would be no harm done to U.S. security because the U.S. arms buildup would proceed on schedule. Finally, the administration thought that previous administrations had done enough to make treaties verifiable. This meant that the administration would be more active in calling attention to what it believed were Soviet violations of past treaties. A major aspect of the Reagan arms control program was to accuse the Soviets publicly of violations. The administration would also insist on new, more stringent means of verification in any new treaties. These new means of verification would include intrusive measures that went well beyond what the Soviets had agreed to in the past.

One result of the Reagan break with the past was that the early 1980s saw a dramatic increase in public concern about the dangers of nuclear war. In part this was caused by the increasing U.S.-Soviet tensions, some loose talk about nuclear war by a few key administration officials, and the lack of progress toward arms control. The result was the growth of a grassroots movement calling for arms control initiatives, and a major increase in congressional concern about arms control. Much of the concern had faded by 1987, however.

It should also be pointed out that in certain ways the Reagan administration's break with the past was not as great as its rhetoric indicated. For example, its policy on intermediate-range nuclear forces (INF) was basically to carry out the decision NATO had agreed to during the Carter administration. In the area of offensive strategic nuclear weapons, the Reagan administration reversed the Carter decision to cancel the B-1 bomber, but Reagan also decided to deploy only half the MX missiles Carter had called for.

In addition, despite Reagan's denunciation of the SALT II Treaty during the 1980 campaign, his administration ultimately decided not to violate the treaty. Instead, it announced that it would take no action that would undercut the treaty, as long as the Soviets did likewise. The effect of this policy was that both superpowers adhered informally to the treaty throughout most of the Reagan administration.

By the middle of 1987, it appeared that the Reagan administration would leave behind a mixed record of accomplishments and disappointments. Until 1985, the administration was very successful in getting the defense budget increases it wanted. After 1985, however, concerns about the growing budget deficit forced cuts in defense spending. The Reagan administration successfully deployed INF missiles in Europe and carried out most elements of its program to modernize U.S. strategic forces. An important exception, however, was the MX missile, whose fate remained very much up in the air by 1987 (see chap. 11). The president's commitment to SDI remained firm, and the program went forward. But by 1987 Congress was making large cuts in the program's budget. Many of the key questions about SDI's cost, effectiveness, and purpose remained unanswered.

In arms control, the Reagan administration succeeded in negotiating an INF Treaty eliminating U.S. and Soviet intermediate-range and short-range missiles in Europe, but no agreement on strategic nuclear weapons was in sight. This was due, in part, to the very different approaches to negotiations on these issues by the superpowers. The United States wanted a new approach to arms control that focused on cutting Soviet missiles. The Soviets wanted arms control based on what had come before — the SALT negotiations. After 1983 the Reagan administration was firmly committed to not negotiating any limits on SDI. For the Soviets negotiated limits on SDI were a priority although in 1987 Gorbachev indicated a willingness to modify Soviet demands regarding SDI.

In addition, in 1987 the Reagan administration was faced with a new situation. The president was weakened by the Iran-Contra scandal. At the same time, the United States was confronted by a vigorous new Soviet leadership.

## THE OFFENSIVE BUILDUP

## The Arms Gap

### *Documents 1 and 2*

In his 1980 campaign for the presidency, Ronald Reagan charged that the Carter administration had neglected U.S. defenses. Reagan's charge played on a widely held belief that the Soviet Union had become militarily superior to the United States. Document 1, from *U.S. News & World Report,* is typical of many of the stories that appeared in the press at the time. It describes a military balance shifting toward the Soviet Union and notes the growing concern in Congress and among the public. Document 2 is taken from a report by one of the most prominent organizations raising the alarm about Soviet military might, the Committee on the Present Danger, a group composed of prominent Democrats and Republicans, many of whom later served in the Reagan administration. The report paints a picture of an increasingly powerful Soviet Union that plans to be able to fight, survive, and win a nuclear war, should one occur. The committee criticizes the Carter defense budget as inadequate for dealing with the growing threat.

### 1 ARMS GAP: HOW RUSSIA STOLE A MARCH ON U.S. November 12, 1979

Fifteen years of miscalculations about Russian military intentions now are catching up with the United States.

That is the conclusion of top defense analysts, a consensus that has come to light in the debate over the new SALT treaty with Moscow. Their findings:

Washington since the mid-'60s has pursued strategic policies based on false assumptions about the Kremlin's aims. As a result, the U.S. has forfeited an enormous arms advantage and has opened the door to a Soviet bid for strategic superiority in the 1980s.

The upshot is a far-reaching reassessment of the U.S. defense posture. There is near unanimity among specialists that major changes in U.S. strategy and substantial increases in Pentagon spending are imperative, whether the Senate approves or rejects the strategic-arms-limitation treaty with Moscow.

Former Secretary of State Henry A. Kissinger is one who warns that the alternative is potential disaster in the decade ahead. His words: "If present trends continue, the '80s will be a period of massive crisis for all of us."

The experts list three basic American assumptions, now exploded by Moscow's actions, that have led to a critical situation.

Assumption No. 1. U.S. policymakers in the 1960s concluded that the Kremlin would settle for permanent strategic inferiority. As Robert McNamara, Secretary of Defense in the Kennedy administration, put it: "There is no indication that the Soviets are seeking to develop a strategic nuclear force as large as ours." McNamara's Pentagon "Whiz Kids," therefore, unilaterally curbed competition with Russia.

In the '70s, officials modified the assessment. Russia, they decided, might close the missile gap but the U.S. could safely live with strategic parity or what now is called "essential equivalence."

Fact: The Russians have spurned permanent strategic inferiority—or even parity. On the contrary, they have mounted a massive buildup that in 10 years has wiped out the huge lead held by the United States at the turn of the decade. Now, the Kremlin is making a strong bid to achieve superiority during the 1980s.

The United States has been slow to respond to this Soviet challenge. Asserts Kissinger: "Rarely in history has a nation so passively accepted such a radical change in the military balance."

Assumption No. 2: Russia would share America's interest in preserving strategic stability. The official U.S. theory: Neither the Americans nor the Russians would have an incentive to build a weapons system that could threaten a knockout attack against its opponent's nuclear forces. Such a threat would create a dangerous, hairtrigger situation in a crisis that both superpowers would seek to avoid.

Kissinger describes it as an "historically amazing theory that vulnerability contributed to peace and invulnerability contributed to the risks of war."

Also, American officials in the 1960s assumed that the Russians would embrace another U.S. concept—the doctrine of "mutually assured destruction." The idea of fighting a nuclear war was ruled out as unthinkable by U.S. defense leaders. The sole aim should be to deter nuclear war by guaranteeing that an aggressor could not escape massive retaliation.

The United States has played by those rules since the 1960s, refraining from building weapons that could threaten a pre-emptive strike against Russian missile forces and from constructing a civil-defense system. It was assumed that the Soviet Union would see a mutual advantage in observing these rules.

Fact. The Russians have shown little interest in the U.S. notion of strategic stability. They are currently building a force of powerful ICBM's that could knock out 90 percent of America's 1,000 Minuteman missiles in a preemptive attack by 1984.

In other ways, too, Moscow has concentrated on plans to fight a nuclear war rather than simply to deter such a conflict. For example: Substantial resources have been devoted to a civil-defense program to protect the population in a nuclear exchange.

A leading French authority on Russia, Michel Tatu, sums up the Kremlin's thinking this way: "Deterrence should be replaced by a capacity for coercion. In other words, American nuclear power should be neutralized in order that Moscow gets a freer hand for military and political manipulations outside Soviet borders.

"For the purpose of neutralizing the American deterrent, the Soviet Union must have a nuclear-war-fighting capability. A nuclear war must be considered a possibility, and Moscow has to be prepared to fight it and win it."

Assumption No. 3. The Russians, U.S. officials believed, had a powerful incentive to cooperate with Washington in negotiations to slow the arms race, curb defense spending and reduce risk of nuclear war. The incentive: The prospect that the Soviet Union would be left far behind in an unrestrained competition, given America's great advantage in technology and a gross national product twice that of Russia's.

Also, Washington officials saw arms negotiations with Russia as the cornerstone of superpower détente, which would insure Soviet good behavior. In the words of *Foreign Policy* magazine: "A decade ago, when the Nixon administration embarked on the long road toward SALT I, the trek was sweetened with visions of American-Soviet harmony and of large domestic dividends from cuts in military spending."

Fact. During 10 years of arms negotiations, marked by two major agreements, the Russians have persisted with a military buildup unparalleled in peacetime. Until recently, the Central Intelligence Agency consistently underestimated the scale and pace of that buildup and the magnitude of Soviet defense spending. Now the CIA estimates that Moscow's military outlays exceed America's by 45 percent.

Defense Secretary Harold Brown describes the Soviet record during SALT negotiations this way: "As our defense budgets have risen, the Soviets have increased their defense budget. As our defense budgets have gone down, their defense budgets have increased again."

Among hawks and doves alike, disenchantment with the SALT process is apparent. Advocates of a more vigorous U.S. defense effort argue that the Soviet Union has exploited the negotiations in their drive for superiority. SALT, they maintain, has been used by the Russians simply as another instrument of strategic planning:

An Australian strategic expert says that "the disillusion of the arms-control enthusiasts is the most bitter of all. SALT has contributed neither to disarmament nor to the stability of the strategic balance, nor even to the preservation of détente."

The theory that SALT negotiations would impose restraint on Kremlin behavior has been exploded by Soviet involvement in military adventures in Angola, the Horn of Africa and the Mideast with the use of Cuban surrogate forces. These are viewed by many experts as samples of what the U.S. can expect in the years ahead.

U.S. defense planners warn of what they describe as "a window of peril" in the early 1980s.

The Soviet Union by then will have attained strategic

nuclear superiority combined with conventional superiority in Europe, plus a blue-water navy and airlift capacity providing a world-wide military reach.

The danger, as these officials see it, is that Moscow will be tempted to exploit its military advantage for political gains before the U.S. can close the gap. Says Gen. Bernard W. Rogers, who recently took over as Supreme Allied Commander, Europe: "We are reaching a critical window. We must be ready to be tested."

How does the U.S. intend to deal with this danger—and 15 years of miscalculations about the Soviets that brought it about?

Largely as a result of the debate over SALT II, a new consensus seems to be emerging in favor of a tougher attitude toward Moscow and a stronger American defense posture.

This new consensus is characterized this way by Prof. Samuel Huntington of Harvard, who served until recently on the President's National Security Council staff: 'The American man in the street is unhappy with what he regards as the decline of U.S. power in the world and demands of his government a more firm attitude, particularly toward the Soviets."

### Senate Waves

Similar sentiments are surfacing in the Senate, where there are demands for a substantial increase in Pentagon spending as the price for approving the new arms treaty with Moscow.

The Carter administration itself is showing signs of responding to the change in national mood in a series of recent decisions.

One is a 33-billion dollar plan to build a powerful mobile MX missile that can be hidden in a collection of shelters situated around a kind of race track. The force as a whole would be designed to survive a Soviet first strike attack.

Another is an administration plan to deploy nearly 600 medium-range missiles in Europe to counter the Soviet Union's nuclear buildup there. The aim is to reinforce the credibility of the American nuclear umbrella that protects Western Europe against a Russian invasion.

A third decision is intended to change the U.S. approach to future arms negotiations with Moscow. A presidential directive seeks to integrate arms-control policy with strategic planning, as the Soviet Union has done all along.

### Spending Pledge

President Carter, at the same time, has given the Senate a guarantee that he will increase defense spending by 3 percent, after allowing for inflation, and he says that he is prepared to go higher if the need can be demonstrated.

Even with these moves, defense analysts warn that the United States will face a time of danger in the early 1980s. It will take at least a decade, they say, to repair the damage of 15 years of strategic blunders in dealing with Russia.

## 2 IS AMERICA BECOMING NUMBER 2? October 5, 1978

The Soviet Union is "our principal national security problem," declares Secretary of Defense Harold Brown in the *Department of Defense Annual Report Fiscal Year 1979,* and "the main objective of our collective security system must be the maintenance of an overall military balance with the Soviet Union."

The debate on the state of the U.S.-Soviet military balance has already produced a consensus judgment that, if present trends continue, the U.S. will soon be in a situation of military inferiority. This judgment was reached by our Committee almost two years ago. Further, it is now widely agreed that such a position of U.S. inferiority would increase instability in international politics by making it possible for the Soviet Union to attempt political coercion backed by the credible threat of superior conventional and nuclear force, and allow Soviet exploitation of "targets of opportunity."

The actions of the Soviet leaders over the last 15 years leave no doubt that they consider the shift in the U.S.-Soviet balance favorable to them and the growth of the Soviet military power—specifically, of Soviet nuclear power—to be basic to all else that has happened, or may happen, in the evolution of world politics. They expect U.S. resistance to the expansion of Soviet influence to be deterred principally by Soviet military power.

U.S. accommodation to the Soviet drive for strategic superiority would confer on the Soviet Union the ability to intimidate and coerce the West into accepting unfavorable bargains. Soviet strategic superiority would give the Soviets dominance in crisis situations; the U.S. would then have to recognize that, if a crisis were to escalate to a strategic nuclear war, the Soviet Union would expect, at a high but perhaps not intolerable cost, to prevail while maintaining a post-war preponderance of global military power.

The Soviet military buildup has been steady, impressive in scale and quality, and dramatic in breadth and depth. It has gone on for more than 15 years and continues steadily at a rate reliably estimated to be between at least four to five percent a year. The Soviet military budget today is far greater than our own—between 40 percent and 60 percent greater. Some estimates go as high as 80 percent.

In the critical area of strategic nuclear strength, Soviet programs confirm beyond any reasonable doubt the rejection of our notions of nuclear stability and sufficiency, and of mutual deterrence. The Soviet buildup reflects the basic doctrinal precepts of Soviet strategy — that strategic nuclear offensive and defensive programs are designed to enable the Soviet Union to fight, survive, and win a nuclear war, should it occur.

The Soviet Union continues to invest heavily in its fixed land-based ICBM force. It is designed for a preemptive strike against U.S. forces, while reserving sufficient forces to hold the U.S. population and industry hostage. It is a formidable threat.

In strategic defense, the Soviet Union, in sharp contrast to the United States, maintains vast air defenses while the U.S. has merely token air defense forces. The Soviets have pursued a vigorous ABM research and development program, one that could provide them with a strategically significant, rapidly deployable "breakout" capability for the aerospace defense of the Soviet Union. They have repeatedly tested an operational anti-satellite system, another capability unmatched by the United States.

In conjunction with these activities, the Soviet Union has been engaged for some time in a comprehensive national civil defense program designed to ensure Soviet nuclear war-survival, recovery, and emergence as the dominant post-war global power.

Against this specter of rapidly expanding Soviet strategic nuclear offensive and defensive capabilities is a U.S. strategic program that is struggling with production and development problems in the TRIDENT program, design and decision programs with basing for a new ICBM, and that has placed enormous faith in the cruise missile program which is still only in development.

In Europe, Soviet forces are designed for surprise attack and the *offensive*. The West is outnumbered in military manpower, reserves, tanks, artillery, and tactical aircraft. Soviet forces are trained and equipped to fight and survive on the nuclear and chemical battlefield and are deployed for a nuclear and chemical blitzkrieg. The Soviets are modernizing their ground, air and naval forces. Present Soviet force modernization programs will be completed well before effective NATO initiatives are fielded. The trends are clearly running in the wrong direction for us and, without an adequate strategy foı European defense, the common argument that NATO quality compensates for Soviet-Warsaw Pact quantity is specious.

There has been significant growth in the offensive capability of Soviet tactical airpower. Deployment of fourth generation aircraft with greater range, payload, and sophisticated weaponry continues. These aircraft can strike all types of targets throughout the European theater and the Middle East.

The Soviet Union is a continental power with secure interior lines of communications and autarkic economic system. The Soviet Navy is designed for offensive political and military operations against our naval forces, our vital sea lines of communication to NATO and our allies in the Pacific, and our access to supplies of raw materials.

The size, sophistication, and rate of growth of Soviet military power far exceeds Soviet requirements for defense. The Soviet military buildup reflects the offensive nature of the Soviet political and military challenge and the Soviet belief that the use of force remains a viable instrument of foreign policy.

While we welcome President Carter's recent strong statements reaffirming our commitment to maintain a balance of power with the Soviet Union, the Defense Budget for the 1979 Fiscal Year is inadequate to meet this objective and will not reverse the adverse trends.

## Plans for a Buildup of Nuclear Forces

### *Document 3*

In document 3, Secretary of Defense Caspar W. Weinberger describes the Reagan administration's plan for a buildup of nuclear forces in testimony to the Senate Armed Services Committee early in the Reagan administration's first term. After noting the buildup of Soviet forces, Weinberger describes planned improvements in each leg of the U.S. triad.

## 3 TESTIMONY TO THE SENATE ARMED SERVICES COMMITTEE

**Caspar W. Weinberger**

**November 3, 4, and 9, 1981**

### Bomber Forces

We plan to take a number of steps to improve our bomber forces. We will develop a variant of the B–1 bomber and procure 100 aircraft, with the first B–1 squadron becoming operational in 1986.

We will continue a vigorous R&D program for an Advanced Technology Bomber (the so-called "Stealth" aircraft). This bomber, under current plans, will be deployed in the 1990's.

Newer B–52s (G and H models) will be modified to carry cruise missiles. Selected aircraft will be modernized to provide added protection against the effects of nuclear explosions (particularly electro-magnetic pulse effects) and to improve their ability to survive against Soviet air defenses (by installation of additional electronic countermeasures equipment).

Older B–52s (D model) will be retired in 1982 and 1983.

Over 3,000 cruise missiles will be deployed on B–

52Gs, B–52Hs, and B–1s. The first squadron of cruise missile-equipped aircraft (B–52Gs) will be operational in 1982.

Finally, existing KC–135 aerial tankers will be outfitted with new engines to increase airborne refueling capabilities.

The previous Administration planned to rely on the aging B–52 force until the "Stealth" bomber become available in the 1990's. We have rejected that approach. We believe that the limitations of the B–52 demand replacement as soon as possible. The B–1 we will deploy, however, is not the same as that cancelled by our predecessors but rather a variant of that design. Its capabilities will be essential in the late 1980's and beyond. In particular, we need the greater B–1 payload, its smaller radar cross section and its improved survivability.

The B–1 offers significant reductions in radar cross section. As you know, the radar cross section of an object is a measure of the relative amount of radar energy reflected by the object. Radar cross section depends on the shape, orientation, and material of an object as well as its physical size, and, the smaller the better. It also varies with the frequency of the radar. Through application of radar absorbing material and redesign of the engine inlets, the radar cross section of the modified B–1 design has been reduced by more than an order of magnitude from the original design.

This reduction is not large enough to prevent detection by Soviet radars. However, it greatly facilitates new techniques in electronic countermeasures: the smaller the radar cross section, the easier it is to hide the bomber and fool the radar. The B–1's combination of lower radar cross section, improved electronic countermeasures, lower penetration altitude and higher penetration speed should enable the B–1 to penetrate Soviet air defenses in the 1980's and into the 1990's. Once the Advanced Technology Bomber is deployed, we plan for the B–1 to become the stand-off cruise missile carrying aircraft. Thus we will be able both to penetrate and stand-off with cruise missiles for the remainder of the century. In addition, the B–1s (and later the Advanced Technology Bombers) optimally employed in concert with our cruise missile carrying B–52 aircraft will impose the ultimate stresses on Soviet air defenses. The synergistic combination of mutually reinforcing penetrating bombers and stand-off cruise missiles will greatly compound the problems and thus dilute the effectiveness of Soviet air defense. Their large investments in air defense can therefore be made obsolescent by our careful mixture of capabilities and tactics offered by the penetrating bombers and cruise missiles.

But penetration will be meaningless if our bombers are destroyed before they can be launched. It is thus essential that our bombers have an adequate margin of safety to survive any Soviet attack on their operating bases. Here too, the B–1 will represent a major improvement.

The B–1 has a much better margin of safety than our B–52s in launch survivability.

It can dash much faster than the B–52 when escaping its base.

It is at least twice as hard as the B–52 to nuclear effects.

Our conclusion is that the B–1 will be an order of magnitude harder to destroy at home than the B–52.

## Land-Based ICBMs

With respect to land-based missiles, we plan a cautious, step-by-step approach. The so-called multiple protective shelter basing scheme favored by our predecessors has been cancelled. This scheme had serious military drawbacks and would not have solved, in the long run, the basic problem: the current vulnerability of the Minuteman and Titan ICBM force. However, we cannot afford to put off deployment of the MX, a much more effective and accurate missile than the existing Minuteman. We will therefore continue development of MX and produce at least one hundred missiles. Some will be deployed in modified Titan and Minuteman silos. We plan now to restructure the silos planned for MX deployment to increase their hardness to nuclear effects and thus to buy time until we have selected and implemented the final MX basing scheme. The harder silos will, in the context of our total force, enhance deterrence during the period before a long-term basing mode for MX becomes available.

For the longer-term, we believe there are alternative basing modes for MX, and vigorous research and development efforts will be initiated on three possibilities. The options we will consider include:

*Continuous Patrol Aircraft.* — This concept would deploy missiles in survivable, long-endurance aircraft, capable of launching the missiles while in flight.

*Ballistic Missiles Defense.* — Under this concept, we would actively defend land-based MX missiles. Research and development efforts for anti-ballistic missile defenses will be increased and the program accelerated. Our efforts will not be directed toward creating an effective city defense, which we continue to believe is not technically feasible. Ultimately, any ground-based scheme may require such a defense, but we are unwilling to commit to ballistic missile defense today because of uncertainties of cost and effectiveness. Any eventual decision to deploy point defenses as an effective defense of our ICBM forces is likely to require alterations to the ABM Treaty. Since the Soviets have been spending far more than we on ballistic missile defense in recent years, any modification to the Treaty must be carefully examined to ensure it is in the net interest of ourselves and our Allies. Thus, this accelerated research is not a decision to begin production and deployment of an ABM system nor to seek abrogation or modification of the 1972 Treaty. We are convinced, however, that the survival and endurance of our land-based nuclear forces is an essential element in the deterrent equation, and that we must explore all options — including ballistic missile defense — which may contribute to that survival.

*Deep Underground Basing.* — Our final alternative, deep underground basing, would entail deployment of MX in survivable locations far underground. If this plan proves feasible and cost-effective, missiles so deployed would be able to survive massive attack and would provide us a true enduring capability.

We will select from among these options as soon as sufficient technical information becomes available and, in any case, no later than 1984. Regardless of the option we select, MX deployment — together with deployment of the Trident II missile at sea — will end the Soviet monopoly on prompt hard target kill capability and thus enhance deterrence.

## Sea-Based Forces

In the area of sea-based forces, we plan three steps.

First, we will continue the production of Trident ballistic missile submarines at a steady rate of one per year. As you know, the first such submarine, the USS *Ohio,* recently completed her initial sea trials and has proven to be even faster and quieter than originally designed.

Second, we will develop a larger, more accurate sea-launched ballistic missile, known as Trident II or the D–5, for deployment on Trident submarines beginning in 1989. Trident II will allow us to take full advantage of the large launch tubes which we have designed into the new *Ohio* class. The new missiles will be larger, have a longer range, have better accuracy and carry either more warheads or larger ones than the Trident I missile. It will represent a significant improvement in capability. The much longer range will double the available patrol area for our Trident submarines, substantially complicating Soviet anti-submarine warfare programs and adding to submarine survivability even in the face of unexpected advances in Soviet anti-submarine warfare technology. The combination of increased accuracy and greater throwweight available with Trident II will allow us to attack any target in the Soviet Union, including hardened missile silos. In deploying Trident II, we will be increasing the total payload of each Trident submarine and thus avoiding any reduction in sea-based capabilities when large numbers of our existing Poseidon submarines are retired in the 1990's.

The third step in the sea-based portion of the Reagan strategic modernization program is the deployment of Tomahawk land-attack cruise missiles on our ships and general purpose submarines. This deployment will begin in mid-1984 aboard submarines.

## Strategic Defense

The final element of our strategic modernization program involves strategic defense.

We plan to upgrade, in coordination with Canada, the North American Air Surveillance Network. The plan will include some combination of new Over-The-Horizon-Backscatter (OTH-B) radars and improved versions of the ground radars that exist today. We will replace five squadrons of aging F-106 interceptors with new F-15s. We will buy at least six additional AWACS airborne surveillance aircraft for North American air defense to augment ground-based radars in peacetime and to provide surveillance and control interceptors in wartime. These aircraft are in addition to those we have programmed for use with NATO forces in Europe.

We will continue to pursue an operational anti-satellite system and, as I discussed a few minutes ago, we will vigorously pursue research and development on ballistic missile defense. Finally, we will improve our civil defense efforts. These steps end years of neglect during which the United States has virtually ignored strategic defense. As a result of all these initiatives, by the end of this decade we will double the number of U.S. warheads which will survive a Soviet attack. Of even greater significance, we will dramatically increase the effectiveness of our forces whether viewed in the context of a surprise attack on our normal day-to-day peacetime posture or of a similar attack when we are at full alert.

## Program Summary and NATO Reaction

In summary, this comprehensive program modernizes all major elements of the U.S. strategic posture, begins to redress the existing imbalances with Soviet forces and signals a national commitment to attain whatever capabilities are needed to counter further growth in Soviet power and global adventurism. It also strengthens and reinforces our extension of our strategic deterrent to our Allies. I am pleased to note in this regard, that I recently briefed the NATO Defense Ministers on the details of our program and on its underlying policy implications. My NATO colleagues endorsed the President's strategic program not only in closed session, but publicly as well. As the communique of the Nuclear Planning Group meeting on October 21 notes, NATO Defense Ministers "expressed their support for the determination of the United States to ensure the deterrent capability of its strategic forces whose importance to the overall defense of the (NATO) alliance is crucial. . . ." Calling U.S. strategic forces "the ultimate guarantee of Western security," the NATO Ministers echoed our view that the U.S. modernization efforts "are intended to maintain an adequate and stable balance of forces at the lowest possible level and do not represent an attempt to achieve strategic superiority."...

**Summary**

In sum, the President's five-part program of strategic force modernization I have discussed today will establish our firm commitment to restore a balance of stable deterrence based on a strategy of prevailing forces and enduring strength. Taken in the aggregate, our strategic programs will greatly enhance our ability to deter Soviet aggression by increasing the flexibility, survivability and endurance of all three legs of our strategic Triad and their supporting command and control system. Further, it strengthens our deterrent guarantees to our NATO Allies in a program which we believe is compatible with the two-track approach to modernization of our long-range theater nuclear forces in Europe. Finally, our commitment to carry forward with these sweeping and comprehensive improvements should strengthen our image in the third world and display our resolve to frustrate any further Soviet adventurism and expansionism in the world. But probably more important, the strategic modernization program will establish a strong foundation for renewed arms control initiatives and provide strong incentives for the Soviets to join with us in meaningful and genuine arms controls and reductions world wide....

## Reagan's View of the Soviet Threat

### *Document 4*

In the middle of his second year, President Reagan made a nationally televised speech to the American people in which he announced: "Today, in virtually every measure of military power, the Soviet Union enjoys a decided advantage." He used charts and graphs to argue that the Soviets were outspending the United States and deploying more systems. He justified his defense buildup as necessary to bring the United States back to a position of parity with the Soviet Union.

### 4 NATIONALLY TELEVISED SPEECH President Ronald Reagan November 22, 1982

You often hear that the United States and the Soviet Union are in an arms race. Well, the truth is that while the Soviet Union has raced, we have not. As you can see from this blue U.S. line in constant dollars, our defense spending in the 1960's went up because of Vietnam. And then it went downward through much of the 1970's.

And now follow the red line, which is Soviet spending. It's gone up and up and up. In spite of a stagnating Soviet economy, Soviet leaders invest 12 to 14 percent of their country's gross national product in military spending. Two to three times the level we invest.

I might add that the defense share of our United States federal budget has gone way down, too. Watch the blue line again. In 1962, when John Kennedy was President, 46 percent, almost half of the federal budget, went to our national defense. In recent years, about one quarter of our budget has gone to defense, while the share for social programs has nearly doubled. And most of our defense budget is spent on people, not weapons.

The combination of the Soviets spending more and the United States spending proportionately less changed the military balance and weakened our deterrent.

Today, in virtually every measure of military power, the Soviet Union enjoys a decided advantage. This chart shows the changes in the total number of intercontinental missiles and bombers. You will see that in 1962 and in 1972, the United States forces remained about the same—even dropping some by 1982. But take a look now at the Soviet side. In 1962, at the time of the Cuban Missile Crisis, the Soviets could not compare with us in terms of strength. In 1972, when we signed the SALT I Treaty, we were nearly equal. But in 1982—well, that red, Soviet bar stretching above the blue, American bar tells the story.

I could show you chart after chart where there is a great deal of red and a much lesser amount of U.S. blue. For example, the Soviet Union has deployed a third more, land-based intercontinental ballistic missiles than we have. Believe it or not, we froze our number in 1965, and have deployed no additional missiles since then. The Soviet Union put to sea 60 new ballistic missile submarines in the last 15 years. Until last year, we had not commissioned one in that same period. The Soviet Union has built over 200 modern Backfire bombers, and is building 30 more a year. For 20 years, the United States has deployed no new strategic bombers. Many of our B-52 bombers are now older than the pilots who fly them.

The Soviet Union now has 600 of the missiles considered most threatening by both sides—the intermediate-range missiles based on land. We have none. The United States withdrew its intermediate-range land-based missiles from Europe almost 20 years ago.

The world has also witnessed unprecedented growth in the area of Soviet conventional forces. The Soviets far exceed us in the number of artillery pieces, aircraft, and ships they produce every year. What is more, when I arrived in this office, I learned that in our own forces we had planes that could not fly and ships that could not leave port mainly for lack of spare parts and crew members.

The Soviet military buildup must not be ignored. We have recognized the problem. And, together with our allies, we have begun to correct the imbalance. Look at this chart of projected, real defense spending for the next several years. Here is the Soviet line. Let us assume the Soviets rate of spending remains at the level they have followed since the 1960s. The blue line is the United States. If my defense proposals are passed, it will still take five yeras before we come close to the Soviet level. Yet, the modernization of our strategic and conventional forces will assure that deterrence works and peace prevails.

## New Soviet Weapon Programs

### *Document 5*

**Beginning in late 1981, the Defense Department has published annual unclassified reports on the Soviet threat. In the 1985 version, the first of President Reagan's second term, it is clear that the Reagan administration believes that there has been no shrinking of the threat. The excerpts from the report in document 5 describe a host of new Soviet weapon programs and warn that the Soviets are cutting into U.S. leads in many critical areas of defense technology.**

### 5 SOVIET MILITARY POWER — 1985 U.S. Defense Department

The forces of the USSR and its allies continue to expand, modernize, and deploy with increasingly capable weapons systems designed for the entire spectrum of strategic, theater-nuclear, and conventional conflict. The Soviet Union has made no secret of certain of these advances. For example, in the autumn of 1984, the Soviet Defense Ministry announced that the USSR was beginning to deploy a new generation of nuclear-armed, air-launched and sea-launched cruise missiles. The Soviets also revealed that nuclear-armed, short-range ballistic missiles had been forward-deployed from the USSR to operational sites in Eastern Europe and that additional ballistic missile submarines were on patrol in the Atlantic and the Pacific. In a speech before the Politburo, General Secretary Chernenko said that further actions would be taken to strengthen the Soviet Union's military capability. These announcements serve notice of the increasingly ambitious Soviet procurement and deployment of major categories of new armaments. The success that the Soviets have achieved in both quantity and quality of systems is based on combining an aggressive R&D program with a systematic effort to target and obtain advanced Western technologies.

Some of the more significant developments reported in this, the fourth edition of *Soviet Military Power,* are:

- Test firings continue for the SS-X-24 and SS-X-25 ICBMs, the new, fifth-generation intercontinental ballistic missiles. The SS-X-25 violates Soviet obligations under SALT II. The level of deployed MIRVed ICBM warheads continues to rise with overall modernization of the Soviet strategic missile force.
- Two units of a new DELTA IV-Class of strategic ballistic missile submarine have been launched; they are the likely platform for the USSR's newest, most accurate submarine-launched ballistic missile (SLBM), the SS-NX-23.
- A third 25,000-ton TYPHOON-Class strategic ballistic missile submarine has completed sea trials, joining the two TYPHOON units already operational, each fitted with 20 SS-N-20 SLBMs, with each missile capable of delivering six to nine MIRVed warheads to ranges of 8,300 kilometers.
- The new supersonic, swing-wing BLACKJACK bomber continues in advanced test and development. New strategic BACKFIRE bombers continue to join operational Soviet forces at a rate of at least 30 a year. New BEAR-H strategic bombers are emerging from Soviet aircraft plants and deploying with the 3,000-kilometer-range, air-launched, nuclear-armed AS-15 cruise missile.
- The USSR is continuing to devote extremely high priority to its military-related space program. A major emphasis is on space systems for long-duration, manned missions engaged in military research. They are developing new heavy-lift launch vehicles, capable of launching 150-ton payloads, for the space shuttle and manned space station programs. The USSR is continuing research on ground-based and space-based high-energy lasers for use in antisatellite roles. The Soviets currently have the world's only deployed antisatellite weapons system that can attack satellites in near-earth orbit.
- The USSR continues to upgrade its heavily layered strategic defenses with expansion of ballistic missile detection and tracking systems and the development of new early warning and air surveillance radars. Silo-based high-acceleration interceptor missiles are replacing older above-ground launchers in the antiballistic missile system ringing Moscow, bringing increased capabilities to the world's only deployed ABM system. A new, large, phased-array radar under construction at Krasnoyarsk violates the ABM Treaty. The USSR may be preparing an ABM defense of its national territory. In addition, the Soviets are actively engaged in extensive research on advanced defenses against ballistic missiles.

Modernization of Soviet forces at the strategic level is mirrored by force improvements at theater-nuclear and conventional levels:

- The Soviets have pressed ahead with construction of new SS-20 missile bases in both the western and eastern USSR, enabling a substantial increase from the 378 MIRVed 5,000-kilometer-range nuclear missiles reported last year to a new total of about 400. In parallel, new SS-21 short-range ballistic missiles are now deployed with Soviet divisions in East Germany, and more accurate 900-kilometer-range SS-22/SCALEBOARD missiles have been forward-deployed to East Germany and Czechoslovakia.

- Soviet Ground Forces, which in 1981 numbered 181 divisions, have now grown to 199 motorized rifle, tank, and airborne divisions. New main battle tanks continue to flow from Soviet factories — some 3,200 in 1984 — upgrading tank division capabilities, which are equipped from an USSR inventory of 52,000 tanks.
- The fourth 37,000-ton KIEV-Class aircraft carrier is fitting out, preparing to join the already operational carriers *Novorossiysk, Minsk,* and *Kiev.* Construction continues on the lead unit of an entirely new class of aircraft carrier that will be about 65,000 tons displacement.
- The second unit of the 28,000-ton nuclear-powered KIROV-Class cruisers has joined the Soviet fleet. A third unit of these heavily armed guided-missile cruisers is on the building ways.
- Nine separate classes of Soviet submarines are in production; these classes include four nuclear-powered attack submarines capable of carrying the new SS-NX-21 land-attack sea-launched cruise missile.
- The Su-27/FLANKER all-weather, air-superiority fighter will soon be deployed, further adding to the capability of Soviet tactical aircraft.

The Soviet military is not a home-based garrison force as attested by the more than 30 ready divisions forward-deployed throughout Eastern Europe, the divisions in combat in Afghanistan, the brigade in Cuba, and military advisers throughout the Third World. The Soviet Navy is the most visible element of the USSR's growing global reach. In Vietnam, for example, the Soviets have transformed Cam Ranh Bay into their largest forward deployment naval base in the world, adding more Tu-16/BADGERs and a squadron of MiG-23/FLOGGER fighters. As the Navy adds to the capabilities of its submarine, surface, and air units, the USSR continues to press for greater access to overseas facilities for its Armed Forces and continues to support the establishment and strengthening of regimes sympathetic to and supportive of Soviet purposes. The continuing flow of increasingly advanced weapons to the Sandinista regime in Nicaragua is a prime example. . . .

It is incumbent upon the United States and its allies to have a full and precise understanding of the Soviet challenge as we take the steps necessary to preserve our freedom, to ensure an effective deterrent to the threat and use of force, and, at the same time, to seek genuine and equitable arms reductions, contributing to global stability and to our transcending goal as a free people — the goal of peace and security.

## Review of the Reagan Buildup

### *Document 6*

These excerpts from a cover story from *Insight,* a weekly magazine published by the conservative *Washington Times,* review the Reagan buildup, describing what was spent and what was bought. The article notes the criticisms of some analysts who claim the huge sums were not spent wisely. The article also describes the problems facing the Reagan Defense Department as Congress looks for ways to trim the federal budget.

## 6 THE SHAPE OF A REARMED PENTAGON
## Philip Gold

Once upon a time, the story goes, a committee of blind men inspected an elephant. Each man grasped a part and decreed it to be something other than what it was. Legs became trees, the trunk became a snake, the tail a rope and so on. Not only did the committee never reach a conclusion, but group discussion was an extremely aggravating business.

For those who have wondered whatever happened to that committee, here is the answer. Its members gained their sight, became experts in national defense and have spent the past six years inspecting an elephant of a different sort: the Reagan rearmament program. Experts in the defense field — inside the Pentagon and out — cannot agree on anything, except that when Ronald Reagan leaves office, he will have spent close to $2 trillion on the nation's defenses. But with the Reagan "modernization program" essentially complete — not by choice but by a change in the political landscape — no one can agree on what the buildup actually accomplished.

Since 1985 the defense budget has effectively been frozen in the $290 billion annual appropriation range. And despite the fact that Defense Secretary Caspar W. Weinberger says, "I don't think the buildup's over," the new Democratic Congress does not seem prepared to support his budget requests any further. In the 1984 election, Reagan ran a campaign bragging about how he had restored U.S. defenses. Apparently, everybody believed him, because right after his landslide election the national consensus on continuing the defense buildup collapsed.

The administration's emphasis on defense spending has been perhaps its most consistent strain (Weinberger is not changing his tune: He is asking for $303 billion in fiscal 1988 and $323 billion for 1989). Reagan was elected in 1980 at least partially on a platform to rearm the United States, whose military force had fallen into severe disrepair during the 1970s. Weinberger has often emphasized what the administration perceived as the criticality of the 1981 situation. "When we came in," he has said, "we found that there was literally nothing we didn't need."

"Perhaps, given their sense of the situtation in 1981, they felt they had no time for strategy, that the important thing was to get the spending program in place as fast as possible," observes analyst Brian McCartan of the Center for Defense Information, a leftist group that has made a career of bashing the Reagan buildup.

The across-the-board shortages may indeed have been as bad in 1981 as Weinberger insists. But now, precisely what was needed and what has been bought remain items of fierce debate, a debate rekindled at the beginning of every budget cycle.

The Department of Defense budget is outlined in the secretary's "Annual Report to the Congress," an unclassified, book-length document issued each January. The report contains not only the budget request but also summaries of work in progress and general policy. A reading of the fiscal 1988 report reveals some remarkable successes, according to the Pentagon.

Although the total uniformed strength of the armed forces has risen only about 100,000 since fiscal 1981 (under President Carter's last budget), the military has grown undeniably stronger. The Army has added two divisions and received thousands of tanks, infantry fighting vehicles, helicopters and other support equipment.

The Navy has grown from 479 deployable battle force ships in 1980 to nearly 600. The Air Force is receiving hundreds of fighter and transport aircraft. The Marine Corps has been fully modernized. In the areas of strategic and theater nuclear weapons, progress is also significant.

The MX missile, the B-1B bomber, the Trident submarine and a whole array of cruise missiles are being deployed. Numerous other initiatives and programs are close to success. All in all, it would seem, the Reagan program has been a great success.

"It's hard," says one analyst, "to spend a trillion and a half dollars on something and not get at least a few results." But more detailed assessment raises troubling questions, from the effectiveness of the weapons being procured to the larger issue of whether the Reagan program has addressed fundamental problems within the defense establishment.

Beyond the matter of individual weapons and systems, three types of critical assessment have emerged.

One criticism is that, despite all the rhetoric, the Reagan program has not been so different from what Jimmy Carter would have done, had he been reelected in 1980. The evidence here comes largely from a comparison of Carter's last Five Year Defense Plan (a standard Pentagon document projecting spending for the next five years, and updated annually) with what the Reagan administration actually did.

In "A Reasonable Defense," a study done for the Brookings Institution, Harvard University Professor and former Pentagon official William W. Kaufmann notes that Carter had planned to ask for $1.276 trillion for fiscal 1982 through 1986, while Reagan actually got $1.46 trillion. The difference: well under $200 billion, measured in current dollars. Kaufmann says that since Congress in the early 1980s was in a profoundly prodefense mood, Carter could have accomplished the same rearmament and well might have, given his "change of heart" about the need for drastically increased military spending after the 1979 Iranian revolution and Soviet invasion of Afghanistan.

Further, concludes Kaufmann, nearly all the systems bought by Reagan were "in the pipeline" during the Carter years. At the conventional level, Reagan pursued a more aggressive shipbuilding program than Carter would have (although more than 20 of "Reagan's" ships were fully funded by Carter), but otherwise, his modernization essentially paralleled Carter's plan. At the strategic level, Reagan did reinstate the B-1 bomber, which Carter canceled, but he also has deployed fewer MX missiles than Carter had planned. (The latter, of course, is not Reagan's doing but that of Congress: if it had been left to his druthers, at least 100 MXs would be deployed by now). . . .

But the contention that the Reagan program represents no fundamental change may be a little disingenuous. The administration has never denied that it has continued Carter initiatives, both by circumstance and by choice. "To change the forces we inherited takes time; we can alter them only incrementally," Weinberger has said. "We are, to a greater extent than we would like, the prisoners of our immediate past."

Beyond this unavoidable continuity — weapons and other systems normally take up to a decade or more to develop — many analysts agree that it makes little sense to measure hypothetical plans against real performance, especially over five years. . . .

Others, under the second type of assessment, believe that the Pentagon under Reagan has made a signal change in the United States' defense posture by trying to improve the nation's offensive capabilities. "What Reagan has done," says Posen, "is to take some tendencies that were inherent in previous administrations and intensify them. Nuclear weapons, for example. Reagan has greatly increased the emphasis on counterforce and nuclear war fighting."

Posen points out that every leg of the so-called nuclear triad — land-based missiles, submarine-based missiles, manned bombers — is now designed to "kill" hard nuclear targets such as missile silos and command bunkers. Hitting these targets requires much greater accuracy and faster response time than are required to hit cities. Reagan has also made major efforts to improve command, control, communications and intelligence — the sine qua non of both nuclear and conventional warfare. "Carter started or developed most of these programs, but it's Reagan who has pushed them." Another analyst agrees. "The current numbers themselves don't tell the whole story. The real impact of the Reagan nuclear program won't be felt until well into the 1990s."

True, strategic deployments are proceeding more slowly than the administration has wished. However, the 1988 report indicates that, by the end of fiscal 1987, 27 MXs should be deployed (10 had been as of Dec. 31), nearly 60 B-1B bombers (28 had been), one more Trident submarine (seven out of a projected 16 are now operational). In addition, 132 B-52s have been equipped with cruise missiles and 108 Pershing 2s and 208 ground-launched cruise missiles have been deployed in Europe.

And beyond these deployments lie the new systems of the 1990s: the extremely accurate D-5 missile for the Trident; the advanced technology bomber, called Stealth; more MXs; Midgetman, the single-warhead, small, mobile ICBM: and perhaps, initial deployment of elements of the Strategic Defense Initiative.

"Reagan may have locked us into an incredible arsenal," says an analyst. "No wonder the Russians are screaming for arms control now."

Another tendency the administration has emphasized is naval power. Some dismiss the push for a 600-ship Navy (a goal the administration says will be met by 1990) as not much more than great salesmanship on the part of Navy Secretary John Lehman, who recently announced his resignation....

Lehman insists that the administration's program is neither arbitrary nor driven by infatuation with high-tech gadgetry. "The number 600 was not plucked out of a hat," he has said. "It is the force structure necessary for the maritime tasks which have been handed to the Department of the Navy." These tasks include delivery of strategic nuclear weapons, control of vital sea-lanes, projecting air power overseas and amphibious operations (landing the Marines).

Pentagon spokesmen admit that the Navy would, of course, be more comfortable with more than 600 ships. But they also assert that a 600-ship Navy, structured around 40 to 44 ballistic missile submarines, 15 large-deck aircraft carriers, four battleships and about 450 other battle force ships (including 100 or so attack submarines), constitutes an adequate force. They also point out that the Soviets have made gigantic strides in naval power over the past decade.

Beyond the question of whether the Reagan buildup has been merely a continuation or a more aggressive permutation lies a third question: Can the administration meet its stated goals now that the free-spending days are over? Here opinion seems relatively clear. The administration lacks, and will never receive from Congress, enough money to complete its plan.

Five years ago, analyst George Kuhn, in a study for the Heritage Foundation, estimated that the administration would never procure more than a fraction of its defense shopping list. A 1986 Senate study estimated the shortfall at around $400 billion. And the current Pentagon budget request, the first two-year budget ever submitted, freely concedes that many purchases will have to be stretched out or delayed....

The Air Force will remain at 37 tactical fighter wings, a unit usually composed of three squadrons, instead of the 40 originally planned. The Navy is asking for 157 fewer aircraft for 1988 and 1989 than originally projected. New ship construction is down about one-third. Nearly all major Army procurement programs are also slowed.

Unfortunately, the effect of these slowdowns will be to increase the ultimate costs of these programs. This phenomenon recurs like a bad dream. In his book "Defense Facts of Life," Pentagon analyst Franklin C. Spinney has demonstrated how, ever since World War II, short-term spending increases have failed to translate into long-term readiness....

And yet, even if the criticisms are valid, it is hard to see how the administration could have done otherwise. "There was a failure," says one administration official who has also worked on Capitol Hill. "But it was a failure of prudence. Reagan should have opted for slow, steady growth, not the 12 to 15 percent jumps during the early years, then the freeze."

Says a prominent neoconservative observer: "Maybe the money wasn't spent as well as it might have been. But the fact of spending it sent a signal that the country was serious about defense again, sent it to the Russians and to allies who'd been wondering how dependable we were."

To complicate the matter further, Congress often cuts requests the Pentagon considers vital, while adding nonessential appropriations to please powerful legislators and their constituents. It is said on Capitol Hill that $20 billion is spent yearly on projects designed to increase employment in representatives' districts or senators' states or else to pay off political debts. Last year, for example, New York Sens. Daniel Patrick Moynihan, a Democrat, and Alfonse M. D'Amato, a Republican, fought ferociously, and successfully, to make the Pentagon continue to buy the T-46 jet trainer, which the Air Force had deemed unnecessary but which is made on Long Island.

Added to this is the congressional penchant for intermittent micromanagement. Not only do the Senate and House Budget, Appropriations and Armed Services committees (and their subcommittees) deal with defense — and the committees on foreign relations, intelligence, commerce and energy routinely get involved — but also, writes Rep. James A. Courter, a Republican from New Jersey, "the congressional appetite for oversight has been growing and shows no sign of abating."

And beyond the question of whether money has been well spent and the annoyances of micromanagement lie larger questions of national strategy.

Only in November 1984 did Weinberger attempt to define criteria for the use of armed force. He now dismisses that attempt — six conditions for the use of force that critics charged harmed deterrence by spelling out the precise conditions for war — as "simplistic." Sensitive to accusations that the administration has no strategy, Weinberger did what Washingtonians do to solve such problems: He appointed a commission on "integrated long-term strategy."

"Astonishing," says analyst Alexis Cain of the Defense Budget Project, a public interest research group. "Six years for a defense-oriented administration to get around to it." Counters a Pentagon official: "Whatever that commission comes up with, it won't have any impact until the 1990s, if then."

To be fair, from time to time the administration has attempted to enunciate something resembling a clear official strategy. In the early 1980s "horizontal escalation" became a fashionable concept. Since the 1950s, U.S. doctrine for defense of Europe has been "forward defense" — to oppose any invasion at the border and escalate "vertically" to first use of tactical nuclear weapons, if necessary.

Horizontal escalation, while not renouncing the battlefield use of nuclear weapons, suggested that aggression in one theater might be met not only by local defense but also by offensive U.S. action in other areas. "I'm not certain if they ever thought it through," says John R. Boyd, a retired Air Force colonel and long a military reform advocate. "If they mean attacking the enemy where he's weak, it's a classic good idea. But it also requires being able to damage the enemy commensurate with what he's doing to us."

The problem, say other analysts, is that commensurate areas may not even exist outside of the Soviet Union. Robert Komer, former under secretary of defense for policy, has said: "It is hard to find any feasible countervailing gains that would compensate strategically for the loss of Persian Gulf oil, Western Europe or Japan. There are only consolation prizes."...

Yet horizontal escalation, at least in the early 1980s, seems to have entailed more than simply "hitting 'em where they ain't." It had two apparent corollaries.

For the conventional defense of Europe, the Pentagon came up with "Deep Strike." Under this concept, NATO forces would absorb the first wave of a Soviet-Warsaw Pact invasion while attacking following echelons east of the inter-German and West German-Czechoslovak borders. . . .

A second corollary to horizontal escalation — some have argued, the essence of the doctrine — is a concept closely associated with the naval buildup. In event of war, officials such as Secretary Lehman have suggested, the Navy could use its carriers to attack the Soviet navy in its home ports or, at the least, before the Soviet fleets could pass the "choke points" and deploy into the open ocean.

Many analysts, among them Komer and naval expert Normal Polmar, have seen this proposal as not much more than an attempt to justify procurement of expensive carrier forces. Carriers attacking Soviet ships and ports would come under attack by Soviet shore-based, long-range naval aviation hundreds of miles before they could launch their aircraft.

Says an active-duty naval officer on the possibility of sailing carrier battle groups up to the Soviet coast and attacking their navy: "I've yet to meet a sailor who wants to make that trip."

In any event, says Cain, "You don't hear much about horizontal escalation anymore."

More recently, Weinberger has suggested a new doctrine of "competitive strategies," whereby the United States gears its programs to eliciting expensive Soviet responses. Weinberger has offered several examples of successful competitive strategies, programs in which the United States uses its technological superiority in an effort to bleed the Soviets economically.

Building advanced submarines compels costly antisubmarine programs. The B-1B and Stealth bombers require and will require major air defense expenditures for the Soviets. And of course (although the administration does not emphasize this aspect), attempting to counter the Strategic Defense Initiative could cost the Soviets enormously.

Says Boyd: "Again, I'm not sure if they've [defense officials] articulated it [competitive strategies] fully. It can make sense. But it can also be just an excuse to go out and buy the things they want to buy."

And that, suggest many analysts, may indeed be the sum and substance of the Reagan administration's strategy: Spend money. One Washington pundit, parodying standard Pentagon obfuscatory terminology, describes it as the $M^3$ approach: money, machines and manipulation. New York Times military correspondent Richard Halloran, in his book "To Arm a Nation," has described Weinberger's concept of his job as analogous to that of a college president: Get out, hustle for money and don't worry too much about what is happening on campus, since success will be measured by the size of the budget.

Or as a cliche inside Washington has it (or had it, until the cancellation of the DIVAD air defense gun program), "Cap Weinberger never met a weapon he didn't like."

Yet the criticism, after six years, begs an essential question: Given the nature of the Pentagon bureaucracy, the accumulated neglect of the 1970s and the perceived need to act quickly, could another administration or a different Pentagon under Reagan have accomplished more?

Certainly Weinberger, an attorney with no military experience save World War II Army service, has never claimed to be a strategist. Nor is any civilian secretary expected to be. Rather, the defense secretary serves as an administrator, arbitrator and advocate. And for six tumultuous years, Weinberger has presided over — and defended — an organization that employs more than 8 million uniformed and civilian personnel, manages more than 5,400 properties and installations, deals with more than 300,000 contractors in 15 million contract actions a year and literally spans the globe.

Given the immensity of the task, perhaps the real evaluation of the program must be not that it accomplished so little, but that it accomplished as much as it has.

## A Soviet View of the Buildup

### *Document 7*

Not surprisingly, the Soviet Union viewed the Reagan buildup quite differently. In this excerpt from *Whence the Threat to Peace,* a pamphlet prepared by the Soviet Ministry of Defense, the Soviets lay out their case: it is the United States that is the enemy of peace; the United States is driving the arms race; the Soviet war threat is a myth.

### 7 WHENCE THE THREAT TO PEACE
### Soviet Ministry of Defense
### 1982

In the 1970s, the relaxation of tensions in relations between states belonging to different socio political systems made the cold war yield ground. The restructuring of international relations on the principles of peaceful coexistence gained momentum. But as the world was entering the 80s, and especially after the change of leadership in the White House, a sharp about-turn occurred in the policy of the United States and a number of other NATO countries. Their ruling circles began to set their sights in international relations on force and force alone. US statesmen and military leaders openly declared that nuclear war, both global and "limited," was thinkable. Large regions of the world thousands of kilometers distant from the United States were proclaimed Washington's spheres of "vital interest".

The present US Administration and its bellicose partners in other NATO countries have set out to upset the military-strategic equilibrium shaped during the past decade between the USSR and the USA, between the Warsaw Treaty Organization and the North Atlantic bloc. To justify their line of securing military superiority over the Soviet Union and the Warsaw Treaty, the myth of a "Soviet war threat" fabricated years ago is being backed up by claims that the USA and NATO as a whole have "fallen behind" in the military field and "windows of vulnerability" have appeared in the US war machine, and the like.

High-ranking political and military members of the US Administration have joined the campaign of inventing and propagating an assortment of various far-fetched conjectures. A special place in the campaign is accorded to a Pentagon pamphlet, entitled *Soviet Military Powers.* Widely advertised by US mass media, it is clearly designed to frighten the public, above all in Western countries, with the military potential of the USSR, and convince it in the compulsive necessity of a further buildup of US and NATO military strength.

The Pentagon pamphlet would not have by itself deserved any special mention if it did not reflect the political tendencies reigning in the United States and directed to torpedoing detente, stoking up tensions in relations between states, and triggering an unbridled arms race.

Inasmuch as the ruling circles of the United States saw fit to publish tendentiously selected and deliberately distorted information about the Armed Forces of the USSR, it became necessary for the sake of objectivity to show the military potential of the other side, so that true conclusions could be drawn on the basis of comparative data.

This book, prepared by competent Soviet quarters, examines the present state and orientation of the armed forces and military-industrial potential of the United States of America, and other elements of the US war machine on which the US Administration relies in its resolve to follow a policy "from positions of strength", and to secure military superiority. In order to provide an objective picture of the strategic situation now prevailing in the world, the book examines the balance of East-West military strength, and the approach of the two sides to international detente and the problems of safeguarding and consolidating peace, and curbing the arms race. . . .

#### IV. Two Trends in World Politics

In recent years two opposite trends have stood out more and more sharply in the approach of the Soviet Union and that of the United States to the solution of international problems.

The determining line in the Soviet Union's foreign policy activities has always been and still is the struggle for peace and security of nations, for detente and curbing of the arms race. Leonid Brezhnev emphasized: "No task is more important today in the international field for our Party, our people, and indeed for all nations on our planet, than to safeguard peace."

It is only natural that the problem of maintaining peace and preventing war is given so high a priority. Man has made unprecedented progress in science, production and culture. On the other hand, however, the great powers have stockpiled weapons the use of which could result in incalculable disasters for mankind and irreparable damage to our civilization. The present situation, with a nuclear sword of Damocles hanging over the nations, is a direct consequence of the arms race which has already been going on for a long time.

The unswerving peaceful line of Soviet foreign policy was reaffirmed at the 26th CPSU Congress, which advanced a series of constructive proposals on the key issues of international life, such as limitation of strategic nuclear arms and medium-range nuclear weapons in Europe; cessation of all tests of nuclear weapons and discontinuation of their manufacture and reduction of stockpiles to the point of their complete liquidation; banning the development and manufacture of all new types of mass destruction weapons; lowering the level of military confrontation in Central Europe; confidence-building measures in the military field; reducing tensions and eliminating hot-beds of conflict over enormous territories, from Central Europe to the Far East, through the Middle East, the Persian Gulf and the Indian Ocean.

All these proposals are motivated by one consideration — that of clearing up the international climate, deepening detente and removing the threat of war. While pressing for a radical improvement in the situation and advancing concrete initiatives, the Soviet Union presents no ultimatums. Its proposals are an invitation to a dialogue and negotiations which can and must cover any possible measures promoting solution of urgent international problems.

United States policy is going the other way. Instead of seeking agreement on the basis of equality and equal security it gives priority to achieving military superiority; instead of curbing the arms race, it talks about rearmament and development of new, still more powerful, mass destruction weapons. Ignoring the realities of the world we live in, the US ruling circles are going out of their way to change in their favor the relation of forces on the world scene. President Reagan admitted in a talk with out-of-town newspaper editors on October 17, 1981, that the US is setting the pace in the arms race and said that the Russians will not be able to catch up with the US.

In actual fact, Washington is doing all it can to kill detente. It has set its sights on achieving domination over other countries and nations, imposing its will on them, exploiting their territories economically and using them for its military-strategic purposes. . . .

# STRATEGIC DEFENSE

## The Launching of the Strategic Defense Initiative

### *Document 8*

In the middle of his first term, President Reagan made a speech to the nation on his defense and arms control policies. Most of the speech reviews the administration's defense programs and describes the growing Soviet threat and the challenge to U.S. interests in Central America. At the end of the speech, the president made a surprising announcement: "I am directing a comprehensive and intensive effort to define a long-term research and development program to begin to achieve our ultimate goal of eliminating the threat posed by strategic nuclear missiles." A year later a new organization was created in the Pentagon — the Strategic Defense Initiative Organization — to develop technologies and systems to be used to defend the United States from Soviet missiles.

### 8 NATIONALLY TELEVISED SPEECH
### President Ronald Reagan
### March 23, 1983

Thus far tonight I have shared with you my thoughts on the problems of national security we must face together. My predecessors in the Oval Office have appeared before you on other occasions to describe the threat posed by Soviet power and have proposed steps to address that threat. But since the advent of nuclear weapons, those steps have been directed toward deterrence of aggression through the promise of retaliation — the notion that no rational nation would launch an attack that would inevitably result in unacceptable losses to themselves. This approach to stability through offensive threat has worked. We and our allies have succeeded in preventing nuclear war for three decades. In recent months, however, my advisers, including in particular the Joint Chiefs of Staff, have underscored the bleakness of the future before us.

Over the course of these discussions, I have become more and more deeply convinced that the human spirit must be capable of rising above dealing with other nations and human beings by threatening their existence. Feeling this way, I believe we must thoroughly examine every opportunity for reducing tensions and for introducing greater stability into the strategic calculus on both sides. One of the most important contributions we can make is, of course, to lower the level of all arms, and particularly nuclear arms. We are engaged right now in several negotiations with the Soviet Union to bring about a mutual reduction of weapons. I will report to you a week from tomorrow my thoughts on that score. But let me just say I am totally committed to this course.

If the Soviet Union will join with us in our effort to achieve major arms reduction we will have succeeded in stabilizing the nuclear balance. Nevertheless it will still be necessary to rely on the specter of retaliation — on mutual threat, and that is a sad commentary on the human condition.

Would it not be better to save lives than to avenge them? Are we not capable of demonstrating our peaceful intentions by applying all our abilities and our ingenuity to achieving a truly lasting stability? I think we are — indeed, we must!

After careful consultation with my advisers, including the Joint Chiefs of Staff, I believe there is a way. Let me share with you a vision of the future which offers hope. It is that we embark on a program to counter the awesome Soviet missile threat with measures that are defensive. Let us turn to the very strengths in technology that spawned our great industrial base and that have given us the quality of life we enjoy today.

Up until now we have increasingly based our strategy of deterrence upon the threat of retaliation. But what if free people could live secure in the knowledge that their security did not rest upon the threat of instant U.S. retaliation to deter a Soviet attack; that we could intercept and destroy strategic ballistic missiles before they reached our own soil or that of our allies?

I know this is a formidable technical task, one that may not be accomplished before the end of this century. Yet, current technology has attained a level of sophistication where it is reasonable for us to begin this effort. It will take years, probably decades, of effort on many fronts. There will be failures and setbacks just as there will be successes and breakthroughs. And as we proceed we must remain constant in preserving the nuclear deterrent and maintaining a solid capability for flexible response. But is it not worth every investment necessary to free the world from the threat of nuclear war? We know it is!

In the meantime, we will continue to pursue real reductions in nuclear arms, negotiating from a position of strength that can be insured only by modernizing our strategic forces. At the same time, we must take steps to reduce the risk of a conventional military conflict escalating to nuclear war by improving our nonnuclear capabilities. America does possess — now — the technologies to attain very significant improvements in the effectiveness of our conventional, nonnuclear forces. Proceeding boldly with these new technologies, we can significantly reduce any incentive that the Soviet Union may have to threaten attack against the United States or its allies.

As we pursue our goal of defensive technologies, we recognize that our allies rely upon our strategic offensive power to deter attacks against them. Their vital interests and ours are inextricably linked — their safety and ours are one. And no change in technology can or will alter that reality. We must and shall continue to honor our commitments.

I clearly recognize that defensive systems have limitations and raise certain problems and ambiguities. If paired with offensive systems, they can be viewed as fostering an aggressive policy and no one wants that.

But with these considerations firmly in mind, I call upon the scientific community who gave us nuclear weapons to turn their great talents to the cause of mankind and world peace: to give us the means of rendering these nuclear weapons impotent and obsolete.

Tonight, consistent with our obligations under the ABM Treaty and recognizing the need for close consultation with our allies, I am taking an important first step. I am directing a comprehensive and intensive effort to define a long-term research and development program to begin to achieve our ultimate goal of eliminating the threat posed by strategic nuclear missiles. This could pave the way for arms control measures to eliminate the weapons themselves. We seek neither military superiority nor political advantage. Our only purpose — one all people share — is to search for ways to reduce the danger of nuclear war.

My fellow Americans, tonight we are launching an effort which holds the purpose of changing the course of human history. There will be risks, and results take time. But with your support, I believe we can do it.

## The Case for Strategic Defense

### *Documents 9, 10, and 11*

The president's speech of March 23, 1983, soon led to a major national debate over SDI, or "Star Wars," as it was often called in the press. The following articles outline some of the key arguments in favor of the president's program. In document 9, Gerald Yonas, a physicist who served as the chief scientist and acting deputy director of the SDI Organization, describes the four tiers or layers of an SDI system: boost phase (attacking an intercontinental ballistic missile soon after it is launched); postboost phase (attacking the ICBM's "bus" that carries its warheads); midcourse (attacking warheads as they travel through space); and reentry (attacking the warheads as they reenter the atmosphere on their way toward U.S. targets). Yonas argues that the technical challenges of SDI can be overcome, though many problems face the program, and he notes that the president requested $26 billion for the first five years of SDI. He concludes that SDI is feasible and can reduce the risks of war. Document 10, an article by George Keyworth, who served as the presidential science adviser during Reagan's first term, argues strongly that SDI will open the way to significant arms control. In document 11, Paul Nitze, the special adviser to the president and the secretary of state on arms control matters, warns that the Soviets already have a program similar to SDI.

## 9 CAN STAR WARS MAKE US SAFE? . . . YES
### Gerald Yonas

In his widely publicized speech of March 23, 1983, President Reagan launched "an effort which holds the promise of changing the course of human history." Having posed the question, "Would it not be better to save lives than to avenge them?" he called upon the scientific and technical community to establish a comprehensive effort to define a research program aimed at eventually eliminating the threat posed by nuclear-armed ballistic missiles.

The President caught many people by surprise, and we find even now, some two years later, that many people still think he called for development or deployment or even an upgrading of a defensive system that they mistakenly think already exists. The fact is that he called for a research program, and we have no deployed system with which to respond to a ballistic-missile attack. The surprise to most people is that we have intentionally placed ourselves in a situation where our only responses to an attack are to either retaliate or surrender, but not protect ourselves. . . .

In contrast to the obvious Soviet commitment to defense, the United States has been pursuing an inadequately supported effort in ballistic-missile-defense (BMD) research. Although we have had an ongoing effort since we signed the treaty, the program has suffered from a lack of definition, technical strategy and goals and could be characterized as consisting of starts and stops that seem to cancel themselves. Despite rather substantial expenditures, the full potential of our ballistic-missile-defense research has not been realized. In addition, our research and development has advanced considerably, in many cases totally independently of the BMD effort, but the nation has not been putting this new capability into acquiring the maximum return on its BMD investments. . . .

Our hopes and expectations that the ABM treaty would lead to strategic arms limitation had been shattered by the realization of the inexorable buildup in Soviet forces. At the same time, we were faced with the fact that, in contrast to our neglect of defense, the Soviets were spending as much on strategic defense as on strategic offense. The President's call to the technical community was the first sign that we might change our course if the community could provide the convincing factual basis to support a decision to move in a new direction.

The next step occurred in April 1983, when the President signed a directive mandating two intensive studies that would develop a plan of research fully consistent with the 1972 ABM treaty and explore policy strategies related to these technologies. The purpose of the technology program was to explore a wide range of concepts and technologies that hold potential for a reliable and effective BMD. The Defensive Technology Study Team (DTST), headed by former NASA Administrator Dr. James Fletcher, produced its report in the fall of 1983 after an intensive review of past work and the full range of proposals for future research. The team consisted of over 50 experts drawn from industry, government, universities and national laboratories. The team represented a wide spectrum of opinion on BMD and fully considered not only the defense approaches but also myriad possible countermeasures to defeat the defense. There was special emphasis on the all-important issue of estimating the cost of various approaches and comparisons with possible costs of countermeasures.

The team agreed from the start that there would not be a "perfect" defense against a determined adversary, but they were instead striving to identify options that would be sufficiently effective and affordable to make a first strike of no military significance (enhance crisis stability) and to so devalue any offensive response (support arms-race stability) to motivate a move toward substantial reductions in armaments.

The DTST chose to adopt a high-payoff, long-range emphasis rather than to identify near-term capabilities that might be more easily attained but might in turn be more easily countered. The research program would emphasize the limits of technologies, not just for the defense but also for the offensive countermeasures. The team decided that the decision process would have to start with a broad range of technologies and approaches, which would then be winnowed down to a concentrated emphasis on a more manageable set, following such criteria as the ability to stay ahead of responses at an affordable cost.

A resolute opponent would attempt to defeat a defense system with countermeasures that might range all the way from directly attacking the defense to massive proliferation of existing weapons. The key was to identify technology options that could advance faster and at a lower cost than the offensive responses. The DTST was fundamentally optimistic about the technologies in the light of the spectacular advances that had taken place over the past two decades in the technologies of sensors, computing hardware and software, optics, beam weapons and propulsion. The team could not foresee fundamental limits in many areas, and in view of the full range of options, there was a general belief that even if certain approaches were eliminated, the overall defense requirements could be met. . . .

The program designed by the DTST is a long-term effort in four phases. The first phase, lasting until the early 1990s, will consist of research. At that time, decisions could be made on whether to begin engineering development of specific weapons. The second phase would focus on systems development, when prototypes of actual defense components would be designed, built and tested, assuming a decision is made to go ahead with this defense. The third phase would be a transition period, with incremental, sequential deployment of defenses, presumably by both the United States and the Soviet Union. At this stage, significant reductions in offensive missile forces could be negotiated. The final phase would be reached when defense deployments are completed and offensive missile forces reach their negotiated low point.

To permit a decision by the early 1990s on whether to advance to the next phase, the Administration requested $1.77 billion for the SDI in fiscal year 1985, up from $0.9 billion in 1984. Ironically, this 1985 request was handed a 20 percent cut by Congress just as the program was getting off the ground in the fall of 1984; thus it began at a level lower than that projected even before the President's speech. The total projected budget for the first five years of the SDI is $26 billion, and the request for fiscal 1986 is $3.7 billion. No attempt was made by the Technology Study Team to estimate the costs for the second phase of the program, but certainly that estimate would play an important role in the decision on whether or not to proceed.

Where might we hope to be in the early 1990s? The tasks faced by any ballistic-missile defense are formidable. To understand the defense concepts and technologies that are being investigated, picture the flight of an intercontinental ballistic missile as passing through four phases — boost, post-boost, mid-course and terminal — each offering different opportunities and challenges to a defense system. A highly effective defense against a massive missile attack would require multiple tiers of defense, countering the offense at each phase until the fraction of warheads remaining was too small to be of military utility.

## The Bright Booster

Boost phase is the ideal time to hit a missile. Here the advantage to the defense is that the bright flame from the booster motors can be easily detected by infrared sensors. It provides an aim point for defense weapons to destroy a booster before any of the independently targeted warheads and decoys are released. The challenge is the short time of less than three minutes, which could become even more stressing if the offense expands its missile force or rebuilds its force with radically different features. The long-term approaches to boost-phase intercept involve extremely bright beam weapons that can operate down into the atmosphere and thus respond to even the most advanced threats.

During the post-boost phase, the defense still has an advantage if it can intercept the vehicle, or "bus," before it releases all of the warheads and decoys. The challenge is that the bus's maneuvering engines are much smaller and more difficult to detect than the plume of the huge booster. Both kinetic-energy and beam weapons can be used to attack, and the combination limits effective responses.

In mid-course, the advantage to the defense is the relatively long period when the warheads and decoys can be located and destroyed by space-based and ground-based interceptors far away from such targets as cities or industrial cites. The challenge is that warheads and effective decoys would look more or less alike to sensors. The sheer number of warheads and decoys could swamp the sensors and interceptors unless the defense can discriminate between them. Here again we think that a combination of beam weapons to assist in discrimination, together with kinetic-energy interceptors, would make mid-course an important layer at which to thwart the attack further.

On reentry, the decoys would be separated from the heavier reentry vehicles or burn up, thereby solving the discrimination problem. There is, however, little time to carry out the interception of the warheads the ballistic-missile defense system has missed in the previous phases before they damage or destroy their targets. Moreover, warheads can be "salvage fuzed" to detonate if struck in the upper atmosphere, aggravating the already difficult job of the terminal sensors. The new technologies here involve the combination of a mobile airborne adjunct, ground-based radar and high-performance nonnuclear homing interceptors.

Many of these boost-phase and reentry-phase technologies are appliable to the shorter range ballistic missiles that pose a threat to our allies as well as to ourselves from submarines off coasts around the world. Despite the much shorter midcourse phase, defense is made simpler by the inability of the offense to field large numbers of decoys in the time available.

Clearly, our present technological capabilities are far from what is needed for a robust defense against plausible Soviet threats and countermeasures in the future. Some of these shortcomings the study teams regarded as critical; unless they could be overcome, there could be no certainty that a robust defense could be achieved. These vital areas include: midcourse discrimination; low-cost interception and destruction, using directed-energy and kinetic-energy weapons in the boost phase; battle-management hardware and software; and survivability of predeployed space assets in the face of direct attack by antisatellite weapons.

By no means does this short list of critical challenges exhaust the range of matters that must and will be addressed in the research program. A whole set of support programs, for instance, must be pursued: determination of generic means for hardening boosters and the lethal effects of various weapons against those means (because we are not likely to get specific engineering design data on Soviet boosters); development of multimegawatt, space-based electrical power supplies, nuclear and non-nuclear, for weapons, sensors and computers; and development of low-cost, heavy-lift space launchers capable of carrying perhaps 100 tons or more to orbit, rather than the space shuttle's current capability of 20 to 30 tons, at one-tenth the cost.

### Come One, Come All

As the research program evolves, new discoveries are likely to be made that may radically change the emphasis of the defense program. It is thus vital to stimulate, encourage and fully investigate innovative approaches as early as possible in the program. These new ideas may arise from totally new sectors of the scientific and technical community, sectors that may not even be aware at the moment of the technical challenges we face. To stimulate the broadest involvement of technical talent from government, industry and universities, the departments of Defense and Energy are providing specially earmarked funds to encourage the investigation of radically different concepts that offer enhanced capabilities, although bearing the admittedly higher risks associated with unexplored approaches. In addition, the Secretary of Defense has given our allies an opportunity to participate in the research, and active discussions to define the appropriate mechanisms for their involvement are under way.

Since our discoveries might aid the offensive countermeasures as well, they could force us to eliminate particular defensive approaches along the way. We need to eliminate all infeasible or impractical defenses as soon as possible in order to focus our efforts. It is therefore essential to approach the overall program at all times with a healthy skepticism, as well as with the creativity associated with the exploration of a new field. With the current pace of technological advancement, and the strong motivation provided by the hope of a more secure and stable future, we believe we are well on our way.

## 10 THE CASE FOR STRATEGIC DEFENSE

## George A. Keyworth III

A number of fundamental issues continue to block the path to meaningful arms control. One is preemptive capability, which the Soviets are determined to retain. And because preemptive capability has now become more a matter of technical quality of missiles (that is, their accuracy and payload flexibility) than of sheer numbers, it is not a property one can necessarily control by fiat.

Another issue is trust. Because the Soviets do not understand us, they do not trust us any more than we trust them. The Soviets suffered staggering losses following the German sneak offensive in June 1941. They have reserved a special place in their preparations for the "surprise" ever since.

In addition, as John Collins says, the Politburo assigns a low priority to sophisticated concepts of limited nuclear war. The Soviets take few risks, and they prefer to employ mass wherever possible to reduce that risk. In Russian methodology, attempts to reduce arms under current circumstances not only raise the risk to them, but compromise their prospects for prompt and conclusive victory as well.

VI

How, then, do we agree on any arms control measures that *matter*? As Admiral Noel Gayler recently commented on Braden and Buchanan's *Cross-Fire* program, today's arsenals are such that one side's strategic advantage of a thousand weapons or so is really lost in the noise. Going further, Carl Sagan postulates that the detonation of just a few hundred weapons would, in his opinion, trigger nuclear winter. Admittedly, Sagan's thesis is undergoing heavy scrutiny and criticism. Both his phenomenology and threshold levels, as well as the winter, or perhaps summer, effect have come under question. But in the end the precise numbers really are not the issue. It is clear that a large portion of the earth's population — perhaps a quarter billion people or considerably more — could die as the result of a global thermonuclear war involving even a fraction of present-day arsenals. . . .

Strategic defenses of the type we can reasonably project — even in their early modes — can be vital catalysts for arms control. Critics are quick to point out that if any defense system is not perfect, some weapons will unquestionably leak through. In fact, early and intermediate defenses will undoubtedly be imperfect, and any nuclear weapon that makes it through to its target will be devastating. While hardened military assets can be very successfully defended by these transition systems, civilian population centers will still be hostage to a determined adversary. Critics cite this as a major failing. In fact, it is crucial to stability during those transition years because as long as there is some leakage in those transition defense technologies, there remains a retaliatory deterrent against first strike.

We will have effectively turned the clock back 20 years. Some will accuse us of returning to an era when weapons were safe but people were not. Perhaps so. But we will once again have a common ground for negotiating real weapons reductions. After all, realistic, survivable, retaliatory arsenals do not have to be enormous, not nearly as large as the arsenals we now require to survive preemptive strikes (or in the Soviet case, to launch them). With the preemptive option clouded, or even removed, we would have an opportunity to negotiate major arms reductions that would still leave each side with a strong retaliatory deterrent.

At that point we would have accomplished two things, two goals that have eluded us for 20 years. We would have reduced both nations' perceptions that the other could launch a successful disarming first strike, and we would have drastically reduced the size of the arsenals.

Achieving these goals could introduce a new transition period during which conventional military technologies and forces would be rebuilt. This will be the price we pay for moving out from under the nuclear umbrella. At the same time, second- and third-generation defensive technologies would become available. This could further reduce the effectiveness of strategic nuclear weapons to the point that civilian targets could become truly viable candidates for defense.

These options will probably become available when the strategic nuclear forces we must build today to maintain our near-term deterrence reach the limits of their operational lifetimes. We then have a new option: rather than replace them, let each side retain only token nuclear forces for their sole remaining purpose — restricted retaliation. . . .

One might conclude that there is absolutely no prospect for the superpowers to negotiate any treaty that would reduce their nuclear arsenals below the uncertain threshold that could cause almost certain annihilation. This reality drives many longtime arms control proponents to an almost "schizophrenic frenzy," in Gray's words. They loudly endorse nuclear disarmament, but then explain that it is necessary to retain massive retaliatory deterrence.

Strategic defense provides the option to break this cycle. Although we cannot disinvent nuclear weapons, and although nations will continue to distrust one another, heavily defended countries could nonetheless realistically enter into treaties to reduce nuclear forces to near zero. The scale of cheating necessary to provide an arsenal capable of successfully engaging several layers of active defenses would be so large as to be impractical within the context of normal intelligence-gathering capabilities.

Strategic defense therefore provides an option for a world effectively disarmed of nuclear weapons, yet still retaining national sovereignty and security. In fact, deployment of strategic defense is the only way in which the superpowers will be able to achieve these very deep arms reductions. It now becomes extremely important to recognize that the ballistic missile and air defenses that might look less than 100 percent perfect in the context of an offensive exchange involving tens of thousands of warheads could be expected to perform magnificently against an attack by only tens, or at the most hundreds, of weapons.

## 11 SDI: THE SOVIET PROGRAM
## Paul H. Nitze
## June 28, 1985

Soviet commentary on the U.S. Strategic Defense Initiative (SDI) research program has been strongly negative. The Soviets have accused us of expanding the arms race into a new area by initiating "the militarization of space." In Geneva, they have demanded a ban on research, development, testing, and deployment of what they call "space-strike arms" and have conditioned progress in the negotiations on offensive nuclear force reductions on prior U.S. acceptance of this ban.

One might conclude from this Soviet commentary that the Soviet Union has no program comparable to our SDI. Such a conclusion would be far from correct.

### Soviet Strategic Defense Efforts

Soviet military doctrine stresses that offensive and defensive forces must interact closely to achieve Soviet aims in any conflict. Accordingly, the Soviets are heavily involved in strategic defense, with programs that go far beyond research. In fact, over the last two decades the Soviet Union has spent roughly as much on strategic defense as it has on its massive offensive nuclear forces. As part of this huge effort, the Soviets have deployed around Moscow the world's only operational antiballistic missile (ABM) system, a system they are currently upgrading with a projected completion date of about 1987. They also have an indepth national air defense force, a vast political leadership survival program, and nationwide civil defense forces and programs.

Further, they have been conducting a number of activities that are inconsistent with and tend to undermine the ABM Treaty. For example, their deployment of a large phased-array ballistic missile tracking radar near Krasnoyarsk in Siberia constitutes a violation of the treaty. We are concerned that, in the aggregate, Soviet ABM-related activities could provide them the basis for deployment of an ABM defense of their national territory, which would also violate the treaty.

Soviet strategic defense programs are not restricted to the more traditional approaches. The Soviets have also been pursuing, since the 1960s, research into advanced technologies for strategic defense. These technologies include high-energy lasers, particle-beam weapons, radio frequency weapons, and kinetic energy weapons. These are the same types of technologies being researched in the U.S. SDI program. Moreover, during this same period, the Soviets have had an active and expanding military space program.

The Soviet version of SDI has been overlooked in the recent public debate. Indeed, taking advantage of the closed nature of Soviet society, Soviet strategic defense efforts have proceeded completely free from debates of the sort that are occurring now in the West over the utility and implications of our program. . . .

### The Soviet Military Space Program

In addition to their huge and comprehensive program of research into advanced strategic defense technologies, the Soviets have the world's most active military space program. This program dominates the Soviet Union's overall space effort. For example, in 1984 the Soviets conducted about 100 space launches. Of these, some 80% were purely military in nature, with much of the remainder serving both military and civil functions. By way of comparison, the total number of U.S. space launches in 1984 was about 20. . . .

### Soviet Disingenuousness

Considering all of the foregoing, it becomes apparent just how preposterous Soviet criticisms of the U.S. SDI program are. The United States is not expanding the military competition into new areas; the Soviets have been researching the same technologies for two decades. Likewise, the United States is not initiating "the militarization of space"; space has been militarized for many years, primarily by Soviet systems and programs. . . .

### Soviet Motives

Why are the Soviets conducting this propaganda campaign? Clearly, they see the potential applications for advanced defensive technologies; otherwise they would not be investing so much effort and so many resources in this area. It is not unreasonable to conclude that they would like to continue to be the only ones pressing forward in this field. At a minimum, they want to keep the United States from outstripping them in such technologies.

In this vein, the Soviet propaganda line against SDI is as predictable as it is hypocritical. The Soviets hope to foster a situation in which we would unilaterally restrain our research effort, even though it is fully consistent with existing treaties. This would leave them with a virtual monopoly in advanced strategic defense research; they see this as the most desirable outcome.

Such a virtual monopoly could be most dangerous for the West. Both sides have recognized for many years that offense and defense are vitally related to each other, that it is the balance between the offense-defense mixes of the sides that is essential to keeping the peace. Unilateral restraint by the United States in the defense area would jeopardize this balance and could, therefore, potentially undermine our deterrent ability.

If the United States proves unwilling to restrain itself unilaterally, the Soviets are prepared to impose an agreed ban on research "designed to create space-strike arms." At worst, a mutually observed ban would leave them where they are today, unthreatened by potential U.S. technological advances and maintaining the only operational ABM and ASAT systems. The Soviets are already positioning themselves, however, to avoid having such a ban apply equally to the research of both sides. They currently deny that any of their efforts fall within their definition of research "designed to create space-strike arms," while asserting that all of the U.S. SDI program fits within that definition. Moreover, even were a research ban to be applied equally to the sides, given its inherent unverifiability and the closed nature of the Soviet Union — and particularly its scientific community compared to ours — the Soviets very well might be able unilaterally to continue their research on a clandestine basis.

### Conclusion

We can expect the Soviets to continue to protest strongly and publicly about SDI and alleged U.S. designs to "militarize space," all the while denying that they are conducting similar programs. We must recognize this propaganda for what it is — the key element of an overall strategy to divide the United States from its allies and elicit from us unilateral concessions. By making clear to the Soviets that we have the political will to maintain the necessary military capabilities effectively to deter them — that is, that their propaganda campaign will not succeed in causing us to exercise unilateral restraint — we can establish the necessary conditions for the Soviets to consider a more forthcoming approach to the negotiations in Geneva. In that event, the United States will be prepared, as it is now, for a serious discussion of how — should new defensive technologies prove feasible — our two sides could move jointly to a more stable strategic relationship, building upon the research efforts of both.

## The Case Against SDI

### *Documents 12 and 13*

In document 12, Hans Bethe, a Nobel prize–winning physicist, argues that SDI is not feasible. Bethe notes that an effective shield against nuclear missiles would have to work perfectly. He says that the Soviets could use countermeasures, such as attacking SDI satellites, that would be relatively easy. He also says that it would be cheaper for the Soviets to deploy more nuclear weapons than it would be for the United States to deploy SDI. Bethe concludes by calling for more research on defensive technologies but no deployment until technical problems have been resolved. In document 13, physicists Sidney Drell and Wolfgang Panofsky point out that SDI would do nothing about nuclear-armed bombers or cruise missiles. They also argue that SDI would make arms control more difficult, if not impossible. The more likely outcome, they say, is a new arms race. They also warn that SDI would make the nuclear balance more dangerous. Finally, they say that although Soviet efforts in the area of strategic defense are significant, they lag behind those of the United States in key areas. Like Bethe, Drell and Panofsky favor research on defensive systems but believe that the massive SDI program is a mistake.

## 12 CAN STAR WARS MAKE US SAFE? . . . NO
## Hans A. Bethe

The Strategic Defense Initiative (SDI) is intended to provide a comprehensive defensive shield for the United States and its allies against a nuclear attack; it is supposed to "render nuclear weapons impotent and obsolete." At first glance, this certainly appears to be desirable goal.

Because of the immense destructive power of nuclear weapons when used against people and cities, and because of the very large number of nuclear weapons the United States and the Soviet Union now have, the degree of perfection required of such a defensive shield is truly staggering. The shield must be capable of intercepting and destroying thousands of ICBMs, SLBMs, cruise missiles and bombers within minutes or even seconds. The intercepts have to be made at sufficient range and altitude to prevent damage from "salvage fuzing" — a term referring to the capability of an ICBM to "sense" when it is being attacked and, upon recognition, being able to detonate its own nuclear explosive. Thus, if such an ICBM is attacked 3 to 12 miles above a city, its nuclear explosion will still do major damage. The number of attacking weapons can be in the range of 10,000; therefore a failure rate of even one in 1,000 on the part of the defense permits a huge amount of damage. And the defense must be able to accomplish all of this in the face of an imposing array of countermeasures available to the attacker. . . .

If someday a near-perfect defense were simultaneously achieved by both sides, then there might be a balance based on defense — one that would be as, or even more, stable than the one we have now based on mutual deterrence. But the transition from our current situation, in which offense dominates, to one in which defense dominates must of necessity pass through a very long phase in which the defense is only partially effective. This transition period would be a time of great strategic instability. A partial defense is likely to be far more effective against a small attack than it is against a large one. In a crisis situation there is therefore a premium in shooting first. If you shoot first, and destroy a reasonable fraction of your opponent's retaliatory force, perhaps your partial defense can cope with the remainder. But if he shoots first, then your remaining forces may not be strong enough to overcome his partial defense; you are destroyed and he survives. In a situation of great tension, there would be immense pressure on each side to shoot first, because of the fear that the other would. In a world without a defense, and with an invulnerable deterrent, such as we have now, no such pressure exists; each side can afford to wait the crisis out. . . .

### Particle Beams at War

Particle beams destroy the ICBM booster by interfering with the electronics in the missile-guidance system. Because the Earth's magnetic field bends charged particles, particle-beam weapons are usually assumed to use beams of neutral atoms in order to be accurately aimed. . . .

All of the boost-phase interception techniques we have described are vulnerable to countermeasures. They require a space-based platform that can be attacked and is far more vulnerable than the ICBM booster itself. It is therefore generally recognized that any space platform will have to defend itself, either with its own weapon or, more likely, with a separate defensive system optimized for that purpose. To avoid the problems of defending the space platform, it is sometimes suggested that a "pop up" scheme be utilized instead, in which the defensive system is launched, probably from a submarine located near the Soviet Union, only after an ICBM attack has begun. The time and weight constraints on such a scheme are, however, extremely severe. Essentially only the X-ray laser, being of low weight, may qualify.

Many of the boost-phase schemes are only effective when the ICBM booster is above the atmosphere. This makes it possible for a potential enemy to adopt a highly effective countermeasure, namely to design boosters that accomplish the boost in a very short time. The Fletcher Committee, appointed by President Reagan to investigate the technical problems of implementing SDI, received a conceptual design of a booster that would attain its full speed in 50 seconds (instead of three to five minutes for present ICBMs) and at a low altitude, about 50 miles. Such a booster would be safe from attack by X-ray lasers, particle beams or homing vehicles. Optical lasers could still attack it, but since the time available for attack would be much shorter, the number of laser space platforms would have to be greatly increased.

Shortening the boost phase would be especially effective against a pop-up scheme, because the popped-up device would not have time to attain sufficient altitude to get a clear, above-the-horizon line of fire to the booster before the booster was burned out. The fast-burn feature is expected to cost only a moderate amount in payload, perhaps 20 percent. That such boosters can be built was demonstrated by Martin Marietta Aerospace in the early 1970s when it built the Sprint missile as part of the U.S. Safeguard hard-point defense system (which was later abandoned as too expensive). The Soviet antiballistic-missile ring around Moscow, the Galosh, is reported to have an even shorter boost phase.

Hardening of ICBM boosters is also possible, again at modest weight penalties, against both optical and X-ray lasers.

### Ultimate Countermeasure

Finally, of course, the ultimate counter-measure consists of building more ICBMs. Unless the incremental cost to the defense of killing an extra ICBM is less than the incremental cost to the offense of building one extra ICBM, the defense loses to proliferation. It is as yet not known, even vaguely, what the defensive schemes that have been proposed would cost. Certainly they are very expensive; estimates by, among others, former Secretaries of Defense Harold Brown and James Schlesinger have ranged up to a trillion dollars. ICBMs, on the other hand, can be built relatively cheaply, especially if they are designed with cost in mind and launched from silos that are not hardened.

Defense during mid-course is somewhat different from defense during boost phase. Mid-course is the phase above the atmosphere, so all of the defensive weapons previously described could, in principle, be relevant. Furthermore, the time and range constraints on the defense are much less stringent. The main problems are the selection of reentry vehicles from decoys and the fact that reentry vehicles are harder to destroy than boosters.

Decoys can be made very effective. For example, at almost no cost in weight, each reentry vehicle can be encased in a balloon, and hundreds of identical balloons without reentry vehicles can be dispensed, too, resulting in a vast number of indistinguishable targets that the defense must cope with. In addition, everything can be enclosed in a cloud of reflecting chaff, depriving the defense of the ability to see individual targets.

Either the defense must shoot at everything, which is difficult with a limited supply of ammunition, or some "active" means of discrimination must be employed. This could entail setting off a nuclear explosion near the targets, sweeping away empty balloons or disturbing each object with a laser and observing how it responds. Again, it will be incremental cost that matters: Can the offense put up more objects more cheaply than the defense can deal with them? . . .

All these difficulties of designing effective defensive weapons pale in comparison with the integration of the defense into a complete system. The battle-management station would have to keep track of some 100,000 objects in mid-course, preferably "from birth to death." It has to assign targets (boosters, warheads, decoys) to individual defensive weapons. And a battle station must assess whether a given target has been destroyed and, if not, "hand it over" from one defensive weapon to the next along the flight path. The computer required for this would be enormously more sophisticated than any yet designed. If it were placed in orbit, it would be susceptible to direct attack, while if it were on the ground, its data link with the enormous establishment of defensive weapons in space could be cut. Furthermore, this entire system could never be tested under circumstances that were remotely realistic.

### Unattainable Goal

Our conclusion from all of this is unequivocal: Even if the concepts now under discussion can be turned into operational devices, they will not be able to overwhelm the countermeasures available to the offense, and they will not, therefore, provide a near-perfect defense. And since a partial defense is more dangerous than no defense at all, we believe that the SDI is a program with a goal that is not attainable unless and until there are technical breakthroughs that have not yet been conceived of. Research on the relevant technologies will, of course, continue even if the SDI is abandoned. If, in the future, this research leads to the possibility of a really viable defense, that will be time enough to decide whether or not we want to replace mutual deterrence by strategic defense. In the meantime, mutual deterrence is all we have and all we can have.

## 13 THE CASE AGAINST STRATEGIC DEFENSE Sidney D. Drell and Wolfgang K. H. Panofsky

### Making Nuclear Weapons Obsolete

A defense meeting the president's vision would require near perfection in performance. If only 1 percent of the approximately 8,000 nuclear strategic warheads in the current Soviet force penetrated a defensive shield and landed on urban targets in the United States, it would cause one of the greatest disasters in recorded history.

To attain such a level of protection, *all* means of delivery of such weapons to the United States must be interdicted with near 100 percent efficiency. This would entail not only defenses against intercontinental and submarine-launched ballistic missiles, but also against strategic aircraft and cruise missiles from air, land, or sea. Even the introduction of "suitcase bombs" would have to be prevented. Yet the Strategic Defense Initiative specifically deals with only the ballistic missile threat.

There is general consensus that U.S. air defenses, largely ignored in recent years, are incapable of dealing with any massive attack from the Soviet strategic air force.

This is true even though the Soviet air force is currently much less capable than the U.S. strategic bomber force, which is now being outfitted with long-range, nuclear-tipped cruise missiles. U.S. air defenses were downgraded in the 1960s when it became clear not only that modernization and maintenance of an effective air defense would be vastly expensive and of dubious technical success, but also that expansion of these air defenses would be a futile gesture against the delivery systems for nuclear weapons then evolving — the intercontinental and submarine-launched ballistic missiles.

By contrast, Soviet air defenses are much more extensive. Several rings of air defenses are emplaced around Moscow, and extensive networks of surface-to-air missiles are deployed throughout the Soviet Union. Soviet air defenses have gone through a number of evolutionary stages, with the new SA-12 being the most capable system. Nonetheless, the U.S. Air Force continues to believe that its manned bombers, the modernized B-52s, would be able to penetrate Soviet air defenses using such diverse penetration tactics as electronic countermeasures and a precursor ballistic missile attack to destroy Soviet surface-to-air missiles prior to the air attack. In addition, cruise missiles can be delivered in the "stand-off" mode, that is, launched from aircraft outside the range of Soviet surface-to-air missiles and beyond the range of most Soviet fighters, a tactic that appears certain to extend the bomber threat against the Soviet Union for the foreseeable future. Moreover, the "stealth" technology being pursued in the United States, which involves measures to reduce the radar cross section of penetrating bombers and of cruise missiles, makes the future air defense task exceedingly, if not prohibitively, difficult.

Conversely, it is indeed hard to imagine that, starting from the minimal system deployed to date, the United States could develop an effective air defense against an opponent determined to counter it. Nor has the administration proposed that such a program be initiated. Yet nuclear weapons could hardly be made "obsolete" unless the air strike "window of vulnerability" is closed.

Potential Soviet cruise missiles pose an even greater threat to the United States. Following the U.S. lead, the Soviets are now acquiring long-range cruise missile technology. During the coming decades we can anticipate that cruise missiles will be deployed on aircraft, on land, and on ships and submarines, unless, of course, such deployments are ruled out by arms control treaties. The technology for defense against cruise missiles is similar in principle to that used against aircraft. However, cruise missiles have smaller radar cross sections and can follow terrain at lower altitudes, which makes them much more difficult to detect and then to destroy. In addition, there is a geographical asymmetry between the United States and the Soviet Union that heightens the danger to the United States: a much larger share of our society is built up near our coastline, within easier range of cruise missiles launched from enemy submarines and aircraft. Finally, the introduction of nuclear explosives into the United States by clandestine transport cannot be prevented by technical means, as has been demonstrated by numerous studies. Although major powers, in particular the Soviet Union, are unlikely to adopt such a tactic, it remains a potential terrorist threat. . . .

## Keeping Pace with Soviet Technology

It has frequently been suggested that the United States should place greater emphasis on ballistic missile defense because the Soviets are undertaking an active program in this area. Yet if the United States concluded that the Soviet effort gave them a significant military edge or threatened strategic stability or U.S. security, the logical U.S. response should be to counter the Soviet threat, not to emulate it. Historically, the Soviet Union has dedicated a much larger fraction of its strategic military effort to defensive programs — motivated in part by the Russian tradition of "protecting the homeland." Yet there is little, if any, disagreement among military analysts that neither the Soviet's extensive air defense nor the Moscow missile defense offers effective protection against U.S. retaliatory forces.

The Soviets are modernizing, within the bounds imposed by the ABM Treaty, the missile defense around Moscow. Specifically, they are replacing the exoatmospheric interceptors deployed since 1970 with a combination of higher performance endoatmospheric and exoatmospheric missiles. In this respect, the Moscow system is acquiring a capability similar to the old U.S. Sentinel and Safeguard systems. One cannot, of course, dismiss the possibility that the new Moscow deployment might form the base of a future nationwide defense. The Soviets have developed modular tracking and missile guidance radars. Coupled with the Moscow system interceptors, these might result in a deployable nationwide defense system. There is no persuasive evidence, however, that the Soviets are in fact preparing for a nationwide deployment, which would constitute a "breakout" from the ABM Treaty. In any event, it would take many years before such a system could reach a level of deployment having potential for significant military effectiveness.

The Soviets have constructed large phased-array radars for early warning at three perimeter locations and have recently closed the remaining gap within this early warning coverage by a further radar of similar design at Krasnoyarsk in Siberia. This radar has probably been under construction since before 1980, but is not yet operating. It has drawn specific attention and raised serious concern because its location — away from Soviet borders, in contrast to the other early warning radars —

constitutes a likely violation of the ABM Treaty. The Soviets state that this radar is designed for space tracking rather than early warning, but this is difficult to reconcile with its characteristics. Be this as it may, the military significance of this radar is minor, although its political significance is important if it does indeed constitute a violation of the treaty.

The Soviet Union has also been pursuing significant research and technology programs for ballistic missile defense, including research on the use of directed-energy weapons for this purpose. Although this Soviet effort has been proceeding steadily for well over a decade, many phases have remained essentially unchanged for some time. Soviet research differs in many details from that pursued by the United States, but its overall quality is comparable to the existing U.S. effort. One should recognize, however, that the Soviet Union lags behind the United States in many of the supporting technologies essential to a successful area defense. This is particularly true in computer hardware and software and in various sensor systems. In short, there is no need for the United States to match the Soviet ABM effort on the basis of its technical merit. Even if it were desirable for purely political reasons to keep pace with the Soviets, it would be difficult to justify an expansion of the current U.S. research and technology effort on that basis. The possibility that the Soviet program might result in new discoveries cannot be ignored, however. Therefore, a deliberate U.S. research and technology program can be justified to allow us to interpret Soviet progress and to prevent "technological surprise."

IV

There is little controversy about whether deliberate research and technology programs on ballistic missile defense should be continued, particularly given the desire to avoid technological surprise. However, the actual magnitude of such a program — and especially public statements referring to its purpose and promise — should be tempered by balancing realistic expectations for a technically functional ballistic missile defense system against the risks of proceeding beyond the research and technology phase, should it appear feasible to do so. Above all, a realistic technical assessment of ballistic missile defense must consider operational limitations, including those stemming from counter-measures by the offense, no matter how successful the technology programs may be. The risks of going forward with deployment include intensified arms competition, a decrease in stability, and abrogration or termination of the ABM Treaty of 1972. These risks will be discussed in the next section.

For as long as there have been ballistic missiles, defenses against them have been studied. This paper can only touch upon some of the generic questions relating to the technical potential of the various defense concepts under consideration in the Strategic Defense Initiative. . . .

V

As noted earlier, an expanded ballistic missile defense effort poses several strategic risks, including potential conflict with arms control treaties and the risk of accelerating arms competition.

## Danger of Confrontation with Arms Control Treaties

The administration has been careful to describe its current program as research, and the activities it proposes for the next fiscal year appear to be in compliance with obligations under existing treaties. However, if the Strategic Defense Initiative were to expand in the future from its current research and technology focus through prototype and systems testing to actual deployment, several arms control treaties would be at risk. These are the 1972 ABM Treaty and its associated 1974 protocol, the 1963 Limited Test Ban Treaty, and the Outer Space Treaty of 1967.

The ABM Treaty explicitly prohibits regional and nationwide ballistic missile defenses, permitting only a single deployment of limited firepower for the defense of the national capital or one designated ICBM complex. Although the treaty permits research and technology, it prohibits a number of new developments, including the development, testing, or deployment of mobile, land-based systems and those based in air, space, or sea. Ambassador Gerard Smith, chief U.S. negotiator of the ABM Treaty, defined the boundary between permitted and forbidden activities during the treaty ratification hearing before the Senate Armed Services Committee in 1972 as follows: "The obligation not to develop such systems, devices or warheads would be applicable only to the stage of development which follows laboratory development and testing. The prohibitions on development contained in the ABM Treaty would start at that part of the development process where field testing is initiated on either a prototype or breadboard model. It was understood by both sides that the prohibition on 'development' applies to activities involved after a component moves from the laboratory development and testing stage to the field testing stage, wherever performed." This interpretation would clearly prohibit prototype and systems testing as well as engineering development.

It has been suggested by some supporters of the Strategic Defense Initiative in and out of government that if confrontations between expanded defense activities and the ABM Treaty were to occur, then the treaty could be renegotiated to accommodate the proposed activities. The ABM Treaty is of indefinite duration and is subject to review every five years. This review, however, does not imply renegotiation, which would be a separate matter. It also contains a provision for either party to abrogate the treaty, after suitable notification, invoking jeopardy to its "supreme interests."

The Strategic Defense Initiative would also violate the Limited Nuclear Test Ban Treaty and the Outer Space Treaty if it moved ahead with tests and operational deployment in space of x-ray lasers pumped by nuclear explosions. The Outer Space Treaty prohibits the placement of weapons of mass destruction, including nuclear weapons, in space. The 1963 Limited Test Ban Treaty prohibits nuclear explosions in the atmosphere, under water, and in outer space. Although this treaty in itself has had only minor impact on the bilateral U.S.-Soviet arms competition, it has reduced worldwide fallout by two orders of magnitude and has been a substantial moral force in the cause of nuclear nonproliferation.

Neither renegotiation nor abrogation of the three treaties mentioned above can be taken lightly for a number of reasons. First, these treaties have served U.S. national security well. Second, should outright abrogation occur the concomitant political price would be heavy. Third, should renegotiation be initiated at the request of the United States, but with the Soviet Union disclaiming interest in such a move, the United States would have to pay a price in concessions to the Soviet Union to arrive at settlement.

The ABM Treaty, in particular, has been of great value to U.S. and NATO security. The treaty has helped limit competitive and escalatory growth of the strategic arsenals, which could well have exceeded current bounds. Furthermore, as documented in the 1972 Moscow summit, the ABM Treaty was enacted by both nations in recognition that peaceful coexistence was a matter of practical necessity. In that spirit, the ABM Treaty is a key step in the political approach to preventing nuclear war. It is much more than just a symbol of arms control hopes. It is not based on idealism; instead it accepts the mutual hostage relationship between the United States and the Soviet Union as a present necessity and as an objective condition, not as an active threat. Although the Soviets have never accepted "deterrence" in precisely the same terms as those used by most U.S. analysts, they have frequently emphasized that under current conditions nuclear war would be tantamount to suicide for both sides. In this sense, deterrence is not based on mutual threats but on prudent reciprocal restraints, such as those embodied in the ABM Treaty, to avoid nuclear war.

The ABM Treaty has also helped to lift the veil of secrecy surrounding the Soviet Union by guaranteeing that satellites and other surveillance tools located outside of national boundaries — the so-called "National Technical Means" of verification — shall not be interfered with in peace time. It also established the Standing Consultative Commission, a generally effective private forum for airing queries and resolving issues of treaty compliance by the United States and the Soviet Union.

In its final 1984 report, the President's Commission on Strategic Forces (the Scowcroft Commission) observed, "Ballistic missile defense is a critical aspect of the strategic balance and therefore is central to arms control . . . no move in the direction of the deployment of active defense should be made without the most careful consideration of the possible strategic and arms control implications."

The Strategic Defense Initiative has not been greeted with expressions of support from the NATO alliance. This is not surprising, as the ABM Treaty is of great value to our nuclear-armed allies — especially the British and French — because it ensures the ability of their missiles to reach their targets. Were the treaty modified or abrogated, resulting in the expansion of Soviet missile defenses, the independent and much smaller deterrent forces of our allies would lose their effectiveness much sooner than would U.S. forces.

Clearly, careful consideration will have to be given to the future of the ABM Treaty should the activities of the Strategic Defense Initiative provide promising results.

## The Risk of Escalation

Whatever the long-range objective of the Strategic Defense Initiative — be it President Reagan's vision of complete protection against nuclear weapons or the more recently stated goal of enhanced deterrence — during the actual deployment of a ballistic missile defense we will face a protracted time during which the offense dominance of the strategic balance is still a reality. Even optimistic projections of the development and deployment of only a partially effective missile defense, ignoring any treaty obstacles, span a decade or more. In contemplating the wisdom of deployment, we must factor in the likely Soviet responses and their impact on stability and escalation of the arms race. . . .

But what about the year after that, and beyond? The announced five-year Strategic Defense Initiative program is both ambitious and expensive, totaling $26 billion from fiscal year 1985 through 1989, as compared with a current spending rate of roughly $1 billion per year. Will this intensified program lead the Soviets to conclude, for example, that the president is really extending hope that the U.S. population can be shielded from the horrors of nuclear attack and is thereby accepting notions of limited nuclear war fighting?

Soviet leaders have continued to emphasize that they will maintain the capacity to retaliate in the face of new U.S. strategic programs. This fact, combined with a "worst case analysis" of the U.S. defense initiative, will surely lead the Soviet Union to drive for expanded offensive programs in addition to specific countermeasures to reduce the effectiveness of the emerging U.S. defenses. This risk is real, and it is futile to believe that economic pressures would coerce the Soviets to moderate their responsive deployments. Strategic nuclear forces are only a fraction, probably much less than one quarter, of the total Soviet military burden. Moreover, the Soviet Union is now spending twice the portion of its gross national product on military programs than is the United States. The Soviet system is more capable of withstanding criticism of this economic drain than is the United States.

A further serious risk is that the effort to neutralize the effect of nuclear weapons by deploying nationwide missile defenses might make the use of such weapons appear to be more acceptable, thereby deflecting efforts to reduce through negotiations the dangers and burdens of arms competition. . . .

We believe that the focus and size of the Strategic Defense Initiative should be restricted to research into new technologies. Such a program would also provide a hedge against Soviet technological breakthroughs or defense developments. The United States should make clear by policy declaration the limited nature of its strategic defense program and should avoid activities leading to erosion of the provisions of the ABM Treaty. It should signal its determination to comply fully with the ABM Treaty and should insist that the Soviet Union join in adhering to the treaty's strict interpretation.

The revived interest in defensive technologies should in no way deflect the nations of the world from giving highest priority to efforts to diminish the risk of nuclear war, to terminate the offensive strategic arms competition, and to reduce the world's nuclear arsenals.

## The ABM Treaty Debate

### *Document 14*

**This article reviews briefly an issue that has become a major part of the SDI debate. The administration argues that a review of the negotiating record of the ABM Treaty proves that the treaty allows the development of antiballistic missile systems as long as they are based on technologies that were not in existence at the time the ABM Treaty was signed (1972). Critics charge that this interpretation is without foundation and that the administration is trying to escape from the ABM Treaty without appearing to. The following report from the *Congressional Quarterly* looks at the critical parts of the ABM Treaty and summarizes the arguments on both sides.**

### 14 THE LEGAL ISSUES IN THE ABM TREATY February 14, 1987

The domestic battle over President Reagan's effort to develop a nationwide anti-missile defense — the strategic defense initiative (SDI) — ultimately will turn on the antagonists' political clout rather than on the niceties of international law.

But both sides in the SDI debate see the issue of legality as a potent one. Both sides are investing a lot of energy in the debate over whether or not Reagan's program is consistent with the 1972 U.S.-Soviet treaty limiting anti-ballistic missiles (ABM) systems.

#### The Texts

Six of the treaty's 16 articles and one appendix are at issue in the debate over SDI:

Article I provides that each of the two countries agrees "not to deploy ABM systems for the defense of the territory of its country and not to provide a base for such a defense and not to deploy ABM systems for defense of an individual region except as provided for in Article III."

Article II defines an ABM system as "a system to counter ballistic missiles or their elements in flight trajectory currently consisting of" radars, interceptor missiles and launchers for the interceptors. In the article's second paragraph, these three kinds of equipment are listed as "ABM system components."

Article III limits each country to two ABM sites, each containing no more than 100 launchers. In 1974, the two governments agreed that each would deploy ABM launchers at only one of the two permitted sites.

Article V provides that the two countries agree "not to develop, test or deploy ABM systems or components which are sea-based, air-based, space-based or mobile land-based."

Article XIV provides that either party may propose amendments to the treaty.

Article XV provides that either country shall "have the right to withdraw from this treaty if it decides that extraordinary events related to the subject matter of this treaty have jeopardized its supreme interests." Six months notice is required for withdrawal.

Agreed Statement D, one of several explanatory statements appended to the treaty, reads:

"In order to ensure fulfillment of the obligation not to deploy ABM systems and their components except as provided in Article III of the treaty, the parties agree that in the event ABM systems based on other physical principles and including components capable of substituting for ABM interceptor missiles, ABM launchers or ABM radars are created in the future, specific limitations on such systems and their components would be subject to discussion," according to provisions of the treaty that provide for amendment by mutual agreement.

#### For What Purpose?

SDI opponents read Article I as a statement that the pact's fundamental purpose is to ban precisely the kind of nationwide population shield Reagan and his aides want. A limited defense of one small region — including either offensive missile sites or the national capital — is permitted by the treaty.

Defense Secretary Caspar W. Weinberger has been particularly insistent during the four-year-long debate over SDI that he and Reagan want the program to defend the American public, not just missile silos. Until late in 1986, Weinberger had rejected any talk of taking the initial step of deploying a partial defense that would protect some U.S. missiles against a Soviet attack.

Of late, Weinberger has begun calling for a phased deployment of anti-missile weapons, but with the stipulation that the initial phase would fit into an ultimate scheme that would defend people, not missiles.

## What Kind of System?

Arms control advocates have insisted, practically since the treaty was signed, that the restrictions in Articles III and V are all-inclusive.

In this view, Article II defines "ABM systems" functionally: anything that can destroy a missile in flight. The reference to missiles, radars and launchers is merely illustrative of what ABM systems were "currently consisting of" at the time the treaty was signed. From this point of view, Agreed Statement D allows only for the possible development of new kinds of ABM weapons if they are land-based and fixed.

In October 1985, the administration presented a contrary position developed by Abraham D. Sofaer, the State Department's senior lawyer. He argued that the treaty consistently used the terms "ABM system" and "component" in contexts that made it clear they referred only to the 1972-style equipment. Accordingly, he reasoned, the limits on ground-based deployment in Article III and the ban on development of space based or mobile systems in Article V applied only to that kind of system. If those restrictions had been intended to apply to novel ABM types as well as the 1970s version, he maintained, there would have been no need for Agreed Statement D.

A review of the negotiations that produced the pact, Sofaer said, showed that Soviet officials expressly rejected the effort of U.S. negotiators to have the treaty ban future types of ABM defenses.

The issue is central to Reagan and Weinberger's insistence that they are not developing a system that would defend only U.S. missile launchers or other military targets. To have any chance of protecting the U.S. population at large, a U.S. defense would have to include some orbiting satellites that could attack Soviet missiles almost as soon as they were launched, before they dispensed their several nuclear warheads and their dozens of decoys.

## How Exotic?

The Pentagon's recent efforts to press for deployment in the early 1990s of a first-phase defense system has raised a new question.

The exotic lasers and particle-beam weapons with which SDI first was associated — the source of its nickname, "star wars" — could not be fielded soon. Deployment in the early 1990s would have to include satellites armed with "kinetic kill vehicles" (KKVs) — small missiles designed to destroy a Soviet missiles by collision. But even under Sofaer's reading of the treaty, these space-based weapons could not be developed unless they depended on "new physical principles" and thus came under the alleged exemption of Agreed Statement D.

Administration officials contend that KKVs differ from earlier ABM interceptor missiles in two respects: They home in on the heat generated by their target instead of being guided by radar, and they destroy their target by colliding with it, at thousands of miles per hour, instead of using the blast of a warhead.

SDI critics ridicule this contention. Heat-seeking missiles have been used by jet fighters for decades, and the principle of destruction by physical impact is as old as the catapult, they insist. The new missiles involve different engineering from that of older ABM weapons, but they are not based on "new physical principles," as, for instance, an anti-missile laser would be.

Even before the administration proposed Sofaer's less-restrictive reading of the treaty, it claimed far more latitude than SDI critics and Soviet officials said was allowed for conducting research on mobile and space-based equipment without violating Article V's ban on "development."

## What Is Development?

The treaty defines neither the term "develop," which is used in the English text, nor the corresponding word in the Russian text, which is translated as "create."

In the political maneuvering before the U.S.-Soviet summit meetings in November 1985 and October 1986, some Soviet officials have insisted that any SDI-related research is banned by the ABM treaty. But from the time the treaty was signed, the most frequently expressed Soviet position on this issue has been that the pact banned experiments that could be observed by the other side by virtue of their being conducted outside a laboratory. During Senate consideration of the treaty in 1972, several Nixon administration officials expressed the same view.

However, in a report to Congress in March 1985, the administration contended that the treaty "does permit research short of field testing of a prototype ABM system or component." Applying that standard, the report described several planned tests that it held to be consistent with the treaty. SDI critics charged that some of the proposed experiments would go far over the line between laboratory research and the kind of field testing that the treaty was intended to preclude.

### What Is a Component?

Paralleling the debate over the meaning of "develop" is a disagreement over the definition of an ABM system "component."

The administration position has been that an element of a future SDI system would be a "component" under the limits of the ABM treaty only if the new item could perform all the functions which, in 1972, were performed by a radar, an interceptor missile or a missile launcher. The 1985 report listed several tests deemed permissible under the treaty since the equipment being tested either was not technically capable of fitting into an ABM system or was tested against an earth-orbiting satellite rather than a ballistic missile. *(1985 Weekly Report p. 1092)*

SDI critics have argued that the administration's narrow definition of "component"—like its definition of "develop"—skirts the treaty's intent.

## SDI: One Technical Evaluation

### *Document 15*

In September 1985 the Office of Technology Assessment, a think tank created and funded by the U.S. Congress, produced a major study of strategic defenses. The 325-page study involved a wide range of experts with many points of view. Document 15 is a brief summary of its findings. Perhaps the most dramatic is that "assured survival of the U.S. population appears impossible to achieve if the Soviets are determined to deny it to us." Protecting population is only possible through a combination of defenses and reductions in offensive forces through arms control. The study also concludes that the technology is now present to allow the building of a defensive system that could offer some protection to U.S. land-based missiles.

### 15 FINDINGS
### Office of Technology Assessment
### September 1985

**1.** Both the capability of a BMD system to defend the United States, and the strategic value to the United States of any given BMD capability, depend on the interaction of all the kinds of the defenses actually deployed with all the kinds of offensive threat against which they must actually defend. In the past, the enormous destructive power of nuclear weapons has meant that offensive strategic technologies have had a large and fundamental advantage over defensive technologies. Unless this imbalance between the offense and defense disappears, strategic defenses might be plausible for limited purposes, such as defense of ICBM silos or complication of enemy attack plans, but not for the more ambitious goal of assuring the survival of U.S. society. This imbalance might be changed either by political decisions of both superpowers to reduce the kinds and levels of offensive deployments to capabilities much less than available technology permits, or by development and deployment of defensive systems able to overcome whatever offenses could be developed and deployed in the same period. While it is certainly possible that defensive technological development could outpace the development of offensive weapons and countermeasures to defenses, this does not appear very likely.

**2.** Assured survival of the U.S. population appears impossible to achieve if the Soviets are determined to deny it to us. This is because the technical difficulties of protecting cities against an all-out attack can be overcome only if the attack is limited by restraints on the quantity and quality of the attacking forces. The Reagan Administration currently appears to share this assessment.

**3.** If the Soviets chose to cooperate in a transition to mutual assured survival, it would probably be necessary to negotiate adequately verifiable arms control agreements on reducing present and restricting future offensive forces and on the manner, effectiveness, and timing of defensive deployments. OTA was unable to find anyone who could propose a plausible agreement for offensive arms reductions and a cooperative transition that could be reached before both the Soviets and the United States learn more about the likely effectiveness and costs of advanced BMD technologies. Indeed, such a transition could hardly be planned until engineering development was well advanced on the actual defensive systems to be deployed. Even then, adequate verification would be difficult. Without such agreement on the nature and timing of a buildup of defensive forces, it would be a radical departure from previous policies for either side to make massive reductions in its offensive forces in the face of the risk that the other side's defenses might become highly effective against the reduced offenses before one's own defenses were ready. Such a transition would be more appealing to both sides if BMD technologies could be developed which cost less to deploy than the offensive countermeasures needed to overcome them than it would be if the historic and current advantages of offense over defense persist. In essence, the question is whether a vigorous U.S. program to develop BMD, and the prospect that both sides might deploy effective BMD, will make the Soviets more willing than they have been in the past (or now say they are) to agree to deep reductions of strategic offensive forces on terms acceptable to the United States.

**4.** There is great uncertainty about the strategic situation that would arise if BMD deployment took place without agreement between the United States and Soviet Union to reduce offensive forces as defensive forces grew. Until the actual offensive systems (including ICBMs, SLBMs, bombers, and cruise missiles) and defensive systems (including BMD and air defenses) were specified and well understood, no one could know with confidence whether a situation of acute crisis instability (i.e. striking first could appear to lead to "victory") could be avoided. A fear on either side that the other could obtain such a first strike capability could lead both sides to build up both their offenses and their defenses. Such buildups would make it even more difficult to negotiate a cooperative transition from offense dominance to defense dominance.

**5.** The technology is reasonably well in hand to build a BMD system that could raise significantly the price in nuclear warheads of a Soviet attack on hardened targets in the United States; such a system, if combined with a re-basing of U.S. ICBMs, could protect a substantial fraction of those U.S. land-based missiles against a Soviet first strike. However, it is not clear whether BMD would be the best way to provide missile survivability, nor is it clear whether the combination of a U.S. program protecting ICBMs and the Soviet response — perhaps expansion of their Moscow defense to other Soviet cities — would on balance strengthen or weaken our deterrent.

**6.** It is impossible to say at this time how effective an affordable BMD system could be. To answer this question requires extensive research on sensor, command and control, and weapons technologies; and on system architecture (including survivability and computer software); on counter-counter-measures. Credible cost estimates based on this research will also be necessary.

**7.** The decision whether to push ahead vigorously with the SDI or to scale back the Administration proposal involves a balancing of opportunities against risks, in the face of considerable uncertainty. The SDI offers an *opportunity* to substantially increase our nation's safety *if* we obtain great technical success and a substantial degree of Soviet cooperation. The argument that sufficiently great U.S. technical success would force the Soviets to cooperate in their own security interests is logically compelling, but there can be no assurance that the Soviets would actually behave as we think they should. The SDI carries a *risk* that a vigorous BMD research program could bring on an offensive and defensive arms race, and a further risk that BMD deployment, if it took place without Soviet cooperation, could create severe instabilities. Whether BMD deployed in the face of intense Soviet efforts to counter it would enhance U.S. security depends on a judgment that decreased Soviet confidence that they could destroy targets in the United States or on allied territory would, in Soviet minds, outweigh their increased confidence that targets in the Soviet Union would survive because of their own BMD.

**8.** Whatever type of BMD research program the United States decides to pursue, it would be prudent to carry out that research in such a way as to minimize Soviet incentives to decide to deploy their own BMD beyond the limits set by the ABM Treaty before the United States has completed the research necessary to make our decision. This might be done by unilaterally restraining our BMD research. We would have greater influence over Soviet actions, however, if we reached agreement with the Soviets regarding disputed interpretations of the ABM Treaty — including the boundaries of permitted research — and regarding the conditions under which future BMD deployments would be desirable. Such an agreement would also reduce Soviet incentives to build up their offensive forces in order to overcome anticipated U.S. defenses. However, it must be recognized that acting to deter a Soviet decision to deploy BMD may require limiting and slowing our own BMD research.

## Soviet Views of SDI

### *Document 16*

**The Soviets have been extremely critical of SDI from the beginning. They have argued that SDI is an attempt by the United States to take the lead in the arms race, and they have said that the real purpose of SDI is offensive. They have also claimed that the Soviet Union would take whatever measures necessary to counter SDI. In addition, they have said that SDI would threaten past arms control agreements and do great harm to U.S.-Soviet relations. The following excerpts from statements by key Soviet leaders contain examples of these themes.**

## 16 SOVIET STATEMENTS ON BMD 1983–1985

The Soviet reaction to President Reagan's March 23, 1983, speech was prompt and strongly negative. Four days after the speech was given, the Soviet President, Yuri Andropov, denounced President Reagan's proposal to develop new types of BMD systems. Andropov said the idea of defensive measures might seem attractive to the uninformed, but:

> . . . In fact, the strategic offensive forces of the United States will continue to be developed and upgraded at full tilt and along quite a definite line at that, namely that of acquiring a nuclear first strike capability. Under these conditions, the intention to secure itself the possibility of destroying, with the help of the ABM defenses, the corresponding strategic systems of the other side, that is, of

rendering it unable to deal a retaliatory strike, is a bid to disarm the Soviet Union in the face of the U.S. nuclear threat. ... [It] is only mutual restraint in the field of ABM defenses that will allow progress in limiting and reducing offensive weapons, that is in checking and reversing the strategic arms race as a whole. Today, however, the United States intends to sever this interconnection. Should this conception be converted into reality, this would actually open the floodgates of a runaway race of all types of strategic arms, both offensive and defensive. Such is the real purport, the seamy side, so to say, of Washington's "defensive conception."[1]

These themes have been reiterated vigorously and persistently ever since by Soviet newspaper commentators, scientists, diplomats, and senior officials.

In August 1983 the Soviet Union formally proposed at the United Nations General Assembly a revised draft treaty on "The Prohibition of the Use of Force in Outer Space and From Space Against the Earth."[2] The provisions of this draft would ban space-based weapons, anti-satellite systems, and military use of manned spacecraft.

Former Soviet President Konstantin Chernenko issued several statements on ballistic missile defense. Following are illustrative excerpts:

We are resolutely against the development of broad-scale antimissile defense systems, which cannot be viewed in any other way than as aimed at the unpunished perpetration of nuclear aggression. There is an indefinite Soviet-American treaty on antimissile defense, prohibiting the creation of such systems. It must be rigorously observed.[3]

Today, no limitation and, all the more, no reduction of nuclear arms can be attained without effective measures that would prevent the militarization of outer space. ... Using the term "defense" is juggling with words. In its substance, this is an ... aggressive concept. The aim is to try to disarm the other side and deprive it of a capability to retaliate in the event of nuclear aggression against it.

To put it simply, the aim is to acquire a capability to deliver a nuclear strike, counting on impunity with an anti-ballistic missile shield to protect oneself from retaliation. ... [U.S. BMD deployment not only would mean] the end of the process of nuclear arms limitation and reduction, but [it] would become a catalyst of an uncontrolled arms race in all fields.[4]

In a lengthy interview on Moscow television January 13, 1985, then Soviet Foreign Minister Andrei Gromyko discussed the results of his January 7-8 meeting with Secretary of State George Shultz. The following excerpts refer to space weapons:

... [It] is impossible to examine either the question of strategic armaments or the question of intermediate-range nuclear weapons without examining the question of ... averting an arms race in space. In the end the American side agreed to adopt such a viewpoint. This fact is a positive one.

... [Preventing "militarization of space" means] arms intended for use against targets in space should be banned categorically and also that arms intended for use from space against. ... targets on the ground, in the sea and in the air should be banned categorically.

[If] accords [on preventing militarization of space] became clear, then it would be possible to move forward also on questions of strategic armaments. The Soviet Union would be willing not only to examine this problem of strategic armaments but would also be willing to reduce them sharply. ... And on the contrary, if there were no movement forward in space questions, then it would be superfluous even to speak about the possibility of a reduction in strategic armaments.

We are told this: After all, the United States does not have the intention of striking a blow at the Soviet Union. We tell them: Well, then, it follows that the Soviet Union must rely on your conscience, on the conscience of Washington. Well, first of all, we are not very convinced that Washington has very great reserves of this merchandise. ... And second, if we were to mentally trade places with you, ... if we were trying to create such a system, corresponding statements, statements to the effect that: You should rely on our conscience. Would they be sufficient for you? Silence. Silence.

[The] chief barrier that separates the policy of the Soviet Union from that of the United States is atomic weapons. ... [Reaching agreement at the Geneva negotiations] would therefore undoubtedly denote a big step forward in matters relating to improving bilateral Soviet-U.S. relations, especially if one takes account of the fact that both sides are major powers with broad-ranging international interests.

In a speech* in May 1985, Soviet General Chairman Mikhail S. Gorbachev said:

There are no people in the world who are not worried by the U.S. plans to militarize space. This worry is well grounded. Let us take a realistic view of matters: the implementation of these plans would thwart disarmament talks.

Moreover, it would dramatically increase the threat of a truly global, all-destroying military conflict. Anyone capable of an unbiased analysis of the situation and sincerely wishing to safeguard peace cannot help opposing "star wars."

In a nationally televised speech June 26, 1985, Chairman Gorbachev said:

We are prepared to seek accord not only about ending the arms race, but about the greatest of arms reductions — right up to general and complete disarmament. At present, as you know, we are holding talks with the United States in Geneva. The task before them, as the

* TASS, May 27, 1985.

Soviet leadership understands it, is to end the arms race on earth and prevent one in space. We embarked upon the negotiations in order to achieve these aims in practice. But all the indications are that this is precisely what the U.S. Administration, and the military-industrial complex which it serves, do not want. The attainment of serious accords evidently does not enter into their plans. They are continuing to implement their gigantic program of forcing through the production of more and more new types of weapons of mass destruction in the hope of achieving superiority over the countries of socialism, and dictating their will to them. The Americans have not only failed to put forward any serious proposals in Geneva for curtailing the arms race, but on the contrary, are taking steps that make such a curtailment impossible. I am thinking of the so-called "star wars" program to create offensive space weapons. Talk of its supposed defensive nature is, of course, a fairy tale for the gullible. The idea is to attempt to paralyze the Soviet Union's strategic arms and guarantee the opportunity of an unpunished nuclear strike against our country.

This is the essence of the matter, and one which we cannot fail to take into account. If the Soviet Union is faced with a real threat from space, it will find a way to effectively counter it. Let no one, and I say this quite definitely, doubt this. For the time being, one thing is clear — that is, that the American program for the militarization of space plays the role of a blank wall, barring the way to the achievement in Geneva of the relevant accords.

By its militarist policy the U.S. Administration is assuming a grave responsibility to mankind. If our partners at the Geneva talks continue with their line of playing for time at the meetings of the delegations, avoiding a solution of the questions for which they have assembled and using this time to push ahead with their military programs in space, on the ground, and at sea, we shall then of course have to assess the whole situation anew. We simply cannot allow the talks to be used again to divert attention and to cover up military preparations, whose purpose is to secure U.S. strategic superiority and achieve world dominance. In rebuffing these schemes, I am confident that we will be supported by the really peace-loving forces throughout the whole world and that we will be supported by the Soviet people.

In a letter[5] sent July 5, 1985, to American scientists, Chairman Gorbachev said:

... On behalf of the Soviet leadership I want to state in all definiteness that the Soviet Union will not be the first to make a step into outer space with weapons. We shall make every effort to convince other countries, and above all the United States of America, not to make such a fatal step which would inevitably increase the threat of nuclear war and would give an impetus to the uncontrolled arms race in all directions.

Proceeding from this goal, the Soviet Union, as you evidently know, has made a radical proposal in the United Nations organization, tabling a draft treaty on the prohibition of the use of force in space and from space against earth. If the United States joined the vast majority of states that have supported this initiative, the issue of space weapons could be closed once and for all.

At the Soviet-American talks on nuclear and space arms in Geneva we are seeking to come to terms on a full ban on the development, testing, and deployment of space attack systems. Such a ban would make it possible not only to preserve outer space for peaceful development, research, and scientific discoveries, but also to launch the process of sharply reducing, then eliminating nuclear weapons.

We have also repeatedly taken unilateral steps which have been called upon to set a good example to the United States. It is for two years now that the Soviet Union has maintained its moratorium on the placement of anti-satellite weapons in outer space, and it will continue abiding by it for as long as the other states will be acting in the same way. Lying on the table in Washington is our proposal for both sides to put a total end to efforts to develop new anti-satellite systems and for such systems already possessed by the U.S.S.R. and the United States, including those whose testing has not yet been completed, to be scrapped. The actions of the American side will show already in the near future which decision the U.S. Administration will prefer.

Strategic stability and trust would, no doubt, be strengthened if the United States agreed together with the U.S.S.R. in a binding form to reaffirm commitment to the regime of the Treaty on the Limitation of Anti-Ballistic Missile Systems, a treaty of unlimited duration.

The Soviet Union is not developing attack space weapons or a large-scale ABM system, just as it is not laying the foundation for such a defense. It strictly adheres to its obligations under the treaty as a whole and, in its particular aspects, unswervingly observes the spirit and the letter of that document of paramount importance. We invite the American leadership to join us in that undertaking, [and] renounce the plans of space militarization that are now in the making, plans which would invariably lead to the breakup of that document — the key link of the entire process of nuclear arms limitations.

The U.S.S.R. proceeds from the premise that the practical fulfillment of the task of preventing an arms race in space and terminating it on earth is possible given the political will and sincere desire of both sides to work toward attaining that historic goal. The Soviet Union has such a desire and such a will. ...

## Notes

1. From *Pravda,* Mar. 27, 1983.
2. U.N. General Assembly Document No. A/38/194.
3. TASS, Dec. 20, 1984
4. "Chernenko Again Warns U.S. on Space Plan," *New York Times,* Feb. 1., 1985, p. 3.
5. "Outer Space Should Serve Peace," article giving text of Mikhail Gorbachev's reply to a message from the Union of Concerned Scientists, TASS, July 5, 1985.

# ARMS CONTROL: FITS AND STARTS

## The Reagan Arms Control Team

### *Document 17*

The Reagan administration came into office with a clear critique of past arms control policy, but it soon had to develop a positive policy of its own. The policy makers were the key members of Reagan's national security bureaucracy, especially the State and Defense departments. In this excerpt from *Deadly Gambits,* a study of arms control in the Reagan administration, author Strobe Talbott describes the important personalities. Talbott notes that the State Department officials seemed more receptive to preserving some continuity in arms control than did key officials at Defense.

### 17 DEADLY GAMBITS
### Strobe Talbott

The top ranks of the Executive Branch had been assembled by a small group of men who had served in Reagan's earlier campaigns and in his gubernatorial administration in California. The principals were Edwin Meese, Michael Deaver, Lyn Nofziger, Caspar Weinberger, and William Clark. They were conservatives from the West Coast with little background or interest in foreign affairs. They represented a geographical as well as ideological break with the East Coast establishment's traditional concerns. The new President's views and those of his closest advisers on foreign policy tended to be simple, with more than a touch of nostalgia for the good old days of global American predominance and the Cold War. They were less impressed than the leaders of previous administrations had been by the differences between Chinese and Soviet Communists; if they saw the Third World at all, it was as an arena of Manichean struggle between the superpowers; they had little understanding of, and even less patience with, Western Europe.

Nonetheless, Reagan's two key appointments in the area of national-security policy were at first reassuring to moderates. Instead of choosing as Pentagon chief one of the many fire-breathing right-wing defense specialists available to him, Reagan picked Weinberger. He was known as "Cap the Knife," and it was governmental fat, not Communist flesh, that had felt his blade. It was hoped by some, feared by others, that he would approach the Defense Department as the ultimate manifestation of federal overspending. A number of conservatives initially worried that Weinberger would be as tough on weapons programs as he had been on social programs during his earlier cabinet assignments as director of the Office of Management and Budget and Secretary of Health, Education, and Welfare in the Nixon Administration.

To compensate for their own lack of experience in foreign affairs, the members of the Reagan inner circle knew they needed a Secretary of State with an established reputation. Alexander Haig looked like a good choice. He was a useful combination of tough guy and good guy—a soldier, a former Supreme Allied Commander in Europe, much respected by the Europeans, and a unique sort of patriotic hero. During Watergate, he had been a White House official whose reputation had actually been enhanced by the scandal. The depiction of him as the man who kept the government from falling apart was not universally credited, but it was widely enough believed to serve Haig well when Ronald Reagan was looking for a Secretary of State.

Despite his credentials, the White House was wary of Haig. For one thing, he had made soundings for a run of his own at the Republican nomination in 1980, deciding against it because of lack of support and poor health (he had undergone open-heart surgery). In his confirmation hearings, he denied categorically that he still harbored any lingering ambitions, but Reagan's men were not so sure. Moreover, Haig had served earlier administrations, and particularly those heavily involved in SALT and détente. The same quality that made him reassuring to the West Europeans and other foreigners made him suspect in Reagan's inner circle.

There was also a historical tension between the White House and the State Department. When a new occupant comes into the White House, he cleans the place out, bringing with him a new staff, made up largely of loyalists known to him or to his closest aides. A new boss at the

State Department, by contrast, changes the names on the doors of a cluster of offices on the seventh floor and a handful on the sixth. The rest of that huge building is populated with career foreign-service officers who have served under earlier administrations and will serve under later ones. The 16,000 or so "working-level" professionals in Foggy Bottom and in diplomatic posts scattered around the world constitute an entrenched bureaucracy that can pose an obstacle to the implementation of bold new policy initiatives.

From John Kennedy to Jimmy Carter, presidents had quickly come to rely on the National Security Council staff, headquartered in the White House basement and next door in the Old Executive Office Building, as a mechanism for managing and often circumventing the State Department. The result was that Assistants to the President for National Security Affairs, who sat near to the Oval Office, ended up as powerful rivals to the Secretary of State.

Reagan was determined to avoid repeating that pattern, partly because any NSC director suffered from a kind of historical guilt by association: Henry Kissinger had achieved the apotheosis of power in that job, and Kissinger was anathema to the new Administration. Reagan deliberately downgraded the NSC staff. The Assistant for National Security Affairs, who also functioned as director of the NSC staff, was Richard Allen, who had served as Reagan's foreign-policy adviser during his campaign for the presidency. Twelve years before, Allen had held the same job in Richard Nixon's entourage, only to end up being elbowed aside by Kissinger. Unlike his predecessors, who had direct access to the President, Allen was to report through Edwin Meese. Meese had cabinet rank and the title of Counselor to the President, but his background was limited to the Governor's office in Sacramento and the Alameda County District Attorney's office. Under Meese and Allen, the NSC staff was weak; it failed to coordinate and synthesize the work of other agencies effectively. It failed particularly to act as a buffer between State and Defense, and thus contributed by default to the tensions that arose between those two departments.

Allen and Meese were bedrock Reaganauts in their view of the world, and accordingly mistrustful of Haig. They were always looking for ways of checking Haig's influence on the President. One opportunity was in filling the job of director of the Arms Control and Disarmament Agency (ACDA). The original candidate for the directorship of ACDA was Edward Rowny. A retired Army general, Rowny had been the military representative on the delegation that negotiated the SALT II treaty; he resigned in protest at the time of its signing by Jimmy Carter and Leonid Brezhnev in 1979, and he campaigned against its ratification. That was enough to earn him a place in the new Administration. But Allen and Meese worried that Rowny would not stand up to Haig. So Allen came forward with a new candidate to head ACDA: Eugene Rostow, an elder statesman, law professor, and leading light of the Committee on the Present Danger, a private group that had fought against SALT II and in favor of new weapons programs.

Thus both the initial and the eventual choices for the leadership of the agency in charge of arms control were men whose principal attraction in the eyes of the White House was their vigorous opposition to arms control as it had been practiced by the preceding three administrations. And of the two, Rostow got the job because he was seen as more likely to counterbalance Haig's suspected softness on the issue. Moreover, because of the shift in the lineup, Rostow was one of the last senior officials designated in 1981. This initial uncertainty over its directorship made the Arms Control Agency even less important than it would have been otherwise at the outset of the Administration. Once confirmed, Rostow did indeed stand up to Haig—and to everyone else, including Reagan, which proved to be his undoing. The bureaucratic combat between Rostow and Haig made for constant friction between their agencies, which further hampered the Administration's ability to make coherent policy.

Another part of the White House effort to keep tabs on the State Department was its pressing for the appointment of Reagan's close friend William Clark as Deputy Secretary of State. Haig agreed to the choice, but Clark then had to pass before the Senate Foreign Relations Committee. His tenure as Governor Reagan's executive secretary in Sacramento and a stint on the California State Supreme Court had not prepared "Judge" Clark, as he would continue to be called, for the oral examination on current events that the senators administered. But they were forgiving; they wished him luck and approved him for the No. 2 job in the State Department. From there, slightly better prepared, he would eventually move to succeed Allen at the NSC.

Haig picked as his own right-hand man a professional foreign-service officer, Lawrence Eagleburger. First Haig made Eagleburger Assistant Secretary of State for European Affairs, then promoted him to be Under Secretary for Political Affairs. Here was yet another reason for the White House to keep a close eye and a short leash on the department. Eagleburger personified what Reagan's men rejected. He was a veteran diplomat who had served every president since Dwight Eisenhower, but had risen to the top working for Henry Kissinger. That was how Haig had come to know and admire him. It was also how Allen had come to resent him: Eagleburger was the man whom Kissinger had assigned the task of easing Allen out of the Nixon Administration.

Haig's choice [to be put in charge of arms control for the State Department] was Richard Burt, a defense intellectual who was then covering national-security affairs for *The New York Times.* Burt had met with Haig on a number of occasions, but the two men did not know each other well. Burt was urged upon Haig by the team that was assembling lists of candidates for subcabinet jobs during the transition between the election and the inauguration. Both the transition team and Haig were attracted to Burt's record of writing and speaking critically about SALT. He had stressed the pitfalls of letting arms control become an end in itself, divorced from the military imperatives of national security.

Burt was put in charge of the Bureau of Politico-Military Affairs, or PM, the State Department's own in-house mini-Pentagon. It was an office charged with coordinating diplomacy with defense — a task that went to the heart of Burt's criticism of SALT. At one of his first meetings with his staff, he declared that his mission was to wage a "one-man crusade" to reintegrate arms-control policymaking with military planning, to turn his bureau into a "bridge" between the State and Defense departments, and to preside over a process that would yield compromises between the two....

Burt was a man of exceptional intelligence. He could talk lucidly, fluently, and persuasively about the most arcane aspects of nuclear arms doctrine, accurately calibrating his presentation to the level of interest and knowledge of his audience. He was also one of the few people in a high position in the new order who respected the need not to tear down the old order. He was genuinely devoted to achieving progress in arms control, and not just for the sake of advancing his own career....

As Eagleburger observed early in 1981, the Reagan Administration had the look of a coalition government. Haig, Eagleburger, and Burt were the leaders of one faction, those who believed that it was critically important to maintain close ties with America's allies and that it was still possible for the U.S. to make agreements with the Soviets that were in the interests of America and the West.

At the other end of the spectrum, and on the other side of the Potomac, were the Pentagon civilians. They put more faith in Fortress America than in the Western alliance, and they tended to the view that the U.S. could not ultimately count on its allies and should not really do business with the Soviet Union. They saw it as self-deluding to think that the West could compromise in the military rivalry. While committed to avoiding, if possible, a nuclear war, they prided themselves on being hard-headed enough to accept the possibility that the planet might not, in the end, be big enough for both superpowers. The principal figure in this camp was Richard Perle.

Just as the State Department had its mini-Pentagon in the Politico-Military Bureau, the Pentagon had its mini-State Department under the Assistant Secretary of Defense for International Security Affairs (ISA). This office was charged with making sure that military procurements and programs fit into the context of U.S. foreign policy — and that the Defense Department had its say in formulating that policy. In the Reagan Administration, ISA was expanded, reorganized, and renamed, and the predominant official was Perle, the Assistant Secretary of Defense for International Security Policy (ISP). He was Richard Burt's Pentagon counterpart. At the beginning of the Administration, both men hoped they would be partners. Perle had been a member of the State Department transition team that helped pick Burt for his job as director of PM. Within a few months, however, the two Richards, as they were soon dubbed, were at loggerheads and would remain so. Much of the story of the Reagan Administration's arms-control policy is the story of the struggle between them.

Perle's many enemies called him the Prince of Darkness, but he was usually the picture of mildness. He had a youthful, almost cherubic face, an easy smile, and a calm, quiet, earnest but soothing manner almost no matter what he was saying....

Perle had spent years working for Senator Henry Jackson, the Democrat from Washington State. With Perle's help, Jackson had become the leading critic of arms control as practiced by Republican and Democratic presidents alike. Jackson's anti-Sovietism and his commitment to unilateralism in defense transcended partisan politics. That made Perle just the sort of Democrat that the Reagan Administration was eager to recruit. It was an ideological administration more than a partisan one: Kissinger Republicans were unwelcome; Jackson Democrats were much in demand. This was the bipartisanship of the right wing on national-security issues, and Perle was a veteran of the cause. He was only six years older than Burt (thirty-nine on taking office), but he had had thirteen years' experience in government — and that was thirteen years more than Burt.

Perle had been a *bête noire* of Henry Kissinger's. In 1974, shortly after Jackson and Perle had struck a crippling blow against détente with a legislative restriction on Soviet-American economic ties, Kissinger, quivering with frustration and anger, remarked, "You just wait and see! If that son of a bitch Richard Perle ever gets into an administration, after six months he'll be pursuing exactly the same policies I've been attempting and that he's been sabotaging."

But Kissinger was wrong....

Perle ended up having more impact on policy in arms control than any other official in the U.S. government, an achievement that was all the more remarkable in that he held a third-echelon job. Part of his success was that he was as personally charming, intellectually brilliant, and politically well connected as he was ideologically self-assured and therefore unyielding. Perle's near-dominance of the arms-control process during the critical first year and a half of the Administration had another explanation as well: he was able to fill the partial vacuum of experience, expertise, and interest in arms control that existed at the highest levels of the government, including on the part of his ultimate superior, Reagan, and his immediate superior, Defense Secretary Weinberger. . . .

Perle's more charitable critics suspected that in pursuing the best in arms control he was making it the enemy of the good. Others occused him of opposing any and all arms control; of propounding principles that were a smokescreen for obstructionism; and of cynically promoting, then defending, proposals that he knew perfectly well were non-negotiable. Perle steadfastly denied that charge many times. . . .

## Public Concern About Nuclear War

### *Document 18*

**The early 1980s saw a dramatic increase in public concern about the dangers of nuclear war. In part this was caused by U.S.-Soviet tensions, some loose talk about nuclear war by a few key government officials, and the Reagan administration's apparent lack of interest in arms control. Many books, movies, and television programs appeared highlighting the horrors of a nuclear war. One of the most influential was *The Fate of the Earth,* a book by Jonathan Schell, which first appeared as a series of articles in the *New Yorker.* As these excerpts show, Schell chillingly describes the potential devastation nuclear weapons could cause and goes on to argue that humankind faces the risk of extinction.**

### 18 THE FATE OF THE EARTH Jonathan Schell

What happened at Hiroshima was less than a millionth part of a holocaust at present levels of world nuclear armament. The more than millionfold difference amounts to more than a difference in magnitude; it is also a difference in kind. The authors of "Hiroshima and Nagasaki" observe that "an atomic bomb's massive destruction and indiscriminate slaughter involves the sweeping breakdown of all order and existence — in a word, the collapse of society itself," and that therefore "the essence of atomic destruction lies in the totality of its impact on man and society." This is true also of a holocaust, of course, except that the totalities in question are now not single cities but nations, ecosystems, and the earth's ecosphere. Yet with the exception of fallout, which was relatively light at Hiroshima and Nagasaki (because both the bombs were air-burst), the immediate devastation caused by today's bombs would be of a sort similar to the devastation of those cities. The immediate effects of a twenty-megaton bomb are not different in kind from those of a twelve-and-a-half-kiloton bomb; they are only more extensive. (The proportions of the effects do change greatly with yield, however. In small bombs, the effects of the initial nuclear radiation are important, because it strikes areas in which people might otherwise have remained alive, but in larger bombs — ones in the megaton range — the consequences of the initial nuclear radiation, whose range does not increase very much with yield, are negligible, because it strikes areas in which everyone will have already been burned or blasted to death.) In bursts of both weapons, for instance, there is a radius within which the thermal pulse can ignite newspapers: for the twelve-and-a-half-kiloton weapon, it is a little over two miles; for the twenty-megaton weapon, it is twenty-five miles. (Since there is no inherent limit on the size of a nuclear weapon, these figures can be increased indefinitely, subject only to the limitations imposed by the technical capacities of the bomb builder — and of the earth's capacity to absorb the blast. The Soviet Union, which has shown a liking for sheer size in so many of its undertakings, once detonated a sixty-megaton bomb.) Therefore, while the total effect of a holocaust is qualitatively different from the total effect of a single bomb, the experience of individual people in a holocaust would be, in the short term (and again excepting the presence of lethal fallout wherever the bombs were ground-burst), very much like the experience of individual people in Hiroshima. The Hiroshima people's experience, accordingly, is of much more than historical interest. It is a picture of what our whole world is always poised to become — a backdrop of scarcely imaginable horror lying just behind the surface of our normal life, and capable of breaking through into that normal life at any second. Whether we choose to think about it or not, it is an omnipresent, inescapable truth about our lives today that at every single moment each one of us may suddenly become the deranged mother looking for her burned child; the professor with the ball of rice in his hand whose wife has just told him "Run away, dear!" and died in the fires; Mr. Fukai running back into the firestorm; the naked man standing on the blasted plain that was his city, holding his eyeball in his hand; or, more likely, one of millions of corpses. For whatever our "modest hopes" as human beings may be, every one of them can be nullified by a nuclear holocaust.

One way to begin to grasp the destructive power of present-day nuclear weapons is to describe the consequences of the detonation of a one-megaton bomb, which possesses eighty times the explosive power of the Hiroshima bomb, on a large city, such as New York. Burst some eighty-five hundred feet above the Empire State Building, a one-megaton bomb would gut or flatten almost every building between Battery Park and 125th Street, or within a radius of four and four-tenths miles, or in an area of sixty-one square miles, and would heavily damage buildings between the northern tip of Staten Island and the George Washington Bridge, or within a radius of about eight miles, or in an area of about two hundred square miles. A conventional explosive delivers a swift shock, like a slap, to whatever it hits, but the blast wave of a sizable nuclear weapon endures for several seconds and "can surround and destroy whole buildings" (Glasstone). People, of course, would be picked up and hurled away from the blast along with the rest of the debris. Within the sixty-one square miles, the walls, roofs, and floors of any buildings that had not been flattened would be collapsed, and the people and furniture inside would be swept down onto the street. (Technically, this zone would be hit by various overpressures of at least five pounds per square inch. Overpressure is defined as the pressure in excess of normal atmospheric pressure.) As far away as ten miles from ground zero, pieces of glass and other sharp objects would be hurled about by the blast wave at lethal velocities. In Hiroshima, where buildings were low and, outside the center of the city, were often constructed of light materials, injuries from falling buildings were often minor. But in New York, where the buildings are tall and are constructed of heavy materials, the physical collapse of the city would certainly kill millions of people. The streets of New York are narrow ravines running between the high walls of the city's buildings. In a nuclear attack, the walls would fall and the ravines would fill up. The people in the buildings would fall to the street with the debris of the buildings, and the people in the street would be crushed by this avalanche of people and buildings. At a distance of two miles or so from ground zero, winds would reach four hundred miles an hour, and another two miles away they would reach a hundred and eighty miles an hour. Meanwhile, the fireball would be growing, until it was more than a mile wide, and rocketing upward, to a height of over six miles. For ten seconds, it would broil the city below. Anyone caught in the open within nine miles of ground zero would receive third-degree burns and would probably be killed; closer to the explosion, people would be charred and killed instantly. From Greenwich Village up to Central Park, the heat would be great enough to melt metal and glass. Readily inflammable materials, such as newspapers and dry leaves, would ignite in all five boroughs (though in only a small part of Staten Island) and west to the Passaic River, in New Jersey, within a radius of about nine and a half miles from ground zero, thereby creating an area of more than two hundred and eighty square miles in which mass fires were likely to break out.

If it were possible (as it would not be) for someone to stand at Fifth Avenue and Seventy-second Street (about two miles from ground zero) without being instantly killed, he would see the following sequence of events. A dazzling white light from the fireball would illumine the scene, continuing for perhaps thirty seconds. Simultaneously, searing heat would ignite everything flammable and start to melt windows, cars, buses, lampposts, and everything else made of metal or glass. People in the street would immediately catch fire, and would shortly be reduced to heavily charred corpses. About five seconds after the light appeared, the blast wave would strike, laden with the debris of a now nonexistent midtown. Some buildings might be crushed, as though a giant fist had squeezed them on all sides, and others might be picked up off their foundations and whirled uptown with the other debris. On the far side of Central Park, the West Side skyline would fall from south to north. The four-hundred-mile-an-hour wind would blow from south to north, die down after a few seconds, and then blow in the reverse direction with diminished intensity. While these things were happening, the fireball would be burning in the sky for the ten seconds of the thermal pulse. Soon huge, thick clouds of dust and smoke would envelop the scene, and as the mushroom cloud rushed overhead (it would have a diameter of about twelve miles) the light from the sun would be blotted out, and day would turn to night. Within minutes, fires, ignited both by the thermal pulse and by broken gas mains, tanks of gas and oil, and the like, would begin to spread in the darkness, and a strong, steady wind would begin to blow in the direction of the blast. As at Hiroshima, a whirlwind might be produced, which would sweep through the ruins, and radioactive rain, generated under the meteorological conditions created by the blast, might fall. Before long, the individual fires would coalesce into a mass fire, which, depending largely on the winds, would become either a conflagration or a firestorm. In a conflagration, prevailing winds spread a wall of fire as far as there is any combustible material to sustain it; in a firestorm, a vertical updraft caused by the fire itself sucks the surrounding air in toward a central point, and the fires therefore converge in a single fire of extreme heat. A mass fire of either kind renders shelters useless by burning up all the oxygen in the air and creating toxic gases, so that anyone inside the shelters is asphyxiated, and also by heating the ground to such high temperatures that the shelters turn, in effect, into ovens, cremating the people inside them. In Dresden, several days after the firestorm raised there by Allied conventional bombing, the interiors of some bomb shelters were still so hot that when they were opened the inrushing air caused the contents to burst into flame. Only those who had fled their shelters when the bombing started had any chance of surviving. (It is difficult to predict in a particular situation which form the fires will take. In actual experience, Hiroshima suffered a firestorm and Nagasaki suffered a conflagration.)

In this vast theatre of physical effects, all the scenes

of agony and death that took place at Hiroshima would again take place, but now involving millions of people rather than hundreds of thousands. Like the people of Hiroshima, the people of New York would be burned, battered, crushed, and irradiated in every conceivable way. The city and its people would be mingled in a smoldering heap. And then, as the fires started, the survivors (most of whom would be on the periphery of the explosion) would be driven to abandon to the flames those family members and other people who were unable to flee, or else to die with them. Before long, while the ruins burned, the processions of injured, mute people would begin their slow progress out of the outskirts of the devastated zone. However, this time a much smaller proportion of the population than at Hiroshima would have a chance of escaping. In general, as the size of the area of devastation increases, the possibilities for escape decrease. When the devastated area is relatively small, as it was at Hiroshima, people who are not incapacitated will have a good chance of escaping to safety before the fires coalesce into a mass fire. But when the devastated area is great, as it would be after the detonation of a megaton bomb, the fires are springing up at a distance of nine and a half miles from ground zero, and when what used to be the streets are piled high with burning rubble, and the day (if the attack occurs in the daytime) has grown impenetrably dark, there is little chance that anyone who is not on the very edge of the devastated area will be able to make his way to safety. In New York, most people would die wherever the blast found them, or not very far from there.

If instead of being burst in the air the bomb were burst on or near the ground in the vicinity of the Empire State Building, the overpressure would be very much greater near the center of the blast area but the range hit by a minimum of five pounds per square inch of overpressure would be less. The range of the thermal pulse would be about the same as that of the air burst. The fireball would be almost two miles across, and would engulf midtown Manhattan from Greenwich Village nearly to Central Park. Very little is known about what would happen to a city that was inside a fireball, but one would expect a good deal of what was there to be first pulverized and then melted or vaporized. Any human beings in the area would be reduced to smoke and ashes; they would simply disappear. A crater roughly three blocks in diameter and two hundred feet deep would open up. In addition, heavy radioactive fallout would be created as dust and debris from the city rose with the mushroom cloud and then fell back to the ground. Fallout would begin to drop almost immediately, contaminating the ground beneath the cloud with levels of radiation many times lethal doses, and quickly killing anyone who might have survived the blast wave and the thermal pulse and might now be attempting an escape; it is difficult to believe that there would be appreciable survival of the people of the city after a megaton ground burst. And for the next twenty-four hours or so more fallout would descend downwind from the blast, in a plume whose direction and length would depend on the speed and the direction of the wind that happened to be blowing at the time of the attack. If the wind was blowing at fifteen miles an hour, fallout of lethal intensity would descend in a plume about a hundred and fifty miles long and as much as fifteen miles wide. Fallout that was sublethal but could still cause serious illness would extend another hundred and fifty miles downwind. Exposure to radioactivity in human beings is measured in units called rems—an acronym for "roentgen equivalent in man." The roentgen is a standard measurement of gamma- and X-ray radiation, and the expression "equivalent in man" indicates that an adjustment has been made to take into account the differences in the degree of biological damage that is caused by radiation of different types. Many of the kinds of harm done to human beings by radiation — for example, the incidence of cancer and of genetic damage — depend on the dose accumulated over many years; but radiation sickness, capable of causing death, results from an "acute" dose, received in a period of anything from a few seconds to several days. Because almost ninety per cent of the so-called "infinite-time dose" of radiation from fallout — that is, the dose from a given quality of fallout that one would receive if one lived for many thousands of years — is emitted in the first week, the one-week accumulated dose is often used as a convenient measure for calculating the immediate harm from fallout. Doses in the thousands of rems, which could be expected throughout the city, would attack the central nervous system and would bring about death within a few hours. Doses of around a thousand rems, which would be delivered some tens of miles downwind from the blast, would kill within two weeks everyone who was exposed to them. Doses of around five hundred rems, which would be delivered as far as a hundred and fifty miles downwind (given a wind speed of fifteen miles per hour), would kill half of all exposed able-bodied young adults. At this level of exposure, radiation sickness proceeds in the three stages observed at Hiroshima. The plume of lethal fallout could descend, depending on the direction of the wind, on other parts of New York State and parts of New Jersey, Pennsylvania, Delaware, Maryland, Connecticut, Massachusetts, Rhode Island, Vermont, and New Hampshire, killing additional millions of people. The circumstances in heavily contaminated areas, in which millions of people were all declining together, over a period of weeks, toward painful deaths, are ones that, like so many of the consequences of nuclear explosions, have never been experienced.

A description of the effects of a one-megaton bomb

on New York City gives some notion of the meaning in human terms of a megaton of nuclear explosive power, but a weapon that is more likely to be used against New York is the twenty-megaton bomb, which has one thousand six hundred times the yield of the Hiroshima bomb. The Soviet Union is estimated to have at least a hundred and thirteen twenty-megaton bombs in its nuclear arsenal, carried by Bear intercontinental bombers. In addition, some of the Soviet SS-18 missiles are capable of carrying bombs of this size, although the actual yields are not known. Since the explosive power of the twenty-megaton bombs greatly exceeds the amount necessary to destroy most military targets, it is reasonable to suppose that they are meant for use against large cities. If a twenty-megaton bomb were air-burst over the Empire State Building at an altitude of thirty thousand feet, the zone gutted or flattened by the blast wave would have a radius of twelve miles and an area of more than four hundred and fifty square miles, reaching from the middle of Staten Island to the northern edge of the Bronx, the eastern edge of Queens, and well into New Jersey, and the zone of heavy damage from the blast wave (the zone hit by a minimum of two pounds of overpressure per square inch) would have a radius of twenty-one and a half miles, or an area of one thousand four hundred and fifty square miles, reaching to the southernmost tip of Staten Island, north as far as southern Rockland County, east into Nassau County, and west to Morris County, New Jersey. The fireball would be about four and a half miles in diameter and would radiate the thermal pulse for some twenty seconds. People caught in the open twenty-three miles away from ground zero, in Long Island, New Jersey, and southern New York State, would be burned to death. People hundreds of miles away who looked at the burst would be temporarily blinded and would risk permanent eye injury. (After the test of a fifteen-megaton bomb on Bikini Atoll, in the South Pacific, in March of 1954, small animals were found to have suffered retinal burns at a distance of three hundred and forty-five miles.) The mushroom cloud would be seventy miles in diameter. New York City and its suburbs would be transformed into a lifeless, flat, scorched desert in a few seconds.

If a twenty-megaton bomb were ground-burst on the Empire State Building, the range of severe blast damage would, as with the one-megaton ground blast, be reduced, but the fireball, which would be almost six miles in diameter, would cover Manhattan from Wall Street to northern Central Park and also parts of New Jersey, Brooklyn, and Queens, and everyone within it would be instantly killed, with most of them physically disappearing. Fallout would again be generated, this time covering thousands of square miles with lethal intensities of radiation. A fair portion of New York City and its incinerated population, now radioactive dust, would have risen into the mushroom cloud and would now be descending on the surrounding territory. On one of the few occasions when local fallout was generated by a test explosion in the multi-megaton range, the fifteen-megaton bomb tested on Bikini Atoll, which was exploded seven feet above the surface of a coral reef, "caused substantial contamination over an area of more than seven thousand square miles," according to Glasstone. If, as seems likely, a twenty-megaton bomb ground-burst on New York would produce at least a comparable amount of fallout, and if the wind carried the fallout onto populated areas, then this one bomb would probably doom upward of twenty million people, or almost ten per cent of the population of the United States. . . .

## Reagan's Proposal to Limit Offensive Nuclear Weapons

### *Document 19*

Spurred in part by public concern about nuclear war, the Reagan administration finally made its first serious proposal to limit offensive nuclear weapons. On May 9, 1982, President Reagan outlined his proposals for the U.S.-Soviet Strategic Arms Reduction Talks (START). He offered the Soviets a two-phase proposal. In the first phase, each side would reduce the numbers of warheads on missiles from 8,000 to 5,000. No more than half of these could be on land-based missiles. In addition, each side would be limited to 850 "deployed ballistic missiles." In the second phase, the two superpowers would agree on an equal ceiling on the throw-weight of all nuclear missiles.

### 19 COMMENCEMENT SPEECH
**President Ronald Reagan**
**Eureka College, Illinois**
**May 9, 1982**

For the immediate future, I am asking my START negotiating team to propose to their Soviet counterparts a practical, phased reduction plan. The focus of our efforts will be to reduce significantly the most destabilizing systems — ballistic missiles — the number of warheads they carry, and their overall destructive potential.

At the end of the first phase of the START reductions, I expect ballistic missile warheads — the most serious threat we face — to be reduced to equal ceilings at least a third below current levels. To enhance stability, I would ask that no more than half of those warheads be land-based. I hope that these warhead reductions, as well as significant reductions in missiles themselves, could be achieved as rapidly as possible.

In a second phase, we will seek to achieve an equal ceiling on other elements of our strategic nuclear forces, including limits on ballistic missile throwweight at less than current American levels. In both phases, we shall insist on verification procedures to insure compliance with the agreement.

The monumental task of reducing and reshaping our strategic forces to enhance stability will take many years of concentrated effort. But I believe that it will be possible to reduce the risks of war by removing the instabilities that now exist and by dismantling the nuclear menace.

I have written to President Brezhnev and directed Secretary Haig to approach the Soviet Government concerning the initiation of formal negotiations on the reduction of strategic nuclear arms — START — at the earliest possible opportunity. We hope negotiations will begin by the end of June.

We will negotiate seriously, in good faith, and carefully consider all proposals made by the Soviet Union. If they approach these negotiations in the same spirit, I am confident that together we can achieve an agreement of enduring value that reduces the number of nuclear weapons, halts the growth in strategic forces, and opens the way to even more far-reaching steps in the future.

I hope the commencement today will also mark the commencement of a new era — in both senses of the word a new start — toward a more peaceful, more secure world.

## The START Negotiations

### *Document 20*

**The START negotiations lasted from June 1982 until November 1983, when they were broken off by the Soviet Union to protest the deployment of new NATO missiles in Western Europe. Document 20 traces the course of the talks and outlines the key issues. Progress was made difficult because the United States wanted a new approach to arms control that focused on cutting Soviet missiles. The Soviet Union wanted to continue in the traditional way, building on the SALT treaties. A new element was added in 1983 when Congress became involved in the negotiations and forced the administration to accept a "build-down" approach to arms reductions.**

### 20 THE STRATEGIC ARMS REDUCTION TALKS (START)
### National Academy of Sciences
### 1985

The Strategic Arms Reduction Talks between the United States and the Soviet Union opened in Geneva, Switzerland, on June 29, 1982. The U.S. negotiating position, which has gone through several revisions, rejects the SALT approach to equal aggregates. Instead, it seeks major reductions, particularly in ICBMs, to establish equal destructive power of U.S. and Soviet missile forces. The Soviet Union continues to support the SALT approach in the START negotiations and seeks modest reductions within the SALT II framework. Despite various revisions in both sides' proposals, there had been little significant progress in narrowing the fundamental differences between the two positions by the end of the fifth round of START. At that point the Soviet negotiators refused to set a date to resume the negotiations, contending that the U.S. deployment of intermediate-range missiles in Europe had created a new strategic situation that had to be reexamined.

#### Background

##### *The Origins*

During the 1980 presidential campaign, candidate Ronald Reagan opposed the unratified SALT II Treaty and promised, if elected, to withdraw the "fatally flawed" treaty from the Senate. He argued that the treaty did not limit throw-weight, the true measure of destructive power, and did not close the "window of vulnerability" caused by accurate Soviet ICBM warheads aimed at U.S. ICBMs. After several months in office the new administration announced that while it reviewed arms control policy, the United States would not undercut the provisions of the SALT II Treaty as long as the Soviet Union did likewise.

The new administration did not initially announce its own approach to strategic arms control, although it did state that a prerequisite for genuine future arms control was to redress the strategic imbalance and restore a margin of safety with the Soviet Union. When the President announced his military program, he called for a 10 percent increase in the military budget over each of the next five years "to restore our defensive forces and to close that window of vulnerability that was opened in recent years with the superiority of Soviet forces." The administration emphasized that it would approach arms control as only a single element in a full range of political, economic, and military efforts. The administration also stressed the need for more effective verification in its new approach to arms control, citing the alleged failure of the Soviet Union to comply with existing agreements.

As domestic and NATO pressure for arms control increased, the President announced in November 1981 that strategic arms talks would possibly begin the following year. He stated that these negotiations, which would be called Strategic Arms Reduction Talks, or START, would have the goal of substantially reducing strategic nuclear arms. Although the negotiations on intermediate-range nuclear forces (INF) began in late November 1981 under strong political pressure from the NATO allies, the START negotiations did not actually begin for another eight months.

The issue of "linkage" of arms control negotiations with the overall U.S.-Soviet relationship, which had been a recurring problem in SALT, arose at the beginning of 1982 in connection with the Polish crisis. This played a role in postponing initiation of the START negotiations. However, by March 1982 the administration came under increasing domestic pressure to initiate negotiations, with nuclear freeze resolutions being introduced in the House of Representatives and the Senate. Shortly afterward the administration, which opposed a nuclear freeze on the grounds that it would leave the United States in a position of strategic inferiority, publicly set forth its preferred approach to nuclear arms control. On March 31, 1982, in his first prime time news conference, the President invited the Soviet Union to join with the United States in negotiations to reduce nuclear weapons substantially. The President also endorsed the Jackson-Warner freeze resolution, which called for reductions to equal levels prior to a freeze. The President contended that since the Soviet Union had "a definite margin of superiority," an immediate freeze would put the United States in a dangerous and disadvantageous position.

### *Initial START Proposals*

President Reagan outlined the elements of the START proposal on May 9, 1982, in an address at Eureka College. In the first phase of the proposal, the United States and the Soviet Union would reduce their arsenals of nuclear warheads on land- and sea-based ballistic missiles from the current levels of around 8,000 to 5,000, with no more than half, or 2,500, of those warheads on land-based missiles. The first phase would also include a limit of 850 on "deployed ballistic missiles," the unit of measure introduced to replace launchers, the SALT II measure of ballistic missiles. In the second phase of the proposal, both nations would accept an equal ceiling on the throw-weight of all nuclear missiles.

The President said that the U.S. goal was to enhance deterrence and achieve stability through significant reductions in "the most destabilizing nuclear systems—ballistic missiles, and especially intercontinental ballistic missiles—while maintaining a nuclear capability sufficient to deter conflict, underwrite our national security and meet our commitment to our allies and friends." Strategic long-range bombers were not included in the President's outline of the START proposals, but under questioning, administration officials said that the United States would be prepared to deal with bombers and cruise missiles throughout both phases of the arms control talks with the Soviet Union.

In declaring a readiness to negotiate an accord with the United States on May 18, 1982, Soviet President Brezhnev stated that the proposed U.S. approach would require a unilateral reduction in the Soviet arsenal. He proposed instead that the accord should either ban or severely restrict the development of all new types of strategic armaments. Brezhnev also called for a nuclear freeze "as soon as the talks begin." When the United States and the Soviet Union simultaneously announced their agreement to begin the START negotiations, President Reagan again pledged to "refrain from actions which would undercut" the unratified SALT II Treaty so long as the Soviets showed the same restraint.

The START negotiations began in Geneva on June 29, 1982. In response to the U.S. proposals, the Soviet Union presented a proposal that included an interim freeze on strategic arms, limits based on the SALT II framework (involving a 20 percent reduction of the SALT II ceilings on the aggregate of central strategic systems from 2,250 to 1,800), and unspecified reductions in the various SALT II subceilings. In presenting this proposal, the Soviet Union emphasized that parity presently existed between both sides' strategic systems. Over the next year the two sides slowly elaborated the details of their proposals, but little progress was made in bridging the gap between the two radically different approaches. . . .

### *The U.S. START Proposal Incorporating Build-Down*

On October 4, 1983, President Reagan announced that the United States would incorporate the build-down concept into the basic U.S. negotiating position. The build-down concept unveiled by the President was much more detailed than the build-down originally proposed by Senator Cohen. The new U.S. position included a proposal that the reduction to 5,000 missile warheads be carried out in whichever of the two following ways produced the greatest annual reduction in warheads: a link between warhead reductions and modernization that would use variable ratios to identify how many existing nuclear warheads must be withdrawn as new warheads of various types are deployed, or a guaranteed annual reduction of 5 percent in the total number of missile warheads. Specifically, the build-down provision reportedly called for the removal of two old warheads for each new MIRVed land-based missile warhead, three old warheads for every two new submarine-based missile warheads, and one old warhead for each new single-warhead land-based missile. In addition, the President stated that the U.S. delegation would be prepared to discuss the build-down of bombers and additional limitations on the air-launched cruise missiles carried by bombers, and to negotiate trade-offs that would take into account Soviet advantages in missiles and U.S. advantages in bombers in ways that would give each side maximum flexibility while maintaining movements toward greater stability. At the same time, the administration made clear that it was keeping intact the main features of the basic U.S. START proposal, including the reduction of missile warheads to 5,000, the limit on deployed ballistic missiles of 1,250, the need to reduce the throw-weight discrepancy between the two sides, and a ceiling of 400 on bombers.

Congressional supporters of the build-down hailed the President's action as a positive move in the arms control process. They stated that it demonstrated the willingness of the United States to make trade-offs between the U.S. lead in bombers and the Soviet lead in missiles. Congressional opponents of the build-down, particularly those who supported the comprehensive nuclear freeze, questioned the President's initiative. They emphasized that it would still allow dangerous, destabilizing first-strike systems to be produced and deployed and that it did not necessarily give the Soviet Union more flexibility in structuring its reductions, since the variable ratios discriminated against the land-based missiles that constitute 70 percent of the Soviet force. On October 31, 1983, the Senate rejected a legislative amendment supporting the comprehensive nuclear feeze and avoided a direct test on the build-down by voting in a parliamentary maneuver to postpone further debate on the approach.

The Soviet reaction to the new initiative was swift. Within a day of the President's offer, the Soviet news agency Tass dismissed the new U.S. proposal as a public relations ploy aimed at securing congressional approval of the MX missile and the planned deployment of medium-range nuclear arms in Europe. The same day as the President's offer, the Soviet Union had proposed at the United Nations a comprehensive nuclear freeze resolution, which was described as not inconsistent with their proposals in Geneva. Several weeks later, in a more detailed editorial on the new build-down initiative, *Pravda* called it entirely one-sided because it aimed chiefly at reducing the number and destructive power of ICBMs. With 70 percent of the Soviet force in ICBMs and only 20 percent of the U.S. force in these systems, *Pravda* stated that the plan was aimed at weakening the Soviet Union while allowing the United States to go ahead with all of its planned deployments for its strategic arsenal.

In Geneva the Soviet delegation reportedly showed no interest in the build-down proposals, arguing that the proposal still focused in a discriminatory manner on slashing Soviet ICBMs. At the end of Round V of START, which followed the Soviet walkout from the INF negotiations, the Soviet delegation did not set a resumption date for the talks, saying that the deployment of Pershing II and cruise missiles in Europe had changed "the overall strategic situation," which had to be reexamined. In response, President Reagan stated that the move was "more encouraging than a walkout" and that he hoped Soviet negotiators would return in 1984.

## U.S. and Soviet START Proposals

Complete descriptions of the U.S. and Soviet negotiating proposals at START have not been made public, but the main elements of the revised U.S. and Soviet START positions at the end of Round V in December 1983 have been announced by the U.S. government or reported authoritatively in the press.

### *The U.S. START Proposal as of December 1983*

The revised U.S. START proposal at the end of Round V included the following elements:

- Reductions to equal levels of 5,000 for both sides in the aggregate number of warheads on land- and sea-based ballistic missiles.
- Equal limits on deployed land- and sea-based ballistic missiles of 1,250 (originally 850).
- Equal ceilings on aggregate missile throw-weight by one of the following approaches: (1) indirectly, by a sublimit of 2,500 on warheads on deployed land-based missiles and sublimits on the number of deployed land-based medium and heavy ballistic missiles (originally the United States proposed a sublimit of 210 on these missiles, of which no more than 110 could be heavy ballistic missiles); (2) by unspecified equal ceilings on overall missile throw-weight that would be substantially below the present Soviet level of 5.6 million kilograms (originally this approach was to be the second phase of the START negotiations); or (3) by an alternative approach to be suggested by the Soviet Union to reduce its superiority in throw-weight.
- The proposed reductions to a ceiling of 5,000 missile warheads would be accomplished in annual increments by whichever of the following two procedures produced the greater annual reduction: (1) guaranteed annual reduction of 5 percent in the number of missile warheads or (2) build-down in missile warheads by reductions linked to any modernization programs by variable ratios defining the number of existing strategic missile warheads that must be withdrawn as new strategic missile warheads are introduced. Reportedly, to encourage modernization toward more stable systems, the build-down would require the removal of two old warheads for each new MIRVed land-based missile warhead, three old warheads for every two new submarine-based missile warheads, and one old warhead for each new single-warhead land-based missile.
- An equal ceiling for both sides of 400 strategic bombers (to include the Soviet Backfire bomber), with a limit of 20 cruise missiles per bomber.
- A willingness by the U.S. delegation to (1) address the build-down of bombers, (2) discuss additional limitations on the air-launched cruise missiles carried by bombers, and (3) negotiate trade-offs that would take into account Soviet advantages in missiles and U.S. advantages in bombers in ways that would give each side maximum flexibility while maintaining movements toward greater stability.

- Unspecified verification measures involving more comprehensive and intrusive measures than in previous agreements to ensure compliance. No encryption of flight test data must be permitted.
- A series of confidence-building measures.

*The Soviet START Proposal as of December 1983*

The revised Soviet START proposal at the end of Round V included the following elements:

- An interim freeze of unspecified coverage on strategic nuclear arms while the negotiations are in progress.
- A limit of 1,800 on the aggregate number of ICBM launchers, SLBM launchers, and heavy bombers (reduced by 20 percent from the SALT II limit of 1,250).
- A limit of 1,200 on MIRVed missile launchers plus bombers equipped with air-launched cruise missiles (reduced from the SALT II limit of 1,320).
- A limit of 1,080 on MIRVed missile launchers (reduced from the SALT II limit of 1,200).
- A limit of 680 land-based MIRVed ICBM launchers (reduced from the SALT II limit of 820).
- Unspecified equal aggregate limits on missile warheads and bomber weapons.
- A number of modernization constraints, including a ban on the deployment of ground- and sea-launched cruise missiles with a range greater than 600 km.
- Corresponding verification provisions.

The Soviet Union also dropped earlier provisions that would have banned the Trident II missile and long-range cruise missiles on aircraft, limited the U.S. deployment of new Trident submarines to four or six, and reduced the number of missiles on future Trident submarines from 24 to 16.

## The Compliance Issue

### *Document 21*

One of the main characteristics of the new Reagan approach to arms control was the belief that the Soviets had violated past arms control agreements and that past administrations had ignored the violations. In this unclassified report to Congress, the administration lays out its case against the Soviets. This was one of several public reports by the administration on alleged Soviet cheating on agreements. This public airing of the compliance issue was a departure in U.S. policy.

### 21 THE PRESIDENT'S REPORT ON SOVIET NONCOMPLIANCE December 23, 1985

In reporting to the Congress on February 1 of this year on Soviet noncompliance with arms control agreements, I have stated that:

> In order for arms control to have meaning and credibly contribute to national security and to global or regional stability, it is essential that all parties to agreements fully comply with them. Strict compliance with all provisions of arms control agreements is fundamental, and this Administration will not accept anything less. To do so would undermine the arms control process and damage the chances for establishing a more constructive U.S.-Soviet relationship.

I further stated that:

> Soviet noncompliance is a serious matter. It calls into question important security benefits from arms control, and could create new security risks. It undermines the confidence essential to an effective arms control process in the future. With regard to the issues analyzed in the January 1984 report, the Soviet Union has thus far not provided satisfactory explanations nor undertaken corrective actions sufficient to alleviate our concerns. The United States Government has vigorously pressed, and will continue to press, these compliance issues with the Soviet Union through diplomatic channels. . . .

At the request of the Congress, I have in the past two years provided three reports to the Congress on Soviet compliance issues. The first, forwarded in January 1984, reviewed seven compliance issues, concluding that the Soviet Union had, in fact, violated a number of important arms control commitments.

In September 1984 I provided, at the request of the Congress, a report on Soviet noncompliance prepared by the independent General Advisory Committee on Arms Control and Disarmament. That report concluded that over a 25-year span the Soviets had violated a substantial number of arms control commitments.

In February 1985, I submitted a report to the Congress updating the Administration's January 1984 report and reviewing 13 issues that could be treated in unclassified terms and an additional group of six issues treated on a classified basis. That report discussed the pattern of Soviet arms control violations, probable violations, or ambiguous activity in seventeen cases. The U.S. Government found seven Soviet violations, three probable violations, one likely and one potential violation. The Soviets were found to be in compliance in two other cases examined.

One of those issues, Yankee-Class submarine reconfiguration, is not addressed in the current report. While a submarine reconfigured to carry long-range cruise missiles constitutes a threat similar to that of the original SSBN, I reported in February that Soviet reconfiguration activities have not been in violation of the SALT I [strategic arms limitation talks] Interim Agreement. This issue, therefore, requires no further judgment in terms of compliance at present.

Public Law 99–145 requires the Administration to

provide on an annual basis by December 1 of each year a classified and unclassified report to the Congress containing the findings of the President and any additional information necessary to keep the Congress informed on Soviet compliance with arms control agreements.

The current report responds to this Congressional requirement. It is the product of months of careful technical and legal analysis by all relevant agencies of the United States Government and represents the Administration's authoritative updated treatment of this important matter.

The current unclassified report examines one new issue and updates all of the issues studied in the classified report of February 1985, except the issue of Yankee-Class submarine reconfiguration. There are violations in nine cases. Of the nine cases involving violations, one SALT II issue — that of Soviet concealment of the association between missiles and their launchers — is examined for the first time. The Soviet Union has now also violated its commitment to the SALT I Interim Agreement through the prohibited use of remaining facilities at former SS–7 ICBM [intercontinental ballistic missile] sites. In addition, Soviet deployment of the SS–25 ICBM during 1985 constitutes a further violation of the SALT II prohibition on a second new type of ICBM. Several other issues involve potential, probable or likely violations.

The current unclassified report reaffirms the findings of the February 1985 classified report concerning ABM [antiballistic missile] issues, making public two of them for the first time. It also reaffirms the February findings concerning SALT II issues involving violations, including one concerning strategic nuclear delivery vehicles, which has not previously been made public. In two SALT II issues with respect to which the Soviets were not judged to be in clear violation in the classified report of last February, the findings are altered or updated. These two issues are the SS–16 and an issue made public for the first time — Backfire Bomber production rate.

The Administration's most recent studies support its conclusion that there is a pattern of Soviet noncompliance. As documented in this and previous reports, the Soviet Union has violated its legal obligation under our political commitment to the SALT I ABM Treaty and Interim Agreement, the SALT II agreement, the Limited Test Ban Treaty of 1963, the Biological and Toxin Weapons Convention, the Geneva Protocol on Chemical Weapons, and the Helsinki Final Act. In addition, the U.S.S.R. has likely violated provisions of the Threshold Test Ban Treaty.

While we remain concerned about Soviet violations of Basket I of the Helsinki Final Act and the Limited Test Ban Treaty, there is no unambiguous evidence of new 1985 Soviet violations of these two treaties. With regard to the Biological and Toxin Weapons Convention, or the Geneva Protocol on Chemical Weapons, there also is no unambiguous evidence of new 1985 Soviet lethal attacks that meets our strict standards of evidence. However, the Soviets clearly remain in violation of the Biological and Toxin Weapons Convention.

## The Significance of Soviet Noncompliance

Through its noncompliance, the Soviet Union has made military gains in the areas of strategic offensive arms as well as chemical, biological and toxin weapons. If the yields of Soviet nuclear tests have been substantially above 150 kilotons, then Soviet testing would allow proportionately greater gains in nuclear weapons development than the U.S. could achieve. The possible extent of the Soviet Union's military gains by virtue of its noncompliance in the area of strategic defense also is of increasing importance and serious concern.

In a fundamental sense, all deliberate Soviet violations are equally important. As violations of legal obligations or political commitments, they cause grave concern regarding Soviet commitment to arms control, and they darken the atmosphere in which current negotiations are being conducted in Geneva and elsewhere.

In another sense, Soviet violations are not of equal importance. While some individual violations are of little apparent military significance in their own right, such violations can acquire importance if, left unaddressed, they are permitted to become precedents for future, more threatening violations. Moreover, some issues that individually have little military significance could conceivably become significant when taken in their aggregate.

### *Telemetry Encryption and Concealment of Missile/Launcher Association*

Two other Soviet violations impede our ability to verify the Soviet Union's compliance with its political commitments. Soviet use of encryption impedes U.S. verification of Soviet compliance and thus contravenes the provision of the SALT II Treaty which prohibits use of deliberate concealment measures which impede verification of compliance by national technical means. A new finding of this report is that current Soviet activities violate the provision of the Treaty which prohibits use of deliberate concealment measures associated with testing, including those measures aimed at concealing the association between ICBMs and launchers during testing. These deliberate Soviet concealment activities impede our ability to know whether a type of missile is in compliance with SALT II requirements. They could also make it more difficult for the United States to assess accurately the critical parameters of any future missile.

Since the SALT I agreement in 1972, Soviet encryption and concealment activities have become more extensive and disturbing. These activities, Soviet responses on these issues, and Soviet failure to take the corrective actions which the United States has repeatedly requested, are indicative of a Soviet attitude contrary to the fundamentals of sound arms control agreements. Soviet encryption and concealment activities present special obstacles to maintaining existing arms control agreements, undermine the political confidence necessary for concluding new treaties, and underscore the necessity that any new agreement be effectively verifiable. Soviet noncompliance, as documented in current and past Administration reports and exemplified by the encryption and concealment issues, has made verification and compliance pacing elements of arms control today.

### *Chemical, Biological and Toxin Weapons*

The Soviet Union's violations of its legal obligations under the Biological and Toxin Weapons Convention and the Geneva Protocol have important political and military implications. The Soviets had a program of biological and toxin weapons before they signed the multilateral Treaty. Upon signing the Treaty, the Soviets not only did not stop their illegal program but they expanded facilities and were instrumental in the use of prohibited agents.

The Soviet Union has a prohibited offensive biological warfare capability which we do not have and against which we have no defense. This capability may include advanced biological agents about which we have little knowledge. Evidence suggests that the Soviets are expanding their chemical and toxin warfare capabilities in a manner that has no parallel in NATO's retaliatory or defensive programs. Even though there has been no unambiguous evidence of lethal attacks during 1985, previous activities have provided testing, development and operational experience.

### *Nuclear Testing*

With respect to the Threshold Test Ban Treaty, Soviet testing at yields above the 150 kiloton limit would allow development of advanced nuclear weapons with proportionately higher yields than the yields of weapons that the U.S. could develop under the Treaty. The U.S. Government judges that Soviet test activities constitute likely violations of the 150 kiloton limit.

### *Other Issues*

Military significance is evidently not necessarily the determining factor in Soviet decisions or actions which violate their arms control commitments. The Soviet Union has also violated or probably violated arms control obligations and commitments from which at present it appears to reap little military gain. The following cases are relevant in this regard:

- the use of remaining facilities at former SS–7 ICBM sites since the February 1985 compliance report (SALT I Interim Agreement);
- exceeding the strategic nuclear delivery vehicle limits (SALT II);
- probable deployment of the SS–16 (SALT II); and
- underground nuclear test venting (Limited Test Ban Treaty).

The 1981 Soviet violation of the military exercise notification provisions of the Helsinki Final Act involved an action contrary to the confidence building measures included in that agreement.

Soviet deployments of Backfire Bombers to Arctic staging bases are inconsistent with the Soviet Union's political commitment to the SALT II Treaty. In addition, while there are ambiguities concerning the data, there is evidence that the production rate of the Backfire Bomber was constant at slightly more than 30 per year until 1984, and slightly less than 30 per year since then. These Soviet Backfire Bomber activities will continue to be monitored and assessed.

## The Soviet Response

At the same time as the Administration has reported its concerns and findings to the Congress, the United States has had extensive exchanges with the Soviet Union on Soviet noncompliance in the Standing Consultative Commission (SCC), where SALT-related issues (including ABM issues) are discussed, and through other appropriate diplomatic channels. I expressed my personal concerns directly to General Secretary Gorbachev during my recent meeting with him in Geneva.

All of the violations, probable violations and ambiguous situations included in this report and previously reported on have been raised with the Soviets, except certain sensitive issues. The Soviet Union has thus far not provided explanations sufficient to alleviate our concerns on these issues, nor has the Soviet Union taken actions needed to correct existing violations. Instead, they have continued to assert that they are in complete compliance with their arms control obligations and commitments.

## U.S. Policy

In contrast with the Soviet Union, the United States has fully observed its arms control obligations and commitments, including those under the SALT I and SALT II agreements. As I stated in my message to the Congress on June 10 of this year concerning U.S. interim restraint policy:

> In 1982, on the eve of the Strategic Arms Reduction Talks (START), I decided that the United States would not undercut the expired SALT I agreement or the unratified SALT II agreement as long as the Soviet Union exercised equal restraint. Despite my serious reservations about the inequities of the SALT I agreement and the serious flaws

of the SALT II agreement, I took this action in order to foster an atmosphere of mutual restraint conducive to serious negotiation as we entered START.

Since then, the United States has not taken any actions which would undercut existing arms control agreements. The United States has fully kept its part of the bargain. However, the Soviets have not. They have failed to comply with several provisions of SALT II, and we have serious concerns regarding their compliance with the provisions of other accords.

The pattern of Soviet violations, if left uncorrected, undercuts the integrity and viability of arms control as an instrument to assist in ensuring a secure and stable future world. The United States will continue to pursue vigorously with the Soviet Union the resolution of our concerns over Soviet noncompliance. We cannot impose upon ourselves a double standard that amounts to unilateral treaty compliance.

On June 10, I invited the Soviet Union to join the United States in an interim framework of truly mutual restraint on strategic offensive arms and to pursue with renewed vigor our top priority of achieving deep reductions in the size of existing nuclear arsenals in the ongoing negotiations in Geneva. I noted that the U.S. cannot establish such a framework alone and that it would require the Soviet Union to take positive, concrete steps to correct its noncompliance, to resolve our other compliance concerns, to reverse its unparalleled and unwarranted military buildup, and actively to pursue arms reduction agreements in the Geneva negotiations.

In going the extra mile, I have made clear that as an integral part of this policy, we will also take those steps required to assure our national security and that of our Allies that were made necessary by Soviet noncompliance. Thus, as I indicated to the Congress on June 10, "appropriate and proportionate responses to Soviet noncompliance are called for to ensure our security, to provide incentives to the Soviets to correct their noncompliance, and to make it clear to Moscow that violations of arms control obligations entail real costs."

As we monitor Soviet actions for evidence of the positive, concrete steps needed on their part to correct these activities, I have directed the Department of Defense to conduct a comprehensive assessment aimed at identifying specific actions that the United States could take to augment as necessary the U.S. strategic modernization program as a proportionate response to, and as a hedge against the military consequences of those Soviet violations of existing arms control agreements which the Soviets fail to correct. We will carefully study this report as soon as it has been completed.

As we press for corrective Soviet actions and while keeping open all programmatic options for handling future milestones as new U.S. strategic systems are deployed, we will continue to assess the overall situation in light of Soviet actions correcting their noncompliance, reversing their military build-up, and promoting progress in Geneva.

I look forward to continued close consultation with the Congress as we seek to make progress in resolving compliance issues and in negotiating sound arms control agreements.

## A Soviet Initiative — Gorbachev's January 1986 Speech

### *Document 22*

Arms control negotiations were broken off until January 1985. When they resumed, both sides made new proposals, but little progress was made. The Soviets finally stopped changing leaders in March 1985, when Mikhail Gorbachev became general secretary. Gorbachev launched new initiatives in many foreign policy areas, including arms control. In January 1986, after his first summit with President Reagan, he made a major speech laying out a plan to eliminate nuclear weapons. This excerpt from a January 1986 article in *Time* discusses the proposal. Gorbachev laid out a timetable for eliminating all nuclear arms and seemed to accept the U.S. zero option (see chap. 10) for eliminating INF missiles in Europe. Gorbachev also suggested new departures on chemical weapons, a nuclear test ban, verification, and controls on conventional forces. The article notes that the Gorbachev proposal caught the Reagan administration off guard and put the United States on the defensive.

### 22 A FAREWELL TO ARMS? January 27, 1986

Soviet diplomats frequently call at the State Department. Particularly since the Geneva summit, there has been a great deal of mid-level diplomacy. So there was no reason to expect anything out of the ordinary when Oleg Sokolov, the Soviet chargé d'affaires in Washington, arrived early last Wednesday morning to see Secretary of State George Shultz. But when Sokolov handed him a lengthy letter from Mikhail Gorbachev to Ronald Reagan, Shultz became the first man in official Washington to be startled by a sweeping and unexpected new arms-control proposal. It was studded with ambiguities and potentially risky approaches, but it also set forth a bold schedule for making the world nuclear-free and left the Administration scrambling for a way to respond. One quick reading of the letter sent Shultz straight to the White House.

Some three hours later in Moscow, the proposal was presented to the world's public — the audience at which it was largely aimed — in typical Soviet fashion. The anchorman on the nightly newscast *Vremya* (Time), his face expressionless, picked up a sheaf of papers and announced, with no more emotion than he might have used to present a weather report, that he had a "statement by the General Secretary of the Communist Party." Then he droned on for half an hour as the news agency TASS distributed the statement around the world.

As many Soviet and American leaders had done before, Gorbachev called for total elimination of nuclear missiles, warheads, bombs and other weapons from the planet. But this was not presented as a vague goal for the future; he proposed a fairly detailed, three-stage timetable culminating at the end of the century. He also offered tantalizing hints about ways to break specific deadlocks. If his plan is adopted, Gorbachev grandly concluded, "by the end of 1999 there will be no nuclear weapons on earth."

Propaganda? Certainly, and very skillful propaganda too. Both its grand vision and many of its specifics are clearly designed to win Moscow public support in Western Europe and around the world while allowing it to retain certain strategic advantages. The plan has a Grammsky-Rudsky appeal, decreeing a timetable for eliminating nuclear weapons the way the Gramm-Rudman Act has decreed a timetable for eliminating the U.S. budget deficit. As with Gramm-Rudman, the cuts proposed by Gorbachev seem to have an easy and automatic simplicity, but the plan ignores the hard and complex choices that will have to be made down the road to preserve the delicate nuclear balance. Indeed, the initial reductions in strategic weapons would tilt the balance dangerously in the Soviets' favor. In addition, the whole scheme appears to hang on a condition that Gorbachev knows Reagan resists: U.S. abandonment of the Strategic Defense Initiative, or Star Wars, whose goal is to develop a defensive shield against nuclear missiles.

But Gorbachev's plan also contains some surprising elements not readily dismissed. Its proposal for the removal of U.S. and Soviet intermediate-range nuclear weapons in Europe is similar to the "zero option" offered by Reagan in 1981. Gorbachev also declared himself ready to accept "on-site inspection" as a means of verifying any agreements. Although it is by no means certain that Moscow will eventually agree to the type and number of inspections necessary to ensure that the Soviets cannot cheat, this represents a concession that Moscow had never made quite so explicitly before.

Gorbachev's proposals caught Washington totally by surprise. At the very moment that Shultz was relaying the Soviet leader's letter to Reagan in the Oval Office, other senior officials were telling journalists in the White House briefing room a few yards away that they expected no significant change in Moscow's negotiating positions until after the Soviet Communist Party Congress next month. The following day, Reagan told reporters, "We are very grateful for the offer." Inexplicably, he added, "It's just about the first time that anyone has ever proposed actually eliminating nuclear weapons"—forgetting not only his own statements identifying that as an ultimate goal but the many similar proposals stretching back over the past four decades.

When Soviet and American bargainers met in Geneva on Thursday to kick off a new round in the arms-control talks that have been recessed since November, Soviet Chief Negotiator Victor Karpov primarily confined himself to a word-for-word repetition of Gorbachev's statement. American negotiators, headed by Max Kampelman, could coax only one elaboration. Asked if the proposal for a ban on Star Wars "development" would forbid research, a Soviet representative referred the Americans to Gorbachev's interview with TIME last August, in which the Kremlin leader said that fundamental research—a term maddeningly difficult to define—might be permitted.

Even more than most Soviet arms-control proposals, Gorbachev's plan is a tantalizing mixture of old and new, ambiguity and detail, apparent concessions and repeated demands. Its distinctive feature is its specific timetable. In the first stage, covering the next five to eight years, Washington and Moscow would agree to and begin a 50% reduction in nuclear weapons capable of striking each other's country. Each side would be limited to 6,000 remaining "nuclear charges" (warheads and bombs), only 3,600 of which could be placed on the long-range land-based missiles that are the backbone of the Soviet arsenal. Washington has also proposed a 50% cut; indeed, Reagan and Gorbachev agreed on one in principle at their November summit meeting. But the U.S. wants to confine the cuts to "strategic" weapons, primarily land-based intercontinental and submarine-launched missiles, while Gorbachev would include America's medium-range bombers based overseas that could hit the Soviet Union.

Gorbachev's first phase would also include an agreement for "elimination" of U.S. and Soviet intermediate-range missiles from the "European zone." At first glance that looks like Reagan's zero option: no U.S. missiles in Western Europe (the U.S. is deploying 108 Pershing II ballistic and 464 Tomahawk cruise missiles in five countries); no Soviet missiles targeted on Western Europe (Moscow has more than 250 mobile, triple-warhead SS-20s in place). Up until last week, the Soviets insisted on keeping enough SS-20s (roughly 140) to equal the number of missiles in the independent British and French nuclear forces. Gorbachev apparently dropped that demand, though on the condition that Britain and France agree not to "build up" their deterrents.

But Gorbachev left it unclear whether the SS-20s to be removed from Europe would be destroyed or simply shuttled into Soviet Asia. From there they could be quickly moved back into Europe during a crisis. In addition, London and Paris are unlikely to halt the scheduled modernization of their nuclear forces.

Another question is whether an agreement on intermediate-range missiles would be conditioned on U.S. renunciation of Star Wars. Negotiator Karpov told journalists in Geneva that elimination of so-called Euromissiles could be negotiated "without links to strategic or space weapons." But Gorbachev's statement asserted that large-scale reductions would be possible "only if the U.S.S.R. and the U.S.A. mutually renounce the development, testing and deployment of space strike weapons."

In the second stage of Gorbachev's program, which would begin by 1990 and last five to seven years, the U.S., the Soviet Union and "other" nuclear powers would make further reductions in intermediate-range missiles and carry out a phased elimination of battlefield nuclear weapons. The problems are obvious: agreement would be required not only from Britain and France but from China, the other known member of the "nuclear club" and a nation that has so far refused to join any nuclear negotiations. An even stickier problem is that the U.S. and its NATO allies depend on nuclear weapons to deter the Soviets from attacking or threatening Western Europe. The Warsaw Pact has a hefty superiority in ground troops and conventional weapons.

Gorbachev's third stage is the most visionary: starting no later than 1995, all nations would get rid of any remaining nuclear weapons and pledge never to build any more. "Mankind [could] approach the year 2000 under peaceful skies and with peaceful space, without fear of . . . annihilation."

Gorbachev also advanced a host of more immediate proposals. In tacit recognition of the link between battlefield nuclear weapons and conventional arms, he called for a speeding up of the negotiations on troop reductions in Europe that have been dragging on in Vienna for twelve years, and matched a Western concession made last December with one of his own on verification. He proposed an agreement on chemical weapons that moved beyond Moscow's previous willingness to destroy only existing stockpiles and called for dismantling production facilities as well. He also extended for three months a Soviet moratorium on weapons tests that began last August and was to have expired on Jan. 1, and he pledged to prolong it further if the U.S. should join. Washington insists it needs to test in order to catch up to Soviet advantages.

Gorbachev is obviously seeking to put Reagan on the defensive, which he has. The Soviet leader's proposal is deftly crafted to appeal immediately to many West Europeans who are anxious about nuclear missiles stationed on their soil or aimed at them. The President will now feel pressure to demonstrate progress toward a deal when the two meet in Washington for their second summit, possibly as early as June.

Gorbachev's initiative will make it ever more difficult for Reagan to put forth a public case for pursuing his Star Wars program. Said the Soviet leader: "Instead of wasting the next ten to 15 years by developing new weapons in space, allegedly designed to make nuclear arms useless, would it not be more sensible to eliminate those arms?" Reagan is caught in a public relations bind: it will be difficult for him to explain convincingly why he is prepared to scuttle a plan to rid the world of nuclear missiles by insisting on the right to build a defensive shield against those missiles. The Soviets are likely to confront Reagan with the somewhat illogical statement he made in his Oct. 31 interview with four Soviet journalists, in which he pledged to seek the elimination of nuclear missiles before deploying a defense against them.

The British, French and West German governments reacted to Gorbachev's proposals about the same way Washington did, expressing both cautious interest and wary skepticism. But one British diplomat ruefully asserted, "It is so simplistic. Good Guy Mikhail offers to get rid of all nuclear missiles while Ron the Hawk lumbers on with his antimissile system. It is going to be a difficult task to explain to public opinion that in the real world it is the small print that really matters, not the grandiose initiatives."

At the moment, Washington is stuck for an effective way to counter Gorbachev's grandiose initiative. Caught off guard, officials have only begun to ponder whether to make a new American proposal, and, if so, what to put in it. The debate is likely to be sharp; the Administration has long been deeply divided over arms control, and previous American proposals have emerged only after prolonged and sometimes heated pulling and hauling.

For now, the U.S. line is simply to insist that Soviet negotiators spell out all the small print in Gorbachev's proposals. So far as it goes, that is logical. For all its ambiguities and propagandistic sweep, the plan hints at enough concessions to spur serious negotiating. Only detailed probing at Geneva will determine how much is real and how much is propaganda, and there is room for healthy skepticism. But the heat will be on Washington — both for the sake of winning the battle for public opinion and, more important, for keeping alive the hope of a genuine arms-control breakthrough — to come up with a response as imaginative as Gorbachev's. In arms-control negotiations, skepticism is always necessary but rarely sufficient.

## Two Views of the Reykjavik Summit

### *Documents 23 and 24*

Soon after the Reykjavik summit began, it became clear that the Soviets had come prepared to deal. They had modified their positions in important ways. They responded by making some compromises, and the two sides made much progress in several of the key areas of arms control, especially in INF and strategic offensive arms. But SDI proved once again to be a stumbling block. The Soviets were adamant about limiting the defensive program the Reagan administration wanted to protect.

President Reagan addressed the nation after the summit. As the excerpts from his speech in document 23 show, he justified his actions in Iceland as being necessary to save SDI, which was vital to U.S. security. In document 24, Strobe Talbott and Michael Mandelbaum review the negotiations at the summit and the other key events in U.S.-Soviet relations that led up to it. They argue that the Soviets sought a "grand compromise": limits on defenses in exchange for limits on offensive forces. They also argue that the Iceland summit, if it had been successful, would have reestablished elements of continuity in the U.S.-Soviet relationship.

## 23 BROADCAST ADDRESS
## President Ronald Reagan
## October 13, 1986

Good evening. As most of you know, I have just returned from meetings in Iceland with the leader of the Soviet Union, General Secretary Gorbachev. As I did last year when I returned from the summit conference in Geneva, I want to take a few moments tonight to share with you what took place in these discussions.

The implications of these talks are enormous and only just beginning to be understood.

We proposed the most sweeping and generous arms control proposal in history. We offered the complete elimination of all ballistic missiles — Soviet and American — from the face of the earth by 1996. While we parted company with this American offer still on the table, we are closer than ever before to agreements that could lead to a safer world without nuclear weapons.

But first, let me tell you that, from the start of my meetings with Mr. Gorbachev, I have always regarded you, the American people, as full participants. Believe me, without your support, none of these talks could have been held, nor could the ultimate aims of American foreign policy — world peace and freedom — be pursued. And it is for these aims I went the extra mile to Iceland.

Before I report on our talks though, allow me to set the stage by explaining two things that were very much a part of our talks, one a treaty and the other a defense against nuclear missiles which we are trying to develop. You've heard their titles a thousand times — the ABM treaty and S.D.I. Those letters stand for anti-ballistic missile and Strategic Defense Initiative.

Some years ago, the U.S. and the Soviet Union agreed to limit any defense against nuclear missile attacks to the emplacement in one location in each country of a small number of missiles capable of intercepting and shooting down incoming nuclear missiles. Thus leaving our real defense a policy called the Mutual Assured Destruction, meaning if one side launched a nuclear attack, the other side could retaliate. This mutual threat of destruction was believed to be a deterrent against either side striking first.

So here we sit with thousands of nuclear warheads targeted on each other and capable of wiping out both our countries. The Soviets deployed the few anti-ballistic missiles around Moscow as the treaty permitted. Our country didn't bother deploying because the threat of nationwide annihiliation made such limited defense seem useless.

For some years now we have been aware that the Soviets have been developing a nationwide defense. They have installed a large modern radar at Krashnoyarsk which we believe is a critical part of a radar system designed to provide radar guidance for anti-ballistic missiles protecting the entire nation. This is a violation of the ABM treaty.

Believing that a policy of mutual destruction and slaughter of their citizens and ours was uncivilized, I asked our military a few years ago to study and see if there was a practical way to destroy nuclear missiles after their launch but before they can reach their targets rather than just destroy people. This is the goal for what we call S.D.I., and our scientists researching such a system are convinced it is practical and that several years down the road we can have such a system ready to deploy. Incidentally we are not violating the ABM treaty, which permits such research. If and when we deploy, the treaty also allows withdrawal from the treaty upon six months' notice. S.D.I., let me make it clear, is not pursuing a non-nuclear defense. . . .

I realize some Americans may be asking tonight: Why not accept Mr. Gorbachev's demand? Why not give up S.D.I. for this agreement?

The answer, my friends, is simple. S.D.I. is America's insurance policy that the Soviet Union would keep the commitments made at Reykjavik. S.D.I. is America's security guarantee — if the Soviets should — as they have done too often in the past — fail to comply with their solemn commitments. S.D.I. is what brought the Soviets back to arms control talks at Geneva and Iceland. S.D.I. is the key to a world without nuclear weapons.

The Soviets understand this. They have devoted far more resources, for a lot longer time than we, to *their own* S.D.I. The world's only operational missile defense today surrounds Moscow, the capital of the Soviet Union. What Mr. Gorbachev was demanding at Reykjavik was that the United States agree to a new version of a 14-year-old ABM treaty that the Soviet Union has already violated. I told him we don't make those kinds of deals in the United States.

And the American people should reflect on these critical questions.

How does a defense of the United States threaten the Soviet Union or anyone else? Why are the Soviets so adamant that America remain forever vulnerable to Soviet rocket attack? As of today, all free nations are utterly defenseless against Soviet missiles — fired either by accident or design. Why does the Soviet Union insist that we remain so — forever?

So, my fellow Americans, I cannot promise, nor can any President promise, that the talks in Iceland or any future discussions with Mr. Gorbachev will lead inevitably to great breakthroughs or momentous treaty signings.

We will not abandon the guiding principle we took to Reykjavik. We prefer no agreement than to bring home a bad agreement to the United States.

And on this point, I know you are also interested in the question of whether there will be another summit. There was no indication by Mr. Gorbachev as to when or whether he plans to travel to the United States, as we agreed he would last year in Geneva. I repeat tonight that our invitation stands and that we continue to believe additional meetings would be useful. But that's a decision the Soviets must make.

But whatever the immediate prospects, I can tell you that I am ultimately hopeful about the prospects for progress at the summit and for world peace and freedom. You see, the current summit process is very different from that of previous decades; it is different because the world is different; and the world is different because of the hard work and sacrifice of the American people during the past five and a half years.

## 24 REYKJAVIK AND BEYOND
## Michael Mandelbaum and Strobe Talbott

The late summer and autumn of 1986 were a busy, confusing and dramatic period in Soviet-American relations. Within four months, the tone and substance of communications between Washington and Moscow oscillated sharply between conciliation and acrimony. At issue was whether there would be a second meeting between Ronald Reagan and Mikhail Gorbachev. If summitry futures had been traded like commodities, fortunes would have been made and lost. The two leaders themselves engaged in a kind of arbitrage, trying to make quick political profits from the swings of the market.

In July and August Reagan and Gorbachev exchanged letters, and each dispatched delegations of arms control experts to the other's capital. Momentum seemed to be building toward a summit in Washington at the end of the year. Then an American journalist was arrested in Moscow. Suddenly the mood soured, and the momentum slowed. But in the midst of what turned out to be a minor crisis, Reagan and Gorbachev made clear first to each other and then to the world that they were determined to proceed with the business between them. They agreed to hold a meeting, which quickly became one of the most extraordinary encounters in the history of relations between their countries, perhaps in the annals of high-level diplomacy.

The two-day meeting in Reykjavik, Iceland, on October 11–12, 1986, broke with virtually all the precedents of U.S.-Soviet relations. There were scarcely any preparations. The meeting that took place was entirely different from the one the Americans had expected. They had anticipated not a full-fledged summit but, in President Reagan's words, "the last base camp" on the way to a Washington summit. Yet the agenda turned out to be much broader, and the issues discussed far more consequential, than even those the Americans had envisioned for the anticipated full summit itself.

In some obvious ways the Reykjavik meeting was a failure. At least in the short term, it derailed the summit process and dramatized the fragility of the U.S.-Soviet relationship. Not since Khrushchev had refused to meet with President Eisenhower in Paris in 1960 and argued with President Kennedy in Vienna the following year had an encounter between the American and Soviet leaders ended so badly. In Iceland, when Reagan emerged from his final session with Gorbachev, his usual jaunty manner was missing; his mood was grim.

In reporting to the press immediately afterward, Secretary of State George Shultz appeared exhausted, dejected and defeated. He had to fight to control his emotions. He repeatedly used the word "disappointment" to describe the weekend. White House Chief of Staff Donald Regan, at an impromptu press conference at Keflavik Airport, lashed out at the Soviets, saying that "they finally showed their hand; it showed them up for what they are." He said that "there will not be another summit in the near future as far as I can see."

Despite the spectacular collapse of the meeting and the ensuing acrimony, there was also significant, if tentative, progress on arms control. In his press conference, Shultz spoke of "potential agreements" that were "breathtaking." The two sides moved closer to accommodation on a number of issues than their top officials had considered possible beforehand.

In violation of all conventional wisdom about sound negotiating tactics and prudent diplomacy, Reagan and Gorbachev engaged each other on the biggest, most difficult issue dividing them — how to structure and limit their huge stockpiles of nuclear weapons — and then proceeded to improvise. Working groups of experts with no clear instructions toiled through the night to hammer out compromises on matters that years of negotiation had failed to resolve. The two leaders themselves spontaneously tabled variations on one of the oldest, most implausible and least productive themes of the nuclear age — general and complete nuclear disarmament. But they also spent considerable time adjusting their proposals for more practical measures that could become part of achievable, verifiable agreements.

They failed at the last minute to overcome the principal obstacle to a treaty that might significantly reduce the levels of offensive weaponry on both sides. They could not resolve the question of how, if at all, to constrain President Reagan's Strategic Defense Initiative. SDI was then, as it had been for several years and promises to be for some time, the most contentious issue in Soviet-American relations. Gorbachev insisted that the program would give the United States military technical superiority and a first-strike capability against the U.S.S.R. President Reagan insisted just as forcefully that SDI would produce a purely defensive shield against all offensive nuclear forces and was, therefore, the moral alternative to traditional deterrence based on mutual assured destruction. Neither leader would accept the other's reasoning.

But the meeting did offer a glimmer of hope of a world in which the United States and its allies would be less threatened by Soviet ballistic missiles. It also demonstrated that SDI gives the United States considerable leverage in the effort to achieve such a world through arms control. . . .

When it came time to make a deal that would be the centerpiece of a summit, Shultz and Shevardnadze were drawn toward INF. That negotiation lent itself to the immediate diplomatic need to achieve concrete agreement far more easily than did START and the space and defense talks, where there were thorny and vitally important military questions at stake, such as whether the United States should spend billions on developing exotic antiballistic missile systems and whether the Soviet Union would have to spend comparable sums on countermeasures.

But when Reagan arrived for the first session in Reykjavik, he found that INF was neither the main item on the agenda nor was it detached from the other, more difficult, strategic issues. Gorbachev had brought with him a briefcase full of papers outlining nothing less than a comprehensive arms control agreement dealing with INF, START and SDI, as well as other issues such as nuclear weapons testing. In the words of one of the President's aides, the Soviet leader was "going for the big casino."

From the beginning it was clear to Reagan that while Gorbachev had come prepared to make some unexpectedly forthcoming concessions, they might all be contingent on some sort of reciprocal American flexibility on SDI, although exactly what that flexibility would have to involve was not at first apparent. Emerging from his first session with Gorbachev to meet with his advisers, President Reagan said, "He's brought at whole lot of proposals, but I'm afraid he's going after SDI."

Gorbachev was proposing a version of what many arms control specialists inside and outside the Administration had long anticipated — and what some had advocated. For many months they had speculated about the possibility of a "grand compromise" in which the United States would accept significant constraints on SDI in exchange for equally significant reductions in Soviet offensive forces. The Soviet incentive for much a compromise was plain. An American defensive system, even if it were not particularly effective, would force the Kremlin into an expensive and potentially disruptive round of the arms race. Moreover, SDI represented a new kind of competition in exotic technology, where the advantage, at least initially, would be with the United States. Those who pondered the possibilities for such a compromise had never been certain about how far the Soviets would go in offering to reduce their most threatening offensive weapons in order to obtain restraints on American defenses.

In Reykjavik Gorbachev and his colleagues moved toward answering that question, although the response that emerged was not conclusive, precise or binding. The exact terms of the tentative accord reached during the weekend were the subject of considerable confusion. There were subsequent disagreements about exactly what had been decided, what conditions had been attached and what timetable had been stipulated. Some reductions were slated to take place over five years, others over the course of ten. Some of the provisions for the second phase seemed more like utopian reveries or pure propaganda than real arms control. In the week after the summit, senior Administration officials launched an intense public relations campaign to reverse the impression that Reykjavik had ended in failure. They engaged in a surreal debate with the Soviets, and sometimes with each other, over whether by 1996 the world was to be free of all nuclear weapons, as the Soviets contended, or only of all ballistic missiles. Neither the President nor Donald Regan was at first quite clear on that point.

During a climactic Sunday session in Reykjavik, President Reagan proposed the elimination of ballistic missiles within ten years. This would have deprived the Soviet Union of its most formidable weapons while leaving the United States with an advantage in nuclear-armed bombers and cruise missiles. Gorbachev countered with a variation of a proposal he had been making since January for the elimination of all nuclear weapons, which would have left the Soviet Union with numerical advantages in conventional forces. Reagan replied, "That suits me fine."

The President subsequently maintained that he had not intended to endorse Gorbachev's call for total nuclear disarmament within ten years; rather, Reagan explained, he had merely meant to reiterate his long-standing hope that a nuclear-free world would be achieved some day. . . .

During their long and tiring sessions in Iceland, Reagan and Gorbachev had apparently been caught up in a make-or-break atmosphere. At the end they had engaged in a bout of feverish one-upmanship, with each trying to outdo the other in demonstrating his devotion to the dream of a nuclear-free world. Each had reverted to his grandiose disarmament appeals of earlier in the year. That part of the documentary record of the weekend appeared destined to recede into the footnotes of history. However, the terms that had been envisioned for the first five-year period were more specific, more modest, and more in line with agreements that the two sides had signed and observed in the past. They were therefore likely to have more staying power.

Detailed negotiations would be necessary to turn the terms to which the two leaders had agreed into a treaty. In the process of conducting such negotiations, the stated goal of a 50-percent across-the-board reduction in strategic weapons might have to be compromised. But an accord along the lines of the Reykjavik agreement would almost certainly compel the Soviets to retire a significant portion of their large, multiple-warhead intercontinental ballistic missiles, including some of their notorious "heavy" SS-18s, which worry the United States because their accuracy, speed and destructive capability make them the potential instruments of a surprise attack. These missiles have been the principal cause of American concerns about a "window of vulnerability," the driving obsession of the American strategic debate for nearly two decades. At Reykjavik, Gorbachev also agreed to consider provisions that would induce both sides to rely more on bombers, cruise missiles and small, single-warhead mobile ICBMs — weapons that are better suited to retaliation and therefore less likely to pose the threat of a first strike.

While the Americans wanted reductions of offensive forces, the chief Soviet goal was restraints on defensive systems — specifically the American SDI. Gorbachev had proposed different kinds of restrictions at different times.

When he assumed power in early 1985, Gorbachev wanted a complete ban on "space-strike arms," including all research. Then, in an interview published in *Time* magazine in September 1985, he said that "fundamental" research might be allowed. Over the following months, he proposed an extension of the 1972 Anti-Ballistic Missile (ABM) Treaty for 15–20 years, then for "up to 15 years."

Meanwhile, in a letter to Gorbachev in July 1986, Reagan had proposed continuing the ABM treaty for seven and a half years. Neither side would be able to withdraw during that period. The question of duration was obviously amenable to compromise: the two could split the difference and arrive at a figure of ten years. So they did at Reykjavik. But that did not resolve the difficult question of what the ABM treaty actually permitted in the way of research, development and testing of high-technology space-based defensive systems. It was over this issue that the Reykjavik meeting collapsed.

Early in the weekend Gorbachev indicated that he was interested in "strengthening" the treaty. However, not until the final unscheduled session on Sunday afternoon did he make clear that by this he meant that research during the ten-year period would have to be confined to the "laboratory." Reagan balked at that formulation. As he told Gorbachev and said repeatedly afterward, he considered this definition of permissible research an attempt to "kill" SDI. When Gorbachev would not budge, the President gathered up his papers and the meeting ended on a note of failure and recrimination.

It was perhaps the most bizarre moment in what was already a peculiar event; the President had not been prepared to deal conclusively or in detail with the vital and immensely complicated question of the future relationship between SDI and the ABM treaty; he had little opportunity to take counsel from his own advisers, not to mention from technical experts and European and congressional leaders, on a subject that had implications spanning both oceans and stretching far into the future. Yet he not only made a critical decision on the spot, he publicized it in a way that froze the two leaders into incompatible positions. Why did he not simply say to Gorbachev, in effect, "This is very interesting, a lot is on the table; we'll have to study it carefully, and we'll get back to you"?

That question was not answered in the immediate post-Reykjavik flurry of official explanation and justification. One conjecture was that Reagan felt under some pressure from the right. If he had appeared even to entertain Gorbachev's proposal, he would have been vulnerable to charges of doing at Reykjavik what he had avoided doing at Geneva the year before: compromising on SDI. Conservative congressmen and columnists had warned him before the meeting not to make any such compromise; they congratulated him afterward for not doing so. Even more important to the President was his deep commitment to the dream of a space shield that would protect the American people from nuclear attack. He sensed that the Soviet leader was trying to get him to give up that dream; he responded by walking away.

From the Soviet point of view, Reagan's position meant that the United States was not willing to pay any appreciable price in defensive restraints to get offensive reductions — at least not yet. Reagan's agreement to delay SDI deployment for ten years and adhere to the ABM treaty depended on the complete elimination of all ballistic missiles within that same ten-year period, something that virtually nobody outside the room in Hofdi House, where the two leaders met, considered even remotely feasible. In any event, the delay hardly represented a concession because SDI would not be ready for full deployment for at least ten years anyway. Moreover, Reagan's understanding of the ABM treaty differed sharply not only from that of the Soviets but from the interpretation of a number of key members of Congress and even of the Americans who negotiated the treaty in the early 1970s.[6]

After the meeting, Administration spokesmen maintained that the treaty gave the United States the right not only to conduct research but also to develop and test an SDI system and its components. So when the ten-year moratorium ended, the United States might have some sort of defensive system ready to put in place. Faced with that prospect, the Soviets would have no incentive to reduce their offensive forces. Quite the contrary, they would have every reason to *increase* their arsenal of offensive weapons; for in order to deter the United States, the Soviets believe, they must be able to penetrate and overwhelm whatever defenses the United States eventually deploys. Thus Reagan's position on the defensive half of the grand compromise at Reykjavik came down to a refusal to accept any of the restraints on SDI that the Soviets sought. . . .

With the Reykjavik meeting, Reagan and Gorbachev were two-thirds of the way to matching the trio of summits that Richard Nixon and Leonid Brezhnev had held during the heyday of détente. Relations between the United States and the Soviet Union were not, however, returning to the conditions of the early 1970s. The political arrangements of that period have sunk into the past, weighted down with controversies and recriminations. The Reagan-Gorbachev relationship, however it turns out, will be different. Moreover, however the bargaining on arms control ends, the interaction of these two leaders, including the roller-coaster course of relations in 1986, demonstrates some enduring principles about the Soviet-American relationship itself. Those principles essentially concern limits — on what the superpowers can do both to each other and with each other.

One is the limit to how far Soviet-American relations can deteriorate. Particularly during his first term, Reagan had been the most anti-Soviet American president in 30 years, perhaps ever. He had aimed not at solidifying the status quo in East-West relations but at overturning it. His rhetoric toward Moscow had been harsh. The Soviet leaders had responded with even harsher language of their own. Each side had tried briefly to impose a diplomatic boycott on the other. Yet at no time, even when relations were at their worst — even after the Korean airliner episode and the Soviet walkout from the Geneva talks in 1983 — had there been a serious danger of war. Moreover, none of the major agreements that had been reached in more cordial times came unstuck. The European settlement that the détente of the early 1970s had produced never even came under critical scrutiny. While the SALT agreements were the objects of a good deal of such scrutiny, they remained in force, at least until late 1986. And in 1985 the two leaders found themselves agreeing to meet regularly. The business they had with each other was too compelling to ignore.

The first half of the 1980s, and the policies that both sides pursued in that period, also showed that neither was likely to gain a decisive advantage over the other. By agreeing in principle to meet on a regular basis and to seek diplomatic accommodation on some of the issues that divided them, the two leaders were implicitly acknowledging the limits of their ability to get their way unilaterally. For both men, this was a lesson that took some time to learn.

In his June 1982 address to the British Parliament, Reagan had called the Soviet Union "inherently unstable" and said that it was facing a "great revolutionary crisis." He had implied that the United States should exploit that instability and aggravate that crisis. By the time he first met with Gorbachev in November 1985, he had ceased to make such claims. He had even signed a presidential directive that concluded that the United States had at best only a very modest ability to influence internal Soviet policy and should focus instead on influencing its external policy.

One way to influence the foreign policy of the Soviet Union was to discourage Soviet expansionism by supporting anti-Soviet insurgencies in the Third World. The Reagan Doctrine, which committed the United States to such support, was still very much in force at the time of Reykjavik. But that hallmark policy of the Administration was encountering difficulties at home. On the issue of Nicaragua, the White House was under public and congressional pressure to couple the military and humanitarian aid for the anti-Sandinista rebels with genuine support for the diplomatic effort to achieve a negotiated settlement, known as the Contadora process.

Meanwhile, there were signs that the Soviets, too, had begun to understand the limits of unilateralism in the nuclear competition. Nikolai Ogarkov, the former chief of the Soviet General Staff, spoke of the fruitlessness of the arms race and said that nuclear superiority was a mirage. Soviet specialists on strategic affairs not only called for a "new way of thinking" about the problems of stability — some of them sometimes also tentatively attempted to think and write in new ways.

Some of the most interesting statements that Gorbachev made during his first 18 months in power concerned what he and other Soviet spokesmen referred to as "common security." At the end of the Geneva summit he expressed his "profound conviction that less security for the United States of America compared to the Soviet Union would not be in our interests, since it could lead to mistrust and produce instability." He elaborated on this theme in his address to the 27th Party Congress three months later:

> The character of present-day weapons leaves a country no hope of safeguarding itself solely with military and technical means. The task of ensuring security is increasingly seen as a political problem, and can be resolved only by political means. . . . Security can only be mutual. . . . It is vital that all should feel equally secure, for the fears and anxieties of the nuclear age generate unpredictability in politics and concrete actions.

Gorbachev's reasurring words may simply have been part of another Soviet campaign to lull and divide the West. But they may also have reflected the beginning of a welcome, if belated, Soviet recognition that the Leninist principle that politics is always a matter of *kto-kogo*—who will prevail over whom—was simply not operative, or for that matter even acceptable, in the strategic nuclear relationship. Gorbachev's words may have bespoken a Soviet conclusion similar to the one strategists in the West had long since reached; however fiercely they may compete elsewhere, in conducting the nuclear arms race the superpowers best serve their own interests by maintaining an equilibrium and jointly fostering the goal of strategic stability. Even though many details remained to be clarified and negotiated, the terms to which the Soviets agreed in Reykjavik suggested that they might be prepared eventually to accommodate some American concerns and cooperate to achieve a more stable nuclear balance.

SDI had undoubtedly played an important part in inducing the Soviet leadership to rethink what common security meant in the strategic nuclear competition. It had forced them to face up to some of the more dangerous consequences of their excessive accumulation of land-based ballistic missile warheads. If they pressed for advantages in the familiar area of offensive weapons, they might find themselves plunging into the unfamiliar and treacherous terrain of high-technology strategic defense. To make matters worse, the Americans would have arrived there first, and would feel much more at home.

Reagan, too, came up against obstacles to altering the nuclear relationship between the superpowers. As he made clearer than ever at Reykjavik, SDI was his bid to change the rules, indeed to change the game itself. But by then, for all his own devotion to SDI and for all the disagreements about how the ABM treaty should be interpreted, he found himself having to offer repeated assurances that the program would proceed under the terms of the treaty. SDI therefore seemed likely to flourish only to the extent that it was compatible with deterrence and arms control. Reykjavik was bound to increase the pressure on him to use it as a "bargaining chip" to get reductions in offensive weapons. That rationale was a far cry from the President's original vision, proclaimed in March 1983, of an impregnable astrodome over the United States that would render nuclear weapons "impotent and obsolete."

Indeed, while Reagan's conduct at Reykjavik demonstrated his continuing belief in that vision, few officials outside the Oval Office of the White House shared his hope. Virtually his entire government either had abandoned the idea of a comprehensive defense that would make traditional deterrence unnecessary or had never subscribed to the idea in the first place.[7]

If the Reagan-Gorbachev relationship demonstrated the limits to both what the superpowers could do to thwart each other and how far their relations could deteriorate, it also illustrated the upper limits on improvement in their relations. The potential accord that was glimpsed in Reykjavik would certainly go beyond the limitations on offensive weapons established by the SALT II treaty of 1979. But the grand compromise, if it ever came about, would scarcely represent a whole new approach to strategic arms control. Quite the contrary, it would reaffirm not only SALT II but SALT I by linking limits on strategic defense with restrictions on strategic offense.

Thus, even as they broke with some of the procedures that their predecessors had followed, Reagan and Gorbachev were moving in the direction of restoring a measure of continuity with the past. Moreover, just as Reagan had learned to live and work with Gorbachev, he was learning to live with the old, familiar problems of asymmetries in force structures, theoretical vulnerabilities and the moral as well as practical dilemmas of deterrence.

If the worst that was likely to happen between the superpowers was not all that bad, the best was not all that good. The fundamental conditions of Soviet-American relations were likely to persist. This, in turn, meant that the ritual of Soviet-American summitry was likely to have a long run, and for all the reasons that had led Reagan and Gorbachev to engage in that ritual themselves, both in the fairly traditional summit at Geneva in November 1985 and in the strange interlude at Reykjavik a year later.

## Notes

6. The ABM treaty had long been understood to permit research but not development or testing of space-based defensive systems utilizing "exotic" technologies. In 1985 some members of the Reagan Administration challenged this traditional, "restrictive" interpretation of the treaty. They advanced a "permissive" interpretation, according to which everything short of actual deployment of SDI could proceed. On this subject see Abram Chayes and Antonia Handler Cheyes, "Testing and Development of 'Exotic' Systems under the ABM Treaty: The Great Reinterpretation Caper"; and Abraham D. Sofaer, "The ABM Treaty and the Strategic Defense Initiative," both in *Harvard Law Review,* June 1986.
7. See Michael Mandelbaum and Strobe Talbott, *Reagan and Gorbachev,* New York: Vintage Books/Random House, 1987, chapter 4.

## Suggestions for Further Reading

Kaufmann, William W. *The 1987 Defense Budget* (Washington, DC: Brookings Institution, 1986). An annual review of the defense budget by one of the United States' most influential defense analysts.

Korb, Lawrence, and Linda Brady, "Rearming America: The Reagan Administration Defense Program," *International Security* 9:3 (Winter 1984–85). A concise description and argument in favor of the Reagan defense buildup.

Posen, Barry R., and Stephen Van Evera, "Defense Policy and the Reagan Administration, Departure from Containment," *International Security* 8:1 (Summer 1983). A critique of the Reagan defense buildup.

Richelson, Jeffrey, "PD-59, NSDD-13, and the Reagan Strategic Modernization Program," *Journal of Strategic Studies* 6:2 (June 1983): 125–46. Puts the Reagan strategic modernization program into the context of the policies of earlier administrations.

Snyder, Craig, ed. *The Strategic Defense Debate: Can Star Wars Make Us Safe?* (Philadelphia: U of Pennsylvania P, 1986). A collection of prominent policy makers and scientists debates the technological feasibility and political desirability of the Strategic Defense Initiative. Includes Richard Pipes, Paul Nitze, Caspar Weinberger, James Schlesinger, and Robert McNamara.

Talbott, Strobe, and Michael Mandelbaum, *Reagan and Gorbachev* (New York: Vintage Books, 1987). This book analyzes superpower summit meetings, Reagan's shifting views of the Soviet Union, and Gorbachev's agenda for the Soviet Union. It also speculates about the future prospects for arms control.

*Thirteen*

# VISIONS OF WAR AND PEACE

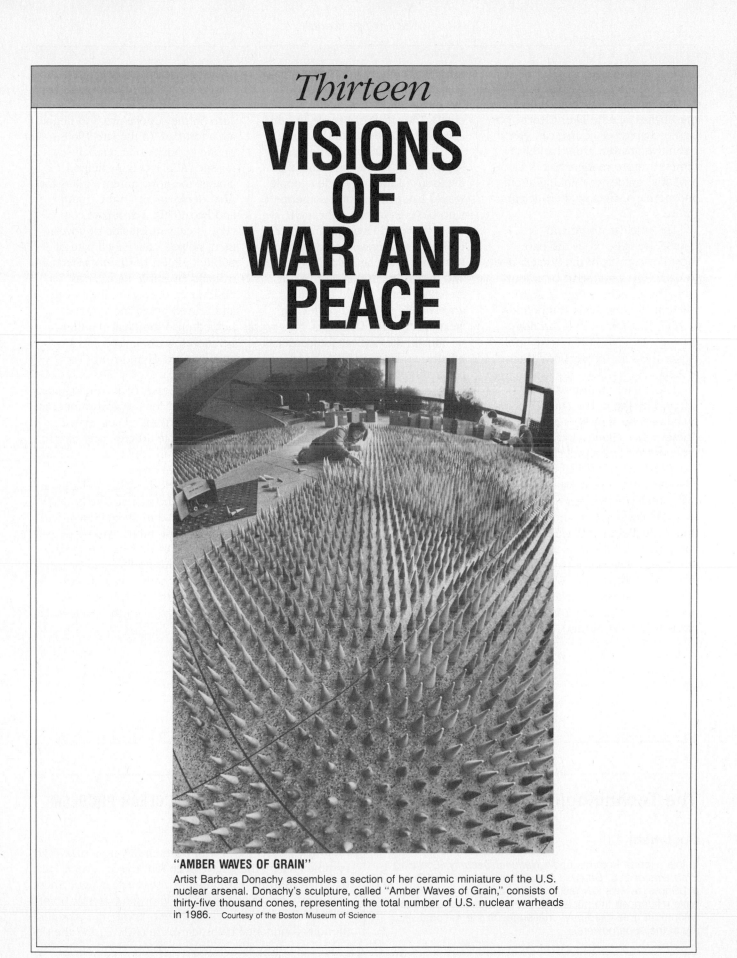

**"AMBER WAVES OF GRAIN"**

Artist Barbara Donachy assembles a section of her ceramic miniature of the U.S. nuclear arsenal. Donachy's sculpture, called "Amber Waves of Grain," consists of thirty-five thousand cones, representing the total number of U.S. nuclear warheads in 1986. Courtesy of the Boston Museum of Science

# INTRODUCTION

What next? What will the future of the nuclear age be like? Clearly, no single chapter or course can give a definitive answer. This chapter attempts a more modest task — to offer some guides to thinking about and perhaps affecting the nuclear future.

The nuclear future will, of course, be affected by the past. Most key aspects of the nuclear age to date will continue to be important. These include the U.S.-Soviet relationship, the arms competition in both numbers and technology, arms control, and the internal politics of the superpowers and their allies.

The nuclear future will also be affected by the policy choices made by key decision makers and others. These policy choices in turn are often determined by differing perspectives on the nuclear age. In this chapter four representative perspectives are reviewed: peace through strength, cooperation and competition, reducing the nuclear danger, and peace and disarmament. We emphasize that these four perspectives are *representative* of the many perspectives people have on the nuclear age. They are not a complete list by any means. In addition, the perspectives are American-oriented. The views of people in other countries may be quite different.

The key point about the perspectives is that they are linked to the kinds of future policies people would like to see. Thus, someone who believes in peace through strength would favor a buildup of U.S. nuclear forces instead of disarmament. Someone holding a peace and disarmament perspective, on the other hand, would urge the U.S. government to get rid of nuclear weapons.

Finally, the nuclear future can be affected by the actions of citizens. After taking an introductory course on the nuclear age, it is easy to feel overwhelmed — weapons systems are so tremendously destructive and complex, arms control agreements are so detailed, the debates are so intense. Moreover, although the threat of nuclear war affects everyone, it can seem that the opinions of the average citizen have little impact on key decisions.

But the history of the nuclear age shows that citizens in the West can understand the issues and affect key decisions about policy. In the late 1950s, for example, the worries of mothers about the health effects of nuclear testing helped put pressure on the superpowers to negotiate a test ban. In the late 1960s, public opposition to antiballistic missile (ABM) systems helped change the government's plans for ABM deployment. In the middle and late 1970s, a group of concerned citizens outside of government helped create a climate of public opinion hostile to arms control and favorable to an arms buildup. In the 1980s, the freeze and related peace movements helped push the Reagan administration toward arms control and changed opinions in Congress.

In each case, concerned citizens did not wait for the government to act. They organized concerned groups, wrote articles, pressured Congress, and voted for candidates sharing their views.

The world has changed a great deal since the first atomic bomb was exploded in 1945. How it will change in the future will be determined in part by what has already happened during the nuclear age. But future changes can also be affected by the wishes of those who must live with the nuclear danger.

# A LOOK BACK

## The Technological Arms Race

### *Document 1*

In this excerpt from his book, *National Security: Enduring Problems of U.S. Defense Policy,* political scientist Donald Snow reviews key technological developments that have influenced the nuclear age. He notes how each development presented new challenges to the national security of the superpowers.

## 1 THE NATURE OF THE NUCLEAR PROBLEM
### Donald Snow

Although it runs the risk of oversimplifying a dizzyingly complex reality, there have been four major "events" that have defined the evolution of the nuclear age. These events are the development of the original atomic bomb, the fabrication of the first hydrogen bomb, the advent of the intercontinental ballistic missile (ICBM), and the development of multiple independently targeted reentry vehicle (MIRV). The future successful completion of an effective system of ballistic missile defense (BMD) would rank as an event of equal importance and, because it is currently under debate, will also be considered.

## The Atomic Bomb

At the most obvious level, the successful development of the original atomic bomb is the seminal event in the nuclear age — there could not have been a nuclear age had this not occurred. Understanding the full significance of this culmination of the efforts of the nuclear physicists, however, requires looking specifically at the physical process involved in a nuclear reaction, what its effects are, and how this development radicalized thinking about warfare generally. . . .

If the atomic bomb revolutionized the ability to kill, the initial question was what to do with it. Brodie and his colleagues had one answer in *The Absolute Weapon*, but there was another alternative.

During the period between the world wars, a number of military thinkers have mused on the impact of aircraft on future wars, and they had devised something known as the theory of strategic bombardment. Pioneers of this theory included the Italian Giulio Douhet, Britain's Hugh Trenchard, and the American Billy Mitchell. They argued that aerial bombardment of the enemy's homeland would be the key to success in future wars. The basis of this contention was their assertion that the ability to wage modern war rests on the industrial capacity to produce the tools of war — what they called the industrial web — and that if that web is destroyed, so is the adversary's ability to fight.

World War II neither conclusively validated nor invalidated strategic bombardment theory. One of the excuses that air power enthusiasts put forward to explain its lack of total success was the lack of adequate munitions to carry out their tasks efficiently. In that regard, the atomic bomb seemed admirably suited to the task of destroying cities (and hence industry), and there was an initial tendency among some to treat it as simply a more efficient means for carrying out the aerial bombardment mission. Civilian authorities resisted the temptation to treat the fission bomb as just another bomb, however, and Brodie's advocacy of the bomb's special character basically prevailed.

The effects of the atomic bomb were unquestionably dramatic, but it was only the first step in the nuclear revolution. Initially, at least, the United States had a monopoly on its possession, and the only means to get it to target was by conventional aircraft that were vulnerable to interception and destruction. A war in which these devices were employed would certainly be far more deadly than anything theretofore experienced, but also one a society could calculate it might be able to survive. Advances in nuclear capability would erode that perception.

## The Hydrogen Bomb

The next major event was the development of the fission-fusion or hydrogen bomb. During the period leading to its successful development, this weapon was known simply as the "Super" to contrast its vastly larger yields with those of even the fission bomb. This form of explosive ultimately would discourage thoughts about the survivability of nuclear conflict. . . .

At the time the hydrogen bomb was being proposed, around 1950, it was highly controversial. Some of the controversy surrounded whether the Super could in fact be built at all. The principles for its operation were known, but it was questionable whether the extremely high temperatures (up to forty million degrees Fahrenheit) necessary to induce fusion could be achieved (traditional fission reactions fell short of the mark). Moreover, there was considerable concern about the political desirability of unleashing this new form of devastation, particularly within that part of the policy community concerned about the growing Soviet-American arms race.

Ultimately, Cold War impulses won out; the Super was first exploded by the United States in 1952 and subsequently by the Soviets in 1953. The political dynamic was straightforward: the hydrogen bomb was built partly because some hoped it would provide military advantage against what was increasingly being perceived as an implacable foe, and partly so that if that adversary should develop his own Super, American possession could act as a deterrent.

The fission fusion bomb had two major effects on the dynamics of the nuclear age. The first arose from its much greater destructive capacity. Whereas it was still possible to contemplate engaging in nuclear war with the Soviets when only fission weapons were available (especially given the lack of Soviet means to deliver those bombs to American soil), such was not clearly the case with the Super. A few atomic bombs might cause significant destruction and suffering, but could be survived. An equal number of hydrogen bombs delivered against urban targets, on the other hand, would cause destruction hardly anyone could regard as tolerable. The fission-fusion bomb, in a phrase, served to strengthen the imperative of deterrence.

The second effect arose from the greater lethal efficiency of the hydrogen bomb. In the late 1940s, great progress in nuclear bomb design had allowed bombs to become considerably lighter and more compact than the original bulky weapons. The hydrogen bomb accelerated this trend; its greater destructive power meant an equivalent explosive effect could be achieved with a lesser amount of fuel. The result was to make nuclear weapons even smaller and lighter. Ultimately, they became compact and light enough to put on the tips of rockets....

The military value of rocketry was questioned at first in the United States. The German programs had not been especially effective against Britain, and many military people tended to dismiss rockets as mere terrorist weapons with marginal military importance. This was especially true in the newly formed U.S. Air Force, which preferred to invest its resources in the development of manned aircraft rather than unmanned rockets.

Events of the 1950s changed that. All the major American services had missile development programs during this period, but the Soviets were concentrating more of their efforts in the area. As a result, they were the first to launch an intercontinental range ballistic missile in 1957, and only months later they launched *Sputnik,* the first manmade satellite, into space. The nuclear rocket age had begun as the United States scrambled to match and surpass the Soviet achievement.

In some ways, the intercontinental ballistic missile represents the single most dramatic element of the nuclear age. Certainly it caught the popular imagination in a way that other aspects of nuclear evolution had not. A fatalistic popular culture about nuclear war emerged in which there was growing consensus that nuclear holocaust was just a matter of time. At the same time, the ICBM sparked the first widespread intellectual examination of the dynamics of the nuclear world. The result was a spate of writing and thinking that many consider to have been the golden age in analyzing nuclear weapons. The centerpiece of that thought was the rediscovery and embellishment of Brodie's emphasis on deterrence.

The major import of the ICBM was total societal vulnerability to nuclear attack. Before the ICBM, it was always possible to calculate surviving a nuclear attack by intercepting and destroying a large proportion of the conventional aircraft carrying the bombs. That problem itself was conventional, even if the weapon was exceptional. The ICBM made the weapon as well as its payload extraordinary.

The reason for this was simple enough: the ICBM was a delivery system against which there were no known defenses. It is true that the theoretical problems of ballistic missile defense had largely been overcome before the first missile was tested, but that was far different from producing an actual workable weapon that could intercept and destroy incoming ballistically delivered warheads....

MIRV represented a considerable refinement of multiple-warhead technology. The key element is something called the MIRV "bus," a cylindrical device in the reentry vehicle that arranges the warheads around its outer wall in much the same way that bullets are held in place in a chamber of a revolver. The bombs can be released individually over a period of time to be sent to differing targets within a defined range known as the MIRV "footprint" (the largest area in which any MIRVed rocket can release its payload). The result is that a number of targets can be attacked by a single rocket — not just a single object, as is the case with single warhead missiles.

The first MIRV was tested by the United States in 1968 on the eve of the opening of the first Strategic Arms Limitation Talks (SALT), and the first MIRVed warheads entered the American arsenal in 1970. The Soviets followed suit by beginning deployment of their own MIRVs in 1975.

The advent of MIRV had three direct effects on nuclear evolution. The first of these was warhead proliferation, a dramatic increase in the number of nuclear bombs in the operational arsenals of both superpowers. This was the case because more warheads can be fitted onto each rocket. The technical term for this is *fractionation,* or the division of the available throw-weight (the amount of weight that can be boosted into space) to allow for additional warheads.

The phenomenon of MIRVing and thus allowing for more warheads occurred during the various SALT talks. Critics of arms control processes often argue that during those talks arsenal sizes grew. This is true in the sense that SALT and MIRVing were occurring simultaneously, but no cause and effect should be inferred. MIRVs were simply not effectively limited by the process.

A second impact of MIRV was to accelerate changes in the weapons balance between the United States and the USSR. The United States held, during the early period of the missile race, a considerable advantage over the Soviets, but a crash program in the Soviet Union began to narrow that gap in 1967. By 1970, the Soviets had more rocket launchers than the United States. The Americans led, thanks to the earlier introduction of MIRV (especially on SLBMs) in total warheads, but Soviet MIRVing promised to change that as well. The reason is that the Soviets have always built much larger rockets than the Americans. In single-warhead days, this meant the Soviets could put much larger bombs on their missiles than could the United States, and with MIRV technology, this translates into the ability to fractionate to a higher degree (put more warheads on a single missile).

The third and most consequential effect of MIRV was to allow the reemergence of thought about counterforce targeting and the possible survivability of nuclear war. Counterforce targeting refers to aiming one's weapons at the adversary's armed forces, generally with the intention of being able to destroy them before they are used, thereby avoiding their destructive effects. (This is known as offensive damage limitation, in the jargon of the trade.)...

## Ballistic Missile Defense

Achievement of a true ballistic missile defense (BMD) system has not as yet occurred, but it would be equally important if it does. Given the current emphasis on the subject by the Reagan administration in promoting its Strategic Defense Initiative (SDI), the general effects of a BMD system warrant some mention; it would constitute a seminal event in the nuclear age.

BMD is a generic term that refers to the range of active measures one might take to intercept and disable or destroy incoming enemy missile warheads. BMD has taken two basic forms to date. The first of these is the antiballistic missile (ABM). An ABM is, as the name suggests, a missile launched with the purpose of intercepting an offensive warhead somewhere in its flight. Thus, one projectile attempts to catch the other, this really means creating an explosion in the path of the incoming missile, and it is the process that led to John Kennedy's bullet analogy. ABMs were initially proposed in the 1960s, and although the only American system deployed at Grand Forks, North Dakota, was deactivated after a brief operational period in 1975, research and development are in advanced stages. The Soviets have the only currently operational ABM system, the Galosh ABM defense of Moscow.

The other form of BMD, much in the public eye since President Reagan's "Star Wars" speech (a designation the president strongly dislikes as suggesting frivolity) of March 23, 1983, are laser and particle-beam defenses. Generically, these two forms of defense are known as directed energy transfer (DET) weapons, and they operate on the principle of aiming an intense stream of light or radioactivity at a warhead and thereby disabling or destroying it. The most publicized version involves the placing of laser stations in space to carry out the mission. . . .

What concerns us now is the impact successful development and deployment of BMD would have on the evolution of the nuclear age. If truly effective systems (systems that could destroy all or virtually all of an enemy's attack) could be devised, the impact could be easily as great as that of the other seminal events.

In the most dramatic prospect, DET-based defenses could render ballistically delivered nuclear weapons obsolete. This has been President Reagan's common theme in his advocacy of the idea, and it has appeared in other public discussions of the prospects over the last decade or so. (These "exotic" defenses have been discussed in the technical, unclassified literature since the mid-1970s.) The basis of such claims is that an effective BMD shield would mean that offensive missiles could not effectively attack and would thus be obsolete; this would free mankind of the "nuclear balance of terror."

Such claims may be excessive: BMD would not, for instance, protect against nuclear delivery by aircraft or cruise missiles. Even if they are, however, BMD could have an effect similar to the impact of MIRV — but without one of the disadvantages.

A BMD system would allow countries possessing the capability to engage in defensive damage limitation options. Just as counterforce capability allows one to contemplate decimating the nuclear forces that could be brought to bear against one by destroying them on the ground, BMD allows a similar calculation: launched forces could be intercepted and destroyed short of their targets. The more effective the system, the greater the diluting effect, and when it approached 100 percent effectiveness, then the claim that it would make nuclear weapons obsolete would become persuasive.

The effects of BMD on the dynamics of nuclear deterrence are controversial. Critics worry that the defensive damage-limitation potential may lull people into believing that a nuclear war could be survived, thereby reducing fears of such a conflict and eroding belief in the need for deterrence. This concern is particularly voiced in regard to even a small overestimation of the system's abilities, since even a small number of nuclear explosions could have absolutely devastating effects.

Proponents argue one or both of two virtues of BMD. On the one hand, some argue that BMD is simply the only responsible insurance one can provide for oneself in a world where deterrence can in fact fail. Since that is the case, the only responsible course is to do everything one can to mitigate the disaster, and diluting the attack through defense is clearly one such measure. On the other hand, other proponents argue that, unlike MIRV, active defenses are inherently stabilizing rather than destabilizing. This is so, they argue, because defensive weapons only threaten the other side's offensive weapons if those forces are launched. Because the extent to which they are effective makes such a first launch futile, incentives to start a war are reduced.

All the developments in the nuclear system are controversial, and they have individually and collectively complicated a system that requires careful management and overview if deterrence is to be maintained. Thought about how to keep deterrence operating has had to evolve along with the weapons, and it is to how adaptation has occurred over time that our attention now shifts. . . .

# Can the U.S. Regain Superiority?

### *Document 2*

Political scientist Richard Smoke looks back at the nuclear age. He argues that a key aspect is that the United States can never again regain the nuclear superiority it enjoyed over the Soviet Union during the 1950s and 1960s. He points out how the numbers of nuclear weapons on both sides have increased, and he does not hold out much hope that the arms race will end any time in the near future.

## 2 THE POST–WORLD WAR II ERA
## Richard Smoke

What observations emerge from viewing this era as a whole? One involves the cycle of American superiority. So noticeable during the first twenty-five years following World War II, the cyclical character of the U.S. arms advantage in the world has *not* continued, at least not at all in the same way. Twice in earlier years an unexpected surge in the Soviet threat seemed to nullify a previously advantageous American position, whereupon a powerful new American effort restored a superior posture — in fact a better one than anticipated. Since about 1970 the stalemate of Mutual Assured Destruction has dampened down this cycle.

Furthermore, at each turn of the wheel the *relative* position of the United States was less advantageous than before. When the era of superiority represented by Massive Retaliation arrived and the Eisenhower administration said the United States would "prevail" in a general war against the USSR (which had only a few atomic weapons and limited ability to deliver them), this was a less desirable situation than the absolute supremacy that had accompanied the American atomic monopoly earlier. When the second (and briefer) era of superiority arrived, the Kennedy administration only explored, with some doubt, the possibility that a counterforce strategy might accomplish some damage limiting in the event of war. This was quite different, and less advantageous, than the Eisenhower administration's belief that damage to the United States would be so slight that America could credibly threaten to *begin* a nuclear war. When these cycles ended, the superpowers found themselves roughly equal in their capacity for Mutual Assured Destruction, an ultimate kind of equivalence that has continued to the present in spite of each side's continual jockeying for minor advantages.

It might be thought that the great Soviet buildup of the 1970s, followed by the American buildup of the 1980s, represents a third cycle in the series. Didn't President Reagan enter office saying the United States was falling behind, and launch a fresh American effort, just as President Kennedy had in 1961?

A minor difference is that the two previous cycles each lasted less than one decade rather than extending over two. A much greater difference is that the previous American efforts had resulted, not very deliberately, in tremendous and very real superiority. Massive Retaliation and counterforce for damage limiting had both put the United States in a position, for a while, that would have been decisive had an all out war occurred. Nothing remotely like this was in prospect for the American buildup that began in the late 1970s and accelerated in the 1980s. The capacity of the USSR to destroy the United States completely could not be challenged. The new American effort was motivated merely by a judgment that the prior and continuing Soviet effort must be matched. A rough balance in forces must be maintained, or in the Reagan administration's perception, restored.

Another observation to be made of the post-World War II era is of a gradual, but more or less steady erosion of what was once the United States' overwhelmingly commanding technological position. America emerged from World War II technologically supreme by a wide margin, not merely by virtue of its atomic monopoly but in many other ways as well. In aircraft design and technology, in electronics, in the size and power of its navy, and in many other respects the United States was far ahead of all other military powers. In the 1950s the Soviets also came to possess nuclear weapons, and were even ahead briefly in building long-range rockets; but the United States retained a commanding lead in other categories. During the 1960s that lead narrowed, and in the 1970s the Soviets caught up in many areas.

Even by the 1980s the *total* breadth and depth of Soviet technological capability had not yet begun to equal that of the United States. The Soviet economy as a whole is technically backward compared to the Western European, Japanese, or American economies. But by concentrating a high fraction of its total technological capabilities into *military* technology, the Soviet Union has succeeded in becoming highly competitive with the United States in weapons.

This dribbling away of the American technological superiority has been the result of two factors, both inevitable. First, it is politically impossible in the United States to spend taxpayers' dollars (particularly as more and more of them would be needed) to remain four or six steps ahead of the nearest competitor. The taxpayer will not pay for more than a moderate advantage. (The United States does remain up to five years ahead of the USSR in some military technologies, primarily those related to electronics.)

Second, the technological progression itself has been relatively homogeneous. The invention of nuclear weapons represented a sharp discontinuity in the evolution of military technology. The nation that possessed them was in a completely different military category from the nation that did not. But it is an accident of nature that no similar discontinuity has appeared since, nor so far as known is any in prospect. Since 1945 the evolution of technology has been homogeneous, each single step ahead in research being marginal. The Soviet leaders were determined to sink all the resources needed into catching up with the United States, and as the USSR is a country of roughly comparable population size, and greater natural resources, in time they were able to do so. Unable to find some new corner to turn into a wholly new technology, and unable to keep many steps ahead in the known technologies, the United States inevitably found itself being overtaken. Henceforward the competition presumably will proceed on a roughly equal basis.

Americans are used to thinking of their country as the strongest military power on earth and have been slow to accept that it is no longer. The breadth and depth of the Soviet technical and industrial base for military programs is now at least equal to America's. The size of the forces the two sides *actually* create will be the result of policy decisions, but broadly speaking, the military *potentials* of the two superpowers are now roughly equal. They will remain so in spite of any effort Americans can make or are likely to try to make. That the USSR no longer *can* be surpassed by any reasonable U.S. effort — as it could be, and twice was — has probably not yet been realized by many Americans.

## The Prospects Ahead

The simplest observation to be made about the last few decades is that the American people now find themselves less secure than they ever have been (except briefly during the most intense cold war crises). The total destructive power the USSR can visit upon the United States, which by the late 1960s was already ample to wipe out every sizable American city, has grown hugely since then and continues to increase. So does the equivalent American power against the Soviet Union. Nothing in the history recounted in this book gives much hope that the mutual piling up of destructive force, or the continuing threat to American security, is likely to be reduced anytime soon.

The "nuclear dilemma"... refers to the fact that the United States dare not, by itself, halt this piling up of weaponry, even though the net effect of both the United States and USSR continuing it is that both are left even less secure. As Americans experience it, the nuclear dilemma is fundamentally this: efforts to increase U.S. nuclear power are matched by Soviet efforts, and both sides end up even more threatened than before; yet for the United States *not* to continue its efforts while the USSR still did obviously would leave America even more vulnerable and insecure.

The prospect is not bright for effective, verifiable agreements between the superpowers to halt the competition together. Unless entirely new social or political forces come into play, or unforeseen events change the world considerably, the long-term trend toward continuing and even increasing insecurity will go on. This book closes with a brief look at the prospect Americans face in the coming years.*

Ever since the commanding superiority of the United States was replaced by the basic stalemate of Mutual Assured Destruction, the best hope for improving Americans' real security — or at least halting the slide toward increasing insecurity — has lain in arms control efforts. As noted earlier, arms control is not an alternative to national security; it is one avenue toward achieving it. The Joint Chiefs of Staff have agreed. They have repeatedly supported the various SALT agreements explicitly on the grounds that limiting Soviet arms would limit the threat to the United States. Arms control becomes a *principal* avenue toward achieving security, when unilateral action to remove the threat is impossible, as it has been between East and West for decades.

But the record of actual arms control achievements, at least to date, is not very satisfying. With the outstanding exception of the ABM treaty, efforts to limit strategic weapons have accomplished little. A decade and a half after SALT began, the Soviet and American arsenals are much larger than they were at the outset! While it is often argued, and may be true, that in the absence of SALT they would have grown even greater, one cannot believe that the arms race is being brought under any effective control when both sides have some five times the number of warheads they had when the effort started. They are also developing new categories of weapons (e.g., cruise missiles). Other efforts to limit arms, conventional as well as nuclear, are also languishing. In the 1980s a mood of pessimism grips many of those who specialize in arms control.

There is reason for pessimism other than the meager results achieved so far. Events of recent years have gone a long way toward undercutting one of the main bases for hope, namely a belief that parity between the superpowers would drain away much of the competitiveness of the arms race.... When national security specialists turned in the early 1960s from grand disarmament schemes to arms control, they did so not only because the grand schemes seemed pointless, but also because they had, or thought they had, positive reason to think that a strategy of slowing and halting the arms race would work. At that time the balance of terror seemed "delicate." Each side's vulnerable forces of bombers and primitive missiles might be wiped out by the other's first strike. Also, the two arsenals were badly "out of synch" in terms of time. First the USSR seemed to be profiting from a "missile gap," then a real missile gap in reverse gave the United States superiority for awhile. Throughout those years many analysts believed that the intensity of

* *Note*: a discussion of future prospects often involves value judgments to a degree greater than a description of past events and conditions. The reader should be aware that in the rest of this chapter the author's values are expressed openly.

the arms race was a product of these imbalances and fears. When the forces facing each other became roughly equivalent in size and were deployed in relatively secure silos and submarines, they thought, the two sides would be able to relax and the competition could be slowed and halted by degrees.

To some small extent this expectation was realized. The SALT process got underway when, and only when, these conditions began to be fulfilled. But events since have suggested that these conditions are *not* enough for the competition to be significantly slowed. Parity, reasonably secure forces, and the more relaxed atmosphere these things helped bring have not led Moscow and Washington to brake the arms race. Instead the competition has continued at a rapid pace. Evidently more conditions, perhaps unknown ones, must also be met before it can be slowed and halted. The hope of the 1960s, a force that launched the whole arms control movement, has been largely dashed.

It is hard to avoid the conclusion, too, that the technology simply moves faster than can efforts to control it. It is true that neither side, and certainly not the United States, pushes weapons technology ahead as rapidly as it *possibly* could, and in that sense the two sides are not "racing" and there is no arms "race." But they push it noticeably faster than they pursue arms control. After SALT I, the rapid deployment of MIRVs forced negotiators to accept much higher force ceilings at Vladivostok. While they were still trying to codify those in a SALT II treaty, the technology was already moving on to cruise missiles and accurate warheads. Before a strong effort could be mounted to control those at the testing stage, they had been tested. The result is that the strategic environment of the 1980s has been greatly complicated. If it was difficult to negotiate meaningful ceilings before, it is doubly hard now.

The onrush of the arms race is all the more troubling because in recent years its underlying character has changed in a way that gives it less and less reasonable relationship to security. Of course any arms race poses dangers. But an element of irrationality has appeared in the Soviet-American competition that it did not used to have. As recently as the mid-1960s much of what was occurring in that arms competition made a considerable amount of sense and, despite the claims of some critics at the time, the forces the two sides were deploying were not wildly excessive. Today that cannot be said. Not everyone understands that in the 1970s, an element of absurdity entered the arms race that had not been present previously.

When the United States built over six hundred B-52 bombers in the 1950s, it was on the assumption that a Soviet sneak attack would destroy some on the ground and others would be shot down by Soviet air defenses. Since destroying the USSR as a modern military and economic power meant destroying several hundred targets inside the Soviet Union, having this many bombers was not extreme.

Even when the United States deployed more than 1,700 missiles in the 1960s, this was originally decided on the basis of a calculation that a Soviet first strike might destroy most of the bombers on the ground, half of the Polaris submarines in port, and a few of the ICBM silos. The missiles of that day were less accurate, and not too reliable; some would fail to put their one warhead near the target, and many would malfunction. The Soviets were beginning an ABM system that might shoot some warheads down. Though all these factors together still left a margin of safety, again the deployment of 1,700 missiles was not too extreme.

Today things are very different. Just two Trident submarines can wreak as much destruction as the entire U.S. missiles force of October 1962, when the Cuban Missile Crisis occurred. One Trident submarine carries twenty-four missiles, each of which has eight warheads for a total of 192 warheads. Three hundred eighty-four warheads on two Trident submarines is approximately the size of the entire American missiles force in October 1962. There are only 218 cities of 100,000 or more population in the whole Soviet Union.

It is true that if one adds significant Soviet military bases and installations (other than missile silos) the number of possible targets increases by several hundred. It increases still further if one adds military targets in Eastern Europe. It is also true that in a war one or more Trident submarines might be sunk before they could fire their missiles.

Even so American striking power is outlandishly excessive, and so is Soviet striking power. Ten Trident submarines are being deployed. In addition, the United States will retain for an indefinite period thirty-one Polaris submarines, each of which carries either 128 or 160 MIRV warheads. There are also 1,000 land-based missiles, more than half of which carry three warheads each. In addition there are over 300 bombers that also carry multiple bombs and warheads. And on top of that the United States will be deploying hundreds, probably thousands, of strategic cruise missiles. Obviously the total destructive power the United States can rain on the Soviet Union is mounting far in excess of the number of feasible targets. The same thing is true of the destructive power the USSR can rain on America. The popular term for this is "overkill."*

* This discussion presumes correct the many scientists who say that actual wartime accuracy would differ considerably from accuracy on test ranges, and hence that neither side could attack the other's ICBM silos with any confidence of destroying most of them. Even on the opposite assumption, the great majority of U.S. missile warheads in the early 1980s are not highly accurate even on test ranges. In any case, both sides' plentiful and secure SLBMs mean that no disarming first strike is possible under any conditions, which leaves little point or purpose even to attempt "silo busting."

A full-scale nuclear war between the superpowers would destroy them utterly and would have the gravest consequences far beyond their borders. This had not been the case in the earlier years of the Soviet-American competition, even though some people were inclined to think so. The general public discovered in the late 1950s that the USSR could launch hundreds of bombers carrying nuclear bombs toward the United States, more than a few of which would get through. Suddenly there was a tendency for Americans' previous feeling of considerable security (which had not been justified) to be replaced by the equally simple, opposite feeling that nuclear war meant the end of the world (which was also not justified). At that time and for a while thereafter, a nuclear war would have been an unprecedented catastrophe but would not have been the equivalent of doomsday.

But more recently the popular fantasy has become essentially true. The armories on both sides have reached a point where a general war — in which nuclear weapons are targeted on cities as well as on military targets — would all but obliterate the United States and the USSR.

In spite of the absurd and dangerous quantity of nuclear weapons, there is hardly any promise of a real braking of the arms race. Rather, the prospect is for its more or less steady continuation in the coming years. The planned cruise missiles probably will be deployed in great numbers, first by the United States and a little later by the USSR. Either or both may deploy mobile ICBMs in quantity, and both are working on weapons for use against targets in space, such as the other side's satellites. Advanced bombers and advanced SLBMs will be deployed, along with other new systems supporting nuclear and other warfare on the ground, on and under the seas, in the air, and quite possibly in outer space.

Some of these systems, certainly the cruises, will be impossible to keep track of by reconnaissance satellites or any other means available. Once they are produced in quantity, no verifiable limit or freeze on their deployment will be possible. Neither side would permit the very extensive and intrusive inspection practices that would be needed to count and track them manually. The first American cruises were deployed in late 1982. These major components of strategic power, and later their Soviet counterparts, can multiply uncontrollably.

Putting a ceiling on the overall total of each side's strategic nuclear forces, then reducing them, was and is the fundamental goal of strategic arms control. At some date in the early to mid-1980s, when the cruises have been deployed in enough numbers to make a difference, that goal will be rendered impossible. It will remain impossible for as far into the future as one can see. Some other nuclear forces may continue to be limited, and certain other measures, such as a comprehensive ban on atomic testing, will still be feasible. But the basic goal of capping and then reducing the two sides' total nuclear striking power will have been lost, perhaps permanently.

Technology itself evidently offers no natural stopping place for the arms competition. There is no reason for it not to go on and on, barring some unpredictable change in underlying Soviet-American hostility, or other unforeseeable event. The prospect before the American people is continuation of the arms race, with all its costs, absurdity, and danger, almost without hope of any end.

## The Soviet Union and Nuclear Weapons

### *Document 3*

**David Holloway, an expert on the Soviet Union, reviews Soviet attitudes toward nuclear weapons and arms control in the nuclear age. He says that Soviet leaders have regarded nuclear weapons as instruments of military power and political influence. But they have also recognized how destructive nuclear weapons could be and have tried to manage the U.S.-Soviet relationship through arms control.**

## 3 THE SOVIET UNION AND THE ARMS RACE

**David Holloway**

I have attempted in this book to explore the historical experience, the policy objectives and the institutions that sustain the Soviet military effort. I have tried to show that Soviet policy has been the product of specific decisions taken in a distinctive institutional setting, under the influence of a particular historical experience. I have not undertaken a comprehensive account of Soviet policy, but have chosen, instead, to explore some specific aspects of Soviet military power. Nor have I sought to provide a history of Soviet military policy: much more research needs to be done — and the Soviet Union needs to be more open about its past decisions — before that becomes possible. Nevertheless I have tried to set my discussion of Soviet military power in its historical context.

One reason why a historical perspective is important is that Soviet policy is not easily explained by the theoretical models of the arms race to be found in the social science literature. There are, it is true, elements of the action-reaction phenomenon (in which each side reacts to actions, or potential actions, by the other side) in the history of Soviet–American nuclear weapons competition, with the Soviet Union less innovative, and therefore more reactive, than the United States. At a broader level too it is possible to identify important points at which American policy seems to have been crucial for Soviet decisions: the atomic bomb decision of 1945; decisions about the development of thermonuclear weapons in the late 1940s and early 1950s; decisions in the early 1960s about strategic forces; decisions about ABM systems and strategic missiles in the years before the SALT I Agreements; and perhaps at the present time too. It is more difficult to trace the interaction for the later decisions than for the earlier ones, but the evidence is strong that interaction exists. It is not helpful, therefore, to view Soviet policy as autistic, unresponsive to external stimuli.

At the same time, however, Soviet decisions cannot be understood only as reactions to Western actions. The Soviet leaders have had their own purposes to pursue, their own conception of what military forces they need in order to pursue those purposes, and their own way of doing things. All these influences have imparted a special quality to Soviet policy and policy-making. Even in the history of the early nuclear program, when the Soviet Union was clearly reacting to developments abroad, the important point to understand is not how Stalin reacted, but why he reacted: what political feelings, what fears and ambitions, lay behind the decisions to enter the nuclear arms race? The answer to this question cannot be provided by the action-reaction model of the arms race, but has to be sought in Soviet history.

The Soviet Union has approached the problem of nuclear war in the way that states have traditionally approached the question of war. It has sought to ensure its own security by increasing its military strength. The Soviet leaders have presented their country as powerful, even to the point of hiding its weakness by deception and bluff, as in the bomber gap episode of the mid-1950s and the missile gap episode of 1959–61. They have not wanted to advertise their vulnerability, and their concern not to do so has contributed to their reluctance to accept mutual deterrence, with its stress on mutual vulnerability, as a sound basis for Soviet–American relations.

The Soviet leaders have treated nuclear weapons like conventional weapons in regarding them as instruments of military power and political influence, and at the same time have recognized their qualitatively new character and the devastation they could bring. The Soviet Union has built up powerful nuclear forces not only in preparation for a possible nuclear war, but also to deprive the United States of any political advantage that superiority might bring. In 1946 Stalin said that it would take at least fifteen years to be ready for all contingencies. But in the nuclear age complete readiness is not possible. The Soviet leaders have been forced to recognize that their relationship with the United States is in reality one of mutual vulnerability to devastating nuclear strikes, and that there is no immediate prospect of escaping from this relationship. Within the constraints of this mutual vulnerability they have tried to prepare for nuclear war, and they would try to win such a war if it came to that. But there is little evidence to suggest that they think victory in a global nuclear war would be anything other than catastrophic.

The Soviet Union has tried to manage the strategic relationship with the United States through arms control negotiations. "Manage" is an ambiguous term here, and appropriately so, for the Soviet commitment to parity is by no means so strong as to rule out the search for unilateral advantage. It is hard to see, however, that arms control, as it has been pursued up to now, will lead to anything better than a regulated arms race.... There is no evidence that the Soviet leaders recognize that this is the best that arms control, as practised in the 1960s and 1970s, can achieve. Nonetheless, arms control has become an important element in the Soviet relationship with the West, and a major arena for pursuing both common goals and conflicting objectives.

The Soviet leaders have valued nuclear weapons not only for their potential military utility, but also for their political effect. When they lacked nuclear weapons they felt themselves to be the targets of "nuclear diplomacy." In the late 1950s and early 1960s Khrushchev tried to extract political gains from the ability the Soviet Union was now acquiring to strike the United States with nuclear-armed missiles. When that failed the Soviet Union pressed ahead with building up its strategic nuclear forces and in the 1970s claimed strategic parity with the United States. Strategic nuclear power is the clearest symbol of Soviet superpower status, and the claim to strategic parity shades into the assertion that the Soviet Union is the United States's political equal. But it is not clear what the Soviet Union means by equality in practical terms, or what it implies for Soviet–American relations: an equal right to intervene in third countries, a Soviet–American condominium, a new world order designed with Soviet participation? If the Soviet claim to equality is to provide the basis for better Soviet–American relations it will have to be explained more fully.

The Soviet leaders have been successful in making their country a military superpower. The defence economy has been able to sustain a high level of military effort, and military R & D has been more effective than its civilian counterpart in generating technological innovation. But the military effort has placed a heavy burden on the economy, absorbing resources that could contribute to economic growth and the welfare of the people. The current economic slowdown will force the Soviet leaders to make difficult choices, not only about the allocation of resources, but also about the system of economic planning and management. The 1980s may see fundamental questions raised about the economic system, and about the ability of the political institutions to cope with change. These questions may become the focus of political conflict during the succession, and, if they do, military policy is likely to be a central issue in the argument. The problems that confront the Soviet leaders are indeed serious, but they are not the portents of imminent collapse; whatever choices the Soviet leaders make, the Soviet Union will remain a great military power and a major force in world politics.

## U.S. Policy Toward the Soviet Union

### Document 4

**Harvard political science professor and national security expert Joseph Nye examines U.S. policy toward the Soviet Union in the nuclear age. He says that the United States has pursued three broad goals: avoiding nuclear war, containing the spread of Soviet power, and encouraging change in the Soviet Union. He argues that U.S. policy has been incoherent and inconsistent, in part because of the U.S. political system.**

## 4 CAN AMERICA MANAGE ITS SOVIET POLICY?

**Joseph S. Nye**

### How Well Have We Done?

At a high level of abstraction, the United States has sought three broad goals in its relationship with the Soviet Union: avoiding nuclear war; containing the spread of Soviet power and ideology; and gradually encouraging change in the nature and behavior of the Soviet Union. It is evident that the United States has been wholly successful in the first of these objectives and successful to a lesser extent in the second and third.

Nuclear war has been avoided, as has all direct armed conflict (though not limited wars with Soviet allies in Korea and Vietnam). Nuclear arsenals on both sides have grown greatly, but there have also been some substantial, if imperfect, efforts at arms control. Most important, the nuclear arms race has not led to nuclear conflict, and both sides have learned some prudent practices of crisis management since the Berlin and Cuba crises of the cold war period. Attributing credit may be difficult. Adam Ulam, for example, argues that what kept the Berlin and Cuba crises from erupting into wars was not only U.S. policies but also Soviet prudence.[1] The fact remains that war has been avoided.

Assessing our success in relation to the second general objective — the containment of Soviet power and ideology — is more debatable. First, there is the undeniable fact of increased Soviet military capability. During the cold war period, the United States enjoyed a distinct nuclear military advantage which it saw as balancing superior Soviet conventional capabilities. This strategic advantage was at its peak after the Kennedy buildup of the early 1960s. Faced with steady Soviet military growth, American policymakers in the mid-1960s concluded that trying to maintain strategic superiority would be both infeasible and too costly to attempt. Subsequently, Vietnam and domestic turmoil diverted resources away from the strategic budget to the point where Soviet gains in some areas, particularly land-based missiles, led some Americans to fear that even rough parity had been lost. While the significance of ICBM vulnerability is highly contested, and few American officials have expressed willingness to trade forces with the Soviet Union, most Americans agreed that Soviet military power had greatly increased since the early 1960s. Where they tended to disagree was over how inevitable that change was and how significant it was for our foreign policy objectives.

American success at political containment is also debated, in part because of ambiguities over whether the goal was the containment of Soviet power or of communist ideology. Some, like Norman Podhoretz, argue that communism is a curse, whether dominated by Moscow or not, and that the cost of our political relationship with China is "the loss of political clarity that it inevitably entails."[2] From this point of view, the existence of Marxist regimes in Angola, Laos, Vietnam, Cambodia, Mozambique, South Yemen, Ethiopia, Afghanistan, and Nicaragua is a serious setback for American foreign policy. Moreover, even those who do not worry about the ideological coloration of poor countries would admit that some of these governments are more susceptible to Soviet than to American influence. This represents an extension of Soviet influence to areas far beyond its borders.

On the other hand, it can be argued that there has been a diffusion of power away from both superpowers since the 1950s. In key areas such as Europe and Japan, the political appeal of Soviet ideology has greatly diminished since the 1940s and 1950s. Yugoslavia began the fracturing of Soviet ideological power, and the Soviets as well as the United States "lost" China. The Soviets as well as the Americans have seen Third World clients collapse and governments turn hostile.[3] Moreover, marginal Third World gains are not nearly as significant to the balance of power in the world as the fact that the key areas of Western Europe, Japan, and the Middle East — though geographically closer to the Soviet Union — have remained politically closer to the United States. In addition, the Soviet empire in Eastern Europe is far from the politically secure bastion that the Soviets might hope it to be. In short, while the United States has not prevented the Soviets from gaining some influence in the Third World, from a geopolitical point of view the Soviets have tended to win the small ones rather than the big ones.

In terms of economic power, while the Soviet economy grew impressively in the postwar period until recently, so also did the American economy. In fact, in recent years the Soviet Union has not closed the economic gap with the United States and the Soviet gross national product still remains at little better than half the size of the American. Khrushchev's 1959 threat to overtake and bury the United States has turned out to be a hollow boast. Although American economic preponderance has declined, with the U.S. share of gross world product dropping from 33 to 22 percent of the total over the past thirty years, this relative decline has not been matched by a commensurate Soviet gain. On the contrary, the Soviet share of gross world product also declined in the past decade from 12.5 to 11.5 percent of the total.[4] Moreover, most of the American loss of relative share in world product went not to the Soviet Union but to our allies in Europe and Japan. The recovery of Europe and Japan was our deliberate foreign policy objective, in part as a means of combatting communist influence, and our success in maintaining those alliances means that our loss has not represented a Soviet gain.

A third general objective of American policy in the postwar period, albeit one that has not been pursued at all times, has been to encourage change in the nature and behavior of the Soviet Union. This has varied, from George Kennan's conception in the 1940s of waiting for Soviet power to mellow, to the Reagan administration's efforts to use economic pressures to accelerate particular types of change inside the Soviet Union. As both Dimitri Simes and Strobe Talbott have described, there have been significant changes in the Soviet Union. Although Lenin's authoritarian party structure remains, Stalin's excesses have been alleviated. Some of these changes have been influenced in part by contacts with Western society. Awareness of Western affluence and ideas stimulates popular expectations and makes it more difficult for Soviet leaders to portray America in terms of simple "demonology." It is far less certain, however, that deliberate American governmental efforts have had significant results in bringing about social change inside the Soviet Union, and in some instances they have had contrary effects. In some cases, efforts to foster emigration, internal liberalization, and human rights through quiet diplomacy or increased contacts have had marginal beneficial effects. But this third objective is a difficult one to manage when dealing with a society like the Soviet Union, and it may be just as well that, with a few exceptions, this objective has tended to rank a distant third in our priorities.

Finally, one could argue that, although oscillations have occurred in U.S. policy toward the Soviet Union, the behavior is not purely cyclical. Things never return to exactly where they were. And oscillations are typical of some aspects of the relationship more than others. For example, if one looks at defense spending or public attitudes of trust in the Soviet Union ... oscillation is quite striking. When one looks at trade and social exchanges ... one sees a continuing upward trend rather than a reversion to the levels of earlier periods. This confirms Samuel Huntington's argument ... that the return to hostility was not exactly the return to cold war that some observers had predicted. On the contrary, a residue of trade and contacts, as well as arms control and crisis management, make the current period of renewed hostility quite different from the 1950s trough in the cycle of attitudes. Thus an optimist could argue that the United States has not done badly in pursuing its major objectives over the past four decades and that there has ever been some progress, albeit glacial, in improving the quality of the relationship. The optimist might argue that American policy has been like a drunk coming home from a bar: he may wander from the path from time to time and follow a circuitous and inefficient route, but the important point is that he eventually reaches home.

## The Costs of the American Policy Process

A pessimist would be less complacent. Maybe we have just been lucky thus far. Some of the wanderings were prolonged and painful detours; and in a nuclear age there is always the danger of a disastrous fall into an open manhole. Moreover, the metaphor can be misleading by implying that there can be an end to the continuing need to be attentive in managing the relationship. Even if one agrees that the postwar record has not been bad, there are significant past and potential costs to a policy marked by incoherence and inconsistency. Certainly the recent experience of negotiating major agreements in trade and arms control and then failing to ratify them, and of applying sanctions inconsistently, make it difficult to build a long-term framework for managing the relationship. There are several reasons why an inefficient process is likely to have a cost, if only the cost of opportunities foregone. It may be that equivalent or better outcomes could be achieved at lower levels of cost to our society if we followed a more coherent and consistent policy process.

First, oscillation and incoherence can be costly in terms of encouraging intransigence in our opponent and wariness about cooperative U.S. positions when we get around to them. Desired Soviet responses to our tactical moves will be delayed if Soviet leaders learn that by simply waiting they can cause the United States to drop the tactic and turn to something else. It is characteristic of U.S.–Soviet negotiations that, after the Soviets reject an American proposal, elements in the American polity proceed to bargain publicly with each other rather than with the Soviet Union.[5]

Indeed, the Soviet Union has had a long time to study American inconsistency and incoherence. During the period of nonrecognition in the 1920s, our policy "came close to being the very opposite from what Washington had intended," and in the 1930s the high expectations held out by both sides at the time of recognition soon eroded in a triumph of domestic over external considerations.[6]

Second and more dangerous, incoherence and inconsistency can lead to Soviet misperceptions of American intentions and concerns. Stalin must certainly have been surprised by Truman's reaction in Korea so soon after the U.S. secretary of state had declared it to be outside our defense perimeter. Khrushchev seems to have been surprised by Kennedy's reaction to the installation of Soviet missiles in Cuba so soon after accepting defeat in the Bay of Pigs episode. In the 1970s, Soviets who argued that the fall of Saigon and the failure of the United States to respond in Angola indicated that the United States was compelled to follow a policy of détente in accordance with the vague Marxist notion of a historical change in the "correlation of forces" between capitalism and socialism may have been surprised by renewed demands in the United States for defense spending and a return to hostility at the end of the decade.

Soviet intentions are opaque to us because of Soviet secrecy. Our intentions may be opaque to them because of incoherence and cacophony. They may be a "black box" to us, but we may confuse them with our "white noise." Efforts to sort out intended from unintended signals and to understand the intentions of our policy must be difficult for the Soviets. For example, even practiced observers of the American scene disagreed on how to interpret American reaction to an alleged Soviet combat brigade in Cuba in 1979 — a clumsily handled incident that set back the ratification of SALT II. Some saw it as an accidental product of the impending electoral process; others believed it was "no accident," but a signal that Carter had turned his back on détente and arms control.[7] Sometimes creating uncertainty in the mind of an adversary can enhance deterrence. But misperceptions may lead to unintended confrontations that can lead to a failure of deterrence and the onset of war. In dealing with a stronger Soviet Union in an age of nuclear parity, the United States may not have as much leeway for incoherence, inconsistency, and inefficiency as we had in earlier periods. In an age when two such disparate societies aim 50,000 nuclear weapons at each other, the costs of miscalculation could be catastrophic.

A third cost of incoherence and inconsistency lies in weakening support from our allies and other countries. This might be called the "third audience problem." Most foreign policy issues involve at least two audiences. Political leaders try to mobilize domestic support for their policies as well as to send signals to foreign governments. But an effective policy toward the Soviet Union involves more than just the U.S. public and the Soviet government. As argued above, success in balancing Soviet power is dependent on allying major countries to the United States rather than to the Soviet Union. And . . . the economic role of other countries is becoming increasingly important. An effective strategy for dealing with the Soviet Union cannot be considered in bilateral terms alone. With reduced American preponderance, more attention must be given to the concerns of allied and other countries. Oscillation and inconsistency confuse, not only the Soviets, but also our allies, and make it more difficult to maintain a common position. It was not only impossible to obtain allied agreement to cancel the natural-gas pipeline from the Soviet Union while the United States lifted its embargo against Soviet grain exports, but the effort to do so managed to turn an East–West issue into a West–West dispute and presented the Soviets with a political windfall. . . . Dividing Western alliances has been a longstanding Soviet foreign policy objective, and maintaining such alliance is a key to an effective policy toward the Soviet Union.

Thus one can agree with the optimist that the overall management of the U.S.–Soviet relationship in the postwar period has not proven disastrous but also agree with the pessimist that the past and potential costs of incoherence and inconsistency are too high to allow one to feel sanguine about the future.

## The Causes of Incoherence and Inconsistency

No foreign policy can be fully consistent. By its nature, foreign policy involves balancing competing objectives in a frustrating and changeable world. Every country faces a problem of relating ends and means — of defining its goals and interests so that they can be met within available levels of resources. The Soviets have not always been consistent or coherent in their policies: Khrushchev was certainly far from clear in his foreign policy signals and eventually was fired for his "harebrained schemes."[8] But . . . the inconsistency and incoherence in American foreign policy are rooted in our political culture and institutions. The eighteenth-century founders of the republic deliberately chose to deal with the danger of tyrannical power by fragmenting and balancing power rather than centralizing and civilizing it. In a sense, a potential degree of incoherence and inconsistency in foreign policy is part of the price we pay for the way we chose to defend our freedoms. In the words of Congressman Barber Conable, "The American people are sufficiently skeptical so that, given the choice between efficiency and impotence, they will usually choose impotence."[9] For better *and* worse, we are a government of "separated institutions and sharing powers."[10]

## Notes

1. Adam Ulam, *The Rivals* (New York: Viking, 1971), p. 389.
2. Norman Podhoretz, *The Present Danger* (New York: Simon and Schuster, 1980), p. 67.
3. Richard Feinberg, *The Intemperate Zone* (New York: Norton, 1981), p. 129.
4. Herbert Block, *The Planetary Product in 1980: A Creative Pause?* (Washington, D.C.: U.S. Department of State, 1980).
5. Congressional Research Service, *Soviet Diplomacy and Negotiating Behavior* (Washington, D.C.: U.S. Government Printing Office, 1979).
6. John L. Gaddis, *Russia, The Soviet Union and The United States* (New York: Wiley, 1978), p. 285.
7. Based on conversations at the Institute of the United States and Canada, Moscow, May 1981. See also Gloria Duffy, "Crisis Prevention in Cuba," in Alexander L. George, ed., *Managing U.S.–Soviet Rivalry* (Boulder, Colo.: Westview Press, 1983), pp. 285–318.
8. Ulam argues that Khrushchev's pressure on Berlin was an invitation to a thoroughgoing accommodation, "but he certainly chose a strange way to pursue these objectives." *The Rivals,* p. 285.
9. Quoted in "What the Next 50 Years Will Bring," *U.S. News and World Report,* May 9, 1983, p. 33.
10. Richard Neustadt, *Presidential Power* (New York: Wiley, 1980), p. 26.

# DIFFERING PERSPECTIVES AND POLICY OPTIONS

## Warriors and Victims

### *Document 5*

In this excerpt from his book, *Weapons and Hope,* Freeman Dyson, a scientist who has consulted for the Pentagon, examines the reasons why people have such differing perspectives on nuclear weapons. He focuses on two different "worlds": that of the warrior and that of the victim. The warrior tends to accept the world as it is and to preserve it, not rebuild it from its foundations. The victims worry about the dangers of the current situation and want to make fundamental changes. The two worlds have such different views that it is difficult for them to communicate. Dyson believes the time is right for a new debate on nuclear weapons but says that there must be an agreed-upon agenda before the debate can be fruitful.

### 5 AGENDA FOR A MEETING OF THE MINDS
### Freeman Dyson

I chose the title *Weapons and Hope* for this book because I want to discuss the gravest problem now facing mankind, the problem of nuclear weapons, from a human rather than a technical point of view. Hope means more than wishful thinking. It means the whole range of positive human responses to intractable problems. Hope is a driving force of political action. The main theme of the book will be the interconnectedness of past and future. I will be exploring the historical and cultural context in which nuclear weapons grew, and at the same time looking for practical ways of dealing with the problem of nuclear weapons in the future. The cultural context provides a basis for hope that we can find practical solutions. Central to my approach is a belief that human cultural patterns are more durable than either the technology of weapons or the political arrangements in which weapons have become embedded. . . .

The world of the warriors is the world I see when I go to Washington or to California to consult with military people about their technical problems. That world is overwhelmingly male-dominated. In spite of Joan of Arc and Margaret Thatcher, soldiering is still a game that only boys are supposed to play. The world of the warriors also includes many people outside the professional military establishments. It includes expert negotiators at the United States Arms Control and Disarmament Agency, and professors of International Affairs at the universities of Princeton and Oxford. It includes doves as well as hawks, scholars as well as generals. It includes the loyal opposition as well as the wielders of power. But all who belong to the world of the warriors share a common language and a common style. Their style is deliberately cool, attempting to exclude overt emotion and rhetoric from their discussions, emphasizing technical accuracy and objectivity, concentrating attention on questions of detail which can be reduced to quantitative calculation. They applaud dry humor and abhor sentimentality. The style of the warriors is congenial to professional scientists and historians, who also base their work on factual analysis rather than on moralistic judgment. The philosophical standpoint of the warriors is basically conservative, even when they consider themselves liberal or revolutionary. They accept the world with all its imperfections as given; their mission is to preserve it and to ameliorate its imperfections in detail, not to rebuild it from the foundations.

John von Neumann was a Princeton mathematician who felt a particularly strong affinity for the warriors' world and became a great expert on weaponry. He liked to shock his friends at Princeton with his version of the warriors' philosophy: "It is just as foolish to complain that people are selfish and treacherous as it is to complain that the magnetic field does not increase unless the electric field has a curl. Both are laws of nature." But Von Neumann was an extreme case, an academic outsider trying to be more military than the military. Real soldiers do not make dogmatic statements about the laws of human nature. Real soldiers know that human nature is unpredictable.

The world of the victims is the world I see when I listen to my wife's tales of childhood in wartime Germany, when we take our children to visit the concentration camp museum at Dachau, when we go to the theater and see Brecht's *Mother Courage,* when we read John Hersey's *Hiroshima* or Masuji Ibuse's *Black Rain* or any of the other books which truthfully record the human realities of war, when we sit with a crowd of strangers in church and hear them pray for peace, or when I dream my private dreams of Armageddon. The world of the victims is not male-dominated. It is, on the contrary, women-and-children-dominated. It is, like the Kingdom of Heaven, difficult to enter unless you come with a child's imagination. It is a world of youth rather than age. It pays more attention to poets than to mathematicians. The warriors' world describes the outcome of war in the language of exchange ratios and cost effectiveness, the victims' world describes it in the language of comedy and tragedy.

I also see the world of the victims when I attend meetings of our local citizens' peace movement in Princeton, the Coalition for Nuclear Disarmament. Our meetings are generally held in rooms belonging to one or another of the local churches. Occasionally we have public sessions with outside speakers. The most memorable of our meetings was an all-day affair which kept the Nassau Presbyterian Church packed from 11 A.M. till 9 P.M. The star of the show was Helen Caldicott, the Australian children's doctor who has become a full-time fighter against nuclear power stations and nuclear weapons. Her medical specialty is cystic fibrosis, but she has also some experience with victims of childhood leukemia, a disease which has a well-documented tendency to occur after children are exposed to excessive doses of nuclear radiation. She began her campaign against nuclear power as an exercise in preventive medicine. Even though childhood leukemia is in many cases a curable disease, the cure is uncertain and the treatment is long and debilitating. Every doctor who has to deal with such diseases knows that prevention is better than cure. In her own mind, Helen Caldicott did not cease to be a doctor when she switched from cure to prevention.

In Australia, Helen Caldicott concentrated her efforts on the local issues of nuclear power and the mining of uranium for export. After she came to America, she became aware that nuclear weapons and nuclear war are a graver public health hazard than nuclear power. "I realize now," she told us in Princeton, "that nuclear power is only the pimple on the pumpkin." She is now a prime mover in the worldwide organization of doctors against nuclear war, Physicians for Social Responsibility. As we listened to her talking in the Presbyterian church, it was easy to understand how she has captured the hearts and minds of people around the world. She is spontaneous, she is articulate, she is witty, and she communicates the anguish of a doctor struggling day after day to find help and comfort for desperately sick children. After you have heard her speak and shaken her hand, you cannot brush aside her message as the emotional outpouring of a fanatic. She speaks from a solid basis of medical experience. She speaks for the victims in a language which all of us should be able to understand.

And yet the world of the warriors goes on its way as if Helen Caldicott had never existed. One week I listen to Helen Caldicott in Princeton. The next week I listen to General So-and-so in Washington. Helen and the general live in separate worlds. In a few minutes of conversation I cannot explain Helen's message to the general or the general's message to Helen. If Helen and the general ever tried to talk directly to each other, it would be a dialogue of the deaf. And that is why I write this book. I know that there are not two separate worlds but only one. Helen and the general, whether they like it or not, live on the same planet. My task is to explain them to each other, to fit together the split halves of our world into a single picture.

Why is it so easy for the warriors to ignore Helen? The warriors do not feel inclined to take her seriously, because she does not play her game according to their rules. Both the style and the substance of her arguments violate the taboos of their profession. Her style is personal rather than objective. The substance of her argument is anecdotal rather than analytical. She is careless about technical details. She does not think naturally in quantitative terms. The qualities that make Helen convincing to an audience of concerned citizens in Princeton, her sincerity and seriousness and down-to-earth goodness, are outweighed in the world of the warriors by her weakness in arithmetic.

If it is difficult to translate Helen's message effectively into the language of the generals, it is even more difficult to translate the legitimate concerns of the generals into a language which pays some respect to ordinary human values and feelings. The deliberately impersonal style of the warriors' world gives outsiders the impression that the warriors are even more inhuman than they actually are. There is prejudice and antipathy on both sides. The military establishment looks on the peace movement as a collection of ignorant people meddling in a business they do not understand, while the peace movement looks on the military establishment as a collection of misguided people protected by bureaucratic formality from all contact with human realities. Both these preconceptions create barriers to understanding. Both preconceptions are to some extent true.

When I was seven years old, I was once reprimanded by my mother for an act of collective brutality in which I had been involved at school. A group of seven-year-olds had been teasing and tormenting a six-year-old. "It is always so," my mother said. "You do things together which not one of you would think of doing alone." That is a piece of my education which I have never forgotten. Wherever one looks in the world of human organization, collective responsibility brings a lowering of moral standards. The military establishment is an extreme case, an organization which seems to have been expressly designed to make it possible for people to do things together which nobody in his right mind would do alone.

Yet military people are, underneath their uniforms, human. The first high-ranking military officer with whom I came into close contact was Air Vice-Marshal Harrison, commanding Number 3 Group of the British Bomber Command in the later stages of World War II. I lived for some weeks at his headquarters in a lovely old country house in the village of Exning in Suffolk. At that time he commanded a force of 290 heavy bombers. His bombers took part in the constant heavy attacks on German cities and oil refineries, and suffered their full share of losses. But 3 Group never hit the headlines. While other bomber groups from time to time carried out individual operations of spectacular folly and heroism, 3 Group preferred to send its bombers to lay mines quietly in German coastal waters. In the pecking order of the six groups of Bomber Command, 3 Group by common consent came last. When I arrived at Harrison's headquarters in Exning, I understood why. I presented my credentials to Harrison as the newly appointed scientific adviser to 3 Group. I came prepared to discuss in detail the technical problems of operating a force of bombers. But Harrison did not want to talk about bombers. He talked only about silkworms. Since I was a scientist, he thought I would appreciate the fine points of silkworms. He took me out to his greenhouses, where his silkworms were feeding on carefully tended mulberry bushes. Silkworms were his passion. I could never get him to talk seriously about anything else.

At that time, when I was trying to give Air Vice-Marshal Harrison unwanted scientific advice, I found it shocking that a man who carried the responsibility for the lives and deaths of thousands should be wasting his time on silkworms. Now, thirty-eight years later, I look back and see Harrison as the wisest of the group commanders. He had probably understood earlier than the others that the area-bombing offensive against Germany was a misguided enterprise unworthy of the heroism of his air crews. He could not hope to challenge or change the overall direction of the campaign. The best he could do was what he did, to drive 3 Group with a light hand and shield his crews so far as possible from deeds of superfluous bravery. The cultivation of silkworms helped to keep him sane.

In every military establishment there are Harrisons to be found, men who obey orders without excessive efficiency, and quietly ameliorate evils which they cannot undo. A few weeks ago, on one of my visits to the warriors' world in Washington, I heard an American general say that he takes for his motto the words of the French diplomat Talleyrand, "Pas Trop de Zèle" — "Not Too Much Enthusiasm." There, I thought, walks the spirit of Air Vice-Marshal Harrison. But the Harrisons, no matter how numerous they may be and no matter how high they rise, are bound by the rules of their profession to keep their skeptical thoughts private. The public voice of the military establishment cannot be critical of its own purposes. The military machine is designed to carry out the missions which it has established for itself, irrespective of the thoughts and feelings of individual commanders.

The responsibility for criticizing and controlling military policies belongs to the political authorities of each country. The political arena is the place where, in theory, the warriors' world and the victims' world should come together, where the claims of generals and pediatricians should be compared and weighed in the balance. Political leaders have the opportunity to hear both sides. If the claims of the generals are found wanting, political leaders have the power to make drastic changes in weapon deployments and in military doctrines. But in the political arena as it actually exists, opportunities for deliberate weighing of alternative philosophical viewpoints rarely arise, and the power to make drastic changes is limited. Every politician knows that drastic change is troublesome and politically costly. Even in countries with a revolutionary political tradition, bureaucratic inertia usually prevails. In the United States, political decisions concerning military policy are almost always made piecemeal, in the course of routine budgetary hearings. Seldom do we see a decision made, as the decision to negotiate and ratify the Test Ban Treaty was made in 1963, with a full public debate allowing proponents and opponents to discuss the long-range historical consequences of the treaty rather than its immediate political costs and benefits.

The time is now ripe for a new public debate, placing in question the fundamental objectives of military policy. This time, the debate must be worldwide. It has already begun in Western Europe and in the United States. The argument centers around the question whether nuclear weapons have any longer a rational military purpose. Helen Caldicott and the European nuclear disarmament movement are a part of the debate. The efforts of my military friends in the Pentagon to find a secure basing mode for their new MX missile are also a part of it. But the argument remains sterile and disjointed because the two sides lack a common language. A debate can be politically effective, like the debate of 1963, giving political leaders courage and strength to make hard decisions which change the world, only if the two sides will listen to each other and understand each other's concerns. There must be an agreed agenda before a fruitful discussion is possible. . . .

## The True Nature of the Soviet Union

### *Document 6*

**In these excerpts from a 1985 article, Midge Decter, an influential neoconservative, lays out some of the basic elements of the peace through strength perspective. Decter criticizes those who assert that "the Soviet Union is only a nation among nations, a power among powers, seeking merely to assure its national self-interest." She argues that the West is not threatened "with the extinction of the planet" but with the collapse of its societies "beneath the weight of that advancing, ponderous barbarism called communism."**

### 6 DEMOCRATIC IDEALS AND THE PROBLEMS OF WAR AND PEACE IN THE NUCLEAR AGE
**Midge Decter**

The "peace movement" of today, in Europe and the United States, is the true spiritual legacy of those much touted and self-deceived young people of the 1960s and 1970s. The "peace movement" does not love peace, it hates the world.

Politicians who wish to display their bona fides as feeling, sensitive souls never refer to the peace movement without pointing out that it is made up of decent people. Particularly when such politicians are engaged in tracing the influence of the Soviet Union on this movement do they seem impelled to express their conviction that most of its members, though perhaps misguided, are moved by the highest motives. The truth is, *they are not decent people.* They may not be Soviet agents, but they are in a certain sense something worse. They are idealists, which is to say, moral evaders, people looking for a quick fix in a situation that offers none — looking for the unattainable because it feels more pleasing to do so, and damn the consequences. Among human transgressions, being idealistic may not rank with murder, but it is anything but noble and, in truth, far from decent.

#### Democratic Realities

Let us, then, set aside any careless impulse to speak of democratic ideals and speak instead of democratic realities. And let us not speak of war and peace but of that messy condition which is neither of these things and which happens to be the state of play between democratic societies and totalitarian ones.

First, as we unhappily do not need to be reminded, the number of nations even attempting to guarantee liberty to their citizens is a small one, whereas the number of nations in the grip of grim and/or bloody totalitarianism appears to grow year by year.

Second, Soviet communism has since its rise to power in Russia been an expansive, aggressive, revolutionary force, seeking by subversion, intimidation, in recent decades nuclear blackmail, and, where necessary or possible, outright military conquest, to achieve hegemony over the world.

Third, the only thing that has stood between the Soviet Union and the realization of its international ambitions has been an alliance headed by the United States and supported by the nations of Western Europe and Japan; Our alliance harbors no such imperialistic ambitions — quite the contrary — and its only *raison d'être* (and that is part of the problem) has been to arrest the spread of Soviet domination.

Fourth, that alliance is now coming unstuck. We might discuss where and how it is coming unstuck in detail, but that has been done in many other forums. Suffice it to say that the West Europeans, not without a great deal of justice, have lost faith in the capacity of the United States to play the role history has handed it, and that the Americans, with equal justice, have lost faith in the West Europeans' commitment to bearing their rightful share of what must be a common burden. The specific charges and counter-charges here are not only divisive, they are *irrelevant.* For our real problem, within ourselves and among us, lies in any case not in our respective shortcomings but in our virtues as societies.

It is not in the nature of Western democratic societies that they remain steadily and staunchly mobilized, as we are now required to do. The liberties we enjoy; the wealth and widespread well-being that only liberty seems able to produce; the notions of equity and civic propriety and private happiness that underlie our political institutions — in short, those things that rightly make us the envy of the whole world — also make us peaceable, unmilitant, and slow to act until we are threatened. There is that in Western democratic man — it is, *up to a point,* an attractive thing to say about him — which does not love to bear or use arms.

Not altogether unlike the youth of the sixties and seventies, we members of democratic societies tend to resist the dirty business that life sometimes imposes upon us. The gaudiest case of this was, of course, to be found in the 1930s, when Britain, France, and the United States, against everything they could see and hear and were actually being told, pretended to themselves that Hitler was only out to rectify a couple of his borders. This trick of self-deception is being repeated in our time in the assertion that the Soviet Union is only a nation among nations, a power among powers, seeking merely to assure its national self-interest. The purpose of this self-deception, like the self-deception of the Allies in the 1930s, is to evade the necessary and possibly politically unpopular need to arm ourselves to the teeth, draw a line, and to say to our enemy and *mean* it, "You step over that line at your grave peril." . . .

## The Defense of Democratic Societies

What, then, are we, disadvantaged as I have said by our very virtues, to do at this most critical juncture of our political existence? What we must do in the first instance is something we must do to ourselves. That is, we must face and admit the cold, brutish truth about our situation. That being accomplished, we shall have far less difficulty dealing with our enemy.

What is that cold, brutal truth? Quite simply, that we are threatened, not, as the "idealists" in our respective countries have been so lustfully declaring, with the extinction of the planet, but with the collapse of our finely and delicately balanced societies beneath the weight of that advancing, ponderous barbarism called communism. Furthermore, this onslaught finds us not — *not yet* — spiritually prepared to save ourselves.

In the perspective of eternity, this is an astonishing thing to recognize. For no one any longer has the right to any illusions about communism. Those who have doomed themselves, or have been doomed by Western cupidity (or stupidity), to live under communist tyranny hate it. No matter how ugly or cruel the government replaced by it, communism has created even greater misery: more poverty, more cynicism, more murder, more despair. As Daniel P. Moynihan once observed, no one has ever climbed into a leaky boat to sail to the Soviet Union, or to Cuba, or for that matter to China. Sixty-five years of hard-won experience by millions upon millions of our utterly hopeless fellow human beings must have left us all perfectly disabused on this point. On the other side are modern Western societies whose discovery of the principle of liberty has provided their citizens not only with freedom, public and private, but with the means to create untold, undreamed of, wealth and to distribute that wealth more broadly, more equitably, than any other societies in human history. There is, as we say in the United States, no contest.

Yet there are those in our societies who ask us not to resist. Some of them, communists themselves, seek no more than to come to power. In this, they need not trouble us. Communists do not come to power by democratic means in democratic societies. The danger they represent lies only in their opportunities to poison the minds and sap the will of others. Such opportunities, however, are being plentifully provided.

They are provided, as I noted earlier, in the repetition of the noxious idea that any society falling short of utopia is not worth defending.

They are provided, far more insidiously, in the idea that international relations is a matter which concerns the behavior of nations understood as nothing more than powers acting as powers, without reference to their internal political morality. Here, of course, I am speaking of that habit of mind that goes by the name of *Realpolitik*. Adherents of *Realpolitik* will tell you that America's commitment to Western Europe at the close of World War II was merely a means of self-interested self-protection (and also, let us never forget, a means of opening up markets). Adherents of *Realpolitik* will tell you that the Soviet Union, too, has interests like any other nation and that these can be traded off, adjudicated, like those of any other nation, through diplomacy.

In the United States (and no doubt also in Western Europe) there has been a thirty-year debate, sometimes friendly, sometimes touched with asperity, between the so-called hard-headed realists and the anticommunist ideologues about the needs and purposes of Western power. The ideologues have been accused by the so-called realists of failing to understand the subtleties and flexibilities of East-West relations, of being crusaders, moralists, of bringing in principle where principle does not apply — of being, in a word, childish. But when the time came, it was the hard-headed people who created the policy of detente — a policy whose intention was to ensnare the Soviet Union in a web of international economic and political entanglements but whose real effect was, on the contrary, to entangle *us* instead. The economic, the political, the technological, not to mention the military, advantages of detente have all moved one way in the wrong direction; at every juncture, we discovered there was to be no *quo* for the *quid*. The debate has been settled. To be an anticommunist ideologue is precisely to be in the position to provide far better, far more practical, hard-headed, serviceable advice about how to understand and deal with the Soviet Union than all the accumulated wisdoms of ordinary statecraft.

All this aside, it is these voices of so-called hard-headedness among us that help to undermine our capacity to face the hard and brutal truth and that provide the richest opportunities of all for those who seek our downfall. Ronald Reagan's use of the simple (*not* simplistic) word "evil" in speaking of the Soviet Union was salutary. Had it not been, neither the Soviets nor the Western press would have been so agitated by it. For in the face of such a word, one is obligated to *do* something: to rouse oneself, to mobilize, and to remain ever alert. It is not the Ronald Reagan who speaks of good and evil who threatens the peace of the world. It is the Ronald Reagan who succumbs to the abuse of the peaceniks, the stridency of the world press, the contempt of the "real-politikers", and the cheap anxieties of his political counsellors and sends his minions to pursue the fruitless expedient of arms control — it is this Ronald Reagan who threatens the peace of the world.

The democratic West, though presently hampered by its reluctance to make hard choices, is far from helpless. We possess that greatest of all assets, a healthy and productive populace. If our elites are decadent — and they are: whose children, after all, march in the streets of Bonn and London and New York demanding our surrender? — our ordinary citizens are not. Our economies, to the extent that they remain free, cannot only out-produce and out-distribute all others; they can also be vibrantly responsive to new demands, to innovation, to the need for moving quickly. Our political institutions, despite all the careless pressure we have put upon them in recent years, are sound. If guns, missiles, planes, tanks, and armies must be maintained in a state of readiness to protect us and to keep the peace, we can admit them to our national lives without fear of corruption. They are costly and inconvenient, to be sure, but they are *not* ignoble.

When we speak of democratic ideals, *true* democratic ideals, we would do well to subsume them all under one emblazoned statement: "The alternative is simply unacceptable." The alternative is unacceptable to us, to those who must languish under it, and to those who will come after us.

"The tree of liberty," it was once long ago said, "is watered by the blood of martyrs." We have no right, and we have no *need,* to let the precious legacy left us by those martyrs — through our own blindness and trembling, and with no thought for the future — slip through our fingers.

## The Failures of Arms Control

### *Document 7*

William R. Van Cleave, a national security specialist and adviser to Ronald Reagan's 1980 campaign, makes the peace through strength case against arms control. Fifteen years of arms control experience, he says, make it clear that arms control with the Soviet Union cannot promote U.S. national security. In fact, arms control is more likely to constrain the United States and lull it into complacency while the Soviet Union continues to build more weapons. Because the United States has lost nuclear superiority, it lacks the leverage to force the Soviets to engage in real arms control.

### 7 THE ARMS CONTROL RECORD: SUCCESSES AND FAILURES
### William R. Van Cleave

There must be national security standards by which to assess the successes or failures of agreements. According to the U.S. Department of State, agreements should make a measurable contribution to national security. But can any recent arms control agreement be said to have made such a clear and significant contribution? Under that demanding standard, agreements that many regard as arms control successes — the Limited Test Ban Treaty, Non-proliferation Treaty (NPT), and SALT I Anti-Ballistic Missile (ABM) Treaty — seem more like failures.

The Limited Test Ban Treaty (1963) accomplished virtually nothing that its supporters had promised. It did not limit or control nuclear armaments. It did not advance the cause of either parity or strategic stability....

I do not know what the NPT (1968) has accomplished, but I doubt that anyone else does either....

Undoubtedly, the SALT I ABM Treaty (1972) has been a "success," if its purpose was to administer the coup de grace to Safeguard and to erase the U.S. advantage in ABM research, development, testing, and engineering. Certainly, many experts regard the agreement that way. On the other hand, the major expectation for the ABM Treaty was that it would reduce requirements for offensive forces. With ABMs stringently limited, neither side would have any incentive to increase its offensive capabilities significantly. An ABM Treaty, then, would lead inexorably to offensive force limitations and reductions. But what happened? The USSR proceeded to increase its offensive force efforts, and Soviet offensive capabilities expanded beyond all expectations.

What the ABM Treaty really did was to encourage Soviet development of a counterforce threat to U.S. land-based deterrent forces. It deprived the United States of a potential means for strengthening ICBM survivability, and it continues to work against that option today. It also allowed the Soviets to gain an edge in ABM technology, and they now have advanced to the potential for a rapidly deployable nationwide system.

If there is no unequivocally successful agreement, what of the value of the arms control process itself? Some commentators, while professing concern over the details of agreements, still argue the importance of the process itself and the utility of agreements in keeping it going. This was a major argument for both SALT I and SALT II. Yet there is no denying that strategic trends accompanying this process have been decidedly adverse to the United States or that the USSR has become increasingly bellicose and threatening. And when one considers the depressant effect of the SALT process on U.S. strategic programs and on the U.S. ability to cope with the Soviet threat, there is surely no evidence that the process has been beneficial to this country. It has not been worthwhile enough to cause us to accept bad agreements and overlook Soviet misbehavior in order to preserve the process.

Nonetheless, faith in arms control negotiations remains strong. Without them, it is argued, there is no chance for arms control. If arms control means only negotiated agreements, useful or harmful, that may be so, but what about no arms control? We should remind ourselves that in the democratic states of the West there is *always* arms control, even without negotiated agreements. Arms are controlled and limited by the West's traditional values, by its political and budgeting processes, and by the influence of the media and of public opinion. Even though not required to do so by arms control agreements, the United States has considerably reduced both the number of its nuclear weapons and the megatonnage of its nuclear stockpile since the late 1960s. The Soviets have expanded both categories severalfold during the period most governed by arms control negotiations.

It is quite difficult to produce an unambiguous example of arms control success during the past twenty years. One may point to agreements on nuclear-free zones — outer space, Antarctica, Latin America — as minor examples (all further examples of the effectiveness of unnecessary agreements). Perhaps the best illustrations of "success" are the few times the U.S. government has been able to use arms negotiations to relieve some short-term political problem — for example, the Mutual and Balanced Force Reductions (MBFR) negotiations to defuse the Mansfield amendment calling for withdrawal of U.S. troops from Europe or flexibility on intermediate-range nuclear forces (INF) to ease public arms control pressures on West European governments beleaguered by Soviet propaganda. Or perhaps, one might see the utility of arms control as giving the U.S. government an excuse for not doing something it does not wish to do, such as, perhaps, deploy Safeguard. This is essentially the view that Lieutenant General Brent Scowcroft (USAF, ret.) seemed to present at a Lawrence Livermore Laboratory arms control conference in 1981. To him, SALT I had been useful because the United States was not competing with the Soviet Union anyway. (He also took the extremely uncritical view "that any kind of an agreement that we have with the Soviet Union is going to be in our interest.")[11]

Everything considered, however, arms control has been a failure. Neither the national security of the United States nor strategic stability has been improved by arms control. To the contrary, the threats to both are far more grave today than before. Arms control policies and their ramifications do bear much of the responsibility for this situation.

I do not wish to examine the arms control record in terms of the details of negotiation and agreements. Rather, I want to address what I perceive to be the general failures and adverse influences of arms control. . . .

Arms control, when combined with related strategic concepts, helped blind Americans to Soviet motivations and objectives. It also led many to disparage the fundamental political and ideological differences between the United States and the USSR. After all, if political differences were irrelevant to agreement on strategic stability, how important could they be?

This can only be regarded as a profound intellectual failure related directly to arms control, and it led to errors in U.S. intelligence estimates and projections throughout the 1960s and well into the 1970s. The U.S. government and its intelligence organizations perceived Soviet objectives in terms of Western concepts. They therefore persisted in interpreting Soviet strategic programs in that context and, *a priori,* resisted evidence that the Soviets had quite different views and more ambitious goals. . . .

. . . Arms control in general, and SALT in particular, have constrained the willingness of the executive branch to pursue and Congress to support programs consistent with U.S. requirements in the face of the Soviet strategic force buildup. As Dr. Kissinger later remarked in Senate testimony on SALT II, "We will not draw the appropriate conclusion if we do not admit that SALT may have had a perverse effect on the willingness of some in the Congress, key opinion makers, and even Administration officials to face fully the relentless Soviet military buildup."[12]

SALT, in other words, has not only failed to achieve the original objectives of the United States in arms control, but it has actually contributed to a worsening of the situation. Arms control has not restrained Soviet strategic programs or counterforce objectives, but arms control has dampened U.S. responses to those programs and objectives. . . .

## Lessons

The proper starting point for arms control is with a clear appreciation of the great difference between U.S. and Soviet political, strategic, and arms control goals. Arms control, as experience shows, cannot be isolated from that context, however fervently earlier theorists believed it could be. The attempted isolation was actually a belief in the congruence of U.S. and Soviet views and goals. The lack of that congruence but continued belief in it resulted in arms control failure.

What other lessons might be derived from the record of arms control failure? Among others, I would suggest the following:

1. Arms control cannot be divorced from politics. It cannot be isolated from Soviet political objectives or from the fundamental political differences between the United States and the USSR or from domestic politics.

2. Arms control agreements will reflect the reality of the existing strategic balance and trends in it. If we are not happy with that situation, we will not be happy with agreements based on it. The strategic situation must be improved before there is much likelihood of satisfactory agreements.

3. The Soviet Union is not interested in arms control to help the United States solve its problems and does not view arms control in terms of stabilizing mutual deterrence. The Soviet approach to arms control and Soviet strategic objectives are not congruent with U.S. arms control goals.

4. Consequently, arms control will not resolve the United States' basic strategic problems. Only a U.S. program can do that. Expecting arms control to produce a stability that does not exist in U.S. programs, or in those of the USSR, is to expect too much.

5. As weak a means to the end of national security as arms control has been, there is still a tendency to regard it as an end in itself. That should be resisted. Arms control should be pursued only to the extent that it may make a meaningful contribution to national security, and its success or failure should be evaluated in those terms.

6. The United States' strategic doctrine and objectives have been established as official expressions of national security requirements and policy. Arms control positions should be in strict concurrence with those requirements and that policy.

7. The United States does not yet have the leverage necessary to interest the Soviet Union in arms control agreements that would be helpful in solving these problems. It may be several years before it does, and by then it may be too late for truly meaningful treaties. The only agreements possible in the near future are cosmetic ones or ones that will be unequal and disadvantageous to the United States. Given the risk of the latter, the United States needs a carefully thought out and tightly controlled "damage-limiting" approach to arms control.

8. Arms control can be harmful to U.S. national security, perhaps less in the direct impact of agreements than in their indirect impact — in the *perverse effect* that agreements or the pursuit of agreements or the general chimera of arms control has on the U.S. ability to produce, support, and sustain necessary force programs and in the self-delusions that promises of arms control inevitably seem to spawn. The more emphasis U.S. leaders place on arms control, the more adverse this impact is likely to be. In addition, overemphasis on arms control can weaken U.S. foreign policy. It can, for example, expand U.S. tolerance of and weaken U.S. responses to Soviet misbehavior, whether it takes the form of noncompliance with agreements, armed aggression, or bestial attacks on commercial airliners.

9. Arms control enthusiasts and politicians have been too careless about the realities of arms control; they have overstated both the possible accomplishments of agreement and the consequences of non-agreement.

10. When both the media and national political leaders engage in this practice, they are following rather than educating, and they increase political pressures for arms control of any sort. National political leaders, in effect, reinforce the political pressures on themselves. pressures that lead them to extol arms control, accommodate to achieve agreements, and then pretend that bad arms control is good arms control. Those same pressures are then brought to oppose necessary defense programs and their proper funding.

## Notes

11. Warren Heckrotti and George Smith, eds. *Arms Control in Transition* (Boulder, Colo.: Westview Press, 1983), pp. 7, 32.

12. The U.S. Congress, Senate. Committee on Foreign Relations, *The SALT II Treaty* (Washington: Government Printing Office, 1979).

## Why Not Superiority?

### *Document 8*

This excerpt from the book *A Strategy for Peace Through Strength* by the American Security Council, a prodefense private group, argues that the United States should regain strategic superiority. This does not necessarily mean a numerical advantage, the authors say, but a technological advantage and a change in strategy. The authors also argue that the Soviet Union now has a strategic superiority.

## 8 DETERRENCE AND DEFENSE
**American Security Council**

The argument against the value of military superiority is especially pernicious because it is always used to justify reducing U.S. military strength. It is never applied against Soviet military power. It is worth remembering that the world was a safer place and Soviet aggression more muted when the U.S. enjoyed overwhelming strategic superiority, because we had a monopoly of nuclear weapons and strategic delivery systems. With a rough U.S.-Soviet parity of numbers and quality of both weapons and means of delivery, the best that can be achieved is some politically useful margin of military superiority.

Current Soviet numerical superiority in strategic weapons, though not sufficient at present to warrant the risk of a first strike, does offer the Soviet Union both military and political advantages. It does not follow that the U.S. should seek superiority merely because it is the Soviet's goal. The initial objective of superiority for the U.S. at the strategic level, based on a unique technological advantage, is to deny the Soviets these advantages.

Those who argue that the U.S. cannot afford superiority tend to picture the U.S. building more and larger weapons of all kinds than the Soviet Union. This is not true, nor is it necessary. Strategic superiority does not demand a numerical advantage. It does demand good strategic thinking and superior science and technology.

Overall military and technological superiority for the U.S. would require fundamentally that we possess unique technological advantages which would: (1) discourage a direct Soviet attack against this country and its principal allies; (2) prevent Soviet coercion of allies; (3) inhibit nuclear proliferation; and, (4) allow us to control the escalation of war begun at a low level of conflict intensity. For the U.S. to control the escalation of war does not require superiority in all categories of conventional weapons. Rather, it requires that we be able to exert a downward pressure against an adversary on the basis of superiority at the high end of the conflict spectrum, strategic power.

At issue, therefore, is whether the U.S. should seek to regain a margin of superiority — or, as the President has called it, a "margin of safety" — by developing unique technological advantages. Advantage need not give the U.S. a first-strike potential, but it should be one that would allow us to control the process of escalation.

The political aspect of strategic superiority is often overlooked by those who seek to downgrade its importance. Third World and uncommitted nations, viewing the Soviet dedication to superiority and measuring their sacrifice, draw the conclusion that the Soviet Union will be the dominant world power in the future. These nations do not engage in academic and moralistic debates about superiority. They simply note the facts objectively, and conclude that their future will be best served by accommodating to the USSR.

The people in the United States who most loudly denounce strategic superiority as a national objective do not recognize — or will not admit — that superiority is the Soviet objective. For years Soviet military officials have publicly denounced U.S. pronouncements about mutual assured destruction as decadent "bourgeois" concepts, not grounded in reality. They have openly declared that they intend to develop superior military power to control the course of history.

First, the Soviets built a large, accurate first-strike offensive force. The Soviet offensive force is designed to give them a disarming capability. It was not designed as a deterrent based on retaliation.

Now, the Soviets are increasing their investment in defense. The Soviets have experimented with anti-aircraft missiles that have an ABM potential, and their experiments have involved netting those weapons in a nationwide array along with acquisition and weapons-control radars. In essence, they have tested the prototype of a nationwide ABM system. Moreover, the Soviets have a large and modern air defense force, supported by a nationwide civil defense structure and program.

Hope for the future lies in what the Joint Chiefs of Staff referred to as "the study of means for defending against strategic nuclear attack." This statement refers to President Reagan's historic speech of March 23, 1983, in which he announced a basic reorientation of our nuclear strategy from Mutual Assured Destruction toward Mutaul Assured Survival. The President called on the scientific community to find ways to make nuclear missiles "impotent and obsolete"; and with that challenge, he renounced the theory of deterrence known as Mutual Assured Destruction (MAD).

Mutual Assured Destruction bases deterrence on the defenselessness of both sides. Conceptually, it places both nations in the position of facing each other with nuclear offensive weapons — nuclear swords, if you will — but without nuclear shields. The Soviets have never accepted this no-defense concept and have made massive investments in ballistic missile defense, anti-bomber defense, and civil defense. Robert Jastrow wrote recently of the Soviet response to MAD:

> It is now clear — in fact it has been clear for a decade — that while for many years the American government adopted the strategy of Mutual Assured Destruction proposed by our scientists and academicians, the Soviet government rejected it. The USSR undertook to do exactly what our strategists say it is supposed not to do: it implemented large programs for defending its citizens from nuclear attack, for shooting down American missiles, and for fighting and winning a nuclear war. The result, as Senator Moynihan has said, is "a policy in ruins, and the greatest peril our nation has faced in its 200-year history."

## Superpowers Have Common Interests

### *Document 9*

Harold Brown's view of the Soviet Union forms part of the competition and cooperation perspective. In this excerpt from his book, *Thinking About National Security,* the former secretary of defense argues that the United States "must keep the Soviets from gaining dominion in the areas that are critical to U.S. security." He adds that the superpowers do have common interests, most importantly in avoiding a nuclear war.

## 9 THE SOVIET UNION
### Harold Brown

The Soviets are likely to pursue an expansionist foreign policy for the rest of this century. Their massive internal and substantial external problems have only intensified the concentration of the leaders on their goals. The first of these goals is maintaining their power at home. They have a good thing going for themselves, and the end of the Stalinist terror and the improvement in economic output over the past few decades have made it better. Their other main goal is to maintain their power along the periphery of the Soviet Union and to extend that power, if possible, to more remote areas as well. Thus the United States and the Soviet Union will continue to be adversaries at least in political terms for the rest of this century.

Nevertheless, the United States and the Soviet Union have some common interests. The first is in avoiding the unimaginably and indeed terminally catastrophic destruction of a nuclear war. The United States ought to aim, and generally has aimed, at a peaceful world system in which the peoples of all countries can determine their own destinies with a minimum of outside coercion and disruption. The Soviet leaders seek, at worst, to gain a dominant position in the world. Both of these aims would be rendered impossible by a nuclear war, so both countries have the strongest possible motivation to prevent a nuclear war.

To say that the Soviets would greatly prefer to gain their ends eventually without a nuclear war and that the United States has as its most important goal the avoidance of a nuclear war is not to say that nuclear war will never happen. But it provides an important basis for pursuing joint policies. Examples are arms limitation, the hot line for communication in a crisis, and nonproliferation policies to increase stability in the rest of the world. In such efforts, each side will try to maximize its own relative advantage even as it attempts to develop some mutually advantageous cooperative policies. The prospects of success will continue to be limited by the adversary relationship and the existence of specific conflicting goals.

U.S. policy toward the Soviet Union must keep the Soviets from gaining dominion in the areas that are critical to U.S. security—specifically, Western Europe, Southwest Asia, including the Middle East, and the Far East. The United States with its friends and allies must be strong enough militarily to prevent a successful Soviet military attack or major political intimidation in those areas and to maintain a dominant military position in the Western Hemisphere. To that end, the United States must build up its political and economic as well as military strength. It must encourage alignments as well as strengthen alliances. At the same time, the industrialized democracies must not forget the factor of Soviet paranoia. An attempt on their part to destabilize Soviet leadership or its dominance of Eastern Europe by economic warfare or subversion would carry grave risks; it should not even be considered except as a response to a clear and direct Soviet threat to an area critical to U.S. security. An attempt to create an explicit military superiority over the Soviet Union of the sort that existed during the 1950s, and the appearance of a military threat to the Soviet Union implicit in such a military posture, would be dangerous and unlikely to succeed.

Given the difference in the ways the United States and the Soviet Union perceive the world, it is not clear that these goals—maintaining enough strength to prevent political intimidation in areas important to the United States while avoiding a threatening appearance to the Soviet Union—are both possible. Seeking to walk that narrow line (if it exists) will challenge U.S. leadership skills to the maximum.

Are there carrots that the United States can dangle before the Soviet leaders to promote a change in the direction of less expansionist and disruptive Soviet policies? There may be. But some earlier carrots have not got the mule pulling in the right direction. The Soviet leaders sought military parity after the Cuban missile crisis. They now have it. The easing of their expansionist and paranoid tendencies that some thought would follow from such parity has not yet appeared. The Soviets want a part at least equal to that of the United States in influencing events all over the world. They have yet to achieve the economic strength or display the political responsibility necessary to lay claim to such a role. The "web of relationships" encouraged by the United States and its allies early in the 1970s, giving the Soviets the promise of economic benefit in return for more responsible political behavior, especially in the Third World, did not come into being—or at least did not produce the hoped-for behavior. But the Soviets have a legitimate argument that the United States reneged on such economic promises as most-favored-nation treatment. It is likely that what they expected from the United States was not what the United States understood by the bargain, nor was what the United States expected from them quite what they understood. Nevertheless, it would be worth trying such an approach again at the right time. But the two parties must be more explicit about the expected behavior of each. Moreover, a schedule of commitment should be included—on the U.S. side, a commitment not to change the economic rules within less than two, three, or even five years, at which time a review would be made; and on the Soviet side, commitments of corresponding duration and specificity.

Such an approach is inevitably a temporizing one. The goal of the United States should be to contain Soviet expansionist tendencies and at the same time to outlast them, hoping for but not assuming an eventual evolution in the Soviet political system or its acceptance of an international order that seeks stability and relative freedom for each country to find its own destiny. The existence of internal contradictions in Soviet policy suggests that over time Soviet motivations and behavior may change for the better. Such a change is rather unlikely in this century, but U.S. attitudes, words, and actions may be able to encourage such a shift in coming decades.

# A Cautious Approach to Arms Control

## *Document 10*

**Richard Burt, a key arms control official in the Reagan administration, makes an argument that fits into the competition and cooperation perspective. He says in this 1982 article that some past arms control agreements have been flawed because they tried to do so much. The United States, Burt says, cannot rely on arms control to protect national security. The continuing challenge from the Soviet Union means the United States must continue to rely on strong nuclear forces.**

## 10 DEFENSE POLICY AND ARMS CONTROL: DEFINING THE PROBLEM
**Richard Burt**

### What Arms Control Can Do

It has now become commonplace for analysts and government officials to argue, as did Leslie H. Gelb, former director of the Bureau of Politico-Military Affairs, recently, that "as a result of specialization of narrow mandate, people all too often focus exclusively either on military programs or on arms control while losing sight of the other. Yet neither new forces nor arms control agreements are an end in itself. They are only means to an end, which is to ensure national security." But recognizing that a sort of analytical and bureaucratic "decoupling" between arms control and defense planning has occurred is only the first step toward finding a solution to the problem Gelb described. The second, more difficult step is to recognize that the conflicts and inconsistencies that plague arms control and defense planning flow, in the main, from misconceptions about what negotiations can accomplish. Thus, while it is now an article of faith that arms control cannot serve as a substitute for an adequate defense posture, U.S. negotiating strategy and conduct in many areas has assumed that this *is* the case. Indeed, some of the basic beliefs that underpin U.S. thinking about arms control seem to rule out the possibility of achieving greater compatibility between negotiating policy and military strategy.

### *The Functions of Arms Control*

A central fallacy of the existing approach to arms control is the belief that the primary function of negotiations is to alleviate sources of military instability. Probably the most conspicuous aspect of the SALT enterprise is the absence of any shared consensus between the two sides over the role and utility of long-range nuclear weapons — in particular, the meaning of "strategic stability." And without such a consensus, negotiators have failed to work out solutions to such problems as ICBM vulnerabilty. In March 1977, for example, the Carter administration tabled a proposal that, from the U.S. perspective, would have restructured both sides' arsenals along more stable lines: the most threatening (and vulnerable) component of both sides' forces — land-based ICBMs — would have been de-emphasized while each would have been free to build up its more secure sea-based and bomber forces.

Although some U.S. officials argued that Moscow's rejection of the so-called "comprehensive proposal" simply reflected a lack of imagination, there were sound strategic reasons for turning the American action down. For a start, given technological and geographical reasons, the idea of placing greater reliance on sea-launched ballistic missiles (SLBMs) and bombers undoubtedly appeared unattractive to Soviet planners. More important, from a doctrinal perspective, the Soviets probably viewed the growing vulnerability of U.S. ICBMs as a stabilizing rather than a dangerous development. What the March 1977 episode, along with the experience at MBFR, reveals is that lacking a consensus among negotiators over what "stability" constitutes, the most likely outcomes of arms control are agreements like the SALT II Treaty — accords that ratify rather than restructure prevailing trends in the military balance. This is surely why the Vienna talks have so far failed to produce an accord; while there are good reasons for the West to insist on manpower parity in the center region, the Soviet Union possesses equally strong incentives for maintaining its existing position of superiority.

The foregoing should not be interpreted to suggest that arms control outcomes do not have a military impact. Agreements, such as the 1972 ABM Treaty, can of course have a major impact on the plans of both sides. But, as in the case of the ABM Treaty, it is probably a mistake to view new agreements as part of a process of doctrinal convergence. The hypothesis that Moscow, by accepting severe restrictions on ABM deployment, agreed, in effect, to a system of "nuclear mutual vulnerability" must be judged against its continuing efforts in the area of air defenses, civil defense, antisubmarine warfare, and antisatellite systems. A much more plausible explanation for Moscow's decision to enter into the treaty is that with the U.S. *Safeguard* system ready to undergo deployment, the Soviet Union made a hardheaded decision to close off competition in ABMs. Again, the lesson is not that arms control outcomes reflect a narrowing of strategic beliefs, but that nations can sometimes reach agreement for very different reasons.

### *Arms Control and Military Change*

A second fallacy that proceeds from the notion of arms control as a solution to defense problems is the idea that military programs that threaten existing negotiations somehow endanger deterrence. As suggested above, the most common result of arms control is not enhanced stability but the registration of reality; agreements are often controversial because, more than anything else, they spotlight military deficiencies. But when looking at the impact of military programs on arms control negotiations, there is a common tendency to confuse means and ends. Weapons that for one reason or another pose threats to existing negotiations are viewed as threatening stability when, in fact, the impact of their deployment might be just the opposite....

### *Disaggregating the Military Balance*

The cruise missile case is also useful in highlighting the tendency of negotiations to distort, simplify, and most important, compartmentalize military reality. As the acronym implies, the SALT process uses as its central organizing principle the idea that there is a distinct class of U.S. and Soviet forces known as "strategic weapons." Although that description of the state of technology was generally accurate during the 1960s, a new class of more accurate and flexible systems, such as the cruise missile, is making the time-honored distinction between "strategic" and "general purpose" forces obsolete. Moreover, new munitions, such as fuel-air explosives and enhanced radiation weapons, are blurring distinctions between nuclear and conventional weapons.

As a result, the preoccupation of the SALT process with the "homeland-to-homeland" nuclear balance between the two superpowers has made it increasingly difficult to cope with weapons technologies that are relevant in both "central strategic" and regional military contingencies. SALT outcomes that limit these systems are unattractive because they foreclose options for upgrading theater defenses. At the same time, agreements that exclude these systems are equally unattractive, because, as the controversy over the *Backfire* at SALT II illustrated, neither side likes the idea of allowing the other to increase its intercontinental-range arsenal under the guise of expanding its theater forces. Because the United States has nuclear commitments to the defense of Western Europe, the notion of a "homeland-to-homeland" balance fostered by SALT has never been terribly attractive. During a period in which the systems limited by the process were not directly relevant to the defense of the theater, bilateral agreements were bearable. But in a period when it no longer is possible to compartmentalize the U.S.-Soviet strategic balance, new SALT agreements seem certain to challenge the military and political cohesion of the Western alliance....

## Finding a New Balance

The central argument of this chapter has been that arms control and defense planning are out of kilter largely because misunderstandings about what can be achieved in negotiations have been reinforced by bureaucratic behavior. There are some ways that these problems might be solved.

### *Scaling Down Ambitions*

The central reality of arms control is that only rarely do negotiated outcomes address pressing military concerns. To reiterate, arms control is primarily useful for registering and codifying an existing balance of forces. This can be a useful outcome. At SALT, the belief that U.S. and Soviet strategic forces are roughly equivalent (at least in size) is probably critical to the maintenance of détente, however tenuous. In the same way, an MBFR agreement that provided for equal manpower ceilings (assuming the use of a mutually acceptable data base) would also create a condition of "optical parity" that would surely enhance political confidence in both Eastern and Western Europe. Moreover, arms control agreements can create a degree of predictability that is useful both politically and militarily. In criticizing arms control, it is easy to lose sight of the uncertainty that plagued political leaders and military planners during the first half of the 1960s. In the early part of the decade the tendency to exaggerate Soviet strategic programs led the United States to rush ahead with programs that by 1965 seemed unnecessary. However, American overreaction in the early 1960s probably fostered a tendency in the latter half of the decade to underestimate Soviet strategic ambitions, an even more dangerous development. Whatever else SALT II does, it will enable political and military authorities to agree on the character of the strategic environment in the mid-1980s.

But "optical parity" and predictability are not the same things as the maintenance of deterrence. In strategic forces, the maintenance of credible deterrence requires the deployment of U.S. land-based systems in a more survivable basing mode and, more controversial, an enhanced ability to threaten hard targets in the Soviet Union. In the European theater, deterrence also requires more survivable nuclear forces. It is possible that many options for bolstering deterrence in these areas could complicate future arms control efforts. There is no obvious solution to this dilemma. Some observers, despite the lessons of SALT II, seem interested in shaping a new set of grandiose goals for a new round of negotiations. In the view of this writer, that would be a major mistake. Asking too much from SALT III not only runs the risk of raising expectations that will surely be disappointed, but also places a national security burden on SALT that it cannot bear.

If there is a solution, it probably lies in asking arms control to do less instead of more. Thus, at SALT III, the United States should not seek severe quantitative reductions or tighter qualitative constraints. An accord that would provide both sides with some flexibilty for dealing unilaterally with their separately perceived military problems might not only be more negotiable but also, probably, more conducive to overall stability. Scaling down ambitions for arms control will not totally eliminate the very real tensions between efforts to achieve "optical parity" at SALT and unilateral efforts to strengthen deterrence. But the first step toward wisdom in this area is to recognize that such tensions exist. . . .

The main way in which defense programs and arms control can interact positively is by enhancing U.S. negotiating leverage. As the ABM case suggests, weapons programs can provide incentives for the Soviet Union to consider negotiating outcomes that do more than simply ratify prevailing strategic trends. It has been suggested, for example, that Carter's MX decision could force the Soviet Union, for the first time, to think seriously about the merit of severe constraints on MIRVed (multiple independently targetable reentry vehicles) ICBMs. Yet, "bargaining chip" negotiating strategies must be approached with caution. In the ABM case, the United States possessed a system that was technologically vastly superior to what Moscow had and, equally important, its deployment lay right around the corner. These conditions are absent in the MX case. First, with the MX only now undergoing full-scale development, it is unrealistic to expect the system to provide the U.S. side with much negotiating leverage in the immediate future. Second, the system's hard-target capability will not be qualitatively different than Soviet systems undergoing deployment at the same time. Thus, it is probably unrealistic to expect that the Soviet Union would react to the threat of MX deployment by agreeing to a scheme for de-emphasizing land-based ICBMs. It would be a much more painful response to the MX if the Soviet Union were to find a more survivable basing mode for its own ICBMs. . . .

# A Cooperation and Competition Arms Control Agenda

## *Document 11*

In the final chapter of their book, *Hawks, Doves, and Owls,* Harvard professors and national security experts Albert Carnesale, Joseph S. Nye, and Graham T. Allison lay out an arms control agenda typical of the cooperation and competition perspective. They list ten principles for avoiding nuclear war, emphasizing modernizing U.S. nuclear forces and building up conventional forces while pursuing limited arms control agreements. They are also skeptical of the Strategic Defense Initiative (SDI). The excerpts here include their list of ten principles and their explanations of the first two.

## 11 AN AGENDA FOR ACTION
## Albert Carnesale, Joseph S. Nye, and Graham T. Allison

Though we consider all of the actions discussed here to be important, some clearly are more consequential than others. Actions also differ in their feasibility and timeliness, and in the degree to which they will prove controversial. Taking these factors into account, we have highlighted under each of the ten principles the two actions — one to be taken and one to be avoided — that we consider most deserving of attention.

### 1. Maintain a Credible Nuclear Deterrent

- DO modernize the strategic triad.
- DON'T adopt a no-first-use policy.

To avoid war, it is necessary (though not sufficient) to maintain the capability of our military forces and the credibility of our political intentions and resolve. Our nuclear arsenal continues to play an important role in deterring aggression against the territory of the United States, our allies, and other areas of vital interest to us. There currently is rough parity in the U.S.-Soviet nuclear balance; but exactly what deters the Soviets is unknown to Americans, and is likely to remain so. Nevertheless, there seems little doubt that deterrence of deliberate nuclear or conventional attack on the American homeland is effective, robust, and stable. No U.S. or Soviet weapons program in progress or on the horizon will significantly alter the likelihood of such attacks, nor are any new capabilities within reach that would give either side a meaningful strategic advantage. Less hardy is deterrence of Soviet aggression against our allies or other areas of vital interest to us, because the threat to use nuclear weapons in response to attacks outside our homeland is inherently less credible. Our suggestions for actions to be taken and actions to be avoided are designed to ensure that Soviet leaders see no advantage in the balance of nuclear forces and to maximize the credibility of our nuclear deterrent.

### *Actions to Take*

• *DO modernize the strategic triad.* The three legs of the strategic triad (land-based missiles, sea-based missiles, and long-range bombers and air-launched cruise missiles) comprise a diverse and redundant retaliatory force. Each component has unique properties, and their collective ability to survive attack and penetrate defenses is greater than that of each leg in isolation. The triad should be modernized as necessary to ensure that an adequate proportion would survive attack and be able to penetrate Soviet defenses. A modern ICBM force, smaller than the other legs of the triad, should be maintained to contribute to deterrence by the threat of reliable prompt use of small numbers of nuclear weapons against virtually any meaningful military targets and as a hedge against possible Soviet breakthroughs in antisubmarine warfare or air defenses. Such capabilities could be acquired by upgrading current Minuteman ICBMs or by deploying new ICBMs or by some combination of these modernizations. Over the longer term, consideration should be given to missile carrying submarines smaller than the current versions.

• *DO put alliance politics first.* Deterrence depends not only on military capabilities, but also on perceived readiness to use force. The political cohesion of an alliance is essential to the credibility of its deterrent. In this connection, it is important for NATO to continue implementation of its intermediate-range nuclear force (INF) modernization program, unless an agreement is reached with the Soviets whereby NATO forgoes some of the planned INF deployments in return for similar reductions of Soviet forces. Political disputes that fractionate the alliance and weaken its resolve can be even more destructive than adverse changes in the military balance.

### *Actions to Avoid*

• *DON'T adopt a no-first-use policy.* Rhetorical removal of the threat of intentional escalation to nuclear war in Europe, the Persian Gulf, or Korea would (if believed) psychologically enhance Soviet advantages in general purpose forces and increase the risk that the Soviets might attempt a conventional attack. If the current imbalance in conventional forces were corrected, so that the West could respond effectively to Soviet offensives without any perceived resort to nuclear weapons, then a strategy of no-first-use would be more attractive. There is no indication, however, that the West is likely soon to build up its conventional forces to that level. For the foreseeable future, a no-first-use declaration would be counterproductive militarily and would undermine essential alliance cohesion. Special effort should be made, however, to eliminate any requirements or operating procedures calling for early use of nuclear weapons in response to conventional aggression.

• *DON'T pursue a comprehensive freeze.* Alarm about the risk of nuclear war has increasingly been expressed in calls for a "comprehensive nuclear freeze." Unfortunately, however, a comprehensive freeze is not a good prescription for avoiding nuclear war. For example, because it is difficult to define and verify a freeze on defensive systems, most so-called "comprehensive" freeze proposals deal only with offensive nuclear weapons. But an agreement that froze only offensive forces and not the corresponding defensive ones (including ballistic missile defenses, air defenses, and antisubmarine warfare) could lead to shifts in the offense-defense balance that would weaken the deterrent value of offensive retaliatory forces. In addition, by prohibiting all modernization of nuclear weapons systems, a comprehensive freeze would preclude changes that would reduce the risk of nuclear war, such as modification of long-range bombers to provide faster takeoff (and thus greater survivability) and replacement of large multiple-warhead ICBMs by small single-warhead models. Partial freezes that impose discriminating restraints on weapons technology can be both feasible and beneficial. The merits of such proposals must, of course, be judged on a case-by-case basis.

• *DON'T confuse MAD with a strategy.* Mutual assured destruction (MAD) describes a condition, not an objective. In this condition, each superpower can absorb a first strike and still retaliate massively against its adversary's population and industry. This condition exists today and is likely to persist for the foreseeable future. But MAD is not an objective of American policy. Its "mutuality" is unattractive to most American policymakers (and presumably to Soviets as well). Nor is MAD a military strategy, for it does not serve to guide U.S. targeting (which focuses primarily on Soviet military forces). Public understanding is not advanced by those who pretend that MAD is America's strategy or goal.

• *DON'T assume that cities can be defended.* In announcing his Strategic Defense Initiative (SDI) on March 23, 1983, President Reagan called for a defensive system that "could intercept and destroy strategic ballistic missiles before they reached our own soil or that of our allies" and thereby render nuclear weapons "impotent and obsolete." The long-term goal is understandable and readily shared, but in all likelihood mutual assured destruction will remain the condition of superpowers for decades to come. Because a substantial portion of each nation's population and industry is concentrated in a relatively small number of cities, and each city can be destroyed by a few nuclear weapons, their protection requires a perfect or near-perfect defense against all forms of nuclear delivery, including long- and short-range ballistic missiles and cruise missiles, manned bombers and, for that matter, fishing trawlers, civilian aircraft, and other means for covert delivery. There are sound military reasons favoring continued research on defensive systems, but it should not be assumed that such research will lead to an effective defense of cities.

## 2. Obtain a Credible Conventional Deterrent

- DO strengthen NATO and the RDF.
- DON'T provoke the Soviet Union.

The non-nuclear forces of the United States and its allies are currently inadequate to deter with high confidence or to defend against Soviet conventional attack in Europe, the Persian Gulf region, and other areas of vital interest. Thus the United States finds itself in effect threatening first use of nuclear weapons to counter conventional aggression. By choosing to rely on early nuclear use, the United States and its European and Japanese allies have opted for defense "on the cheap." Current political preferences make an early reversal of this policy unlikely, but it is not unaffordable. The Soviet Union enjoys no economic advantage over the United States. Quite the reverse: the U.S. gross national product (GNP) is roughly twice that of the Soviet Union. Moreover, the United States and its allies enjoy a combined GNP more than four times that of the Soviet Union and its allies. If the Western democracies and Japan rely on a cheaper, more dangerous, more nuclear-weapons-dependent defense, it is because they choose to accept that risk. Insufficient resources are not a plausible excuse.

*Actions to Take*

• *DO strengthen NATO and the RDF.* Because threats to use conventional force are more credible than threats to use nuclear weapons, improved general purpose forces would enhance deterrence even between the nuclear superpowers. The United States and its allies, each paying its fair share, should continue those conventional force improvements that reduce the chances that the Soviets could achieve rapid victory conventionally in vital areas like Europe and the Persian Gulf. Such improvements include the acquisition of a militarily meaningful Rapid Deployment Force (RDF) and additional airlift and sealift capacities, and upgrading of air defenses in Europe. Our objective should be to escape from the position in which we have to threaten escalation to nuclear use; greater conventional capabilities will strengthen deterrence of Soviet aggression and reduce the dangers of conventional and nuclear war.

• *DO raise the nuclear threshold.* By developing and deploying conventional weapons systems capable of performing some of the functions now assigned to battlefield nuclear weapons, the United States and its allies can raise their threshold of nuclear use. This transition would be complemented by a reversal of the United States' practice of integrating battlefield nuclear weapons with general purpose forces. It must be recognized, however, that conventional forces alone cannot eliminate the risk of nuclear war. After all, the Soviets could choose to use nuclear weapons first.

*Actions to Avoid*

• *DON'T provoke the Soviet Union.* As the United States and its allies expand and improve their conventional forces, they should be wary of the dangers of threatening vital Soviet interests. Regardless of the peacefulness of the West's intentions, our offensive conventional capabilities should not be strong enough to pose plausible threats to Eastern Europe and the Soviet homeland. NATO should continue to adhere to a military strategy consistent with the fundamentally defensive character of its current forces. An offensive force posture and strategy, whether based on nuclear or advanced conventional technologies, even though intended to enhance deterrence could increase the risk of nuclear war by provoking the Soviets to preempt or by lowering their threshold for nuclear use.

• *DON'T pretend that nuclear weapons deter only nuclear war.* The proposition that the only military purpose of nuclear weapons is to deter the adversary's use of nuclear weapons is gaining acceptance as a new conventional wisdom. But we believe it is wrong. So long as nuclear forces are deployed in substantial numbers, they present an inescapable risk that any conventional war might escalate by design or by accident to a nuclear one. How much the United States should rely on the risk of nuclear escalation to deter conventional war is an appropriate topic for debate. That discussion is not advanced, however, by denying that the danger of nuclear escalation affects the calculations of a potential aggressor.

## 3. Enhance Crisis Stability

- DO take decapitation seriously.
- DON'T adopt a launch-on-warning policy. . . .

## 4. Reduce the Impact of Accidents

- DO reduce reliance on short-range theater nuclear weapons.
- DON'T use nuclear alerts for political signaling. . . .

## 5. Develop Procedures for War Termination

- DO plan for ending a war if it begins.
- DON'T plan for early use of nuclear weapons. . . .

### 6. Prevent and Manage Crises

- DO prepare decision-makers to deal with nuclear crises.
- DON'T engage American and Soviet forces in direct combat. . . .

### 7. Invigorate Nonproliferation Efforts

- DO maintain security gurantees.
- DON'T be fatalistic about proliferation. . . .

### 8. Limit Misperceptions

- DO meet regularly with Soviet leaders.
- DON'T treat nuclear weapons like other weapons. . . .

### 9. Pursue Arms Control Negotiations

- DO preserve existing arms control agreements.
- DON'T oversell arms control. . . .

### 10. Reduce Reliance on Nuclear Deterrence over the Long Term

- DON'T assume that nuclear deterrence will last forever.
- DO intensify the search for alternatives to deterrence. . . .

## Reducing the Nuclear Danger — The Catholic Bishops' View

### *Document 12*

In 1983 the United States Conference of Catholic Bishops took a close look at the morality of nuclear deterrence and nuclear war. They produced a pastoral letter, "The Challenge of Peace: God's Promise and Our Response." In these excerpts from the letter, the bishops make clear that nuclear war of any kind is immoral and that nuclear deterrence is acceptable only as a way to prevent nuclear war. The bishops call for a halt to the deployment of first-strike weapons and emphasize the urgent need for major steps to stop the arms race.

## 12 PASTORAL LETTER ON WAR AND PEACE U.S. Catholic Bishops 1983

### The Just-War Criteria

(80) The moral theory of the "just-war" or "limited-war" doctrine begins with the presumption which binds all Christians: We should do no harm to our neighbors; how we treat our enemy is the key test of whether we love our neighbor; and the possibility of taking even one human life is a prospect we should consider in fear and trembling. How is it possible to move from these presumptions to the idea of a justifiable use of lethal force?

(81) Historically and theologically the clearest answer to the question is found in St. Augustine. Augustine was impressed by the fact and the consequences of sin in history — the "not yet" dimension of the kingdom. In his view war was both the result of sin and a tragic remedy for sin in the life of political societies. War arose from disordered ambitions, but it could also be used in some cases at least to restrain evil and protect the innocent. The classic case which illustrated his view was the use of lethal force to prevent aggression against innocent victims. Faced with the fact of attack on the innocent, the presumption that we do no harm even to our enemy yielded to the command of love understood as the need to restrain an enemy who would injure the innocent.

(82) The just-war argument has taken several forms in the history of Catholic theology, but this Augustinian insight is its central premise.[13] In the 20th century, papal teaching has used the logic of Augustine and Aquinas[14] to articulate a right of self-defense for states in a decentralized international order and to state the criteria for exercising that right. The essential position was stated by Vatican II: "As long as the danger of war persists and there is no international authority with the necessary competence and power, governments cannot be denied the right of lawful self-defense, once all peace efforts have failed."

(84) The determination of *when* conditions exist which allow the resort to force in spite of the strong presumption against it is made in light of *jus ad bellum* criteria. The determination of *how* even a justified resort to force must be conducted is made in light of the *jus in bello* criteria. We shall briefly explore the meaning of both.[15]

(85) *Jus ad Bellum:* Why and when recourse to war is permissible.

(86) a. Just Cause: War is permissible only to confront "a real and certain danger," i.e., to protect innocent life, to preserve conditions necessary for decent human existence and to secure basic human rights. As both Pope Pius XII and Pope John XXIII made clear, if war of retribution was ever justifiable, the risks of modern war negate such a claim today.

(87) b. Competent Authority: In the Catholic tradition the right to use force has always been joined to the common good; war must be declared by those with responsibility for public order, not by private groups or individuals. . . .

(92) c. Comparative Justice: Questions concerning the means of waging war today, particularly in view of the

destructive potential of weapons, have tended to override questions concerning the comparative justice of the positions of respective adversaries or enemies. In essence: Which side is sufficiently "right" in a dispute, and are the values at stake critical enough to override the presumption against war? The question in its most basic form is this: Do the rights and values involved justify killing? For whatever the means used, war by definition involves violence, destruction, suffering and death. . . .

(95) d. Right Intention: Right intention is related to just cause—war can be legitimately intended only for the reasons set forth above as a just cause. During the conflict, right intention means pursuit of peace and reconciliation, including avoiding unnecessarily destructive acts or imposing unreasonable conditions (e.g., unconditional surrender).

(95) e. Last Resort: For resort to war to be justified, all peaceful alternatives must have been exhausted. There are formidable problems in this requirement. No international organization currently in existence has exercised sufficient internationally recognized authority to be able either to mediate effectively in most cases or to prevent conflict by the intervention of U.N. or other peacekeeping forces. Furthermore, there is a tendency for nations or peoples which perceive conflict between or among other nations as advantageous to themselves to attempt to prevent a peaceful settlement rather than advance it. . . .

(98) f. Probability of Success: This is a difficult criterion to apply, but its purpose is to prevent irrational resort to force or hopeless resistance when the outcome of either will clearly be disproportionate or futile. The determination includes a recognition that at times defense of key values, even against great odds, may be a "proportionate" witness.

(99) g. Proportionality: In terms of the *jus ad bellum* criteria, proportionality means that the damge to be inflicted and the costs incurred by war must be proportionate to the good expected by taking up arms. Nor should judgments concerning proportionality be limited to the temporal order without regard to a spiritual dimension in terms of "damage," "cost" and "the good expected." In today's interdependent world even a local conflict can affect people everywhere; this is particularly the case when the nuclear powers are involved. Hence a nation cannot justly go to war today without considering the effect of its action on others and on the international community.

## *Jus in Bello*

Even when the stringent conditions which justify resort to war are met, the conduct of war (i.e., strategy, tactics and individual actions) remains subject to continuous scrutiny in light of two principles which have special significance today precisely because of the destructive capability of modern technological warfare. These principles are proportionality and discrimination. In discussing them here we shall apply them to the question of *jus ad bellum* as well as *jus in bello;* for today it becomes increasingly difficult to make a decision to use any kind of armed force, however limited initially in intention and in the destructive power of the weapons employed, without facing at least the possibility of escalation to broader, or even total, war and to the use of weapons of horrendous destructive potential. . . .

(103) Response to aggression must not exceed the nature of the aggression. To destroy civilization as we know it by waging a "total war" as today it *could* be waged would be a monstrously disproportionate response to aggression on the part of any nation.

(104) Moreover, the lives of innocent persons may never be taken directly, regardless of the purpose alleged for doing so. To wage truly "total" war is by definition to take huge numbers of innocent lives. Just response to aggression must be discriminate; it must be directed against unjust aggressors, not against innocent people caught up in a war not of their making. . . .

When confronting choices among specific military options, the question asked by proportionality is: Once we take into account not only the military advantages that will be achieved by using this means, but also all the harms reasonably expected to follow from using it, can its use still be justified? We know, of course, that no end can justify means evil in themselves, such as the executing of hostages or the targeting of non-combatants. Nonetheless, even if the means adopted is not evil in itself, it is necessary to take into account the probable harms that will result from using it and the justice of accepting those harms. . . .

In terms of the arms race, if the *real* end in view is legitimate defense against unjust aggression and the means to this end are not evil in themselves, we must still examine the question of proportionality concerning attendant evils. . . . Do the exorbitant costs, the general climate of insecurity generated, the possibility of accidental detonation of highly destructive weapons, the danger of error and miscalculation that could provoke retaliation and war—do such evils or others attendant upon and indirectly deriving from the arms race make the arms race itself a disproportionate response to aggression? Pope John Paul II is very clear in his insistence that the exercise of the right and duty of a people to protect their existence and freedom is contingent on the use of proportionate means.[16]

(107) Finally, another set of questions concerns the interpretation of the principle of discrimination. The principle prohibits directly intended attacks on non-combatants and non-military targets. It raises a series of ques-

tions about the term "intentional," the category of "non-combatant" and the meaning of "military. . . ."

These two priniciples in all their complexity must be applied to the range of weapons—conventional, nuclear, biological and chemical—with which nations are armed today. . . .

(139) . . . As bishops we see a specific task defined for us in Pope John Paul II's 1982 World Day of Peace Message:

> Peace cannot be built by the power of rulers alone. Peace can be firmly constructed only if it corresponds to the resolute determination of all people of good will. Rulers must be supported and enlightened by a public opinion that encourages them or, where necessary, expresses disapproval.[17]

The pope's appeal to form public opinion is not an abstract task. Especially in a democracy, public opinion can passively acquiesce in policies and strategies or it can through a series of measures indicate the limits beyond which a government should not proceed. The "new movement" which exists in the public debate about nuclear weapons provides a creative opportunity and a moral imperative to examine the relationship between public opinion and public policy. We believe it is necessary for the sake of prevention to build a barrier against the concept of nuclear war as a viable strategy for defense. There should be a clear public resistance to the rhetoric of "winnable" nuclear wars, or unrealistic expectations of "surviving" nuclear exchanges and strategies of "protracted nuclear war." We oppose such rhetoric. . . .

(141) Charting a moral course in a complex public policy debate involves several steps. We will address four questions, offering our reflections on them as an invitation to a public moral dialogue:

1. The use of nuclear weapons;
2. The policy of deterrence in principle and in practice;
3. Specific steps to reduce the danger of war;
4. Long-term measures of policy and diplomacy.

*C. The Use of Nuclear Weapons:* Establishing moral guidelines in the nuclear debate means addressing first the question of the use of nuclear weapons. . . .

(147) *1. Counterpopulation Warfare:* Under no circumstances may nuclear weapons or other instruments of mass slaughter be used for the purpose of destroying population centers or other predominantly civilian targets. Popes have repeatedly condemned "total war," which implies such use. For example, as early as 1954 Pope Pius XII condemned nuclear warfare "when it entirely escapes the control of man" and results in "the pure and simple annihilation of all human life within the radius of action."[18]

(148) Retaliatory action, whether nuclear or conventional, which would indiscriminately take many wholly innocent lives, lives of people who are in no way responsible for reckless actions of their government, must also be condemned. This condemnation, in our judgment, applies even to retaliatory use of weapons striking enemy cities after our own have already been struck. No Christian can rightfully carry out orders or policies deliberately aimed at killing non-combatants. . . .

(150) *2. The Initiation of Nuclear War:* We do not perceive any situation in which the deliberate initiation of nuclear warfare on however restricted a scale can be morally justified. Non-nuclear attacks by another state must be resisted by other than nuclear means. Therefore, a serious moral obligation exists to develop non-nuclear defensive strategies as rapidly as possible. . . .

(152) Whether under conditions of war in Europe, parts of Asia or the Middle East, or the exchange of strategic weapons directly between the United States and the Soviet Union, the difficulties of limiting the use of nuclear weapons are immense. A number of expert witnesses advise us that the commanders operating under conditions of battle probably would not be able to exercise strict control; the number of weapons used would rapidly increase, the targets would be expanded beyond the military and the level of civilian casualties would rise enormously.[19] No one can be certain that this escalation would not occur even in the face of political efforts to keep such an exchange "limited." The chances of keeping use limited seem remote, and the consequences of escalation to mass destruction would be appalling. Former public officials have testified that it is improbable that any nuclear war could actually be kept limited. Their testimony and the consequences involved in this problem lead us to conclude that the danger of escalation is so great that it would be morally unjustifiable to initiate nuclear war in any form. The danger is rooted not only in the technology of our weapons systems, but in the weakness and sinfulness of human communities. We find the moral responsibility of beginning nuclear war not justified by rational political objectives. . . .

(154) At the same time we recognize the responsibility the United States has had and continues to have in assisting allied nations in their defense against either a conventional or a nuclear attack. Especially in the European theater, the deterrence of a *nuclear* attack may require nuclear weapons for a time, even though their possession and deployment must be subject to rigid restrictions.

(155) The need to defend against a conventional attack in Europe imposes the political and moral burden of developing adequate, alternative modes of defense to present reliance on nuclear weapons. Even with the best coordinated effort—hardly likely in view of contemporary political division on this question—development of an alternative defense position will still take time.

(156) In the interim, deterrence against a conventional attack relies upon two factors: the not inconsiderable conventional forces at the disposal of NATO and the recognition by a potential attacker that the outbreak of large-scale conventional war could escalate to the nuclear level through accident or miscalculation by either side. We are aware that NATO's refusal to adopt a "no first use" pledge is to some extent linked to the deterrent effect of this inherent ambiguity. Nonetheless, in light of the probable effects of initiating nuclear war, we urge NATO to move rapidly toward the adoption of a "no first use" policy, but doing so in tandem with development of an adequate alternative defense posture.

(157) *3. Limited Nuclear War:* It would be possible to agree with our first two conclusions and still not be sure about retaliatory use of nuclear weapons in what is called a "limited exchange." The issue at stake is the real as opposed to the *theoretical* possibility of a "limited nuclear exchange."

(158) We recognize that the policy debate on this question is inconclusive and that all participants are left with hypothetical projections about probable reactions in a nuclear exchange. While not trying to adjudicate the technical debate, we are aware of it and wish to raise a series of questions which challenge the actual meaning of "limited" in this discussion.

- Would leaders have sufficient information to know what is happening in a nuclear exchange?
- Would they be able under the conditions of stress, time pressures and fragmentary information to make the extraordinarily precise decision needed to keep the exchange limited if this were technically possible?
- Would military commanders be able in the midst of the destruction and confusion of a nuclear exchange to maintain a policy of "discriminate targeting"? Can this be done in modern warfare waged across great distances by aircraft and missiles?
- Given the accidents we know about in peacetime conditions, what assurances are there that computer errors could be avoided in the midst of a nuclear exchange?
- Would not the casualties, even in a war defined as limited by strategists, still run in the millions?
- How "limited" would be the long-term effects of radiation, famine, social fragmentation and economic dislocation?

(159) Unless these questions can be answered satisfactorily, we will continue to be highly skeptical about the real meaning of "limited." One of the criteria of the just-war tradition is a reasonable hope of success in bringing about justice and peace. We must ask whether such a reasonable hope can exist once nuclear weapons have been exchanged. The burden of proof remains on those who assert that meaningful limitation is possible.

(160) A nuclear response to either conventional or nuclear attack can cause destruction which goes far beyond "legitimate defense." Such use of nuclear weapons would not be justified. . . .

Without making a specific moral judgment on deterrence, the council clearly designated the elements of the arms race: the tension between "peace of a sort" preserved by deterrence and "genuine peace" required for a stable international life; the contradiction between what is spent for destructive capacity and what is needed for constructive development.

In the post-conciliar assessment of war and peace and specifically of deterrence, different parties to the political-moral debate within the church and in civil society have focused on one or another aspect of the problem. For some, the fact that nuclear weapons have not been used since 1945 means that deterrence has worked, and this fact satisfies the demands of both the political and the moral order. Others contest this assessment by highlighting the risk of failure involved in continued reliance on deterrence and pointing out how politically and morally catastrophic even a single failure would be. Still others note that the absence of nuclear war is not necessarily proof that the policy of deterrence has prevented it. Indeed, some would find in the policy of deterrence the driving force in the superpower arms race. Still other observers, many of them Catholic moralists, have stressed that deterrence may not morally include the intention of deliberately attacking civilian populations or non-combatants.

The statements of the NCCB-USCC [National Conference of Catholic Bishops-U.S. Catholic Conference] over the past several years have both reflected and contributed to the wider moral debate on deterrence. In the NCCB pastoral letter "To Live in Christ Jesus" (1976), we focused on the moral limits of declaratory policy while calling for stronger measures of arms control.[20] In 1979 Cardinal John Krol, speaking for the USCC in support of SALT II ratification, brought into focus the other element of the deterrence problem: The actual use of nuclear weapons may have been prevented (a moral good), but the risk of failure and the physical harm and moral evil resulting from possible nuclear war remained.

"This explains," Cardinal Krol stated, "the Catholic dissatisfaction with nuclear deterrence and the urgency of the Catholic demand that the nuclear arms race be reversed. It is of the utmost importance that negotiations proceed to meaningful and continuing reductions in nuclear stockpiles and eventually to the phasing out altogether of nuclear deterrence and the threat of mutual-assured destruction."[21]

These two texts, along with the conciliar statement, have influenced much of Catholic opinion expressed recently on the nuclear question.

In June 1982, Pope John Paul II provided new impetus and insight to the moral analysis with his statement to the U.N. Second Special Session on disarmament. The pope first situated the problem of deterrence within the context of world politics. No power, he observes, will admit to wishing to start a war, but each distrusts others and considers it necessary to mount a strong defense against attack. He then discusses the notion of deterrence:

> Many even think that such preparations constitute the way — even the only way — to safeguard peace in some fashion or at least to impede to the utmost in an efficacious way the outbreak of wars, especially major conflicts which might lead to the ultimate holocaust of humanity and the destruction of the civilization that man has constructed so laboriously over the centuries.
>
> In this approach one can see the "philosophy of peace" which was proclaimed in the ancient Roman principle: *Si vis pacem, para bellum.* Put in modern terms, this "philosophy" has the label of "deterrence" and one can find it in various guises of the search for a "balance of forces" which sometimes has been called, and not without reason, the "balance of terror."[22]

(173) Having offered this analysis of the general concept of deterrence, the Holy Father introduces his considerations on disarmament, especially, but not only, nuclear disarmament. Pope John Paul II makes this statement about the morality of deterrence:

> In current conditions "deterrence" based on balance, certainly not as an end in itself but as a step on the way toward a progressive disarmament, may still be judged morally acceptable. Nonetheless in order to ensure peace, it is indispensable not to be satisfied with this minimum, which is always susceptible to the real danger of explosion.[23]

(174) In Pope John Paul II's assessment we perceive two dimensions of the contemporary dilemma of deterrence. One dimension is the danger of nuclear war with its human and moral costs. The possession of nuclear weapons, the continuing quantitative growth of the arms race and the danger of nuclear proliferation all point to the grave danger of basing "peace of a sort" on deterrence. The other dimension is the independence and freedom of nations and entire peoples, including the need to protect smaller nations from threats to their independence and integrity. Deterrence reflects the radical distrust which marks international politics, a condition identified as a major problem by Pope John XXIII in "Peace on Earth" and reaffirmed by Pope Paul VI and Pope John Paul II. Thus a balance of forces, preventing either side from achieving superiority, can be seen as a means of safeguarding both dimensions.

(175) The moral duty today is to prevent nuclear war from ever occurring and to protect and preserve those key values of justice, freedom and independence which are necessary for personal dignity and national integrity. . . .

(178) Targeting doctrine raises significant moral questions because it is a significant determinant of what would occur if nuclear weapons were ever to be used. Although we acknowledge the need for deterrent, not all forms of deterrence are morally acceptable. There are moral limits to deterrence policy as well as to policy regarding use. Specifically, it is not morally acceptable to intend to kill the innocent as part of a strategy of deterring nuclear war. The question of whether U.S. policy involves an intention to strike civilian centers (directly targeting civilian populations) has been one of our factual concerns.

(179) This complex question has always produced a variety of responses, official and unofficial in character. The NCCB committee has received a series of statements of clarification of policy from U.S. government officials.[24] Essentially these statements declare that it is not U.S. strategic policy to target the Soviet civilian population as such or to use nuclear weapons deliberately for the purpose of destroying population centers.

These statements respond, in principle at least, to one moral criterion for assessing deterrence policy: the immunity of non-combatants from direct attack either by conventional or nuclear weapons.

(180) These statements do not address or resolve another very troublesome moral problem, namely, an attack on military targets or militarily significant industrial targets could involve "indirect" (i.e., unintended) but massive civilian casualties. We are advised, for example, that the U.S. strategic nuclear targeting plan (SIOP — Single Integrated Operational Plan) has identified 60 "military" targets within the city of Moscow alone, and that 40,000 "military" targets for nuclear weapons have been identified in the whole of the Soviet Union.[25] It is important to recognize that Soviet policy is subject to the same moral judgment; attacks on several "industrial targets" or politically significant targets in the United States could produce massive civilian casualties. The number of civilians who would necessarily be killed by such strikes is horrendous. This problem is unavoidable because of the way modern military facilities and production centers are so thoroughly interspersed with civilian living and working areas. It is aggravated if one side deliberately positions military targets in the midst of a civilian population.

In our consultations, administration officials readily admitted that while they hoped any nuclear exchange could be kept limited, they were prepared to retaliate in a massive way if necessary. They also agreed that once any substantial numbers of weapons were used, the civilian casualty levels would quickly become truly catastrophic and that even with attacks limited to "military" targets the number of deaths in a substantial exchange would be almost indistinguishable from what might occur if civilian centers had been deliberately and directly struck. These possibilities pose a different moral question and are to be judged by a different moral criterion: the principle of proportionality.

(181) While any judgment of proportionality is always open to differing evaluations, there are actions which can be decisively judged to be disproportionate. A narrow adherence exclusively to the principle of noncombatant immunity as a criterion for policy is an inadequate moral posture for it ignores some evil and unacceptable consequences. Hence, we cannot be satisfied that the assertion of an intention not to strike civilians directly or even the most honest effort to implement that intention by itself constitutes a "moral policy" for the use of nuclear weapons.

(182) The location of industrial or militarily significant economic targets within heavily populated areas or in those areas affected by radioactive fallout could well involve such massive civilian casualties that in our judgment such a strike would be deemed morally disproportionate, even though not intentionally indiscriminate.

(183) The problem is not simply one of producing highly accurate weapons that might minimize civilian casualties in any single explosion, but one of increasing the likelihood of escalation at a level where many, even "discriminating," weapons would cumulatively kill very large numbers of civilians. These civilian deaths would occur both immediately and from the long-term effects of social and economic devastation.

(184) A second issue of concern to us is the relationship of deterrence doctrine to war-fighting strategies. We are aware of the argument that war-fighting capabilities enhance the credibility of the deterrent, particularly the strategy of extended deterrence. But the development of such capabilities raises other strategic and moral questions. The relationship of war-fighting capabilities and targeting doctrine exemplifies the difficult choices in this area of policy. Targeting civilian populations would violate the principle of discrimination — one of the central moral principles of a Christian ethic of war. But "counterforce targeting," while preferable from the perspective of protecting civilians, is often joined with a declaratory policy which conveys the notion that nuclear war is subject to precise rational and moral limits. We have already expressed our severe doubts about such a concept. Furthermore, a purely counter-force strategy may seem to threaten the viability of other nations' retaliatory forces, making deterrence unstable in a crisis and war more likely.

(185) While we welcome any effort to protect civilian populations, we do not want to legitimize or encourage moves which extend deterrence beyond the specific objective of preventing the use of nuclear weapons or other actions which could lead directly to a nuclear exchange.

(186) These considerations of concrete elements of nuclear deterrence policy, made in light of John Paul II's evaluation, but applying it through our own prudential judgments, lead us to a strictly conditioned moral acceptance of nuclear deterrence. We cannot consider it adequate as a long-term basis for peace.

(187) This strictly conditioned judgment yields criteria for morally assessing the elements of deterrence strategy. Clearly, these criteria demonstrate that we cannot approve of every weapons system, strategic doctrine or policy initiative advanced in the name of strengthening deterrence. On the contrary, these criteria require continual public scrutiny of what our government proposes to do with the deterrent.

(188) *On the basis of these criteria we wish now to make some specific evaluations:*

1. If nuclear deterrence exists only to prevent the use of nuclear weapons by others, then proposals to go beyond this to planning for prolonged periods of repeated nuclear strikes and counterstrikes, or "prevailing" in nuclear war, are not acceptable. They encourage notions that nuclear war can be engaged in with tolerable human and moral consequences. Rather, we must continually say no to the idea of nuclear war.
2. If nuclear deterrence is our goal, "sufficiency" to deter is an adequate strategy; the quest for nuclear superiority must be rejected.
3. Nuclear deterrence should be used as a step on the way toward progressive disarmament. Each proposed addition to our strategic system or change in strategic doctrine must be assessed precisely in light of whether it will render steps toward "progressive disarmament" more or less likely.

(189) Moreover, these criteria provide us with the means to make some judgments and recommendations about the present direction of U.S. strategic policy. Progress toward a world freed of dependence on nuclear deterrence must be carefully carried out. But it must not be delayed. There is an urgent moral and political responsibility to use the "peace of a sort" we have as a framework to move toward authentic peace through nuclear arms control, reductions and disarmament. Of primary importance in this process is the need to prevent the development and deployment of destabilizing weapons systems on either side; a second requirement is to ensure that the more sophisticated command and control systems do not become mere hair triggers for automatic launch on warning; a third is the need to prevent the proliferation of nuclear weapons in the international system.

(190) In light of these general judgments *we oppose* some specific proposals in respect to our present deterrence posture:

1. The addition of weapons which are likely to be vulnerable to attack, yet also possess a "prompt hard-target kill" capability that threatens to make the other side's

retaliatory forces vulnerable. Such weapons may seem to be useful primarily in the first strike;[26] we resist such weapons for this reason and we oppose Soviet deployment of such weapons which generate fear of a first strike against U.S. forces.

2. The willingness to foster strategic planning which seeks a nuclear war-fighting capability that goes beyond the limited function of deterrence outlined in this letter.
3. Proposals which have the effect of lowering the nuclear threshold and blurring the difference between nuclear and conventional weapons.

(191) In support of the concept of "sufficiency" as an adequate deterrent and in light of the present size and composition of both the U.S. and Soviet strategic arsenals, *we recommend:*

1. Support for immediate, bilateral, verifiable agreements to halt the testing, production and deployment of new nuclear weapons systems.[27]
2. Support for negotiated bilateral deep cuts in the arsenals of both superpowers, particularly those weapons systems which have destabilizing characteristics: U.S. proposals like those for START (Strategic Arms Reduction Talks) and INF (Intermediate-Range Nuclear Forces) negotiations in Geneva are said to be designed to achieve deep cuts; our hope is that they will be pursued in a manner which will realize these goals.
3. Support for early and successful conclusion of negotiations of a comprehensive test ban treaty.
4. Removal by all parties of short-range nuclear weapons which multiply dangers disproportionate to their deterrent value.
5. Removal by all parties of nuclear weapons from areas where they are likely to be overrun in the early stages of war, thus forcing rapid and uncontrollable decisions on their use.
6. Strengthening of command and control over nuclear weapons to prevent inadvertent and unauthorized use.

(192) These judgments are meant to exemplify how a lack of unequivocal condemnation of deterrence is meant only to be an attempt to acknowledge the role attributed to deterrence, but not to support its extension beyond the limited purpose discussed above. Some have urged us to condemn all aspects of nuclear deterrence. This urging has been based on a variety of reasons, but has emphasized particularly the high and terrible risks that either deliberate use or accidental detonation of nuclear weapons could quickly escalate to something utterly disproportionate to any acceptable moral purpose. That determination requires highly technical judgments about hypothetical events. Although reasons exist which move some to condemn reliance on nuclear weapons for deterrence, we have not reached this conclusion for the reasons outlined in this letter. . . .

## Notes

13. Augustine called it a Manichean heresy to assert that war is intrinsically evil and contrary to Christian charity, and stated: "War and conquest are a sad necessity in the eyes of men of principle, yet it would be still more unfortunate if wrongdoers should dominate just men" (*The City of God,* Book IV, C. 15). Representative surveys of the history and theology of the just-war tradition include: F. H. Russell, *The Just War in the Middle Ages* (N.Y.: 1975); P. Ramsey, *War and the Christian Conscience* (Durham, N.C.: 1961), *The Just War: Force and Political Responsibility* (N.Y.: 1968); J. T. Johnson, *Ideology, Reason and the Limitation of War* (Princeton: 1975), *Just War Tradition and the Restraint of War: A Moral and Historical Inquiry* (Princeton: 1981); L. B. Walters, "Five Classic Just-War Theories" (Ph.D. Dissertation, Yale University, 1971); W. O'Brien, *War and-or Survival* (N.Y.: 1969), *The Conduct of Just and Limited War* (N.Y.: 1981); J. C. Murray, "Remarks on the Moral Problem of War," *Theological Studies* 20 (1959) pp. 40–61.
14. Aquinas treats the question of war in the *Summa Theologica,* II-IIae, q. 40; also cf II-IIae, q. 64.
15. For an analysis of the context and relationship of these principles cf: R. Potter, "The Moral Logic of War," *McCormick Quarterly* 23 (1970) p. 203–233; J. Childress in Shannon, cited, p. 40–58.
16. John Paul II, World Day of Peace Message, 1981, 12.
17. John Paul II, World Day of Peace Message, 1982, 6, cited, p. 476.
18. Pius XII, Address to the VIII Congress of the World Medical Association, in Documents, p. 131.
19. Testimony given to the NCCB Committee during preparation of this pastoral letter.
20. USCC, "To Live in Christ Jesus" (Washington: 1976) p. 34.
21. Cardinal John Krol, Testimony on SALT II, *Origins* (1979), p. 197.
22. John Paul II, Message U.N. Special Session, 1982; 3.
23. Same, 8.
24. Particularly helpful was the letter of Jan. 15, 1983, of William Clark, national security adviser, to Cardinal Bernardin. Clark stated: "For moral, political and military reasons, the United States does not target the Soviet civilian population as such. There is no deliberately opaque meaning conveyed in the last two words. We do not threaten the existence of Soviet civilization by threatening Soviet cities. Rather, we hold at risk the war-making capability of the Soviet Union — its armed forces, and the industrial capacity to sustain war. It would be irresponsible for us to issue policy statements which might suggest to the Soviets that it would be to their advantage to establish privileged sanctuaries within heavily populated areas, thus inducing them to locate much of their war-fighting capability within those ur-

ban sanctuaries." A reaffirmation of the administration's policy is also found in Secretary Weinberger's Annual Report to the Congress (Caspar Weinberger, Annual Report to the Congress, Feb. 1, 1983, p. 55): "The Reagan administration's policy is that under no circumstances may such weapons be used deliberately for the purpose of destroying populations." Also the letter of Weinberger to Bishop O'Connor of Feb. 9, 1983, has a similar statement.

25. S. Zuckerman, *Nuclear Illusion and Reality,* (N.Y.: 1982); D. Ball, cited, p. 36; T. Powers, "Choosing a Strategy for World War III," *The Atlantic Monthly* (November 1982) p. 82–110.

26. Several experts in strategic theory would place both the MX missile and Pershing II missiles in this category.

27. In each of the successive drafts of this letter we have tried to state a central moral imperative: that the arms race should be stopped and disarmament begun. The implementation of this imperative is open to a wide variety of approaches. Hence we have chosen our own language in this paragraph, not wanting either to be identified with one specific political initiative or to have our words used against specific political measures.

## A Nuclear Freeze

### *Document 13*

**In 1980, Randall Forsberg, an arms control expert, drafted and circulated a pamphlet, *Call to Halt the Nuclear Arms Race,* which became the basis of a grass-roots movement to freeze the arms race. In these excerpts from a 1983 article in *Scientific American,* Forsberg says that a U.S.-Soviet freeze on the development and production of all nuclear weapons systems is urgently needed. Without a freeze, according to Forsberg, the technological arms race will continue, increasing the chances of nuclear war.**

### 13 A BILATERAL NUCLEAR-WEAPON FREEZE November 1982

The proposal of a bilateral nuclear-weapon "freeze" by the U.S. and the U.S.S.R. has excited wide public discussion in this country during the past year. The idea is to stop the nuclear arms race quite literally, by stopping the development and production of all nuclear-weapon systems in the two countries. Public interest (expressed, for example, by votes in numerous town meetings) brought the proposal in the form of an advisory resolution before the U.S. Congress. Whereas a vote on it was blocked in the Senate, it lost in the House in August by the narrow margin of 204 to 202. The proposal is now on the ballot as a referendum question in impending congressional and local elections in enough cities and states to put it before nearly a fourth of the country's population. Next to the depressed state of the economy, the nuclear freeze is said to be the warmest current issue in the country's politics.

First put forward in the "Call to Halt the Nuclear Arms Race" drafted by me and published in April, 1980, by several public-interest groups, the freeze goes beyond other arms-control measures proposed in the past 25 years to put a stop to the production, testing and, implicitly, development of nuclear weapons as well as their deployment. By the same simplicity that has given it wide popular appeal the freeze proposal responds directly to an ominous turn in the arms race. The bilateral freeze would preclude the production of a new generation of "counterforce" weapons by the U.S. and the U.S.S.R. These are weapons designed to attack the opponent's nuclear forces. In the ultimate scenario they would disarm the other nation and hold its population hostage. The quest for improved counterforce capability has driven the arms race far past the point where each contender can destroy the other's society and much else besides. The production of counterforce weapons would increase the risk of a nuclear war. Their deployment would put pressure on leaders to launch their weapons first in time of crisis, before they were attacked, and perhaps to place their nuclear forces in an automatic "launch on warning" status in peacetime. A freeze would prevent these dangerous developments.

A freeze would help to accomplish other desirable goals. The U.S. and the U.S.S.R., by fulfilling the pledge they made in the 1970 Nonproliferation Treaty to stop the arms race, would help to brake the spread of nuclear weapons to countries that do not already have them. A freeze would create an opportunity for the nations of the world to make further progress in arms control and other global issues. It would also save billions of dollars.

The time is propitious for a bilateral freeze. Today the U.S. and the U.S.S.R. are closer to parity in nuclear arms than they have been at any time since World War II. The U.S.S.R. has advantages in some elements of nuclear weaponry, the U.S. has advantages in others. The most frequently cited statistics compare the numbers of "strategic" ballistic missiles and bombers and the numbers of nuclear warheads and free-fall bombs they carry. The U.S.S.R. has more strategic missiles: 1,398 land-based intercontinental ballistic missiles (ICBM's) compared with 1,052 for the U.S. and 950 submarine-launched ballistic missiles (SLBM's) compared with 520 for the U.S. In addition a recent buildup has brought the strategic force of the U.S.S.R. abreast of that of the U.S. in the arming of these missiles with multiple independently targetable reentry vehicles (MIRV's). The land-based

ICBM's of the U.S.S.R. carry more warheads and larger ones. On the other hand, the U.S. has more warheads in total, owing to the larger number of warheads on its SLBM's. The U.S. also has many more intercontinental bombers, with much larger payloads, and a five-to-10-year lead in the new technology of small, long-range, low-flying cruise missiles.

More meaningful than comparisons of numbers of weapons is the fact that both countries have acquired enormous "overkill," that is, each has many times the number of weapons necessary to annihilate the other's urban population. Thus even if the U.S.S.R. destroyed all U.S. ICBM's, all U.S. bombers and all U.S. submarines in port, the U.S. would still have about 2,400 nuclear warheads on submarines at sea, completely invulnerable to such preemptive attack. This is several times the number needed to destroy the 300 largest cities and towns in the U.S.S.R., which have one-third of the population and three-fourths of the industry. Conversely, a U.S. attack on ICBM's, bomber bases and submarine ports in the U.S.S.R. would leave an estimated 1,200 strategic warheads, more than enough to inflict equivalent damage on U.S. urban centers.

The bilateral freeze would preserve this parity. It would prevent the emergence of a new, destabilizing U.S. advantage in counterforce capability, projected in the buildup planned by the Reagan Administration. And it would forestall the inevitable effort by the U.S.S.R. to match U.S. developments.

As spelled out in the "Call to Halt the Nuclear Arms Race," a freeze on both sides would stop the following: the production of fissionable material (uranium 235 and plutonium) for nuclear weapons; the fabrication, assembly and testing of nuclear warheads; the testing, production and deployment of missiles designed to deliver nuclear warheads, and the testing of new types of aircraft and the production and deployment of any additional aircraft designed primarily to deliver nuclear weapons.

In order to achieve its promise as a new departure in arms control the freeze must be complete. One reason is to facilitate its verification. In all arms-control agreements to date the parties have relied primarily on "national" methods of verification, that is, methods that can be managed independently, without cooperation. This has meant principally surveillance by satellites. For this reason some have argued that the freeze should be limited to the deployment of large nuclear-weapon delivery systems, an activity that is confidently subject to satellite surveillance. Such a freeze would be better than none at all. There are, nonetheless, persuasive arguments in favor of a freeze that covers production as well as deployment and small systems as well as large.

If production is not banned, the military on both sides is likely to argue that missiles and bombers, warheads and bombs should continue to be produced, if only for storage in warehouses. Thus the 1963 Partial Test-Ban Treaty was followed by more vigorous testing underground than had ever been conducted aboveground, and the 1972 Anti-Ballistic-Missile Treaty has sheltered intensive developmental testing of those weapons. A "production but not deployment" race would continue the buildup on both sides, and along with it the confrontation, the cost and the growing destructive potential.

This line of reasoning suggests that any freeze agreement should incorporate objectives such as the production ban that, although they may be less independently verifiable, define the intent and interpretation of the more verifiable parts. A full statement of intent has force in other realms of domestic and international law.

In fact, as has been established by three decades of experience with demonstrated modes of verification, production activities are not hidden but are well known. The brochure *Soviet Military Power,* produced by the U.S. Department of Defense, gives a summary of what is known about the weapon-production complex in the U.S.S.R.:

"The military production industry includes 135 major final assembly plants involved in producing weapons as end products. Over 3,500 individual factories and related installations provide support to these final assembly plants."

A map in the brochure shows the military products manufactured in 14 regions of the U.S.S.R. Tables give the annual production of every type of weapon system, including small arms. This detailed information has been pieced together in spite of complete Russian secrecy about military production.

The production facilities for nuclear weapons are known at least as well as those for conventional weapons. Nuclear warheads are fabricated and assembled at just a handful of facilities in the U.S.S.R., which were identified in the 1950's, soon after they were established and years before the introduction of reconnaissance satellites. The closing down of these facilities could be monitored with high confidence from satellites; it would be no easier to replicate them secretly than it was to keep their construction secret the first time.

A long and well-worn production path precedes the deployment of nuclear-weapon systems. It begns with the production of fissionable material at specialized, highly visible plutonium-production reactors and uranium-enrichment plants. The fissionable materials go on to the factories that fabricate and assemble the components of missile warheads and free-fall bombs. The components are then transported to other factories where they are fitted in the nose cones of missiles or the casings of bombs. The nuclear missiles and bombs go on to deployment or to storage depots. All these activities proceed at plants and along transportation routes identified by the special equipment and procedures required for handling nuclear-weapon materials and for security. Possible new production facilities and transport routes can be kept under satellite scrutiny, as the old ones have been.

A variety of nonintrusive on-site verification measures can supplement satellite observation. They can take such forms as occasional, unannounced inspections or continuously monitored, sensor-equipped, secure "black boxes" installed in shut-down or controlled factories. The U.S.S.R., reluctant to agree to on-site verification in the past, has recently shown signs of greater flexibility on this point in the negotiation of a comprehensive nuclear test ban.

In the end there would be little to gain and much to lose in any clandestine attempt to violate an agreement banning production. In the view of most people the only value of nuclear weapons is as a deterrent to war. In order to play this role effectively nuclear arsenals must be known to exist and must be deployed in relatively usable form. Nuclear weapons made "in secret" and stored in warehouses or caves do not contribute to nuclear deterrence. Moreover, the number of weapons that could be produced clandestinely would be very small (some tens or hundreds) with respect to the size of the current arsenals (20,000 to 30,000 warheads, including those stockpiled but not deployed). Thus it is highly unlikely that either party would take the risk of trying to construct a nuclear-weapon production system in secret.

Most of these arguments support extending the bilateral freeze to intermediate-range and battlefield nuclear delivery systems. Like large strategic systems, smaller nuclear-weapon systems call for special security, handling and command-and-control procedures. These activities, signaling the presence of nuclear weapons, have made it relatively easy for each side to keep track of the other's arsenal of tactical nuclear weapons throughout the period since World War II.

More important, as long as new nuclear warheads continue to be manufactured for small delivery vehicles, the entire nuclear-weapon production chain will be operational. A cutoff of warhead production, which would be relatively easy to monitor if it were complete, would be difficult or impossible to verify if it were only partial. Stopping production completely, particularly the production of all nuclear warheads, would therfore make the verification of a freeze more reliable than would be the case if the freeze were limited to testing and deployment activities.

A strictly enforced freeze that includes production and testing as well as deployment could lead after some years to a decline in the reliability and readiness of existing nuclear armaments. Such incidental or inadvertent disarmament may be the only way the world will ever get rid of nuclear weapons, or so George B. Kistiakowsky, science adviser to President Eisenhower, has observed. A freeze should probably be designed and implemented, nonetheless, to avert an automatic decrease in nuclear-weapon stockpiles. Responsible officials will object to a situation in which the choice of what to reduce and when has been preempted by purely technical considerations that may not weigh equally on both parties to the freeze. What is more, even though reduced confidence in the nuclear arsenal may decrease the likelihood of nuclear war and make nuclear weapons seem less relevant to security, uncertainty in this regard is bound to make most people feel less secure rather than more so. Hence a freeze should be defined to allow the maintenance of existing nuclear forces until reductions can be agreed on with due deliberation.

Various factors in the aging of nuclear weapons must therefore be dealt with. For example, the tritium modules that initiate the fusion reaction in thermonuclear explosives must be replaced every few years. This implies that the freeze should allow the operation of tritium-component assembly facilities and the running of perhaps one military nuclear reactor to produce tritium. Special safeguards will be needed to ensure that the reactor does not produce plutonium for new warheads.

Among strategic delivery systems, submarines most clearly have a limited service life, generally estimated at 30 years. The "Call to Halt the Nuclear Arms Race" specifically excludes submarines from the freeze. It allows their replacement but requires the installation of existing missiles rather than new ones so that the quantitative and technical threat does not grow.

In principle aircraft and missiles have a shorter service life than submarines. In practice aircraft and missiles can be maintained indefinitely in good operating condition simply by the replacement of parts during regular maintenance and major overhauls. The B-52G's and B-52H's, the last of the B-52 series delivered to the U.S. Air Force in 1960-62, are expected to remain serviceable through the 1990's and even into the next century. With new engines and updated electronic gear installed and major structural elements replaced and reinforced, the aircraft are physically different entities from those originally delivered. The useful life of the planes is limited only by the availability of spare parts. Although some parts now being cannibalized from retired older-model B-52's may run out, new production lines could be opened.

Even missiles sitting in their silos deteriorate to some extent. The stored fuel can be corrosive and is subject to decomposition; the gyroscopes and electrical systems are in constant operation. By replacement of worn-out parts, however, missiles too can be maintained for long periods.

Tactical or battlefield nuclear weapons present much

the same picture with respect to maintenance, except for supersonic fighters and attack aircraft subject to wear from high stress; they are replaced at the rate of about 10 percent of the inventory per year. For the administration of a nuclear freeze, tactical aircraft present a special problem because they are "dual capability" systems, intended to deliver conventional munitions as well as nuclear ones. The "Call to Halt the Nuclear Arms Race" would allow their continued production, but only with conventional capability. The verification of such a limitation might require on-site inspection. An alternative arrangement might allow the production of dual-capability systems to replace existing stocks on a one-for-one basis. The difficulty here is that there is no generally accepted accounting of such weapons today. A final possibility is to exclude these vehicles from the freeze and rely on the control of the nuclear warheads that can be carried by them. To be effective this would require not only a cutoff in the production of new nuclear warheads but also a complete accounting of existing warheads and of fissionable material in storage.

Some have argued that if offensive nuclear-weapon systems are frozen, a country's existing weapons will gradually become vulnerable to the improved defenses and countermeasures of its opponent. The U.S.-U.S.S.R. strategic competition, however, pits the offense not so much against the defense as against the opposing offense, keeping up, as it were, with the Joneses. In ICBM technology no technical improvements are needed to ensure the penetration of defenses as long as the treaty prohibiting anti-ballistic-missile (ABM) systems is kept in force. (Reagan Administration officials are, to be sure, considering the abrogation of the treaty in order to provide ABM defense of MX-missile sites.)

In the case of strategic submarines the U.S.S.R. has not yet initiated any programs that might threaten U.S. submarines in the way that U.S. antisubmarine forces currently threaten the strategic submarines of the U.S.S.R. Exploiting geographic advantages, the U.S. has spread vast underwater sonar arrays in friendly waters in the North Atlantic and North Pacific, and the U.S. fleet of 80 (expanding soon to 90) "hunter-killer" submarines, assisted by several hundred P-3C maritime patrol aircraft (with similar aircraft flown by Japan and Britain), keeps tabs on any strategic submarines that venture out of home waters. Apart from Cuba, the U.S.S.R. has no access to land near U.S. strategic submarine ports that it might rely on for comparable antisubmarine operations. In the event that the U.S.S.R. did begin to construct similar sonar arrays and expand its fleets of hunter-killer submarines and antisubmarine aircraft, the buildup would take 20 years and would be highly visible.

In the competing technologies of bomber aircraft and antiaircraft defenses there is relatively intense interaction between the offense and the defense. Relevant technical advances are likely to continue in conventional equipment even in the event of a nuclear freeze. Bombers, however, represent a nonessential supplement to strategic missile forces. They do introduce uncertainty and compel the opponent to plan and budget for defense, but for this purpose they do not need high penetration capability. The U.S. B-52's and the much less capable Russian Tu-95's and Mya-4's have always constituted an element of uncertainty in the strategic calculation and will continue to do so, regardless of improvements in air defenses.

The advances in the technology of anti-ballistic-missile systems, anti-submarine warfare and air defense that can be foreseen for the remainder of this century will do little to decrease the capacity for devastation that exists in the offensive strategic nuclear forces of the two sides today. In fact, most of the technical advances planned for the offensive forces are not intended to offset improvements in defenses. They seek increases in offensive power only — in yield, accuracy and numbers.

The new MX ICBM of the U.S. is a case in point. The missile is expected to have 10 warheads with a yield of 600 kilotons each and an accuracy of 400 feet. (The accuracy refers to the radius within which half of the warheads would be expected to land.) Thus the warheads could be highly effective against hardened targets. The deployment of the MX would not reduce the vulnerability of U.S. ICBM forces to attack from the U.S.S.R.; it would simply raise the vulnerability of the ICBM's on the other side of the North Pole.

The way to reduce the vulnerability of land-based systems, of course, is not to give them a first-strike potential; that only increases their priority as targets. The wisest course would be to eliminate them altogether. This cheap measure, if taken by the U.S., would deprive the U.S.S.R. of its alleged advantage in counterforce capability and render militarily worthless its recent large investment in accurate, MIRVed ICBM's.

Although the U.S. and the U.S.S.R. both have many times over the power to destroy the population of the other, neither commands the capability to threaten a disarming counterforce attack. The proposed freeze would secure the parity to which their competition has brought them.

Under a freeze the U.S. would retain the preponderance that the evidence indicates it holds in short-range tactical nuclear weapons. Because they do less injury to nearby civilian populations and friendly troops (in military jargon "collateral damage") the lower-yield tactical nuclear weapons fielded by the U.S. are said to increase the credibility of a threat of "controlled" escalation up from conventional war. This dubious "advantage" would not change if the U.S. were prevented from manufacturing new eight-inch and 155-millimeter rocket-assisted nuclear artillery shells, with a range of from 20 to 30 miles, and new warheads for an entire panoply of tactical weapons. Under a freeze the U.S.S.R. would also stop the manufacture of new SS-21, SS-22 and SS-23 battlefield weapons and artillery with a nuclear capability.

In intermediate-range weapons a freeze would prevent the U.S. from deploying in Europe the new Pershing 2 ballistic missiles (the first ballistic missiles with terminal guidance) and the first generation of ground-launched cruise missiles (GLCM's). The deployment of these new weapons has been justified as being necessary to offset the estimated 900 warheads on the U.S.S.R.'s new SS-20 intermediate-range missiles. The SS-20's are already offset, however, by a comparable number of missile warheads aimed at the U.S.S.R.: 64 warheads on British submarines, 98 on French land- and submarine-launched missiles, 640 on four U.S. Poseidon strategic submarines assigned to the North Atlantic Treaty Organization (NATO) and 75 on Chinese land-based missiles.

The new SS-20's actually reduce the nuclear threat to Western Europe compared with the old SS-4's and SS-5's they are replacing. The older missiles carried bigger warheads, 1,000 kilotons compared with the 150 kilotons on the SS-20's. The SS-4's, which constituted 80 percent of the original force, are above-ground missiles with nonstorable liquid fuel; they were "sitting ducks" for a preemptive attack. The U.S.S.R. has thus replaced a destabilizing "first strike" force, which would have had to be used first if it were not to be destroyed, with a less vulnerable force that can be held back and launched on warning of attack. The greater accuracy of the SS-20's gives them a higher "kill probability" against the few hardened targets in Western Europe (nuclear storage depots and command-and-control centers). Their yield is not low enough however, to present a credible threat of a "controlled" counterforce attack that would not kill millions in the densely populated Western European theater.

Concerning intercontinental strategic weapons, it is alleged that the U.S.S.R. now has ICBM's with an unparalleled first-strike counterforce capability against U.S. ICBM's. This claim applies particularly to a new 10-warhead version of the large SS-18 and an improved, six-warhead version of the SS-19, both estimated to have 550-kiloton warheads, 800-to-900-foot accuracy and a kill probability against U.S. ICBM silos of slightly more than 60 percent. There is evidence, however, that the instrumentation providing high accuracy is not yet installed in most of the missiles but is being backfitted into 308 SS-18's in 1982 and 1983 and will be incorporated in 60 new SS-19's and 300 existing SS-19's in 1984 and 1985.

At the same time, the U.S. Mark 12A warhead, recently backfitted into the Minuteman 3's, has a comparable theoretical kill probability of about 60 percent against the hardest of the U.S.S.R.'s silos. The yield of the Mark 12A is 335 kilotons and the accuracy is 700 feet. On both sides the calculated kill probability depends on the estimated hardness, or blast resistance, of the opponent's ICBM silos. The hardness is not known precisely even for the U.S. silos, much less for those of the U.S.S.R., but it is assumed in these estimates that the silos can withstand a blast pressure of 2,000 pounds per square inch. Current plans call for 300 Minuteman 3's with 900 Mark 12A warheads to be deployed by the end of this year. This is enough to send a single warhead against each of the 818 MIRV-capable silos in the U.S.S.R., or two warheads against the majority of the 658 silos estimated to contain MIRVed missiles. Since these 658 missiles carry nearly three-fourths of the U.S.S.R.'s strategic warheads, a hypothetical U.S. first strike conducted against them in late 1982 would be more devastating to them than a U.S.S.R. first strike against U.S. ICBM's.

Moreover, as many as 600 improved Minuteman 3's with 1,800 Mark 12A warheads (enough to put two of these warheads on each MIRV-capable silo) could be deployed by the mid-1980s, that is, by the time the U.S.S.R. is expected to have warheads with comparable counterforce potential deployed in significant numbers. There is no plan, however, to deploy all 600 improved Minuteman 3's — perhaps because these missiles would obviate the military requirement for the new MX ICBM, with its even more devastating countersilo capabilities. If the U.S. were to forgo the installation of the MX and the additional 300 improved Minuteman 3's under the terms of the freeze, it would still be secure in its large and invulnerable submarine-based forces. For its part the U.S.S.R. would have to halt the deployment of the 10-warhead version of the SS-18 and the more accurate six-warhead SS-19. It would also forgo production of a new single-warhead ICBM now under development.

Although the U.S.S.R. has 62 strategic submarines with 950 SLBM's (about twice as many as the U.S.), it keeps only nine or 10 submarines with about 225 warheads at sea in range of targets, leaving the other 52 submarines in just two ports, where they could be destroyed by a few nuclear bombs. Given the surveillance and trailing capabilities of the U.S. and its allies, the number of strategic submarines the U.S.S.R. keeps at sea and in port would allow constant surveillance, making most if not all of these vessels vulnerable to preemptive attack. In contrast, 16 of the 32 U.S. *Lafayette*- and *Ohio*-class submarines, with about 2,400 warheads, are kept at sea at all times. As far as is known, no U.S. strategic submarine in normal operating condition has ever been detected or trailed by the much more limited antisubmarine forces of the U.S.S.R.

Under the bilateral freeze the U.S. would retain its advantage in submarine-based weapons with their invulnerability to counterforce attack. It would, however, set aside plans to develop a submarine-based counterpart to the MX: the Trident 2. The U.S.S.R. would stop the rearming of its strategic submarines with the seven-MIRV SS-N-18 and stop production of the new 10-MIRV SS-N-20. In addition it would halt the deployment of the SS-N-19 cruise missile and stop the production of new submarine- and ship-based nuclear antisubmarine weapons.

To the extent that bombers carry weight in the nuclear balance, the U.S. clearly has the advantage. Its 330 B-52's and 60 FB-111's are superior in performance as well as numbers to the 154 antiquated bombers deployed by the U.S.S.R. In a U.S. first strike the Russian bomber force would be destroyed on the ground because it is not kept on quick-reaction alert. In contrast, a third of the U.S. bombers are kept on eight-minute alert at all times. Moreover, the entire force is about to be fitted with its fifth generation of electronic jamming and penetration equipment. The freeze would spare the U.S. the immense outlays planned for production of the B-1 bomber and the development of its Stealth successor. On the Russian side it would stop production and deployment of the Tu-26 "Backfire" intermediate-range bomber and the development of a new intercontinental bomber.

Even if U.S. land-based ICBM's are or become more vulnerable to preemptive attack than those of the U.S.S.R. (a disputable point), this would be offset by the invulnerability of U.S. bombers and submarines. On the U.S.S.R. side the high vulnerability of its strategic bomber and submarine forces is offset by the size of its ICBM force. Without a bilateral freeze this relatively stable balance will be eroded by the weapon programs planned for the next decade.

As an innovative approach to arms control, the freeze differs in crucial respects from the position of the Reagan Administration outlined in its proposals for the Strategic Arms Reduction Talks (START) and the negotiations on Intermediate-Range Nuclear Forces (INF). The Administration has inaccurately characterized its position as "reduce first, then freeze," to contrast it with the freeze proposal to "freeze first, then reduce." What the Administration proposes is a freeze in numbers only, not in technology or production. Its START proposal would limit U.S. and U.S.S.R. strategic warheads at a level about a third below their present number. Within this numerical constraint it would allow the replacement of existing missiles by new and more capable ones. Thus Trident 2 SLBM's could replace Poseidon and Trident 1 missiles on submarines, and new MX ICBM's could replace Minuteman 3 missiles on land, thereby raising the theoretical kill probability of U.S. missiles against land-based ICBM silos in the U.S.S.R.

The U.S. nuclear weapons to be built during the 1980's have been mistakenly characterized as "bargaining chips." This implies that there is some concession for which the weapons would be traded away. In the INF talks the Administration has in fact offered not to deploy the Pershing 2 ballistic missile and ground-launched cruise missiles in Europe if the U.S.S.R. will dismantle its SS-20's (including those aimed at China as well as those aimed at Europe). The Administration has not, however, put the MX, the Trident 2, the B-1 bomber, the air- and submarine-launched cruise missiles or the many thousands of new battlefield nuclear weapons on either the INF or the START agenda. The freeze proposal would ban the manufacture of all these new weapon systems and their counterparts in the U.S.S.R.

The Administration presents itself as advocating "not merely a freeze, but more: reductions." Even in the category of intercontinental strategic weapons, however, a comprehensive accounting shows the Administration proposing a new increase in the number of nuclear weapons, at least on the U.S. side. The START proposal would reduce ballistic-missile warheads on each side by about 2,500 but would place no limits on strategic cruise missiles. During the 1980's the U.S. plans to deploy about 3,000 air-launched cruise missiles on B-52G's (while putting the existing B-52G payload on new B-1's) and in addition more than 1,000 Tomahawk strategic cruise missiles on surface ships and submarines. The START proposal would therefore result in a net increase of at least 1,500 warheads in the U.S. strategic arsenal. Since the U.S.S.R. has not developed small, long-range cruise missiles that can be deployed in large numbers, the effect of the START proposal is to invite the U.S.S.R. to reduce its arsenal while the U.S. increases its own.

Under the Administration's proposals the technological arms race would continue indefinitely. The U.S. and the U.S.S.R. would operate a large nuclear-weapon industry, go on testing new warheads and missiles, and cultivate advances in the many old and new technologies associated with nuclear-weapon systems. Under the freeze proposal the nuclear part of the military industry would be closed down and there would be no future generations of nuclear weapons.

The freeze would not eliminate the existing capacity of the U.S. and the U.S.S.R. to bring about a global nuclear holocaust. As few as 100 nuclear weapons on each side, half of 1 percent of the current arsenals, could devastate the U.S. and the U.S.S.R. beyond any previous historical experience and perhaps beyond recovery as industrial societies. To end the danger of nuclear war the nations must not merely freeze nuclear weapons but abolish them. The freeze represents a modest but significant step toward abolition. It would terminate the technological arms race and shut down entirely this wasteful and dangerous form of human competition.

## A Call for Dramatic Measures to Stop the Arms Race

### *Document 14*

This brief article by George Kennan, the author of the containment doctrine and one who has studied and participated in U.S.-Soviet relations for more than fifty years, demonstrates some of the key aspects of the reducing the nuclear danger perspective. Kennan emphasizes the dangers of the nuclear arms race, he says that it is not just the "supposed wickedness of our opponents" that has caused the current situation, and he calls for dramatic measures to stop the arms race. In particular, Kennan calls for the superpowers to reduce their nuclear arsenals by 50 percent across the board.

## 14 A MODEST PROPOSAL
## George Kennan

Adequate words are lacking to express the full seriousness of our present situation. It is not just that we are for the moment on a collision course politically with the Soviet Union, and that the process of rational communication between the two governments seems to have broken down completely; it is also — and even more importantly — the fact that the ultimate sanction behind the conflicting policies of these two governments is type and volume of weaponry which could not possibly be used without utter disaster for us all.

For over 30 years wise and far-seeing people have been warning us about the futility of any war fought with nuclear weapons and about the dangers involved in their cultivation. Some of the first of these voices to be raised were those of great scientists, including outstandingly that of Albert Einstein himself. But there has been no lack of others. Every president of this country, from Dwight Eisenhower to Jimmy Carter, has tried to remind us that there could be no such thing as victory in a war fought with such weapons. So have a great many other eminent persons.

When one looks back today over the history of these warnings, one has the impression that something has now been lost of the sense of urgency, the hopes, and the excitement that initially inspired them, so many years ago. One senses, even on the part of those who today most acutely perceive the problem and are inwardly most exercised about it, a certain discouragement, resignation, perhaps even despair, when it comes to the question of raising the subject again. The danger is so obvious. So much has already been said. What is to be gained by reiteration? What good would it now do?

Look at the record. Over all these years the competition in the development of nuclear weaponry has proceeded steadily, relentlessly, without the faintest regard for all these warning voices. We have gone on piling weapon upon weapon, missile upon missile, new levels of destructiveness upon old ones. We have done this helplessly, almost involuntarily: like the victims of some sort of hypnotism, like men in a dream, like lemmings heading for the sea, like the children of Hamlin marching blindly along behind their Pied Piper. And the result is that today we have achieved, we and the Russians together, in the creation of these devices and their means of delivery, levels of redundancy of such grotesque dimensions as to defy rational understanding.

I say redundancy. I know of no better way to describe it. But actually, the word is too mild. It implies that there could be levels of these weapons that would not be redundant. Personally, I doubt that there could. I question whether these devices are really weapons at all. A true weapon is at best something with which you endeavor to affect the behavior of another society by influencing the minds, the calculations, the intentions, of the men that control it; it is not something with which you destroy indiscriminately the lives, the substance, the hopes, the culture, the civilization, of another people.

What a confession of intellectual poverty it would be — what a bankruptcy of intelligent statesmanship — if we had to admit that such blind, senseless acts of destruction were the best use we could make of what we have come to view as the leading elements of our military strength!

To my mind, the nuclear bomb is the most useless weapon ever invented. It can be employed to no rational purpose. It is not even an effective defense against itself. It is only something with which, in a moment of petulance or panic, you commit such fearful acts of destruction as no sane person would ever wish to have upon his conscience.

There are those who will agree, with a sigh, to much of what I have just said, but will point to the need for something called deterrence. This is, of course, a concept which attributes to others — to others who, like ourselves, were born of women, walk on two legs, and love their children, to human beings, in short — the most fiendish and inhuman of tendencies.

But all right: accepting for the sake of argument the profound iniquity of these adversaries, no one could deny, I think, that the present Soviet and American arsenals, presenting over a million times the destructive power of the Hiroshima bomb, are simply fantastically redundant to the purpose in question. If the same relative proportions were to be preserved, something well less than 20 percent of those stocks would surely suffice for the most sanguine concepts of deterrence, whether as between the two nuclear superpowers or with relation to any of those other governments that have been so ill-advised as to enter upon the nuclear path. Whatever their suspicions of each other, there can be no excuse on the part of these two governments for holding, poised against each other and poised in a sense against the whole northern hemisphere, quantities of these weapons so vastly in excess of any rational and demonstrable requirements.

How have we got ourselves into this dangerous mess?

Let us not confuse the question by blaming it all on our Soviet adversaries. They have, of course, their share of the blame, and not least in their cavalier dismissal of the Baruch Plan so many years ago. They too have made their mistakes; and I should be the last to deny it.

But we must remember that it has been we Americans who, at almost every step of the road, have taken the lead in the development of this sort of weaponry. It was we who first produced and tested such a device; we who were the first to raise its destructiveness to a new level with the hydrogen bomb; we who introduced the multiple warhead; we who have declined every proposal for the renunciation of the principle of "first use"; and we alone, so help us God, who have used the weapon in anger against others, and against tens of thousands of helpless noncombatants at that.

I know that reasons were offered for some of these things. I know that others might have taken this sort of a lead, had we not done so. But let us not, in the face of this record, so lose ourselves in self-righteousness and hypocrisy as to forget our own measure of complicity in creating the situation we face today.

What is it then, if not our own will, and if not the supposed wickedness of our opponents, that has brought us to this pass?

The answer, I think, is clear. It is primarily the inner momentum, the independent momentum, of the weapons race itself—the compulsions that arise and take charge of great powers when they enter upon a competition with each other in the building up of major armaments of any sort.

This is nothing new. I am a diplomatic historian. I see this same phenomenon playing its fateful part in the relations among the great European powers as much as a century ago. I see this competitive buildup of armaments conceived initially as a means to an end but soon becoming the end itself. I see it taking possession of men's imagination and behavior, becoming a force in its own right, detaching itself from the political differences that initially inspired it, and then leading both parties, invariably and inexorably, to the war they no longer know how to avoid.

This is a species of fixation, brewed out of many components. There are fears, resentments, national pride, personal pride. There are misreadings of the adversary's intentions—sometimes even the refusal to consider them at all. There is the tendency of national communities to idealize themselves and to dehumanize the opponent. There is the blinkered, narrow vision of the professional military planner, and his tendency to make war inevitable by assuming its inevitability.

Tossed together, these components form a powerful brew. They guide the fears and the ambitions of men. They seize the policies of governments and whip them around like trees before the tempest.

Is it possible to break out of this charmed and vicious circle? It is sobering to recognize that no one, at least to my knowledge, has yet done so. But no one, for that matter, has ever been faced with such great catastrophe, such inalterable catastrophe, at the end of the line. Others, in earlier decades, could befuddle themselves with dreams of something called "victory." We, perhaps fortunately, are denied this seductive prospect. We have to break out of the circle. We have no other choice.

How are we to do it?

I must confess that I see no possibility of doing this by means of discussions along the lines of the negotiations that have been in progress, off and on, over this past decade, under the acronym of SALT. I regret, to be sure, that the most recent SALT agreement has not been ratified. I regret it, because if the benefits to be expected from that agreement were slight, its disadvantages were even slighter; and it had a symbolic value which should not have been so lightly sacrificed.

But I have, I repeat, no illusion that negotiations on the SALT pattern—negotiations, that is, in which each side is obsessed with the chimera of relative advantage and strives only to retain a maximum of the weaponry for itself while putting its opponent to the maximum disadvantage—I have no illusion that such negotiations could ever be adequate to get us out of this hole. They are not a way of escape from the weapons race; they are an integral part of it.

Whoever does not understand that when it comes to nuclear weapons the whole concept of relative advantage is illusory—whoever does not understand that when you are talking about absurd and preposterous quantities of overkill the relative sizes of arsenals have no serious meaning—whoever does not understand that the danger lies not in the possibility that someone else might have more missiles and warheads than we do but in the very existence of these unconscionable quantities of highly poisonous explosives, and their existence, above all, in hands as weak and shaky and undependable as those of ourselves or our adversaries or any other mere human beings: whoever does not understand these things is never going to guide us out of this increasingly dark and menacing forest of bewilderments into which we have all wandered.

I can see no way out of this dilemma other than by a bold and sweeping departure—a departure that would cut surgically through the exaggerated anxieties, the self-engendered nightmares, and the sophisticated mathematics of destruction, in which we have all been entangled over these recent years, and would permit us to move, with courage and decision, to the heart of the problem.

President Reagan recently said, and I think very wisely, that he would "negotiate as long as necessary to reduce the numbers of nuclear weapons to a point where neither side threatens the survival of the other."

Now that is, of course, precisely the thought to which these present observations of mine are addressed. But I wonder whether the negotiations would really have to be at such great length. What I would like to see the President do, after due consultation with the Congress, would be to propose to the Soviet government an immediate across-the-boards reduction by 50 percent of the nuclear arsenals now being maintained by the two superpowers — a reduction affecting in equal measure all forms of the weapon, strategic, medium-range, and tactical, as well as all means of their delivery — all this to be implemented at once and without further wrangling among the experts, and to be subject to such national means of verification as now lie at the disposal of the two powers.

Whether the balance of reduction would be precisely even — whether it could be construed to favor statistically one side or the other — would not be the question. Once we start thinking that way, we would be back on the same old fateful track that has brought us where we are today. Whatever the precise results of such a reduction, there would still be plenty of overkill left — so much so that if this first operation were successful, I would then like to see a second one put in hand to rid us of at least two-thirds of what would be left.

Now I have, of course, no idea of the scientific aspects of such an operation; but I can imagine that serious problems might be presented by the task of removing, and disposing safely of, the radioactive contents of the many thousands of warheads that would have to be dismantled. Should this be the case, I would like to see the President couple his appeal for a 50 percent reduction with the proposal that there be established a joint Soviet-American scientific committee, under the chairmanship of a distinguished neutral figure, to study jointly and in all humility the problem not only of the safe disposal of these wastes but also the question of how they could be utilized in such a way as to make a positive contribution to human life, either in the two countries themselves or — perhaps preferably — elsewhere. In such a joint scientific venture we might both atone for some of our past follies and lay the foundation for a more constructive relationship.

It will be said: this proposal, whatever its merits, deals with only a part of the problem. This is perfectly true. Behind it there would still lurk the serious political differences that now divide us from the Soviet government. Behind it would still lie the problems recently treated, and still to be treated, in the SALT forum. Behind it would still lie the great question of the acceptability of war itself, any war, even a conventional one, as a means of solving problems among great industrial powers in this age of high technology.

What has been suggested here would not prejudice the continued treatment of these questions just as they might be treated today, in whatever forums and under whatever safeguards the two powers find necessary. The conflicts and arguments over these questions could all still proceed to the heart's content of all those who view them with such passionate commitment. The stakes would simply be smaller; and that would be a great relief to all of us.

What I have suggested is, of course, only a beginning. But a beginning has to be made somewhere; and if it has to be made, is it not best that it should be made where the dangers are the greatest, and their necessity the least? If a step of this nature could be successfully taken, people might find the heart to tackle with greater confidence and determination the many problems that would still remain.

It will also be argued that there would be risks involved. Possibly so. I do not see them. I do not deny the possibility. But if there are, so what? Is it possible to conceive of any dangers greater than those that lie at the end of the collision course on which we are now embarked? And if not, why choose the greater — why choose, in fact, the greatest — of all risks, in the hopes of avoiding the lesser ones?

We are confronted here, my friends, with two courses. At the end of the one lies hope — faint hope, if you will — uncertain hope, hope surrounded with dangers, if you insist. At the end of the other lies, so far as I am able to see, no hope at all.

Can there be — in the light of our duty not just to ourselves (for we are all going to die sooner or later) but of our duty to our own kind, our duty to the continuity of the generations, our duty to the great experiment of civilized life on this rare and rich and marvelous planet — can there be, in the light of these claims on our loyalty, any question as to which course we should adopt?

In the final week of his life, Albert Einstein signed the last of the collective appeals against the development of nuclear weapons that he was ever to sign. He was dead before it appeared. It was an appeal drafted, I gather, by Bertrand Russell. I had my differences with Russell at the time as I do now in retrospect; but I would like to quote one sentence from the final paragraph of that statement, not only because it was the last one Einstein ever signed, but because it sums up, I think, all that I have to say on the subject. It reads as follows:

> We appeal, as human beings to human beings: Remember your humanity, and forget the rest.

# The Urgent Need for Peace and Disarmament

### *Document 15*

In this excerpt from her book *Missile Envy,* Dr. Helen Caldicott, former president of the Physicians for Social Responsibility, makes several arguments that are consistent with a peace and disarmament framework. She criticizes traditional arms controllers for being ineffective and calls for replacing arms control with "rapid bilateral nuclear disarmament." She indicates that part of the problem is that the United States has a wartime economic system. It must be converted to a peace economy if disarmament is to come. She refers to the distorted U.S. view of the Soviet Union and says that Americans must reach out to the Soviets, "who are people like ourselves." Finally, she calls for a moral crusade to eliminate nuclear weapons.

## 15 THERAPY
## Helen Caldicott

Because the planet is terminally ill, there is a grave urgency about our work. In the past, traditional arms control negotiators sometimes have stopped single weapons systems, but on the whole they have just sanctified and justified continuation of the arms race on both sides. They and their colleagues in the Pentagon and the corporations also have developed an obscure mystical language for the arms race to confuse the public. Because of patient demands, physicians recently have learned to demystify the language of medicine so that patients become adequately informed about their illnesses. Similarly, it is time to demystify the arms race. There are no professional "arms controllers." If there were, surely we would have had real arms reductions by this time.

It also is time to change our way of thinking about arms control. I prefer not to use this phrase at all. Let's talk about rapid bilateral nuclear disarmament and abolition of nuclear weapons. It must be rapid because even if we achieve a freeze we still have fifty thousand nuclear weapons; even if we move down to five thousand within five years, that still is ample to killl most people in the world. (Carl Sagan's data imply that a hundred megatons could destroy the earth.) Physicians treating a terminally ill patient never compromise. They work on that patient twenty-four hours a day for weeks or months, and occasionally the patient survives. A similar degree of dedication must be shown by the world leaders and their people if we are to save the earth.

After the Pentagon prepared its Five-Year Defense Guidance Plan for protracted winnable nuclear war, I prepared a five-year plan for rapid nuclear disarmament. It has three phases (the last two are adopted from a proposal made by George Kennan):

- a bilateral verifiable freeze on production, deployment, and testing of any more nuclear weapons or delivery systems, to be achieved by the superpowers within one year
- 50 percent across-the-board cuts in all nuclear weapons and delivery systems; each superpower can select which bombs it chooses to discard — to be completed within two years
- two-thirds cuts in the remainder of nuclear weapons and delivery systems bilaterally — to be completed in two years

At the end of five years, the United States would have five thousand bombs and the Soviet Union three thousand. This still is not enough of a reduction, but I would hope that the momentum and goodwill generated would be sufficient by the end of that time to proceed rapidly to zero.

Some people say I am naïve to suggest this time frame and such a severe degree of disarmament. I believe it is naïve to suggest that the world will continue unscathed by nuclear holocaust. We must implement such a plan immediately. It is important to define an objective goal. People tend to procrastinate unless they have a defined time limit, and there is no time to waste. Only if the superpowers begin to exert nuclear self-discipline will they be in a position to exert pressure on other nuclear nations and to lobby to prevent further proliferation of nuclear weapons.

Roger Fisher, a lawyer at Harvard, has suggested a scheme that may help prevent nuclear war. He advises that the codes the president needs to start a nuclear war be buried in the pericardium of the heart of one of the men who normally carries the "football" (the case containing the nuclear war codes) behind the president. Should the president decide to start a nuclear war, he would have to slice open the man's chest to retrieve the codes. Apparently some military people were horrified at this suggestion and said, aghast, "But that would mean killing a man if the president wanted to start a nuclear war."

### Conversion from a War Economy to a Peace Economy

After World War II, America took the initiative and quickly converted its economy to peacetime uses. It also behaved in a mature, statesmanlike way on the international scene when it instituted the Marshall Plan, which helped revivify the disastrous economic situations of the European Allies. It also instigated programs that have allowed Japan to develop one of the most successful peacetime economies in the world.

The American corporations that are involved in the arms race are run by very intelligent people who will quickly perceive that the people of America will not allow the wartime economic system to continue to flourish. They will put their heads together and will be motivated to design equipment that will be used to the benefit of people both in the United States and internationally.

The world urgently needs adequate production and equitable distribution of food. It needs vast production of medicines and vaccines, and redistribution of medical expertise and medical supplies to the millions of suffering people in the Third World. Adequate distribution of birth-control techniques is required to prevent an increase in global population growth from 4.5 billion now to 6 billion in 2000. Reforestation of many areas of the world is a mandatory priority, since trees currently are used to provide fuel for the poor countries, and trees recycle carbon dioxide to produce oxygen. The riches of the sea must be equitably distributed among all nations on earth and must not be mined only by those few Western nations that currently possess the technology and expertise to do so. All the world's natural resources must be shared and used for the benefit of the family of man and not hoarded and wasted on production of weapons. Millions of the world's people must be delivered from their situation of illiteracy and poverty — a vicious cycle that perpetuates endemic overpopulation and hunger.

The air and the water of America and large ports of the world are fast becoming irretrievably polluted with carcinogenic and mutagenic poisons produced by industry to make profits. There are 4.5 million known toxic chemicals, and 375,000 new ones are produced annually. Most have never been adequately tested for carcinogenicity, and most are released to the environment, often illegally. Many of these chemicals are by-products of industries that produce plastic throwaway materials we don't need.

America needs to tighten its belt. My husband and I visited Cuba in November 1979. Before the revolution, malaria, hook-worm, tuberculosis, and gastrointestinal disease were endemic there. Cuba now has one of the best medical schemes in the world — so good that Dr. Julius Richmond, President Carter's surgeon general, visited Cuba to develop ideas for America's health-care systems. Prerevolution illiteracy was about 40 percent; now it is almost negligible. The education programs are excellent. Nevertheless, life is still spare. There is no choice of clothes in the shops — one type of shoe, one type of trousers — and a limited variety of foods. The government has helped its people enormously, and the people are grateful.

We returned to Christmas in America with the stores just dripping with luxury and affluence. We knew then that if America redefined its priorities, it could help feed many of the world's people. Americans do not have a God-given right to be the wealthiest people in the world to the detriment of millions of others. These poor countries are now developing their own nuclear weapons, and they are justifiably angry. Who will they drop them on?

Men are very smart — so smart that they have learned to destroy themselves. They could with a little effort and ingenuity develop a global economic system (excluding the production and sales of weapons) that would benefit the Western corporations, as well as all the countries on earth. For several years, the Third World has been pleading for such a move, but the selfish Western nations have refused to cooperate or to contemplate ways to alleviate the plight of the poor. Yet it is obvious that the global situation is all interconnected and relevant to prevention of nuclear war.

All such a scheme would take is creative initiative with the right motivation. If people see that in the end, they, too, will benefit as wealth is equitably shared around the world, thus making the world a safer place, they will become enthusiastic about such an endeavor. This is not pie-in-the-sky talk; it is pragmatic and ultimately reasonable and rational. It will take place only if the people in the wealthy Western democracies educate themselves about the plight of mankind and decide for their own well-being that they and their politicians will create the solutions. The powerful politicians who met in Williamsburg in 1983 to discuss the global economic crisis behaved like emasculated pawns. They made soothing noises but did absolutely nothing to change the situation.

Conversion of a corporation from war to peace can be achieved not just by a decision of the corporate heads but also by initiative from the workers. In England, the Lucas Aerospace Industry used to make parts for missiles. After many years, the workers became concerned about the global implications of their work. They called in some consultants and asked, "With our technical skills, what can we make that would benefit mankind?" So the consultants designed electric cars, dialysis machines, and mass-transit systems. The workers then took these plans to the management and said, "We are not going to make missiles anymore. We are going to make this equipment."...

We must reach out to the Soviets, who are people like ourselves. We must demystify the Soviet culture, as they must learn to understand ours. Cultural exchanges and scientific exchanges must increase, and trade between the superpowers must become the utmost priority. The USSR for years has been begging to become a major trading partner of the United States. Let's do it. Let's move toward them as Richard Nixon once did with that long-hated enemy, Red China. Overnight, China became an ally and a major trading partner. If we did the same thing with the Soviet Union, weapons involving our two countries would become anachronistic. It is simple, obvious, and easy. We must drop our ancient need for a tribal enemy and grow up and become responsible nations....

It is time for people to rise to their full moral and spiritual height, to take the world on their shoulders like Atlas, forgetting all other priorities in their lives, and to say, "*I* will save the earth." Each person can be as powerful as the most powerful person who ever lived. I have achieved a lot in a foreign country. I am an Australian and a woman, but neither of these factors has been an impediment. Think how much Americans could achieve by using and working through the democracy they have inherited from their forebears. All it takes is willpower and determinaiton.

This quest is a spiritual adventure. It is time for mankind to achieve spiritual fulfillment. Each person has much to offer. However, it is imperative that the ego be controlled. Ego needs are enormous and can be extremely destructive when working with others. I have learned in this work that if my ego becomes dominant and I engage in negative thoughts, things always go wrong. If I meditate or pray and decide simply to do what is right — not because it *feels* right but because it *is* right — and I drop my own egocentric needs, things always fall into place in the most amazing way. Such action is enormously rewarding. As we work with others, we must remember only one thing, and that is our final common goal: elimination of nuclear weapons. We don't need our egos fulfilled; we need only to fulfill our destiny on the planet in the twentieth century: to save the world. We must learn to reinforce and support one another. True happiness lies in helping one another. We are all sons and daughters of God, and under the universal horror of the nuclear Sword of Damocles, we will be united to work together in mutual respect and peace.

No other generation has inherited this enormous responsibility. We have been given the privilege of saving all past and all future generations, all animals, all plants. Think of the enormous variety of delicate butterflies; think of the gorgeous birds of the earth, of the endless designs of fish in the sea; think of the beautiful and exotic flowers with their gorgeous and seductive perfumes; think of the proud lions and tigers and of the wondrous prehistoric elephants and hippopotamuses; think of what we are about to destroy.

Rapid nuclear disarmament is the ultimate issue of preventive medicine.

It is the ultimate parenting issue.

It is the ultimate Republican and the ultimate Democratic issue.

It is the ultimate patriotic issue.

Above all, it is the ultimate religious issue.

We are the curators of life on earth; we hold it in the palms of our hands. Can we evolve spiritually and emotionally in time to control the overwhelming evil that our advanced and rational intellect has created? We will know the answer to this question in our lifetime. This generation will die having discovered the answer.

## Only Disarmament Will Prevent Nuclear Winter

### *Document 16*

This excerpt from *Nuclear Winter,* by British analysts Owen Greene, Ian Percival, and Irene Ridge, argues that humankind faces the real danger of extinction unless nuclear weapons are abolished. Even deep cuts in the superpowers' arsenals will leave so many weapons that a nuclear war might cause a nuclear winter that could wipe out all human life.

### 16 POLICY IMPLICATIONS
### Owen Greene, Ian Percival, and Irene Ridge

The recent research outlined in this book shows that the combination of the Earth's climatic system and the nuclear weapons stockpile might be a *Doomsday machine.*

Readers who have seen the film *Dr. Strangelove* have already come across the notion of a Doomsday machine. It is a hypothetical device whose only function is to automatically destroy most, if not all, human life if ever deterrence fails. The classic machine would be wired to go off as soon as nuclear weapons detonate over the homeland. The so-called *Doomsday-in-a-hurry* version would be triggered by a lesser provocation such as an attack on an ally. At first sight such devices would seem to be the ultimate deterrent.

The concept of a Doomsday machine was formulated by Herman Kahn, a strategist and systems analyst working at the RAND Corporation in the USA.[28] Writing in 1960, Kahn thought that the device would probably involve "the creation of really large amounts of radioactivity or the *causing of major climatic changes* or, less likely, the extreme use of thermal effects."[29] At the time the most likely candidate seemed to be a giant cobalt bomb which, when detonated, would send vast quantities of long-lived radioactive cobalt around the world.

Kahn considered whether a Doomsday machine might be built inadvertently, but ruled it out on the grounds that decision makers were now alerted to the possibility and would make sure it never happened.[30] Now it looks as if he might have been proven wrong in this last respect. If the recent scientific research is even approximately correct, there have been more than enough nuclear weapons to trigger a climatic catastrophe since the late 1950s.

Unlike the classic Doomsday device, nuclear winter is not an inevitable consequence of nuclear war. It is only a possibility, and the triggering mechanism is complex and poorly understood. Nevertheless the similarities are striking. Humankind might have built itself a Doomsday machine over a quarter of a century ago without even realizing it.

This raises some key questions. How should we react to this possibility? What implications should it have for public policy and personal action? This chapter sets out to provide some initial answers. . . .

### Uncertainties

There are real uncertainties involved in the nuclear winter predictions. They are based on models of poorly-understood processes. Many of the complex scientific problems will take many years to resolve and some of the key uncertainties will remain unless there is a nuclear war. Science cannot provide certainty on this issue. However, one doesn't require certainty to take decisions about risks.

Manufacturers of dangerous chemicals have to show that there is no significant risk of a catastrophic accident. People who object to the prospect of living around the site of a chemical plant are not required to prove that such an accident is inevitable: if the risk is high, the plant should not be built.

Nevertheless, with chemical plants people can live with some chance of an accident. In this case, humanity can learn from its past mistakes. With nuclear winter there would be no second chance. The potential costs are so enormous that it hardly matters for our argument whether the probability that the nuclear winter predictions are basically correct is 10 per cent, 50 per cent, or 90 per cent. As the report of the Royal Society of Canada said: "We conclude that the nuclear winter hypothesis does indeed modify the global strategic position . . . At some point the strategists have to accept the probability of the predicted consequences, and incorporate that judgement into this thinking."[31]

This risk of a nuclear winter means that the present nuclear weapon arsenals are unacceptable.

### What Should Be Done?

Granted that the possibility of nuclear winter undermines present nuclear weapons policies, how should they be changed?

The fundamental task, in our view, is to ensure that no nuclear war can occur at all by securing verified complete global nuclear disarmament, while reducing the role of military force in international relations. However that can only be achieved, if at all, as a result of a long process. So in the first instance, the nuclear winter predictions mean that we must ensure that any nuclear war would not trigger climatic catastrophe.

## Notes

28. Herman, Kahn, *On Thermonuclear War,* London: Oxford University Press, 1960.
29. H. Kahn, p. 145
30. H. Kahn, p. 150
31. The Royal Society of Canada, *Nuclear Winter and Associated Effects* (Report of the Committee on the Environmental Consequences of Nuclear War, Royal Society of Canada, Ottawa: 31 January, 1985) pp. 5 and 7.

# Some Soviet Perspectives

## *Documents 17 and 18*

Document 17 contains excerpts from a survey on Soviet perceptions of the United States done by the Office of Research, U.S. International Communications Project in 1983. Not surprisingly, Soviets tend to blame the United States for bad U.S.-Soviet relations. They believe the United States does not accept the Soviet Union's right to an equal place in the world and that U.S. policy toward the Soviet Union has been inconsistent. The Soviets have a healthy fear of U.S. military might and worry that the U.S. is "trigger-happy."

In document 18, Georgi Arbatov, the most senior Soviet expert on the United States, says that the American public does not have an accurate view of the Soviet Union. He blames much of this on the influence of the U.S. "military business" sector. He also says that its historical isolation from other nations makes the United States susceptible to distorted and oversimplified views of the Soviet Union.

## 17 SOVIET PERCEPTIONS OF THE U.S. 1984

### General Observations

Soviets at all levels[32] see Soviet-American relations as their most critical international relationship. This perception appears to be shared by both those who hope for a cooperative relationship and those who fear or desire a confrontational relationship.

In general, Soviets believe that the U.S. does not attach as great a significance to the relationship as they do. They are disappointed that the perceived mutual benefits of détente were never realized, but they see this as the fault of the American side. Even before Afghanistan they felt that little more could be lost in the relationship, because they were convinced that the U.S. was not going to deliver its share of the bargain. This attitude makes it possible to fit almost any American action into a pattern of anti-Soviet behavior, and greatly blurs the perception of linkages between Soviet and American behavior.

The present crisis has not greatly diminished the traditional and widely held perception of the U.S. and the USSR as natural allies — which may arise from a desire to be associated with the industrial West as well as from a visceral intolerance of non-whites.

At the same time, elements hostile to a cooperative relationship with the U.S. have emerged from hiding with what is basically an "I told you so" message. Those who have staked their professional careers and reputations on a cooperative relationship with the U.S. appear to be taking a more defensive position and modifying some of their earlier views — at least for public consumption. For example, leading Americanists have taken the opportunity to point out to American contacts the basic hostility of the U.S. toward the Soviet experiment even from its beginning.

Rarely if ever do Soviets see their own actions as precipitants of U.S. action. Soviet foreign policy remains a sacred cow internally. Given their history, Soviets find it difficult to believe that they would take offensive actions, but are inclined to view each action as defensive in a hostile world. This unwillingness to be critical of their own actions makes it very difficult for them to understand other countries' actions which are predicated on a view that the Soviet Union is a military threat to their security.

## Power Politics

Ideology clearly plays a role in Soviet views of the U.S. Yet, when Soviets discuss the relationship with Americans, the terms are usually non-ideological and framed much more within the context of power politics. Soviets say that world peace ultimately depends on the U.S. and the Soviet Union working together. They appear to desire the establishment of a Soviet-American co-dominion to stabilize a frightening world and avoid what is most feared: a third-party problem escalating into a superpower confrontation.

Soviets believe that a superpower has and should have the right to act in areas of its perceived national interest. While Soviets express a willingness to recognize that the U.S. has this right, they feel that the U.S. is unwilling to reciprocate. They are quick to draw a distinction between verbal abuse for a particular action — which they see as a normal part of the game — and actual retaliatory measures.

Nonetheless, Soviets still speak of the U.S. as a potential, if erratic, "partner" in resolving the problems of world peace. They believe that they have a longer-term view of the problems besetting the relationship and hope that American leaders will recognize its true importance. There is a strong feeling that the continuity in Soviet leadership requires of them a patient policy of educating each successive American administration to the real significance of the relationship.

## The Question of Equality

Coupled with a feeling that world peace rests on the ability of the U.S. and the Soviet Union to work together, there is considerable sentiment that the U.S. is unwilling to recognize the legitimate place of the Soviet Union in the world of nations. For the most part Soviets see the U.S. as unwilling to acknowledge its loss of economic and political preeminence, and unable to accept the ascendance of the Soviet Union. The desire for U.S. recognition of Soviet equality and legitimacy is palpable in most conversations with Soviets.

Consonant with the official line, there is a strong feeling that the Soviet Union as a superpower must be involved in the resolution of any major international issue. Soviet isolation from the Middle East peace process is seen as evidence of American unwillingness to accord the Soviets their rightful status.

Soviets want American recognition of their equality on the international scene, but barring that recognition they appear willing to demonstrate this equality through unilateral action. Even those who are skeptical about the wisdom of the Afghanistan venture seem, nonetheless, pleased that the USSR acted as they perceive a superpower ought to act.

Many Soviets believe that the U.S., in failing to accept their equality and legitimacy, focuses in communication with the Soviet Union only on the negative and does not place disagreements in an "appropriate" context of mutual respect and recognition.

## American Foreign Policy

There are some consistent strains in Soviet views of recent U.S. foreign policy, even though the level of sophistication and information is quite varied. Ideological jargon and categories are used significantly less than one might assume in discussions of American foreign policy.

They see recent American foreign policy as inconsistent and, as they like to say, "zig-zaggy."[33] They claim to find the U.S. unpredictable and unreliable. To the extent that they see consistency, they see it as anti-Soviet. The wellsprings of this "anti-Sovietism" are seen variously as the President and his administration, the pressure of the "military-industrial complex," the imperatives of domestic politics, and/or the need for distractions from American foreign policy failures elsewhere.

Most Soviets believe that over the past few years there have been diminishing returns from the Soviet-American relationship, for which they blame the U.S. They see the U.S. backing away from earlier promises. For example, many who know the inner workings of the Soviet system argue that it was an uphill fight to increase emigration, but they did it, perceiving it to be a quid pro quo for better relations. But, they found that rather than receiving MFN and increased trade, their efforts went unappreciated.

Similarly they see SALT II as another instance of U.S. reluctance to enter fully into the relationship. It is commonly believed that the President had retreated from his initial support of the treaty — further evidence of a perceived unwillingness to treat the Soviet Union as an equal. They see this treaty as a benefit to both countries and the cause of world peace, as well as recognition of the military parity that the Soviet Union has achieved. They feel that the U.S. thought it was doing the Soviet Union a favor by signing the agreement. On those terms, American discussion of the treaty was perceived as offensive. . . .

### American Military Power and Political Resolve

Soviets at most levels have a very healthy regard for American military strength. Recent American debates concerning military weakness are viewed as a pretext for reasserting American military superiority. Their views of the military balance are made more salient by an overwhelming preoccupation with the issue of war and peace.

While some Soviets believe that they have achieved military equality, most face the future with ambivalence. They, including the military, view American technology with awe, fearing that the U.S. could, if it chooses, unleash its productive capacity and eliminate the Soviets' hard-earned relative gains. This attitude is reenforced by other considerations.

First, most Soviets are convinced that they would not be the first to attack, but that their actions are defensive in nature. They find it difficult to believe that the U.S. sees the Soviet Union as a threat. But, they fear that the U.S., untempered by the horrors of war on its own territory, might be tempted to attack or that war might arise out of a third-country conflict.

Second, they view the U.S. as "trigger happy" and erratic, willing to commit its military strength much more readily than the Soviet Union — this even after Afghanistan. Such "militarism" is even more dangerous in Soviet eyes if the U.S. perceived itself to be losing preeminence around the world.

Third, even those insulated from economic sacrifices by virtue of their own privileged positions are aware of the society's vulnerabilities, especially economic. They fear that a new arms race will be severely detrimental to their own society and that they may not be able to keep up with the U.S.

These feelings are somewhat balanced by a view that they are more disciplined and willing to sacrifice for a perceived national interest than are Americans. Nonetheless, the situation is perceived as very dangerous. Soviets talk about the possibility of war with visceral emotion. While clearly they will continue to probe American strength and resolve, direct confrontation appears to be an unthinkable thought.

## Notes

32. Although the study focused on elites, respondents mentioned that some specific views seemed to be shared by all of their contacts. In the report these views are indicated by a phrase such as "Soviets at all levels."

33. There is a striking congruence between the views discussed here and the Soviet official line as expressed publicly and privately.

## 18 ACCURACY OF U.S. PERCEPTIONS
## Georgi Arbatov, Soviet Expert on U.S. 1984

*1. Does the American public have an accurate perception of the Soviet Union, its people, and its leaders?*

I think it does not — even on the problems which are of high importance to the U.S. itself, its national interests and the formulation of its foreign policy. Inaccuracy of many American perceptions of the Soviet Union is hardly surprising given the fact there may be no other country in the world the U.S. perceptions of which have for such a long time been formed on the basis of so one-sided and distorted information. That is why they are so tinted with strong bias and prejudices.

Due to détente in Soviet-U.S. relations and the increase in contacts, exchanges and tourism that accompanied the process since early 1970 there were signs of change for the better in this field. Of late, however, one sees in the United States intensified efforts not only to slow down this process but also to reverse it.

*2. On the basis of what information and as a result of what psychological, social, and political forces is American public opinion toward the Soviet Union formed?*

The bulk of information the Americans get about the Soviet Union is secondhand, being delivered to the American public through American intermediaries (journalists, experts, politicians, reports by the CIA and other governmental and private organizations). To a certain extent this is probably the case with any other country. But in informing the U.S. public about the Soviet Union, these American intermediaries display very often a particular bias. This is the result of personal ideological prejudices characteristic of many of them and of direct or indirect pressure of the forces that have vested interests in creating a distorted picture of the Soviet Union.

I have in mind first and foremost the economic forces. The biggest business in the U.S. is military business. For the past several decades, together with the entire military establishment, this business has been thriving in the climate of distorted ideas about the Soviet Union, artificially bloated fears of the "Soviet military threat" and continuously fanned animosity and distrust toward the USSR. It is common knowledge that blatant disinformation is being fed to the American public (as well as to the lawmakers) in the interests of these forces, but the existing norms of American politics for some reason make a serious discussion of this (e.g. in U.S. Congress) look almost indecent.

The U.S. is hardly comparable to any other country in the world in terms of the extent to which special interests affect national policy and the concepts that underlie it. Among those vitally interested in the distortion of the American perception of the USSR are the military-industrial complex, the ultraconservative elements, groups benefitting from the cold war, organizations representing anti-Communist emigration from Eastern Europe, the Israeli lobby, and others. In fact, it is hardly necessary to tell the U.S. Senators about this influence on the American public opinion and even on the opinions of the U.S. legislators on issues regarding the Soviet Union.

What ideological and psychological patterns of American thinking are being used to achieve this end? First of all, one should mention anti-Communism which has been cultivated for a long time as well as fears generated by it. With some it is fear of Communism itself, with others, fear of seeming "soft on Communism."

A major psychological role is played by an inertia of thinking and by a difficult problem of adjusting to new realities of the time, and more specifically, of shaking off the burden of the old perceptions inherited from the "cold war."

The strength of these perceptions lies in their simplicity and easiness to comprehend — there is a concrete enemy who is the source of all evils; there is a clear aim — to fight this enemy with all available means; and there are well-established and tested methods of such a fight. It is easy, within the framework of these perceptions, to stir emotions deeply rooted in the psychology of many people — the feeling of national superiority, jingoism, suspicion and hostility towards everything unusual or strange. These perceptions also tend to shape specific norms of political behavior which identifies political courage with "toughness" and intolerance, political wisdom — with the skill to overwhelm the opponent in the dangerous game of who chickens out first.

The philosophy of détente, of peaceful coexistence, is much more sophisticated. It deals with coexistence, establishing good relations and cooperation between the states that truly differ in their social systems, political institutions, values, sympathies, and antipathies. It is not so easy to realize that relations between them are not a "zero sum game" in which one side gains exactly what the other loses, that notwithstanding all the differences and contradictions they might have common interests, that irrespective of their sympathies and antipathies they have to live together on one planet. It is even more difficult to understand that the source of troubles could be not only the actions of the other side but also miscalculations and mistakes in one's own policy, saying nothing of objective processes taking place in the world. It is not very easy to realize that under present conditions restraint, moderation and willingness to compromise take not only more wisdom, but more political courage, than "tough play." The accommodation to these new and much more complicated realities and perceptions is a serious and, as L. I. Brezhnev once said, difficult process.

The negative role of the inertia of thinking reveals itself in other problems as well. Americains, for instance, have grown accustomed to a sense of almost national security. Over the centuries this has been instilled in them by the almost insurmountable barriers of the two oceans, and in the first post-war decades by their confidence in the overwhelming U.S. military supremacy. Now the situation has changed, and America finds herself not only at a rough parity with the USSR militarily but absolutely equal with other countries in terms of her own vulnerability to a holocaust should a war break out. This is a new situation for Americans. It is undoubtedly not easy to get used to it, not easy to get along with it. It nurtures not only a climate for more panicking about the "Soviet threat" but also a permanent temptation to follow those who promise an act of magic — a return to past invulnerability if only a sufficient amount of dollars is allocated and an adequate number of weapons systems are produced.

What makes Americans susceptible to one-sided, simplified, and just incorrect perceptions of the world at large (USSR included) are in my opinion certain other peculiarities of their history and traditions. One may take, for instance, the very fact of the U.S. remoteness, almost complete self-sufficiency and isolation that for a long time did not encourage much interest in the outside world but resulted instead in a particular concentration of things domestic. That is why Americans are not particularly prone to scrutinize the intricacies of international scene, and that is why foreign policy so often falls a prey to domestic politicking. There is also a firm belief characteristic of many Americans dating back to the Pilgrims that it was in their country that a new civilization was born bearing closest resemblance to the Promised Land, free from the sins that had engulfed the Old World. Lately, this belief and the resulting messianism together with the faith in America's "Manifest Destiny," her right and even an obligation to carry the light of truth and American values to other countries, have been badly shattered.

But the underlying sentiments have not vanished. Facts show that they can be quite easily stirred, given the double standards brought to life by messianism and the traditional inability (and, at times, plain unwillingness) to understand a different country, a different nation, to realize that it may have her own values and ideals and to imagine how the other side feels about a given issue. Evidence of this is provided not only by the human rights campaign but also by many American interpretations of the security problem.

Currently, for instance, concern is often expressed in the United States that the Soviet military might exceeds the "legitimate defense needs." But has any American, while gauging these needs, attempted to position himself in our place and to realize that the USSR has to simultaneously confront a potential threat from the three largest military capabilities of the world: those of the U.S., Western Europe, and China?

I could continue citing all the forces and factors which prevent Americans from getting a correct perception of the Soviet Union, its people, its leaders, and its policies. They are quite formidable and if there were nothing to resist them, there would not be much hope left for normal relations between our two countries. Fortunately, this does not seem to be the case. On many issues of the U.S. policy toward the Soviet Union a majority of Americans voice sound, realistic judgments. They favor an improvement in Soviet-American relations, détente, arms limitation agreements, and development of trade. In any case this is borne out by U.S. public opinion polls.

This is probably explained by accurate American perceptions — but not so much of the Soviet Union as of the U.S. own interests — by common sense akin to Americans, their healthy instincts, their ability to draw the right conclusions from past experiences. One more aspect seems important to me in this regard. The Americans who realistically appraise Soviet-American relations are much more vocal these days in the U.S. than was the case 10 or 20 years ago. These Americans include those who far from being sympathetic with Communism or Soviet domestic ways take real American national interests close to heart.

## WHAT CITIZENS CAN DO

## Nuclear Protest

### *Document 19*

This excerpt from a 1982 article in the *New York Times Magazine* describes the growth in the early 1980s of a grass-roots movement favoring arms reductions. It discusses the impact of church groups, pro–arms control groups such as the Physicians for Social Responsibility and the Union of Concerned Scientists, and the nuclear freeze campaign. The article concludes that "the movement has clearly had an impact on President Reagan, affecting his policy if not personal thinking."

### 19 ANATOMY OF A NUCLEAR PROTEST
**Fox Butterfield**

Randall Forsberg was born in Alabama with "a few Georgia plantations ravaged by Sherman's troops floating around in my past." She graduated from Barnard College in the mid-1960s and became an English teacher at the proper Baldwin School in Bryn Mawr, Pa. There was little in her background to suggest that one day she would produce the idea that has turned the esoteric art of nuclear-arms control into an explosive popular issue.

Alan F. Kay graduated from the Massachusetts Institute of Technology, served in Army intelligence during World War II and got a Ph.D. in math at Harvard. He founded and eventually sold two highly profitable electronics companies, one of which worked for the Pentagon, before retiring to his home in Weston, a green-carpeted expanse of multiacre houses that is Boston's wealthiest suburb. There was little in his biography to suggest that he would provide the first key infusion of cash that enabled Miss Forsberg to translate her potent idea into action.

It was in 1980 that the retired businessman heard the

former school teacher, now a student of the arms race, make her proposal. She was calling for a freeze — a mutual and verifiable freeze by the United States and the Soviet Union — on the testing, production and deployment of all nuclear weapons. It was a very simple idea — too simple, some critics contended, since it did not allow for the staggering complexities of the arms race. But Mr. Kay recognized that its simplicity could also be a strength: It sidestepped the old hard-to-understand arguments about MIRVs, megatonnage, throw weight and inspection that had long baffled the public. So Mr. Kay contributed the money that set the freeze campaign in motion — $5,000 to help organize the first national conference of peace groups in Washington in March 1981, where it was decided to concentrate on promoting the freeze as a common strategy. He would eventually add a quarter of a million dollars, spread among several antinuclear-war groups.

In the year since that first meeting, the freeze idea has reached what some activists like to call critical mass, borrowing from the lexicon of atomic physics. A poll last spring by The New York Times and CBS News found that 72 percent of Americans favor a nuclear freeze. It has been endorsed by hundreds of town meetings, dozens of city councils and nine state legislatures. Last month, it was approved by the House Foreign Affairs Committee in a nonbinding resolution.

The freeze idea has provided a spark, but it is only part of a larger story, an extraordinary grass-roots, nationwide movement to stop the nuclear arms race. The movement has even influenced President Reagan, leading him to soften his longtime opposition to arms-control talks and inspiring him to offer several sweeping proposals to negotiate sharp reductions in nuclear arsenals with the Soviet Union.

The movement's scope was dramatically illustrated by last Month's [June 1982] disarmament rally in New York City, in which an estimated 700,000 people participated, making it the largest political demonstration in the history of the United States. And there are a growing number of politicians in Washington who believe the antinuclear arms issue may play an important role in this November's Congressional elections and the 1984 Presidential contest. Two weeks after the New York rally, the Democratic Party, at its midterm convention in Philadelphia, endorsed a carefully worded freeze resolution that had been drafted by aides to the party's leading Presidential contenders.

The profile of this latest of protests is a far cry from that of the powerful antiwar demonstrations of the late 1960s. The leaders are not bearded radicals but middle-aged and middle-class men and women, many accustomed to positions of responsibility and prestige. They include doctors, lawyers, nurses, scientists, teachers and priests. Their chief battles have been fought, not in street confrontations, but at sermons and lectures, in books and pamphlets.

The history of the new movement offers special insights into the American political process and the state of the public mind and character. It also suggests how disparate ideas and people can be successfully joined, given good timing, a willingness to learn the hard lessons of modern political organizing and the presence of a powerful catalyst. In this case, the catalyst was a President whose continuous preaching about the need for a massive buildup of American nuclear forces aroused the fears of an already anxious nation.

The anxiety began with the scientists who built the bomb and then sought to place it under international controls. It surfaced publicly in the late 1950s and early '60s with the controversy over fallout from nuclear testing in the atmosphere. And it reappeared in the late '60s with public worry over the Pentagon's plans to build an antiballistic missile system in heavily populated areas.

These movements faded once they seemed to achieve their objectives, but they left a heritage of fear about nuclear peril. In 1978, a small peace group, the Institute for World Order, commissioned Yankelovich, Skelly and White, the polling organization, to study why more people don't join peace groups. Yankelovich's conclusion was that there was both widespread ignorance about what nuclear weapons do and deep latent concern about them.

"They became very interested in the problem and began talking about where can we sign up to stop this madness," recalled Greg Martire, a vice president of the Yankelovich organization. "They were not unaware of the dangers of nuclear war, but they had felt it was beyond their control."

Based on this study and another Yankelovich did in 1980 for a second peace group, the polling organization predicted that many people would join up if the issue was explained to them in understandable terms and if they could be shown how they could be effective. Today, speaking of the sudden growth of the antinuclear-arms movement, Mr. Martire says, "It doesn't surprise me. When we wrote those reports two years ago, it was clear the potential was there." . . .

Henry W. Kendall, yet another M.I.T. physicist and one-time consultant to the Defense Department, helped found the Union of Concerned Scientists in 1969 to lead the battle against the ABM. He was elated when he won that struggle, but increasingly frustrated as he watched public interest in disarmament decline while the weapons race intensified. As Professor Kendall, a soft-spoken man dressed in an old dark gray wool suit and moccasins, analyzed the situation, the average citizen was put off by the "forbidding complexity of nuclear arms. They have been hidden behind the combined shroud of technology and national security."

During the 1970s, his organization, with headquarters in Harvard Square, switched its focus to the then more popular issue of nuclear power. The Union of Concerned Scientists grew rapidly, and by the time of the serious accident at the Three Mile Island nuclear power plant in 1979, the group had 100,000 contributors. But Professor Kendall was dissatisfied. "The dangers of nuclear power are so small compared with nuclear war," he explained, "it seemed to me like a tangential issue." So in 1980 he pushed to return the organization to its original purpose, nuclear-arms control.

His timing was excellent. "The real hard-line voice about nuclear weapons had emerged and started to really scare people," he said. "There was Reagan talking about fighting and winning a limited nuclear war and handing out his laundry list of building up every conceivable nuclear weapon because he claimed we were behind the Russians. It brought out the latent anxiety."

Basing its strategy on one of the Yankelovich studies, the Union of Concerned Scientists set about organizing a series of teach-ins at what the group thought would be two dozen colleges last Nov. 11, [1981,] Veterans Day. Eventually, 150 schools participated. "We hit a nerve," a professor at the University of Texas said afterward. "And this is Texas, not the Northeast." The Veterans Day events proved an important turning point, attracting widespread attention in the press and from television, focusing still more public interest on the issue.

While Professor Kendall in Cambridge was trying to reorient the Union of Concerned Scientists back to nuclear war, Dr. Bernard Lown was part of a similar attempt across the Charles River in Boston — with a group he had started in his living room in 1961, Physicians for Social Responsibility. One of the world's most distinguished cardiologists and a professor at the Harvard School of Public Health, Dr. Lown had pioneered the use of coronary-care units and much of the technology to help prevent sudden death from heart attack. An intense, articulate and precise man, he became concerned about the arms race after hearing a lecture on nuclear holocaust in 1959. He proceeded to organize a group of fellow physicians and to publish a series of papers on the medical consequences of thermonuclear war in the New England Journal of Medicine, one of the country's leading medical bulletins, in 1962. It remains the classic work on the total inadequacy of any medical response in an American city hit by a nuclear bomb.

After the partial Test Ban Treaty in 1963, however, the physicians' group atrophied. Seated in the wood-paneled Harvard Club in Boston's Back Bay section, Dr. Lown recalled that the organization was not really revived until 1980, when Mr. Reagan's campaign rhetoric rekindled the old fears. Dr. Lown calculated that doctors might accomplish what the physicists had never been able to do — arouse the public. "After all," he said, "if you have a serious problem, where do you go? In a secular age, the doctor has become priest, rabbi, counselor. Then, too, the doctor brings all the credentials of a scientist."

One of the key new activists in the Physicians for Social Responsibility was Dr. Helen M. Caldicott, an outspoken Australian-born pediatrician. She had been passionately involved in the antinuclear movement since she read the novel "On the Beach" as a teen-ager in Melbourne. The book, set in Australia, describes the end of the world in a nuclear war. She became president of the group in 1979 and resigned her practice and a teaching job at the Harvard Medical School.

Since then, Dr. Caldicott, who is 43 years old, has toured the country showing the film "The Last Epidemic," which describes in chilling detail exactly what would happen to San Francisco in a nuclear attack. She sees her work as a logical extension of the practice of medicine: "It is the ultimate form of preventive medicine. If you have a disease and there is no cure for it, you work on prevention."

The Physicians for Social Responsibility has increased its membership from 3,000 a year ago to 16,000 today. Thomas A. Halsted, the group's director, who once worked for the Arms Control and Disarmament Agency under the Carter Administration, says that it is now gaining more than 300 new adherents a week. The doctors' main organizational tactic until recently has been their careful field work, conducting day-long educational symposiums for groups of 1,500 to 3,000 doctors in a dozen cities around the country. But P.S.R., as it is called, has also begun adopting direct-mail appeals. . . .

Another important factor in convincing middle-class and middle-aged citizens to join the movement have been American churches — particularly the Roman Catholic Church, which has experienced a critical transformation.

According to Bishop Thomas J. Gumbleton, Roman Catholic auxiliary Bishop of Detroit, the change began during the Vietnam War, "though not many bishops publicly identified with it at the time." In 1968, he recalled, the National Conference of Catholic Bishops had written a pastoral letter outlining the possibility "of a conflict between a person's conscience and what the Government asks you to do." This, Bishop Gumbleton said, "highlighted a problem that had been there for many Catholics. We had a heritage as an immigrant church. We tended to overcompensate for this by our patriotism. As Francis Cardinal Spellman used to say, 'My country, right or wrong.' "

But as the Vietnam War continued, the bishops began to reexamine the old arguments concerning a just war. And, as Bishop Gumbleton pointed out, the church's reevaluation of the relationship between the individual and the state intensified with the Supreme Court decision allowing abortion in 1973.

In November 1980, with the collapse of the SALT II treaty and Mr. Reagan's campaign rhetoric about the need to increase America's nuclear arsenal, the Catholic bishops conference began work on a pastoral letter on the arms race. It is due to be issued this fall. Bishop Gumbleton, who is head of the American branch of Pax Christi, a Roman Catholic peace group, would not comment on its contents. But he referred to a statement made last year by Archbishop John R. Roach, president of the bishops conference, in which he proclaimed that "the most dangerous moral issue in the public order confronting us is the arms race." The nuclear freeze has been endorsed by 133 of the nation's 280 active Roman Catholic bishops.

An important facet of the peace movement has been the degree to which Boston and Cambridge have been its breeding ground. With the exception of Ground Zero, in Washington, and the church organizations, most of the major antinuclear-war groups have their headquarters in the Boston area or started there, including the freeze campaign itself. That is a traditional role for an area that has long been a center of liberal political thought and activity. And Bernard Feld of M.I.T. offers another explanation. He talks about "the critical mass effect": "We have so many universities around here that people don't feel isolated and can talk to each other without feeling strange."

For Randall Forsberg, though, the transformation from private school teacher to peace activist began elsewhere. It was in 1967, at the height of the Vietnam War, that Miss Forsberg married a young Swedish student and moved to Stockholm. The Swedish Government had decided one contribution it could make to world peace would be to monitor the arms race. So, in 1966, it had established the Stockholm International Peace Research Institute. Because the organizers wanted an international staff, Miss Forsberg was able to walk in off the street and get a job as a typist. (The institute was organized with the stated goal of providing independent analysis of the United States-Soviet balance of power. Within the last year, it has become a target of criticism, accused of issuing findings that tend to favor the Soviet point of view.)

Miss Forsberg's introduction to the complexity of the nuclear-weapons race came when she began reading what she was typing. She couldn't believe that the 1963 talks on a comprehensive test ban treaty had broken down over the dispute between Washington's demand for seven onsite inspections a year and the Russians' limit of three. Why not compromise on five, she wondered. Soon she was writing her own research papers on the arms race.

In 1974, divorced and the mother of a 5-year-old daughter, Miss Forsberg moved to Boston where she started graduate work in arms control at M.I.T. A few years later, she set up her own small agency, the Institute for Defense and Disarmament Studies, in suburban Brookline.

Miss Forsberg describes how she arrived at her freeze proposal: "I came to the conclusion that after the failure of the comprehensive test ban talks in 1963, the arms-control experts gave up on complete disarmament, even on substantial reductions in nuclear and conventional forces. What replaced it was the idea of managing a permanent arms race, the goal being to keep things relatively equal. The buzz word was stability, to avoid destabilizing weapons." Then when President Reagan began talking about a $240 billion buildup in MX missiles, cruise missiles and Trident submarines, she became convinced that "the United States was giving up even this limited goal."

The answer, Miss Forsberg felt, was an idea that would be simple enough to involve the public and that would actually lead to reductions in nuclear stockpiles and stop the introduction of ever newer, more lethal weapons — the mutual and verifiable freeze. And that would be equitable, she felt, because she was convinced, as are many supporters of the freeze today, that the United States nuclear arsenal is at least the equal of the Soviet arsenal, notwithstanding President Reagan's claims to the contrary.

Miss Forsberg herself believes the freeze idea has been "the single most important factor" in the sudden growth of the movement over the past year. She and other activists cite several additional key factors that have stimulated the movement: the Senate's failure to ratify the 1979 SALT II Treaty limiting strategic offensive nuclear weapons, President Reagan's talk about fighting and surviving a limited nuclear war and the Reagan Administration's push for a vastly increased Pentagon budget at a time when the economy is in recession. Each of these increased anxiety to the point where, for many people, Miss Forsberg feels, curbing the arms race no longer seemed a partisan political issue.

She does not, however, believe the explosion of the peace movement in Europe over the last two years has been important for its American counterpart. "The Europeans are reacting to a very specific problem," she said. "They don't want new American nuclear weapons deployed in their backyards, making them a target for the Russians. But this is not the issue for Americans; they aren't particularly concerned about what the Western Europeans are feeling."

Yet, as the American public has awakened to the antinuclear-weapons question, each new event has added to the movement's momentum, like the publication in The New Yorker of Jonathan Schell's series which has now become a best-selling book, *The Fate of the Earth.* In California, Harold Willens, A Los Angeles millionaire, has led a drive which got more than 700,000 signatures, far more than needed, to put the freeze on the state's November ballot. And during one week in April, Ground Zero got a million Americans to watch films, listen to debates or circulate petitions in 650 towns and cities, 350 colleges and more than 1,200 high schools. . . .

But the movement has clearly had an impact on President Reagan, affecting his policy if not his personal thinking. The first significant change took place back in November, not long after the widespread teach-ins on Veterans Day, when he proposed to the Soviet leader Leonid I. Brezhnev that Washington would forgo placing its new Pershing 2 and cruise missiles on European soil if Moscow would scrap its SS-20 missiles, already targeted on Western Europe.

Mr. Reagan appeared to be trying to outflank the burgeoning antinuclear-arms movement by being conciliatory instead of combative. Then last month he signaled a major switch away from his hard-line policy of linking arms control talks with Soviet aggression around the world. In a commencement speech at Eureka College in Illinois, he proposed a two-step plan in which the United States and the Soviet Union would initially reduce by one-third their inventories of nuclear warheads on land- and sea-based ballistic missiles.

Yet many peace activists remain skeptical about Mr. Reagan's sincerity in wanting nuclear-arms control. At the same time he was making his latest offer to Moscow, the Pentagon, under Secretary of Defense Caspar W. Weinberger, was drafting a five-year plan for fighting nuclear war against the Soviet Union "over a prolonged period." It has also not gone unnoticed that Mr. Reagan's choice to head the United States delegation to the new talks on reducing strategic arms, which began in Geneva on June 29, is a conservative, retired Army lieutenant general, Edward L. Rowny. General Rowny, who resigned from the American SALT II negotiating team to protest what he felt were too great concessions by the Carter Administration to the Soviet Union, has charged that a freeze would lock the United States into an inferior position.

Despite the rapid spread of the antinuclear-arms movement, there is still far from a consensus about how the United States should proceed or whether the freeze proposal itself is a good plan. More than twenty-five different resolutions to end the arms race have been introduced in Congress, and a freeze resolution was rejected by the Republican-controlled Senate Foreign Relations Committee.

Even some of the most active members of the movement worry that the freeze is too simplistic and impractical. Roger C. Molander, the founder of Ground Zero and a former National Security Council staff member, asks: "Freeze what? Does it mean freezing every last vehicle that is rigged up to deliver nuclear weapons, like the A-6's on aircraft carriers?"

"The freeze campaign is a good way for people to express their concern about the dangers of nuclear war," he continues, " but the lesson we can learn from the last twenty years is that focusing exclusively on arms-control agreements or the development of new weapons is not enough. The hard thing to face up to is that you can't get real arms control without improving relations with the Soviet Union."

Mr. Molander is concerned that Americans are deceiving themselves by concentrating only on affecting United States Government policy. "There is a little too much of the feeling that the whole problem is in this country and that if we can just get our act together, the Russians will go along."

But many of the activists are heartened by their sudden success, particularly as seen in the huge New York rally. Joan Baez, the folk singer and a leader of civil-rights and anti-Vietnam War protests of the 1960s, remarked in New York: "I have been on peace marches since I was probably 14 years old. But never in all those years did I feel the kind of encouragement I do now." Dr. James Muller, secretary of the International Physicians for the Prevention of Nuclear War and an assistant professor of cardiology at the Harvard Medical school, was euphoric after the big rally. "It was far more people than we expected," he said.

## Moving the Public Debate Toward Peace Through Strength

### *Documents 20 and 21*

Documents 20 and 21 illustrate two ways in which conservative groups influence public thinking about the key issues of the nuclear age. Document 20's excerpts from a 1984 article in the *Christian Science Monitor* describe how the influential conservative think tank, the Heritage Foundation, provides key Washington policy makers with information and opinions. Document 21, taken from a 1987 issue of *High Frontier Newswatch,* the newsletter of a prominent pro-SDI group, describes how grass-roots groups are being set up around the country to "keep their Senators and Congressmen on track on SDI."

### 20 YOUNG, BRASH AND CONSERVATIVE
**Jim Bencivenga**

When William F. Buckley Jr. was fresh out of Yale, he wrote a book that rocked his alma mater. As a young man he expressed his patriotism by working for the Central Intelligence Agency and then starting his own conservative journal of opinion (National Review).

Thanks to his brash, combative style, the flavor of conservatism has never been the same since.

If he were graduating today, Mr. Buckley just might join the Heritage Foundation.

Thanks to this foundation, Washington think tanks—conservative or liberal—will never be quite the same again, either.

Heritage hit the policy beaches of Washington 11 years ago, the intellectual equivalent of the US Marines. Provocative as a commando raid in broad daylight, it seized an ideological beachhead and started making the case for slashing government spending, cutting regulations, and rebuilding the military.

Its goal has been not so much to think about conservative policies as to help turn them into marching orders—a goal that sets Heritage starkly apart from the less advocacy-oriented think tanks.

Also setting Heritage apart is the tone of its approach: a certain self-assured bravado, a confidence that it can make a difference in the marketplace of ideas and that it can get the government to buy its policies, not sometime in the future, but right now.

A stream of policy papers, books, monographs, newsletters, and reviews on domestic and foreign policy issues pours from its offices—on average 60 to 100 of them annually. Some are written in-house, others by outside scholars commissioned by Heritage. All are geared to exploit conservative policy opportunities whenever possible. To this end they are often hand-delivered to nearly 1,000 policymakers in Congress and the administration. In addition, they are mailed out to some 6,000 journalists, editors, academics, and contributors.

True to its "travel light and fight hard" philosophy, more than 70 percent of these publications must pass what Herbert B. Berkowitz, vice-president of Heritage, calls the briefcase test:

"Can it be read," he asks, "in the back seat of a limousine on the way to giving testimony before some congressional committee in the time it takes [approximately 20 minutes] to drive from National Airport to Capitol Hill?" If not, "then probably the American Enterprise Institute should write it," he says with a chuckle.

"We want to see conservative scholarship have an impact on Washington," Mr. Berkowitz says. "People on college faculties write the books. We read, digest, synthesize, and adapt them to the real world as public policy."

In 1979, in keeping with its aggressive style, Heritage's leadership correctly assessed the chances a conservative Republican would have to be elected president in 1980. And the foundation was ready with a detailed, nitty-gritty, sleeves-rolled-up study of how to effect policy change in Washington. The report, "Mandate for Leadership"—all 1,093 pages of it, was published soon after Ronald Reagan entered the White House.

President Reagan has praised the foundation on several occasions, referring to it as "that feisty new kid on the conservative block" and crediting Heritage as a source of the ideas used in his administration's policy-making process. In the world of think tanks, such an endorsement is almost better than a blank check from the US Treasury.

The rise of Heritage to this level of influence has been nothing less than meteoric—especially considering that, unlike other think tanks, which employ senior policymakers and veteran strategists, its staff is almost totally composed of people under age 40. But access to power has in no way mellowed its brashness. Heritage gave the White House only a 62 percent "compliance rating" on major conservative issues at the end of Mr. Reagan's first 12 months in office.

Foundation president Edwin J. Fuelner Jr. received a "Dear Ed" letter from President Reagan saying that the criticism was well taken and that ". . . I am grateful for your dedication and am looking forward to working with you and the members of this team in pursuit of our common goals for a better America."

Heritage's financial fortunes have also risen sharply during the unabashedly patriotic Reagan years. Founded in 1973 with $250,000 from Colorado brewer Joseph Coors, Heritage could list revenues at a little more than $1 million by 1975. Money flowing into the coffers has gone up 40 percent a year since 1976, totaling $10 million in 1983. That year Heritage moved its headquarters from a suite of offices in a run-down, out-of-the-way building in northeastern Washington (it once housed a Korean grocery store and a halfway house for drug addicts) to a new, eight-story, $9.5 million office building on Capitol Hill.

In addition to its in-house staff, Heritage taps a network of conservatives at some 450 research groups, as well as about 1,100 scholars and public-policy experts in universities. It helps bring a number of these individuals to Washington to testify as expert witnesses at congressional and administrative agency hearings.

A former Heritage fellow, along with a scholar who was a contract researcher for Heritage, now work for the influential editorial page of the Wall Street Journal. And Adam Meyerson, formerly on the Journal's editorial board, now edits Heritage's Policy Review magazine.

The 35 resident scholars and 75 supporting staff take a free-market approach to domestic and economic policy studies. On foreign policy and defense, Heritage takes a strong pro-national-security position.

Moreover, Heritage, unlike such gloomy prognosticators as the Club of Rome, believes in a future that works. One of its more controversial studies predicts less crowding (despite continued population growth), less pollution, and fewer people living at the economic margin by the year 2000 than today.

In the area of civil rights, Heritage is strongly opposed to racial quotas. Its publication "Agenda for '83" seeks to redefine "discrimination." Position papers argue that the Justice Department should switch from civil rights lawsuits to prosecuting affirmative-action violations based on quotas. The think tank seems to have had an impact in this area, to judge from Reagan administration policies on this issue and the kind of suits filed recently by the Justice Department.

On the Mideast, Heritage is pro-Israel. In fact, an Israeli general is here as a visiting fellow. "No other think tank has someone like that on their staff," says Mr. Berkowitz. "We thought looking at the Middle East the way a military commander does would be helpful." Officers from the US military also serve as visiting fellows at Heritage, a practice also common at other think tanks.

One of Heritage's hardest-hitting publications, "A World Without the UN," characterizes the international organization as a forum for attacks on Western interests and democratic values and suggests that it makes world conflicts worse rather than helping to resolve them. The paper calls for US withdrawal from the organization unless broad changes are made. "Far from cooling passions," the study states of anti-Western rhetoric, "the techniques of name-calling and lying are intended to mobilize the Assembly on the side of the speaker, to discredit and isolate adversaries, and to cultivate climates of opinion inhospitable to rational argument."

If Walter Mondale is searching for the "beef" in Ronald Reagan's program for a second administration, the Heritage Foundation would be a good place to start. "Mandate for Leadership II," just as detailed and specific as its predecessor, is in the final stages now and will be released shortly after the November election.

## 21 COMMITTEES TO SECURE THE HIGH FRONTIER 1984

Several months ago, High Frontiersmen around the country began organizing support for SDI in their Congressional Districts by forming bipartisan committees to help keep their Senators and Congressmen on track on SDI.

Called the Committees to Secure the High Frontier, each organization is co-chaired by a Democrat, a Republican, and frequently, an Independent—and that is enough to start. Some chapters have named a coordinator and a legislative director, and several committees have even formed strategic advisory boards and engineering and science advisory boards comprised of local retired military personnel, engineers, scientists, and college professors.

Thus far, 42 Congressional Districts throughout the nation are organized and keeping close watch on their Washington representatives. They monitor votes and write letters of either approval or dismay, and urge Congressional support of early deployment of SDI. The committees will also periodically issue press releases detailing the SDI voting records of their Senators and Congressmen and write letters to local editors to make their sentiments known.

Louisiana's Sixth District was the first Committee formed. Districts in Alabama, Alaska, California, Florida, Georgia, Hawaii, Maryland, Tennessee, and Texas are organized and ready to go. Others in Arizona, Connecticut, Indiana, Kansas, Maine, Missouri, New Jersey, New York, Ohio, Oregon, Pennsylvania, South Carolina, Vermont, Virginia, and Wisconsin are well on their way.

The Committees' National Director will regularly send committee members news packets containing information on political and technological developments related to SDI and distribute other information of interest to committees around the country.

For more information about the Committee in your district; how to organize one; or volunteer to serve on an advisory board, call High Frontier at (202) 737-4979.

# Getting Involved

### *Documents 22 and 23*

There are a great many groups covering a wide range of perspectives that citizens who want to affect the future of the nuclear age can join. Documents 22 and 23 offer examples. Document 22 is taken from the 1986 edition of the *Peace Resource Book,* published annually by the Institute for Defense and Disarmament Studies. It lists a few of what the *Peace Resource Book* calls "national peace groups." Document 23 is taken from the 1986 edition of *The Washington Directory,* published by the Conservative Network. It lists a few national groups that are skeptical of arms control and believe the United States must build up its defenses.

## 22 NATIONAL PEACE GROUPS 1986

AMERICAN FRIENDS SERVICE COMMITTEE (AFSC)
Peace Education Division
1501 Cherry St.
Philadelphia, PA 19102 215/241-7000
Activist Group
Focus: Pacifism, Nonintervention
Founded: 1917 ML: 72,000
*Quaker Service Bulletin,* 3/yr, $5

Works for peace, justice, and equality. Worldwide programs are based on the conviction that there is that of God in every human being, and that nonviolent solutions can be found to problem situations.

COMMON CAUSE
Fred Wertheimer, President
2030 M St., NW
Washington, DC 20036 202/833-1200
Lobby Group
Focus: Arms Control
Founded: 1970 Mbr: 250,000 ML: 250,000
*Common Cause,* 6/yr, $20 ($30 family, $10 student)

Lobbies against private interest and for public accountability in government. Supports a bilateral nuclear-weapon freeze and opposes the MX.

GREENPEACE USA
2007 R St., NW
Washington, DC 20009 202/462-1177
Activist Group
Focus: Arms Control, Safe Environment
Founded: 1970 ML: 80,000
*Greenpeace Examiner Quarterly,* 4/yr, $.75

International environmental organization which uses nonviolent direct action to promote a more ecologically safe world. Addresses issues of whaling, toxic pollution, nuclear weapons testing, and offshore oil development.

NATIONAL NUCLEAR WEAPONS FREEZE CAMPAIGN
Jane Gruenebaum, Director
220 I St., Suite 130
Washington, DC 20002 202/544-0880
Activist Group
Focus: Disarmament
Founded: 1981
*Local Organizers Mailing,* 24/yr, $15

Works to support passage of bilateral nuclear-weapon freeze in Congress, to build diverse, broad based grass-roots movement, and to assist international efforts to halt the nuclear arms race and end military intervention.

PEACE LINKS: WOMEN AGAINST NUCLEAR WAR
Laurie Fulton, Director
747 8th St., SE
Washington, DC 20003 202/544-0805
Activist Group: Women
Focus: Disarmament
Founded: 1982 Mbr: 20,000 ML: 20,000
*Connection,* 4/yr, Free

Works through traditional community groups to foster women's awareness and participation in organizing to prevent nuclear war.

SANE: COMMITTEE FOR A SANE NUCLEAR POLICY
David Cortright, Director
711 G St., SE
Washington, DC 20029 202/546-7100
Activist Group
Focus: Disarmament
Founded: 1957 ML: 90,000
*Sane World,* 12/yr, $10
*Sane Action,* Irregular

Provides information and education on disarmament, arms control, and economic conversion. Lobbies Congress and monitors congressional action.

SIERRA CLUB DISARMAMENT COMMITTEE
Madge Strong, Co-chair
530 Bush St.
San Francisco, CA 94108 415/653-6148
Activist Group: Environmentalists
Focus: Safe Environment
Founded: 1892 ML: 350,000
*Sierra,* 6/yr, $2

Lobbies and educates on environmental issues, including wilderness protection, and air and water quality. Sponsors nature appreciation activities. Supports a nuclear weapons freeze.

UNITED CAMPUSES TO PREVENT NUCLEAR WAR (UCAM)
Sanford Gottlieb, Director
1346 Connecticut Ave., Suite 706
Washington, DC 20036 202/223-6206
Activist Group: Students-College, Educators
Focus: Arms Control
Founded: 1982 ML: 1500
*Network News,* 12/yr, $20 ($10 students)

Network of contacts at 600 colleges and universities involved in arms control, education, and action. Produces curriculum development materials and resources on US-USSR relations; government decision-making on nuclear war; and successful campus organizing techniques. Promotes courses on nuclear war and lobbies for issues.

## 23 GROUPS FOR DEFENSE BUILDUP 1986

AMERICAN DEFENSE FOUNDATION
P.O. Box 2497
Washington, DC 20013-2497 (202) 544-4704
Head(s) of Washington Office
Capt. Eugene McDaniel, Chairman
Dorthy McDaniel, Director
Number of Staff in Washington Office — 7
Has 35,000 members nationwide

Issue(s) of Interest and Respective Contacts
Key Issue — Defense budget
S.D.I.
Voter registration
Newsletters
A.D.F. newsletter
Frequency of Publication — Quarterly
Publications
Alerts
Defense Alerts
Description of Organization
The American Defense Foundation tries to increase public awareness, as well as that of congressional leaders, in the need for increased National Defense.

AMERICAN DEFENSE LOBBY
7015 Old Keene Mill Road, #203
Springfield, VA 22150 (703) 866-0344
Head(s) of Washington Office
Michael W. Thompson, Chairman
Chadwick R. Gore, Executive Director
Number of Staff in Washington Office — 6
Has 25,000 members nationwide
Issue(s) of Interest and Respective Contacts
Key Issue — Full Funding of S.D.I
Defense Budget in General — Chadwick Gore
Grace Commission — Chadwick Gore
Packard Commission — Chadwick Gore
Freedom Fighters — Chadwick Gore
Newsletters
Defense Issues, Editor — Richard Mesmer
Frequency of Publication — Bi-Monthly
Seminars — Informational
"Staff Defense Forum," Contact — Office
Description of Organization
Anti-Communist pro-defense grass roots lobby committed to Peace Through Strength. Generated public pressure through Radio/TV program on specific legislative initiatives.

AMERICAN SECURITY COUNCIL
499 S. Capitol Street, SE #500
Washington, DC 20003 (202) 484-1676
Head(s) of Washington Office
John M. Fisher, President
Greg Hilton, Director
Number of Staff in Washington Office — 12
Has 260,000 members nationwide
Issue(s) of Interest and Respective Contacts
Key Issue — President Reagan's Defense and Foreign Policy Agenda
Defense Budget & U.S. Soviet Strategic Balance — Gregg Hilton
Soviet Union & Eastern Europe — Thomas B. Smith
Central America — Col. Samuel T. Dickens
African Affairs — John Blumer
Conventional Weapons — Bob Hanrahan
Newsletters
Peace Through Strength Report, Editor — Greg Hilton
Frequency of Publication — Monthly
Publications
Various studies on defense and foreign policy
Description of Organization
A pro-defense citizens lobby established in 1955. ASC serves as the Legislative Coordinator of the bi-partisan Coalition for Peace Through Strength. ASC is dedicated to a strong American defense and sound pro-American foreign policy.

AMERICANS FOR A SOUND FOREIGN POLICY
418 C Street, NE
Washington, DC 20070-0287 (202) 546-3224
Head(s) of Washington Office
Phillip Abbott Luce, Chairman
Number of Staff in Washington Office — 1
Has 10,000 members nationwide
Issue(s) of Interest and Respective Contacts
Key Issue — Salt
Foreign Policy
S.D.I.
Contra Aid
Newsletters
Frontline, Editor — Phillip Abbott Luce
Frequency of Publication — Quarterly
Publications
Specials on various issues
Description of Organization
A Mainstream Conservative group with a large number of volunteer advisors with a great deal of flexibility to mobilize on issues.

CONSERVATIVE ACTION FOUNDATION
1326 G Street, SE
Washington, DC 20003 (202) 547-0200
Head(s) of Washington Office
Lee Bellinger, President
Jeff Pandin, Executive Director
Number of Staff in Washington Office — 8
Has 4,000 members nationwide
Issue(s) of Interest and Respective Contacts
Key Issue — Reducing trade between the U.S. and the Soviets
Human Rights
Support Democratization of World
U.S. Campaign Academy
Foreign Policy
Newsletters
Frontline, Editor — John Scanlon
Frequency of Publication — Bi-monthly

Publications
Manuscripts
Policy Monitor's
Seminars — U.S. Campaign Academy
Educating potential candidates, Contact — John Scanlon
Description of Organization

C.A.F., formed in 1983, is an activist oriented conservative organization focusing on matters of foreign policy, activist tactics drawing public attention on foreign policy of U.S., and human freedom worldwide.

U.S. DEFENSE COMMITTEE
3238 Wynford Dr.
Fairfax, VA 22031 (703) 281-5517

Head(s) of Washington Office
Huck Walther, President
Number of Staff in Washington Office — 15
Has 143,000 members nationwide
Issue(s) of Interest and Respective Contacts
Key Issue — SDI–Central America–UN
All defense and foreign policy
Export Administration
Foreign aid
Newsletters
Defense Watch, Editor — Michael I. Rothfeld
Frequency of Publication — 6 per year
Description of Organization

The United States Defense Committee lobbies on behalf of a strong national defense and foreign policy.

## Suggestions for Further Reading

Cromelin, Quentin, Jr., and David S. Sullivan. *Soviet Military Supremacy: The Untold Facts About the New Danger to America* (Washington, DC: Citizen's Foundation, 1985). As its title implies, this book provides a good example of the peace through strength perspective.

Harvard Nuclear Study Group, *Living with Nuclear Weapons* (New York: Bantam Books, 1983). A widely read introduction to the nuclear age. For the most part, it presents a competition and cooperation perspective.

Joseph, Paul, and Simon Rosenblum, eds. *Search for Sanity: The Politics of Nuclear Weapons and Disarmament* (Boston: South End Press, 1984). Peace researchers and activists present their views on the history of the nuclear arms race, the likelihood of nuclear war, and strategies for disarmament.

McNamara, Robert, *Blundering into Disaster — Surviving the First Century of the Nuclear Age* (New York: Pantheon, 1986). A concise statement of reducing the nuclear danger perspective.

Public Agenda Foundation, *The Superpower — Nuclear Weapons and National Security* (Dayton, OH: Domestic Policy Association, 1987). A discussion of four perspectives on superpower relations and nuclear weapons. The perspectives differ somewhat from the ones presented in this course.

Sharp, Gene. *Making Europe Unconquerable: The Potential of Civilian-Based Deterrence and Defense* (Philadelphia: Taylor and Francis, 1985). A proposal to defend Europe through civilian resistance instead of relying on nuclear weapons.

# CREDITS AND PERMISSIONS

### Chapter 1 Dawn

1. Joseph E. Davies, *Mission to Moscow.* Copyright © 1941 by Joseph E. Davies, copyright renewed 1969 by Eleanor Davies Dtizen, Rahel Davies Broun, and Emlen Davies Grosjean. Reprinted by permission of Simon & Schuster.

2. Copyright © 1943 by Time, Inc. Reprinted by permission from *Life,* Mar. 29, 1943, vol. 14, no. 13, p. 18.

3. Reprinted from *Vital Speeches of the Day,* vol. 9, no. 3.

4. From George F. Kennan, *Memoirs, 1925–1950.* Copyright © 1967 by George F. Kennan; reprinted by permission of Little, Brown & Company in association with The Atlantic Monthly Press.

5. Reprinted from *Witness to History,* 1929–1969 by Charles E. Bohlen, by permission of W. W. Norton and Co., Inc., Copyright © 1973 by W. W. Norton and Co., Inc.

6. Franklin D. Roosevelt, "Address to Congress on the Crimean Conference," Washington, DC, Mar. 1, 1945.

7. From Spencer R. Weant and Gertrude Szilard, eds., *Leo Szilard: His Version of the Facts* (Cambridge, MA: MIT Press, 1978).

8. Manhattan Engineer District Records, Top Secret of Special Interest to General Groves files, folder no. 4, Trinity Test, National Archives.

9. Alice Kimball Smith, *A Peril and a Hope.* Copyright © 1965 (Chicago: U of Chicago P).

10. Copyright ©1945 by The New York Times Company. Reprinted by permission.

11. John Hersey, *Hiroshima* (New York: Knopf, 1946).

12. Reprinted by permission from *The New Republic.* Copyright © 1981 by The New Republic, Inc.

13. U.S. Strategic Bombing Survey, *Japan's Struggle to End the War,* Washington, DC (1946).

14. From *Strategies of Containment: A Critical Appraisal of Postwar American National Security Policy* by John Lewis Gaddis. Copyright © 1982 by Oxford University Press, Inc. Reprinted by permission.

15. Richard Smoke, *National Security and the Nuclear Dilemma* (New York: Knopf, 1984).

16. Harry S Truman, *Memoirs,* vol. 1, *Year of Decision* (New York: Doubleday, 1956). Used by permission of Margaret Truman Daniel.

17. *Foreign Relations of the United States, 1945,* vol. 2 (Washington, DC, 1971).

18. From B.J. Bernstein and A.J. Matuson, eds., *The Truman Administration: A Documentary History* (New York: Harper & Row, 1966), pp. 215–219.

19. U.S. Department of State, *Documents on Disarmament: 1945–1959,* vol. 1, 1945–1956 (Washington, DC: U.S. Government Printing Office, 1960).

20. Reprinted with permission from the *Bulletin of the Atomic Scientists,* a magazine of science and world affairs. Copyright © 1946 by the Educational Foundation for Nuclear Science.

### Chapter 2 The Weapon of Choice

1. Harry S Truman, "The Truman Doctrine Speech," Mar. 12, 1947.

2. *Department of State Bulletin,* vol. 14, no. 415 (June 15, 1947).

3. U. N. General Assembly, *Official Records,* Plenary Meetings, Verbatim Record (Sept. 18, 1947).

4. Reprinted with permission from *Foreign Affairs* (July 1947).

5. Myron Rush, ed., Professor of Government, Cornell University, *The International Situation and Soviet Foreign Policy: Reports of Soviet Leaders.* Copyright © 1970.

6. Secretary of State Dean Acheson, "The Meaning of the North Atlantic Pact," Mar. 18, 1949.

7. "Memorandum of the Soviet Government on the North Atlantic Treaty," Mar. 31, 1949, printed in *The Foreign Policy of the Soviet Union.*

8. Richard Smoke, *National Security and the Nuclear Dilemma* (New York: A. Knopf, 1984).

9. Reprinted by permission of New York University Press from *The Truman Administration: its Principles and Practice,* Louis W. Koenig, ed. Copyright © 1956 by New York University.

10. *Foreign Relations of the United States: 1949,* vol. 2, Washington, DC.

11. *Foreign Relations of the United States: 1950,* vol. 1, Washington, DC.

12. *Foreign Relations of the United States: 1949,* vol. 2, Washington, DC.

13. From Herbert F. York, "The Debate Over the Hydrogen Bomb." Copyright © 1975 by Scientific American, Inc. All rights reserved.

14. R.C. Williams and P.L. Cantelon, eds., *The American Atom: Documentary History of Nuclear Policies from the Discovery of Fission to The Present: 1939–1984* (New York: Doubleday, 1984).

15. *Public Papers of the President, Harry S Truman, 1950* (Washington, DC: U.S. Government Printing Office, 1965).

16. *United States Policy in the Korean Crisis* (Washington, DC: Department of State, 1950).

17. Reprinted from B.J. Bernstein & A. Matuso, eds., *The Truman Administration: A Documentary History* (New York: Harper & Row, 1966).

18. Harry S Truman, "Speech to the Nation," Radio address, Apr. 10, 1951.

19. Reprinted from *The Saturday Evening Post.* Copyright © 1950 by The Curtis Publishing Co.

20. From *The Wilson Quarterly* (Summer 1978). Copyright © 1978 by The Woodrow Wilson International Center for Scholars.

### Chapter 3 A Bigger Bang for the Buck

1. From Louis J. Halle, *The Cold War as History,* pp. 276–282. Copyright © 1967 by Louis J. Halle. Reprinted by permission of Harper & Row, Publishers, Inc.

2. *Department of State Bulletin,* vol. 30, no. 761 (Jan. 25, 1954).

3. CJCS 381, Sept. 11, 1954, Washington, DC.

4. From Howard L. Rosenberg, *Atomic Soldiers* (Boston: Beacon Press, 1980).

5. Reprinted with permission from the *Bulletin of the Atomic Sciences,* a magazine of science and world affairs, Copy-

right © 1955 by the Educational Foundation for Nuclear Science.

6. *Nuclear Arms Control: Background and Issues,* Copyright © 1985 by the National Academy of Sciences.

7. Jerome H. Kahan, *Security in the Nuclear Age,* (Washington, DC: The Brookings Institution, 1975).

8. Reprinted by permission from *Air Force* magazine. Copyright © 1957 by the Air Force Association.

9. "The Gaither Report," Nov. 7, 1957, Security Resources Panel of the Science Advisory Committee.

10. Copyright © 1960 by The New York Times Company. Reprinted by permission.

11. Copyright © 1960 by The New York Times Company. Reprinted by permission.

12. *Congressional Record,* 86th Cong., 2nd Sess., 1960, CVI, pt. 3.

13. "Question and Answer Period Conducted by General LeMay," March 1957; declassified top-secret document.

14. Charles J. V. Murphy, *Fortune.* Copyright © 1959 by Time Inc. All rights reserved.

15. From David Alan Rosenberg, *International Security* (Spring 1983) vol. 7, no. 4. Copyright © 1983. Reprinted by permission of the author.

16. *The Public Papers of the Presidents: 1960–61,* Washington, DC, 1961.

17. Herbert York, *Race to Oblivion,* (New York: Simon & Schuster, 1970).

### Chapter 4 Europe Goes Nuclear

1. From Louis J. Halle, *The Cold War as History,* pp. 184–186. Copyright © 1967 by Louis J. Halle. Reprinted by permission of Harper & Row, Publishers, Inc.

2. From *Strategies of Containment: A Critical Appraisal of Postwar American National Security Policy* by John Lewis Gaddis. Copyright © 1982 by Oxford University Press, Inc. Reprinted by permission.

3. John Foster Dulles, "Statement by the Secretary of State to the North American Council Closed Ministerial Session, Paris," Apr. 23, 1954.

4. "Letter from Prime Minister Eden to President Eisenhower," July 18, 1956, Eisenhower Library, Whitman File, International File. Secret; personal.

5. "The Revolt of Common Sense," *The New Statesman,* (editorial) May 10, 1958.

6. *Manifesto der Kampf dem Atomtod,* reprinted in James L. Richardson, *Germany and the Atlantic Alliance* (Cambridge, MA: Harvard UP, 1966).

7. Reprinted from Margaret Gowing, ed., *Independence and Deterrence: Britain and Atomic Energy, 1945–1952,* vol 1, (London: Macmillan, 1974).

8. From "Science and the Citizen: Britain's Bomb" and "British Bomb." Copyright © 1952 by Scientific American, Inc. All rights reserved.

9. Lawrence Freedman, *The Evolution of Nuclear Strategy.* U.S. and Canadian copyrights © 1983 by Lawrence Freedman. (New York: St. Martin's Press, 1983) and (London: Macmillan London Ltd.).

10. Reprinted from *Orbis,* a journal of world affairs, published by the Foreign Policy Research Institute, Philadelphia, PA.

11. *Documents on Disarmament, 1964,* Washington, DC.

12. Translated and reprinted in *Survival* (February 1968).

13. Secretary of State Dean Acheson, "German Rearmament and Problems of the Defense of Europe," Internal Memorandum (July 6, 1951).

14. U.S. Senate, Foreign Relations Committee Documents on Germany, 1944–1970, 92nd Cong. 1st Sess. (May 1971).

15. Reprinted with permission from *New Times,* no. 21 (Moscow: TRUD, 1955).

16. *Statement on Nuclear Defense Systems,* Dec. 21, 1962 (Washington, DC: U.S. Government Printing Office).

17. *Speeches and Press Conferences,* no. 185, Jan. 14, 1963, (New York: *French Embassy Press and Information Service).*

18. From Marsha McGraw Olive and Jeffrey D. Porro eds., *Nuclear Weapons in Europe* (Lexington, MA.: Lexington Books, D.C. Heath), copyright © 1983 by D.C. Heath and Company. Reprinted by permission of the publisher.

### Chapter 5 At the Brink

1. *Department of State Bulletin,* Oct. 1, 1962.

2. Reprinted from *U.S. News & World Report* (Sept. 10, 1962). Copyright © 1962.

3. From Strobe Talbott, trans. and ed., *Khrushchev Remembers.* Copyright © 1970 by Little, Brown and Company.

4. *Thirteen Days: A Memoir of the Cuban Missile Crisis* by Robert F. Kennedy, by permission of W. W. Norton and Co., Inc. Copyright © 1968 by McCall Corporation.

5. *Public Papers of the Presidents, John F. Kennedy, 1962,* Washington, DC.

6. Reprinted from *U.S. New & World Report* (Nov. 5, 1962). Copyright © 1962.

7. Copyright © 1962 by The New York Times Company. Reprinted by permission.

8. Translation copyright © 1963 by The Current Digest of the Soviet Press, Columbus, Ohio. Reprinted by permission of the Digest.

9. Copyright © 1962 by The New York Times Company. Reprinted by permission.

10. *Department of State Bulletin* (Nov. 12, 1962).

11. *Public Papers of the Presidents, John F. Kennedy, 1962,* Washington, DC.

12. *Department of State Bulletin* (Nov. 12, 1962).

13. *Ibid.*

14. *Thirteen Days: A Memoir of the Cuban Missile Crisis* by Robert F. Kennedy, by permission of W. W. Norton and Co., Inc. Copyright © 1968 by McCall Corporation.

15. From Strobe Talbott, trans. and ed., *Khrushchev Remembers.* Copyright © 1970 by Little, Brown and Company.

16. *Arms Control and Disarmament Agreements* (Washington, DC.: U.S. Government Printing Office).

17. *Nuclear Arms Control: Background and Issues,* Copyright © 1985 by the National Academy of Sciences.

18. Reprinted by permission from *Time.* Copyright © 1982 by Time Inc. All rights reserved.

19. *Thirteen Days: A Memoir of the Cuban Missile Crisis* by Robert F. Kennedy, by permission of W. W. Norton and Co., Inc. Copyright © 1968 by McCall Corporation.

### Chapter 6 The Education of Robert McNamara

1. Reprinted with permission from *Foreign Affairs,* (January 1959). Copyright © 1959 by the Council on Foreign Relations, Inc.

2. *Public Papers of the President, John F. Kennedy, 1961,* no. 99.

3. Reprinted by permission from *Time.* Copyright © 1962 by Time Inc. All rights reserved.

4. Richard Smoke, *National Security and the Nuclear Dilemma* (New York: Knopf, 1984).

5. Jerome H. Kahan, *Security in the Nuclear Age* (Washington, DC.: The Brookings Institution, 1975).

6. Reprinted from *U.S. News & World Report* (Sept. 3, 1962). Copyright © 1986.

7. Reprinted with permission from *Life* (Sept. 15, 1961), vol. 15, no. 11. Copyright © 1961 by Time Inc.

8. William W. Kaufmann, *The McNamara Strategy* (New York: Harper & Row, 1964).

9. Reprinted from *Vital Speeches of the Day,* vol. 28.

10. V.D. Sokolovskiy, *Soviet Military Strategy,* trans. and ed. Harriet Fast Scott (Arlington, VA: SRI International).

11. Reprinted from *The Saturday Evening Post.* Copyright © 1962 by The Curtis Publishing Co.

12. From Robert S. McNamara, *The Essence of Security: Reflections in Office,* pp. 51–55. Copyright © 1968 by Robert S. McNamara. Reprinted by permission of Harper & Row, Publishers, Inc.

13. Ashton B. Carter and David N. Schwartz, *Ballistic Missile Defense* (Washington, DC: The Brookings Institution, 1984).

14. Reprinted from *Vital Speeches of the Day,* vol. 33, no. 24.

15. Reprinted from *International Affairs,* vol. 10, no. 10, Moscow, October 1964).

16. Richard L. Garwin and Hans Bethe, "Anti-Ballistic-Missile Systems." Copyright © March 1968 by Scientific American, Inc. All rights reserved.

17. Reprinted with permission from *Foreign Affairs* (April 1969). Copyright © 1969 by the Council on Foreign Relations, Inc.

### Chapter 7 One Step Forward . . .

1. Thomas C. Schelling and Morton H. Halperin, *Strategy and Arms Control* (Washington, DC: Pergamon-Brassey's Classic, 1985).

2. Reprinted with permission from Donald M. Snow, *National Security: Enduring Problems of U.S. Defense Policy.* Copyright © 1987 by St. Martin's Press, Inc.

3. *Strategies of Containment: A Critical Appraisal of Postwar American National Security Policy* by John Lewis Gaddis. Copyright © 1982 by Oxford University Press, Inc. Reprinted by permission.

4. Copyright © 1972 by The New York Times Company. Reprinted by permission.

5. From ed. and intros., Alvin Z. Rubinstein, *The Foreign Policy of the Soviet Union,* 3rd ed. (New York: Random House, 1972).

6. From *Selected Speeches and Writings on Foreign Affairs* (Oxford, England, and Elmsford, NY: Pergamon Press), pp. 32–33.

7. Copyright © 1973 by John Newhouse.

8. Copyright © 1968 by *The New Yorker.* Reprinted by permission.

9. Ashton B. Carter and David N. Schwartz, *Ballistic Missile Defense* (Washington, DC: The Brookings Institution, 1984).

10. "Military Implications of the Treaty on the Limitations of Anti-Ballistic Missile Systems and the Interim Agreement on Limitation of Strategic Offensive Arms," 92nd Cong., 2nd Sess., 1972 (Washington, DC: U.S. Government Printing Office).

11. *Congressional Action,* Public Law, 92–448, Washington, DC.

12. *Congressional Record,* 92nd Cong., 2nd Sess. (1972), vol. 118, no. 130, pp. S13467–S13469, and vol. 118, no. 138, pp. S14280–S14283.

13. © 1972 by National Review, Inc., 150 East 35th Street, New York, NY 10016. Reprinted with permission.

14. From Joseph S. Nye, Jr., ed., *The Making of America's Soviet Policy,* (New Haven, CT: Yale UP, 1984).

15. Gerard Smith, *Doubletalk* (New York: Doubleday, 1980).

16. Bernard T. Feld, "Looking at SALT II." Reprinted with permission from the *Bulletin of the Atomic Scientists.* Copyright © 1972 by the Educational Foundation for Nuclear Science.

17. Reprinted from *International Security* (Fall 1979), vol. 4, no. 2, by permission of The MIT Press. Copyright © by the President and Fellows of Harvard College.

### Chapter 8 Haves and Have-Nots

1. Leonard S. Spector, *The New Nuclear Nations* (New York: Vintage, Random House, 1985).

2. Department of State Publication no. 5314 (Washington, DC. U.S. Government Printing Office, 1953).

3. *Public Papers of the President* (Washington, DC: U.S. Government Printing Office, 1977).

4 Reprinted from "Nuclear Proliferation and World Politics," by Lewis Q. Dunn, in Volume 430 of THE ANNALS of The American Academy of Political and Social Science.

5. *Nuclear Arms Control: Background and Issues.* Copyright © 1985 by the National Academy of Sciences.

6. *Documents on Disarmament* (Washington, DC: U.S. Government Printing Office, 1967).

7. *Documents on Disarmament* (Washington, DC: U.S. Government Printing Office, 1967).

8 *Preventing Nuclear Weapons Proliferation* (Stockholm: Stockholm International Peace Research Institute).

9. *Documents of Disarmament* (Washington, DC: U.S. Government Printing Office, 1968).

10. From Leonard S. Spector, *Going Nuclear: The spread of Nuclear Weapons 1986–1987.* Copyright 1987 by Carnegie Endowment for International Peace. Reprinted with permission from Ballinger Publishing Company.

11. Reprinted with permission from the *Bulletin of the Atomic Scientists.* Copyright © 1987 by the Educational Foundation for Nuclear Science. *Who's Next,* Copyright © 1965 by Tom Lehrer. Used by permission.

12. *Documents on Disarmament 1964* (Washington, DC: U.S. Government Printing Office, 1964).

13. *Documents of Disarmament 1967* (Washington, DC: U.S. Government Printing Office, 1967).

14. *Ibid.*

15. *Documents of Disarmament 1974* (Washington, DC: U.S. Government Printing office, 1974).

16. Reprinted with permission from United Media.

17. Reprinted with permission from *Time.* Copyright © 1976 by Time Inc. All rights reserved.

18. From Leonard S. Spector, *Going Nuclear: The Spread of Nuclear Weapons 1986–1987.* Copyright © 1987 by Carnegie Endowment for International Peace. Reprinted with permission from Ballinger Publishing Company.

### Chapter 9 Carter's New World

1. From *Strategies of Containment: A Critical Appraisal of Postwar American National Security Policy* by John Lewis Gaddis. Copyright © 1982 by Oxford University Press, Inc. Reprinted by permission.

2. David Holloway, *The Soviet Union and the Arms Race,* (New Haven, CT: Yale UP, 1983). Copyright © 1983 by The Yale University Press.

3. Richard Smoke, *National Security and the Nuclear Dilemma* (New York: Knopf, 1984).

4. *Public Papers of the President: Jimmy Carter,* Book 1, (Washington, DC, 1977).

5. Dennis Ross, "The Ideas of March: Incremental vs. Comprehensive SALT," *Arms Control Today* (May 1979). Copyright 1979 by The Arms Control Association.

6. Reprinted with permission from *SALT Hand Book: Key Documents and Issues, 1972–1979,* published by the American Enterprise Institute for Public Policy Research.

7. Copyright © 1978 by The New York Times Company. Reprinted by permission.

8. Richard Pipes, "Why the Soviet Union Thinks it Could Fight and Win a Nuclear War," *Commentary,* (July 1977).

9. Raymond C. Garthoff, *Detente and Confrontation* (Washington, DC: The Brookings Institution, 1985).

10. Reprinted with permission from *SALT Hand Book: Key Documents and Issues 1972–1979,* published by the American Enterprise Institute for Public Policy Research.

11. From Franqis Sauzey, ed., *Trialogue* (Fall 1978), no. 19, published by the Trilateral Commission.

12. Courtesy *Aviation Week and Space Technology.* Copyright © 1979 McGraw-Hill, Inc. All rights reserved.

13. Reprinted from the March 12, 1979 issue of *Business Week* by special permission. Copyright © 1979 by McGraw-Hill Inc.

14. Copyright © 1979 by The New York Times Company. Reprinted by permission.

15. U.S. Department of State, *Current Policy,* no. 72 A, Senate Testimony (Washington, DC: U.S. Government Printing Office, 1972).

16. *Ibid.*

17. Copyright © 1978 by The Progressive, Inc. Reprinted by permission from *The Progressive,* Madison, WI 57303.

18. Reprinted by permission of *The Wall Street Journal,* © Dow Jones & Company, Inc., 1979. All rights reserved.

19. *The SALT II Treaty,* "Hearings before the Committee on Foreign Relations," U.S. Senate, First Session on Example Y, 96–1, pt. 1.

20. Reprinted with permission from the *Bulletin of the Atomic Scientists.* Copyright © 1979 by the Educational Foundation for Nuclear Science.

## Chapter 10 Zero Hour

1. Reprinted from *International Security* (Summer 1979), vol. 4, no. 11, by permission of The MIT Press. Copyright © by the President and Fellows of Harvard College.

2. From *Survival* (November/December 1979). Published by the International Institute for Strategic Studies, London.

3. McGeorge Bundy, "The Future of Strategic Defense," *Survival* (November/December, 1979). Published by the International Institute for Strategic Studies, London.

4. Leon V. Sigal, *Nuclear Forces in Europe: Enduring Dilemmas, Present Prospects* (Washington, DC: The Brookings Institution, 1984).

5. Gregory Treverton, "Nuclear Weapons in Europe," *Adelphi Paper* (1981) no. 168. Published by the International Institute for Strategic Studies, London.

6. Reprinted from *Survival* (January/February 1978). vol. 20, no. 1. Published by the Institute of Strategic Studies.

7. "Communiqué Issued at a Special Meeting of the NATO Foreign and Defense Ministers in Brussels on December 12, 1979" (Washington, DC: U.S. Government Printing Office, 1979).

8. "The Modernization of NATO's Long-Range Theater Nuclear Forces," House Committee on Foreign Affairs, 96th Cong., 2nd Sess., Dec. 31, 1980 (Washington, DC: U.S. Government Printing Office, 1981).

9. From Malvern Lumsden, "Nuclear weapons and the new peace movement," *SIPRI Yearbook.* (1983).

10. Reprinted from Robert Schuil, *The Times* of London, (Nov. 23, 1981).

11. Copyright © 1983 by The New York Times Company. Reprinted by permission.

12. Reprinted from *Survival* (November/December 1979). Published by the Institute of Strategic Studies, London.

13. David Holloway, *The Soviet Union and the Arms Race* (New Haven, CT: Yale UP, 1983). Copyright © 1983 by The Yale University Press.

14. Reprinted from *Vital Speeches of the Day,* vol. 48, no. 4

15. *Nuclear Arms Control,* Study by the National Academy of Sciences (Washington, DC: National Academy Press, 1985).

16. Raymond L. Garthoff, "The Gorbachev Proposal and Prospects for Arms Control," *Arms Control Today* (January/February 1986). Copyright 1986 by The Arms Control Association.

17. Copyright © 1987 by The New York Times Company. Reprinted by permission.

## Chapter 11 Missile Experimental

1. Annual Defense Department Report, FY 1976 and FY 1977 (Washington, DC: U.S. Government Printing Office).

2. Office of Technology Assessment (Washington, DC: U.S. Government Printing Office, May 1980).

3. From *The Use of Force* (Lanham, MD: University Press of America).

4. Reprinted from *Survival* (March/April 1980), Institute of Strategic Studies, London.

5. Report of the Secretary of Defense to the Congress on the FY 1982 Budget, FY 1983 Authorization Request and FY 1982–1986, Jan. 19, 1981 (Washington, DC: U.S. Government Printing Office, 1981).

6. Office of Technology Assessment (Washington, DC: U.S. Government Printing Office, May 1980).

7. From Strobe Talbott, *Endgame: The Inside Story of SALT II,* pp. 180–181. Copyright © 1979 by Strobe Talbott. Reprinted by permission of Harper & Row, Publishers, Inc.

8. Dennis A. Williams et al., "MX Spells Trouble Out West," *Newsweek* (Feb. 11, 1980).

9. Copyright © 1981 by The New York Times Company. Reprinted by permission.

10. Reprinted from *Vital Speeches of the Day* (Dec. 15, 1982) vol. 49, no. 5.

11. Reprinted with permission from *Time.* Copyright © 1983 by Time Inc. All rights reserved.

12. Reprinted by permission of *The New Republic,* © 1982 by The New Republic, Inc.

13. "Report of the President's Commission on Strategic Forces," Brent Scowcroft, Chairman, Apr. 6, 1983 (Washington, DC: U.S. Government Printing Office, 1983).

14. Reprinted by permission of the publisher, from *American Defense Annual 1986–1987,* Joseph Kruzel, ed. (Lexington, MA: Lexington Books, D.C. Heath), Copyright © 1986 by D.C. Heath and Company.

15. Reprinted by courtesy of *Aviation Week and Space Technology.* Copyright © 1987 by McGraw-Hill, Inc. All rights reserved.

16. Reprinted by permission of Les Aspin, "Why we need a Small Missile," *Issues in Science and Technology* (Summer 1986) vol. 2, no. 4. Copyright © 1986 by the National Academy of Sciences, Washington, DC.

17. Reprinted by permission of Pete Wilson, "Midgetman: Small at any cost," *Issues in Science and Technology* (Summer 1986). vol. 2, no. 4. Copyright © 1986 by the National Academy of Sciences, Washington, DC.

18. John C. Baker and Joel S. Wit, "Mobile Missiles and Arms Control," *Arms Control Today,* 1985. Copyright © 1985 by The Arms Control Association.

19. Scott L. Berg, "Midgetman: The Technical Problems," *Arms Control Today* (November/December 1985). Copyright © 1985 by The Arms Control Association.

## Chapter 12 Reagan's Shield

1. Copyright © 1979 by *U.S. News & World Report.*

2. Report issued Oct. 5, 1978 (Washington, DC.: The Committee on the Present Danger).

3. Hearings Before the Senate Committee on Foreign Relations, 97th Cong., 1st Sess., pt. 1, Nov. 3, 4, and 9, 1981 (Washington, DC.: U.S. Government Printing Office)

4. Reprinted from *Vital Speeches of the Day,* vol. 49, no. 9.

5. *Soviet Military Power, 1985,* 4th ed., (April 1985), U.S. Department of Defense, Washington, DC.

6. Reprinted from *Insight* (Mar. 9, 1987), vol. 3, no. 10.

7. *Whence the Threat to Peace,* U.S.S.R. Ministry of Defense (Moscow: Military Publishing House, 1982), pp. 3–4, 72–76.

8. Reprinted from *Vital Speeches of the Day,* (Apr. 15, 1983).

9. Permission granted by Gerald Yonas, Titan Technologies.

10. Reprinted with permission from George A. Keyworth III, "The Case for Strategic Defense: An Option for a World Disarmed," *Issues in Science and Technology,* vol. 1, no. 1. Copyright © 1984 by the National Academy of Sciences, Washington, DC.

11. *Department of State Bulletin* (Washington, DC.: U.S. Government Printing Office, 1985).

12. Hans A. Bethe and Fred Zathariasen, in *Science Digest* (September 1983).

13. Reprinted with permission from Sidney D. Drell and Wolfgang K. H. Panofsky, "The Case Against Strategic Defense: Technical and Strategic Realities", *Issues in Science and Technology,* vol. 1, no. 1. Copyright © 1984 by the National Academy of Sciences, Washington, DC.

14. *Congressional Quarterly* (Feb. 14, 1987), Washington, DC.

15. Office of Technology Assessment, *Strategic Defenses: Ballistic Missile Defense Technologies, Anti-Satellite Weapons, Countermeasures, and Arms Control.* Copyright © 1986 by Princeton University Press.

16. *Ibid.*

17. Strobe Talbott, *Deadly Gambits* (New York: Knopf, 1984).

18. Johathan Schell, *The Fate of the Earth* (New York: Knopf, 1984).

19. Reprinted from *Vital Speeches of the Day,* vol. 48, no. 16.

20. Committee on International Security and Arms Control, *...uclear Arms Control: Background and Issues* (Washington, ... National Academy Press, 1985).

... *Department of State Bulletin* (February 1986), Washing-...

...rinted by permission of *Time.* Copyright © 1986 by ... rights reserved.

...d from *Vital Speeches of the Day,* vol. 53, no. 2.

...endelbaum and Strobe Talbott, "Reykjavik ... *Affairs* (Winter 1986/1987). Reprinted by permission of *Foreign Affairs.* Copyright © 1986 by the Council on Foreign Relations, Inc.

## Chapter 13 Visions of War and Peace

1. From *National Security: Enduring Problems of U.S. Defense Policy* by Donald M. Snow. Copyright © 1987 by St. Martin's Press, Inc. Used with publisher's permission.

2. Richard Smoke, *National Security and the Nuclear Dilemma* (New York: Knopf, 1984).

3. David Holloway, *The Soviet Union and the Arms Race* (New Haven, CT: Yale UP, 1983). Copyright © by The Yale University Press.

4. Joseph S. Nye, Jr., ed., *The Making of America's Soviet Policy* (New Haven, CT: Yale UP, 1984).

5. From Freeman J. Dyson, *Weapons and Hope,* pp. 3–9. Reprinted by permission of Harper & Row, Publishers, Inc.

6. From James E. Dougherty, *Ethics, Deterrence, and National Security* (Oxford: Pergamon Press, Ltd., 1985).

7. Reprinted from *Arms Control: Myth Versus Reality,* Richard F. Starr, ed., with permission of Hoover Institution Press. Copyright © 1984 by the Board of Trustees of the Leland Stanford Jr. University.

8. "A Strategy for Peace Through Strength" by the American Security Council Foundation.

9. Harold Brown, *Thinking About National Security* (Boulder, CO: Westview Press, 1982).

10. Richard Burt, ed. *Arms Control and Defense Postures in the 1980s* (Boulder, CO: Westview Press, 1982).

11. *An Agenda for Avoiding Nuclear War,* by Graham T. Allison, Albert Carnesale, and Joseph S. Nye, Jr., Editors by permission of W. W. Norton and Co. Inc., Copyright © 1985, by Graham T. Allison, Albert Carnesale, and Joseph S. Nye.

12. Excerpts from "The Challenge of Peace: God's Promise and Our Response," copyright © 1983 by the United States Catholic Conference, Washington, DC. Used with permission.

13. Randall Forsberg, "A Bilateral Nuclear Weapons Freeze." Copyright © 1982 by Scientific American, Inc. All rights reserved.

14. George F. Kennan, "A Modest Proposal," ed., Bruce Weston, *Toward Nuclear Disarmament and Global Security: A Search for Alternatives* (Boulder, CO: Westview Press, 1984).

15. From Dr. Helen Caldicott, *Missile Envy: The Arms Race and Nuclear War,* pp. 298–313. Copyright © 1984 by Helen Caldicott. By permission of William Morrow and Company.

16. From *Nuclear Winter,* reprinted with permission from Basil Blackwell Ltd., Oxford, England.

17. Bruce Weston, ed., *Toward Nuclear Disarmament and Global Security: A Search for Alternatives* (Boulder, CO: Westview Press, 1984).

18. *Ibid.*

19. Copyright © 1982 by The New York Times Company. Reprinted by permission.

20. Jim Bencivenga, "Young, brash, and conservative," Reprinted by permission from *The Christian Science Monitor* © 1984 by The Christian Science Publishing Society. All rights reserved.

21. *High Frontier Newsletter,* vol. 4, no. 10, publisher Lt. Gen. Daniel O. Graham (USA-Ret.).

22. From Bernstein, et al, *Peace Resource Book; A Comprehensive Guide to Issues, Groups and Literature,* 1986. Copyright by the Institute for Defense & Disarmament Studies (Cambridge, MA: Ballinger Publishing, 1986).

23. From *The Washington Directory* (1986), Conservative Network, Washington, DC.

DC:
21.
ton, DC.
22. Rep
Time Inc. All
23. Reprinte
24. Michael M
and Beyond," *Foreig*